TEACHER'S EDITION

PRENTICE HALL
WRITING AND GRAMMAR

WG

GRADE TEN

Copyright © 2008 by Pearson Education, Inc., publishing as Pearson Prentice Hall, Boston, Massachusetts 02116. All rights reserved. Printed in the United States of America. This publication is protected by copyright, and permission should be obtained from the publisher prior to any prohibited reproduction, storage in a retrieval system, or transmission in any form or by any means, electronic, mechanical, photocopying, recording, or likewise. For information regarding permission(s), write to: Rights and Permissions Department, One Lake Street, Upper Saddle River, New Jersey 07458.

Pearson Prentice Hall™ is a trademark of Pearson Education, Inc.
Pearson® is a registered trademark of Pearson plc.
Prentice Hall® is a registered trademark of Pearson Education, Inc.

Boston, Massachusetts
Upper Saddle River, New Jersey

ISBN 0-13-200974-9

2 3 4 5 6 7 8 9 10   10 09 08 07

Program Authors

The program authors guided the direction and philosophy of *Prentice Hall Writing and Grammar: Communication in Action.* Working with the development team, they contributed to the pedagogical integrity of the program and to its relevance to today's teachers and students.

Joyce Armstrong Carroll

In her forty-year career, Joyce Armstrong Carroll, Ed.D., has taught on every grade level from primary to graduate school. In the past twenty years, she has trained teachers in the teaching of writing. A nationally known consultant, she has served as president of TCTE and on NCTE's Commission on Composition. More than fifty of her articles have appeared in journals such as *Curriculum Review, English Journal, Media & Methods, Southwest Philosophical Studies, Ohio English Journal, English in Texas,* and the *Florida English Journal.* With Edward E. Wilson, Dr. Carroll co-authored *Acts of Teaching: How to Teach Writing* and co-edited *Poetry After Lunch: Poems to Read Aloud.* Beyond her direct involvement with the writing pedagogy presented in this series, Dr. Carroll guided the development of the Hands-on Grammar feature. She co-directs the New Jersey Writing Project in Texas.

Edward E. Wilson

A former editor of *English in Texas,* Edward E. Wilson has served as a high-school English teacher and a writing consultant in school districts nationwide. Wilson has served on the Texas Teacher Professional Practices Commission and on NCTE's Commission on Composition. With Dr. Carroll, he co-wrote *Acts of Teaching: How to Teach Writing* and co-edited the award-winning *Poetry After Lunch: Poems to Read Aloud.* In addition to his direct involvement with the writing pedagogy presented in this series, Wilson provided inspiration for the Spotlight on Humanities feature. Wilson's poetry appears in Paul Janeczko's anthology *The Music of What Happens.* Wilson co-directs the New Jersey Writing Project in Texas.

Gary Forlini

Gary Forlini, a nationally known education consultant, developed the grammar, usage, and mechanics instruction and exercises in this series. After teaching in the Pelham, New York, schools for many years, he established Research in Media, an educational research agency that provides information for product developers, school staff developers, media companies, and arts organizations, as well as private-sector corporations and foundations. Mr. Forlini was co-author of the *S.A.T. Home Study* program and has written numerous industry reports on elementary, secondary, and post-secondary education markets.

National Advisory Panel

The teachers and administrators serving on the National Advisory Panel provided ongoing input into the development of *Prentice Hall Writing and Grammar: Communication in Action.* Their valuable insights ensure that the perspectives of teachers and students throughout the country are represented within the instruction in this series.

Dr. Pauline Bigby-Jenkins
Coordinator for Secondary English
  Language Arts
Ann Arbor Public Schools
Ann Arbor, Michigan

Lee Bromberger
English Department Chairperson
Mukwonago High School
Mukwonago, Wisconsin

Mary Chapman
Teacher of English
Free State High School
Lawrence, Kansas

Jim Deatherage
Language Arts Department
  Chairperson
Richland High School
Richland, Washington

Luis Dovalina
Teacher of English
La Joya High School
La Joya, Texas

JoAnn Giardino
Teacher of English
Centennial High School
Columbus, Ohio

Susan Goldberg
Teacher of English
Westlake Middle School
Thornwood, New York

Jean Hicks
Director, Louisville Writing Project
University of Louisville
Louisville, Kentucky

Karen Hurley
Teacher of Language Arts
Perry Meridian Middle School
Indianapolis, Indiana

Karen Lopez
Teacher of English
Hart High School
Newhall, California

Marianne Minshall
Teacher of Reading and Language Arts
Westmore Middle School
Columbus, Ohio

Nancy Monroe
English Department Chairperson
Bolton High School
Alexandria, Louisiana

Ken Spurlock
Assistant Principal
Boone County High School
Florence, Kentucky

Cynthia Katz Tyroff
Staff Development Specialist
  and Teacher of English
Northside Independent School District
San Antonio, Texas

Holly Ward
Teacher of Language Arts
Campbell Middle School
Daytona Beach, Florida

Grammar Review Team

The following teachers reviewed the grammar instruction in this series to ensure accuracy, clarity, and pedagogy.

Kathy Hamilton
Paul Hertzog
Daren Hoisington
Beverly Ladd

Karen Lopez
Dianna Louise Lund
Sean O'Brien

CONTENTS IN BRIEF

Note: Some features of the *Writing
and Grammar* Student Edition do not
appear in the Handbook Edition.
Please consult the Handbook table of
contents for more information.

CONTENTS
PART 1: WRITING

Chapter 1
The Writer in You 2

Chapter 2
A Walk Through the Writing Process 12

Chapter 3
Sentences, Paragraphs, and Compositions
Structure and Style 28

viii • Contents

INTEGRATED SKILLS

INTEGRATED SKILLS

INTEGRATED SKILLS

Chapters begin on the following
pages in the Handbook Edition:

Chapter 4 32

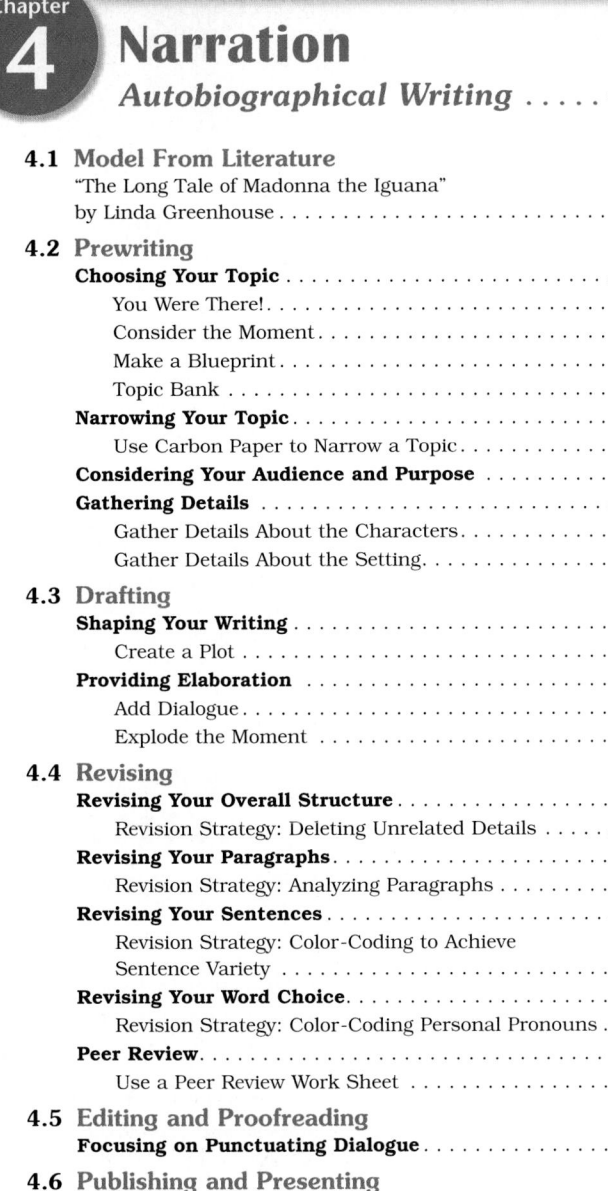

Chapter 4 Narration
Autobiographical Writing 48

INTEGRATED SKILLS

Contents • **ix**

5 Narration

Short Story 76

INTEGRATED SKILLS

x • Contents

Chapters begin on the following pages in the Handbook Edition :

Chapter 6 62

Chapter 6

Description 100

Student Work
IN PROGRESS

Featured Work:
"Phantom Finish"
by Leslie Harris
Sunnyslope High School
Phoenix, Arizona

INTEGRATED SKILLS

Contents • **xi**

Chapters begin on the following pages in the Handbook Edition ⊞:

Chapter 7 76

xii • Contents

Chapter 8 Persuasion

Advertisement 152

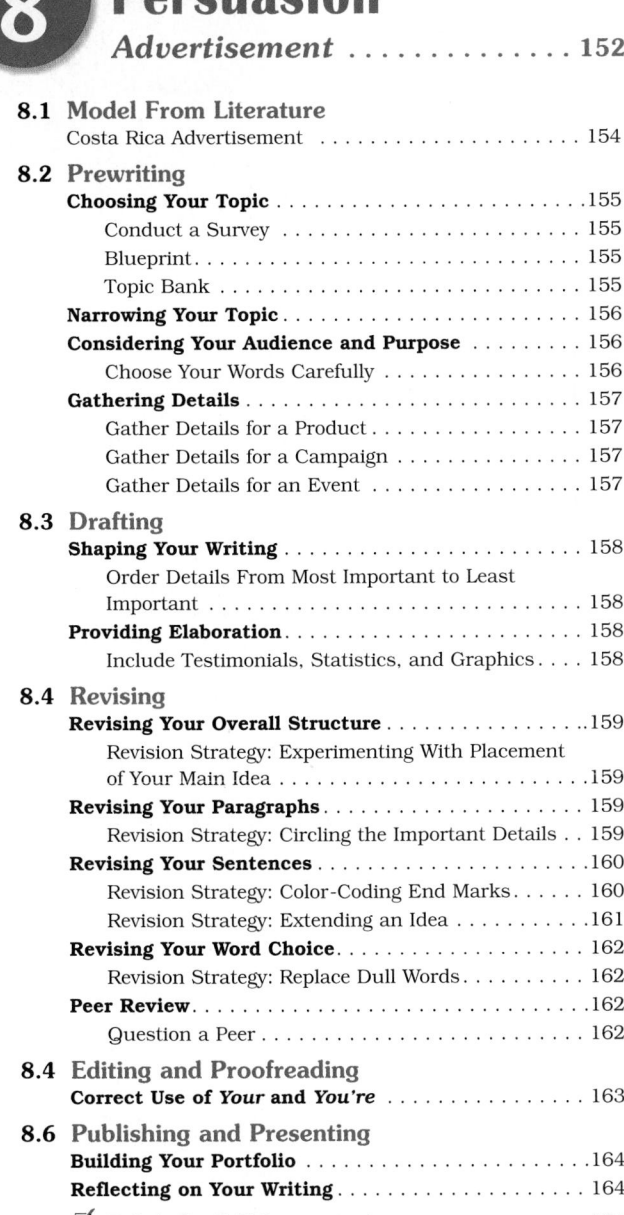

Student Work
IN PROGRESS

INTEGRATED SKILLS

Contents • **xiii**

Chapters begin on the following pages in the Handbook Edition🄷:

Chapter 9 106

xiv • Contents

Chapter 10

Exposition
Cause-and-Effect Essay 196

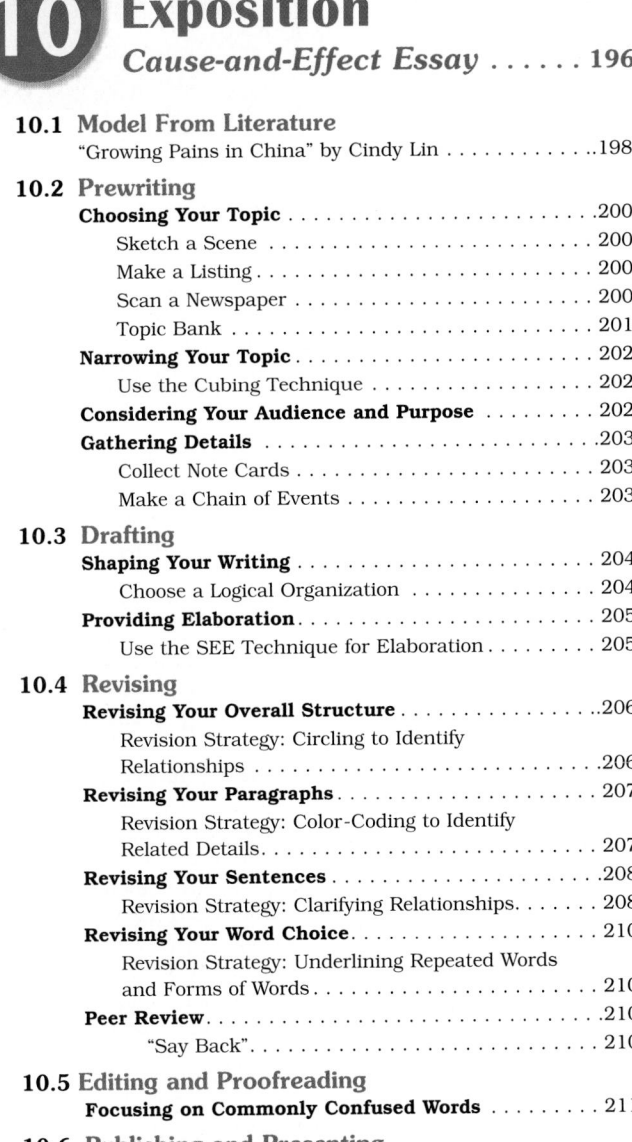

Student Work
IN PROGRESS

Featured Work:
"El Niño"
by Jennifer Hoss
Bel Air High School
El Paso, Texas

INTEGRATED SKILLS

Contents • **xv**

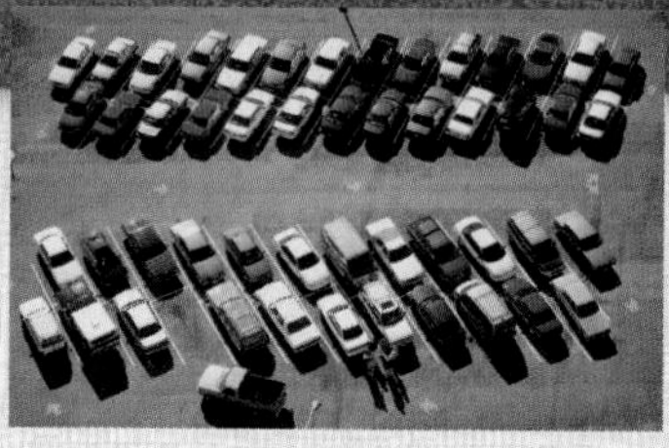

Chapter

11 Exposition
Problem-and-Solution Essay . . 220

Student Work
IN PROGRESS

Featured Work:
"Parking Permits Needed to
Regulate Student Parking"
by Patrick Swan
Muncie Central High School
Muncie, Indiana

INTEGRATED SKILLS

Chapter 12 Research Writing . . . 244

INTEGRATED SKILLS

Contents • **xvii**

Chapters begin on the following pages in the Handbook Edition🄷:

Chapter 13 176

Chapter 13 Response to Literature 276

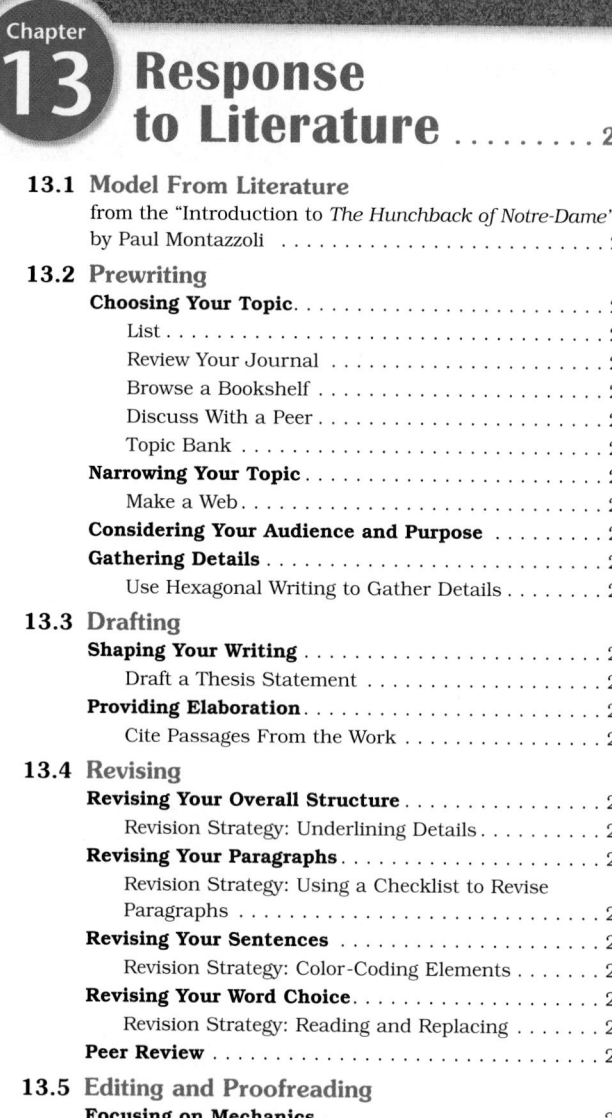

Student Work
IN PROGRESS

Featured Work:
"Telemachus in
Homer's *Odyssey*"
by Sheetal Wadera
Hightower High School
Missouri City, Texas

INTEGRATED
SKILLS

Chapter 14 Writing for Assessment 304

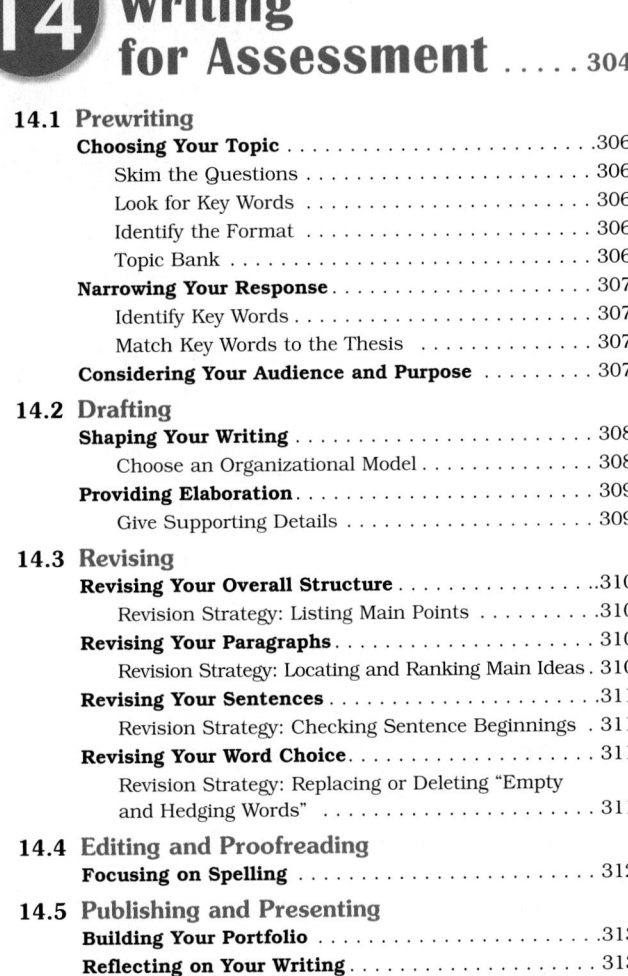

Student Work
IN PROGRESS

Featured Work:
　"Why the United States
　Entered World War I"
　by Tricia Bushnell
　Buena High School
　Ventura, California

Elaborating With
Supporting Details 309
Deleting Empty and
Hedging Words 311
Final Draft **314**

INTEGRATED SKILLS

▶ **Grammar in Your Writing**
Spelling *ie* and *ei* Words . . 312

▶ **Spotlight on the Humanities**
Recognizing the Varieties of
Media

Focus on Film:
The Last Emperor 318

▶ **Media and Technology Skills**
Taking Computerized Tests

Activity: Share Test-Taking
Strategies 319

▶ **Standardized Test
Preparation Workshop**
Analyzing Errors in
Writing 320

Contents • **xix**

INTEGRATED SKILLS

Chapters begin on the following pages in the Handbook Edition :

Chapter 16

Nouns, Pronouns, and Verbs 338

Chapter 17

Adjectives and Adverbs 368

Chapter 18

Prepositions, Conjunctions, and Interjections 390

Contents • xxi

Chapter 19

Basic Sentence Parts 410

Chapter 20

Phrases and Clauses 440

Chapters begin on the following
pages in the Handbook Edition🄷:

Chapter 21 338
Chapter 22 366
Chapter 23 386

Chapters begin on the following
pages in the Handbook Edition H:

Chapter 24 404
Chapter 25 424
Chapter 26 438

Chapter 27

Chapter 28

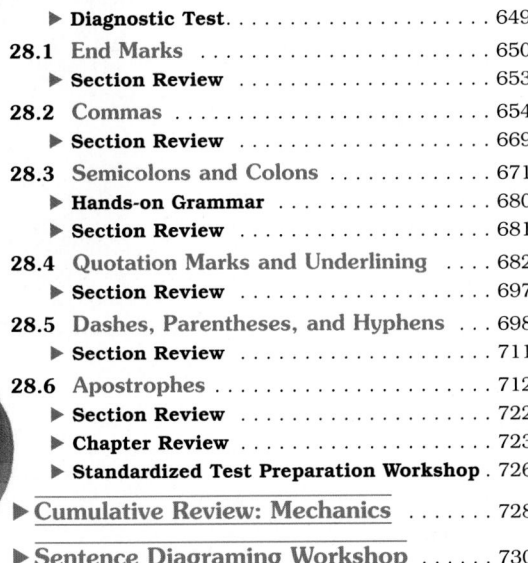

Contents • **xxv**

PART 3: ACADEMIC AND WORKPLACE SKILLS

Chapters begin on the following
pages in the Handbook Edition :

Chapter 32 608
Chapter 33 628

What's new

Prentice Hall Writing and Grammar now includes:

- **Online Essay Scorer – see page T29**

  Save time while helping your students become better writers. The Prentice Hall Online Essay Scorer provides instant holistic essay scoring along with analytical feedback and multiple opportunities for revision.

- **Test Preparation Handbook – see page T34**

  Prepare your students for success on high-stakes standardized tests with the new Test Preparation Handbook in the Student Edition—**a Prentice Hall exclusive!**

- **TeacherEXPRESS™ – see page T36**

  Everything you need to teach your class! TeacherEXPRESS™ includes a robust lesson planner that automatically adds lessons to your calendar with links to every printable resource you need!

- **Exam*View*® Test Bank – see page T36**

  From customized, multi-version tests in minutes to LAN-based assessment and reporting, the new **Exam*View*®** Test Bank does it all!

Clear, consistent organization

Prentice Hall Writing and Grammar **develops and reinforces skills through easy-to-follow chapter organization**

Writing

Guided writing instruction walks students through each step of the writing process.

Correlated to the Six Traits Model

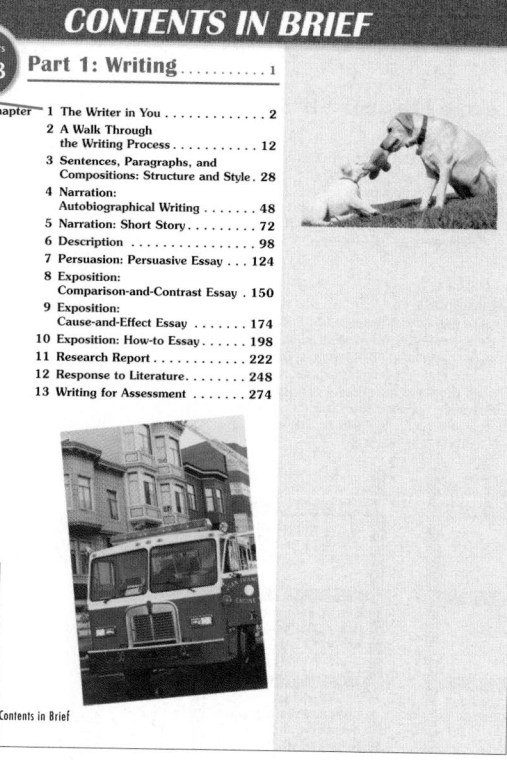

Contents in Brief

Contents in Brief • vii

Grammar, Usage, and Mechanics

Comprehensive grammar instruction, practice, and ongoing diagnostics ensure skills mastery.

Academic and Workplace Skills

Help students develop real-world skills for success in school and beyond.

T27

Guide students through every step of the writing process

7.4 Revising

Once you've written your first draft, look for ways to make it better. Start by reviewing the overall structure of your essay and paragraphs.

Revising Your Overall Structure

Analyze the Organization

As you reread your draft, look at the arrangement of your main points. Is it logical? Is it effective? Do your main points build toward a climax, with your strongest point last? Each point in your essay is like a rung in a ladder leading readers to your viewpoint—each must be in the proper position. To check your organization, highlight your main points.

▶ **REVISION STRATEGY**
Highlighting Main Points

Highlight the main points you have used to convince your readers. Then, number each in order. Next, look at the connections between your main points. For instance, will readers understand main point 3 if you haven't explained main point 4? If not, you should probably move point 4 before point 3. Write down any changes you need to make to the order of your points in the margin of your draft. Refer to this chart for more ideas about how points might connect.

⚙ Technology Tip

If you are using a word processor, highlight or use boldface type for your main ideas so that you can more easily review your organization and supporting arguments.

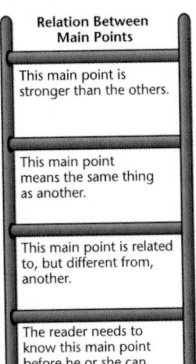

Relation Between Main Points	Possible Revision
This main point is stronger than the others.	Save this main point until the very end of the essay.
This main point means the same thing as another.	If found in different paragraphs, combine the paragraphs.
This main point is related to, but different from, another.	Make sure that the paragraphs in which you discuss the two are next to each other.
The reader needs to know this main point before he or she can understand a second one.	Make sure the first main point comes before the second.

134 • Persuasive Essay

Hands-on Strategies

Writing and Grammar provides systematic, hands-on strategies for every step of the writing process and comprehensive support in areas where students struggle most.

7.2 Prewriting

Choosing Your Topic

To create a powerful persuasive essay, write on an issue about which you care. Use the following strategies to choose a good topic. (Remember, your issue must have more than one side.)

Interactive Textbook

Try it out! Use the interactive Quicklist in **Section 7.2**, online or on CD-ROM.

Strategies for Generating a Topic

1. **Round Table** With a group of classmates, hold a round-table discussion of problems in your school and community. Raise as many different issues as possible. Jot down topics on which you have strong feelings. Choose among these subjects for your essay topic.
2. **Media Flip-Through** Your city government announces a budget crisis. A slumping basketball team trades its key forward. Every day, controversies blare from newspapers and television sets. Over the course of a few days, flip through newspapers, watch TV, and listen to the radio for possible topics. Choose one that interests you.
3. **Quicklist** Fold a piece of paper lengthwise in three. In the first column, write a list of issues and ideas that interest you. In the second, write a descriptive word for each. In the third, give an example supporting that description. Review your list, and decide which topic interests you most.

Authentic Student Models

Authentic student models in every chapter track the development of one student's writing through a specific writing mode, illustrating writing techniques in action.

Student Work
IN PROGRESS

Name: Josh McWhirter
College Station Junior High
College Station, TX

Using a Quicklist

Here's the quicklist Josh McWhirter used to choose his topic:

Topic	Descriptive Word	Examples
After-school clubs	helpful	Mr. Heisen's Math Club
Sports on TV	action-packed	table-tennis championships
Television comedies	stupid	Honey, I'm Home!
Mountain climbing	thrilling	weekend backpack trip with Dad
Computers	neat	program I wrote in Basic
Homelessness	sad	high rents
Global warming	scary	hole in the ozone over Australia

128 • Persuasive Essay

Prentice Hall Online Essay Scorer

Help your students become better writers while
providing valuable practice in writing on demand!
Our Online Essay Scorer provides:

- Instant essay scoring and analytical feedback

- Summaries of misspelled words, grammatical errors, and redundant sentences

- Scoring rubrics

- Sample scored essays

- Interactive model essays and graphic organizers

- Writing and grammar tips along with frequently asked questions

Comprehensive grammar instruction

Ensure mastery of grammar skills

Section 15.2 Linking Verbs

Some verbs do not show action. Instead, they link two parts of a sentence. These *linking verbs* thus show a relationship between words in a sentence.

KEY CONCEPT A **linking verb** connects a noun or pronoun with a word that identifies or describes it. ■

EXAMPLES: New York *is* a city.

The best swimmers *were* Margie and Pia.

Lucy *seems* unhappy.

Linking verbs act almost as equal signs. *City* identifies *New York; Margie* and *Pia* identify the *swimmers; unhappy* describes *Lucy.*

The Most Common Linking Verb

In English, the most common linking verb is *be.* This verb has many forms.

FORMS OF *BE*		
am	can be	have been
are	could be	has been
is	may be	had been
was	might be	could have been
were	must be	may have been
am being	shall be	might have been
are being	should be	must have been
is being	will be	shall have been
was being	would be	should have been
were being		will have been
		would have been

Exercise 10 Writing Sentences With Linking Verbs Write a sentence using each form of *be* listed below.
1. might have been
2. should have been
3. could be
4. were being
5. will be
6. has been
7. shall be
8. is being
9. would be
10. had been

Theme: Immigration
In this section, you will learn about linking verbs. The examples and exercises in this section are about immigration.

Cross-Curricular Connection: Social Studies

320 • Verbs

Step-by-step Teaching Guides

Key concepts are introduced, modeled, and practiced.

25.1 SUBJECT AND VERB AGREEMENT

Hands-on Grammar

Subject-Verb Agreement Color Match

Cut three strips of paper of equal length. Draw a blue line across the center of one. Draw a red line across the center of the other. Fold the strip into thirds, as shown in the illustration. Then, write a sentence with a singular subject, a singular verb form, and a phrase across the blue line. Write the subject in the first fold, the verb in the second, and the remaining words in the third fold. Write the same sentence on the strip with the red line, but use a plural subject and plural verb form. Next, cut each strip on the folds. Finally, try to line up the parts of the sentence. You will find that you can't create a color match between a singular subject and a plural verb form.

The Minister	attends	every session

The Ministers	attend	every session

The Ministers	attends	every session

Find It in Your Reading Do this activity with a sentence from the Grammar in Literature passage from "Glory and Hope," on page 578. If the sentence has too many phrases, just use the subject and verb.

Find It in Your Writing Review a recent piece of writing in your portfolio. Use this activity with several sentences from the piece.

Subject and Verb Agreement • 581

Exclusive Hands-on Grammar Exercises

Our unique interactive exercises encourage active learning and reinforce grammar concepts.

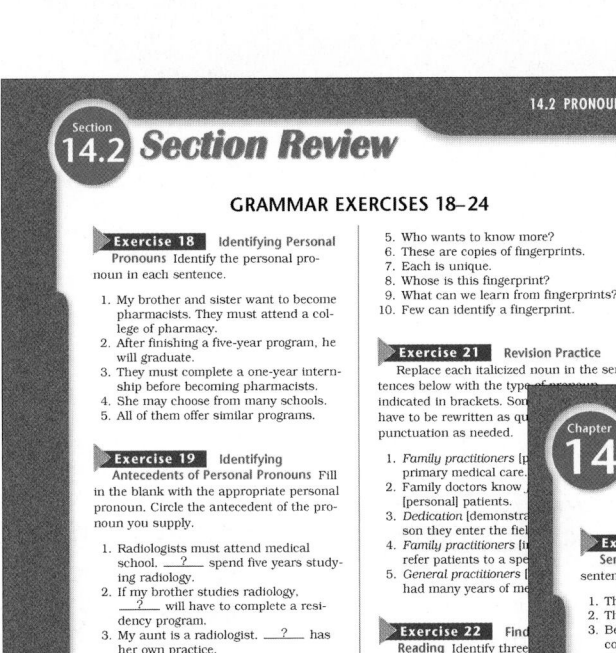

Section 14.2 Section Review

GRAMMAR EXERCISES 18–24

Exercise 18 Identifying Personal Pronouns Identify the personal pronoun in each sentence.

1. My brother and sister want to become pharmacists. They must attend a college of pharmacy.
2. After finishing a five-year program, he will graduate.
3. They must complete a one-year internship before becoming pharmacists.
4. She may choose from many schools.
5. All of them offer similar programs.

Exercise 19 Identifying Antecedents of Personal Pronouns Fill in the blank with the appropriate personal pronoun. Circle the antecedent of the pronoun you supply.

1. Radiologists must attend medical school. __?__ spend five years studying radiology.
2. If my brother studies radiology, __?__ will have to complete a residency program.
3. My aunt is a radiologist. __?__ has her own practice.
4. After completing __?__ residency, radiologists may decide to specialize.
5. __?__ may choose to teach instead.

Exercise 20 Recognizing Types of Pronouns Identify each of the pronouns in the sentences below as *personal*, *demonstrative*, *interrogative*, or *indefinite*.

1. My brother is in high school. He wants to study forensic medicine.
2. That is the study of medical evidence.
3. It helps police officers solve crimes.
4. You may have seen popular shows about "crime doctors."

5. Who wants to know more?
6. These are copies of fingerprints.
7. Each is unique.
8. Whose is this fingerprint?
9. What can we learn from fingerprints?
10. Few can identify a fingerprint.

Exercise 21 Revision Practice Replace each italicized noun in the sentences below with the type of pronoun indicated in brackets. Som... have to be rewritten as qu... punctuation as needed.

1. *Family practitioners* [p... primary medical care.
2. Family doctors know... [personal] patients.
3. *Dedication* [demonstra... son they enter the field.
4. *Family practitioners* [i... refer patients to a spe...
5. *General practitioners* [... had many years of me...

Exercise 22 Find... Reading Identify three... nouns in the excerpt from... Thought She Was a Dog .

Exercise 23 Find... Writing In your own w... least one example of each...

Exercise 24 Writ... Write a brief descriptio... in a job that interests you... kinds of pronouns you us...

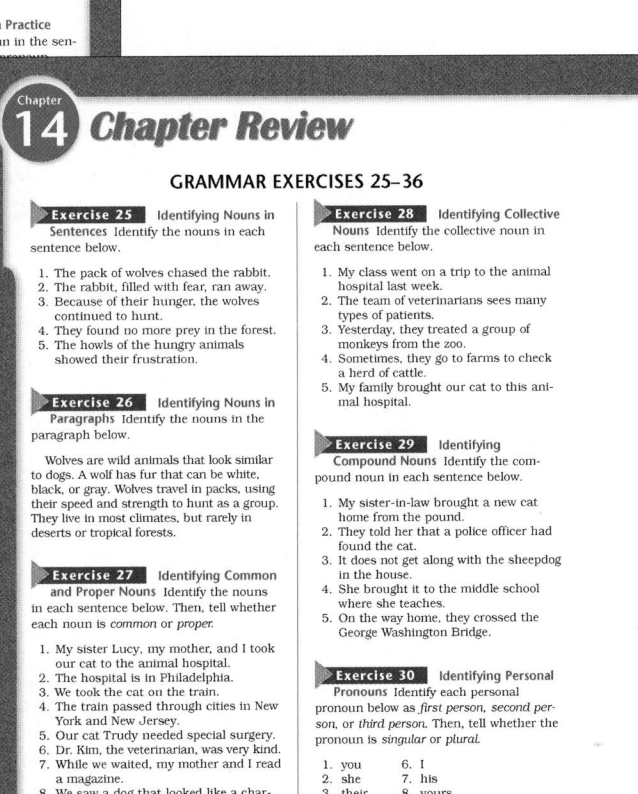

Chapter 14 Chapter Review

GRAMMAR EXERCISES 25–36

Exercise 25 Identifying Nouns in Sentences Identify the nouns in each sentence below.

1. The pack of wolves chased the rabbit.
2. The rabbit, filled with fear, ran away.
3. Because of their hunger, the wolves continued to hunt.
4. They found no more prey in the forest.
5. The howls of the hungry animals showed their frustration.

Exercise 26 Identifying Nouns in Paragraphs Identify the nouns in the paragraph below.

Wolves are wild animals that look similar to dogs. A wolf has fur that can be white, black, or gray. Wolves travel in packs, using their speed and strength to hunt as a group. They live in most climates, but rarely in deserts or tropical forests.

Exercise 27 Identifying Common and Proper Nouns Identify the nouns in each sentence below. Then, tell whether each noun is *common* or *proper*.

1. My sister Lucy, my mother, and I took our cat to the animal hospital.
2. The hospital is in Philadelphia.
3. We took the cat on the train.
4. The train passed through cities in New York and New Jersey.
5. Our cat Trudy needed special surgery.
6. Dr. Kim, the veterinarian, was very kind.
7. While we waited, my mother and I read a magazine.
8. We saw a dog that looked like a character from the movie *Benji*.
9. A poodle sat on a chair next to us.
10. Before we returned home, we stopped to see the Liberty Bell.

Exercise 28 Identifying Collective Nouns Identify the collective noun in each sentence below.

1. My class went on a trip to the animal hospital last week.
2. The team of veterinarians sees many types of patients.
3. Yesterday, they treated a group of monkeys from the zoo.
4. Sometimes, they go to farms to check a herd of cattle.
5. My family brought our cat to this animal hospital.

Exercise 29 Identifying Compound Nouns Identify the compound noun in each sentence below.

1. My sister-in-law brought a new cat home from the pound.
2. They told her that a police officer had found the cat.
3. It does not get along with the sheepdog in the house.
4. She brought it to the middle school where she teaches.
5. On the way home, they crossed the George Washington Bridge.

Exercise 30 Identifying Personal Pronouns Identify each personal pronoun below as *first person*, *second person*, or *third person*. Then, tell whether the pronoun is *singular* or *plural*.

1. you
2. she
3. their
4. our
5. them
6. I
7. his
8. yours
9. mine
10. we

Develop Skills through Meaningful Practice

Provide the practice your students need to improve their grammar skills and apply them in both writing and speaking.

And for even more practice:

- **Interactive Textbook** features thousands of interactive grammar exercises with instant feedback.

- The **Grammar Exercise Workbook** provides hundreds of grammar exercises for your students

- **Extra Grammar and Writing** give students additional practice in both grammar and writing.

- The **Daily Language Practice Book** offers brief, daily activities that sharpen students' proofreading skills.

- The **Hands-on Grammar Activity Book** offers easy-to-use templates for every Hands-on Grammar Activity in the Student Edition.

Grammar Exercise Workbook

PRENTICE HALL
WRITING AND GRAMMAR

Academic and workplace skills

Prepare students for the world beyond school!

Writing and Grammar's Academic and Workplace Skills chapters provide solid instruction in and hands-on practice with real-world skills.

Developing a Multimedia Presentation

In most multimedia presentations, the presenter gives an oral report, illustrating the main points with media selections. This type of presentation can be effective and memorable if it is well planned and executed.

KEY CONCEPT Multimedia presentations supply information through a variety of media, including text, slides, videos, music, maps, charts, and art. ■

Tips for Preparing a Multimedia Presentation

- Create an outline of your report first, and then decide which parts to illustrate through the use of media.
- Choose a medium that is suited to your topic. For example, if you were discussing the art of Leonardo da Vinci, reproductions of his artwork and music selections from his time would enhance your presentation.
- Evenly space the media within your presentation. Don't bunch them up at the beginning or end of your presentation.
- Check to ensure that the media you've selected will be able to be seen or heard by everyone. A postage stamp, for example, is too small to be held up in front of a large audience. It would be better to photocopy it and enlarge the image.
- Before the presentation, check your equipment—slide projectors, overhead projectors, microphones, cassette players—to be sure that they are in working condition.
- Always have a backup plan in case anything goes wrong with the equipment.
- Plan to rehearse with the equipment the day before the presentation. Be sure you know the location of all controls—for focus or for volume, for example—and understand their use.

Exercise 13 Preparing a Multimedia Presentation Read through the saved writings in your portfolio. Select one that could be made into a multimedia presentation. Then, using an outline, select the media you'd like to include, and decide on the sequence of your presentation.

Viewing

Section 28.2 Viewing and Representing Skills

Visual representation is an important way to communicate. Television programs, textbooks, and works of art are common types of media that use images to expand your view of the world. Graphic organizers, multimedia presentations, and performances are ways in which you can express yourself to the world. In this section, you will learn how to receive—and provide—information through visual representations.

Interpreting Maps, Graphs, and Photographs

Any map, graph, or photograph can provide a wealth of information. The key to the information these representations hold is your ability to interpret them.

KEY CONCEPT Use your knowledge of the features of maps, graphs, and photographs to get information visually. ■

Follow these general guidelines when reading a visual aid:

- **Determine Your Purpose** Knowing your purpose helps you focus on the information you need.
- **Read the Title, Caption, and Labels** The title or caption tells you what kind of information to expect.
- **Decode Symbols** Symbols are sometimes used to give information. Find out what they represent.
- **Look for Notable Features** Areas that stand out usually contain important information.
- **Link Information to Text** Determining the relationship between the visual elements and the text allows you to use the text to understand the visual elements better and vice versa.

Maps A map can do more than simply indicate the location of a state capital. For example, maps can identify population clusters, clarify wartime battle activities, and report weather forecasts.

Use these steps when interpreting maps:
1. Familiarize yourself with the map.
2. Find out which way is north on the map.
3. Look at the distance scale (usually found at the bottom of the map).

Graphs There will be times when you have to get information from graphs. Graphs provide a quick and easy way to compare several pieces of related information.

Viewing a

Speaking, Listening, Viewing, and Representing

Develop effective communication skills with a wide variety of exercises and activities.

Section 29.3 Studying Word Parts and Origins

Using Roots

Learning roots, the most basic parts of words, will help you learn the meanings of groups of words. For example, if you know that the root -gress means "to step or move forward," you have a key to the meaning of the following words: *regress, progress, retrogress, transgress, egress,* and *digress.*

KEY CONCEPT A **root** is a word part that determines an important part of the meaning of a word. ■

FIVE COMMON ROOTS		
Root	Meaning	Example
-mit- (-mis-)	to send	dismiss (to *send* away)
-mov- (-mot-)	to move	motion, *movement*
-ven- (-vent-)	to come	convene (to *come* together)
-vert- (-vers-)	to turn	reversal (*turning* around)
-vid- (-vis-)	to see	vision (ability to *see*)

Exercise 7 Learning Word Roots Match the words in the first column with the words in the second column that appear to have the same root. Look up each pair of words in a dictionary. Identify the root they share, and write its meaning.
1. reflect   a. manuscript
2. motivate   b. deflect
3. dimension   c. centipede
4. pedal   d. immense
5. hapless   e. modify
6. model   f. happiness
7. manufacture   g. motion
8. picture   h. circumstance
9. distance   i. assent
10. sentence   j. depict

Exercise 8 Using Roots to Determine the Meaning of Words Match each word in the first column with its definition in the second column. Explain how the roots you learned in the previous exercise helped you to determine each answer.
1. motility   a. person walking
2. pedestrian   b. by hand
3. manual   c. one of a set of units
4. module   d. unfortunate accident
5. mishap   e. ability to move on one's own

▶ **More Practice**
Academic and Workplace Skills Activity Book
• pp. 22–23

Vocabulary and Spelling

Expand students' vocabulary and improve their spelling with exercises using context, word structure and origins, reference tools, and spelling tips.

Reading Skills

Teach students how to use reading skills to improve their comprehension of materials they read in or out of school.

Section 30.2 Reading Nonfiction Critically

Nonfiction is writing that is based on fact. When you read nonfiction critically, you examine and question the ideas the author presents. You learn to distinguish between fact and opinion, to identify the author's purpose, and to recognize when language is being used to distort your understanding of the text. This section will guide you through a number of reading strategies that you can use to become a critical reader.

Comprehending Nonfiction

Before you begin to read a text critically, you need to have a general understanding of it. This process involves finding and interpreting important information, identifying the author's purpose, and understanding the relationship the material has to what you are studying.

KEY CONCEPT Comprehending nonfiction involves understanding the author's purpose as well as the information presented in the writing. ■

Locate Main Ideas and Major Details The main ideas are the key points an author wishes to convey. The major details explain and support these main points.

Interpret What You Are Reading Paraphrase, or state in your own words, the information in the text, starting with the main ideas and major details. This technique will help you to remember ideas and their relationship to each other.

Identify the Author's Purpose for Writing After you have a general idea of the content, examine the writer's choice of words and details to determine the author's purpose. As you continue to read, look for additional information that supports this purpose.

Reflect on What You Have Read After you have finished reading, take a moment to think about what the author has written. Consider the following questions: How does the information relate to what you are studying? How does this information relate to your life?

► Exercise 6 Comprehending Nonfiction Use the strategies mentioned above to read a chapter from one of your textbooks. Then, answer these questions: What main points and major details did you locate? What was the author's purpose? What details did you use to identify it? What is the importance of the information you read?

⊘ Learn More

These critical reading skills are also helpful when revising the ideas in your own writing. See Chapters 1, 2, and 3.

► More Practice

Academic and Workplace Skills Activity Book
• pp. 38–39

Taking Notes

Taking good notes is an important and useful study skill. Taking notes in class helps you remember what you heard, and taking notes while reading helps you remember what you read. Later, you can use your notes to study for a test or just to review the information you have learned.

TIPS FOR TAKING NOTES

• Don't record every word; focus on capturing main ideas.
• Label your notes with the topic and date.
• Keep notes for different subjects in separate notebooks or in separate sections of a general notebook.

Modified Outlines One note-taking device that you can use to sort out main ideas and major details is a *modified outline*. List each main idea, and underline it. Place major details below the main idea, and number them. Jot down supporting details under each major detail.

SAMPLE MODIFIED OUTLINE

```
○  Solar System ─────────── Main idea
   1. Sun ─────────────── Major detail
      A star ──────────── Supporting details
      Center of the solar system
   2. Planets
      Nine planets
      Orbit the sun in west to east direction
      Most have moons or satellites
   3. Asteroids, Meteoroids, and Comets
      Asteroids—fragments of rock
      Meteoroids—the result of asteroid collisions
      Comets—solid nucleus surrounded by
○            frozen gases and dust particles
```

Summaries Writing a *summary* is another way of organizing information you've learned. After reading a chapter or attending a class, write one or more paragraphs stating the key points covered and explaining how the ideas are connected.

► Exercise 4 Making a Modified Outline and a Summary Create a modified outline and a summary of a chapter in your science or social studies textbook.

31.3

Answering Different Types of Questions

If you are familiar with the different kinds of questions that are frequently asked on tests, you may improve your performance. It is also important to know various strategies for answering the different kinds of questions.

Answering Multiple-Choice Questions This kind of question asks you to choose from several possible responses.

EXAMPLE:
What is a URL?

a. an Internet service provider   c. a universal reference
b. an Internet Web site address   d. a periodical index

In the preceding example, the answer is *b*.

ANSWERING MULTIPLE-CHOICE QUESTIONS

1. Try answering the question before looking at the choices. If your answer is one of the choices, select that choice.
2. Eliminate the obviously incorrect answers, crossing them out if you are allowed to write on the test paper.
3. Change a question into a statement by inserting your answer to see whether the statement makes sense.

Answering Matching Questions Matching questions ask that you match items in one group with items in another.

EXAMPLE:

___ 1. negligible   a. causing fear or dread
___ 2. formidable   b. difficult to understand
___ 3. inscrutable   c. small or unimportant

In the preceding example, the answers are *c*, *a*, and *b*.

ANSWERING MATCHING QUESTIONS

1. Count each group to see whether items will be left over. Check the directions to see whether items can be used more than once.
2. Read all the items before you start matching.
3. Match the items you know first. If you can write on the paper, cross out the items when you use them.
4. Match remaining items about which you are less certain.

💻 Internet Tip

You can find additional information, strategies, and practice on test-taking on the Internet.

► More Practice

Academic and Workplace Skills Activity Book
• p. 59–60

Study, Reference, and Test-taking Skills

Help students make the most of their study time with study and note taking tips, research skills, and test-taking strategies.

Help your students succeed on high-stakes assessments

Prentice Hall's exclusive Test Preparation Handbook features detailed instruction—along with ample practice questions and essays in standardized test format—in reading comprehension, grammar, and writing on demand.

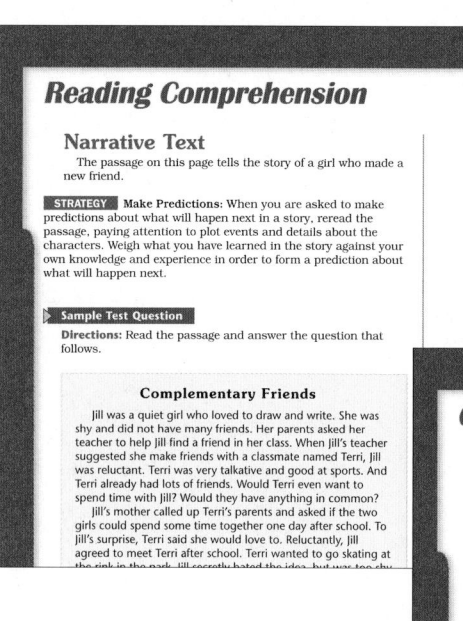

Reading Comprehension

Improve students' reading comprehension scores with step-by-step guides to answering comprehension questions and a variety of sample passages and questions.

Grammar

Reinforce students' mastery of commonly tested grammar and usage concepts with brief review and test-formatted exercises.

Writing on Demand

Strengthen students' writing skills with tips, sample prompts, annotated student essays, and writing exercises in test format.

Additional support throughout the Student Edition

Standardized Test Preparation Workshops

Standardized Test Preparation Workshops after each chapter provide comprehensive preparation for the PSAT, SAT, ACT, AP*, state, and local standardized tests.

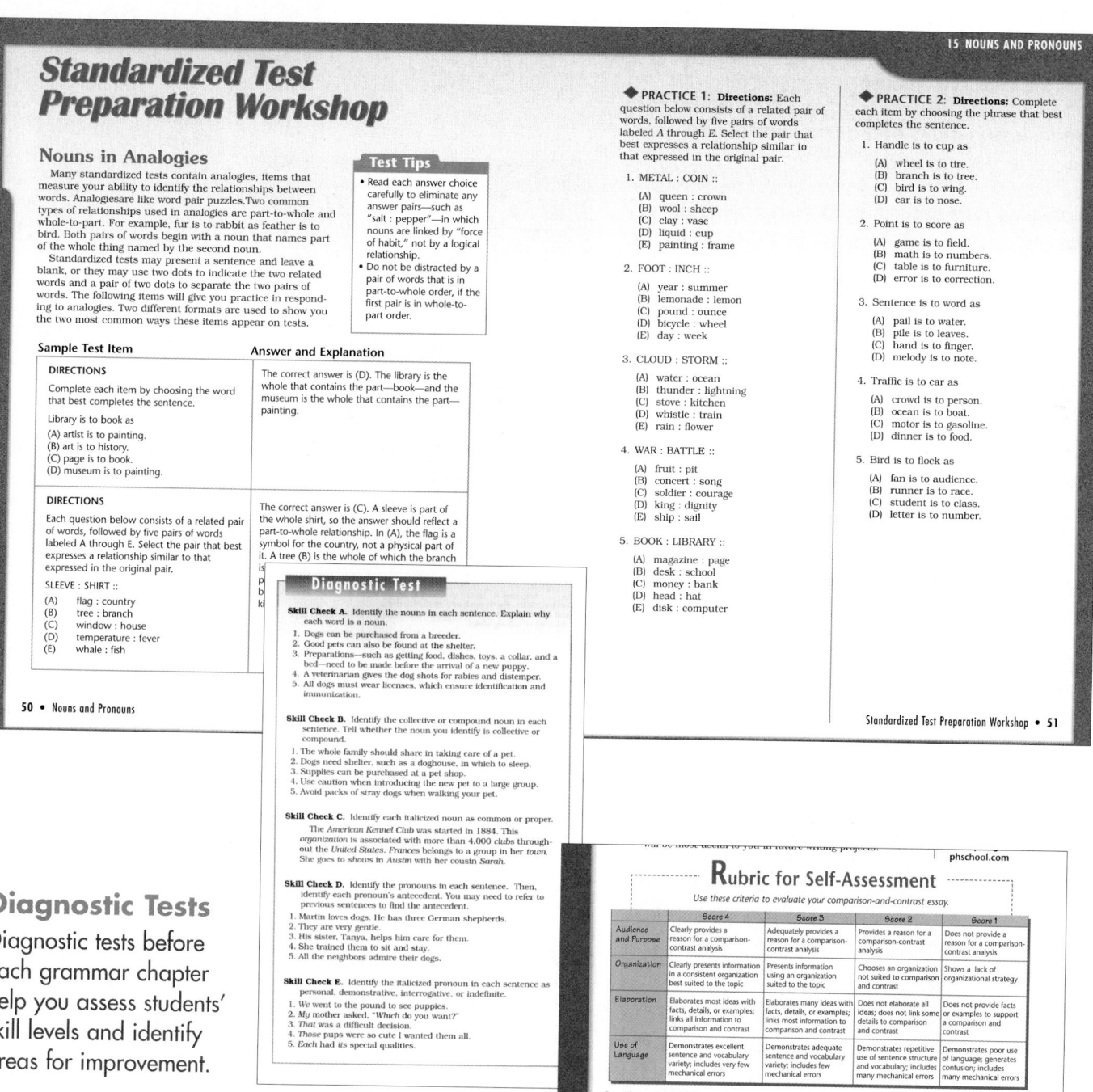

Diagnostic Tests

Diagnostic tests before each grammar chapter help you assess students' skill levels and identify areas for improvement.

Rubrics for Self-Assessment

Rubrics for Self-Assessment with each writing lesson help build critical thinking skills as students evaluate their own work.

Teaching resources

Powerful tools for powerful results

TeacherEXPRESS™

One-stop classroom management!

- Access, search, and print any teaching resource with the click of a mouse

- Create lesson plans and automatically add lessons to your calendar

- Customize tests according to skills objectives and ability level with **Exam**_View_® Test Bank

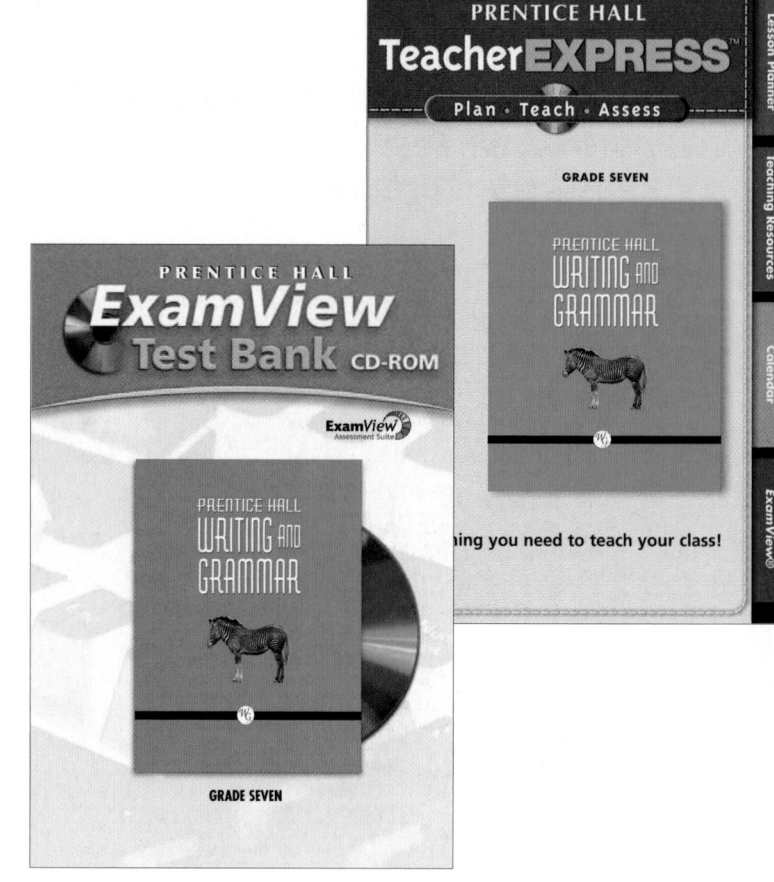

Exam_View_® Test Bank CD-ROM

Powered by **Exam**_View_® test generator!

- Easy to use and teacher–friendly

- Easily create and customize tests, worksheets, and study guides in minutes

- Create paper, LAN–based, and Internet tests

Writers at Work DVD

Demonstrate the real-world relevance of the writing process as professionals explain how they incorporate the writing process into their daily lives.

Interactive Textbook—Available online or on CD-ROM

Take the weight off their shoulders! The Interactive Textbook provides the same trusted content as your textbook without the weight in the backpack, and includes:

- **Online Essay Scorer**—The Prentice Hall Online Essay Scorer provides instant holistic essay scoring along with analytical feedback and multiple opportunities for revision.

- **Interactive writing and grammar exercises**—Web codes throughout the Student Edition allow students to quickly access interactive online grammar exercises, reviews, writing tools, and tutorials—all with instant feedback.

- **Diagnostic tests**—Instantly assess student readiness to learn new skills.

- **Scoring rubrics and scored student models**— Reliable, scored essays use a 4- or 6-point rubric with specific suggestions for improved writing.

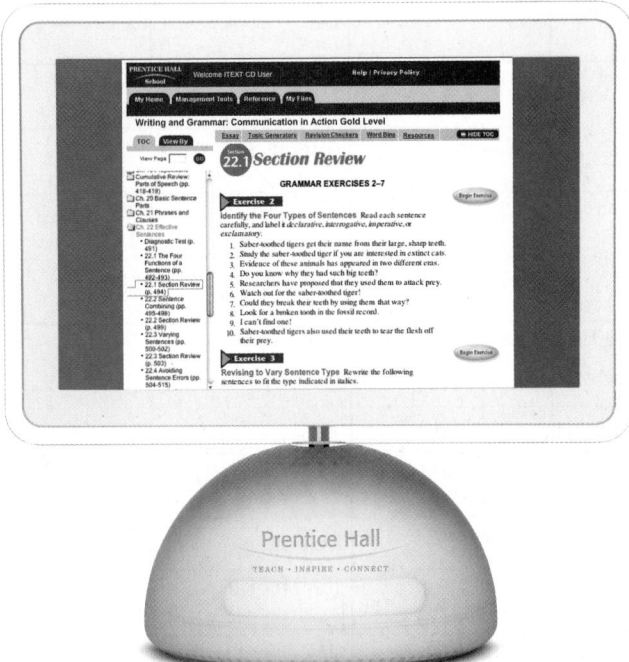

Writing and Grammar Components

Student Edition
Interactive Textbook
Student Handbook Edition
Teacher's Edition
Spanish Speakers' Handbook

Teaching Resources
Teaching Resources:
  Writing Support Activity Book
  Topic Bank for Heterogeneous Classes
  Grammar Exercise Workbook Teacher's Edition
  Daily Language Practice
  Hands-on Grammar Activity Book
  Academic and Workplace Skills Activity Book Teacher's Edition
  Vocabulary and Spelling Workbook Teacher's Edition
  Reading Support Practice Book Teacher's Edition
  Standardized Test Preparation Workbook Teacher's Edition
  Writing Assessment and Portfolio Management
  Formal Assessment Book
SuccessNet Teacher Access Pack
Scoring Rubrics on Transparency

Assessment
Formal Assessment Book
Standardized Test Preparation Workbook
Standardized Test Preparation Workbook Teacher's Edition
Writing Assessment and Portfolio Management

Grammar, Usage, and Mechanics
Grammar Exercise Workbook
Grammar Exercise Workbook Teacher's Edition
Extra Grammar and Writing Exercises
Grammar Exercises Answers on Transparencies
Hands-on Grammar Activity Book
Hands-on Grammar Activity Book Teacher's Edition
Daily Language Practice
Daily Language Practice Transparencies

Writing
Writing Support Activity Book
Writing Support Activity Book Teacher's Edition
Writing Support Transparencies
Topic Bank for Heterogeneous Classes

Academic and Workplace Skills
Academic and Workplace Skills Activity Book
Academic and Workplace Skills Activity Book Teacher's Edition

Reading, Vocabulary, and Spelling
Reading Support Activity Book
Reading Support Activity Book Teacher's Edition
Vocabulary and Spelling Workbook
Vocabulary and Spelling Workbook Teacher's Edition

Technology
TeacherEXPRESS™
Exam*View®* Test Bank CD-ROM
StudentEXPRESS™
Writers at Work DVD

Correlation to the Six Traits Analytic Model

Chapter	Ideas	Organization	Voice	Word Choice	Sentence Fluency	Conventions
1 The Writer in You	7	7	7	7	7	7
	H3	H3	H3	H3	H3	H3
2 A Walk Through the Writing Process	14–17; 18; 24	18–20		21		22
	H6–9; 10	H10–12		H13		H14
3 Sentences, Paragraphs, and Compositions: Structure and Style	33–35; 37; 44	36–37; 39	42	31; 42–43	29–32; 42	31
	H21–23; 25	H24–25; 27	H30	H19; 30–31	H17–20; 30	H19
4 Narration: Autobiographical Writing	50–61; 68–72	50–53; 68–71		63	62	64; 66
	H34–41			H43	H42	H44; 46
5 Narration: Short Story	78–83; 85–86; 92–96	78–79; 84; 86; 92–95		89	87	88; 90
	H50–53; 55–56	H54; 56		H59	H57	H58; 60
6 Description	102–107; 109; 116–119; 120	109; 116–119	108	102–103; 108; 110; 112; 116–119		111; 114
	H64–67; 69	H69	H68	H68; 70; 72		H71; 74
7 Persuasion: Persuasive Essay	126–134; 136–137; 144–148	126–129; 135; 144–147		126–129; 141; 146–147	138; 140; 144–147	139; 142
	H78–82; 84–85	H83		H89	H86; 88	H87; 90
8 Persuasion: Advertisement	154–159; 165–168	159; 165–167		162; 165–167	160–161	161; 163
	H94–99; 105	H99; 105		H102; 105	H100–101	H101; 103
9 Exposition: Comparison-and-Contrast Essay	174–179; 181; 184; 189–192	174–175; 180; 182–183; 189–191		162	184	185; 187
	H108–111; 113; 116; 121	H112; 114; 121		H102	H116	H117; 119
10 Exposition: Cause-and-Effect Essay	198–203; 205; 207; 213–216	198–199; 204; 206; 213–215		210	208	209; 211
	H124–127; 129; 131; 137	H128; 130; 137		H134	H132	H133; 135
11 Exposition: Problem-and-Solution Essay	222–227; 229; 231; 237–240	222–223; 228; 230; 237–239	237–239	234; 237–239		232–233; 235
	H140–143; 145; 147; 153	H144; 146; 153	H153	H150; 153		H148–149; 151
12 Research Writing	246–253; 255; 259; 265–272	246–249; 254; 256–257; 260; 267–271	268	246–249; 263	261	262; 264–265
	H156–159; 161; 165; 171–175	H160; 162–163; 166; 173–175	H174	H169	H167	H168; 170–171
13 Response to Literature	278–285; 287; 289; 295–300	278–281; 286; 288; 295–299		292; 295–299	290	291; 293
	H178–181; 183; 185; 191–193	H182; 184; 191–193		H188; 191–193	H186	H187; 189

Correlation to the Six Traits Analytic Model

Chapter	Ideas	Organization	Voice	Word Choice	Sentence Fluency	Conventions
14 Writing for Assessment	306–307; 309–310; 314–318	308; 314–317		311	311	312
	(H)196–197; 199–200	(H)198		(H)201	(H)201	(H)202
15 Workplace Writing	324–327; 332	324–329		324–325		
	(H)206–209	(H)206–211		(H)206–207		
16 Nouns, Pronouns, and Verbs						340–366
						(H)216–239
17 Adjectives and Adverbs						370–387
						(H)242–257
18 Prepositions, Conjunctions, and Interjections						392–405
						(H)260–271
19 Basic Sentence Parts						412–437
						(H)274–297
20 Phrases and Clauses						442–481
						(H)300–337
21 Effective Sentences					489–499	486–488; 500–513
					(H)343–353	(H)340–342; 354–365
22 Verb Usage			534–537; 539	534–537; 539	534–537; 539	520–539
			(H)382–385	(H)382–385	(H)382–385	(H)368–385
23 Pronoun Usage						544–561
						(H)388–403
24 Agreement						566–585
						(H)406–423
25 Using Modifiers					597–598	590–603
					(H)433–434	(H)426–437
26 Miscellaneous Problems in Usage						608–625
						(H)440–455

Correlation to the Six Traits Analytic Model

Chapter	Ideas	Organization	Voice	Word Choice	Sentence Fluency	Conventions
27 Capitalization						632–645
						⊞458–469
28 Punctuation						650–725
						⊞472–543
29 Speaking, Listening, Viewing, and Representing	746–748	746–748	746–748	746–748	746–748	
	⊞548–550	⊞548–550	⊞548–550	⊞548–550	⊞548–550	
30 Vocabulary and Spelling	771			768–771; 773–777		778–787
	⊞571			⊞568–571; 573–577		⊞578–587
31 Reading Skills	798–807		807	802–803; 807		807
	⊞596–605		⊞605	⊞600–601; 605		⊞605
32 Study, Reference, and Test-Taking Skills						
33 Workplace Skills and Competencies						

PRENTICE HALL
WRITING AND GRAMMAR

Grade Ten

PEARSON

Prentice
Hall

Upper Saddle River, New Jersey
Boston, Massachusetts

WRITING AND GRAMMAR

Grade Ten

Pearson Prentice Hall™ is a trademark of Pearson Education, Inc.
Pearson® is a registered trademark of Pearson plc.
Prentice Hall® is a registered trademark of Pearson Education, Inc.

ISBN 0-13-200964-1

1 2 3 4 5 6 7 8 9 10   10 09 08 07 06

Go Online
PHSchool.com

Use  **Interactive Textbook** *Writing and Grammar,* your textbook online!

(Includes every grammar exercise in this book!)

- instant feedback on interactive grammar exercises
- interactive writing tools and writing tutorials
- access to the *Prentice Hall Online Essay Scorer*

Interactive Textbook is also available on CD-ROM.

Go on-line to get instant help on the Writing and Grammar Web site!

- additional grammar practice opportunities
- scoring rubrics with scored student models for different modes of writing

Here's how to use the Writing and Grammar Web site:

Look for these Web Codes in your book:

eek-1001
eek-1002

Here's how to use Web Codes:

1. Go on-line. Enter URL: PHSchool.com

2. If you want instant feedback on interactive grammar exercises, enter Web Code: eek-1002

   Choose the appropriate chapter from the menu that appears.

3. If you want to review writing rubrics and scored student models, enter Web Code: eek-1001

   Choose the appropriate chapter from the menu that appears.

iii

Objectives

1. To understand writing as a recursive process and to develop ownership of one's own writing process

2. To write in a variety of forms, including narrative, descriptive, persuasive, expository, and literary texts, and to develop skills in writing for assessment

3. To analyze works of literature and student drafts as models and examples of specific writing strategies

4. To develop voice and adjust one's writing to various audiences and purposes

5. To develop research skills and to use writing as a tool for learning

6. To apply specific prewriting strategies for generating and narrowing writing topics

7. To use graphic organizers and other methods for organizing and supporting ideas in drafting

8. To approach revision in a systematic way in terms of overall structure, paragraphs, sentences, and word choice

9. To edit and proofread drafts to ensure appropriate usage and accuracy in spelling and the conventions and mechanics of written English

10. To understand rubrics and to use them to evaluate one's own writing and the writing of others

Writing

Femme Cousant, Henri Lebasque, Christie's Images

Responding to Fine Art

Femme Cousant by Henri Lebasque

Use this artwork to start a discussion about the process of writing.

1. Have students examine Lebasque's painting. You might use the following questions to prompt discussion:

   Does this scene seem to be set in a public or a private space?

   What do you think the woman in the painting is doing?

   What is she thinking?

2. Ask students how they would describe the mood of this scene. Do students find some moods and locations more conducive than others to writing?

3. The woman at the table seems to be alone. Ask students to explain how writing is simultaneously a private exercise and a public one. How does writing affect our relationship with the world?

About the Artist

Henri Lebasque (1865–1937) was born in Maine-et-Loire, France, and made his way to Paris in 1886 to study painting. There he encountered the work of Pissarro, a founder of the Impressionist movement, with whom he shared an interest in the new style of painting. Like the work of other impressionists, Lebasque's paintings were lighter and more freely rendered than those of more traditional artists. His work focused on the lives of ordinary working people in humble surroundings, rather than on portraits of the rich and famous or on classical or biblical scenes. Though he lived and painted in many outdoor locations, there often seems something domestic about virtually all of Lebasque's subjects. So intimate is he with his subject that whether he depicts a quiet workroom, a child on a park bench, or people sitting in a lovely garden, he seems to transform each location into an interior.

In-Depth Lesson Plan

	LESSON FOCUS	PRINT AND MEDIA RESOURCES
DAY 1	**Introduction to Writing** Students discuss the value of writing in everyday life. (p. 2/H2)	*Writers at Work* **DVD**, selected segments *Writing and Grammar* **Interactive Text**, Ch. 1
DAY 2	**Developing Your Writing Life; Sharing Your Work** Students identify strategies for generating and organizing ideas for writing. Coverage of organizing includes notebooks, clipping files, portfolios, and journals. Students also recognize the value of sharing their work. (pp. 3–6)	*Writing and Grammar* **Interactive Text**, Ch. 1 **Teaching Resources** *Writing Support Transparencies,* 1-A–B; *Writing Support Activity Book,* 1–1
DAY 3	**Qualities of Good Writing; Reflecting on Your Writing** Students identify qualities of good writing and write a reflective response on their own writing practices. (p. 7/H3)	*Writing and Grammar* **Interactive Text**, Ch. 1 **Teaching Resources** *Formal Assessment,* Ch. 1

Accelerated Lesson Plan

	LESSON FOCUS	PRINT AND MEDIA RESOURCES
DAY 1	**Introduction Through Sharing Your Work** Students learn strategies for generating and organizing ideas and recognize the value of sharing their work. (pp. 2–6/H2)	*Writers at Work* **DVD**, selected segments *Writing and Grammar* **Interactive Text**, Ch. 1 **Teaching Resources** *Writing Support Transparencies,* 1-A–B
DAY 2	**Qualities of Good Writing; Reflecting on Your Writing** Students identify qualities of good writing and write a reflective response on their own writing practices. (p. 7/H3)	*Writing and Grammar* **Interactive Text**, Ch. 1 **Teaching Resources** *Formal Assessment,* Ch. 1

Options for Adapting Lesson Plans

HOMEWORK

Have students complete any stage of the lesson for homework.

FEATURES

Extend coverage with Spotlight on the Humanities (p. 8), Media and Technology Skills (p. 9), and the Standardized Test Preparation Workshop (p. 10).

TECHNOLOGY

Students can complete any stage of the lesson on the computer, using *Writing and Grammar* Interactive Text or a word-processing program. Have them print out their completed work.

Writing and Grammar Handbook Alignment

Page numbers in Step-by-Step Teaching Guides in this Teacher's Edition refer to pages from the full student text. Handbook page references, indicated with this icon 🄷, are provided in Time and Resource Manager boxes and at the bottom of each Teacher's Edition page.

INTEGRATED SKILLS COVERAGE

Viewing and Representing
Critical Viewing, SE pp. 2, 5, 6, 8/🄷2
Analyzing How Meaning Is Communicated Through the Arts, SE p. 8; ATE p. 8

Grammar
ATE p. 7

Vocabulary
ATE p. 4

Real-World Connection
ATE p. 6

Workplace Skills
ATE p. 9

ASSESSMENT SUPPORT

Standardized Test Preparation Workshop, SE p. 10
Standardized Test Preparation Workbook, pp. 1–2
Formal Assessment, Ch. 1

MEETING INDIVIDUAL NEEDS

Less Advanced Students ATE p. 11. See also Ongoing Assessment ATE p. 4.
ESL Students ATE p. 7
More Advanced Students ATE pp. 6, 11
Gifted and Talented Students ATE p. 9

BLOCK SCHEDULING

Pacing Suggestions
For 90-minute Blocks
• Assign a topic and have students complete the Prewriting and Drafting stages in a single period.
• Focus one class period on Revising and Editing and Publishing and Presenting. Allow at least 30 minutes for peer revision.

Resources for Varying Instruction
• *Writers at Work* DVD Show selected segments in class.

Professional Development Support
• *How to Manage Instruction in the Block* This teaching resource provides management and activity suggestions.

MEDIA AND TECHNOLOGY

For the Teacher
• *Writers at Work* DVD
• Teacher**EXPRESS** CD-ROM

WRITING AND GRAMMAR ON-LINE

Interactive Text (On-line or on CD-ROM)
• Easily navigable instruction with interactive Revision Checkers
• Full use of e-rater™, the essay-scoring system (on-line only)

Companion Web Site PHSchool.com
• Scoring rubrics with models (use Web Code eek-1001)

See the Go On-line! feature, SE p. iii.

Lesson Objectives

1. To understand the purposes and significance of writing in everyday life
2. To identify the qualities of good writing, including organization, voice, word choice, sentence fluency, and appropriate usage
3. To compile and represent information in a variety of ways
4. To use writing as a study tool to clarify and remember information
5. To analyze strategies that writers in different fields use to compose
6. To explore options for working together, including group brainstorming and peer reviews
7. To examine possible outlets for publishing written material

Critical Viewing

Classify Possible questions to ask: How often do you write? What kinds of writing do you do? How do you begin a writing project? What is the easiest part about writing for you? The most difficult?

Chapter 1 The Writer in You

▲ Critical Viewing Suppose you wanted to interview this student about her writing habits. Name three questions you might ask. [Classify]

You weren't born knowing how to speak. You learned to speak by listening to others and, eventually, by using words yourself. The more you spoke, the better you became at it. The same is true of writing. The best way to discover the writer in you is, naturally, to write!

Writing in Everyday Life

Writing is already and will continue to be an important part of your everyday life. The writing you do can be as simple as jotting down a phone message or writing yourself a quick reminder or as complex as developing a research paper on a historical event or preparing a science lab report. You probably do some form of writing—either simple or complex—just about every day. In this chapter, you will learn strategies to help you fully take advantage of each writing opportunity so that you can continue to develop your skills as a writer.

2 • The Writer in You

⏱ TIME AND RESOURCE MANAGER

Resources
Print: *Writing Support Transparencies*, 1-A–B; *Formal Assessment*, Ch. 1
Technology: *Writers at Work* DVD, selected segments

Using the Full Student Edition	Using the Handbook🄷
• Cover pp. 2–7 in class. • Have students name career fields that depend on good writing skills. • Preview segments of the *Writers at Work* DVD.	• Cover pp. 2–3 in class. • Have students name career fields that depend on good writing skills. • Preview segments of the *Writers at Work* DVD.

Why Write?

Being a writer helps you respond to the world. Writing is often the most effective way to communicate. Suppose you read an article in a newspaper that makes you feel angry or frustrated. Writing a thoughtful letter to the editor can help you express and share your feelings. Writing can also bring you surprising insights into yourself. For example, when you gather facts for an essay, you might discover interests you never knew you had.

Developing Your Writing Life

One of the keys to improving as a writer is to develop an approach to writing that works for you. Your approach includes where, when, and how you write.

Keep Track of Your Ideas

Experiment with different ways of generating and keeping track of writing ideas. Following are a few techniques you might consider:

Notebook Carry a small notebook with you and record in it anything that captures your interest—places that you visit, events that you witness, interesting news stories. Whenever you need a writing idea, look through your notebook for possibilities.

Clipping File Look through books, magazines, Web pages—even calendars and travel brochures. Capture the interesting pieces of information you come across by keeping a clipping file—a folder containing clippings from the sources you've consulted.

Style Journal Use a style journal to experiment with different writing styles or goals. You might try writing the opening sentence for three different kinds of novels. Or you might take a line of dialogue and write it in four or five different styles. Look at the examples on this page.

Writers in
ACTION

Doris Lessing, who has written dozens of widely admired books, stories, and nonfiction works, offers this advice:
"In the writing process, the more the story cooks, the better. The brain works for you even when you are at rest. I find dreams particularly useful.... You can only learn to be a better writer by actually writing."

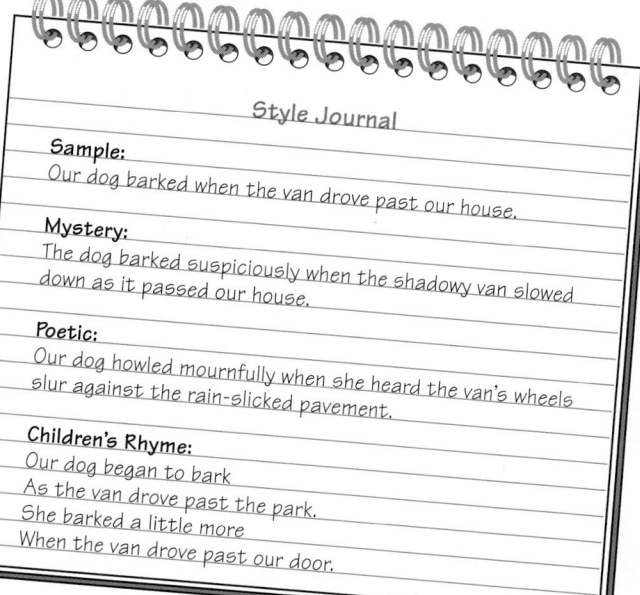

Style Journal

Sample:
Our dog barked when the van drove past our house.

Mystery:
The dog barked suspiciously when the shadowy van slowed down as it passed our house.

Poetic:
Our dog howled mournfully when she heard the van's wheels slur against the rain-slicked pavement.

Children's Rhyme:
Our dog began to bark
As the van drove past the park.
She barked a little more
When the van drove past our door.

The Writer in You • 3

PREPARE and ENGAGE

Interest GRABBER Ask students to imagine that they have suddenly lost the ability to write. What would they miss? How would their lives change? What other methods of communication could they use?

Activate Prior Knowledge

Have students think about their writing when they were in middle school. In what ways has their writing changed since then? What do they do now that makes them better writers?

More About the Writer

Born in Iran and raised in Zimbabwe before moving to England, Doris Lessing explores the inner lives and identities of her characters in her mostly autobiographical five-volume *Children of Violence*.

TEACH

Step-by-Step Teaching Guide

Keep Track of Your Ideas

Teaching Resources: Writing Support Transparencies, 1-A

1. Discuss the three strategies for keeping track of ideas. Ask questions like these:

   Which of these strategies do you use already? Which ones help? Should you keep your idea notebook at home? (No. It won't be handy as ideas occur.)

   How can you keep clippings from library books or from textbooks? (Students could make photocopies of them.)

   How could keeping a style journal help nonprofessional writers? (It could help them to be flexible in writing.)

2. Display Transparency 1-A. After reviewing the sample, write a declarative sentence on the board. Then, ask students to rewrite this sentence in three styles.

Keep Track of Your Writing and Reading

1. Show student writing samples collected from the beginning and from the end of a school year. Ask the class to point out the improvements they notice. You may wish to take note of any grammar or spelling errors that still need attention.

2. Have students begin their writing portfolios. Discuss how often they should review the contents. Set up some class time each month to complete this review.

3. Invite students to share examples of their writing in small groups.

Integrating Vocabulary Skills

Point out that students are likely to learn interesting new words as they read. Encourage them to add these words to their reader's journals, along with the definitions, which they might need to verify in a dictionary.

Try Different Approaches

1. To explore the approaches, ask students the following questions.

   Which writing materials do you prefer? Why?

   What time of day is the best for you to write?

   Is it possible to spend too much time revising?

   How can you tell when your writing is the best it can be?

2. Ask students if they always approach a writing task the same way. What are the advantages of experimenting? (Writers need to know different strategies so they can use them for different kinds of tasks.)

1

Keep Track of Your Writing and Reading

Writing Portfolio Writing is a permanent form of communication. Unlike speech, the writing projects you complete are lasting. You can return to them at any time. Maintaining a writing portfolio of your past works is the best way to monitor your progress as a writer. You can include your favorite writing—whether it is a particularly effective poster or a complete autobiographical narrative. For a longer work, consider including several preliminary drafts to give a snapshot of your writing process in action.

No matter what you include in your portfolio, it will be useful only if you actually reread and review the materials inside. Schedule time at least once a month to review the contents of your portfolio. At that time, you can add new materials or remove those you no longer feel represent your best work.

Reader's Journal When you come across quotations from other writers that strike you as memorable, write them down. Someday, they might be useful for a piece of your own writing.

Try Different Approaches

Selecting Writing Materials The materials you use to write can affect your writing. You might use a pen or pencil and paper or a computer. For some writers, a word processor is an ideal tool for drafting a lengthy report, but a simple pen and pad works best for generating ideas for a poem.

Evaluating Your Writing Time Some writers are more productive in the morning; others work best at night. Learn your time preference by writing the time and date at the beginning of each writing session. When you review your work, look for trends. You might find that your drafting improves in the afternoon, but you get your best prewriting ideas before breakfast.

Improving Your Work Writers' revision strategies vary greatly. You might rewrite obsessively, as Gore Vidal says he does. On the other hand, you might agree with Elie Wiesel, who feels that writing "is more like sculpture where you remove, you eliminate in order to make the work visible." When you revise, you could combine both theories, adding some ideas and taking others away.

Experiment

Discover your own most effective strategies by experimenting. Try new approaches, and then reflect on their success. When you find a technique that works, add it to your set of writing tools.

☑ ONGOING ASSESSMENT: Monitor and Reinforce

If students often imitate the textbook examples or other examples you show the class, try this strategy.

Have students work in small groups to answer questions or complete exercises. The discussion and interaction should encourage students to	rely more on their own ideas and strategies. The stimulation from their peers should lead to more original ideas and less imitation.

Planning to Write

Some writing occurs almost automatically. You can fill out a form or leave a phone message without much thought. Other writing requires careful planning. Suppose you are working on an investigative report or a personal essay. If you skip the planning, you might end up frustrated, anxious, or short of time. Structuring your writing life can help you avoid these setbacks.

Organize Your Environment

You need to find and create an environment that supports your writing process.

Choose a Conducive Location Select a place to work where you know you can write productively. Consider each element of your writing environment: the materials available, the mood or feeling of the place, and the presence of distractions or potential inspirations. Of course, you may not always be able to set up the perfect writing environment, so learning to adapt is another important writer's skill. For example, if you have to work in a noisy cafeteria, listening to quiet music on headphones might help you block out the distractions.

Budget Your Time A deadline may be inspiring or intimidating. To make a long-term deadline work for you instead of against you, it is important to break it down into short-term goals. Estimate the amount of time you will need for each step of the writing process. Allow enough time in your schedule for stages that take more time than expected. You may want to include group conferences or peer-review meetings in your deadline schedule, but remember to notify others of any changes.

Stop When You Still Have Something to Say When working on a long project, stop working when you still have some ideas left. If you do, you will know exactly where to begin when you start again. Ernest Hemingway described this strategy by saying that he "learned never to empty the well of [his] writing, but always to stop when there was still something there in the deep part of the well, and let it refill at night from the springs that fed it." Jot down a few notes on your plans; then, return to them when you are fresh and ready to write more.

▲ **Critical Viewing**
How might an audiocassette recorder help you collect and develop ideas? **[Analyze]**

Deadlines for Investigative Report

Sept. 18: Brainstorming session with team.

Sept. 20: Choose topic and begin research.

Sept. 27: Complete research. Assemble notes.

Sept. 29: Develop outline.

Oct. 1: Finish first draft.

Oct. 3: Review draft with peer-review team.

Oct. 4: Finish revising report. Proofread draft.

Oct. 8: Report due.

The Writer in You • 5

Sharing Your Work

Work With Others

You will often want to include other people in your writing process. From equal collaborators to helpful peer reviewers, other people can invigorate and improve your writing skills.

Group Brainstorming Writer's block can be frustrating and numbing. If you're stuck for an idea, it can be difficult to find one on your own. Try brainstorming with a group to generate potential ideas. The key to successful brainstorming is not to be critical. Let ideas flow, good and bad. You can always evaluate them later.

Collaborative Writing Writing collaboratively means sharing the steps of the writing process. You might divide jobs for a long project, such as researching and organizing. You can also work more closely, cooperating on each necessary step. Discuss your choices carefully, and make sure each team member has equal input.

Peer Reviewing An "outsider" can often catch mistakes and confusing statements that you, as the writer, may be too close to the project to see. Ask a peer reviewer—a fellow student—to help you catch mistakes and point out parts of your writing that need further elaboration, as well as passages that are particularly strong.

Publish

Sharing your work with an audience can be a satisfying conclusion to any writing project. Your work in print might even inspire other young writers to reach new writing goals. A number of organizations and groups publish the works of students. Look for opportunities to publish your writing, whether through a student Web site or a magazine contest. Ask your librarian or teacher for suggestions, or consult the list of publications on page 901.

Writers in ACTION

> *Editors can help a writer identify passages that aren't working. Author Toni Morrison thinks of a good editor as a "third eye." She praises an editor's ability to be "cool" and "dispassionate" because he or she is not as involved as the writer. "Sometimes it's uncanny: the editor puts his or her finger on exactly the place the writer thought it might fly, but wasn't sure. Good editors identify that place, and sometimes make suggestions."*

▼ **Critical Viewing** Suppose that this group of students is collaborating on a literary analysis. How might they divide their writing tasks? **[Analyze]**

What Are the Qualities of Good Writing?

Ideas Strong ideas are the starting point for good writing. Try to begin each piece of writing by focusing on a topic that interests you. In addition, consider whether an idea you are writing about will interest your audience. If not, you may want to consider writing about something else.

Organization Present your ideas and details in a consistent, organized manner that will be easy for readers to follow. Often, your topic and the type of writing that you are doing will dictate a particular method of organization. For example, if you are telling a story, you'll probably want to present events in the order in which they occur.

Voice Voice refers to all of the qualities that make your writing different from that of others. It includes the way you use words and sentences, the types of topics you write about, and the perspective that you bring to those topics. Whenever you write, let your personal voice come through in your writing.

Word Choice Words are the building blocks of a piece of writing. The stronger each block is, the stronger the finished piece will be. Carefully choose each word you use. Make sure that it conveys your intended meaning as precisely as possible. In addition to conveying your meaning, your words should also capture your attitude toward your subject.

Sentence Fluency Read your work aloud to see that each sentence flows smoothly from one to the next. Use transitions to connect your sentences, and vary the length and structure of your sentences to help build a rhythm.

Conventions Don't let errors spoil the impact of your work. Take care to ensure that you have followed the conventions of English grammar, usage, mechanics, and spelling.

Reflecting on Your Writing

Self-questioning is useful for honing your writing skills. Here are some questions that can lead you to discover more about the writer in you:

- Which of your recent writing projects was most successful? Why did you connect so well with this project?
- What specific obstacles have you faced when writing? What strategies might you use to overcome these obstacles?
- What writers do you admire? How does reading their work suggest ideas you can apply to your own writing?

The Writer in You • 7

Integrating Grammar Skills

Stress that writers must have good grammar skills. If they do not, readers might not be able to understand their ideas. Challenge students to review the basic grammar rules when revising their writing.

Lesson Objectives

1. To use writing to discover, organize, and support what is known and what needs to be learned about a topic
2. To recognize how visual and sound techniques or design convey messages in media
3. To write in a voice and a style appropriate to audience and purpose

Analyzing How Meaning Is Communicated Through the Arts

1. Review each of the six art forms with the class. Poll students about their interests in each of the areas.

2. Ask for specific examples of several of these art forms and have students offer their thoughts about what ideas or moods are conveyed by the specific pieces. Alternatively, you might bring in and share such well-known works as Van Gogh's *Starry Night* or Tchaikovsky's "1812 Overture" and have students discuss the meaning they find in these works.

3. Divide the class into groups according to students' interest in one of the art forms. Students should find specific examples of the art form and explain how meaning is created. Give students the initiative to find the necessary books, videotapes, or pictures.

4. Have each group share its findings with the class.

Viewing and Representing

Activity Give interested students the opportunity to share their journal entries with the class. If they were inspired by a work of art, film, or music, suggest that they incorporate a visual or audio portion of the work as part of their presentation.

Analyzing How Meaning Is Communicated Through the Arts

Overview

In the chapters that follow, you'll learn a wide variety of ways to express yourself through writing. You can also express yourself through other art forms. Below are some of these art forms.

- **Fine Art** creates meaning through color, line, texture, and subject. Paintings, sketches, sculpture, and collage can convey literal or abstract ideas.

- **Photography** uses still images to create meaning. While a photograph captures still images on film, photographers express ideas through subject, composition, and lighting.

- **Theater** is designed to be performed by actors on a stage. Using props, scenery, sound effects, and lighting, drama brings a story to life. In some cases, music, songs, and dance are incorporated into the story line. For example, in an opera, the story is told completely through song.

- **Film** captures sound and motion to convey an idea. Like dramatic theater, most film tells a story and uses setting, costumes, and characterization to develop a story. A filmmaker can portray a unique point of view using camera angles, lighting, and sound techniques.

- **Music** uses sound to impart meaning. Whether presented as a clarinet solo, an operatic performance, or a symphony, music can create moods or present variations on a theme.

- **Dance** displays meaning through organized movement. It can be performed by a single person, a pair, or large groups.

Introducing Spotlight on the Humanities In the Spotlight on the Humanities features, you will discover how all art is connected—layer upon layer—and how the inspiration that moved the hearts and minds of artists in the past continues to touch artists today.

Writing Activity

Think of a time when you felt inspired to create. Whether it was something artistic or practical, write a journal entry describing your experience as you remember it.

▲ **Critical Viewing**
What ideas can be expressed through a dance like the one shown here?
[Analyze]

Critical Viewing

Analyze Students may mention that specific dances are representative of certain cultures. Also, dance often conveys a mood or attitude and may even relate stories.

Media and Technology Skills

▶ *Lesson Objectives*

1. To use a variety of forms and technologies to communicate specific messages
2. To use technology for aspects of creating, revising, editing, and publishing

Making Technology Work for You

Activity: Experiment With a Variety of Tools

Technology can help you develop effective writing strategies. Familiarize yourself with the tools available in your classroom, computer lab, library, and home. Here are a few types of technology that many writers employ.

Word-Processing Software Using a word processor simplifies many basic writing tasks. For example, moving a sentence from the beginning to the end of a paragraph is a simple cut-and-paste operation. This chart shows some common word-processing features.

Search and Replace	Also known as a "global replace," this tool can help you quickly change a recurring word.
Spelling and Grammar Check	Many word processors include tools to check your spelling and grammar. These can find many errors, but they do not replace proofreading.
Undo/Redo	These functions allow you to change your mind when you are writing or revising.

Desktop-Publishing Software You might decide to design a newsletter, flyer, brochure, or other work that combines graphics and text. Desktop-publishing software helps you design your project from beginning to end. You can enter text and style fonts. You can also add original art, clip art from professional sources, or photographs.

The Internet The Internet is a worldwide network of computers. When you sign on, you connect your computer to this network and can collect information from sources throughout the world. The Internet is a valuable research tool that contains millions of pages of information on every subject from Abigail Adams to Zoology.

E-mail You might use e-mail (electronic mail) to keep in touch with friends or students at other schools. You can also share samples of your writing through e-mail attachments, allowing a student hundreds of miles away to help you revise a draft. E-mail is also a useful way to request information from businesses or government organizations.

Media and Technology Skills • 9

A Few Good Tools

Using tools can help you expand your idea of what a writer does. Consider these possibilities:

- Audiocassette recorders can capture brainstorming sessions or group improvisations.
- Videocassette recorders can collect images for multimedia presentations.
- Scanners allow you to convert photos and artwork into electronic files for use in word-processing or desktop-publishing files.
- Digital cameras take photographs that can be included in computer documents.
- Film cameras take pictures that can be included in brochures or newspapers. You can also have film developed as electronic files. Ask your photo developer for more information.

Step-by-Step Teaching Guide

Making Technology Work for You

1. Invite students to share their experiences with the technology described on this page, especially desktop publishing or locating information through Internet searches. Perhaps some students have experience in creating a personal Web page.

2. Encourage students to describe any times they have used scanners or digital cameras. If possible, have knowledgeable students demonstrate how to use technology to help with an aspect of writing.

3. Discuss how new technologies change the way we get information and also how we understand that information once we have it. Ask students to contrast word processing with typing, for example, and printing presses with Internet publishing.

Customize for
Gifted and Talented Students

Encourage students to use desktop publishing to create a publicity piece for an upcoming school or community event. Have them incorporate clip art or a scanned photograph, if possible. Encourage students to consider how they will present their information. Will they write a list or an essay?

Integrating Workplace Skills

Ask students to consider the importance of computer skills in today's workplace. How important will these skills be in the future? How might gaining more knowledge of technology affect their value to an employer? How might learning new computer skills affect the number or kinds of jobs open to them?

Lesson Objectives

1. To write a response to a test prompt
2. To organize ideas in writing to ensure coherence, logical progression, and support for ideas
3. To demonstrate control over grammatical elements

Step-by-Step Teaching Guide

The Writer in You

Teaching Resources: Standardized Test Preparation Workbook, pp. 1–2

1. Emphasize to students that their key to success in most standardized essay tests is to address the question being asked. Students should read the questions carefully and confine their answers to the topic area indicated.

2. Remind students that preliminary drafting for essays need not be extensive. Often, it is enough to jot down several key words that will help them remember their main points.

3. Reassure students that while neatness counts, examiners understand that the time constraints prevent most standardized tests of this kind from being finished products.

4. As practice for a writing test, have students write in response to the sample prompt on this page.

Standardized Test Preparation Workshop

The Writer in You

Writing is an important part of many standardized tests. On such tests, you will be given a prompt or topic about which to write. When responding to this prompt, you will often have to work within a set time period.

When your work is evaluated, the scorers will look to see that

- you have responded directly to the prompt and performed all of the activities it includes.
- your writing is well-organized and easy-to-follow.
- you have presented and developed a main point and thoroughly supported your main point with facts, examples, and other types of details.
- you have used lively, engaging language.
- you have avoided errors in grammar, usage, mechanics, and spelling.

The process of writing for a test, or any kind of writing, can be divided into stages. Plan to use a specific amount of time for prewriting, drafting, revising, and proofreading.

Following is an example of one type of writing prompt you might find on a standardized test. Use the suggestions on the following page to help you respond. The clocks next to each stage suggest a plan for organizing your time.

Test Tip

Read the test prompt carefully and focus your preparation on the answer. Then, analyze the prompt to provide the types of detail and explanation required.

Sample Prompt

Respond to the following questions in a brief essay. Back up each of your points with examples drawn from your own experience.

In your experience as a writer up to this point, which techniques have you found to be most effective? Why? Which techniques have you found to be less effective? Why?

 TEST-TAKING TIP

Suggest that students allow a few minutes to think about their writing plan before they set down a timeline.

Explain to students that, because tests are timed, it is important to organize their points during the prewriting stage since there will not be time to go back and reorganize what they

want to say. This will also make drafting the final paper much easier.

Reassure students that, though they should try to be as neat as possible, examiners understand that tests will probably contain crossed-out lines and insertions.

Prewriting

Allow about a quarter of your time for prewriting.

Prepare a List Quickly list various techniques you have used as a writer, and note why these have or have not been effective.

Review Your List and Narrow Your Focus Review your list, and circle the techniques that you consider most and least effective. Then, arrange the techniques in order from least to most effective. Begin with techniques that you did not find effective.

Drafting

Allow about half of your time for drafting.

Write More Slowly Than Usual You may be working within a set time frame. However, it is important to draft slowly and carefully when you are writing an essay for a standardized test because you will have less time to revise than you will in other writing situations. Review your notes and think through each sentence as you write it so that you can minimize the number of changes you will have to make.

Establish Your Main Points In your introduction, briefly touch on each of the techniques that you will be discussing. Also, try to begin with an attention-grabbing opening sentence.

Elaborate Devote one paragraph to each technique. Elaborate on the technique by providing detailed examples from your own experience. Describe each example as thoroughly as possible, and explain the outcome of using each technique.

Leave a Lasting Impression End with a conclusion that sums up your writing experiences. Consider offering predictions about what you expect to learn as you continue to develop as a writer. Try to end with a concluding sentence that will leave a lasting impression on those who will evaluate your work.

Revising, Editing, and Proofreading

Allow about a quarter of your time to revise, edit, and proofread your work.

Check for Missing Details Review your essay to see whether you have left out any important details. If you find that you have, add the details. Do so neatly, using a caret [^] to indicate where the added material is to be inserted.

Eliminate Errors Check your work carefully for errors in grammar, usage, mechanics, and spelling. These types of errors can hurt your test score.

Time and Resource Manager

In-Depth Lesson Plan

	LESSON FOCUS	PRINT AND MEDIA RESOURCES
DAY 1	**Introduction to the Writing Process** Students become familiar with the modes of writing and the five stages of the writing process. (pp. 12–13/⊞4–5)	*Writing and Grammar* Interactive Text, Ch. 2, Introduction **Teaching Resources** *Writing Support Transparencies*, 2-A
DAY 2	**Prewriting** Students learn strategies for choosing and narrowing a topic, considering audience and purpose, and gathering details. (pp. 14–17/⊞6–9)	*Writing and Grammar* Interactive Text, Section 2.1 **Teaching Resources** *Writing Support Transparencies*, 2-B–F; *Writing Support Activity Book*, 2-1–3
DAY 3	**Drafting** Students learn strategies for shaping their writing and providing elaboration. (p. 18/⊞10)	*Writing and Grammar* Interactive Text, Section 2.2 **Teaching Resources** *Writing Support Transparencies*, 2-H
DAY 4	**Revising** Students learn strategies for revising sentences, paragraphs, and overall structure. (pp. 19–21/⊞11–13)	*Writing and Grammar* Interactive Text, Section 2.3 **Teaching Resources** *Writing Support Transparencies*, 2-I
DAY 5	**Editing and Proofreading; Publishing and Presenting** Students learn strategies for checking their work and presenting their final drafts. (pp. 22–23/⊞14–15)	*Writing and Grammar* Interactive Text, Sections 2.4–5 **Teaching Resources** *Writing Support Transparencies*, 2-J; *Formal Assessment*, Ch. 2

Accelerated Lesson Plan

	LESSON FOCUS	PRINT AND MEDIA RESOURCES
DAY 1	**Introduction to the Writing Process; Prewriting** Students become familiar with the five steps of the writing process and learn strategies for prewriting. (pp. 12–17/⊞4–9)	*Writing and Grammar* Interactive Text, Ch. 2, Introduction through Section 2.1 **Teaching Resources** *Writing Support Transparencies*, 2-A–F; *Writing Support Activity Book*, 2-1–4
DAY 2	**Drafting Through Presenting** Students learn strategies for drafting, revising, editing, and presenting their writing. (pp. 18–23/⊞10–15)	*Writing and Grammar* Interactive Text, Sections 2.2–5 **Teaching Resources** *Writing Support Transparencies*, 2-G–K; *Formal Assessment*, Ch. 2

Options for Adapting Lesson Plans

HOMEWORK

Have students complete any stage of the lesson for homework.

FEATURES

Extend coverage with Spotlight on the Humanities (p. 24), Media and Technology Skills (p. 25), and the Standardized Test Preparation Workshop (p. 26).

TECHNOLOGY

Students can complete any stage of the lesson on the computer, using *Writing and Grammar* Interactive Text or a word-processing program. Have them print out their completed work.

Writing and Grammar Handbook Alignment

Page numbers in Step-by-Step Teaching Guides in this Teacher's Edition refer to pages from the full student text. Handbook page references, indicated with this icon 🄷, are provided in Time and Resource Manager boxes and at the bottom of each Teacher's Edition page.

INTEGRATED SKILLS COVERAGE

Viewing and Representing
Critical Viewing, SE pp. 12, 24/🄷4
Comparing Themes in Different Media, SE p. 24
ATE p. 24

Speaking and Listening
ATE pp. 16, 21

Technology
SE pp. 22, 25/🄷14; ATE p. 25

Workplace Skills
ATE p. 14

Real-World Connection
ATE p. 22

ASSESSMENT SUPPORT

Standardized Test Preparation Workshop, SE p. 26; ATE p. 21
Standardized Test Preparation Workbook, pp. 3–4
Formal Assessment, Ch. 2

MEETING INDIVIDUAL NEEDS

Less Advanced Students ATE pp. 15, 27. See also Ongoing Assessments, ATE pp. 16, 20.
More Advanced Students ATE pp. 17, 27
ESL Students ATE pp. 14, 19, 23
Gifted and Talented Students ATE p. 18
Interpersonal Learners ATE p. 19
Logical/Mathematical Learners ATE p. 22

BLOCK SCHEDULING

Pacing Suggestions
For 90-minute Blocks
• Have students complete the Introduction and the Prewriting and Drafting strategies in a single period.
• Focus one class period on Revising, Editing and Proofreading, and Publishing and Presenting strategies.

Resources for Varying Instruction
• *Writing and Grammar* Interactive Text A 90-minute block provides an ideal opportunity for students to work on the computer.

Professional Development Support
• *How to Manage Instruction in the Block* This teaching resource provides management and activity suggestions.

MEDIA AND TECHNOLOGY

For the Student
• *Writing and Grammar* Interactive Text, Ch. 2

For the Teacher
• Teacher**EXPRESS**™ CD-ROM

WRITING AND GRAMMAR ON-LINE

Interactive Text (On-line or on CD-ROM)
• Easily navigable instruction with interactive Revision Checkers
• Full use of e-rater™, the essay-scoring system (on-line only)

Companion Web Site PHSchool.com
• Scoring rubrics with models (use Web Code eek-1001)

See the Go On-line! **feature, SE p. iii.**

▶ Lesson Objectives

1. To write in a variety of forms for various audiences and purposes
2. To analyze strategies that writers in different fields use to compose
3. To use prewriting strategies to generate ideas, develop voice, and plan
4. To use writing to formulate questions, refine topics, and clarify ideas
5. To organize ideas in writing to ensure coherence, logical progression, and support for ideas
6. To represent information in a variety of ways, such as graphics, conceptual maps, and learning logs
7. To develop and revise drafts in terms of structure, paragraphs, sentences, and word choice
8. To edit and proofread to ensure standard English usage and grammar
9. To respond productively to peer review of one's own work
10. To refine selected work for publication

Critical Viewing

Analyze Students will observe that the on-line catalog helps them find more and more varied sources for writing.

Chapter 2 — A Walk Through the Writing Process

Writing, in one form or another, is an essential component of your daily life. Whatever your final product, the writing process—a systematic approach to writing—can help you achieve it. From prewriting to publishing and presenting, being familiar with and using the stages of the writing process will help you write better.

▲ **Critical Viewing** Identify one way in which computers in the library can improve your writing process. **[Analyze]**

Types of Writing

There are many types of writing. The various types can be grouped into **modes**, a word that refers to the central purpose of a piece of writing. The chart at right shows the modes you'll encounter in this book.

Writing can also be divided into two broader categories: reflexive and extensive, based on the source of inspiration and audience for a piece of writing. When you write reflexively, you choose what to write, what format to use, and whether to share your writing with others. **Reflexive writing**—such as a journal entry, a personal essay, or a list—is writing you do for yourself. **Extensive writing**, which focuses on topics outside of your imagination and experience, is writing that you do for others. Examples of extensive writing include research papers, persuasive essays, and book and theater reviews.

The Modes of Writing
- Narration
- Description
- Persuasion
- Exposition
- Research
- Response to Literature
- Assessment
- Workplace

12 • A Walk Through the Writing Process

⏱ TIME AND RESOURCE MANAGER

Resources
Print: *Writing Support Transparencies,* 2-A

Using the Full Student Edition	Using the Handbook🕀
• Cover pp. 12–13 in class.	• Cover pp. 4–5 in class.
• Ask students to describe the differences between extensive and reflexive kinds of writing.	• Ask students to describe the differences between extensive and reflexive kinds of writing.
• Use Transparency 2-A to give students an overview of the writing process.	• Use Transparency 2-A to give students an overview of the writing process.

The Process of Writing

The process of writing occurs in several stages:

- **Prewriting** includes exploring topics, choosing a topic, and beginning to gather and organize details before you write.
- **Drafting** involves getting your ideas down on paper in roughly the format you intend for the finished work.
- **Revising** is the stage in which you rework your first draft to improve its content and structure.
- **Editing and proofreading** involve correcting errors in grammar, spelling, and mechanics.
- **Publishing and presenting** are the sharing of your work with others.

These stages may appear to follow a set sequence, but as writers work, they often skip stages or shift back to earlier stages. For example, as you draft, you may begin making revisions in your work; or as you revise, you may discover that you need to go back and gather more ideas.

A Guided Tour

Use this chapter as a guided tour of the stages of the writing process. Familiarize yourself with the activities of writing. Learn new strategies, look at the way other effective writers employ them, and try them out yourself. In the chapters that follow, you'll see how to apply these and other strategies to specific types of writing.

A Walk Through the Writing Process • 13

 Interest GRABBER Have students write brief descriptions of themselves, not including their names, but including any details that they think might help someone guess their identity. This could include favorite clothes, friends, hobbies, clubs, best subjects, or where they live. Collect papers and hand them out randomly, and then have students guess whose description they received. Then, ask students how they decided which details to include and how to organize them.

Activate Prior Knowledge

Ask students to discuss recent occasions when they have written either formally or informally. Remind them that diaries, employment applications, letters, and e-mails are all forms of composition. List examples students share on the board under the headings "Extensive Writing" and "Reflexive Writing." Discuss each type of writing with the class.

Step-by-Step Teaching Guide

The Process of Writing

Teaching Resources: Writing Support Transparencies, 2-A

1. After students have reviewed the different types of writing, ask them to share what they know or have experienced of the writing process.

2. You may wish to introduce students to the *Writers at Work* DVD, which also covers the modes of writing.

3. Display the transparency and ask students why they think the process is shown as a circle (a writer might need to go through the process more than once, revisiting steps as work takes shape).

4. Explain that this chapter will introduce them to sample strategies that can help them accomplish each of the stages in the process.

☑ **ONGOING ASSESSMENT: Diagnose**

Use one of the following options to diagnose students' current level of familiarity with the writing process.

Option 1 Ask each student to bring in the strongest sample of his or her writing from last year. Hold conferences in which you review each student's work. Use the conferences to determine which students will need extra support.

Option 2 Ask students to describe their bedrooms. Have them detail their furniture, "toys," clothing, and so on. Students who have difficulty completing this exercise may need extra help.

Prewriting: Choosing Your Topic

Teaching Resources: Writing Support Transparencies, 2-B

1. Explain to students that blueprinting is only one possible strategy among many. These strategies are designed to help trigger ideas for writing.

2. Using Transparency 2-B, point out the level of detail in the sample blueprint. Show that there is some detail, but that students may add more, if it helps them think of topics. Also explain that these "blueprints" could be done for other rooms, such as students' bedrooms, or for parks, neighborhoods, or stores. The objective is to generate topic ideas.

3. Give students the option of working in pairs to generate this first blueprint. When students have begun to work, ask volunteers for permission to share some of their works in progress. Students should reflect on the level of detail, both in the shared work and in their own.

Customize for
ESL Students

As you cover the prewriting strategies, define each term. You may wish to show pictures of blueprints or demonstrate the looping strategy. Then, clarify how the strategies help in the prewriting stage. Encourage students to translate the definitions of these terms into their first languages and record them in their writers' notebooks.

Integrating Workplace Skills

Explain that, while it might seem as though choosing topics is a skill limited to the classroom, it is an ability that often helps in the workplace. Work assignments may be based on an employee's ability to define a topic he or she would like to pursue or to identify what issues need discussion.

2.1 *What Is Prewriting?*

Most writers feel challenged when faced with a blank sheet of paper. Writers may grapple with what topic to write about, or they may wonder just how much they have to say about a subject. The prewriting stage helps to get a writer's creative juices flowing. Just as musicians prepare for a performance by practicing, you can warm up to write with your own set of prewriting strategies and techniques.

Choosing Your Topic

To begin writing, you must have a topic. Usually, it is best to write about what you know or about what you find interesting. Take time to explore subjects, issues, and experiences that are meaningful to you. You can use a wide variety of strategies to generate topics. Try this sample strategy:

SAMPLE STRATEGY

Blueprinting When you blueprint, you draw a map of a place you know well. To try this strategy, draw a floor plan of a classroom in your school. Fill in the room plan with symbols for desks, chairs, computers, chalkboards, bookshelves, windows, doorways, pictures, and whatever else is appropriate. Think about significant events that this room calls to mind, and list the ideas on your blueprint. From that list, select a topic to develop.

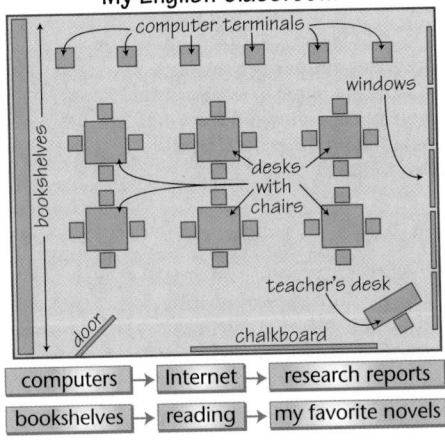

My English Classroom

computers → Internet → research reports
bookshelves → reading → my favorite novels

Learn More

For additional prewriting strategies suited to specific writing tasks, see Chapters 4–15.

⏱ TIME AND RESOURCE MANAGER

Resources
Print: *Writing Support Transparencies, 2-B–F; Writing Support Activity Book, 2-1-3*

Using the Full Student Edition	Using the Handbook Ⓗ
• Cover pp. 14–17 in class. • Work through the four sample strategies, using the transparencies as needed. • Have students complete the Applying the Prewriting Strategies activities (p. 17) in class.	• Cover pp. 6–9 in class. • Work through the four sample strategies, using the transparencies as needed. • Have students complete the Applying the Prewriting Strategies activities (p. 9) in class.

Narrowing Your Topic

Once you have selected a writing topic, make sure it is not so general that you can't cover it thoroughly in a short piece of writing. Consider whether you can narrow your topic by focusing on a single subtopic or aspect of it. One strategy you might use is shown below.

SAMPLE STRATEGY

Looping to Narrow a Topic Looping is a way of discovering and focusing on the features of a topic that are most important or interesting to you. Begin by freewriting on a general topic, such as sports, friends, or favorite books. Write for five minutes. Then, review what you have written. Circle the most important or significant word. Next, freewrite based on that word for five more minutes. Once again, circle the most important or significant word, and freewrite about it. Continue looping until you are satisfied that your topic is narrow enough. Look at this example:

Looping

Broad topic: Reading
I think I enjoy the time I spend reading because it is private time.

Reading is something I can really get lost in. When I'm reading a

great book, not much can distract me.

Reading gives me an alternative to the everyday realities of my own

life and is a great way to disregard anything that annoys me.
Great book:
Novels especially appeal to me for lots of reasons. Sometimes

characters seem really strange and foreign to me, and other times

I can really relate to them. I like to be pulled into the life of another

character, to feel like I'm experiencing the world being presented in

that novel, and to learn new things.
Narrowed topic:
The characters in novels make reading appealing to me.

Prewriting: Narrowing Your Topic

Teaching Resources: Writing Support Transparencies, 2-C

1. Explain to students that narrowing a topic is not always necessary. Sometimes, students' first topic is an ideal length for research. Sometimes, however, an interesting topic is too broad for treatment in an essay. For example, "National Parks of the U.S." would be a suitable topic for an entire book, while "My Week at Yellowstone" or "The History of Old Faithful" might be better suited to an essay.

2. Display Transparency 2-C to illustrate how looping may be used to narrow a topic. Show how the general topic, reading, has been expanded through freewriting and then how the key ideas have been circled, with "loops" connecting ideas and leading to the final, narrowed topic ("The characters in novels make reading appealing to me").

3. Have students freewrite for five minutes. Have them circle key words or ideas and then repeat the process, freewriting about the key words or ideas they circled. Ask volunteers to share some of their narrowed topics.

4. If students need a topic suggestion to get them started, provide them with a general one such as "school" or "leisure," which allows broad latitude for students to find their own direction.

Customize for
Less Advanced Students

After students freewrite, have them work with a partner to identify the key ideas. They may continue their freewriting based on those ideas and then discuss the next level of the process with their partners, again helping one another identify key ideas in what is written.

Prewriting: Considering Your Audience and Purpose

Teaching Resources: Writing Support Transparencies, 2-D; Writing Support Activity Book, 2-1

1. Review page 16 with students. Discuss how identifying and understanding your readers can affect what you write for them. (The age, background, or experience of your intended audience should determine the language and level of detail that you employ.)

2. Write the following questions on the board.

   Are there terms or concepts I will need to explain?

   Do I need to "win over" the audience, or are they already interested in the topic?

   What do I want my audience to do, think, or feel after reading this?

3. Identify several different audiences (examples: a parent group, elementary-school children, peers) on the board. Ask students to suggest sample topics, such as the Internet, conflict resolution, or school dress codes. Have them discuss the purposes they might have for writing about these topics and how their writing might differ for the audiences listed.

Integrating Speaking and Listening Skills

Explain to students that considering audience and purpose is also vital in spoken communication. When students speak to friends, the vocabulary and tone they use will differ from those they use when speaking with a parent. Considering audience and purpose is vital in situations such as a job interview, when success depends on speaking carefully, precisely, and appropriately and in listening carefully for feedback.

Considering Your Audience and Purpose

After you've narrowed your topic, identify your audience—the person or people who will read your work—and your purpose—what you want your writing to accomplish. Your audience and purpose will affect the type of language you use and the types of information you present.

Considering Your Audience It is best not to develop a piece of writing without thinking about who is going to read it. Consider your audience's age, interests, and knowledge of your subject. If you are writing for young children who know little about your topic, use simple language and include the most basic details. If, on the other hand, you are writing for experts or enthusiasts in the field, use sophisticated language and leave out extended explanations of basic details.

Develop an audience profile by asking and answering questions about your audience, such as those on the notepad below. Refer back to your audience profile as you develop your writing.

Considering Your Purpose Identify what you hope to accomplish with your writing. You may be writing to persuade, to entertain, to inform, or to achieve a variety of other specific purposes. Keep your purpose in mind as you decide which details to include, which to leave out, and what type of language to use.

Audience Profile

1. What does my audience already know?

2. What do they need to know?

3. What details will interest or influence my audience?

16 • A Walk Through the Writing Process

☑ ONGOING ASSESSMENT: Monitor and Reinforce

If you observe that students are having difficulty identifying their audience, try one of the following options.

Option 1 Suggest that students write to a very specific audience of one person—an older relative or a younger student.	**Option 2** Have students write down a brief profile of their intended audiences, including their level of education, background knowledge of the topic, and interest in the topic.

Gathering Details

Regardless of your subject, it is essential that you back up the points you make with examples, facts, and details. Generally, it is most effective to take some time to gather details before you begin writing. This may involve research in the library or on the Internet or interviews with experts. Consider these strategies for gathering details:

SAMPLE STRATEGY

Using Hexagonal Writing

Hexagonal writing helps you gather details about a literary work in order to write a well-balanced, complete analysis. Create a chart like the one at right. Then, follow the directions shown here to fill it out.

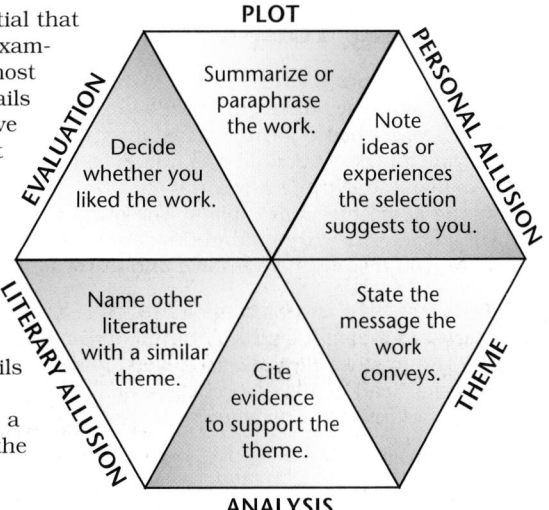

PLOT — Summarize or paraphrase the work.

PERSONAL ALLUSION — Note ideas or experiences the selection suggests to you.

EVALUATION — Decide whether you liked the work.

THEME — State the message the work conveys.

LITERARY ALLUSION — Name other literature with a similar theme.

ANALYSIS — Cite evidence to support the theme.

SAMPLE STRATEGY

Generating Sensory Word Bins When you are writing description, the words you use create an image for your reader. Identify your topic, and then list words that appeal to each of the senses. Look at this example:

Sensory Word Bin: A Summer Storm				
SIGHTS	**SOUNDS**	**SMELLS**	**TASTES**	**PHYSICAL SENSATIONS**
glistening foggy murky	thunder splashes muffled	freshness springlike		heat breeze

▶ **APPLYING THE PREWRITING STRATEGIES**

1. Construct a blueprint of a special place. Then, use your blueprint to identify potential writing topics.
2. Use looping to narrow a topic generated by your blueprint.
3. Identify two different audiences, and devise corresponding audience profiles for an account of a memorable vacation.
4. Use hexagonal writing to gather details about a short story or novel you have recently read.

 Internet Tip

Using an Internet browser, you can conduct a keyword search on your topic. Be as specific as possible when entering key words, so that you don't come up with more information than you can manage.

Step-by-Step Teaching Guide

Prewriting: Using Hexagonal Writing

Teaching Resources: Writing Support Transparencies, 2-E; Writing Support Activity Book, 2-2

1. Discuss with students the prompts on the six sides of the hexagon.
2. Explain that they will not always have responses for all six prompts in the hexagon, but students should consider each when planning a writing project.
3. Hand out the activity sheet (2-2) and have students work through the six strategies, using a story that the class has recently read.

Step-by-Step Teaching Guide

Prewriting: Generating Sensory Word Bins

Teaching Resources: Writing Support Transparencies, 2-F; Writing Support Activity Book, 2-3

1. Display Transparency 2-F to show students how to generate lists of sensory words. Give students copies of the blank organizer (2-3).
2. Ask students to fill out the word bin based on a topic of their choice. Ask volunteers to read their words to the class.

Customize for
More Advanced Students

Students may want to demonstrate their proficiency in other prewriting strategies. Allow them to choose one of the four steps (*choose a topic, narrow a topic, consider audience and purpose, gather details*) and present their own strategies to the class.

⏱ TIME SAVERS!

 Writing Support Transparencies
Use the transparencies for Chapter 2 to facilitate the teaching of strategies.

 Writing Support Activity Book
Use the graphic organizers for Chapter 2 to facilitate student planning.

Drafting: Shaping Your Writing

1. Ask students to discuss some of the forms they may have used for writing and to describe the advantages and disadvantages of each.

2. Explain that a good lead need not always be arresting, but it must let the reader know that there is a good reason to continue, such as learning something they want to know or finding out how the story resolves.

Drafting: Using the SEE Method

Teaching Resources: Writing Support Transparencies, 2-H

1. Explain to students that the "statement" identified as the first element of the SEE method is a statement of a main idea or topic for a paragraph. For example, "Poodles are great pets."

2. Extending the topic involves expanding or restating the topic idea. For example, the extension might be, "These dogs are ideal in situations where other dogs might be unsuitable."

3. Explain that in elaboration the "evidence" given is information that either explains or supports the topic. To continue the example, "Because poodles have fur instead of hair, they don't shed. People who are allergic to other dogs usually aren't allergic to poodles. They are among the most intelligent of all dog breeds and are very brave, having originally been bred as hunting dogs."

Customize for
Gifted and Talented Students

Write a range of initial statements on cards, using topics with which students are likely to be familiar. Challenge students to extend and elaborate these statements in improvised monologues. Allow them one minute to consider and plan what they are going to say and then have them deliver a brief monologue on the topic described on their card.

2.2 What Is Drafting?

Shaping Your Writing

Match Purpose and Form Each form of writing is linked to a specific purpose. Make sure that your purpose in writing matches that of your chosen form. For instance, if you are writing an editorial, your purpose should be to influence the way others think or act. If you are writing a report or how-to essay, your purpose should be to inform or explain. The purpose of your chosen form will shape your writing, from the details you include to the organization you use. Keep your form and purpose in mind as you draft.

Pull Readers In With an Enticing Lead Begin with an interest-grabbing first paragraph to attract your audience's attention and to stoke their desire to keep reading. To hook with a powerful "lead," employ a controversial quotation, a little-known fact, a bizarre bit of dialogue, or a striking description.

Providing Elaboration

As you draft, elaborate on your main ideas, providing supporting facts, examples, statistics, and other details to help readers understand and accept your points. The SEE method is one strategy that you can use for elaboration.

SAMPLE STRATEGY

Using the SEE Method To use the SEE method (Statement, Extension, and Elaboration), begin each paragraph with a statement that conveys a main idea. Extend that idea by restating or explaining the first sentence. Elaborate on your explanation or restatement by providing supporting details.

STATEMENT: Family reunions can be fun.

EXTENSION: When you get together with relatives, you can enjoy the funny stories they tell.

ELABORATION: No matter how many times you hear about your brother's first report card, you'll still find the exaggerations of the story amusing.

▶ **APPLYING THE DRAFTING STRATEGIES**

1. Write a humorous or startling lead sentence for a description of a basketball game.
2. Complete the following statements. Then, use the SEE technique to elaborate your ideas.
   My favorite actor is ___?___.
   I'd like to travel to ___?___.

18 • A Walk Through the Writing Process

🔊 Learn More

You can learn about all of the various forms of writing in the writing chapters that follow.

⏱ TIME AND RESOURCE MANAGER	
Resources	
Print: *Writing Support Transparencies,* 2-H	
Using the Full Student Edition	**Using the Handbook H**
• Cover p. 18 in class.	• Cover p. 10 in class.
• Demonstrate and discuss the SEE Method.	• Demonstrate and discuss the SEE Method.
• Assign the Applying the Drafting Strategies activities to be completed in class.	• Assign the Applying the Drafting Strategies activities to be completed in class.

2.3 *What Is Revising?*

Using a Systematic Approach to Revision

Revision is probably the most important stage of the writing process. However, many writers also find it to be the most difficult. In this textbook, you will learn a systematic approach to revision called **ratiocination** (rash´ ē äs ə nā´shen). In everyday use, *ratiocination* refers to the process of reasoning using formal logic. In writing, it refers to the use of a logical step-by-step process to color-code, analyze, evaluate, and rework your writing.

Start by evaluating the overall structure of your work. Then, look at paragraphs, sentences, and words. Throughout the process, use a simple system of highlighting and color-coding to draw your attention to areas that need improvement.

Revising Your Overall Structure

There are a variety of things to look for when revising the overall structure of your work, including the following:

- Check to see that your organization makes sense and that it is consistent. You may find it necessary to reorganize parts of your paper.

- Make sure that your introduction will grab your readers' interest and that your conclusion will leave a lasting impression.

- Determine whether you have provided enough support for your main idea. One strategy you can use for this purpose is shown next.

SAMPLE STRATEGY

▶ **REVISION STRATEGY**
Color-Coding Support for Your Main Point

With a red pencil, underline the sentence or sentences that convey the main point of your paper. Then, use a blue pencil to underline the support you've provided for your main point. Once you've finished, you should find that much of your paper is underlined in blue. If not, you probably don't have enough support for your main point. Add more facts, details, or examples to strengthen your writing. In addition, you may want to consider whether all of the passages you have not underlined are necessary.

Writers in ACTION

In The Elements of Style, *William Strunk, Jr., and E. B. White say:*
"Revising is a part of writing. Few writers are so expert that they can produce what they are after on the first try."

What Is Revising? • 19

Step-by-Step Teaching Guide

Revising: Using a Systematic Approach to Revision

1. Explain to students that *ratiocination* means "exact thinking," or a "reasoned train of thought."

2. Point out that, while up until now the objective has been to simply get ideas and information down on paper, the revision stage is when they can fine-tune the structure and artistry of their writing.

3. Explain that the strategies for revision will help them identify the places where improvements can be made to a piece of writing.

4. Using a sample paragraph from a book or newspaper, demonstrate the color-coding strategy to show students how they can identify the support for the main idea(s) of their papers. Encourage students to take advantage of the revision stage to make certain their ideas are well supported.

Customize for *ESL Students*

Pair students with partners who are more fluent in English. Have them work together on the revision strategies in this section. Color-coding words and passages with a partner will provide students with practice and reinforcement of their reading skills. Suggestions and assistance from the more fluent partner will add to students' vocabulary, making it easier for them to avoid repetition in sentence leads or word choices.

Customize for *Interpersonal Learners*

Have students create examples, either from an article or from an item from their writing portfolios, of the revision techniques explained in this section, and have them demonstrate them for the class. Encourage students to give precise instructions on how writing can be improved by revising structure, paragraphs, sentences, or words.

⏱ TIME AND RESOURCE MANAGER

Resources
Print: *Writing Support Transparencies,* 2-1

Using the Full Student Edition	Using the Handbook🄗
• Cover pp. 19–21 in class.	• Cover pp. 11–13 in class.
• Using the chalkboard or an overhead projector, demonstrate the strategies used throughout this section.	• Using the chalkboard or an overhead projector, demonstrate the strategies used throughout this section.
• Assign the Applying the Revision Strategies activity, to be completed in class.	• Assign the Applying the Revision Strategies activity, to be completed in class.

Step-by-Step Teaching Guide

Revising: Using Steps, Stacks, Chains, and Balances

1. Ask students to identify things they have read, in class and out, that either used, or would benefit from using, one of these four strategies (examples: steps—a how-to manual or a recipe, as well as chronological narratives; stacks—informative essays, research papers; chains—persuasive writing, cause-and-effect writing; balances—movie reviews, product reports, comparison-and-contrast essays).

2. Explain that what matters most is that the chosen strategy works for whatever is being written. Transition words, such as *first, in addition,* or *however,* are simply methods of helping the reader follow the writer's ideas or arguments.

Step-by-Step Teaching Guide

Revising: Bracketing Sentence Openers

1. Explain that an important element of writing style is sentence variety. If all sentences have similar beginnings, the reader may lose interest.

2. Point out that bracketing sentence openers makes it obvious whether or not there is variety or repetition.

3. Write the following on the board, and lead students through the process of bracketing the openers and revising the sentences.

   I like going to the forest preserve. I love the trees and wildflowers. I also like the trails that run through the woods. I stop to watch the frogs by the pond.

4. Students will probably note that every sentence begins with "I." This paragraph can be strengthened by changing some openers. Sample rewrite:

   I like going to the forest preserve. The trees and wildflowers delight me. Trails lead me among the trees. At the side of a pond, I stop to watch the frogs.

Revising Your Paragraphs

Once you've reviewed the structure of your draft, check to see that each paragraph focuses on a single aspect of your topic and that all of the sentences within a paragraph relate to one another. Eliminate any sentences that are not clearly related to the others, and look for places where transitions can link the ideas within a paragraph.

SAMPLE STRATEGY

▶ **REVISION STRATEGY**
Using Steps, Stacks, Chains, and Balances

- **Steps** When a paragraph presents a series of events or explains a series of steps, check to see that you have used transitions to make the sequence clear to readers. If not, add words such as *first, then,* and *finally.*

- **Stacks** When a paragraph presents a series of related ideas, add transitions such as *in addition* and *as well as.* If certain ideas are more important than others, make sure that you have indicated this with transitions such as *most important.*

- **Chains** When a paragraph explains a cause-and-effect relationship, add transitions such as *consequently* and *as a result* to clarify the relationships among your details.

- **Balances** When the paragraph shows contrast or choice, add words such as *similarly, however, although,* and *rather.*

Revising Your Sentences

Next, study your sentences. Check to see that you have varied their length and structure. Using too many sentences of the same types can make your writing sound choppy.

SAMPLE STRATEGY

▶ **REVISION STRATEGY**
Bracketing Sentence Openers

Use a colored pen to bracket the first three words of each sentence. Review your paper, focusing only on the bracketed words. If you have begun most of your sentences in the same way, rework some of them to produce greater variety.

20 • A Walk Through the Writing Process

🔵 Learn More

You will learn more about how to achieve greater sentence variety in Chapter 21.

☑ **ONGOING ASSESSMENT: Monitor and Reinforce**

If you observe that students are having difficulty with the revising stage, use the following strategy.

After students have bracketed sentence openers and/or repeated words in their drafts, have them exchange their drafts with a partner. Have the partners discuss the sentences or phrases that are bracketed, looking for ways to make them clearer or more interesting. This may involve making suggestions or asking questions for clarification. Remind students that, as they answer questions, they should jot down notes, since these answers may be useful in revising their drafts.

Revising Your Word Choice

Complete the process of revision by analyzing words you have used. Look for places where you can replace vague or general words with ones that more precisely convey your meaning. Also, check to see whether you have overused certain words. The following strategy will help:

SAMPLE STRATEGY

▶ **REVISION STRATEGY**
Highlighting Repeated Words

Use a highlighter to mark any words you have used more than once. Review the words that you have marked, and consider replacing some to make your writing more lively. Look at this example:

Peer Review

Once you've finished revising on your own, you may want to enlist the help of classmates. Often, others can see problems that are hard for the writer to identify. Use these tips to get the specific feedback you want:

EVALUATING REPEATED WORDS

~~first flakes of snow began drifting down from the sky~~
The ~~snow began falling~~ early in the morning.
By early afternoon, the ground was covered with
fluffy white crystals
several inches of ~~snow.~~ When evening came,
it was still snowing heavily
~~the snow was still falling,~~ and by that time, ~~there~~
the landscape
was layered with at least a foot of soft white powder
~~was at least a foot of snow on the ground.~~

Focusing Peer Review	
Purpose	**Ask**
Evaluate introduction	What part of the introduction was most interesting?
Test argument	Which reason was most convincing?
	Which point was least compelling?

▶ **APPLYING THE REVISION STRATEGIES**

Select a piece of writing you did last year. Use the revision strategies presented here to make improvements in this piece. Identify four changes the strategies helped you make.

⬚ STANDARDIZED TEST PREPARATION WORKSHOP

Correcting Run-ons
Standardized tests may require students to recognize or correct run-on sentences.

Read the following sentences. Which one is not a run-on?

A The sky was covered with clouds it began to rain.

B The sky was covered with clouds, it began to rain.

C The sky was covered with clouds, and it began to rain.

D The sky was covered with clouds and it began to rain.

Students should recognize that **C** is not a run-on sentence. A comma itself cannot join two sentences, but a comma with a coordinating conjunction (and) can.

Step-by-Step Teaching Guide

Revising: Highlighting Repeated Words

Teaching Resources: Writing Support Transparencies, 2-I

1. Tell students that there are times when repeating a word is necessary, as with the use of technical terms, and times when it is a good strategy, as when driving home a point. Usually, however, the repeated use of a word or words becomes tedious for the reader.

2. Point out that students can use revision as an opportunity to learn new words as they research ways of saying things differently.

3. Using Transparency 2-I, point out how the passage on snow was made more descriptive. Note how each change not only uses different words but adds to the image of snow (*fluffy white crystals, soft white powder*).

4. Reassure students that they do not have to make every word different, as in this example, but they should aim for variety of expression.

Step-by-Step Teaching Guide

Revising: Peer Review

1. Have students choose a selection from their portfolios and write five questions to ask a peer reviewer.

2. Have students trade papers and question lists. When they finish reading, have them answer the questions and return papers and answers to their owners.

3. Reassure students that the writer has the last word on revisions. While they should consider comments from a peer reviewer, they are not required to incorporate them.

Integrating Speaking and Listening Skills

Students may benefit from seeing the peer review process modeled, so they know how to word their suggestions. Role-play a peer review conference with another teacher or with a student familiar with the peer review process.

Editing and Proofreading

Teaching Resources: Writing Support Transparencies, 2-J

1. Ask students to think about the disadvantages of having run-on sentences in their writing. (Run-on sentences make writing more difficult for the reader to follow. Run-on sentences show careless construction, and readers may think the writing is unreliable.)

2. Discuss what makes the first example sentence a run-on (the lack of transition between the two parts of the sentence).

3. Point out that the run-on sentence may be corrected by breaking it into two shorter sentences or by providing a transition word.

4. You may wish to point out that another way of modifying the sentence might be

   Some whales weigh as much as twenty elephants and have blood vessels wide enough for a trout to swim through.

   Here, the subject, *whales*, has two verbs, *weigh* and *have*; the second subject, *they*, is gone.

Real-World Connection

Proofreading is especially important in contexts such as advertisements, cover letters, and résumés. In these types of writing, the writer not only conveys information, but gives an impression of how thoughtful and thorough he or she has been about presenting the information.

Customize for
Logical/Mathematical Learners

Students who are learning to proofread may find it easier to mark changes if they use standard proofreading symbols such as delete marks, insertion marks, transposing symbols, and so on.

2.4 What Are Editing and Proofreading?

Once you have finished revising for content, proofread your work carefully to find and eliminate errors in grammar, usage, mechanics, and spelling. These types of errors will distract readers and may cause them to respond negatively to your work—even if the content is excellent.

Focusing on Proofreading

To check your writing for errors, get in the habit of reviewing your draft several times. Each time, focus on a specific proofreading topic. Consider these key areas:

Scrutinize Your Spelling The spell-check function of a word-processing program is never fully dependable. Refer to a dictionary to check the spelling of questionable words.

Follow the Conventions of Grammar, Usage, and Mechanics Apply these conventions to everything you write. Examine each sentence, and correct capitalization and punctuation. Check your grammar and usage, and eliminate problematic language or grammatical structures.

Eliminate Run-on Sentences One specific type of error that you may uncover while proofreading is a run-on sentence—two main clauses that are not adequately separated by punctuation. Look at this example:

CORRECTING RUN-ON SENTENCES

> Some whales weigh as much as twenty elephants, they have blood vessels wide enough for a trout to swim through!

Below are two ways to correct a run-on sentence:
- Break it into two simple sentences.

> Some whales weigh as much as twenty elephants. They have blood vessels wide enough for a trout to swim through!

- Rewrite it as a compound sentence.

> Some whales weigh as much as twenty elephants, and they have blood vessels wide enough for a trout to swim through!

▶ APPLYING THE EDITING
AND PROOFREADING STRATEGIES

With a partner, identify two grammar, usage, or mechanics errors in a recent piece of your writing. Then, discuss ways to locate and correct such problems during the proofreading stage.

22 • A Walk Through the Writing Process

Technology Tip

If your word processor has a spell-check feature, use it, but don't expect it to do the job of a good proofreader. Both *where* and *wear* will pass a spell check, but you may not have used the word you wanted.

⏱ TIME AND RESOURCE MANAGER

Resources
Print: *Writing Support Transparencies*, 2-J; *Formal Assessment*, Ch. 2
Technology: *Writing and Grammar* Interactive Text, Section 2.4

Using the Full Student Edition	Using the Handbook Ⓗ
• Cover pp. 22–23 in class. • Assign the Applying the Strategies activities to be completed in class. • Brainstorm for a list of ways to publish student writing.	• Cover pp. 14–15 in class. • Assign the Applying the Strategies activities to be completed in class. • Brainstorm for a list of ways to publish student writing.

2.5 What Are Publishing and Presenting?

Moving Forward

This preview of the writing process provides just a glimpse of the strategies and techniques you can employ in your writing process. Each lesson in this section provides specific strategies that will aid you as you write.

Building Your Portfolio Your finished writing products are valuable, so be sure to organize and save them in a folder, a box, or some other secure place. View your portfolio as a record of your development as a writer. Occasionally, you may return to it to compare your latest writing with something you wrote a while ago.

You can also use your portfolio as a repository for future writing ideas, including unfinished writing and thought-provoking photographs or clippings.

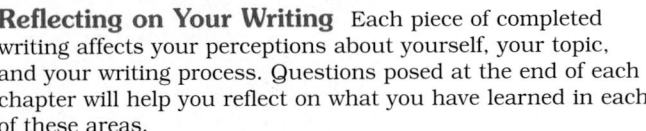

PORTFOLIO

Reflecting on Your Writing Each piece of completed writing affects your perceptions about yourself, your topic, and your writing process. Questions posed at the end of each chapter will help you reflect on what you have learned in each of these areas.

Assessing Your Writing A rubric, or set of criteria, on which your work can be evaluated is offered at the end of each chapter. To ensure that you are addressing the main points of the particular mode, refer to the rubric throughout the writing process.

▶ **APPLYING THE PUBLISHING AND PRESENTING STRATEGIES**

1. Reexamine the prewriting activities you used in this introduction to the writing process. Choose one you want to work into a fully developed piece of writing at a later time. Place it in your portfolio. Speak with a writing partner about what made you choose that particular activity.
2. In your writing journal, reflect on your writing process by responding to the following questions:

   • Which techniques helped you the most? Explain.
   • What are your strengths as a writer?

What Are Publishing and Presenting? • 23

Publishing and Presenting

1. After students read the information on portfolios, reflection, and assessment, discuss their thoughts, past experiences, and expectations regarding each.
2. Ask students to generate a list of questions or create a checklist of elements that they might want to look for in their writing as they reflect on it over time.
3. Encourage students to review and discuss the main points of this chapter in small discussion groups.
4. Make a class summary of the key ideas that emerged from the smaller groups.

Customize for
ESL Students

Encourage students to reflect on their writing in their first languages if that feels most comfortable to them. For many students, this will stimulate deeper insights.

ASSESS and CLOSE

Assessment

Teaching Resources: Formal Assessment, Ch. 2

1. Have students answer the questions in Activity 2 in Applying the Strategies on this page.
2. Discuss students' reflections on the writing process. What strategies or techniques did they find most helpful?
3. You may wish to assign one of the assessment options in the Ongoing Assessment chart on this page. You may also consider the following:

   • review the Standardized Test Preparation Workshop on pages 26–27, and have students respond to the writing prompt within a set time limit.
   • administer the Chapter 2 assessment from *Formal Assessment* in the Teaching Resources to measure students' grasp of concepts presented.

☑ **ONGOING ASSESSMENT: Assess Mastery**

Use one of the following options to assess students' understanding of the writing process.

Option 1 Ask students to describe in their own words each step in the writing process and explain why each one is important. Also have them name the most important writing tip or strategy they learned in this chapter.	**Option 2** Have students choose one of the steps in the writing process and make a list of three to five helpful strategies for this step. Suggest that students combine the best strategies into a class reference booklet for the writing process.

Lesson Objectives

1. To recognize distinctive and shared characteristics of cultures through reading
2. To analyze relationships, ideas, and cultures as represented in various media
3. To use prewriting strategies to generate ideas
4. To use writing to formulate questions, refine topics, and clarify ideas

---

Step-by-Step Teaching Guide

Comparing Themes in Different Media

1. Ask students whether they are familiar with the play *Romeo and Juliet*. If possible, show excerpts from one of the several filmed versions of the play and have students discuss how they think actors prepare for plays.

2. You may also want to show excerpts from a video of the ballet version of *Romeo and Juliet*. Discuss how the techniques by which dance communicates emotion differ from those used in a play.

3. To carry the comparison of themes further, you may want to have students research the real rivalries between the Italian families that inspired Shakespeare to write his play.

4. There is a story, too, behind Dumas's novel *Camille,* one that involves the author. Students may wish to look into his inspiration for this tragic tale.

Viewing and Representing

Writing Activity Offer students an opportunity to share their lists of ideas with the class. Discuss similarities or differences among lists.

Critical Viewing

Interpret Students may observe that Duse appears reflective, resigned, or melancholy.

Comparing Themes in Different Media

Focus on Film: Eleonora Duse

When you approach the writing process, you choose your topic, develop your idea, and decide how you want to present the topic to your audience, much like an actor would go about choosing and crafting a role. Considered one of the foremost actors of her time, Italian Eleonora Duse (1858–1924) first attracted attention in 1873 when she played Juliet in Shakespeare's *Romeo and Juliet*. Widely known for her sense of realism, immense emotion, and the poetic spirit in her acting, Duse went on to earn international acclaim as one of the finest dramatic actors of her day. Her work has had great influence.

Dance Named after Eleonora Duse, American ballerina Nora Kaye (1920–1987) was known as the "Duse of Dance." After dancing with the Metropolitan Opera Ballet as a child, Kaye studied with the renowned Russian choreographers Michel Fokine and George Balanchine. In 1939, she joined the American Ballet Theatre. Her performance in the ballet *Pillar of Fire* in 1942 brought her international fame.

Literature Connection Eleonora Duse's premiere performance in New York City was in the play *La dame aux camélias* by the French novelist and playwright Alexandre Dumas (1824–1895). The drama came from his first novel, *Camille,* which appeared in 1848. Born in Paris, Dumas wrote his first volume of poetry in 1847. His feeling for drama and dialogue also made him a first-rate dramatist; his popular plays centered on social and moral problems of the middle class. His father, Alexandre Dumas (1802–1870) was the author of such novels as *The Count of Monte Cristo* and *The Three Musketeers.*

Writing Process Activity: Brainstorming for Ideas

Choose a film, television show, or a song you enjoy. Using it as an inspiration, list several ideas for writing projects. Keep this list in your portfolio for later development.

▲ **Critical Viewing** What emotion does this photograph of Eleonora Duse convey? Explain. **[Interpret]**

Media and Technology Skills

▶ **Lesson Objectives**
1. To use technology for aspects of creating, revising, editing, and publishing texts
2. To compile information in systematic ways using available technology

Building an Electronic Portfolio

Activity: Setting Up Your Portfolio

Writing on a computer can help you maintain an organized writing portfolio. Your portfolio can include copies of your writing in several subject areas, as well as your writing and notes for future projects. Keeping an organized electronic portfolio can help you find your past and current projects; it can also help you evaluate your progress as a writer. In some cases, you might decide to revise files that you once thought were in final form.

Learn About It Your computer system, or platform, uses a specific method of organizing files. Although systems vary, many use the terms *file* and *folder* as organizational tools. Each separate work is a file; you can group one or more files into a folder. For example, a folder labeled *Social Studies* might contain all of the files you prepared for that subject.

Structure It Choose a structure that matches the writing you plan to do. Devising a directory structure will help you find your work quickly. Your folder headings should reflect the kinds of writing you do.

- 📁 Writing Notes
- 📁 Fiction
- 📁 Poetry
- 📁 Nonfiction
  - Literature
  - History
  - Spanish
  - Geometry
- 📁 English Class
- 📁 Civics
- 📁 Algebra I
- 📁 Physics
- 📁 Journal

Use It When you start a new file or document, save it in the appropriate folder in your portfolio. When you decide to revise the document, save your first draft by pasting the writing into a new file. Amend the file name to show that it is a revision. Here is one system you might use:

Essay 1	(first draft)	Essay 3	(third draft)
Essay 2	(second draft)	Essay x	(final draft)

Maintain It Adjust your portfolio structure as you use it. You might decide to place early drafts in a separate folder or split one overloaded folder into three smaller categories.

Computer Tips

- If you store your portfolio on a hard drive, regularly back it up on a disk or CD-R.
- Store disks and CDs away from heat or magnetic sources.
- Label disks clearly.
- If possible, protect your files with a password that will prevent others from reading them.
- Use your computer system's Search or Find to locate a file that isn't where you thought it was.

Step-by-Step Teaching Guide

Building an Electronic Portfolio

Teaching Resources: Writing Support Transparencies, 2-K

1. Discuss with students the benefits of maintaining an electronic portfolio. Review the techniques listed in the sidebar box for organizing, accessing, and moving files.

2. Ask students to mention any particular techniques they use to organize files. Display Transparency 2-K to show students one system for setting up their folders.

3. If possible, bring students to the computer lab and have them set up portfolios to use for the year.

4. If students encounter difficulties, ask them to explain them in class so that you or other class members can help to solve them.

Integrating Technology Skills

Remind students to keep hard copies of all important documents and to back up electronic files on disk, too. This way, they will have insurance against possible system errors.

Lesson Objectives

1. To write a speech appropriate to audience and purpose
2. To organize ideas in writing to ensure coherence, logical progression, and support for ideas
3. To present and advance a clear thesis and logical points, claims, or arguments to support messages
4. To use appropriate appeals to support claims and arguments

Step-by-Step Teaching Guide

Using the Writing Process to Respond to Test Prompts

Teaching Resources: Standardized Test Preparation Workbook, pp. 3–4

1. Students might not be accustomed to using prewriting strategies when taking tests. They might be hesitant to take time away from drafting. Explain that their drafts will be much more thorough and clear if they take the time to organize their thoughts before beginning to write.

2. Have students read the sample writing prompt, and ask them to restate the issue in their own words.

3. Remind students to state their position clearly in their opening sentence. They can think of this as a topic sentence; it should introduce the main idea of the essay.

Standardized Test Preparation Workshop

Using the Writing Process to Respond to Test Prompts

Using the writing process helps writers produce well-organized, interesting, and coherent works. When responding to a test prompt for a standardized test, use the writing process to construct an effective response. You will be evaluated on your ability to do the following:

- Choose a logical, consistent organization.
- Elaborate with the appropriate amount of detail for your specific audience and purpose.
- Use appropriate transitions so ideas flow together coherently.
- Use complete sentences and follow the rules of grammar.
- Use correct spelling and grammar.

As you learned in this chapter, the process of writing for a test or any kind of writing can be divided into stages. Plan to use a specific amount of time for each task—prewriting, drafting, revising, and proofreading.

Following is an example of one type of writing prompt that you might find on a standardized test. Use the suggestions on the following page to help you respond. The clocks next to each stage show a suggested plan for organizing your time.

Test Tip

When trying to be persuasive, it is important to write convincingly. Support your argument with clear, concise examples. Make sure you draw a persuasive conclusion to your argument.

Sample Writing Situation

One of the educational topics under discussion addresses whether or not students should attend school year round with only a month off during the summer. Supporters argue that increasing the number of days students attend school will increase student performance. Those who disagree with the idea of year-round schooling argue that the current system is working and that it is unfair to expect teachers to work more days without additional compensation. Which side do you support? Write an essay in which you present your position and provide evidence to support it.

TEST-TAKING TIP

Tell students that when they are asked to choose a side or a position in a writing prompt, there is no "right answer." They should simply choose the position they feel most strongly about, for then they will be able to make their argument more sincerely and persuasively. Their essay will be scored, not on the basis of which side they chose, but on how well they presented and supported their position.

Prewriting

Allow about one quarter of your time for prewriting.

Make a Chart of Pros and Cons Create a simple chart with two columns. On one side, list the arguments for a longer school year; on the other side, list arguments against a longer school year. Review your chart, and choose a side.

Develop a Thesis Statement Your thesis statement is a one- or two-sentence explanation of the main idea that you will present in your essay. Before you begin writing, draft a thesis statement in which you sum up your position on an extended school year.

Gather Support Jot down specific facts and examples that you can use to back up your thesis. For example, you may have a friend whose grades improved greatly after attending summer school.

Drafting

Allow approximately half of your time for drafting.

Organize Your Ideas Present your arguments in the order of their importance. Begin with your least important argument and move toward your most important one.

Develop a Strong Introduction and Conclusion Start with an introduction in which you grab readers' interest with a thought-provoking statement, a quotation, or a surprising observation. Your introduction should also include your thesis statement. End with a conclusion in which you restate your thesis and offer final thoughts that will leave a lasting impression.

Write Thoughtfully Because you have less time to revise than you might in other writing situations, write slowly and carefully. Focus on choosing words that convey your exact meaning and on using transitions to connect your ideas.

Revising, Editing, and Proofreading

Allow about one quarter of your time to revise, edit, and proofread your paper.

Clean It Up Review your essay. Neatly cross out any details that will not influence your audience, and add support for your argument wherever possible. Also, check for errors in spelling. If you are unsure of the spelling of a word, consider replacing it with one you know better. If you are crossing out or erasing, do so neatly.

Customize for
Less Advanced Students

Explain to students that if their pro-and-con chart contains more cons than pros, they might consider changing their position. They should argue for the idea that they can most skillfully and emphatically defend.

Customize for
More Advanced Students

Remind students that when they write an essay, they should include a lead that immediately grabs the reader's attention. Suggest that they consider beginning with a hypothetical question in order to get the reader actively involved. Or, they might use a short, relevant anecdote.

In-Depth Lesson Plan

	LESSON FOCUS	PRINT AND MEDIA RESOURCES
DAY 1	**Sentence Combining; Main Idea and Topic Sentence** Students practice sentence combining, review samples from literature, and learn how to identify and write topic sentences. (pp. 28–34/⊞16–22)	*Writing and Grammar* Interactive Text, Ch. 3, Introduction through Section 3.1; Section 21.2
DAY 2	**Supporting Sentences and Paragraph Organization** Students examine strategies for supporting the main idea of a paragraph and learn a basic pattern of organization. (pp. 35–36/⊞23–24)	*Writing and Grammar* Interactive Text, Section 3.1 **Teaching Resources** *Writing Support Transparencies,* 3-A; *Writing Support Activity Book,* 3-1
DAY 3	**Unity and Coherence** Students learn the importance of unity in a paragraph and study organizational strategies and transitions that create coherence. (pp. 37–38/⊞25–26)	*Writing and Grammar* Interactive Text, Section 3.1
DAY 4	**Parts of a Composition; Types of Paragraphs** Students plan a composition, examine functional and block paragraphs, and review an example of functional paragraphs in literature. (pp. 39–41/⊞27–29)	*Writing and Grammar* Interactive Text, Section 3.2 **Teaching Resources** *Writing Support Transparencies,* 3-B; *Writing Support Activity Book,* 3-2
DAY 5	**Writing Style** Students discover how sentence variety, diction, and tone contribute to style, and when to use formal and informal English. (pp. 42–43/⊞30–31)	*Writing and Grammar* Interactive Text, Section 3.4 **Teaching Resources** *Writing Support Transparencies,* 3-C; *Formal Assessment,* Ch. 3

Accelerated Lesson Plan

	LESSON FOCUS	PRINT AND MEDIA RESOURCES
DAY 1	**Sentence Combining Through Paragraph Organization** Students review sentence combining and paragraph structure and utilize the TRI pattern. (pp. 28–36/⊞16–24)	*Writing and Grammar* Interactive Text, Ch. 3, Introduction through Section 3.1; Section 21.2 **Teaching Resources** *Writing Support Transparencies,* 3-A; *Writing Support Activity Book,* 3-1
DAY 2	**Unity and Coherence Through Writing Style** Students review coherence and paragraph types, and they discuss style and language. (pp. 37–43/⊞25–31)	*Writing and Grammar* Interactive Text, Sections 3.1–4 **Teaching Resources** *Writing Support Transparencies,* 3-B–C; *Writing Support Activity Book,* 3–2; *Formal Assessment,* Ch. 3

Options for Adapting Lesson Plans

HOMEWORK
Have students complete any stage of the lesson for homework.

FEATURES
Extend coverage with Spotlight on the Humanities (p. 44), Media and Technology Skills (p. 45), and the Standardized Test Preparation Workshop (p. 46).

TECHNOLOGY
Students can complete any stage of the lesson on the computer, using *Writing and Grammar* Interactive Text or a word-processing program. Have them print out their completed work.

Writing and Grammar Handbook Alignment

Page numbers in Step-by-Step Teaching Guides in this Teacher's Edition refer to pages from the full student text. Handbook page references, indicated with this icon **H**, are provided in Time and Resource Manager boxes and at the bottom of each Teacher's Edition page.

INTEGRATED SKILLS COVERAGE

Integrating Grammar
Formal and Informal English, SE p. 43/**H**31

Viewing and Representing
Critical Viewing, SE pp. 28, 29, 35, 37, 41, 43, 44/**H**16, 17, 23, 25, 29, 31
Analyzing Culture as Presented in Media, SE p. 44
Recognizing the Varieties of Media, SE p. 45
ATE p. 44

Speaking and Listening
SE p. 36/**H**24, ATE p. 38

Writing
Collaborative Writing, SE p. 34/**H**22
Writing Activity, SE p. 44

Vocabulary
ATE p. 35

Real-World Connection
ATE p. 42

Workplace Skills
ATE p. 37

ASSESSMENT SUPPORT

Standardized Test Preparation Workshop, SE p. 46; ATE pp. 36, 41

Standardized Test Preparation Workbook, pp. 5–6

Formal Assessment, Ch. 3

MEETING INDIVIDUAL NEEDS

Less Advanced Students ATE pp. 34, 36, 47. See also Ongoing Assessments, ATE pp. 32, 35, 38, 43.
Linguistic Learners ATE p. 34
More Advanced Students ATE pp. 35, 47
Gifted and Talented Students ATE p. 38
ESL Students ATE pp. 37, 42
Logical/Mathematical Learners ATE p. 41

BLOCK SCHEDULING

Pacing Suggestions
For 90-minute Blocks
- Follow the Accelerated Lesson Plan, covering topic and support sentences and paragraph organization in one class period and compositions and writing style in a second class period.
- Allow class time for students to complete and discuss exercises in lesson.

Resources for Varying Instruction
- *Writing and Grammar* Interactive Text A 90-minute block provides an ideal opportunity for students to work on the computer.
- *Writers at Work* DVD Show the Description segment in class.

Professional Development Support
- *How to Manage Instruction in the Block* This teaching resource provides management and activity suggestions.

MEDIA AND TECHNOLOGY

For the Student
- *Writing and Grammar* Interactive Text, Ch. 3

For the Teacher
- *Writers at Work* DVD, Description
- **Teacher EXPRESS** CD-ROM

WRITING AND GRAMMAR ON-LINE

Interactive Text (On-line or on CD-ROM)
- Easily navigable instruction with interactive Revision Checkers
- Full use of e-rater™, the essay-scoring system (on-line only)

Companion Web Site PHSchool.com
- Scoring rubrics with models (use Web Code eek-1001)

See the Go On-line! **feature, SE p. iii.**

Lesson Objectives

1. To practice sentence-combining skills to improve sentence style and fluidity
2. To write in a variety of forms, in a voice and style appropriate to audience and purpose
3. To use prewriting strategies to generate ideas and to plan
4. To organize ideas in writing to ensure coherence, logical progression, and support for ideas
5. To use writing to discover, organize, and support what is known and what needs to be learned about a topic
6. To analyze strategies that writers in different fields use
7. To evaluate writing for both mechanics and content

Critical Viewing

Connect Creating a garden requires careful selection and placement of elements in a coherent and unified setting. Similarly, an effective paragraph contains carefully selected and arranged elements such as words, phrases, and sentences.

Chapter 3

Sentences, Paragraphs, and Compositions
Structure and Style

What Are Sentences, Paragraphs, and Compositions?

A *sentence* is a group of words with a subject and a predicate that expresses a complete thought. Sentences are the building blocks of your writing.

A *paragraph* is a group of related sentences that presents a unit of thought. Paragraphs provide organization and focus to your writing. When you read, a new paragraph is indicated by visual clues, such as the indentation of the first word of the first sentence or an extra line of space between lines of text.

A *composition* is a connected series of paragraphs on a single topic. There are many types of compositions, including essays, research papers, and workplace writing. The specific types of compositions will be covered in later chapters.

▲ **Critical Viewing** Explain how creating a garden is like constructing an effective paragraph. **[Connect]**

28 • Sentences, Paragraphs, and Compositions

⏱ TIME AND RESOURCE MANAGER

Resources
Print: *Grammar Exercise Workbook*, pp. 85–86; *Extra Grammar and Writing Exercises*, pp. 21, 27–29
Technology: *Writing and Grammar* Interactive Text, Section 21.2

Using the Full Student Edition	Using the Handbook Ⓗ
• Read and discuss pp. 28–32 in class. • Have students work through Exercises 1–4 in class. Discuss their responses.	• Read and discuss pp. 16–20 in class. • Have students work through Exercises 1–4 in class. Discuss their responses.

3.1 *Sentence Combining*

Writing Effective Sentences

Effective sentences are the key to appealing and interesting writing. A sentence that is effective by itself, however, may seem uninteresting if it is one in a series of short sentences. Such a series can produce a choppy, repetitive effect.

To keep your sentences interesting, you need to consider sentence variety. By combining two or more short sentences, you can vary your sentences. At the same time, you can show connections between events, stress important information, and create a smooth flow of ideas.

Inserting Words and Phrases

You may combine two related sentences by taking key information from one and inserting it into the other. The information to be inserted may be a word or it may be a phrase. To combine sentences successfully, you may have to change the form of the words and use additional punctuation.

EXAMPLE:	The Spanish artist Joan Miró worked in many different media. <u>Miró is a world-famous artist.</u>
INSERTING A WORD:	The **world-famous** Spanish artist Joan Miró worked in many different media.
EXAMPLE:	Miguel de Cervantes was born outside Madrid. <u>He is the author of *Don Quixote*.</u>
INSERTING A PHRASE:	Miguel de Cervantes, **the author of *Don Quixote*,** was born outside Madrid.

▶ **Exercise 1** Combining With Words and Phrases
Combine each pair of sentences by inserting key information from one sentence into the other. Add commas as necessary.

1. Antoni Gaudí was a famous architect. He was from Spain.
2. Gaudí is probably best known for the Church of the Sagrada Familia in Barcelona. It is unfinished.
3. The Prado contains collections of paintings by artists such as El Greco, Velázquez, and Goya. The Prado is located in Madrid, Spain.
4. The Canary Islands are located in the Atlantic Ocean off the coast of Africa. They are part of Spain.
5. The wild canary bird is generally green, unlike the canaries bred as pets. It takes its name from the islands on which it lives.

▼ **Critical Viewing**
How is constructing a building, such as this building by Antoni Gaudí, like combining sentences in a paragraph? **[Connect]**

Sentence Combining • 29

Answer Key

▶ **Exercise 1**

Possible answers:

1. Antoni Gaudí was a famous Spanish architect.
2. Gaudí is probably best known for the unfinished Church of the Sagrada Familia in Barcelona.
3. The Prado, located in Madrid, Spain, contains collections of paintings by artists such as El Greco, Velázquez, and Goya.
4. The Canary Islands, located in the Atlantic Ocean off the coast of Africa, are part of Spain.
5. The wild canary bird, taking its name from the islands on which it lives, is generally green, unlike the canaries bred as pets.

Critical Viewing

Analyze Possible answer:
In making a building or writing a paragraph, you must fit parts together to make a whole.

PREPARE and ENGAGE

☀ **Interest GRABBER** Write these sentences on the board:

Spanish painters have contributed great works to world culture. Spanish writers have also contributed great works to world culture. El Greco is a great Spanish painter. Juan Gris is a great Spanish painter. Miguel de Cervantes is one great Spanish writer. Miguel de Unamuno is another.

Challenge students to combine all six sentences into one coherent sentence. (Possible response: Spanish painters, including El Greco and Juan Gris, and Spanish writers, including Miguel de Cervantes and Miguel de Unamuno, have contributed great works to world culture.)

Activate Prior Knowledge

Remind students that adjectives are words that modify (make more specific) the meaning of a noun and that an adjective can appear before or after the noun it modifies, as in these sentences:

The boy is <u>good</u>.
The <u>good</u> boy runs an errand.

TEACH

Step-by-Step Teaching Guide

Inserting Words and Phrases

1. Explain to students that writers often combine sentences by taking key adjectives from one and inserting them in the other. Point out that in the first example on page 29, the adjective *world-famous* has been taken from one sentence and inserted in another.

2. Explain to students that to combine two sentences, they may also rewrite one sentence as a phrase. Write the following sentences on the board:

   Miguel de Cervantes wrote Don Quixote. *By writing this book, he invented the modern novel.*

3. Then, write the following phrase:

   inventing the modern novel

   Note that this phrase contains the main idea of the second sentence. Ask students to add this phrase to the first sentence. (*Miguel de Cervantes wrote* Don Quixote, *inventing the modern novel.*)

Using Compound Elements

1. Explain that the subjects, verbs, or objects in a sentence may be compound, consisting of two or more subjects, verbs, or objects joined together. Write the following example on the board:

   (S)   (S)   (V) (Obj.).
   José and Juanita buy fish and

   (Obj.)   (V)
   squid at the port and sell them in the marketplace.

2. Using the examples on page 30, guide students to see that they can use compound verbs or objects to combine sentences.

3. Remind students that a preposition is a word that links a noun or pronoun to other words in a sentence. Use the example on page 30 to demonstrate the use of compound prepositional phrases for sentence combining.

Answer Key

▶ **Exercise 2**

Possible answers:
1. Seville and Córdoba are cities in southern Spain.
2. Catalan, a Romance language, is spoken in Catalonia and Roussillon.
3. Spain is known for its sunny climate and its beautiful castles and cathedrals.
4. Spanish fishers catch squid, sardines, tuna, and octopuses.
5. The entertainers in the café danced the flamenco and played the guitar.
6. The Prado, Madrid's great museum, and El Escorial, a palace outside Madrid, are main attractions for visitors.
7. The Spanish are the inventors of *paella,* a rice-based dish, and *gazpacho,* a cold tomato soup.
8. The Spanish parliament, known as the Cortes, is divided into two houses and has more than 500 members.
9. The Spanish people elect members of the Chamber of Deputies, the lower house of the Cortes, and of the Senate, the upper house.
10. You can see traces of Spain's history in the ruins left by the ancient Romans and in the alcazars (palaces) built by the Moors of North Africa.

Using Compound Elements

Related sentences may be combined by joining elements from each to form compound subjects, verbs, or objects.

EXAMPLE:	<u>Spain</u> is on my list of places to go on vacation. <u>Gibraltar</u> is also on my list.
COMPOUND SUBJECT:	**Spain and Gibraltar** are on my list of places to go on vacation.
EXAMPLE:	We <u>visited the Alhambra</u> in Granada, Spain. Then, <u>we toured the gardens and parks</u>.
COMPOUND VERB:	We **visited the Alhambra** and **toured the gardens and parks** in Granada, Spain.
EXAMPLE:	In the Straits of Gibraltar, tourists can see <u>dolphins</u>. They can also see <u>whales.</u>
COMPOUND OBJECT :	In the Straits of Gibraltar, tourists can see **dolphins and whales.**
EXAMPLE:	Gibraltar is famous <u>for its caves.</u> It is also known <u>for the wild Barbary apes.</u>
COMPOUND PREPOSITIONAL PHRASE:	Gibraltar is famous **for its caves and the wild Barbary apes.**

▶ **Exercise 2** Using Compound Sentence Elements Combine each pair of sentences using compound elements.

1. Seville is a city in southern Spain. Córdoba is another city in southern Spain.
2. Catalan, a Romance language, is spoken in Catalonia. It is also spoken in Roussillon.
3. Spain is known for its sunny climate. It is also known for its beautiful castles and cathedrals.
4. Spanish fishers catch squid and sardines. They also catch tuna and octopuses.
5. The entertainers in the café danced the flamenco. They played the guitar, too.
6. The Prado, Madrid's great museum, is a main attraction for visitors. El Escorial, a palace outside Madrid, is another.
7. The Spanish are the inventors of *paella*, a rice-based dish. They also invented *gazpacho*, a cold tomato soup.
8. The Spanish parliament, known as the Cortes, is divided into two houses. It has more than 500 members.
9. The Spanish people elect members of the Chamber of Deputies, the lower house of the Cortes. They also vote for the Senate, the upper house of the Cortes.
10. You can see traces of Spain's history in the ruins left by the ancient Romans. You can also see them in the alcazars (palaces) built by the Moors of North Africa.

Ⓠ **Learn More**

For additional information about objects, see Section 19.3; for additional information about prepositional phrases, see Section 20.1.

Customize for
Bodily/Kinesthetic Learners

Provide students with pairs of short sentences on strips of paper. The two sentences in each pair should have the same subject or verb. Have students combine pairs by selecting one sentence pair, cutting out the words it shares with the other, and, using tape, patching them into the other sentence to form compound subjects, verbs, or objects. Guide students to make any necessary changes to the form of words or to punctuation.

Forming Compound Sentences

A **compound sentence** consists of two or more independent clauses joined by a comma and a **coordinating conjunction** (*and, but, for, nor, or, so,* or *yet*) or by a semicolon.

EXAMPLE: Soccer is the most popular sport in Spain. Many cities have soccer stadiums that seat tens of thousands of spectators.

COMBINED: Soccer is the most popular sport in Spain, **and** many cities have soccer stadiums that seat tens of thousands of spectators. (comma and coordinating conjunction)

You may also use a semicolon or a semicolon and a transition word called a **conjunctive adverb,** such as *however, nevertheless,* and *consequently.* Notice that you are not simply linking two ideas: You are expressing a relationship between them.

EXAMPLE: We were exhausted after six days of touring. We went on to Madrid anyway.

COMBINED: We were exhausted after six days of touring; **nevertheless,** we went on to Madrid. (semicolon and conjunctive adverb)

To Combine Independent Clauses
Use a coordinating conjunction and a comma.
Coordinating Conjunctions: and, but, for, nor, or, so, yet
Use a semicolon and a conjunctive adverb.
Conjunctive Adverbs: consequently, furthermore, however, otherwise, therefore

Exercise 3 **Forming Compound Sentences** Using the strategy in parentheses, combine each pair of sentences to form a compound sentence.

1. The Strait of Gibraltar connects the Mediterranean Sea with the Atlantic Ocean. The Suez Canal links the Mediterranean Sea with the Red Sea. (comma and coordinating conjunction)
2. Spain is only eight miles from Morocco across the Strait of Gibraltar. The two countries lie on different continents. (semicolon and conjunctive adverb)
3. Rabat is the capital of Morocco. Casablanca is the largest city in Morocco. (comma and coordinating conjunction)
4. Arabic-speakers make up nearly 65 percent of Morocco's population. Berber-speakers constitute the rest of the population. (semicolon)
5. Morocco exports leatherwork and rugs. It imports oil. (comma and coordinating conjunction)

Learn More

For additional information about compound sentences, see Section 21.2; for additional information about using semicolons, see Section 28.3.

Sentence Combining • 31

sing Subordination

Write the following sentence on the board, underlining the subordinate clause.

When people travel in the Sahara, they usually go by camel.

Guide students to recognize that the clause functions as an adverb: It modifies the verb *go* by telling *when* people go by camel.

Write the following sentences on the board:

We went to Algeria. Then, we traveled to Libya.

Demonstrate how these sentences can be combined by rewriting one of them as an adverb clause:

After we went to Algeria, we traveled to Libya.

Explain that an adjective clause is another type of subordinate clause; it tells more about a person or thing mentioned in a sentence. Adjective clauses begin with words such as *that, who,* and *which*.

Write the following sentences on the board:

Our guide was helpful. He came from Algiers.

Guide students to see that these sentences can be combined by rewriting one as an adjective clause. Write the combined sentence:

Our guide, who came from Algiers, was helpful.

Answer Key

Exercise 4

Possible answers:

1. The northernmost point in continental Africa is in Tunisia, which is bordered on the north and east by the Mediterranean Sea.
2. Most people who live in the Sahara use camels for transpor–tation because camels can travel far without food or water.
3. When camels use the fatty tissue in the hump for energy, the hump gets smaller and softer.
4. Scientists believe that camels originated in North America, although there are no native camels in North America today.
5. Our trip to Algeria ended with a visit to the city of Algiers, which is my parents' city of origin.

3.1

Using Subordination

When one sentence explains more about an idea in another sentence, you can combine the two sentences by rewriting the first sentence as a subordinate clause. Although a **subordinate clause** has a subject and a verb, it cannot stand by itself as a sentence. An **adjective clause** is a subordinate clause that modifies a noun or pronoun by telling *what kind* or *which one*, using a relative pronoun such as *who, whom, whose, which,* or *that*.

EXAMPLE: The Sahara is the world's largest desert. The Sahara includes portions of eleven countries.

COMBINED: The Sahara, **which includes portions of eleven countries,** is the world's largest desert.

An **adverb clause** is a subordinate clause that answers the question *where, when, in what way,* or *why*. All adverb clauses begin with subordinating conjunctions such as *after, although, as, because, before, if, in order that, unless, until, where,* or *wherever*.

EXAMPLE: Most of Libya is covered by the Sahara. For this reason, most of Libya is uninhabitable.

COMBINED: Most of Libya is uninhabitable **because it is covered by the Sahara.**

Subordinating Conjunctions			
after	because	in order that	unless
although	before	since	until
as	even though	so that	when
as if	if	than	while

▶ **Exercise 4**   Using Subordination   Combine each pair of sentences using subordinate clauses.

1. The northernmost point in continental Africa is in Tunisia. Tunisia is bordered on the north and east by the Mediterranean Sea. (adjective clause)
2. Most people who live in the Sahara use camels for transportation. Camels can travel far without food or water. (adverb clause)
3. Sometimes, camels use the fatty tissue in the hump for energy. Then, the hump gets smaller and softer. (adverb clause)
4. Scientists believe that camels originated in North America. There are no native camels in North America today. (adverb clause)
5. Our trip to Algeria ended with a visit to the city of Algiers. Algiers is my parents' city of origin. (adjective clause)

32 • Structure and Style

ⓛ Learn More

For additional information about clauses, see Section 20.2; for additional information about pronouns, see Section 16.2.

☑ **ONGOING ASSESSMENT: Monitor and Reinforce**

If students have difficulty understanding subordination, try the following option.

Have students in small groups construct brief narratives using only simple sentences. One student should start by writing a sentence, and each should add a sentence telling what happens next. They should continue until their narratives have grown to eight to ten sentences. Then, list several subordinating conjunctions on the board: *after, because, before, until,* and *when*. Guide students to use the subordinating conjunctions to show connections between

events. Model the process using this example:

I got up this morning. The dog was barking.

Show students that these sentences might be combined in a number of ways, including:

When I got up this morning, the dog was barking.

I got up this morning because the dog was barking.

Have students use as many different subordinating conjunctions as they can.

3.2 *Writing Effective Paragraphs*

Main Idea and Topic Sentence

In a good paragraph, all of the sentences work together to present and develop one main idea. Often, the main idea is directly stated in a single sentence called the *topic sentence.* All of the other sentences in the paragraph support the topic sentence with examples, details, facts, or reasons.

Sometimes, a paragraph's main idea is *implied*, not directly stated. In such cases, all of the sentences work together to develop the main idea and communicate it to readers.

WRITING MODELS

from The Cabuliwallah
by Rabindranath Tagore
Translated From the Bengali Language

Mini, my five-year-old daughter, cannot live without chattering. I really believe that in all her life she has not wasted one minute in silence. Her mother is often vexed at this and would stop her prattle, but I do not. To see Mini quiet is unnatural, and I cannot bear it for long. Because of this, our conversations are always lively.

> In this paragraph, the stated topic sentence is shown in blue italics. The other sentences support, develop, and illustrate the topic sentence.

from Imitating Nature's Mineral Artistry
Paul O'Neil

The chemical ingredients for a man-made gem are easy to obtain, since most gems consist of relatively common chemical compounds. The art of gem synthesis lies in the technique by which the gem material is liquefied, in a melt or a solution, and then allowed to crystallize slowly and evenly.

> Notice that this paragraph does not contain a topic sentence. Instead, all of the sentences work together to communicate an implied main idea: Creating synthetic gems is an art that requires expertise.

Writing Effective Paragraphs • 33

⏱ TIME AND RESOURCE MANAGER

Resources
Print: *Writing Support Transparencies, 3-A; Writing Support Activity Book, 3-1*
Technology: *Writing and Grammar* Interactive Text, Section 3.1

Using the Full Student Edition	Using the Handbook Ⓗ
• Cover pp. 33–38 in class. • Read the Writing Models (p. 33) in class, and use the Step-by-Step Teaching Guide. • Read through pp. 34–38 in class. • Have students work through Exercises 5–11 in class.	• Cover pp. 21–26 in class. • Read the Writing Models (p. 21) in class, and use the Step-by-Step Teaching Guide. • Read through pp. 22–26 in class. • Have students work through Exercises 5–11 in class.

PREPARE and ENGAGE

✦ Interest GRABBER Ask students how they would introduce themselves at a party if they could use only one sentence. (Possible answer: *I am [name of student]*.) Explain that the topic sentence of any paragraph is like this sentence. It briefly identifies the subject of the paragraph. The other sentences in the paragraph give further details. Similarly, a person at a party might go on to tell more about him- or herself after exchanging introductions.

Activate Prior Knowledge

Ask students to think about the last time they read something that had a very strong message. They may have heard a speech or read a self-help magazine article, newspaper exposé, poem, or note from a friend. What strategies did the writer use to make the composition effective?

TEACH

Step-by-Step Teaching Guide

Main Idea and Topic Sentence

1. After students read the Writing Models, use questions like these to prompt discussion:

   In Tagore's piece, what idea unifies the writing?

   What makes O'Neil's piece coherent?

2. Ask students to compare the two pieces. How are they different? (Tagore has stated his main idea in a topic sentence, while O'Neil has implied his main idea.)

More About the Writers

Sir Rabindranath Tagore (1861–1941) was an Indian writer and philosopher who studied law in England. He won the Nobel Prize for Literature in 1913 and was knighted in England in 1915. Later, he founded a school in India that focused on social reform.

Paul O'Neil (1909–1988) spent his life writing. His freelance writing career followed thirty years of staff writing for *Time, Sports Illustrated,* and *Life* magazines. O'Neil also authored or contributed to books on topics such as America's West.

Exercise 5

The stated topic sentence is the first sentence : "A medieval feast was designed to appeal to the senses."

Exercise 6

Sample implied topic sentence: Much time and effort go into a successful pep rally.

Step-by-Step Teaching Guide

Writing Topic Sentences

1. Pick a familiar topic for students to write about, such as school rules or new movies. Have several students go to the board and list items within that topic.

2. Ask students to make positive or negative statements about their topics. Have them give reasons for their ideas.

3. After each student has taken a stand on a topic, have them write topic sentences that reflect their opinions. (Example: "Students should be required to recycle notebook paper, because it will help save our environment.")

4. Have students review each other's topic sentences and look for clearly stated topics.

Customize for
Linguistic Learners

Verbal students may find Exercise 5 more helpful if they work on it orally before they write. Read the excerpt out loud. Ask students to summarize what they have heard. Then ask them to look at the text and choose one sentence that best fits their summaries.

Customize for
Less Advanced Students

Read the excerpt in Exercise 6 aloud. Ask students to suggest topics that this paragraph is *not* about (or prompt them with questions about these nontopics). For instance, it is not about the band or about Helen and Alex being friends. Ask students to complete the sentence: "This paragraph is about . . ."

Exercise 5 Identifying a Stated Topic Sentence Identify the stated topic sentence of the following paragraph:

A medieval feast was designed to appeal to the senses. The dishes were colorful, such as green eel stew, and highly spiced, such as rabbit seasoned with ginger, cinnamon, saffron, sugar, cloves, and nutmeg. Regarding flavor, two words that appeared often in medieval cooking were *aigre*, a popular sour flavor, and *doux*, meaning "not salty."

Exercise 6 Identifying an Implied Main Idea Identify the implied main idea of the following paragraph:

We arrived at the gym an hour before the pep rally started. Helen and I hung red and white streamers from the bleachers, while Alex hung posters from the chalkboards. After twenty minutes, the band filed in, pumping marching music with a rhythmic beat. Next, the bell rang, and suddenly the entire class was piling in, stepping clunkily onto the bleachers. Once everyone was seated, the state champion soccer team stormed the floor, and the crowd went wild.

Writing Topic Sentences

In most of the writing you'll do in school—with the exception of stories and other types of creative writing—you will want to focus on writing paragraphs that contain topic sentences. Following are some tips for writing strong topic sentences:

TIPS FOR WRITING TOPIC SENTENCES

1. Review the details you've gathered for a piece of writing.
2. Identify groups of details to focus on specific topics or subtopics.
3. Jot down a few words to capture the main idea that connects each group of details.
4. Develop a sentence that thoroughly and concisely captures the main idea of a group of details.
5. Once you've completed a paragraph, review your topic sentence, and make sure it still sums up the main idea expressed in the other sentences. Revise it if necessary.

Exercise 7 Writing Topic Sentences Write a topic sentence for a paragraph on each of the following topics:
1. How computers have changed the quality of life
2. The value of holding a position in student government
3. Building-accessibility for the physically challenged
4. Funding for boys' and girls' sports
5. The high cost of concert tickets

Answer Key

Exercise 7

Answers will vary. Examples:

1. Computers have reduced people's physical and social activities.
2. Working in student government can help students develop communication skills.
3. It is important that public buildings be accessible to everyone.
4. Fairness requires that boys' and girls' sports be funded equally.
5. Costly ticket prices are preventing families from attending concerts.

Writing Supporting Sentences

A paragraph's topic sentence should be accompanied by a series of sentences that develop, explain, or illustrate. These other sentences are called *supporting sentences*. Following are some of the types of information that you can include in your supporting sentences:

Use Facts Facts are statements that are provable. They support your key idea by offering backup or proof.

TOPIC SENTENCE: Our car is almost ready for "retirement."

SUPPORTING FACT: Our state has just instituted a strict, new automobile inspection policy.

Use Statistics A statistic is a fact stated with numbers.

TOPIC SENTENCE: Our car is almost ready for "retirement."

SUPPORTING STATISTIC: It has 235,000 miles on it, and we've owned it for 12 years.

Use Examples, Illustrations, or Instances An example, illustration, or instance is a specific person, thing, or event that demonstrates a point.

TOPIC SENTENCE: Our car is almost ready for "retirement."

ILLUSTRATION: Last week, the car broke down, and we had to have it towed.

Use Details Details are the specifics—the parts of the whole. They make your main idea or key point clear by showing how all the pieces fit together.

TOPIC SENTENCE: Our car is almost ready for "retirement."

DETAIL: When our car broke down on the highway last week, it sputtered, slowed down, and finally came to a complete standstill. While we waited for the tow truck, we felt isolated on the highway and annoyed with ourselves for not listening to our trusted mechanic's advice.

▲ **Critical Viewing**
What topic sentence and supporting sentences would you use to describe this car? **[Describe]**

▶ **Exercise 8** Writing Supporting Sentences Write two supporting sentences for each of the following topic sentences. Use a variety of types of support.
1. The library is a place in which people should gather.
2. Many college students choose a vegetarian diet.
3. It's important to drink plenty of water when you exercise.
4. Music can be beneficial for both the mind and the body.
5. Being on a team builds self-esteem.

Writing Supporting Sentences

1. Ask students to read through the different types of supporting sentences. Ask them why writers would use the supporting sentences. (Writers use supporting sentences to develop, explain, illustrate, or prove their main idea.)

2. Have students write supporting sentences for the topic sentences in Exercise 8. Encourage students to vary the types of supporting sentences they use.

Answer Key

▶ **Exercise 8**

Ask volunteers to share some of their supporting sentences. Having more than one volunteer respond for each topic will illustrate how varied support can be for some topics.

Customize for
More Advanced Students

Ask students to choose two topic sentences in Exercise 8 and use them to write complete paragraphs. Between the two paragraphs, all four different types of supporting sentences should be used at least once.

Integrate Vocabulary Skills

Have students look up the word *support* in a variety of dictionaries. They should find a variety of meanings, including "to uphold or defend," "to serve as a foundation," and "to assist." Ask students to apply these different definitions to the uses of supporting sentences. (Example: Using a fact might defend a topic sentence, while using details might assist the reader in understanding the author's topic sentence.)

Critical Viewing

Describe Students' responses may range from the advantages of a large car for a big family to questions about fuel economy for larger cars.

☑ **ONGOING ASSESSMENT: Diagnose**

Use one of the following options to diagnose student's current level of proficiency in writing effective paragraphs.

Option 1 Ask students to select two strong paragraphs they have written recently. They might choose from class assignments or personal writing. Ask them to be prepared to describe, in a conference setting, how their paragraphs are organized and why they are effective. Use the conference to determine which students will need extra help.

Option 2 Ask students to write an informational paragraph about a sport, hobby, place, or event with which they are familiar. Have them include a topic sentence and at least three supporting sentences in their paragraphs. Plan extra help for those students who have difficulty completing this assignment.

aching Resource: Writing Support ansparencies 3-A; Writing Support tivity Book, 3-1

Display Transparency 3-A to demonstrate how the TRI pattern (Topic, Restatement, Illustration) has been used to organize the parts of the paragraph.

Have students practice creating variations by reading the sentences aloud in different orders. Note that, sometimes, different transition words will need to be added.

Explain that this pattern can be used for building paragraphs, as well as for analyzing them. Have students brainstorm for a question or topic, then "build" a paragraph as a class using one of these patterns.

Customize for
Less Advanced Students

Less advanced students may have difficulty rearranging the sentences in Exercise 9. To make the exercise more concrete, give students strips of paper. Have students rewrite each of the three sentences on a separate paper strip. Then, have them experiment with the TRI variations. Ask students to discuss the arrangement they like best. Why do they think this arrangement is effective?

Answer Key

Exercise 9

The third sentence is the topic sentence. The second is the restatement, and the first is the illustration. Tell students that they may modify sentences when trying variations of the TRI pattern. After they have completed the exercise, discuss how the TRI pattern worked for them.

3.2

Placing Topic Sentences

Most often, topic sentences appear at the start of a paragraph. They can also be placed in the middle or at the end of a paragraph to create different effects. Place a topic sentence

- **at the beginning of a paragraph** so that readers will immediately see the focus of the paragraph and know what to expect in the sentences that follow.

- **in the middle of a paragraph** when you need to provide sentences that lead into or introduce your topic sentence.

- **at the end of a paragraph** when you want to drive home your main point, leaving the point fresh in readers' minds.

Paragraph Patterns Paragraphs can follow a variety of different patterns, depending on the placement of the topic sentence. One common pattern is called TRI (Topic, Restatement, Illustration). A TRI paragraph begins with a topic sentence, which is followed by a restatement of the main idea and one or more sentences illustrating the main idea through facts and examples. The elements of a TRI paragraph can be reorganized to follow other patterns, such as ITR and TIR.

T R I	Planting perennial beds, borders, or gardens is an investment in years of floral beauty. Most perennial varieties multiply annually, so the initial costs and efforts of planting reap incremental returns in years to come. Under favorable conditions, daffodils, for instance, can cover almost twice as much space in the garden in their second year.

I T R	Daisies standing guard along the garden border, snapdragons peeking out between holly bushes, and cosmos waving near the side of the house are arranged in colorful groupings. Masses of lavender, lilacs, and forsythia add a brilliant backdrop. The garden is a bright spot in the yard. It presents a splash of color against the expanse of green.

Exercise 9 Placing a Topic Sentence Arrange the sentences below into a TRI pattern. Add transitions as necessary. Then, add two new sentences. Next, reorganize the sentences into a new pattern. Explain the effect created by each pattern.

- Some students do spend hours alone with their computers.
- The fear is that these students will become so used to predictable machines that they will be unable to function with real, fallible human beings.
- Many people think that computers isolate students.

36 • Structure and Style

Speaking and Listening Tip

To experiment with different placements of topic sentences, read your paragraphs aloud. Often, your ear can help you judge the effectiveness of different placements.

⬦ STANDARDIZED TEST PREPARATION WORKSHOP

Organize and Plan Standardized tests may require students to answer questions about how to organize paragraphs. Here is an example:

Andy wrote several statements to support his topic sentence, "Of all dogs, Labrador retrievers make the best pets for families." Here are his supporting statements. Use them to answer the question.

Labrador retrievers are gentle with children. Just the other day, our Lab helped the family by bringing in the newspaper. Labradors can jump about four feet. Labradors bond to more than one person in the family.

Which statement is not related to Andy's topic sentence?

A Labrador retrievers are gentle with children.
B Just the other day, our Lab helped the family by bringing in the newspaper.
C Labradors can jump about four feet.
D Labradors bond to more than one person in the family.

Students should recognize that **C** is the unrelated statement. B is an example and A and D are facts that support the topic statement.

Unity and Coherence

Maintain Unity

A paragraph has unity when all of the sentences support, illustrate, explain, or develop the topic sentence or main idea. To ensure unity as you draft, think about whether each sentence you write connects clearly and logically to the paragraph's topic sentence. When you revise, strengthen the unity of each paragraph by deleting those details or sentences that do not contribute to the support, development, or explanation of the main idea. Look at this example:

The Russian Revolution resulted in the destruction of the monarchy. During the February Revolution of 1917, Czar Nicholas II was forced to leave the throne of Russia. ~~The term Soviet Union was not used until 1917.~~ With the removal of Nicholas's family, the Romanov dynasty was erased. The Russian Empire had been ruled by czars for hundreds of years; it ended when the reign of Nicholas II ceased. ~~Nikolai Lenin died seven years after the revolution, in 1924.~~

▶ **Exercise 10** **Revising for Unity** On a separate sheet of paper, copy the following paragraph. Mark for deletion the two sentences that interfere with the unity of the paragraph.

The communist government recognized the need for a strong military. Russia signed a treaty with Germany in 1918. There were factions across Russia that did not readily support the new regime. Officials foresaw rebellion and resistance among these groups and needed a well-trained, powerful military force to oppose and put down resisters. To this end, the Red army was established; participation in it became compulsory for city workers and peasants. More than 20 million Russians died during the civil war, which lasted from 1918 to 1921.

▼ **Critical Viewing**
What can you infer, or conclude, about Russian Czar Nicholas II based on this picture? **[Infer]**

Writing Effective Paragraphs • 37

Step-by-Step Teaching Guide

Maintain Unity

1. To give a concrete example of unity, show students three related objects and one unrelated object. (For example: you could use a pen, pencil, piece of chalk, and a book.) Ask students to identify the unrelated object and explain why it is not related. (For the example above, they might say that the book is unrelated because people do not use it to write or because it is not cylindrical.)

2. Explain that all the sentences in a paragraph must be related, just as the objects were related to each other. Unrelated sentences should be taken out.

3. Read the example paragraph aloud, and then ask students why two sentences were marked for deletion.

Answer Key

▶ **Exercise 10**

The two sentences that should be marked for deletion are "Russia signed a treaty with Germany in 1918." and "More than 20 million Russians died during the civil war, which lasted from 1918 to 1921."

Critical Viewing

Infer Students' responses will likely focus on either the formality and elegance of the Czar's appearance or on the fact that he was apparently a family man.

Integrating Workplace Skills

In many businesses, employees communicate by memo (short for "memorandum"). Memos can be formal business documents or short e-mail messages. Because memos often require action on the part of the recipient, they need to be unified and coherent. An effective memo expresses ideas or requests without creating confusion.

Customize for
ESL Students

Students who have not yet had a world history class in English may be unfamiliar with the English names of countries. Identifying Russia on a map may help them begin to understand the topic.

Create Coherence

1. Explain that writing gains strength from being coherent—that is, by having ideas clearly and logically linked. Organization is the key to coherence.

2. Review the different purposes for the different organizational strategies. Explain that, whichever strategy is used, a writer should use it consistently throughout the passage.

3. Review the chart of transition words with students, explaining that these are words that are used to make connections clear or to establish the direction in which topics flow.

Answer Key

▶ **Exercise 11**

Sample revision: The view was the most beautiful thing Rebecca had ever seen. <u>Finally</u>, she remembered her hiking companion. She <u>immediately</u> looked back down the trail to see Jim. Hot and tired, he trudged toward her. He was never going to let her talk him into a "little hike" again.

Integrating Speaking and Listening Skills

Ask students to take turns telling about something that happened to them during the day, such as what they had for lunch or breakfast. The students listening should count the number of transition words the speaker uses. To increase difficulty, try making words and phrases such as "um," "like," and "you know" off limits.

Customize for
Gifted/Talented Students

Have students rewrite a well-known fairy tale using each of the bulleted organization strategies. For example, "Little Red Riding Hood" might be revised with comparison-and-contrast organization by having alternating paragraphs told from the wolf's and then from Red Riding Hood's point of view. Challenge students to maintain the plot and tone of the story.

3.2

Create Coherence

For a paragraph to have coherence, the supporting ideas must be arranged in a logical order and the sentences must be clearly connected. Following are common organizations:

- **Chronological order** places details in time order.
- **Spatial order** arranges details according to the position in which they appear.
- **Order of importance** presents details from most to least important, or vice versa.
- **Comparison-and-contrast order** discusses all of the details related to one subject, followed by a discussion of all the details related to the other subject; or two or more items are compared point by point.

In addition to using a consistent organization, use transitions to show connections among details.

COMMON TRANSITIONS

To Show Chronological or Sequential Relationships	To Show Spatial Relationships	To Show Comparison-and-Contrast Relationships	To Show Logical Relationships
first	through	along with	if
second	next to	together with	whether
then	above	as well as	unless
next	below	also	therefore
finally	in front of	by the same token	thus
before	behind	similiarly	hence
after	connected to	although	henceforth
at the same time	north	though	in fact
later	south	however	albeit
immediately	inside	despite	
soon	outside	yet	
daily	centered	but	
frequently	middle	on the other hand	
recently	on	in contrast	
when	at the top of	except for	
	at the bottom of		

▶ **Exercise 11** **Revising for Coherence** Revise this paragraph to create coherence. Reorganize sentences and add transitions.

The view was the most beautiful thing Rebecca had ever seen. He was never going to let her talk him into a "little hike" again. She remembered her hiking companion. Hot and tired, he trudged toward her. She looked back down the trail to see Jim.

38 • Structure and Style

🔍 **Learn More**

To learn more about creating coherence in various types of writing, see Sections 4.4, 6.4, and 10.4.

☑ ONGOING ASSESSMENT: Monitor and Reinforce

If you observe that students are having a problem with unity and coherence in their paragraphs, try these strategies.

Option 1 Have students work with paragraphs they have written recently. Ask them to add a concluding sentence to each that summarizes the information contained in the paragraph as succinctly as possible.	**Option 2** Have students work with news analysis stories from the newspaper to determine how specific paragraphs are organized. Ask them to find examples of paragraphs that are organized in chronological or developmental order, order of importance, spatial order, or cause-and-effect order.

3.3 *Paragraphs in Essays and Other Compositions*

Writers rarely use paragraphs in isolation. Most writing consists of a series of connected paragraphs that work together to form a composition, such as an essay or a research paper, or another type of writing, such as a short story or an anecdote.

The Parts of a Composition

As you'll learn in the chapters that follow, there are many types of compositions. Compositions include just about any type of writing you do in school, aside from creative writing. While compositions can vary widely in form and purpose, they generally consist of the following elements:

The Introduction

Usually the first paragraph of a composition, the *introduction* introduces the topic, hooks the reader's interest, and presents the thesis statement. The *thesis statement* is a one- or two-sentence summary of the key point of the essay. The thesis statement may be accompanied by a few sentences outlining the subtopics to be covered in the body of the essay.

SAMPLE THESIS STATEMENTS

- Mikhail Gorbachev's policies of openness during the 1980's paved the way for the dismantling of the Soviet Union.
- Hitting a golf ball effectively involves choosing the correct club, assuming the proper position, and swinging smoothly and evenly.

The Body

The *body* of an essay consists of two or more paragraphs that develop and support the thesis. Each body paragraph should focus on a single subtopic and should provide examples, details, facts, reasons, and other types of support. Most often, each body paragraph should include a topic sentence that clearly indicates the subtopic being developed.

The Conclusion

The *conclusion* is the essay's final paragraph. It should reinforce or restate the thesis and offer readers final thoughts on the topic. Ideally, the final sentence should be a forceful, witty, or memorable statement called a *clincher*.

> **Exercise 12** Analyzing a Composition Find an article in a newsmagazine that follows the preceding format. Explain each element.

🕮 **Learn More**

To learn more about writing introductions, body paragraphs, and conclusions for various types of compositions, see Sections 10.4 and 13.4.

Step-by-Step Teaching Guide

The Parts of a Composition

1. After students have reviewed the parts of a composition, ask them how the organization of a composition is similar to that of a paragraph. How is it different? (Like a paragraph, it starts with a topic and adds support. Unlike a paragraph, it is longer and has a conclusion.)

2. Point out that an outline can often help make the parts of a composition clearer. Tell students that, once they decide on an organizational strategy, they can create a simple outline. Demonstrate the outline form if necessary.

3. Suggest that students work first on the thesis statement, then outline the points they need to support the thesis statement. After some research is done, it will be easier to go back and create an introduction and conclusion that tie all the points together.

Answer Key

> **Exercise 12**

This may be done in class or as homework. Ask students to share some of the observations they made while analyzing the articles they found.

🕐 TIME AND RESOURCE MANAGER

Resources
Print: *Writing Support Transparencies*, 3-B; *Writing Support Activity Book*, 3-2

Using the Full Student Edition	Using the Handbook 🄷
• Use the Writing Model to demonstrate the technique of using functional paragraphs to arouse or sustain interest or to create emphasis. • Work through Exercises 12–13 with the entire class.	• Use the Writing Model to demonstrate the technique of using functional paragraphs to arouse or sustain interest or to create emphasis. • Work through Exercises 12–13 with the entire class.

Types of Paragraphs

1. Point out that topical paragraphs are what students have been studying thus far—paragraphs with main ideas to be supported.

2. Explain that not all paragraphs are topical. Some paragraphs are functional, designed to create an effect.

3. Write on the board the three purposes of functional paragraphs (indicate dialogue, make a transition, create emphasis).

4. After reading the model, ask students why the author chose to use such a brief paragraph here? (The brevity contrasts with the rest of the piece, which places emphasis on the short paragraph. This contrasting paragraph also adds interest to the story.)

5. Explain that using a paragraph to make a transition is a way of turning the reader's attention to a different location, character, situation, or point without losing continuity.

Teaching From the Model

You can use this Writing Model to show students the purpose of a functional paragraph. In the model paragraph, the author uses direct language and brevity to make his point. Have students find the shortest sentence in the paragraph. (*I think not.*) What effect does this sentence have? What other paragraph topics could benefit from this type of short, direct statement?

More About the Writer

Heinrich Böll (1917–1985) was a German novelist and short-story writer. Böll was a reluctant soldier in Hitler's war machine, and much of his writing explores the horror, guilt, and moral implications of Germany's role in World War II. He won the Nobel Prize for Literature in 1972.

Types of Paragraphs

There are a number of types of paragraphs you can use in compositions and pieces of creative writing.

Topical Paragraphs

A topical paragraph consists of a topic sentence and several sentences that support or illustrate it. All of the paragraphs on the preceding pages are examples of topical paragraphs.

Functional Paragraphs

Functional paragraphs are used to achieve a specific purpose in an extended piece of writing. Unlike topical paragraphs, they often do not contain a topic sentence. In addition, they are often shorter than topical paragraphs—in some cases, they are only a single sentence. Functional paragraphs may do the following:

- **Indicate dialogue.** One of the conventions of written dialogue is that a new paragraph begins with each change of speaker.

- **Make a transition.** A short paragraph can help a reader move between the ideas of two topical paragraphs.

- **Create emphasis.** A paragraph of a sentence or two that reinforces a main point in a piece of writing will leave a lasting impression with readers. (See the example below.)

WRITING MODEL

from **The Laugher**
Heinrich Böll

I go through life with an impassive expression, from time to time permitting myself a gentle smile, and I often wonder whether I have ever laughed. I think not. My brothers and sisters have always known me for a serious boy.

So I laugh in many different ways, but my own laughter I have never heard.

Because the second paragraph is so brief and direct, it emphasizes the contradiction at the heart of the excerpt: This man goes through life wearing a serious expression, but he laughs inwardly in many different ways.

Paragraph Blocks

Occasionally, you may have so much information that you will need to develop a single idea over several paragraphs. Such "blocks" of paragraphs all support the same main idea or topic sentence. By separating the development of the contributing ideas into paragraph blocks, your ideas become clearer and more accessible.

Topic Sentence → The unexpected weather patterns seemed to result from both natural and artificial, or man-made, factors.

Natural Factor 1 with elaboration

Natural Factor 2 with elaboration

Artificial Factor 1 with elaboration

Artificial Factor 2 with elaboration

Four paragraphs working as a block

▶ **Exercise 13** Analyzing Functional Paragraphs and Paragraph Blocks Choose a descriptive essay or factual report. Then, choose a story containing dialogue. In both, locate examples of functional paragraphs that create emphasis, indicate dialogue, and make transitions. Also, locate an example of a paragraph block. Explain to a partner how the functional paragraphs and the paragraph block work within the context of the longer pieces of writing.

▼ Critical Viewing
What topic sentence might you come up with if you were writing a description of this storm? **[Describe]**

Paragraphs in Essays and Other Compositions • 41

Paragraph Blocks

Teaching Resources: Writing Support Transparencies, 3-B; Writing Support Activity Book, 3-2

1. Display Transparency 3-B to show students how the paragraphs all relate to the main idea. Ask students to identify the main idea of the paragraph block and to identify how the other paragraphs contribute to the main idea.

2. Tell students that each paragraph in a block needs to follow immediately after the preceding one.

3. Explain that, just as all the statements within a paragraph should support the topic, all the information in a paragraph block should support the topic paragraph.

Critical Viewing

Describe Responses may relate some aspect of what the storm looks like, may ask a question about the origin or effect of the storm, or may comment on weather in general.

Answer Key

▶ **Exercise 13**

Ask volunteers to share examples of the functional paragraphs and paragraph blocks they found.

Customize for
Logical/Mathematical Learners

Students may get more out of the exercise if they serve as statistical recorders. After the class completes Exercise 13, have interested students record how many times each type of paragraph occurs. Have these students report to the whole class about which types of paragraphs were the most common, which types were the least common, and why they think this distribution occurred.

✎ STANDARDIZED TEST PREPARATION WORKSHOP

Standardized tests may require students to identify the main idea of a story or paragraph.

It's hard to imagine a plant eating a bug, but the truth is that some do. These plants are called "carnivorous plants." Examples of carnivorous plants are the sundew, pitcher plant, and Venus' flytrap. Why do these plants eat bugs? Carnivorous plants grow in poor soils, so they cannot get enough nutrients. Instead, their leaves and stems trap insects. They digest their prey slowly to get the nutrients they need to live.

Which sentence best describes the main idea of this paragraph block?

A Most people don't think about plants.

B Carnivorous plants are plants that eat bugs.

C Some plants get their nutrients in unexpected ways.

D Plants digest their prey over a long period of time.

Students should see that **C** is the correct answer. A is not really supported by the paragraph. B and D give supporting points of the main idea.

Developing Style

Teaching Resources: Writing Support Transparencies, 3-C

1. Display Transparency 3-C to help students visualize how writing style evolves out of several factors, including sentence variety, diction, and tone.

2. Remind students that sentences can vary not only in length, but in subject-verb order, function, and complexity. Varying sentences not only creates style, it also keeps the writing interesting.

3. Point out that tone can be subtle or obvious, depending on the author's purpose.

Answer Key

▶ **Exercise 14**

Discuss the style of the excerpts in class. Have students exchange paragraphs with partners, examining the parallels they observe with the models.

Real-World Connection

There are few lines of work in which diction and tone are not important writing tools. In business writing, in particular, it is vital to choose the right words and express the right tone for each situation, whether it is giving instructions to a subordinate or asking advice of a supervisor.

Customize for
ESL Students

Students learning English as a second language may have difficulty using variety in diction. Students may use some English words repetitively because they are sure of their meaning. Encourage students to generate word lists in their first languages and then brainstorm for synonyms, which they can translate into English with the help of a dictionary.

⏱ **TIME SAVERS!**

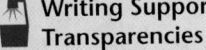 **Writing Support Transparencies**
Use the transparencies for Chapter 3 to facilitate the teaching of strategies.

3.4 Writing Style

Developing Style

You express yourself through your "personal style." It includes your music preferences, the way you dress, how you speak. Style also refers to how you express yourself in writing. These elements work together to determine your writing style:

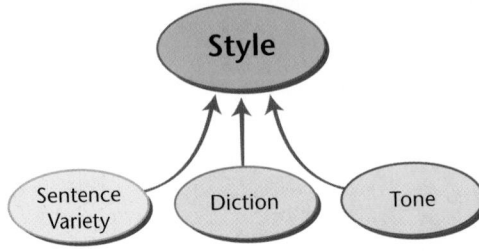

Sentence Variety One of the keys to developing a strong writing style is learning to vary the length and structure of your sentences. Sentences that are all short will sound choppy to readers; sentences that are all very long or all begin in the same way will become boring or hard to follow. Use a mixture of short and long sentences to create a rhythm and emphasize key points. For instance, you can follow a series of long sentences with a short one to drive home an important idea.

Diction Diction refers to a writer's choice of words. When you write, choose your words carefully to have the effect you desire. For example, if you are writing an essay about a serious topic, you will want to use formal language that will command your reader's respect. If, on the other hand, you are writing an amusing story for your friends, you will want to use informal language that matches the way you speak.

Tone The tone of your writing is your attitude toward your subject. Your tone may be formal or informal, friendly or distant, personal or impersonal. A writer offering advice on a serious topic may still choose a lighthearted, amusing tone. When expressing intense personal thoughts about an important topic, however, a writer's tone might reflect awe or respect.

▶ **Exercise 14** Analyzing Sentence Variety Read the Writing Models on pages 33 and 40. Compare and contrast the sentence lengths and structures, the word choice, and the tone of each. Then, write paragraphs of your own, modeled on the style of each piece.

42 • Structure and Style

🔵 Learn More

When you revise, you can often achieve better sentence variety by combining your short sentences into longer ones. For instruction on combining sentences, see Sections 21.2 and 21.3.

⏱ **TIME AND RESOURCE MANAGER**

Resources
Print: *Writing Support Transparencies*, 3-C; *Formal Assessment*, Ch. 3
Technology: *Writing and Grammar* Interactive Text, Section 3.3

Using the Full Student Edition	Using the Handbook Ⓗ
• Work through pp. 42–43 in class.	• Work through pp. 30–31 in class.
• Have students complete Exercise 14 individually.	• Have students complete Exercise 14 individually.
• Assign Exercise 15 for small groups. Have the groups compare their revised sentences.	• Assign Exercise 15 for small groups. Have the groups compare their revised sentences.

Formal and Informal English

Standard English can be either formal or informal. It is best to use formal English for serious or academic purposes. Informal English is appropriate for stories and casual writing.

Formal English

Formal English should be used for essays, newspaper articles, formal reports, speeches, letters of application, and most school assignments. When using formal English,

- Avoid contractions.
- Do not use slang.
- Use standard English and grammar.
- Use a serious tone and sophisticated vocabulary.

Informal English

The "everyday" English we speak is informal English. You can use informal English when you write dialogue, stories, personal essays, poems, letters to friends, and journal entries. Writing informally allows you to

- Use contractions.
- Use slang and popular expressions, especially to capture the natural sound of speech.

FORMAL ENGLISH:	Sumo wrestling, a special Japanese form of wrestling, may be the most Japanese sport of all. Wrestlers perform ceremonial actions that have traditional significance, like squatting deeply to show respect.
INFORMAL ENGLISH:	I don't think I've ever seen people so crazy about baseball. There's a game every night of the week! It's excellent watching games with a crowd that's totally psyched!

▲ **Critical Viewing** How would you describe this platter of sushi using informal English? How would you describe it using formal English? **[Describe, Compare and Contrast]**

> **Exercise 15** Using Formal and Informal English Rewrite the following sentences. Use formal English for those written in informal English. Use informal English for those written in formal English.

1. In Japan, the contrast of old and new is very striking.
2. This week, I checked out Tokyo.
3. Sushi and sashimi, two types of raw fish dishes, are eaten with soy sauce.
4. Some people are grossed out by the idea of eating raw fish.
5. If you've never tried sushi or sashimi, you may be floored to discover that they don't have a fishy taste.

Writing Style • 43

Lesson Objectives

1. To write an expository essay appropriate to audience and purpose
2. To analyze relationships, ideas, and cultures as represented in various media
3. To deconstruct media to get the main idea of the message's content

---

Step-by-Step Teaching Guide

Analyzing Culture as Presented in Media

1. Students may want to divide into small groups to discuss Native American dance as it has been represented in literature and film. Have them locate Scott S. Warren's book *Desert Dwellers: Native People of the Southwest*, as well as additional books and films, in the school or local library.

2. Bring in recordings of Native American music. Discuss the distinctive rhythmic patterns of the voices and instruments. Compare and contrast the musical style with other styles of music.

3. Interested students may decide to pursue sources that focus on specific Native American dances, their purposes, and accompanying costumes. Looking at detailed, authentic illustrations would be valuable background material for their expository essays.

Viewing and Representing

Activity After students have watched the film *Dances With Wolves*, they can discuss its message and dance images in small groups. Have them present their finished essays orally in these same groups, showing scenes from the film to demonstrate their points.

Critical Viewing

Interpret Students should be as specific as possible in describing the dancers' costumes, body decorations, and types of movement. Ask them to tell at what point in the movie's plot this scene takes place and what the purpose of the dance is.

Spotlight on the Humanities

Analyzing Culture as Presented in Media

Focus on Dance: Native American Dancing

Just as pieces of writing follow a structure consisting of an organized series of paragraphs, dances follow a structure consisting of an organized pattern of steps. In addition, certain dances involve special costumes.

For Native Americans, dance is highly symbolic and can represent actions by people or events in nature. The costume for the men's traditional dance may include a single bustle with eagle feathers or a breastplate of animal bones. Eagle feathers are sacred to Native Americans and are awarded for bravery. In the women's traditional dance, the costume may include a fringed shawl and a feather fan.

The movements in women's traditional dance are focused; the women move their feet close to the ground, keeping the rhythm of the drum. More complex dances by the men require stamina and athletic ability. Advanced dancing requires the dancer to keep the feathers moving at all times throughout a song. Native American dance has served as a source of inspiration for films and literary works.

Film Connection The 1990 film *Dances With Wolves* uses the image of Native American dance to tell the story of a Civil War soldier and his relationship with a Sioux Indian tribe. Directed by Kevin Costner, the film won seven Academy Awards, including Best Picture, Best Director, and Best Cinematography.

Literature Connection In his book *Desert Dwellers: Native People of the Southwest*, Scott S. Warren captures the costumes and customs of Native American dance in colorful photographs and elaborates on the meaning of movements in dance among the Pueblo, Navajo, and Hopi.

Writing Activity: Composition About a Film

Watch the film *Dances With Wolves*. Write a composition explaining how the image of dance is used in the film to convey a message to the audience. Share your exposition with other class members.

▲ **Critical Viewing** What does this photograph reveal about Native American dance? **[Interpret]**

Media and Technology Skills

Recognizing the Varieties of Media Sources of Information

Activity: Keep a Media Log

We receive information from an astonishing variety of media sources. Once, the printed book was the primary source of recorded information. Today, news and other data are stored in newspapers, magazines, network and cable television broadcasts, radio transmissions, and computers connected via the Internet.

You may not be aware of the many sources you use to collect information every day. Keeping a media log will help you assess the channels you use. It might even encourage you to broaden the sources you frequently use.

Think About It Your media log will list the information sources you use every day for one week. Begin by making some predictions about your day-to-day reference sources. Which source do you think you use most often? Write your predictions at the beginning of your media log.

Collect It Keep track of the media sources you use each day. Include everything—from watching television news to getting information from a telephone call. You can organize your list chronologically or by type of media.

Annotate It After you collect your information, use a rating scale to tell how useful each source was. Devise your own rating scale, such as one to five, with five being the highest. Create a code that indicates what each rating means.

Reflect on It When you have completed entries for one week, take time to review your original predictions. Evaluate your use of media sources, and consider making goals for your future research. For example, you might decide to get more information from the Internet.

Varieties of Print Media

When looking for information, be sure to consult a wide variety of print resources. In addition to books, magazines, and newspapers, the following sources of information may contain the facts you need:

- pamphlets and brochures
- government bulletins and documents
- local newsletters
- catalogs and product information sheets
- instruction manuals
- product labels
- direct mail and advertisements

Tuesday

TV:	evening news
Newspaper:	The Washington Post (news)
Radio:	morning weather
Telephone:	record release dates and musician interviews
Internet:	information from poison hotline
	more information about household poisons
CD-ROM:	record reviews
Magazines:	looked up poisons in encyclopedia
	Time magazine (news and reviews)
	Scientific American

---

1. To collect and analyze a variety of media sources used each day
2. To distinguish the purposes of various media forms and to recognize genres
3. To compare, contrast, and critique various media coverage of the same event, such as in newspapers, television, and on the Internet

Step-by-Step Teaching Guide

Recognizing the Varieties of Media Sources of Information

Teaching Resources: Writing Support Transparency 3-D

1. Using the previous day as a starting point, have students volunteer any types of media they used and for what purpose. Discuss the types used most frequently and which were most useful.

2. Display Transparency 3-D to show students how they might record their information about media sources. As they create their own charts, students will need to decide whether they want to record their information chronologically or by type of media.

3. As students collect their information during the week, they might want to observe the media activity of an adult in their household, as well. In this way, they could compare and contrast media use by age group or occupational focus, as well as add to their list of possible media sources.

4. Have students reflect on their completed charts in small groups. They should analyze whether or not their sources were the most effective for their intended purposes and come up with possible alternatives.

Step-by-Step Teaching Guide

Strategy, Organization, and Style

Teaching Resources: Standardized Test Preparation Workbook, pp. 5–6

1. Discuss with students the qualities of an effective paragraph. They should mention a clear topic sentence, several specific supporting details, and a logical concluding statement.

2. Remind students that in evaluating writing style, they should try to identify the writer's purpose and intended audience. This will help them evaluate whether diction, tone, sentence variety, and word choice seem appropriate or whether they need to be changed.

3. Go over the Sample Test Item with students. (Point out that this sample is a partial paragraph; students should focus on aspects of sentences and language, not on paragraph form.) In their analysis of the possible answers, students should notice that the correct response includes all of the details within one clearly written sentence.

4. Ask students if they can think of other ways that the repetition of "Vietnam" could have been avoided in this sample. (Examples: it could have been left in two sentences, but the second sentence might have been started with "It" or "This ancient land.")

Standardized Test Preparation Workshop

Strategy, Organization, and Style

Your knowledge of how to write and revise effective paragraphs is often measured on standardized tests. These types of test items consist of a paragraph in which each sentence is numbered and specific questions based on the passage. These test questions often ask about the writer's strategy, organization, sequence of sentences, choice of words, and overall style. The following are three types of questions that you will need to answer:

- **Strategy questions** ask whether a given revision is appropriate in the context of the essay.

- **Organization questions** ask you to choose the most logical sequence of ideas or to decide whether a sentence should be added, deleted, or moved.

- **Style questions** focus on assessing the writer's point of view and the use of appropriate and effective language for the intended audience.

The sample test item that follows will give you practice in answering questions on writing strategy, organization, and style.

Test Tip

Before reading the questions, read the paragraph, noting any places where the text does not flow or seems incorrect. Refer back to this as you answer the questions.

Sample Test Item

Directions: This passage is part of a report that Brooke has written for her geography class. As part of a peer conference, you are asked to read the report and think about suggestions you might make. When you finish reading the report, answer the multiple-choice question that follows.	A Vietnam is a tropical country in Southeast Asia, and Vietnam extends south from China in a long, narrow S-curve.
1 Vietnam is a tropical country in 2 Southeast Asia. Vietnam extends 3 south from China in a long, narrow 4 S-curve. 1 What is the BEST way to combine the sentences in lines 1–4? ("Vietnam . . . S-curve.")	B A tropical country in Southeast Asia, Vietnam extends south from China in a long, narrow S-curve. C Vietnam is located in Southeast Asia and has an unusual shape. D Make no change
	Answer and Explanation The correct answer is *B*. Combining the sentences in this way eliminates the unnecessary repetition of the word *Vietnam*.

✏ TEST-TAKING TIP

Emphasize the importance of reading the entire passage before moving on to the test questions. Tell students that they should trust their initial reactions to sentences that seem out of order, unnecessarily complicated, repetitive, or choppy.

Tell students that in evaluating the appropriate use of words, they should focus on specificity. That is, they should ask themselves whether or not the chosen word gives them specific information or whether it is too vague and general.

Practice 1 **Directions:** This paragraph is part of a report that Lauren has written for her art class. As part of a peer conference, you are asked to read the report and think about suggestions you might make. When you finish reading the report, answer the multiple-choice questions that follow.

1 Although Degas is considered one of
2 the Impressionist painters, he did not
3 share their thing about light and color.
4 Instead of concentrating on color and
5 light, he focused on composition, drawing,
6 and form. He created many sculptures.
7 Some of them are quite nice. These were
8 "practice works." They made Degas one
9 of the most important modern sculptors.

1 What is the BEST change, if any, to make the language more appropriate for a formal piece of writing in the sentence in lines 1–3? ("Although . . . color.")

  A Change *thing* to *enthusiasm.*

  B Remove the comma after *painters.*

  C Remove *Impressionist.*

  D Make no change.

2 What is the BEST way, if any, to rewrite the sentence in lines 4–6? ("Instead . . . form.")

  A He didn't want to focus on color and light because he focused on composition, drawing, and form.

  B Instead, he focused on composition, drawing, and form.

  C To focus on color and light was not his primary interest.

  D Make no change.

3 Which sentence would BEST add information about Degas to the passage?

  A Painting and sculpture are powerful art forms.

  B Degas is a well-known painter.

  C Impressionist painting was an important art form.

  D Degas created sculpture to study form and body movements.

4 What is the BEST way to combine the last two sentences? ("These . . . sculptors.")

  A These were "practice works," and they made Degas one of the most important modern sculptors.

  B These practice works made Degas one of the most important modern sculptors.

  C Degas was made one of the most important modern sculptors by these practice works.

  D One of the most important sculptors of our time was Degas.

5 Which of the following sentences, if any, would be the BEST choice to be removed from the passage?

  A Although Edgar Degas is considered one of the Impressionist painters, he did not share their thing about light and color.

  B They made Degas one of the most important sculptors in modern times.

  C Some of them are quite nice.

  D Make no change.

Answer Key

Practice 1

1. A
2. B
3. D
4. B
5. C

Customize for
Less Advanced Students

Tell students to focus their concentration, especially in test situations, on the main idea of the paragraph. Some response choices may be eliminated based on their weak support of the main idea. After doing this as a timed test, go through the questions one at a time in class, explaining why the choices identified as best are, in fact, best of those offered.

Customize for
More Advanced Students

These students might try, in the practice passage, reading through all of the responses to a question before referring back to the passage. They might be able to eliminate several responses at once. You may want to challenge these students to rewrite the paragraph completely, making not only the suggested changes, but adding any other refinements they feel would improve it.

Chapter 4

Time and Resource Manager

In-Depth Lesson Plan

	LESSON FOCUS	PRINT AND MEDIA RESOURCES
DAY 1	**Introduction to Autobiographical Writing** Students learn key elements of autobiographical writing and analyze the Model From Literature. (pp. 48–53/H32–33)	*Writers at Work* **DVD**, Narration *Writing and Grammar* **Interactive Text,** Ch. 4, Introduction
DAY 2	**Prewriting** Students choose and narrow a topic, consider their audience and purpose, and gather information. (pp. 54–57/H34–37)	**Teaching Resources** *Writing Support Transparencies,* 4-A–D; *Writing Support Activity Book,* 4-1–2; *Topic Bank for Heterogeneous Classes,* Ch. 4 *Writing and Grammar* **Interactive Text,** Section 4.2
DAY 3	**Drafting** Students organize their ideas and write their first drafts. (pp. 58–59/H38–39)	**Teaching Resources** *Writing Support Transparencies,* 4-E–F; *Writing Support Activity Book,* 4-3 *Writing and Grammar* **Interactive Text,** Section 4.3
DAY 4	**Revising** Students revise their drafts in terms of overall structure, paragraphs, sentences, and word choice. (pp. 60–65/H40–45)	**Teaching Resources** *Writing Support Transparencies,* 4-G–I; *Writing Support Activity Book,* 4-4 *Writing and Grammar* **Interactive Text,** Section 4.4
DAY 5	**Editing and Proofreading; Publishing and Presenting** Students check their work for accuracy and correctness and present their final drafts. (pp. 66–67/H46–47)	**Teaching Resources** *Scoring Rubrics on Transparency,* Ch. 4; *Writing Assessment and Portfolio Management; Formal Assessment,* Ch. 4 *Writing and Grammar* **Interactive Text,** Sections 4.5–6

Accelerated Lesson Plan

	LESSON FOCUS	PRINT AND MEDIA RESOURCES
DAY 1	**Introduction Through Drafting** Students review characteristics of autobiographical writing, select topics, and write drafts. (pp. 48–59/H32–39)	**Teaching Resources** *Writing Support Transparencies,* 4-A–E; *Writing Support Activity Book,* 4-1–4 *Writing and Grammar* **Interactive Text,** Ch. 4, Introduction through Section 4.3
DAY 2	**Revising Through Presenting** Students work individually or with peers to revise, edit, and proofread their work for presentation. (pp. 60–67/H40–47)	**Teaching Resources** *Writing Support Transparencies,* 4-F–G; *Scoring Rubrics on Transparency,* Ch. 4; *Writing Assessment and Portfolio Management; Formal Assessment,* Ch. 4 *Writing and Grammar* **Interactive Text,** Sections 4.4–6

Options for Adapting Lesson Plans

HOMEWORK

Have students complete any stage of the lesson for homework.

FEATURES

Extend coverage with Connected Assignment (p. 71), Spotlight on the Humanities (p. 72), Media and Technology Skills (p. 73), and the Standardized Test Preparation Workshop (p. 74).

TECHNOLOGY

Students can complete any stage of the lesson on the computer, using *Writing and Grammar* Interactive Text or a word-processing program. Have them print out their completed work.

Writing and Grammar Handbook Alignment

Page numbers in Step-by-Step Teaching Guides in this Teacher's Edition refer to pages from the full student text. Handbook page references, indicated with this icon Ⓗ, are provided in Time and Resource Manager boxes and at the bottom of each Teacher's Edition page.

INTEGRATED SKILLS COVERAGE

Integrating Grammar
Nominative and Objective Cases of Pronouns, SE p. 64/Ⓗ44
Paragraphing and Punctuating Dialogue, SE p. 66/Ⓗ46

Reading/Writing Connection
Recognize the Author's Purpose, SE p. 50
Writing Application, SE p. 53

Viewing and Representing
Critical Viewing, SE pp. 48, 51, 52, 61, 68, 70, 71, 72/Ⓗ32, 41
Appreciating the Arts, SE p. 72
Creating a Video Journal, SE p. 73; ATE p. 73

Technology SE pp. 56, 58/Ⓗ36, 38

Speaking and Listening ATE p. 53

Collaborative Writing SE p. 59/Ⓗ39

Workplace Skills ATE p. 52

Real-World Connection ATE p. 51

ASSESSMENT SUPPORT

Standardized Test Preparation Workshop SE p. 74; ATE pp. 56, 63
Standardized Test Preparation Workbook, pp. 7–8
Scoring Rubrics on Transparency, Ch. 4
Formal Assessment, Ch. 4
Writing Assessment and Portfolio Management

MEETING INDIVIDUAL NEEDS

Less Advanced Students ATE pp. 58, 61, 75. See also Ongoing Assessments ATE pp. 57, 59, 64.
More Advanced Students ATE p. 75
Gifted and Talented Students ATE p. 62
ESL Students ATE pp. 52, 53, 59
Spatial Learners ATE p. 55
Linguistic Learners ATE pp. 65, 69
Bodily/Kinesthetic Learners ATE p. 70
Musical Learners ATE pp. 52, 57

BLOCK SCHEDULING

Pacing Suggestions
For 90-minute Blocks
- Have students complete the Prewriting and Drafting stages in a single period.
- Focus one class period on Revising and Editing and Publishing and Presenting. Allow at least 30 minutes for peer revision.

Resources for Varying Instruction
- *Writing and Grammar* Interactive Text A 90-minute block provides an ideal opportunity for students to work on the computer.
- *Writers at Work* DVD Show the Narration segment in class.

Professional Development Support
- *How to Manage Instruction in the Block* This teaching resource provides management and activity suggestions.

MEDIA AND TECHNOLOGY

For the Student
- *Writing and Grammar* Interactive Text, Ch. 4
- *On-line Exercise Bank*, Section 4.4

For the Teacher
- *Writers at Work* DVD, Narration
- **Teacher**EXPRESS™ CD-ROM

WRITING AND GRAMMAR ON-LINE

Interactive Text (On-line or on CD-ROM)
- Easily navigable instruction with interactive Revision Checkers
- Full use of e-rater™, the essay-scoring system (on-line only)

Companion Web Site PHSchool.com
- Scoring rubrics with models (use Web Code eek-1001)

See the Go On-line! **feature, SE p. iii.**

LITERATURE CONNECTIONS

Related selections from *Prentice Hall Literature, Penguin Edition*, Grade 10:
Professional Model from *Desert Exile: The Uprooting of a Japanese-American Family,* Yoshiko Uchida, SE p. 53
Topic Bank Option "Occupation: Conductorette," Maya Angelou, SE p. 55/Ⓗ35

Lesson Objectives

1. To write an autobiographical narrative appropriate to audience and purpose
2. To read to appreciate a writer's craft and to discover models for writing
3. To use prewriting strategies to generate ideas, develop voice, and plan
4. To develop and revise drafts in terms of structure, paragraphs, sentences, and word choice
5. To compose increasingly more involved sentences
6. To edit and proofread to ensure standard English usage and grammar
7. To use technology for aspects of creating, revising, editing, and publishing texts
8. To evaluate writing for both mechanics and content
9. To respond productively to peer review of his/her own work
10. To refine an autobiographical narrative for publication

Critical Viewing

Analyze Students may observe that the boys look tidy but a bit shabby, as well as a little sad. Unless they know about shoe-shine boys and the poverty that drove these youngsters to the streets of big cities, they may not guess many details of their lives. You may want to share some details with the class.

Chapter
4 Narration
Autobiographical Writing

A Tough Story, John G. Brown, North Carolina Museum of Art

▲ Critical Viewing
Judging from the details in this piece of fine art, what sort of life story might these boys have to tell? [**Analyze**]

Autobiographical Narration in Everyday Life

Think for a moment about a typical school day. To whom do you talk? What do you say? Chances are, you probably talk with friends about your experiences since you last met. When you tell a friend about what you did during the weekend or describe a funny thing that happened to you, you are engaging in **autobiographical narration**—telling a story from your own life. These stories may be funny or sad, short or long.

Autobiographical narration sometimes takes written form. You may, for example, write a letter to a cousin about a concert you heard, or you may relate a story about yourself on a job or college application.

48 • Narration

⏱ TIME AND RESOURCE MANAGER

Resources
Technology: *Writers at Work* DVD, Narration; *Writing and Grammar* Interactive Text, Ch. 4

Using the Full Student Edition	Using the Handbook Ⓗ
• Cover pp. 48–49 in class. • Show the Narration section of the *Writers at Work* DVD. • Read the Model From Literature (pp. 50–53) in class, and use it to discuss elements of autobiographical narrative. • Discuss examples of autobiographical writing with which students are familiar.	• Cover pp. 32–33 in class. • Show the Narration section of the *Writers at Work* DVD. • Discuss examples of autobiographical writing with which students are familiar.

What Is Autobiographical Writing?

Autobiographical writing tells a story about an event or experience in the writer's own life. An autobiographical narrative can be as simple as a description of a recent car trip or as complex as the entire story of a person's life.

Autobiographical writing usually includes

- the writer as the main character.
- a sequence of events.
- conflict or tension between characters or between a character and an outside force.
- an insight gained by the writer.

To preview the criteria on which your autobiographical narrative may be evaluated, see the Rubric for Self-Assessment on page 67.

Types of Autobiographical Writing

Following are some types of autobiographical writing:

- **Eyewitness accounts** are retellings of events personally witnessed by a writer.

- **Personal narratives** are stories that reveal a writer's opinions, feelings, and insights about an experience.

- **Autobiographical incidents** tell of a memorable or pivotal event in a writer's life.

- **Memoirs** contain a writer's reflections on an important person or event from his or her own life.

- **Anecdotes** are brief, true, and usually humorous stories that contain a definite conclusion.

PREVIEW
Student Work
IN PROGRESS

Erica Jackson, a student at Boone County High School in Florence, Kentucky, wrote a personal narrative called "The Ultimate Challenge." Follow along as she prewrites, drafts, and revises her work. You can read her completed narrative at the end of the lesson.

Writers in ACTION

American writer and poet Muriel Rukeyser understood the importance of storytelling. In "The Speed of Darkness," she observed the following:

"The universe is made of stories, not of atoms."

PREPARE and ENGAGE

Interest GRABBER Ask students to remember the funniest thing that has ever happened to them. Ask students to consider what made the situation funny. Did they think it was funny at the time? Have they ever shared the story with others? Have students jot down notes about their experiences, then ask volunteers to share their narratives in class.

Activate Prior Knowledge

Ask students to recall an autobiographical anecdote they have heard recently, perhaps on television or radio, or in conversation with friends. Ask students what characteristics made the story memorable. Note to students that the ability to tell anecdotes effectively is not only valuable in writing, it is also a useful social skill.

More About the Writer

Muriel Rukeyser (1913–1980) was a writer and teacher whose work played a part in the development of contemporary American writing. Rukeyser was as well known for her social activism as for her writing. The issues that concerned her most included women's rights, civil rights, anti-Semitism, and environmentalism. Her first award-winning book of poetry was written while she was a college student. Rukeyser felt that poetry had a central role in a democratic society, a view that she explores at length in *The Life of Poetry*.

4.1 Model From Literature

Linda Greenhouse is a journalist who covers the Supreme Court for The New York Times. *The following article was published in* The New York Times Magazine.

Reading Strategy: Recognize the Author's Purpose As you read, think about why the author is writing and how he or she wants you to respond. For example, an author may want to warn you about something or to persuade you to think in a specific way. As you read this narrative, examine Greenhouse's word choice and selection of details to identify her purpose for writing.

The Long Tale of Madonna the Iguana

Linda Greenhouse

Madonna the Iguana came into our life when my daughter, Hannah, was 9 years old, desperately wanting a house pet but allergic to almost anything with fur or hair. The little lizard was like a tiny green jewel, small enough to fit in my hand and so fragile I worried each breath might be its last. Five years later, she (we deemed it a female, but we were never really sure) was a muscular, fully grown adult. Five feet long, she had outgrown three enclosures, the last the size of a stall shower, a two-level contraption with sliding glass doors.

She had also outgrown the affections of a teenage girl whose friends now shuddered at the sight of her huge reptilian roommate. I understood Hannah's embarrassment, but I was proud that while the great majority of iguanas die in their first year as house pets, Madonna was thriving. Without my wanting it to happen, this iguana had found a place in my heart.

So that became our story. A pet outgrew a girl. A girl outgrew her pet. And a mother tried, probably for longer than she should have, to hold on to both.

50 • Autobiographical Writing

Notice the play on words in the title. "Tale" could be changed to "tail".

Greenhouse provides a vivid description of the iguana.

Greenhouse herself is the "I" in the story.

"But Madonna doesn't do anything!" Hannah would sometimes say. That was true; these big lizards just bask in the sun munching on leaves and flowers. Visitors often asked if iguanas were smart. Smart enough, was all I could say of a species that had flourished through many millenniums. "Does Madonna love me?" my daughter asked early on. I don't really think so, I replied. "Well, at least does she like me?"

Yet my relationship with Madonna was not just a one-way street. She perked up when I came into the room. She let me peel off her shedding skin like a giant green sunburn, stripes and all. The skin of her feet sometimes came off like a delicate glove, a mysterious artifact from a distant time and place.

At first she wouldn't eat while I watched, and I would peer from the hallway as she delicately picked through her dish to find her favorites—broccoli, green beans and carrots always disappeared before collard greens or kale. Eventually, she ate in front of me. She liked pansies, which I grew as a special treat.

When the window was open, she would climb up the screen and hold herself upright, listening to the birds and watching the breeze intently. I half hoped that the sight of this enormous reptile would terrify someone, but no one noticed.

She did give us a scare when an ice storm knocked out our electricity, forcing us to vacate the house. Not knowing what else to do, we covered Madonna in a towel and left her lying still. Each day for three days, I came back to the cold, dark house to check on her. A mammal might well have died. But her cold blooded reptilian body simply slowed down to the minimum. When the heat came back on, Madonna warmed up and within hours was back to normal, with no damage done.

▶ **Critical Viewing** What might account for the popularity of iguanas as house pets? **[Generalize]**

Dialogue such as this helps bring characters and situations to life for readers.

The autobiographical narrative is told in chronological order, progressing forward in time.

Model From Literature • 51

Integrating Workplace Skills

Encourage students to think about jobs that might involve being able to handle an iguana (pet store owner, veterinarian, zoo keeper, naturalist, animal behavior researcher). Ask them to think about the skills these jobs would have in common (love of animals, knowledge of how to keep animals healthy). In what ways might theses jobs differ? (Students may cite differing levels of physical activity, differing levels of education).

Customize for
ESL Students

Many cultures have strong traditions of storytelling. Ask students if there are stories they have heard from friends and relatives while they were growing up. Encourage them to think of this tradition of sharing personal history as they approach their autobiographical narratives, since the forms are related in many respects.

Customize for
Musical Learners

From old ballads to country and western music to popular songs, music has long been a way that autobiographical narratives have been shared with an audience. Encourage students to bring in recordings of songs that tell stories about the people who wrote them. If possible, allow time for listening to some of the selections. Alternatively, you can select and play music that you know will be acceptable, to illustrate songs as a medium for stories.

Critical Viewing

Analyze Answers will depend on students' feelings about lizards, but will likely include descriptions of skin texture, color, eyes, and body shape.

▲ Critical Viewing What descriptive words would you choose to paint a verbal portrait of this iguana? [**Analyze**]

When the end came, it was without warning. Just as our Thanksgiving guests were due to arrive, we heard a huge crash from Hannah's room. We raced up the stairs to find the plate glass of Madonna's enclosure shattered. Madonna, uninjured, seemed just as surprised as we were. A random flick of that powerful tail probably hit the glass at a vulnerable point.

The glass could have been replaced. But to me, the message was clear. It was time. Hannah barely blinked. "I'll get a sofa for that corner, where I can stretch out," she said.

An hour on the telephone the next morning confirmed that zoos have no interest in the outgrown pets of families who should have known better in the first place. But we did find a local pet shop that had an empty iguana habitat. Madonna would live there or be placed for adoption in a qualified home.

This event triggers the resolution of the story.

52 • Autobiographical Writing

We were at the shop within half an hour, Madonna struggling in the unfamiliar surroundings of a plastic recycling bin. But she didn't fight as the clerk lifted her into her new home, taller and deeper than the one she left behind. She scampered up the climbing log and stared at us, breathing heavily.

I cried on the way home, embarrassed at my inability to stop my tears. "I can't believe I'm crying over an iguana!" I managed to say. "She wasn't just an iguana to you," my husband said. "You took responsibility for her."

I suddenly remembered a scene from "The Little Prince," in which a fox asks a boy to tame him. But why should you want me to tame you? the boy asks. Because, the fox replies, "you become responsible, forever, for what you have tamed."

I never really tamed Madonna, of course, as the fading scars on my arms demonstrate—any more than I can hope to tame my lovely, headstrong 14-year-old daughter, who picked out a new couch before I had even dismantled Madonna's enclosure. A tamed teenager would be as unnatural a creature as a tamed iguana. Both in their natural states are prickly, wary, and inexorably growing into a strength under which things can shatter unexpectedly. In our iguana-less family, as Hannah reclaims her bedroom and looks beyond its walls to the world outside, I will try to remember what Madonna taught: that with responsibility, and love, comes the moment for letting go.

Writing Application: Choose Details to Achieve Purpose As you prepare to write your autobiographical narrative, identify your purpose for writing and think about the types of details that will help you achieve that purpose.

LITERATURE

Desert Exile by Yoshiko Uchida is another example of autobiographical writing. You can find a selection from the work in *Prentice Hall Literature, Penguin Edition*, Grade 10.

This allusion or reference is both literary and personal.

In the story's last sentence, Greenhouse reveals the insight she gained from her experience.

Model From Literature • 53

Integrating Speaking and Listening Skills

Explain to students that it is not only in writing that we communicate autobiographical information. When people talk to friends, to an individual they just met, or a small group of people, it is important they be able to communicate autobiographical data in an interesting, concise, and easy-to-follow manner. Encourage students to pick an incident, event, or memory from their lives and relate it to a small group in the form of an anecdote. Suggest that they briefly sketch out the important points first, to help them organize what they want to say.

Customize for
ESL Students

Suggest that students bring in an autobiographical story of someone from their home country. If they can find the story in both their first language and in English, that would be ideal. Ask them to discuss how the story relates details not only of the person's life but of the culture with which the student is familiar. What details speak most clearly to the student? How would they describe differently those elements with which they are familiar?

Reading\Writing Connection

Writing Application: Choose Details to Achieve Purpose

Explain to students that different types and levels of details accomplish different things. For example, if they are interested in entertaining, amusing anecdotes are more entertaining than detailed facts. However, detailed facts are vital if they are trying to persuade. Remind students that their writing can have more than one purpose, but that there should be one primary purpose that they can identify.

Prewriting: You Were There!

1. Suggest that students jot down notes about a variety of interesting things they have seen.

2. Have students narrow their lists to things about which they remember the most details. Explain that, if something was exciting but they remember little about it, it may not be suitable for a narrative. Details are what draw others into a story.

3. If students have trouble thinking of details, suggest they close their eyes and "relive" the event.

Prewriting: Consider the Moment

1. Give students time to make their lists. Remind them that simple things can be interesting if they are things with which readers can identify. Remind them that the story of the iguana was not "exciting," but people who have had similar experiences would appreciate it.

2. As students narrow their lists, suggest that they consider the details they can share, since details are important to narrative.

3. Encourage students to choose the topic that pleases them most. No matter what the story is, it will be better if the *writer* likes it.

Prewriting: Make a Blueprint

Teaching Resources: Writing Support Transparencies, 4-A

1. Tell students that they may narrow this down to a specific room. For example, a student's bedroom might contain gifts, friendship rings, posters, or other memory triggers.

2. Point out that the important thing is to have enough detail in the blueprint to trigger memories of things they've done. Using the transparency, point out how Erica used her blueprint to trigger a memory of water-skiing.

4.2 Prewriting

Choosing Your Topic

Choose a topic for your autobiographical narrative that you find important or interesting. Following are some ideas for generating topics:

Strategies for Generating Topics

1. **You Were There!** Choose as a topic an exciting event that you witnessed. For example, you could tell about a championship playoff game you attended or about a fantastic concert you heard.

2. **Consider the Moment** Write the following words on a sheet of paper: *Funny, Exciting, Interesting, Puzzling.* Then, try to recall moments in your life that fit each of these categories. Finally, choose one of these moments as the basis of your narrative.

3. **Make a Blueprint** Draw a floor plan of a significant place in your life. Label the rooms or areas, and, if you like, draw in details like furniture or trees. Then, make a list of words, phrases, sentences, names, or activities that come to mind as you "walk through" this special place. Review your ideas, and choose one as the basis of your narrative.

Try it out! Use the interactive Blueprinting activity in **Section 4.2**, on-line or on CD-ROM.

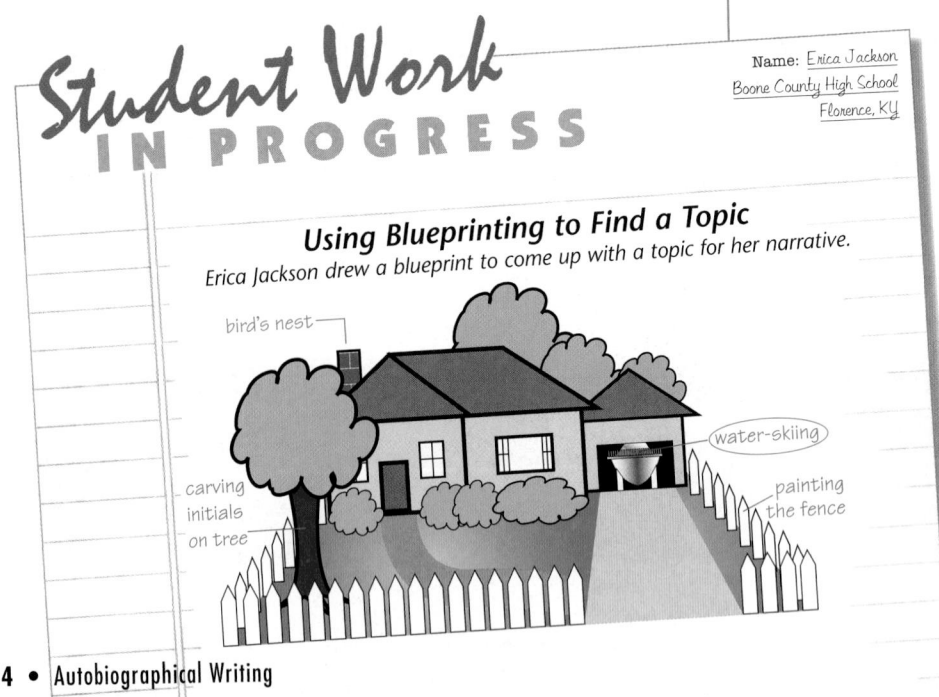

Student Work
IN PROGRESS

Name: Erica Jackson
Boone County High School
Florence, KY

Using Blueprinting to Find a Topic
Erica Jackson drew a blueprint to come up with a topic for her narrative.

bird's nest

water-skiing

carving initials on tree

painting the fence

54 • Autobiographical Writing

⏱ **TIME AND RESOURCE MANAGER**

Resources
Print: *Writing Support Transparencies,* 4-A–D; *Writing Support Activity Book,* 4-1–2
Technology: *Writing and Grammar* Interactive Text, Section 4.2

Using the Full Student Edition	Using the Handbook🄷
• Cover pp. 54–57 in class. • Work through the Prewriting strategies with the class. • Use the Responding to Fine Art transparency to help students generate additional topics.	• Cover pp. 34–37 in class. • Work through the Prewriting strategies with the class. • Use the Responding to Fine Art transparency to help students generate additional topics.

TOPIC BANK

Consider these suggestions if you are having difficulty coming up with your own topic:

1. **Anecdote About a Surprise** Recall a time when you were truly surprised. In a brief anecdote, tell the story of the situation and your actions.

2. **Memoir** Think of a person who has influenced your life in a positive way. In a memoir, recount one incident that shows why that person is a worthy role model.

3. **Personal Narrative About a Time of Change** Write about a period of transition in your own life. Describe fully the people and events that prompted such a change.

Responding to Fine Art

4. Look closely at *Backgammon* by Jane Freilicher. Why might the scene pictured inspire a piece of autobiographical writing? Study the setting and characters in the painting, and write an autobiographical narrative that comes to mind.

Backgammon, 1976, Jane Freilicher, Utah Museum of Fine Arts

Responding to Literature

5. "Occupation: Conductorette" is a real-life story taken from the autobiography of writer Maya Angelou. After reading the story, recall some of the goals you've struggled to achieve. Write an autobiographical essay about one of these goals and how you dealt with the obstacles in your path. You can find "Occupation: Conductorette" in *Prentice Hall Literature, Penguin Edition,* Grade 10.

🕐 Timed Writing Prompt

6. There is an old saying that "Laughter is the best medicine." A good joke or funny incident can pull us out of a bad mood or turn around a difficult situation. Write an autobiographical narrative about a moment when something humorous happened to you. **(30 minutes)**

Prewriting • 55

Step-by-Step Teaching Guide

Responding to Fine Art

Backgammon by Jane Freilicher

Teaching Resources: Writing Support Transparencies, 4-B

1. Display the transparency (4-B) and engage students in a discussion about it. You may ask questions like these to prompt discussion:

   How does the painting make you feel?

   What does it make you think of?

   Does the picture suggest an experience in your own life?

2. Brainstorm for ideas that the image might trigger (visits in the country, friendship, learning backgammon, summer vacation, and so on).

3. Students may wish to add these ideas to their topic banks.

Customize for
Spatial Learners

Some might find it easier to find a topic by responding to fine art than by responding to literature. If they do not identify well with the artwork on this page, show them some other pieces in art books from your school library. Encourage them to think about how the colors, brush strokes, or characters make them feel, and write about a time they have felt similarly.

🕐 Timed Writing Prompt

• To help students come up with humorous anecdotes, discuss different types of humor, such as slapstick, puns, and witty comebacks. Also, have students come up with examples of self-deprecating humor.

• Suggest that students allow five minutes for prewriting, twenty minutes for writing, and five minutes for reviewing and proofreading.

Prewriting: Use Carbon Paper to Narrow a Topic

1. Explain that this is a type of freewriting activity. The idea is to get down as many ideas about a topic as possible. The advantage to using the carbon paper for "invisible writing" is that the writing can't be seen and judged until the exercise is over.

2. An alternative would be to type on a computer with the monitor covered or turned off.

3. Tell students that no one will be looking at their "invisible writing," so they need not be concerned about style or neatness.

4. Suggest that, once they remove the carbon paper, students circle details or ideas that interest them, to see if there is a pattern that can help them focus their topics.

Prewriting: Considering Your Audience and Purpose

Teaching Resources: Writing Support Transparencies, 4-C; Writing Support Activity Book, 4-1

1. Brainstorm with students for a list of potential audiences and purposes. Some audiences might be friends, classmates, teachers, young children, or potential employers. Some purposes are to inform, to entertain, to persuade, or to work through an issue.

2. Give students copies of the graphic organizer (4-1), or have them create their own charts. Remind them to make sure that the audience and purpose work together logically. For example, the purpose of a story for young children will probably differ from one for a potential employer.

Customize for
Less Advanced Students

Work through the process of picking an audience, purpose, and strategy for several narrative ideas suggested by students. Then have students break into groups and work together to determine audience and purpose for each student who is having difficulty deciding.

4.2

Narrowing Your Topic

Once you have chosen your topic, narrow it so that the scope of your narrative is manageable. Use the following technique for narrowing the scope of your topic.

Use Carbon Paper to Narrow a Topic

1. Insert carbon paper between two sheets of notepaper.
2. Using an empty pen or a pen that is "unclicked," write on the top sheet anything that comes to mind about your topic. Write for at least five minutes.
3. Remove the top sheet and the carbon paper, and review what you wrote. Choose the aspect of your topic that interests you most.

Considering Your Audience and Purpose

Your audience and purpose for writing will have an impact on the details that you choose to include and the type of language that you use. The following chart highlights strategies for achieving your purpose, depending on your audience.

Type of Narrative	Audience	Purpose	Strategy
Anecdote about a humorous event	Classmates	To entertain	• Use lighthearted, informal language • Emphasize or exaggerate absurd or comical situations
Memoir about an influential friend	General audience	To inform	• Include ample background information since the audience may not be familiar with the subject • Develop details about the subject that explain his or her actions

56 • Autobiographical Writing

 Technology Tip

If you are working on a computer, use the following strategy to narrow your topic:
1. Open up a word-processing document on your computer.
2. Turn off the monitor so that you can't see the document.
3. Freewrite about your general topic for five minutes. Type anything that comes to mind.
4. Turn the monitor back on, and review what you wrote. Choose the aspect of your topic that interests you most.

◇ STANDARDIZED TEST PREPARATION WORKSHOP

Organize and Plan Standardized tests may require students to answer questions about how to organize a narrative.

Tessa wrote an outline for a report on her first day of high school. The major headings are shown below; use them to answer the question.

I Bus Ride to School   IV Finding My Locker

II Winter Break   V First Day Homework

III Meeting My Teachers

Which item does not fit the topic of "My First Day of High School"?

A I   D IV

B II   E V

C III

Students should recognize that **B** is the item that does not belong with the rest of the headings. "Winter Break" would not be a suitable subheading for the topic "My First Day of High School."

Gathering Details

Begin gathering details that are necessary to the narrative and interesting to the reader.

Gather Details About the Characters

Before you write your autobiographical narrative, gather details about your characters that will help bring them to life for your readers. Use a character profile like the one that follows to help you gather details about characters—the people in your narrative.

CHARACTER PROFILE

- What is the character's name, age, profession, and background?

- How would you describe the character's personality, habits, and likes or dislikes?

- What dreams or goals does this character have?

- What has this character achieved in life?

- What do other characters in your narrative think about this character?

- Why is the character important to the narrative you are going to relate?

Gather Details About the Setting

The setting is the time and place in which the events of the narrative unfold. The setting locates your reader in your narrative, explaining when and where the action of the story takes place. Fill out a setting chart like the one that follows to help you get started.

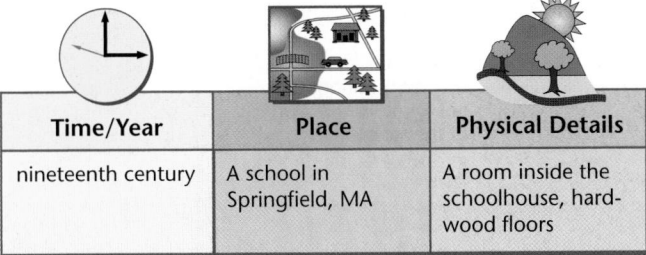

Time/Year	Place	Physical Details
nineteenth century	A school in Springfield, MA	A room inside the schoolhouse, hardwood floors

Try it out! Use the interactive Setting Chart in **Section 4.2,** on-line or on CD-ROM.

Prewriting: Gathering Details

Teaching Resources: Writing Support Transparencies, 4-D; Writing Support Activity Book, 4-2

1. Explain that details are what really help the reader get inside a story. Not everything in a narrative must be described, but enough details must be included so that the reader can recognize the people, places, reactions.

2. Remind students that, when they are doing character profiles, they should answer the questions for themselves, too. As the pivotal "character" in an autobiography, the writer needs to include details that help the reader understand what the writer is experiencing, thinking, feeling.

3. Discuss with students the importance of setting. Ask them what sort of actions can happen anywhere, and which might be dependent on setting.

4. Display Transparency 4-D to show students how a chart might help them develop their setting. Distribute copies of the graphic organizer (4-2) or have students create their own charts using details about setting for the topic they have selected.

Customize for
Musical Learners

If students work on this exercise for homework, encourage them to choose a piece of music that reminds them of the time and place they are writing about. Explain that music is often a powerful tool for unlocking details and memories about a certain time. Have them play the music while they gather details for their narratives.

☑ ONGOING ASSESSMENT: Monitor and Reinforce

If students are having difficulty gathering relevant details to include in their narratives, try the following strategy.

Have students meet and briefly discuss their topics with partners. Then have the partner write three or four questions that will elicit more information about the topic. The questions should elicit important information that the writer omitted in the initial discussion. As the writers answer the questions they will probably find that their answers contain details that they can use in their narratives.

TIME SAVERS!

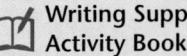 **Writing Support Transparencies**
Use the Transparencies for Chapter 4 to facilitate the teaching of strategies.

Writing Support Activity Book
Use the graphic organizers for Chapter 4 to facilitate student planning.

Drafting: Create a Plot

Teaching Resources: Writing Support Transparencies, 4-E; Writing Support Activity Book, 4-3

1. Point out to students that the conflicts they choose do not have to be major external events. They can be internal conflicts, such as when a character struggles to understand a person or an event in a new way. Writers can make these conflicts exciting through the use of such techniques as tension and elaboration.

2. Once they have identified the major conflict in the narrative, have them fill in the events before and after it on the plot diagram. The conflict should cause some type of change in or for the main character. This change should be evident by reading the completed plot diagram.

3. If students are having trouble identifying the conflict and the way it affects the main character, work with them to fill in the plot diagram for the excerpt from "The Long Tale of Madonna the Iguana" or another selection they've read this year as an example.

Customize for
Less Advanced Students

As a class, discuss a popular movie with which most students are familiar, then fill in a plot diagram. Make sure to include the major conflict and how it affects the main characters. Explain that there might also be minor characters who experience conflicts that relate in some way to the main conflict of the story.

---

④.③ Drafting

Shaping Your Writing

During the drafting stage, give your narrative its shape. Decide where and how to begin and end it, which characters to develop fully, and which events to highlight.

Create a Plot

Just like fictional stories, autobiographical stories should capture and hold the readers' interest. Think about your real-life story as if it were fiction. To do so, identify the timeline of events and decide on where to begin and end your story.

- List the events, and identify the climax, or high point of interest, in the story.
- Then, arrange the rest of the events so that they follow the structure of a plot diagram.

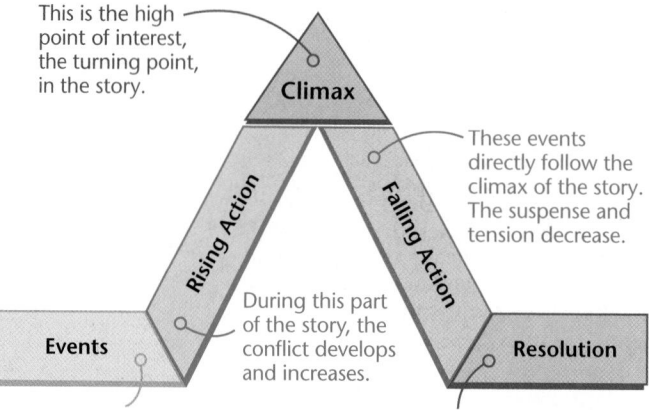

This is the high point of interest, the turning point, in the story.

Climax

Rising Action

Falling Action

These events directly follow the climax of the story. The suspense and tension decrease.

Events

During this part of the story, the conflict develops and increases.

Resolution

Introduce the characters, setting, and conflict. *Conflict* refers to a struggle that takes place in the story. It can occur between characters, between a character and a force of nature (such as a tornado), or within a character's mind.

Loose ends are tied up and questions are answered in this part of the story.

Technology Tip

In your word-processing program, write several ending paragraphs for your narrative, and then cut and paste each one in your narrative. Which one ties up the loose ends most effectively? Choose one that leaves readers with the strongest image.

⏱ TIME AND RESOURCE MANAGER

Resources
Print: *Writing Support Transparencies, 4-E–F; Writing Support Activity Book, 4-3*
Technology: *Writing and Grammar* Interactive Text, Section 4.3

Using the Full Student Edition	Using the Handbook🄷
• Work through the Create a Plot strategy and have students write a plot chart in class. • Demonstrate the techniques of adding dialogue and exploding the moment and have students add dialogue and details in class.	• Work through the Create a Plot strategy and have students write a plot chart in class. • Demonstrate the techniques of adding dialogue and exploding the moment and have students add dialogue and details in class.

Providing Elaboration

To *elaborate* means "to develop in detail." Make your narrative compelling to readers by using elaboration.

Add Dialogue

One way to add interest to your narrative is to provide dialogue that re-creates conversations or that reveals the thoughts that went through your head while you were in a particular situation. As you draft, develop your character and the characters of others through dialogue.

Explode the Moment

In everyday life, a moment of time passes quickly; there's little opportunity to observe it in detail. In a narrative, a moment can be "exploded." As a writer, you have the luxury of putting it under a magnifying glass, turning it upside down and inside out, and examining it from a variety of angles. Asking questions about an action or event is one way to get started.

Collaborative Writing Tip

Work with a partner to help you explode a moment in your writing. Describe a moment to your partner. Then, have your partner ask you questions about the moment. Use the details that answer the questions to help you explode the moment.

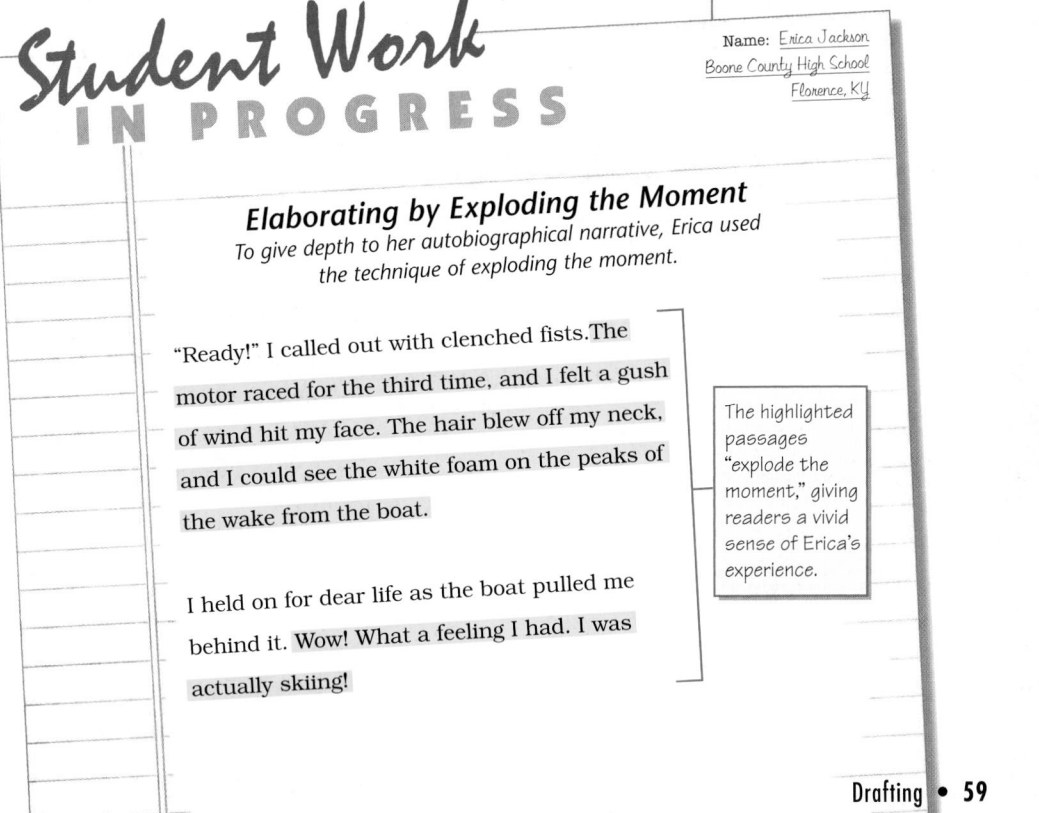

Student Work IN PROGRESS

Name: Erica Jackson
Boone County High School
Florence, KY

Elaborating by Exploding the Moment

To give depth to her autobiographical narrative, Erica used the technique of exploding the moment.

"Ready!" I called out with clenched fists. The motor raced for the third time, and I felt a gush of wind hit my face. The hair blew off my neck, and I could see the white foam on the peaks of the wake from the boat.

I held on for dear life as the boat pulled me behind it. Wow! What a feeling I had. I was actually skiing!

The highlighted passages "explode the moment," giving readers a vivid sense of Erica's experience.

Drafting • 59

Step-by-Step Teaching Guide

Drafting: Providing Elaboration

Teaching Resources: Writing Support Transparencies, 4-F

1. Explain that dialogue can add interest by breaking up the narrative and by letting characters express their own emotions.

2. Use the transparency (4-F) to show students how "exploding the moment" might look in practice. Point out that the author "exploded the moment" to help the reader experience it in greater detail.

3. Explain that "exploding the moment" makes writing much more interesting. It helps the reader feel the intensity of important moments in a narrative.

4. Suggest that students look at the climactic moments in the narratives they have written. Are the moments as exciting as they could be? If not, encourage students to "explode the moment."

Customize for
ESL Students

Students might have trouble writing authentic-sounding dialogue in English. Encourage them to write dialogue in their native language and then work with a more-fluent English speaker to translate it into English. Their partners can help answer questions about word choice, common expressions, and the connotations of various words.

☑ ONGOING ASSESSMENT: Monitor and Reinforce

If you observe that students are having difficulty completing their plot diagrams, try the following strategy.

Have students list, in no particular order, the major events in their stories. Have them identify which event is the climax of the story, and enter it at the top of the diagram. Then ask them to divide the remaining events into two sub-lists: events that occur before the climax and those that come after. Breaking down events in the plot into smaller groups should make it easier for students to decide where they might place events in their diagrams.

Revising: Deleting Unrelated Details

Teaching Resources: Writing Support Transparencies, 4-G

1. Work with students to make a list of qualities that define a relevant detail. For example, a detail may be relevant if it moves the action forward, makes the plot or characters more vivid, or reveals something about the plot or characters.

2. Have students evaluate the details of their stories. If they are unsure whether a detail is necessary, have them consider whether it serves any of the functions on their list.

3. Show the transparency (4-G) and point out how Erica deleted an unrelated detail in her story.

4. You may want to allow students to discuss their drafts with a partner after they've searched for unrelated details. Often, it is difficult for a writer to realize that an unrelated detail is irrelevant. A reader new to the tale can spot unrelated items more easily.

4.4 Revising

Revising Your Overall Structure

A first draft is not a final product. To make it into something wonderful, you need to trim, shape, and polish it. Following are some aspects you should look at as you begin to revise your narrative:

Create Unity

Review the individual elements of your autobiographical narrative to make sure they are unified and that they work together. Each paragraph should help develop the overall impression you want to leave with your readers. Sentences within each paragraph should work to develop the paragraph's main idea.

▶ **REVISION STRATEGY**
Deleting Unrelated Details

Each sentence in the narrative should have a clear relationship to the sentences around it. Delete those sentences or details that do not move events forward or create an image for the readers.

Interactive Textbook

Get instant help! For assistance in creating unity, use the Unity and Coherence Revision Checker, accessible from the menu bar, on-line or on CD-ROM.

Timed Writing Hint

When writing under timed conditions, spend a few minutes revising to delete unrelated details.

Student Work IN PROGRESS

Name: Erica Jackson
Boone County High School
Florence, KY

Deleting Unrelated Details

When Erica reviewed her draft for unity, she discovered that she had included some unrelated details. When she deleted them, her narrative became more focused.

Because these details stray from the main idea of the paragraph, Erica deleted them.

"Are you ready?" my sister shouted from the boat. ~~My sister is an expert water-skier. She's won several local competitions over the years for swimming, diving, and water skiing.~~ I paused for a moment, swallowed hard, and nodded.

60 • Autobiographical Writing

⏱ TIME AND RESOURCE MANAGER

Resources
Print: *Writing Support Transparencies, 4-G–I; Writing Support Activity Book, 4-4*
Technology: *Writing and Grammar* Interactive Text, Section 4.4

Using the Full Student Edition	Using the Handbook🄷
• Work through the Revision strategies with the class (pp. 60–65). • Assign Grammar in Your Writing (p. 64). • Allow time in class for the peer review process.	• Work through the Revision strategies with the class (pp. 40–45). • Assign Grammar in Your Writing (p. 44). • Allow time in class for the peer review process.

Revising Your Paragraphs

Form Functional Paragraphs

As you revise, make sure that your paragraphs perform specific narrative functions. Following are major functions your paragraphs might serve:

▶ **REVISION STRATEGY**
Analyzing Paragraphs

To sustain interest: Reread the longer paragraphs in your work to evaluate their ability to hold the readers' interest. If necessary, revise these paragraphs by breaking them into shorter ones that keep the readers involved in the story.

To achieve desired effects: Intersperse short one- or two-sentence paragraphs with longer ones to achieve desired effects, such as indicating a shift in time, a change in mood, or the occurrence of a major event.

To signify a change in speaker: Indicate which character is speaking by beginning a new paragraph each time a different character begins to speak. Because these paragraphs show that another character is speaking, they allow you, the writer, to avoid repeating "he said" or "she said." In the following example, a long paragraph was made into shorter, functional paragraphs.

Draft: In this version, an exchange of dialogue appears in a single paragraph. It is dense to read and doesn't have much of an impact.

> As Bryan and I rode up the mountain in the chair lift, I peppered him with questions about skiing. "What trail should we take?" I asked. "Can I handle an intermediate trail?" "Well," Bryan replied, "we'll just see what's there when we jump off the lift." "Jump off the lift?" I said. "You mean the lift doesn't stop for us?" "No," Bryan said, "the lift keeps moving and you jump off." "Oh," I said, in a small voice.

Revision: By breaking the large paragraph into smaller paragraphs, it's easier to follow the exchange of dialogue. The final line spoken by the narrator has more impact because it stands alone.

> As Bryan and I rode up the mountain in the chair lift, I peppered him with questions about skiing. "What trail should we take?" I asked. "Can I handle an intermediate trail?"
>
> "Well," Bryan replied, "we'll just see what's there when we jump off the lift."
>
> "Jump off the lift? You mean the lift doesn't stop for us?"
>
> "No," Bryan said, "the lift keeps moving and you jump off."
>
> "Oh," I said, in a small voice.

✿ Grammar and Style Tip

Avoid stringing together too many short sentences with the words *and* or *but*. Varying connecting words is just as important as varying sentence length and structure.

▼ **Critical Viewing**
If this were a movie scene, what lines of dialogue might these skiiers be speaking? **[Speculate]**

Revising: Analyzing Paragraphs

1. Remind students that, as they learned in Chapter 3, functional paragraphs accomplish different things than topical paragraphs do.

2. Encourage students to analyze where they need to "pick up the pace." A very long paragraph can sometimes slow down the narrative, while breaking it up can add interest and make the writing flow more freely.

3. Suggest that students identify places in their drafts where there is a change in time, mood, or location, and consider how a transition paragraph might help make the transition smoother.

4. Review the examples of dialogue in the text. Point out how much easier it is to recognize that speakers are changing in the revised dialogue. Also note that the writer was able to delete an extra "I said," since the paragraph breaks indicate the change of speaker. This helps to cut down on the number of times a writer has to tell you who is speaking, while still making it clear to the reader.

5. Allow students time to check their paragraphs for the possible inclusion of more functional paragraphs.

Critical Viewing

Speculate Answers will largely depend on the types of movies students prefer, and could range from skiing instruction to a spy selling information to a happy couple speaking of love.

Customize for
Less Advanced Students

Have students exchange papers with a partner. Have them make notes (in pencil) in the margin or on self-sticking notes that can be easily removed, identifying places that they think functional paragraphs might be useful. Then, have partners discuss their ideas and talk through how the desired changes could be made.

Color-Coding to Achieve Sentence Variety

1. Tell students that sentence length is a significant factor in sustaining readers' interest.

2. Point out that short, choppy sentences may fail to provide enough information or create a strong enough rhythm to sustain a reader's interest. Similarly, sentences that are too long may overwhelm a reader who is not yet intrigued by the subject matter.

3. A combination of short and long sentences is an effective way to sustain readers' interest. In addition, sentence length can reflect subject matter. For example, a narrative about a long, drawn-out event could include long, drawn-out sentences. An action-packed event might be written with many short, breathless sentences.

Customize for
Gifted and Talented Students

Encourage students to find other ways to add variety to their sentences. Inverting subject and verb order can create interest. The beginnings of sentences can be another area where variety can be added. Suggest that students avoid beginning sentences repetitively ("first I, then I, and then I"). Tell them to be as creative as possible while still observing proper English usage and grammar.

4.4

Revising Your Sentences
Vary Your Sentence Lengths

In narrative writing, variety in sentence length can "spice up" your narrative. Make your writing more expressive by breaking up passages that have consecutive short sentences or consecutive long sentences. Use different sentence types to help make your writing more interesting and mature.

▶ **REVISION STRATEGY**
Color-Coding to Achieve Sentence Variety

Review your draft, and use a blue pencil to highlight sentences of six words or less. Highlight longer sentences in green. Then, examine the balance of sentence lengths and make the following revisions, if necessary.

* Short, simple sentences, which contain only one complete idea, can be combined into compound and complex sentences.

* Long compound and complex sentences can be split into two or three simple sentences.

Simple Sentences: Express only one main idea.		The students wanted to play football. The hailstorm made it impossible to play.
Compound Sentences: Contain two or more complete ideas.	Ideas are joined with the words *and, but, or,* or a semicolon.	The students wanted to play football, **but** the hailstorm made it impossible to play. The students wanted to play football; the hailstorm made it impossible to play.
Complex Sentences: Contain an independent clause with one main idea and one or more subordinate clauses with less important ideas.	Subordinate clauses are introduced by conjunctions, such as *although, because, before, since,* and *while.*	**Although** the students wanted to play football, the hailstorm made it impossible to play.

62 • Autobiographical Writing

Get instant help! For assistance in revising sentences, use the Sentence Length Revision Checker, accessible from the menu bar, on-line or on CD-ROM.

Revising Your Word Choice

Evaluate Your Use of *Me, Myself,* and *I*

When you are writing a narrative from the first-person point of view—such as a *memoir, personal narrative,* or *eyewitness account*—you will probably use the personal pronouns *me* and *I*. It's particularly important, therefore, to make sure that you use these pronouns correctly. *I* and *we* are **subject pronouns;** they act as the subjects of a sentence. *Me* and *us* are **object pronouns;** these pronouns receive the action of the verb.

▶ **REVISION STRATEGY**
Color-Coding Personal Pronouns

Read through your draft, and circle each use of the personal pronouns *I, myself,* and *me.* Then, examine each usage, and make sure that you've chosen the correct pronoun based on its function in the sentence. A chart explaining the nominative case and objective case of pronouns appears on the following page.

Student Work
IN PROGRESS

Name: Erica Jackson
Boone County High School
Florence, KY

Color-Coding Personal Pronouns

Erica checked her use of personal pronouns and corrected an error she had made. She also deleted an unnecessary use of the word myself.

He had been wanting me to try the whole summer, but ⓘ hadn't gotten up the nerve to do it. (My) sister and ~~me~~ had always been competitive, and she was an expert water-skiier. Also, the thought of making a fool of (myself) in front of everyone didn't sound appealing. At first, ⓘ was unsure ~~myself~~ whether ⓘ really wanted to undertake skiing, but what did ⓘ have to lose? . . .

Revising • 63

Revising: Color-Coding Personal Pronouns

Teaching Resources: Writing Support Transparencies, 4-H

1. Using Transparency 4-H, discuss how Erica identified the use of *I, me,* and *myself* in this paragraph. Ask students why the changes were necessary (*me* is wrong, since it's part of the subject, which means it takes the nominative case; *myself* is simply unnecessary).

2. Explain that an easy way to chose between *me* and *I* when students are writing about more than one person is to rephrase the sentence using only the pronoun. "He gave it to Bill and I" may not sound so bad, but "He gave it to I" is obviously wrong, so the pronoun should be *me.* Similarly, in Erica's draft, "me had always been competitive" would have alerted her that *I* was the correct pronoun.

3. Point out to students that, while *I, me,* and *myself* are often the most common pronouns in an autobiographical narrative, they are not the only ones. They should be aware of their use of other personal pronouns as they write.

4. Remind students that they should also be aware of pronoun antecedents. A reader should always be able to tell to whom a pronoun refers.

🖉 STANDARDIZED TEST PREPARATION WORKSHOP

Sentence Structure Standardized test questions may require students to identify the various types of sentence structures. Provide students with opportunities to practice identifying simple, compound, and complex sentences.

Identify the correct sentence structure in the following example.

The students wanted to ride the bus, but they were too late.

A Simple   C Complex
B Compound   D Compound-Complex

Students should recognize that **B** is the correct answer. Two complete ideas, "The students wanted to ride the bus," and "They were too late," are combined by a comma and the conjunction *but.* Each is equally important; neither is dependent upon the other.

Pronoun Case

1. Ask volunteers to define *subject* and *predicate nominative*. You may need to identify *predicate nominative* as *predicate noun*, since that is often the way students learn the term. (*Subject:* person, place, or thing that the sentence is about; *predicate nominative:* noun or pronoun that appears with a linking verb and renames, identifies, or explains the subject.)

2. Review direct and indirect objects, reminding students that only a sentence with a direct object can have an indirect object.

3. Ask students to name several prepositions in addition to the one in the example.

4. Have students suggest sentences to illustrate each of the uses, but with a different pronoun than the one used in the text.

Find It in Your Reading

The examples that students identify will vary, but all should explain why *I* or *me* was used. Examples: "I understood Hannah's embarrassment"—nominative case is used because it's the subject. "Does Madonna love me?"—objective case is used because speaker is the direct object.

Find It in Your Writing

Have students review their narratives for personal pronouns. Sometimes the correct choice does not "sound right" to students. Suggest that they consider rephrasing these sentences. For example: It is correct to answer the phone, "This is I." However, it might not sound realistic to students. Advise them that they can resolve the problem by writing, "This is Jack."

4.4

Grammar in Your Writing
Pronoun Case

Case is the form of a noun or pronoun that indicates its use in a sentence. Use the **nominative case** for the subject of a verb and for a predicate nominative. Use the **objective case** for the object of any verb, preposition, or verbal.

Nominative Pronouns	Examples
Subject	*She* is the president of the class. *I* gave my coat to the clerk.
Predicate Nominative	The president is *she*.
(Formal Usage)	It is *I.*
(Informal Usage)	It is *me.*

Objective Pronouns	Examples
Direct Object	Our family praised *her.*
Indirect Object	The organization gave *us* a check.
Object of Preposition	Between *us,* there are no secrets.
Object of Participle	The noise scaring *them* was outside.
Object of Gerund	Helping *them* was my foremost thought.
Object of Infinitive	They want to ask *me* to lead the team.

Find It in Your Reading Read through "The Long Tale of Madonna the Iguana" on pages 50–53. Write down three sentences in which the author uses the personal pronouns *I,* and *me.* Then, explain why each is *nominative case* or *objective case.*

Put It in Your Writing Review your draft to see whether you've used the objective case of a pronoun following a linking verb. If so, replace the objective case pronoun with a subject pronoun and examine the effect on your writing. Decide which better suits your audience and purpose.

For more on pronoun usage, see Chapter 23.

☑ ONGOING ASSESSMENT SYSTEM

Prerequisite Skills If students have difficulty with the nominative and objective cases of pronouns, you may find it helpful to refer them to the following materials to assure coverage of prerequisite skills.

In the Textbook	Print Resources	Technology
Direct and Indirect Objects, and Predicate Nominatives, Sections 19.3–19.4 Prepositional Phrases, Section 20.1	*Grammar Exercise Workbook,* pp. 51–58	*On-Line Exercise Bank,* Section 4.4

Peer Review

Use a Peer Review Work Sheet

A peer reviewer can help you assess the clarity and effectiveness of your narrative and spot any errors that you have missed.

- Make a Peer Review work sheet like the one below.
- Photocopy the work sheet and distribute it to peer reviewers, along with a copy of your narrative.
- Have reviewers respond by filling in the work sheet.
- Consider the comments of your peer reviewers as you prepare your final draft.

Title_____	
Intended Audience_____ **Intended Purpose**_____	

Question:	**Response/Suggestions for Improvement**
Does the opening of the story grab your interest? Would you read on if you came across this story in a magazine?	
Are the characters and settings described well? Why or why not?	
Are the language and details in the story appropriate for the intended audience?	
Are there any story passages that get bogged down in unnecessary detail?	
Are there any other areas that need improvement or other suggestions that you would make?	

interactive
Textbook

Try it out! Use the interactive Peer Review Work Sheet in **Section 4.4**, on-line or on CD-ROM.

Revising: Use a Peer Review Work Sheet

Teaching Resources: Writing Support Transparencies, 4-I; Writing Support Activity Book, 4-4

1. Begin the peer review process by inviting students to identify a draft's strengths before focusing on its drawbacks.

2. Remind students to use the work sheet or a separate sheet of paper for peer editing rather than making corrections on the original draft. Though students are encouraged to consider seriously the opinions and observations that arise during the peer review, ultimately, the author decides whether to make any changes.

3. Remind students that some errors will be corrected at the proofreading stage, and that the focus here should be on content, dialogue, and character.

Customize for
Linguistic Learners

Suggest that students read their narratives aloud. This will allow them to emphasize certain words and to insert dramatic pauses. Students may also find passages that they choose to rewrite, adding or deleting for dramatic effect, once they hear the narratives read aloud.

Editing and Proofreading

1. Explain to students that editing and proofreading is an essential part of the writing process. Suggest that students check their punctuation paragraph by paragraph.

2. Tell students to check for one type of error at a time. This will prevent them from feeling bogged down by trying to spot all possible errors at once.

Paragraphing and Punctuating Dialogue

1. Write the following sentences on the board.

   Get out of the car before it explodes shouted the emergency worker.

   I am ready for my check said the woman to the waiter.

2. Have students punctuate the sentences on the board. ("Get out of the car before it explodes!" shouted the emergency worker. "I am ready for my check," said the woman to the waiter.)

3. Point out that the first sentence requires an exclamation point to show emotion. In the second sentence, the tone of the woman's remark depends upon whether a comma or an exclamation point is used.

Find It in Your Reading

By scanning for quotation marks, students should readily find two examples of dialogue from the five instances in Greenhouse's narrative.

Find It in Your Writing

If students have no dialogue in their narratives, encourage them to find at least one occasion to add dialogue.

4.5 Editing and Proofreading

Before sharing your narrative, check it for errors in grammar, spelling, punctuation, and capitalization. Since most narratives contain a lot of details involving characters, make sure that you have used pronouns consistently and correctly. Then, use the following strategy to give your narrative a final polish.

Focusing on Punctuating Dialogue

Review the use of dialogue in your draft to be sure you've punctuated dialogue correctly. Use the tips below for further help:

Timed Writing Hint

If you are given thirty minutes to complete an essay, plan to spend three to five minutes proofreading for punctuation and spelling errors.

Grammar in Your Life
Paragraphing and Punctuating Dialogue

Quotation Marks Dialogue should be set off with quotation marks. Begin a new paragraph with each new speaker. Look at this example:

"These students are very bored," I said. "They need interesting games that they can play inside in the winter."

"Well, then, perhaps you could invent a new game," the doctor replied.

Punctuation Marks Place punctuation marks that indicate the way in which the dialogue is spoken inside the final quotation mark:

"How about that!" exclaimed Judy.

"Who's there?" asked the leader.

Find It in Your Reading Find two examples of dialogue within "The Long Tale of Madonna the Iguana" on pages 50–53. Think about why the dialogue is punctuated as it is.

Find It in Your Writing Review the use of dialogue in your narrative. Be sure that you've correctly punctuated each instance of dialogue. Also, check to be sure that you've begun a new paragraph with each new speaker.

For more on the use of quotation marks, see Chapter 28.

⏱ TIME AND RESOURCE MANAGER

Resources
Print: *Scoring Rubrics on Transparency,* Ch. 4; *Writing Assessment and Portfolio Management; Formal Assessment,* Ch. 4
Technology: *Writing and Grammar* Interactive Text, Section 4.5

Using the Full Student Edition	Using the Handbook🄗
• Review p. 66 in class, including Grammar in Your Writing. • Analyze the Final Draft (pp. 68–70). • Have students edit and proofread their narratives in class.	• Review p. 46 in class, including Grammar in Your Writing. • Have the students edit and proofread their narratives in class.

4.6 Publishing and Presenting

When you've completed your narrative, share it with others and save a copy for yourself. Following are additional ideas for publishing and presenting your writing:

Building Your Portfolio

1. **Publish in a Print Medium** Submit your narrative to a school newspaper or to a national magazine that publishes student writing. Consult your teacher or librarian to find out about publications that might publish your narrative.

2. **Tell Your Story** Rehearse reading your story aloud. Mark up a copy of the story, and underline words that you plan to emphasize. Also, mark passages you'd like to read more slowly or more quickly. Finally, assemble a group of peers or family, and tell your story to them.

Reflecting on Your Writing

Think for a moment about what it was like to create a piece of autobiographical writing. Then, respond to the following questions, and save your responses in your portfolio.

- As you wrote, what insights did you gain about yourself?
- What "tricks of the trade" did you learn about telling a good story?

Internet Tip

To see model narratives scored with this rubric, go on-line:
PHSchool.com
Enter Web Code:
eek-1001

Rubric for Self-Assessment

Evaluate your autobiographical narrative using the following criteria.

	Score 4	Score 3	Score 2	Score 1
Audience and Purpose	Contains details that engage the audience	Contains details appropriate for an audience	Contains few details that appeal to an audience	Is not written for a specific audience
Organization	Presents events that create an interesting narrative; told from a consistent point of view	Presents a clear sequence of events; told from a specific point of view	Presents a confusing sequence of events; contains a point of view that is inconsistent	Presents no logical order; is told from no consistent point of view
Elaboration	Contains details that create vivid characters; contains dialogue that develops characters and plot	Contains details that develop character and describe setting; contains dialogue	Contains characters and setting; contains some dialogue	Contains few or no details to develop characters or setting; no dialogue provided
Use of Language	Use of language creates a tone; contains no errors in grammar, punctuation, or spelling	Uses vivid words; contains few errors in grammar, punctuation, and spelling	Uses clichés and trite expressions; contains some errors in grammar, punctuation, and spelling	Uses uninspired words; has many errors in grammar, punctuation, and spelling

Publishing and Presenting • 67

Publishing and Presenting

1. After reviewing presentation options on page 67, encourage students to consider other places to share their work. (Examples: related Web sites, writing contests, the school library, or with family and friends.)

2. In preparing their narratives for publication, students may wish to add illustrations, diagrams, or photos to their narratives. Ask them to extend the process of composition by considering which of these items would help a reader most.

ASSESS and CLOSE

Assessment

Teaching Resources: Scoring Rubrics Transparency, 4; Writing Assessment and Portfolio Management; Formal Assessment, Ch. 4

1. Display the Scoring Rubric transparency and review the criteria in class.

2. Before students proceed with self-assessment, you may wish to review Erica's final draft on pages 68–70. Have students score the Final Draft in one or more of the rubric categories.

3. In addition to student self-assessment, you may wish to use the following assessment options:

   - score student essays yourself, using the rubric and scoring models from *Writing Assessment and Portfolio Management.*

   - review the Standardized Test Preparation Workshop on pages 74–75 and administer a timed writing assignment.

   - administer the Chapter 4 assessment from *Formal Assessment* in the Teaching Resources to measure students' grasp of concepts presented.

☑ ONGOING ASSESSMENT: Assess Mastery

Use one of the following options to assess final drafts of students' autobiographical narratives.

Self-Assessment Ask students to score their narratives using the rubric provided. Then, have students write a single paragraph reflecting on the most valuable thing they learned in completing this narrative.

Teacher Assessment You may wish to use the rubric and the scoring models provided in *Writing Assessment and Portfolio Management* in the Teaching Resources to score the autobiographical narratives.

Final Draft

1. Help students see that "The Ultimate Challenge" incorporates key elements of the auto-biographical narrative.

   • The topic sustains readers' interest and is manageable in scope.

   • Audience and purpose have been carefully considered.

   • The topic appeals to anyone who has ever experienced sibling rivalry or wrestled with a personal drive for perfection.

   • The introduction engages the reader immediately with an effective interjection.

   • The body of the narrative presents an accurate physical sensation of the water skiing experience, drawing the reader into the narrative.

   • The conclusion ties up loose ends by clearly stating the lesson learned.

2. Ask students if there are any changes they would recommend to make the narrative flow better or to fine-tune the language. How might they apply these suggestions to their own writing?

Critical Viewing

Interpret Students' responses may range from fear to exhilaration.

FINAL DRAFT

◀ **Critical Viewing** What words would you use to describe the moment captured in this photograph? **[Interpret]**

The Ultimate Challenge

Erica Jackson
Boone County High School
Florence, Kentucky

Splash!

The water smacked the sides of the boat as it slowed to a stop while the sun beat down on the vinyl seats. The humidity made the atmosphere stifling, and the water was as smooth as silk. The lake was so transparent you could see your whole body while taking a refreshing swim. The beaches on either side of me were long and sandy, and towering above them the trees rustled with the slightest breeze. I was relaxing in the front of the boat, sunbathing, when I heard footsteps growing near.

This narrative opens in an attention-getting way.

"Erica, are you ready to try water-skiing?" my dad asked.

He had been wanting me to try the whole summer, but I hadn't gotten up the nerve to do it. My sister and I had always been competitive, and she was an expert water-skiier. Also, the thought of making a fool of myself in front of everyone didn't sound appealing. At first, I was unsure whether I really wanted to undertake skiing, but what did I have to lose? I grabbed my life jacket and put it on.

By this time, my knees were trembling and my heart was pounding. Thoughts raced through my mind. Balancing on the side of the boat as it rocked back and forth, I jumped into the lake. The water engulfed my body, but in the blink of an eye I was back up again.

My dad threw the skis to the left of me, and the rope was thrown in next. I realized it was drifting away quickly. This was the big moment. The temperature of my body seemed to drop suddenly, but I guess that was because I was so nervous.

I maneuvered myself into the skiing position, but my legs wouldn't cooperate. My body went one way, my skis the other. It was such an awkward position that I started laughing at how contorted my body was. Gallons of water went down my throat, and I began gasping for air. I struggled to keep my head above water. When I had finally composed myself, I positioned myself once again for skiing.

I clasped the rope with my left hand and placed it between my skis, which were unmanageable and bobbing up and down with the incoming waves. The rope straightened out and dragged me forward. No turning back now!

"Are you ready?" my sister shouted from the boat. I paused a moment, swallowed hard, and nodded. The knot in my throat was growing as the time drew nearer.

"Ready," I replied, questioning my own decision. I heard the engine roar, and a wall of water blocked my view of the boat. I rocked and then dove forward, still grasping the rope. As my skis flew off my feet, I fell face first into the water.

Smack! My stomach was the first to hit and a throbbing pain ran down my body. Everyone's eyes were on me, staring. I let go of the rope.

"Let the rope pull you up," everyone kept telling me. That was easier said than done.

The rope came around again, and I clenched hard. It straightened out again and I yelled, "Ready!" This time I was positive I would get up. Once again the engine roared, and I was pulled up,

Erica used chronological organization in her personal narrative.

Throughout the narrative, Erica maintains the first-person point of view. Erica is "I," the main character in the narrative.

Use of dialogue helps bring Erica's story to life.

Teaching From the Final Draft

Students should understand that the personal reflections that the author makes are in retrospect. The advantage of writing a personal narrative is the chance to explore and learn from experience. The author would not have time to formulate such self-reflective feelings at the time of the event. It is only in retrospect that she is able to gain insight about the situation. Have students review their work for personal reflections. Are these as effective as they might be?

Customize for
Linguistic Learners

Invite a student with dramatic flair to read the narrative to the class. There is ample opportunity for bringing the excitement and nervousness of the character to life with a live reading. Students with verbal strengths will appreciate the power of specific interjections, such as "Splash!" and "Smack!" This exercise will help them to identify areas in their own writing where they can strengthen the moment with added verbal emphasis.

Have students think about how they could relate an event from their lives without writing about it. This might involve doing a painting, creating a collage, building a diorama, or even creating a graph that charts their progress in some area. Encourage students to bring to class a photograph or other image that would help them share with others something they have experienced. If students bring an image that is related to the narrative they have written, they might consider incorporating it into the story when they publish it.

Customize for
Bodily/Kinesthetic Learners

Have students create a mime skit about an incident in their lives. It could be a special event, such as a party, or an everyday occurrence, such as doing chores. Ask students to guess what they are doing, suggesting ways in which the incident or action could be described if it were being written about.

Critical Viewing

Speculate Answers will vary. Students may mention the risks of colliding with other skiers, boats, swimmers, or even the shoreline.

along with the rope. The wall of water hit my body and my legs flew out into a straddle position. My body was screaming out in pain. I let go of the rope and and plunged into the water head first. By this point, I was frustrated. If this is as easy as everyone says it is, then why can't I do it?

My determination took over. Once again, the boat circled around me, and I grabbed the rope. My muscles were tight, but I maneuvered my body into skiing position. It was now or never.

"Ready," I called out with clenched fists. The motor raced for the third time, and I felt a gush of wind hit my face. The hair blew off my neck, and I could see the white foam on the peaks of the wake from the boat. I held on for dear life as the boat pulled me behind it. Wow! What a feeling I had. I was actually skiing!

Learning to ski was not just for my own self-fulfillment. I discovered that nobody is perfect at everything they do. If you learn to accept imperfection, you will still succeed at what you do. This was a lesson that was hard for me to learn, but eventually I learned it was the truth.

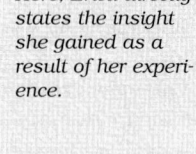

Here, Erica directly states the insight she gained as a result of her experience.

◄ **Critical Viewing** Judging from the clues in this photograph, what risks might a water-skiier face? **[Speculate]**

Connected Assignment
Firsthand Biography

One step away from telling your own life story—an autobiography—is telling the life story of someone you know well. In a **firsthand biography,** you use your special view to recount important moments from this person's life. You include your own experiences and interactions with the person to give the biography an intimate and accessible tone. As with any other biography, include facts and descriptive background gained from research.

Use the writing process steps outlined below to write a firsthand biography about someone you know.

Prewriting Choose someone you know well as the subject of your firsthand biography. You may choose as a subject a person in your family or someone from your school and community who has strongly influenced your life.

Drafting As you draft, focus on bringing your subject to life for your audience. Include examples, dialogue, and vivid descriptions that reveal your subject's personality and life story. Write in the first person to give your biography an "I was there" feeling.

Revising and Editing If possible, have the subject of your firsthand biography read your draft and comment on the truthfulness of the story as it is written. Then, revise your draft, reorganizing events or adding new transitions as necessary. Make sure you've kept consistently to the first-person point of view.

Publishing and Presenting Add photographs or artwork to enhance the text of your firsthand biography. Then, print out a neat copy, and bind it with a cover. You may present your firsthand biography as a gift to its subject, or you may prefer to share it with others who know and appreciate him or her.

▲ **Critical Viewing**
What interviewing skills does this student seem to be using as she collects details for her firsthand biography? **[Analyze]**

Connected Assignment: Firsthand Biography • 71

► **Lesson Objectives**
1. To write a firsthand biography
2. To organize material to ensure support for ideas
3. To use writing processes to develop and revise drafts

Step-by-Step Teaching Guide

Firsthand Biography

1. Discuss biographies students have read. Were any firsthand biographies?
2. Suggest that students review strategies from Chapter 4.
3. Have students give examples of possible subjects. They should choose someone they know well and, preferably, someone who will be available to interview.
4. Instruct students to work through all the stages of creating an essay, using care in organization, structure, and word choice.
5. Have students read each other's first drafts. Did readers get a clear picture of the subject? Did they want to know more about particular incidents?
6. Students might want to include a photograph of the subject about whom they are writing in their biographies.

Critical Viewing

Analyze Students may comment on the fact that she seems well prepared, is taking notes, is appropriately dressed, and is looking directly at the person being interviewed.

☑ **ONGOING ASSESSMENT: Prerequisite Skills**

Students may find the following resources from Chapter 4 particularly helpful in completing their firsthand biographies.

In the Textbook	Print Resources	Technology
Considering Your Audience and Purpose, Section 4.2 Create a Plot, Section 4.3 Explode the Moment, Section 4.3	*Writing Support Transparencies,* 4-E–F *Writing Support Activity Book,* 4-1, 4-3	*Writing and Grammar* Interactive Text, Sections 4.2–3

Lesson Objectives

1. To deconstruct media to get the main idea

2. To analyze ideas as presented in various media

3. To recognize how visual and sound techniques convey messages in media

4. To write in a variety of forms, such as autobiographical narrative

Step-by-Step Teaching Guide

Appreciating the Arts

1. Focus on one of the Spotlight elements for class discussion, or allow students to work in small groups or individually on the elements of their choice.

2. Ask students whether they are familiar with any of the writers mentioned. Have they seen *A Star Is Born* or any of the movies based on Lillian Hellman's work?

3. Point out that, since most movies tell stories, most are narratives. Ask students to talk about movies they have seen that have been biographical in nature, whether fiction or nonfiction. What elements of the film did they feel contributed most toward moving the story forward?

4. Ask students whether they have seen any movies based on literature. Encourage them to find out, either by reading the original book or by finding reviews of the movie, how closely the movie followed the original story.

Viewing and Representing

Activity Give interested students an opportunity to share their autobiographical accounts with the class.

Critical Viewing

Distinguish The elegance of the train might be a clue, but the clothing is the primary indicator that this story is set in a different time. The uniforms show that the scene takes place outside the United States.

Spotlight on the Humanities

Appreciating the Arts

Focus on Film: *Julia*

Narrative writing is writing that tells a story, and one of the most popular forms of twentieth-century storytelling is filmmaking. Nominated for eight Academy Awards, the 1977 film *Julia* is the true story of the friendship between playwright Lillian Hellman and her lifelong friend Julia. Involved with the anti-Nazi movement in Europe in the 1930's, Julia needs Hellman's help to assist in her work. Hellman comes to the aid of her friend and risks her own life in the process. Winner of three Oscars, the film version of *Julia* not only is a study of true friendship and courage, but it is also a dramatic look at the triumph of the human spirit.

Theater Connection American playwright Lillian Hellman (1905–1984) started her writing career composing book reviews for the *New York Herald Tribune* in the mid-1920's. Her powerful plays embodied strong messages of human courage and determination. The dramas became landmarks in the American theater and are still popular today. Among Hellman's best works are the dramas *The Children's Hour* (produced when she was twenty-eight), *The Little Foxes*, and *Watch on the Rhine*. All were made into films.

Literature Connection Author Dorothy Parker (1893–1967) was with Lillian Hellman in Europe as she traveled toward Nazi Germany for her friend Julia. Born in West End, New Jersey, Parker became known for being the only female founding member of the famous Algonquin Round Table in New York. Located in the Algonquin Hotel, such noted authors as Robert Sherwood, James Thurber, and George Kaufman would gather, creating a literary circle. Dorothy Parker was a drama critic, screenwriter, and book reviewer. She won an Academy Award for her screenplay of the film *A Star Is Born*.

Narrative Writing Activity: Autobiographical Incident

Risking one's life for a friend is an extreme example of helping a friend in need, but at one time or another, we all lend a helping hand to a troubled friend. Write an autobiographical incident about a time that you either helped a friend in need or were helped by a friend.

▲ **Critical Viewing** What details in this film still from the movie *Julia* reveal the time and place in which the story is told? **[Distinguish]**

Media and Technology Skills

Creating a Video Journal

Activity: Record a Trip

A video camera can help you capture the most exciting sights and sounds from any trip—whether you are traveling to a local amusement park, a state fair, or a relative's office. Your video journal will help you remember your trip and share your experience with an audience.

Think About It Choose a specific trip you would like to record with a video camera. Focus on one event from a longer journey. For example, rather than trying to capture an entire trip to New York City, you might create a video journal of your visit to the Statue of Liberty.

Set It Up One key to an effective video journal is to set up imaginative and revealing shots. Don't rely on point-and-shoot views to create an interesting video. Take a few moments to find an unusual angle or an especially powerful view.

Set up and shoot a variety of different shots. You might use:
- long shots to show scenery
- close-ups to show details
- panning shots to show motion or a vast scene
- interviews to share people's reactions

Also, remember that a video camera captures sounds, so background noise—such as birds, traffic, or even wind—can add to the atmosphere of your video.

  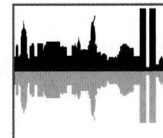

| Close Up | Long Shot | Panned Shot | People's Reactions |

Enrich It Your video camera may offer a variety of special effects, such as titles, unusual fades, color tints, or black-and-white options. Read the manual, and experiment to find new ways to enrich your journal.

Edit It After shooting your video, edit it to create a concise and engaging video journal. Use your camera's editing function, or use a double-deck videocassette recorder. Keep your audience in mind as you edit. Try to create a tape that will make your viewers feel as if they were actually along for the ride.

Media and Technology Skills • **73**

> **Some Things to Include**
> - People: Look for opportunities to film friends, relatives, and people you meet while traveling.
> - Signs and plaques can help to identify settings.
>
> **Some Things to Avoid**
> - Long, static shots of scenery are boring.
> - Close-ups that are too close may prevent your audience from knowing what it's looking at.
> - Shaky camera work may make your audience dizzy. Try using a tripod to get an extra-steady image.

▶ *Lesson Objectives*

1. To recognize how visual and sound techniques convey messages in media

2. To use a variety of forms and technology, including videotape and photographs, to communicate a specific message

3. To use a range of techniques to plan and create a media text and reflect critically on the work produced

Step-by-Step Teaching Guide

Creating a Video Journal

1. If students have no trips planned, discuss ways they can "relive" a trip on video. Possible strategies might include filming souvenirs and photos, and interviewing others who went along.

2. Draw students' attention to the graphic on page 73 that illustrates some of the techniques for making a video more interesting. Ask students to think of other techniques they may have seen in movies.

3. Discuss how students will handle titles—will information be announced for the soundtrack, or will they create printouts of information that they can film as part of the video.

4. Assign students to complete their storyboards before they begin filming.

5. If students do not have access to video equipment, suggest they try to come up with an idea for a video project that can be done at school, if equipment is available on-site.

6. When student videos are finished, create a presentation schedule for students willing to present their work to the class.

Lesson Objectives

1. To write a narrative appropriate to audience and purpose
2. To organize ideas and details to ensure coherence
3. To use effective sequences and transitions
4. To demonstrate control over grammatical elements

Responding to Narrative Writing Prompts

Teaching Resources: Standardized Test Preparation Workbook, pp. 7–8

1. Students taking a writing test must first identify the type of writing they are being asked to do. Remind students that narrative has a story-like structure, and that this piece will be a narrative.

2. Students should spend part of their prewriting time jotting down ideas and focusing their topics.

3. Emphasize the importance of having a clear purpose and a specific audience in mind. These will help students identify which points to highlight, what language to use, and what terms might need to be defined.

4. Discuss how a narrative essay intended as a letter would differ from a narrative essay intended as an editorial. Who is the audience for each?

5. Review the basic drafting procedure. Emphasize the importance of leaving time to proofread and edit.

Standardized Test Preparation Workshop

Responding to Narrative Writing Prompts

The writing prompts on standardized tests often measure your ability to write using the elements of narrative writing. The following criteria upon which your writing will be evaluated include:

- details suitable for the audience and purpose named in the prompt
- a method of organization that allows you to organize details in a meaningful and coherent sequence
- appropriate transitions that help your narrative achieve unity and coherence
- effective use of description, characterization, and other details
- correct grammar, spelling, and punctuation

When writing for a timed test, plan to devote a specified amount of time to prewriting, drafting, revising, and proofreading. Following is an example of a narrative writing prompt. Use the suggestions on the following page to help you respond. The clocks next to each stage show a suggested percentage of time to devote to each stage.

Test Tip

When sharing your experiences, include only details that relate to the purpose of your response.

Sample Writing Situation

The Internet is rapidly becoming a primary source of research and communication. It is also becoming an easy and time-saving way to make purchases. Because the Internet is still relatively new, many people are wary of using it for this purpose. Using your own experiences working on the Internet, respond to one of the following prompts:

- Write a letter to a family member who is not familiar with shopping on the Internet. Draw on your own experiences to convince him or her to use the Internet to do some shopping.

- Write an editorial for your town paper directed at working parents on the ease of using the Internet for shopping. Draw on your own experiences to convince them of its many benefits.

74 • Autobiographical Writing

✍ TEST-TAKING TIP

A clear understanding of the writing prompt is the first step to success on a written test. Tell students to make sure to identify the exact words in the prompt that specify audience, purpose, topic, and form. They might find it useful to mark these words in the prompt before they begin to plan their responses.

Ask students to pick out the key words in the Sample Writing prompts on this page.

Prompt 1: letter, family member, not familiar with Internet, your experience, convince

Prompt 2: editorial, town paper, working parents, ease of using Internet, your experiences, convince

Prewriting

Allow close to one quarter of your time for prewriting.

Consider Your Audience Although each prompt is directed at an audience that does not use the Internet to shop, avoid getting caught up in defining technical terms or providing directions on navigation. Use language that is appropriate for your audience. For example, if you are writing to a family member, you may use less formal language and shorter sentences. If you are writing an editorial, you should use more formal language and longer, complex sentences.

Consider Your Purpose Your purpose is to persuade your audience to shop using the Internet. Make a T-chart listing any negative aspects on the left side and positive aspects on the right side. Then, as you make your argument, show how the negative aspects can be overcome.

Gather Details Begin to gather information from your personal experiences of using the Internet for browsing or shopping. List details about your own experiences and the many different types of shopping offered.

Drafting

Allow almost half of your time for drafting.

Elaborate As you draft, give specific details that support your ideas. For example, you may include details from your personal experience, an anecdote about a friend's experience, and factual data about how long it took you to place an order on-line.

Make Clear Connections In order for your audience to follow your ideas, use transitions that indicate the logical connections between ideas. For example, *first*, *second*, *after*, and *then* indicate the time that events occurred, while *most importantly* and *less importantly* indicate order of importance.

Revising, Editing, and Proofreading

Allow almost one quarter of your time to revise and edit. Use the last few minutes to proofread your work.

Make Corrections Review your response for errors. Neatly cross out any details that do not support your purpose. Change language that is inappropriate for your audience, and make sure that transitions keep ideas flowing smoothly. Check for errors in spelling, grammar, and punctuation. When making changes, place one line through text that you want eliminated and place it in brackets. Use a caret [^] to indicate the places you wish to add words.

Customize for
Less Advanced Students

Students may not be comfortable with writing about the Internet. Encourage them to come up with another topic to write about, so they can still gain confidence writing, even if they do not have computer expertise.

Customize for
More Advanced Students

Have students extend the prompt by researching specific sites on the Internet that might help people become more comfortable using the Internet. These might include the user-friendly assisted search sites or on-line courses that demonstrate surfing skills. Have students create a handout of tips on using the Internet, along with a list of these sites.

Time and Resource Manager

In-Depth Lesson Plan

	LESSON FOCUS	PRINT AND MEDIA RESOURCES
DAY 1	**Introduction to the Short Story** Students learn about elements and types of short stories and analyze the Model From Literature. (pp. 76–79/H48–49)	*Writers at Work* **DVD**, Narration *Writing and Grammar* **Interactive Text**, Ch. 5, Introduction
DAY 2	**Prewriting** Students choose and narrow a topic, consider their audience and purpose, and gather details. (pp. 80–83/H50–53)	**Teaching Resources** *Writing Support Transparencies*, 5-A–D; *Writing Support Activity Book*, 5-1 *Writing and Grammar* **Interactive Text**, Section 5.2
DAY 3	**Drafting** Students shape their writing with a plot diagram and provide elaboration through dialogue as they write their first drafts. (pp. 84–85/H54–55)	**Teaching Resources** *Writing Support Transparencies*, 5-E; *Writing Support Activity Book*, 5-2 *Writing and Grammar* **Interactive Text**, Section 5.3
DAY 4	**Revising** Students revise their drafts in terms of overall structure, paragraphs, sentences, and word choice. (pp. 86–89/H56–59)	**Teaching Resources** *Writing Support Transparencies*, 5-F–H; *Writing Support Activity Book*, 5-3–4 *Writing and Grammar* **Interactive Text**, Section 5.4
DAY 5	**Editing and Proofreading; Publishing and Presenting** Students check their short stories for accuracy and correctness and present their final drafts. (pp. 90–93/H60–61)	**Teaching Resources** *Scoring Rubrics on Transparency*, Ch. 5; *Writing Assessment and Portfolio Management; Formal Assessment*, Ch. 5 *Writing and Grammar* **Interactive Text**, Sections 5.5–6

Accelerated Lesson Plan

	LESSON FOCUS	PRINT AND MEDIA RESOURCES
DAY 1	**Introduction Through Drafting** Students review characteristics of short stories, select topics, and write drafts. (pp. 76–85/H48–55)	**Teaching Resources** *Writing Support Transparencies*, 5-A–E; *Writing Support Activity Book*, 5-1–2 *Writers at Work* **DVD**, Narration *Writing and Grammar* **Interactive Text**, Ch. 5, Introduction through Section 5.3
DAY 2	**Revising Through Presenting** Students work individually or with peers to revise, edit, and proofread their short stories for presentation. (pp. 86–93/H56–61)	**Teaching Resources** *Writing Support Transparencies*, 5-F–H; *Writing Support Activity Book*, 5-3–4; *Scoring Rubrics on Transparency*, Ch. 5; *Writing Assessment and Portfolio Management; Formal Assessment*, Ch. 5 *Writing and Grammar* **Interactive Text**, Sections 5.4–6

Options for Adapting Lesson Plans

HOMEWORK

Have students complete any stage of the lesson for homework.

FEATURES

Extend coverage with Connected Assignment (p. 94), Spotlight on the Humanities (p. 96), Media and Technology Skills (p. 97), and the Standardized Test Preparation Workshop (p. 98).

TECHNOLOGY

Students can complete any stage of the lesson on the computer, using *Writing and Grammar* Interactive Text or a word-processing program. Have them print out their completed work.

Writing and Grammar Handbook Alignment

Page numbers in Step-by-Step Teaching Guides in this Teacher's Edition refer to pages from the full student text. Handbook page references, indicated with this icon **H**, are provided in Time and Resource Manager boxes and at the bottom of each Teacher's Edition page.

INTEGRATED SKILLS COVERAGE

Integrating Grammar
Verbs: Active and Passive Voice, SE p. 88/**H**58
Formatting and Punctuating Dialogue, SE p. 90/**H**60

Reading/Writing Connection
Predict, SE p. 78
Writing Application, SE p. 79

Viewing and Representing
Critical Viewing, SE pp. 76, 79, 85, 92, 94, 96/**H**48, 55
Recognizing the Oral Tradition, SE p. 96
Using Media to Convey Ideas, SE p. 97

Vocabulary Skills ATE p. 85

Speaking and Listening ATE pp. 81, 93

Technology Skills SE p. 90/**H**60

Real-World Connection ATE p. 86

BLOCK SCHEDULING

Pacing Suggestions
For 90-minute Blocks
- Have students complete the Prewriting and Drafting stages in a single period.
- Focus one class period on Revising and Editing and Publishing and Presenting. Allow at least 30 minutes for peer revision.

Resources for Varying Instruction
- *Writing and Grammar* Interactive Text A 90-minute block provides an ideal opportunity for students to work on the computer.
- *Writers at Work* DVD Show the Narration segment in class.

Professional Development Support
- *How to Manage Instruction in the Block* This teaching resource provides management and activity suggestions.

ASSESSMENT SUPPORT

Standardized Test Preparation Workshop SE p. 98; ATE pp. 84, 87
Standardized Test Preparation Workbook, pp. 9–10
Formal Assessment, Ch. 5
Scoring Rubrics on Transparency, Ch. 5
Writing Assessment and Portfolio Management

MEDIA AND TECHNOLOGY

For the Student
- *Writing and Grammar* Interactive Text, Ch. 5
- *On-line Exercise Bank*, Section 22.2

For the Teacher
- *Writers at Work* DVD, Narration
- **TeacherEXPRESS** CD-ROM

MEETING INDIVIDUAL NEEDS

Less Advanced Students ATE pp. 82, 97, 99. See also Ongoing Assessments ATE pp. 81, 83, 88.
More Advanced Students ATE p. 99
ESL Students ATE pp. 85, 93
Spatial Learners ATE p. 84
Bodily/Kinesthetic Learners ATE p. 83
Logical/Mathematical Learners ATE p. 87

WRITING AND GRAMMAR ON-LINE

Interactive Text (On-line or on CD-ROM)
- Easily navigable instruction with interactive Revision Checkers
- Full use of e-rater™, the essay-scoring system (on-line only)

Companion Web Site PHSchool.com
- Scoring rubrics with models (use Web Code eek-1001)

See the Go On-line! feature, SE p. iii.

LITERATURE CONNECTIONS

Related selections from *Prentice Hall Literature, Penguin Edition*, Grade 10:
Professional Model from "The Leap," Louise Erdrich, SE p. 79
Topic Bank Option from "The Monkey's Paw," W. W. Jacobs, SE p. 81/**H**51

▶ **Lesson Objectives**

1. To write a short story appropriate to audience and purpose
2. To read to appreciate a writer's craft and to discover models for writing
3. To use prewriting strategies to generate ideas, develop voice, and plan
4. To develop and revise drafts in terms of structure, paragraphs, sentences, and word choice
5. To edit and proofread to ensure standard English usage and grammar
6. To evaluate writing for both mechanics and contents
7. To refine a short story for publication

Critical Viewing

Speculate The storyteller might be relating a mystery or ghost story, as evidenced by his body language and the listeners' facial expressions.

Chapter 5 *Narration*
Short Story

Short Stories in Everyday Life

Storytelling is a part of everyday life. Some stories are true: They relate what happens in the lives of our friends and family. Other stories are fictional: They may teach or caution or amaze the listener. These are the stories you read at bedtime and tell around the campfire. These stories, although fictional, say something about the teller's beliefs, hopes, and ideas of truth and beauty.

▲ **Critical Viewing**
What sort of story might this storyteller be relating? Explain. **[Speculate]**

76 • Narration

🕐 **TIME AND RESOURCE MANAGER**	
Resources **Technology:** *Writers at Work* DVD; *Writing and Grammar* Interactive Text, Ch. 5	
Using the Full Student Edition	**Using the Handbook🄷**
• Cover pp. 76–77 in class. • Show the Short Story section of the *Writers at Work* DVD. • Read the Model From Literature (pp. 78–79) in class, and use it to brainstorm for short-story ideas with students.	• Cover pp. 48–49 in class. • Show the Short Story section of the *Writers at Work* DVD.

What Is a Short Story?

Narration is writing that tells a story. A **short story** is a particular kind of narration. It is always fictional and always brief. These stories are meant to be read in a single sitting. Using relatively few words, the writer of a short story aims to create a powerful impression on the reader. Most short stories contain

- a main character, who undergoes a change or learns something during the course of the story.
- a setting, the time and location in which the story takes place.
- a single plot, or series of events, which leads to a climax, or high point of interest.
- a theme, or main message, that is revealed by the story's end.

To preview the criteria on which your short story may be evaluated, see the Rubric for Self-Assessment on page 91.

Types of Short Stories

Although a short story is a specific type of literature, the stories themselves, like longer fictional works, vary widely. Following are a few examples:

- **Adventure stories** keep readers in suspense as they follow the plot twists and turns to the final outcome.
- **Fantasies** depart from reality to explore worlds and characters that stem from the writers' imaginations.
- **Fables** often contain animals as characters, and they convey a specific lesson or observation about life.
- **Science-fiction stories** combine elements of fiction and fantasy with scientific fact.

PREVIEW
Student Work
IN PROGRESS

In this chapter, you'll follow the progress of Ian Venokur, a student at Columbia High School in Maplewood, New Jersey, as he drafts his suspenseful short story "Horror Movie." The final draft of "Horror Movie" appears at the end of the chapter.

Writers in ACTION

Writer Maxine Hong Kingston finds that the process is similar for creating both fiction and nonfiction narratives:

"Narration has to do with movements and story and events and the adventures that we all have in our lives. There's an ongoing movement through time. And when I am writing a story, I am very aware of action that happens now—and then what? Then what happens next? And this way we keep moving."

Interest GRABBER Ask students to brainstorm for the most interesting stories that their family members tell about their lives. After they jot down notes about their stories, ask volunteers to share them. Discuss what makes each story so interesting.

Activate Prior Knowledge

Challenge students to make a list of every story they've heard in the past week. If they claim they have not heard any, remind them that stories are everywhere: in movies, in the newspaper, on television, at the dinner table, in books, and so on. Ask students why they think so many people enjoy listening to and telling stories.

More About the Writer

Maxine Hong Kingston is an influential Asian American writer. She was born in California to Chinese immigrants. Kingston tells both the stories of her childhood in America and the stories of her ancestors' experiences in China. Her first and most famous book is *The Woman Warrior: Memories of a Girlhood Among Ghosts*. The companion novel *China Men* tells her family's stories from the male point of view.

Reading\Writing Connection

Reading: Predict

Explain to students that *predicting* involves noticing the details in a story that provide clues to the story's outcome. Ask students to name details that give them clues about what will happen to the mouse in "Maud Martha Spares the Mouse."

Step-by-Step Teaching Guide

Engage Students Through Literature

1. Read this excerpt aloud, or have a prepared student read it.

2. After the reading, ask students to discuss the excerpt. You can use questions such as these to prompt discussion:

   How does Maud Martha feel when she first catches the mouse? (She is happy to have finally caught it after weeks of trying.)

   What makes Maud Martha change her mind about killing the mouse? (She thinks about the mouse's family responsibilities and the things the mouse enjoys in life.)

   What does Maud Martha learn about herself at the end of the story? (She learns that she is a good person.)

3. Ask students to brainstorm for other short-story topics that involve Maud Martha, the mouse, or both. Here are some possibilities:

   The mouse tells the story of its escape to its children.

   Maud Martha adopts the mouse or another animal.

   The mouse family gets too big and Maud Martha has to run them out of the house.

   The mouse family decides to move outside to a field when Maud Martha gets a cat.

   Students may add these to their own short-story ideas in their topic banks.

5.1 Model From Literature

Gwendolyn Brooks is a prolific poet and writer of short stories. Her work often focuses on family and the city of Chicago, where she grew up. Her first collection of poetry, A Street in Bronzeville, describes her childhood in that city. Brooks was the first African American woman to receive the Pulitzer Prize for Poetry.

Reading | Writing Connection

Reading Strategy: Predict In the following short story, the main character catches a mouse and muses about its life. As you read, use clues in the text to **predict** what will happen to the mouse.

Maud Martha Spares the Mouse

from Maud Martha

Gwendolyn Brooks

There. She had it at last. The weeks it had devoted to eluding her, the tricks, the clever hide-and-go-seeks, the routes it had in all sobriety devised, together with the delicious moments it had, undoubtedly, laughed up its sleeve—all to no ulti-mate avail. She had that mouse.

It shook its little self, as best it could, in the trap. Its bright black eyes contained no appeal—the little creature seemed to understand that there was no hope of mercy from the eternal enemy, no hope of reprieve or postponement—but a fine small dignity. It waited. It looked at Maud Martha.

She wondered what else it was thinking. Perhaps that there was not enough food in its larder. Perhaps that little Betty, a puny child from the start, would not, now, be getting fed. Perhaps that, now, the family's seasonal house-cleaning, for lack of expert direction, would be left undone. It might be regretting that

The story's two characters, Maud Martha and the mouse, are introduced in the opening paragraph.

By describing Maud Martha's speculations about the mouse's thoughts, Brooks helps reveal Maud Martha's personality to readers.

78 • Short Story

☑ ONGOING ASSESSMENT: Diagnose

Use one of the following strategies to diagnose students' current level of proficiency in short-story writing.

Option 1 Ask students to select their best example of narrative writing from last year. Have students reread it and write down its strongest quality and the one that needs the most improvement. Have individual conferences with students to discuss what they need to focus on in this chapter.

Option 2 Draw a plot diagram on the board and ask students to copy it into their notebooks and label the five plot elements. Students who remember these elements from previous years can help classmates fill in the diagram and discuss what each plot point means.

◀ **Critical Viewing**
Why might a person want to spare the life of a mouse such as the one pictured? **[Relate]**

LITERATURE

"The Leap" by Louise Erdrich is another short story that revolves around a character's decisions. You can find this story in *Prentice Hall Literature, Penguin Edition*, Grade 10.

young Bobby's education was now at an end. It might be nursing personal regrets. No more the mysterious shadows of the kitchenette, the uncharted twists, the unguessed halls. No more the sweet delights of the chase, the charms of being unsuccessfully hounded, thrown at.

Maud Martha could not bear the little look.

"Go home to your children," she urged. "To your wife or husband." She opened the trap. The mouse vanished.

Suddenly, she was conscious of a new cleanness in her. A wide air walked in her. A life had blundered its way into her power and it had been hers to preserve or destroy. She had not destroyed. In the center of that simple restraint was—creation. She had created a piece of life. It was wonderful.

"Why," she thought, as her height doubled, "why, I'm good! I am *good*."

She ironed her aprons. Her back was straight. Her eyes were mild, and soft with a godlike loving-kindness.

The plot, which revolves entirely around Maud Martha's decision, reaches its climax when she decides to free the mouse.

The story's theme is revealed as the readers discover the impact that Maud Martha's decision has on her life.

Writing Application: Help Your Readers Make Predictions What clues in the story's text helped you **predict** the mouse's fate? If you were to write a story about a fateful decision, what details might you include to help your readers predict the story's outcome?

Model From Literature • **79**

Prewriting: Sketch a Character or Setting

1. Have each student fold a piece of paper in half, then draw a character or setting on one side of the page and jot down story ideas on the other.

2. Students may also exchange papers after they draw their characters or settings so that they create story ideas from others' sketches.

Prewriting: Browse Through Quotations

1. Divide the class into small groups and supply each group with a book of quotations such as *Bartlett's Familiar Quotations*.

2. Have one student look through the book to find an interesting quotation, and then have each group member write it down at the top of a sheet of paper. Then, have them freewrite about it for three minutes.

3. Repeat the process three or four times, with a different student choosing the quotation each time.

Prewriting: Freewrite

Teaching Resources: Writing Support Transparencies, 5-A

1. Display Transparency 5-A and discuss how Ian used freewriting to develop short story topics.

2. Before students freewrite, remind them that the goal of this exercise is to record as many ideas as possible by writing freely about whatever comes to mind.

3. Explain to students that they probably will not discover the entire plot for a short story in their freewrites. Instead, they might find something minor like a character's reaction or an intriguing setting. Often, a small but interesting detail can play an important role in a story.

5.2 Prewriting

Choosing Your Topic

Sometimes, ideas for stories come easily and quickly to writers; other times, writers use various strategies to come up with ideas. Below are several strategies you can use to generate ideas for your short story:

Strategies for Generating Topics

1. **Sketch a Character or Setting** Use your imagination to sketch a character or setting. Then, review your sketch, and jot down story ideas that stem from it. Choose one idea to develop into your short story.

2. **Browse Through Quotations** "There is nothing to fear but fear itself!" "One is the loneliest number." Sometimes, looking through a book of quotations can provide you with a theme for a story. Find a quotation or theme that intrigues you, and then build a story around it.

3. **Freewrite** Freewrite for ten minutes about whatever pops into your mind. Review what you have written, looking for an interesting theme or idea. Then, develop your short story around that idea.

Interactive Textbook

Try it out! Use the interactive Freewriting activity in **Section 5.2**, on-line or on CD-ROM.

IN PROGRESS

Name: *Ian Venokur*
Columbia High School
Maplewood, NJ

Freewriting to Discover a Topic

Ian Venokur decided to freewrite about events in his own life to find inspiration for his short story. He began by writing about the events of the previous weekend. When he reviewed his prewriting, he found that a number of details in his freewriting were like elements of a scary movie. Because he was working to catch ideas quickly, Ian's freewriting included sentence fragments. These sentence errors can be corrected in a final draft.

The weekend. After school Friday went skateboarding, dull. Was (home alone) at night. Mom and dad went out. Gave me the usual business about (locking up) etc., etc., etc., Rented a couple (horror) movies.

A horror story about watching horror movies!

⏱ TIME AND RESOURCE MANAGER

Resources
Print: *Writing Support Transparencies, 5-A–D; Writing Support Activity Book, 5-1*
Technology: *Writing and Grammar* Interactive Text, Section 5.2

Using the Full Student Edition	Using the Handbook Ⓗ
• Work through the strategies for generating topics with the class (p. 80). • Use Responding to Fine Art and Responding to Literature to generate more ideas.	• Work through the strategies for generating topics with the class (p. 50). • Use Responding to Fine Art and Responding to Literature to generate more ideas.

TOPIC BANK

For more specific story ideas, consider the possibilities below:

1. **Story With a Theme** Write a short story around the theme "All's well that ends well." The theme may be implied or directly stated.

2. **Story About a Struggle With Nature** Conflict is the heart of a short story. Develop a conflict between a character and a dangerous foe—nature. Hurricanes, anacondas, a sudden flash flood along a remote hiking trail—you choose the specific force with which the character clashes.

Responding to Fine Art

3. Study the images presented in *Students of Modeling and Painting,* shown at right. Use the characters or setting within the painting to spark story ideas.

Responding to Literature

4. "The Monkey's Paw" by W. W. Jacobs is a chilling short story. First, read the story. Then, write your own short story in response. Your story may update the original version or continue Jacobs's story. "The Monkey's Paw" appears in *Prentice Hall Literature, Penguin Edition,* Grade 10.

Students of Modeling and Painting Anonymous, Private Collection

🕐 Timed Writing Prompt

5. Some of the greatest writers have followed the advice, "Write what you know." Now it's your turn. Write a short story set in your hometown. Use the streets and buildings that you see everyday and other details from your hometown to make the story believable. **(30 minutes)**

✓ ONGOING ASSESSMENT: Monitor and Reinforce

If you observe that some students are having difficulty generating or selecting a topic, use one of the following strategies.

Option 1 If ideas in the Topic Bank are too difficult for students, give them suggestions from the *Topic Bank for Heterogeneous Classes* in the Teaching Resources.	**Option 2** Have the entire class work on one idea from the Topic Bank. For example, you might assign all students to write an "All's well that ends well" story, or a story based on another quotation that you or the class chooses. When they finish, the class can compare the stories that result.

Responding to Fine Art

Students of Modeling and Painting, Anonymous

Teaching Resources: Writing Support Transparencies, 5-B

1. Display the transparency and engage students in a discussion about it. You may use questions such as these to prompt discussion:

   What do you think the people are doing?

   Where do you think this scene takes place?

2. Ask students to brainstorm for short-story ideas suggested by this piece of art. Here are some possibilities:

   The characters in the painting are going to work for a world-famous painter.

   A mysterious stranger is going to visit the characters. He will be carrying a priceless painting.

   Students may include these topic ideas along with their own suggestions in their topic banks.

🕐 Timed Writing Prompt

- To generate ideas about their hometowns, ask students to think about what they see on their way to and from school each day. Ask them to describe one place that stands out in their minds, such as buildings, landscapes, monuments, or storefronts.

- Suggest that students allow five minutes for prewriting, twenty minutes for writing, and five minutes for reviewing and proofreading.

Integrating Speaking and Listening Skills

Briefly remind students of the plot of a well-known fairy tale such as "Little Red Riding Hood." Ask students to take turns orally retelling the end of the story. In each retelling, the main character should make a different decision at the end. Remind students that this is only one way to alter an existing story. Other ideas include telling it from a different perspective or placing it in a different period or location.

Step-by-Step Teaching Guide

Prewriting: Narrowing Your Topic

1. Explain to students that the question "What is the main character's problem?" is actually asking them to describe the conflict in the story. The main character should play a major role in the story's central struggle.

2. Tell students that a good story is sometimes said to involve these three steps: getting the character stuck in a tree, throwing things at him, and then getting him down. Ask students to explain what they think this metaphor means (introduce the conflict, add more twists to it, and then figure out a way to solve it).

3. Ask students to identify these steps in stories that they've read this year. How would a story be affected if any of these steps were missing?

Step-by-Step Teaching Guide

Prewriting: Create a Purpose Planner

Teaching Resources: Writing Support Transparencies, 5-C; Writing Support Activity Book, 5-1

1. After students fill out their purpose planners, have them meet with other students whose stories have the same purpose. Give them time to discuss the ways they plan on achieving that purpose.

2. Remind students to keep their purpose planners in their notebooks and refer to them as they write their stories. This will help keep them focused as they choose details and events to include.

Customize for
Less Advanced Students

Before students fill out their own purpose planners, complete the purpose planner for "Maud Martha Spares the Mouse" or "The Leap." Have students determine the purpose of each story and supply details from the text to support their answers.

Narrowing Your Topic

A short story has to be short, containing a single main character, a limited setting, and a focused plot. To ensure that your story will be narrow and focused, answer the following questions as you plan your story. Refer to your answers to help you draft and revise.

- Who is the main character?
- What is the main character's problem?
- Will the main character solve the problem?
- What does he or she learn during the course of the story?

Considering Your Audience and Purpose

Though your general purpose for writing a short story is probably to entertain, you should focus on a more specific purpose as well. This purpose will affect the language and details you choose.

Create a Purpose Planner

Because short stories are meant to convey a single strong impression, think about the impression you want your story to leave on the reader. This will become your purpose for writing. Once you identify your purpose, develop a plan for achieving that purpose.

Create a purpose planner like the one below. Use the purpose planner as you gather details for your short story.

Purpose	Details to Achieve This Purpose
To amuse	Create eccentric characters; use exaggeration
To teach	State your theme; use main character as example
To horrify	Create a mood of horror through word choice; leave things unsaid and mysterious; create suspense by foreshadowing, or by dropping hints about the story's outcome

⏱ Timed Writing Hint

When writing under timed conditions, focus your story on one main character. If you introduce other characters, you may not have time to develop them.

82 • Short Story

Gathering Details

While the plot is the "engine" of your story, details help to develop the characters, and setting helps to bring your short story to life for your readers. Before you begin drafting your story, gather details about your characters and setting.

Gathering Details About Characters Characters are people, animals, alien life forms, or other creatures that take part in the action of a narrative. Effective characters are memorable, believable, and understandable. Before you begin drafting, jot down details about each character.

Gathering Details About Setting The setting is the time and place in which story events unfold. It includes the historical period, year, season, and time of day; it also includes the planet, country, city, block, or building, as well as specific physical features—such as furniture, plants, and weather conditions. To gather details about the setting, make a setting chart like the one shown below.

Try it out! Use the interactive Setting Chart in **Section 5.2,** on-line or on CD-ROM.

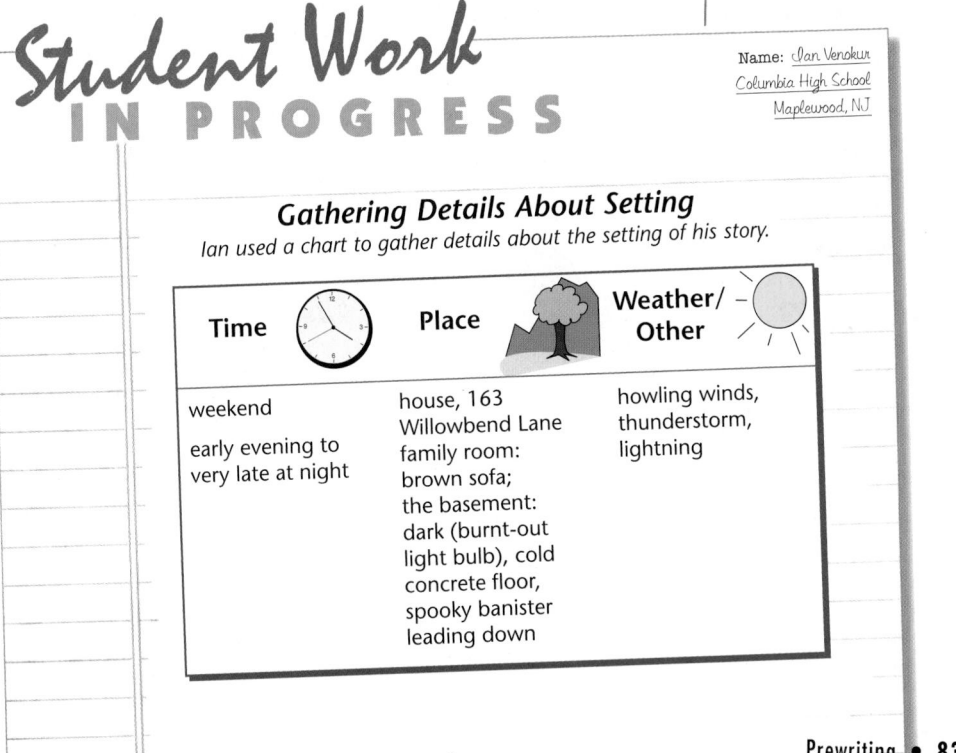

Student Work
IN PROGRESS

Name: *Ian Venokur*
Columbia High School
Maplewood, NJ

Gathering Details About Setting

Ian used a chart to gather details about the setting of his story.

Time	Place	Weather/ Other
weekend	house, 163 Willowbend Lane family room: brown sofa; the basement: dark (burnt-out light bulb), cold concrete floor, spooky banister leading down	howling winds, thunderstorm, lightning
early evening to very late at night		

Prewriting • 83

If students are having difficulty gathering details about their main characters, try the following strategy.

Give students a copy of a "personality test" from a magazine. Have them answer all of the questions based on the personality of their main character. This will help them think through the ways this character thinks, feels, and acts in many different situations.

Prewriting: Gathering Details About Character

1. Have each student fold a piece of paper in half, and then in half again, so that they create four columns. Students should label the columns "Name/Age," "Personality," "Goals," and "Other."

2. Ask students to pick one of the story topics from their topic banks and fill out a chart for each character.

3. Encourage students to write five more questions that will elicit important details about characters. Then, have them trade papers with a partner and answer the questions he or she devised.

Prewriting: Gathering Details About Setting

Teaching Resources: Writing Support Transparencies, 5-D

1. Use the transparency (5-D) to show students how a chart of details might look.

2. Explain that using details makes a setting more vivid to the reader. Have students identify vivid details from the setting of "The Leap." Then, have them explain how these details contribute to the story.

3. Ask students to choose one of the topics from their topic banks and fill out the chart for the setting. Remind them to include these details when they begin drafting their stories.

Customize for
Bodily/Kinesthetic Learners

Have students act out what their characters would do in the following situations: getting stuck in an elevator, watching a sports event, taking a very hard test, and starting school in a new town. Then, have them discuss the characters' actions. What important details did they learn about the characters by how they acted in each situation?

Drafting: Make a Plot Diagram

Teaching Resources: Writing Support Transparencies, 5-E; Writing Support Activity Book, 5-2

1. Display Transparency 5-E to demonstrate how Ian plotted his story as a diagram. Give students copies of the blank diagram (5-2) to plan their own stories.

2. Following Ian's example, have students write a brief summary for each stage of the plot.

3. Encourage students to invent new scenes in their stories if they cannot complete one of the sections of the plot diagram. Tell them to make sure that these new scenes fit logically with the rest of the story.

Customize for
Spatial Learners

Some students may find it easier to visualize a plot than to write it. Instead of written descriptions for each of the plot points, have students sketch the action that will occur at each point. Then, have them go back and describe each sketch in words. Tell students that filmmakers often use a similar technique to help visualize each scene in relation to the scenes around it. The technique is called *storyboarding*.

5.3 Drafting

Shaping Your Writing

As you draft your narrative, keep your central conflict in mind and shape the story around it. You may want to use a plot diagram to plan the events leading up to and following the climax of your plot.

Make a Plot Diagram

A plot usually contains the following elements:

- In the **exposition**, the characters and setting are introduced, as is the **conflict**—the struggle between characters or between a character and some other force.

- During the **rising action**, the tension builds as the conflict becomes more evident.

- The **climax** is the high point of interest in the story, during which one of the battling forces wins and the conflict is resolved.

- The **falling action** refers to the events that immediately follow the climax.

- The section of the story in which loose ends are tied up is called the **resolution.**

Timed Writing Hint

When writing with a deadline, use a diagram like the one on this page to shape your plot quickly.

CLIMAX — Doug's parents arrive home just as Doug panics.

RISING ACTION

FALLING ACTION

EXPOSITION — Doug's parents go away, leaving Doug alone for the first time.

Doug watches horror movies. He wakes up, alarmed at a noise. He decides to check the basement door. He gets locked in the basement.

Doug explains to his parents why he was in the basement.

RESOLUTION — Doug realizes that he learned an important lesson about himself.

84 • Short Story

⏱ TIME SAVERS!

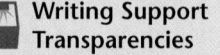 **Writing Support Transparencies**
Use the transparencies for Chapter 5 to facilitate the teaching of strategies.

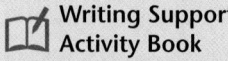 **Writing Support Activity Book**
Use the graphic organizers for Chapter 5 to facilitate student planning.

✎ STANDARDIZED TEST PREPARATION WORKSHOP

Organize and Plan Standardized tests may require students to be familiar with the various points of a plot.

Arrange these plot points in logical order for a story: exposition, rising action, climax, falling action, resolution.

a. Jane goes shopping with a new friend.

b. Jane's friend returns the sweater but refuses to be Jane's friend anymore.

c. Jane learns that real friends don't put each other in dangerous situations.

d. Jane is afraid the store owner will think she stole the sweater, so she confronts her friend.

e. Jane's friend steals a sweater from the store.

Which order is correct?

A a, b, c, e, d   **D** e, a, c, d, b

B c, a, d, b, e   **E** d, a, b, e, c

C a, e, d, b, c

Students should recognize that **C** is the most logical order for a story.

Providing Elaboration

Use Dialogue to Develop and Reveal Character

Often, the most effective way to convey the traits and attributes of your characters is through dialogue. Dialogue is the exact words that your characters say aloud or think to themselves. Through dialogue, you show rather than tell readers about the characters in your story. As you draft, look for opportunities to use dialogue rather than description.

Telling Through Description

Terence caught sight of Pat and enthusiastically greeted him in the hallway. Pat, feeling acutely embarrassed, tried to avoid his friend but had no choice. At first, Terence noticed nothing unusual about his friend's behavior, but puzzled by Pat's reluctance to talk, Terence eventually left.

Showing Through Dialogue

"Hey, pal! Great to see you!" boomed Terence, catching sight of Pat.

"Yeah," Pat said weakly, "great to see you too."

"What luck, running into you here and all."

"Yeah, luck, . . . huh?"

"Anything wrong, Pat? You seem kinda quiet."

"No, no, . . . everything's okay."

"Right," said Terence uneasily, "I guess I'll catch you later."

▲ **Critical Viewing**
If you were to write dialogue to accompany the scene pictured, what would it say? [Analyze]

Use Dialogue to Further the Plot Events

When drafting your story, avoid always having your narrator explain what events happened next. Instead, let the dialogue sometimes reveal what happened to whom.

Description of Plot Events

Jenny was very angry with her friend Bob for forgetting to drive her to the cast party after the show. After all, Jenny was in the play and had worked hard all month during rehearsal. Now, she just wanted to cry.

Plot Events Revealed Through Dialogue

"Bob! How *could* you leave me behind? I've worked so hard all month, rehearsing and rehearsing this play so I'd be good in it. And you leave for the cast party without me! I could just cry."

Drafting • 85

⏱ **TIME AND RESOURCE MANAGER**

Resources
Print: *Writing Support Transparencies,* 5E; *Writing Support Activity Book,* 5-2
Technology: *Writing and Grammar* Interactive Text, Section 5.3

Using the Full Student Edition	Using the Handbook Ⓗ
• Work through the plot diagram with the class.	• Work through the plot diagram with the class.
• Demonstrate the technique of using dialogue to reveal character and further plot events.	• Demonstrate the techniques of using dialogue to reveal character and further plot events.

Revising: Identifying the Purpose of Plot Events

Teaching Resources: Writing Support Transparencies, 5-F; Writing Support Activity Book, 5-3

1. To give them practice with filling out a plot analyzer, work with students to analyze the plot events in "Maud Martha Spares the Mouse" or "The Leap."

2. Next, have students analyze their own stories in a chart like the one shown on page 86. Encourage them to eliminate any plot events that do not seem pertinent.

3. Encourage students to think about characters in a similar fashion. Do all of the minor characters have a purpose in the story? Can they name the purpose of each one?

Revising: Using Contractions in Dialogue

1. Have students read through all the dialogue in their stories, circling each word pair that could be made into a contraction.

2. Ask students to evaluate their circled words. Ask them whether the dialogue would sound more realistic if these were contractions. If so, have the students rewrite the words as contractions.

Real-World Connection

Reporters must be careful to write down exactly what people say. Not only does this make the reporter's story more realistic and interesting, it helps the reporter write an accurate story.

5.4 Revising

Revising Your Overall Structure

Critically examine your short story to ensure that it's fast-moving and interesting. The following strategies will help you evaluate the plot of your story.

▶ **REVISION STRATEGY**
Identifying the Purpose of Plot Events

Short stories that contain too many plot events may be slow-moving and boring. Stories containing plot events that are not clearly connected to the rest of the story may be confusing and hard to follow. Review your draft critically, examining your story's plot events. Then, fill in a chart like the one at right, in which you identify plot events and evaluate their usefulness to the plot. Cut plot events that do not further the plot, and make clear connections between the other plot events to show readers how they relate to each other.

PLOT ANALYZER

	How Does It Further Plot?	What Is Its Purpose?
Event A:		

Revising Your Paragraphs

Revise the Dialogue to Make It Realistic

The challenge in writing dialogue is to make it sound as if your characters are real people, speaking as they would in the real world. For example, in the real world, people often use sentence fragments and slang in conversation. Use the following strategy to help make your dialogue more realistic:

▶ **REVISION STRATEGY**
Using Contractions in Dialogue

Only in rare situations would you encounter someone who avoids contractions in everyday speech. When revising your dialogue, combine word pairs, such as *I will* and *have not*, to make contractions.

I would have tried to go, but it is not possible now. ⟷ I would've tried to go, but it's not possible now.

🕐 TIME AND RESOURCE MANAGER

Resources
Print: *Writing Support Transparencies, 5-F–H; Writing Support Activity Book, 5-3–4*
Technology: *Writing and Grammar* Interactive Text, Section 5.4

Using the Full Student Edition	Using the Handbook🖽
• Work through pp. 86–89 in class.	• Work through pp. 56–59 in class.
• Use the Grammar in Your Writing lesson (p. 88) to review active and passive voice.	• Use the Grammar in Your Writing lesson (p. 58) to review active and passive voice.
• Have students revise their stories in class.	• Have students revise their stories in class.

Revising Your Sentences

Change the Passive Voice to Active Voice

Your short story should engage and hold the interest of your readers. One way to do this is to write it in the active voice. The active voice, in which the subject performs the action, is livelier and more direct than the passive voice, in which the action is performed on the subject. The use of too many passive sentences may result in clunky and lifeless writing.

▶ **REVISION STRATEGY**
Color-Coding Passive Sentences

Use a colored highlighter to mark instances of passive voice in your narrative. Passive verbs always have two parts: a form of *be* plus the past participle of a transitive verb. Once you've color-coded passive voice passages, review them carefully. If your use of the passive voice is unintentional, revise the passage to be in the active voice.

 **Learn More**

For more instruction on passive and active voice, see the Grammar in Your Writing feature on page 88.

Student Work
IN PROGRESS

Name: Ian Venokur
Columbia High School
Maplewood, NJ

Color-Coding Passive Sentences

Ian color-coded the passages containing the passive voice. To give his story energy and interest, he changed the passive voice to active voice.

his parents left him alone
It was the first time ~~he had been left alone by his parents~~ for a night. Doug couldn't be happier. He had prepared for it all week by picking out the movies he wanted to see and the junk food he wanted to eat. "Now, the doors
keep
~~should be kept~~ locked,........."

Revising • 87

Step-by-Step Teaching Guide

Revising: Color-Coding Passive Sentences

Teaching Resources: Writing Support Transparency, 5-G

1. Use Transparency 5-G to show how Ian color-coded his story for passive voice. Discuss the effect of changing passive voice to active voice in the passage. (The passage becomes more direct and livelier.)

2. Have a volunteer read aloud a paragraph from his or her story that contains passive voice. Write these sentences on the board and have students suggest ways to revise them.

3. Give students time to color code their stories and make the necessary revisions. Students who are having trouble may want to work with partners on this exercise.

Customize for
Logical/Mathematical Learners

Let students predict the ratio of passive to active voice passages in their stories. Then, have them count the instances of passive and active voice and calculate the ratio. Have students revise to lower the ratio of passive to active voice in their stories.

✎ STANDARDIZED TEST PREPARATION WORKSHOP

Active and Passive Voice Standardized test questions may require students to identify whether a verb is in active or passive voice.

Which sentence below contains passive voice?

A She was driving home from school.

B She drove home from school.

C She really enjoys drama club at school.

D She was driven home by her best friend.

Students should recognize that **D** is written in passive voice. The subject, *She*, receives the action, *was driven*. In the other sentences, the subject, *She*, performs the action.

⏱ TIME SAVERS!

 Writing Support Transparencies
Use the transparencies for Chapter 5 to facilitate the teaching of strategies.

 Writing Support Activity Book
Use the graphic organizers for Chapter 5 to facilitate student planning.

Verbs: Active and Passive Voice

1. Have students note that it is not always incorrect to use passive voice; it simply serves a different function than the active voice. *Passive voice* is used when the writer wishes to emphasize the receiver of the action rather than the performer, or when the performer is unknown.

2. Give students copies of a short article from a magazine. Have them underline the verbs and classify them according to voice. Have them share their answers.

3. Next, have the class write all the verbs in the article in passive voice. Compare this revision with the original. This will emphasize that the active voice makes the writing more lively and direct.

Find It in Your Reading

Students may note that the speculations about the mouse's family in the third paragraph (page 78) are written in the passive voice.

Find It in Your Writing

Remind students that if they decide to use passive voice, they should be doing so for a specific reason: to emphasize the receiver of the action or to acknowledge that the performer of the action is unimportant or unknown.

5.4

Grammar in Your Writing
Verbs: Active and Passive Voice

Differences Between Active and Passive Voice

There are two voices in English: **active** and **passive.** Only action verbs show voice; linking verbs do not. The voice is determined by the relationship between the subject and the verb. In a sentence in the active voice, the subject performs the action expressed by the verb. In the sentence below, the subject is *balloonists*.

                   S

Active Voice: Two balloonists sought the trophy.

In a sentence in the passive voice, the subject receives the action expressed by the verb. In the sentence below, the subject is *trophy*. Note that a passive voice verb contains a form of the helping verb *be* and the past participle of the main verb.

               S

Passive Voice: The trophy was sought by two balloonists.

Use Voice Correctly

Because the active voice is more direct and lively, you should generally use it in your writing. However, if you want to emphasize the receiver of the action rather than the performer of an action, use the passive voice.

Use the passive voice to emphasize the receiver of the action: George Ramirez was awarded Student of the Year by school officials.

The passive voice is also effective when the performer of the action is not important or is not known.

Use the passive voice when the performer of the action is unknown: The mysterious package was left in the cafeteria.

Find It in Your Reading Find two examples of active voice in "Maud Martha Spares the Mouse" on pp. 78–79. Explain how the passages would differ if they had been written in the passive voice.

Find It in Your Writing Find an instance of passive voice in your short story. Then, decide whether its meaning would be better served in the passive voice or if the passage would have more impact if written in the active voice.

For more on passive and active voice, see Chapter 22.

☑ ONGOING ASSESSMENT: Prerequisite Skills

If students have difficulty with active and passive voice, you may find it helpful to refer them to the following materials to ensure coverage of prerequisite knowledge.

In the Textbook	Print Resources	Technology
Active and Passive Voice, Sections 22.1–22.2	*Grammar Exercise Workbook,* pp. 121–124	*On-Line Exercise Bank,* Section 22.2

Revising Your Word Choice

▶ **REVISION STRATEGY**
Evaluating the Use of Tag Words

Tag words describe the way a character in a narrative speaks. For example, "he *said*" and "they *whispered*" are examples of tag words. When the same tag words are used repeatedly, writing may get repetitive and dull. On the other hand, the overuse of tag words or too large a variety of tag words may be annoying to readers. Keep the following tips in mind as you revise your draft:

- Rely mainly on *said* as a tag word, and let the actual dialogue convey the *emotion*—the way the line would be stated:

EXAMPLE:　　"Are you coming?" Stephen asked. "It's getting late, and I'm rather tired."

　　　　　　"Yes, I'm coming" Miranda said.

- Try to limit the use of tag words in extended passages of dialogue. It has to be clear to readers, however, who is addressing whom.

EXAMPLE:　　Stephen and Miranda discussed leaving the party.

　　　　　　"Are you coming? It's getting late, and my dad needs the car back."

　　　　　　"Yes, I'm coming."

- Vary the use of tag words to avoid repetition:

EXAMPLE:　　"Are you coming?" Stephen demanded. "It's getting late, and my dad needs the car back."

　　　　　　"Yes, I'm coming," sulked Miranda.

Peer Review

Consult with peer reviewers as you revise your short story. Use the "Say Back" Sheet for getting useful feedback from peer reviewers.

"Say Back"

Assemble a group of four or five peer reviewers. Read your story aloud to them once. Then, distribute a work sheet to them like the one shown at right. Read your story again to the group, and instruct them to fill out the work sheet. Consider the comments of your peer reviewers as you revise your short story a final time.

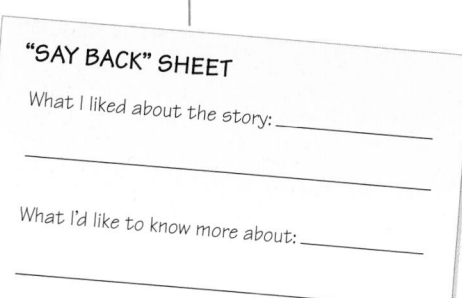

"SAY BACK" SHEET

What I liked about the story: _____

_____

What I'd like to know more about: _____

_____

Interactive Textbook

Try it out! Use the interactive "Say Back" Sheet in **Section 5.4**, on-line or on CD-ROM.

Revising • 89

1. Remind students that the editing and proofreading phases are essential parts of the writing process.

2. Check that students look carefully at dialogue and at active and passive voice. Is the dialogue punctuated correctly? Are there any uses of passive voice that make the writing dull or unclear?

Step-by-Step Teaching Guide

Formatting and Punctuating Dialogue

1. Write the following passage from "Maud Martha Spares the Mouse" on the board:

   go home to your children she urged to your wife or husband she opened the trap

2. Without allowing students to look at the story, challenge them to punctuate the dialogue correctly. Encourage them to consult the list of rules on page 90. (*"Go home to your children," she urged. "To your wife or husband." She opened the trap.*)

3. Explain to students that "To your wife or husband" is punctuated like a sentence, though it is just a phrase. This is acceptable because it is a direct quotation from the character.

Find It in Your Reading

To extend the activity, ask students to review passages that show what characters are thinking without using dialogue. Have students rewrite the paragraph as dialogue to practice formatting and punctuating dialogue.

Find It in Your Writing

Remind students that just as they should not depend on tags to convey emotion, they also should not depend on exclamation points. Instead, they should focus on conveying emotion through the dialogue itself.

5.5 Editing and Proofreading

An error-free, clearly written story will be easier for readers to follow and enjoy. When you have finished revising your narrative, check for errors in grammar, spelling, and punctuation.

Focusing on Punctuation

Check your short story to be sure that you have correctly punctuated passages of dialogue. First, read through your draft and locate all opening quotation marks. Then, make sure that for each opening quotation mark, there is a closing quotation mark. Also, check to see that you have correctly placed end marks in passages of dialogue.

⊚ Technology Tip

Use the Find feature of your computer's word-processing program to quickly locate all opening quotation marks. Then, check to see that each has a corresponding closing quotation mark.

Grammar in Your Writing
Formatting and Punctuating Dialogue

Because short stories often make extensive use of dialogue, it's particularly important to understand how to format and punctuate it correctly.

- A character's exact words are enclosed in quotation marks.
- Commas separate quotations from words that identify the speaker. The comma always appears inside the closing quotation mark.
- A new paragraph begins each time the speaker changes.
- When a paragraph ends while a character is still speaking, quotation marks do not appear at the end of that paragraph. However, quotation marks do appear at the beginning of the next paragraph.

Find It in Your Reading Find an example of dialogue in "Maud Martha Spares the Mouse" on pages 78–79. Explain the conventions used for punctuating and formatting the character's dialogue.

Find It in Your Writing Find the first passage of dialogue in your short story. Look at the end punctuation to be sure that it matches the way in which a character is speaking. For example, if the character is surprised, use an exclamation mark. Then, check to be sure that the dialogue is punctuated and formatted correctly.

For more on punctuating and formatting dialogue, see Chapter 28.

90 • Short Story

⏱ TIME AND RESOURCE MANAGER

Resources
Print: *Scoring Rubrics on Transparency*, Ch. 5; *Writing Assessment and Portfolio Management*; *Formal Assessment*, Ch. 5
Technology: *Writing and Grammar* Interactive Text, Section 5.5

Using the Full Student Edition	Using the Handbook🄷
• Review pp. 90–93 in class, including Grammar in Your Writing. • Analyze the Final Draft (pp. 92–93). • Have students edit and proofread their stories in class.	• Review pp. 60–61 in class, including Grammar in Your Writing. • Have students edit and proofread their stories in class.

5.6 Publishing and Presenting

Following are a few ideas for publishing and presenting your short story:

Building Your Portfolio

1. **Verbal Sharing** With a partner, take turns reading your narratives aloud or organize a reading in which several people read their short stories. Place a copy of the story or a tape of the reading into your portfolio.
2. **Anthology** Present your short story as part of a larger collection of short stories. In your anthology, include works written by your classmates. Organize the stories by theme.

Reflecting on Your Writing

Think back for a moment about your experience writing a short story. Then, answer the following questions, and save your responses in your portfolio.

- Which part of writing a story appealed to you most? Why?
- If you were to write another short story, on which stage of the writing process would you spend more time?

 **Internet Tip**

To see model stories scored with this rubric, go on-line: PHSchool.com Enter Web Code: eek-1001

Rubric for Self-Assessment

Use the following criteria to evaluate your short story.

	Score 4	Score 3	Score 2	Score 1
Audience and Purpose	Contains details that engage and impact the audience	Contains details that appeal to an audience	Contains few details that contribute to its purpose or that appeal to an audience	Contains no purpose; is not written for a specific audience
Organization	Presents events that create an interesting, clear narrative; told from a consistent point of view	Presents sequence of events; told from a specific point of view	Presents a confusing sequence of events; contains inconsistent points of view	Presents no logical order; is told from no consistent point of view
Elaboration	Contains details that provide insight into characters; contains dialogue that reveals characters and furthers the plot	Contains details and dialogue that develop characters	Contains characters and setting; contains some dialogue	Contains few or no details to develop characters or setting; no dialogue provided
Use of Language	Uses word choice and tone to reveal story's theme; contains no errors in grammar, punctuation, or spelling	Uses interesting and fresh word choices; contains few errors in grammar, punctuation, and spelling	Uses clichés and trite expressions; contains some errors in grammar, punctuation, and spelling	Uses uninspired word choices; has many errors in grammar, punctuation, and spelling

Publishing and Presenting • **91**

Use one of the following options to assess final drafts of students' short stories.

Self-Assessment Ask students to score their stories using the rubric provided. Then, have them write a single paragraph reflecting on the most valuable thing they learned in completing their stories.	**Teacher Assessment** You may wish to use the rubric and the scoring models provided in *Writing Assessment and Portfolio Management* in the Teaching Resources to score students' short stories.

Publishing and Presenting

1. Encourage students to brainstorm for a list of more places to share their work (on related Web sites, in the school library, or with family and friends).
2. In preparing their short stories, students may wish to add illustrations or photos to their work. Ask them to extend the process of composition by considering which of these items would help the reader most.
3. Suggest that students laminate or cover their narratives with clear plastic adhesive so that they will withstand handling. Suggest the class create a classroom anthology of short stories, so that classmates can read each other's work.

ASSESS and CLOSE

Assessment

Teaching Resources: Scoring Rubrics on Transparency, Ch. 5; Writing Assessment and Portfolio Management; Formal Assessment, Ch. 5

1. Display the Scoring Rubric transparency and review the criteria with students.
2. Before students proceed with self-assessment, you may wish to review the Final Draft of the Student Work in Progress on pages 92–93.
3. In addition to student self-assessment, you may wish to use the following assessment options:
   - score student essays yourself, using the rubric and scoring models in *Writing Assessment and Portfolio Management*.
   - review the Standardized Test Preparation Workshop on pages 98–99 and administer a timed writing assignment.
   - administer the Chapter 5 assessment in *Formal Assessment* to measure students' grasp of the concepts presented.

Final Draft

1. Help students see that "Horror Movie" incorporates key elements of the short story.

   • The topic has been well chosen and the incidents are high interest.

   • Audience and purpose have been considered carefully. The story appeals to other young people who may in the past have had experiences like Doug's.

   • The introduction tells the readers everything they need to know to get involved in the story.

   • The body of the short story clearly relates the events of Doug's evening.

   • Dialogue and vivid description provide an engrossing narration.

   • Finally, a short conclusion is given. It tells what Doug has learned from his experiences.

2. Ask students whether they can imagine how Doug feels when he goes to check the basement door. Explain that carefully crafted description gives the reader a feeling of being involved in the incidents described and engages the reader in the story.

3. Ask students whether there are any other changes they would recommend to make the narrative flow better. How might they apply these suggestions to their own writing?

Critical Viewing

Analyze Students may say that the photograph evokes a sense of mystery or suspense. The door slightly ajar, the light within the room, and even the camera angle all contribute to the mood.

5.7 *Student Work*
IN PROGRESS

FINAL DRAFT

Horror Movie

Ian Venokur
Columbia High School
Maplewood, New Jersey

It was the first time his parents had left him home alone for a night, and Doug couldn't have been happier. He had prepared for it all week by picking out the movies he wanted to see and the snack food he wanted to eat. "Now keep the doors locked, go to bed before midnight, and be *safe*," Doug's parents reminded him at least five hundred times while they walked toward the car.

"I can handle it, Mom." Doug responded. It frustrated him that his mother refused to accept the fact that he was grown up. "Have fun! I'll be fine!" Doug yelled to his parents as they pulled out of their driveway.

"Finally," Doug said to himself. What to do first? The possibilities seemed endless to the new king of 163 Willowbend Lane. The microwave clock read 7:00 P.M. "Perfect! Movie time." Doug dashed to the kitchen table where the Movie-Town bag lay on its side. Doug popped in *Hangman Twelve* and sat down on the family couch in the television room.

Two bags of corn chips, a bowl of popcorn, and three movies later, Doug lay with a stomachache and heavy eyelids. He decided to go to his royal bathroom to brush his teeth and flop in bed.

92 • Short Story

◄ **Critical Viewing**
What mood or atmosphere does this photograph evoke in you? What details contribute to that mood? **[Analyze]**

In the exposition, Ian has introduced everything his readers need in order to get involved in the story—the characters, the setting, and a situation to which they can relate.

Ian included variety in his tag words, such as "responded" and "yelled."

By using dialogue here, Ian reveals Doug's inner thoughts and personality.

Around 2:00 A.M., Doug woke up. Still groggy, he wondered what disturbed him, and he strained his ears to listen. The basement door was locked . . . right? I remembered to do that. But he crept downstairs to check it anyway.

The whole house was dark, but Doug's eyes were focused on the door to the basement, which was open a crack. Everything inside of him told him to turn back, but for some reason Doug continued until he stood directly in front of the door. By this time, he was sweating and his heart was racing. As fate would have it, the light bulb was burnt out. "It'll only take a minute . . . ," Doug reassured himself as he took the first step into the darkness.

He reached out and grabbed the banister. It would be his only guide, because it was pitch black and he was alone. Doug's foot touched the cold concrete floor. He knew that the outside basement door was only about ten feet from where he stood, but he could not see it. "I have nothing to worry about, I'll be back upstairs in a minute," Doug proclaimed to his audience of none.

Doug's forehead was the first thing to reach the door; the rest of his body followed. He fumbled for the handle and then the lock.

The familiar click of the key turning put his fears to rest. Smiling to himself, Doug began backtracking toward the stairs. Step by step, Doug's triumph grew larger and larger, and greater and greater, until he reached the doorway back to the kitchen.

The door was stuck. Suddenly, Doug was shocked back to reality as he pulled the metal handle with all his might. He fought back his rising horror as best he could. But it was no good. Doug sank weakly on the top stair. To keep his fears aways, he loudly began reciting nursery rhymes. "Hey diddle, diddle, . . ."

Without warning, the door gave way behind his back. His mother gasped and shouted, "Douglas! What are you *doing*?"

"I knew he wasn't ready to stay home alone," Doug's dad chipped in.

"I couldn't sleep," Doug said.

"But why are you in the basement?"

"It's all right, Mom. I came down to lock the basement door, and I just felt like staying down here." Doug did not allow himself to tell the whole story.

"As long as you're OK."

"I'm fine, Mom." And Doug knew that next time, he would be.

Details about the setting ("pitch black," "cold concrete floor") contribute to the atmosphere of suspense.

The climax of the story occurs as Doug realizes he is locked in the basement.

The final statement of the story reveals what Doug, the main character, learns from his experience.

Integrating Speaking and Listening Skills

It is not only in writing that we tell short stories about real or imagined characters. When students talk to someone they have recently met, it is important to be able to communicate short anecdotes in an interesting and concise manner. Challenge students to pick a topic related to their short story and tell it to a peer or small group in the form of a short anecdote.

Customize for
ESL Students

As they read, have students make a list of unfamiliar words. If they cannot determine their meaning from context clues, have them look up these words in the dictionary. Challenge students to use at least one of these new words in their own stories.

Step-by-Step Teaching Guide

Drama

Teaching Resources: Writing Support Transparencies, 5-I; Writing Support Activity Book, 5-5

1. Read aloud the excerpt from *Invasion From Mars*, and identify character names and stage directions. Have additional plays available for students to use as models.

2. Suggest that students review writing strategies from Chapter 5. See the chart below for specific suggestions.

3. Encourage students to think about familiar people, conflicts, and settings as they begin to brainstorm for ideas. Remind them that specific details make a drama come alive.

4. Provide time for students to perform their dramas for the class or in small groups.

continued

Critical Viewing

Interpret Students will probably say that it is a rehearsal because of the way the people are sitting together as an ensemble.

Connected Assignment
Drama

Like a short story, **drama** contains characters who face a problem or conflict. The major difference is that drama is written to be performed by actors on a stage. Costumes, lighting, music, and sound effects add to the total effect of drama.

▲ **Critical Viewing** Judging from the details in this photograph, would you think this was an audition or a rehearsal? Explain. **[Interpret]**

Most dramas

• are generated in a script format.

• contain stage directions to indicate props, movements, and information about characters' motives.

• contain dialogue that develops characters and furthers the plot.

The following excerpt is from a radio play—a type of drama. It contains a typical script format and basic elements of a drama.

MODEL

from *Invasion From Mars*
Howard Koch

OPERATOR FIVE. This is 8X3R . . . coming back at 2X2L.

OPERATOR FOUR. How's reception? How's reception? K, please. Where are you, 8X3R?

What's the matter? Where are you?

[*Bells ringing over city gradually diminishing*]

ANNOUNCER. I'm speaking from the roof of Broadcasting Building, New York City. The bells you hear are ringing to warn the people to evacuate the city as the Martians approach.

---

94 • Short Story

☑ ONGOING ASSESSMENT: Prerequisite Skills

Students may find the following resources particularly helpful in completing their scripts.

In the Textbook	Print Resources	Technology
Create a Purpose Planner, Section 5.2 Make a Plot Diagram, Section 5.3	*Writing Support Transparencies,* 5-C, 5-E *Writing Support Activity Book,* 5-1–2	*Writing and Grammar* Interactive Text, Sections 5.2–3

Prewriting Choose an idea to center your drama around. Following are some suggestions to help you come up with an idea for a drama:

- **Start with a character.** Jot down a description of your main character: his or her appearance, goals, problem, family life, and dreams.

- **Start with a conflict.** Choose an exciting or a thought-provoking problem that your characters will grapple with during the course of your drama.

- **Start with a theme.** Decide on a main message that you would like to convey through your drama.

- **Start with a setting.** Create a wild, unique, beautiful, or realistic setting to act as a backdrop for your characters. Your setting might also play a role in your drama if you pit your characters against some force of nature, like a typhoon.

Gather Details Once you have a basic story idea, gather details about the setting, characters, and plot. Then, bring your characters to life by listing details about them, such as name, age, job, education, physical appearance, mannerisms, views, and especially speech style.

Drafting As you draft, tell the story of your drama. Elaborate by writing dialogue that develops characters and furthers the action of the drama. Also, insert stage directions that give information about the set, actors' movements, and characters' motivations. The diagram shown here indicates the correct terms to describe stage locations, as seen from the stage.

The Stage

Wings (offstage)	Upstage Right	Upstage Center	Upstage Left	Wings (offstage)
	Right	Center	Left	
	Downstage Right	Downstage Center	Downstage Left	

The Audience

Revising and Editing Read your drama aloud to friends. Ask them to note and correct any dialogue that seems stilted, inconsistent, or unrealistic. If appropriate, use phrases or informal slang to add realism to the dialogue. If needed, add stage directions to more specifically describe the characters' actions or moods, along with the use of props or sound effects.

Publishing and Presenting Cast the parts in your play, and read it for the class. Decide whether you will include lighting and sound effects or whether you would rather assign an actor to read stage directions aloud.

Connected Assignment: Drama • 95

Step-by-Step Teaching Guide continued

5. Display Transparency 5-I as you go over the section on drafting with the class. You may wish to point out that the terms *upstage* and *downstage* originated when actual stages used to slope toward the audience, so that people could see everything at the back. *Stage left* and *stage right* are always determined from the perspective of the actor on stage facing the audience, not from the audience's point of view.

6. Distribute copies of the stage location diagram (5-5) so that students can block out movements of their characters, jot down notes for scenery details, and so on.

Teaching From the Model

You may wish to note that when Howard Koch's *Invasion from Mars* was first broadcast, it created widespread panic. Despite many disclaimers in the broadcast that *Invasion* was a drama, not an actual event, thousands of listeners poured into streets in fear of Martians. What details in this excerpt create a sense of realism? How might students add such realism to their own scripts?

Lesson Objectives

1. To recognize and interpret a speaker's message
2. To listen and respond to a song
3. To write a short story based on song lyrics

Step-by-Step Teaching Guide

Recognizing the Oral Tradition

1. Have students gather different versions of the John Henry story in music, prose, and visual art. Compare and contrast them in terms of audience appeal.

2. Bring in additional ballads in song or written form. Discuss their narrative qualities.

3. Students will enjoy examining the entire picture book, *John Henry*, as retold by Julius Lester. Jerry Pinkney has illustrated more than 75 children's books and has received numerous awards. What qualities of his artistic style might draw a young reader into the folktale? How does Pinkney's artwork enhance this tall tale?

4. Show an excerpt from the film *2001: A Space Odyssey*, in which the computer Hal has a conversation with a human. Whom do students think will prevail?

Viewing and Representing

Activity Some students may want to present their narrative writing activity by reading aloud their short story and playing a recording of the song on which it is based.

Critical Viewing

Connect Responses will vary. Students might refer to the character's expressive face and the realistic rendering of his body to show his strength.

Recognizing the Oral Tradition

Focus on Music: "The Ballad of John Henry"

Some stories are told through music. Embedded in the roots of American folklore, "John Henry, the Steel Driving Man" is a ballad—a narrative set to music—about an African American railroad worker who was seven feet tall and as strong as thirty men. Renowned for his superhuman strength, Henry, using only his hammer, raced a mechanical steam drill to cut a railroad tunnel through a mountain. John Henry won the race, but after the tremendous exertion, his heart gave out, and he lost his life. Many different forms of this ballad exist, with the oldest printed copy dated around 1900. This ballad has been sung by such notables as Woody Guthrie, Pete Seeger, and Burl Ives.

Art Connection Various artists have captured through clay, paint, and watercolor the hero John Henry. Jerry Pinkney (born 1939) created a watercolor of John Henry for the jacket illustration of the book by Julius Lester. The 1994 watercolor captures the herculean features of John Henry as well as the rough landscape of the railroad man's life.

Film Connection The legendary John Henry pitted his strength against that of a machine. This conflict—"man against the machine"—has been explored a number of times throughout the years. A notable and memorable example of this theme is presented in *2001: A Space Odyssey*, in which an astronaut matches wits with a computer named Hal.

Narrative Writing Activity: Short Story Based on a Favorite Song

Select a favorite song from an artist or a band you enjoy. Then, write a short story based on the lyrics of the song. Add details and additional information that will make your song a compelling short story.

He Laid Down His Hammer and Cried, 1944-47, Palmer C. Hayden, Museum of African American Art, Los Angeles, CA

▲ Critical Viewing
What details in this painting help convey John Henry's legendary strength? [Connect]

Media and Technology Skills

Using Media to Convey Ideas
Activity: Video Adaptation of a Short Story

A short video can bring to life the action, mood, theme, and style of a story. A viewer audience receives more sensory information than a reader does: The film uses motion and imagery to provide a narrative.

Many effective film adaptations change the time or place of a story. Your adaptation might reset a historical tale in modern times or change characters from adults to high-school students.

Think About It Select a short story to adapt that has a concise plot and interesting characters. Look especially for a story that has a strong visual element—for instance, a vivid setting.

Storyboard It Sketch a storyboard to plan your film. A storyboard is an illustrated sequence of sketches that shows the scenes in order. You can include ideas for camera angles, close-ups, distance shots, and fades.

Susan sends an e-mail. | Fade out. | Zoom in on Hillary's desk. | Hillary runs in and signs onto the Net.

Script It Developing a storyboard will help you decide what scenes and dialogue you need for your film. Write a shooting script by indicating the location of each scene and the characters' dialogue. Try improvising scenes to help give each character a distinctive voice.

Design It Create the sets and costumes you will need. Remember that costumes provide important information about the characters' personalities and preferences. You may need to find or build specific props that are key to your story's development.

Shoot It Use your storyboard to guide the filming. Shoot several versions, or takes, of each scene. Then, use your camera's or videocassette recorder's editing functions to select the best takes, and copy them onto a new tape. During editing, you can also add titles and music to polish your video.

Media and Technology Skills • 97

Step-by-Step Teaching Guide

Using Media to Convey Ideas

Teaching Resources: Writing Support Transparencies, 5-J; Writing Support Activity Book, 5-6

1. Ask students to think of books they are familiar with that were made into films. Discuss specific visual aspects of the films that are especially effective in bringing the story to life.

2. Using Transparency 5-J, demonstrate a storyboard plan. You might use a simple story, such as a fairy tale, with which all students are familiar. Include some specific ideas for film techniques, set, and costumes.

3. Have students work on their storyboards using copies of the organizer (5-6). Students could exchange them with partners and discuss changes for improvement before filming.

4. Provide opportunities for students to view the completed videos.

Customize for
Less Advanced Students

Some students may prefer adapting a children's book, in which the elements of plot, setting, theme, and character are less complex than in a short story.

Lesson Objectives

1. To write a cohesive response to a specific question about a short story

2. To use prewriting, organizing, and proofreading strategies

3. To demonstrate control over grammatical elements and spelling

4. To evaluate writing for both mechanics and content

Step-by-Step Teaching Guide

Responding to Questions About Short Stories

Teaching Resources: Standardized Test Preparation Workbook, pp. 9–10

1. Tell students that in a test situation, they should decide quickly the question to which they will respond. It will help to write one or two sentences that describe their general response. This will become their main idea.

2. When students have compiled their list of supporting details and begun writing paragraphs, remind them to explain how the details support their main idea.

3. Tell students to use clear transitional words and phrases that link one idea to the next. Give them some examples.

4. Walk students through a response to one of the questions. Brainstorm for supporting details and organize them into logical groups.

Standardized Test Preparation Workshop

Responding to Questions About Short Stories

Knowing how the elements of a short story work helps you write about short stories. Some standardized tests require you to write a short response about a story you have read. Before responding to a test prompt on a short story, think about how its narrative elements contribute to the story's effectiveness. Take the following elements into consideration: **plot**—the story's sequence of events; **characters**—people, animals, or other beings who perform the action; **setting**—time and place in which the story takes place; and **theme**—the story's central message. The following are some of the criteria upon which your response will be evaluated:

• a clear and logical organization of ideas

• details and precise language that fully develop your ideas

• a focused purpose for writing

• correct spelling, capitalization, punctuation, grammar, usage, and sentence structure

Choose one of the following sample prompts for the short story "Maud Martha Spares the Mouse," and write a short response.

Sample Writing Situations

> Read this quote:
>
> "A life had blundered its way into her power and it had been hers to preserve or destroy. She had not destroyed. . . . She had created a piece of life. It was wonderful."

> What does the quotation above reveal about how Maud views her decision? Describe a time when you made a decision that made you feel good about yourself, and compare it to Maud Martha's decision and her feelings. Use details and information from the story to support your answer.

> The quotation from "Maud Martha Spares the Mouse" reveals a message or theme to readers. Explain how the story's narrative elements—character, plot, and setting—help to convey its theme. Use details and information from the story to support your answer.

98 • Narration: Short Story

Test Tips

• When writing about a short story, be careful not to simply retell the story. Instead, focus on responding to the prompt.

• When writing for a timed test, plan to devote a certain amount of time to prewriting, drafting, revising, and proofreading.

✎ TEST-TAKING TIP

When responding to a prompt, students need to be sure they understand each part of the task. Tell students that often they will find writing prompts that contain more than one question or topic to be addressed. For example, in the first prompt, students are asked to discuss both their own feelings about a decision and Maud Martha's feelings about a decision, and then to compare and contrast them. In the second prompt, students will need to explain the theme itself before moving on to explain how the narrative elements support it.

Customize for
Less Advanced Students

Help students organize their supporting details by putting them into visual formats such as simple outlines, webs, or charts.

Customize for
More Advanced Students

Students may want to revise their topic sentence as they work. They should be careful, however, to stay with their original main idea.

Prewriting

Allow close to one fourth of your time for prewriting.

Gather Details Respond to the prompt by listing several details that support your response. For example, you may jot down lines from the story, references to other stories, and personal observations. If you are comparing and contrasting two or more ideas, you may use a Venn diagram as you gather similarities and differences between ideas.

Organize Details Organize your details in a logical and effective order. If you are discussing plot events, you may want to organize them chronologically, or in time order. If you are comparing and contrasting, you may use point-by-point or subject-by-subject organization. If you are discussing a single element of literature, you may want to use order of importance to organize your paragraphs.

Drafting

Allow almost half of your time for drafting.

Write a Topic Sentence Write a topic sentence that tells specifically what the main idea and purpose of your response will be.

Use the Story as Support Develop your short response using details from the story and your own experience to elaborate upon your topic sentence.

Conclude Effectively Write a concluding sentence in which you sum up the main idea of your response.

Revising, Editing, and Proofreading

Allow almost one fourth of your time to revise and edit. Use the last few minutes to proofread your work.

Check Language and Details After you have drafted your response, read through it again to make sure that you have included only those details that directly support the main point of your response. Eliminate those details that do not.

Make Corrections Review your response for errors. Neatly cross out details that do not support your purpose. Eliminate language that is vague, and replace it with precise, strong words. Check for errors in spelling, grammar, and punctuation. When making changes, draw a line through text that you want eliminated. Use a caret [^] to indicate the places that you are adding or revising words.

Time and Resource Manager

In-Depth Lesson Plan

	LESSON FOCUS	PRINT AND MEDIA RESOURCES
DAY 1	**Introduction to Description** Students learn key elements of description and analyze the Model From Literature. (pp. 100–103/Ⓗ62–63)	*Writers at Work* DVD, Description *Writing and Grammar* Interactive Text, Ch. 6, Introduction
DAY 2	**Prewriting** Students choose and narrow a topic, consider their audience and purpose, and gather information. (pp. 104–107/Ⓗ64–67)	**Teaching Resources** *Writing Support Transparencies*, 6-A–D; *Writing Support Activity Book*, 6-1 *Writing and Grammar* Interactive Text, Section 6.2
DAY 3	**Drafting** Students organize their ideas and write their first drafts. (p. 108/Ⓗ68)	**Teaching Resources** *Writing Support Transparencies*, 6-E; *Writing Support Activity Book*, 6-2 *Writing and Grammar* Interactive Text, Section 6.3
DAY 4	**Revising** Student revise their drafts in terms of overall structure, paragraphs, sentences, and word choice. (pp. 109–113/Ⓗ69–73)	**Teaching Resources** *Writing Support Transparencies*, 6-F–G; *Writing Support Activity Book*, 6-3 *Writing and Grammar* Interactive Text, Section 6.4
DAY 5	**Editing and Proofreading; Publishing and Presenting** Students check their work for accuracy and correctness and present their final drafts. (pp. 114–117/Ⓗ74–75)	**Teaching Resources** *Scoring Rubrics on Transparency*, Ch. 6; *Writing Assessment and Portfolio Management; Formal Assessment*, Ch. 6 *Writing and Grammar* Interactive Text, Sections 6.5–6

Accelerated Lesson Plan

	LESSON FOCUS	PRINT AND MEDIA RESOURCES
DAY 1	**Introduction Through Drafting** Students review characteristics of description, select topics, and write drafts. (pp. 100–108/Ⓗ62–68)	**Teaching Resources** *Writing Support Transparencies*, 6-A–E; *Writing Support Activity Book*, 6-1–2 *Writing and Grammar* Interactive Text, Ch. 6, Introduction through Section 6.3
DAY 2	**Revising Through Presenting** Students work individually or with peers to revise, edit, and proofread their work for presentation. (pp. 109–117/Ⓗ69–75)	**Teaching Resources** *Writing Support Transparencies*, 6-F–G; *Writing Support Activity Book*, 6-4; *Scoring Rubrics on Transparency*, Ch. 6; *Writing Assessment and Portfolio Management; Formal Assessment*, Ch. 6 *Writing and Grammar* Interactive Text, Sections 6.4–6

Options for Adapting Lesson Plans

HOMEWORK

Have students complete any stage of the lesson for homework.

FEATURES

Extend coverage with Connected Assignment (p. 118), Spotlight on the Humanities (p. 120), Media and Technology Skills (p. 121), and the Standardized Test Preparation Workshop (p. 122).

TECHNOLOGY

Students can complete any stage of the lesson on the computer, using *Writing and Grammar* Interactive Text or a word-processing program. Have them print out their completed work.

Writing and Grammar Handbook Alignment

Page numbers in Step-by-Step Teaching Guides in this Teacher's Edition refer to pages from the full student text. Handbook page references, indicated with this icon ⬚, are provided in Time and Resource Manager boxes and at the bottom of each Teacher's Edition page.

INTEGRATED SKILLS COVERAGE

Integrating Grammar
Dangling and Misplaced Modifiers, SE p. 111/⬚71
Using Commas Correctly, SE p. 114/⬚74; ATE p. 114

Reading/Writing Connection
Envision, SE p. 102
Writing Application, SE p. 103

Viewing and Representing
Critical Viewing, SE pp. 100, 102, 108, 113, 116, 117, 118, 120/⬚62, 68, 73
Making Cultural Connections, SE p. 120
Evaluating Images, SE p. 121; ATE p. 121

Speaking and Listening ATE p. 106

Vocabulary ATE pp. 101, 107, 117, 119

Real-World Connection ATE p. 103

Workplace Skills ATE p. 103

BLOCK SCHEDULING

Pacing Suggestions
For 90-minute Blocks
• Have students complete the Prewriting and Drafting stages in a single period.
• Focus one class period on Revising and Editing and Publishing and Presenting. Allow at least 30 minutes for peer revision.

Resources for Varying Instruction
• *Writing and Grammar* Interactive Text A 90-minute block provides an ideal opportunity for students to work on the computer.
• *Writers at Work* DVD Show the Description segment in class.

Professional Development Support
• *How to Manage Instruction in the Block* This teaching resource provides management and activity suggestions.

ASSESSMENT SUPPORT

Standardized Test Preparation Workshop SE p. 122; ATE p. 111
Standardized Test Preparation Workbook, pp. 11–12
Scoring Rubrics on Transparency, Ch. 6
Formal Assessment, Ch. 6
Writing Assessment and Portfolio Management

MEDIA AND TECHNOLOGY

For the Student
• *Writing and Grammar* Interactive Text, Ch. 6

For the Teacher
• *Writers at Work* DVD, Description
• Teacher**EXPRESS** CD-ROM

MEETING INDIVIDUAL NEEDS

Less Advanced Students ATE p. 123. See also Ongoing Assessments ATE pp. 105, 109.
ESL Students ATE pp. 111, 112
More Advanced Students ATE pp. 119, 123
Musical Learners ATE p. 108
Intrapersonal Learners ATE p. 109
Interpersonal Learners ATE p. 105

WRITING AND GRAMMAR ON-LINE

Interactive Text (On-line or on CD-ROM)
• Easily navigable instruction with interactive Revision Checkers
• Full use of e-rater™, the essay-scoring system (on-line only)

Companion Web Site PHSchool.com
• Scoring rubrics with models (use Web Code eek-1001)

See the Go On-line! feature, SE p. iii.

LITERATURE CONNECTIONS

Related selections from *Prentice Hall Literature, Penguin Edition*, Grade 10:
Topic Bank Option "Jazz Fantasia," Carl Sandburg, SE p. 105/⬚65

Lesson Objectives

1. To write a description that is appropriate to audience and purpose
2. To read to appreciate a writer's craft and to discover models for writing
3. To use prewriting strategies to generate ideas and to plan
4. To use writing to refine topics, clarify ideas, and discover, organize, and support what is known and what needs to be learned about a topic
5. To develop and revise drafts in terms of structure, paragraphs, sentences, and word choice
6. To edit and proofread to ensure standard English usage and grammar
7. To evaluate writing for both mechanics and content
8. To refine a description for publication and produce error-free writing in the final draft

Critical Viewing

Interpret Students may suggest words such as *cold, snowy, frozen, white,* or *sunny.*

Chapter 6 Description

▲ **Critical Viewing**
If you were to describe the scene pictured above, what words would you select? Why? **[Interpret]**

Description in Everyday Life

Before you leave your home each day, you probably use description. For example, you might describe how well you slept or how a new cereal tasted. Through description, patients tell doctors about their illnesses, travel agencies tempt homebodies to new horizons, victims lead detectives to criminals, and screenwriters portray environments for movie producers to build or find.

Description also takes written form. For example, you might write a description about last night's championship game in an e-mail to a friend, or you might describe a chemical reaction in a report for your chemistry class. In the workplace, too, description plays a vital role. Precise descriptions may convey company procedures, explain benefits packages, or provide detailed instructions for accessing a phone-mail system.

100 • Description

⏱ **TIME AND RESOURCE MANAGER**	
Resources **Technology:** *Writers at Work* DVD, Description; *Writing and Grammar* Interactive Text, Ch. 6	
Using the Full Student Edition	**Using the Handbook🅗**
• Cover pp. 100–101 in class. • Show the Description section of the *Writers at Work* DVD. • Read the Model From Literature (pp. 102–103) in class and use it to brainstorm for description ideas with students. • Discuss examples of description that you or your students bring to class (journal entries, excerpts from novels, poems, and so on).	• Cover pp. 62–63 in class. • Show the Description section of the *Writers at Work* DVD. • Discuss examples of description that you or your students bring to class (journal entries, excerpts from novels, poems, and so on).

What Is Description?

You experience your world through your senses: sight, hearing, taste, smell, and touch. **Description** is writing that enables you to re-create your experiences vividly and share them with others. Most descriptive writing contains

- sensory language that shares what the writer sees, hears, tastes, smells, and touches.

- precise language, including vivid verbs and precise nouns.

- figurative language, such as personification, exaggeration, simile, and metaphor.

- a logical organization, such as chronological or spatial order.

To see the criteria on which your final essay may be evaluated, preview the Rubric for Self-Assessment on page 115.

Types of Description

Most writing contains description. Following are a few types of writing that depend heavily on descriptive language:

- **Descriptions of a person, place, or thing** contain sensory details that bring to life actual people, places, and things.

- **Observations** describe an event the writer has witnessed. Often, the event takes place over an extended period of time.

- **Travel brochures** contain factual information as well as persuasive language to encourage tourism.

- **Character sketches** describe fictional characters—their appearances, personalities, hopes, and dreams.

Writers in
ACTION

Colleen J. McElroy, poet and author, often uses descriptive details in her writing. Like most writers, she understands the power of description. She has the following to say about finding inspiration for writing a description:

"What makes a description good for me is not so much reporting it, but finding the impression. You're looking for that thing that's in the corner of the eye— or that smell that sort of drifts by— and it reminds you of some place."

PREVIEW
Student Work
IN PROGRESS

Leslie Harris, a student at Sunnyslope High School in Phoenix, Arizona, wrote a description of her impressions during the seconds before the start of a footrace. Follow along as Leslie plans, drafts, and revises her writing. A final draft of her description appears at the end of the chapter.

Description • 101

PREPARE and ENGAGE

Interest GRABBER Ask students to consider their favorite or least favorite foods. Have them write a detailed description of their ideal fantasy meal as it might appear on a menu at an elegant restaurant. Ask volunteers to read their menus aloud.

Activate Prior Knowledge

Ask students to think about how they would describe a school or social event to a friend who missed it. What kinds of details are their friends likely to be curious about? As a class, have students generate questions that a friend might use to elicit detailed descriptions.

More About the Writer

Colleen J. McElroy is a poet and short-story writer of African American heritage. She has received an American Book Award for her novel *Queen of the Ebony Isles* and a Fulbright Creative Writing Fellowship to Madagascar.

Integrating Vocabulary Skills

The word *describe* (of which *description* is a form) comes from Latin: *de* means "about" and *scribere* means "write." In Latin, describing something meant writing about it. Can students think of other types of descriptions?

☑ ONGOING ASSESSMENT: Diagnose

Use one of the following options to diagnose students' current level of proficiency in descriptive writing.

Option 1 Suggest that each student select an example of his or her descriptive writing from the previous year's writing portfolio. You may wish to hold brief conferences with each student to review and assess these samples.	**Option 2** Ask students to write a descriptive paragraph about the scene outside the classroom window. Students who do not include sufficient supporting descriptive detail may need extra help.

Reading\Writing Connection

Reading: Envision

Ask students to visualize or make a "movie in their minds" as they read this letter. Point out that Loffler helps us envision the scenes by extensively reporting the sights, sounds, sensations, and other details in his descriptive piece.

Step-by-Step Teaching Guide

Engage Students Through Literature

1. After students read the Model From Literature, use questions such as this one to prompt discussion:

   What impression do you get of the writer's surroundings?

   How is the writer's attitude revealed?

2. Encourage students to consider additional descriptive elements such as attitudes, facts, and geography contained in the description.

3. Students may add these elements to their topic banks. Remind students that their topic banks can reflect their own experiences and environments, as well.

Teaching From the Model

You can use the Model From Literature to show students how to find a topic for a descriptive essay. In the model, the writer is far from home in an unfamiliar environment. He uses writing as a way to share his experiences with people he cares about. Have students consider occasions when they had experiences apart from friends and family.

Critical Viewing

Analyze Students may say that the tension on the soldier's face suggests a dangerous situation.

 # 6.1 Model From Literature

Dear America: Letters Home From Vietnam is a collection of actual letters written by various American soldiers while they were posted in Vietnam during the war. The following letters were written in the spring of 1967 by Richard Loffler, Sp/4, 36th Sig. Bn., 2nd Sig Gp., Long Binh, Bear Cat, 1966–1967.

Reading Writing Connection

Reading Strategy: Envision When you envision a writer's words, you mentally picture what is being described. As you read these letters, pay attention to the descriptive details to help you envision the scenery and the experiences of the author.

from Letters Home From Vietnam

March 26, 1967
Dear Folks,

New place, new faces, a few old. I've been transferred to a region near Bien Hoa, almost 20 miles southeast of Saigon. Our base is about one mile square. Scraped out of the jungle, with the name of Bear Cat; it's the code name for the home base of the Big Red "One" (First Infantry Division).

We came by chopper. Ride was all vibration—hot, noisy, kerosene smell, door open wide, man at machine-gun–ready. This camp has dust over everything. A beige landscape. It's a fine powder that blows at the slightest breeze. Clouds of it blow into the mess hall while you're eating and get in your food, mouth—gritty, gritty.

I'm with a signal company again and still have my draftsman's job—doing charts, etc.

I've heard the camp has been shelled in the past. This means a red alert is in progress. You have to grab your flak jacket, rifle and ammo, and go stand at a post for a half hour or so until the "danger" is over. 105-millimeter cannons surround the perimeter of the camp and go off any time and rumble the tents, and the middle of your stomach. It's not bad, though. 242 days to go.

▲ **Critical Viewing**
What situation might the soldier pictured be facing? Explain why you think as you do. **[Analyze]**

The opening of the letter contains both factual details and figurative language.

This paragraph is full of descriptive details such as "hot," "noisy," "beige," and "gritty."

102 • Description

April 15, 1967

Dear Folks,

This is your "on the spot" correspondent in the BIG NAM reporting. . . .

Answers to pertinent questions first. Yes, we sleep on cots. One can buy mattresses and pillows at a Vietnamese store outside our base. I have a towel for a pillow and roll myself in the blanket. Just not energetic enough to get sheets and pillow.

On a trip to Vung Tau, I noticed red flowers abundant. Small, white, bell-shaped type are shaped by kids into garlands for the neck. They sell for five piasters. Trees are scrubby junk or a banana type. Soil is really hard as rock for about three feet down, then becomes sandy.

Well, guard duty is a drag. We go to a commercial post (a solitary telephone sitting on a bench) at 2:30 P.M. for instructions, then are driven out to the bunkers—sandbag shelters with broken cots inside. There are peepholes for observation. Chow is brought out to us at dusk. Three guys to a bunker. Two stay awake at all times. We eat, and sit, and sit, and sit. Then the cannons start.

Here are the noises of the ritual of firing one round: Whhiirrrrrrr-klick. Sskkllaannkkk. WWhhiiirrr-kkllaannk. That was the charge and shell being loaded into the breech. More whirring follows; asimuth and elevation controls are set. Then a guy gives a short "yell" and then an instant's silence. Then a BAM-BOOM-TTHHAATT sound combination that bounces the ground, the cot, and you. Maybe a half hour of this is followed by an hour and a half of silence. Then BBAAMM, BAAAMM for another half hour. This goes on all night. Flares can be seen nearby, fired off when somebody sees "sumthin out dare." There [are] the whining choppers slipping by, landing lights glowing red. Mice and rats squeak, and the night goes on.

Well, the routine goes on. We're just "paper soldiers," that is, the people doing administration, although somebody has got to do it. The "roughness" we endure is only the water rationing, being hot, and the somewhat dreary atmosphere of it all. Dirty Boy Scouts moved up a notch.

Hope all are in good health.

Sp/4 Richard Loffler, 36th Sig. Bn., 2nd Sig. Gp., Long Binh, Bear Cat, 1966–1967.

Because the audience for this letter is the soldier's family, the soldier uses slang and informal language.

Onomatopoeia—the use of words that imitate sounds—makes this descriptive paragraph a vivid re-creation of the sounds of battle.

Writing Application: Envision Before you begin writing your description, envision your subject and think of words and phrases that will help you to convey that vision to readers.

Model From Literature • 103

More About the Writer

Richard Loffler was in Vietnam from November 1966 to October 1967. He served in the army as a draftsman and supply clerk. After the war, he became an architectural draftsman in Little Neck, New York.

Real-World Connection

Point out to students that for young people who study, travel, or take jobs far from home, letters are an important tool for keeping in touch with friends and family. The ability to describe experiences and feelings in vivid, precise language can ease the loneliness of being away from home and bridge time and distance. Ask students to consider which details they would include in letters to friends or relatives whom they have not seen in some time.

Integrating Workplace Skills

Precise description is a skill central to report writing. Report writing is vital to many professional or managerial jobs. Encourage students to brainstorm for attributes and skills needed to work in a managerial position. Personal attributes may include patience, being a good communicator, and being organized. Skills may include good written and oral communication, time management, and conflict resolution.

Reading\Writing Connection

Writing Application: Envision

Have students reread the excerpt and jot down descriptive details that Loffler used to set the scene for his family. Ask students to order each detail in a graphic organizer labeled *Taste, Sight, Touch, Smell,* and *Sound.* Which of the five senses is represented most? Does this suggest anything to students about what Vietnam was like?

Prewriting: Draw or Sketch

1. Provide students with a supply of pencils, thin- and thick-lined markers, and drawing paper. Make sure to draw your own sketch. Your involvement will give students encouragement and support to take risks.

2. Group students with one or two others and give them time to review their sketches with peers.

Prewriting: Browse in a Calendar

Teaching Resources: Writing Support Transparencies, 6-A

1. Refer students to Transparency 6-A. Discuss why they think each item was listed. (The events tell us about the student's hobbies, interests, and family.)

2. Once students have labeled their most significant events, encourage them to make a list of the five to ten most vivid or interesting events. Students should then put stars by the three events that provide the best topics to write about. Encourage students to talk over their choices with peers or with you. You may want to remind them that the best topics are those they remember in great detail and are enthusiastic about sharing.

Prewriting: Make a Blueprint

1. Ask students to brainstorm for their own places to diagram.

2. Show students examples of blueprints. Explain that blueprints generally use an overhead perspective. Discuss how blueprints show general views rather than complete representations.

3. Encourage students to annotate or label their blueprints to remind themselves of ideas or memories they can use in their writing.

6.2 *Prewriting*

Choosing Your Topic

Memorable people, remarkable places, unusual events, and intriguing ideas all make great topics for description. Following are more ideas for coming up with a topic for description.

Strategies for Generating Topics

1. **Draw or Sketch** Use a drawing pencil and paper to sketch a person, place, thing, or event you find interesting. Your sketch may be as abstract or realistic as you like. When you are finished sketching, choose an aspect of the drawing to develop into a description.

2. **Browse in a Calendar** Look through this year's or last year's calendar or date book to spark memories of people and events of the past year. For example, a certain date might remind you of someone you met, a game you played, or your grandfather's birthday party. Choose one of those memories to form the heart of your description.

3. **Make a Blueprint** Draw the floor plan of a place you know well. Next, label each room or area with a name that makes it personal for you, such as *My Studio*, *Kai's Hideout*, or *Mom's Den*. Also, jot down memories or ideas you associate with each room. Then, select the most interesting idea, and make it the topic of your description.

⏱ TIME AND RESOURCE MANAGER

Resources
Print: *Writing Support Transparencies, 6-A–D; Writing Support Activity Book, 6-1*
Technology: *Writing and Grammar* Interactive Text, Section 6.2

Using the Full Student Edition	Using the Handbook Ⓗ
• Work through the sketch, calendar, or blueprint strategy with the class (p. 104). • Use the Responding to Fine Art transparency to generate additional topics.	• Work through the sketch, calendar, or blueprint strategy with the class (p. 64). • Use the Responding to Fine Art transparency to generate additional topics.

TOPIC BANK

To get more specific writing ideas for a description, read the following suggestions:

1. **Describe an Idea: Democracy** Think about the concept of democracy and the images it conjures up for you. For example, you may think of a person voting, a town meeting, or a king losing his crown. Then, develop this idea, and write a description of "democracy."

2. **Recall a Challenging Moment** What was the last big challenge you faced? Write some adjectives or sensory images that arise from your memory of facing that challenge. Then, work your ideas into a description.

Responding to Fine Art

3. *Studio Interior* by Jane Freilicher depicts a picture within a picture. Imagine yourself in the artist's studio, and write a description of what you see, as though speaking to a friend far away. You may describe what is actually in the picture or what you imagine lies beyond the window.

Studio Interior, 1982, Jane Freilicher, Tibor De Nagy

Responding to Literature

4. In "Jazz Fantasia," the poet Carl Sandburg uses vivid descriptive language to bring to life jazz music. Write a description in response to this poem by bringing to life your ideas about jazz or any other type of music you like. "Jazz Fantasia" appears in *Prentice Hall Literature, Penguin Edition,* Grade 10.

🕐 Timed Writing Prompt

5. Write a description of your favorite place in the world. It can be anywhere from a corner of your room to an interesting place you once visited. Use sensory details to create a sense of your chosen place for your reader. **(35 minutes)**

✓ ONGOING ASSESSMENT: Monitor and Reinforce

You may wish to explore the elements of descriptive writing in greater depth with students who have difficulty generating topics.

Option 1 Supply students with examples of descriptive writing to jog their imaginations. See "The Apple Tree" by Katherine Mansfield or the excerpt from *My Left Foot* by Christy Brown. Both may be found in *Prentice Hall Literature, Penguin Edition,* Grade 10.

Option 2 If items in the Topic Bank seem too difficult for some students, offer suggestions from the *Topic Bank for Heterogeneous Classes* in the Teaching Resources.

Step-by-Step Teaching Guide

Responding to Fine Art
Studio Interior by Jane Freilicher
Teaching Resources: Writing Support Transparencies, 6-B

1. Display the transparency (6-B) and invite students to discuss what they notice. Here are some questions to stimulate discussion:

   What do the details of the painting tell you about the artist's studio?

   How would it feel to work there?

   What might these details suggest about the artist?

2. Have students consider the different ways this piece of art can prompt writing. You may wish to suggest the following to show how they can use the painting to generate topics:

   Take a point of view other than your own, that of the artist's mother, for example. How does this place look through her eyes?

   Speculate about things just outside the picture. What else do you think may be in the room?

   Students may include these topic ideas along with their own suggestions in their topic banks.

🕐 Timed Writing Prompt

• Ask students to identify the sense (or senses) that seem most alive in their favorite place. Discuss why that sense seems to be most prevalent.

• Remind students that the prompt calls for a description, not simply a summary. Student responses should include details about what they see, hear, touch, taste, or smell in that place.

• Suggest that students allow five minutes for prewriting, twenty-five minutes for writing, and five minutes for reviewing and proofreading.

Customize for
Interpersonal Learners

Ask pairs of students to study an object and write a list of descriptive words about it. Then, group them with another pair of classmates. Pairs exchange lists and review the similarities and differences in the details chosen to describe the object.

Prewriting: Narrowing Your Topic

Teaching Resources: Writing Support Transparencies, 6-C; Writing Support Activity Book, 6-1

1. Using Transparency 6-C, show how subtopics can be expanded: Use *her life* as the center of a new web and have students suggest details to go with the subtopics of *Rhodes Scholar, historian,* and *world traveler.*

2. Point out that narrowing the topic does not mean excluding all details in other subtopics. For example, details about Aunt Bertie's appearance and personality may still appear, even if the topic is narrowed to one country she visited during her travels.

3. Distribute copies of the graphic organizer (6-1) and assign students to record their subtopics in it.

Prewriting: Considering Your Audience and Purpose

1. Have students talk about strategies a writer might use when trying to impress friends. Ask students how these strategies were employed in the example.

2. Ask how the purpose and audience in the second description have affected the writing. (Since the audience is a doctor, details about the injury are most useful.)

3. Ask students to summarize the differences in purpose, detail, and tone between the descriptions in a two-column chart.

Integrating Speaking and Listening Skills

Ask students to write a short but detailed description of someone or something with which they are familiar. Have a volunteer read a description to the class, then have the class try to recall as many details as possible. Record their responses on the board, then compare responses to the description. How close is the match? Repeat if desired.

6.2

Narrowing Your Topic

Use a topic web to explore several aspects of a topic. Then, choose the aspect that most interests you to write about.

Make a Web

Write your broad topic at the top of a piece of paper, and then write subtopics in circles connected to your broad topic by lines. Following is an example:

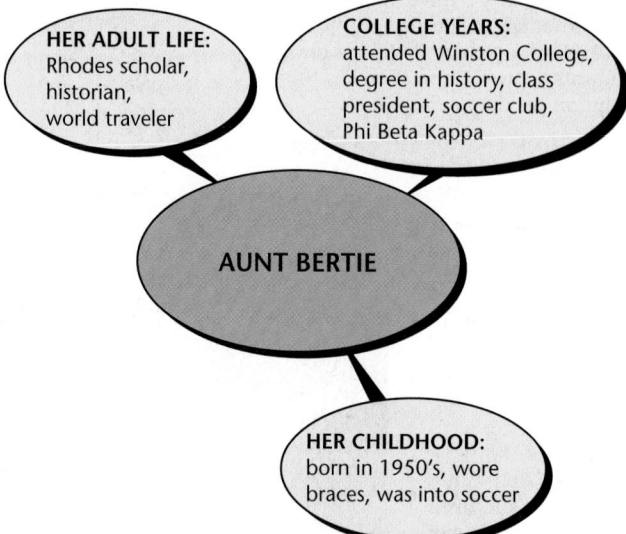

Considering Your Audience and Purpose

Choose details for your description that your audience will understand and appreciate. Your choice of details and your tone, or attitude toward your subject, will also help you to achieve your purpose, your overall reason for writing. In the following example, the details and writer's tone vary because the audiences and purposes differ.

Audience: Friends
Purpose: To impress

I lunge through the pressing cluster of runners near the finish line. I push so hard I twist my right ankle. Despite the shooting pain, I manage to limp over the finish line first.

Audience: Doctor
Purpose: To diagnose

The right Achilles tendon is so tight and numb that my foot will flex no more than an inch. Inward and outward motion of the foot is difficult, and I feel a shooting pain with each slow step.

⏱ Timed Writing Hint

When you are given a prompt, read it carefully to determine the audience for your writing.

Gathering Details

Gather a wide range of descriptive details using the cubing technique, which is explained below.

Use the Cubing Technique

Just as a cube has six sides or aspects, so may your description topic have different aspects. Following are six ways to look at your topic. Jot down your responses to the directions. Then, use your responses as you draft your description.

1. **Describe It** Provide details about your subject's appearance, importance, or personality.

2. **Associate It** Tell what related thoughts come to mind when you think of your subject.

3. **Apply It** Provide examples of what you can do with or learn from your subject.

4. **Analyze It by Breaking It Into Parts** Describe your subject aspect by aspect, using factual terms.

5. **Compare or Contrast It** Tell what your subject is similar to or different from.

6. **Argue for or Against It** Give details that explain your subject's value or problems.

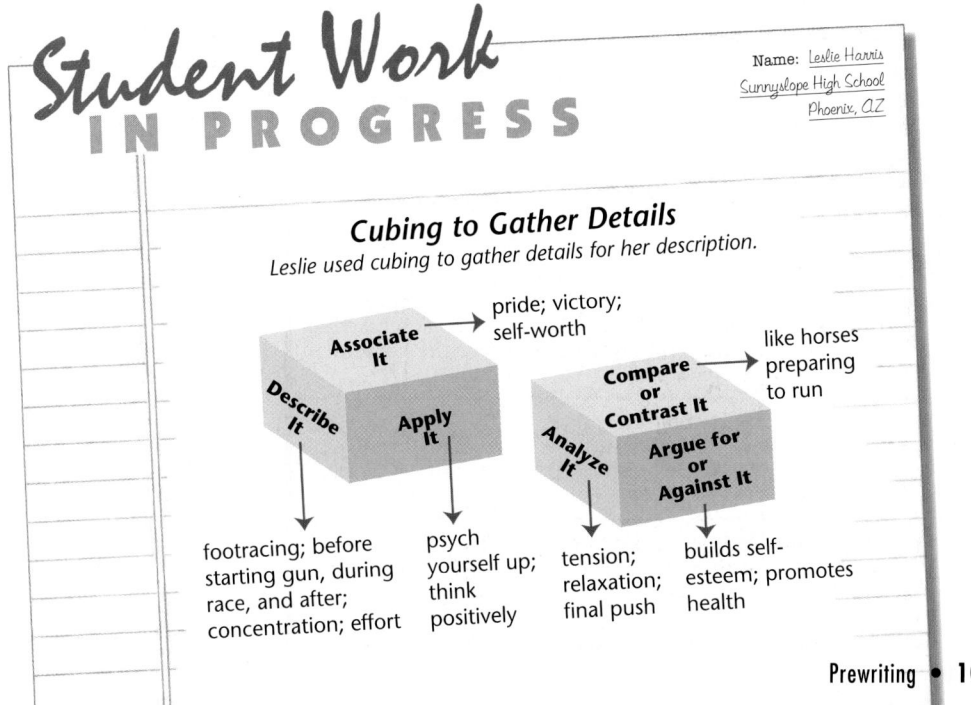

Student Work IN PROGRESS

Name: Leslie Harris
Sunnyslope High School
Phoenix, AZ

Cubing to Gather Details
Leslie used cubing to gather details for her description.

Associate It → pride; victory; self-worth

Describe It

Apply It

Compare or Contrast It → like horses preparing to run

Analyze It

Argue for or Against It

footracing; before starting gun, during race, and after; concentration; effort

psych yourself up; think positively

tension; relaxation; final push

builds self-esteem; promotes health

Prewriting • 107

Step-by-Step Teaching Guide

Prewriting: Use the Cubing Technique

Teaching Resources: Writing Support Transparencies, 6-D

1. Begin by defining the terms with students. Compile a mini-glossary on the board of such terms as *Associate, Apply, Compare,* and *Contrast.* Have students construct their own working definitions of these terms on which you can all agree.

2. Refer students to Transparency 6-D. Discuss each of the examples generated by the topic, *A Footrace.*

3. Encourage students to choose a preliminary topic for their descriptions. Ask them to record this topic on a piece of paper and be prepared to share it. This will help them have definite images in mind as they begin to create a "cube" of their own.

4. Invite students to share examples generated from their preliminary description topics. (Example: "Describe It" asks students to share details about the appearance or personality of their chosen subject.)

Integrating Vocabulary Skills

Using a Journal This cubing exercise involves working with terms such as *contrast* and *associate.* These terms might be unfamiliar to students, and they have a special definition in this context. Remind students that recording definitions in a journal or log can be a powerful aid in vocabulary development.

 **TIME SAVERS!**

Writing Support Transparencies
Use the transparencies for Chapter 6 to facilitate teaching of strategies.

Writing Support Activity Book
Use the graphic organizers for Chapter 6 to facilitate student planning.

Drafting: Create a Mood

1. Ask the class to read the "Joyous Mood" and "Awed Mood" passages and identify the words and phrases that help create the mood in each.

2. Have students generate phrases and words that would reflect the mood of someone who doesn't like snow and someone who has never seen snow before. Record these words and phrases on the board. This will give students practice with applying these concepts.

Drafting: Create Figurative Language

Teaching Resources: Writing Support Transparencies, 6-E; Writing Support Activity Book, 6-3

1. Point out that students hear or use figurative language often. Stories, movies, poems, songs, and familiar sayings usually rely on figurative language.

2. Use Transparency 6-E to review figurative language terms, offering some additional examples.

3. Invite students to share and generate their own examples. Distribute copies of the organizer (6-3) or have students create their own figurative language chart.

Customize for
Musical Learners

Song lyrics are usually filled with figurative language. Encourage students to perform or play recordings of examples that they have found and identify the type of figurative language used in each example.

Critical Viewing

Analyze Students may feel the photo conveys a homey, domestic mood or a lonely mood.

6.3 Drafting

Shaping Your Writing
Create a Mood

Once you have gathered a wide range of details that appeal to the senses, choose the ones that create an overall mood, or atmosphere. The mood your description provides will add to your readers' understanding and to their enjoyment of your writing.

In the following models, the choice of descriptive details gives each description a definite mood:

Joyous Mood The morning sunlight hit the window above my bed and sent dizzying rays of light dancing over the wall. I sprang up and looked outside. The whiteness was almost blinding in its brilliance. It had snowed!

Awed Mood The morning sun was different that morning. It was shining, clear and true, throwing intricate, mysterious patterns onto the wall. With bemused anticipation, I sat up and peered out the window. Snow had fallen overnight, transforming the town into a heartbreakingly beautiful wonderland.

Providing Elaboration
Create Figurative Language

As you draft, use figurative language to make your description memorable and unique. Following are some commonly used types of figurative language:

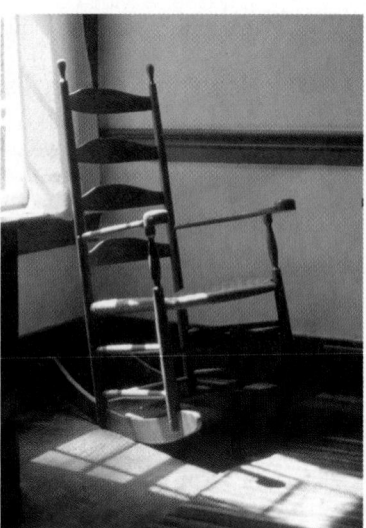

▲ **Critical Viewing**
What mood does the image in this photograph convey? Explain. **[Analyze]**

Simile	A simile compares two unlike things using the words *like* or *as*.	The dog was *as fast as a rocket.*
Metaphor	A metaphor compares two unlike things by stating that one thing *is* the other.	The *ball of fire* rises each morning over the horizon.
Hyperbole	Hyperbole is exaggeration that is usually used to create a comic effect.	The guard was *twelve feet tall, with muscles of steel.*
Personification	Personification applies human qualities or behavior to something nonhuman.	The washing machine *danced* across the basement floor!

108 • Description

TIME AND RESOURCE MANAGER

Resources
Print: *Writing Support Transparencies, 6-E–G; Writing Support Activity Book, 6-3*
Technology: *Writing and Grammar* Interactive Text, Section 6.3

Using the Full Student Edition	Using the Handbook🄷
• Discuss strategies for creating figurative language (p. 108), and then have students begin drafting. • Cover revising strategies (pp. 109–113) in class and assign Grammar in Your Writing. • Have students work in groups for the peer revision activity.	• Discuss strategies for creating figurative language (p. 68), and then have students begin drafting. • Cover revising strategies (pp. 69–73) in class and assign Grammar in Your Writing. • Have students work in groups for the peer revision activity.

6.4 Revising

Revising Your Overall Structure

Review your description to be sure that you've used a consistent, logical, and effective structural organization.

▶ **REVISION STRATEGY**
Outlining Details to Check Your Organization

Create an outline to show the content and order of each paragraph in your description. Then, review your outline and rearrange paragraphs, if necessary, to make your description more effective. Following are some organizational strategies you might want to use as you reorganize your description:

- **General to Specific** Use this structure when describing a person, thing, or an idea.
- **Chronological Organization** Use chronological, or time, order to bring events to life for readers.
- **Spatial Organization** Use spatial organization to describe where things are located in relation to each other; for example, a place, a building, or an object.

Revising Your Paragraphs

Check Unity

Review the paragraphs in your description to be sure that the main idea of each describes an aspect of your overall topic. Also, make sure that individual sentences within a paragraph support the topic sentence.

▶ **REVISION STRATEGY**
Color-Coding to Check Unity

With a highlighter, color-code the main idea of each paragraph. If any main ideas do not support the topic of your description, rewrite or delete them. Then, use a different-colored highlighter to call out the sentences within each paragraph that support the main idea. Rewrite or delete sentences that stray from the paragraph's main idea.

Jasmine's singing voice had the power to enthrall an audience. Her voice range was impressive, spanning three octaves. An octave is a set of eight notes on a diatonic scale. An easy way to remember what an octave is is the song "Do, a deer." But it was the bell-like quality of her voice that truly set Jasmine apart as a singer.

Get instant help! To create your outline, use the Essay Builder, accessible from the menu bar, on-line or on CD-ROM.

Revising • 109

Revising: Adding Modifiers

Teaching Resources: Writing Support Transparencies, 6-F

1. Using the transparency, point out to students how Leslie added modifiers to her draft.

2. Ask students to identify whether any modifiers are misplaced or dangling.

3. Challenge students to suggest more modifying words and phrases that could be added to Leslie's draft.

Integrating Grammar Skills

Point out that modifiers may be words, phrases, or clauses. They give further detail about nouns and pronouns (adjectives) or verbs, adjectives, and adverbs (adverbs). Sometimes modifiers are less obvious than *big* or *quickly*. For example, verbals are verb forms that can be used as modifiers (the *blazing* sun).

6.4

Revising Your Sentences
Add Modifiers to Enhance Your Description

Enliven your description by adding modifiers to dull sentences. Through the use of modifiers, you give more information about the subject or verb of a sentence. Modifiers may be single words (adjectives and adverbs) or they may be in the form of a phrase (adjectival and adverbial phrases and clauses).

▶ **REVISION STRATEGY**
Adding Modifiers

First, read through your draft and circle any passages that seem terse, dull, or incomplete. Then, add descriptive details, answering the questions *Who? What? Where? When? Why?* and *How?* through the use of modifiers. Your modifiers may be single words, phrases, or clauses.

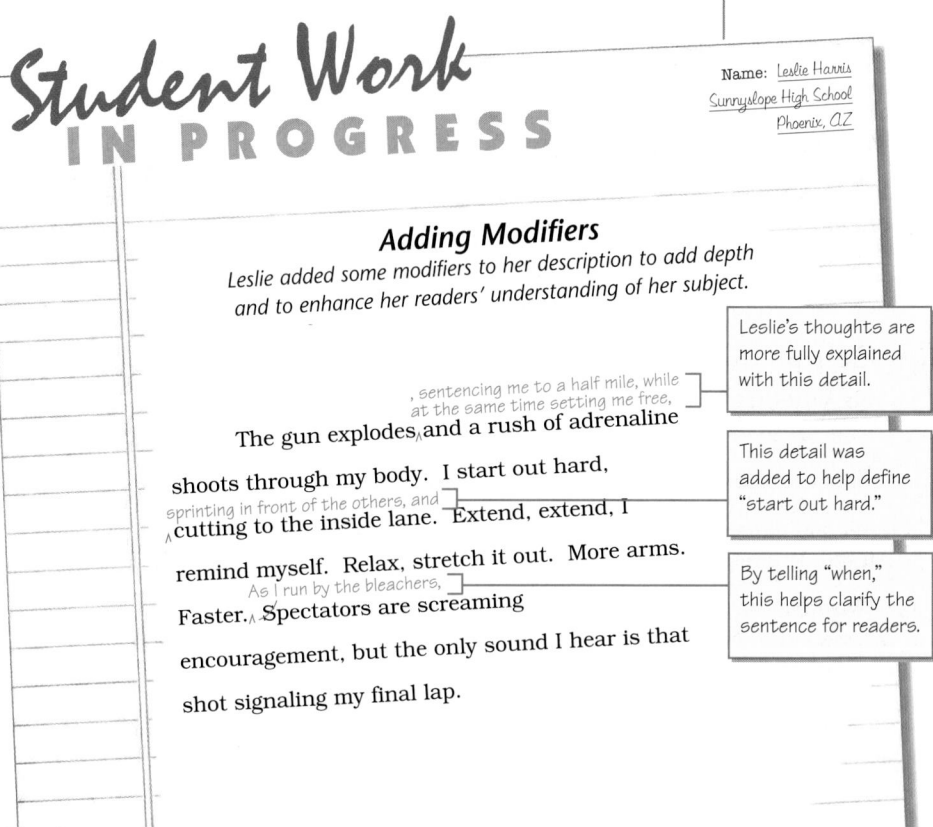

Student Work
IN PROGRESS

Name: *Leslie Harris*
Sunnyslope High School
Phoenix, AZ

Adding Modifiers

Leslie added some modifiers to her description to add depth and to enhance her readers' understanding of her subject.

The gun explodes, *, sentencing me to a half mile, while at the same time setting me free,* and a rush of adrenaline shoots through my body. I start out hard, *sprinting in front of the others, and* cutting to the inside lane. Extend, extend, I remind myself. Relax, stretch it out. More arms. Faster. *As I run by the bleachers,* Spectators are screaming encouragement, but the only sound I hear is that shot signaling my final lap.

> Leslie's thoughts are more fully explained with this detail.

> This detail was added to help define "start out hard."

> By telling "when," this helps clarify the sentence for readers.

110 • Description

⏱ **TIME SAVERS!**

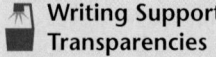 **Writing Support Transparencies**
Use the transparencies for Chapter 6 to facilitate teaching of strategies.

📖 **Writing Support Activity Book**
Use the graphic organizers for Chapter 6 to facilitate student planning.

110 • 70🄷

Grammar in Your Writing
Dangling and Misplaced Modifiers

A **modifier** is a word or phrase that helps describe nouns or verbs in a sentence. An essential ingredient of clear writing is effectively placed modifiers. A modifier should be placed as close as possible to the word it modifies.

Misplaced Modifiers

A **misplaced modifier** appears to modify the wrong word in a sentence. In the sentence below that contains the misplaced modifier, the reader may at first think that "we" were covered with cobwebs and mold, not the cabinet.

Sentence with misplaced modifier: Covered with cobwebs and mold, we cleaned the old cabinet.

Corrected sentence: We cleaned the old cabinet that was covered with cobwebs and mold.

Dangling Modifiers

A **dangling modifier** appears to modify either the wrong word or no word at all because the word it should logically modify is missing. In the sentence below that contains the dangling modifier, the reader may wonder what, exactly, is "pistoning like spark plugs"?

Sentence with dangling modifier: Pistoning like spark plugs in a human engine, the track was pounded.

Corrected sentence: Pistoning like spark plugs in a human engine, the runner's feet pounded the track.

Find It in Your Reading Read the excerpt from *Letters Home From Vietnam* on pages 102–103. Locate three sentences that contain modifiers. On a separate sheet of paper, circle each modifier and the word it modifies. Observe where the modifier appears in relation to the word it modifies. Then, answer the following question for each word-modifier combination you identified. Could the modifier be closer to the word it modifies, or does the sentence work fine as is?

Find It in Your Writing Review your draft to identify and correct any dangling or misplaced modifiers. Be sure you have placed your modifiers near their subjects. Be particularly careful about sentences that contain passive voice; they are more likely to contain dangling modifiers.

For more on misplaced and dangling modifiers, see Chapter 21.

Dangling and Misplaced Modifiers

1. Have students note that dangling and misplaced modifiers cause confusion or, sometimes, unintentional hilarity.

2. To give students additional experience with dangling or misplaced modifiers, have them rewrite the following sentences. Write on the chalkboard:

   Ringing loudly, I reached for the alarm clock.

   (I reached for the alarm clock, which was ringing loudly *or* I reached for the loudly ringing alarm clock.)

   The area attracts many birds with idyllic weather.

   (The area's idyllic weather attracts many birds.)

Find It in Your Reading

Encourage students to experiment with rewriting some sentences to place the modifiers in different places, or to change the form of the modifier.

Find It in Your Writing

Review with students the concept of passive voice. (Example: The party was enjoyed by everyone.) Ask students how this can be rewritten in active voice. (Everyone enjoyed the party.) The subject of the sentence (party) and the "actor" of the action (everyone) have been reversed, which can make it more difficult to identify what is being modified.

Customize for
ESL Students

The concept of misplaced and dangling modifiers may be challenging for English language learners. Languages other than English use a variety of different word order conventions. When writing examples on the board, use a different-colored chalk or marker to identify modifiers and the words they modify.

✎ STANDARDIZED TEST PREPARATION WORKSHOP

Punctuation Standardized test questions may require students to recognize incorrect punctuation.

1. Correctly punctuate this sentence.
   Write about a time when you had a happy unexpected thrilling surprise.

   A Write about, a time, when you had a happy, unexpected, thrilling, surprise.

   B Write about a time when you had a happy, unexpected, thrilling surprise.

   C Write about a time when you had a happy unexpected thrilling surprise.

   D Write about a time when, you had a happy, unexpected thrilling surprise.

   Students should recognize that **B** is correct. They should be able to explain that commas belong after *happy* and *unexpected* because these words are multiple adjectives of equal rank.

Revising: Replace Vague Words

Teaching Resources: Writing Support Transparencies, 6-G

1. Explain that, though vague words are useful when discussing generalities, they are not helpful in descriptions.

2. Write on the board: I ate ___. Explain that "some food" would complete the thought, but not precisely. Suggest that a writer could be humorous (I ate what?!?), boastful (I ate fourteen hard-boiled eggs), enticing (I ate a juicy hamburger with all the fixings), and so on.

3. Point out that sometimes the more precise element will be a single word (*sterilized* instead of *cleaned; granite* for *rock*) or a phrase (*below zero* for *cold; on a 45-degree angle* for *steep*).

4. Review the Student Work In Progress. Ask students to identify how the new words add more information.

5. Ask students to use the checklist on the chart to critique their own drafts. Have them share precise words they have used (either originally or to replace vague words during revision).

Customize for
ESL Students

Making language more concrete, specific, and precise offers English language learners a good opportunity to learn new vocabulary words. Pair students with more experienced English-speakers as they generate alternatives to vague words and phrases.

6.4

Revising Your Word Choice
Replace Vague Words

A vague word—whether it is a noun, a verb, or a modifier—cannot communicate your unique experience. Reread your draft, and replace words that are vague with more precise words.

Vague Words	Precise Words
good	delicious, excellent, well-mannered
looked	stared, glanced, peered, squinted
store	grocery, delicatessan, boutique
cold	freezing, chilly, brisk, frigid

▶ **REVISION STRATEGY**
Circling and Replacing

Read through your description, and circle words that are vague, dull, or inaccurate. Then replace those circled words or phrases with choices that better reflect what it is you are describing.

Student Work
IN PROGRESS

Name: *Leslie Harris*
Sunnyslope High School
Phoenix, AZ

Replacing Vague Words
Leslie replaced vague words with more precise words to make her narrative more engaging.

I am ⟨sure⟩ that I am going to win. All the way
determined

through, I ⟨think⟩ run all the way through the
mentally chant

finish line. And then, as ⟨soon⟩ as I started, I am
abruptly

⟨done⟩, drained of nervousness and the ability to
finished

remain standing. I open my eyes, knowing that I

am now ⟨ready⟩ and confident enough to run.
prepared

Peer Review

One way to get feedback on your description is to work with a group of peers and have them comment on the effectiveness of your writing. Use the following activity as you edit your description.

Create a Plus-and-Minus Chart

Use the following guidelines as you work with your peers to revise your description:

1. Work in a group of three to five students.
2. Prepare a chart like the one shown, and give copies to peers.
3. Read your description aloud to your peers.
4. Then, read the first entry on the chart, and ask your peers to make a thumbs-up sign if their response is positive and a thumbs-down sign if their response is negative. Enter your peers' responses on your chart.
5. Review the responses, and make revisions to your draft as necessary.

▲ Critical Viewing
Why is it useful to compare and contrast reviewers' reactions to your writing? **[Apply]**

Plus-and-Minus Chart

	Reviewer #1	Reviewer #2	Reviewer #3
1. The title is appropriate and interesting.	+	+	-
2. The description contains details like vivid verbs and precise nouns.	-	-	+
3. The description creates a definite mood, or atmosphere.	-	-	-
4. The writing is unified.	+	+	+
5. Each sentence is clear, with no misplaced or dangling modifiers.	+	+	-

Revising: Peer Review

Teaching Resources: Writing Support Transparencies, 6-H; Writing Support Activity Book, 6-4

1. Before students begin peer review, note that writers should ask for the feedback most useful to them. They should feel free to direct their reviewers to pay special attention to a particular aspect of the writing.

2. Display Transparency 6–H to demonstrate one method writers can use to chart the responses of their reviewers. Distribute copies of the organizer (6-4), and encourage students to ask friends and family from outside the class to respond to their writing.

3. Peer reviewers should focus on the most vivid impressions they got from the writing. This will tell the writers which descriptive details were most successful.

4. Have reviewers ask questions about the parts they found unclear. This will cue the writer to focus on places where point of view or other details may be confusing.

Critical Viewing

Apply Students should recognize that comparing and contrasting responses to their writing can give them a wider perspective on whether their writing is successful, and with what kind of readers.

Editing and Proofreading

1. Point out that the editing and proofreading phase is the appropriate time to focus on punctuation. Ask students to check their punctuation paragraph by paragraph.

2. Encourage students to pay attention to their commas. When they fixed dangling modifiers, were commas moved? Do commas set off nonessential phrases, such as "for example"? Do introductory adverbial phrases have needed commas?

Using Commas Correctly

1. Remind students that before this final stage, writers might frequently need to add clauses and rearrange sentences. Therefore, it is most efficient to do a final check once the wording of a piece is finalized, rather than before.

2. To make certain students understand the use of serial commas, adjectives of equal rank, and adjectives of unequal rank, ask them to suggest additional sentences to illustrate each usage.

Find It in Your Reading

Ask students to find the following sentence in the model.

It's a fine powder that blows at the slightest breeze.

Ask students to identify the adjectives in the sentence. Ask them why the writer does not need commas to separate adjectives in this sentence. (The adjectives appear singly.)

Find It in Your Writing

Ask volunteers to share samples of adjectives from their writing. Use a student's sentence as a model, writing it on the board. Ask students to identify the adjectives as equal or unequal in rank and tell whether the punctuation is correct.

6.5 Editing and Proofreading

Before you share your description with others, take time to polish it. Correct errors in grammar and punctuation, and make sure that you have spelled everything correctly.

Focusing on Commas

Review your description carefully, and check to be sure that you have correctly used commas to separate adjectives of equal rank and to separate a series of adjectives.

🕐 **Timed Writing Hint**

When you write quickly, you may make careless punctuation errors. Allow two or three minutes to check your writing for correct use of commas and other punctuation.

Grammar in Your Writing
Using Commas Correctly

Commas are used to separate items in a series and to separate certain kinds of adjectives.

Serial commas: Use commas to separate three or more words, phrases, or clauses in a series. In the example below, the first two adjectives are followed by a comma. The third adjective does not need a comma.

Example: The restless, tired, and hungry crowd gathered near the mountaintop.

Adjectives of equal rank: Use commas to separate adjectives of equal rank, called coordinate adjectives. In the sentence below, the adjectives *moist* and *delicious* could be switched without changing the meaning.

Example: The moist, delicious pie was a hit after dinner.

Adjectives of unequal rank: If one adjective has a closer relationship to the noun than the other, no comma appears between them. Below, the adjective *talented* has a closer relationship to *acrobats* than does *twenty*.

Example: Twenty talented acrobats appeared in the circus ring.

Find It in Your Reading Read through the excerpt from *Letters Home From Vietnam* on pages 102–103, and find adjectives that the writer does not separate with commas. Explain why commas are not needed.

Find It in Your Writing Check your description to make sure that you have used commas with adjectives correctly. Find items in a series of adjectives. If there are none, challenge yourself to add a series of adjectives.

To learn more about the correct use of commas, see Chapter 28.

114 • Description

🕐 TIME AND RESOURCE MANAGER

Resources
Print: *Scoring Rubrics on Transparency,* Ch. 6; *Writing Assessment and Portfolio Management; Formal Assessment,* Ch. 6
Technology: *Writing and Grammar* Interactive Text, Section 6.5

Using the Full Student Edition	Using the Handbook🄷
• Review pp. 114–115 in class, including Grammar in Your Writing.	• Review pp. 74–75 in class, including Grammar in Your Writing.
• Have students edit and proofread their essays in class.	• Have students edit and proofread their essays in class.
• Have students present their final drafts.	• Have students present their final drafts.

6.6 Publishing and Presenting

Use the following ideas for sharing your description with others:

Building Your Portfolio

1. **Display** Request a bulletin board at school where you can post your description. Place photos or illustrations around your paper to further enhance its effectiveness.

2. **Audiotape** Capture your description on audiotape. First, rehearse yourself reading your paper. Mark on your copy where you will pause and what words require special emphasis. Then, record your reading. Play the tape back for family and friends.

Reflecting on Your Writing

After you have finished your description, think about the experience of writing it. Use these questions to direct your reflection, and record your responses in your portfolio.

- What did you learn about the subject you chose?
- Which strategy for choosing a topic would you use for a future descriptive essay?

🖥 Internet Tip

To see descriptions scored with this rubric, go on-line:
PHSchool.com
Enter Web Code:
eek-1001

Rubric for Self-Assessment

Use the following criteria to evaluate your description.

	Score 4	Score 3	Score 2	Score 1
Audience and Purpose	Contains details that work together to create a tone	Creates a tone through use of details	Contains extraneous details that detract from the tone	Contains details that are unfocused and create no tone
Organization	Is organized consistently, logically, and effectively	Is organized consistently	Is organized, but not consistently	Is disorganized and confusing
Elaboration	Contains creative use of figurative language, creating interesting comparisons	Contains figurative language that creates comparisons	Contains figurative language, but the comparisons are not fresh	Contains no figurative language
Use of Language	Contains sensory language that appeals to the five senses; contains no errors in grammar, punctuation, or spelling	Contains some sensory language; contains few errors in grammar, punctuation, and spelling	Contains some sensory language, but it appeals to only one or two of the senses; contains some errors in grammar, punctuation, and spelling	Contains no sensory language; contains many errors in grammar, punctuation, and spelling

Publishing and Presenting • 115

Step-by-Step Teaching Guide

Publishing and Presenting

1. Make sure to give students a say in how or if their work will be displayed. Not all students are comfortable displaying their work in public.

2. If the technology is available at your school, you may wish to have students make video tapes of their presentations.

ASSESS and CLOSE

Step-by-Step Teaching Guide

Assessment

Teaching Resources: Scoring Rubrics on Transparency, Ch. 6; Writing Assessment and Portfolio Management; Formal Assessment, Ch. 6

1. Display the Scoring Rubric transparency and review the criteria in class.

2. Before students proceed with self-assessment, you may wish to review the Final Draft of the Student Work in Progress on pages 116–117.

3. In addition to student self-assessment, you may wish to use the following options:

- score student essays yourself, using the rubric and scoring models in *Writing Assessment and Portfolio Management*.

- review the Standardized Test Preparation Workshop on pages 122–123 and administer a timed writing assessment.

- administer Chapter 6 assessment from *Formal Assessment* in the Teaching Resources to evaluate students' grasp of the concepts presented.

Step-by-Step Teaching Guide

Final Draft

1. Help students see that "Phantom Finish" incorporates key elements of the descriptive essay.

   • The title is appropriate and interesting.

   • The description contains vivid language. We "feel" Leslie's exertions around the track.

   • The description conveys a distinctive mood of tension and eagerness by means of figurative language and vivid modifiers.

   • The ideas in the piece are unified.

   • Sentences are clear and avoid misplaced and dangling modifiers.

   • The audience has been carefully considered. The narrative is addressed to all people who have anxiously waited for something to begin.

2. Ask students to discuss the ideas, elements, or approaches the writer uses in this model that they might incorporate into their own drafts.

3. Ask students whether there are revisions, deletions, or additions that they would make to this essay to make it more effective. Which of these suggestions seem especially applicable to their own writing?

Critical Viewing

Relate Answers will vary, but students should supply descriptive details about the kind of concentration each sport requires.

FINAL DRAFT

◀ **Critical Viewing** What sports require the kind of concentration you see on the face of this athlete? Explain. **[Relate]**

Phantom Finish

Leslie Harris
Sunnyslope High School
Phoenix, Arizona

Fears sprout wings, taking flight in the depths of my stomach, and my mutinous mouth refuses to swallow. Breathe, I tell myself. Settle down. Every logical part of me assures myself that it's no big deal; I have nothing to be afraid of. But my stomach will not stop its incessant churning, and my chest is tight with anticipation. Realizing that no one else can calm my fears, I slowly exhale, forcing myself to relax and focus on the event ahead. Closing my eyes, I envision myself at the starting line, feeling vul-

Sensory details like "taking flight" and "churning" help readers understand Leslie's experience.

116 • Description

nerable and uncertain of my abilities. Faceless competitors surround me, jumping, stretching, and talking amongst themselves. Each of us presents a recognized threat to the other, and good luck wishes fill the air like cheap perfume. I am quiet and withdrawn, mentally preparing and hoping that hours of painful training will pay off. Too soon come those haunting words: "On your mark." My heart beats wildly in opposition with my stiffened and tense body. The gun explodes, sentencing me to a half mile, while at the same time setting me free, and a rush of adrenaline shoots through my body. I start out hard, sprinting in front of the others, and cutting to the inside lane. Extend, extend, I remind myself. Relax, stretch it out. More arms. Faster. As I run by the bleachers, spectators are screaming encouragement, but the only sound I hear is that shot signaling my final lap. "Faster" it screams, and I obey its command. Pounding footsteps on my heels torture me, and the visible shadows of opponents barely behind, force my straining body to test its limits. Final 200, final 200. I sprint harder than ever before; I am determined that I am going to win. All the way through, I mentally chant: "Run all the way through the finish line." And then, as abruptly as I started, I am finished, drained of nervousness and the ability to remain standing. I open my eyes, knowing that I am now prepared and confident enough to run. Just then, a competitor compliments me: "You're always so calm before you run." At this I simply smile; little does she know.

This metaphor compares insincere good luck wishes to cheap perfume filling the air.

Chronological organization carries the readers along with Leslie through the race.

Here, Leslie uses vivid, precise words like "pounding" and "force" to create a specific mood.

◀ **Critical Viewing**
What qualities are needed to be a successful runner like the ones pictured? **[Analyze]**

Teaching From the Final Draft

So vivid is Leslie's description that you may need to remind students that she is describing a "phantom" race, envisioning the event before it actually occurs. Ask students what difficulties Leslie might encounter if she extended her description to include the actual race. (Students may recognize that it would be difficult to make the "real" race more vivid and exciting than the imaginary one she has presented. A second race might be repetitive and anticlimactic.)

Integrating Vocabulary

Verbs and Adverbs Remind students that a vivid description is conveyed through effective word choice. Note that in describing an athletic event, Leslie appropriately relies on verbs and adverbs to capture the action. Have students identify words and phrases from "Phantom Finish" that they find particularly effective.

Critical Viewing

Analyze Students may mention talent, discipline, and endurance are needed to be a successful runner.

Lesson Objectives

1. To write a poem
2. To use prewriting strategies to generate ideas, develop voice, and plan
3. To respond productively to peer review of his/her own work

Step-by-Step Teaching Guide

Poem

Teaching Resources: Writing Support Transparencies, 6-I; Writing Support Activity Book, 6-5

1. Review the format for haiku and point out that some haiku, like these, vary from the standard 5-7-5 syllabic pattern. Students should organize their haiku as follows: Line 1: what or who; Line 2: an action or description; Line 3: summary.

2. Point out that free verse, as illustrated by "Night Clouds," is not restricted by line length or rhyme scheme.

3. Suggest that students review strategies from Chapter 6. See the chart below for resources.

4. Use Transparency 6-I to show students how to record and organize sensory images.

5. Review poetic devices such as simile, metaphor, alliteration, and onomatopoeia. Have students find some of each in the example poems. Give students copies of the organizer (6-5) for their own use in gathering sensory images.

6. When students form groups for their readings, instruct them to discuss which descriptive elements in each poem are particularly effective, and why.

Critical Viewing

Relate Answers will vary, but should describe or evoke the scene pictured.

Connected Assignment
Poem

Like writers of description, poets carefully choose words. In their **poems**, they use words to create images, moods, sounds, and to communicate ideas. Some poems tell a story; others describe something or express a feeling or an idea. Poems come in many forms: some are epic in length, and others are a few lines long. Some poems have rigid structures and rhyming rules, and others do not. Below are examples of two types of poems: haiku and free verse.

Write your own poem, following the writing process suggestions outlined on the page at right.

▲ **Critical Viewing**
If you were to write a poem inspired by this photograph, what would be its title? **[Analyze]**

MODEL

Bashō
Translated by Harold G. Henderson

The sun's way:
Hollyhocks turn toward it
Through all the rain of May.

Poverty's child—
He starts to grind the rice,
And gazes at the moon.

Night Clouds
Amy Lowell

The white mares of the moon rush along the sky
Beating their golden hoofs upon the glass Heavens;
The white mares of the moon are all standing on their hind
        legs
Pawing at the green porcelain doors of the remote Heavens.
Fly, Mares!
Strain your utmost.
Scatter the milky dust of stars,
Or the tiger sun will leap upon you and destroy you
With one lick of his vermilion tongue.

118 • Description

Prewriting Before you begin writing your poem, take some time to decide on its format, subject matter, and the impact you want to have on your readers.

Choose a Format Sometimes, it helps to choose a format for a poem before you choose its subject. Select a format that you like, such as a haiku or limerick. Read a few examples to remind yourself of the format's line structure and rhythm. Then, sort through recent experiences for moments that captivated your senses.

Select Subject Matter Think about what you want the subject of your poem to be. For example, you may want to explore what it feels like to be a turnip, or you may want to tell the story of your ninth birthday party.

Gather Details With a format and topic in hand, brainstorm for images that will convey ideas about your poem's subject. Record sensory images in a chart like the one below, that lists sights, sounds, tastes, smells, and touch.

SENSORY CHART				
Sight	**Sound**	**Taste**	**Smell**	**Touch**
bright	musical	salty	foul	rough
beautiful	noisy	sour	fragrant	bumpy
hazy	echoing	spicy	fresh-baked	furry

Drafting Let your chosen format help you draft and guide the number of syllables, lines, or stanzas that you write. Then, give your imagination license to run free. Experiment with unexpected word order, and create unusual metaphors. Include sound devices such as alliteration (repeated beginning consonants) and onomatopoeia (words that sound like their meaning) to support the desired mood.

Revising and Editing Read your poem aloud to a friend or to yourself. Listen for the sound, of the words, and picture the images. Add or change wording to make your images more vivid and powerful. Rearrange words to catch the desired rhythm.

Publishing and Presenting Hold a poetry reading with a group of peers. Take turns reading your poems aloud. Then, following the reading, discuss your experiences as poets and your ideas for upcoming poems.

Connected Assignment: Poem • **119**

Customize for
More Advanced Students

Encourage students to choose a form that is suitable for their topic. For instance, if their poem tells a story, they might choose limerick, ballad, or free-verse form, not haiku form. If it describes a quick impression, haiku would be more appropriate than ballad form.

Integrating Vocabulary Skills

Encourage students to use strong, vivid verbs instead of relying too heavily on adverbs. For example, instead of writing *walked slowly,* they might write *ambled, sauntered,* or *strolled.*

☑ **ONGOING ASSESSMENT: Prerequisite Skills**

Students may find the following resources from Chapter 6 particularly helpful in composing their poems.

In the Textbook	Print Resources	Technology
Choosing your Topic, Section 6.2 Considering Your Audience and Purpose, Section 6.2 Gathering Details, Section 6.2	*Writing Support Transparencies,* 6-A, 6-D–E; *Writing Support Activity Book,* 6-1–3	*Writing and Grammar* Interactive Text, Section 6.2

Lesson Objectives

1. To write a descriptive essay
2. To recognize distinctive and shared characteristics of cultures through reading
3. To evaluate artistic performances of peers, public presenters, and media presentations
4. To analyze relationships, ideas, and cultures as represented in dance

Step-by-Step Teaching Guide

Making Cultural Connections

1. Interested students might find examples of Diego Rivera's artwork to show the class. Discuss how the artist communicated cultural details through his painting.

2. Read aloud Pat Mora's poem. Have students describe the baker's actions as he works. Ask students how the poet's use of language evokes dancing.

3. Students might locate additional information about flamenco dancing in a library or on the Internet. Ask students to think of other styles of dancing they have seen or know about. Are any of the dances associated with a particular culture or country?

4. Discuss dances students have seen on stage, television, or in a film. Brainstorm for descriptive verbs and adverbs that apply to their topic. Remind students to include, in addition to describing the action, details of the dancers' appearance and surroundings.

Viewing and Representing

Activity Give interested students the opportunity to share their dance descriptions in small groups. They might provide visual representations, such as relevant artwork or video clips, to represent the dance they described in writing.

Spotlight on the Humanities

Making Cultural Connections
Focus on Dance: Flamenco

If you were going to describe a dance performance to a friend, you would use vivid verbs and adverbs to paint a picture of the performance. In the fifteenth century, flamenco arose as a popular art form among the people of southern Spain. A type of folk-loric dance, flamenco is a combination of singing, dancing, and guitar music. The complicated footwork mirrors its complex rhythms, making it challenging for the dancer and exciting for an audience to watch.

Art Connection Born in Mexico, Diego Rivera (1886–1957) is considered one of the great artists of the twentieth century. As in the painting at right, Rivera often used Hispanic dancers as the subject of his paintings, capturing the costumes and flavor of Mexican culture in his work. Rivera will forever be remembered for his great mural paintings, which captured the essence of Mexican society.

Portrait of Dolores Olmedo, Diego Rivera

Literature Connection In her poem "Mexican Magician," twentieth-century American poet Pat Mora compares the daily activities of a baker with the movements of a Mexican dance.

> All day the panadero
> in white apron and call cap,
> stirs flour, eggs and sugar
> then salsas with his broom. . . .
> His hips sway while he sprinkles
> cookies with sweet confetti,
> dance-dancing panadero,
> magician with a flair.

Pat Mora, a native Texan, continues to write books for children and adults. Recipient of a Poetry Fellowship from the National Endowment for the Arts in 1994, she currently lives in New Mexico.

Description Writing Activity: Dance Description

Describe a dance performance that you've seen recently. Use descriptive details and vivid verbs to bring the dance to life for your readers—but do so without naming the type of dance you are describing. Share your dance description with your class, and see whether they can guess the type of dance you described.

120 • Description

▲ **Critical Viewing** Why might female folkloric dancers, like the one pictured, wear flowing skirts? **[Speculate]**

Critical Viewing

Speculate Students might point out aspects of folkloric dancing, such as dipping and twirling movements, that would be accentuated by full, colorful skirts.

Media and Technology Skills

Evaluating Images

Activity: Rating a News Set

The production values of any television program send carefully planned messages to viewers. Designers work with producers to create sets, lights, costumes, and logos that project the desired "look." A passive television audience can be unconsciously manipulated by these carefully constructed images. You can easily see through these images by becoming an active, analytical viewer.

Think About It Consider the messages sent by your preferred television news program. Write down four or five words that describe the overall feeling or tone of the program. These words may help you understand your unconscious impression. Next, you will become an active viewer and take a close look at the production elements that might contribute to your perception.

Describe It Watch the program you have selected, and create a chart describing each of these production elements.

LOGO	SETS	PROPS	COSTUMES	LIGHTING
First-Witness News	Small set, very sparsely furnished	Only a long desk	Anchors are wearing serious business suits	Very bright lighting

Use specific descriptive language to help you analyze each element. You might find it useful to turn the sound down or off so that you are focusing primarily on the images.

Rate It Review your descriptions to make specific generalizations about the way the news program uses images to create a look or identity. Refer to your initial impressions to see whether your previous perceptions match the results of your analysis.

After analyzing the production elements, you can share your evaluation by giving the news program a rating. You might use a letter grade (*A*, *B*, *C*, etc.) or a five-star scale. You may wish to give ratings for a variety of aspects, such as overall appearance, professional feeling, or attitude.

Media and Technology Skills • 121

Identifying Image Trends

Being an active viewer includes recognizing various uses of images in film and video. Think about which of these trends you have noticed and whether or not you find them effective:

- Fast-cutting techniques appear often in music videos.
- Some stations place their logo in a corner of the screen at all times.
- Some commercials or promotional spots use quirky camera angles and speeded-up or unfocused footage.

▶ **Lesson Objectives**

1. To recognize how visual techniques convey messages in media
2. To evaluate informative and persuasive media presentations
3. To recognize genres such as nightly news, newsmagazines, and documentaries and identify the unique properties of each
4. To examine the effect of media on constructing one's perception of reality

Step-by-Step Teaching Guide

Evaluating Images

Teaching Resources: Writing Support Transparencies, 6-J; Writing Support Activity Book, 6-6

1. Discuss the major news programs on television and students' general impressions of these programs.
2. Use Transparency 6-J to show students how to set up a chart of production elements. Begin by writing general categories such as set, lighting, camera angles, newscasters' appearance, or logos.
3. Point out the list of image trends in the sidebar. Have students refer to their small-group discussions as they come up with particular impressions created by the production techniques.
4. Give students copies of the blank chart (6-6) to use in analyzing their news program.
5. Suggest that students create a rubric for rating the news program. The rubric should identify the categories rated and what constitutes a high or low "grade." These categories could correlate with those on their chart of production elements.
6. Have students divide into groups based on which news program they analyzed, consolidate their results, and compare their conclusions with those of other groups.

121

Step-by-Step Teaching Guide

Strategy, Organization, and Style

Teaching Resources: Standardized Test Preparation Workbook, pp. 11–12

1. Remind students that writing strategy relates to author's purpose. Does the information in the passage fit the writer's main idea? Do ideas build logically? Is the language specific and appropriate to the topic?

2. Tell students that reading the whole passage before choosing an answer will give them a better idea of the writer's topic and purpose.

3. In reviewing the sample test item, point out that the question focuses on organization. The reader would better understand the sequence of events after revision *A*.

Standardized Test Preparation Workshop

Strategy, Organization, and Style

On a standardized test, you may be asked to read a descriptive passage in which each sentence is numbered. Following the passage will be several multiple-choice questions based on the reading.

The following are three types of questions that you will need to answer:

- **Strategy questions** ask whether a given revision is appropriate in the context of the essay.
- **Organization questions** ask you to choose the most logical sequence of ideas.
- **Style questions** focus on conveying the writer's point of view and the use of appropriate and effective language.

Test Tip

Skillful test takers read questions twice. Scan questions before reading the passage, and then examine them closely before answering.

Sample Test Item	Answer and Explanation

Directions: Read the passage, and then answer the questions that follow.
 	
1 The original garden plan had no fence.
2 Several rabbit families resided in our back-
3 yard. Mark was able to build a picket fence
4 to enclose the raised beds. Even so, the
5 baby rabbits were able to get into the garden.
 	
1 Which of the following is the **BEST** revision of lines 1 to 3?
 	
  A The original garden plan had no fence; then, we learned that several rabbit families resided in our backyard.
 	
  B The original garden plan had no fence and several rabbit families resided in our backyard.
 	
  C The original garden plan had no fence, and lots of rabbits lived there.
 	
  D Correct as is.
	The correct answer is *A*. The transition word *then* links the two clauses and alerts the reader to the chronological order of the passage.

TEST-TAKING TIP

Point out to students that by reading quickly through the questions about a passage before reading the passage itself, they may be better able to focus on relevant ideas. Suggest that students try different ways to approach these kinds of test questions to find which method works best for them.

Before choosing an answer, students should reread the questions to be sure they understand exactly what they are being asked to evaluate. If the relevant area does not stand out on the first reading, it is likely that no change needs to be made.

Practice 1 **Directions:** Read the passage, and then answer the questions that follow. Choose the letter of the **BEST** answer.

1 There are woods surrounding poet Carl
2 Sandburg's home, in Flat Rock, North
3 Carolina. They are thick with young
4 pines, and old rhododendrons. The
5 beautiful mountainside property is now
6 a national park. A small parking lot
7 limits the number of guests in the park.
8 A long trail climbs up the hill parallel
9 to an enormous grassy expanse of lawn.
10 The park offers several benches along the
11 many hiking trails, as well as many direc-
12 tional signs to help trail-weary hikers
13 find their way around the property.

14 For small children and animal lovers,
15 perhaps the main attractions are the
16 barns and fields. Park patrons are
17 invited to enter the fenced meadows
18 where the nanny goats and kids wan-
19 der. The more aggressive billy goats are
20 penned separately. Mrs. Sandburg ded-
21 icated much of her time to raising
22 several kinds of goats.

23 The house itself sits about two thirds of
24 the way up the mountain. Across the
25 lawn from the trail is an outdoor
26 amphitheater with wooden benches
27 and a small wooden stage. Behind the
28 large white house are several out-
29 buildings, including the park ranger's
30 residence, and several barns that used
31 to house the Sandburg vehicles.

1 Which of the following is the **BEST** order for the paragraphs?
A 3,2,1
B 2,3,1
C 1,3,2
D Correct as is.

2 Which of the following would be the best way to write lines 1–3?
F There are woods surrounding poet Carl Sandburg's home, in Flat Rock, North Carolina, they are thick with young pines and old rhododendrons.
G The woods surrounding poet Carl Sandburg's home, in Flat Rock, North Carolina, are thick with young pines and old rhododendrons.
H There are woods surrounding poet Carl Sandburg's home, in Flat Rock, North Carolina; they are thick with young pines and old rhododendrons.
J The thick woods surrounding poet Carl Sandburg's home, in Flat Rock, North Carolina, have many young pines and old rhododendrons.

3 If the author wanted to include more information about what adults might enjoy at the park, which of the following would be an appropriate addition?
A Mr. and Mrs. Sandburg loved their home in Flat Rock.
B There are currently many goats living at the Sandburg Park.
C Sandburg wrote the poem *Skyscraper*.
D The samples of Sandburg's poetry are displayed in his own unique handwriting.

4 Which of the following words, if any, would be more descriptive than the word *small* in line 27?
F little
G tiny
H miniature
J Correct as is.

5 Which sentence should be deleted to eliminate irrelevant information?
A the sentence in lines 1–2
B the sentence in lines 6–7
C the sentence in lines 14–16
D the sentence in lines 20–22

Practice 1
1. C
2. G
3. D
4. J
5. D

Customize for
Less Advanced Students

Encourage students to read the passage slowly and carefully for meaning, and to resist the urge to race ahead. Evaluation of this kind requires full comprehension of the passage.

Customize for
More Advanced Students

As students read the passage, they should keep in mind the writer's emerging purpose, the quality of organization, and the language style. This focus could help them predict possible questions.

Time and Resource Manager

In-Depth Lesson Plan

	LESSON FOCUS	PRINT AND MEDIA RESOURCES
DAY 1	**Introduction to Persuasive Essays** Students learn key elements of persuasive writing and analyze the Model From Literature. (pp. 124–129/H76–77)	*Writers at Work* **DVD**, Persuasion *Writing and Grammar* **Interactive Text,** Ch. 7, Introduction
DAY 2	**Prewriting** Students choose and narrow a topic, consider their audience and purpose, and gather information. (pp. 130–134/H78–82)	**Teaching Resources** *Writing Support Transparencies, 7-A–E; Writing Support Activity Book, 7-1–2; Topic Bank for Heterogeneous Classes, Ch. 7* *Writing and Grammar* **Interactive Text,** Section 7.2
DAY 3	**Drafting** Students organize their ideas and write their first drafts. (pp. 135–136/H83–84)	**Teaching Resources** *Writing Support Transparencies, 7-F* *Writing and Grammar* **Interactive Text,** Section 7.3
DAY 4	**Revising** Students revise their drafts in terms of overall structure, paragraphs, sentences, and word choice. (pp. 137–141/H85–89)	**Teaching Resources** *Writing Support Transparencies, 7-G–I* *Writing and Grammar* **Interactive Text,** Section 7.4
DAY 5	**Editing and Proofreading; Publishing and Presenting** Students check their work for accuracy and correctness and present their final drafts. (pp. 142–145/H90–91)	**Teaching Resources** *Scoring Rubrics on Transparency, Ch. 7; Writing Assessment and Portfolio Management; Formal Assessment, Ch. 7* *Writing and Grammar* **Interactive Text,** Sections 7.5–6

Accelerated Lesson Plan

	LESSON FOCUS	PRINT AND MEDIA RESOURCES
DAY 1	**Introduction Through Drafting** Students review characteristics of persuasive writing, select topics, and write drafts. (pp. 124–136/H76–84)	**Teaching Resources** *Writing Support Transparencies, 7-A–F; Writing Support Activity Book, 7-1–2* *Writers at Work* **DVD**, Persuasion *Writing and Grammar* **Interactive Text,** Ch. 7, Introduction through Section 7.3
DAY 2	**Revising Through Presenting** Students work individually or with peers to revise, edit, and proofread their work for presentation. (pp. 137–145/H85–91)	**Teaching Resources** *Writing Support Transparencies, 7-G–I; Scoring Rubrics on Transparency, Ch. 7; Writing Assessment and Portfolio Management; Formal Assessment, Ch. 7* *Writing and Grammar* **Interactive Text,** Sections 7.4–6

Options for Adapting Lesson Plans

HOMEWORK

Have students complete any stage of the lesson for homework.

FEATURES

Extend coverage with Connected Assignment (p. 146), Spotlight on the Humanities (p. 148), Media and Technology Skills (p. 149), and the Standardized Test Preparation Workshop (p. 150).

TECHNOLOGY

Students can complete any stage of the lesson on the computer, using *Writing and Grammar* Interactive Text or a word-processing program. Have them print out their completed work.

Writing and Grammar Handbook Alignment

Page numbers in Step-by-Step Teaching Guides in this Teacher's Edition refer to pages from the full student text. Handbook page references, indicated with this icon ⊞, are provided in Time and Resource Manager boxes and at the bottom of each Teacher's Edition page.

INTEGRATED SKILLS COVERAGE

Integrating Grammar
Adding Parallel Clauses, SE p. 139/⊞87
Words That End in *-ance* and *-ence*, SE p. 142/⊞90

Reading/Writing Connection
Identify the Author's Main Points, SE p. 126
Writing Application, SE p. 129

Viewing and Representing
Critical Viewing, SE pp. 124, 126, 129, 136, 137, 141, 144, 148/⊞76, 84, 85, 89
Recognizing Messages in Art, SE p. 148
Recognizing Persuasion in Media, SE p. 149

Speaking and Listening ATE p. 136

Research Skills ATE p. 129

Workplace Skills ATE p. 128

Real-World Connection ATE p. 128

ASSESSMENT SUPPORT

Standardized Test Preparation Workshop SE p. 150; ATE p. 139
Standardized Test Preparation Workbook, pp. 13–14
Scoring Rubrics on Transparency, Ch. 7
Formal Assessment, Ch. 7
Writing Assessment and Portfolio Management

MEETING INDIVIDUAL NEEDS

Less Advanced Students ATE pp. 137, 145, 147, 151. See also Ongoing Assessments ATE pp. 126, 131, 136.
More Advanced Students ATE pp. 147, 151
ESL Students ATE pp. 141, 145, 147
Gifted and Talented Students ATE p. 147
Musical Learners ATE p. 133
Linguistic Learners ATE pp. 138, 140

BLOCK SCHEDULING

Pacing Suggestions
For 90-minute Blocks
• Have students complete the Prewriting and Drafting stages in a single period.
• Focus one class period on Revising and Editing and Publishing and Presenting. Allow at least 30 minutes for peer revision.

Resources for Varying Instruction
• *Writing and Grammar* Interactive Text A 90-minute block provides an ideal opportunity for students to work on the computer.
• *Writers at Work* DVD Show the Persuasion segment in class.

Professional Development Support
• *How to Manage Instruction in the Block* This teaching resource provides management and activity suggestions.

MEDIA AND TECHNOLOGY

For the Student
• *Writing and Grammar* Interactive Text, Ch. 7
• *On-line Exercise Bank*, Section 20.2

For the Teacher
• *Writers at Work* DVD, Persuasion
• **TeacherEXPRESS** CD-ROM

WRITING AND GRAMMAR ON-LINE

Interactive Text (On-line or on CD-ROM)
• Easily navigable instruction with interactive Revision Checkers
• Full use of e-rater™, the essay-scoring system (on-line only)

Companion Web Site PHSchool.com
• Scoring rubrics with models (use Web Code eek-1001)

See the Go On-line! feature, SE p. iii.

LITERATURE CONNECTIONS

Related selections from *Prentice Hall Literature, Penguin Edition,* Grade 10:

Professional Model "Keep Memory Alive," Elie Wiesel, SE p. 127

Topic Bank Option Nobel Lecture, Alexander Solzhenitsyn, SE p. 131/⊞79

▶ *Lesson Objectives*

1. To write a persuasive essay appropriate to audience and purpose

2. To read to appreciate the writer's craft and to discover models for writing

3. To use prewriting strategies to generate ideas and plan

4. To research topics using texts and technical resources

5. To represent information in a variety of ways, including graphics

6. To develop and revise drafts in terms of structure, paragraphs, sentences, and word choice

7. To edit and proofread to ensure standard English usage and grammar

8. To evaluate writing for both mechanics and content

9. To refine selected work for publication

Critical Viewing

Connect Students may suggest that persuasive skills are needed to help people of many different backgrounds and cultures work together and understand one another.

Chapter 7 Persuasion
Persuasive Essay

▲ Critical Viewing Kofi Annan, pictured above, is giving a speech in his role as Secretary General of the United Nations. Why might a member of the United Nations find persuasive skills useful? [Connect]

Persuasion in Everyday Life

The art of persuasion—getting others to do something or to think as you do—is a part of daily life. Persuasion may involve convincing a friend to see a movie with you or bargaining over the cost of a comic book at a flea market. Persuasion sometimes is verbal, sometimes visual, sometimes written, and often a combination of all these elements.

Persuasion is often a part of various types of writing, as well as a type of writing itself. For example, a character in a short story may speak persuasively to a group of friends, or a poem may contain a plea to readers about an important issue. Persuasive writing gives you an opportunity to make your voice heard and to express your opinion on an issue about which you feel strongly. In this chapter, you'll learn how to create a persuasive essay that is clear, organized, and forceful.

124 • Persuasion

🕐 **TIME AND RESOURCE MANAGER**	
Resources **Technology:** *Writers at Work* DVD, Persuasion; *Writing and Grammar* Interactive Text, Ch. 7	
Using the Full Student Edition	**Using the Handbook** 🔢
• Read and discuss pp. 124–125 in class. • Show the Persuasion section of the *Writers at Work* DVD. • Read the Model From Literature (pp. 126–129) and discuss possible essay topics. • Discuss examples of persuasive writing that you or your students bring to class.	• Read and discuss pp. 76–77 in class. • Show the Persuasion section of the *Writers at Work* DVD. • Discuss examples of persuasive writing that you or your students bring to class.

What Is a Persuasive Essay?

A **persuasive essay** is a piece of writing that tries to convince readers to accept a particular viewpoint or to take a certain action. Most effective persuasive essays contain

- a clearly stated opinion or argument on an issue that has more than one side.
- evidence to support the opinion or argument.
- memorable and convincing details and vivid, persuasive language.
- an effective, logical organization.

To preview the criteria on which your persuasive essay may be evaluated, see the Rubric for Self-Assessment on page 143.

Types of Persuasive Essays

In addition to persuasive essays, there are many other forms of persuasion:

- **Editorials and letters to the editor** appear in newspapers. Editorials express the newspaper's stand on a current issue; letters to the editor present readers' viewpoints.
- **Persuasive speeches** are an oral form of a persuasive essay. They often contain allusions and sound devices to make them stirring and memorable.
- **Position papers** address one side of a controversial issue. They are often directed at a person or group with some power to shape policy on a particular issue.
- **Grant proposals** make a request for financing a program or a project of the writer's. They are usually addressed to members of a government agency or private corporation.

Writers in **ACTION**

Dean Rusk, *former secretary of state, shares the following insight about the art of persuasion:*

"One of the best ways to persuade others is with your ears—by listening to them."

PREVIEW *Student Work* **IN PROGRESS**

In this chapter, you'll follow the work of Sharon Goldberg, a student at Miami-Palmetto High School in Pinecrest, Florida, as she drafts a persuasive essay that expresses her opinion on the importance of volunteerism. Sharon's completed essay appears at the end of the chapter.

Persuasive Essay • **125**

PREPARE and ENGAGE

Interest GRABBER Bring in a copy of a recent editorial from your school or local newspaper. Have students read it, decide whether or not they agree with it, and then write down three reasons to support their opinions. Next, have students share their opinions and use their three reasons to try to persuade others of their thinking.

Activate Prior Knowledge

Ask students to recall the most effective television advertisement they have seen. What did it aim to sell? What persuasive techniques did the presenter use? Why were these techniques so effective? Have students share their answers and discuss how these techniques can be used in persuasive writing.

More About the Writer

(David) Dean Rusk (1909–1994) was born in Cherokee County, Georgia. The son of a Presbyterian minister, he studied politics at Oxford University as a Rhodes scholar, and then taught political science on his return to the United States. Rusk joined the U.S. State Department after World War II and became assistant secretary for Far Eastern affairs from 1950–1951. He served as secretary of state for presidents Kennedy and Johnson.

✓ ONGOING ASSESSMENT: Diagnose

Use one of the following options to diagnose students' current level of proficiency in persuasive writing.

Option 1 Ask each student to select the strongest example of his or her persuasive writing from last year. Review each student's sample and determine which students will need extra support in developing persuasive essays.	**Option 2** Ask students to write a sample invitation to an upcoming school event, such as a fund-raiser or a dance. Have them include three reasons the invitees should attend. If students have difficulty completing this exercise, you will need to devote more time to Gathering Evidence (p. 134) and Providing Elaboration (p. 136).

Reading: Identify the Author's Main Points

Encourage students to jot down each of the authors' main points while reading. They might benefit by organizing the notes in a two-sided chart, labeled *Agree* and *Disagree*. This will enable them to form an opinion about each point based on the evidence presented.

Step-by-Step Teaching Guide

Engage Students Through Literature

1. Read the Model From Literature and use questions such as the following to prompt discussion of the essay.

   What are the authors' main arguments for who should have final custody of the boy?

   Which of the main arguments is the strongest, and why?

   Which is the weakest, and why?

2. Ask students why they think the arguments are arranged in the order that they appear. How would the essay be affected if the order were changed?

3. Point out to students that it is often effective to build up to the most important point. That way, the essay gets stronger rather than fading away.

Critical Viewing

Make a Judgment Answers will vary. Encourage students to think of circumstances that might change their responses.

7.1 Model From Literature

Ellen Goodman is a newspaper columnist based at the Boston Globe. She won the Pulitzer Prize for Distinguished Commentary in 1980.

George F. Will won the Pulitzer Prize for Commentary in 1977. In addition to authoring a syndicated newspaper column, he is a commentator for a network news program.

Reading Writing Connection

Reading Strategy: Identify the Author's Main Points As you read a persuasive essay, look for the **main points** the author provides to support his or her argument. If those main points are few or weak, you should consider seriously whether to agree with his or her viewpoint.

Two Views

The following persuasive articles were written in response to a controversial issue: A twelve-year-old boy, Walter Polovchak, wanted to stay behind in the United States when his parents decided to move back home—to the Soviet Union. Americans were sharply divided on the issue. Some felt that keeping the Polovchak family together was most important; others thought that Walter should have the right to live in a free country.

The State's Nose in Family Life
Ellen Goodman

Imagine that you, a parent of sound mind and body, are moving cross-country. You've had enough of California and want to try New England.

The children, however, don't want to move. They like the weather, their friends, the school, the usual.

You argue about it, of course; that's what families do. Eventually, you decide that the 17-year-old has a right to stay with her aunt and uncle because she is, after all, one year away from being on her own. But the 12-year-old must come along.

▲ **Critical Viewing** This photograph shows Walter Polovchak walking to a press conference. Would you consider a boy this age able to make life decisions? Why or why not? **[Make a Judgment]**

Goodman opens her persuasive essay by comparing the Polovchaks' situation with a situation to which her readers can relate.

126 • Persuasive Essay

☑ ONGOING ASSESSMENT: Monitor and Reinforce

While reading the Model From Literature, some students may have difficulty with some of the words. Use one of the following options.

Option 1 If students read the model independently, have them make a list of unfamiliar words. Then, go over pronunciations and definitions in class.	**Option 2** If you or a prepared student reads aloud in class, take time to define unfamiliar words as you come across them. Words such as *asylum, disillusioned, defector,* and *totalitarian* may need definition.

More About the Writers

Ellen Goodman has been an associate editor and columnist with the *Boston Globe* since 1967. Her columns are widely syndicated, and other writing has appeared in *Life, Ms., The New York Times Book Review, Savvy, The Los Angeles Times Book Review,* and *Working Woman.* Goodman's reporting earned her the American Society of Newspaper Editors Distinguished Writing Award and a Pulitzer Prize for Commentary in 1980.

George F. Will was a professor of political philosophy until his interests drew him to Washington, D.C., where he joined a congressional staff and became Washington editor for *National Review* magazine. Will is currently a television commentator and a contributing editor for *Newsweek.* Will was awarded the Pulitzer Prize for Commentary in 1977.

Rebelling, the boy runs away. But when the state finds him, they do not return him. Instead, they grant your son asylum in California.

Asylum from you.

Or maybe it wasn't California. Perhaps you have emigrated to a socialist country and seven months later, disillusioned, want to come home. But this time the state grants your 12-year-old political asylum to save him from a lifetime of materialism, capitalism—who knows what?—in the United States.

If you can imagine these situations, you can feel what has happened to the Polovchak family of Chicago and the Ukraine. The Polovchaks, five of them, emigrated to this country, apparently encouraged by a family member who promised them a leg up into American life. Now, disappointed, the parents want to go back, taking Walter and his younger brother with them.

But the U.S. government has offered Walter asylum and a lawyer and the temporary custody of the state. Two parents, who have neither abused nor neglected their son, have temporarily lost their right to make decisions for their boy, for reasons that are blatantly political.

If it happened to an American family, it would be an outrage. If it happened to an American family in the Soviet Union, it would make furious headlines. It goes against the basic American principle of keeping the state—whenever possible—out of family life.

"There is nothing that any of us would find in the current situation to justify the state entertaining this case," says Yale Law School's Joseph Goldstein, who has written extensively about parents' and children's rights. "We don't put someone else in the place of the parents unless they are disqualified. These parents did not abuse or neglect their children."

Psychiatrist Allen Stone, who teaches family law at Harvard, had very much the same reaction: "This is totally outside the range of what family law and family courts ought to be doing. The notion that they would interfere in an ongoing, intact family boggles the mind. It just boggles the mind."

The fact is that we have given much more weight to this Ukrainian boy's testimony than to any American boy of the same age. We have given his parents' views much less weight, because they want him to return with them to the Soviet Union.

But it is almost impossible to assess the boy's own frame of mind and values. Is he a 12-year-old who merely likes the ice cream and bicycles of America? "There is lots of food here," he said. "You can buy many things and I liked school."

For another example of persuasive writing, read "Keep Memory Alive" by Elie Wiesel. The essay appears in *Prentice Hall Literature, Penguin Edition,* Grade 10.

This expert testimony, in the form of a quotation, helps support Goodman's argument.

Goodman includes quotations from Walter to emphasize how immature he really is.

Connections With Literature

If students read "Keep Memory Alive" by Elie Wiesel, have them identify his key arguments and the evidence he gives for his position.

Model From Literature • 127

Real-World Connection

Political reform is always a relevant topic for policy makers in Washington, D.C. Lobbyists present a proposal to a legislator in the hopes of someday having the idea turned into law. But these legislators are unable to promote every good idea that is presented to them. A proposal must be very persuasive in order to capture the attention and support of a policy maker. Have students look in the newspaper for articles on recent political reforms. Have them come up with persuasive reasons for or against the new policy or proposal.

Integrating Workplace Skills

Encourage students to do some research on the job of a lobbyist. Then, have them brainstorm for personal attributes and skills needed to become a successful lobbyist. Their answers may include persistence, determination, excellent speaking skills, and a passion for a cause.

Is he, like so many his age, testing the limits, tasting his first tidbits of rebellion? Or can he be mature enough to choose political freedom above family?

It is equally difficult to determine what is best for the boy. There are psychological terrors as well as exhilarations for a child who "wins" such an early and terminal battle with his parents. There are also troubles ahead for a child who returns unwillingly, an embarrassment, to the Ukraine.

But our laws assume (except in rare instances) that the parent is best judge of the state of mind, the needs and the future of the child. Whether we approve or not, we do not interfere unless they have been proven unfit.

No matter what fantasies we have about rescuing Walter Polovchak, no matter how certain we are that his parents are wrong, we can't have two standards of law—one for Americans and one for Soviet immigrants.

In a Chicago courtroom on Aug. 4, Judge Joseph Mooney ruled that the boy should remain in the custody of the state, and the care of his aunt and uncle, for five more weeks. But his intention is clearly to reunite this family, "whatever the political consequences." And he is right.

The irony is that we criticize, even denounce, the power of the state in the Soviet Union, the way it interferes in private lives. We pride ourselves on being different, pride ourselves on protecting the integrity of the family from the state. But in the case of Walter Polovchak we very nearly lost that difference.

"The Littlest Defector" Deserves Asylum
George Will

Washington—The case of Walter Polovchak, "the littlest defector," dramatized the difficulties, logical and political, that occur when people do not take seriously the radical evil of totalitarian states. Americans who oppose Walter's plea for political asylum are disregarding the premise of the United States, or the manifest nature of the USSR, or both.

Eight months ago Walter, 12, and his family emigrated from the Soviet Union to Chicago. The father is unhappy and wants to return with his wife, Walter, and another son, 6. His daughter, 17, has her own visa and has no intention of leaving the United States. She and Walter are staying with relatives in Chicago, pending disposition of Walter's case.

People opposed to the Illinois court's intervention say the case is "political." Usually that adjective is used to imply that there are

Parallel structure helps makes Goodman's point memorable and effective.

In his opening paragraph, George Will uses powerful words and phrases such as "radical evil" and "totalitarian states" to make his opinion clear.

◀ Critical Viewing What message do you think this photograph of Walter conveys? Explain. [Interpret]

no legal standards to control judgment, or that the Constitution commits disposition of such matters to another branch of government. Whatever constitutional problem, if any, lurks here, most of those who complain that Walter's case is "political" seem to mean something else.

They seem to mean only that if Walter were resisting return to, say, Denmark rather than to a closed, totalitarian society, the court probably would not have given Walter a hearing. To which, the answer is: Of course. Justice cannot be done here without taking cognizance of the two regimes, under one of which Walter will live.

Many who oppose granting asylum say Walter is not "mature enough" to choose freedom above family. And they stress American respect for parental authority.

But the fundamental question pertains to claims that are being made to rights that are not contingent upon maturity: Should Walter's parents have the right to choose for him a future in which the possibility of freedom is foreclosed? A nation that asserts that fundamental rights are "inalienable" should not spurn the pleas of a boy whose parents are asserting a right to alienate his fundamental rights, permanently.

In his final paragraph, Will makes his strongest argument: Should Walter's future freedom be decided for him by his parents?

Writing Application: **Include Main Points**
As you prepare to write your persuasive piece, think about the main points you will make to support your opinion or viewpoint.

Model from Literature • 129

Critical Viewing

Interpret Students may mention that the photograph conveys a sense of Walter's stress and perhaps his distance from other family members.

Integrating Research Skills

Students may be interested in further researching some aspect of this story, such as what life was like in the Soviet Union at the time, or the eventual outcome of the situation. They might also investigate more recent situations in which parent-child issues became embroiled in international politics. (Students will discover that Walter Polovchak remained in the United States. He and his wife and son live in a suburb of Chicago, IL; his sister lives nearby. Polovchak's parents returned to the Ukraine.)

Reading\Writing Connection

Writing Application: Include Main Points

Review with students the main points cited by Goodman and Will to support their distinctly opposed positions. Ask them to think about how each writer built a case for his or her point of view. Remind them that, while they may choose topics based on their opinions about a subject, they will still need to convince their readers by supplying facts.

129

Step-by-Step Teaching Guide

Prewriting: Scan Newspapers

1. Distribute newspapers in class, or assign students to go to the library or read a paper at home.

2. After students choose topics, have them meet in small groups and share their ideas. Group members can help each student brainstorm for persuasive arguments.

3. The opinions of group members who disagree with the topic being presented are valuable. A strong persuasive essay will acknowledge the opposing viewpoint and then explain why the writer disagrees with it.

Step-by-Step Teaching Guide

Prewriting: Make a Quicklist

1. You may want to do this exercise as a class. Have students brainstorm for issues of which they are aware, and list their suggestions on the board.

2. Have students choose the issues that mean the most to them or for which they think they can find the most supporting detail.

Step-by-Step Teaching Guide

Prewriting: Use Sentence Starters

Teaching Resources: Writing Support Transparencies, 7-A

1. Encourage students to think carefully about realistic ideas when completing their sentence starters. They must be able to defend and support their ideas.

2. Display Transparency 7-A to show how Sharon used sentence starters to focus on an issue.

Choosing Your Topic

To write a powerful persuasive essay, start with a topic that is important to you. For help in generating topics, use the strategies below:

Strategies for Generating Topics

1. **Scan Newspapers** Scan a newspaper, looking for stories that matter to you on a personal level. What do you see that makes you angry, strikes you as unfair, or cries out "this needs to be changed"? Use one of the news stories to provide you with a topic for your persuasive essay.

2. **Make a Quicklist** Come up with a topic for your persuasive writing by listing types of issues. For example, write headings like Community Issues, Political Issues, and Social Issues at the top of a sheet of paper, and quickly list ideas inspired by each. Review your lists, and choose the issue that interests you most as the topic of your persuasive essay.

3. **Use Sentence Starters** To come up with a topic, copy the following sentence starters and fill in the blanks. Then, review your completed sentences. Choose one issue as the topic of your persuasive essay.

   • If I became (mayor/president/school principal), the first thing I would do is ___?___ .

   • Something that needs to be changed at this school is ___?___ .

   • Teenagers today should ___?___ .

Interactive Textbook

Get instant help! To make your Quicklist, use the Essay Builder, accessible from the menu bar, on-line or on CD-ROM.

Student Work IN PROGRESS

Name: *Sharon Goldberg*
Miami-Palmetto High School
Pinecrest, FL

Using Sentence Starters to Choose a Topic

Using sentence starters helped Sharon Goldberg focus on an issue that was important to her.

• Something that needs to be changed at this school is *cafeteria food*

• Teenagers today should *help others*

130 • Persuasive Essay

⏱ TIME AND RESOURCE MANAGER

Resources
Print: *Writing Support Transparencies, 7-A–E; Writing Support Activity Book, 7-1–2; Topic Bank for Heterogeneous Classes,* Ch. 7
Technology: *Writing and Grammar* Interactive Text, Section 7.2

Using the Full Student Edition	Using the Handbook ⊞
• Work through the Prewriting strategies in class.	• Work through the Prewriting strategies in class.
• Use the Responding to Fine Art transparency to generate additional topic ideas.	• Use the Responding to Fine Art transparency to generate additional topic ideas.
• Read and discuss pp. 130–134.	• Read and discuss pp. 78–82.

TOPIC BANK

If you are having difficulty finding a suitable topic for your persuasive piece, use one of the following:

1. **Persuasive Speech** Choose a global issue—child labor laws or deforestation, for example—about which you would like to take a stand. Write and deliver a persuasive speech in which you support your opinion.

2. **Persuasive Essay** Write an essay in which you support one candidate over another. Candidates may be actual, perhaps someone running for student council president, or imaginary, as in Hero of the Year.

Responding to Fine Art

3. Study *Arrivals and Departures* by Chester Arnold. Determine what you think the artist's message is. Then, write a persuasive essay in which you agree or disagree with that message.

Responding to Literature

4. In his Nobel lecture, Alexander Solzhenitsyn argues that writers have the power and responsibility to change the world by telling the truth. Read the speech and write a persuasive essay in which you agree or disagree with Solzhenitsyn's assertion. You can find the speech in *Prentice Hall Literature, Penguin Edition,* Grade 10.

Arrivals and Departures, 1999, Chester Arnold, The Seven Bridges Foundation, Greenwich, CT

Timed Writing Prompt

5. Some people argue that no one under the age of twenty-one should be allowed to drive. They cite statistics that show teenaged drivers are involved in more accidents than older drivers. Write a persuasive essay explaining why you agree or disagree with this position. Use examples from your personal experience and the experience of people you know to support your argument. **(35 minutes)**

Prewriting • 131

Step-by-Step Teaching Guide

Responding to Fine Art
Arrivals and Departures,
by Chester Arnold
Teaching Resources: Writing Support Transparencies, 7-B

1. Use this artwork as a starting point to help students find relevant topics for persuasive essays.

2. Display Transparency 7-B and ask students what specific impressions they have from the image.

3. Ask students to brainstorm for persuasive essay ideas suggested by this piece of art. Here are some possibilities:

   A proposal is drafted to have a new garbage dump or landfill created in your community.

   City funds have decreased and the recycling program is in danger of being terminated.

Students may add these topic ideas to their own suggestions in their topic banks.

Timed Writing Prompt

- To help students think about the issue, have them think of at least one argument for and one argument against driving before the age of twenty-one. Tell students to consider how driving can be helpful as well as harmful. Ask how each student's desire to drive while still a teenager influences his or her opinion.

- Remind students that to answer the prompt, they should decide whether they think the driving age should be changed.

- Suggest that students allow five minutes for prewriting, twenty-five minutes for writing, and five minutes for reviewing and proofreading.

✓ ONGOING ASSESSMENT: Monitor and Reinforce

If you observe that some students are having difficulty coming up with a topic, use one of the following options.

Option 1 Suggest that students choose an idea from the Topic Bank. If many students have difficulty, work with the whole class on one of the ideas from the Topic Bank or from ideas suggested by students.	**Option 2** If Topic Bank ideas seem too difficult, offer suggestions from the *Topic Bank for Heterogeneous Classes* in the Teaching Resources.

Prewriting: Narrow a Topic by Looping

Teaching Resources: Writing Support Transparencies, 7-C

1. Remind students that this writing will not be evaluated for grammar, usage, or structure. Its function is simply to generate and explore ideas. Therefore, students should let their ideas flow freely without worrying about writing style.

2. Display Transparency 7-C. Show students how Sharon selected one element of her original freewriting, and then expanded on that one element in order to narrow her topic.

3. If students have trouble deciding which parts of their freewriting are best suited for a topic, have them share their ideas with a partner. Talking about a topic may help them realize which idea is of most interest, or the partner's questions may help them focus on the most intriguing item.

7.2

Narrowing Your Topic

Once you've chosen a general topic, narrow it into one you can argue effectively. Looping is one strategy you can use to ensure that your topic isn't too broad.

Narrow a Topic by Looping

1. Write freely on your general topic for about five minutes.
2. Read what you have written. Circle the most important idea.
3. Write freely on that idea for about five minutes.
4. Repeat the process until you have found a topic that is narrow enough to address in your persuasive essay.
5. If you keep writing, you may even be able to identify a thesis statement, or main idea, that you want your persuasive essay to communicate.

Student Work
IN PROGRESS

Name: *Sharon Goldberg*
Miami-Palmetto High School
Pinecrest, FL

Looping to Narrow a Topic
Sharon used looping to narrow her broad persuasive topic.

Broad Topic: Helping Others
It's important to help others. Those in service industries—like nursing and the fire and police departments—devote their lives to the public. Some people prefer to help in other ways. From retirees who help care for children in need to families who donate food to the hungry to teenagers who work in their communities, everyone can make a difference.

More Narrowed Topic: Everyone Can Make a Difference
Working with others gives volunteers a sense of perspective. Volunteering their extra time keeps teens focused and gives them a sense of responsibility and accomplishment. Schools should offer course credit to teens who take on a volunteering role in the community. Everyone in the community—from elementary-school children to people who have retired—should take time to help others.

Thesis Statement: Volunteerism is vital.

132 • Persuasive Essay

Considering Your Audience and Purpose

As you draft, identify your audience and their opinions. This will help you achieve your purpose—to persuade them.

Write for Various Audiences

A hostile audience is one that will not be immediately receptive to your argument. A friendly audience is one that is likely to be more sympathetic. Depending on whether you expect your audience to be hostile, friendly, or a mix, vary your argument accordingly.

EXAMPLE: Imagine that you are writing an editorial calling for a ban on bicycle traffic from a park pathway.

Hostile Audience: Bicycle Riders

Emphasize alternative paths that would remain available for people who ride bicycles.

Friendly Audience: Families With Small Children

Emphasize the dangers that are posed when bikes and pedestrians mix.

Create a Purpose Planner

Ultimately, you hope your persuasive writing will change the thinking or behavior of your audience. To do so, choose details that will lead your audience to think or behave in a certain way. A purpose planner can help you achieve your particular goals. Use the following purpose planner as a guide for making your own.

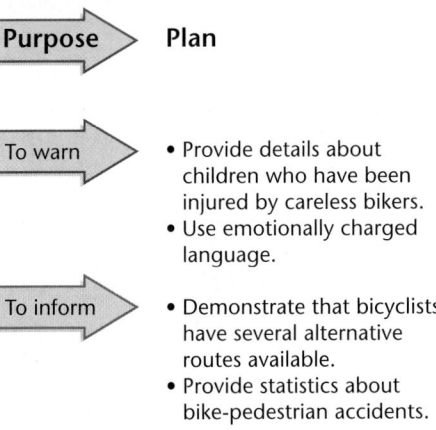

Purpose ▷ **Plan**

To warn ▷
• Provide details about children who have been injured by careless bikers.
• Use emotionally charged language.

To inform ▷
• Demonstrate that bicyclists have several alternative routes available.
• Provide statistics about bike-pedestrian accidents.

⏱ Timed Writing Hint

Read the prompt carefully at least twice to make sure you understand the purpose of your writing and its audience.

Prewriting: Write for Various Audiences

Teaching Resources: Writing Support Transparencies, 7-D; Writing Support Activity Book, 7-1

1. Give students a list of topics for persuasive essays and have them list examples of hostile and friendly audiences for each. Some examples of topics are year-round school, banning the designated hitter in baseball, shorter terms in the Senate, and raising the minimum driving age.

2. Have students meet in small groups and fill out a purpose planner chart for one of the topics listed in Step 1. Display Transparency 7-D to demonstrate a purpose planner, and then distribute copies of the organizer (7-1) for their own use.

3. Then, have students work individually to fill out a purpose planner for their own topics. Remind them to keep these charts so they can determine whether they've achieved their purpose when they reach the revision stage.

Customize for
Musical Learners

Explain to students that political issues commonly find voice in song. For centuries, ideas, ideals, and opinions have been passed along in ballads, spirituals, folk tunes, and protest songs. Encourage students to research a song associated with a political situation, whether from the American Revolution, the Civil War, or the Vietnam conflict. Have students share the song they select with the class. You may even encourage students to write their own song about an issue that is important to them.

Step-by-Step Teaching Guide

Prewriting: Find Unbiased Research

1. Point out to students that, because everyone has an opinion, it is important to examine more than one source. It is also important to separate a writer's feelings from stated facts ("I believe" vs. "research shows").

2. Remind them that, even when checking credible sources, they should look at both sides of an issue. It will strengthen their support to know all the facts.

Step-by-Step Teaching Guide

Prewriting: Conduct Interviews

1. Point out to students that many experts are eager to make the time for an interview. If they are passionate about their area of expertise, they will likely want to share it with young people.

2. Have students prepare questions prior to the interview. A little research on the topic will help them ask informed, meaningful questions.

3. Suggest that students tape-record interviews, with permission, so that the student will not have to slow the pace of the interview in order to take notes.

Step-by-Step Teaching Guide

Prewriting: Make a Pro-and-Con Chart

Teaching Resources: Writing Support Transparencies, 7-E; Writing Support Activity Book, 7-2

1. Explain to students that looking at both sides of an issue will allow them to strengthen their position by anticipating the views of the opposition.

2. Display Transparency 7-E to model a T-Chart, or distribute copies of the blank form (7-2). Encourage students to write down all opposing arguments and come up with at least one way to respond to each.

Gathering Evidence

You'll need facts and details from a variety of sources to support your position. Follow these strategies as you gather the evidence you need:

1. **Find Unbiased Research** The foundation of an effective persuasive essay should contain reliable evidence in support of its position. Evidence from biased or unreliable sources will weaken your argument. As you perform research for your editorial, find sources of information that are objective and bias-free.

2. **Conduct Interviews** For some issues, the most powerful evidence you can use to support your argument is evidence that you collect yourself. Interview an expert in that field. His or her words will prove more persuasive than a quotation from an unqualified person.

3. **Make a Pro-and-Con Chart** Make a chart to help you see both sides of an issue. In the left column, list your arguments, or "pros"; in the right column, list opposing arguments, or "cons." When it's complete, note the evidence in the "Opposing" column. Brainstorm for ways to counter-argue the evidence listed there.

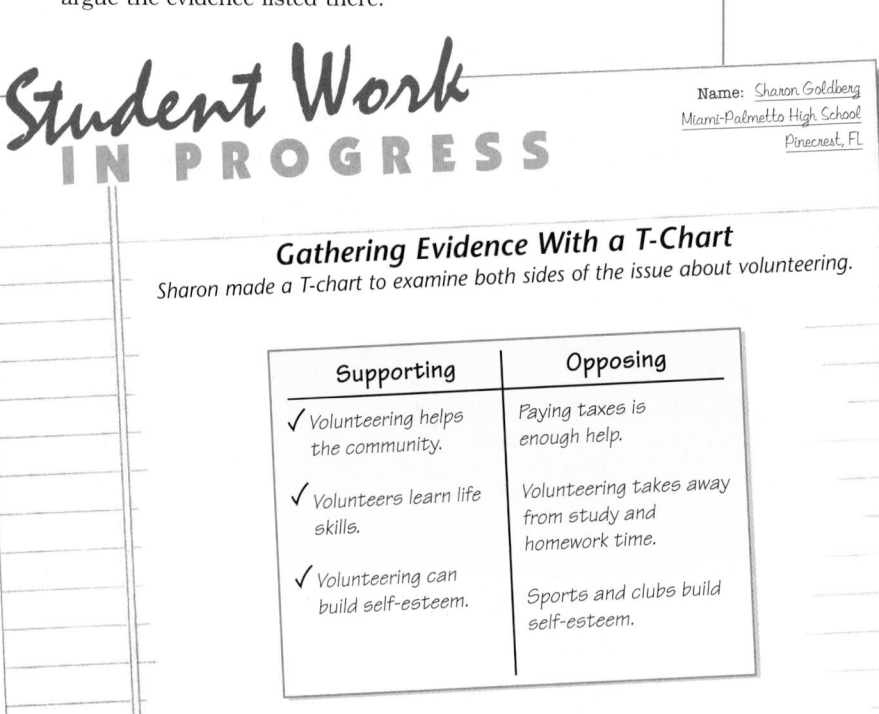

Student Work IN PROGRESS

Name: Sharon Goldberg
Miami-Palmetto High School
Pinecrest, FL

Gathering Evidence With a T-Chart

Sharon made a T-chart to examine both sides of the issue about volunteering.

Supporting	Opposing
✓ Volunteering helps the community.	Paying taxes is enough help.
✓ Volunteers learn life skills.	Volunteering takes away from study and homework time.
✓ Volunteering can build self-esteem.	Sports and clubs build self-esteem.

134 • Persuasive Essay

7.3 Drafting

Shaping Your Writing

Structure your persuasive writing in the way that best suits your argument and your evidence.

Use TRI/PS/QA to Structure Paragraphs

As you draft paragraphs, think first about what you want to say and then choose a logical organization for each. Following are some ideas for organizing your paragraphs:

TRI stands for **T**opic, **R**estatement, **I**llustration. This type of organization helps readers follow along as you explain your ideas. The elements TRI can occur in any order within a paragraph (TIR). You could also include two illustrations, or even three, within the same paragraph (TRII).

T—
R— **Example:** Ursuline Avenue should and must be converted to a one-way street. It cannot support two-way traffic because it is too narrow and it has too much traffic.

I— For example, in a three-month period last year, there were eleven accidents on Ursuline Avenue and at least thirty traffic tie-ups caused by traffic-flow problems.

PS stands for **P**roblem and **S**olution. This type of organization emphasizes the problem-and-solution relationship between the facts you are presenting. To use this type of structure, begin by stating a problem. Follow it with one or more solutions to that problem.

P— **Example:** Our town has been severely damaged by floods over the past ten years. Local officials must look

S— into the solutions of people in areas that have experienced similar problems. Starting from scratch won't gain us anything. We must use the knowledge and experience of others as a starting point so that we can solve our flooding problems soon.

QA stands for **Q**uestion and **A**nswer. Use this method of organization when you anticipate that your audience will have specific questions about your topic. Begin by posing a question or problem. Then, present your answer or answers in response to the question.

Q— **Example:** Why is it necessary to build a new computer laboratory? The future is now. Students must become

A— familiar with current technology in order to better their chances of developing viable work skills. Current software applications will not run on our old computers, so many students miss out on becoming familiar with those all-important workplace tools.

Drafting • 135

Drafting: Use TRI/PS/QA to Structure Paragraphs

Teaching Resources: Writing Support Transparencies, 7-F

1. Discuss the TRI/PS/QA strategies in class. Display Transparency 7-F, and read aloud some sample paragraphs from students' work. Challenge students to correctly associate each paragraph with one of the listed strategies.

2. As students look over their drafts, have them find examples of these paragraph patterns in their own writing.

3. Point out that, in addition to being a method of analyzing paragraphs, these patterns can help students build paragraphs. Suggest that, if students are having trouble organizing information in a paragraph, they consider the information to be presented. If they can identify a problem, a question, or a topic statement, they can then work to fill in the rest of the elements appropriate to the paragraph structure that suits the information.

⏱ TIME AND RESOURCE MANAGER

Resources
Print: *Writing Support Transparencies*, 7-F
Technology: *Writing and Grammar* Interactive Text, Section 7.3

Using the Full Student Edition	Using the Handbook
• Read and discuss pp. 135–136 in class, and use the corresponding transparency. • Give students time to organize and elaborate on their essays in class.	• Read and discuss pp. 83–84 in class, and use the corresponding transparency. • Give students time to organize and elaborate on their essays in class.

⏱ TIME SAVERS!

Writing Support Transparencies
Use the transparencies for Chapter 7 to facilitate the teaching of the strategies.

Writing Support Activity Book
Use the graphic organizers for Chapter 7 to facilitate student planning.

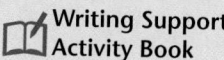

Drafting: Build Your Argument With Evidence

1. Help students distinguish between pertinent and irrelevant evidence. Students might be tempted to include detailed evidence that interests them, regardless of its effectiveness or relevance. Remind them that irrelevant detail is a distraction from the essay, no matter how interesting it may be.

2. Have students use the following criteria to evaluate the details they might add.

   Does the detail relate to the main idea?

   In what way does the detail strengthen the argument?

   According to the chosen method of organization, what is the best place for this detail?

Integrating Speaking and Listening Skills

Encourage students to brainstorm for ideas for a fifteen-second persuasive radio commercial on their topics. Which details do they find indispensable? Which would they omit? By condensing their topics into a short time frame, they will quickly discover which details and arguments are the most important.

If possible, have them record their commercials and share them with the class.

Critical Viewing

Relate Answers will vary. Students might mention personal enjoyment, school credit, and so on.

Providing Elaboration

Elaborate on your ideas by providing details that explain, restate, illustrate, or expand on them.

Build Your Argument With Evidence

As you draft, build and support your argument by providing evidence or support. Choose details of various types from various sources. Following are types of evidence you should consider including in your persuasive essay:

- **Historical details** may be provided through excerpts from government records, war records, and almanacs.

  EXAMPLE: The Central School Stage Band has been in existence since 1922.

- **Statistical information** may be researched or gathered firsthand. This type of information may come from results of surveys, polls, scientific data, and weather records.

  EXAMPLE: Four out of five high-school musicians go on to higher education.

- **Expert testimony** is provided by someone who is considered extremely knowledgeable about or familiar with your topic.

  EXAMPLE: Dr, Rita Sohns, head of the American Student Agenda, strongly advocates music programs in schools. She said, "There is no better way to learn discipline, art, and camaraderie, than through participation in music programs."

- **Textual evidence** may come from literature, letters, and personal documents.

  EXAMPLE: In an open let-ter to Principal Ordonez, the band request-ed "funding for new sheet music and new instruments."

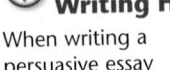

Timed Writing Hint

When writing a persuasive essay under timed conditions, include strong examples to support your argument.

▼ Critical Viewing If you were to persuade someone to take up a musical instrument, what reasons would you give? **[Relate]**

☑ ONGOING ASSESSMENT: Monitor and Reinforce

If you observe that students are having trouble providing elaboration for their topics, try the following strategy.

Have students meet with partners and exchange drafts. After the partners read the draft, have them write five questions about it. The questions should elicit information they thought was missing from the draft. Students will find that the answers to these questions will probably be details that can be included in their essays.

7.4 *Revising*

Revising Your Overall Structure

Once you've completed your first draft, make sure that it contains the details needed to be effective. Also, check to be sure that you develop and support your argument in the body of your paper.

▶ **REVISION STRATEGY**
Color-Coding to Identify Support

Reread your essay to see whether you have included enough supporting details to make your argument successful. As you read, use a colored pencil to circle each topic sentence. Then, use a different-colored pencil to circle supporting details.

Next, review your markings. If a topic sentence has fewer than two supporting details, add more evidence to support it or reconsider whether the point is worth including.

▲ **Critical Viewing**
In what ways can hospital volunteers improve the quality of patient care? **[Speculate]**

Step-by-Step Teaching Guide

Revising: Color-Coding to Identify Support

Teaching Resources: Writing Support Transparencies, 7-G

1. If you choose to use this strategy in class, you may need to provide colored pencils or highlighters.

2. Display Transparency 7-G. Discuss how Sharon inserted a quotation to provide support for her topic.

3. Discuss with students other types of details that can be useful in a persuasive essay. (Examples might include quotations from experts or printed materials, statistics, personal experience or observation, and so on.)

Critical Viewing

Speculate Hospital volunteers might free medical staff to do more serious tasks, or they might provide special services for patients.

Customize for
Less Advanced Students

If students are having trouble identifying where they need additional support, have them work with partners or in small groups. Have partners point out places that need to be strengthened or ask questions about items that are not supported. Encourage students to consider adding support to paragraphs that elicited comments.

Student Work IN PROGRESS

Name: *Sharon Goldberg*
Miami-Palmetto High School
Pinecrest, FL

Color-Coding to Identify Support

Sharon used color-coding to identify the types of support she used in her essay. She revised accordingly and added a different type of support—a quotation—to give this paragraph more depth.

Not only is it necessary to perform community-service hours to graduate from high schools, but it is also essential to provide time and commitment voluntarily to the surrounding community. Young students, for example, should assist at a hospital or a nursing facility as much as possible without interfering with their schoolwork. These services should provide the satisfaction of knowing that the volunteers have made a difference in someone's life.

"Don't give until it hurts, but give until it feels good" is a statement that accurately describes how an individual should volunteer.

Revising • 137

⏱ TIME AND RESOURCE MANAGER

Resources
Print: *Writing Support Transparencies, 7-G–I*
Technology: *Writing and Grammar* Interactive Text, Section 7.4

Using the Full Student Edition	Using the Handbook 🖽
• Work through revising strategies in class. • Review the concept of parallel clauses, and have students check for parallelism in their essays.	• Work through revising strategies in class. • Review the concept of parallel clauses, and have students check for parallelism in their essays.

Revising: Forming Parallel Structures

Teaching Resources: Writing Support Transparencies, 7-H

1. Point out to students that parallelism can add richness to their writing by creating a rhythm and by emphasizing a point through the repetition of a sound.

2. Display Transparency 7-H, and point out how Sharon strengthened her introduction by adding parallelism.

3. Allow students time to check their essays for opportunities to build parallelism into the sentence structure.

4. Tell students that most great writers have relied on parallelism to make a passage memorable. You may wish to quote examples. "The Gettysburg Address" is notable for its use of parallelism.

Customize for
Linguistic Learners

Many speeches rely heavily on parallel structure and repetition. One reason is because it is easier for both speakers and listeners to remember the ideas when there is a rhythm to them and when they are repeated. Have students find a copy of such a speech and challenge them to memorize a section of it.

7.4

Revising Your Paragraphs

Make the main points in your essay memorable by using *parallelism*—the use of patterns or repetitions of grammatical structures. Parallelism adds rhythm and balance to your writing. Use it to emphasize important points and to forge links between related ideas.

▶ **REVISION STRATEGY**
Forming Parallel Structures

To form parallel structures in your draft, locate an important word, phrase, clause, or question. Then, experiment with building upon that word, phrase, clause, or question to make it into a passage containing parallelism.

PARALLEL QUESTIONS: Who will step up first? Who will lead the way? Who will win the day?

PARALLEL PHRASES: If you care, if you can, and if you would, lend a hand now.

PARALLEL CLAUSES: Although we strive for greatness, although we work hard, although we deserve the best, sometimes, it's just not enough.

Student Work
IN PROGRESS

Name: *Sharon Goldberg*
Miami-Palmetto High School
Pinecrest, FL

Making Use of Parallelism

As she revised, Sharon made use of parallelism to make her introduction more memorable and stirring.

cap Reading a book to a blind person. ~~At a nursing home,~~
at a nursing home.
feeding a debilitated patientᴧ Tutoring a younger child.
These are examples of community service projects that provide the performer of such deeds with feelings of self-worth and gratification. By serving others in the community, the individual is helping himself or herself to grow and to acquire knowledge and wisdom.

138 • Persuasive Essay

☑ ONGOING ASSESSMENT: Prerequisite Skills

If students have difficulty identifying parallel structure, you may find it helpful to refer them to the following materials to ensure coverage of prerequisite knowledge.

In the Textbook	Print Resources	Technology
Clauses, Section 20.2	*Grammar Exercise Workbook,* pp. 75–80	*On-Line Exercise Bank,* Section 20.2

Grammar in Your Writing
Adding Parallel Clauses

A **clause** is a group of words with its own subject and verb. One way to make your persuasive essay memorable is by adding **parallel clauses.** These are clauses within a sentence that have matching grammatical forms or patterns.

Following are some tips for revising your sentences to form parallel clauses.

1. Make sure that the verbs in each clause are in the same tense.

NOT PARALLEL:	The Garden Group planted, the Garden Group hoed, the Garden Group was persevering, and the Garden Group triumphed.
PARALLEL:	The Garden Group planted, the Garden Group hoed, the Garden Group persevered, and the Garden Group triumphed.

2. Don't change the subject in subsequent clauses.

NOT PARALLEL:	After his efforts on our behalf, after Matt's sacrifices on our behalf, and after his achievements on our behalf, isn't it time to elect him president of the class?
PARALLEL:	After Matt's efforts on our behalf, after his sacrifices on our behalf, and after his achievements on our behalf, isn't it time to elect him president of the class?

3. Always use the same type of subordinate clause:

NOT PARALLEL:	The corporation will sponsor only those projects that are worthy and it thinks have a chance at winning awards.
PARALLEL:	The corporation will sponsor only those projects that are worthy and that might win awards.

Find It in Your Reading Find an example of parallelism in the essay by Ellen Goodman on pages 126–128. Explain the impact that parallelism has on the passage.

Find It in Your Writing As you revise your essay, look for two examples of parallel clauses. If you cannot identify any, revise to insert them.

For more on parallel clauses, see Chapter 20.

Adding Parallel Clauses

1. Point out to students that parallel clauses can make their writing more complex and rich in texture. Faulty parallelism can weaken their writing and confuse the reader.

2. Do students have too many short, choppy sentences in their work? If so, remind them that creating a series of parallel clauses is one method of combining sentences.

3. Point out that simple parallelism— making certain that verbs and structures remain parallel in a sentence, is always desirable. However, a series of parallel clauses is particularly emphatic, and should be reserved for where it will have the greatest effect. Using it repeatedly will lessen the impact.

Find It in Your Reading

Sample answer: "If it happened to an American family, it would be an outrage. If it happened to an . . ." The phrasing adds more emphasis and power to the passage.

Find It in Your Writing

Ask volunteers to share examples of parallel structure that they found in or added to their drafts. Discuss what they think it accomplishes in their essays.

STANDARDIZED TEST PREPARATION WORKSHOP

Parallelism Standardized test questions may require students to identify parallel structure.

Read the following sentence and choose the version of it below that contains parallel structure.

Jamie washed her car, waxed it, and then was drying it in the driveway.

A Jamie washed and waxed her car and then was drying it in the driveway.

B No revision needed.

C Jamie washed her car, waxed it, and then dried it in the driveway.

D Jamie was washing her car, waxed it, and then was drying it in the driveway.

Students should recognize that the correct answer is **C**. All of the verbs are in the same form.

Revising: Color-Coding Clues to Sentence Types

Teaching Resources: Writing Support Transparencies, 7-I

1. Remind students that *exclamatory* sentences create a sense of urgency. (Example: *Yes! Watch out!*) *Interrogative* sentences ask questions. (Example: *When will this end?*) *Imperative* sentences give orders. (*Write this down.*)

2. Remind students not to use too many imperative, exclamatory, or interrogative sentences. This will lessen the impact of each one. Encourage them to use these types of sentences judiciously, to make their writing more interesting.

3. Display Transparency 7-I to analyze how Sharon varied types of sentences in her drafts.

Customize for
Linguistic Learners

Students who have a flair for the dramatic will enjoy the challenge of converting sentences to the exclamatory and interrogative forms. Ask them to read and act out their changes to the class. The oral demonstration will emphasize to other students the way that these types of sentences can enliven writing.

7.4

Revising Your Sentences
Add Variety to Your Sentences

Writing is much more persuasive if it is interesting. One way to add interest to your writing is to use a variety of sentence types and lengths. Review your draft, and analyze the sentences you have used. If you tend to use too many sentences of one type and of one average length, revise to make your writing more interesting to read and hear.

▶ **REVISION STRATEGY**
Color-Coding Clues to Sentence Types

Use this strategy to analyze the sentence variety in your writing:

1. Read through your essay. Underline declarative sentences in red, interrogative sentences in green, exclamatory sentences in blue, and imperative sentences in black.

2. Review the underlined material. If you have little or no variety in sentence types, revise to make your writing more interesting.

🔵 **Learn More**

To learn more about revising to create effective sentences, see Chapter 21.

Student Work
IN PROGRESS

Name: *Sharon Goldberg*
Miami-Palmetto High School
Pinecrest, FL

Color-Coding Sentence Types
When Sharon discovered that she used only declarative sentences in this paragraph, she revised a sentence to provide sentence variety. Her revised sentence is circled.

"Don't give until it hurts, but give until it feels good" is a statement that accurately describes how an individual should volunteer. These services should provide the satisfaction of knowing that the volunteer has made a difference in someone's life. Similarly, community service activities serve as a learning tool for those involved. *Why* Although traditional teaching techniques require students to sit in a classroom and study from books or that which is written on a traditional chalkboard *when* community service projects give individuals hands-on experiences?

Revising Your Word Choice

Revise Informal Language

The words you choose can influence the power of your essay. Using slang and informal language can mean that your writing may not be taken seriously. Instead, use formal language that reflects the seriousness of your topic.

Informal Language	**Formal Language**
The town dump has to be cleaned up before it makes everyone really sick.	Conditions at the town's garbage collection center must be made more sanitary before it poses a health risk for residents.

Peer Review

Use Point/Counterpoint

Anticipating counterarguments can strengthen your editorial. Share your revised draft with a partner who takes on the role of the opposition. Together, make a list of the main points in your writing. Then, ask your partner to come up with counterpoints, or opposing arguments for these points.

When your partner has finished, find evidence to weaken the opposition's argument. Incorporate that evidence into your draft to strengthen your own argument.

⚙ Grammar and Style Tip

Use a thesaurus to come up with alternative, more formal word choices for your persuasive writing.

▶ **Critical Viewing**
Why is it useful to work with a peer while revising? **[Reflect]**

Revising • 141

Editing and Proofreading

1. Remind students that careless errors can undermine their arguments, no matter how persuasive they are.

2. Point out that using a computer spell-check program is an excellent way to eliminate many spelling errors. However, remind them that it is not foolproof. Misused words will not be caught as long as they are spelled correctly. (For example: The movie was *to* long.)

3. Students might make unintentional spelling errors by typing incorrectly. The best way to ensure proper spelling is to proofread carefully.

Words That End in -*ance* and -*ence*

1. Read the Grammar in Your Writing section to the class and challenge students to add extra -*ance* and -*ence* words to the list.

2. Encourage students to use a dictionary when proofreading their work.

Find It in Your Reading

Students may cite *instances, consequences, difference* (p. 128), and *cognizance* (p. 129).

Find It in Your Writing

After students have checked their drafts, ask them to share some of the words they found. Discuss how they might remember the correct spelling (for example, *to radiate* creates *radiance*—both have *a's*).

7.5 # Editing and Proofreading

Before you revise your final draft, proofread your writing, and correct errors in grammar, spelling, and punctuation.

Focusing on Spelling

Your readers will equate careless writing with a careless argument. Make sure that your persuasive essay is free of spelling errors. As you proofread, look for words you frequently misspell, as well as words with tricky endings, such as -*ance* and -*ence*.

Grammar in Your Writing
Words That End in -*ance* and -*ence*

Word endings that sound similar are sometimes difficult to spell. Among the most misspelled word endings are -*ance* and -*ence*.

If a noun ends in -*ance*, the corresponding adjective will end in -*ant*. If the noun ends in -*ence*, the corresponding adjective will end in -*ent*.

abundance/abundant   independence/independent

> **Common Words Ending in -*ance*:** abundance; acquaintance; appearance; brilliance; defiance; importance; radiance; resonance; romance; tolerance

> **Common Words Ending in -*ence*:** absence; convenience; correspondence; difference; excellence; independence; patience; presence; reference; violence

Find It in Your Reading Read the persuasive essays by Ellen Goodman and George Will on pages 126–129. Within them, find two words that end in -*ance* and two that end in -*ence*. Practice writing and spelling those words.

Find It in Your Writing As you proofread your essay, check to be sure that you have spelled words ending in -*ance* and -*ence* correctly.

For more on spelling word endings, see Chapter 30.

⏱ TIME AND RESOURCE MANAGER

Resources
Print: *Scoring Rubrics on Transparency,* Ch. 7; *Writing Assessment and Portfolio Management,* Persuasive Essay; *Formal Assessment,* Ch. 7
Technology: *Writing and Grammar* Interactive Text, Section 7.5

Using the Full Student Edition	Using the Handbook🄷
• Cover pp. 142–145 in class. • Give students time in class to work on the activities on p. 143. • Read and discuss the Final Draft on pp. 144–145.	• Cover pp. 90–91 in class. • Give students time in class to work on the activities on p. 91.

7.6 Publishing and Presenting

Building Your Portfolio

The purpose of persuasive writing is to influence your audience. To achieve this goal, find a way to share your work with others. Below are a few possibilities for presenting your finished work:

1. **School Paper** If the topic of your persuasive writing is school- or community-related, publish it in your school newspaper.
2. **Local Newspaper** The editorial page of your local newspaper is a place to make your voice heard. Contact the paper for the proper procedures for submitting a letter to the editor, and revise your writing to conform to the newspaper's guidelines.

Reflecting on Your Writing

Once you have completed your persuasive essay, reflect on the experience of writing it. Answer the following questions, and record your responses in your portfolio:

- What did you discover about your topic as you wrote about it?
- What did you learn about the process of writing persuasively? Can you apply what you learned to other types of writing?

Internet Tip

To see persuasive essays scored with this rubric, go on-line:
PHSchool.com
Enter Web Code:
eek-1001

Rubric for Self-Assessment

Use the following criteria to evaluate your persuasive writing:

	Score 4	Score 3	Score 2	Score 1
Audience and Purpose	Demonstrates effective word choice; clearly states focus on persuasive task	Demonstrates good word choice; states focus on persuasive task	Shows some good word choices; minimally states focus on persuasive task	Shows lack of attention to persuasive task
Organization	Uses clear, consistent organizational strategy	Uses clear organizational strategy with occasional inconsistencies	Uses inconsistent organizational strategy; illogically presented	Lacks organizational strategy
Elaboration	Provides specific, well-elaborated reasons that support the writer's position	Provides two or more moderately elaborated reasons to support the writer's position	Provides several reasons, but only one is elaborated	Provides no specific reasons or elaboration
Use of Language	Incorporates many transitions to provide clarity of expression; has very few mechanical errors	Incorporates some transitions to help flow of ideas; has few mechanical errors	Incorporates few transitions; does not connect ideas well; has many mechanical errors	Fails to connect ideas; has many mechanical errors

Publishing and Presenting • 143

Final Draft

1. Help students see that the final draft of the student sample incorporates key elements of the persuasive essay.

   • The topic is clearly presented and supported by relevant details.

   • The organizational style is based on order of importance.

   • The conclusion clearly explains why volunteering is important.

2. Point out that, even though the essay is well supported by facts, the author includes some of her personal views in the piece, making it more personal and passionate. The author gives a balanced mix of facts and personal opinions. Encourage students to do the same in their own persuasive essays.

3. Ask students whether they have any ideas for improving the essay. How might they apply these suggestions to their own writing?

Critical Viewing

Evaluate Possible answers: The work seems to be getting done, each volunteer appears to be doing his or her task, and so on.

7.7 *Student Work*
IN PROGRESS

FINAL DRAFT

Volunteering Is Vital

Sharon Goldberg
Miami-Palmetto High School
Pinecrest, Florida

Reading a book to a blind person, feeding a debilitated patient in a nursing home, and tutoring a young child are all examples of community service projects. Such projects not only help others, they also help build feelings of self-worth and gratification in the volunteer. By serving others, volunteers acquire knowledge and wisdom. In fact, volunteering is an important part of life and growing up.

The importance of volunteerism is starting to catch on. Many local high schools, for example, are making volunteer service in a community project a requirement for graduation. In one scenario, students may assist at a hospital or nursing facility. In another, students may help refurbish a local playground. Students are encouraged to work as much as possible, as long as it does not interfere with their schoolwork. As the saying goes, "Don't give until it hurts; give until it feels good!"

144 • Persuasive Essay

▲ **Critical Viewing**
How well do the volunteers in this photograph seem to be working as a team? Explain. **[Evaluate]**

Using parallel structure in the essay's opening sentence helps Sharon grab the attention of her audience. Her main point is revealed at the end of the introduction.

Sharon gives examples to illustrate the types of community service projects that exist.

Similarly, community service projects serve as learning tools for those involved. Although classroom study is important, community service projects give individuals hands-on experience. Through such experiences, volunteers learn about real-life situations. How so? For example, helping to build a house for an impoverished family gives the volunteer a greater sense of what it is like to give (the volunteering experience) and to receive (the thanks of the new homeowner). At the same time, volunteers are acquiring life skills, such as learning how to put up drywall and how to operate a power saw. Learning to work as part of the home-building team provides the volunteer with an experience that will most likely be cherished forever.

In addition, the performance of community service provides students with the opportunity to become familiar with potential careers. If a student wanted to pursue an acting career, what could be more appropriate than volunteering at a local theater? If a teenager is interested in becoming a veterinarian, why not spend time working in an animal shelter? Volunteering is like a blank canvas; how one fills the space for the enrichment of others can be determined only by the interests of the giver and the needs of the community.

Although many people associate volunteering with working at a hospital, anyone can use a helping hand. People do not need to be poor or infirm to welcome assistance. A beautification project in which community members assist the police department in painting over graffiti is an example, as is helping out at a soup kitchen or tutoring younger children.

Some people avoid community service; they would rather give money and not get personally involved. Community service, however, can furnish volunteers with self-fulfillment, gratification, and peace, knowing that they have helped to make a difference. This is one reason that so many people take part in volunteering activities in later life. Volunteerism provides senior citizens with a purpose, which, in turn, promotes their happiness and satisfaction with life even after retirement.

Just think how wonderful your community could be if you and your peers take the time to volunteer. Serve meals to the hungry. Plant a tree in the park. Pick up garbage by the lake. Aside from feeling great about yourself, you will have helped someone in need, helped your community look better, and helped yourself become a mature, contributing member of society.

Specific examples of the benefits of volunteering help Sharon support her argument.

This essay is organized aspect by aspect: Sharon examines different aspects of the benefits of volunteering in successive paragraphs.

Using sentences of various lengths helps keep Sharon's writing interesting.

In the essay's final paragraph, Sharon sums up her argument and restates her main idea—that volunteerism is an important part of life.

Customize for
Less Advanced Students

For students who have difficulty editing another student's work, help guide them by focusing on a specific skill they have recently learned. Guide them through an editing session, searching specifically for parallel structure or formal language.

Customize for
ESL Students

The concepts of self-worth, satisfaction with life, and quality of life are all subjective ideas that might be difficult to explain to English-language learners because they are abstract. Try to give specific, concrete examples of each.

Lesson Objectives

1. To write an editorial
2. To organize ideas in writing to ensure support for ideas
3. To use prewriting strategies to generate ideas, develop voice, and plan
4. To develop drafts by organizing and reorganizing content
5. To refine selected pieces for general and specific audiences

Step-by-Step Teaching Guide

Editorial

Teaching Resources: Writing Support Transparencies, 7-J

1. Encourage students to watch television news shows and read newspaper pages for editorials about current events. This way, students can become familiar with editorial styles and inform themselves about events that might make good topics.

2. Suggest that students review their prewriting notes from pages 130–134. Did students generate any ideas that they did not choose for their persuasive essay that would make a good topic for an editorial? See the chart below for additional resources from Chapter 7.

3. Before they begin to write, remind students that newspaper editorials are typically quite short. Urge students to pay attention to their introductions and make sure that they set out their arguments in ways that quickly grab the reader's attention.

4. Display Transparency 7-J to discuss specific editing tips for editorials.

Connected Assignment
Editorial

Like persuasive essays and speeches, **editorials** are a form of persuasion that allows people to share their opinions. In editorials, writers express their ideas about current events or political issues. In some instances, editorials are written to reveal an organization's official position on an issue. Editorials may appear in newspapers, in journals, on radio, or on television.

WPLIX - EDITORIAL

An effective editorial
- clearly states the writer's position on an issue.
- contains details that support the writer's opinion.
- uses a respectful yet persuasive tone.
- is brief and to the point.
- is logically and effectively organized.

Write your own editorial on a current issue that interests you. Use the following strategies to help you:

Prewriting

Choosing Your Topic To find a topic for your editorial, scan the editorial page of the newspaper or listen to an editorial on the television news. You can also talk to family members or friends about issues currently in the news. Think about the opinions people present, and note your reactions. Then, review the issues, and choose one to form the heart of your editorial.

Narrowing Your Topic Your topic should be narrow enough to address fully in your editorial. For example, you should be able to reveal your opinion in a single thesis statement. For help narrowing your topic, make a list of the various aspects of your broad topic. Then, choose one of those aspects as your focus.

Gathering Details Once your topic is narrow enough, gather details to support your opinion or main idea. If you quote outside sources, make sure that they are reputable and unbiased. To add variety to the details you use as support, find examples of the following: quotations, historical events, statistical data, expert testimonies, and personal observations.

146 • Persuasive Essay

☑ ONGOING ASSESSMENT: Prerequisite Skills

Students may find the following resources from Chapter 7 particularly helpful in completing their editorials.

In the Textbook	Print Resources	Technology
Use Sentence Starters, Section 7.2 Make a Pro-and-Con Chart, Section 7.2 Color-Coding to Identify Support, Section 7.4	*Writing Support Transparencies,* 7–A, D–E *Writing Support Activity Book,* 7-2	*Writing and Grammar* Interactive Text, Sections 7.2–3

Drafting Adopt a firm and persuasive tone as you draft. Keep your audience in mind by defining any terms readers may not know and providing necessary background information. Refer to your prewriting plan as you present your position, and support it with details. Show that you care about your topic by bringing it to life with vivid verbs and precise nouns.

Revising and Editing Check your editorial to be sure that it is free of faulty logic such as bandwagon appeals (Everyone's doing it, so you should too!); circular reasoning (Rain forests should be preserved because it's important to preserve them.); and loaded language (Don't be a loser; buy Chooser!).

Read your editorial critically, and add details where needed. Delete details if they are unnecessary or beside the point. To get a fresh perspective on the effectiveness of your writing, consult a peer editor, and take his or her comments into consideration as you revise.

Carefully proofread your editorial, and correct any errors you find in grammar, spelling, and punctuation. Also, check to be sure that you have cited the quotation correctly and consistently and correctly spelled the names of experts or sources. Use the chart at right to help guide your editing.

Publishing and Presenting Neatly print out a copy of your editorial. Share it with friends, or send it to the editors of your school newspaper and ask them to publish it on their Op Ed page.

Editing Tips

☑ **Experts:** *If you quoted experts in your editorial, be sure their names, positions, and organizational affiliations are properly spelled and capitalized.*

☑ **Titles:** *Whether it's a newspaper, book, or periodical, make sure that any titles you mentioned are formatted correctly.*

☑ **Names: Edwin or Edward?** *Don't take a guess at people's names. Be sure instead. If necessary, call back interview subjects to double-check spellings and personal information.*

☑ **Addresses:** *Confirm that all addresses are correct and properly punctuated.*

Customize for
More Advanced Students

Do students know whether television editorials have ever prompted the public to take action about something? Assign students to research this question and report on it in class.

Customize for
Less Advanced Students

Have students compile a list of vocabulary words they might use in their editorial essays. You may wish to have students work in groups to create word banks. If you have newspapers in class, have the groups scan the headlines and editorials to highlight nouns and verbs that they can add to their word banks.

Customize for
ESL Students

Suggest that students try to find news from their family's homeland and write an editorial about an aspect of a situation with which they may be more familiar.

Customize for
Gifted and Talented Students

Encourage students to put together a presentation as if they were an on-the-scene news correspondent. Have them describe the things they would be seeing and hearing, as well as other facts, such as statistics. Offer interested students the opportunity to present their "up-close and personal" view of the issue on which they are writing.

Lesson Objectives

1. To evaluate media presentations
2. To analyze relationships, ideas, and cultures as represented in various media
3. To prepare, organize, and present a persuasive message effectively

Step-By-Step Teaching Guide

Recognizing Messages in Art

1. Have students explain how a painting such as *Snap the Whip* can transmit a message.

2. Ask students to think of other visual forms of persuasion they've seen. (Advertisements for car safety or against smoking are possibilities. Most advertisements, in fact, rely in some way on visual images).

3. Discuss in class why fiction can be a useful tool of persuasion and reform. (People read a story for pleasure, become attached to the characters, and then become very concerned for what happens to them.)

4. Play a song that has been part of a period of change. For example, "Follow the Drinking Gourd" was an encouragement for slaves to head north before the Civil War. Ask students to discuss how music affects them. Can they think of words or tunes they just can't get out of their heads? How can this help get a message across?

Viewing and Representing

Activity Allow students the opportunity to make class presentations of their multi-genre projects. Students who listen to the presentation should provide feedback about which genre was most convincing and why.

Critical Viewing

Interpret Students may mention that the interlocking hands signify unity, while the boys' facial expressions indicate a sense of freedom and enjoyment.

Spotlight on the Humanities

Recognizing Messages in Art

Focus on Art: *Snap the Whip*

Persuasion comes in many forms—speeches, essays, television ads, and even works of art. One such persuasive painting is *Snap the Whip* by Winslow Homer. It was painted in 1872, after the Civil War. During this time, reformers in education promoted free, unbridled development of children, as opposed to strict discipline and demands for obedience. Homer's message in *Snap the Whip* reflects this new ideology of the educational reformers. In the painting, the boys are running free, and the little red schoolhouse in the background symbolizes a more innocent era.

Snap the Whip, 1872, Winslow Homer

▲ **Critical Viewing**
What overall message is conveyed in this painting? **[Interpret]**

Literature Connection Authors throughout the years have used the pen to address injustices and to advocate reform. Charles Dickens was among the most influential novelists to use his novels and characters to make persuasive points. In *Hard Times*, for example, Dickens lampoons the educational practices of the day through the characters of Gradgrind and M'Choakumchild.

Music Connection Persuasive messages are often transmitted through song. From "Yankee Doodle," which dates back to the Revolutionary War, to the sixties anthem "The Times They Are A-Changin'," songs combine the power of music with the power of words, giving listeners something to think about.

Persuasive Writing Application: Multigenre Persuasive Message

Persuasion can appear in art, music, song, and poetry. Think of a persuasive message you would like to convey about an issue that matters to you. Do research on the issue. Then, produce a multigenre project in which you convey your message in three or more forms. For example, you may create a piece of art that conveys your persuasive theme, design a public-service announcement that has the same message, and follow up with a poem exploring that same idea. Share your multigenre persuasive project with others in your class.

148 • Persuasive Essay

Media and Technology Skills

► *Lesson Objectives*

1. To distinguish the purposes of various media forms
2. To deconstruct media to get the main idea of the message's content
3. To evaluate and critique the persuasive techniques of media messages

Recognizing Persuasion in the Media

Activity: Identify Persuasive Strategies in Commercials

Media researchers estimate that the average American views close to 20,000 television commercials every year. Even if you watch less television than most people, chances are good that you sit through thousands of carefully produced advertisements. Identifying the persuasive techniques in commercials can help you become an active viewer and resist the powerful pull of these advertisements.

Think About It Think about the last five items you purchased. Consider how your buying decisions were affected by advertising. Then, evaluate your satisfaction with each product. Compare your expectations with the actual performance of each item.

Describe It Conduct a viewing survey of at least five television commercials. Begin by describing the basic elements of each commercial. Use a chart like the one below to help you.

Product	Setting	Actors	Events/Plot	Special Features
Stone-washed jeans	A high-school parking lot after school	Five teenagers, all wearing the product	Kids are carrying backpacks and kidding around.	Camera keeps shifting back to the jeans; emphasizes that the jeans make the kids popular

Analyze It After describing each commercial, study how the elements work together to persuade an audience. Draw a conclusion about why the advertisers chose this strategy to appeal to an audience. You may analyze commercials that use some of these strategies:

- **Testimonials** add glamour to a product's image. Recommendations from "real-life" people make an ad's claims seem more believable.

- **Bandwagon appeals** rely on peer pressure to encourage buyers to join a trend.

- **Identity advertising** promotes specific appeals that have more to do with lifestyles than with product qualities.

Publish It Start a Media Watch column for your class or school newspaper. Each column can analyze current commercials and expose the persuasive techniques at work.

Media and Technology Skills • 149

Check Your TV Pulse

Find out how your viewing habits compare with those of the average American teenager. Keep an exact record of your television viewing for one week. Then, compare your results with the information in the chart below.

TV Viewing Habits/Ages 12–17
- M–F, 10 A.M. to 4:30 P.M.: 1 hr., 46 min.
- M–F, 4:30 P.M. to 7:30 P.M.: 2 hr., 51 min.
- M–Sun, 8 P.M. to 11 P.M.: 6 hr., 2 min.
- Sat. 7 A.M. to 1 P.M.: 38 min.
- M–F, 11:30 P.M. to 1 A.M.: 46 min.
* Source: World Almanac Book of Facts, 1999

Step-By-Step Teaching Guide

Recognizing Persuasion in Media

Teaching Resources: Writing Support Transparencies, 7-K; Writing Support Activity Book, 7-3

1. Ask the class to consider items they or someone they know has purchased. Why did they choose to buy a particular item?

2. Display Transparency 7-K. Work with the students to fill in the chart for one or two well-known commercials.

3. Give students a copy of the blank organizer (7-3). Have them continue the survey of commercials on their own or with a partner, incorporating their findings on a chart.

4. Have the class develop a list of techniques used to persuade people in different kinds of advertisements. Lead them to see such techniques as testimonials, bandwagon appeals, and identity advertising. Ask the class whether these techniques vary in different types of media.

5. Allow students the opportunity to create their own commercial for an item, applying techniques that they feel will be most effective to persuade an audience.

Responding to Persuasive Writing Prompts

Teaching Resources: Standardized Test Preparation Workbook, pp. 13–14

1. Review the four bulleted points with students. Remind students that the success of their persuasive writing depends on their ability to do these four things.

2. Direct students to the sample prompt on this page. Help them evaluate the prompt to find these key points that should focus what they write:

   Form: *Letter*

   Purpose: *State a position and support it with convincing reasons.*

   Audience: *School Board*

3. Remind students to pace themselves as they work, allowing time for each stage of the writing process. Rushing ahead will not help them. The few minutes they spend organizing may actually save them time in the drafting stage.

4. Have students write an essay in response to the prompt on this page. Using the strategies and guidelines on page 151, set a time limit for this task in order to give students practice "writing against the clock."

Standardized Test Preparation Workshop

Responding to Persuasive Writing Prompts

Some persuasive writing prompts on standardized tests examine your ability to present, argue, and defend a position. You must clearly state your position and support it with specific examples, reasons, or details. You will be evaluated on your ability to do the following:

- Develop a clearly stated position in response to the essay prompt.

- Identify and include compelling details suited to the essay's audience and purpose.

- Organize ideas in a logical way, and express them with effective language.

- Use correct grammar, spelling, and punctuation.

As you generate standardized test responses, rely on the basic writing process stages—prewriting, drafting, revising, editing, and proofreading—to lead you through the task. Be aware, however, of how much time you are allotted for completing your response.

Below is an example of a typical standardized test persuasive writing prompt. Before developing your response, read the tips on the next page. Also, note the time-planning suggestions on the clocks next to each stage.

Test Tip

When writing a persuasive test response, make sure to state your position clearly. Choose reasons and language that are appropriate to the specified audience.

Sample Writing Situation

Many schools have budget issues that require a choice to be made between one service or program and another. Your school board is planning to cut one school program in order to stay within next year's budget. In a letter to the board, explain which program you think is least valuable and might be cut in order to maintain other programs. Support your position with convincing reasons, facts, and examples.

150 • Persuasive Essay

◊ TEST-TAKING TIP

It is important that students are aware of the language they use when writing. When writing persuasive essays, students need to remember not to present opinions as facts. All statements should be well supported, and the difference between fact and opinion should be clear. Also, remind students that language should be formal in an essay of this nature, so they should avoid slang and contractions, and make certain that they keep their audience in mind.

Prewriting

Allow about one quarter of your time for shaping your argument and identifying supporting details.

Look at Both Sides Quickly jot down your ideas in a pro-and-con chart to help you see both sides of the issue. This will help you solidify your own argument and develop reasons that address those who would argue in favor of keeping the program you suggest eliminating.

Support Your Ideas Look at your notes to identify details that will influence your audience of board members. Your goal is to persuade your audience to agree with your ideas, not to attack people who hold opposing views. Come up with supporting details or reasons that are specific and effective but not inflammatory.

Drafting

Allow about half of your time for drafting. Leave space for text you may want to insert when revising.

Begin, Develop, and Conclude As you draft, write an introduction that reveals your purpose and main idea. Also, in your introduction, establish your tone and get the audience "on your side." Then, in the body of the essay, develop your argument. Give reasons that your audience should agree with you. Summarize your most important points, and restate your main idea in your conclusion.

Craft Your Language Effective persuasion contains not only credible ideas but high-impact language. Choose vivid verbs, nouns, and adjectives that engage readers in your essay. Mix punchy, short sentences with longer, more elaborate language for variety.

Revising, Editing, and Proofreading

Allow almost one quarter of your time for revising and editing. In the last few minutes, proofread carefully.

Verify Your Response Reread the test prompt to be sure that you have fully and completely responded to it. If you have not, revise your letter to make sure that it addresses the prompt.

Review Your Tone Read over your work, and listen to its tone. Replace words that have negative connotations, and delete critical language that may alienate undecided readers. If time allows, recopy your work neatly. Otherwise, carefully insert changes to your draft.

Correct the Errors Work steadily and carefully to review your essay for spelling and punctuation errors. Sometimes, reading backward makes these errors easier to spot. Make all changes with proofreader's marks and neatly drawn deletion lines.

Time and Resource Manager

In-Depth Lesson Plan

	LESSON FOCUS	PRINT AND MEDIA RESOURCES
DAY 1	**Introduction to Advertisements** Students learn key elements of an advertisement and analyze the Model From Literature. (pp. 152–154/H92–94)	*Writers at Work* DVD, Persuasion *Writing and Grammar* Interactive Text, Ch. 8, Introduction
DAY 2	**Prewriting** Students choose and narrow a topic, consider their audience and purpose, and gather information. (pp. 155–157/H95–97)	**Teaching Resources** *Writing Support Transparencies*, 8-A; *Topic Bank for Heterogeneous Classes*, Ch. 8 *Writing and Grammar* Interactive Text, Section 8.2
DAY 3	**Drafting** Students organize their ideas and write their first drafts. (p. 158/H98)	**Teaching Resources** *Writing Support Transparencies*, 8-B *Writing and Grammar* Interactive Text, Section 8.3
DAY 4	**Revising** Students revise their drafts in terms of overall structure, paragraphs, sentences, and word choice. (pp. 159–162/H99–102)	**Teaching Resources** *Writing Support Transparencies*, 8-C *Writing and Grammar* Interactive Text, Section 8.4
DAY 5	**Editing and Proofreading; Publishing and Presenting** Students check their work for accuracy and correctness and present their final drafts. (pp. 163–165/H103–105)	**Teaching Resources** *Scoring Rubrics on Transparency*, Ch. 8; *Writing Assessment and Portfolio Management; Formal Assessment*, Ch. 8 *Writing and Grammar* Interactive Text, Sections 8.5–6

Accelerated Lesson Plan

	LESSON FOCUS	PRINT AND MEDIA RESOURCES
DAY 1	**Introduction Through Drafting** Students review characteristics of an advertisement, select topics, and write drafts. (pp. 152–158/H92–98)	**Teaching Resources** *Writing Support Transparencies*, 8-A–B *Writing and Grammar* Interactive Text, Ch. 8, Introduction through Section 8.3
DAY 2	**Revising Through Presenting** Students work individually or with peers to revise, edit, and proofread their work for presentation. (pp. 159–165/H99–105)	**Teaching Resources** *Writing Support Transparencies*, 8-C *Scoring Rubrics on Transparency*, Ch. 8; *Writing Assessment and Portfolio Management; Formal Assessment*, Ch. 8 *Writing and Grammar* Interactive Text, Sections 8.4–6

Options for Adapting Lesson Plans

HOMEWORK

Have students complete any stage of the lesson for homework.

FEATURES

Extend coverage with Connected Assignment (p. 166), Spotlight on the Humanities (p. 168), Media and Technology Skills (p. 169), and the Standardized Test Preparation Workshop (p. 170).

TECHNOLOGY

Students can complete any stage of the lesson on the computer, using *Writing and Grammar* Interactive Text or a word-processing program. Have them print out their completed work.

Writing and Grammar Handbook Alignment

Page numbers in Step-by-Step Teaching Guides in this Teacher's Edition refer to pages from the full student text. Handbook page references, indicated with this icon **H**, are provided in Time and Resource Manager boxes and at the bottom of each Teacher's Edition page.

INTEGRATED SKILLS COVERAGE

Integrating Grammar
The Four Functions of Sentences, SE p. 161/H101
Homophones, SE p. 163/H103

Reading/Writing Connection
Recognize Figurative Language, SE p. 154/H94
Use Figurative Language, SE p. 154/H94

Viewing and Representing
Critical Viewing, SE pp. 152, 166, 168/H92
Recognizing Theater Connections, SE p. 168
Using Technology to Extend Meaning, SE p. 169; ATE p. 157

Real-World Connection ATE p. 165

Workplace Skills ATE p. 153

Language Skills ATE p. 165

Technology Skills SE p. 167

ASSESSMENT SUPPORT

Standardized Test Preparation Workshop, SE p. 170; ATE pp. 157, 161

Standardized Test Preparation Workbook, pp. 15–16

Scoring Rubrics on Transparency, Ch. 8

Formal Assessment, Ch. 8

Writing Assessment and Portfolio Management

MEETING INDIVIDUAL NEEDS

Less Advanced Students ATE p. 171. See also Ongoing Assessments ATE pp. 156, 159.
More Advanced Students ATE pp. 155, 171
ESL Students ATE pp. 156, 160, 163
Gifted and Talented Students ATE p. 161
Linguistic Learners ATE p. 157

BLOCK SCHEDULING

Pacing Suggestions
For 90-minute Blocks
• Have students complete the Prewriting and Drafting stages in a single period.
• Focus one class period on Revising and Editing and Publishing and Presenting. Allow at least 30 minutes for peer revision.

Resources for Varying Instruction
• *Writing and Grammar* **Interactive Text** A 90-minute block provides an ideal opportunity for students to work on the computer.
• *Writers at Work* DVD Show the Persuasion segment in class.

Professional Development Support
• *How to Manage Instruction in the Block* This teaching resource provides management and activity suggestions.

MEDIA AND TECHNOLOGY

For the Student
• *Writing and Grammar* **Interactive Text**, Ch. 8

For the Teacher
• *Writers at Work* DVD, Persuasion
• **TeacherEXPRESS** CD-ROM

WRITING AND GRAMMAR ON-LINE

Interactive Text (On-line or on CD-ROM)
• Easily navigable instruction with interactive Revision Checkers
• Full use of e-rater™, the essay-scoring system (on-line only)

Companion Web Site PHSchool.com
• Scoring rubrics with models (use Web Code eek-1001)

See the Go On-line! **feature, SE p. iii.**

LITERATURE CONNECTIONS

Related selection from *Prentice Hall Literature, Penguin Edition,* Grade 10:
Topic Bank Option *Antigone,* Sophocles, SE p. 155/H95

▶ **Lesson Objectives**

1. To write a persuasive advertisement appropriate to audience and purpose

2. To read to appreciate the writer's craft and to discover models for writing

3. To use prewriting strategies to generate ideas and to plan

4. To test and revise a project using questionnaires, group discussions, and feedback forms

5. To use writing to formulate questions, refine topics, and clarify ideas

6. To develop and revise drafts in terms of structure, paragraphs, sentences, and word choice

7. To edit and proofread to ensure standard English usage and grammar

8. To evaluate writing for both mechanics and content

9. To refine selected work for publication

Critical Viewing

Connect Students will probably comment on the fact that, because there is so much advertising, eye-catching ads are more likely to get noticed.

Chapter 8 Persuasion
Advertisement

Advertisements in Everyday Life

Advertisements are all around you. For example, when you watch television, you probably spend at least fifteen minutes every hour watching commercials—advertisements of various companies pitching their products. Advertisements also appear on magazines and billboards and even on T-shirts and hats. In recent years, ads have become common sights on the Internet as well, blinking and winking to grab the attention of those surfing the Web.

▲ **Critical Viewing** Judging from this photograph, why might it be important for an advertisement to be eye-catching? **[Connect]**

🕐 **TIME AND RESOURCE MANAGER**

Resources
Technology: *Writers at Work* DVD, Persuasion; *Writing and Grammar* Interactive Text, Ch. 8

Using the Full Student Edition	Using the Handbook 🄷
• Cover pp. 152–154 in class. • Show the Persuasion section of the *Writers at Work* DVD. • Read the Model From Literature in class, and use it to brainstorm for advertisement ideas with students.	• Cover pp. 92–94 in class. • Show the persuasion section of *Writers at Work* DVD. • Read the Model From Literature in class, and use it to brainstorm for advertisement ideas with students.

What Is an Advertisement?

An **advertisement** is a persuasive message paid for by an individual or company. Ads attempt to persuade people to buy something, accept an idea, vote for a candidate, or support a cause.

Advertisements take many forms—from media ads on television and radio to print ads in newspapers, magazines, and flyers to creative visual ads, such as skywriting or walking billboards.

Most effective advertisements contain

- a slogan or catchy phrase that grabs the audience's attention.
- reasons the customer should purchase the product or service.
- details that tell who to call or where to purchase the product or service.

To preview the criteria upon which your advertisement may be evaluated, see the Rubric for Self-Assessment on page 164.

Types of Advertisements

Although most people think of advertising as only commercial ads used to sell consumer products, advertisements can take many forms:

- **Public-service announcements,** sent out by nonprofit organizations, discuss topics such as public safety or health.
- **Merchandise ads** are print, broadcast, or visual messages about products that consumers can purchase.
- **Service ads** are print, broadcast, or visual messages about services—cleaning, entertaining, or self-improvement.

PREVIEW
Student Work
IN PROGRESS

In this chapter, you'll follow the progress of Ever Chapa, a student at La Joya High School in La Joya, Texas, as he drafts an advertisement for a college fair. Follow along as Ever uses prewriting, drafting, and revising strategies to develop his ad. Ever's completed advertisement appears at the end of the chapter.

Writers in ACTION

As a person who did fund-raising for and advanced the ideas of the Asia Society in New York City, Sayu Bhojwani has firsthand experience writing persuasively:

"The most important aspect of persuasive writing is to be able to convey to your reader a certain emotion or concept. In the type of work that I do, it's usually a concept.... We want to convey a sense of innovation and newness, to get a reader in."

Advertisement • **153**

PREPARE and ENGAGE

Interest GRABBER Name several products that are widely advertised and ask students to identify the image or slogan that the product uses. Have students suggest some favorite television ads. What do they like about these advertisements?

Activate Prior Knowledge

Ask students to recall the last time they bought something. Did they hear or see an advertisement for the product in a magazine, on the radio, on television, or in the store where they bought the item? What steps and techniques did the advertiser use to make the advertisement interesting and appealing? After discussing these methods, refer students to the characteristics of advertisement writing in the text.

More About the Writer

The Asia Society, where Sayu Bhojwani is the program associate, has been described as "America's preeminent organization linking Asians and Americans" by former U.S. Secretary of State Warren Christopher. The society is responsible for promoting public awareness of the more than thirty countries in the Asia-Pacific region, including Japan, China, Korea, India, New Zealand, Australia, and the Pacific Islands.

Integrating Workplace Skills

Have students create a list of personal attributes and skills needed to work in an advertising agency. (Students may cite creativity, self-motivation, and ability to work with others.)

✓ ONGOING ASSESSMENT: Diagnose

Use one of the following options to diagnose students' current level of proficiency in persuasive writing.

Option 1 Ask each student to select the strongest example of his or her persuasive advertisement from last year. Hold conferences in which you review each student's sample. Use conferences to determine which students will need extra support in developing a persuasive advertisement.	**Option 2** Ask students to write a topic sentence advertising an ice-skating rink. Have them list three words or items of evidence that support the topic sentence. If students have difficulty completing this exercise, you will need to devote more time to the gathering evidence and narrowing your topic phases of the process.

Reading\Writing Connection

Reading: Creative Language

Tell students that most advertisements are designed to express as much as possible in the fewest possible words. Ad writers choose their words for maximum impact and persuasive appeal. As students analyze the Costa Rica advertisement, have them note how the words and images creatively spring from an unlikely pattern: a recipe.

Step-by-Step Teaching Guide

Engage Students Through Literature

1. Ask students what they noticed first about this advertisement. Do they find it appealing?

2. Have students discuss how photographs and text work together in the ad. Why are both necessary?

3. Have students identify the metaphor used in the ad (Costa Rica is a wonderful dish with "no artificial ingredients").

4. Explain that an essential factor of a successful advertisement is that readers or viewers remember what the product is. Ask students whether they feel that the Costa Rica advertisement is successful in this regard.

Reading\Writing Connection

Writing Application: Use Creative Language

As students begin to plan their advertisements, ask them to strive to use language creatively. This involves not only word choice, but the inventive use of metaphors and other figurative language.

8.1 Model From Literature

The following advertisement appeared in a magazine about nature and travel.

This advertisement contains an interesting use of language. The text is like a recipe that creates something wonderful—Costa Rica.

This statistic is presented in an appealing way.

Parallel structure runs through this advertisement: Each sentence is an imperative.

The ad's tag line—no artificial ingredients—continues the recipe metaphor.

Writing Application: Use Creative Language
You'll notice that the ad above contains creative use of language. As you prepare to write your own ad, think about creative ways you can use language.

154 • Advertisement

8.2 Prewriting

Choosing Your Topic

You can write an advertisement for a product, a political candidate, or a service. Use the following strategies to help you come up with a topic for your advertisement:

Strategies for Generating Topics

1. **Conduct a Survey** Ask the following survey question: What gift would you most like to receive for your birthday? Review the responses, and choose one to form the topic of your advertisement.

2. **Blueprint** Draw the floor plan of a room in your everyday environment. Fill the room of your drawing with appropriate gadgets, clothes, or art objects. As you draw the items, decide which object appeals to you most. Make that one the subject of your advertisement.

TOPIC BANK

If you need a specific topic for your advertisement, follow these suggestions:

1. **Advertisement for a School Function** Write and design a poster publicizing a school music festival.

Responding to Literature

2. In the ancient Greek tragedy *Antigone*, a woman defies the order of a stern king and gives her dead brother an appropriate burial. Think of images from this or another play that would make an exciting poster for a theatrical production. Then, create such a poster. You can read *Antigone* in *Prentice Hall Literature, Penguin Edition*, Grade 10.

🕐 Timed Writing Prompt

3. Everyone has a favorite class in school. Write a letter to your principal that explains why you enjoy your favorite class. Describe what makes your favorite class educational and enjoyable. **(35 minutes)**

Try it out! Use the interactive Blueprint activity in **Section 8.2**, on-line or on CD-ROM.

Prewriting: Strategies for Generating Topics

1. For the survey strategy, suggest that students interview family members, friends, and classmates.

2. For the blueprint strategy, point out that the more details students include in the blueprint, the more likely they are to find something that they would want to advertise.

Customize for *More Advanced Students*

Have students create a grid that includes space for background information about survey subjects as well as their answers. Background information might include the subject's age, gender, profession, and hobbies. Encourage students to survey a broad range of people. This background information will help them when they begin to consider the audience for their advertisements.

🕐 Timed Writing Prompt

- To help students generate ideas, have them discuss what makes a class enjoyable. For instance, ask them if they believe two classes can be taught differently but still be equally fun to attend. They could also discuss how a class's subject matter affects their opinions about it. Finally, talk about how the level of student interaction affects a class's atmosphere.

- Suggest that students allow five minutes for prewriting, twenty-five minutes for writing, and five minutes for reviewing and proofreading.

🕐 TIME AND RESOURCE MANAGER

Resources
Print: *Writing Support Transparencies*, 8-A
Technology: *Writing and Grammar* Interactive Text, Section 8.2

Using the Full Student Edition	Using the Handbook🄷
• Work through pp. 155–157 in class. • Work through the Conduct a Survey and Blueprint strategies with the class. • After covering prewriting strategies, have students begin work on their advertisements in class.	• Work through pp. 95–97 in class. • Work through the Conduct a Survey and Blueprint strategies with the class. • After covering prewriting strategies, have students begin work on their advertisements in class.

Step-by-Step Teaching Guide

Prewriting: Narrowing Your Topic

1. Have students pick two or three topics from their topic bank. For each topic, have students think about what is being offered to potential customers.

2. Point out that many advertisements not only describe the product, but also focus on how the item or service will improve the customer's life.

Step-by-Step Teaching Guide

Prewriting: Choose Your Words Carefully

1. Point out how the perfume advertisements shown on this page are designed to appeal to quite different audiences.

2. Ask students whether they think they would ever find a perfume ad that proclaims, "It Smells." What connotation would this slogan have? Point out that, generally, coffee ads speak of *aroma*, room fresheners speak of *scent*, and perfumes speak of *fragrance*, though all these words refer to how something smells.

Customize for
ESL Students

Have students work in groups to brainstorm for words that describe the product a student has chosen. Then, have more-fluent students explain the connotation of any words suggested, as well as alternative words that may not have the same connotation. (A thesaurus may be helpful for finding alternative words, and dictionaries often identify words with strong connotations.)

Narrowing Your Topic

An advertisement should almost always have a narrow focus: Most effective ads are short and memorable. To narrow your topic for your advertisement, answer the following questions:

- What product/person/service am I selling or promoting?
- What is the one thing I'd like to communicate to my audience about this product/person/service?

As you draft your ad, refer to your responses to ensure that your focus has remained narrow.

Considering Your Audience and Purpose

As you think about the advertisement you are going to write, consider whom it is you are trying to persuade. Then, decide on the language and details that will impress them most.

Choose Your Words Carefully

One way to achieve your purpose is to choose words that will most appeal to your audience. Select your words carefully, taking into consideration their denotation and connotation. A word's *denotation* is its dictionary meaning. Its *connotation* is the positive or negative association the word conjures up. In your ad, take advantage of a word's connotation as well as its denotation.

156 • Advertisement

☑ ONGOING ASSESSMENT: Monitor and Reinforce

If you observe that some students are having difficulty determining their audience, use one of the following options.

Option 1 Suggest that students prepare their advertisements for a very specific audience (a friend, an aunt or uncle, a parent).	**Option 2** Have students write down a brief profile of their intended audience, including their interest in the topic, their background, and their education.

Gathering Details

Put yourself in the place of your audience. Then, answer the questions you, as the audience, have about the product, service, or person you are promoting. Be sure to answer those questions somewhere in the advertisement you write.

Gather Details for a Product

- What is it?
- What makes it special or different?
- How much does it cost?
- Where can I buy it?

Gather Details for a Campaign

- What are his or her qualifications?
- What is his or her stand on ___?___ ?
- Who else supports this candidate?

Gather Details for an Event

- Who is sponsoring the event?
- Where is the event to be held? At what time?
- How much is the cost of admission?

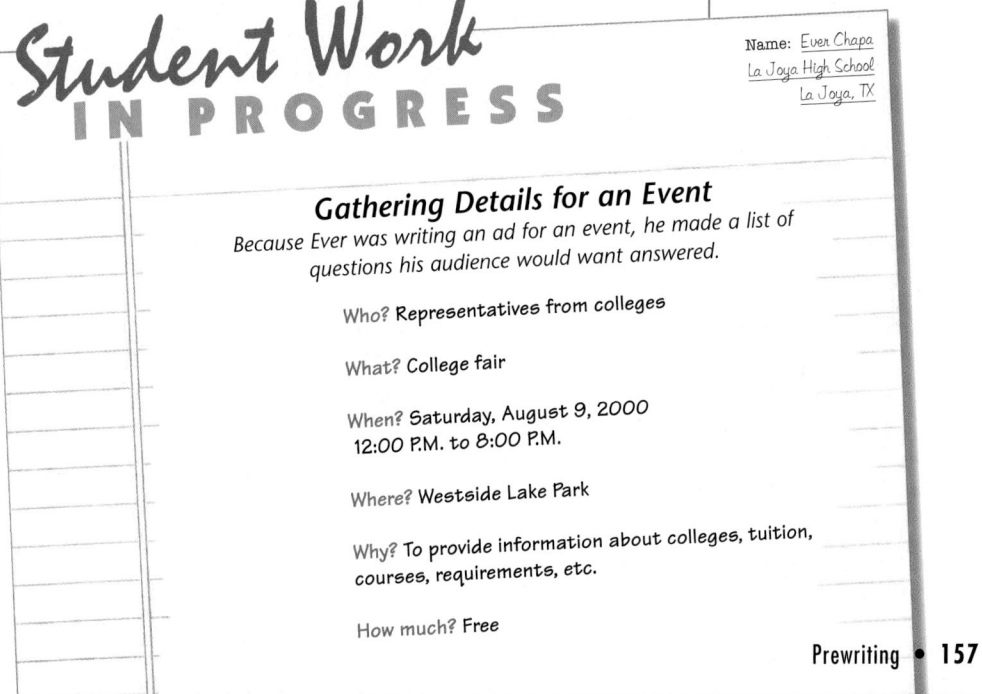

Student Work
IN PROGRESS

Name: Ever Chapa
La Joya High School
La Joya, TX

Gathering Details for an Event
Because Ever was writing an ad for an event, he made a list of questions his audience would want answered.

Who? Representatives from colleges

What? College fair

When? Saturday, August 9, 2000
12:00 P.M. to 8:00 P.M.

Where? Westside Lake Park

Why? To provide information about colleges, tuition, courses, requirements, etc.

How much? Free

Prewriting • 157

Drafting: Order Details From Most Important to Least Important

1. Ask students to explain the reason the writer used the word order shown in the lawn service advertisement. (The first item is the service itself, followed by "Half Price," the strongest selling point. Referrals, while important to business, are not key to the ad.)

2. Have students list the details they have gathered for their advertisements and then rank them from most important to least.

3. If students are having trouble ranking details, ask, "Which would you choose if you could have only one? If you had to cut one?"

4. Point out that there may be several details that are similarly ranked. For example, in the lawn service ad, while price is the key element, the next three items are similar in importance and could be moved around without hurting the ad.

Drafting: Include Testimonials, Statistics, and Graphs

1. Point out that each elaboration technique is suited to many, but not all products. Testimonials work well to establish durability, for example: "My watch lasted for fourteen years." For medicine, statistics would be more reassuring than hearing one person say, "Well, I felt better."

2. Ask students to consider which technique is most appropriate for their advertisement. Which one would they be most likely to value if they were buying this product?

8.3 Drafting

Shaping Your Writing

When drafting your ad, be sure to grab the audience's attention right away. To do this, start with the most appealing characteristic of the product.

Order Details From Most Important to Least Important

Know what is most important to your audience, and tell them about that up front. Then, follow with details that your audience will also want to know.

In the advertisement at right, details are arranged in descending order of importance: The most important detail is that the lawn service is half price. The least important detail is that referrals are available.

Providing Elaboration

Include Testimonials, Statistics, and Graphics

Elaborate your advertisement, using pictures, quotations, and facts that will convince your audience of your product's superiority:

Testimonials are quotes from satisfied users:

Mary Kay Louis of Denver, Colorado, says "I'll never leave home without my Timetip wristwatch!"

Statistics are numerical facts that favor the use of the product or service being advertised:

More than 70 percent of the people polled by Dennton University say that they'd like to try a Timetip wristwatch.

Attractive graphics could include photographs of people using your product or service, diagrams that show the benefits of your product, or illustrations of the product or service.

Lawn Service at HALF PRICE

☑ **Cart-Away Clippings**
☑ **State-of-the-Art Equipment**
☑ **Courteous Service**
☑ **Referrals Available**

1/2 PRICE

158 • Advertisement

⏱ **TIME AND RESOURCE MANAGER**

Resources
Print: *Writing Support Transparencies*, 8-B–C
Technology: *Writing and Grammar* Interactive Text, Section 8.3

Using the Full Student Edition	Using the Handbook🄷
• Cover pp. 158–162 in class. • Demonstrate the techniques of providing elaboration through testimonials, statistics, and graphics. • Work through revising strategies as a class. • Have students revise their advertisements in class.	• Cover pp. 98–102 in class. • Demonstrate the techniques of providing elaboration through testimonials, statistics, and graphics. • Work through revising strategies as a class. • Have students revise their advertisements in class.

8.4 Revising

Revising Your Overall Structure

Prominently Place the Main Idea

In most advertisements, the most important idea occupies the most prominent place. (If your advertisement is written for radio, you will probably want to lead off with your most important idea.)

▶ **REVISION STRATEGY**
Experimenting With Placement of Your Main Idea

Critically examine the layout of your advertisement, and juggle the placement of your most important idea until it achieves the maximum impact.

Revising Your Paragraphs

▶ **REVISION STRATEGY**
Circling the Important Details

Trim unnecessary information from your paragraphs so that every detail and concept is essential to the message and its delivery. To do this, circle the most important details and delete uncircled material.

Technology Tip

Explore formatting options your word-processing program has to offer. Then, experiment with formats as you revise your advertisement. Choose the format that best suits your purpose.

Student Work IN PROGRESS

Name: _Ever Chapa_
La Joya High School
La Joya, TX

Circling Important Details

Ever Chapa circled the most important details in his advertisement. Then, he deleted or rewrote the uncircled details.

(Attention all SENIORS!) ~~You know who you are.~~ (Come join the fun) at the first annual Bash at the Lake. ~~Who said getting the scoop on what colleges have to offer you has to be boring?~~ (Come out and learn more about local scholarships and grants.)

Revising • 159

Revising: Color-Coding End Marks

Teaching Resource: Writing Support Transparencies, 8-C

1. Use Transparency 8-C to show how Ever's draft is color-coded for declarative, interrogative, exclamatory, and imperative sentences.

2. Allow students time to check their own drafts for these four types of sentences.

3. Explain that checking end marks helps, but students still need to be alert to sentence type. Remind students that, while declarative sentences end in periods and exclamatory sentences end in exclamation marks, imperative sentences can end in either.

4. After students have color-coded their advertisements, ask them to determine whether there is enough variety, and then revise if necessary.

Customize for
ESL Students

Like many advertisements, Ever's draft uses idiomatic expressions that may puzzle students learning English. You may need to clarify the meanings of *bash* and *scoop* for students.

8.4

Revising Your Sentences
Vary Sentence Types

Any writing is more enjoyable and engaging when its rhythms vary. By varying sentence type, you vary the rhythm of your prose. There are four basic sentence types: declarative, interrogative, exclamatory, and imperative.

▶ **REVISION STRATEGY**
Color-Coding End Marks

Read through your draft, and use a colored pen or pencil to call out various end marks. By doing this, you'll be able to see whether, for example, you have mostly declarative or imperative sentences, interrogative sentences, or exclamatory sentences.

First, draw a circle around periods, a square around question marks, and triangles around exclamation marks. Then, review your draft. If you have too many end marks of one shape, you may want to vary your sentence types to make your advertisement more interesting to read.

Timed Writing Hint

When revising your writing under timed conditions, check that you have varied sentence types and lengths to engage your reader.

Student Work
IN PROGRESS

Name: Ever Chapa
La Joya High School
La Joya, TX

Coding to Identify Sentence Types

When Ever reviewed his draft, he found that too many of his sentences were declarative. He made the following changes to enliven his writing and keep the interest of his audience.

BASH AT THE LAKE

Attention all seniors!

What's happening with your future?

Come to the first annual Bash at the Lake to find out!
Learn about various colleges and what they have to offer

YOU.

Why not Get the *real scoop* on local

scholarships and grants?

Create Parallel Structure

Although it can be effective to vary your sentence types in an advertisement, you can make your advertisement memorable if you create parallel structure by repeating sentence types for effect. In the following example, three interrogative sentences are followed by an exclamatory sentence to create an impact.

EXAMPLE: Is your breakfast cereal boring? Is it bland? Is it full of sugar? Then, try Crackle, a new type of cereal that is sure to enliven your mornings!

▶ **REVISION STRATEGY**
Extending an Idea

Read through your draft, and locate an idea that you'd like to emphasize. Then, build on that idea by creating short sentences of the same type to make the idea memorable to readers.

Grammar in Your Writing
The Four Functions of Sentences

Just as sentences can have varied structures, they can have varied functions as well. Try to include declarative, interrogative, exclamatory, and imperative sentences in your writing.

The Four Functions of Sentences Every sentence fulfills one of the following four functions:

Declarative—a sentence that makes a statement
Example: This product whitens and brightens your teeth.

Interrogative—a sentence that asks a question
Example: Do you need a new bicycle?

Exclamatory—a sentence that expresses strong emotion
Example: Try our great-tasting soup!

Imperative—a sentence that gives a command
Example: Be the first to buy this product.

Find It in Your Writing Review your draft to identify sentences that fulfill each of the four functions. Be sure that you have used the appropriate end marks. If you cannot identify all four functions, challenge yourself to add at least one more to your writing.

To learn more about types of sentences, see Chapter 21.

Revising • 161

Step-by-Step Teaching Guide

The Four Functions of Sentences

1. Review with students the function of each of the four types of sentences.

2. Explain that, while declarative sentences are common in advertising, exclamatory (*It's new! It's improved!*) and imperative (*Buy this. Try this.*) sentences become more prominent.

3. Give students two or three samples of advertisements from magazines or newspapers. Have them identify the function of each sentence in the ads.

Find It in Your Writing

Ask students which sentences were most common in their advertisements. Discuss with students why they think some sentence functions seem more useful in advertisements than in other forms of writing.

Customize for
Gifted and Talented Students

Suggest that students consider preparing their ads for more than one medium. For example, in addition to a print ad, which might include a graphic element, suggest they prepare a radio ad that has to get the message across without an image. Television, billboards, and Internet banners are other advertising media they might consider.

STANDARDIZED TEST PREPARATION WORKSHOP

Punctuation Standardized test questions may require students to identify whether a sentence is declarative, interrogative, imperative, or exclamatory. Use the following example to demonstrate.

Which sentence is interrogative and requires a question mark at the end?

A I've never been so angry in my life

B She was very angry

C Have you ever been so angry

D Don't get so angry

Students should recognize that the correct answer is **C**. A is not the right answer as it is an exclamatory sentence. B is not the correct answer as it is a declarative sentence. D is not the correct answer as it is an imperative sentence.

Step-by-Step Teaching Guide

Revising: Replace Dull Words

1. Explain that verbs help stimulate people's imaginations, and vivid verbs are more stimulating.

2. Point out in the text how much more energetic *jump in* sounds than *get in,* and how much more exciting and active *relive* is than *see.*

3. Point out that context affects which verbs you can use. In the Williamsburg example, *see* is replaced by two different verbs, making the message more precise as well as more interesting.

4. Have students scan their drafts for verbs. Do they notice that some verbs are more interesting than others? Encourage them to find places in their advertisements to add vivid verbs.

Step-by-Step Teaching Guide

Revising: Peer Review

1. Begin the peer review process by asking student reviewers to identify a draft's strengths before commenting on its weaknesses.

2. Remind students that the focus here should be on clarity, appealing language, and effectiveness.

3. Ask students to be as specific as possible when they make suggestions. "I don't like it" is not helpful, while "Perhaps you could make the following verbs more vivid" is helpful.

Revising Your Word Choice

In advertising, you want to keep your sentences short and powerful. You don't want to use too many words, so choose carefully. Verbs, especially, can help you stimulate the readers' imagination or motivate them to do something.

▶ **REVISION STRATEGY**
Replace Dull Words

When you want to attract attention, use verbs that vividly describe the action you want readers to take.

	DULL VERBS	VIVID VERBS
Example:	*Get* into our car.	*Jump* into our car.
Example:	*See* Williamsburg, Virginia, and *see* the eighteenth century.	*Come* to Williamsburg, Virginia, and *relive* the eighteenth century.

Peer Review

Question a Peer

With a partner, exchange advertisement drafts. Then, have your partner answer the following questions, or create questions of your own that you'd like to have answered.

- What is the main idea conveyed by my advertisement?

- Do any images within the ad seem distasteful? If so, which?

- Which words seem weak or inappropriate? What replacements do you suggest?

- Is any information left out of the ad that you would like to know? If so, what?

- Does my ad need to be enlivened with graphics, charts, or photographs? What type would be effective?

- If you could change one thing about my advertisement, what would it be?

Review the responses of your partner. Then, incorporate changes into your ad, and review it again.

Timed Writing Hint

It is fine to cross out unnecessary words neatly when you revise your timed writing.

Get instant help! For assistance in replacing dull words, use the Word Bins, accessible from the menu bar, on-line or on CD-ROM.

8.5 Editing and Proofreading

Correct Use of *Your* and *You're*

Homophones—words that sound the same—are sometimes used incorrectly. For example, you might write the contraction *you're* instead of the possessive *your*. Read through your advertisement carefully to make sure that you have chosen the correct homophones.

EXAMPLE: These walking shoes are made for you're comfort.
CORRECT: These walking shoes are made for your comfort.

EXAMPLE: Your going to notice the cushioned insole.
CORRECT: You're going to notice the cushioned insole.

Grammar in Your Writing
Homophones

Homophones are words that sound the same but have different spellings and meanings. Some homophones that are commonly confused include the following:

It's	Its	
By	Buy	
Who's	Whose	
To	Too	Two

Find It in Your Reading Find a homophone in the advertisement on page 154. Then, write down the related homophones and their meanings.

Find It in Your Writing As you proofread your advertisement, check that you have written all homophones correctly.

For more on spelling homophones, see Chapter 30.

Editing and Proofreading • 163

Publishing and Presenting

1. If students' ads are for actual products (fund raising, upcoming events), help them think of places to share their ads (school, community center, churches, stores).

2. If the ads are for products the students are not actually promoting, discuss appropriate outlets (part of portfolio, school career fair).

ASSESS and CLOSE

Assessment

Teaching Resources: Scoring Rubrics on Transparency, Ch. 8; Writing Assessment and Portfolio Management; Formal Assessment, Ch. 8

1. Display the Scoring Rubric transparency and review the criteria in class.

2. Before students proceed with self-assessment, you may wish to review the Final Draft of the Student Work in Progress on page 165.

3. In addition to student self-assessment, you may wish to use the following assessment options:

   - score student ads yourself, using the rubric and scoring models from *Writing Assessment and Portfolio Management*.

   - review the Standardized Test Preparation Workshop on pages 170–171 and have students complete the practice items.

   - administer the Chapter 8 assessment from *Formal Assessment* in the Teaching Resources to measure students' grasp of the concepts presented.

8.6 Publishing and Presenting

Building Your Portfolio

Use the following suggestions for sharing your advertisement:

1. **Post It** If your advertisement is for a real product or service, get permission to post it throughout your school or in your community.

2. **Record It** Rework your advertisement for radio presentation. Add sound effects and tape-record your efforts. Play the ad for your peers.

Reflecting on Your Writing

Consider the experience of writing your advertisement. Then, answer the following questions, and record your responses in your portfolio.

- In the process of writing, what did you learn about how you relate to your audience?

- Which strategies for prewriting, drafting, revising, or editing might you recommend to a friend?

🖥 Internet Tip

To see an advertisement scored with this rubric, go on-line:
PHSchool.com
Enter Web Code:
eek-1001

Rubric for Self-Assessment

Use the following criteria to evaluate your advertisement.

	Score 4	Score 3	Score 2	Score 1
Audience and Purpose	Presents effective slogan; clearly addresses persuasive task	Presents good slogan; addresses persuasive task	Presents slogan; minimally addresses persuasive task	Does not present slogan; shows lack of attention to persuasive task
Organization	Uses clear, consistent organizational strategy	Uses clear organizational strategy with few inconsistencies	Uses inconsistent organizational strategy; creates illogical presentation	Demonstrates lack of organizational strategy; creates confusing presentation
Elaboration	Successfully combines words and images to provide convincing, unified support for a position	Combines words and images to provide unified support for a position	Includes some words or images that detract from a position	Uses words and images that do not support a position
Use of Language	Successfully communicates an idea through clever use of language; includes very few mechanical errors	Conveys an idea through adequate use of language; includes few mechanical errors	Misuses language and lessens impact of ideas; includes many mechanical errors	Demonstrates poor use of language and confuses meaning; includes many mechanical errors

164 • Advertisement

☑ ONGOING ASSESSMENT: Assess Mastery

Use one of the following options to assess final drafts of students' persuasive advertisements.

Self-Assessment Ask students to score their advertisements using the rubric provided. Then, have students write a single paragraph reflecting on the most valuable thing they learned in completing this advertisement.	**Teacher Assessment** You may wish to use the rubric and the scoring models provided in *Writing Assessment and Portfolio Management* in the Teaching Resources to score students' advertisements.

8.7 Student Work
IN PROGRESS

FINAL DRAFT

Ever Chapa
La Joya High School
La Joya, Texas

BASH AT THE LAKE

Come join the fun at the first annual **BASH AT THE LAKE.**

Learn about various colleges and what they have to offer **YOU.**

Get the *real scoop* on local scholarships and grants.

Attention all seniors!

Representatives from more than ninety colleges!
Five hot bands!
Food!

Westside Lake Park
Saturday, August 9, 2000
12:00 P.M. to 8:00 P.M.

Free of charge for everyone

High-school seniors are encouraged to attend.
(10 Senior Points for those who come!!!)
Parents are also encouraged to attend.

Capital letters emphasize the main idea.

Details that make the event more attractive are featured to the side of the main ad.

Colorful text emphasizes the time and place of the event.

Ever used boldface text to highlight the fact that the event is free.

Colloquial terms like "real scoop" appeal to the audience of high-school students.

Final Draft

1. Help students understand how this advertisement uses the key elements of ad creation.
   - The topic is of interest to target audience.
   - The ad engages the reader and relates the important details.
   - A variety of sentences and phrases keeps it interesting.
2. Explain that carefully chosen words and an appealing layout contribute to making this advertisement effective.
3. Ask students whether there are any revisions that would make the ad more appealing, the language more vivid, or the details clearer. How might theses suggestions improve their own advertisements?

Real-World Connection

Most invitations to big events, such as fundraisers, political rallies, or business conferences, are written by event planners. An event planner's job is to make an event successful. The goal of the invitations is to get as many people as possible to attend. Ask students what they would look for in sample invitations if they were hiring an event planner. (Sample invitations should be clear, vivid, error free, appropriate for the event, and appealing to the eye).

Integrating Language Skills

Students should know that ads often don't use complete sentences. Point out that full sentences and fragments alternate in the Final Draft. Ask students to explain why the writer (and real advertisers) use fragments. (Fragments keep ads from being too wordy. Fragments make it easier for the reader to notice important details.)

1. To create media products, including a flyer, to engage a specific audience
2. To use prewriting strategies to generate ideas
3. To distinguish the purposes of various media forms

Step-by-Step Teaching Guide

Flyer

Teaching Resources: Writing Support Transparencies, 8-D; Writing Support Activity Book, 8-1

1. Have students give examples of flyers they have seen in the mail, on billboards, or in school hallways. Discuss the kinds of things that are advertised. Point out that flyers are often used to promote a service or an upcoming event.

2. Refer students to the example on page 166 and use it to discuss the elements of a good flyer: it immediately identifies the "product," includes all the necessary information, and uses organization and design elements (particularly type size) to highlight key elements and get the reader's attention.

3. Point out that, as with most flyers, the message is dependent on organization, information, and appropriate highlighting of key elements, rather than the glitz, gloss, and artwork of more expensive advertising forms.

4. Suggest that students review strategies they've learned in this chapter before creating their own flyers. See the chart below.

continued

Critical Viewing

Connect Students may suggest that a flyer could attract visitors to specific exhibitors and job opportunities.

Connected Assignment
Flyer

A flyer is an advertisement that is printed on a sheet of paper. Flyers vary in complexity from a simple photocopied piece of paper to a high-gloss, printed color piece, but the basic features are the same. Flyers are delivered by hand or through the mail. They convey current information about a product or service and seek to grab readers' attention on the spot.

An example of a flyer appears below. Use the writing process tips suggested on the next page to create your own flyer.

▲ **Critical Viewing**
What use would a flyer, such as the one shown here, serve at a job fair? **[Connect]**

GET YOUR CAR WASHED!

On Saturday, May 15th, come over to Yallum High School to get your car washed.

From 10:00A.M. to 4:00P.M.
South Parking Lot
(behind the stadium)
Each car wash costs $5.00

Proceeds benefit the High-School Marching Band.
We need: New uniforms, Sheet music, Money for our band trip...

Sponsored by the Music Boosters Assoc.

166 • Advertisement

✓ ONGOING ASSESSMENT: Prerequisite Skills

Students may find the following resources from Chapter 8 particularly helpful in completing their flyers.

In the Textbook	Teaching Resources	Technology
Gathering Details for an Event, Section 8.2 Providing Elaboration, Section 8.3	*Writing Support Transparencies,* 8-A–B	*Writing and Grammar* Interactive Text, Sections 8.2–3

Prewriting Skim through the handouts you've received at school this week, or ask the office to show you some examples. Then, think about activities or events that you might need to advertise to others. Also, think about products or services available that classmates might find useful.

Having no more space available than a page printed on both sides, you must give your message a focus. Use an inverted pyramid chart to narrow your topic until you can state the main message in one sentence. Then, brainstorm for adjectives and vivid verbs that capture the excitement of your product or service.

Mindy's is a great new restaurant serving our town. It offers wonderful burgers and shakes. Its prices are reasonable, and the service is terrific.

Mindy's has great food and service.

Eat at Mindy's.

Drafting People will look at your flyer for just a second before deciding to read it or toss it. Grab them in that instant with powerful language and engaging visuals. Reshape your prewriting sentence into a slogan or headline. Then, use sound devices such as alliteration (repeated initial consonants) to help your message stick with your readers.

Revising and Editing Study your flyer from a distance to make sure that its visual appeal works. Make sure that your text is large enough to read quickly and that all the key information is easily accessible. Add vivid verbs that lend zest to your language and present your product or service in the most positive light.

Publishing and Presenting Photocopy your flyer. Then, hand out copies to friends, and get their reactions to the information printed on it.

 Technology Tip

Become familiar with the features of your word-processing software. Then, use features like centering text, boldfacing, and adding bullets to enhance the appearance of your flyer.

5. Display Transparency 8-D to show students how they can use an inverted pyramid strategy to help them narrow their ideas. Remind them that all the information with which they start may still appear on the flyer, but "getting to the point" gives them a key element to highlight.

6. Hand out copies of the activity sheet (8-1), or have students create their own pyramid charts, using them to focus the topics of the product or service they want to advertise.

7. Students might get ideas for catchy phrases and visuals by looking at magazine advertisements and television commercials. Discuss current advertisements that they find especially effective, and why.

8. Post the finished flyers around the room and discuss initial reactions to them. If flyers have been created for real services or events, encourage students to find other places to post them.

1. To create a print ad to engage specific audiences
2. To analyze ideas and cultures as represented in various media
3. To investigate the source of a media production

Recognizing Theater Connections

1. Discuss with students why modern writers might turn for inspiration to a millennia-old playwright, such as Plautus. Ask them to think about the ideas, truths, or theatrical elements that would appeal to audiences of any era (love, bravery, treachery, justice, action, human foibles, happy endings, and so on).

2. Students might want to find additional information about the playwright Plautus, as well as descriptions of his plays, to share with the class.

3. Students might wish to locate illustrations of the Roman Forum or Romulus' tomb to help them visualize the surroundings that influenced Plautus.

4. To prepare for writing a film or play advertisement, have students bring in examples from newspapers or magazines. In small groups, students can discuss the elements they might want to consider for their own advertisements.

Viewing and Representing

Activity Give interested students the opportunity to present and/or post their advertisements in class.

Critical Viewing

Speculate Students might note that the characters' costumes and the setting suggest that the play is probably set in ancient Roman times. Ask whether anything in the photo suggests that the play is a comedy.

Spotlight on the Humanities

Recognizing Theater Connections

Focus on Theater: *A Funny Thing Happened on the Way to the Forum*

Before a play or film opens, it is usually backed by an ad campaign promoting it to guarantee that an audience will support it. In fact, one of the most successful forms of persuasion is advertising—convincing an audience that a performance or product is something they must see or purchase. Winner of five Tony Awards, the musical *A Funny Thing Happened on the Way to the Forum* opened on Broadway on May 8, 1962. Based on the writings of the ancient Roman playwright Plautus, the music and lyrics were written by Stephen Sondheim, and the book was created by Burt Shevelove and Larry Gelbart. The writers, hoping to give Broadway a taste of what once delighted ancient Roman audiences, carefully studied all twenty-one of Plautus' surviving comedies and then created their own original story, drawing characters and situations freely from many of the old scripts.

▲ Critical Viewing
Judging from this photograph, what sort of play is *A Funny Thing Happened on the Way to the Forum?* Explain. [**Speculate**]

Literature Connection Born Titus Maccius Plautus (ca. 254–184 B.C.), this Roman playwright first worked as a stagehand. He may have acted, also. At least 130 plays were attributed to Plautus, and 21 of these were authentically his own.

Art Connection The Forum Romanum in the city of Rome lies between the Palatine and Capitoline hills. Used as a location for public meetings and courts of law, the Forum was also a center for shopping and open-air markets. It was also the site of several monuments. Among the monuments lies the tomb of Romulus, the founder of Rome.

Persuasive Writing Activity: Advertisement for Current Play or Film

A Funny Thing Happened on the Way to the Forum enjoyed another successful run on Broadway in 1997 and 1998, thanks to its reputation and an aggressive advertising campaign that boasted top-name celebrities in the title roles. Choose a film or play that is currently being performed, and write an advertisement for it that will be sure to bring audiences flocking to the theaters.

Media and Technology Skills

Using Technology to Extend Meaning

Activity: Enhance a Print Piece

In bookstores, thousands of books compete for your attention. An effective cover can make one book stand out from the crowd. You can apply visual strategies to enhance any writing project. A word processor or page-layout program can help you to increase visual impact and appeal. To enhance an advertisement, brochure, or other writing, become familiar with the features offered by the programs you use most frequently.

Think About It Choose a writing project that you would like to publish in a more elaborate format. Think about how visual imagery can help you reach a wider audience, and choose a relevant format. For example, you might turn a personal advertisement into a brochure or a short story into a small booklet.

Lay It Out Choose a layout that is appropriate for the format you have chosen. You might consider these layouts:

- newspaper style, with headlines and several articles per page
- magazine style, with headlines and one article per page
- brochures, created by folding two-sided printouts
- newsletter style, with headlines and two or three columns of text

Display It After choosing your layout, decide what type styles, or fonts, you will use. Some fonts are designed to be used for headlines; others are best used for running text. Headline fonts are often more detailed or ornate; text fonts should be clear and easy to read even in small sizes.

Example Font

Example Font

Illustrate It You can import a variety of images to add visual appeal. Consider importing digital photographs or artwork. You can create your own artwork using a graphics program, or you can find ready-made art in a clip art source.

Printing Formats

You can turn an 8-1/2" x 11" sheet of paper into a professional-looking brochure by printing on both sides and then folding it. If you are planning to fold your work, lay out the columns so that they will follow the correct order when folded.

► Lesson Objectives

1. To refine selected pieces to publish
2. To use technology for aspects of creating, revising, editing, and publishing texts
3. To use a range of techniques to plan and create a media text

Step-by-Step Teaching Guide

Technology and Meaning

1. Bring to class a few examples of the layouts described in the textbook, including magazines, newspapers, brochures, and newsletters. Have students compare and contrast each type of layout, and then discuss how each layout suits the particular purpose of the information being conveyed.

2. Point out the examples of fonts pictured in the student text. Encourage students to check the fonts list on their computers, to find out what fonts are available to them for this project, and which ones they like. Remind them that fonts need to be readable as well as eye-catching, so some of the wilder fonts won't work well for the body of the text.

3. Once students have chosen the writing project they want to publish in a new format, they should decide which layout best suits its purpose. Remind students to consider their intended audience, as well.

4. Students might enjoy sharing their finished products with classmates. If possible, have them bring the writing project in its original form, for comparison.

Lesson Objectives

1. To distinguish the purposes of various media forms, such as advertisements
2. To deconstruct media to get the main idea of the message's content
3. To evaluate and critique the persuasive techniques of media messages

Step-by-Step Teaching Guide

Analyzing Persuasive Texts

Teaching Resources: Standardized Test Preparation Workbook, pp. 15–16

1. Go over the bulleted evaluating strategies with students. Students may need to review the following terms:
   - *Overgeneralization* (an inference too broad or sweeping for its limited supporting evidence)
   - *Loaded language* (words or phrases that have strong emotional connotations, either positive or negative)
   - *Circular reasoning* (an argument that attempts to prove its point by restating it in other words)
   - *Questionable cause-and-effect reasoning* (statements that mistake a time-order relationship for a cause-and-effect relationship)
   - *Either/or argument* (oversimplified argument that offers a choice of only two extremes)
   - *Bandwagon appeal* (a statement based on the desire of people to conform or be part of a group)

2. Emphasize to students that uncovering the whole truth in an advertisement usually takes careful reading, with special attention to specific words and phrases.

3. Discuss the sample test items and their answers and explanations. Tell students that the key to analyzing persuasive texts effectively is to read carefully and objectively.

4. Assign the practice test. After checking students' answers, discuss any items that gave students trouble.

Standardized Test Preparation Workshop

Analyzing Persuasive Texts

Standardized test questions often measure your ability to evaluate an advertisement. All advertisements, whether for political campaigns or consumer products, have the same goal—to get you to act. As an educated reader, you must look past the attempts to persuade to find the factual, relevant information. The following methods will help you evaluate an advertisement:

- Search for facts.
- See whether the argument or claim is supported.
- Check for missing information, vague statements, or partial truths.
- Recognize false conclusions and oversimplifications, such as overgeneralizations, loaded language, circular reasoning, questionable cause-and-effect statements, either/or arguments, or bandwagon appeals.

The following sample test items will give you practice with these types of questions.

Test Tip

When evaluating an advertisement, it is just as important to consider whether information has been left out as it is to weigh information that has been included.

Sample Test Items	Answers and Explanations
Directions: Read the passage, and then choose the best answer to each question. This week, only at Athletes' World locations in Dallas: *Striker* Athletic Shoes on sale! With *Striker* on your feet, you'll be a starter on your team! **1** What important information has been left out of this advertisement? A name brand of the shoes B time frame of the sale C name of the store where the sale is D price of shoes on sale	The correct answer is *D*. The price of the shoes is not given in the ad.
2 What type of unreasonable appeal does "With *Striker* on your feet, you'll be a starter on your team!" exemplify? A circular reasoning B bandwagon appeal C questionable cause and effect D overgeneralization	The correct answer is *C*. The ad implies that the reader need only wear *Striker* shoes to be one of the best players on a sports team.

170 • Advertisement

TEST-TAKING TIP

When analyzing a persuasive advertisement, students should be alert to clues that identify overgeneralizations, bandwagon appeals, and loaded language. Statements like "neglecting our children" are loaded. Who wants to say that they are neglecting their children? Words like "a new craze" make it sound like "everyone is doing it," which makes this a bandwagon appeal.

In addition, there is a decided absence of hard facts or useful information in the item. This also should make a reader look further into an issue. Perhaps everything that is said is true, but the ad doesn't prove it. Suggest that students jot down questions as they read, noting information that should reasonably be included but isn't.

▶ **Practice 1** **Directions:** Read the passage, and then choose the letter of the best answer to each question.

There is a new craze hitting Harleville: RECYCLE TODAY!!! Before you throw away that soup can, before you trash that newspaper—think about our children. Money earned from recycling could be put toward a new city park. The Mayor, the City Council, and the Police Chief have all endorsed our new recycling program. Remember, neglecting our environment is neglecting our children! Let's all RECYCLE TODAY to give our children a new park tomorrow.

1 You can tell the writer is
  A indifferent to recycling
  B in favor of recycling
  C opposed to recycling
  D trying to endorse town officials

2 Which of the following is an example of loaded language—appealing to readers' fears or prejudices?
  F "... and the Police Chief have all endorsed ... "
  G "Money earned from recycling could be put toward a new city park."
  H "... neglecting our environment is neglecting our children!"
  J none of the above

3 The author implies that the town of Harleville is
  A refusing to recycle
  B building a recycling plant
  C earning money from recycling
  D none of the above

4 Which of the following statements is an example of a partial truth?
  F "Let's all RECYCLE TODAY to give our children a new park tomorrow."
  G "before you trash that newspaper— think about our children"
  H "The City Council, . . . all endorsed our new recycling program."
  J none of the above

5 The statement, "There is a new craze hitting Harleville: RECYCLE TODAY!!!" is an example of which of the following types of persuasive reasoning?
  A circular reasoning
  B either/or argument
  C questionable cause and effect
  D bandwagon appeal

6 What fact does the author state in the article?
  F Money from recycling will be spent a new park.
  G Everyone in Harleville recycles.
  H The Police Chief has endorsed Harleville's recycling program.
  J A large amount of money will be earned from the recycling program.

7 What conclusion is NOT supported by information given in the article?
  A Some citizens of Harleville are recycling.
  B The recycling program includes tin cans and newspapers.
  C The author would like to raise money to build new parks.
  D The mayor of Harleville wants to use recycling revenue to build new parks.

Answer Key

▶ **Practice 1**

1. B
2. H
3. C
4. F
5. D
6. H
7. D

Customize for
Less Advanced Students

Students may need more help recognizing types of faulty logic, such as bandwagon appeal or circular reasoning, in order to evaluate a persuasive advertisement. You may want to do the practice test as a group, discussing each of the questions and how students might recognize the best answers. You may also want to discuss how specific items could have been written to make them more precise.

Customize for
More Advanced Students

Ask students to discuss the connotations of the following words: *craze, children, neglecting.* Ask students to describe their reaction to the use of capitalization and exclamation points. Are they effective, and what do they convey? Then ask students, if the ad writer had included images with the ad, what they think he or she might have chosen.

Chapter 9 Time and Resource Manager

In-Depth Lesson Plan

	LESSON FOCUS	PRINT AND MEDIA RESOURCES
DAY 1	**Introduction to Comparison-and-Contrast Essays** Students learn key elements of a comparison-and-contrast essay and analyze the Model From Literature. (pp. 172–175/H106–107)	*Writers at Work* DVD, Exposition *Writing and Grammar* Interactive Text, Ch. 9, Introduction
DAY 2	**Prewriting** Students choose and narrow a topic, consider their audience and purpose, and gather information. (pp. 176–179/H108–111)	**Teaching Resources** *Writing Support Transparencies*, 9-A–D; *Writing Support Activity Book*, 9-1–2; *Topic Bank for Heterogeneous Classes*, Ch. 9 *Writing and Grammar* Interactive Text, Section 9.2
DAY 3	**Drafting** Students organize their ideas and write their first drafts. (pp. 180–181/H112–113)	**Teaching Resources** *Writing Support Transparencies*, 9-E–F; *Writing Support Activity Book*, 9-3 *Writing and Grammar* Interactive Text, Section 9.3
DAY 4	**Revising** Students revise their drafts in terms of overall structure, paragraphs, sentences, and word choice. (pp. 182–186/H114–118)	**Teaching Resources** *Writing Support Transparencies*, 9-G–I *Writing and Grammar* Interactive Text, Section 9.4
DAY 5	**Editing and Proofreading; Publishing and Presenting** Students check their work for accuracy and correctness and present their final drafts. (pp. 187–188/H119–120)	**Teaching Resources** *Scoring Rubrics on Transparency*, Ch. 9; *Writing Assessment and Portfolio Management; Formal Assessment*, Ch. 9 *Writing and Grammar* Interactive Text, Sections 9.5–6

Accelerated Lesson Plan

	LESSON FOCUS	PRINT AND MEDIA RESOURCES
DAY 1	**Introduction Through Drafting** Students review characteristics of comparison-and-contrast writing, select topics, and write drafts. (pp. 172–181/H106–113)	**Teaching Resources** *Writing Support Transparencies*, 9-A–F; *Writing Support Activity Book*, 9-1–3 *Writing and Grammar* Interactive Text, Ch. 9, Introduction through Section 9.3
DAY 2	**Revising Through Presenting** Students work individually or with peers to revise, edit, and proofread their work for presentation. (pp. 182–188/H114–120)	**Teaching Resources** *Writing Support Transparencies*, 9-G–I; *Scoring Rubrics on Transparency*, Ch. 9; *Writing Assessment and Portfolio Management; Formal Assessment*, Ch. 9 *Writing and Grammar* Interactive Text, Sections 9.4–6

Options for Adapting Lesson Plans

HOMEWORK

Have students complete any stage of the lesson for homework.

FEATURES

Extend coverage with Connected Assignment (p. 191/H121), Spotlight on the Humanities (p. 192), Media and Technology Skills (p. 193), and the Standardized Test Preparation Workshop (p. 194).

TECHNOLOGY

Students can complete any stage of the lesson on the computer, using *Writing and Grammar* Interactive Text or a word-processing program. Have them print out their completed work.

Writing and Grammar Handbook Alignment

Page numbers in Step-by-Step Teaching Guides in this Teacher's Edition refer to pages from the full student text. Handbook page references, indicated with this icon 🖥, are provided in Time and Resource Manager boxes and at the bottom of each Teacher's Edition page.

INTEGRATED SKILLS COVERAGE

Integrating Grammar
Conjunctions, SE p. 185/🖥117
Punctuating Compound Sentences, SE p. 187/🖥119;
ATE p. 187

Reading/Writing Connection
Reading Strategy: Recognize Patterns, SE p. 174
Writing Application, SE p. 175

Viewing and Representing
Critical Viewing, SE pp. 172, 174, 181, 189, 192/🖥106, 113
Examining Cultures Through Film, SE p. 192
Analyze Relationships Between Media, SE p. 193

Technology Skills SE pp. 179, 187, 188, 193/🖥111, 119, 120

Research Skills ATE pp. 179, 190

Vocabulary Skills ATE p. 184

ASSESSMENT SUPPORT

Standardized Test Preparation Workshop, SE p. 194; ATE p. 186

Standardized Test Preparation Workbook, pp. 17–18

Scoring Rubrics on Transparency, Ch. 9

Formal Assessment, Ch. 9

Writing Assessment and Portfolio Management

MEETING INDIVIDUAL NEEDS

Less Advanced Students ATE pp. 178, 195. See also Ongoing Assessments ATE pp. 177, 181, 183.

ESL Students ATE pp. 177, 184, 190

More Advanced Students ATE pp. 185, 193

Spatial Learners ATE p. 195

BLOCK SCHEDULING

Pacing Suggestions
For 90-minute Blocks
• Have students complete the Prewriting and Drafting stages in a single period.
• Focus one class period on Revising and Editing and Publishing and Presenting. Allow at least 30 minutes for peer revision.

Resources for Varying Instruction
• *Writing and Grammar* Interactive Text A 90-minute block provides an ideal opportunity for students to work on the computer.
• *Writers at Work* DVD Show the Exposition segment in class.

Professional Development Support
• *How to Manage Instruction in the Block* This teaching resource provides management and activity suggestions.

MEDIA AND TECHNOLOGY

For the Student
• *Writing and Grammar* Interactive Text, Ch. 9
• *On-line Exercise Bank,* 18.2

For the Teacher
• *Writers at Work* DVD, Exposition
• **Teacher**EXPRESS™ CD-ROM

WRITING AND GRAMMAR ON-LINE

Interactive Text (On-line or on CD-ROM)
• Easily navigable instruction with interactive Revision Checkers
• Full use of e-rater™, the essay-scoring system (on-line only)

Companion Web Site PHSchool.com
• Scoring rubrics with models (use Web Code eek-1001)

See the Go On-line! **feature, SE p. iii.**

LITERATURE CONNECTIONS

Related selections from *Prentice Hall Literature, Penguin Edition,* Grade 10:

Professional Models Book Review, Franco Ferrucci, SE p. 175

Book Review, Anatole Broyard, SE p. 175

Topic Bank Options "Touch the Top of the World," Erik Weihenmayer, SE p. 177/🖥109

Swimming to Antarctica, Lynne Cox, SE p. 177/🖥109

Lesson Objectives

1. To write a comparison-and-contrast essay appropriate to audience and purpose

2. To analyze text structures such as compare and contrast for how they influence understanding

3. To read to appreciate a writer's craft and to discover models for writing

4. To use prewriting strategies to generate ideas, develop voice, and plan

5. To develop and revise drafts in terms of structure, paragraphs, sentences, and word choice

6. To represent information in a variety of ways such as graphics, conceptual maps, and learning logs

7. To edit and proofread to ensure standard English usage and grammar

8. To evaluate writing for both mechanics and content

9. To refine a comparison-and-contrast essay for publication

Critical Viewing

Analyze Shoppers might be comparing style, size, price, fabric, or overall quality.

Exposition
Comparison-and-Contrast Essay

▲ **Critical Viewing**
What sort of features or qualities might these shoppers be comparing and contrasting? **[Analyze]**

Comparing and Contrasting in Everyday Life

Comparing and contrasting are processes that you perform every day. Whether you're deciding which movie to see or which jacket to buy, you analyze the similarities and differences between the choices and make judgments about the positive qualities or shortcomings of each one.

Developing your ability to compare and contrast is useful any time you have to make a major decision. When the time comes to decide which college to attend or which job offer to accept, being able to clearly assess your options will help you take the best possible course of action.

172 • Exposition

⏱ TIME AND RESOURCE MANAGER

Resources
Technology: *Writers at Work* DVD, Exposition; *Writing and Grammar* Interactive Text, Ch. 9

Using the Full Student Edition	Using the Handbook 🄷
• Read and discuss pp. 172–173 in class. • Read the Model From Literature (pp.174–175) in class and use it to teach patterns of organization. • Discuss examples of comparison-and-contrast writing you or your students bring to class.	• Read and discuss pp. 106–107 in class. • Discuss examples of comparison-and-contrast writing you or your students bring to class.

What Is a Comparison-and-Contrast Essay?

To *compare* is to show how two or more things are similar. To *contrast* is to show how two or more things are different. An essay exploring the similarities and differences between two or more subjects is a **comparison-and-contrast essay.**

Most effective comparison-and-contrast essays contain

- two or more subjects that are being compared and contrasted.
- details that reveal the similarities and differences between the subjects.
- transitions that make relationships between the subjects clear.
- an effective structure, such as point-by-point or subject-by-subject organization.

To preview the criteria on which your comparison-and-contrast essay may be evaluated, see the Self-Assessment Rubric on page 188.

Types of Comparison-and-Contrast Essays

Topics for a comparison-and-contrast essay range widely. Following are some examples:

- significant events from history
- works of art, literature, or music
- lives and achievements of historical figures
- effects of different laws or policies

PREVIEW
Student Work
IN PROGRESS

Follow the progress of Emily Agy, a student at Pleasant Valley High School, in Pleasant Valley, Iowa, as she drafts a newspaper article that explores the similarities and differences between life in the United States and life in England. The completed article appears at the end of the chapter.

Writers in ACTION

Journalist and author Joseph Epstein considers himself lucky to have discovered at an early age that essay-writing was his preferred form of expression. He reveals the following insight about what makes essay-writing so appealing:

"Writing an essay has for me tended to be an act of self-discovery. By this I mean that I come to the writing of an essay not knowing what I think of the subject, except in an [unformed] way; or if I believe I know what I think, the writing itself leads me into aspects of the subject whose importance or even existence I hadn't earlier recognized."

PREPARE and ENGAGE

Interest GRABBER Ask students to quickly indicate by a show of hands which they would prefer in each instance if given the following choices:

- *cola drink or fruit juice?*
- *beach vacation or mountain vacation?*
- *rice or potatoes?*

Next, ask for a student to volunteer the reasons behind one of his or her choices. The answer will most likely include a comparison of the features of the two options. If it does not, ask the student to tell what the two options have in common and what makes one more appealing than the other. Explain that in this chapter, they will learn to incorporate such comparisons and contrasts in essay form.

Activate Prior Knowledge

Explain to students that we compare and contrast information as we make choices in our lives. We weigh the options and try to distinguish among them as we plan what to wear, eat, or study. Since many students will receive their driver's licenses soon, ask them to compare the relative advantages of cars and trucks. Ask them to list similarities and differences between the two. Have students share their results. (Students may mention cost, mileage, passenger space, vehicle image, and cargo space.)

More About the Writer

Joseph Epstein was born and raised in Chicago, Illinois. He has published more than 1,700 essays. He was editor of *The American Scholar* for twenty-two years and has lectured at Northwestern University since 1974. When recently asked why the essay form is thriving at the moment, he responded, "because there are a number of people who are good at [it]. . . Then again, [it] may have something to do with the diminishing national attention span."

Reading: Recognize Patterns

Explain to students that looking for organizational patterns in someone else's writing will help them with their own writing. Have them skim the essay to determine that Zinsser organized his evidence chronologically and in a point-by-point manner.

Step-by-Step Teaching Guide

Engage Students Through Literature

1. After reading the essay, ask the students the following questions.

   Whose primary job is that of writing?

   What is Dr. Brock's primary job?

   What is Dr. Brock's view of writing?

   What is the author's view of writing?

   What is the doctor's view of revising written work?

   What is the author's view?

2. Have students consider why the points of view differ. (The doctor writes as a hobby, so he takes it less seriously; the author writes for a living, so he is very concerned about writing well.)

Critical Viewing

Assess The fountain pen might be used for writing a letter or signing an important document.

9.1 Model From Literature

William Zinsser was for thirteen years an editor, critic, and editorial writer with the New York Herald Tribune. *He now teaches writing at the New School in New York City.*

Reading Writing Connection

Reading Strategy: Recognize Patterns Recognizing how material is organized can help you to understand and evaluate it. As you read this essay, look at each paragraph's first line to see if the essay is ordered chronologically or in order of importance.

Two Writing Processes

William Zinsser

A school in Connecticut once held "a day devoted to the arts," and I was asked if I would come and talk about writing as a vocation. When I arrived I found that a second speaker had been invited—Dr. Brock (as I'll call him), a surgeon who had recently begun to write and had sold some stories to magazines. He was going to talk about writing as an avocation. That made us a panel, and we sat down to face a crowd of students and teachers and parents, all eager to learn the secrets of our glamorous work.

Dr. Brock was dressed in a bright red jacket, looking vaguely bohemian, as authors are supposed to look, and the first question went to him. What was it like to be a writer?

He said it was tremendous fun. Coming home from an arduous day at the hospital, he would go straight to his yellow pad and write his tensions away. The words just flowed. It was easy. I then said that writing wasn't easy and wasn't fun. It was hard and lonely, and the words seldom just flowed.

Next Dr. Brock was asked if it was important to rewrite. Absolutely not, he said. "Let it all hang out," he told us, and whatever form the sentences take will reflect the writer at his most natural. I then said that rewriting is the essence of writing. I pointed out that professional writers rewrite their sentences over and over and then rewrite what they have rewritten.

▲ **Critical Viewing** For what type of writing might you use the type of pen pictured? Why? **[Assess]**

Early in the essay, it becomes apparent that Zinsser and Brock have different ideas about what it means to be a writer.

174 • Comparison-and-Contrast Essay

☑ ONGOING ASSESSMENT: Diagnose

Use one of the following options to diagnose students' current understanding of comparison-and-contrast essays.

Option 1 Ask each student to select an article from a newspaper, magazine, or textbook that compares and contrasts two or more things or ideas. Ask each student to draw a Venn diagram to represent the two things or ideas. Students who have trouble with this exercise may need extra support.	**Option 2** After they read the essay, have students write two short paragraphs: one that outlines Zinsser's views on writing, and one that outlines Brock's views. Review students' paragraphs and make sure they included at least three differences between the authors' points of view.

"What do you do on days when it isn't going well?" Dr. Brock was asked. He said he just stopped writing and put the work aside for a day when it would go better. I then said that the professional writer must establish a daily schedule and stick to it. I said that writing is a craft, not an art, and that the man who runs away from his craft because he lacks inspiration is fooling himself. He is also going broke.

"What if you're feeling depressed or unhappy?" a student asked. "Won't that affect your writing?"

Probably it will, Dr. Brock replied. Go fishing. Take a walk. Probably it won't, I said. If your job is to write every day, you learn to do it like any other job.

A student asked if we found it useful to circulate in the literary world. Dr. Brock said he was greatly enjoying his new life as a man of letters, and he told several stories of being taken to lunch by his publisher and his agent at Manhattan restaurants where writers and editors gather. I said that professional writers are solitary drudges who seldom see other writers.

"Do you put symbolism in your writing?" a student asked me.

"Not if I can help it," I replied. I have an unbroken record of missing the deeper meaning in any story, play or movie, and as for dance and mime, I have never had any idea of what is being conveyed.

"I *love* symbols!" Dr. Brock exclaimed, and he described with gusto the joys of weaving them through his work.

So the morning went, and it was a revelation to all of us. At the end Dr. Brock told me he was enormously interested in my answers—it had never occurred to him that writing could be hard. I told him I was just as interested in *his* answers—it had never occurred to me that writing could be easy. Maybe I should take up surgery on the side.

As for the students, anyone might think we left them bewildered. But in fact we probably gave them a broader glimpse of the writing process than if only one of us had talked. For there isn't any "right" way to do such personal work. There are all kinds of writers and all kinds of methods, and any method that helps you to say what you want to say is the right method for you. . . .

Reading \ Writing Connection

Writing Application: Use Patterns Before you draft your essay, decide on a method of organization to help your readers follow along.

Here, it becomes clear that Zinsser is comparing and contrasting the writing methods of two writers: himself and Dr. Brock.

Two book reviews written by Franco Ferrucci and Anatole Broyard comment on a work by Italo Calvino. The essays appear in *Prentice Hall Literature, Penguin Edition,* Grade 10.

Transitions such as "At the end" help readers follow Zinsser's thoughts.

The essay contains a clear and logical organization— point-by-point organization—that is consistent throughout.

Teaching From the Model

You can use this model as a way to illustrate point-by-point organization. Have students note how the point-by-point comparison structure is an effective way to arrange an argument made up of many ideas. It neatly conveys two different points of view without being confusing.

Connections With Literature

Ask students to find comparing and contrasting passages in the literary reviews by Franco Ferrucci and Anatole Broyard in *Prentice Hall Literature, Penguin Edition,* Grade 10.

More About the Writer

William Zinsser, a nonfiction writer and author of writing reference books, feels that after teaching writing for over thirty years, he is still learning and evolving as a writer. In the bestseller *On Writing Well,* he states, "A clear sentence is no accident. Few sentences come out right the first time, or even the third time." He also believes that no amount of time spent perfecting a paragraph or a sentence was ever wasted.

Reading\Writing Connection

Writing Application: Use Patterns

Review with students the structure of Zinsser's point-by-point organization. Explain to them that the choice between point-by-point and subject-by-subject will depend in large part on their purpose. Once committed to a particular pattern, they should use it consistently.

9.2 Prewriting

Choosing Your Topic

Choose two or more subjects to explore in a comparison-and-contrast essay. For help getting started, consider the strategies below:

Strategies for Generating Topics

1. **Freewrite** Freewrite for five minutes about recent decisions you have made. For example, have you recently purchased one brand of clothing over another brand? If so, why? Review your freewriting, and use an idea from it to form the basis of your comparison-and-contrast essay.

2. **List** First, choose a broad subject area, such as music, art, history, sports, or characters in a novel. Then, list items that come to mind within that subject area—your favorite examples or ones that you find particularly interesting. Finally, examine your list to find connections between the two or more items you recorded. Strong connections between items indicate that they might be effective subjects for a comparison-and-contrast essay. If so, choose those items and build your comparison-and-contrast essay around them. Here's an example:

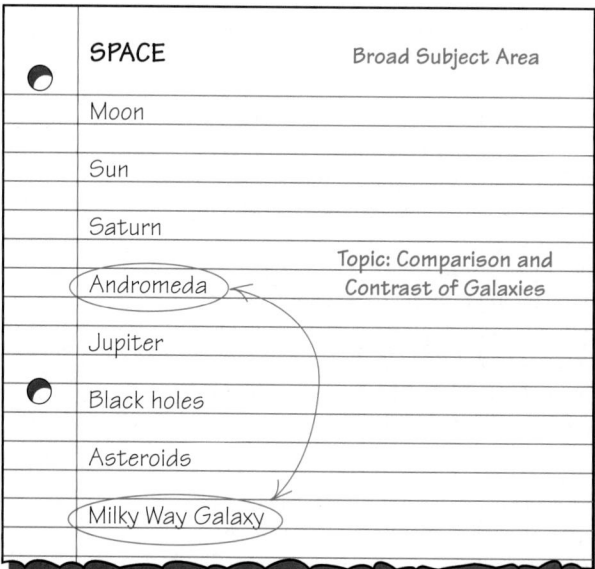

Get instant help! Freewrite or list your items using the Essay Builder, accessible from the menu bar, on-line or on CD-ROM.

176 • Comparison-and-Contrast Essay

⏱ TIME AND RESOURCE MANAGER

Resources
Print: *Writing Support Transparencies, 9-A–D; Writing Support Activity Book, 9-1–2*
Technology: *Writing and Grammar* Interactive Text, Section 9.2

Using the Full Student Edition	Using the Handbook Ⓗ
• Work through the Freewrite or Listing strategies with the class (p. 176).	• Work through the Freewrite or Listing strategies with the class (p. 108).
• Review the Topic Bank to help generate additional topics (p. 177).	• Review the Topic Bank to help generate additional topics (p. 109).
• Work through strategies for Considering Your Audience and Purpose and Gathering Details (pp. 178–179).	• Work through strategies for Considering Your Audience and Purpose and Gathering Details (pp. 110–111).

TOPIC BANK

For more specific suggestions for your comparison-and-contrast essay, consider the following ideas:

1. **Historical and Current Situations** Write an essay in which you compare and contrast an event or situation from history with one that is occurring today. For example, you could compare and contrast the Information Age with the Industrial Revolution.

2. **Two Products** Select two competing products that you would consider buying. In your essay, focus on the merits or shortcomings of each one. Finally, provide the reader with a recommendation about which one is the better product or the better value.

*Responding to Fine Art*

3. Study *Minor League*, by Clyde Singer. Then, write a comparison-and-contrast essay about two favorite athletes or baseball today compared with baseball of the 1920's.

Responding to Literature

4. Compare and contrast the excerpts from "Touch the Top of the World" by Erik Weihenmayer and "Swimming to Antarctica" by Lynne Cox. You can find both selections in *Prentice Hall Literature, Penguin Edition*, Grade 10. Focus on the similarities and differences in the narrators, the dangers they face, and the character traits they exhibit.

🕐 **Timed Writing Prompt**

5. Write an essay in which you explain to an eighth grader the differences and similarities between middle school and high school. Identify two ways in which middle school and high school are similar and two ways in which they are different. **(40 minutes)**

Minor League, Clyde Singer, Butler Institute of American Art

Responding to Fine Art

Minor League by Clyde Singer

Teaching Resources: Writing Support Transparencies, 9-B

1. Display Transparency 9-B and have students examine the artwork. Point out that the prompt suggests comparing and contrasting two favorite athletes or baseball's past with its present. Ask students what types of comparisons and contrasts could be made with these ideas.

2. Encourage students to volunteer additional topic ideas suggested by this piece of art. Students may include these topic ideas in their topic banks.

🕐 **Timed Writing Prompt**

• To help students remember their eighth-grade experiences, have each try to recall his or her class schedule from that year. Ask them to walk through that schedule briefly in their minds and think of teachers, fellow students, and other important people from that year.

• Suggest that students allow five minutes for prewriting, thirty minutes for writing, and five minutes for reviewing and proofreading.

Customize
for ESL Students

Some students may benefit from using sources that are written in their first language. Students who are recent arrivals to the United States may feel comfortable comparing and contrasting their lives before and after coming to the United States. Another approach is to have them work with their expectations before they came versus the reality they have experienced.

✓ **ONGOING ASSESSMENT: Monitor and Reinforce**

If your students are having difficulty coming up with topics, try one of the following strategies.

Option 1 If students have difficulty selecting a topic, offer suggestions from the *Topic Bank for Heterogeneous Classes* in the Teaching Resources.	**Option 2** Have students choose an idea from the Topic Bank on this page. You might assign all students to write a product comparison. When students turn in their work, the class can compile a "consumer's guide" and read each other's work.

Evaluating Your Topic

Evaluate your topic to make sure the subjects you have chosen share a valid basis for comparison. Don't compare dissimilar subjects, such as the work of an artist with that of a musician, unless you have a compelling reason for doing so.

Also, make sure that the focus of your comparison isn't too broad. For example, the complete body of work of two writers is too much to handle in a single essay; two of their works or characters is a much more manageable challenge.

Use a Venn Diagram

To evaluate whether or not your subjects have enough points of comparison and contrast, use a Venn diagram.

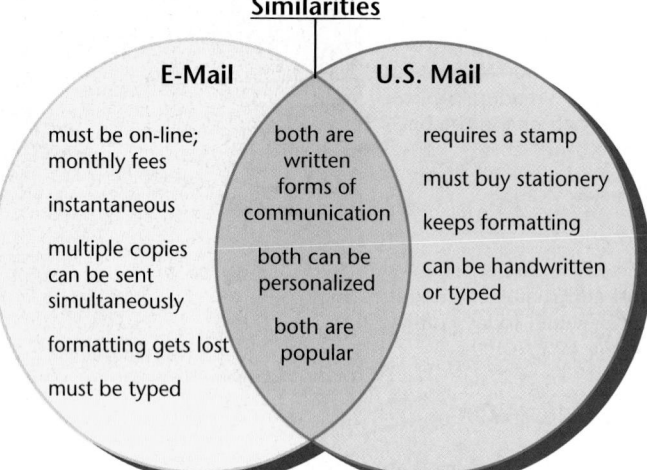

Similarities

E-Mail
- must be on-line; monthly fees
- instantaneous
- multiple copies can be sent simultaneously
- formatting gets lost
- must be typed

both are written forms of communication

both can be personalized

both are popular

U.S. Mail
- requires a stamp
- must buy stationery
- keeps formatting
- can be handwritten or typed

Considering Your Audience and Purpose

The audience and purpose for your essay will affect the type of information you include in it. Use these questions to help you consider your audience:

- Who will read your essay? Peers? A review panel?
- How familiar will they be with the topic? What aspects of the topic will be most interesting to them?

Use these questions to help you consider your purpose:

- What aspects of the topic are most important to emphasize?
- How will your audience use the information you are providing?

178 • Comparison-and-Contrast Essay

Try it out! Use the interactive Venn Diagram in **Section 9.2**, on-line or on CD-ROM.

Gathering Details

Gather enough details, descriptions, facts, examples, and reasons to provide your audience with a clear understanding of each subject being compared and to support your statements about the similarities and differences between them. Below are three ways to gather details:

Use Personal Experience

Experience counts. Use yours if you are comparing products, places, or things with which you have direct experience or if you are comparing works of art, literature, or music. For example, if you are comparing two products, use your own experience with each of them as evidence.

Use Primary Sources

Primary sources include original documents, such as scientific reports, company brochures, speeches, diary entries, journals, letters, or interview responses. Primary source material provides the words or works of people who were participants in or eyewitnesses to an event.

Use Secondary Sources

Secondary sources come from a published work in which the writer presents ideas about a subject based on evidence from several primary sources. For example, a biography of a president of the United States would be a secondary source. To write one, its author would draw upon primary sources, including letters from the president and interviews with people who worked with the president.

The following chart gives examples of different types of details gathered in various ways:

Subjects	Personal Experience	Primary Source	Secondary Source
two mountain-bike models	your experience riding each model	specification sheets from the manufacturers	newspaper article on this year's mountain-bike models
tornadoes and hurricanes	your experience with those types of weather phenomena	interviews with people who survived a category 5 hurricane	encyclopedia entry on hurricanes

🖳 Internet Tip

If you are comparing and contrasting two or more products in your essay, take advantage of official company Web sites. Many companies maintain Web sites with detailed information (including technical specifications) about their products. Use a search engine to find the company's URL, or web address.

Step-by-Step Teaching Guide

Prewriting: Gathering Details

Teaching Resources: Writing Support Transparencies, 9-D; Writing Support Activity Book, 9-2

1. Explain to students that, in order to demonstrate that there are both similarities and differences between their subjects, they will need to collect details—facts, examples, descriptions, ideas. Details provide credibility and give writers something to compare and contrast.

2. Display Transparency 9-D and go over with students the three basic sources students can use as support (personal experience, primary sources, secondary sources).

3. Explain that personal experience refers to one's own experience with the subject. Ask students which types of details can be gathered from personal experience, and which types have to be gathered from other sources.

4. Explain that there are advantages to both primary and secondary sources. Primary sources give you actual impressions and experiences of the people involved. Secondary sources may offer a broader scope by including the impressions of several people.

Integrating Research Skills

Allow students class time to use the school library or Internet to research their subjects. Have them print out the source material they plan to use so that it can be referenced in class. Let them know that, if both are available, primary sources will make their essays more credible than secondary sources.

⏱ TIME SAVERS!

 Writing Support Transparencies
Use the transparencies for Chapter 9 to facilitate the teaching of strategies.

 Writing Support Activity Book
Use the graphic organizers for Chapter 9 to facilitate student planning.

Drafting: Shaping Your Writing

Teaching Resources: Writing Support Transparencies, 9-E

1. Explain that comparison-and-contrast essays are generally organized either subject by subject or point by point.

2. Remind students of the truck vs. car activity they completed on p. 175. If a subject-by-subject organizational approach were used, the writer would have addressed all the information about one vehicle before addressing all the information about the other. If they chose a point-by-point organizational approach, the writer would make comparisons on an element-by-element basis, such as comparing ride, then price, then handling, and so on.

3. Display the transparency (9–E) for an example of point-by-point organization. Remind them that the Model From Literature, "Two Writing Processes," is also organized point by point.

4. Ask students to choose the method of organization appropriate to their purpose and begin drafting their essays.

9.3 Drafting

Shaping Your Writing

An effective comparison-and-contrast essay is usually organized in one of two ways:

Use Subject-by-Subject Organization

In a subject-by-subject organization, first discuss all the aspects of one subject and then discuss all the aspects of the second subject. For example, you could discuss figure skating first and then discuss hockey skating.

Use Point-by-Point Organization

In a point-by-point organization, each aspect or point of comparison and contrast is discussed in turn. You might, for instance, discuss the cost of product A and the cost of product B, and then discuss the appearance of product A and that of product B, and so on.

Timed Writing Hint

Make a quick outline based on the subject-by-subject or the point-by-point organization to plan your essay under timed conditions.

Interactive Textbook

Try it out! Use the interactive Point-by-Point activity in **Section 9.3**, on-line or on CD-ROM.

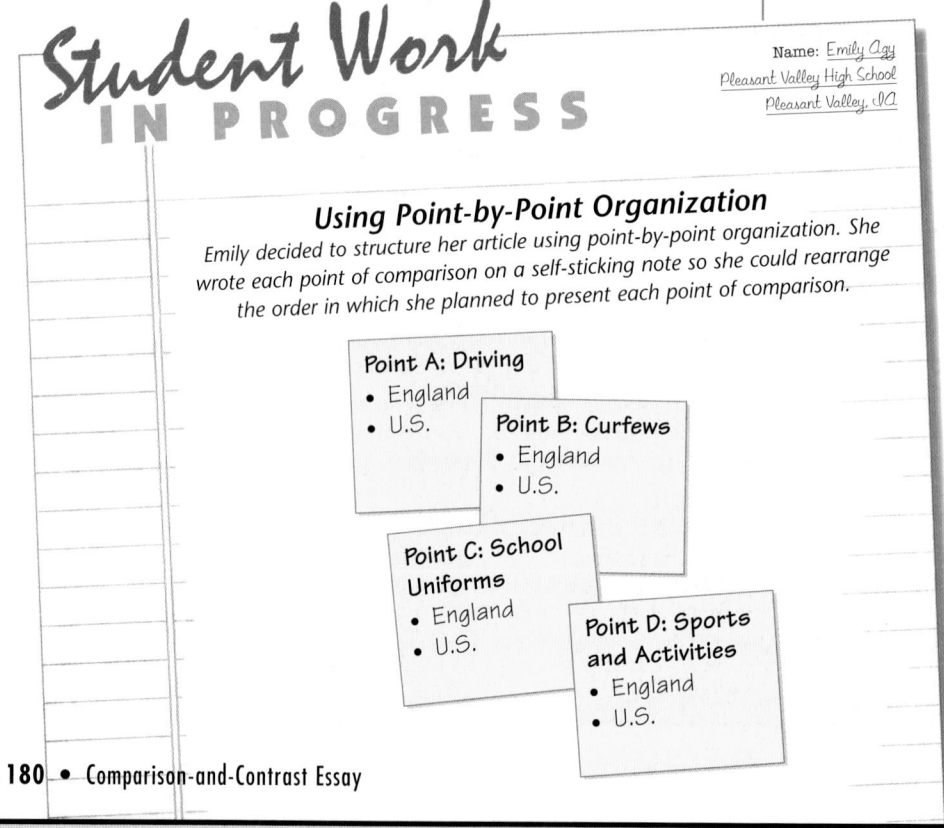

Student Work
IN PROGRESS

Name: *Emily Agy*
Pleasant Valley High School
Pleasant Valley, IA

Using Point-by-Point Organization

Emily decided to structure her article using point-by-point organization. She wrote each point of comparison on a self-sticking note so she could rearrange the order in which she planned to present each point of comparison.

Point A: Driving
- England
- U.S.

Point B: Curfews
- England
- U.S.

Point C: School Uniforms
- England
- U.S.

Point D: Sports and Activities
- England
- U.S.

180 • Comparison-and-Contrast Essay

⊘ TIME AND RESOURCE MANAGER

Resources
Print: *Writing Support Transparencies, 9-E–F; Writing Support Activity Book, 9-3*
Technology: *Writing and Grammar* Interactive Text, Section 9.3

Using the Full Student Edition	Using the Handbook⊞
• Review both subject-by-subject and point-by-point organizational forms (p. 180). • Have students write their comparison-and-contrast drafts in class. • Review elaboration strategies (p. 181).	• Review both subject-by-subject and point-by-point organizational forms (p. 112). • Have students write their comparison-and-contrast drafts in class. • Review elaboration strategies (p. 113).

Providing Elaboration
Give Examples

During the drafting process, make sure you provide support for each of the statements you make about your subjects. Elaborate on your points by providing specific details and examples that clarify the similarities and differences between the subjects.

Provide Facts

Provide facts to give your readers a clear understanding of each subject under discussion.

EXAMPLE: Bike 3000 is suitable for the toughest terrain. It is tough enough to handle boulder-strewn trails and has special gearing for handling steep inclines. Advanced brakes help riders make quick stops on wet surfaces.

Cite Quotations and Figures

Use quotations and statistical or numerical figures to lend authority to the points you make in your comparison-and-contrast essay.

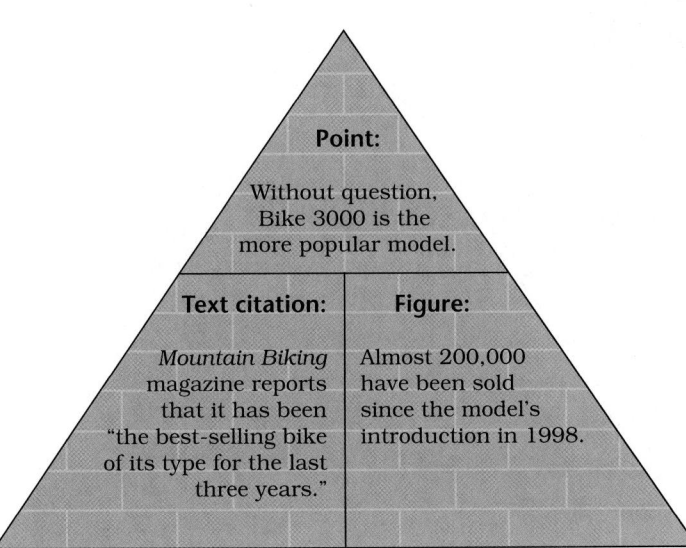

Point:

Without question, Bike 3000 is the more popular model.

Text citation:	**Figure:**
Mountain Biking magazine reports that it has been "the best-selling bike of its type for the last three years."	Almost 200,000 have been sold since the model's introduction in 1998.

▲ **Critical Viewing**
If you were thinking of purchasing a bike like the one shown, about what features would you want to know? **[Relate]**

Drafting • 181

Step-by-Step Teaching Guide

Drafting: Providing Elaboration

Teaching Resources: Writing Support Transparencies, 9-F; Writing Support Activity Book, 9-3

1. Emphasize that students must support all statements made about a subject with details or examples that prove the point. (Example: when stating that one car is more expensive than another, it is appropriate to cite the actual cost of each vehicle from a source such as the newspaper, the Internet, or a conversation with a dealer.)

2. Explain that details and examples about a subject are necessary for elaboration. Providing facts rather than opinions lends credibility to an argument. (An exception is an expert's opinion, such as a scientist's or scholar's observations.)

3. Display Transparency 9-F. Discuss how a text citation and sales figures are used to support the point.

Critical Viewing

Relate Students might mention price, size, durability, speed, and maintenance requirements of a bike.

☑ **ONGOING ASSESSMENT: Monitor and Reinforce**

If your students are having difficulty determining how to organize their drafts, try the following strategy.

Suggest that students try using an outline, a diagram, a chart, or a graph to organize evidence. Students who find that their material will fit in a time line, for example, may see that their drafts could be organized on a point-by-point basis, with comparisons and contrasts on the topic being made over time. Other students might construct a T-chart in which they can enter details about the subjects they are comparing. This can help students see similarities and differences that can help them construct a subject-by-subject organization.

Revising: Color-Coding by Subject

Teaching Resources: Writing Support Transparencies, 9-G

1. Remind students that organization is important in communicating ideas in an essay. Balance is also important; equally important points deserve equal treatment.

2. Display Transparency 9-G and show students how color-coding can be used to check organization and balance.

3. Have students read through their drafts, highlighting all information that pertains to one subject in one color and to the other subject in another color.

4. After students finish, have them examine the color pattern that results. Is the pattern balanced? Too much of one color may indicate that one subject is covered in greater depth than the other.

5. Explain that colors don't have to balance perfectly, but if one color predominates, the draft might be unbalanced or biased.

Integrating Grammar Skills

Transitions Point out to students that transitions can play an important part in making comparisons and contrasts. Transitional words or phrases help the reader realize that you are speaking about a different subject. *Now, on the other hand, in comparison, similarly,* and other words or phrases can help make transitions clear.

9.4 Revising

Revising Your Overall Structure

Because your essay has two or more subjects, it's particularly important to make sure that its structure is sound. If the structure of the essay is disorganized, a reader may become confused about which subject you are discussing. You also need to ensure that your essay is balanced—that equal space is devoted to each subject.

▶ **REVISION STRATEGY**
Color-Coding by Subject

Using a highlighter of one color, go through your essay and mark each detail you have included about subject A. Then, use a highlighter of a second color to mark each detail you have included about subject B. Examine the essay. Is there a lot of one color and just a little of the other? If so, add more information about the other subject.

Also, check to be sure that your essay consistently follows either point-by-point or subject-by-subject organization. If the essay is well structured, your highlighted body paragraphs will form a pattern of color.

Student Work IN PROGRESS

Name: Emily Agy
Pleasant Valley High School
Pleasant Valley, IA

Color-Coding to Check Structure

Emily highlighted information about England and the U.S. in different colors to make sure she had included sufficient details about both countries.

There are many differences when it comes to extracurricular school-sponsored activities. "Here there are all kinds of activities: football teams, field hockey teams, language clubs, etc. In England, we don't have extra-curricular activities at school. If you want to play sports, you have to find the time to do it yourself...."

182 • Comparison-and-Contrast Essay

⏲ TIME AND RESOURCE MANAGER

Resources
Print: *Writing Support Transparencies,* 9-G–I
Technology: *Writing and Grammar* Interactive Text, Section 9.4

Using the Full Student Edition	Using the Handbook🄷
• Work through revising strategies (pp.182–186) in class.	• Work through revising strategies (pp. 114–118) in class.
• Have students participate in Peer Review in class (p.186).	• Have students participate in Peer Review in class (p. 118).

Revising Your Paragraphs

Once you've evaluated the balance and structure of your essay, analyze your writing at the paragraph level. You may want to reorganize some of your paragraphs to give your essay variety and to make it more interesting to read. Read the following examples to come up with ways to structure your paragraphs.

▶ **REVISION STRATEGY**
Using TRI/PS/QA

TRI: *TRI* stands for Topic, Restatement, and Illustration.

Michael Jordan has had a serious impact on the American economy. Some estimate that the "Jordan Effect" reached as high as $10 billion dollars over the course of his career. If that seems high, consider $165 million in basketball tickets, the $230 million worldwide gross of the movie he starred in, and almost $3 billion in Jordan-related merchandise.

> Topic
> Restatement
> Illustration

PS: *PS* stands for Problem and Solution. In this kind of structure, both a problem and a solution are presented.

> PROBLEM

A mountain bike must be able to withstand repeated bumps and jolts as it navigates the trails. Bike 3000 handles this requirement by incorporating a special frame geometry that disperses shocks more efficiently than conventional bikes.

> SOLUTION

QA: *QA* stands for Question and Answer. Using this organization, a paragraph poses and answers a question.

> QUESTION

How did Tiger Woods gain so much acclaim, so quickly? The answer is a stunning string of victories in both his amateur and professional careers.

> ANSWER

Revising • **183**

Step-by-Step Teaching Guide

Revising: Using TRI/PS/QA

Teaching Resources: Writing Support Transparencies, 9-H

1. Explain that sticking to one main idea per paragraph helps to create an organized essay, which is easier for a reader to follow.

2. Point out that there are many ways to organize the information within a paragraph, but three common types of paragraph structure are Topic, Restatement, and Illustration (TRI), Problem and Solution (PS), and Question and Answer (QA).

3. Display Transparency 9-H to show students how these three structures can be put into practice.

4. You may wish to refer to the Model From Literature (pp. 174–175) and have students look for different paragraphs that illustrate TRI or QA structure.

5. Have students check their own work. Ask which structures they used. If paragraphs appear to be unstructured, encourage students to rewrite them using one of the presented structures.

☑ **ONGOING ASSESSMENT: Monitor and Reinforce**

If you observe that students are supporting their opinions with more opinions, use the following strategy.

Select two newspaper letters to the editor, each expressing a different point of view on a current topic. With the class, label each sentence fact or opinion. Compare how the use of opinions and facts contributes to making the arguments either stronger or weaker. Then, have students label their own drafts the same way, to determine whether there are enough facts to support opinions.

⏱ **TIME SAVERS!**

📰 **Writing Support Transparencies**
Use the transparencies for Chapter 9 to facilitate the teaching of strategies.

📖 **Writing Support Activity Book**
Use the graphic organizers for Chapter 9 to facilitate student planning.

Revising: Using Conjunctions to Combine Sentences

Teaching Resources: Writing Support Transparencies, 9-I

1. Ask students to explain the function of a conjunction in a sentence. (A conjunction connects words or groups of words.) Ask for examples of conjunctions *(and, but, or, because, so)*.

2. Explain that choosing appropriate conjunctions helps to express relationships clearly and accurately. Write on the board

   I like you and . . .

   I like you but . . .

   Ask students how the different conjunctions change the meaning and tone of these phrases.

3. Display Transparency 9-I and point out how Emily added conjunctions to make her writing flow more freely.

4. Ask students to reread their drafts and determine whether there is an interesting variety of constructions and lengths of sentences. Suggest that they add conjunctions to add interest or smooth the flow of their writing.

Integrating Vocabulary Skills

Word Choice Point out that, in addition to varying sentence length, varying words can add interest to any writing. Instruct students to be aware of repetition in their writing and to vary their word choice to make the essay less redundant.

Customize for
ESL Students

Students may have difficulty if they know only a few conjunctions, or if they are uncertain of how to use them. Pair these students with more-fluent speakers who can help them find alternative words and show how they can be worked into the essay.

9.4

Revising Your Sentences

Read your comparison-and-contrast essay carefully, examining the sentences you have written. Correct run-ons and fragments by joining or breaking up groups of words as needed. Also revise complete sentences to create variety within your essay. Make sure that your sentences flow smoothly and connect ideas.

Improve Connections Between Ideas

Review your draft, paying special attention to how well your ideas connect and flow together. If your sentences are choppy and unconnected, consider combining them. When combining sentences, use appropriate conjunctions to clearly indicate how the ideas within them are related.

▶ **REVISION STRATEGY**
Using Conjunctions to Combine Sentences

Read your draft critically to make sure that your ideas flow smoothly and logically. Whenever you find a passage that contains short, choppy sentences, combine the sentences and use a conjunction within the sentence to indicate relationships. Use a coordinating conjunction to link ideas of equal importance. Use a subordinating conjunction to indicate that one idea within a sentence is dependent upon another.

Student Work
IN PROGRESS

Name: *Emily Agy*
Pleasant Valley High School
Pleasant Valley, IA

Adding Conjunctions to Connect

After reviewing her opening paragraph, Emily decided that her sentences were too short and choppy. She decided to add conjunctions to connect her ideas more smoothly.

It's one thing to move from one state to another. ~~To~~ but to move from a different country to the United States must certainly be a challenge. Michael Johnson, a fifteen-year-old sophomore recently moved from Southend-on-Sea, England. Johnson was recently interviewed at a journalism club meeting where ~~students.~~ ~~During the interview,~~ he explained the differences between life in the United States and life in England.

184 • Comparison-and-Contrast Essay

Grammar in Your Writing
Conjunctions

A conjunction is a word used to connect other words or groups of words. In English, there are three main kinds of conjunctions: *coordinating conjunctions*, *correlative conjunctions*, and *subordinating conjunctions*.

Coordinating conjunctions connect similar kinds or groups of words. There are seven coordinating conjunctions: *and, but, or, nor, for, yet,* and *so.*

Examples:

The golfers **and** basketball players arrived at the tournament.

The carryall bag given out to students was sturdy **yet** lightweight.

Carry the picnic basket **or** the blanket outside.

Correlative conjunctions are used in pairs to connect similar words or groups of words. Examples of correlative conjunction pairs include *neither/nor, just as/so, both/and,* and *whether/or.*

Examples:

Neither thunder **nor** lightning had much of an effect on our sleepy cat.

Both Charles **and** Ed promised to help us get ready for the dance.

Just as bees fly to honey, **so** my car gravitates to potholes.

Subordinating conjunctions connect two complete ideas by placing one idea below the other in rank or importance. Commonly used subordinating conjunctions include *after, before, because, even if, since, so that, unless, until, when,* and *while.*

Examples:

He achieved a great deal of success **because** he practiced regularly.

We can go to the park today, **even if** it rains.

Now that the show is over, you can go home.

Find It in Your Reading Find an example of a coordinating conjunction and of a subordinating conjunction in "Two Writing Processes" on pages 174–175. Then, explain how the conjunctions help to show the relationships between the ideas being connected.

Find It in Your Writing As you revise your comparison-and-contrast essay, look for one example of each type of conjunction. Examine each conjunction to make sure it shows the relationship you intend. If you can't find any, challenge yourself to combine ideas with conjunctions.

For more on conjunctions, see Chapter 18.

Revising • 185

Conjunctions

1. Review with students the three types of conjunctions and their roles.

2. Distribute copies of a newspaper or magazine article to the class. Ask them to highlight all conjunctions in the article.

3. Ask volunteers to read aloud a sentence in which they have highlighted one or more conjunctions. Then, ask them to restate the information given in the sentence without using any conjunctions.

4. Ask students how they think conjunctions might contribute to the clarity of a compare-and-contrast essay. (Conjunctions clarify the relationship between sentences.)

Find It in Your Reading

Ask students to explain how each conjunction connects pairs of ideas in the Model From Literature. Ask how a different conjunction or no conjunction would have affected the connected ideas. Would the connection still have been clear?

Find It in Your Writing

Suggest that students make notes of the conjunctions they use and how they contribute to the meaning or flow of their writing. These notes might help with later revising phases.

Customize for
More Advanced Students

Have students write sentences that correctly use more than one type of conjunction. (Example: Both Jane and Maria called because they had heard that I was sick.) Then, have them explain which ideas or things are being connected and why.

☑ **ONGOING ASSESSMENT: Prerequisite Skills**

If students are having difficulty in identifying conjunctions, you may find it helpful to refer them to the following materials to ensure coverage of requisite skills.

In the Textbook	Print Resources	Technology
Conjunctions, Section 18.2	*Grammar Exercise Workbook,* pp. 35–40	*On-Line Exercise Bank,* Section 18.2

Step-by-Step Teaching Guide

Revising: Add Transitions to Clarify Relationships

1. Explain to students that transitions help readers follow the logic and organization of a written work. They can also clarify meaning.

2. Point out that "I went to school. I went to the store" might appear confusing. Adding a transition clarifies this: "I went to school. *Later*, I went to the store."

3. Have students suggest examples using some of the transitions in the chart, placing them at both the beginning of and within the sentence. ("I took math *as well as* history" or "I took German for two years. *Next*, I tried French.") Make sure they offer examples for all four types of relationships in the chart.

Step-by-Step Teaching Guide

Reading Aloud

1. Direct students to read pairs of sentences aloud to themselves or a partner, pausing to look for logical connections and making sure these connections are obvious.

2. Encourage students to add transitions to improve the logic, clarity, and flow of the writing.

Step-by-Step Teaching Guide

Revising: Peer Review

1. As students think about the questions they want to ask, suggest they scan the chapter for ideas of things they should consider, including audience, using conjunctions or transitions, appropriate organization, logic, balance, and structure.

2. Direct students to read each other's drafts carefully and to answer the questions thoughtfully, providing useful input rather than "yes" or "no" answers.

Revising Your Word Choice
Add Transitions to Clarify Relationships

Transitions indicate relationships. You can improve the clarity of your writing by adding transitions that express the relationships between the ideas in your essay.

Common Transitions			
Time Relationships	Spatial Relationships	Comparison-and-Contrast Relationships	Logical Relationships
before; during after; first; second; last; next; then; when; at the same time; now; later; immediately; soon; recently	above; below; behind; in front of; alongside; next to; north; south; east; west; inside; outside; beneath; at the top of; at the bottom of	along with; together with; as well as; also; similarly; although; though; however; nevertheless; yet; but; on the other hand; in contrast	if; whether; unless; therefore; thus; hence; in fact; in essence; for example; for instance

▶ **REVISION STRATEGY**
Reading Aloud

Read aloud pairs of sentences in your draft. For example, read the first and second sentence, then the second and third sentence, and so on. Pause after each pair and ask: Would adding transitions clarify the relationship between the two sentences? If so, add a transition from the chart above. Reread the sentence to be sure that the transition works well.

Peer Review
Ask Questions

Work with a peer to revise your essay. Write down five questions about your essay that you would like your peer reviewer to answer. Then, exchange drafts and questions with your peer reviewer. Take your peer's comments into consideration as you prepare a final draft.

Sample Questions:

- What types of details would enhance my essay?
- Have I provided a balanced treatment of the two subjects?
- What aspects of the essay need improvement? Why?

186 • Comparison-and-Contrast Essay

⏱ Timed Writing Hint

Adapt the read-aloud strategy in an exam by reading silently to yourself. "Hear" how your sentence pairs sound and improve them when necessary.

 STANDARDIZED TEST PREPARATION WORKSHOP

Vocabulary Standardized tests often require students to recognize synonyms and antonyms. They often provide more than one possible answer, although only one is the best answer. Remind students that they are to choose the best answer. Write the following statements on the board.

The best synonym for the word *now* is ___.
A then   **B** soon   **C** immediately   **D** first
Students should recognize that **C** is the best synonym.
The best antonym for the word *now* is ___.
A next   **B** during   **C** when   **D** later
Students should recognize that **D** is the best antonym.

9.5 Editing and Proofreading

Before sharing your comparison-and-contrast essay with others, proofread it carefully to correct errors in spelling, punctuation, and grammar.

Focusing on Punctuation

Because comparison-and-contrast essays discuss two or more subjects, they often contain compound sentences. Pay close attention to your punctuation of compound sentences to ensure that you have correctly used commas within them.

📀 Technology Tip

Use the Find feature of your word-processing software to locate conjunctions like *and, but,* and *yet.* When each is found, examine the sentence to see if it is compound. If so, make sure that it has a comma before the conjunction.

Grammar in Your Writing
Punctuating Compound Sentences

A **compound sentence** consists of two or more independent clauses joined by a comma and a coordinating conjunction or by a semicolon. Use the following rules for properly punctuating compound sentences:

- Use a comma before the conjunction that joins the clauses of a compound sentence.

  Eighteen tourists remained on the island, **but** most were safely evacuated before the hurricane struck.

- Use a semicolon when no conjunction is used to join closely related independent clauses.

  The tour bus was forced to take a detour; mudslides had made the main road impassable.

Find It in Your Reading Find three examples of compound sentences in "Two Writing Processes," on pages 174–175. Explain the rules for punctuating them.

Find It in Your Writing As you proofread your comparison-and-contrast essay, check to be sure that you have punctuated all compound sentences correctly.

For more on compound sentences, see Chapter 20.

Editing and Proofreading • **187**

Editing and Proofreading: Punctuating Compound Sentences

1. Ask students to define "independent clause" (a clause that can stand by itself as a complete sentence).

2. Point out that, in both rules, the first thing to note is whether or not the ideas are related closely enough to be linked. If not, make two separate sentences. If they are related, then there are only two rules to follow: A comma comes before a coordinating conjunction, and a semicolon appears only if there is no conjunction.

3. Write the following sentences on the board as examples. Have students explain the use of the comma and the semicolon.

   Shopping at the mall can be fun, but it is very time-consuming.

   Shopping on-line can be fun and fast; you don't have to walk from store to store.

Find It in Your Reading

There are several examples of compound sentences in the Model From Literature, but they all use commas and conjunctions. Ask students how the sentences would be different if Zinsser had used semicolons.

Find It in Your Writing

Suggest that students correct their drafts using colored ink or pencil, so that the corrections stand out and can serve as a model for them in the future.

⏱ TIME AND RESOURCE MANAGER

Resources
Print: *Scoring Rubrics on Transparency,* Ch. 9; *Writing Assessment and Portfolio Management; Formal Assessment,* Ch. 9
Technology: *Writing and Grammar* Interactive Text, Section 9.5

Using the Full Student Edition	Using the Handbook🄷
• Review pp.187–188 in class, including Grammar in Your Writing. • Have students edit and proofread in class. • Have students select a method of publishing and presenting their work. • Analyze the Final Draft on pp.189–190.	• Review pp. 119–120 in class, including Grammar in Your Writing. • Have students edit and proofread in class. • Have students select a method of publishing and presenting their work.

Publishing and Presenting

1. If students decide to do oral presentations, remind them to check pronunciation of any difficult words beforehand, and to speak clearly.

2. Allow students time in class to reflect and write about creating their essays. To prompt further reflection, you could ask the following questions, in addition to those in the text:

   Did writing this essay change your opinion about either of your subjects? How?

   What was the most difficult element of writing this essay?

ASSESS and CLOSE

Assessment

Teaching Resources: Scoring Rubrics on Transparency, Ch. 9; Writing Assessment and Portfolio Management; Formal Assessment, Ch. 9

1. Display the Scoring Rubric transparency and review the criteria.

2. Before students proceed with self-assessment, review the Final Draft of the Student Work in Progress on pages 189–190. Have students score it in one or more of the rubric categories.

3. In addition to student self-assessment, you may wish to use the following assessment options:

   • score student essays yourself, using the rubric and scoring models from *Writing Assessment and Portfolio Management*.

   • review the Standardized Test Preparation Workshop on pages 194–195 and administer a timed writing assignment.

   • administer the Chapter 9 assessment from *Formal Assessment* in the Teaching Resources to measure students' grasp of the concepts presented.

9.6 Publishing and Presenting

Consider the following possibilities for publishing and presenting your comparison-and-contrast essay:

Building Your Portfolio

1. **Presentation** Present your comparison-and-contrast essay to the class. Gather or create visual aids such as photographs and charts, and decide on the order in which you'll present them. Rehearse your presentation to give it polish.

2. **Electronic Essay** Add to the details in your essay with digitized photographs, sound or video clips, or other multimedia elements. Share your essay with others by posting it on a Web site or uploading it onto a classroom computer.

Reflecting on Your Writing

Think back on your writing experience. Then, answer the following questions and save your responses in your portfolio.

• What surprises did you encounter while gathering details for your essay?

• If you could start over, would you choose the same subjects to compare and contrast? Why or why not?

💻 Internet Tip

To see model essays scored with this rubric, go on-line:
PHSchool.com
Enter Web Code:
eek-1001

Rubric for Self-Assessment

Use the following criteria to evaluate your comparison-and-contrast essay:

	Score 4	Score 3	Score 2	Score 1
Audience and Purpose	Chooses details and language that engage audience and achieve purpose	Chooses details and language appropriate for audience and purpose	Chooses details that mostly suit audience and purpose	Chooses details inappropriate for audience and that do not fulfill any purpose
Organization	Clearly presents information in a consistent organization best suited to the topic	Presents information using an organization suited to the topic	Chooses an organization not suited to comparison and contrast	Shows a lack of organizational strategy
Elaboration	Elaborates several ideas, with facts, details, or examples; links all information to comparison and contrast	Elaborates most ideas with facts, details, or examples; links most information to comparison and contrast	Does not elaborate all ideas; does not link some details to comparison and contrast	Does not provide facts or examples to support a comparison and contrast
Use of Language	Demonstrates excellent sentence and vocabulary variety; includes very few mechanical errors	Demonstrates adequate sentence and vocabulary variety; includes few mechanical errors	Demonstrates repetitive use of sentence structure and vocabulary; includes many mechanical errors	Demonstrates poor use of language; generates confusion; includes many mechanical errors

188 • Comparison-and-Contrast Essay

☑ ONGOING ASSESSMENT: Assess Mastery

Use one of the following options to assess final drafts of student's comparison-and-contrast essays.

Self-Assessment Ask students to score their essays using the rubric provided. Then, have them write a single paragraph reflecting on the most valuable thing they learned in completing this essay.	**Teacher Assessment** You may wish to use the rubric and the scoring models provided in *Writing Assessment and Portfolio Management* in the Teaching Resources to score the comparison-and-contrast essays.

9.7 Student Work IN PROGRESS

FINAL DRAFT

▲ **Critical Viewing**
In what ways are these groups of students similar and different? **[Compare and Contrast]**

Life in Britain Versus Life in the U.S.

Emily Agy
Pleasant Valley High School
Pleasant Valley, Iowa

It's one thing to move from one state to another, but to move from a different country to the United States must certainly be a challenge. Michael Johnson, a fifteen-year-old sophomore, recently moved here from Southend-on-Sea, England. Johnson was interviewed by students taking a journalism course, to whom he explained the differences between the United States and England.

Emily clearly identifies the subjects of the comparison—life in the United States and in England.

Step-by-Step Teaching Guide

Final Draft

1. Remind students to keep in mind the key elements of the comparison-and-contrast essay as they review Emily's final draft.
   • Is the topic well defined and sufficiently focused?
   • Are there points of both comparison and contrast?
   • Are main ideas supported by details and examples?
   • Is the information logically organized?
   • Do transitions make relations between ideas clear?
   • Was the research done with primary or secondary sources? (primary)
   • How are individual paragraphs structured? (a combination of TRI and QA)
   • What is the conclusion/ summarizing transition in the last paragraph? ("all in all")

2. Suggest that students consider these elements when revising their own essays.

Critical Viewing

Compare and Contrast Students will observe that one group of students is casually dressed as if for sports, while the other group wears jackets and ties. The groups are similar in that both are all male, and at least one member of each group is carrying books.

189

When asked to name a few differences, Johnson replied, "Petrol (gasoline) is a lot more expensive at home and brand names of clothing are more expensive." He was eager to point out that living in England certainly isn't without its major benefits, though. "I think I've a lot less freedom here than in England. For example, in England, teenagers are treated more like adults. They are less supervised by parents and teachers."

Is driving on the right side of the street hard to get used to? This question was of great interest to the students. "Surprisingly, no," answered Michael. The steering wheel and driving controls are the same in both countries. But they are located on the left side in American cars and on the right side in British cars. If you simply remember that the driver always should be closer to the road's center than the passenger, you're all right."

Another main question was whether the school system was the same as in the United States. There are some similarities. For example, students attend school for the same number of years, and the school year is about the same length. They also study the same basic disciplines such as math, science, and literature. The major difference was that the classes are not structured the same in England. "Teenagers in England have more of a choice of what classes we take, and the schedule varies daily," Johnson said. In the United States, students may choose only one or two classes, and the schedule for classes is set.

Another difference is the school uniform. While it isn't uncommon to have a school uniform in the United States, we do not wear uniforms in Pleasant Valley High School. A typical school  uniform for boys in England consists of, "Shoes, blue pants, shirt, tie, and blazer," Johnson said.

Although both American and English students love team sports, there are many differences when it comes to extracurricular school-sponsored activities. "Here, there are all kinds of activities: football teams, field hockey teams, language clubs, and so on. In England, we don't have extracurricular activities at school. If you want to play sports, you have to find the time to do it yourself. There *are* sports, but they aren't this big; for instance, we haven't got a stadium like you have."

All in all, we, the journalism students, learned that despite the differences, teenagers in England and teenagers in the United States have more in common than we originally believed. Long live the Queen!

Point-by-point organization makes this essay easy to follow.

Emily chooses details that will interest her audience, such as school clothing and class structure.

Supporting details such as these help explain the similarities and differences.

Connected Assignment *Consumer Report*

When you want to compare and contrast several products or services, you can read a **consumer report.** In these reports, writers analyze different features of the products or services being discussed and come up with a recommendation. Consumer reports often take readers step by step through data such as user polls, expert opinions, and test results. They may use tables, graphs, or charts to show at a glance how the products or services compare and contrast.

Write your own consumer report about a product or service you know well. Use the writing process tips outlined below to help you.

Prewriting Decide on two or more products or services to compare and contrast. To come up with an idea, think about products you are interested in buying or a service, such as car washes, that you have used.

Before you draft, collect details that describe the features of the products or services about which you are writing. Use a chart like this one to help you organize the information as you find it.

PACKAGING	
Product A	Product B

Drafting Open your draft with a general statement about the product type and a quick explanation of the features you will be examining. Refer to the chart often as you address each feature and evaluate the pros and cons of each product example. Close with a recommendation about which product or service you find superior.

Revising and Editing Check for consistency in your organization. For example, if have used point-by-point organization, don't switch to subject-by-subject organization later in the report. Confirm that all product names are accurate and correctly spelled. Strengthen your conclusion by correcting wordiness and adding persuasive modifiers.

Publishing and Presenting Make a neat copy of your consumer report, and post it for others to read. If time allows, collect consumer reports from your peers and assemble them into a binder for classmates to use as a reference.

Connected Assignment: Consumer Report • 191

▶ **Lesson Objectives**

1. To write a consumer report in a voice and style appropriate to audience and purpose
2. To develop drafts by organizing and reorganizing content
3. To compile written ideas and representations into reports, and to draw conclusions

Step-by-Step Teaching Guide

Consumer Report

1. Help students choose topics. Discuss products and services they have seen in advertisements, have directly experienced, or would like to purchase.

2. Direct students' attention to the chart on this page. Point out that packaging is only one possible point of comparison between two products. Using a specific example, such as two portable CD players, have students name other important points of comparison (features, durability, price, sound quality).

3. Before students begin to write their essays, they should decide how they want to organize them. See the chart below for useful resources from Chapter 9.

4. When they finish, have students share their work. You might compile all the essays into a "consumer's guide" for the class or the school.

☑ **ONGOING ASSESSMENT: Prerequisite Skills**

Students may find the following resources from Chapter 9 particularly helpful in writing their reports.

In the Textbook	Print Resources	Technology
Use a Venn Diagram, Section 9.2 Use Point-by Point Organization, Section 9.3	*Writing Support Transparencies,* 9-C *Writing Support Activity Book,* 9-1	*Writing and Grammar* Interactive Text, Sections 9.2–3

Lesson Objectives

1. To analyze ideas, relationships, and cultures as represented in various media
2. To compile information from primary and secondary sources using available technology
3. To write a response to a film based on a story or novel

Step-by-Step Teaching Guide

Examining Cultures Through Film

1. Choose one of the Spotlight elements for class discussion, or have students work individually or in groups on one of the elements.
2. Students who read Pearl Buck's *The Good Earth* should also be encouraged to view the film, which is readily available on video.
3. Interested students may research traditional Chinese art in local libraries or on the Internet. Encourage them to bring photographs or posters of examples to share with the class.

Viewing and Representing

Activity If students present their responses to a favorite film in class, encourage them to show clips from the movie to illustrate their points.

Critical Viewing

Compare and Contrast Students may note that modern movie posters, like *The Good Earth* poster shown, often depict settings and main characters from the film, with an emphasis on actors' faces. Modern posters might not use such heavy typeface as this 1937 example, nor do they emphasize cast and production details. Current posters often include a slogan or catch phrase from the movie.

Spotlight on the Humanities

Examining Cultures Through Film

Focus on Film: *The Good Earth*

Through the magic of cinema, you may experience a world other than your own and compare and contrast the characters' experiences with your own. Released in 1937, *The Good Earth* is considered by many movie fans to be one of the best films ever made. Based upon the novel by Pearl Buck, the motion picture stars legendary actor Paul Muni and actress Luise Rainer. The film follows an Asian rice-farming family through their reverence for the land and the fortunes and misfortunes that overtake their lives. Luise Rainer won an Academy Award for Best Actress, and the film also won an Oscar for Best Cinematography.

Literature Connection American author Pearl S. Buck (1892–1973) is one of only nine women to win the Nobel Prize for Literature. She was not only an author, but also a philanthropist, editor, and crusader for women's rights. After growing up in China with her missionary parents, Buck returned to the United States to attend college. She later returned to China and traveled the countryside acting as an interpreter for her husband, Dr. John Lossing Buck. Her novel *The Good Earth* sold over 1,800,000 copies in 1931 and was awarded the Pulitzer Prize in 1932. *The Good Earth* has been translated into thirty languages.

Art Connection Nature and the importance of the land appear consistently in traditional Chinese art. The land is represented distinctively in hanging scrolls, usually done with ink on paper, showing images of rocks, trees, and the outline of distant mountains. These hanging scrolls were common in the eleventh, twelfth, thirteenth, and fourteenth centuries in China.

Writing Application: Response to a Favorite Film
You've probably seen many wonderful films based on novels that moved you to tears or made you laugh out loud until your stomach ached. Choose one of your favorite movies that was based on a short story or novel, and write a response to it. In your response, tell what you liked about the film and, if you read the story as well, whether you preferred the film or the book and why.

▲ Critical Viewing
In what ways is this movie poster similar to or different from movie posters of today? [**Compare and Contrast**]

192 • Comparison-and-Contrast Essay

Media and Technology Skills

Analyze Relationships Between Media

Activity: Compare Versions of a News Story

Different media have different strengths and weaknesses. Imagine that a flood takes place in a nearby town. A newspaper could present in-depth coverage of the event, including several first-person accounts, photographs, and a comparison with earlier floods in your region. A television report would be shorter, but its video footage helps viewers understand the tragedy of the event.

Think About It You can discover a lot about a medium's strengths and the producer's perspectives by comparing two different versions of the same news story. Choose a local, state, or national story and compare the way it is presented in your local newspaper and on a local television broadcast.

Summarize It Begin by summarizing the coverage presented in each source. You may want to use a chart like this one to collect details about each story.

	Newspaper Report	Television Report
Facts		
Images		
Sources Cited		
Length (estimated word count; length of time)		
Position (front page/ back page; first in program, and so on)		

Compare It After reviewing both sources, consider their similarities and differences. Ask questions such as the following:

- Which source assigned greater importance to the story?
- How did each source adapt the story to suit the needs of its medium?
- Which source gave its audience more information?

Write a review in which you compare and contrast the two stories. You may wish to provide a rating for each source, indicating which source you find more reliable.

Comparing Other Media Sources
Extend your comparison to include one or more of the following sources of information. Review the medium's coverage of the same story:
- radio newscast
- weekly newsmagazine
- Internet news resource or on-line newspaper

From Page to Screen
Reading television transcripts can help you evaluate the difference between the written material spoken during a news report and the completed report with video and audio. Write to a network program to request a transcript from a specific program. After reading the transcript, share your reactions with your class.

---

1. To compare, contrast, and critique various media coverage of the same event
2. To examine the effect of media on constructing one's own perception of reality
3. To write a compare-and-contrast review of two types of news coverage

---

Step-by-Step Teaching Guide

Analyze Relationships Between Media

Teaching Resources: Writing Support Transparencies, 9-J; Writing Support Activity Book, 9-4

1. Bring in samples of newspaper articles about a recent local or national event. If possible, bring in clips from television news coverage, too.

2. Display Transparency 9-J or distribute copies of the organizer (9-4). Compare and contrast the newspaper and television coverage of the event, and have students fill in the chart during the discussion.

3. Tell students that to choose a news event to analyze, they might watch an evening news program and then check the next morning's paper for coverage of the same event. Remind them that they should jot down notes about each of the categories in the chart as they watch television news.

4. Before students begin writing, they should decide on a plan for organizing their information.

5. Have students share their information. You might organize a class debate on the relative merits of newspaper and television news coverage.

Customize for
More Advanced Students

Have students repeat the activity, this time comparing newspaper versus magazine or television versus radio coverage of the same event. Have them share their findings with the class.

► Lesson Objectives

Lesson Objectives

1. To write a comparison-and-contrast essay

2. To organize ideas in writing to ensure coherence, logical progression, and support for ideas

3. To use prewriting strategies to generate ideas, develop voice, and plan

4. To demonstrate control over grammatical elements

Step-by-Step Teaching Guide

Responding to Comparison-and-Contrast Prompts

Teaching Resources: Standardized Test Preparation Workbook, pp. 17–18

1. Have students read the sample prompt. Then, have them choose two characters from a novel or short story they read in class this year. Work with them to identify possible points of comparison between the characters.

2. Point out that in a comparison-and-contrast essay, it is useful to collect and organize supporting details before writing. Students should choose several points of comparison and two or three supporting details for each point. If they cannot find enough details, they might choose to focus on a different point of comparison.

3. In order to arrive at a clear thesis, students should reread details they have collected and look for patterns.

4. Assign the writing prompt to be completed within one class period. Make sure students use characters different from the two you just used as an example.

Standardized Test Preparation Workshop

Responding to Comparison-and-Contrast Prompts

On a standardized test, you may be asked to analyze literature, evaluate ideas, or make a judgment and explain your reasons. In responding to these types of prompts, you will often compare and contrast characters, concepts, or choices. You will be asked to identify similarities and differences. You may also be asked to develop a position or draw a conclusion based on the similarities and differences you identify. You will be evaluated on your ability to do the following:

- recognize similarities and differences among the two or more choices

- structure your ideas in a format appropriate for comparing and contrasting

- choose supporting details that develop your ideas

- use correct spelling, language, and grammar

Use the basic writing process stages—prewriting, drafting, revising, editing, and proofreading—as you prepare your test responses. As part of your strategy, plan to devote a set amount of time for each stage of the writing process.

Below is an example of a standardized test writing prompt that involves comparing and contrasting. Develop a response, using the suggestions on the next page for guidance. The clock next to each stage shows a suggested portion of your time to devote to that stage.

Sample Writing Situation

Read "The Masque of the Red Death" by Edgar Allan Poe. Then, respond to the following prompt.

In "The Masque of the Red Death," the people inside the abbey have a very different life from the people outside the abbey. In an essay, explain how this contrast and the common fate that the characters share reveal the theme of the story.

194 • Comparison-and-Contrast Essay

Test Tip

When writing a comparison-and-contrast essay about a creative work, make sure to provide sufficient context for readers who may be unfamiliar with the work. Also, choose items for comparison and supporting details that are appropriate to the specified audience.

✍ TEST-TAKING TIP

Explain to students the importance of creating a context for their readers. For example, if they are discussing the different ways two characters acted in a certain situation, it would be helpful to briefly describe the situation. Discuss some examples using movie characters, political figures, etc.

Point out that the implied audience for essays on standardized tests are well-educated adults. Students should choose points of comparison and supporting details that are appropriate for this audience. They should use formal language and a formal tone unless otherwise noted.

Prewriting

Allow about one quarter of your time for finding a specific topic and identifying comparison-and-contrast details.

Gather Details Use a Venn diagram to jot down the similarities and differences between the Prince's party and the situation of the common people (as described in the opening of the story and as you infer from details in the story.) For example, Poe describes the music and dancing within the abbey. The contrasting detail might be the crying and suffering outside the abbey.

Organize Details Study the details you collected, and decide on a method of organization that will help you achieve your purpose of showing the theme. You might find subject-by-subject organization the most effective method for showing an overall contrast between the rich and the poor. In this case, write about all the details on one side of your Venn diagram before moving on to the other side.

Drafting

Allow about half of your time for drafting. Write neatly, and leave space for text you may want to insert when revising.

Write an Introduction, Body, and Conclusion
Use a traditional format for your comparison-and-contrast essay. In your introduction, you should state your thesis, or main point, so a sentence that states how the contrast in the story illustrates its theme. (Whenever you respond to a prompt, reread the prompt to be sure that your thesis statement addresses the prompt.) Then, develop your ideas in the body of your essay. Conclude by restating your thesis, and leave your readers with a powerful image from the story, such as the clock or the strange visitor.

Revising, Editing, and Proofreading

Allow about one quarter of your time for revising. Allow about five minutes to check your work for spelling, punctuation, or grammar errors.

Close the Gaps Read through your essay, and look for places where you can elaborate further. If you have written that the party was extravagant, make sure you have included several details that show how extravagant the party was. If you have not included several such details, add them at this time. Also, add transitions, if necessary, to indicate places that you change from describing life inside the abbey to life outside the abbey.

Reread After making your revisions, spend a few minutes checking that you have used capitals for characters' names and the beginnings of sentences. Double-check your use of end marks and commas as well. Correct as necessary.

Customize for
Less Advanced Students

Have students meet in small groups before they draft their essays. This will give them a chance to discuss the characters and the points of comparison they have chosen. It might help them to clarify or extend their ideas.

Customize for
Spatial Learners

Encourage students to create a chart or other graphic organizer to keep track of their main points and supporting details. They might make a two-column chart, writing the characters' names in the top row and exploring a different point of comparison in each subsequent row.

Time and Resource Manager

In-Depth Lesson Plan

	LESSON FOCUS	PRINT AND MEDIA RESOURCES
DAY 1	**Introduction to the Cause-and-Effect Essay** Students learn key elements of cause-and-effect essays and analyze the Model From Literature. (pp. 196–199/H122–123)	*Writers at Work* DVD, Exposition *Writing and Grammar* Interactive Text, Ch. 10, Introduction
DAY 2	**Prewriting** Students choose and narrow a topic, consider their audience and purpose, and gather information. (pp. 200–203/H124–127)	**Teaching Resources** *Writing Support Transparencies,* 10-A–D; *Topic Bank for Heterogeneous Classes,* Ch. 10 *Writing and Grammar* Interactive Text, Section 10.2
DAY 3	**Drafting** Students organize their ideas and write their first drafts. (pp. 204–205/H128–129)	**Teaching Resources** *Writing Support Transparencies,* 10-E *Writing and Grammar* Interactive Text, Section 10.3
DAY 4	**Revising** Students revise their drafts in terms of overall structure, paragraphs, sentences, and word choice. (pp. 206–210/H130–134)	**Teaching Resources** *Writing Support Transparencies,* 10-F–G *Writing and Grammar* Interactive Text, Section 10.4
DAY 5	**Editing and Proofreading; Publishing and Presenting** Students check their work for accuracy and correctness and present their final drafts. (pp. 211–214/H135–136)	**Teaching Resources** *Scoring Rubrics on Transparency,* Ch. 10; *Writing Assessment and Portfolio Management; Formal Assessment,* Ch. 10 *Writing and Grammar* Interactive Text, Sections 10.5–6

Accelerated Lesson Plan

	LESSON FOCUS	PRINT AND MEDIA RESOURCES
DAY 1	**Introduction Through Drafting** Students review characteristics of cause-and-effect essays, select topics, and write drafts. (pp. 196–205/H122–129)	**Teaching Resources** *Writing Support Transparencies,* 10-A–E *Writing and Grammar* Interactive Text, Ch. 10, Introduction through Section 10.3
DAY 2	**Revising Through Presenting** Students work individually or with peers to revise, edit, and proofread their work for presentation. (pp. 206–214/H130–136)	**Teaching Resources** *Writing Support Transparencies,* 10-F–G; *Scoring Rubrics on Transparency,* Ch. 10; *Writing Assessment and Portfolio Management; Formal Assessment,* Ch. 10 *Writing and Grammar* Interactive Text, Sections 10.4–6

Options for Adapting Lesson Plans

HOMEWORK

Have students complete any stage of the lesson for homework.

FEATURES

Extend coverage with Connected Assignment (p. 215/H137), Spotlight on the Humanities (p. 216), Media and Technology Skills (p. 217), and the Standardized Test Preparation Workshop (p. 218).

TECHNOLOGY

Students can complete any stage of the lesson on the computer, using *Writing and Grammar* Interactive Text or a word-processing program. Have them print out their completed work.

Writing and Grammar Handbook Alignment

Page numbers in Step-by-Step Teaching Guides in this Teacher's Edition refer to pages from the full student text. Handbook page references, indicated with this icon 🄷, are provided in Time and Resource Manager boxes and at the bottom of each Teacher's Edition page.

INTEGRATED SKILLS COVERAGE

Integrating Grammar
Transitional Phrases, SE p. 209/🄷133
Using *Since, Because, Then,* and *Than* Correctly, SE p. 21/🄷135
Grammar and Style, SE p. 210/🄷134

Reading/Writing Connection
Question, SE p. 198
Writing Application, SE p. 199

Viewing and Representing
Critical Viewing, SE pp. 196, 199, 204, 213–216/🄷122, 128
Examining Images, SE p. 216
Examining the Effect of Media on Perceptions of Reality, SE p. 217

Speaking and Listening Skills ATE pp. 204, 214

Viewing and Representing Skills ATE p. 214

Spelling Skills ATE p. 207

Technology Skills SE pp. 203, 211, 212/🄷127, 135, 136

Real-World Connection ATE p. 199

Workplace Skills ATE p. 206

ASSESSMENT SUPPORT

Standardized Test Preparation Workshop SE p. 218; ATE p. 208
Standardized Test Preparation Workbook, pp. 19–20
Scoring Rubrics on Transparency, Ch. 10
Formal Assessment, Ch. 10
Writing Assessment and Portfolio Management

MEETING INDIVIDUAL NEEDS

Less Advanced Students ATE pp. 203, 208, 219. See also Ongoing Assessments ATE pp. 198, 201, 205, 207.
ESL Students ATE p. 210
More Advanced Students ATE p. 219
Spatial Learners ATE p. 202
Musical Learners ATE p. 217

BLOCK SCHEDULING

Pacing Suggestions
For 90-minute Blocks
• Have students complete the Prewriting and Drafting stages in a single period.
• Focus one class period on Revising and Editing and Publishing and Presenting. Allow at least 30 minutes for peer revision.

Resources for Varying Instruction
• *Writing and Grammar* **Interactive Text** A 90-minute block provides an ideal opportunity for students to work on the computer.
• *Writers at Work* **DVD** Show the Exposition segment in class.

Professional Development Support
• *How to Manage Instruction in the Block* This teaching resource provides management and activity suggestions.

MEDIA AND TECHNOLOGY

For the Student
• *Writing and Grammar* **Interactive Text,** Ch. 10
• *On-line Exercise Bank,* Section 20.1

For the Teacher
• *Writers at Work* **DVD,** Exposition
• **Teacher**EXPRESS™ **CD-ROM**

WRITING AND GRAMMAR ON-LINE

Interactive Text (On-line or on CD-ROM)
• Easily navigable instruction with interactive Revision Checkers
• Full use of e-rater™, the essay-scoring system (on-line only)

Companion Web Site PHSchool.com
• Scoring rubrics with models (use Web Code eek-1001)

See the Go On-line! **feature, SE p. iii.**

LITERATURE CONNECTIONS

Related selections from *Prentice Hall Literature, Penguin Edition,* Grade 10:

Professional Model "Like the Sun," R. K. Narayan, SE p. 199

Topic Bank Option "Tides," Joseph D. Exline, et al., SE p. 201/🄷125

Lesson Objectives

1. To write a cause-and-effect essay that is appropriate to audience and purpose

2. To read to appreciate a writer's craft and to discover models for writing

3. To analyze text structures such as cause and effect to determine how they influence understanding

4. To use prewriting strategies to generate ideas, develop voice, and plan

5. To use texts and technical resources to research self-selected topics

6. To develop and revise drafts in terms of structure, paragraphs, sentences, and word choice

7. To edit and proofread to ensure standard English usage and grammar

8. To respond productively to peer review of his/her own work

9. To refine a cause-and-effect essay for publication

Critical Viewing

Relate Student responses may address the causes and effects of any exploration: the desire for food, land, knowledge, or wealth leads to a quest; establishing settlements may lead to conflicts.

Chapter

10 Exposition
Cause-and-Effect Essay

▲ Critical Viewing
When you look at this picture, what causes and effects come to mind? [Relate]

Cause-and-Effect Relationships in Everyday Life

Identifying causes and effects is a part of daily life. Giving advice to a friend based on the effects you predict, fireproofing a potential fire hazard, and arguing about the best way to solve a problem—all these activities show an awareness of cause-and-effect relationships.

Cause-and-effect relationships are also explored in writing. Feature articles in your daily newspaper often describe causes and effects related to politics, crime, or the environment. History textbooks are primarily focused on causes and effects, as well. Even something as common as a recipe may describe a cause-and-effect process.

196 • Exposition

⏱ TIME AND RESOURCE MANAGER

Resources
Technology: *Writers at Work* DVD, Exposition; *Writing and Grammar* Interactive Text, Ch. 10

Using the Full Student Edition	Using the Handbook🄷
• Cover pp. 196–197 in class. • Show the Exposition section of the *Writers at Work* DVD. • Read the Model From Literature (pp. 198–199) in class, and use it to brainstorm for cause-and-effect essay ideas with students.	• Cover pp. 122–123 in class. • Show the Exposition section of the *Writers at Work* DVD.

What Is a Cause-and-Effect Essay?

Exposition is writing that informs or explains. A **cause-and-effect essay** is a piece of exposition that describes the relationship between an event or circumstance and its causes. Good cause-and-effect essays contain

- a clearly stated topic that explains what cause-and-effect relationships will be explored.
- an effective and logical method of organization.
- details and examples that elaborate upon the writer's statements.
- transitions that smoothly and clearly connect the writer's ideas.

To preview the criteria on which your cause-and-effect essay may be evaluated, see the Rubric for Self-Assessment on page 212.

Types of Cause-and-Effect Essays

Cause-and-effect relationships are explored in many types of writing, including the ones listed below:

- **Historical articles** explain how events in history contributed to or resulted in other events.
- **Process explanations** take readers step by step through a process, such as a math formula or a scientific technique.
- **Predictions** make educated guesses about future events based on knowledge of cause-and-effect relationships.

PREVIEW
Student Work
IN PROGRESS

In this chapter, you'll follow the progress of Jennifer Hoss, a student at Bel Air High School in El Paso, Texas, as she writes a cause-and-effect essay entitled "El Niño." At the end of the chapter, you can read Jennifer's completed work.

Writers in ACTION

Writer Rudolfo Anaya discusses the process of writing an expository essay:

"In expository writing you're guided by an idea that you want to develop. It may be a paragraph, it may be ten pages, but what you really have is a subject, and you want to convey it. . . ."

PREPARE and ENGAGE

Interest GRABBER Have students choose an item on their desk, such as a pencil. Challenge them to trace back, as far as possible, the chain of events that caused the item to appear on their desks. (Example: student bought it from store, store bought it from distributor, distributor bought it from pencil factory, pencil factory bought wood from lumber company, and so on.)

Activate Prior Knowledge

Ask students to think of a recent accomplishment, such as learning a new chord on the guitar or earning a driver's license. Have them list the various causes that led up to this event. Point out that a single event often has more than one cause.

More About the Writer

A champion of Hispanic literature, Rudolfo Anaya has written novels, short stories, essays, journals, and children's books. His best-known novel, *Bless Me, Ultima,* earned him the *Premio Quinto Sol* Award, a major award for Chicano literature, in 1972. Much of Anaya's inspiration came from his early childhood in the small village of Pastura, New Mexico.

Reading Strategy: Question

Questioning an author's work will help students establish a criterion for credibility. Have students write down at least three questions that come to mind as they read this selection. (Example: What is the author's argument? Does she validate this position?)

Step-by-Step Teaching Guide

Engage Students Through Literature

1. After students have read the essay, ask them to summarize the factors that have contributed to China's growing pains (changes in government, economy, jobs).

2. Point out that an effect can, in turn, become the cause of another effect. Also, some causes have more than one effect, and some effects have more than one cause.

3. Write on the board the following causes (or others you noticed) and have students identify the effects.

   Cause—the government owned and controlled everything (Effects—food and clothing rationed, foreign imports restricted, economy stagnates)

   Cause—U.S.-China trade resumes (Effects—skyscrapers, American products, economic growth.)

   Cause—government reforms (Effects—farmers can keep some of what they grow, foreign investment is encouraged, money flows in)

   Cause—money flows in (Effects—growing middle class, more consumer goods are available)

Critical Viewing

Speculate Students may suggest a flourishing economy or favorable government policies.

10.1 Model From Literature

California native Cindy Lin attended Columbia University's Graduate School of Journalism. Following a two-year period teaching high school in Japan, Lin now reports for an educational news station in New York City.

Reading Writing Connection

Reading Strategy: Question As you read works of nonfiction such as the following, question the author's statements, and check to be sure they are supported with evidence.

▲ **Critical Viewing**
What might be the causes of urban development such as you see in the background of this photograph? **[Speculate]**

Growing Pains in China

Cindy Lin

If you go to the big cities in China today, you'll see skylines teeming with new skyscrapers and stores filled with consumer goods like refrigerators and designer handbags. You'll see a lot of billboards and ads for American products, and people dressed in Western clothes. In fact, they look like many big cities in the United States.

But as recently as the 1980's, things in China were very different. Few people owned televisions, and even fewer people had cars. There wasn't much choice in what you could buy, because food and clothing were rationed and foreign imports were restricted. The government owned and controlled everything, including deciding which products got made and in what quantities. The result was massive state-run companies that, while usually not profitable or efficient, employed thousands of people for life.

That all began to change in the early 1980's, after diplomatic relations with the U.S. and China resumed in 1979. China's leaders instituted reforms, such as allowing farmers to keep a small portion

In the opening paragraph, Lin describes the effect—China's newfound prosperity—that she plans to explore.

Transitions such as "because" help readers make connections between causes and effects.

198 • Cause-and-Effect Essay

✓ ONGOING ASSESSMENT: Monitor and Reinforce

After previewing the Model From Literature, you might anticipate some students' difficulty with some of the vocabulary. Use the following options.

Option 1 If students read the model independently, have them list any unfamiliar words they encounter. These words can be listed on the board and discussed as a group.	**Option 2** If you or a prepared student reads the model aloud in class, define unfamiliar words as they appear. Words such as *teeming, rationed,* and *privatization* may need explanation.

of what they grew to sell on their own, inviting foreign investment and encouraging the privatization of state-owned companies. Money from foreign investors flowed into China—$67 billion in the last two years alone—as companies hurried to establish their products in a market with 1.25 billion people.

Now, 93 percent of Chinese households have a television set, and other goods such as washing machines and refrigerators are becoming common as well. But not everyone is benefiting from the changes in China—an estimated 100 million people are unemployed in China's cities and more than 80 million peasants in the country live in poverty, earning less than $100 a year.

SO WHO WINS AND WHO LOSES?

China's emerging middle class is reaping the benefits of change in China. They are the educated ones—usually in the cities—who can adjust to change and take the opportunity to start their own business or move into a management position at the growing numbers of new, privately owned businesses.

Those with little skills or education, who expected to work for a lifetime doing the same job, are now the ones who struggle. As state-owned companies have shut down or laid them off, the unskilled laborers become part of the staggering numbers of unemployed. Elderly retirees who exist on tiny government pensions also can't keep up with the changes, and people in the country who are too far from the big job markets of the cities continue to be mired in poverty.

For much of this century, Americans also expected to work at the same job or company for their entire careers. While American companies may be privately run, competition from other companies both domestically and abroad (such as in the auto industry) led to a spate of layoffs and factory closings in the late 1980's and early 1990's. People have since discovered that the more varied skills and education they have, the easier it will be for them to find work—especially in the event of change.

Reading \ Writing Connection Writing Application: **Answer Readers' Questions** As you prepare to write your cause-and-effect essay, think about the questions your readers may ask. Be sure you answer those questions as you draft your essay.

A chronological organization helps Lin trace the various causes leading to China's present-day conditions.

Statistical details such as the ones in this paragraph support Lin's ideas.

R. K. Narayan's "Like the Sun" traces the effects of one man's attempts to tell the truth. The short story appears in *Prentice Hall Literature, Penguin Edition,* Grade 10.

In her concluding paragraph, Lin notes that the cause-and-effect relationships that existed in China also hold true in the United States.

▲ **Critical Viewing** Would you say that the photograph shows a town with a healthy economy or a poor one? Explain. **[Make a Judgment]**

Teaching From the Model

Have students examine the essay's organization. Point out that in the first half of the essay, Lin begins with a major effect and then goes back and builds a history of smaller influences that become the cause of the effect she first described. Ask students how Lin shows the connections between causes and effects. *(Sometimes words like because point out the connection; at other times, facts simply follow an initial point, and it is left to the reader to make the connection.)*

More About the Writer

Cindy Lin has been to more than twenty countries on four continents. Degrees in communications and psychology (University of Pennsylvania) came before her journalism degree—all of which helped prepare her for a varied career as teacher, Web page designer, writer, and editor.

Real-World Connection

Medical science is one field in which noticing cause-and-effect relationships is a key element of the job. Epidemiologists (people who study and try to stop the spread of disease) are trained to find the causes behind epidemics.

Reading\Writing Connection

Writing Application: Answer Readers' Questions

Remind students that as they read, they automatically ask themselves questions about the text. Tell them that as they write, they should put themselves in their readers' place and anticipate their questions, particularly about causes and effects.

Critical Viewing

Make a Judgment Students may say the economy is healthy because of the many customers and the abundance of goods.

Choosing Your Topic

Choose a topic for your cause-and-effect essay that you find interesting and that centers around a cause-and-effect relationship.

Strategies for Choosing a Topic

1. **Sketch a Scene** Draw a scene from the world of nature. Review your sketch to find interesting details that make a good writing topic. For example, you might draw a field of dandelions and clover that has a pond in the middle of it. You might then decide to write about the effects of last year's drought on local flowers and crops.

2. **Make a List** List interesting events or scientific phenomena. After five minutes, circle the one you find most interesting. Then, write for another five minutes, listing any causes and effects that spring to mind when you think of that topic. Review what you wrote, and develop your topic into a cause-and-effect essay. If you find that your topic doesn't have a strong enough cause-and-effect relationship, continue the listing process until you find one that does.

3. **Scan a Newspaper** Scan a newspaper, looking for topics that you can link to causes or effects. Keep a list of the possible topics as you come across them. Then, review your list, and choose as a topic the item you find most interesting.

Get instant help! Make your list using the Essay Builder, accessible from the menu bar, on-line or on CD-ROM.

IN PROGRESS

Name: *Jennifer Hoss*
Bel Air High School
El Paso, TX

Doing a Newspaper Scan to Find a Topic
Jennifer Hoss found her topic by flipping through a newspaper. She jotted down articles that explained causes and effects and chose the one she liked the best as her topic.

1. Academic scores rise dramatically
2. Indonesia elects a new president
3. Scientists analyze tissue from a twenty-five-thousand-year-old frozen woolly mammoth
4. El Niño crop failure blamed for high cost of chilies

200 • Cause-and-Effect Essay

⏱ TIME AND RESOURCE MANAGER

Resources
Print: *Writing Support Transparencies,* 10-A–D
Technology: *Writing and Grammar* Interactive Text, Section 10.2

Using the Full Student Edition	Using the Handbook🄷
• Work through the Sketching, Listing, and Newspaper Scan strategies with the class.	• Work through the Sketching, Listing, and Newspaper Scan strategies with the class.
• Use the Responding to Fine Art transparency to generate additional topics.	• Use the Responding to Fine Art transparency to generate additional topics.
• Use the Cubing technique as part of a group assignment.	• Use the Cubing technique as part of a group assignment.

TOPIC BANK

If you are having difficulty finding a specific topic for your cause-and-effect essay, use the following ideas:

1. **Influences of the Blues on Popular Music** Write an essay that reveals how blues instruments, blues singers, and recurring themes in blues songs affect music today.

2. **Causes of Changes in Rain Forests** In a cause-and-effect essay, explore the various factors that have led to the rain forest's acreage being decreased. You can find information about deforestation in current periodicals available at the library.

Responding to Fine Art

Rolling Power, Smith College Museum of Art

3. *Rolling Power* depicts a close-up view of the workings of a locomotive. Write a cause-and-effect essay, explaining how steam engines propel locomotives. As an alternative, explore the cause-and-effect relationship between the development of the railroad and patterns of settlement westward across the United States.

Responding to Literature

4. Read the technical article "Tides" by Joseph D. Exline and others. Using this selection as a model, research and write an essay in which you explain the causes of another natural phenomenon, such as the northern lights. You can find the article in *Prentice Hall Literature, Penguin Edition*, Grade 10.

⏱ Timed Writing Prompt

5. Write an essay in which you introduce a historical event and discuss its causes and effects. Identify at least two causes for the historical event you have chosen. Then, explain at least two effects that resulted from the historical event. Write this essay for a reader who knows nothing about the historical event you are discussing. **(40 minutes)**

Responding to Fine Art

Rolling Power

Teaching Resources: Writing Support Transparencies, 10-B

1. Display Transparency 10-B and engage students in discussion. You might use questions about what contributed to the invention of the locomotive or what impact its invention had.

2. Ask students to brainstorm for additional ideas. Students could move from a discussion of transportation and technology topics of the past to current or future transportation (high-speed trains, electric cars, space exploration).

3. Appoint a student to serve as a recorder of ideas raised in discussion. From the list, have students select the most appealing topics for cause-and-effect essays.

⏱ Timed Writing Prompt

- To help students focus on a topic, ask volunteers to name an event in history that stands out in their minds. Suggest influential people in history to help generate ideas. Discuss what caused each event to happen and what the lasting effects are.

- Remind students that to answer the prompt, they must provide two causes and two effects of this historical event.

- Suggest that students allow five minutes for prewriting, thirty minutes for writing, and five minutes for reviewing and proofreading.

✓ ONGOING ASSESSMENT: Monitor and Reinforce

If you observe that some students are having difficulty choosing a topic, use one of the following strategies.

Option 1 Recommend that students choose an idea from the Topic Bank. If many students have difficulty, have the entire class work on a single topic. Try to generate ideas by discussing issues of importance at your school.

Option 2 Have students make a list of areas that interest them (sports, dating, dress codes, authority figures). Remind students that their sources of information are what they know, what they observe, and/or what they can find out. Be sure the topic they select will provide them with sources.

⏱ TIME SAVERS!

 **Writing Support Transparencies**
Use the transparencies for Chapter 10 to facilitate the teaching of strategies.

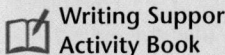 **Writing Support Activity Book**
Use the graphic organizers for Chapter 10 to facilitate student planning.

Prewriting: Use the Cubing Technique

Teaching Resources: Writing Support Transparencies, 10-C
Writing Support Activity Book, 10-1

1. Point out to students that when they answer the questions associated with each strategy, they will generate details that can help give direction and focus to their essay topics.

2. Model for students how cubing to narrow a topic can help them begin to compose a thesis statement. For example, if the general topic is "The Future of Railroads," an answer to the "Apply It" questions might be, "Railroads are an important part of the history of the United States," and an answer to the "Associate It" question might be, "Railroads help reduce air pollution and traffic congestion."

Customize for
Spatial Learners

It may help students to have a physical cube to work with. Cubes of styrofoam could be used, with tape for attaching questions to the six sides. Students add comments to each side and can readily see which sides have the most detail.

Prewriting: Considering Your Audience and Purpose

1. Explain that, though the example identifies a specific audience, an audience is often defined more generally, by interests (e.g., people who are interested in education) and levels of knowledge (novice to expert).

2. State that, while for cause-and-effect essays, purposes will be demonstrating connections or predicting effects, the more basic purposes of essays are to entertain, inform, or persuade. Ask what the basic purpose of the example is *(persuade—don't cut funding)*.

10.2

Narrowing Your Topic

Once you have a general idea for a topic, work with the material until it is narrow enough to cover effectively within the scope of your essay. Cubing is one narrowing technique that you can use.

Use the Cubing Technique

Cubing lets you focus on details by helping you identify six perspectives or aspects of your topic. Answer the six questions, and decide to focus your essay on one or two of the perspectives or aspects you explored.

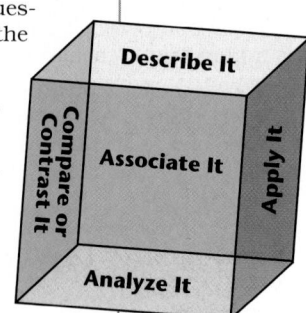

1. **Describe It** How would you describe your topic to someone who is unfamiliar with it?
2. **Associate It** What other situations or events does your topic bring to mind?
3. **Apply It** Why is your topic important? Why is it useful to explore?
4. **Analyze It** Where is it? When did it happen? Why might it happen again? Can anything stop it from happening?
5. **Compare or Contrast It** How does your topic compare and contrast with similar topics?
6. **Argue for or Against It** What are the positive and negative effects of your topic?

Considering Your Audience and Purpose

Before you gather details, identify your audience and your purpose. Your audience and purpose will affect your word choice, the details you include, and the way in which you present those details. For help identifying the types of details and style of language that will be most effective, devise a plan like the one that appears below.

Audience:	School Board
Purpose:	To explain effects of decreased music funding
Details:	Facts and statistics; cause-and-effect chart; examples
Style of Language:	Formal word choice; vivid persuasive language; tone of respect

Gathering Details

Before you draft, collect and organize details for your cause-and-effect essay. Following are two methods for collecting and organizing details:

Collect Note Cards

When you research a topic, it's important to keep note cards for each cause-and-effect idea and its source. Before you begin to draft your essay, collect note cards from at least three or four sources either at home or at the library. On each note card, record the quotation or the idea you want to include in your report. Mark the note card with a number that identifies its source and the page number(s) on which the information can be found.

As an alternative, photocopy source pages and highlight the information you use.

Chart Causes and Effects

On a sheet of paper, write the effect, or event, that is your subject. Then, use arrows and boxes to show events or conditions that are caused by or result from your topic. If one event has several different effects, use a separate arrow to point to each.

 **Technology Tip**

If you find information on the Internet, print out the pages containing the information you plan to use. Make sure to print out or write down the Web address, too.

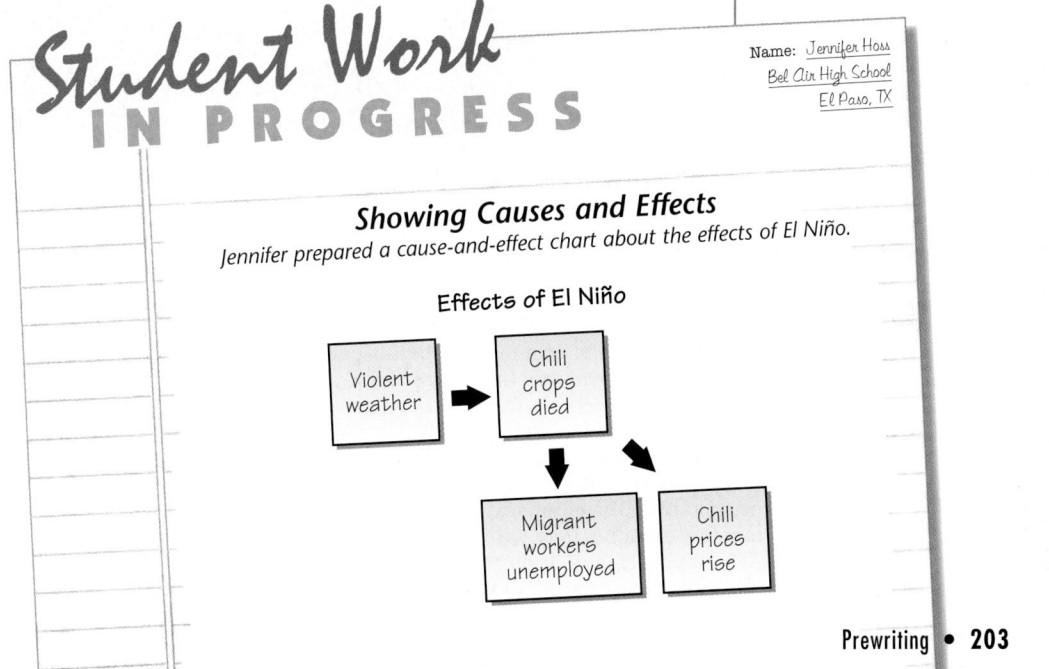

Student Work **IN PROGRESS**

Name: *Jennifer Hoss*
Bel Air High School
El Paso, TX

Showing Causes and Effects
Jennifer prepared a cause-and-effect chart about the effects of El Niño.

Effects of El Niño

Violent weather → Chili crops died → Migrant workers unemployed / Chili prices rise

Prewriting • **203**

Step-by-Step Teaching Guide

Prewriting: Collect Note Cards

1. Explain to students that note cards listing related details can be spread out and reordered to help with planning and organization.

2. Remind students that source citations require the title and author of the work, publisher, copyright date, and place of publication. Also, page references are helpful if the information has to be checked.

3. If students choose to do some of their research on the Internet, remind them that they will still need to note the source information and include the URL (Internet address).

4. If possible, schedule a class period in the library for research.

Step-by-Step Teaching Guide

Prewriting: Chart Causes and Effects

Teaching Resources: Writing Support Transparencies, 10-D
Writing Support Activity Book, 10-2

1. Display Transparency 10-D and point out how Jennifer created a chain of events, or series of causes and effects, of which El Niño was the original cause.

2. Explain that, if there are other effects, other chains can connect with any of the squares, and that some causes have more than one direct effect. Assure students that chains will differ.

3. Have students write their essay topic on a sheet of paper and create a chain for causes and effects using the blank organizer (10-2).

Customize for
Less Advanced Students

If students are having difficulty connecting causes and effects, explain that the cause is the "why," and the effect is the "result." Provide examples. Check their work frequently and offer suggestions for less-obvious or more-complex causes for the main effect.

Drafting: Choose a Logical Organization

1. Ask students why chronological order might be a logical choice for a cause-and-effect essay (causes always precede effects).

2. Ask when order of importance might be a more useful way to organize writing (when there are several causes and/or effects, or when some causes are more important than others).

3. Have students review their chain-of-events assignment and determine which order of presentation would be most effective. Then, have students write an outline to help them organize details before drafting their essays.

4. Allow time for students to complete their first drafts in class.

Critical Viewing

Analyze Students will observe the effects of corrosion and decay on the *Titanic*.

Integrating Speaking and Listening Skills

Ask students to record their drafts on tape and then focus on what the writing sounds like as they listen to the recording. They can note corrections as they listen to the playback. If time permits, students can do this activity in pairs and stop the tape to discuss points.

10.3 *Drafting*

Shaping Your Writing

Now that you have gathered details on your topic, shape the structure of your essay. Choose a logical method of organization for your cause-and-effect essay.

Choose a Logical Organization

Chronological Organization Chronological, or time, organization is a logical choice for structuring a cause-and-effect essay. You can start either with the effect and go back through its causes one at a time, in chronological order, or you can start with the cause and proceed to describe its effects in time order.

Effects Organized Chronologically:

After the *Titanic* sank, new marine regulations were put into effect. The tragedy of the *Titanic* caused mariners to firm up regulations about radio contact and lifeboats. Marine regulations instituted after the *Titanic* included these mandates: constant radio contact between vessels and sufficient lifeboats to hold all passengers.

Order-of-Importance Organization Order-of-importance organization allows you to build an argument or to present various causes or effects in the order of their relative importance. You can either begin with the most important detail and end with the least important detail or reverse it, beginning with the least important detail and ending with the most important detail.

Effects Organized in Order of Importance:

The *Titanic*'s voyage proved to be a disaster because of many causes. Chief among them was the failure of the crew to navigate around the iceberg. The resulting damage to the ship's hull made its sinking inevitable. . . .

Another contributing cause was the lack of adequate lifeboats and safety instruction. Because the *Titanic* was "unsinkable," the company that made the ship did not provide enough safety equipment to ensure the safety of passengers and crew.

The weather conditions certainly did not help. . . .

▼ **Critical Viewing** What effect has time had on the *Titanic*, shown in this recent photograph? **[Analyze]**

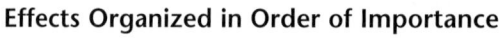

204 • Cause-and-Effect Essay

⏱ TIME AND RESOURCE MANAGER

Resources
Print: *Writing Support Transparencies*, 10-E
Technology: *Writing and Grammar* Interactive Text, Section 10.3

Using the Full Student Edition	Using the Handbook Ⓗ
• Work through Choose a Logical Organization with the entire class.	• Work through Choose a Logical Organization with the entire class.
• Have students determine the organizational pattern they intend to use.	• Have students determine the organizational pattern they intend to use.
• Have students write their first drafts in class.	• Have students write their first drafts in class.

Providing Elaboration

Elaborate as you draft to add depth and detail to your cause-and-effect essay. Types of elaboration include examples, statistics, quotations, and other types of details that support your ideas. Use the following strategy to help you elaborate:

Use the SEE Technique for Elaboration

Use the SEE technique to layer, or give depth, to your writing as you draft. First, write a basic statement about your topic. Next, write a sentence that extends that statement. Finally, write a sentence that elaborates on the extension.

STATEMENT:	**State the main idea of the paragraph.** Exercise is beneficial to your health.
EXTENSION:	**Restate the idea.** People who exercise regularly live longer, fuller lives.
ELABORATION:	**Add information that further explains or defines the main idea.** For example, a person who works out for twenty minutes three times a week is often in far better shape than a person who has no regular routine.

Drafting: Use the SEE Technique for Elaboration

Teaching Resources: Writing Support Transparencies, 10-E

1. Display Transparency 10-E and point out how Jennifer used the SEE technique to elaborate on her original statement about El Niño.

2. Write on the board the following main idea from the second paragraph of Cindy Lin's essay on China:

   Statement: As recently as the 1980's, things in China were very different [from what they are today].

   Beneath it, write

   Extension:

   Elaboration:

3. Ask students what the extension and elaboration might have been for this statement. (Possible answer:

   Extension: *Few people owned televisions or cars. There wasn't much choice in what you could buy.*

   Elaboration: *Clothing was rationed, imports restricted, and the government owned and controlled production.*)

4. Have students review their drafts to see whether the main ideas of their paragraphs have been extended and elaborated. Suggest that they elaborate as necessary, to make sure ideas and points are adequately supported.

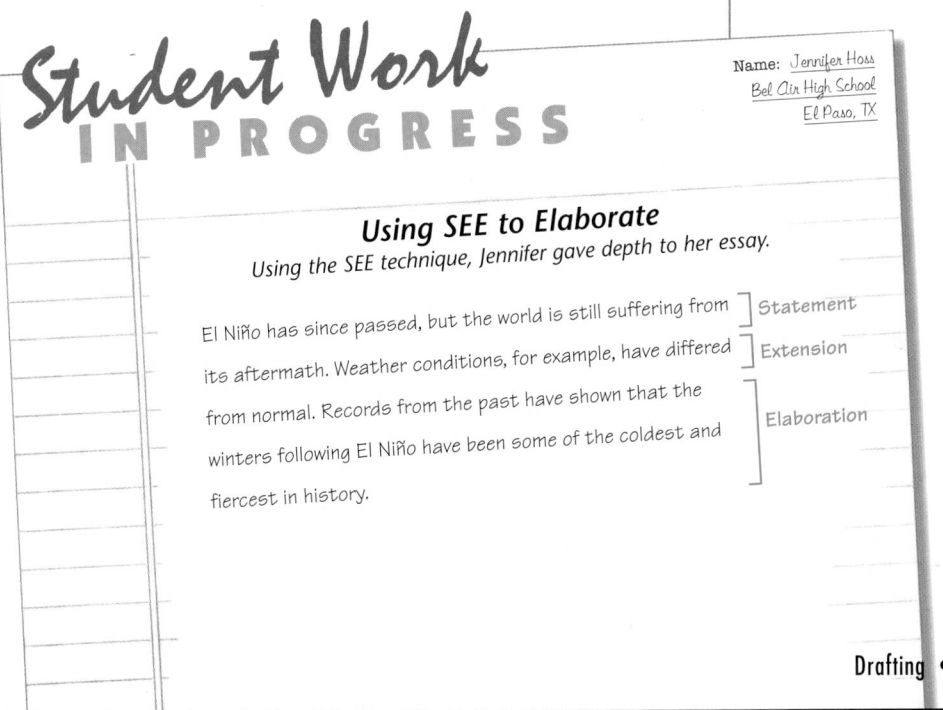

Student Work IN PROGRESS

Name: Jennifer Hoss
Bel Air High School
El Paso, TX

Using SEE to Elaborate
Using the SEE technique, Jennifer gave depth to her essay.

El Niño has since passed, but the world is still suffering from } Statement

its aftermath. Weather conditions, for example, have differed } Extension

from normal. Records from the past have shown that the } Elaboration

winters following El Niño have been some of the coldest and

fiercest in history.

Drafting • 205

☑ **ONGOING ASSESSMENT: Monitor and Reinforce**

If you observe that some students are having difficulty elaborating on their topic, use one of the following options.

Students may have difficulty recognizing the strengths and weakness of their evidence. If you observe this, try the following strategy.

Have students work in pairs using questions such as the following to identify the main elements required to make the essay successful.

Can the reader identify the thesis statement and purpose of the essay?

Is the organization of the support (causes or effects) clear and effective? Is there a better way to organize, or can students find better supporting details?

Are students' resources reliable?

Revising: Circling to Identify Relationships

1. After students read the sample paragraphs, discuss how the conclusion restates the main idea.

2. Point out that, in a cause-and-effect essay, the final paragraph should reaffirm the original statement, confirming the relationship between the cause and the effect or predicted effect.

3. You may wish to point out that the ending in the Model From Literature might have been strengthened if Lin had related the paragraph about the United States to the rest of the article. Ask students to suggest a sentence that might tie together the whole article (e.g., "Changes like those in China can carry important lessons for us and for people in other nations.").

4. Have students read their introductions and circle the statement that presents the main idea of the essay.

5. Have students then move to the conclusion. Have them circle the restatement of the main idea.

6. If students cannot identify a clear relationship between the introduction and the conclusion, encourage them to rewrite either the introduction or the conclusion.

Integrating Workplace Skills

Explain to students that cause-and-effect writing is common in the business world. In order to create new products, revise strategies, or improve methods, companies need to know how things happen and how they might be affected by various changes. A clear statement of cause and effect (from environmental impact to estimated sales figures), with appropriate details and logical organization, is vital to business writing.

Revising

Revising Your Overall Structure

As you look at the structure of your essay, make sure that the ideas you've presented appear in logical order and are clearly connected to each other.

Strengthen Your Introduction and Conclusion

In your introduction, clearly present the main idea of your cause-and-effect essay. You may also mention reasons for your choice of topic and give readers an idea about why it is interesting or important.

▶ **REVISION STRATEGY**
Circling to Identify Relationships

To make sure that your introduction and conclusion "match up," circle the main idea you present in your introduction. Then, find and circle in your conclusion a restatement of that main idea. If your conclusion does not contain such a restatement, either rewrite your introduction or rewrite your conclusion so that they work together effectively.

Following is an example of the circling strategy:

INTRODUCTION

The ancient Peruvian society was based upon agriculture. As a result, their need for social cooperation was great. For instance, crops needed to be gathered and stored so that all the people could eat them. Just as important were the division of labor among farming, home-building, child-rearing, and hunting. When the Incas conquered Peru's tribes, the Incas continued to support the existing social structure.

CONCLUSION

With a brilliant government strategy, the Incas maintained the social structures the conquered tribes already had in place and expanded them to include an empire. Because of the Incas' wise and thoughtful governing methods, they went on to rule a peaceful and prosperous society for more than a thousand years.

206 • Cause-and-Effect Essay

Timed Writing Hint

As you revise your timed writing, make sure that your introduction states your main idea in a clear and compelling way.

⏱ TIME AND RESOURCE MANAGER

Resources
Print: *Writing Support Transparencies,* 10-F–G
Technology: *Writing and Grammar* Interactive Text, Section 10.4

Using the Full Student Edition	Using the Handbook🄷
• Work through Revision strategies with the entire class, pp. 206–208. • Have students work in groups for the peer review activity.	• Work through Revision strategies with the entire class, pp. 130–132. • Have students work in groups for the peer review activity.

Revising Your Paragraphs

Review your paragraphs to be sure that each develops a single idea and that the paragraphs themselves flow together smoothly. Check to be sure that topical paragraphs—those that contain a topic sentence—are unified.

Strengthen the Unity of Paragraphs

Revise your topical paragraphs to make them unified—to make sure that each has a topic sentence and that the other sentences within the paragraph support or develop the main idea expressed in the topic sentence.

▶ **REVISION STRATEGY**
Color-Coding to Identify Related Details

Circle each topic sentence in every topical paragraph. (Functional paragraphs—those that perform a specific function—do not have topic sentences.) Then, using a pencil of a different color, circle the details that support the topic sentence. Examine sentences you have *not* circled. If they do not support the topic sentence, either rewrite or delete them.

 **Learn More**

To learn more about unified paragraphs, see Chapter 3.

Student Work
IN PROGRESS

Name: *Jennifer Hoss*
Bel Air High School
El Paso, TX

Color-Coding to Identify Related Details
To make her writing more unified, Jennifer deleted an unrelated detail.

Because of adverse weather conditions brought on by El Niño, the Southwest's world-famous chili crops began to die. ~~The Southwest is in an area comprising New Mexico, Arizona, Texas, and California.~~ This in turn put many migrant workers, who harvest chili peppers, out of work and it raised the price of chili to much higher than it had been before. What was once affordable by the pound became a precious commodity. The Southwestern tradition of having a delicious red or green chili with every meal or as a staple ingredient was now not possible for some people until the prices fell.

Revising • **207**

Revising: Clarifying Relationships

Teaching Resources: Writing Support Transparencies, 10-G

1. Use the transparency (10-G) to generate discussion on how transitions improve the flow of writing.

2. Point out that, not only did Jennifer add transitions, but she also exchanged the conjunction *and* for *but*, to agree with the transition *not only*.

3. If students need help in generating words or phrases that will help in clarifying relationships, refer them to the chart of common transitions and transitional phrases in Chapter 9.

4. Have students reread their essays, independently or with a partner, to identify places where transitions might clarify the relationship of one idea, cause, detail, or statement to another.

Customize for
Less Advanced Students

Students frequently need help staying focused throughout the writing process. Provide them with a list of steps needed to complete the assignment, which, when completed, can be used to help evaluate their efforts.

10.4

Revising Your Sentences

Now that your paragraphs are unified, look even more closely at your writing. Within each sentence, check to see that the relationships are logical.

▶ **REVISION STRATEGY**
Clarifying Relationships

Within each sentence, make sure that the connections among words, phrases, and clauses are clear. Read each sentence carefully. If there is more than one thought within the sentence, you may have to add a transition to show how those thoughts are related. Some transitions indicate meaning or clarify the significance of a detail. For example, the phrase *not only* indicates that a detail is just one of many.

🕐 **Timed Writing Hint**

When you write quickly, you may neglect clear transitions. As you revise, add transition words as needed.

Student Work
IN PROGRESS

Name: *Jennifer Hoss*
Bel Air High School
El Paso, TX

Clarifying Relationships With Transitions
To make the relationships more clear, Jennifer added several transitions to her draft.

Because of adverse weather conditions the Southwest's world-famous chili crops began to die, and harvesting was delayed. This *not only* put many migrant workers out of work *but* and it also raised the price of chili to much higher amounts than it had been before. What was once affordable by the pound *now* became a precious commodity. The Southwestern tradition of having a delicious red or green chili with every meal or as a staple ingredient was put on the shelf for some people until the prices fell.

The phrase not only alerts readers that there is more than one effect being discussed.

By changing and to but, Jennifer clarifies the importance of the second detail in the sentence.

The word now was added to make the cause-and-effect relationship more clear.

208 • Cause-and-Effect Essay

🎸 STANDARDIZED TEST PREPARATION WORKSHOP

Phrases as Transitions Standardized test questions may require students to recognize the type of phrase used to join two sentences.

A transitional phrase has been inserted to clarify the relationship of the two sentences. Identify the type of phrase inserted.

The pilgrims' voyage was long and hard. Many died during the first winter.

The pilgrims' voyage was long and hard. Weakened by the journey, many died during the first winter.

A gerund   **C** infinitive
B participial   **D** prepositional

Students should recognize that **B** is the correct answer because the phrase "weakened by the journey" begins with a participle and functions as an adjective. Gerunds are verbals that function as nouns, so answer A is not correct. C is incorrect because the phrase does not contain the word *to* or an implied *to*. D is incorrect because the word *weakened* is not a preposition.

Grammar in Your Writing
Transitional Phrases

A **phrase** is a group of words without a subject and verb. In your cause-and-effect essay, use transitional phrases to show connections between ideas. A phrase may appear at the beginning of the sentence, between the subject and the verb, or at the end of a sentence:

Beginning:
After lunch, we worked enthusiastically.

Between the Subject and Verb:
We, after eating lunch, worked enthusiastically.

End:
We worked enthusiastically after eating lunch.

There are many types of phrases that you can use as transitions, connecting ideas in your writing.

A **prepositional phrase** is a group of words made up of a preposition and a noun or pronoun, called the object of the preposition:

Inside the studio, the sound engineers began mixing the demo.

A **participial phrase** is a participle modified by an adverb or adverb phrase or accompanied by a complement. The entire phrase acts as an adjective:

Using a high-powered lens, Annette could just make out the letters.

An **infinitive phrase** is an infinitive with modifiers, complements, or a subject, all acting together as a single part of speech:

To avoid the iceberg, the captain had to steer hard to starboard.

Find It in Your Reading   Read through "Growing Pains in China" by Cindy Lin, on pages 198–199. Identify three sentences that contain transitional phrases—phrases that connect ideas. Explain the ways in which those phrases help to clarify the relationships within the essay.

Find It in Your Writing   Review your draft to identify where you have used phrases to show transitions. If you cannot identify six phrases, challenge yourself to add at least one more to your writing. Notice the improvement.

For more on phrases, see Chapter 20.

Transitional Phrases

1. Explain that there are two ways to create a transition. One is by combining two sentences with related ideas, and the other is by adding a transitional phrase to a sentence.

2. Offer the following examples of the two ways to create transitional phrases.

   Combining:

   We took a walk in the country. We found a nice spot. We had a picnic.

   We took a walk in the country. At a nice spot, we had a picnic.

   or Walking in the country, we found a nice spot. We had a picnic there.

   Adding:

   The snow fell thick and soft. I was safe and warm.

   The snow fell thick and soft. Inside the cabin, I was safe and warm.

3. Have students work in pairs to create groups of sentences, similar to those above, that can benefit from the use of transitions.

Find It in Your Reading

Point out that the exercise does not require students to identify the types of transitional phrases. The transitional phrases in the essay do not all fit into the three categories defined here. You may want to have students look for all the transitions in the essay, rather than just the transitional phrases. You may wish to direct attention to specific paragraphs or sentences to help less advanced students.

Find It in Your Writing

Have students read their own essays, scanning for transitional phrases. If students find few, encourage them to add at least one participial and one infinitive phrase to the essay. Remind them that the objective is to make relationships between ideas clear.

☑ ONGOING ASSESSMENT: Prerequisite Skills

If students have difficulty with transitional phrases, you may find it helpful to refer them to the following materials to ensure coverage of prerequisite knowledge.

In the Textbook	Print Resources	Technology
Phrases, Section 20.1	*Grammar Exercise Workbook,* Phrases, pp. 57–74	*On-line Exercise Bank,* Section 20.1

Revising: Underlining Repeated Words and Forms of Words

1. Read and discuss the material on page 210, emphasizing the examples of useful and careless repetition.

2. Have students read through their drafts to look for repeated words or forms of words.

3. Tell students that reading out loud, even if to themselves, can make the repeated words more obvious, since the ear is often more sensitive to repetition than the eye.

4. Point out that the examples are not the only types of repetition that occur. Common repetitions may be sentence openers, such as "There is . . ." or "There are . . . ."

Customize for
ESL Students

Students who are learning English are likely to repeat the words with which they are most familiar. Pair up students with more fluent speakers who can help them find (and explain) suitable replacements for repeated words in their essays.

Revising: Peer Review

1. If students are reluctant to read their own essays aloud, allow group members to read others' work.

2. If you feel your students would benefit from prompts, offer the following questions on the chalkboard.

   • Does the introduction grab your attention?

   • Are the ideas well supported?

   • Does the conclusion clearly restate the position?

   • Is the tone appropriate for the audience and purpose?

10.4

Revising Your Word Choice
Review Your Word Choice

If you use the same word or form of it several times within a passage, your writing can sound tedious and awkward. Learn to distinguish between useful repetition and careless repetition. Useful repetition helps to emphasize a point or to make a passage memorable. Careless repetition creates a dull impression on the reader.

USEFUL REPETITION:	In the 1920's, people *flocked* to theaters to see plays; in the 1930's, they *flocked* to theaters to see movies.
CARELESS REPETITION:	Because I have always loved the *theater,* I'm studying *theater* and *theater* arts in school.

▶ **REVISION STRATEGY**
Underlining Repeated Words and Forms of Words

Read through your draft, and underline repeated words or forms of words. Then, review your draft. If passages containing repetition are not intended, replace some of the repeated words with synonyms, words with the same meaning.

OVERUSED WORD:	They *housed* the furniture for the *house* in a shed out back.
VARIED WORDS:	They *stored* the furniture for the *house* in a shed out back.
OVERUSED WORD:	We tried to *locate* a better *location* for our party.
VARIED WORDS:	We tried to *find* a better *location* for our party.

Peer Review
"Say Back"

Work with a small group of peers to get feedback on your writing.

• Read your paper aloud to your peer editors twice.

• Have peers jot down two positive comments and three constructive comments for improvement.

• One by one, have your peers read aloud their comments to you.

• Take their comments into consideration as you prepare your final draft.

⚙ Grammar and Style Tip

If there is a thesaurus in your word-processing program, use it to locate alternative word choices.

10.5 Editing and Proofreading

Reread your cause-and-effect essay carefully, correcting any mistakes you find in spelling, punctuation, and grammar. Double-check statistics or other details you present as fact.

Focusing on Commonly Confused Words

Proofread your essay carefully. Make sure you've correctly used the following commonly confused words: *since, because, then,* and *than.*

Technology Tip

Use the Find feature of your word-processing program to locate the words *since, because, then,* and *than.* Once you've located those words, check to be sure your usage of them is correct.

Grammar in Your Writing
Using *Since, Because, Then,* and *Than* Correctly

As you proofread, make sure that you have used these words appropriately.

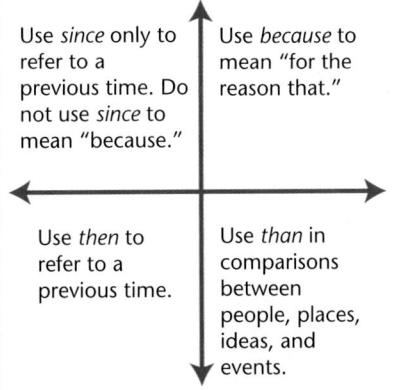

Use *since* only to refer to a previous time. Do not use *since* to mean "because."

Use *because* to mean "for the reason that."

Use *then* to refer to a previous time.

Use *than* in comparisons between people, places, ideas, and events.

Find It in Your Reading In "Growing Pains in China," which appears on pages 198–199, Cindy Lin correctly uses the word *since.* Find the usage, and explain why her choice was correct.

Find It in Your Writing As you proofread your cause-and-effect essay, check to be sure you have used the words *since, because, then,* and *than* correctly. If you have not used any of those words, challenge yourself to add them to make clear connections between your ideas.

For more on word usage, see Chapter 26.

Editing and Proofreading • 211

Step-by-Step Teaching Guide

Editing and Proofreading

1. Remind students that editing and proofreading should be viewed as a vital part of the writing process.

2. Suggest that students check their punctuation carefully, paying particular attention to the commas, which are commonly misused.

Step-by-Step Teaching Guide

Using *Since, Because, Then,* and *Than* Correctly

1. Referring students to the chart in the text, explain that these four words are often misused. To make certain readers know what is meant (and have a good opinion of the writer), it is important to use the right word when writing—and when speaking.

2. Ask students to write sentences that use these four words correctly, and scan their essays for occurrences of these words, to check their use.

Find It in Your Reading

Challenge students to find examples of *because, then,* and *than* in "Growing Pains in China." Ask students to explain why each usage is correct.

Find It in Your Writing.

Have students swap their drafts with a classmate. Have each student read the draft to see whether these common words have been used correctly. Have the reader and the writer discuss the findings and, if necessary, have the writer make revisions.

⏱ TIME AND RESOURCE MANAGER

Resources
Print: *Scoring Rubrics on Transparency,* Ch. 10; *Writing Assessment and Portfolio Management; Formal Assessment,* Ch. 10
Technology: *Writing and Grammar* Interactive Text, Section 10.5

Using the Full Student Edition	Using the Handbook Ⓗ
• Review p. 211 in class, including Grammar in Your Writing. • Analyze the Final Draft of "El Niño." • Have students edit and proofread their essays in class.	• Review p. 135 in class, including Grammar in Your Writing. • Have students edit and proofread their essays in class.

Publishing and Presenting

1. Encourage students to seek audiences in their families, community, or even on the Internet.

2. Discuss how students might use visuals to further enhance their essays. What kinds of information are best presented visually?

ASSESS and CLOSE

Assessment

Teaching Resources: Scoring Rubrics Transparency, Ch. 10; Writing Assessment and Portfolio Management; Formal Assessment, Chapter 10

1. Display the Scoring Rubric transparency and review the criteria in class.

2. Before students proceed with self-assessment, you may wish to review the Final Draft of the Student Work in Progress on pages 213–214. Have students score the Final Draft in one or more of the rubric categories.

3. In addition to student self-assessment, you may wish to use the following assessment options:

   • score student essays yourself, using the rubric and scoring models from *Writing Assessment and Portfolio Management*.

   • review the Standardized Test Preparation Workshop on pages 218–219, and have students respond to a cause-and-effect writing prompt.

   • administer the Chapter 10 assessment from *Formal Assessment* in the Teaching Resources to measure students' grasp of concepts presented.

10.6 Publishing and Presenting

When you are finished writing your cause-and-effect essay, share it with others. Following are some ideas for sharing your writing:

Building Your Portfolio

1. **Presentation** Use your essay as the basis of a cause-and-effect presentation. Use photographs, charts, and diagrams as you explain the topic of your essay. Save the essay and visuals in your portfolio.

2. **E-mail** Share your essay electronically. Type the essay using word-processing software. Then, attach the file to an e-mail to a friend or relative.

Reflecting on Your Writing

Think back on your experience of writing a cause-and-effect essay. Then, respond to the following questions, and save your responses in your portfolio.

• During the process of writing, what did you learn about the subject you chose?

• Which strategy for writing a cause-and-effect essay might you recommend to someone as being most useful? Why?

Internet Tip

To see model essays scored with this rubric, go on-line: PHSchool.com Enter Web Code: eek-1001

Rubric for Self-Assessment

Use the following criteria to evaluate your cause-and-effect essay:

	Score 4	Score 3	Score 2	Score 1
Audience and Purpose	Consistently targets an audience through word choice and details; clearly identifies purpose in thesis statement	Targets an audience through most word choice and details; identifies purpose in thesis statement	Misses target audience by including a wide range of word choice and details; presents no clear purpose	Addresses no specific audience or purpose
Organization	Presents a clear, consistent organizational strategy to show cause and effect	Presents a clear organizational strategy with occasional inconsistencies; shows cause and effect	Presents an inconsistent organizational strategy; creates illogical presentation of causes and effects	Demonstrates a lack of organizational strategy; creates a confusing presentation
Elaboration	Successfully links causes with effects; fully elaborates connections among ideas	Links causes with effects; elaborates connections among most ideas	Links some causes with some effects; elaborates connections among most ideas	Develops and elaborates no links between causes and effects
Use of Language	Chooses clear transitions to convey ideas; presents very few mechanical errors	Chooses transitions to convey ideas; presents few mechanical errors	Misses some opportunities for transitions to convey ideas; presents many mechanical errors	Demonstrates poor use of language; presents many mechanical errors

212 • Cause-and-Effect Essay

☑ ONGOING ASSESSMENT: Assess Mastery

Use one or both of the following options to assess mastery of the cause-and-effect essay.

Self-Assessment Ask students to score their essays using the rubric provided. In a single paragraph, have students reflect on the most valuable thing they learned in completing this assignment.

Teacher Assessment You may use the rubric and scoring models provided in *Writing Assessment and Portfolio Management* in the Teaching Resources to score students' essays.

10.7 Student Work IN PROGRESS

FINAL DRAFT

El Niño

Jennifer Hoss
Bel Air High School
El Paso, Texas

For the past year or so, El Niño has been a troublemaking culprit, causing mischief and mayhem with the chili pepper crop in the United States Southwest. In addition to causing local trouble, El Niño has been the cause of terrible occurrences around the globe, and it is not the innocent-faced little boy the direct Spanish translation suggests. In fact, the awful effects of El Niño may be yet to come.

El Niño is a weather pattern that brings with it rain, wind, drought, thunderstorms, heat, and other examples of Mother Nature's fury. Past El Niños have occurred in 1953, 1957–58, 1965, 1972–73, 1976–77, and 1982. To put it in simple terms, El Niño is caused by a cooling of the waters in the Peru Current off the coast of South America. The change in temperature occurs because for most of the year, the east Pacific is cooler than the west Pacific. The trade winds drag the warmer water west, and it "piles up" on the ocean's surface, resulting in heavy rainfall. The opposite situation exists on the eastern boundary: The cooler waters experience relatively dry weather. During El Niño, this situation is upset. The water on the west comes back east in big waves and the west becomes dry, whereas the east experiences heavy rainfall.

The El Niño weather pattern produces more than violent weather, however: It also has had a huge effect here in the United States, wreaking havoc on the chili crops of western Texas and southern New Mexico.

▲ Critical Viewing
What weather conditions might have caused the situation pictured? **[Connect]**

The first paragraph of Jennifer's essay reveals her topic: the causes and effects of El Niño.

In the second paragraph, Jennifer discusses some causes of the El Niño weather pattern.

Jennifer's essay is logically organized: The first half explains causes of El Niño; the second half explains the effects of El Niño.

Student Work in Progress • 213

Step-by-Step Teaching Guide

Final Draft

1. Read the essay aloud, pointing out these key elements of a cause-and-effect essay:
   - The topic has been well chosen.
   - The topic is focused and manageable.
   - Audience and purpose have been carefully considered.
   - The tone of the essay is appropriate to the audience.
   - The introduction engages the reader and gives the reader a good idea of what is to come.
   - The body of the essay clearly identifies causes and effects.
   - The essay is logically organized.
   - The conclusion restates the essay's main idea.

2. Tell students to pay particular attention to Jennifer's use of transitions. The relationships of ideas are closely tied together by transitions. Have students find examples of two or three transitions and describe what they connect.

3. Ask whether the students feel confident that the author understood her topic. Did she supply enough detail to make her conclusion credible?

4. Ask students to review this essay in terms of the first two bulleted points. Suggest that students use all eight points as a checklist when revising their own essays or when conducting reviews.

Critical Viewing

Connect Students will observe that flooding often follows heavy rain, or in some locations, an earthquake.

Teaching From the Final Draft

Explain that sometimes, in a longer work, more than just a word or a phrase is needed to show the relation between events or thoughts. Point out that at the bottom of page 213, Jennifer uses an entire paragraph ("The El Niño weather patterns . . .") to create a transition between the first part of the essay, which describes El Niño, and the second half of the essay, which relates the effects.

Integrating Viewing and Representing Skills

Ask students to create pictures or collages that illustrate a cause-and-effect relationship. Tell them that, if they wish, they may use mixed media in their representation. For example, they might show an image of someone smoking followed by a chart that shows increased incidence of lung cancer.

Integrating Speaking and Listening Skills

Challenge students to jot down a list of the main points, summarizing the cause-and-effect theme and details of the model. Ask each student to use these notes to prepare for an oral report. Ask volunteers to give their oral reports to the class.

Critical Viewing

Analyze The crop appears unhealthy because of its withered stalks and its wilted, tattered leaves.

▼ **Critical Viewing**
Is the crop pictured a healthy one? Why or why not? **[Analyze]**

Because of adverse weather conditions brought on by El Niño, the Southwest's world-famous chili crops began to die. This not only put many migrant workers out of work, but it also raised the price of chili much higher than it had been before. What was once affordable by the pound became a precious commodity. The southwestern tradition of having a delicious red or green chili with every meal or as a staple ingredient was now not possible for some people until the prices fell.

While chili-loving patrons from across the globe may have suffered, chili farmers have suffered even more. Acres of crops were ruined or even killed by extremely high winds and excessive rain storms. If that weren't enough, the winds and rain brought along with them a virus that added to the devastation of the chili crops. Millions of dollars washed away with the rain, leaving farmers, families, and migrant workers without a means of making a living.

This year's El Niño has passed, but the world is still suffering from its aftermath. Records from the past have shown that the winters following El Niño have been some of the coldest and fiercest in history. In fact, some scientists argue that El Niño and the ice ages may actually be connected. Cold winters often signal the coming of poor summer crops, so perhaps the worst effects of El Niño have yet to be seen.

Transitions like "because" and "in turn" help connect the ideas in this paragraph.

Jennifer provides specific examples to support her statement that chili farmers have suffered more than others.

In the last paragraph, Jennifer concludes with a chilling prediction: El Niño's worst effect may be yet to come.

Connected Assignment   Documentary

What Is a Documentary?

Documentaries are films that focus on real-life people and issues. Because they often deal with specific problems or issues, they usually demonstrate or track cause-and-effect relationships. An overarching narrative often ties all the pieces together and emphasizes cause-and-effect links.

The basis for a documentary is a script, written in stage format with stage directions and dialogue. In such a script, stage directions indicate the sequence of elements and camera shots along with any of the actors' movements.

Write your own documentary script. Use the following writing process guidelines:

Prewriting Find a topic by thinking about your community and its history or problems. Look for trends that you can explain and new developments you can track to their results.

Research your topic at the library and through visits to locations. Conduct tape-recorded interviews, and take notes about your observations. Then, jot down your ideas for ways to present your findings visually. Also, look for existing visuals such as film clips. Generate index cards for each key idea, and note possible ways to express it. Then, focus on structuring the cause-and-effect relationship you want to show.

Drafting As you draft, bring your vision to life. Mix voice-over narration and still images (shots of letters or the outside of a building, for example) with live action scenes. When you're happy with the sequence and blend of visuals, write the narration in the dialogue portion of the script. Within the narrative, provide any necessary background information, identify people and places, and highlight cause-and-effect links.

Revising and Editing Mentally "view" your documentary as you read your script. Improve clarity by adding explanations, and strengthen connections by adding transitional sentences or phrases.

Publishing and Presenting Film your documentary, or a portion of it, and hold a screening for friends, peers, teachers, and relatives. Have a question-and-answer session following the screening.

▲ **Critical Viewing**
Judging from this photograph, does the person who's filming seem experienced? Explain why or why not. **[Make a Judgment]**

Connected Assignment: Documentary • 215

Examining Images

1. After students have read this page, review the wide influence of the story of Tristan and Isolde. Have students discuss why they think the tale of Tristan and Isolde has had such an impact on artists, writers, and composers.

2. Assign students to further research and explore the original Celtic tale of Tristan and Iseult, and the story's role as an influence on Richard Wagner and Ferdinand Leeke.

3. Have students present their findings to the class.

4. To prepare students for the Writing Activity, create an annotated timeline with the class using information from the students' presentations.

Viewing and Representing

Activity When students present their findings from the research activity, have them add to an annotated timeline describing the events of the specific time period they have researched.

Critical Viewing

Assess Students may mention that the figures seem romanticized because their actions and dress appear ceremonial and highly dramatic.

Spotlight on the Humanities

Examining Images

Focus on Art: *Tristan and Isolde*

Powerful stories can have a ripple effect through the ages. For example, artist Ferdinand Leeke painted his famous rendition of Tristan and Isolde in 1889. His depiction was inspired by composer Richard Wagner's opera *Tristan and Isolde*, which, in turn, was inspired by the centuries-old legend of Tristan and Iseult.

Literature Connection Known as one of the world's greatest love stories, the Celtic tale of Tristan and Iseult was written in the mid-twelfth century by a French poet. The tale centers on a princess and a knight, who accidentally drink a love potion and immediately fall in love. When Tristan is wounded, he calls for Iseult because he believes only she can save him. Another woman, Iseult of the White Hands, tells him deceivingly that the first Iseult refused his request. Tristan dies of a broken heart. When the first Iseult hears what has happened, she also dies of a broken heart. Tristan and Iseult were buried side by side. A vine grew from Tristan's grave, and a rose grew from Iseult's. The vine and rose met, entwined, and never separated.

Music Connection Between 1857–1859 German composer Richard Wagner wrote the words and music for his opera *Tristan and Isolde*. The three-act opera tells of the fatal love of the Irish princess Isolde and the Cornish knight Tristan. Wagner had to wait six years before he found a patron—King Ludwig II of Bavaria—to finance the production of the opera. Its leading roles are considered very difficult to perform.

Cause-and-Effect Writing Activity: Annotated Timeline of a Story's History

Throughout the ages, popular stories have developed and then were told and retold time and again. Choose one such story, and trace its history. Develop an annotated timeline in which you chronicle the story's history, the differences among versions, and the cultural and historical influences that might be the cause of such variations. Include visuals, and post your finished timeline in the classroom.

Tristan and Isolde, 1912, John Duncan, City of Edinburgh Museums and Art Galleries

▲ **Critical Viewing**
Do the figures in this painting seem romanticized or realistic? Explain. [Assess]

Media and Technology Skills

Examining the Effects of Media on Perceptions of Reality

Activity: Prepare a Multimedia Evaluation

Television viewers often unconsciously absorb the images and ideas broadcast day and night. You can analyze the effects of specific television genres or programs to understand how people's choices and attitudes are influenced by what they view.

Situation comedies, or sitcoms, are one of television's most successful genres. By carefully analyzing today's most popular sitcoms, you can uncover ways in which these programs shape viewers' perspectives.

Learn About It Begin by finding out which current sitcoms are most popular. An entertainment magazine might report weekly Nielsen ratings, which describe television viewing patterns. If you prefer, conduct your own survey to discover which television programs are most popular.

Record It Record and view several episodes of the program you plan to evaluate. Make an annotated episode log to help you remember the original broadcast date and theme or topic of each episode.

Date Aired	Plot Summary	Theme
3/21/00	George gets fired.	Have a backup plan.

Evaluate It After viewing three or four episodes, evaluate the program's underlying principles. To think about how the program might affect viewers, ask questions such as the following:

- What beliefs or values do most of the characters share?
- Have any of the characters' clothing styles become popular because of this series?
- What recurring motifs or events occur on almost every episode?
- Are there any "catch phrases" or familiar sayings associated with this show?
- Which specific scenes best reflect the program's attitudes?

Present It Recap your analysis for your class in a multimedia presentation. Select brief scenes from the episodes you recorded that illustrate your evaluation. You can use video editing to create a highlights tape or simply cue up desired scenes. Allow time for your audience to share their insights into each program's effects.

Media and Technology Skills • **217**

▶ Lesson Objectives

1. To deconstruct media to get the main idea of the message's content
2. To examine the effect of media on constructing his/her own perception of reality
3. To focus attention, interpret, respond, and evaluate a speaker's message
4. To use a range of techniques to plan and create a media text and reflect critically on the work produced

What You'll Need
- Television
- Videocassette Recorder (editing features optional)

Perspective on the Past
- Viewing television programs of the past can help you understand how these sources influence people.

Step-By-Step Teaching Guide

Examining the Effect of Media on Perceptions of Reality

Teaching Resources: Writing Support Transparencies, 10-H; Writing Support Activity Book, 10-1

1. Review popular sitcoms with the class, and draw conclusions about how these programs influence people's attitudes.
2. Have students consider the questions in Evaluate It as they prepare their multimedia evaluations.
3. Allow students the opportunity to offer ideas and insights into each program's effects.

Customize for
Musical Learners

Have students evaluate the theme music of the sitcom they have chosen. As they evaluate the program's underlying principles, have students analyze the appropriateness of the sitcom's theme music. They may choose to include it as a supporting detail in their multimedia presentation. If they think the music is inappropriate, have them describe or select music that would better fit the show.

Standardized Test Preparation Workshop

Analyzing Cause-and-Effect Relationships

On some standardized tests, you will be prompted to evaluate and show your understanding of various cause-and-effect relationships. These prompts measure your ability to identify, analyze, and explain in writing the causal relationship between two or more events or circumstances. You will be tested on your ability to

- Clearly answer or respond to the prompt.

- Provide sufficient details that elaborate upon and support your statements.

- Organize details in a clear and coherent format.

- Use correct grammar, spelling, and punctuation.

As you draft your response to a writing prompt, follow the stages of the writing process. Devote sufficient time to prewriting, drafting, revising, and proofreading, bearing in mind the time constraints of a standardized test.

Following is an example of a cause-and-effect writing prompt. Use the suggestions on the following page to help you respond. The clocks next to each stage show the suggested percentage of time to devote to each stage.

Sample Writing Situation

Read the following writing prompt, and draft a response. Use specific details to support your ideas.

Suppose it is discovered that the planet Mars is able to support human life. How might things change on Earth in terms of global politics, science, education, social programs, and so on? Give specific examples of the changes you foresee.

 **TEST-TAKING TIP**

Remind students that transitional words often help to make connections in writing clear to the reader. Because cause-and-effect processes are best described using chronological-order organization, transitional words and phrases can help the reader know where he or she is in the cause-and-effect process. When writing a cause-and-effect essay, students should use transitional words and phrases such as these: *as a result, consequently, because,* and *therefore.*

Prewriting

Allow one quarter of your time for prewriting.

Gather Information Quickly jot down ideas that you have in response to the writing prompt. When finished, review your list to decide on a focus for your response. For example, you may want to focus on how world governments will decide on "ownership" of Mars territory.

Organize Your Ideas Once you have focused your ideas, decide on the most effective and logical organizational method. Because you will be discussing cause-and-effect relationships, you may consider chronological organization—showing the flow of causes and effects—or you may choose to examine multiple effects of a single cause.

Drafting

Allow approximately half of your time for drafting.

Elaborate As you draft your response, include various types of supporting details. For example, you could cite historical similarities that give your prediction believability or you could use statistical figures to explain your ideas in depth. Also, give examples of how you think people will behave following the announcement that people will be able to live on Mars.

Create a Tone Choose your words carefully as you draft, to create a tone or to reveal your attitude about your subject. In this response, you are revealing a prediction; therefore, your tone should be convincing and authoritative.

Revising, Editing, and Proofreading

Allow one quarter of your time to revise and proofread your response.

Strengthen Unity Read through your response to make sure that each paragraph addresses the prompt. Revise or delete paragraphs that stray from your main point. Also, check details within paragraphs to make sure they support each paragraph's main idea. If you find a detail that does not, either rewrite it or delete it.

Check Verb Tense Be especially careful to review your use of verb tense throughout your response. Because you are writing a prediction, you probably will make use of the future tense as well as the present and past tenses.

Correct Errors Proofread carefully to locate and correct any and all errors you have made in grammar, spelling, and punctuation. Also, check to be sure that you have indented each paragraph and that you have titled and signed your response.

In-Depth Lesson Plan

	LESSON FOCUS	PRINT AND MEDIA RESOURCES
DAY 1	**Introduction to Exposition: Problem-and-Solution Essays** Students learn key elements of problem-and-solution essays and analyze the Model From Literature. (pp. 220–223/⊞138–139)	*Writers at Work* DVD, Exposition *Writing and Grammar* **Interactive Text**, Ch. 11, Introduction
DAY 2	**Prewriting** Students choose and narrow a topic, consider their audience and purpose, and gather information. (pp. 224–227/⊞140–143)	**Teaching Resources** *Writing Support Transparencies*, 11-A–D; *Writing Support Activity Book*, 11-1; *Topic Bank for Heterogeneous Classes*, Ch. 11 *Writing and Grammar* **Interactive Text**, Section 11.2
DAY 3	**Drafting** Students organize their ideas and write their first drafts. (pp. 228–229/⊞144–145)	**Teaching Resources** *Writing Support Transparencies*, 11-E–F; *Writing Support Activity Book*, 11-2 *Writing and Grammar* **Interactive Text**, Section 11.3
DAY 4	**Revising** Students revise their drafts in terms of overall structure, paragraphs, sentences, and word choice. (pp. 230–234/⊞146–150)	**Teaching Resources** *Writing Support Transparencies*, 11-G–J *Writing and Grammar* **Interactive Text**, Section 11.4
DAY 5	**Editing and Proofreading; Publishing and Presenting** Students check their work for accuracy and correctness and present their final drafts. (pp. 235–238/⊞151–152)	**Teaching Resources** *Scoring Rubrics on Transparency*, Ch. 11; *Writing Assessment and Portfolio Management; Formal Assessment*, Ch. 11 *Writing and Grammar* **Interactive Text**, Sections 11.5–6

Accelerated Lesson Plan

	LESSON FOCUS	PRINT AND MEDIA RESOURCES
DAY 1	**Introduction Through Drafting** Students review characteristics of problem-and-solution essays, select topics, and write drafts. (pp. 220–229/⊞138–145)	**Teaching Resources** *Writing Support Transparencies*, 11-A–F; *Writing Support Activity Book*, 11-1–2 *Writing and Grammar* **Interactive Text**, Ch. 11, Introduction through Section 11.3
DAY 2	**Revising Through Presenting** Students work individually or with peers to revise, edit, and proofread their work for presentation. (pp. 230–238/⊞146–152)	**Teaching Resources:** *Writing Support Transparencies*, 11-G–J; *Scoring Rubrics on Transparency*, Ch. 11; *Writing Assessment and Portfolio Management; Formal Assessment*, Ch. 11 *Writing and Grammar* **Interactive Text**, Sections 11.4–6

Options for Adapting Lesson Plans

HOMEWORK

Have students complete any stage of the lesson for homework.

FEATURES

Extend coverage with Connected Assignment (p. 239/⊞153), Spotlight on the Humanities (p. 240), Media and Technology Skills (p. 241), and the Standardized Test Preparation Workshop (p. 242).

TECHNOLOGY

Students can complete any stage of the lesson on the computer, using *Writing and Grammar* Interactive Text or a word-processing program. Have them print out their completed work.

Writing and Grammar Handbook Alignment

Page numbers in Step-by-Step Teaching Guides in this Teacher's Edition refer to pages from the full student text. Handbook page references, indicated with this icon 🄷, are provided in Time and Resource Manager boxes and at the bottom of each Teacher's Edition page.

INTEGRATED SKILLS COVERAGE

Integrating Grammar
The Six Tenses of Verbs, SE p. 233/🄷149
Restrictive and Nonrestrictive Clauses, SE p. 235/🄷151

Reading/Writing Connection
Evaluate the Author's Message, SE p. 222
Writing Application, SE p. 223

Viewing and Representing
Critical Viewing, SE pp. 220, 222, 230, 234, 237, 238, 239, 240/🄷138, 146, 150, 153
Appreciating the Arts, SE p. 240

Speaking and Listening
SE p. 235/🄷151; ATE pp. 229, 238

Technology
Using Technology to Find Answers, SE pp. 236, 241/🄷152

Real-World Connection, ATE p. 225

Research Skills, ATE p. 227

Organization Skills, ATE p. 230

ASSESSMENT SUPPORT

Standardized Test Preparation Workshop SE p. 242; ATE p. 232
Standardized Test Preparation Workbook, pp. 21–22
Scoring Rubrics on Transparency, Ch. 11
Formal Assessment, Ch. 11
Writing Assessment and Portfolio Management

MEETING INDIVIDUAL NEEDS

Less Advanced Students ATE p. 243. See also Ongoing Assessments ATE pp. 222, 225, 226, 229, 231.
More Advanced Students ATE pp. 228, 243
ESL Students ATE pp. 224, 231
Interpersonal Learners ATE p. 226
Spatial Learners ATE pp. 230, 232, 238

BLOCK SCHEDULING

Pacing Suggestions
For 90-minute Blocks
• Have students complete the Prewriting and Drafting stages in a single period.
• Focus one class period on Revising and Editing and Publishing and Presenting. Allow at least 30 minutes for peer revision.

Resources for Varying Instruction
• *Writing and Grammar* **Interactive Text** A 90-minute block provides an ideal opportunity for students to work on the computer.
• *Writers at Work* **DVD** Show the Exposition segment in class.

Professional Development Support
• *How to Manage Instruction in the Block* This teaching resource provides management and activity suggestions.

MEDIA AND TECHNOLOGY

For the Student
• *Writing and Grammar* **Interactive Text,** Ch. 11
• *On-line Exercise Bank,* Section 22.1

For the Teacher
• *Writers at Work* **DVD,** Exposition
• **Teacher EXPRESS** CD-ROM

WRITING AND GRAMMAR ON-LINE

Interactive Text (On-line or on CD-ROM)
• Easily navigable instruction with interactive Revision Checkers
• Full use of e-rater™, the essay-scoring system (on-line only)

Companion Web Site PHSchool.com
• Scoring rubrics with models (use Web Code eek-1001)

See the Go On-line! **feature, SE p. iii.**

LITERATURE CONNECTIONS

Related selections from *Prentice Hall Literature, Penguin Edition,* Grade 10:

Professional Model "A Problem," Anton Chekhov, SE p. 223
Topic Bank Option "The Dog That Bit People," James Thurber, SE p. 225/🄷141

▶ *Lesson Objectives*

1. To write a problem-and-solution essay appropriate to audience and purpose
2. To read to appreciate the writer's craft and to discover models for writing
3. To use prewriting strategies to generate ideas and plan
4. To research self-selected topics using texts and technical resources
5. To represent information in a variety of ways, including graphics
6. To develop and revise drafts in terms of structure, paragraphs, sentences, and word choice
7. To edit and proofread to ensure standard English usage and grammar
8. To evaluate writing for both mechanics and content
9. To refine selected work for publication

Critical Viewing

Speculate Students might say that the people in the photograph are cleaning up after a storm or some other type of disaster.

11 Exposition
Problem-and-Solution Essay

▲ Critical Viewing
What problem might the people in this photograph be working together to solve? **[Speculate]**

Problem-and-Solution Essays in Everyday Life

Tackling difficult problems can help you develop powerful and effective strategies for daily life. As the poet Jean Toomer said, "We learn the rope of life by untying its knots." Writing about problems and solutions can help you find innovative solutions to your problems and allow you to share your discoveries with an audience. You might write a letter to a relative suggesting a way to resolve a family conflict or share your new solution to a school dilemma in a newspaper editorial.

220 • Exposition

⏱ TIME AND RESOURCE MANAGER

Resources
Technology: *Writers at Work* DVD, Exposition; *Writing and Grammar* Interactive Text, Ch. 11

Using the Full Student Edition	Using the Handbook🄷
• Cover pp. 220–221 in class. • Discuss examples of problem-and-solution essays with which you and your students are familiar. • Read the Model From Literature (pp. 222–223) and use it to brainstorm for essay ideas with students.	• Cover pp. 138–139 in class. • Discuss examples of problem-and-solution essays with which you and your students are familiar.

What Is a Problem-and-Solution Essay?

Exposition is writing that explains or informs. A **problem-and-solution essay** is a specific type of exposition that identifies a problem and presents one or more potential solutions. An effective problem-and-solution essay

- clearly states a specific, real-life problem.
- identifies the most important aspects of the problem.
- presents one or more possible solutions.
- supports each solution with specific details and logical reasons.

To preview the criteria on which your problem-and-solution essay may be evaluated, see the Rubric for Self-Assessment on page 236.

Types of Problem-and-Solution Essays

Problem-and-solution essays may address a wide variety of issues. Following are some of the specific types of issues they can address:

- **Consumer issues** include problems with products or services and how they can be remedied.
- **Local issues** may be problems facing your community, such as issues of school funding and library staffing.
- **Business issues** involve problems facing a company or business, such as budget shortages or schedule delays.

PREVIEW
Student Work
IN PROGRESS

Patrick Swan, of Muncie High School in Muncie, Indiana, realized that the parking situation at his school was out of control. Follow along as he uses prewriting, drafting, and revising techniques to develop an essay that analyzes the problem and proposes a solution. A final version of Pat's problem-and-solution editorial appears at the end of the chapter.

Writers in ACTION

Without challenges, life would become too predictable and even a bit boring. Author Marsha Sinetar acknowledges the importance of working on hard challenges:

"Rather than denying problems, focus inventively, intentionally on what solutions might look or feel like. . . . Our mind is meant to generate ideas that help us escape circumstantial traps—if we trust it to do so."

Problem-and-Solution Essay • 221

Reading: Evaluate the Author's Message

Tell students that as they read a problem-and-solution essay, they should evaluate the validity of the writer's proposed solutions. What details support the writer's ideas? Is there a sufficient quantity of support? Does each solution directly relate to the problem? How do the problem and proposed solutions compare with similar situations you know of or have read about? Have students keep those questions in mind as they read Mark Carwardine's essay.

Step-by-Step Teaching Guide

Engage Students Through Literature

1. After reading the essay, use questions such as these to prompt discussion about it:

   What are some of the obstacles to whale conservation?

   What encouraging trends are taking place? (Many whale species are thriving; public awareness is increasing.)

   What are conservation organizations accomplishing? (They are cultivating politicians and fishers, educating children about conservation, and developing action plans for endangered species.)

2. Allow students to make other observations about the passage.

3. Ask students to brainstorm for related problem-and-solution essay topics. Here are some possibilities:

   Other endangered species

   Countries that still hunt whales, and why

   Increasing environmental consciousness in your school

Critical Viewing

Connect Students might note that the majesty of the whale makes it seem worth protecting, and its disappearing into the waves might represent escaping or seem to signal a possible farewell.

11.1 Model From Literature

Mark Carwardine has a degree in zoology from London University. Since 1986, he has been a writer, consultant, lecturer, and broadcaster.

Reading Writing Connection

Reading Strategy: Evaluate the Author's Message When you read a problem-and-solution essay, don't accept a proposed solution unless the author has included thorough support.

from
Caring for Whales, Dolphins, and Porpoises

Mark Carwardine

The final death toll is shocking: about a million sperm whales, at least half a million fin whales, more than 350,000 blue whales, nearly a quarter of a million humpbacks, and literally hundreds of thousands of others. Two million whales were killed in the Southern Ocean alone. Some years were particularly bad: In the 1930–31 season, 28,325 blue whales were killed; more than 30 years later, in 1963–64, no fewer than 29,255 sperm whales met their death—we still had not learned the lessons of the past. Today, we are left with merely the tattered remnants: In most cases, no more than 5–10 percent of the original great whale populations remain.

By the time the animals were given official protection, it was almost too late and, indeed, some species may never recover. . . . But there is some good news, as well. Against all the odds, several species appear to be bouncing back. The gray whale is the ultimate success story. The North Atlantic stock was probably wiped out by early whalers, and only a remnant population survives in the western North Pacific. But in the eastern North Pacific, it has made such a dramatic recovery that it is now believed to be at least as abundant as in the days before whaling. Meanwhile, there

222 • Problem-and-Solution Essay

▲ **Critical Viewing** Why is this photograph an appropriate choice for a problem-and-solution essay about whaling? **[Connect]**

Carwardine begins with a direct statement of the problem. Next, he uses detailed statistics to elaborate on the situation.

Carwardine points out that some progress has been made already in addressing the problem.

☑ ONGOING ASSESSMENT: Monitor and Reinforce

Some students will take an interest in learning more about the Southern Ocean Whale Sanctuary and the Whale and Dolphin Conservation Society. Try these strategies.

Option 1 Have interested students conduct research in the school library or on the Internet. Have them make fact sheets about each topic and share them with the class.	**Option 2** Students might make illustrated posters on these topics. Have them compile facts, drawings, and copies of photographs on posterboard and display them in the classroom for their peers to learn from and enjoy.

has been a dramatic increase in blue whale numbers off the coast of California, where about 2,000 animals gather for the summer and autumn. Humpbacks and southern right whales are also making a comeback in many places.

It is only natural that, from time to time, everyone involved in whale conservation feels a sense of despair and helplessness. But progress is being made, albeit slowly, and the attitudes of governments and other key decision makers are gradually changing. In the past decade, there have been many success stories, from the establishment of the Southern Ocean Whale Sanctuary, surrounding Antarctica, to the passing of a new law to ban dolphin hunting in Peru. . . .

There are no easy solutions to most of the problems facing whales, dolphins, and porpoises. The issues are complex and there are often many vested interests involved. Solutions do exist, but they are often complex themselves and it may be many long years before they are put into effect.

The work undertaken by organizations such as the British-based Whale and Dolphin Conservation Society, the largest charity of its kind dedicated to the conservation, welfare, and appreciation of cetaceans, is necessarily wide ranging. It includes anything from the development of good working relationships with key politicians to working toward a feeling of mutual respect and cooperation with local fishers.

It involves encouraging and assisting schoolchildren to take an interest in conservation, and focusing world attention on key issues, such as commercial whaling and destructive fishing methods. It entails producing action plans for saving endangered species, or populations, and developing realistic economic alternatives to hunting and killing. It involves undercover operations to gather important information on a wide range of illegal activities, improving the enforcement of existing laws and regulations, and much more. Above all, constant vigilance is essential because, even when important progress has been made, it can always be weakened or revoked.

Writing Application: Provide Support for Your Message When you write your problem-and-solution essay, provide thorough support for the solution you propose.

Carwardine does not oversimplify the solutions. Because the problem is a large and complex one, the solutions are detailed and complex.

Here, Carwardine acknowledges that the solutions must work for all involved and be reached through cooperation between conservationists and fishers.

In the final paragraph, Carwardine organizes proposed actions in order of importance. He concludes by pointing out that the solutions must be realistic and sustainable.

In Anton Chekhov's "A Problem," relatives disagree about the right way to solve a family dilemma. You can find the story in *Prentice Hall Literature, Penguin Edition,* Grade 10.

Teaching From the Model

Have students offer their opinions on the introductory paragraph. Some will find the list of statistics dramatic and moving; others may find it impersonal and distant. Have students write and share alternative introductions to this essay.

More About the Writer

British zoologist Mark Carwardine describes himself as a "whale addict." A photographer and researcher, Carwardine travels the world studying whales and other creatures. He is a BBC radio broadcaster with a weekly nature show and is the author of numerous books on animals, especially whales.

Reading\Writing Connection

Writing Application: Provide Support for Your Message

Explain that there are a variety of ways to support a proposed solution. One might be pointing out similar situations in which the idea has worked. Another might be showing how the steps taken will reverse the process that caused the problem. The key is in providing adequate detail and showing a clear connection between the cause of the problem and the proposed solution.

Connections With Literature

If students have read "A Problem," discuss how a solution to the problem of a family dilemma is pursued in this story.

Teaching Resources: Writing Support Transparencies, 11-A; Writing Support Activity Book, 11-1

1. Display Transparency 11-A and discuss one of the problems listed in the chart on this page. Distribute copies of the chart (11-1) for student use.

2. Challenge students to add at least two problems to each of the four categories in the chart.

3. Remind students that the best essays often arise from subjects that are important to the writer. Encourage students to list and discuss issues they really care about.

Prewriting: Use Sentence Starters

1. After students have jotted down multiple endings for each sentence, have students share their endings in class.

2. Encourage students to jot down the ideas of their classmates to use as springboards for their own ideas.

3. Next, have students circle the idea they find most interesting.

4. Give students five minutes to freewrite about this idea. If students have trouble with this, they might need to learn more about their topic or choose a different one.

Customize for
ESL Students

Suggest that students address problems they have faced and have overcome, or that they are currently facing, such as learning a new language or adjusting to an unfamiliar culture. Choosing a well-known problem may enable them to focus more of their attention on the mechanics of the essay.

11.2 *Prewriting*

Choosing Your Topic

Begin by identifying an important problem about which you feel strongly. Your essay will be more effective if you choose a significant and meaningful problem rather than a simple one that can be solved easily. Use these strategies to find a topic you would like to develop:

Strategies for Generating Topics

1. **Talk With a Peer** Talking with a partner can help you identify important problems in your school and community. You can also talk about state or national problems. Begin by working together to brainstorm for a list of problems. As you work, use a chart like the one below to gather ideas. When your chart is completed, choose the item you find most interesting to become the topic for your problem-and-solution essay.

School	City	Nation	World
Overcrowded classes	Dangerous intersection at Elm and Watson	Highway safety	International policies
Chaotic parking lot		Government corruption	Diminishing resources
	Zoo closing	Campaign financing	World hunger

2. **Use Sentence Starters** Complete the sentence starters below to help you come up with a topic. Don't stop with one response. Try to come up with three or four endings for each sentence. Then, review your ideas to find a problem that is important to you.

Possible Sentence Starters
- The biggest problem facing students today is . . .
- The world would be a much better place if we could solve the problem of . . .
- I wish that we could eliminate the problem of . . .
- One problem we could solve if we all work together is . . .

Interactive Textbook

Try it out! Use the interactive Sentence Starters activity in **Section 11.2**, on-line or on CD-ROM.

224 • Problem-and-Solution Essay

⏱ TIME AND RESOURCE MANAGER

Resources
Print: *Writing Support Transparencies*, 11-A–D; *Writing Support Activity Book*, 11-1
Technology: *Writing and Grammar* Interactive Text, Section 11.2

Using the Full Student Edition	Using the Handbook⊞
• Work through the Prewriting strategies in class.	• Work through the Prewriting strategies in class.
• Use the Responding to Fine Art transparency to generate additional topics.	• Use the Responding to Fine Art transparency to generate additional topics.
• Work with students to narrow their topics and gather information.	• Work with students to narrow their topics and gather information.

TOPIC BANK

Consider these suggestions if you are having difficulty coming up with your own topic:

1. **Solution to a Math Problem** Write an essay in which you explain a complex math problem and its solution.

2. **Editorial Addressing a Local Issue** Choose a problem that faces your school or neighborhood, and write an editorial presenting a solution.

Responding to Fine Art

3. *Unloading the Cargo*, by Ralston Crawford, depicts the unloading of a ship's cargo. What sorts of problems might such a task involve overcoming? Write a problem-and-solution essay that describes one such problem and details the solution.

Unloading the Cargo, 1942, Ralston Crawford

Responding to Literature

4. In James Thurber's humorous story "The Dog That Bit People," the characters are confronted with a dog's behavior problems. Write a problem-and-solution essay proposing steps that could be taken to change the dog's behavior. You can find "The Dog That Bit People" in *Prentice Hall Literature, Penguin Edition,* Grade 10.

⏱ Timed Writing Prompt

5. Write a letter to the school board requesting a new facility for your school, such as an auditorium, a sports facility, or a science lab. Include clear examples of how your proposed facility would improve the school. **(40 minutes)**

Prewriting • 225

☑ ONGOING ASSESSMENT: Monitor and Reinforce

If you observe that some students are having difficulty coming up with a topic, use one of the following options.

Option 1 Suggest that students choose an idea from the Topic Bank. If many students have difficulty, work with the whole class on one idea selected from the Topic Bank or from ideas suggested by students.

Option 2 If Topic Bank ideas seem too difficult, give students suggestions from the *Topic Bank for Heterogeneous Classes* in the Teaching Resources.

Step-by-Step Teaching Guide

Responding to Fine Art

Unloading the Cargo, by Ralston Crawford

Teaching Resources: Writing Support Transparencies, 11-B

1. Display Transparency 11-B and ask questions such as these to prompt a discussion about the art:

   How does the artist portray the heavy, complex job of unloading cargo from a ship? What elements of the process are shown?

   What difficulties or hazards might workers need to deal with in doing this task?

   What difficulties might occur when shipping goods by sea?

   What other jobs are part of the shipping industry, and what sorts of problems may workers in these other industries face?

2. Ask students to brainstorm for other work-related problem-and-solution topics. They might start by considering problems they have faced at work. Or, they might interview friends or family members about on-the-job problems.

⏱ Timed Writing Prompt

- To help students identify improvements, discuss problems they face using the facilities at their school. Does the auditorium need repairs? Is the sports equipment in good shape? Are classes overcrowded?

- Suggest that students allow five minutes for prewriting, thirty minutes for writing, and five minutes for reviewing and proofreading.

Real-World Connection

Explain to students that many workers use various forms of the problem-and-solution essay every day. Some examples are politicians who deliver speeches that identify civic problems and offer solutions, and social workers who keep records on the ways they try to help families solve problems. Challenge students to name more examples.

Prewriting: Use Looping to Narrow Your Topic

Teaching Resources: Writing Support Transparencies, 11-C

1. Draw students' attention to the example of looping on the page, or refer to Transparency 11-C.

2. Discuss how the author narrowed her topic from "pollution," to "water pollution," to "water pollution in a local stream." Ask students why this is a better topic than "pollution."

3. Have students use looping to narrow their own topics. You may want to walk students through an example on the board before having them work on their own.

Prewriting: Considering Your Audience and Purpose

1. Have students jot down the problem they will be writing about.

2. Then, have them brainstorm for a list of possible audiences for their essays. The audience should consist of people who might be able to contribute to solving the problem.

3. Have students choose one group for their intended audience. Then, have them figure out how much the audience knows about the topic. This way, they will know how much detail they should include in their explanation of the problem.

Customize for
Interpersonal Learners

Have students meet in small groups, with group members taking turns role-playing each writer's intended audience. Their goal is to help the writer learn about the audience's knowledge of the topic, their attitude toward it, and the questions they might ask about it.

Narrowing Your Topic

If your topic is broad, narrow it so that you can focus on presenting a solution to a single problem.

Use Looping to Narrow Your Topic

Looping can help you focus on key aspects of your topic. Begin by writing freely on your topic for about five minutes. Read what you have written, and circle the most interesting or important idea. Then, write about that idea for five minutes. Repeat this process until you arrive at a topic narrow enough to address thoroughly in your essay.

Problem: Pollution

I think pollution is a big problem. Soon, we won't be able to enjoy the environment because it will be so polluted. It's not just the land, it's the (water) and air, too.

Water Pollution: Acid rain is a problem. And oil spills in oceans. Even our (local stream) has suds in it. Lakes can get polluted, too.

Miller Stream: The stream behind the school is unsafe because of phosphates dumped into it from local businesses.

Considering Your Audience and Purpose

The type of language you use will depend on the audience for your problem-and-solution essay. Some audiences, such as a group of friends, will relate best to informal language. Many other audiences, however, will respond better if you use formal language to communicate your ideas.

FORMAL LANGUAGE	INFORMAL LANGUAGE
The parking situation in the eastern lot is dangerous.	The parking lot is a mess.
The most effective solution to the problem of truancy is to make the issue of attendance important to students.	The best way to stop kids from cutting class is to make them feel that attendance is a big deal.

226 • Problem-and-Solution Essay

⏱ Timed Writing Hint

Pay close attention to all the details in a writing prompt. Read the prompt carefully twice to determine the purpose and the audience for your writing.

☑ **ONGOING ASSESSMENT: Monitor and Reinforce**

If students have trouble seeing their topic from the perspective of their audience, try the following strategies.

Option 1 Have each student write and answer five to ten questions about his or her audience. Questions should cover the audience's level of education, skills, knowledge of the topic, attitude toward the topic, and more. This will make their audience seem more concrete and real.

Option 2 If possible, have students discuss their topic with a member of the intended audience. Have them prepare specific questions before the telephone conversation or meeting.

Gathering Information

To develop a successful essay, you need a strong set of facts, statistics, and other types of support. Most likely, you'll find it necessary to conduct research in the library or on the Internet to gather the material you need.

Gather Various Types of Details

As you gather details, look to find those that fully explain the problem you are proposing to solve and the steps or aspects of the solution.

- **Cite examples:** Give examples from research or real life to explain the problem and its history.
- **Interview:** Talk to people who have a deep knowledge of the problem or who have definite ideas on how to solve it.
- **Survey:** Create and distribute a survey that probes for ideas about the problem and possible solutions. Tabulate the responses, and cite the results in your essay.

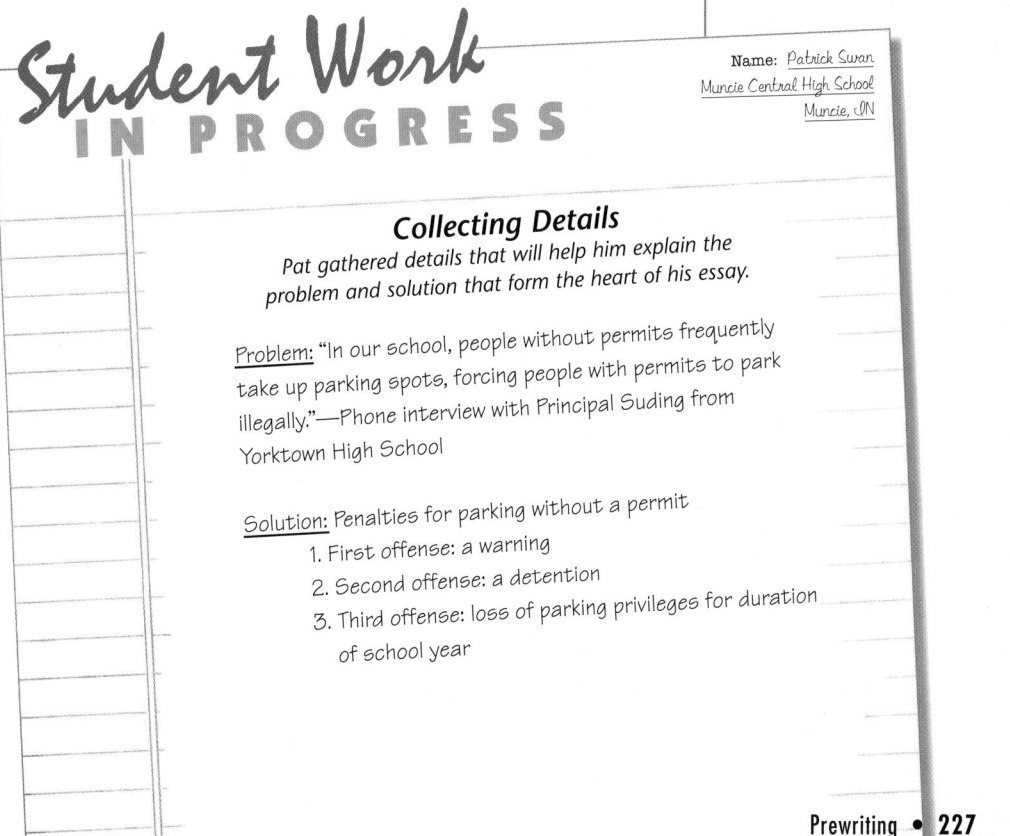

Student Work
IN PROGRESS

Name: Patrick Swan
Muncie Central High School
Muncie, IN

Collecting Details

Pat gathered details that will help him explain the problem and solution that form the heart of his essay.

Problem: "In our school, people without permits frequently take up parking spots, forcing people with permits to park illegally."—Phone interview with Principal Suding from Yorktown High School

Solution: Penalties for parking without a permit
  1. First offense: a warning
  2. Second offense: a detention
  3. Third offense: loss of parking privileges for duration of school year

Prewriting: Gather Various Types of Details

Teaching Resources: Writing Support Transparencies, 11-D

1. Ask students why it is important to explain the problem in a clear and thorough manner. (Readers will be reluctant to support a solution if they are not aware of the magnitude of the problem.)

2. Bring in newspaper or magazine articles that use examples and interviews to explain a problem. Read and discuss them with students. This will give students ideas about how to work this information into their essays.

3. Explain to students that a survey can be a powerful tool in a problem-and-solution essay. Readers are likely to support a solution that a majority of people believes is sensible and realistic.

Integrating Research Skills

Explain to students that information found in books and periodicals is often considered more credible than some sources on the Internet. Remind students to evaluate their sources carefully. They should double-check any information they find on the Internet or in print sources whose reputation is not firmly established.

TIME SAVERS!

 Writing Support Transparencies
Use the transparencies for Chapter 11 to facilitate teaching of strategies.

 **Writing Support Activity Book**
Use the graphic organizers for Chapter 11 to facilitate student planning.

Drafting: Using an Outline

Teaching Resources: Writing Support Transparencies, 11-E; Writing Support Activity Book, 11-2

1. Show Transparency 11-E and discuss the two types of outlines for problem-and-solution essays.

2. Have students look at the information they have gathered and decide which organizational method will be most suitable. If they plan to offer more than one solution, they should probably choose the method on the right.

3. Give students copies of the organizer (11-2), and then have them complete their outlines. Encourage them to circle any points that need more information. They can address these weak spots in the strategy for providing elaboration on the next page.

Customize for
More Advanced Students

Ask students to explain the quotation from Charles Kettering on this page: "A problem well stated is a problem half solved." Why does Kettering consider it so important to state a problem clearly? (Students might say that this implies a clear understanding of the problem and its sources. This is a requisite step in finding effective solutions.)

11.3 Drafting

Shaping Your Writing
Start With the Problem

As inventor Charles Kettering once said, "A problem well stated is a problem half solved." Your problem-and-solution essay should begin with a detailed description of the problem. Make sure your audience understands all of the important aspects of your problem. Once the problem is clear, you can write about the solution or solutions you propose.

Using an Outline An outline can help you organize your ideas before you begin to draft. Look at the examples below. The first example shows how to organize an essay presenting a single solution to a problem. The second example shows how to organize an essay proposing more than one solution. Use the organization that fits your topic.

Get instant help! To create your outline, use the Essay Builder, accessible from the menu bar, on-line or on CD-ROM.

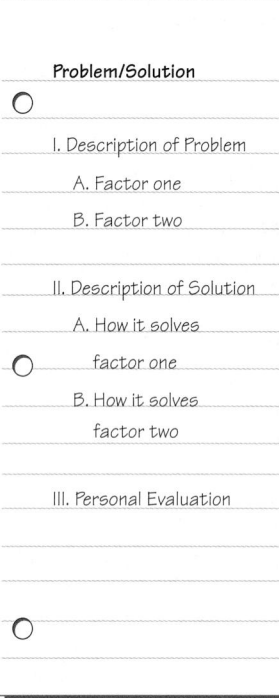

Problem/Solution

I. Description of Problem
   A. Factor one
   B. Factor two

II. Description of Solution
   A. How it solves factor one
   B. How it solves factor two

III. Personal Evaluation

Problem/Solution/Solution

I. Description of Problem
   A. Factor one
   B. Factor two

II. First Solution
   A. Advantages
   B. Disadvantages

III. Second Solution
   A. Advantages
   B. Disadvantages

IV. Personal Evaluation

228 • Problem-and-Solution Essay

⏱ TIME AND RESOURCE MANAGER

Resources
Print: *Writing Support Transparencies, 11-E–F; Writing Support Activity Book,* 11-2
Technology: *Writing and Grammar* Interactive Text, Section 11.3

Using the Full Student Edition	Using the Handbook🄷
• Work through the drafting strategies in class. • On the board, demonstrate the technique for expanding on points in an outline. • Let students begin drafting in class. • Address individual drafting questions as needed.	• Work through the drafting strategies in class. • On the board, demonstrate the technique for expanding on points in an outline. • Let students begin drafting in class. • Address individual drafting questions as needed.

Providing Elaboration

Following your outline, begin writing your first draft. Support each major point in your outline by adding facts and other details, expanding on ideas, and discussing important related concepts. This elaboration will help you convince readers of the soundness of your solution.

Expand on Your Outline

Support each major point in your essay by providing clear and relevant details. Doing so will help readers understand and accept the solution you are proposing.

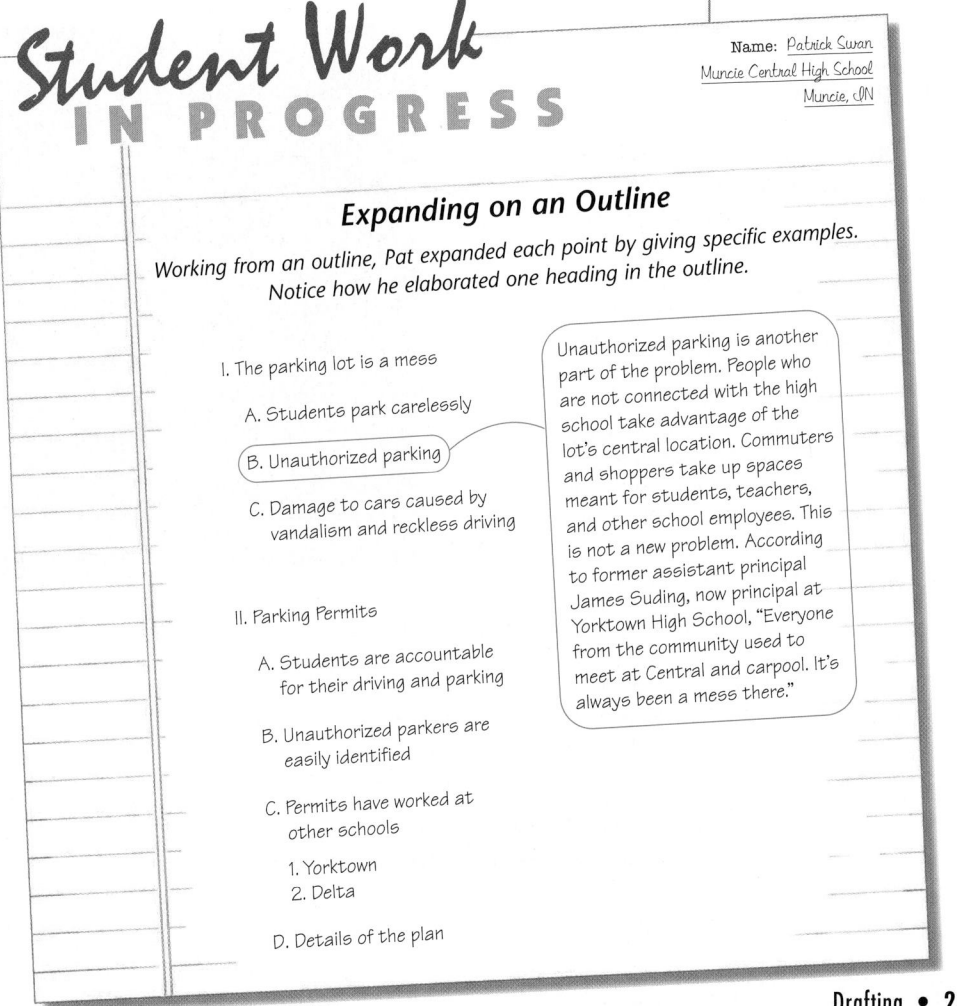

Student Work
IN PROGRESS

Name: *Patrick Swan*
Muncie Central High School
Muncie, IN

Expanding on an Outline

Working from an outline, Pat expanded each point by giving specific examples. Notice how he elaborated one heading in the outline.

I. The parking lot is a mess

  A. Students park carelessly

  B. Unauthorized parking

  C. Damage to cars caused by vandalism and reckless driving

II. Parking Permits

  A. Students are accountable for their driving and parking

  B. Unauthorized parkers are easily identified

  C. Permits have worked at other schools

    1. Yorktown
    2. Delta

  D. Details of the plan

> Unauthorized parking is another part of the problem. People who are not connected with the high school take advantage of the lot's central location. Commuters and shoppers take up spaces meant for students, teachers, and other school employees. This is not a new problem. According to former assistant principal James Suding, now principal at Yorktown High School, "Everyone from the community used to meet at Central and carpool. It's always been a mess there."

Drafting • **229**

Drafting: Expand on Your Outline

Teaching Resources: Writing Support Transparencies, 11-F

1. Explain to students that drafting from an outline will help them write their essays in an organized manner. If the material is arranged logically in outline form, it will also be clear and logical in essay form.

2. As they elaborate on each point, students should make sure to include specific examples and supporting details. If they have not, they should find more evidence to support their ideas or make a different point that is supported by the evidence they have.

3. Encourage students to keep the main point in mind when they elaborate, and resist the temptation to digress. Irrelevant or unhelpful information distracts readers.

Integrating Speaking and Listening Skills

After students have written their drafts, let them choose one paragraph they believe needs more elaboration. Have them read it aloud to a partner. The partner can then help the writer decide whether it needs more elaboration and, if so, how to provide it.

☑ **ONGOING ASSESSMENT: Monitor and Reinforce**

If your students have difficulty deciding which examples to include in their essays, try the following strategy.

Have students work in pairs. Each student should write his or her supporting points on note cards and have the other arrange them from strongest to weakest. Students can then discuss the effectiveness of each supporting point and the advisability of adding it to the essay.

Revising: Connecting Ideas

Teaching Resources: Writing Support Transparencies, 11-G

1. Emphasize the importance of having a solution for each problem and revising or deleting solutions that do not fit problems.

2. If students find that many parts of the problem do not have corresponding solutions, they might choose one of these approaches: do research to obtain more information, further narrow the topic, or choose a new topic.

Customize for
Spatial Learners

Students might benefit from making a visual representation, such as a T-chart, for this exercise. On the left, have them write down the elements of the problem. On the right, have them write the corresponding solutions. Show them an example on the board.

Integrating Organization Skills

During the prewriting and drafting stages, students will collect a range of materials. Encourage students to keep their notes organized in notebooks, folders, or boxes. Ask volunteers to demonstrate their methods of organizing research materials. Remind students that this will make it easier to find needed information during the drafting and revision stages.

Critical Viewing

Analyze Students are likely to identify loose or slippery rocks, the difficulty of walking on uneven ground, or the potential dangers of turning ankles or falling in the water.

---

⑪.④ Revising

As you review your first draft, you will find many ways to improve your writing. You might begin by focusing on the overall structure to make sure the whole essay "hangs together." After that, look at each paragraph, sentence, and word to sharpen your work.

Revising Your Overall Structure
Solve the Problem

The success of a problem-and-solution essay depends on two things: You need to clearly define the problem, and you need to describe a specific and effective solution. The structure of your essay should make it easy to see how your solution answers every aspect of the problem.

▶ **REVISION STRATEGY**
Connecting Ideas

Use a highlighter to connect parts of the problem to related parts of the solution.

- Highlight or underline each problem or part of a problem and label it *P.*

- Highlight or underline each solution. Label it *S.* Connect related problems and solutions.

If you find a problem that has no matching solution, you need to expand your solutions. If you find a solution that doesn't fit part of the problem, it is probably unnecessary. You should consider cutting it.

▼ Critical Viewing
What sort of problems might someone encounter while wading this stream? **[Anayze]**

CONNECTING PROBLEMS TO SOLUTIONS

P ... A primary cause of the pollution is restaurants that use phosphates in their dishwashing liquids. Acid rain also contributes to the poor water quality. ...

S Requiring all local businesses to use phosphate-free detergents will greatly improve the water quality of Hawkins Stream. These detergents are slightly more expensive but clean equally well. ...

230 • Problem-and-Solution Essay

⏱ TIME AND RESOURCE MANAGER

Resources
Print: *Writing Support Transparencies,* 11-G–J
Technology: *Writing and Grammar* Interactive Text, Section 11.4

Using the Full Student Edition	Using the Handbook⒣
• Work through revising strategies in class. Use Transparencies 11-G–J to demonstrate them. • Review the six tenses of verbs. • Have students revise their essays in class.	• Work through revising strategies in class. Use Transparencies 11-G–J to demonstrate them. • Review the six tenses of verbs. • Have students revise their essays in class.

Revising Your Paragraphs

Focus Each Paragraph on a Single Topic

Every paragraph in your problem-and-solution essay should develop a single idea or topic. You can test each paragraph by asking questions as you revise.

▶ **REVISION STRATEGY**
Questioning Your Paragraph Choices

Review your essay, and evaluate each paragraph as a separate unit. When you come to the end of a paragraph, pause to ask yourself why you grouped these sentences together.

- **Does the paragraph focus on one idea?** State the idea, and describe how each sentence expands on, supports, or clarifies that idea.

- **Does every sentence relate to the main idea?** If you find sentences on different topics, consider cutting them or moving them to other, more appropriate paragraphs.

- **Do two paragraphs discuss the same topic?** Consider combining the paragraphs to improve the flow of ideas.

🕐 **Timed Writing Hint**

When revising your essay in timed conditions, it is fine to add words and sentences neatly and to cross out sentences or words that you want to delete.

Student Work IN PROGRESS

Name: *Patrick Swan*
Muncie Central High School
Muncie, IN

Focusing a Paragraph

Pat made several adjustments after considering the paragraphs in his problem-and-solution essay.

This solution has worked well at two local high schools. Both Yorktown and Delta high schools require students and faculty members to display parking permits. ~~The parking lots at these school are always filled to capacity.~~ The lots are patrolled periodically to identify cars without permits on display.

Administrators at both schools report that the permits have been popular and effective. Consequences have been created for students who fail to purchase a permit.

Revising: Questioning Your Paragraph Choices

Teaching Resources: Writing Support Transparencies, 11-H

1. Display Transparency 11-H to demonstrate how to focus each paragraph on a single topic. Discuss how Pat's changes improved his essay.

2. Have students reread their drafts, underlining the main idea in each paragraph. Have them check the other sentences in each paragraph to see whether they relate to the main idea. Encourage students to combine paragraphs that relate to the same topic.

Customize for
ESL Students

Students might find it easier to take notes on their paragraphs in their first language. This way, they can concentrate on evaluating the content of each paragraph without having to worry about finding the words to explain their evaluations.

✓ **ONGOING ASSESSMENT: Monitor and Reinforce**

If you observe that students have trouble evaluating their paragraphs, try the following strategy.

Have them show the troublesome paragraph to a partner, but omit the topic sentence. After reading the paragraph, have the partner try to write a topic sentence about it. If he or she cannot identify the intended topic of the paragraph, it is likely that it needs revision. Students might need to add relevant details or delete irrelevant ones.

⏲ **TIME SAVERS!**

 Writing Support Transparencies
Use the transparencies for Chapter 11 to facilitate the teaching of strategies.

Revising: Fix Unnecessary Shifts in Tense

Teaching Resources: Writing Support Transparencies, 11-I

1. Discuss with students the reasons that the paragraph with consistent verb tenses is easier to understand.

2. Use Transparency 11-I to discuss how Pat revised his essay to keep verb tense consistent.

3. Have students go over their own writing, highlighting each verb and labeling its tense.

4. Have students modify their verbs as necessary.

Customize for
Spatial Learners

Have students draw a chart and label each column with a different verb tense. Then, have them choose a paragraph from their essays and place every verb in the corresponding column in the chart. This will make it easier to see which verbs are inconsistent.

Revising Your Sentences
Fix Unnecessary Shifts in Tense

Your sentences should use verb tenses to indicate clearly when an event occurred. It is often best to stay with a single tense. For example, if you are writing about a problem in the past, make sure that all your verbs are in the past tense.

Mixed Tenses

The stream <u>has contained</u> high levels of dangerous chemicals. The surrounding ecosystem <u>will be</u> greatly affected. Fish living in the stream <u>suffered</u> because of the poor water quality. Birds that eat these fish <u>have gotten</u> sick, too.

Consistent Tense

The stream <u>contains</u> high levels of dangerous chemicals. The surrounding ecosystem <u>is</u> greatly affected. Fish living in the stream <u>suffer</u> because of the poor water quality. Birds that eat these fish <u>get</u> sick, too.

▶ **REVISION STRATEGY**
Naming Each Tense

Read through your draft. Find each verb, and name the tense. If you find more than one verb tense in a sentence or paragraph, make sure that the tense shift is necessary. If it is not, revise accordingly.

Student Work
IN PROGRESS

Name: *Patrick Swan*
Muncie Central High School
Muncie, IN

Fixing Verb Tenses
Pat revised this paragraph to put each verb in the future tense.

will be able to
Unauthorized parking will also be greatly reduced. Administrators ~~can~~

won't
recognize unauthorized cars because those cars ~~don't~~ have permits.

will also help
The plan ~~would also have helped~~ our school identify potential suspects

in cases of damaged and vandalized automobiles.

232 • Problem-and-Solution Essay

Verb Tense Standardized test questions may require students to identify whether verb tense is consistent in a sentence or paragraph.

Which choice below is the best revision of the underlined verb?
Many fish suffered when they <u>swim</u> into the oil slick. The disaster killed thousands of marine creatures.

A had swum   **C** were swimming

B swam   **D** no revision needed

Students should recognize that **B**, which is the past tense, is the correct answer. *Suffered* and *killed* are both in the past tense as well.

Grammar in Your Writing
The Six Tenses of Verbs

There are six verb tenses. Each tense has a basic form, as shown in this chart.

Basic Forms

Present	I *look* for a solution.
Past	I *looked* for a solution yesterday.
Future	I *will look* for a solution tomorrow.
Present Perfect	I *have looked* for a solution before.
Past Perfect	I *had looked* for a solution until I almost gave up.
Future Perfect	I *will have looked* for a solution by the end of next week.

Each tense also has a progressive form, ending in *-ing.*

Progressive Forms

Present Progressive	I *am looking* for a solution.
Past Progressive	I *was looking* for a solution yesterday.
Future Progressive	I *will be looking* for a solution tomorrow.
Present Perfect Progressive	I *have been looking* for a solution since last week.
Past Perfect Progressive	I *had been looking* for a solution when I found the answer.
Future Perfect Progressive	I *will have been looking* for a solution for two weeks.

Find It in Your Reading Review "Caring for Whales, Dolphins, and Porpoises" on pages 222–223. Choose one paragraph, and identify the tense of each verb. Explain the reason for any shifts in tense that you find.

Find It in Your Writing Identify the tense of each verb in your draft. Highlight paragraphs that have more than one verb tense. Evaluate whether or not each shift in tense is necessary.

To learn more about verb tenses, see Chapter 22.

Revising • 233

Step-by-Step Teaching Guide

The Six Tenses of Verbs

1. Students should note that verb tense shows when an event occurred. This can be especially important in problem-and-solution essays, which often track the development of a problem over time.

2. Review with students the six tenses of verbs. If necessary, choose a verb and have students write one sentence using each tense.

3. Remind students that some verbs are irregular. An irregular verb is one whose past and past participle are not formed by adding *–ed* or *–d* to the present form.

4. Below are some examples of irregular verbs. Challenge students to think of more examples, and remind them to use a dictionary when they are not sure how to form a certain verb tense. (Examples: *arise–arose; eat–ate; keep–kept; take–took*)

Find It in Your Reading

Sample answer:
First paragraph verb tenses:
Is–present; *were killed*–past perfect; *were*–past; *were killed*–past perfect; *met*–past; *had learned*–past perfect; *are*–present; *remain*–present
The writer uses both past and present tenses because he is describing the way past events affect the present whale population.

Find It in Your Writing

Have students trade papers with a partner to check consistency in verb tense.

☑ **ONGOING ASSESSMENT: Prerequisite Skills**

If students have difficulty recognizing and using consistent verb tenses, you might find it helpful to refer them to the following materials to ensure coverage of requisite skills.

In the Text	Print Resources	Technology
Verbs Tenses, Sections 22.1–22.2	*Grammar Exercise Workbook,* pp. 107–120	*On-Line Exercise Bank,* Section 22.1

Revising Your Word Choice

Revise Your Word Choice to Create a Tone

The words you select help set the tone of your writing—the attitude toward your subject that you convey to your readers. Decide on a tone you would like to convey, and revise your choice of words to help you achieve that tone.

The following chart shows how an alteration in word choice can affect the tone of a piece of writing.

Optimistic Tone	Discovering an effective solution will be most challenging.
Pessimistic Tone	Reaching a workable solution will be extremely difficult.
Informal Tone	Getting at a decent answer will be really hard.

▶ **REVISION STRATEGY**
Highlighting Key Words

Changing just a few words can adjust or heighten the tone you want to develop. Highlight two or three key words in each paragraph, and brainstorm for ideas for words that might replace them. Weigh your choices carefully, and then make any desired changes.

Peer Review

Key Questions

The actor Robert Redford has said that "problems can become opportunities when the right people come together." Revising your problem-and-solution essay with a partner is an excellent way to use teamwork to make effective changes. Have a partner or group read your problem-and-solution essay. Use these questions as a starting point for your discussion:

▼ Critical Viewing Do the students in the photograph seem to be working well together? Explain. [Analyze]

- How complete is the description of the problem?
- How well does the solution match the problem?
- Are there any important parts of the problem that are not discussed?

After listening to your classmates, consider using their suggestions to improve your work.

11.5 Editing and Proofreading

Because spelling and grammar errors can make your writing confusing and distract your readers' attention, make sure that your essay is error-free.

Focusing on *That* and *Which*

The words *that* and *which* are often misused, even by experienced writers. As you check your essay for errors, look to see whether you have used *that* and *which* correctly. Highlight each use of both words, and decide whether or not you have chosen the appropriate word.

Use the following information to help you determine whether your use of *that* and *which* is correct.

Speaking and Listening Tip

It is often helpful to read your writing aloud to check for errors. If you stumble over words while reading, look to see whether you have come across a typographical error or an error in punctuation.

Grammar in Your Writing
Restrictive and Nonrestrictive Clauses

Adjective clauses often begin with *that* or *which*. You can decide which word to use by deciding whether the clause is restrictive or nonrestrictive.

A **restrictive clause** contains information that is essential to the meaning of the noun it modifies. It can expand, limit, or define the noun. Begin a restrictive clause with *that*:

The essay that I wrote was published in the school newspaper.
I found a solution that was simple and effective.

A **nonrestrictive clause** contains information that is not essential to the meaning of the noun it modifies. Begin a nonrestrictive clause with *which*. Set off a nonrestrictive clause with commas:

The mayor's speech, which was about crime, was quite rousing.
"How to Stop Litter," which I wrote last year, won first prize in an essay contest.

Find It in Your Writing As you proofread, locate instances in which you used *that* and *which*. Then, check to be sure you've used those words correctly.

For more on restrictive and nonrestrictive clauses, see Chapter 20.

Editing and Proofreading • **235**

Step-by-Step Teaching Guide

Editing and Proofreading

1. Help students edit in an organized manner by brainstorming with them for a list of specific problems to check for. Examples include inconsistent verb tense, confusing organization, and lack of elaboration on an idea.

2. Refer students to the discussion of *that* and *which*. Challenge them to add this concept to the list of problems to monitor as they proofread.

Step-by-Step Teaching Guide

Restrictive and Nonrestrictive Clauses

1. Write the following sentences on the board.

   They paused at the next photograph, which had won an award.

   They stopped at the next photograph that had won an award.

2. Ask students to explain the difference in meaning between the two sentences. (The first sentence implies that the photograph "they" stopped at won an award. The second implies that they kept walking until they came to another award-winning photo.)

3. This will demonstrate how misusing *that* and *which* can alter the meaning of a sentence.

Find It in Your Writing

Ask students to work with partners to check that they used the words *which* and *that* correctly. In addition, they should make sure they set off nonrestrictive clauses with commas.

⏱ TIME AND RESOURCE MANAGER

Resources
Print: *Scoring Rubrics on Transparency,* Ch. 11; *Writing Assessment and Portfolio Management; Formal Assessment,* Ch. 11
Technology: *Writing and Grammar* Interactive Text, Section 11.5

Using the Full Student Edition	Using the Handbook🄷
• Review the use of *that* and *which* (p. 235) in class.	• Review the use of *that* and *which* (p. 151) in class.
• Have students edit and proofread their problem-and-solution essays in class.	• Have students edit and proofread their problem-and-solution essays in class.
• Give students time to complete the Reflecting on Your Writing and Rubric for Self-Assessment activities.	• Give students time to complete the Reflecting on Your Writing and Rubric for Self-Assessment activities.

Publishing and Presenting

1. Encourage student participation in a discussion of the problem-and-solution essays. Their interactions about this type of writing should prove lively and interesting, especially for problems related to their school or town.

2. For issues that generate a lot of discussion, you might want to organize a formal class debate.

3. Encourage students to submit their essays to magazines, Web sites, and writing contests that accept student work.

ASSESS and CLOSE

Assessment

Teaching Resources: Scoring Rubrics on Transparency, Ch. 11; Writing Assessment and Portfolio Management; Formal Assessment, Ch. 11

1. Display the Scoring Rubric transparency and review the criteria in class.

2. Before students proceed with self-assessment, you may wish to review the Final Draft of the Student Work in Progress on pages 237–238. Have students score the Final Draft in one or more of the rubric categories.

3. In addition to student self-assessment, you may wish to use the following assessment options:

   • score student essays yourself, using the rubric and scoring models from *Writing Assessment and Portfolio Management.*

   • review the Standardized Test Preparation Workshop on pages 242–243 and administer a timed writing assignment.

   • administer the Chapter 11 assessment from *Formal Assessment* in the Teaching Resources to measure students' grasp of concepts presented.

11.6 Publishing and Presenting

Once you have polished and completed your problem-and-solution essay, share your final draft with an audience. Your readers will enjoy learning about your solutions, and you will have the satisfaction of knowing that you have made a helpful proposal.

Building Your Portfolio

1. **Encourage Responses** Sponsor a group read-aloud of several problem-and-solution essays. Take time to discuss the proposed problems and solutions in each essay.

2. **Submit Your Essay** Send your essay to the editors of a magazine or Web site that accepts student writing. Use writers' directories to help you locate addresses.

Reflecting on Your Writing

Reflect on your writing experience by answering these questions. Save your responses in your portfolio.

• Which was more difficult to write about, the problem or the solution? Why?

• What strategies did you use to make sure that your solution was complete and effective?

 **Internet Tip**

To see model essays scored with this rubric, go on-line: PHSchool.com
Enter Web Code: eek-1001

Rubric for Self-Assessment

Use the following criteria to evaluate your problem-and-solution essay.

	Score 4	Score 3	Score 2	Score 1
Audience and Purpose	Contains language and details to engage audience and accomplishes purpose	Contains language and details appropriate for audience and that help contribute to purpose	Contains some language and details not suited for audience; contains some details that detract from purpose	Contains language and details that are not geared for a particular audience; has an unclear purpose
Organization	Is organized consistently, logically, and effectively	Has consistent organization	Has some organization, but its organization is not consistent	Is disorganized and confusing
Elaboration	Has a solution that is clearly laid out, along with details that support or explain	Has a solution that is supported with details	Has a stated solution, but it contains few details to support it	Has unclear solution, and no details are given to support it
Use of Language	Contains language that helps the writer achieve an effective tone; contains no errors in grammar, punctuation, or spelling	Contains language that creates a tone; contains few errors in grammar, punctuation, and spelling	Contains few examples of language that create tone; contains some errors in grammar, punctuation, and spelling	Demonstrates no attempt to create tone through word choice; contains many errors in grammar, punctuation, and spelling

236 • Problem-and-Solution Essay

✓ ONGOING ASSESSMENT: Assess Mastery

Use one the following options to assess final drafts of students' problem-and-solution essays.

Self-Assessment Ask students to score their essays using the rubric provided. Then, have students write a single paragraph reflecting on the most valuable thing they learned in completing this essay.	**Teacher Assessment** You might wish to use the rubric and the scoring models provided in *Writing Assessment and Portfolio Management* to score the problem-and-solution essays.

11.7 Student Work IN PROGRESS

FINAL DRAFT

Parking Permits Needed to Regulate Student Parking

Patrick Swan
Muncie Central High School
Muncie, Indiana

Our parking lot is a mess.

Students drive in from all angles and park anywhere. Because school starts earlier this year, many student drivers are even more rushed, to avoid being tardy. Their haste adds to the parking lot chaos.

Unauthorized parking is another part of the problem. People who are not connected with the high school take advantage of the lot's central location. Commuters and shoppers take up spaces meant for students, teachers, and other school employees. This is not a new problem. According to former assistant principal James Suding, now principal at Yorktown High School, "Everyone from the community used to meet at Central and carpool. It's always been a mess there."

The parking lot has become unsafe for both cars and pedestrians. There has been a noticeable increase in vandalism, damage to cars, and small fender benders. If you park in our lot, you are lucky if your car leaves without being nicked, scratched, painted, or dented.

Although there is assistance from administration members and security guards to control traffic after school, there is no master plan to indicate who is parking where and for what reason.

An informal statement of the problem grabs readers' attention in the essay's first sentence. Pat then describes the problem more fully, using formal language.

Pat quotes a knowledgeable source, a high-school principal, to further explain the problem.

Final Draft

1. Help students see that "Parking Permits Needed to Regulate Student Parking" incorporates the key elements of the problem-and-solution essay.

   • The parking problem is well defined.

   • The audience is anyone familiar with the school's parking problem, including administrators who can solve it.

   • The purpose is to propose an answer to the parking problem.

   • The solution is well supported and clear.

2. Ask students to look in the essay for three reasons that the parking problem is an urgent one. Then, have them find three reasons why parking permits are a practical solution. Are students convinced that permits are a good idea? Why?

3. Ask students whether there are any suggestions they would make to improve this essay. How might they apply these suggestions to their own writing?

Critical Viewing

Analyze Students might note that the lot is full, so drivers might be so intent on finding a parking spot that they could forget to pay attention to other cars or to pedestrians.

We think we have a solution.

It only makes sense that students, faculty, and staff members ought to be issued parking permits, which will be kept on file in the front office. Using this plan, administrators can easily find the owner of any car that is improperly parked. If students know that they can easily be traced, they will drive and park more carefully.

Unauthorized parking will also be greatly reduced. Administrators will be able to recognize unauthorized cars because those cars won't have permits. The plan will also help our school identify potential suspects in cases of damaged and vandalized automobiles.

This solution has worked well at two local high schools. Both Yorktown and Delta high schools require students and faculty members to display parking permits. The lots are patrolled periodically to identify cars without permits on display. Administrators at both schools report that the permits have been popular and effective.

Consequences have been created for students who fail to purchase a permit. The first offense results in a warning, followed by a detention for the second offense, and the third results in loss of parking privileges for the remainder of the year. However, according to Suding, "We haven't had much trouble with students parking in reserved spots or not getting a pass."

Yorktown High School also uses the permits as an extra source of revenue. Students there have the opportunity to buy reserved spots at the front of the parking lot, near the building. The school uses the money as a fund-raising opportunity for any club or organization. At a cost of five dollars per semester, 64 students have reserved spots for this fall. Other parking passes cost the students one dollar for general parking outside the reserved area.

We can take a tip from our neighboring high schools and organize the parking situation at Central High School. One dollar is a low price to pay for keeping your car and its contents safe.

Pat clearly indicates the structure of the essay by announcing that he will discuss the solution.

Each part of the solution corresponds to part of the problem identified earlier in the essay.

Pat's word choices help him create a formal, direct tone. Doing so helps ensure that Pat's audience will take his ideas seriously.

The closing statement helps convince Pat's audience that his solution is a good one.

◀ **Critical Viewing** Give two reasons for the importance of having an organized parking lot such as the one pictured. [Apply]

238 • Problem-and-Solution Essay

Connected Assignment *Advice Column*

One way to solve a problem is to seek expert advice. You can often find expert advice in question-and-answer forums or in advice columns in magazines or newspapers. Topics may range from gardening to computer use to chess strategies to parenting. In such a column, one writer presents a problem and another writer responds with a proposed solution. Sometimes, however, the columnist presents both aspects after receiving an inquiring letter.

Write your own advice column, inventing the problem and coming up with a solution. Use the writing process skills outlined below to guide you.

Prewriting Make a T-chart of problems you've recently encountered. In the left-hand column, write down possible problems that an advice-seeker might have. In the right-hand column, jot down the solutions, or advice, you would give to address each problem.

Review your chart, and choose as a topic the advice you feel most confident about giving.

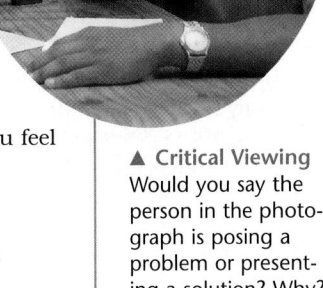

▲ **Critical Viewing**
Would you say the person in the photograph is posing a problem or presenting a solution? Why? **[Speculate]**

Problem	Solution
noise	ear plugs
	white-noise machine

Drafting Keep your audience—the advice-seeker and your readers—in mind as you draft your advice column. For example, you may want to adopt a friendly and persuasive tone as you present your solution. As you give advice, support it with examples, quotations, and other types of evidence.

Revising and Editing Review your advice column to ensure that both the problem and the solution are clearly stated. Add to or modify your language to create an upbeat and positive tone, especially in the advice portion.

Publishing and Presenting Share your advice column with others. Ask them whether or not they agree with the advice you have given.

▶ *Lesson Objectives*
1. To write an advice column appropriate to audience and purpose
2. To use prewriting strategies to generate ideas, develop voice, and plan
3. To refine selected pieces to publish for general and specific audiences

Step-by-Step Teaching Guide

Advice Column

1. Students are probably familiar with advice columns in newspapers and magazines. Ask them to bring samples to class and explain what kind of advice the columnist specializes in (etiquette, romance, car problems, technology problems). Have students meet in small groups and read each other's columns.

2. Students might have difficulty choosing a problem to write about. If so, have each student write a question and place it in a box. Students can draw a question from the box to use as their topic.

3. Allow students time to brainstorm in small groups for solutions to the problems they plan to write about. They can then decide individually which solution (or solutions) to use.

4. When they finish, have volunteers share their columns. Have them submit their work to the school newspaper.

Critical Viewing

Speculate Answers will vary. The student looks thoughtful and deliberative, so he might be envisioning solutions.

Lesson Objectives

1. To recognize distinctive and shared characteristics of cultures through reading

2. To analyze relationships, ideas, and cultures as represented in various media

3. To represent information in a variety of ways, such as graphics

Step-by-Step Teaching Guide

Appreciating the Arts

1. Have students research one of the Spotlight elements. For example, they might rent the 1972 film version of *Man of La Mancha*. Have them watch it and share their reactions with the class. They might focus on Don Quixote's approach to problems.

2. Students might be interested in listening to the music from *Man of La Mancha*. Have volunteers play selections for the class and lead a discussion on how the music enhances the ideas in the story.

3. Students who are interested in classical music might study Richard Strauss's tone poem. Have them look up the definition of a tone poem. They can play excerpts for the class and explain how the music relates to the plot and characters.

4. Students might do research on the life and work of Cervantes. Have them analyze excerpts from *Don Quixote de La Mancha* and share their findings with the class.

Viewing and Representing

Activity Have students choose one entry from their charts and develop it into a brief oral presentation, with visual aids, that they can present to the class or to school administrators.

Critical Viewing

Distinguish Don Quixote is on the left and Sancho Panza is on the right. Quixote wears a helmet (because he believes himself to be a knight) and rides a horse, while Sancho Panza rides a lowly donkey.

240

Spotlight on the Humanities

Appreciating the Arts

Focus on Theater:
Man of La Mancha

If only there were a solution to every problem in life, as legendary fictitious hero Don Quixote believed. The musical *Man of La Mancha*, whose main character is Don Quixote, premiered on the Broadway stage in 1965. With music by Mitch Leigh, lyrics by Joe Darion, and book by Dale Wasserman, the musical ran for six years on Broadway. The show won six Tony Awards, including Best Musical of the 1965–1966 season, and the New York Drama Critics Circle choice for Best Musical.

▲ **Critical Viewing** Can you tell from this photograph which figure is Don Quixote and which is Sancho Panza, his servant? Explain. **[Distinguish]**

Literature Connection Written by Miguel de Cervantes Saavedra in 1605, *Don Quixote de la Mancha* is one of the most famous books in literature. The novel tells the story of Don Quixote, who decides to right the wrongs of the world. He is so taken with the concept of romanticized chivalry, however, that he becomes blind to the world around him. He soon believes that windmills are giants and flocks of sheep are armies. Cervantes's novel was first translated into English in 1616.

Music Connection German composer Richard Strauss (1864–1949) wrote a tone poem in 1897 based on Cervantes's *Don Quixote de la Mancha*. The tone poem is considered to be one of Strauss's most important orchestral pieces.

Problem-and-Solution Writing Activity:
Solutions to Problems at School

Perhaps students in your school are constantly complaining about the quality of their school lunches. Maybe your school could use several "late buses" to accommodate students participating in after-school activities. Create a chart that vividly illustrates several problems you perceive and how you would solve each one. Color-code or illustrate your chart to make problems stand out from solutions. Post your completed chart in your classroom.

Media and Technology Skills

Using Technology to Find Answers

Activity: Create a Research Quiz

Research today may involve a wide variety of media sources, from books and magazines to software and the Internet. Using a variety of sources will increase your ability to locate the information you need efficiently. Using several different information sources, create a challenging quiz for your classmates to solve.

Think About It Choose a format and topic for your research quiz. Your quiz format may be multiple choice, true or false, short answer, or a combination of formats.

Research It Plan to use at least three different sources of information to collect facts and details for your challenge. You might use any of these sources:

- **CD-ROMs:** CD-ROMs contain many types of media, such as music, art, photographs, and illustrations.

- **Software tools:** Many software programs come with built-in tools that can provide valuable information. For example, most word processors include a thesaurus and a spell checker.

- **Internet search engines:** The Internet contains millions of pages of information, but finding the facts you need can be difficult. Search engines help you find sites that mention specific topics.

Write It Create your research challenge by writing eight to ten questions. Make sure that the information required is found in a variety of different sources. In addition to the questions, prepare a hint sheet that lists the information sources you used to write the questions. Fold the hint sheet, and place it in an envelope.

Hint Sheet

1. Internet
2. Encyclopedia

Swap It Exchange quizzes and hints with another classmate or team. Keep track of the sources you use to solve each question. Refer to the hint sheet if you have difficulty answering a question. Score one another's tests, and discuss what you learned about conducting research.

Using Internet Search Engines

Use these tips to help you use search engines effectively:

- Always try more than one search engine. Because the indexes and methods differ, you may get very different results at each site.

- If a search generates too many hits, or matches, try a more specific search. Add one or more words to narrow your search.

- To search for a multi-word name or phrase, enclose all the words in quotation marks.

- Many search engines allow you to use the words *AND, OR,* and *NOT* when searching for information. Click on Advanced Search options to learn how to use these features.

Step-by-Step Teaching Guide

Using Technology to Find Answers

1. Some students will be more adept than others with each of the research sources. If possible, bring students to the computer lab to demonstrate each one. Have students who are experts help you with your presentation.

2. Before students begin to make a quiz for their classmates, have them come up with a specific topic on which to focus. Some examples are sports, fine art, movies, American or world history, and famous writers.

3. After students write their quizzes and hint sheets, have them exchange them with a classmate who wants to learn more about the subject of the quiz. Make sure students keep a list of answers so that they can check one another's work.

4. Have students discuss what this activity taught them about doing research. They might add helpful hints to the list in the sidebar on this page.

Media and Technology Skills • 241

Standardized Test Preparation Workshop

Responding to Problem-and-Solution Prompts

Problem-and-solution prompts, in which you are asked to propose a solution to a stated problem, appear on some standardized tests. They measure your ability to analyze a problem, identify and propose an arguable solution, and defend that solution with specific reasons. You will be evaluated on your ability to do the following:

- organize your ideas and information in a clear and coherent manner
- include specific and compelling details tailored to the specific audience and purpose
- generate well-paced and engaging arguments
- apply grammar, spelling, and punctuation conventions

Writing for a test differs from other writing primarily in the time limitation placed upon your writing. You can still, however, apply the writing process stages—prewriting, drafting, revising, editing, and proofreading—to ensure that your writing is as effective as it can be.

Below is an example of one kind of problem-and-solution prompt that might appear on a standardized test. Let the writing process steps on the next page guide you in generating a response. Check the clocks next to each stage for ideas on how much time to allow along the way.

Sample Writing Situation

> More and more young people are leaving your community after high school. What can be done to change this? Write a letter to the community government proposing a solution to this troubling problem. Discuss the roots of the problem as you see them, and cite specific reasons why your proposed solution will improve the situation. Make sure that you explain any steps needed to implement the solution you are proposing.

Prewriting

Allow about one fourth of your time for developing your solution and identifying supporting reasons.

Identify a Solution First, identify the solution to the problem posed in the prompt. When proposing a solution, it's critical that it be possible, practical, and realistic. Readers will ignore your proposal if they find it irresponsible. Before you begin drafting, evaluate whether or not your solution is realistic.

Drafting

Allow approximately half of your time for drafting. Write neatly and leave space to insert revisions later.

Organize Ideas Use a T-chart to organize information about both the problem and your proposed solution. Identify specific details concerning the problem, such as financial costs, human impact, and community response.

Stay Upbeat As you propose solutions, stress their benefits to the community. Briefly outline exactly how the solution will function and how it will solve the problem. Make sure you stress why the problem should be solved.

Revising, Editing, and Proofreading

Allow about one fourth of your time for revising and editing, and about five minutes for proofreading. Make changes neatly with a proofreader's insertion mark [^] or, if time permits, rewrite your work.

Rearrange Details Examine your draft to be sure that you have chosen a logical and effective organizational strategy. If not, rearrange details to more clearly show the relationship between the problem you have outlined and the solutions you are proposing.

Add Details Reread your essay. Look for places where an added step will clarify exactly how the solution will solve the problem. Insert transition words or rearrange sentences to reinforce the cause-and-effect link you are making.

Fix the Errors Proofread carefully to fix errors in grammar, spelling, and punctuation. Cross out errors with a single line, and neatly write in your correction above the line.

Customize for
Less Advanced Students

After students read the sample writing situation, have them brainstorm in small groups for possible solutions. Then, they can work independently to choose the most realistic solution and develop it into a coherent essay.

Customize for
More Advanced Students

Students might find that they complete their essays before the allotted time period has ended. If so, provide them with strategies for using this extra time wisely. For example, they might devote more time to revising and proofreading. Or, they might insert a paragraph that addresses and refutes a possible challenge to their proposed solution.

In-Depth Lesson Plan

	LESSON FOCUS	PRINT AND MEDIA RESOURCES
DAY 1	**Introduction to Research Writing** Students learn key elements of research writing and analyze the Model From Literature. (pp. 244–249/H154–155)	*Writers at Work* **DVD**, Research Writing *Writing and Grammar* **Interactive Text**, Ch. 12, Introduction
DAY 2	**Prewriting** Students choose and narrow a topic, consider their audience and purpose, and gather information. (pp. 250–255/H156–161)	**Teaching Resources** *Writing Support Transparencies*, 12-A–C; *Writing Support Activity Book*, 12-1; *Topic Bank for Heterogeneous Classes*, Ch. 12 *Writing and Grammar* **Interactive Text**, Section 12.2
DAY 3	**Drafting** Students organize their ideas and write their first drafts. (pp. 256–258/H162–164)	**Teaching Resources** *Writing Support Transparencies*, 12-D–F *Writing and Grammar* **Interactive Text**, Section 12.3
DAY 4	**Revising** Students revise their drafts in terms of overall structure, paragraphs, sentences, and word choice. (pp. 259–263/H165–169)	**Teaching Resources** *Writing Support Transparencies*, 12-G–I *Writing and Grammar* **Interactive Text**, Section 12.4
DAY 5	**Editing and Proofreading; Publishing and Presenting** Students check their work for accuracy and correctness and present their final drafts. (pp. 264–269/H170–175)	**Teaching Resources** *Scoring Rubrics on Transparency*, Ch. 12; *Writing Assessment and Portfolio Management; Formal Assessment*, Ch. 12 *Writing and Grammar* **Interactive Text**, Sections 12.5–6

Accelerated Lesson Plan

	LESSON FOCUS	PRINT AND MEDIA RESOURCES
DAY 1	**Introduction Through Drafting** Students review characteristics of research writing, select topics, and write drafts. (pp. 244–258/H154–164)	*Writers at Work* **DVD**, Research Writing **Teaching Resources** *Writing Support Transparencies*, 12-A–F; *Writing Support Activity Book*, 12-1 *Writing and Grammar* **Interactive Text**, Ch. 12, Introduction through Section 12.3
DAY 2	**Revising Through Presenting** Students work individually or with peers to revise, edit, and proofread their work for presentation. (pp. 259–269/H165–175)	**Teaching Resources** *Writing Support Transparencies*, 12-G–I; *Scoring Rubrics on Transparency*, Ch. 12; *Writing Assessment and Portfolio Management; Formal Assessment*, Ch. 12 *Writing and Grammar* **Interactive Text**, Sections 12.4–6

Options for Adapting Lesson Plans

HOMEWORK

Have students complete any stage of the lesson for homework.

FEATURES

Extend coverage with Connected Assignment (p. 270), Spotlight on the Humanities (p. 272), Media and Technology Skills (p. 273), and the Standardized Test Preparation Workshop (pp. 274–275).

TECHNOLOGY

Students can complete any stage of the lesson on the computer, using *Writing and Grammar* Interactive Text or a word-processing program. Have them print out their completed work.

Writing and Grammar Handbook Alignment

Page numbers in Step-by-Step Teaching Guides in this Teacher's Edition refer to pages from the full student text. Handbook page references, indicated with this icon ⊞, are provided in Time and Resource Manager boxes and at the bottom of each Teacher's Edition page.

INTEGRATED SKILLS COVERAGE

Integrating Grammar
Special Problems With Agreement, SE p. 262/⊞168
Citing Sources, SE p. 265; ATE, pp. 265, 271/⊞171

Reading/Writing Connection
Reread to Find Context Clues, SE p. 246
Writing Application, SE p. 249

Viewing and Representing Skills
Critical Viewing, SE pp. 244, 246, 249, 252, 255, 267, 269, 270, 272/⊞154, 158, 161, 173, 175
Recognizing Musical Achievements, SE p. 272
Using Media to Produce a Documentary, SE p. 273

Technology Skills SE pp. 259, 266/⊞165, 172

Workplace Skills ATE p. 255

Research Skills SE p. 255/⊞161

Real-World Connection ATE p. 268

ASSESSMENT SUPPORT

Standardized Test Preparation Workshop SE p. 274; ATE p. 263
Standardized Test Preparation Workbook, pp. 23–24
Scoring Rubrics on Transparency, Ch. 12
Formal Assessment, Ch. 12
Writing Assessment and Portfolio Management

MEETING INDIVIDUAL NEEDS

Less Advanced Students ATE pp. 252, 254, 258, 259, 269, 271, 275. See also Ongoing Assessments ATE pp. 247, 251, 257, 260.
More Advanced Students ATE pp. 253, 271, 275
ESL Students ATE pp. 250, 258, 263, 268
Gifted and Talented Students ATE p. 248
Spatial Learners ATE p. 261

BLOCK SCHEDULING

Pacing Suggestions
For 90-minute Blocks
• Have students complete the Prewriting and Drafting stages in a single period.
• Focus one class period on Revising and Editing and Publishing and Presenting. Allow at least 30 minutes for peer revision.

Resources for Varying Instruction
• *Writing and Grammar* Interactive Text A 90-minute block provides an ideal opportunity for students to work on the computer.
• *Writers at Work* DVD Show the Research Writing segment in class.

Professional Development Support
• *How to Manage Instruction in the Block* This teaching resource provides management and activity suggestions.

MEDIA AND TECHNOLOGY

For the Student
• *Writing and Grammar* Interactive Text, Ch. 12
• *On-line Exercise Bank,* Sections 24.1, 28.4

For the Teacher
• *Writers at Work* DVD, Research Writing
• Teacher**EXPRESS** CD-ROM

WRITING AND GRAMMAR ON-LINE

Interactive Text (On-line or on CD-ROM)
• Easily navigable instruction with interactive Revision Checkers
• Full use of e-rater™, the essay-scoring system (on-line only)

Companion Web Site PHSchool.com
• Scoring rubrics with models (use Web Code eek-1001)

See the Go On-line! **feature, SE p. iii.**

LITERATURE CONNECTIONS

Related selections from *Prentice Hall Literature, Penguin Edition,* Grade 10:

Professional Model "Making History With Vitamin C," Penny Le Couteur and Jay Burreson, SE p. 247
Topic Bank Option "The Marginal World," Rachel Carson, SE p. 251/⊞157

Lesson Objectives

1. To write a research paper appropriate to audience and purpose
2. To read to appreciate a writer's craft and to discover models for writing
3. To use prewriting strategies to generate ideas and plan
4. To use writing to formulate questions, support what is known, and compile information
5. To represent information in a variety of ways such as graphics and conceptual maps
6. To develop drafts by organizing content to suit purpose
7. To edit and proofread to ensure standard English usage and grammar
8. To evaluate writing for both mechanics and content
9. To refine selected work for publication

Critical Viewing

Analyze Students might suggest such research topics as the history of Easter Island, Easter Island today, or other ancient mysteries, such as Stonehenge, explaining that they recognize these statues as those of ancient but uncertain origin found on Easter Island.

Chapter 12 Research Writing

▲ **Critical Viewing**
What three research ideas does this photograph inspire? Why? [**Analyze**]

Researching in Everyday Life

Our era has been called the Age of Information because there are so many different sources of information—from traditional print sources, like books and magazines, to multimedia sources, including film and video, CD-ROMs, and the Internet. You conduct research every time you tap into any information source. For example, you become a researcher when you look up a telephone number, talk to your doctor about nutrition, or read about the life of a favorite celebrity.

Research often serves as a foundation for writing. For an end-of-semester essay, for example, you might incorporate historical research. Later in life, you may find that researching skills help you to produce business reports, write historic plays, or re-create historic homes.

244 • Research Writing

⏱ TIME AND RESOURCE MANAGER

Resources
Technology: *Writers at Work* DVD, Research Writing; *Writing and Grammar* Interactive Text, Ch. 12

Using the Full Student Edition	Using the Handbook 🅗
• Review pp. 244–245 in class. • Show the Research Writing section of the *Writers at Work* DVD. • Read the Model From Literature (pp. 246–249) with students, and use it to discuss the characteristics and types of research writing.	• Review pp. 154–155 in class. • Show the Research Writing section of the *Writers at Work* DVD.

What Is Research Writing?

Research writing—writing based on information gathered from outside sources—gives you the power to become an expert on any subject. This focused study of a topic helps you to explore and connect ideas, make discoveries, and share your findings with an audience. Effective research writing

- focuses on a specific, narrow topic, which is usually summarized in a thesis statement.
- presents relevant information from a wide variety of sources.
- structures the information logically and effectively.
- identifies the sources from which the information was drawn.

To preview the criteria on which your research writing may be evaluated, see the Rubric for Self-Assessment on page 266.

Types of Research Writing

Besides the formal research report, there are many other specialized types of writing that depend on accurate and insightful research:

- **Multimedia presentations** support written information with a variety of media, including slide shows, videos, audio recordings, and fine art.
- **Statistical reports** explore a subject through numerical data.
- **Annotated bibliographies** are a compilation and evaluation of resources available about a specific subject.
- **Experiment journals** are a record of the process and results of an experiment.

Writers in ACTION

Authors of all types of writing recognize the usefulness of research. Author N. Scott Momaday, for example, has the following to say about the importance of research:

"Research is absolutely essential to me as a writer. . . . In the case of The Way to Rainy Mountain, *I needed additional information. I needed to know about the history and the pre-history of the Kiowa people. And so I made the migration trip myself. . . . I saw firsthand the landscape that they had passed through, and I imagined —with the help of the stories—what it must have been like to come across this vast sea of plains."*

PREVIEW

IN PROGRESS

While taking a class in photography, Michael S. Dougherty, a student at Central Bucks West High School in Doylestown, Pennsylvania, became interested in war photographers. In this chapter, you will see how he applied his curiosity about this subject to develop a strong piece of research writing. His completed report appears at the end of this chapter.

Research Writing • 245

PREPARE and ENGAGE

Interest GRABBER Mention a well-known movie that is set in the past (or ask students for suggestions), and discuss with students how they think the screenwriter learned so much about the period. Ask students what other elements, beside the story line, they think needed to be researched (costumes, language, how people behaved, sets).

Activate Prior Knowledge

Ask students to name sports figures, movie stars, singers, or other popular figures about whom they have at some time tried to get more information. Ask how they learned more about these individuals (magazines, TV, the Internet, other people). Did they share the information with others who had the same interest? Explain that many of these skills can be applied to doing research for a paper.

More About the Writer

N. Scott Momaday is a Kiowa Indian who says that he feels "fortunate to have the heritage I have." A Pulitzer Prize-winning novelist and Regents Professor of English at the University of Arizona, Momaday is also a painter who has exhibited his work in the United States and abroad. The son of two teachers, he grew up in the Southwest, living on Navajo, Apache, and Pueblo reservations before his family settled in New Mexico. He has a Ph.D. from Stanford University and was the first professor to teach American literature at the University of Moscow, Russia. Of his own books, *The Way to Rainy Mountain* is a favorite because of its reflection of Kiowa culture at its height.

☑ ONGOING ASSESSMENT: Monitor and Reinforce

Use one of the following options to diagnose students' current level of proficiency in descriptive writing.

Option 1 Ask students to select a piece of writing from the previous year that demonstrates their ability to research and write. Review each student's work to determine who may need extra assistance to develop a research paper.

Option 2 Have students read a magazine article that includes cited references, and then write a summary of it. Determine whether they can state the author's main point and supporting details without plagiarizing. If students have difficulty completing this activity, they may need extra help with gathering information, drafting, and providing documentation.

Reading: Reread to Find Context Clues

Tell students that, when reading research writing, they may have to reread passages to clarify unknown terms. Let students know that a careful examination of words and phrases surrounding unfamiliar terms can provide valuable clues to meaning. Encourage students to consult a dictionary or glossary to confirm their guesses.

Step-by-Step Teaching Guide

Engage Students Through Literature

1. Elicit discussion about the essay with questions such as these:

   What effect does citing sources have on the reader? (Such citation provides evidence and allows the reader to pursue more information.)

   What kinds of sources does the author use? (The author uses texts about arts and crafts and Native American cultural history.)

2. Have students review the text and note the words and phrases the author uses to informally cite sources ("Haury 233–245") and how they are formally listed at the end of the piece.

3. Encourage students to think about the resources that are available to them as they choose a topic for their own research writing.

Critical Viewing

Interpret Responses will vary. Encourage students to do research on common stories told in Pueblo culture.

Model From Literature

Barbara Babcock is a Professor of English at the University of Arizona. She has published and lectured frequently on the subject of Pueblo ceramics. Guy and Doris Monthan, a husband-and-wife photographer-writer team, have for many years collaborated on writing about Native American art.

Reading Strategy:
Reread to Find Context Clues Reports involving research may sometimes contain specialized language with which you are unfamiliar. If you come across unfamiliar terminology, reread confusing passages to clarify their meaning.

▲ **Critical Viewing**
If they could speak, what story might these Storyteller figures have to tell? Explain. [Interpret]

from

The Figurative Tradition

**Barbara A. Babcock and
Guy and Doris Monthan**

In April 1981, the Third Annual Storyteller Show opened at the Adobe Gallery in Albuquerque, and, in contrast to the gallery's first show in 1979, in which the work of ten Rio Grande Pueblo potters was represented, there were over two hundred figures by sixty-three potters. When I reported this substantial development in the Storyteller revolution to Cochiti potter Helen Cordero, she replied, "See, I just don't know. I guess I really started something" (Cordero). And so, indeed, she did. When Helen Cordero shaped the first Storyteller doll in 1964, she made one of the oldest forms of Native American self-portraiture her own, reinvented a long-standing but moribund Cochiti tradition of figurative pottery, and engendered a revolution in Pueblo ceramics comparable to the revivals begun by Nampeyo, the Hopi-Tewa potter of Hano, and Maria Martinez of the Tewa Pueblo of San Ildefonso. In the last

The introduction begins with a recollection of an actual event in Babcock's life. By sharing this information, Babcock draws the reader into the report.

A quotation from an interview is placed in quotation marks.

two decades, Pueblo figurative pottery has been rediscovered, redefined, and reinvented by both producers and consumers. The "little people" that Helen Cordero has created have become prize-winning and world-famous collectors' items, and by the mid-1980's Storytellers and related figures were being made by more than 175 potters throughout the New Mexico Pueblos. In addition, figurines were being judged in categories other than "Pottery, Miscellaneous" and were regularly winning prizes at the Santa Fe Indian Market, sponsored by the Southwestern Association on Indian Affairs (SWAIA), and other major arts and crafts fairs throughout the Southwest; and galleries throughout the United States were having shows devoted entirely to figurative pottery. In the late 1970's and early 1980's, Sotheby Parke Bernet auctioned off old Cochiti figures for four-digit figures; and, for the first time in several centuries, Pueblo ceramic figurines began to be valued and respected as art.

Pueblo culture, which has endured in the southwestern United States for almost two thousand years, is distinguished both by its instinct for survival and its capacity to revitalize itself (Dozier; Ortiz). Without pottery to store water and grain, settled Puebloan existence as it developed in the first centuries A.D. and was lived until the last decades of the nineteenth century would have been literally inconceivable. In the twentieth century, pottery has rarely been used for the storage, preparation, and consumption of food-stuffs, but it has become increasingly important symbolically and economically as a form of Pueblo cultural identity and survival (Brody, *The Creative Consumer* 70–84: Brody, *Pueblo Fine Arts* 603–608). The invention of the Storyteller and the attendant revival and expansion of figurative pottery making epitomize this capacity for revitalization, and the pages which follow document and describe these important changes and significant develop-ments in the shape of Pueblo pottery.

Archaeologists conjecture that ceramic technology was intro-duced into what is now the American Southwest from Mesoamerica about 500 B.C. Within centuries, pottery making had become an integral element of the three major prehistoric sedentary cultures: the Hohokam of the southern Arizona desert; the Mogollan of mountainous eastern Arizona and southwestern New Mexico; and the Anasazi in the high plateau country of northern Arizona and New Mexico and southern Utah and Colorado. In addition to utility ware, these Puebloan predecessors shaped and painted ceramic images of themselves, their gods, and the animals around them. The representative impulse in prehis-toric pottery takes several forms: fetish, figurine, and effigy or

Like most writings based on research, this piece contains formal language.

Background informa-tion contained in this paragraph helps the audience under-stand Babcock's subject more fully.

"Making History With Vitamin C" by Penny Le Couteur and Jay Burreson is an essay based on research that details the importance of vitamin C to the sailor's diet during the Age of Discovery. The selection appears in *Prentice Hall Literature, Penguin Edition,* Grade 10.

Model From Literature • 247

More About the Writer

Professor Barbara A. Babcock has earned an international reputation for her groundbreaking scholarly work on links between literary and anthropological theory—the recognition that oral traditions reflect solid historical insights. She has published widely in folklore, symbolic anthropology, literary criticism, and women's studies. In the last decade, her writing and research has focused on the art and experience of Pueblo potter Helen Cordero, on the work of women anthropologists in the Native American Southwest, and on representations of Pueblo women and their crafts.

Connections With Literature

If students have read "Making History With Vitamin C" by Penny Le Couteur and Jay Burreson, have them identify passages in which the authors provide necessary background information for readers.

☑ ONGOING ASSESSMENT: Monitor and Reinforce

If students need additional help understanding the concept of documentation, try the following strategy.

Using local magazines or newspapers, show students examples of researched essays or articles. Point out, or help students locate, examples of people, books, and organizations that served as documented sources of information. Make sure students take note of the language the authors use in referring to these sources.

Teaching From the Model

Have students note that after the author first cites an authoritative source within the text, she continues to cite the same source in later passages. Point out how her sources are listed on page 249 (in alphabetical order by author's last name; underscore or italics for titles of books, periodicals, and newspapers; quotation marks used for titles of chapters, articles, and short stories; and so on). For more in-depth information about citing sources and listing bibliographies, you may wish to equip your classroom with the latest edition of the University of Chicago's *A Manual of Style,* or another reference guide of your choice.

Customize for
Gifted and Talented Students

Ask students to imagine that they are to prepare this report as a feature article in a general interest magazine. What additional photographs are needed? Where should they appear? Have students sketch a layout for the report, showing how text and photographs would appear.

effigy vessel, as well as both three-dimensional appliquéd figures and two-dimensional, painted figures on nonfigurative and figurative shapes. . . .

Both fired and unfired ceramic figurines of animals, birds, and humans have been found throughout the prehistoric Southwest, widely distributed in space and time. Morss has argued that "the earliest known occurrence of figurines . . . in the whole Southwest is in the early pit house village of the Hilltop Phase known as Bluff Ruin, in Forrestdale Valley in eastern Arizona, which is rather closely dated by a good cluster of tree-ring dates falling between A.D. 287 and 312 (Morss 27). Haury, however, dates Hohokam figurines found at Snaketown from the earliest, or Vahki, phase of the Pioneer Period, 300 B.C.–A.D. 100 (233–245). While the baseline for the figurine complex in the Southwest is debatable, there is no question that among the Anasazi true figurines were an integral element of Basketmaker III culture (A.D. 400–A.D. 650) and that the most common forms were human females. Most of these figurines consist of a minimally modeled slab or cylinder of clay no longer than six inches, with frontal orientation and perforated or appliquéd features; rarely are they painted or fired. The most interesting and elaborately modeled of Anasazi Basketmaker figurines are the Pillings figurines from northeast Utah described by Morss. . . .

Like figurines, human and animal effigy vessels have been found in three prehistoric southwestern cultures. The largest numbers of such forms are Anasazi in origin and date from Pueblo II and III (A.D. 900–A.D. 1300). In addition to effigy-handled vessels—such as mugs, pitchers, and jars, as well as ladles with "babe-in-cradle" handles—the most common effigy vessels are bird forms (Morss 27; Hammack 33–34). Inevitably, analyses of representational prehistoric art in general and of effigy vessels in particular lead archaeologists to look south, not only to the figurine complexes of the high cultures of Mesoamerica, but to Casas Grandes, the great trading center in what became northern Chihuahua. The largest community in the Southwest, Casas Grandes developed in the eleventh and twelfth centuries; between A.D. 1060 and A.D. 1340, it produced the finest of painted prehistoric effigy jars. The work of eleventh-century Casas ceramists was widely traded; Casas pottery (and its influence) has been found as far north as the great Anasazi Pueblo of Mesa Verde. Most of these polychrome figurative vessels are human, and in both their modeled form and painted decoration bear a striking resemblance to historic Pueblo figurines and effigies, especially

Babcock gives specific dates and other factual details she found while researching.

Transitions such as "in addition to" help to connect Babcock's ideas.

Source information appearing in parentheses follows details that Babcock found from outside sources.

those produced at Cochiti Pueblo in the last half of the nineteenth century. It does not seem possible that almost a thousand years elapsed between effigies such as the Casas mother and child and the "Madonna" or "Singing-Mother" figures produced at Cochiti in the late 1800's and early 1900's (DiPeso 32–37, 90). . . .

The figure of a woman holding or carrying a child or two, which Cochiti potters called a "Singing Mother" or "Madonna," was the most popular human form made at Cochiti between 1920 and 1960. But only a few women, such as Teresita Romero, Damacia Cordero, and Laurencita Herrara, made them, and, as Helen Cordero has said, "for a long time pottery was silent in the Pueblo" (Cordero). In the mid-1980's, when pottery was anything but silent at Cochiti and over fifty potters were making Storytellers and related figurines, many potters would tell you that their mother or aunt or grandmother "made Storytellers a long time ago." They were referring, I have discovered, not to the Storyteller as later conceived and made popular by Helen Cordero, but to this Cochiti traditional of pottery mothers singing to their children.

Works Cited

Brody, J. J. "The Creative Consumer: Survival, Revival, and Invention in Southwest Indian Arts." *Ethnic and Tourist Arts*. Ed. Nelson Graburn. Berkeley: University of California Press, 1976. 70–84.

Brody, J. J. "Pueblo Fine Arts." *Handbook of North American Indians*, Vol. 9. (1979): 603–608.

Cordero, Helen. Personal Interview. 1981.

Di Peso, Charles C. "Casas Grandes Effigy Vessels". *American Indian Art* 2:4 (1977): 32–37, 90.

Dozier, Edward P. *The Pueblo Indians of North America.* New York: Holt, Rinehart and Winston, 1970.

Haury, Emil. "Figurines and Miscellaneous Clay Object." *Medallion Papers*. Vol. 25 (1937): 233–245.

Hammack, Laurens C. "Effigy Vessels in the Prehistoric American Southwest." *Arizona Highways* 50:2 (1974): 33–34.

Morss, Noel. "Clay Figurines of the American Southwest." *Papers of the Peabody Museum* 49:1. Cambridge, Mass.: Peabody Museum Press, 1954. 27.

Ortiz, Alfonso, ed. "The Dynamics of Pueblo Cultural Survival." American Anthropological Association Meeting. Washington, D.C. 1976.

Writing Application: Give Context Clues As you prepare to write a research paper, think about the types of terminology that your audience may find baffling and the context clues you could use to help them understand those terms.

▼ Critical Viewing
What value would you place on a piece of art like this one? Why? **[Make a Judgment]**

Babcock wraps up her report by returning to the subject of Storyteller pottery as it is today.

A works-cited list provides complete information about the source material Babcock used.

Critical Viewing

Make a Judgment Responses will vary. Make sure that students explain the reasons behind the value they would assign the piece of art.

Reading\Writing Connection
Writing Application: Give Context Clues

Remind students to keep context clues in mind as they write. Specialized words should either be defined or used in context, so the reader can figure out their meaning by analyzing context clues. In addition, use of context clues in writing will make students' writing more coherent and unified and make their main ideas more convincing.

Step-by-Step Teaching Guide

Prewriting: Refer to a Map, Globe, or Atlas

1. Depending on the number of maps, globes, and atlases available, this can be done individually or in small groups.

2. Start this activity by writing the name of one country on the board and having the class brainstorm for topics from that country.

Step-by-Step Teaching Guide

Prewriting: Scan Headlines

1. Bring magazines or newspapers to class. Ask students to select one and scan for headlines that suggest possible topics.

2. Ask students to look for wordplay and other creative elements in the headlines. Encourage students to analyze each headline and any photographic material that accompanies it.

Step-by-Step Teaching Guide

Prewriting: Make a Celebrity List

1. Discuss the list of celebrities in the text, and encourage students to notice how they are grouped.

2. You may wish to have individuals generate their own ideas for categories and fill them in.

3. As an alternative, you could have the whole class generate celebrity categories in addition to those in the text. Write the new categories on the board. Then, have students suggest celebrities for each category.

Choosing Your Topic

Choosing a subject for research writing is a matter of following your instincts and interests. Consider as a topic anything you would like to know more about, from antibiotics to zoology. These strategies can help you find topics to explore:

Strategies for Generating Topics

1. **Refer to a Map, Globe, or Atlas** A map, globe, or atlas can be a useful springboard to a world of research topics in geography, social studies, history, and other areas. Turn to a random page of an atlas or spin a globe of the world, and see where your finger lands; or open to a region you want to visit or know more about, and really inspect the surrounding terrain. Make a list of potential topics, and then evaluate your list. Choose one item as the topic for your research.

2. **Scan Headlines** A newspaper or magazine can provide many inspirations for subjects that connect to contemporary issues. Use a marker or self-sticking notes to indicate intriguing headlines or articles. Review your notes to find a topic you want to investigate in a research report.

3. **Make a Celebrity List** Biographical research can give you remarkable insights into the people you admire and respect. Make a list of celebrities about whom you would like to know more. You might organize your list into categories of accomplishment, such as athletes, actors, politicians, philanthropists, scientists, or philosophers. Review your list, and select the person you find most interesting to research. A sample listing of possible research subjects appears below:

Artists	Authors	Composers and Musicians
Diego Rivera	Michael Crichton	Duke Ellington
Henri Matisse	Mark Twain	Edith Piaf
Georgia O'Keeffe	Edith Wharton	Wolfgang Amadeus Mozart
Charles Schultz	George Eliot	George Gershwin
Mary Cassatt	John Updike	Elvis Presley
Jan van Eyck	Agatha Christie	Suzanne Vega
Camille Pissarro	Carl Sagan	Lyle Lovett
Henry Moore	Jamaica Kincaid	Paul McCartney

Interactive Textbook

Try it out! Use the interactive Make a Celebrity List activity in **Section 12.2**, on-line or on CD-ROM.

Customize for
ESL Students

Suggest that students consider exploring a familiar aspect of their culture or history that they find interesting.

⏱ TIME AND RESOURCE MANAGER

Resources
Print: *Writing Support Transparencies*, 12-A–C; *Writing Support Activity Book*, 12-1
Technology: *Writing and Grammar* Interactive Text, Section 12.2

Using the Full Student Edition	Using the Handbook 🄷
• Work through the Strategies for Generating Topics with the class as a whole, or divide students into three groups and ask each to use one of the strategies.	• Work through the Strategies for Generating Topics with the class as a whole, or divide students into three groups and ask each to use one of the strategies.
• Use the Topic Bank ideas, Responding to Fine Art, and Responding to Literature to generate additional topics.	• Use the Topic Bank ideas, Responding to Fine Art, and Responding to Literature to generate additional topics.

TOPIC BANK

Use these topics to help launch your research writing.

1. **Essay on a Historical Personality** Choose an influential historical personality, such as Genghis Khan, Joan of Arc, or Henry VIII. Begin by reading an encyclopedia entry to get a helpful overview, and choose one specific aspect of the person's life to research.

2. **Investigation of a Scientific Phenomenon** Select a unique occurrence on Earth or in space, such as fjords, coral atolls, or the aurora borealis. Browse through a science textbook to find a topic and some initial information. Use several additional sources to help you present a complete explanation for your audience.

Responding to Fine Art

3. List the historical conflicts that come to mind as you study the painting *Federal Brigade Commanded by General Winfield Scott* by Julian Scott. Choose one of these conflicts to research.

Responding to Literature

4. Read "The Marginal World" by Rachel Carson, a description of the ecology of the edge of the sea. Identify a topic she discusses that interests you and write a research report on it. The selection appears in *Prentice Hall Literature, Penguin Edition,* Grade 10.

Federal Brigade Commanded by General Winfield Scott, Julian Scott, Smithsonian Institution

 Timed Writing Prompt

5. Write an essay about a topic that you would like to investigate. Identify three questions about the topic that you would like to answer through research. Then, discuss what resources you would use to conduct your research. **(45 minutes)**

Responding to Fine Art

Federal Brigade Commanded by General Winfield Scott by Julian Scott

Teaching Resources: Writing Support Transparencies, 12-A

1. Display Transparency 12-A and ask students what the painting suggests to them. Perhaps General Scott himself would make an interesting topic.

2. If students like the painting, suggest that they research other works by the artist.

 Timed Writing Prompt

- To help students generate topics for their essays, discuss hobbies or interests that they have outside of school, such as music, sports, writing, art, or movies. Have them list three things they would like to research about a certain hobby or interest. Students should use their lists to write their essays.

- Remind students that the prompt asks them to include the types of resources they would use. Discuss the types of reference materials students have used in the past for research.

- Suggest that students allow five minutes for prewriting, thirty-five minutes for writing, and five minutes for reviewing and proofreading.

☑ ONGOING ASSESSMENT: Monitor and Reinforce

If you observe that students have difficulty coming up with a topic, use one of the following options.

Option 1 If many students have difficulty, work with the whole class on one idea selected from the Topic Bank or from an idea suggested by students.	**Option 2** If Topic Bank ideas seem too difficult, offer suggestions from the *Topic Bank for Heterogeneous Classes* in the Teaching Resources.

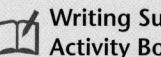 **TIME SAVERS!**

Writing Support Transparencies
Use the transparencies for Chapter 12 to facilitate the teaching of strategies.

Writing Support Activity Book
Use the graphic organizers for Chapter 12 to facilitate student planning.

Narrowing Your Topic

If your topic is not narrow enough to be covered fully within the space limitations of your essay, narrow it before you begin your research.

Use Research Clues to Narrow Your Topic

Use library or Internet sources for ideas on ways to divide subjects for a narrower focus.

- **Look at encyclopedia entries,** which often include sub-headings and highlighted key words. Both of these features can help you identify narrower topics you might consider.

- **Read the table of contents** of books and the title and sub-headings of magazine articles and Web pages to get ideas about different aspects of your topic.

- **Scan book indexes** to find groupings of related ideas.

Considering Your Audience and Purpose

As you gather details for your research report, choose words and details that will appeal to your audience and help you to accomplish your purpose for writing.

Use Formal Language

To reflect a serious tone, most writers of research reports use formal language. The features of formal language include sophisticated vocabulary, sentences with varied structures, and avoidance of slang and con-tractions. As you gather details about your topic, keep in mind that your details and word choice should be precise and formal.

▼ **Critical Viewing** How is the scene in this illustration simi-lar to and different from modern work-day conditions? **[Compare and Contrast]**

Informal Language	Formal Language
Back in the 1850's and later, things changed a great deal for lots of women, especially in New England. Factories began to make the same stuff that women made at home. So the women didn't have any choice. They had to take factory jobs.	During the second half of the nineteenth century, the lives of many New England women changed dramatically. As factories began to compete with home industries, many women who had earned money by sewing and knitting at home were compelled to take factory jobs for the first time.

252 • Research Writing

Gathering Information

Make a research plan to find the information you need from the wide array of sources available.

Perform Library Research

Historian Barbara Tuchman acknowledges, "To a historian, libraries are food, shelter, and even muse." Develop your library skills to help you use your library time effectively.

- Discover how your library is organized. Use the catalog to search for titles. Remember that books are organized by categories, so when you find a useful volume, be sure to explore the nearby titles as well.

- Use indexes like the *Readers' Guide to Periodical Literature* and bibliographies to find information about publications related to specific types of subjects.

- Many libraries today offer Internet access so that you can search for topics on the World Wide Web. Use key words to focus and speed your research.

To organize your library research plan, make a K-W-L Chart, filling in what you **k**now, what you **w**ant to know and what you **l**earned during your research.

Student Work IN PROGRESS

Name: *Michael S. Dougherty*
Central Bucks West High School
Doylestown, PA

Guiding Research With a K-W-L Chart

After narrowing the subject of war photography to focus on one photographer, Robert Capa, Michael used a K-W-L chart to guide his library research.

Know	Want to Know	What I Learned
Robert Capa was a successful war photographer.	How did he get his start?	At the age of 18, he worked as a darkroom apprentice in Berlin.
Capa was often present during war battles.	How did he feel about being at battle scenes?	"It is not always easy to stand aside and be unable to do anything except record the suffering around one."

Prewriting • 253

Prewriting: Perform Library Research

Teaching Resources: Writing Support Transparencies, 12-B; Writing Support Activity Book, 12-1

1. Schedule a library orientation for the students. Make certain they are shown where resources are located and how they are used.

2. Allow time for students to do some preliminary research on their topics.

3. Display Transparency 12-B and show students how Michael used the K-W-L Chart to guide his library research.

4. Have students use their preliminary research to create the "Know" column and to help them formulate items for the "Want to Know" column.

5. Encourage students to use their K-W-L Charts to help them pursue further research on their topics. Suggest that, as they learn new things, they add new "want to know" items suggested by their research.

Customize for
More Advanced Students

To help these students take their research to a higher level, have them evaluate their sources in terms of:

- the author's authority—What are his or her credentials? What makes him or her an authority on the subject?

- the reliability of the source

- the timeliness of the source (Internet sources may be more current than encyclopedias.)

- the objectivity of the source

- validity—Does the same information appear in more than one source?

Make students aware that evaluating sources is particularly important on the Internet. Anyone can post information on the Internet, and not every source is reliable.

Prewriting: Take Organized Notes

Teaching Resources: Writing Support Transparencies, 12-C

1. Display Transparency 12-C and point out the elements of the two different types of cards.

2. Make certain that students realize the number on the note card (1) refers to the source card (for *Lights, Camera, War*). This cross referencing will help them go back to get additional information, if necessary, and will also help them when they cite references.

3. Advise students to write down all of the details about a source so that they will not have to relocate it for additional information when they are compiling a bibliography or works-cited page. Review the needed information (author, title, publisher, date and place published, page numbers where a quotation or detail was found).

4. Warn students about inadvertent plagiarism. Encourage them to take information out of its source and put it on a note card in their own words, rather than photocopying material, and to acknowledge the source of all ideas they use when they write.

5. Schedule a research day or days in the library for students to complete their information gathering.

Customize for
Less Advanced Students

Students may have a difficult time understanding paraphrasing. Give them practice by providing a passage from a book or article. Have them read through the passage at least twice, once silently as you read aloud and once independently. Ask students to identify the main ideas. Then, have students turn away from the passage and summarize the key points. Encourage them to use their own words.

12.2

Take Organized Notes

One major challenge of conducting research is keeping track of all the information you discover. Use the following tips to organize your material.

Source cards list the publication information for each source you consult. When you find a source that you might use, make a source card for it and assign it a number.

Note cards list specific details for use in your writing, such as direct quotations or summaries of important facts.

Photocopy and highlight pages from sources you plan to use. Also, photocopy copyright information to use in your works-cited list.

Print copies of on-line source information for later reference. Be sure that the Web address can be clearly seen in the printout.

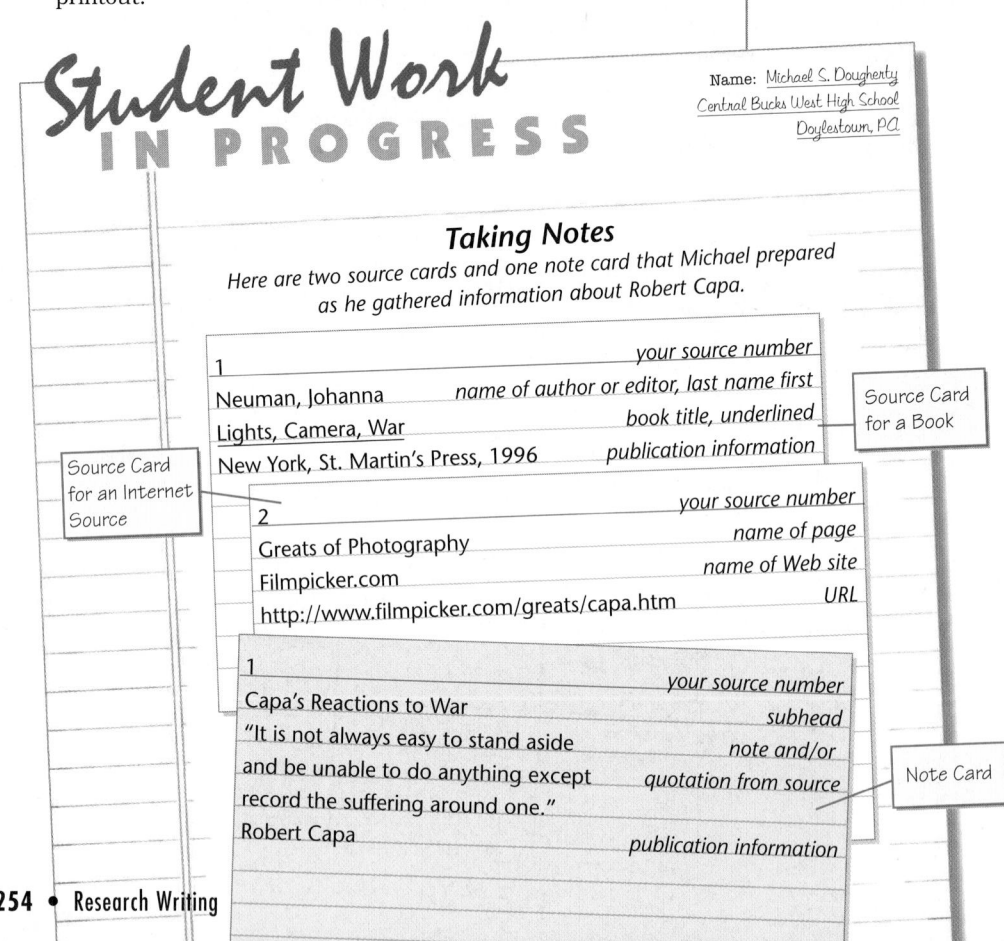

Student Work IN PROGRESS

Name: Michael S. Dougherty
Central Bucks West High School
Doylestown, P.A.

Taking Notes

Here are two source cards and one note card that Michael prepared as he gathered information about Robert Capa.

1 — *your source number*
Neuman, Johanna — *name of author or editor, last name first*
Lights, Camera, War — *book title, underlined*
New York, St. Martin's Press, 1996 — *publication information*

Source Card for a Book

Source Card for an Internet Source

2 — *your source number*
Greats of Photography — *name of page*
Filmpicker.com — *name of Web site*
http://www.filmpicker.com/greats/capa.htm — *URL*

1 — *your source number*
Capa's Reactions to War — *subhead*
"It is not always easy to stand aside and be unable to do anything except record the suffering around one." — *note and/or quotation from source*
Robert Capa — *publication information*

Note Card

Doing Investigative Research

Consider supplementing the information that you collect from published sources with your own investigative research. Conducting your own interviews, polls, and surveys can make your writing uniquely powerful: You can present facts and quotations that no one else can.

- **Interviews** Conduct an interview to get information directly from a primary source. Prepare for your interview by finding out about the subject you will interview. Familiarize yourself with the person's background so that you can ask informed questions. Be sure to compile a list of questions beforehand, but feel free to depart from your list when additional questions arise naturally.

Interview Tips

√ Prepare questions in advance.

√ Avoid asking "yes" and "no" questions.

√ Wait for answers. Don't interrupt the interviewee.

√ Ask permission to tape the interview.

- **Polls and Surveys** Use polls and surveys to gather information about public opinion. Write survey questions that are unbiased and easy to tabulate. Choose a random sample for your target group. Be careful when you interpret your poll results. Your group may not be representative of a larger population. For example, if you interview only seniors at your school, their opinions will not reflect those of all students in the school.

- **Experiments** Conduct experiments to test theories in science or social sciences. For example, to test a theory about student alertness, you might give different groups of students the same quick quiz early in the morning and late in the afternoon to see which group does better.

Whenever you conduct your own investigations, take careful notes using source cards and note cards. You may want to include information about your interviews or polls in your bibliography.

🔲 Research Tip

To write an effective survey, provide a limited number of responses. For example, ask people to rate their opinions using a 1–10 scale or to categorize their feelings according to terms like "strongly support," "support," "oppose," and "strongly oppose."

▼ **Critical Viewing**
What sort of research is the pictured student performing? Explain. **[Analyze]**

Critical Viewing

Analyze Students will probably say that the student is taking some kind of poll or survey, as evidenced by her use of the clipboard for taking notes.

Step-by-Step Teaching Guide

Prewriting: Doing Investigative Research

1. After they have read the text material on interviewing, have students write up three interview questions to ask a partner, and then have partners interview each other. Next, have them comment on the questions they were asked and answers they received. How could they improve the interview?

2. Have the class brainstorm for the types of people they might interview (parents, doctors, local business owners, librarians, teachers, police officers).

3. Encourage students to prepare and ask questions, if appropriate, for their topics. Suggest that, if they are slow at note taking, they consider taping the interviews, and then adding later to their written notes.

4. Remind students that an interview involves a resource, and that they should fill out a resource card with the person's name and job.

5. Ask students to suggest the types of topics that lend themselves to a poll or survey (topics that involve or affect a lot of people, such as viewing habits, taxes, education, etc.).

6. Ask students to think about the kinds of experiments that might be useful in helping them gain additional information on their topics. Make sure students present their ideas to you, and get permission to carry out any experiments that might involve other classes or school facilities.

Integrating Workplace Skills

Interviews are an important part of getting hired in today's work force. Professional appearance, self-confidence, a cooperative spirit, integrity, and initiative are some of the attributes employers look for. Encourage students to research other aspects of the interview process that might make a job interview go more smoothly.

Drafting: Arrange Your Findings

1. Have students sort their cards by subtopic, and then have them pick one subtopic and spread out those note cards, moving them around to help them decide on the order in which the information should be presented.

2. Consider collecting note cards for evaluation. Although reviewing note cards can be time-consuming, it will help ensure that information and sources are adequate.

Drafting: Choose an Organizational Strategy

Teaching Resources: Writing Support Transparencies, 12-D

1. Explain to students that an important part of creating their outlines is determining how they will organize information.

2. Point out that the advantage to picking an organizational strategy and sticking with it is that it will help readers follow the flow of information. This does not mean elements cannot be combined (for example, one could give a brief timeline for one part within a part-to-whole organization); it means that writers shouldn't change directions mid-report.

3. Discuss in class which strategies might work for a variety of topics. Encourage students to suggest their actual topics if they are having trouble determining which organizational pattern to use.

4. Have students make any necessary adjustments to their outlines.

12.3 Drafting

Shaping Your Writing

Research writing needs an effective organization in order to communicate clearly with an audience.

Arrange Your Findings

Use your note cards or photocopied materials to identify major aspects of your topic. Gather related notes together, and consider their relationships. Arranging your notes on a table or adjusting their arrangement in a stack can help you try out different organizations.

Choose an Organizational Strategy

One of the most important decisions you will make as you draft is how to organize your information. A carefully planned structure can make the difference between powerful writing and confusing disorder. The chart below shows several common ways of organizing research writing. Choose a logical organization that matches the content and purpose of your writing.

Description	Uses
Chronological Order: Events are presented in time order.	Chronological order is useful for research reports on historical topics and for experiment journals. For example, if you were writing about a time in history, you could trace actual events.
Part-to-Whole Order: Aspects or parts of a larger topic are described one by one to build a complete picture.	Use this organization to examine the categories that make up a whole. For example, if you were writing about volcanoes, you could show how the location of volcanoes and volcanic eruptions have helped scientists learn about the Earth's interior.
Order of Importance: Details are presented from most important to least important or from least important to most important.	Order of importance can help you build an argument. To write about safety and skiing, you might begin with the least important or most obvious—wearing warm gloves—and end with the most important safety factor—avoiding restricted zones.

⏱ **Timed Writing Hint**

Pay close attention to the way a prompt is written. The prompt will often suggest which organizational strategy you should use.

⏱ TIME AND RESOURCE MANAGER

Resources
Print: *Writing Support Transparencies,* 12-D–F
Technology: *Writing and Grammar* Interactive Text, Section 12.3

Using the Full Student Edition	Using the Handbook🄷
• Work through drafting strategies with the class. • Have students determine the organizational pattern that they intend to use. • Have students elaborate using their own ideas.	• Work through drafting strategies with the class. • Have students determine the organizational pattern that they intend to use. • Have students elaborate using their own ideas.

Prepare an Outline

Prepare an outline to organize the details you have gathered. Begin by reviewing the notes or research materials you have photocopied and grouped. Then, use Roman numerals to indicate major sections of your report. Use capital letters to indicate subsections of each major section, and use Arabic numbers to indicate specifics you plan to discuss within each subsection. As you develop an outline, the entries at each level should be nearly equal in importance.

Your outline may be as broad or detailed as you like. Following are two types of outlines you may like to consider:

- A "sentence outline" can be used to help you rough out your ideas.

- A traditional outline will help you determine the major sections of your topic and will guide you as you write.

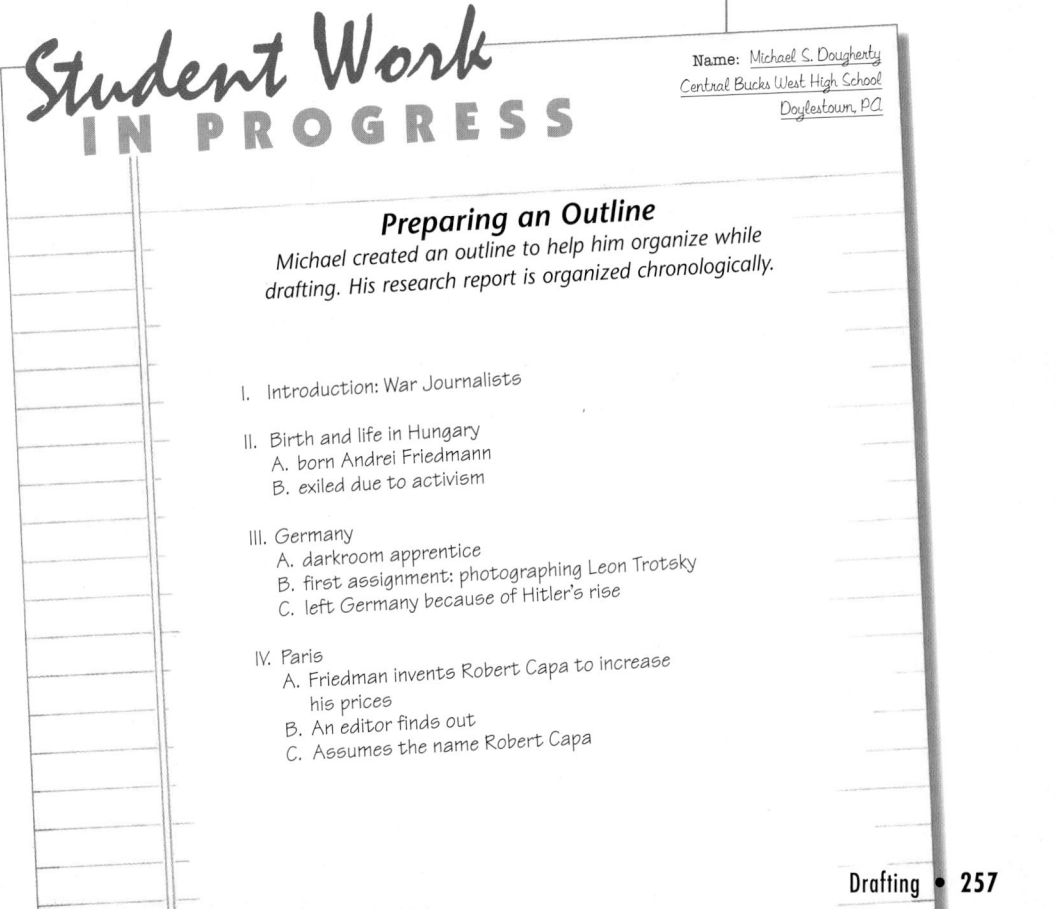

Student Work
IN PROGRESS

Name: Michael S. Dougherty
Central Bucks West High School
Doylestown, PA

Preparing an Outline

Michael created an outline to help him organize while drafting. His research report is organized chronologically.

I. Introduction: War Journalists

II. Birth and life in Hungary
   A. born Andrei Friedmann
   B. exiled due to activism

III. Germany
   A. darkroom apprentice
   B. first assignment: photographing Leon Trotsky
   C. left Germany because of Hitler's rise

IV. Paris
   A. Friedman invents Robert Capa to increase his prices
   B. An editor finds out
   C. Assumes the name Robert Capa

Drafting • 257

Drafting: Prepare an Outline

Teaching Resource: Writing Support Transparencies, 12-E

1. Display Transparency 12-E and point out how Michael has created an outline of the major subjects for his topic.

2. Review the details of constructing an outline. (There is no *I* without a *II*, no *A* without a *B*, and, moving down for more detail, no *1* without a *2*, and no *a* without a *b*.)

3. Suggest that, after they decide on the major sections (using Roman numerals), students can use their organized note cards to help them determine the next level of points in their outlines.

4. You may want to cover organizational strategies before you have students finalize their outlines, since the strategy they select will affect how they outline their information.

Integrating Grammar Skills

Parallel structure is key in aligning ideas of equal importance in an outline. Explain that *parallel structure* means using equivalent structures of words, phrases, and clauses to emphasize the similarities or differences among items. For example, "I. Education's Strengths; II. Education's Weaknesses; III. Education's Future" exhibits parallel construction. "I. Education's Strengths; II. Some Classes I Like; III. Why Can't They Improve Cafeteria Food?" does not exhibit parallel construction. Refer to the Student Work In Progress for another example (Birth and Life in Hungary; Germany, Paris). Have students suggest other examples.

☑ ONGOING ASSESSMENT: Monitor and Reinforce

Students may have problems recognizing the strengths and weaknesses of their evidence. If you think this is the case, try the following strategy.

Pair students and have them exchange note cards, asking each to place a check mark in pencil on the upper right corner of their partner's cards to identify what they think are the strongest points. Students can then discuss their thoughts on supporting points before continuing to draft.

Drafting: Providing Elaboration

Teaching Resources: Writing Support Transparencies, 12-F

1. Remind students that they do not want their papers to be only a series of quotations and facts.

2. Display Transparency 12-F and discuss how Michael has woven his own reactions and observations into his work (for example, the observation that "photographing . . . never an easy task for Capa" that introduces the direct quotation).

3. Point out that, even when he paraphrases information, Michael cites the source for his facts.

Integrating Grammar Skills

Remind students of the basic rules for direct quotations (quotation marks enclose only the exact words; attribution is set off by a comma, whether it precedes or follows the quotation). More guidelines for usage of quotation marks can be found in Chapter 28.

Customize for
Less Advanced Students

Remind students to create introductions that use primarily their own observations and thoughts on the subject. A good direct quotation can be included, but most of the information in the introduction should be in the student's own "voice." Remind students to include their thesis statement in the introduction and to restate the thesis in the conclusion.

Customize for
ESL Students

Putting information in "their own words" may not be easy for some students. Have students do most of the initial writing in class so that you can help them rephrase facts. You might want to pair them with more-fluent English speakers, and have the pairs work together to find other words for ideas and information.

12.3

Providing Elaboration
Elaborate on Notes

As you draft, refer to your note cards or photocopies of source material to provide facts, statistics, and quotations you have discovered. In addition to citing your findings, also provide your own ideas, examples, and analyses as you weave together the information you found while researching. For example, if you give a statistic, also tell why you find the statistic interesting or significant.

Be sure to paraphrase the words of a source unless you plan to put the person's exact words within quotation marks. All source material, whether taken word for word or paraphrased, must be cited in your report.

Student Work
IN PROGRESS

Name: *Michael S. Dougherty*
Central Bucks West High School
Doylestown, PA

Elaborating on Notes

Michael referred to his notes as he drafted his report on Robert Capa. In addition to using the facts he found in his notes, Michael added his own insights to elaborate on what he found.

He was the sole photographer of the bloodiest landing, Omaha Beach, and took 106 photographs in what he considered to be an outstanding personal victory. Unfortunately, a darkroom assistant turned on too much heat while developing the pictures and destroyed all but eight. Despite such setbacks, Capa remained dedicated to photographing the war effort, making several other parachute landings as well (Stein 189).

> Although Michael paraphrased his source material, he was careful to include an in-text citation to credit the source's information.

Although his talents as a war journalist were outstanding, photographing the frightening images of war was never an easy task for Capa. As he once said, "It is not always easy to stand aside and be unable to do anything except record the suffering around one." Capa's humanity and compassion shine through his powerful photographs.

> Michael used what he found out about Capa to come up with this analysis.

258 • Research Writing

12.4 Revising

Writer E. B. White once commented, "When you say something, make sure you have said it. The chances of your having said it are only fair." During revision, you have the opportunity to make sure that you have said what you wanted to say. You can make adjustments in your paper's organization, presentation of ideas, and language.

Revising Your Overall Structure

Create Unity

The first step in revising is to consider the "big picture." Your research writing needs to show unity, that is, a sense that the entire work relates to one specific subject. While you were drafting, your primary goal was to get the words down on paper. During revision, you take a close look at those words to make sure that you haven't strayed from your main idea, added empty padding to fill space, or used an illogical organization that is certain to baffle your audience.

▶ **REVISION STRATEGY**
Using Marginal Notes to Identify the Structure

Review the major sections and subsections in your report by writing notes about the main points of each paragraph. To make these notes stand out, work with a red pen or place self-sticking notes in the margins of your draft. After writing marginal comments or descriptions, read them from beginning to end to make sure that the flow makes sense. You might consider rearranging sections that flow awkwardly or cutting sections that stray from the central topic.

In the example at right, one unrelated section of a research paper about the Channel was deleted and another was moved to a more appropriate position.

💿 Technology Tip

If you are working electronically, boldface any passages that are word-for-word quotations from a source. When you revise, you can quickly proofread those passages against the original source to check for accuracy.

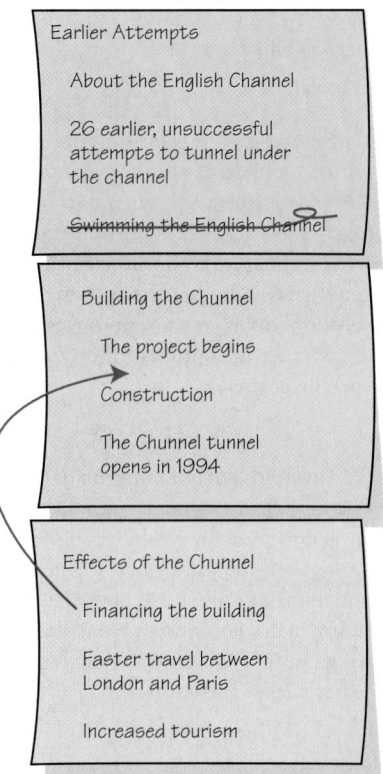

THE ENGLISH CHANNEL TUNNEL

Earlier Attempts

About the English Channel

26 earlier, unsuccessful attempts to tunnel under the channel

~~Swimming the English Channel~~

Building the Chunnel

The project begins

Construction

The Chunnel tunnel opens in 1994

Effects of the Chunnel

Financing the building

Faster travel between London and Paris

Increased tourism

Revising • 259

⏱ TIME AND RESOURCE MANAGER

Resources
Print: *Writing Support Transparencies,* 12-G–I; *Writing Support Activity Book,* 12-2
Technology: *Writing and Grammar* Interactive Text, Section 12.4

Using the Full Student Edition	Using the Handbook 🄷
• Work through the Revision strategies on pp. 259–263 with the class. • Use the relevant transparencies to demonstrate the strategies for Marginal Notes (p. 259), Coding Structure (p. 260), and Color-Coding Agreement (p. 261). • Have students do the Grammar in Your Writing activity (p. 262).	• Work through the Revision strategies on pp. 165–169 with the class. • Use the relevant transparencies to demonstrate the strategies for Marginal Notes (p. 165), Coding Structure (p. 166), and Color-Coding Agreement (p. 167). • Have students do the Grammar in Your Writing activity (p. 168).

Step-by-Step Teaching Guide

Revising: Using Marginal Notes to Identify the Structure
Teaching Resources: Writing Support Transparencies, 12-G

1. Explain that marginal notes should parallel the paragraphs of an essay: one note for each paragraph.

2. Display the transparency and point out how the needed changes stand out more in this "bare bones" format than they would in full sentences.

3. Explain that the point of creating unity within any piece of writing is that it makes the writing stronger. It also makes it more likely that readers will be able to understand the writer's ideas and conclusions.

4. To clarify the strategy further, you might want to discuss in class what marginal notes might look like for the first paragraph of the student essay on the opposite page.

5. Provide students with colored pens or self-sticking notes and give them time to get started making marginal notes on their drafts. Tell them that they are not required to find changes; this exercise can also help confirm good structure. However, most writers will find something to change at this stage.

6. Encourage students to revise their drafts if marginal notes reveal items that need to be moved or deleted.

Customize for
Less Advanced Students

Explain that *plagiarism* is taking credit for work produced by another person. Both words and ideas can be plagiarized. One might easily plagiarize a source without meaning to, by writing about ideas found during research without taking the time to say, "As Smith has shown, . . . " Encourage students to cite references for ideas or facts taken from specific sources, even when they are paraphrased.

Revising: Coding to Identify Structure

Teaching Resources: Writing Support Transparencies, 12-H

1. Using Transparency 12-H, demonstrate how the Topic, Restatement, Illustration pattern has been used to identify the parts of the paragraph about the California gold rush.

2. Next, review the PS and QA patterns.

3. Explain that all three types of paragraph organization can appear in the same piece of writing. The point is that each paragraph has its own organization, with a key idea and supporting information.

4. Explain that these tools can be used for building paragraphs as well as for analyzing them. If students are not entirely certain how to present information, they can refer to these models and use them as guidelines for developing their own paragraphs.

5. Have students read through their drafts and identify the TRI, PS, and QA patterns in their paragraphs.

6. Encourage students to revise paragraphs that are not well organized.

12.4

Revising Your Paragraphs

Every paragraph you write should have a clear organization that explains a single idea.

▶ **REVISION STRATEGY**
Coding to Identify the Structure

There are many different patterns you can use to organize your paragraphs. Three of the most common patterns are identified by the initials *TRI*, *PS*, and *QA*. Read through each paragraph in your research writing, and identify its structure. Revise paragraphs so that each is structured effectively.

T R I

When almost 100,000 people flooded to California in search of gold in 1848 and 1849, some cities grew almost instantly. } Topic
These cities were known as "boom towns." } Restatement
One city on the Yuba River had only two houses in September 1848. A year later, those two houses had expanded into a city of 1,000 inhabitants. } Illustration

P S

Scientists are searching for new ways to handle epidemics that are spread by insects like mosquitoes. Spraying can often kill the insects, but it affects other animals and the } Problem
environment as well. Intervention on the genetic level may offer the most promising solution. Soon, researchers might be able to generate mosquitoes that cannot carry specific germs. } Solution

A

How did *gerrymandering* get its name? } Question
Elbridge Gerry, an early Massachusetts governor, redivided election districts to strengthen his party. Artist Gilbert Stuart noticed that one of the new districts had the shape of a salamander. He drew a head, wings, and a tail onto the map. A newspaper editor added the caption "Gerrymander." } Answer

(?) Learn More

To learn more about writing effective paragraphs, see Chapter 3.

✓ **ONGOING ASSESSMENT: Monitor and Reinforce**

If students are having difficulty identifying the structure of their paragraphs, use the following strategy.

Provide students with sample paragraphs that illustrate each of the patterns, and work through identifying the organization types in class. If students are still unclear about the concepts, provide only topic, problem, or question statements. When students can effectively identify them, add the support.

Revising Your Sentences

When most of the sentences within a written work are similar in length, type, or structure, it can have a numbing effect on the audience. Read through your draft carefully, and vary the length, type, and structure of your sentences to ensure that your writing is lively.

Invert Some Sentences for Variety

Most sentences contain a subject followed by a verb. To add variety to your sentences, you may want to invert the order of the subject and verb. As you do so, be careful not to introduce an error in subject-verb agreement.

▶ **REVISION STRATEGY**
Color-Coding to Identify Subject-Verb Patterns

First, circle the subjects and verbs in each sentence. Review your draft. If every sentence contains the traditional subject-verb order, invert a sentence to add variety to your writing.

Student Work
IN PROGRESS

Name: Michael S. Dougherty
Central Bucks West High School
Doylestown, PA

Color-Coding to Identify Patterns

While revising, Michael noticed that he always used a subject-verb pattern. He inverted a sentence in this paragraph to add variety to his writing.

Americans honor and respect the brave citizens who, over the years, have fought for their country. They have ensured the tranquillity of our people by bearing arms against the ever-changing threats to our nation's security. Often overlooked, however, are Scores of men and women who have gone into battle defenseless against enemy attacks are often overlooked however: wartime journalists. With only a camera or a pad and pencil in hand, they live a soldier's life while working a civilian job. Looking danger in the face, this unarmed crew records the dramatic details of war to inform people at home, as well as generations to come.

Revising • 261

Step-by-Step Teaching Guide

Revising: Invert Some Sentences for Variety

Teaching Resources: Writing Support Transparencies, 12-I

1. Display Transparency 12-I and point out how Michael changed one sentence to create variety. Show that he inverted the subject and verb in the sentence.

2. Tell students that subjects and verbs can be inverted in a variety of ways. For example, Michael simply moved the verb and its modifier and added the transition word *however.* Another way is to begin a sentence with *here* or *there,* which causes a verb-subject inversion. A prepositional phrase may also help create an inversion (for example, *By the stream stood four trees*).

3. Caution students about subject-verb agreement in inverted order sentences (see page 262 for more details on this).

4. Have students color-code their paragraphs.

5. Encourage students to consider changing the word order of at least one sentence. Tell students that, while using passive voice too often weakens writing, the occasional use of passive voice is another way to add variety, and can help emphasize different elements than active voice does.

Customize for
Spatial Learners

As students complete their final drafts, have them design a graphic aid to complement their work. They might create a graph or line drawing, or incorporate pictures, if appropriate. The graphic aid should complement the project and illustrate or clarify a main point of the paper.

Special Problems With Agreement

1. Point out that, while they are creating variety in their writing, students need to be aware of problems they are creating in verb-subject agreement. When sentences are inverted, the correct verb may sound odd, since it doesn't follow the subject. Care must be used.

2. Show students that a compound noun can further complicate things when subject and verb are inverted. (Example: I opened the door, and there were Bill and June.)

3. Explain that one way to avoid the confusion that occurs with collective nouns is to further modify the phrase. (Example, "Faculty members discuss . . .").

4. Remind students that some words are the same in the singular and plural, such as *sheep, fish,* and *deer*. In these cases, it is the verb that makes the difference clear (*deer is; deer are*). Readers will know if the word is plural only if the correct verb is used.

5. Have students write a sample sentence for each of the three situations described in the text.

Find It in Your Reading

Students may mention *pottery* as a collective noun. *United States*, as used in the first sentence of the second paragraph on page 247, is plural in form but singular in meaning, as is *ceramics*.

Find It in Your Writing

If students find no examples of confusing subject-verb agreement, challenge them to create an inverted order sentence so that they can practice this skill.

12.4

Grammar in Your Writing
Special Problems With Agreement

All sentences contain at least one subject and one verb. The subject and verb pairs should agree in number. In some instances, knowing how to make the subject and verb agree may not be immediately clear.

Inverted Sentences

When a verb precedes its subject in a sentence, the sentence is said to be inverted. A subject that comes after its verb must agree with it in number:

Under the boardwalk **was** a tiny **crab.**

There **are** no more **seats** left in the auditorium.

Collective Nouns

Collective nouns—such as *audience, class, couple, crowd, faculty, group,* and *team*—can be either singular or plural depending upon how they are used.

If a collective noun refers to a whole group, use a singular verb:

The **army approaches** the border.
The **jury listens** to the evidence.

If a collective noun refers to individual group members, use a plural verb:

The **faculty discuss** the proposal.
The **jury are** unable to reach a consensus.

Confusing Plurals

Some nouns are plural in form but singular in meaning. Many of these nouns name branches of knowledge: *ethics, mathematics, physics, politics, social studies*. Others name a single unit or idea: *measles, news, series*.

If a noun is plural in form but singular in meaning, use a singular verb:

Physics is an interesting subject.
The **news** today **seems** good.

Find It in Your Reading Review the excerpt from *The Figurative Tradition* on pages 246–249 of this chapter. Within it, identify one collective noun and one noun that is plural in form but singular in meaning.

Find It in Your Writing Review the subject-verb agreement in your sentences, paying close attention to your use of collective nouns and plurals. Circle any subject-verb pairs that you want to reconsider. Discuss circled pairs with a peer reviewer.

To learn more about agreement, see Chapter 24.

☑ ONGOING ASSESSMENT: Prerequisite Skills

If students have difficulty with agreement, refer them to the following materials to ensure coverage of prerequisite knowledge.

In the Textbook	Print Resources	Technology
Agreement, Section 24.1	*Grammar Exercise Workbook,* pp. 133–138	*On-Line Exercise Bank,* Section 24.1

Revising Your Word Choice

Delete Instances of Wordiness

Direct writing is more effective and interesting than writing that is weighed down with unnecessary words. Review your draft, and eliminate instances of wordiness.

WORDY: As a matter of fact, there are many qualities in Capa's photographs that are beautiful, despite the fact that they depict war.

CONCISE: Many of Capa's photographs are beautiful, even though they depict war.

▶ **REVISION STRATEGY**
Deleting Empty Words

This chart shows some common phrases that are often unnecessary. Read through your draft to locate the following phrases. If the phrase does not help connect ideas, delete it.

EMPTY WORDS AND PHRASES

as a matter of fact	in my opinion	to the extent that
as I said before	it is a fact that	the reason was that
by way of	it is also true that	there is/there are
despite the fact that	needless to say	the thing is
given the fact that	of course	the type of
indeed	on account of the fact that	what I mean is

Peer Review

Review With a K-W-L Chart

Determine how effectively your research writing meets your audience's needs by asking a peer reviewer or review team to complete a K-W-L chart as they review your work. Briefly describe the topic, and have your reviewers write what they **k**now about the topic and what they **w**ant to know. After reading your essay, reviewers complete the chart by adding what they **l**earned.

Use the charts to focus a group discussion. Then, incorporate appropriate suggestions from your peers as you revise your research writing.

🕐 **Timed Writing Hint**

When revising under timed conditions, it is fine to cross out empty words and rewrite sentences. Do so neatly so that your reader will not be confused.

Step-by-Step Teaching Guide

Revising: Deleting Empty Words

1. Point out that the phrases shown on the chart are often empty, but not always. Sometimes, an interjection such as *indeed* or *of course* adds emphasis. Save them for when they will be effective.

2. Write the following examples on the board to show students how empty words can be eliminated.

   It is a fact that dogs like bones.

   Dogs like bones.

   The reason he went to the store was that . . .

   He went to the store because . . .

3. Have students exchange papers with a partner and underline any words that they think are unnecessary.

4. Encourage students to eliminate empty phrases or words from their drafts.

Step-by-Step Teaching Guide

Revising: Peer Review

1. Review the K-W-L chart. Use Transparency 12-B or give students copies of the blank chart (12-1).

2. Have each student write his or her topic on the chart.

3. Have students exchange charts and give a brief description of the topic to their partners. Allow time for reviewers to complete the charts.

4. Have students read the essays and fill in the chart.

5. Encourage students to consider peer suggestions as they revise their essays.

🎸 STANDARDIZED TEST PREPARATION WORKSHOP

Agreement Standardized test questions about subject-verb agreement may require students to identify sentences in which the subject-verb usage is correct.

Identify the sentence that contains appropriate subject-verb agreement.

A There is a man and a woman waiting for a taxi.

B At the bottom of Mammoth Cave, lives blind fish.

C In the box were a cat and three kittens.

D The new series are not funny.

Students should recognize that *C* is the correct response; *cat and three kittens* is a compound noun that requires a plural verb. Item *A* is incorrect because the subject—*a man and a woman*—is plural, but the verb is singular. *B* is incorrect because *fish* is a plural subject, but the verb *lives* is singular. *D* is incorrect because *series* is plural in form but singular in meaning; it requires a singular verb.

Customize for
ESL Students

For the peer review, pair students with partners who can help make concrete suggestions about language, style, and organization.

169 H • 263

Preparing a Reference List

1. Make certain as students begin to work on their reference lists that they know which format for bibliographic information you prefer or which style guide carries information on your preferences.

2. Review the differences in formatting for the major types of entries students might use (books, encyclopedias, journals or periodicals, and electronic sources).

3. Cover the additional material on citing sources on page 265 before students finalize their references.

4. Have students use their source note cards, placed in alphabetical order by author, to begin the process of creating a works-cited page. Remind students that alphabetical order is based on the last name of each author listed.

Focusing on Proofreading

1. Suggest that students read through their work more than once, checking for a different element each time.

2. Have students check for any other elements (such as use of informal language) about which you are specifically concerned.

12.5 Editing and Proofreading

Before you hand in your final draft, prepare a works-cited list, and proofread your draft to correct errors in spelling, grammar, and punctuation.

Preparing a Reference List

No research paper is complete without a reference list. Before you turn in your paper, compile a works-cited list on which you completely and accurately document the source material for your research paper. Check with your teacher to confirm the type of format your works-cited list should take.

Following is a list of style manuals you may want to consult as you put together your works-cited list:

- *Modern Language Association Handbook* (MLA)
- *American Psychological Association Handbook* (APA)
- *The Chicago Manual of Style* (CMS)

Focusing on Proofreading

Proofread to make sure all quoted passages, book titles, author names, and page references within parenthetical citations and on your works-cited page are correct. Also, check to be sure that your use of colons, commas, and other punctuation symbols conforms to a specific style of citation.

- Underline the titles of long written works and the titles of publications that are printed as a single work.
- Also, underline the titles of movies, TV and radio series, lengthy works of music, paintings, and sculptures.
- Use quotation marks around the titles of short works.
- Use quotation marks to set off titles of photographs.

Research writing often refers to titles of works, from books and articles to artworks and Internet sites. Check that you have capitalized and punctuated each title correctly.

Remember to capitalize the first, last, and key words in a title. Conjunctions and prepositions shorter than four letters are not considered key words.

⏱ TIME AND RESOURCE MANAGER

Resources
Print: *Scoring Rubrics on Transparency*, Ch. 12; *Writing Assessment and Portfolio Management*; *Formal Assessment*, Ch. 12
Technology: *Writing and Grammar* Interactive Text, Section 12.5

Using the Full Student Edition	Using the Handbook🄷
• Review pp. 264–265 in class.	• Review pp. 170–171 in class.
• Have students analyze their rough drafts and create final drafts.	• Have students analyze their rough drafts and create final drafts.
• Complete the Portfolio Building and Reflecting on Your Writing exercises on p. 266.	• Complete the Portfolio Building and Reflecting on Your Writing exercises on p. 172.

Grammar in Your Writing
Citing Sources

In your research paper, be sure to credit the sources of information. To do this, include endnotes, footnotes, or internal citations within the text. Also, prepare a bibliography or works-cited list that will appear on the last page of your writing.

Footnotes and Endnotes When using footnotes and endnotes to provide internal documentation, include full details about the source and cite the page number. Indicate a footnote or an endnote by placing a number at the bottom of the page on which the information cited appears; for an endnote, place the documentation in numerical order on a page preceding the reference list.

> **Example footnote:** Bruce Goldfarb, *King of the Desert* (New York: Leland, 1999)

Parenthetical Documentation Using parenthetical references allows readers to learn about sources quickly and easily, without having to refer to a footnote. A parenthetical reference usually includes the author's last name and the page numbers from which the information is taken. The full publication information about each source to which you refer in parentheses will appear on your works-cited list.

> **Example:** Two thirds of employed actors appear only in commercials (Fleming 55).

Works-Cited List A works-cited list appears at the end of a piece of research writing and includes the publication information for any source used or quoted. Titles are usually arranged in alphabetical order by author's last name and are underscored or italicized. Your source cards will have all of the information you need to include on this list.

Bibliography Present your sources in a standardized format based on the type of resource referenced. Include the author's names, source title, place of publication, publisher, and date of publication.

> **Example entry:** Dryson, Edna. *Knowing a Thing or Two*. Chicago: Tower, 2000.

Find It in Your Reading Review the works-cited list in the excerpt from *The Figurative Tradition* on pages 246–249. Explain why each title is underlined or set in quotation marks.

Find It in Your Writing Check the punctuation of the titles in your research writing. Make sure that you have used capitalization, underlining, and quotation marks correctly.

To learn more about punctuating cited sources, see Citing Sources and Preparing Manuscript on pp. 848–854.

Editing and Proofreading • 265

Citing Sources

1. Review the different ways source information can be cited in a paper. Explain to students that not all forms appear in any one paper.

2. You may wish to have students turn to the Final Draft of the Student Work in Progress as an example of references noted parenthetically within the body of the paper.

3. Determine which types of documentation you want students to use, and focus on those during your review. Make sure students know your preferences.

4. When students have finished their works-cited pages, have them work with partners to check their work.

Find It in Your Reading

Students should respond that book titles and names of magazines are underlined, and article or chapter titles are in quotation marks. Ask students to explain the use of numbers in cited material.

Find It in Your Writing

Even if there are no quotations in students' papers, point out that all the entries in their source lists will require care. If students need additional information, you can refer to Chapter 27 for capitalization or Chapter 28 for punctuation.

☑ ONGOING ASSESSMENT: Prerequisite Skills

If students have difficulty with punctuating titles, you may find it helpful to refer them to the following materials to ensure coverage of prerequisite knowledge.

In the Textbook	Print Resources	Technology
Punctuating Titles, Section 28.4	*Grammar Exercise Workbook*, pp. 175–180	*On-Line Exercise Bank*, Section 28.4

Publishing and Presenting

1. Discuss in class the definition of an anthology, and how students think it might be organized (by subject area, organizational strategy, and so on).

2. Ask students to suggest audiences to whom they can present their material (clubs, other classes, friends, and family members).

3. If your school supports a Web site that accepts student work, encourage students to post their essays. If sharing their writing on the Internet, they may want to consider adding graphic elements of some sort, from colored type for subheads to graphs or pictures.

ASSESS and CLOSE

Assessment

Teaching Resources: Scoring Rubrics on Transparency, Chapter 12; Writing Assessment and Portfolio Management; Formal Assessment, Ch. 12

1. Display the Scoring Rubric transparency and review the criteria in class.

2. Before students proceed with self-assessment, you may wish to review the Final Draft of the Student Work in Progress on pages 267–269. Have students score the Final Draft in one or more of the rubric categories.

3. In addition to student self-assessment, you may wish to use the following assessment options:

   • score student essays yourself, using the rubric and scoring models from *Writing Assessment and Portfolio Management*.

   • administer the Chapter 12 assessment from *Formal Assessment* in the Teaching Resources to measure students' grasp of the concepts presented.

12.6 Publishing and Presenting

Following are some ways to share your research writing:

Building Your Portfolio

1. **Class Anthology** Assemble an anthology of essays by combining your class's examples of research writing. Discuss the organization and title of the anthology, and work together to write an introduction or foreword explaining the project. Bind the anthology, and make it available to classmates.

2. **Internet Publication** Use the Internet to share your research writing. Send your finished draft to a friend or relative by e-mail, or submit your writing to a Web site that publishes student writing.

Reflecting on Your Writing

Think over your research writing experience. Then, answer the following questions, and record your responses in your portfolio.

• Where did you find the most useful information?

• Which writing strategies worked so well that you would like to try them again?

🖥 Internet Tip

To see model research papers scored with this rubric, go on-line: PHSchool.com Enter Web Code: eek-1001

Rubric for Self-Assessment

Evaluate your research writing using the following criteria.

	Score 4	Score 3	Score 2	Score 1
Audience and Purpose	Focuses on a clearly stated thesis, starting from a well-framed question; gives complete citations	Focuses on a clearly stated thesis; gives citations	Focuses mainly on the chosen topic; gives some citations	Presents information without a clear focus; few or no citations
Organization	Presents information in logical order, emphasizing details of central importance	Presents information in logical order	Presents information logically, but organization is poor in places	Presents information in a scattered, disorganized manner
Elaboration	Draws clear conclusions from information gathered from multiple sources	Draws conclusions from information gathered from multiple sources	Explains and interprets some information	Presents information with little or no interpretation or synthesis
Use of Language	Shows overall clarity and fluency; contains few mechanical errors	Shows good sentence variety; contains some errors in spelling, punctuation, or usage	Uses awkward or overly simple sentence structures; contains many mechanical errors	Contains incomplete thoughts and mechanical errors that make the writing confusing

266 • Research Writing

☑ ONGOING ASSESSMENT: Assess Mastery

Use one or both of the following options to assess the final drafts of students' research essays.

Self-Assessment Ask students to score their essays using the rubric provided. In a single paragraph, have students reflect on the most valuable thing that they learned in completing this paper.

Teacher Assessment You may use the rubric and scoring models provided in *Writing Assessment and Portfolio Management* in the Teaching Resources to score students' research essays.

12.7 Student Work IN PROGRESS

FINAL DRAFT

Robert Capa

Michael S. Dougherty
Central Bucks West High School
Doylestown, Pennsylvania

Americans honor and respect the brave citizens who, over the years, have fought for their country. They have ensured the tranquillity of our people by bearing arms against the ever-changing threats to our nation's security. Often overlooked, however, are scores of men and women who have gone into battle defenseless against enemy attacks: wartime journalists. With only a camera or a pad and pencil in hand, they live a soldier's life while working a civilian job. Looking danger in the face, this unarmed crew records the dramatic details of war to inform people at home, as well as generations to come. The public certainly owes much to these brave and loyal workers. One of the most renowned of these war journalists was a photographer named Robert Capa, who dedicated his life to capturing the essence of war on film.

Capa was born Andrei Friedmann in Budapest, Hungary, in 1913. Little is known about his childhood, except that he did not have formal training in photography. Indeed, he taught himself everything that he learned in this field (Adato 98). While a high-school student in Hungary, he was exiled because of his political beliefs. Leaving his home country would have a strong influence on his life and career as a photographer.

In 1931, Friedmann got a job with a picture agency in Berlin, where he took his first assignment. He traveled to Copenhagen to photograph Russian Communist leader Leon Trotsky. Upon completing this assignment, he returned to Germany but was driven out by Hitler's menacing regime. Cast out from his second home, Friedmann found a new, more welcoming home in Paris, France.

While he was in Paris, Friedmann's career began to flourish, but not without an initial struggle. Even at the start of

Michael builds his opening paragraph to a thesis statement that describes the topic of his essay.

▼ **Critical Viewing**
What type of personality might you guess Capa to have had, based on this photograph? Explain. **[Speculate]**

Integrating Grammar Skills

Suggest that students use participial phrases and subordinate clauses at the beginning of sentences, in addition to inverting subject-verb order, to add variety. Alternatively, have students search Michael's final draft to find examples of sentences that have inverted subject-verb order, participial phrases as openers, and subordinate clauses as openers.

Customize for
ESL Students

If students are writing on a topic relating to their homeland, they may use words from their first languages. Encourage students to use context clues in their writing so that readers can make good guesses about the meanings of such words. If you have not already done so, you might wish to provide the classroom with a bilingual dictionary.

Real-World Connection

Writing a research paper is a task that some students may think only students have to do. Have students brainstorm for other occupations that might require a person to do research and document the sources and findings (scholars, scientists, reporters, lawyers, writers, politicians). Discuss in class how these research papers would be similar to, and different from, student research papers. (Possible answers might include: use of more primary sources or experimentation, might be more likely to use surveys and polls.)

---

his year in Paris, Friedmann was proud of the powerful images he was creating. However, he was dismayed that they were not selling for very much money, so he devised a plan that would benefit him and his wife financially. In order to sell prints for higher prices, Friedmann posed as the assistant to a completely fictitious American photographer named Robert Capa. For a while, he and his wife, who pretended to be the famous American's secretary, were making a substantial profit with this scheme. Unfortunately, in 1936, an editor recognized their fraud and threatened to expose them. Instead of abandoning the name, as the editor suggested, Friedmann decided to resolve the situation by adopting it. For the rest of his life, Andrei Friedmann was known as Robert Capa.

Later the same year, a conflict in Spain began to attract some of the world's attention away from the rising Nazi regime. Attracted by the limitless possibilities that war-field photography offered, Capa got a job with *Life* magazine and left France to cover the war. It was here that he developed a knack for war photography that made him famous. By shooting such remarkable images as "Death of a Loyalist Militiaman Frederico Borrell García, Cerro Muriano (Córdoba Front), 1936," Capa's reputation steadily grew until the European and American Press circles named him the "greatest war photographer in the world" (Emery 538).

In the following years, Robert Capa spent time covering China's war with Japan. He documented this war, but he was given his greatest opportunity when the Allied Forces declared war against Hitler's Axis Powers, which signaled the beginning of World War II.

As a Hungarian citizen based in America during this war, Capa suffered greatly. Because the Allies had declared war against the Axis, many Americans felt angry with Middle Europeans. Capa, a citizen of a country united with others against America, was categorized as an enemy alien. He was fired from his job at *Life* and found it difficult to make ends meet (Lande 251).

Finally in 1943, Capa was hired to cover the war overseas for *Collier's* magazine. His first assignment was the North African invasion. Dodging bullets as he traveled across the countryside, Capa was always in the center of the action. He made many friends, but he was eventually fired from *Collier's* for pooling, or sharing, his pictures with them. Scrambling for a new assignment, Capa took a job once again for *Life*. He was assigned to fill in for a sick man who was scheduled to jump out of a plane with a squad of paratroopers. Although he was nervous, Capa showed his dedication to his job by hurling himself from the plane into the African canopy (Stein 188).

Michael clearly and effectively organizes his paper using chronological organization of details.

Parenthetical documentation is used to name the sources of information. The full citation for the source appears at the end. The numbers indicate the page number.

Michael uses formal language to share the facts and details he discovered during research.

Michael italicized the titles of magazines. He proofread his writing carefully to make sure that it was free of distracting errors.

Capa's success was capped, however, when he was selected as one of four photographers who would make the D-Day landing in Normandy. He was the sole photographer of the bloodiest landing, Omaha Beach, and took 106 photographs in what he considered to be an outstanding personal victory (Neuman 85). Unfortunately, a darkroom assistant turned on too much heat while developing the pictures and destroyed all but eight. Despite such setbacks, Capa remained dedicated to photographing the war effort, making several other parachute landings as well (Stein 189).

Although his talents as a war journalist were outstanding, photographing the frightening images of war was never an easy task for Capa. As he once said, "It is not always easy to stand aside and be unable to do anything except record the suffering around one." Capa's humanity and compassion shine through his powerful photographs.

World War II eventually ended, but Capa's career moved forcefully ahead. After only three years, a conflict between the Israelis and Arabs broke out. Capa was one of the first men there and one of the first in Indochina to record fighting between the French and the Viet Minh.

Tragically, covering this event in 1954, Robert Capa was killed after stepping on a land mine. He had lived for forty years and covered four major wars. By capturing the horrifying and moving images of war, Robert Capa served America and its journalism well, eventually sacrificing his life for a profession he loved.

▲ **Critical Viewing**
This photograph shows the Normandy invasion in action. If the invasion were to take place today, how would it be similar and different? Explain. **[Modify]**

Michael closes with a strong restatement of his opening thesis.

Works Cited

Adato, Allison. "The Double Life of a Legendary War Photographer." *Life*, March 1997: 98–103.

Emery, Edwin. *The Press and America: An Interpretive History of the Mass Media*. 3rd Edition. Englewood Cliffs, NJ: Prentice Hall, Inc., 1972.

Lande, Nathaniel. *Dispatches from the Front: News Accounts of American Wars, 1776–1991*. New York: Henry Holt and Company, 1995.

Neuman, Johanna. *Lights, Camera, War*. New York: St. Martin's Press, 1996.

Stein, M. L. *Under Fire: The Story of American War Correspondents*. New York: Julian Messner, 1968.

Lesson Objectives

1. To write a documented essay appropriate to audience and purpose
2. To compile information from primary and secondary sources in systematic ways using available technology
3. To compile written ideas and representations into reports, summaries, or other formats and draw conclusions

Step-by-Step Teaching Guide

Documented Essay

1. Review the description of a documented essay with students, emphasizing that research sources are placed in parentheses within the text, not in a list at the end of the essay.
2. Have students brainstorm for topics connected to recent news events, perhaps in the sciences, the arts, politics, or sports. Encourage students to choose a topic in which they are genuinely interested.
3. Suggest that students review strategies from Chapter 12. See the chart below for suggestions.
4. Remind students that charts, graphs, and photographs can add to the appeal of a documented essay.
5. After students have published and presented their essays, they can be added to their portfolios.

Critical Viewing

Hypothesize Students might say that articles in newspapers, news magazines, science magazines, or on the Internet would contain information about the Hubble Telescope.

Connected Assignment
Documented Essay

In a **documented essay,** a thesis or main idea is presented and supported with evidence that comes in part from research. A documented essay is generally less formal than a traditional report. It also may contain fewer research sources and focus on a contemporary topic. Evidence within a documented essay might include more immediate or subjective information, such as interviews rather than just factual data. Also, sources are cited in full in parentheses immediately following appropriate text; no works-cited list is provided. Finally, like a magazine article, a documented essay may reflect a more informal tone than a traditional research paper.

▲ Critical Viewing What sources might you use to find information about the Hubble Telescope, pictured here? **[Hypothesize]**

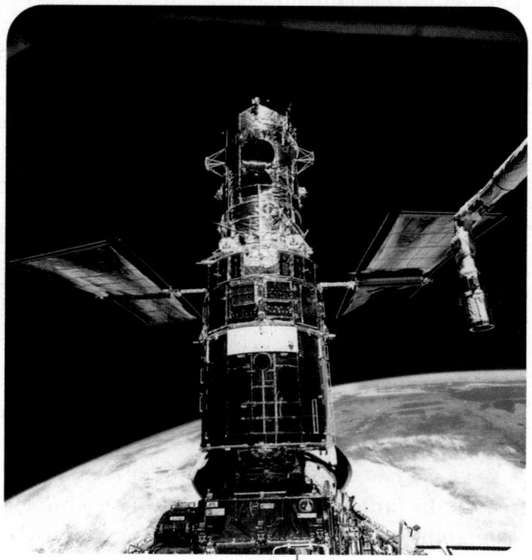

An effective documented essay contains

- a thesis or main idea.
- evidence or details to support that main idea.
- language appropriate for its audience and purpose.
- an effective and logical organization.
- parenthetical citations that reveal source information.

Develop your own documented essay, using the writing process skills that follow:

Prewriting

Choosing Your Topic Make sure to choose a topic you're genuinely interested in—you'll need to immerse yourself in it to write a successful documented essay. Listen to or watch the day's headline news, read the school's newspaper, or exchange ideas with a friend.

Narrowing Your Topic Once you have chosen a topic, narrow it so that you can discuss it fully within the space limitations of your essay. To narrow your topic, make a web by writing your broad topic in the center. Then, list related subtopics around the broad topic. Choose one of the subtopics as the focus for your documented essay.

ONGOING ASSESSMENT: Prerequisite Skills

Students may find the following resources from Chapter 12 particularly helpful in preparing their documented essay.

In the Textbook	Print Resources	Technology
Guiding Research With a K-W-L Chart, Section 12.2 Taking Notes, Section 12.2	*Writing Support Transparencies,* 12-B–C *Writing Support Activity Book,* 12-1	*Writing and Grammar* Interactive Text, Section 12.2

Gathering and Organizing Details Gather details from a variety of sources to support the main idea of your documented essay. Some details you may research in books or on-line; some you may discover for yourself by interviewing or conducting surveys. Take careful notes as you gather details. Be sure that you accurately copy down all the source information you will use in parenthetical documentation.

Once you have a body of facts and examples, decide on the most effective way in which to present them. Develop an outline like the one that follows to organize your documented essay.

I. Hubble Telescope

  A. History & Development
    1. Invention team
    2. Sponsor

  B. Current Mission
    1. Successes
    2. Failures

  C. Future Missions
    1. Goals
    2. Next generation

Drafting Open your essay by stating your thesis or main idea. You may also want to grab the interest of your audience by sharing an interesting anecdote or posing an interesting question. In the body of the essay, weave illustrative examples with explanatory text. Refer to your outline to ensure that your essay is logically organized. Insert parenthetical documentation of source material as you draft.

Revising and Editing Ask a peer to read your essay aloud. Listen for and correct any inconsistencies in tone or attitude toward your subject. Add or clarify details by scanning your notes. Double-check all details for accuracy, and proofread carefully. Where appropriate, consider putting large blocks of data into a chart or graph to make your presentation more appealing.

Publishing and Presenting Hand write or print out a neat copy of your documented essay. Add photographs, charts, and other visuals to enhance the information within the text. Then, share your essay with peers or family members.

✹ Grammar and Style Tip

As you draft, use transitions such as *then, since,* and *however* to make connections between your ideas.

Customize for
Less Advanced Students

If students seem confused about how to organize their drafts, suggest that they try using an outline, a diagram, a chart, or a graph to organize details. Students who find that their material will fit in a time line, for example, may see that their drafts should follow chronological order. Other students might construct a T-chart headed "Events" and "Effects," which may suggest a cause-and-effect organization for their drafts. A web diagram labeled in the center with the name of a broad topic can help students organize and order the many details surrounding it and encourage them to consider a part-to-whole structure for their essays.

Integrating Grammar Skills

Punctuation Point out the difference between using direct quotes and paraphrasing. Remind students that they need not use quotation marks when they paraphrase from a source. However, they must cite those sources with the same accuracy as they would a direct quote.

Customize for
More Advanced Students

Encourage students to investigate two or three different news sources on the Internet. Have them compare the various articles on their topics. Encourage them to evaluate the information they gather. Do different sources share the same conclusions? Ask students to consider what they would do if they found conflicting research.

Lesson Objectives

1. To analyze relationships and ideas as represented in various media
2. To compile information from primary and secondary sources in systematic ways using available technology
3. To produce reports and research projects in varying forms for audiences

Recognizing Musical Achievements

1. Choose, or have students choose, one of the Spotlight elements to research and discuss.

2. Interested students might research additional information about Franz Schubert. Tell them that *lied* (rhymes with *heed*) means "song" in German. Students will find that despite Schubert's short life, he was able to compose about six hundred songs, nine symphonies, and piano music, masses, operas, and chamber music.

3. Students interested in Goethe might enjoy reading his short novel, *The Sorrows of Young Werther*. Have them note possible connections between this novel and the music of Schubert.

4. Students might do research on Wolfgang Amadeus Mozart (1756–1791), who also had a relatively short life. He composed over six hundred works, including many operas.

Viewing and Representing

Activity If students present their reports on Schubert in class, encourage them to enrich their presentations by playing selected recordings of his music.

Critical Viewing

Distinguish Most students will say that the orchestra appears to be performing since the conductor and members of the orchestra are dressed formally.

Spotlight on the Humanities

Recognizing Musical Achievements

Focus on Music: Franz Schubert

Research allows you to study the past as well as the present, finding out about famous people and events of centuries ago. Born in Vienna, Franz Schubert (1797–1828) grew up in a musical family but remained a fairly unknown composer throughout his lifetime. The lyrical quality of Schubert's work made it compatible with the music form known as the *lied*. Later in his life, he composed pieces inspired by the nineteenth-century poet Johann Wolfgang von Goethe. Schubert's expressive music reflected the poetry of writers such as Goethe. Schubert established the German *lied* as a new art form in the nineteenth century.

▲ Critical Viewing
Does this photograph depict a rehearsal or a performance? How do you know?
[Distinguish]

Film Connection The rivalry between Wolfgang Amadeus Mozart and Schubert's teacher Antonio Salieri is the focus of the film *Amadeus* (1984). Originally a Broadway play by Peter Shaffer, the film won eight Academy Awards, including Best Picture, Best Director, and Best Actor.

Literature Connection Franz Schubert was inspired by the words of poet and writer Johann Wolfgang von Goethe (1749–1832), who was at the center of the literary movements during the "Age of Goethe" in Germany (1770–1832). The poetry, dramas, novels, and essays of Goethe have influenced writers of such esteem as Samuel Taylor Coleridge, Percy Bysshe Shelley, Henry Wadsworth Longfellow, and Harriet Beecher Stowe.

Research Writing Activity:
Research Report on Franz Schubert

It may have surprised you to read that Schubert was a relatively unknown composer throughout his lifetime. For other interesting facts and anecdotes about Schubert's life and works, research him at your local library or on the Internet. Then, write a research report on Schubert's life and inspirational works. Share your research paper with your classmates.

272 • Research Writing

Media and Technology Skills

Using Media to Produce a Documentary

Activity: Produce a Video Report

Documentaries are nonfiction films that share many kinds of information with an audience. You can use a video camera to produce a well-researched and effective documentary that uses images, sounds, and narration to communicate ideas.

Think About It Shoot a 5–6 minute documentary based on research into a topic. As you select a topic, consider the possibilities that video offers. For example, you may want to include interviews with local experts or family members. The people available to you may suggest suitable topics or themes.

Research It Use a variety of sources to collect information for your documentary. Look for opportunities to expand your research to include the Internet, CD-ROMs, and other media.

Storyboard It While you gather facts, you will begin to plan your documentary. A storyboard will help you plan the sequence of shots. It might also help guide your research by suggesting new directions or missing elements.

Introduction:
Our Local Fire Department

Narrated history, with photographs

Interview with Captain Isaiah Acevedo

Script It Once you have determined the flow of elements, write the script for the documentary's narration. Use a direct, explanatory tone. Practice reading your script several times, looking for phrases that sound awkward or confusing.

Produce It Shoot your documentary. Film several versions of each scene to be sure you have one that is clear and effective. During editing, follow the sequence of your storyboard, adding titles to clarify ideas or identify sources or settings.

Media and Technology Skills • 273

Lesson Objectives

1. To proofread writing for appropriateness of organization, content, style, and conventions

2. To produce legible work that shows accurate spelling and correct use of the conventions of punctuation and capitalization

3. To demonstrate control over grammatical elements such as subject-verb agreement, pronoun-antecedent agreement, verb forms, and parallelism

Step-by-Step Teaching Guide

Applying Revising and Editing Skills to Writing

Teaching Resources: Standardized Test Preparation Workbook, pp. 23–24

1. Go over the bulleted items with students, and then ask them to read and respond to the sample test item.

2. If students missed the agreement problem with *involve* in the first line, emphasize that they should read test items carefully when asked to revise and edit a passage.

3. Assign Practice 1, and then review the answers.

4. If a substantial number of students missed a particular item, reteach the necessary skills.

Standardized Test Preparation Workshop

Applying Revising and Editing Skills to Writing

Your skills at revising and editing a passage will be assessed on some standardized tests. These skills are also useful to have when you are writing a research paper. When you are prompted to revise and edit, these strategies will assist you in formulating your answers:

- Check that the writer has not strayed from the main idea of the passage.
- Analyze the passage for sentences that seem misplaced or that contain details insignificant to the rest of the passage.
- While reading, think of suitable ways to clarify the structure of the paragraphs and sentences.
- Check for correct grammar and punctuation.
- Check for the proper use of verb tenses.
- When deciding how to best reword a sentence, be certain to avoid redundancies, jargon, and padded phrases.

The following is a sample prompt for revising and editing:

Test Tip

Always read the questions carefully, and make sure you comprehend what is being asked.

Sample Test Item	Answer and Explanation
Directions: Read the passage, and choose the best answer to each question: [1]Irony is the literary technique that involve surprising, interesting, or amusing contradictions at work. [2]These differences can result from clashes between what a character believes and what is actually the case. [3]Irony might also result from clashes between what a character expects to happen and what actually happens.	

1 What is the most fitting change to make to the preceding passage?
 	
  A Part 1: change <u>involve</u> to <u>involves</u>
 	
  B Part 2: insert a <u>comma</u> after <u>and</u>
 	
  C Part 3: change <u>expects</u> to <u>expected</u>
 	
  D Make no change
	The answer is *A*. This question addresses subject-verb agreement. In this case, the subject of the sentence, *literary technique,* is singular. Therefore, the verb should be in a singular form: *involves.*

274 • Research Writing

✎ TEST-TAKING TIP

Encourage students to concentrate on the organization of a test passage in addition to noting grammar, usage, and mechanics errors. Do some sentences seem unrelated to the topic? Could details be ordered differently? Should choppy sentences be combined?

Instruct students to look for odd shifts in verb tense. For example, if in part 10 of the practice item, the verb *to be* had appeared in the present tense, it would be an error since the sentence refers to events in the past.

> **Practice 1** Directions: Read the passage, and choose the best answers to the following questions.

¹The ancient Greek dramatist Sophocles wrote one hundred plays, but only seven remains in existence. ²The most famous are the three dealing with Oedipus and his children: *Oedipus Rex (Oedipus the King), Oedipus at Colonus,* and *Antigone.* ³Today, there are many stage actors who vie for the role of Oedipus. ⁴This trilogy was written over a span of forty years. ⁵Born in Colonus, near Athens, Sophocles was one of the most respected Greek dramatists of his time. ⁶He was admired not only for his poetic and dramatic skills, but also for his good looks and musical talent. ⁷Sophocles frequently won first place in the competitions of plays performed in the Dionysian festivals. ⁸With his first tragedy, written at age twenty-seven, he defeated the highly respected Aeschylus. ⁹Sophocles made some changes to the traditions of Greek theater. ¹⁰One of the most important changes, was to increase the size of the chorus.

1 What is the best change to make to part 1?

  A Change <u>dramatist</u> to <u>Dramatist</u>.

  B Change <u>ancient</u> to <u>Ancient</u>.

  C Change <u>remains</u> to <u>remain</u>.

  D Make no change

2 Which of the following changes, if any, is needed in the passage?

  A Delete part 3.

  B Delete part 6.

  C Delete part 4.

  D Make no change.

3 Which of the following should have a comma deleted?

  A Part 1

  B Part 10

  C Part 6

  D Make no change

4 Which is the best way to combine the sentences in part 9 and part 10?

  A Sophocles made some changes to the traditions of Greek theater, and one of the most important changes was to increase the size of the chorus.

  B Such as Sophocles made, one of the most important changes to Greek theater was an increase in the size of the chorus.

  C Sophocles, who had made some changes to the traditions of Greek theater, made one of the most important changes, which was to increase the size of the chorus.

  D An increase in the size of the chorus is one of the most important changes Sophocles made to Greek theater, among the other changes he made.

5 Which of these sentences would best fit after part 5?

  A Sophocles passed through life virtually unnoticed, and not accepted by Greek society.

  B Sophocles lived a long, healthy life, and died before Athens fell from glory.

  C Of the major Greek tragedy writers of his time, Sophocles is the only one not mocked in the comedies of Greek playwright Aristophanes.

  D His works, however, are not worthy enough of being deemed scholarly nor classical.

6 Which of the following changes, if any, is needed in part 2?

  A Place the comma inside the parentheses.

  B Replace the colon with a comma.

  C Change <u>King</u> to <u>king</u>.

  D Make no change

> **Practice 1**

1. C
2. A
3. B
4. A
5. C
6. D

Customize for
Less Advanced Students

Assure students that they needn't be knowledgeable about the content area of a test such as this one. Students are asked only to note errors; they do not need background knowledge about Sophocles or his works.

Customize for
More Advanced Students

Students might review previously graded papers and note the types of errors they need to work on. They can study more effectively for a test of this type if they know their weaknesses.

13 Time and Resource Manager

In-Depth Lesson Plan

	LESSON FOCUS	PRINT AND MEDIA RESOURCES
DAY 1	**Introduction to Response to Literature** Students learn key elements of writing responses to literature and analyze the Model From Literature. (pp. 276–281/Ⓗ176–177)	*Writers at Work* DVD, Response to Literature *Writing and Grammar* Interactive Text, Ch. 13, Introduction
DAY 2	**Prewriting** Students choose and narrow a topic, consider their audience and purpose, and gather information. (pp. 282–285/Ⓗ178–181)	**Teaching Resources** *Writing Support Transparencies*, 13-A–C; *Writing Support Activity Book*, 13-1–2 *Writing and Grammar* Interactive Text, Section 13.2
DAY 3	**Drafting** Students organize their ideas and write their first drafts. (pp. 286–287/Ⓗ182–183)	**Teaching Resources** *Writing Support Transparencies*, 13-D–E *Writing and Grammar* Interactive Text, Section 13.3
DAY 4	**Revising** Students revise their drafts in terms of overall structure, paragraphs, sentences, and word choice. (pp. 288–292/Ⓗ184–188)	**Teaching Resources** *Writing Support Transparencies*, 13-F–G *Writing and Grammar* Interactive Text, Section 13.4
DAY 5	**Editing and Proofreading; Publishing and Presenting** Students check their work for accuracy and correctness and present their final drafts. (pp. 293–294/Ⓗ189–190)	**Teaching Resources** *Scoring Rubrics on Transparency*, Ch. 13; *Writing Assessment and Portfolio Management; Formal Assessment*, Ch. 13 *Writing and Grammar* Interactive Text, Sections 13.5–6

Accelerated Lesson Plan

	LESSON FOCUS	PRINT AND MEDIA RESOURCES
DAY 1	**Introduction Through Drafting** Students review characteristics of a response to literature, select topics, and write drafts. (pp. 276–287/Ⓗ176–183)	*Writers at Work* DVD, Response to Literature **Teaching Resources** *Writing Support Transparencies*, 13-A–E; *Writing Support Activity Book*, 13-1–2 *Writing and Grammar* Interactive Text, Ch. 13, Introduction through Section 13.3
DAY 2	**Revising Through Presenting** Students work individually or with peers to revise, edit, and proofread their work for presentation. (pp. 288–294/Ⓗ184–190)	**Teaching Resources** *Writing Support Transparencies*, 13-F–G; *Scoring Rubrics on Transparency*, Ch. 13; *Writing Assessment and Portfolio Management; Formal Assessment*, Ch. 13 *Writing and Grammar* Interactive Text, Sections 13.4–6

Options for Adapting Lesson Plans

HOMEWORK

Have students complete any stage of the lesson for homework.

FEATURES

Extend coverage with Connected Assignment (p. 298), Spotlight on the Humanities (p. 300), Media and Technology Skills (p. 301), and the Standardized Test Preparation Workshop (p. 302).

TECHNOLOGY

Students can complete any stage of the lesson on the computer, using *Writing and Grammar* Interactive Text or a word-processing program. Have them print out their completed work.

Writing and Grammar Handbook Alignment

Page numbers in Step-by-Step Teaching Guides in this Teacher's Edition refer to pages from the full student text. Handbook page references, indicated with this icon 🕀, are provided in Time and Resource Manager boxes and at the bottom of each Teacher's Edition page.

INTEGRATED SKILLS COVERAGE

Integrating Grammar
Pronouns and Antecedents, SE p. 291/🕀187
Styling Titles of Poems, Stories, and Novels, SE p. 293/🕀189
Grammar and Style, SE p. 299
ATE p. 293

Vocabulary Skills ATE pp. 288, 297

Reading/Writing Connection
Identify Support for the Author's Points, SE p. 278
Writing Application, SE p. 281

Viewing and Representing
Critical Viewing, SE pp. 276, 278, 279, 280, 292, 295, 296, 298, 300/🕀176, 188, 191, 192
Appreciating Performing Arts, SE p. 300
Movie Review, ATE p. 298

Speaking and Listening Skills ATE p. 283

Technology Skills
Responding Using Technology, SE pp. 282, 301/🕀178

Real-World Connection ATE p. 280

ASSESSMENT SUPPORT

Standardized Test Preparation Workshop SE p. 302; ATE p. 292
Standardized Test Preparation Workbook, pp. 25–26
Scoring Rubrics on Transparency, Ch. 13
Formal Assessment, Ch. 13
Writing Assessment and Portfolio Management

MEETING INDIVIDUAL NEEDS

Less Advanced Students ATE pp. 289, 303. See also Ongoing Assessments ATE pp. 283, 285.
More Advanced Students ATE pp. 280, 286, 300, 303
Gifted and Talented Students ATE p. 283
ESL Students ATE pp. 279, 284, 289, 299, 301

BLOCK SCHEDULING

Pacing Suggestions
For 90-minute Blocks
• Have students complete the Prewriting and Drafting stages in a single period.
• Focus one class period on Revising and Editing and Publishing and Presenting. Allow at least 30 minutes for peer revision.

Resources for Varying Instruction
• *Writing and Grammar* Interactive Text A 90-minute block provides an ideal opportunity for students to work on the computer.
• *Writers at Work* DVD Show the Response to Literature segment in class.

Professional Development Support
• *How to Manage Instruction in the Block* This teaching resource provides management and activity suggestions.

MEDIA AND TECHNOLOGY

For the Student
• *Writing and Grammar* Interactive Text, Ch. 13
• *On-line Exercise Bank,* Sections 24.1–2

For the Teacher
• *Writers at Work* DVD, Response to Literature
• Teacher**EXPRESS** CD-ROM

WRITING AND GRAMMAR ON-LINE

Interactive Text (On-line or on CD-ROM)
• Easily navigable instruction with interactive Revision Checkers
• Full use of e-rater™, the essay-scoring system (on-line only)

Companion Web Site PHSchool.com
• Scoring rubrics with models (use Web Code eek-1001)

See the Go On-line! **feature, SE p. iii.**

LITERATURE CONNECTIONS

Related selections from *Prentice Hall Literature, Penguin Edition,* Grade 10:

Professional Model from *In Commemoration: One Million Volumes,* Rudolfo A. Anaya, SE p. 281
Topic Bank Option "The Masque of the Red Death," Edgar Allan Poe, SE p. 283/🕀179

▶ *Lesson Objectives*

1. To write a response to literature appropriate to audience and purpose

2. To read to appreciate a writer's craft and to discover models for writing

3. To analyze literary elements for their contributions to meaning in literary texts

4. To use prewriting strategies to generate ideas, develop voice, and plan

5. To develop and revise drafts in terms of structure, paragraphs, sentences, and word choice

6. To edit and proofread to ensure standard English usage and grammar

7. To evaluate writing for both mechanics and content

8. To refine selected work for publication

Critical Viewing

Make a Judgment Students may note that the reader looks absorbed. The comfortable position in which she is reading might suggest that she's reading for pleasure.

Chapter
13 Response to Literature

Responding to Literature in Everyday Life

You probably respond to literature in everyday life more often than you realize. For example, when you lend a book to a friend with a comment like "It's really funny," or when you summarize the plot of a favorite childhood story, you are responding to literature. Other ways of responding to literature in everyday life include silently identifying with a character in a book you're reading or sharing your views about a story or poem with a teacher or friend.

Responses to literature also appear in written form in everyday life. For example, your morning newspaper may contain a review of a new novel or collection of poetry. On-line, Web sites may be devoted to sharing readers' responses to a particular author's works or to a genre of literature.

▲ **Critical Viewing**
What clues indicate that this student is enjoying what she is reading? Explain.
[Make a Judgment]

276 • Response to Literature

⏱ TIME AND RESOURCE MANAGER	
Resources **Technology:** *Writers at Work* DVD, Response to Literature; *Writing and Grammar* Interactive Text, Ch. 13	
Using the Full Student Edition	**Using the Handbook** Ⓗ
• Read and discuss pp. 276–281 in class. • Analyze the Model From Literature. • Share journal responses to literature from other classes.	• Read and discuss pp. 176–177 in class. • Share journal responses to literature from other classes.

What Is a Response to Literature?

A **response to literature** is a reader's reaction to any aspect of the literature he or she is reading. Some responses are formal and academic in tone; others are informal and more personal. Most responses to literature contain

- a reaction to a poem, story, essay, or other work of literature.
- references to or passages from works that support the writer's main points.
- personal and literary allusions, quotations, and other examples that support the writer's opinions.
- an effective and logical organization.
- a conclusion or evaluation that sums up the writer's response to the work.

To preview the criteria on which your response to literature may be evaluated, see the Rubric for Self-Assessment on page 294.

Types of Responses to Literature

Readers can respond to literature in various ways:

- **Journal entries** contain a reader's unique responses. They are generally informal and not shared with others.
- **Critical reviews** discuss various elements of a literary work—characters, plot, theme—and offer opinions about the work's effectiveness.
- **Literary analyses** examine various aspects of a work of literature. Often, an analysis compares the work with other works and offers an opinion of the work's literary importance.

PREVIEW

Student Work
IN PROGRESS

Follow the progress of Sheetal Wadera, a student at Hightower High School in Missouri City, Texas, as she drafts her response to Homer's *Odyssey*. Sheetal's completed response appears at the end of this chapter.

Writers in ACTION

Literature is meant to be read, shared, and responded to. For Miguel Algarín, teacher and poet, responding to literature is a way of life:

"A lot of the responding I do is face-to-face. It's people bringing their work and looking for me to respond while they're here. . . . I've made a passionate life out of talking about how other people have written . . . and talking to other people through my writing about how I felt it."

Response to Literature • 277

PREPARE and ENGAGE

Interest GRABBER Write on the board: *Laugh, Cry, Think, Question, Remember.* Ask students to suggest stories, poems, or plays that they have read for which these were their reactions. Did more than one of these apply to a single literary work? Ask them to identify other emotional and intellectual reactions to reading that they have had. Write these on the board. Have students suggest why they think such responses are both common and important to the reading experience. (The objective of writing is to share experiences, ideas, and truths. Writing is intended to make the reader respond; without a response, the connection between reader and writer has not been made.)

Activate Prior Knowledge

Ask students to think of elements of fiction. List them on the chalkboard as they respond (*characters, setting, plot, theme*). Next, ask them to think of a novel or short story that they have particularly enjoyed. Have them write the title and author, and then write one sentence each describing their favorite character and the setting, one or two sentences summarizing or describing the plot, and one sentence stating a theme. Explain that one type of response to literature is a critical review that discusses these components and offers opinions about the effectiveness of the work. Refer students to the other types of literature responses on this page.

More About the Writer

Miguel Algarín, a poet, critic, and entrepreneur, was the father of the contemporary Latino literary movement and the founder of New York's landmark Nuyorican Poet's Café. He has written several award-winning poetry collections, including *Love Is Hard Work*.

ONGOING ASSESSMENT: Diagnose

Use one of the following options to diagnose students' current level of proficiency in writing responses to literature.

Option 1 Have students select their strongest example of a response to literature essay from last year. Read their samples to determine which students need extra support in developing a response essay.	**Option 2** Ask students to list one or two of the most challenging aspects they encounter when writing response essays. (For example, understanding the ideas in literature or providing sufficient evidence to support a main point.) Use their responses to assess which part of the writing process you will want to emphasize.

Paul Montazzoli is a graduate of Rutgers University. He works in New York City as a freelance editor and book reviewer.

Reading ← Writing Connection

Reading Strategy: Identify Support for the Author's Points As you read nonfiction essays like this response to literature, look for examples, quotations, and other types of details that support the author's points. If there are few supporting details, you should question the author's ideas.

▲ **Critical Viewing** What sort of story would you set in Notre-Dame, pictured here? Why? **[Relate]**

from the *Introduction to The Hunchback of Notre-Dame*

Paul Montazzoli

The Victor Hugo who wrote *The Hunchback of Notre-Dame* was a twenty-nine-year-old firebrand burning at full blaze—sure of his own genius, gripped by an epic vision of Homeric proportions, and in no mood to bow down to church, state, or public taste. . . . Indeed, *The Hunchback of Notre-Dame* must have irked even some of Hugo's fellow Romantics, for it does not show that favorite period of Romantic nostalgia—the Middle Ages—as they liked to show it: a soft-focus tableau of saints, lords, ladies, and knights. Medieval life in this prose epic is as full of squalor as of splendor, and far too dynamic ever to hold still for a tableau. The book gives its specific setting—fifteenth-century Paris—all the variety and danger, the dash and the dreariness, that great cities have always had.

In the introduction, Montazzoli reveals his topic: his response to The Hunchback of Notre-Dame.

One way to respond to literature is to compare it with other works of the same period or literary movement.

278 • Response to Literature

Imagine yourself living in this city—it is not difficult. You swing around a drab, dirty corner—and your head is thrown back by the vision of the exalted towers of Notre-Dame. You stand on your toes and peer above the heads of a jeering crowd in a square—and catch sight of an impossibly deformed creature with bristling red hair, writhing and sweating in the sun as he is turned slowly on a pillory. You loll about the plaza in front of the cathedral, watching the gaudily dressed passersby—and are jostled by a priest in somber clothes and with a somber face, who is walking quickly—almost ferociously—through the crowd. Before he disappears into it, you make out in his eyes glimmers of complicated secrets that you want to know and fear to know.

No doubt the central figure of the book is that horrendous one you saw on the turning wheel. Why did Hugo make him *so* horrendous—with his crooked legs, enormous hump, and eye covered by a pronounced wart? To shock us, undoubtedly—though, since we are not dealing with a horror movie but with a tragic novel, the shock is not meant to vibrate in us for a minute and then pass, but to lead us to pity and wonder. The pity is for Quasimodo, the hunchback, and the wonder is for Fate, which made him what he is.

"Oh! Why am I not of stone, like thee?" Quasimodo asks one of the sculpted goblins in the cathedral. His question curiously inverts one that King Lear asks the dead Cordelia in the last scene of Shakespeare's play: "Why should a dog, a horse, a rat, have life,/ And thou no breath at all?" The tragic substance of the two questions is the same: life is given or denied by Fate with no regard for justice or the needs of the human heart.

In Quasimodo's disharmonious features, Hugo embodied the chaos of the world as he perceived it—a world of plague, riot, and passion, of titanic clashing energies both psychic and material. In those same features he also imaged the deformities in the soul of that priest who jostled you in the crowd, and who happened to be Quasimodo's beloved master, the

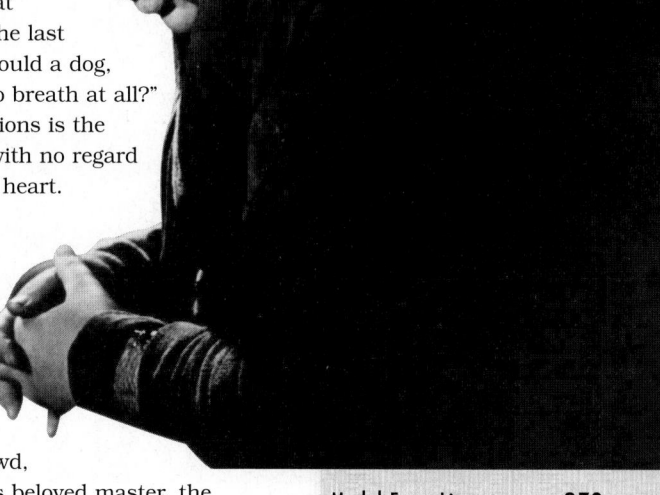

Here, Montazzoli uses his own imagination as he responds to Hugo's work.

▼ **Critical Viewing**
How well does this actor's makeup and costume convey Hugo's Quasimodo? Explain. **[Criticize]**

Customize for
ESL Students

Read Montazzoli's essay to the class, clarifying the text and explaining vocabulary as needed. As the essay is read, have students list the new words and write a synonym or short definition for each.

More About the Writer

Born in France in 1802, Victor Hugo published his first collection of poems when he was seventeen. Before long, he was also a successful playwright. The introduction to his 1827 drama *Cromwell* became the manifesto for Romanticism. In contrast to the ruling classical ideal, Romanticism called for writing that reflected reality and showed both good and evil, beauty and ugliness, tears and laughter. Hugo's grief at the death of his daughter in 1843 prompted him to begin *Les Misérables*. Revolution brought fourteen years of exile. When Hugo was finally able to return to France, in 1871, he was viewed as a hero, as much for his political activism and writing about freedom and justice as for his fame as a novelist, poet, and playwright.

Critical Viewing

Criticize Students may note that the actor's appearance corresponds to Montazzoli's description of Hugo's Quasimodo. You may wish to note that the actor shown is Charles Laughton, the first and best known of film Quasimodos.

Model From Literature • 279

archdeacon Claude Frollo. This soul is an impressive one, however bent and twisted: Claude is no stage villain, but a complex mixture of overardent intellectuality, misguided generosity, and undeterable spite.

Another intention behind the hunchback's singular grotesqueness is less obvious. In Quasimodo's body, chaos meets order and the inhuman confronts the human. The mystical vision also admits a joining of opposites—all the contraries of the world blending into a whole, though the result is not disharmony but harmony. In a skewed, ironic way, the figure of Quasimodo alludes to mysticism. Thus, his close relation to the cathedral of Notre-Dame—a sublime vision in stone—and to its awesome bells seems oddly appropriate at the same time that it arrestingly contrasts the ugly and the beautiful.

Looked at another way, Quasimodo represents a crossing of the human into the bestial, or the bestial into the human. Here is a glimpse at one of the chief underlying patterns of the book: the crossing of boundaries. For example, in Book II, the poet Pierre Gringoire—bumbling innocent that he is—crosses unawares into the Court of Miracles, the center of the Vagabonds' domain of illegality, where the king's writ does not run.

There are many less literal but more dramatic examples. Spurred

This response to literature is well organized: Each paragraph explores a specific aspect of the author's response.

▼ **Critical Viewing** Explain the ways in which this scene illustrates "chaos meeting order." [Connect]

on by passion, the characters in the book again and again take up the dare of a society that confines its members to specialized roles in rigid hierarchies, and grants outsiders no respect at all. . . .

The society these characters struggle against represented, for Hugo, an attempt to create a zone of reason and order within a world tending naturally to blind conflict and chaos. This attempt—and perhaps all such attempts—he regarded as futile. For example, *The Hunchback of Notre-Dame* shows us a Paris made up of a patchwork of many judicial sovereignties, whose boundaries and prerogatives often blur together. Where so many are responsible, none are responsible, and the city seems to live under no law at all. The justice that *is* dispensed tends to be laughable or lamentable. As for the supreme judge, Louis XI, his arbitrary cruelty mimics that of Fate itself. . . .

While the characters are driven by passions ranging from the merely fierce to the berserk, and an already weak social fabric is torn and mangled by violence, the voice that conveys this anguishing picture is surprisingly calm and detached. It is as if the narrator were determined to keep his balance at the edge of the abyss of unreason opened up by his own tale. His favorite approaches include dry reportage, enthusiastic lecturing, suave irony, and poetic whimsy, all of which provide satisfying counterpoint to the stupendous flux of the action. Unlike many narrators in nineteenth-century fiction, only occasionally and moderately does he exhibit astonishment or pity. Generally he leaves these emotions to the characters and the reader. For example, his accounts of the four appalling deaths in Book IX are sharply focused and unflinching, and he does not pause to sympathize, eulogize, or blame. In one case, he dryly provides one exact, hair-raising detail after another until the effect is excruciating.

The author of *The Hunchback of Notre-Dame* desired not to soothe and lull his audience with confections, but to move and disturb it with tragedy. The book shows man as a victim or a victimizer in society, and a victim and an orphan in the cosmos. Significantly, the main characters include three actual orphans, one foundling, and one kidnapped child. There is no hedging of the truth. Into this gorgeous, savage, and wholly unconsoling masterpiece, Victor Hugo put all the candor as well as all the intensity of his youthful genius.

Writing Application: Identify Support for Your Points In your response to literature, include direct quotations as well as paraphrased descriptions of events, settings, characters, and ideas.

Specific allusions to elements from The Hunchback of Notre-Dame *support Montazzoli's ideas.*

The example given in this paragraph is an effective type of elaboration.

The conclusion to Montazzoli's response restates his thesis and adds a powerful insight: Hugo's novel is a masterpiece, a work of genius.

In his memoir *In Commemoration: One Million Volumes,* Rudolfo A. Anaya discusses the impact that literature has had on his personal growth. You can find an excerpt from Anaya's memoir in *Prentice Hall Literature, Penguin Edition,* Grade 10.

Model From Literature • 281

Integrating Grammar Skills

Punctuation Call students' attention to the use of dashes in the essay and review the following guidelines.

1. A dash may be used after a series if a summary statement follows. (Example: Hamlet, Macbeth, and Julius Caesar—these are some of Shakespeare's best-known characters.)

2. A long phrase that interrupts a sentence can be set off by dashes instead of commas.

3. Dashes are sometimes used in place of commas to set off appositives, especially when there are commas within the appositive. (Example: Three countries—Russia, Germany, and Italy—have contributed great music to the world.)

4. A dash may be used when special emphasis is needed for an appositive or phrase. (Example: This day—it had been an exhausting one—was almost over.)

Reading\Writing Connection

Writing Application: Identify Support for Your Points

Have students write the points they want to make at the top of separate sheets of paper. As they gather details for their essays, students can list the information under the point it supports. If their research turns up an additional point they want to make, they can start another sheet.

Prewriting: List

1. Ask students what they know about Prince Prospero, the main character in Poe's "The Masque of the Red Death." (He is wealthy, eccentric, and trying to escape a plague.) Would students have chosen this character or someone else on the list? Why?

2. Ask students to brainstorm for a list of characters from literature whom they have found interesting, either individually or as a class. Have them select one to add to a topic bank.

Prewriting: Review Your Journal

1. If students have kept a reading journal, have them review their journals and choose two interesting ideas as possible topics.

2. Ask them to write a short journal response for each topic. These could later be developed into an essay.

Prewriting: Browse a Bookshelf

1. You might want to schedule a visit to the school library for this strategy.

2. As an alternative, you might suggest that students browse through the table of contents of their literature textbooks.

Prewriting: Discuss With a Peer

1. Tell students that they need not limit their discussion strictly to recently read titles, but they may discuss any books or poems they have read that have made a significant impression.

2. Suggest that students keep pencil and paper handy to jot down anything they say during the discussion that they realize might work as an essay topic.

13.2 Prewriting

Choosing Your Topic

The best topic for a response to literature is a work about which you have strong ideas. Use the following strategies to come up with a topic for your response to literature:

Strategies for Generating Topics

1. **List** Begin by listing characters from literature whom you find interesting. These characters should belong to the stories and poetry about which you have the most to say. Review your list, and choose as a topic the character or work that you find most intriguing.

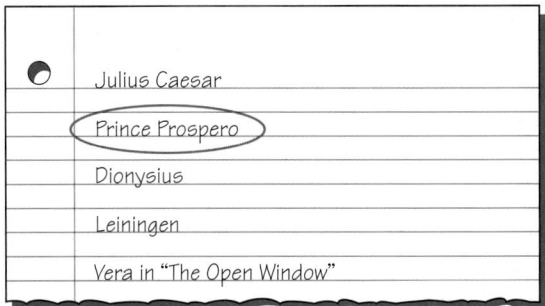

Julius Caesar

Prince Prospero

Dionysius

Leiningen

Vera in "The Open Window"

2. **Review Your Journal** In your reading journal, you may have recorded quotes from literature or themes, plots, and imagery that intrigued you. Look through your journal, and put self-sticking notes on pages that contain interesting ideas. Revisit the pages you marked, and choose one entry for your response to literature.

3. **Browse a Bookshelf** Go to the library or to a bookstore, and browse through the bookshelves to get writing ideas. Jot down titles of literature that you have read, authors you like, and literature that you would like to read. Review your notes, and choose as a topic for your response to literature a book you have already read, a comparison of two works by the same author, or a review of a book that you found while browsing.

4. **Discuss With a Peer** Discuss with a peer the books and poems you have recently read. Notice the topics you discuss the longest: Those are probably the ones for which you have the most to say. Choose one of those discussion points to form the basis of your response to literature.

ⓘnteractive Textbook

Get instant help! Make your list of characters using the Essay Builder, accessible from the menu bar, on-line or on CD-ROM.

⏱ TIME AND RESOURCE MANAGER

Resources
Print: *Writing Support Transparencies,* 13-A–C; *Writing Support Activity Book,* 13-1–2
Technology: *Writing and Grammar* Interactive Text, Section 13.2

Using the Full Student Edition	Using the Handbook Ⓗ
• Cover pp. 282–285 in class.	• Cover pp. 178–181 in class.
• Allow students to discuss with classmates the books or poems they have recently read.	• Allow students to discuss with classmates the books or poems they have recently read.
• Do the webbing activity in class.	• Do the webbing activity in class.
• Demonstrate the use of hexagonal writing and monitor students as they create hexagons for their topics.	• Demonstrate the use of hexagonal writing and monitor students as they create hexagons for their topics.

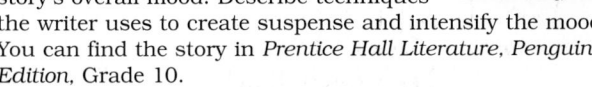

TOPIC BANK

If you are having difficulty choosing a topic for your response to literature, look at these suggestions:

1. **Critical Review** Write a review of the last work you read. Because it's fresh in your mind, this piece will be a good subject for you. Freewrite until you settle on a specific aspect of the work that interests you, such as character, theme, setting, or plot.

2. **Comparison and Contrast** Choose two poems by a favorite poet. Then, compare and contrast the elements the poems have in common—speaker, theme, imagery, or structure, for example.

Responding to Fine Art

3. Study the character and setting of *Children Dancing* by Robert Gwathmey. Then, write a response to the painting in which you explore your reactions to the mood and subject matter of the work.

Responding to Literature

4. Write an analysis of "The Masque of the Red Death" by Edgar Allan Poe. Discuss the central conflict in the story and the story's overall mood. Describe techniques the writer uses to create suspense and intensify the mood. You can find the story in *Prentice Hall Literature, Penguin Edition*, Grade 10.

Children Dancing, Robert Gwathmey, Butler Institute of American Art

Timed Writing Prompt

5. Write an essay in which you introduce your favorite book to your classmates. Clearly identify the book and its author. Then, discuss why the book was so compelling to you. Share the literary features—for example, the theme or the plot—that you found most interesting. Aim to convince your classmates that this is a book worth reading. **(45 minutes)**

Prewriting • 283

☑ ONGOING ASSESSMENT: Monitor and Reinforce

If students are having difficulty developing a topic, try one of the following strategies.

Option 1 Work as a class to generate additional topics. Ask students for titles of works they have enjoyed. Why did they like these? What was memorable about them? Encourage students to add to their topic banks during the discussion.	**Option 2** If possible, question students individually about what they have read. Speaking is a stimulus to thinking, so encourage them to talk about their reading as much as possible.

Step-by-Step Teaching Guide

Responding to Fine Art

Children Dancing, by Robert Gwathmey

Teaching Resources: Writing Support Transparencies, 13-A

1. Display Transparency 13-A and discuss the mood of the work and how it was created.

2. Ask students to write one adjective describing their overall reaction to *Children Dancing*. Then, ask students to brainstorm for a list of adjectives that could describe the scene and choose one as the focus for a descriptive paragraph.

⏱ Timed Writing Prompt

- Ask volunteers to describe their favorite books. Use these examples as the basis for a discussion of why certain literary elements appeal to them.

- Remind students that they should convince readers that the books are worth reading. Their essays should include statements that reflect on the theme, characters, plot, or author's writing style.

- Suggest that students allow five minutes for prewriting, thirty-five minutes for writing, and five minutes for reviewing and proofreading.

Integrating Speaking and Listening Skills

Ask students to choose a favorite book and create a two- to three-minute sales presentation to convince other students to read the book. Encourage the listeners to give the speaker feedback on how convincing he or she was, or whether the sales pitch was effective.

Customize for
Gifted and Talented Students

Ask students to list titles of literary works that the class is likely to have read and to create a matching game by writing statements or phrases that describe a character, setting, or incident from these works. The statements will later be read to a student contestant, who should answer by giving the character's name or the title of the work. Play the game in class to help all students generate additional topics.

Prewriting: Make a Web

Teaching Resources: Writing Support Transparencies, 13-B; Writing Support Activity Book, 13-1

1. Display the transparency (13-B) and discuss how the subtopics are related to the main points in a web.

2. Choose a title from literature that the students have read and, with the class, create a web on the board as another example. Develop a list of topics from the web and challenge students to make an even narrower topic web.

3. Ask students to choose a literary work from their topic banks and create a web. You may wish to pass out copies of the web organizer (13-I). This activity can be done as a homework exercise.

Prewriting: Considering Your Audience and Purpose

1. Ask students to think about possible audiences they might reach (friends, family, readers of a magazine or Web site where they might publish).

2. Ask students what purposes they might have for writing a response to literature essay (sharing, encouraging others to read the book, supporting opinions).

3. Ask students to list their topic, audience, and purpose at the top of a sheet of paper and then make notes about how they can modify their writing to reach their audiences and accomplish their purposes.

Customize for

ESL Students

Allow students to choose a literary work they have read in their home language and create a web for it. The web can then be translated into English with the help of a dictionary and a student volunteer who is proficient in English.

Narrowing Your Topic

Before you write your response to literature, narrow your topic so that you will be able to develop your ideas fully within the space limitations. Making a web is an effective way to narrow a response to literature.

Make a Web

Make a web like the one below, changing heads and categories as you see fit. Then, review your web, and choose as your narrowed topic one of the subtopics you wrote down.

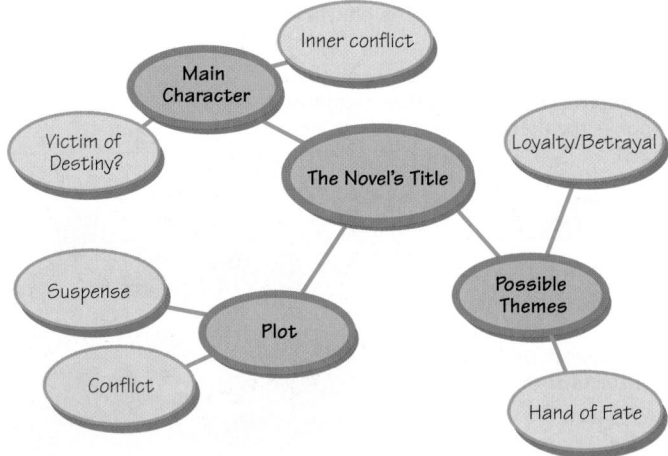

Considering Your Audience and Purpose

Responses to literature may be read by audiences of any age and may vary widely in their purpose. Choose details that will appeal to your audience and that will help you achieve your purpose.

Type of Response	Language and Details
Journal	Informal language: details that vary
Critical Review	Formal language: details that illustrate the work's strengths and weaknesses; excerpts from the work
Literary Analysis	Very formal language: details that prove your ideas about the work; excerpts from the work; excerpts from, or allusions to, other literary works

⏱ Timed Writing Hint

When writing under timed conditions, make a quick web to plan your essay.

Gathering Details

Once you have a narrowed topic, gather details to support your purpose and main idea and give depth to your writing.

Use Hexagonal Writing to Gather Details

One way to ensure that you have considered all the various aspects of a literary work is to use the technique of hexagonal writing. A hexagon is a six-sided geometrical figure. With hexagonal writing, you explore six aspects (one per side) of a work of literature.

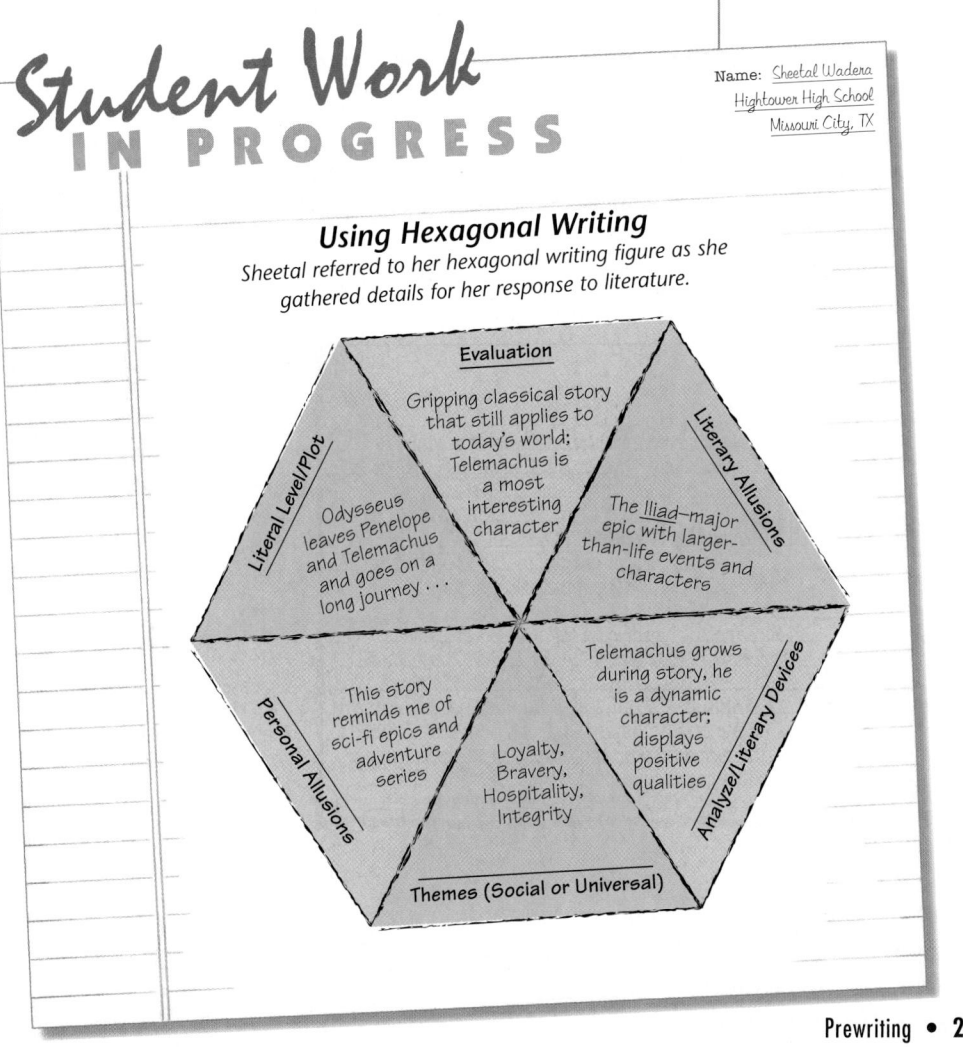

Student Work
IN PROGRESS

Name: *Sheetal Wadera*
Hightower High School
Missouri City, TX

Using Hexagonal Writing

Sheetal referred to her hexagonal writing figure as she gathered details for her response to literature.

Evaluation
Gripping classical story that still applies to today's world; Telemachus is a most interesting character

Literary Allusions
The Iliad–major epic with larger-than-life events and characters

Literal Level/Plot
Odysseus leaves Penelope and Telemachus and goes on a long journey . . .

Analyze/Literary Devices
Telemachus grows during story, he is a dynamic character; displays positive qualities

Personal Allusions
This story reminds me of sci-fi epics and adventure series

Themes (Social or Universal)
Loyalty, Bravery, Hospitality, Integrity

Prewriting • 285

Step-by-Step Teaching Guide

Prewriting: Use Hexagonal Writing to Gather Details

Teaching Resources: Writing Support Transparencies, 13-C; Writing Support Activity Book, 13-2

1. With students, examine the hexagonal writing chart. Display Transparency 13-D during the discussion and explain to students that the hexagonal writing strategy helps Sheetal explore her topic from many angles.

2. Define *allusion* and ask students to share some examples of personal allusions for books they have read. (Example: This story reminded me of the time I . . .)

3. Explain that writers frequently make literary allusions to Greek or Roman mythology, the Bible, and Shakespeare's plays. (Example: The title of Stephen Vincent Benet's story "By the Waters of Babylon" is an allusion to Psalm 137 in the Bible.) Explain that recognizing allusions makes it easier to understand and appreciate literature.

4. Discuss the Evaluation component of the hexagon and tell students to avoid making empty generalizations, such as, "It was a wonderful book." Encourage them to make an evaluation that can be supported with details.

5. Allow class time for students to create a hexagon chart for their topics and discuss their charts with each other.

⏱ **TIME SAVERS!**

Writing Support Transparencies
Use the transparencies for Chapter 13 to facilitate the teaching of strategies.

Writing Support Activity Book
Use the graphic organizers for Chapter 13 to facilitate student planning.

Drafting: Draft a Thesis Statement

Teaching Resources: Writing Support Transparencies, 13-D

1. Ask students to consider why organization in writing is important and list their responses on the board.

2. Display Transparency 13-D to show students how the supporting details elaborate upon the thesis statement.

3. Ask students to write their thesis statements at the top of a sheet of paper and list the major supporting details. Use Transparency 13-D as a model.

4. Have students use an organizational method such as a topic or sentence outline to organize their response.

Connections With Literature

Ask a student who has read *The Tragedy of Julius Caesar* to briefly summarize the plot for the class. You could also provide a summary on the board if a student summation is not available.

Customize for
More Advanced Students

Challenge students to explore Shakespearean comedy by researching some of the comedic devices Shakespeare used. Ask students to read *As You Like It* or *A Midsummer Night's Dream*. Have them see the appropriate film version and write a response comparing and contrasting the play and the film.

13.3 Drafting

Shaping Your Writing

Take the details you have collected during prewriting, and organize them logically as you draft your response to literature. One way to do this is to develop a thesis statement and support it with details you've gathered.

Draft a Thesis Statement

The **thesis statement** is the main message of your essay, which you will support with various kinds of details. To come up with a thesis statement, review your notes, and answer the following:

> **Out of all that I have learned, the most important point I would like to make about [the work of literature] is ___?___ .**

Then, use the following tips to draft your thesis statement:

- Write your thesis statement at the top of a sheet of paper.

- Refer to your prewriting notes, and list all the major details that help support your thesis statement.

- When the list is complete, decide on an organizational method that will present those details most effectively.

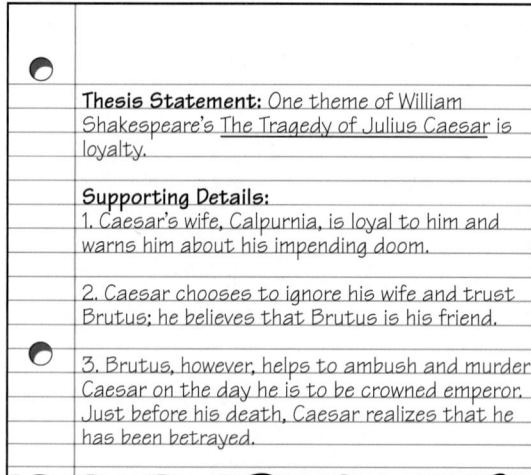

Thesis Statement: One theme of William Shakespeare's The Tragedy of Julius Caesar is loyalty.

Supporting Details:
1. Caesar's wife, Calpurnia, is loyal to him and warns him about his impending doom.

2. Caesar chooses to ignore his wife and trust Brutus; he believes that Brutus is his friend.

3. Brutus, however, helps to ambush and murder Caesar on the day he is to be crowned emperor. Just before his death, Caesar realizes that he has been betrayed.

The Tragedy of Julius Caesar appears in Prentice Hall Literature, Penguin Edition, Grade 10.

286 • Response to Literature

⏱ TIME AND RESOURCE MANAGER	
Resources	
Print: *Writing Support Transparencies,* 13-D–E	
Technology: *Writing and Grammar* Interactive Text, Section 13.3	
Using the Full Student Edition	**Using the Handbook🄷**
• Cover pp. 286–287 in class.	• Cover pp. 182–183 in class.
• Show several examples of well-written thesis statements.	• Show several examples of well-written thesis statements.
• Supervise as students write thesis statements and list supporting details.	• Supervise as students write thesis statements and list supporting details.
• Show examples of paragraphs in which cited passages are used.	• Show examples of paragraphs in which cited passages are used.

Providing Elaboration
Cite Passages From the Work

As you draft your response to literature, cite words, lines, or passages from the work to which you are responding. Doing so will help you make your points, as well as give your readers specific examples. Enclose cited passages within quotation marks, and indicate where the passage is in the literature. If you are citing a large passage of the work, indent your left and right margins, and type the excerpt in a separate paragraph. Quotation marks are not necessary when excerpts are set off this way.

Student Work IN PROGRESS

Name: *Sheetal Wadera*
Hightower High School
Missouri City, TX

Citing Passages From Literature
Sheetal supported her main points by citing specific passages from the Odyssey.

In ancient Greek culture, women had few legal rights, and if their husbands passed away or went to war and never returned, they were expected to remarry. Because of this, Telemachus' house was constantly overrun with suitors who wished to court his mother. Although Telemachus wanted to get rid of the suitors, he did not possess the power to do so. "For he, too, was sitting there, unhappy among the suitors, a boy, daydreaming" (19–21).

In the course of the story, Telemachus makes many moral decisions that help the readers see that he truly knows the difference between right and wrong. A prime example of this is at the beginning of the epic, when Athena is talking to Telemachus about the obnoxious suitors, and she tells him, "You need not bear this insolence of theirs; you are a child no longer" (76–77).

Sheetal used quotations from the Odyssey to make her ideas clear for readers.

Drafting • 287

Drafting: Cite Passages From the Work

Teaching Resources: Writing Support Transparencies, 13-E

1. Display Transparency 13-E and point out the quotations Sheetal included in the two paragraphs.
2. Explain that quotations can be a writer's strongest supporting points for a thesis. They supply the reader with evidence showing how the essay writer reached his or her conclusions.
3. Ask students to suggest other sources that might be quoted when writing about a piece of literature (book reviews, scholarly essays about the work).
4. Point out that although both quotations in the example are single sentences, shorter and longer passages can be quoted, too.
5. Encourage students to select quotations carefully, so that they truly support the topics with which they appear.

Integrating Grammar Skills

Quotations Review with students the important elements of formatting quotations. Key elements include, of course, punctuation (how to use quotation marks, when to use single versus double quotes, when end marks go inside quotes), indenting longer quotations, using ellipses when words are omitted, and using brackets around words that are added or changed to clarify meaning.

Revising: Underlining Details

Teaching Resources: Writing Support Transparencies, 13-F

1. Display Transparency 13-F and discuss how Sheetal underlined important details. Point out to students that underlining details in introductions and conclusions allows writers to see whether their introductory ideas are addressed in the conclusion.

2. Tell students to underline or highlight the sentences in their drafts that contain supporting details or examples for their main points. Ask students to read their drafts silently and then reread the introductions and conclusions.

3. Allow time for students to underline the thesis statements in their introductions and the sentences in the conclusions that restate the main idea. Have them revise if the two do not match.

4. Ask student partners to read at least one paragraph to each other and exchange feedback on the structure of the paragraph and the adequacy of supporting details.

Integrating Vocabulary Skills

Synonyms Ask students to circle words in their drafts that are used frequently. Encourage them to consult a dictionary and, if necessary, a thesaurus to make sure they are precise and varied in their word choice.

Revising Your Overall Structure

Make Your Introduction and Conclusion Match

Review the overall structure of your response to literature to be sure that it is clear and effective. An effective essay usually contains an introduction, a body, and a conclusion. In your introduction, be sure you have presented the main message of your response. Your conclusion should restate that main idea and reveal additional insights you may have about your topic.

▶ **REVISION STRATEGY**
Underlining Details

Read through your introduction, and underline important points you make there, as well as questions you raise. Then, read your conclusion, and underline its important details. Review your introduction and conclusion to be sure that they match. If they do not, make necessary revisions.

Name: *Sheetal Wadera*
Hightower High School
Missouri City, TX

Underlining Details

Sheetal underlined important details in her introduction and conclusion to make sure that her response ended where she began. She decided to add a sentence to her introduction to make her overall intent more clear.

> **Introduction**
> The *Odyssey* mainly <u>focuses upon</u> the <u>character of Odysseus</u>, telling of his wartime adventures as an epic hero. Odysseus' son, <u>Telemachus, the secondary hero, also plays a vital role</u> in the *Odyssey*; the reader sees him grow from a young boy to a fully grown man, and this maturity comes from the fact that Telemachus has had to learn to fend for himself during his father's absence. ∧
>
> *In fact, tracing the growth of Telemachus during the Odyssey shows what qualities the ancient Greeks considered noble and admirable in a man.*

> **Conclusion**
> All in all, <u>Telemachus is a very interesting character.</u> Not only do we see him as a young child, <u>but as time progresses,</u> as an intelligent young man. He plays a vital role in the *Odyssey*. His heroic actions, gestures, and thoughts make him a hero of great renown.

288 • Response to Literature

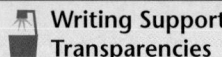 **Writing Support Transparencies**
Use the transparencies for Chapter 13 to facilitate the teaching of strategies.

⏱ TIME AND RESOURCE MANAGER

Resources
Print: *Writing Support Transparencies*, 13-F–G
Technology: *Writing and Grammar* Interactive Text, Section 13.4

Using the Full Student Edition	Using the Handbook🄷
• Cover pp. 288–292 in class.	• Cover pp. 184–188 in class.
• Work through the revising strategies with students.	• Work through the revising strategies with students.
• Have students revise their drafts in class.	• Have students revise their drafts in class.
• Allow time for peer reviews.	• Allow time for peer reviews.

Revising Your Paragraphs

Polish Your Paragraphs

To be effective, a topical paragraph should have a single main idea that is supported by various types of information. An effective functional paragraph should perform a specific function, such as indicating a transition or emphasizing a point.

▶ **REVISION STRATEGY**

Using a Checklist to Revise Paragraphs

Use these questions to help you analyze and revise the topical paragraphs in your response to literature. Complete the checklist, and revise your paragraphs accordingly.

1. Does the topic sentence clearly express the main idea of the paragraph?
2. Does the paragraph contain various types of support in the form of examples, quotations, and reasons?
3. Is any of the supporting information weak, repetitive, or inappropriate?
4. Does the supporting information pertain to the main idea of the paragraph?
5. Is the supporting information presented logically? Could the supporting information be organized more effectively?
6. Do transitions connect the ideas within your paragraph?

EXAMPLE

~~In this story,~~ the narrator ^of "Axolotl"^ reflects on his fascination with axolotls, which he defines as "the larval stage" (provided with gills) of a species of salamander. By the end of the first paragraph, ^the narrator^ ~~he~~ has summarized the whole plot: He saw some axolotls in an aquarium, he watched them ~~a lot~~, and thought a lot about them, and now he has become one. The plot sounds almost like a joke, like one of those cartoons in which a person and his or her pet start to look more and more alike. ~~I think Cortazar is making a point about how people become what they are.~~

> This correction makes the main idea of the paragraph more clear.

> This phrase was deleted to avoid unnecessary repetition.

> This sentence belongs in another paragraph, because it deals with the story's theme, not with its plot.

🔄 Learn More

To learn more about effective paragraphs, see Chapter 3.

Revising • 289

Step-by-Step Teaching Guide

Revising: Using a Checklist to Revise Paragraphs

1. You may first want to review the three types of paragraphs (topical, functional, and block; see Chapter 3 for more details).

2. Point out that the checklist strategy given here is for topical paragraphs.

3. Read the checklist in the student text out loud, or ask a volunteer to read it, adding any comments or insights you have after each point.

4. Ask students to examine the revised paragraph in the text. Have them identify revisions that relate to any of the items on the checklist.

5. Discuss how the revisions improved the paragraph. Ask whether students have any questions about why some of the changes were made.

6. Encourage students to go over their own drafts using the checklist.

Customize for
Less Advanced Students

Students may have difficulty recognizing elements that need revision. Allow students to work with partners, discussing their drafts paragraph by paragraph. Encourage partners to ask questions about things that are not clear, or to point out elements that might benefit from revision. This should give students additional insight into how to revise their work.

Customize for
ESL Students

Revision may be difficult for some students, since writing problems may be related to language skills rather than to any difficulty with the writing process. Give them additional attention during the revision stage, or pair them with a more fluent English speaker. Additionally, encourage them to use this as an opportunity to increase vocabulary and to use a dictionary and thesaurus to increase variety in word choice.

Revising: Color-Coding Elements

Teaching Resources: Writing Support Transparencies, 13-G

1. Display the transparency (13-G) and point out how Sheetal color-coded subjects to make sure they were clear.

2. Point out that the two changes that were made clarify who is speaking or being spoken to. Explain that "the young prince" would be an excellent substitution for "Telemachus" in a paragraph where only Telemachus is discussed, but here, there are several people being discussed, so the reference is unclear.

3. Distribute colored highlighters and ask students to highlight sentence subjects, focusing on characters. Suggest that students also highlight all pronouns, whether they are the subject or not, and decide whether the antecedents are clear. (You may want to review "Grammar in Your Writing" on p. 291 before having students do this.)

4. Ask for volunteers to share their reactions to this strategy and give examples of how it was helpful.

5. Have students discuss how pronouns that do not have clear antecedents can create confusion.

6. Have students check their drafts for clarity and revise as needed.

13.4

Revising Your Sentences
Revise for Clarity

One of the problems that can occur when writing about literature is confusion about who or what is being discussed. This is especially true when you are discussing several characters, works, themes, or writers. Read through your draft, and make sure that each sentence has a clear subject.

▶ **REVISION STRATEGY**
Color-Coding Elements

Use a colored pen or highlighter to call out each character reference in your draft. Use a different color for each character. Then, locate personal pronouns that stand in for character names, and circle or highlight each using its appropriate color. If you experience confusion figuring out which color to use, the pronoun's antecedent is probably unclear. In that case, replace the pronoun with the proper noun.

Student Work
IN PROGRESS

Name: *Sheetal Wadera*
Hightower High School
Missouri City, TX

Color-Coding Characters to Check for Clarity
Sheetal used color-coding to make sure that each character reference was clear and that when she used personal pronouns, they had clear antecedents.

Unaware of his visitor's identity, Nestor invites Telemachus to join the feast of Poseidon, the blue-maned god. After the feast, Nestor he calls Telemachus and asks him who he is. The young prince Nestor tells him that he is Odysseus' lost soldier and asks him if he knows anything about his lost father. "Nestor is full of praise for the lost soldier, and he quickly recognizes the heroic qualities of the son" (188–190). Nestor also praises Telemachus himself saying, "Your manner of speech couldn't be more like his; one would say No; no boy could speak so well" (191–192).

Grammar in Your Writing
Pronouns and Antecedents

In your response to literature, you may have used many **pronouns** to refer to characters or elements within the work. A pronoun is used in place of a noun. The noun the pronoun replaces is its **antecedent.**

Nouns and Pronouns

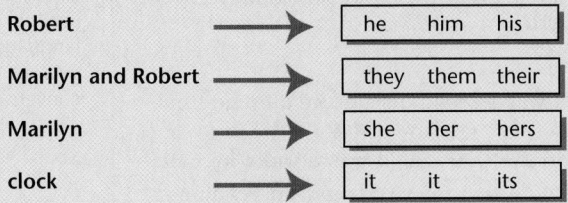

Robert	→	he	him	his
Marilyn and Robert	→	they	them	their
Marilyn	→	she	her	hers
clock	→	it	it	its

Fixing Unclear Pronouns

Because pronouns can be used in place of nouns, you can use them to help you avoid repeating a character or person's name over and over. However, when several characters are being discussed, it may be ambiguous or unclear to whom the pronoun refers. Ambiguous pronoun references can be fixed in two ways.

In the following example, the antecedent of *he* is unclear because two masculine nouns precede the masculine pronoun. The problem is eliminated by repeating Steve's name.

Unclear: Joe and Steve discussed the novel. They both enjoyed the characters and plot, but he didn't like the setting.

Clear: Joe and Steve discussed the novel. They both enjoyed the characters and plot, but Steve didn't like the setting.

In the next example, the antecedent is unclear because readers don't know whether Joe or Mike returned from vacation. The error is corrected by revising the sentence so that it is clear that Joe returned from vacation.

Unclear: Joe told Steve to read the book after he returned from vacation.

Clear: After Joe returned from vacation, he told Steve to read the book.

Find It in Your Reading Review the excerpt from the "Introduction to *The Hunchback of Notre-Dame*" on pages 278–281 of this chapter. Find three examples of pronouns, and identify their antecedents.

Find It in Your Writing Identify three examples of pronouns that refer to characters in your response to literature. If you cannot find three examples, challenge yourself to add some. Use pronouns to avoid repetition of the characters' names.

For more on pronouns and antecedents, see Chapters 16 and 23.

Revising • 291

Step-by-Step Teaching Guide

Revising: Use Formal Language

1. Discuss the difference between formal and informal language. Ask students to suggest examples of both.

2. Ask students to discuss when each type of language is acceptable. (Formal language is preferred for formal responses such as essays and in almost all business communications; informal language is acceptable with friends or in some creative writing, especially in dialogue that establishes the personality of the character.)

3. Discuss with students some of the problems that slang or idioms can create in writing. (Some people will be unfamiliar with the terms and won't understand what is being said. Slang goes out of fashion quickly. A work that includes slang doesn't seem serious, and readers may discount what is said.)

Step-by-Step Teaching Guide

Revising: Peer Review

1. Pick one of the two strategies listed for peer review, and allow time for students to carry out the strategy.

2. Encourage students always to identify a paper's strengths before commenting on weaknesses.

3. Ask students to make practical and specific suggestions for improvement.

4. Remind each writer to consider peer suggestions objectively before making changes. Sometimes a suggestion is a step toward finding a solution, but not the best fix. Remind students that the writer is the person responsible for making choices and decisions about his or her own work.

Critical Viewing

Generalize Students might mention errors in spelling, syntax, and punctuation. They might also note repetitive words or rhythms.

Revising Your Word Choice

Review your draft to be sure that you've used words correctly. Also, check your word choice, making sure that any informal words were used intentionally.

Use Formal Language

In fiction writing and journal writing, you may use informal language—language that contains conversational expressions such as slang and idioms. In an academic report, however, you should use formal English.

EXAMPLES:

SLANG: There is no way I would discourage a friend from reading the *Odyssey*. It was **way cool.**

IDIOM: When I read the *Odyssey*, it was **a wake-up call.**

FORMAL: I would never discourage a friend from reading the *Odyssey*. It was excellent.

▶ **REVISION STRATEGY**
Reading and Replacing

Read through your draft, paying particular attention to the types of words you have chosen to convey your ideas. Rewrite contractions as full words, and replace slang and idioms with more formal word choices. Also, delete instances of informal phrases such as *like, you know,* and *kind of.*

Peer Review

Work with a peer to review the level of formality of the language in your response to literature. Following are two strategies for working with peers:

- Exchange papers with a partner, and review each other's language to make sure that the level is appropriate for an academic report. Make a list of informal expressions and contractions. Help replace these with formal language.

- Read your paper aloud to a small group, and ask them to stop you whenever they hear informal English. Discuss the language and possible revisions to use formal English.

🕐 Timed Writing Hint

When writing for an exam, it is wise to use formal, academic language unless a prompt asks for a conversational style.

▼ **Critical Viewing**
What sorts of mistakes are you likely to catch when reading a draft aloud? **[Generalize]**

✏️ STANDARDIZED TEST PREPARATION WORKSHOP

Standardized test questions may require students to identify the correct use of the pronouns *who* and *whom.* Provide students with opportunities to practice using these pronouns correctly.

Which pronoun best completes this sentence?

This is my new friend Nancy ___ I met on vacation this summer.

A who	**C** whose
B whom	**D** who's

Students should recognize that **B** is the correct answer because it is the object of the verb *met* in the subordinate clause.

13.5 Editing and Proofreading

Proofread your response to literature carefully, looking for any errors in grammar, spelling, and punctuation.

Focusing on Mechanics

In a response to literature, you will probably refer to the authors and titles of the works you are discussing. Make sure that you spell, capitalize, and style these names and titles correctly.

Grammar in Your Writing
Styling Titles of Poems, Stories, and Novels

Use the following rules for styling titles of literary works:

- Always capitalize the first and last words in the title, including articles and prepositions. Do not capitalize articles or prepositions with fewer than four letters, unless they are the first or last word of the title.
  Of Mice and Men   John Steinbeck
  "Through the Tunnel"   Doris Lessing

- The titles of short works—such as poems, songs, and short stories—are enclosed in quotation marks.
  "The Dog That Bit People"   James Thurber
  "After Apple-Picking"   Robert Frost

- The titles of long works—such as novels, plays, and epic poetry—are set in italics or underlined. Newspaper, magazine, movie, painting, and sculpture titles are also treated this way.
  the *Iliad*   Homer
  The New York Times
  Mona Lisa   Leonardo da Vinci

Find It in Your Reading Find a book title in the excerpt from Paul Montazzoli's "Introduction to *The Hunchback of Notre-Dame*" on pages 278–281. Tell why the title is styled as it is.

Find It in Your Writing As you proofread your response to literature, check to be sure that you have written and styled all titles correctly.

For more on styling titles, see Chapter 28.

⏱ TIME AND RESOURCE MANAGER

Resources
Print: *Scoring Rubrics on Transparency,* Ch. 13; *Writing Assessment and Portfolio Management; Formal Assessment,* Ch. 13
Technology: *Writing and Grammar* Interactive Text, Section 13.5

Using the Full Student Edition	Using the Handbook🄷
• Cover pp. 293–294 in class. • Discuss the difference between revising and editing. • Analyze the Final Draft (pp. 295–297) in class. • Have students edit and proofread their essays in class.	• Cover pp. 189–190 in class. • Discuss the difference between revising and editing. • Analyze the Final Draft (pp. 191–193) in class. • Have students edit and proofread their essays in class.

Step-by-Step Teaching Guide

Editing and Proofreading

1. Encourage students to proofread their drafts several times, concentrating on spelling in one reading, punctuation in another, and so on.

2. Review Grammar in Your Writing (see below) for a specific focus on styling titles.

Step-by-Step Teaching Guide

Styling Titles of Poems, Stories, and Novels

1. After reviewing the three rules in this lesson, write the following titles on the board and have students style them.

   The Daily News

   To Kill a Mockingbird

   The Tragedy of Julius Caesar

   The Tell-Tale Heart

   The Bean Eaters

   (The first three titles—a newspaper, a novel, and a play—should be underlined or set in italics. The last two—a short story and a poem—should be enclosed in quotation marks.)

2. Remind students that commas and periods are always placed inside the closing quotation mark, and colons and semicolons are always placed outside the quotation marks.

Finding It in Your Reading

The title *"The Hunchback of Notre-Dame"* appears in the first two sentences on page 278. It is in italics because it is the title of a novel.

Finding It in Your Writing

Ask students to look through their portfolios or journals to see whether they have styled titles correctly. Have them make corrections if necessary.

1. Discuss with students options for publishing that are available at your school, such as those listed in the text.

2. Encourage students who have previously published their work in any of the suggested ways to share their experiences with the class.

ASSESS and CLOSE

Assessment

Teaching Resources: Scoring Rubrics on Transparency, Ch. 13; Writing Assessment and Portfolio Management; Formal Assessment, Ch. 13

1. Display the Scoring Rubric transparency and review the criteria in class.

2. Before students proceed with self-assessment, you may wish to review the Final Draft of the Student Work in Progress on pages 295–297. Have students score the Final Draft in one or more of the rubric categories.

3. In addition to student self-assessment, you may wish to use the following assessment options:

   • score student essays yourself, using the rubric and scoring models from *Writing Assessment and Portfolio Management.*

   • review the Standardized Test Preparation Workshop on pages 302–303 and administer a timed writing assignment.

   • administer the Chapter 13 assessment from *Formal Assessment* in the Teaching Resources to measure students' grasp of the concepts presented.

13.6 Publishing and Presenting

Once you have completed your response to literature, share it with others.

Building Your Portfolio

1. **Student Newspaper or Web Site** You could publish in a student paper or on a student Web site a review of a work of literature that has deeply affected you. First, check with the editor for submission requirements and deadlines.

2. **Book Club** Share your critique of a work of literature with a small group that meets regularly to discuss books they are reading. Prepare organized notes to which you can refer as you speak.

Reflecting on Your Writing

Pause to think about what you experienced as you wrote your response to literature. Then, answer the following questions, and put a copy of your responses in your portfolio.

• In the process of writing, what did you learn about how you value literature?

• Which strategy for prewriting, drafting, revising, or editing would you recommend to a friend?

Internet Tip

To see model essays scored with this rubric, go on-line: PHSchool.com
Enter Web Code: eek-1001

Rubric for Self-Assessment

Use these criteria as you evaluate your response to literature:

	Score 4	Score 3	Score 2	Score 1
Audience and Purpose	Presents sufficient background on the work(s); completely achieves purpose	Presents background on the work(s); achieves purpose	Presents some background on the work(s); partially achieves purpose	Presents little or no background on the work(s); does not achieve a purpose
Organization	Presents points in logical order, smoothly connecting them to the overall focus	Presents points in logical order and connects them to the overall focus	Organizes points poorly in places; connects some points to an overall focus	Presents information in a scattered, disorganized manner
Elaboration	Supports reactions and evaluations with elaborated reasons and well-chosen examples	Supports reactions and evaluations with specific reasons and examples	Supports some reactions and evaluations with reasons and examples	Offers little support for reactions and evaluations
Use of Language	Shows overall clarity and fluency; language is appropriate; makes few mechanical errors	Shows good sentence variety; language is mostly appropriate; makes some mechanical errors	Uses awkward or overly simple sentence structures and vague evaluative terms; makes many mechanical errors	Presents incomplete thoughts; makes mechanical errors that cause confusion

294 • Response to Literature

☑ ONGOING ASSESSMENT: Assess Mastery

Use one or both of the following options to assess final drafts of students' essays.

Self-Assessment Ask students to score their essays using the rubric provided. Have students write a paragraph in which they reflect on the most valuable thing that they learned in completing this paper.	**Teacher Assessment** You may use the rubric and scoring models provided in *Writing Assessment and Portfolio Management* in the Teaching Resources to score students' work.

13.7 Student Work IN PROGRESS

FINAL DRAFT

Penelope at the loom and Telemachus, Museo Nazionale, Chiusi, Italy

Telemachus in Homer's Odyssey

Sheetal Wadera
Hightower High School
Missouri City, Texas

The *Odyssey* focuses mainly on the character of Odysseus, telling of his wartime travels and adventures as an epic hero. Odysseus' son, Telemachus, the secondary hero, also plays a vital role in the *Odyssey*; the reader sees him grow from a young boy to a fully grown man, and this maturity comes from the fact that Telemachus has had to learn to fend for himself during his father's absence. In fact, tracing the growth of Telemachus during the *Odyssey* shows what qualities the ancient Greeks considered noble and admirable in a man.

◀ **Critical Viewing**
This urn displays an image of characters from Homer's *Odyssey.* Why might artists have chosen to decorate items such as urns with scenes from literature? **[Speculate]**

Sheetal reveals her thesis—the essay's main idea—in the final sentence of her introduction.

Final Draft

1. Point out to students that the Final Draft incorporates key elements of a response to literature.
   - The thesis is succinctly stated in the introduction.
   - Audience and purpose have been carefully considered.
   - The body paragraphs provide support for the thesis statement.
   - Sheetal uses quotations to provide elaboration on her main points.
   - Her conclusion repeats the main idea expressed in the thesis.

2. Ask students to identify the thesis statement. *"In fact, tracing the growth of Telemachus during the* Odyssey *shows what qualities the ancient Greeks considered noble and admirable in a man."*

3. Ask a volunteer to read the conclusion aloud. Which sentence repeats the main idea expressed in the thesis? *(Telemachus . . . embodies many qualities prized in Greek culture.)*

4. Ask students whether there are any changes they would recommend for this essay. How might they apply these suggestions to their own writing?

Critical Viewing

Speculate Students may say that these scenes would be understood by people who couldn't read; these stories were an important part of the culture, and people wanted to remember them; it honored their heroes, as we do today with stamps, magazines, and movies.

More About the Writer

Homer was evidently a blind bard, a singer who usually made up verses as he sang, and although he is a major figure in ancient Greek literature, little is known about his life. His name was attached to the epic poems the *Iliad* and the *Odyssey* by the Greeks themselves. The *Iliad* tells how the Greeks besieged and took the city of Troy in Asia Minor, and the *Odyssey* recounts the adventures of the hero Odysseus as he returns to his homeland after the siege of Troy.

Integrating Grammar Skills

Ask students to find examples of compound sentences in Sheetal Wadera's essay and note the punctuation. Ask them to also find examples of sentences with compound verbs. Discuss the difference between a compound sentence and a simple sentence with a compound verb. Ask volunteers to create sentences illustrating both and put them on the board.

Critical Viewing

Analyze The beard, robes, and general appearance of the character on the right (probably Odysseus) seem to be those of someone considerably older than the whiskerless, and perhaps shorter, figure on the left (probably Telemachus).

Telemachus' father, Odysseus, left home to go to war, leaving his very young son, Telemachus, and his beautiful wife, Penelope, behind. Since that fateful day, twenty years have passed, and young Telemachus has had to grow up and become sole protector of his mother and himself.

In ancient Greek culture, women had few legal rights, and if their husbands passed away or went to war and never returned, they were expected to remarry. Because of this custom, Telemachus' house was constantly overrun with suitors who wished to court his mother. Although Telemachus wanted to get rid of the suitors, he did not possess the power to do so. "For he, too, was sitting there, unhappy among the suitors, a boy, daydreaming" (19–21).

Telemachus takes his first steps toward becoming a man—and developing positive character traits—when he first visits his father's old friend Nestor, king of Pylos and a hero of the Trojan War, to tell him of the suitors' rude comments. Unaware of his visitor's identity, Nestor invites Telemachus to join the feast of Poseidon, the blue-maned god. After the feast, Nestor calls Telemachus over and asks him who he is. Telemachus tells him that he is Odysseus' lost soldier and asks Nestor if he knows anything about his lost father. "Nestor is full of praise for the lost soldier, and he quickly recognizes the heroic qualities of the son" (188–190). Nestor also

In this paragraph, Sheetal gives background information about Telemachus and his mother, Penelope.

Because this is an important event in the development of the character of Telemachus, Sheetal explains in detail what happened.

Ulysses and his son Telemachus, Kunsthistorisches Museum, Antikensammlung, Vienna, Austria

◀ **Critical Viewing** Using details in this mosaic, decide which character is Odysseus (Ulysses) and which is Telemachus, his son. **[Analyze]**

296 • Response to Literature

praises Telemachus outright, saying, "Your manner of speech couldn't be more like his; one would say No; no boy could speak so well" (191–192). Nestor then tells Telemachus to visit Menelaus for further news.

Obedient and determined to learn more, Telemachus arrives at Menelaus' palace, which catches the eye with shining gems and precious metals such as gold, bronze, amber, silver, and ivory. The vision is more dazzling than anything Telemachus has seen before, and he immediately senses the power and wealth that Menelaus must have. Menelaus begins to tell his young visitor old war stories, and Telemachus finds Odysseus' name mentioned many times. Although this pleases Telemachus and reminds him of his father, the tribute brings tears to his eyes. At this instant, Menelaus and Helen (the lady whose elopement with the prince of Troy started the Trojan War) recognize their guest. "Never anywhere have I seen so great a likeness in man or woman, but it is truly strange! This boy must be the son of Odysseus, Telemachus . . ." (236–240)

Telemachus also displays hospitality on several occasions. The first time we see this is when Athena appears to have been waiting. "Straight to the door he came, irked with himself, to think a visitor had been kept there waiting" (26–27). In Greek culture, it was not unusual to invite visitors to feast without knowing anything about them. In fact, it was, on many occasions, expected. Much later in the story, Telemachus is visited by a stranger. Not realizing that the beggar is his father in disguise, Telemachus says, "Friend, sit down; we'll find another chair in our own hut" (1414–1415). In Greek epic poems, one can always spare a moment to help someone or feed someone.

Perhaps the most important quality displayed by the maturing Telemachus, however, is his sense of loyalty—to the memory of his father and to his mother. For example, he doesn't force his mother to choose among the raucous suitors; he respects her desires and wishes. To his father, too, Telemachus displays touching faith and loyalty. Although he was an infant when Odysseus left, his son is proud of his father and eager to preserve his reputation.

Telemachus, as portrayed by Homer, embodies many qualities prized in Greek culture. As he grows, he shows initiative and develops a keen sense of kindness and loyalty. His heroic actions, gestures, and thoughts make him a hero in his own right—one who reflects many qualities considered ideal by ancient Greek culture, and indeed, by cultures far and wide.

This paragraph helps support Sheetal's thesis. It reveals further qualities of Telemachus' character.

Throughout this response to literature, Sheetal has used formal language appropriate for her audience and purpose.

In this paragraph, Sheetal cites examples from the text of the Odyssey to support her main point— that Telemachus displays hospitality throughout the Odyssey.

In her conclusion, Sheetal restates her thesis and adds a further observation about connections among cultures.

Discuss with students the meaning of the following words as they are used in the essay: *fend, sole, fateful, raucous.* Ask students to write each word in a sentence. Remind them to include context clues for each of the words.

The following names are mentioned in Sheetal Wadera's response to literature. Have students look up these character names and provide pronunciation respellings and brief descriptions of each. (Answers given.)

Odysseus (ō dis´ ē əs): the master strategist who devised a way to conquer Troy by tricking the Trojans with a giant wooden horse.

Telemachus (tə lem´ ə kes): son of Odysseus.

Penelope (pə nel´ ə pē): wife of Odysseus.

Menelaus (men ə lā´ əs): King of Sparta. His wife, Helen, was kidnapped by Paris, a prince of Troy, sparking the Trojan War.

Helen: wife of Menelaus. Considered the most beautiful woman in the world, hers was "the face that launched a thousand ships."

Poseidon (pə sīd´ 'n): the god of the sea, earthquakes, and horses. He was the father of the one-eyed monster, the Cyclops, who fights Odysseus.

Athena (ə thē´ na): the goddess of war and wisdom. She supported the Greeks and championed Odysseus.

Aphrodite (a´ frə dī´ tē): the goddess of love. She supported Paris and the Trojans.

Lesson Objectives

1. To write a movie review
2. To organize ideas in writing to ensure coherence, logical progression, and purpose
3. To recognize how visual and sound techniques or design convey messages in media, such as special effects and cinematography

Step-by-Step Teaching Guide

Movie Review

Teaching Resources: Writing Support Transparencies, 13-H; Writing Support Activity Book, 13-3

1. Bring to class reviews of current movies from a variety of sources. If possible, collect several reviews of the same movie by different reviewers. Have volunteers read these reviews aloud and note differences and similarities in opinions and how they are supported.

2. Point out that, while movie reviews include some facts, such as who directed the film and what effects were most current, most of a movie review is opinion. Emphasize that it is, however, well-supported opinion. Reviewers include supporting details about pacing, performances, plot, and the likely overall effect of the movie on viewers.

3. Remind students that it is possible to dislike a movie that is very well made and to like one that might show room for improvement. Emphasize to students the importance of choosing a film about which they can write with enthusiasm, even if they are enthusiastically critical.

continued

Critical Viewing

Evaluate Answers will vary, but may include elements that are dated (not splashy, no "teaser" lines) and those that seem contemporary ("nothing cut but the price").

Connected Assignment
Movie Review

Just like the more formal responses to literature that you write for school, a movie review discusses strengths and weaknesses of a work. Movie critics usually begin a review by briefly summarizing the plot of the movie that is being discussed. Then, they analyze creative elements in the film and cite specific scenes or features to support their reactions. Usually, a movie review contains an opinion or recommendation for readers to view or avoid the film.

An effective movie review should do the following:

- clearly state the criteria on which the movie is being evaluated

- state a main idea and develop it, citing details from the movie

- include details that explain or illustrate ideas

- have a clear and logical organization

- make a recommendation about the movie's effectiveness and importance

Write your own movie review about a film you've seen recently. Follow the writing process suggestions as you draft.

Prewriting

Choosing Your Topic To come up with a topic for your movie review, think about the films you've seen in recent months. As an alternative, ask the local video store to print out your rental record or scan a movie book to stir up memories. Also, consider films you've seen in school as well as those viewed on recreational time. Then, choose to review a film about which you have a lot to say.

Focusing Your Response Before you begin drafting, identify your response to the movie you plan to review. Take time to pinpoint specific reasons for your positive or negative reactions. For example, you may identify weak acting as a major reason for your dislike of a movie or you may feel that a movie's special effects help it overcome a weak plot. Then, draft a statement about the movie that sums up or provides a focus for your response. Keep this focus in mind as you gather details for your movie review.

▲ Critical Viewing Would this movie poster be effective as a selling tool in today's market? Why or why not? **[Evaluate]**

298 • Response to Literature

✓ ONGOING ASSESSMENT: Prerequisite Skills

Students may find the following resources from Chapter 13 particularly helpful in completing their movie reviews.

In the Textbook	Print Resources	Technology
Narrowing Your Topic, Section 13.2 Using Hexagonal Writing, Section 13.2	*Writing Support Transparencies*, 13-B–C *Writing Support Activity Book*, 13-1–2	*Writing and Grammar* Interactive Text, Section 13.2

Gathering Details After choosing your film and deciding on a focus, recall it carefully or view it several times. Jot down the key cast and crew members for accurate reference. Take notes about elements within the movie that you find especially effective or unsuccessful. You may want to prepare a chart like the one below to use as your watch the movie.

Actor's Performance:

Special Effects:

Symbolism:

Cinematography:

Soundtrack:

Drafting Invite readers into your movie review by offering your recommendation in the first paragraph. Provide any necessary background information your audience will need to understand and appreciate your review. Outline the elements you plan to discuss, and name the work's key creative forces. (In a film, these are probably the director, screenwriter, and central performers.) Briefly summarize the film's plot—without giving away the ending. In the body paragraphs, address each selected element with a general statement supported by specific examples from the film.

Revising and Editing Reread your review objectively. Make sure that you clearly indicate what is fact and what is opinion in the review. Wherever necessary, strengthen your main idea by adding supporting details. Also, review your word choice, and replace overly harsh or imprecise words with better word choices.

Publishing and Presenting Make a neat copy of your movie review, and post it in the classroom for others to read. If other classmates have written movie reviews, you may want to gather and bind them together, assembling a film anthology to share with others.

Grammar and Style Tip

Movie reviews vary widely in tone, depending on the author's attitude toward the film. When you write your review, select words and phrases that mirror your attitude toward the movie.

4. Display Transparency 13-H and discuss with students the kind of information they would be likely to include in a movie review. Pick a well-known recent movie and ask students to comment on the performances, special effects, symbolism, or other elements in the movie.

5. Distribute copies of the blank organizer (13-3) for students to use as they watch the movie; students might also develop their own charts.

6. Schedule time in class for students to present their reviews. If several students have selected the same film, you may wish to set up small-group discussions, as well.

Customize for
ESL Students

Suggest that students watch a favorite film in their first languages. They can gather details and then translate them before or as they write their reviews. If the film has subtitles in English, encourage students to include comments about the translation. Do they think it was accurate? Did it come at the right time for the action? What word play or nuances were lost in translation?

Step-by-Step Teaching Guide

Appreciating Performing Arts

1. Choose one of the Spotlight elements for class discussion, or have students work individually or in groups on the elements of their choice. Encourage students to research and share information about Sarah Siddons and her world.

2. Interested students might find reproductions of the portraits of Joshua Reynolds, including his portrait of Sarah Siddons, and present them to the class.

3. Students will enjoy watching a videotape of *All About Eve,* which is widely available for rental. Ask students whether the world of the theater as seen in the film seems very different from what they know of the theater today.

Viewing and Representing

Activity If the technology is available to students, they may wish to record the awards ceremony they will be reviewing. The videotape will enable them to make accurate references to the events in their reviews. If students present their reviews in class, encourage them to use video clips from the events as part of their presentations.

Critical Viewing

Speculate Students may suggest any of the plays mentioned in the text about Siddons's roles.

Spotlight on the Humanities

Appreciating Performing Arts

Focus on Theater: Sarah Siddons

A theater review is a kind of response to literature, and a positive, glowing review is what every actor and actress desires. Considered the greatest English tragic actress of the eighteenth and nineteenth centuries, Sarah Siddons (1755–1831) made her acting debut in London in 1775 at the Drury Lane Theatre as Portia in *The Merchant of Venice* by William Shakespeare. Her performance, however, was so unsuccessful she spent the next seven years performing in smaller theaters. In 1782, she again appeared at the Drury Lane Theatre, but this time her success in Thomas Southerne's *The Fatal Marriage* made her a star. She went on to play Shakespearean roles for most of her career; her best role was that of Lady Macbeth in Shakespeare's *Macbeth.*

Film Connection Winner of six Academy Awards, including Best Film and Best Screenplay, *All About Eve* is the story of a young actress who moves into the life of a Broadway star in a secret effort to find stardom for herself. With its sharp, witty dialogue and strong characterization, the film has become a classic since its release in 1950. The beginning and ending scenes of the film are set at a ceremony for the Sarah Siddons Awards—Broadway theater's top honors.

Art Connection Creator of a portrait of Sarah Siddons as the Tragic Muse in 1784, Sir Joshua Reynolds (1723–1792) was an influential English painter. Reynolds completed more than 2,000 portraits in his lifetime. His work was noted for its classical references, full color, and realistic representation of his subject. In 1764, he began the Literary Club in England with artists and writers such as Samuel Johnson and James Boswell.

Response to Literature Writing Activity: Review of an Awards Ceremony

The classic film *All About Eve* won six Academy Awards in 1950 and continues to place highly on "Best Ever" film lists of today. Recall or review an awards ceremony, like the Academy Awards, in which film, music, or artists are honored for their contributions. Then, write a review of that event, taking into account its script, music or dance performances, variety of presenters, and so on. Share your finished review with classmates.

300 • Response to Literature

▲ Critical Viewing
For what role might Sarah Siddons have worn this costume? Explain. [Speculate]

Customize for
More Advanced Students

Challenge these students to research information about the Academy Awards and present the information to the class. This will not only allow them to use their skills to explore a subject, but it will also give them an opportunity to practice their public-speaking skills.

Media and Technology Skills

Responding Using Technology

Activity: Share Your Impressions

Use the Internet to share your responses to literature with readers around the world. With one click of the mouse, you can share your response with a friend in another town or participate in a discussion group hosted by an author. How you use the Internet depends on the audience you want to reach.

Think About It Think of ways to share your ideas about literature. For example, you might e-mail an informal note to a friend about a poem you like. You might monitor a university's lecture series on literature via the Internet or go to an author's Web page and contribute questions or comments.

Log Onto It

- To send an e-mail, log onto your service provider. Then, copy and paste your response onto an e-mail template or attach your response to a brief e-mail note. Type in the address of the recipient, and send it off.

- Comb the newspapers for advertisements about author seminars and readings offered by bookstores and publishers. Often, these seminars and readings take place on-line. Log onto the Web site as advertised and participate as much as you want in the discussion.

Post It Electronic bulletin boards are public forums in which any computer user can read messages posted by others and respond to them. You can find bulletin boards through search engines, your Internet Service Provider, and school Web sites. Because most bulletin boards focus on a specific topic, find one that is related to your response. Keep these suggestions in mind when posting to a bulletin board:

- Read several messages and responses to evaluate the tone of the board before you add your own messages.

- Keep postings relatively short. You may want to post an edited or condensed version of your original writing.

- Use a subject heading that clearly describes your message so that readers know what to expect when they open your posting.

A Home Page of Your Own

Another way to share your views with readers on the Internet is to design your own Web literary page. Most Web pages use a computer language called HTML. You can learn the basic HTML codes fairly quickly, or use a Web design software that writes the necessary codes for you.

Here are just a few elements you might include on your home page:

- Images: Include digital photographs and/or computer artwork.
- Text: Include your stories, essays, or poems.
- Lists of favorites: Describe your favorite books, movies, songs, performers, or television shows.
- Links: Add links to your favorite Web sites.

Lesson Objectives

1. To write a response to literature within a time limit

2. To use prewriting strategies to generate ideas, develop voice, and plan

3. To produce legible work that shows accurate spelling and correct use of the conventions of punctuation and capitalization, and to demonstrate control over grammatical elements

Step-by-Step Teaching Guide

Responding to Literature-Based Prompts

Teaching Resources: Standardized Test Preparation Workbook, pp. 25–26

1. Go over the bulleted criteria with students.

2. Have students read the sample writing situation. Define and clarify terms such as *counted, sorest, purple Host, forbidden ear,* and *strains.*

3. To make sure students understand the assignment, have them rephrase it in their own words.

4. Assign the sample writing situation for completion within a set time period.

Standardized Test Preparation Workshop

Responding to Literature-Based Prompts

This chapter explores the many ways that you can respond to a literary work. Often, standardized test questions evaluate the way you respond to literature by measuring your ability to do the following:

- Respond directly to the prompt.

- Organize your ideas so that they are clear and easy to follow.

- Develop your ideas thoroughly by using appropriate details and precise language.

- Communicate effectively by using correct spelling, capitalization, punctuation, and grammar.

Following is an example of one type of writing prompt you might find on a standardized test. Use the suggestions on the following page to help you respond. The clocks next to each stage show a suggested plan for organizing your time.

Test Tip

When writing a response to literature, don't simply summarize the piece of literature. React to it by giving opinions, examining the author's style, and connecting it to your life.

Sample Writing Situation

Read the poem "Success is counted sweetest" by Emily Dickinson. Then, respond to the prompt that follows this poem:

Success is counted sweetest

Success is counted sweetest
By those who ne'er succeed.
To comprehend a nectar
Requires sorest need.

5 Not one of all the purple Host
Who took the Flag today
Can tell the definition
So clear of Victory

As he defeated—dying—
10 On whose forbidden ear
The distant strains of triumph
Burst agonized and clear!

In "Success is counted sweetest," Dickinson communicates a message about success and failure. Write an essay identifying the poem's message and explaining how the message relates to the lives of high-school students. You may use examples and details from real life, books, movies, television shows, and from the selection you just read.

✎ TEST-TAKING TIP

Explain that a good essay begins with a clear and strong introduction and thesis statement. Direct students to state a main idea. The rest of the essay should be devoted to that main idea.

Students should provide specific details and quotes supporting their thesis statements. Remind them that when they use quotes, they must explain how the quotes back up their arguments, rather than simply citing them.

Prewriting

Allow close to one quarter of your time for prewriting.

Identify Your Response Reread the prompt and identify what, exactly, it asks you to do. Then, reread the poem and develop a response to the prompt. As you develop your response, refer to the prompt often, to be sure you don't stray from the specified task.

Gather Details for Support To gather details for your response to literature, take notes about the poem's message and the way Dickinson gets her message across. Then, include details from your own knowledge, experience, and observations.

Drafting

Allow almost half of your time for drafting.

Develop a Thesis Statement Write a thesis statement that conveys the main idea of your response, and support it with various kinds of details. As you draft, refer to your thesis statement and make sure that all your details support it.

Elaborate When writing your response, include specific descriptions from the poem. Then, elaborate on them by adding your own insights and conclusions. You may also include details that define, explain, or illustrate the points you are making.

Use Formal Language When drafting your response, use formal language. Formal language does not contain contractions, slang, or colloquial language. For example:

Informal: I thought the theme was a *cool idea* for a poem.
Formal: The theme of the poem was an *interesting choice.*

Revising, Editing, and Proofreading

Allow close to one quarter of your time for revising, editing, and proofreading.

Check Support Review your response for details that do not directly support your thesis statement, and remove them. Make sure that you include the title of the poem in the first line, and double-check all quotations to make sure they match the poem exactly.

Make Corrections Proofread carefully to find and correct errors in grammar, spelling, and punctuation. When making changes, place a line through text that you want eliminated and place it in brackets. Use a caret [^] to indicate places where you are adding words.

Chapter 14 Time and Resource Manager

In-Depth Lesson Plan

	LESSON FOCUS	PRINT AND MEDIA RESOURCES
DAY 1	**Introduction to Writing for Assessment** Students learn key elements of writing for assessment. (pp. 304–305/⊞194–195)	*Writers at Work* DVD, Practical and Technical Writing *Writing and Grammar* Interactive Text, Ch. 14, Introduction
DAY 2	**Prewriting** Students choose and narrow a topic, consider their audience and purpose, and gather information. (pp. 306–307/⊞196–197)	**Teaching Resources** *Topic Bank for Heterogeneous Classes* *Writing and Grammar* Interactive Text, Section 14.1
DAY 3	**Drafting** Students organize their ideas and write their first drafts. (pp. 308–309/⊞198–199)	**Teaching Resources** *Writing Support Transparencies,* 14-A–B *Writing and Grammar* Interactive Text, Section 14.2
DAY 4	**Revising** Students revise their drafts in terms of overall structure, paragraphs, sentences, and word choice. (pp. 310–311/200–201)	**Teaching Resources** *Writing Support Transparencies,* 14-C *Writing and Grammar* Interactive Text, Section 14.3
DAY 5	**Editing and Proofreading; Publishing and Presenting** Students check their work for accuracy and correctness and present their final drafts. (pp. 312–315/⊞202–203)	**Teaching Resources** *Scoring Rubrics on Transparency,* Ch. 14; *Writing Assessment and Portfolio Management; Formal Assessment,* Ch. 14 *Writing and Grammar* Interactive Text, Sections 14.4–5

Accelerated Lesson Plan

	LESSON FOCUS	PRINT AND MEDIA RESOURCES
DAY 1	**Introduction Through Drafting** Students review characteristics of writing for assessment, select topics, and write drafts. (pp. 304–309/⊞194–199)	**Teaching Resources** *Writing Support Transparencies,* 14-A–C *Writing and Grammar* Interactive Text, Ch. 14, Introduction through Section 14.2
DAY 2	**Revising Through Presenting** Students revise, edit, and proofread their work for presentation. (pp. 310–315/⊞200–203)	**Teaching Resources** *Scoring Rubrics on Transparency,* Ch. 14; *Writing Assessment and Portfolio Management; Formal Assessment,* Ch. 14 *Writing and Grammar* Interactive Text, Sections 14.3–4

Options for Adapting Lesson Plans

HOMEWORK

Have students complete any stage of the lesson for homework.

FEATURES

Extend coverage with Connected Assignment (p. 316), Spotlight on the Humanities (p. 318), Media and Technology Skills (p. 319), and the Standardized Test Preparation Workshop (p. 320).

TECHNOLOGY

Students can complete any stage of the lesson on the computer, using *Writing and Grammar* Interactive Text or a word-processing program. Have them print out their completed work.

Writing and Grammar Handbook Alignment

Page numbers in Step-by-Step Teaching Guides in this Teacher's Edition refer to pages from the full student text. Handbook page references, indicated with this icon ⊞, are provided in Time and Resource Manager boxes and at the bottom of each Teacher's Edition page.

INTEGRATED SKILLS COVERAGE

Viewing and Representing
Critical Viewing, SE pp. 304, 307, 310, 315, 316, 318/⊞194, 197, 200
Analyze Ideas Represented in Various Media, SE p. 318
Using Technology to Respond to a Variety of Test Formats, SE p. 319
ATE p. 309

Spelling Skills
Spelling *ie* and *ei* Words, SE p. 312/⊞202

Test-Taking Skills
ATE p. 319

Vocabulary Skills
ATE p. 311

Speaking and Listening Skills
ATE p. 315

Real-World Connection
ATE p. 315

ASSESSMENT SUPPORT

Standardized Test Preparation Workshop SE p. 320; ATE p. 311
Standardized Test Preparation Workbook, pp. 27–28
Scoring Rubrics on Transparency, Ch. 14
Formal Assessment, Ch. 14
Writing Assessment and Portfolio Management

MEETING INDIVIDUAL NEEDS

Less Advanced Students ATE pp. 308, 310, 317. See also Ongoing Assessments ATE pp. 307, 309.
More Advanced Students ATE pp. 309, 315, 317, 321
ESL Students ATE pp. 306, 321
Spatial Learners ATE p. 308

BLOCK SCHEDULING

Pacing Suggestions
For 90-minute Blocks
• Have students complete the Prewriting and Drafting stages in a single period.
• Focus one class period on Revising and Editing and Publishing and Presenting.

Resources for Varying Instruction
• *Writing and Grammar* **Interactive Text** A 90-minute block provides an ideal opportunity for students to work on the computer.
• *Writers at Work* **DVD** Show the Response to Literature segment in class.

Professional Development Support
• *How to Manage Instruction in the Block* This teaching resource provides management and activity suggestions.

MEDIA AND TECHNOLOGY

For the Student
• *Writing and Grammar* **Interactive Text**, Ch. 14

For the Teacher
• *Writers at Work* **DVD**, Practical and Technical Writing
• **Teacher EXPRESS** CD-ROM

WRITING AND GRAMMAR ON-LINE

Interactive Text (On-line or on CD-ROM)
• Easily navigable instruction with interactive Revision Checkers
• Full use of e-rater™, the essay-scoring system (on-line only)

Companion Web Site PHSchool.com
• Scoring rubrics with models (use Web Code eek-1001)

See the Go On-line! feature, SE p. iii.

► Lesson Objectives

1. To write for assessment, organizing ideas in writing to ensure coherence, logical progression, and support for ideas

2. To use prewriting strategies to generate ideas and plan

3. To develop drafts by organizing content to suit purpose

4. To revise drafts in terms of structure, paragraphs, sentences, and word choice

5. To edit and proofread to ensure standard English usage and grammar

6. To evaluate writing for both mechanics and content

7. To produce error-free writing in the final draft

Critical Viewing

Analyze These students are probably taking multiple-choice tests. They are marking their answers on a bubble sheet.

Chapter 14 Writing for Assessment

Assessment in School

Being evaluated is a part of life. For example, a music teacher may measure how much you have improved as a trombone player in the course of a year, or a track-and-field coach may assess your hurdling technique to help you prepares for an upcoming meet.

In class, evaluations help teachers assess how much students have learned and how well their students' progress compares with that of other students—in their own school and all over the nation. Teachers use various kinds of assessment tools, from pop quizzes to questions in class to essay assignments and special projects.

▲ **Critical Viewing**
What kind of test might these students be taking? How do you know? **[Analyze]**

304 • Writing for Assessment

⏱ TIME AND RESOURCE MANAGER

Resources
Technology: *Writers at Work* DVD, Practical and Technical Writing; *Writing and Grammar* Interactive Text, Ch. 14

Using the Full Student Edition	Using the Handbook🄷
• Cover pp. 304–305 in class. • Show the Practical and Technical Writing section of the *Writers at Work* DVD. • Discuss the ways in which work is assessed in school and on the job.	• Cover pp. 194–195 in class. • Show the Practical and Technical Writing section of the *Writers at Work* DVD. • Discuss the ways in which work is assessed in school and on the job.

What Is Assessment?

Assessment is evaluation. In life, people may be assessed by anyone, from parents to employers. In school, however, assessment is used to gauge the depth of students' knowledge, their ability to learn, and their problem-solving abilities.

Most educators who make assessments of students' work look for

- answers or responses that match the questions asked.
- clearly stated main points that are supported with details.
- writing that is organized logically and effectively.
- correct grammar, spelling, and punctuation.

To preview the criteria on which your essay may be evaluated, see the Rubric for Self-Assessment on page 313.

Types of Assessment

Many types of tests and essays allow teachers and other educators to assess their students' progress. Following are some assessment tools commonly used by educators:

- **Timed tests** assess students' familiarity with the tested topics.
- **Short-answer tests** require brief answers, ranging from a word or phrase to a few sentences for each question.
- **Analyses** are critical papers in which the structural components of a work are examined and evaluated.
- **Comparison-and-contrast essays** provide detailed information about the similarities and differences among two or more people, places, things, or ideas.
- **Personal essays** reveal the unique experiences and insights of the writer.

PREVIEW
Student Work
IN PROGRESS

Follow along as Tricia Bushnell, a student at Buena High School in Ventura, California, drafts and revises an essay about World War I for assessment. A completed draft appears at the end of this chapter.

Writers in ACTION

Emile-Auguste Chartier, renowned French philosopher, understood the importance of arriving at truths. He had the following to say about his methods:

"Every idea I get I have to deny. That's my way of testing it."

Writing for Assessment • **305**

Prewriting: Choosing Your Topic

1. Discuss the strategies for choosing a topic by asking the following questions:

   What can happen if you just choose the first question and try to answer it? (It may be more difficult for you than later questions; your answer might not be an accurate reflection of your general knowledge of the topic.)

   Why is it important to identify key words? (This will ensure that students address every part of the question and use the proper tone and method of organization.)

2. Ask students to think about which formats seem more comfortable to them. Have them explain why.

3. Have students identify the required format for each topic in the Topic Bank.

Customize for
ESL Students

Offer one or more of the following questions for students to answer:

Explain conditions that make it easy to move from one country to another.

What is a misconception, positive or negative, that people in the United States have about your country of origin? Explain why you think this misconception exists and what could be done to correct it.

Compare and contrast the average student's attitude toward school in the United States and in your country of origin. Use examples to support your main points.

14.1 Prewriting

Choosing Your Topic

You may be asked to write an essay to evaluate your understanding of a subject. In many cases, more than one essay question is provided, and you will be asked to choose one on which to write your essay. For help with choosing a topic for an essay test, follow these guidelines:

- **Skim the Questions** Quickly read the questions, and eliminate those about which you have limited knowledge. One quick way to measure your knowledge is to think of at least three details that you could use immediately in answering an essay question. If you cannot easily come up with three supporting points, choose another question to answer.

- **Look for Key Words** As you read through the essay questions, look for key words that reveal what your response must address. Key words can include *examine the causes, analyze, compare and contrast, distinguish between, identify,* and *evaluate.* Choose to answer the question that you feel most prepared to answer in full.

- **Identify the Format** Analyze the questions, and note the format your response will require. For example, a question may ask you to compare and contrast, trace the causes of something, or argue persuasively. If you feel especially confident with any one format over the others, choose to answer the question that requires that format.

TOPIC BANK

Following are some sample essay-test questions. If you plan to practice writing for assessment, choose one of these or ask your teacher to provide you with one.

1. Explain the conditions that must exist in order for a hurricane to occur.

2. Which American president governed most effectively? Give reasons to support your opinion.

3. If you had a motto in life, what would it be? Explain, using examples from experience, literature, and the media.

4. Define the concept of globalization, and give examples of it in action.

5. Discuss the causes of the bubonic plague epidemics in Europe and the effects the epidemics had on people's behavior and beliefs.

306 • Writing for Assessment

⏱ TIME AND RESOURCE MANAGER

Resources
Print: *Topic Bank for Heterogeneous Classes*
Technology: *Writing and Grammar* Interactive Text, Section 14.1

Using the Full Student Edition	Using the Handbook H
• Cover pp. 306–307 in class. • Have students choose a writing prompt from the Topic Bank. • If students create their own topics, approve them before they continue with the Prewriting strategies.	• Cover pp. 196–197 in class. • Have students choose a writing prompt from the Topic Bank. • If students create their own topics, approve them before they continue with the Prewriting strategies.

Narrowing Your Response

Narrow your response by identifying your main point. To do this, note specifically what the essay question is asking of you. For example, are you going to defend a position, show the causes of something, or make a prediction? For help narrowing your topic, use the strategies that follow.

Identify Key Words

Reread the question you're answering, and find key words within it that indicate the form your response should take. Key words may include *predict, trace, compare, analyze, evaluate, support,* and *criticize.*

Once you have identified exactly what the question is asking, stay within those limits to keep your topic narrow and focused.

Match Key Words to the Thesis

To narrow your topic, find the key words in an essay question, and write a thesis statement that answers the question. Use that thesis statement as a guide when you draft your essay. This will help you to keep your topic focused and to answer effectively and completely the question that is being asked.

QUESTION: Who do you predict will have a more lasting reputation as a poet: Emily Dickinson or Elizabeth Barrett Browning? Why?

THESIS: I predict that Emily Dickinson will have a more lasting literary reputation because . . .

Elizabeth Barrett Browning
1803–1861, Field Talfourd

Emily Dickinson, artist unknown

Considering Your Audience and Purpose

Before you begin drafting, take time to identify for whom you are writing and your purpose for writing. In most assessment situations, your audience and purpose are predetermined: You will write for evaluators and teachers, and your purpose will be to show them how well you understand your subject.

To impress your audience and achieve your purpose, choose details that support your main points and use a style of language that is formal and respectful.

▲ Critical Viewing
What similarities and differences can you identify between the styles of portraits shown here?
[Compare and Contrast]

Prewriting • 307

1. Ask students why it's important to narrow an essay topic (to make sure the idea is not too broad to cover in a short essay).

2. Have students share other key words they've noticed in essay-test questions. Define any words they do not understand.

3. Discuss the definition of *thesis* with the class. Explain that a thesis is a statement that expresses the main point of a piece of writing.

4. Have students work in pairs to write thesis statements for the questions in the Topic Bank.

Critical Viewing

Compare and Contrast Both portraits emphasize the heads of the subjects, and in both the subject is gazing forward. Students may note slight differences in pose and facial expression.

Prewriting: Considering Your Audience and Purpose

1. Explain that essay-test questions are similiar to other essays students have written for class. They both require a formal tone and a strong grasp of the subject matter.

2. Ask students to name ways of creating a formal tone (using formal language, including statistics, quoting experts).

☑ **ONGOING ASSESSMENT: Monitor and Reinforce**

If some students are having difficulty selecting a topic, use one of the following options.

Option 1 If many students are having difficulty, work with the whole class on one idea selected from the Topic Bank or from ideas suggested by students.	**Option 2** If the Topic Bank ideas seem too difficult, offer suggestions from the *Topic Bank for Heterogeneous Classes* in the Teaching Resources.

Drafting: Choose an Organizational Method

Teaching Resources: Writing Support Transparencies, 14-A

1. Ask students why it is important to choose an organizational method before they begin writing (to save time; to make sure they have enough information to write a complete and thorough essay).

2. Have students imagine they are writing an essay that compares and contrasts middle school and high school. Ask them to fill in both types of comparison-and-contrast organization based on this topic. Which do they prefer and why?

3. Display Transparency 14–A on Nestorian Organization. Ask a volunteer to express the concept in his or her own words.

4. Invite students to suggest appropriate topics for all three organizational methods.

Customize for
Spatial Learners

Ask students to create a graphic organizer to illustrate the concept of chronological organization. To make this task more concrete, you might give them a specific essay question. Then, they can make a visual representation of the answer to this question.

Customize for
Less Advanced Students

Remind students that the answer to an essay question should include an introduction, a body, and a conclusion, just like a typical essay.

14.2 Drafting

Shaping Your Writing
Choose an Organizational Method

Take time to organize your thoughts and to plan a structure for your essay. Doing so now will cut down on the amount of revision you will have to do later.

Comparison-and-Contrast Organization Use this method of organization to show how two or more subjects are alike and different. This organizational method can take two forms: subject by subject or point by point.

Chronological Organization Use chronological organization—time order—when you're asked to trace causes and effects, examine the history of something, or tell a personal story.

Nestorian Organization Use Nestorian organization when you want to build an argument or end your paper in the strongest possible way. In this method, you lead off with your second-most important point, and present the remaining points in increasing order of importance to end with your strongest observation.

Point-by-Point Organization	Subject-by-Subject Organization
Point A	Subject A
subject A	point A
subject B	point B
Point B	point C
subject A	Subject B
subject B	point A
	point B
	point C

NESTORIAN ORGANIZATION

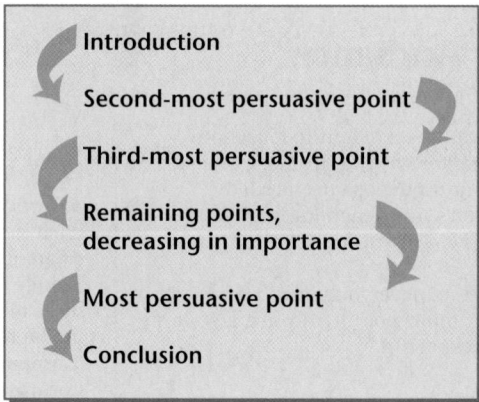

Introduction

Second-most persuasive point

Third-most persuasive point

Remaining points, decreasing in importance

Most persuasive point

Conclusion

⏱ TIME AND RESOURCE MANAGER

Resources
Print: *Writing Support Transparencies, 14-A–B*
Technology: *Writing and Grammar* Interactive Text, Section 14.2

Using the Full Student Edition	Using the Handbook🄷
• Cover pp. 308–309 in class.	• Cover pp. 198–199 in class.
• Give students time to choose an organizational method and write a first draft.	• Give students time to choose an organizational method and write a first draft.
• Have partners exchange first drafts and mark places that are unclear or need elaboration.	• Have partners exchange first drafts and mark places that are unclear or need elaboration.

Providing Elaboration

As you draft, make your writing convincing and give it depth by providing supporting details. The supporting details you choose should define, restate, explain, or illustrate your main points.

Give Supporting Details

Examples may include illustrations, instances from real life, and allusions (references) to literary works or actual experiences.

Quotations may come from a well-known person or from a literary work.

Comparisons may be drawn from the past, the present, reality, or fiction. Comparisons help your readers understand vague or unfamiliar ideas.

Personal observations may include your opinions and experiences. You might also draw upon books you've read or movies you have seen.

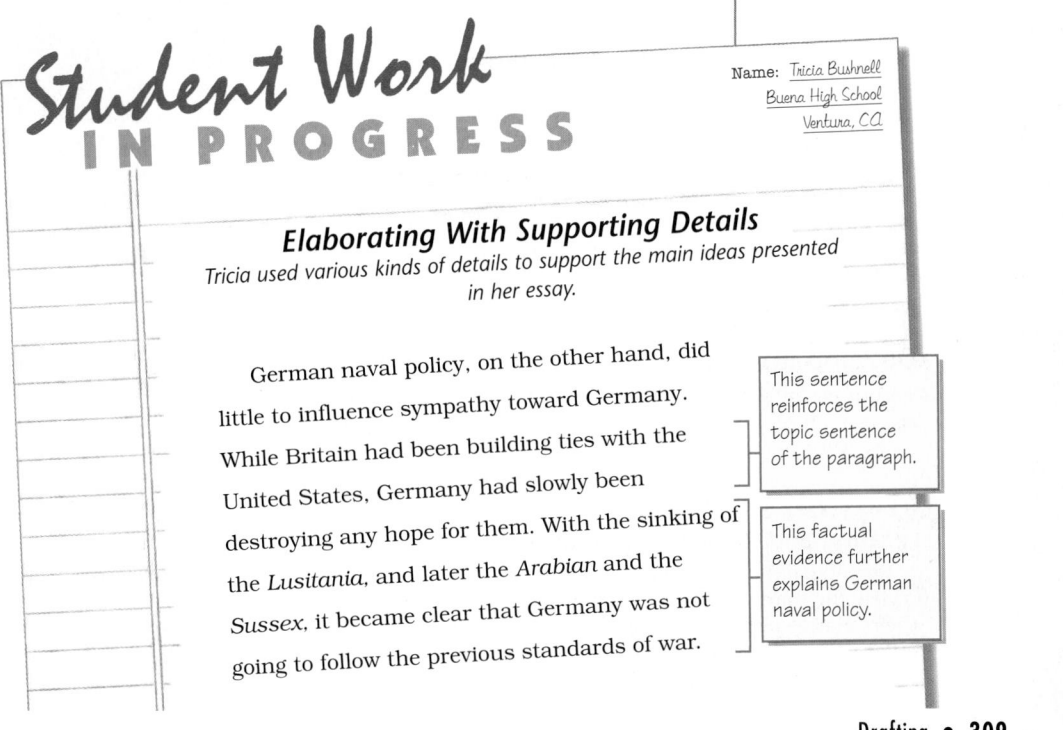

Student Work IN PROGRESS

Name: *Tricia Bushnell*
Buena High School
Ventura, CA

Elaborating With Supporting Details

Tricia used various kinds of details to support the main ideas presented in her essay.

German naval policy, on the other hand, did little to influence sympathy toward Germany. While Britain had been building ties with the United States, Germany had slowly been destroying any hope for them. With the sinking of the *Lusitania*, and later the *Arabian* and the *Sussex*, it became clear that Germany was not going to follow the previous standards of war.

> This sentence reinforces the topic sentence of the paragraph.

> This factual evidence further explains German naval policy.

Drafting • 309

Drafting: Providing Elaboration

Teaching Resources: Writing Support Transparencies, 14-B

1. After students read about the methods of providing elaboration, display Transparency 14-B. Ask students the following questions:

   What methods does Tricia use to provide elaboration? (She offers supporting details.)

   What other supporting details might she add? (She might add statistics about the deaths on the ships that sank or quotations from German or American leaders.)

2. Invite volunteers to read from their drafts, showing how they used a certain kind of elaboration to support a point.

Customize for *More Advanced Students*

Ask students to read a recent article from the school or local newspaper. Have them identify the thesis and three supporting details. Then, have students suggest at least one other detail the author could have included to make the argument more interesting and convincing.

Integrating Viewing and Representing Skills

Ask students to recall an advertisement they have seen or heard. What kinds of elaboration were included to make the sales pitch more convincing? Did it include personal observations from a famous athlete? Did it offer statistics from government studies? Discuss the effectiveness of these types of elaboration in convincing people to buy a product.

☑ ONGOING ASSESSMENT: Monitor and Reinforce

Students sometimes have difficulty recognizing the strengths and weaknesses of their supporting evidence. If this is the case, try the following strategy.

Have each student consider his or her thesis statement and write five supporting points on separate note cards. Pair students and have them exchange cards. The receiving partner will order the cards from the strongest point to the weakest. Have pairs discuss their reasons for ordering the cards as they did. Suggest that students eliminate the one or two weakest points.

⏱ TIME SAVERS!

 **Writing Support Transparencies**

 Use the transparencies for Chapter 14 to facilitate the teaching of concepts.

Revise your writing as best you can, given the time allotted. Following are several strategies for revising your essay.

Revising Your Overall Structure
Make the Introduction and Conclusion Match

Review your essay to be sure your introduction and conclusion match. Your introduction should state your thesis or main idea and preview the contents of the essay. Your conclusion should reinforce the ideas presented in the introduction.

▶ **REVISION STRATEGY**
Listing Main Points

Read through your introduction, and list the main points you made there. Then, list the main points that you made in your conclusion. If the majority of the main points on your lists do not match, revise either the introduction or your conclusion so that they match more closely.

The following introduction and conclusion work well together. The introduction states the main points, and the conclusion reiterates them and gives readers more to think about.

Introduction
✓ 1. Superhighways changed how we live.
✓ 2. Cars promoted urban flight.
   3. Suburbs became desirable places to live.

Conclusion
✓ 1. Cars and the development of highway systems had a huge impact on American life.
✓ 2. The rise of suburbs led to the fall of cities.
   3. Will the coming of virtual offices promote flight to exurbs?

Revising Your Paragraphs
Develop and Build Your Argument or Thesis

Your essay should build an argument or develop your thesis, or main point. Make sure that the paragraphs in your essay work together, building to your conclusion.

▶ **REVISION STRATEGY**
Locating and Ranking Main Ideas

Reread each paragraph, and jot down its main idea. Then, review the main ideas, and assign them a ranking based on their relative importance. Review your list, and switch the order of paragraphs, if necessary, to build or develop your argument or thesis.

▲ **Critical Viewing**
What dominant impression is revealed in this photograph? **[Analyze]**

Revising Your Sentences

Create Sentence Variety

Review your draft to be sure that your sentences begin in a variety of ways.

▶ **REVISION STRATEGY**
Checking Sentence Beginnings

Read quickly through your draft, and look at the beginnings of your sentences. If more than three sentences in a row begin the same way, rewrite or combine some of them to break up the pattern and add interest and variety to your writing.

Revising Your Word Choice

▶ **REVISION STRATEGY**
Replacing or Deleting "Empty and Hedging Words"

Locate "empty words" and "hedging words" (words that take away from meaning) in your essay, and replace or delete them. The chart at right contains words and phrases you should eliminate from your essay:

Empty Words/ Hedging Words
by way of; despite the fact that; what I mean is; in my opinion; needless to say; to the extent that; there are; the reason was that; the thing is; almost; it seems; kind of; quite; rather; somewhat; sort of; tends; nearly

Student Work
IN PROGRESS

Name: *Tricia Bushnell*
Buena High School
Ventura, CA

Deleting Empty and Hedging Words
After closely examining her draft, Tricia deleted some words that added nothing.

Although President Wilson proclaimed neutrality at the start of the war, it soon became ~~somewhat~~ clear that the U.S.'s economic heart belonged to Britain and the Allies. Impeded by the British blockade, Americans, ~~needless to say,~~ found it substantially harder to trade with Germany.

Revising • 311

Empty Words Standardized tests might require students to identify empty and unnecessary words. For example, which word or words in the following sentence provide no additional information?

In my opinion, I believe that poverty is the greatest contributing factor to crime.

A greatest   **C** to crime

B In my opinion   **D** contributing factor to

Students should recognize that **B** is the correct answer. "I believe that" and "In my opinion" say the same thing; one of these phrases should be eliminated.

Revising: Checking Sentence Beginnings

1. Write the following paragraph on the board. Ask students to revise it, focusing on adding variety to sentence beginnings.

   Fossil fuels are also called nonrenewable fuels. Fossil fuels are used up much faster than they are produced far underground. Fossil fuels pollute the air when they are burned.

   Possible revision: *Fossil fuels, also called nonrenewable fuels, are used up much faster than they are produced far underground. Another problem is that burning these fuels pollute the air.*

2. Provide time for students to add variety to the beginnings of the sentences in their own essays.

Integrating Vocabulary Skills

Point out that a thesaurus can help students add variety to their sentences. Encourage students to use a thesaurus to replace repeated words with appropriate synonyms.

Revising: Replacing or Deleting "Empty and Hedging Words"

Teaching Resources: Writing Support Transparencies, 14-C

1. Have students read the list of empty and hedging words. Have them add more examples to the list.

2. Display Transparency 14-C to demonstrate how Tricia deleted words from her draft.

3. Give students time to eliminate similar empty words from their essays. Remind them that sometimes, entire sentences can be empty if they offer no new information.

Editing and Proofreading

1. Invite students to identify groups of words or spelling patterns that they find challenging.

2. Encourage students to share ways they remember spelling patterns. One might be short sayings that aid memory. For example: *The principal is my pal.*

3. Discuss ways to check spelling, such as reading sentences backward. If students are running out of time while answering an essay question, urge them to concentrate on writing accurate and complete answers, not on spelling.

Spelling *ie* and *ei* Words

1. Encourage students to use the dictionary to check *ie* and *ei* spellings whenever possible. There are many exceptions to the rule, so the dictionary is more dependable than the rule.

2. For the next week, have students look for exceptions to the rule while reading. Have them share their findings in class.

Find It in Your Writing

Have students share the words in their essays that contain *ie* or *ei*. Write them on the board under the headings *ie* or *ei*, eliminating duplications. Have students examine the class list and identify the words that follow the traditional spelling rule and those that do not.

14.4 Editing and Proofreading

Misspellings indicate sloppiness or carelessness on the writer's part. Be sure you correct misspellings before you hand in your essay.

Focusing on Spelling

For Open-Book and Nontimed Essays Use a dictionary to check the spellings of words about which you are unsure. If you are working electronically, use a spell-check feature to help you catch errors. Don't, however, rely on spell-checks to catch all typographical errors. A spell-check, for instance, will not catch the mistaken use of "he" for "the" or "you" for "your."

For Timed-Test Essays If you are aware of mistakes you often make in spelling, scan your writing for such mistakes now. Otherwise, check for common errors, such as misspellings in "*i* before *e* words" and homophones such as *to, too, two; its, it's;* and *there, they're,* and *their.*

Grammar in Your Writing
Spelling *ie* and *ei* Words

Use the traditional rule for spelling words with an *ie* or *ei* combination: "Use *i* before *e* except after *c* or when sounded like *a*, as in *neighbor* or *sleigh.*"

chief   ceiling   freight   tier

The most common exception to this rule involves words that contain the *sh* sound spelled with a *c*.

ancient   conscience

Following are some more exceptions to the rule:

either   foreign   heir   height   seize   neither   forfeit   their

Find It in Your Writing Read through your essay to be sure you've correctly spelled words containing either *ei* or *ie*.

To learn more about spelling rules, see Chapter 30.

⏱ TIME AND RESOURCE MANAGER

Resources
Print: *Scoring Rubrics on Transparency,* Ch. 14; *Writing Assessment and Portfolio Management; Formal Assessment,* Ch. 14
Technology: *Writing and Grammar* Interactive Text, Section 14.4

Using the Full Student Edition	Using the Handbook⒣
• Cover pp. 312–313 in class. • Have students edit and proofread their essays in class. • Have students complete the Rubric for Self-Assessment, p. 313.	• Cover pp. 202–203 in class. • Have students edit and proofread their essays in class. • Have students complete the Rubric for Self-Assessment, p. 203.

14.5 Publishing and Presenting

Building Your Portfolio

1. **Portfolio** Save your completed essay in your portfolio. Attach a small note on which you describe when and where you took this test.
2. **Guidance Counselor** Give a copy of your writing for assessment to your guidance counselor for his or her review. Then, make an appointment with the counselor to discuss how to best take advantage of your writing skills.

Reflecting on Your Writing

Take a few moments to think about writing for assessment. Then, answer the following questions, and save your responses in your portfolio.

- Were you satisfied with the question you chose to answer? Why or why not?
- If you were to coach someone on how to write effectively for assessment, what points would you emphasize? Why?

 Internet Tip

To see essays scored with this rubric, go on-line:
PHSchool.com
Enter Web Code:
eek-1001

Rubric for Self-Assessment

Use the following criteria to evaluate your writing for assessment:

	Score 4	Score 3	Score 2	Score 1
Audience and Purpose	Uses appropriately formal tone; clearly addresses writing prompt	Uses mostly formal tone; adequately addresses prompt	Uses some informal tone; addresses writing prompt	Uses inappropriately informal tone; does not address writing prompt
Organization	Presents an effective, consistent organizational strategy	Presents a clear organizational strategy with few inconsistencies	Presents an inconsistent organizational strategy	Shows a lack of organizational strategy
Elaboration	Provides several ideas to support the thesis; elaborates each idea; links all information to support thesis	Provides several ideas to support the thesis; elaborates most ideas with facts, details, or examples; links most information to thesis	Provides some ideas to support the thesis; does not elaborate some ideas; does not link some details to thesis	Provides no thesis; does not elaborate ideas
Use of Language	Uses excellent sentence and vocabulary variety; includes very few errors	Uses adequate sentence and vocabulary variety; includes few errors	Uses repetitive sentence structure and vocabulary; includes many errors	Demonstrates poor use of language; generates confusion; includes many errors

Publishing and Presenting • 313

Step-by-Step Teaching Guide

Publishing and Presenting

1. Encourage students to add other essay tests to their portfolios if they are not already doing so.
2. Have them make sure each essay is dated so they can track their progress in improving their writing.

ASSESS and CLOSE

Step-by-Step Teaching Guide

Assessment

Teaching Resources: Scoring Rubrics on Transparency, Ch. 14; Writing Assessment and Portfolio Management; Formal Assessment, Ch. 14

1. Display the Scoring Rubric transparency and review the criteria in class.
2. Before students proceed with self-assessment, you may wish to review the Final Draft of the Student Work in Progress on pages 314–315.
3. In addition to student self-assessment, you may wish to use the following options:
   - score student essays yourself, using the rubric and scoring models.
   - review the Standardized Test Preparation Workshop on pages 320–321 and assign the practice items.
   - administer the Chapter 14 assessment from *Formal Assessment* in the Teaching Resources to evaluate students' grasp of the concepts presented.

☑ **ONGOING ASSESSMENT: Assess Mastery**

Use one of the following options to assess final drafts of students' essays.

Self-Assessment Ask students to score their essays using the rubric on page 313. Then, have them write a paragraph reflecting on the most valuable thing they learned in completing this essay.	**Teacher Assessment** Use the rubric and scoring models provided in *Writing Assessment and Portfolio Management* to score essays.

Final Draft

1. Read the Final Draft. Ask students the following questions to prompt discussion about it.

   Which of the three influences listed in the question did Tricia decide to assess? (She assesses American economic interests, German naval policy, and Allied propaganda.)

   Where did she first list these influences? (She lists them at the end of the first paragraph.)

   Why did Tricia place them there? (She probably did so to introduce the points she will cover.)

2. Explore the purpose of the three middle paragraphs in Tricia's essay. (They each cover one of her main points.)

3. Help students identify and discuss the organizational method that Tricia used. (Tricia's points are arranged roughly in chronological order. She does not argue that one point is the most important; rather, she explains how each influenced the United States to enter the war.)

4. Ask students to analyze the kinds of elaboration used in each paragraph. Which paragraph do they consider the strongest? Why?

5. Ask students to compare Tricia's introduction and conclusion. Do the main points match?

6. Challenge students to find any empty or hedging words that could have been deleted from the essay.

14.6 *Student Work*

IN PROGRESS

FINAL DRAFT

Why the United States Entered World War I

Tricia Bushnell
Buena High School
Ventura, California

> Assess the relative influence of THREE of the following in the American decision to declare war on Germany in 1917.
>
> - German naval policy
> - Woodrow Wilson's idealism
> - Allied propaganda
> - America's claim to world power
> - American economic interests

When the United States entered World War I, despite protests from Secretary of State William Jennings Bryan, America's seemingly nonchalant view of the war turned to one of excitement. Led by President Wilson's promise of "a war to end all wars," citizens of the United States quickly answered Herbert Hoover's calls for "Wheatless Wednesdays" and Victory Gardens. However, it was not Wilson's idealistic policies that persuaded the United States to enter the war on the side of the Allies; rather, it was a combination of economic ties, German naval policy, and Allied propaganda.

Although President Wilson proclaimed neutrality at the start of the war, it soon became clear that the economic heart of the United States belonged to Britain and the Allies. Impeded by the British blockade, Americans found it substantially harder to trade with Germany. Furthermore, when Germany and Britain began searching and seizing goods from American ships, Britain continued to pay for all seized items. However, the greatest economic tie came with the labors of American banker J. P. Morgan. Through his efforts, various loan agreements were made between U.S.

Tricia's thesis statement appears in the last sentence of her introduction.

Tricia's essay is clearly organized: She uses transitions, such as "furthermore" and "however" to connect the supporting details she provides.

banks and Allied powers. As a result, much of America's money lay in Allied hands; therefore, it was seemingly important that America enter the war to protect its investments.

German naval policy, on the other hand, did little to influence sympathy toward Germany. While Britain had been building ties with the United States, Germany had slowly been destroying any hope for them. With the sinking of the *Lusitania*, and later the *Arabian* and the *Sussex*, it became clear that Germany was not going to follow the previous standards of war. Germany declared unlimited submarine warfare, an idea never fathomed before. Americans were alarmed.

Further influencing American ties with the Allies was various anti-German propaganda. Commonly referred to as the "Huns," German soldiers were depicted committing violent crimes on civilians. Furthermore, Britain controlled the transatlantic cable, making it much easier for pro-British propaganda to find its way to the United States.

It seemed the Central Powers had little hope for help from the United States, and American-German economic ties appeared impossible to forge. The Americans were busy feeding on anti-German propaganda. They were all too eager to believe what they read because they were still angry over the sinking of American ships. Add to this Wilson's idealism and his 14-point plan, and the American entrance to the "Great War" on the side of the Allies was inevitable.

The conclusion to Tricia's essay sums up the main points she has already developed in the body of her writing.

▶ Critical Viewing Why might the sinking of a ship like the *Lusitania*, pictured, provoke outrage? [**Connect**]

Integrating Speaking and Listening Skills

Ask the class to listen closely as a volunteer reads the Final Draft aloud. Discuss how they might change this essay if it were to be presented orally instead of in writing. (Some of the sentences might be shorter; the speaker might add visual aids, such as an overhead transparency of the three main points or an example of Allied propaganda.)

Customize for
More Advanced Students

Invite students to explain whether they agree with Tricia's assessment of the influences on the American decision to declare war on Germany in 1917. Would they have discussed any other influences listed in the question? Why or why not?

Real-World Connection

Explain to students that essay writing, especially under time pressure, is good practice for writing in the workplace. On a job, workers might have to write a memo or report in a limited time period. It is important to get accustomed to working with deadlines.

Critical Viewing

Connect The sinking of the *Lusitania* provoked outrage because of the loss of innocent human lives. It also provoked fear, because the U.S. was not prepared to defend itself against similar attacks.

315

316

Lesson Objectives

1. To write an essay for a take-home test
2. To organize ideas in writing to ensure coherence, logical progression, and support for ideas
3. To proofread writing for appropriateness of organization, content, style, and conventions

Step-by-Step Teaching Guide

Take-Home Test

Teaching Resources: Writing Support Transparencies, 14-D; Writing Support Activity Book, 14-1

1. Review the basic essay format: introductory paragraph with thesis statement; body paragraphs that contain main ideas and supporting details; and conclusion, which restates the thesis. See the chart below for resources from Chapter 14.

2. Tell students that even though they will be writing this essay at home, they should prepare as they would for an in-class essay. This involves consolidating and clarifying their ideas about the topic and reviewing textbooks and notes.

3. Display Transparency 14-D to show students how to use a topic web as part of the prewriting process. Point out that they might use this kind of web to explore the details of each paragraph.

4. Suggest that before students begin drafting, they check their webs and other notes against the test question to ensure accurate and complete coverage.

Critical Viewing

Make a Judgment Answers will vary. Students should support their answers with specific reasons.

Connected Assignment
Take-Home Test

Writing for assessment doesn't always take place in a controlled classroom environment. Sometimes, you will be asked to complete a test at home. A take-home test requires many of the same skills you use for an in-class test—careful time planning, clear and brief writing, attention to accuracy, and adequate supporting details. It also asks for a few added skills: You must monitor your time, stay focused, and follow guidelines about acceptable reference use.

Practice writing for a take-home test by following the writing process skills steps.

Prewriting

Choosing Your Topic Most essay tests, at home or in school, will usually offer a choice of topics. When given a choice, focus on the topic you know most about and find most interesting.

Focusing Your Topic Even when topics are predetermined, you can focus your response on an engaging aspect of the topic. Take a few moments to prepare a topic web, on which you quickly sketch various aspects of your topic. Then, if it suits the test question, choose one specific aspect of your topic on which to focus your response.

▲ **Critical Viewing** Do you prefer working at home as the student here is doing or working in a classroom or library? Why? **[Make a Judgment]**

TOPIC WEB

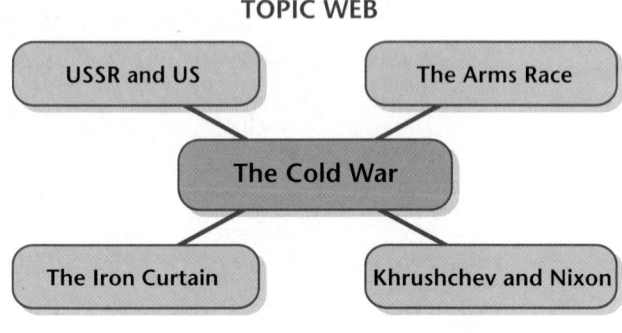

316 • Writing for Assessment

☑ **ONGOING ASSESSMENT: Prerequisite Skills**

Students may find the following resources from Chapter 14 particularly helpful in completing their open-book tests.

In the Textbook	Print Resources	Technology
Choose an Organizational Method, Section 14.2 Providing Elaboration, Section 14.2	*Writing Support Transparencies,* 14-A–B	*Writing and Grammar,* Interactive Text, Section 14.2

Gathering Your Details Before you start drafting, follow these steps:

- Double-check the test rules.

- Assemble all allowed materials in a quiet location.

- Set a timer, if appropriate.

- Once you have set up a test environment, review what you know about the chosen topic, scanning study materials for ideas and grouping details in logical categories. Develop a thesis, and briefly outline your essay.

Drafting State your thesis in the opening paragraph. As you elaborate with key points and supporting details, capitalize on any allowable references by including facts and quotations you might not be able to quote in a traditional test. Let the more relaxed test environment ease your writing process—walk around or speak aloud, if this will help you draft a more effective response.

Revising and Editing

Answering the Question Review your writing to make sure that you've answered the test question. If not, rework the details, as well as your introduction and conclusion, to better answer the question.

Review Organization Review the overall organization of your essay to be sure that it is consistent and effective. Move paragraphs around to better achieve your purpose or to clarify relationships among your ideas. Also, check to ensure that your introduction and conclusion "match up."

Checking Your Facts Check the accuracy of details in your writing. You may use allowed references to confirm their accuracy. Add details if your ideas need more support. Delete details that are unnecessary.

Improve the Language Review your essay to eliminate any words that may be too informal for a test situation. Also consider making these corrections to language:

- Define words that your reader may not know. The brief explanations you provide may make your essay stronger.

- Assess evaluative language. If your response requires you to express an opinion, check that you have conveyed your feelings clearly.

Publishing and Presenting
Type out a new copy of your writing, and review it carefully. Check to be sure that you have corrected all errors in spelling, grammar, and punctuation. Also, check to see that your paragraphs are indented and that you've correctly cited quotations or other source information.

When you are satisfied that your essay is the best it can be, hand it in. Keep a copy for your portfolio.

**Grammar
and Style Tip**

Choose formal words and phrases to create an academic tone in your writing.

**Customize for
*Less Advanced Students***

Remind students that open-book tests do not mean they don't have to prepare. Before the test day, they should become familiar with the books they are permitted to use. This way, they won't have to waste time searching for relevant quotations and examples.

**Customize for
*More Advanced Students***

Tell students that developing techniques for taking open-book, take-home essays will be especially useful for preparing for college-level examinations. Explain that Advanced Placement examinations in the humanities commonly provide students with passages of text to use in constructing an essay.

Step-by-Step Teaching Guide

Recognizing the Varieties of Media

1. Read and discuss the Focus on Film, Dance Connection, and Art Connection sections. Have students summarize what they've learned about the Ch'ing Dynasty and its last emperor, Henry P'u-i. Then, have them make a list of five things they'd like to learn about this subject.

2. Have interested students watch *The Last Emperor* and share what they've learned with the class.

3. Have students do research to determine the role of the emperor. Does he really rule, or is his power symbolic? How can a three-year-old be an emperor?

4. Students should use this information to begin their discussion of the role of an American president. What are some important characteristics of a presidential candidate? Have students share their ideas.

Viewing and Representing

Activity Allow students the opportunity to share their lists of requirements needed to run for and be elected president. You may wish to encourage them to present their laws as a poster or to create a parchment-like document resembling the Constitution.

Spotlight on the Humanities

Recognizing the Varieties of Media

Focus on Film: *The Last Emperor*

Although the Ch'ing Dynasty may seem to you like the subject for a perfect essay-test question, such subjects may also be used as a springboard for creative work. Film director Bernardo Bertolucci released his cinematic masterpiece *The Last Emperor* in 1987. The film tells the true story of China's last emperor, Henry P'u-i (1906–1967) of the Ch'ing Dynasty, who ascended to the throne at age three. Although the young emperor was forced to renounce his throne in 1912 at five years of age, he continued to live within the walls of the Forbidden City in Peking for many years.

Dance Connection Early in the Ch'ing Dynasty, a team of dancers from the province of Fuzhou was invited to perform the Dragon Dance for the emperor in Peking. After being praised by the Ch'ing emperor for their work, they became famous throughout the country. The Dragon Dance continued to be an integral part of Chinese culture for hundreds of years. The colors of the dancing dragon are symbolic, with green suggesting great harvests, red representing excitement, and yellow symbolizing the empire. A dancing dragon is divided into nine sections and is approximately 112 feet long.

Art Connection The Ch'ing Dynasty to which the Last Emperor belonged cultivated Chinese art and culture. Artists often performed research by comparing the etchings on stone tablets and bronze vessels with the writings of ancient texts. The inscriptions helped inspire a new form of calligraphy, called *k'ao-cheng-hsueh*, which was highly defined and detailed. It allowed painters to experiment more intently with brushwork.

Assessment Writing Activity: Election Laws

Imagine the citizens of this country electing a three-year-old to be president! Fortunately, election laws in the United States specify an age requirement, but in monarchies, this is not the case. Think about the requirements you think are necessary to be president. Then, write a set of laws regarding presidential elections and the requirements needed to run for and be elected president.

The Emperor Ch'ien Lung (1736–1795) as a Young Man, Ch'ing Dynasty, Metropolitan Museum of Art

▲ **Critical Viewing** Emperor Chien Lung of the Ch'ing Dynasty is featured in this painting. What can you tell about Chinese ideas of art and beauty by looking at this painting? **[Analyze]**

Critical Viewing

Analyze The painting displays almost perfect symmetry. It creates a sense of stillness and balance.

Media and Technology Skills

► *Lesson Objectives*

1. To learn strategies for taking computerized tests
2. To compare computerized tests with print tests and to become familiar and comfortable with elements of both
3. To use technology for aspects of creating texts

Taking Computerized Tests

Activity: Share Test-Taking Strategies

Many tests today are conducted using computers. In some cases, you might be given a choice of taking a print test or a computerized test; in others, only the computerized version is available. Expand your test-taking strategies to include methods and approaches for taking these tests.

Think About It Review your own experiences with computerized tests or tutorials. Think about what features helped ensure your success. List three points you would like to share during a team discussion.

Discuss It Share your ideas about computerized tests with a group of peers. In addition to talking about ideas, discuss these strategies:

- **Practice.** Take a practice test or tutorial, if available. Doing so will help you to become familiar and comfortable with the test-taking process itself.

- **Read instructions and tips carefully.** Take time to read the test rules and any suggestions provided. Also familiarize yourself with the keyboard commands you may need to use.

- **Use a pen and notepad.** You may want to jot down notes, even though they will not be recorded as part of the test.

- **Ask questions.** If you are unclear about how to finish the test, ask your teacher or media center worker for assistance.

- **Print out results.** After taking a test, print out the results so that you can review them later.

- **Prepare.** You still need to know the content before you take a computerized test, so allow yourself sufficient study time to ensure that you will be ready.

Compare It Identify how computerized tests differ from print tests. During your discussion, compare related strategies for each type of test. For example, you can preview a printed test quickly by flipping through the pages to see how long it will be. Many computerized tests offer you the same ability by letting you scroll or click through the test items.

List It Summarize your discussion by making a list of your most effective test-taking strategies. Share the list with your class in a presentation. Include examples that demonstrate how each strategy helps you to succeed.

Working at the Computer

Sitting at a computer terminal for more than thirty minutes can make you feel stiff. Discomfort can distract you and prevent you from doing your best work. Follow these strategies any time you are working at the computer:

- Take time to stretch your hands and fingers every fifteen minutes.
- Relax your fingers as you take the test. Try not to clench or tense your muscles.
- Stretch your arms, legs, and fingers before the test begins. Stand up and stretch briefly every half hour.

Media and Technology Skills • **319**

Step-by-Step Teaching Guide

Taking Computerized Tests

1. Ask students whether they have taken tests on a computer. If so, have them describe the experience.

2. On the board, draw a two-column chart, labeling one column "Similarities" and the other "Differences." Have students list the ways in which taking a computerized test is similar to and different from taking a print test. Ask students which method they prefer, and why.

3. Have students write down three effective strategies to apply when taking a computerized test. Have them share their answers one at a time, trying not to duplicate anything already mentioned.

4. Students may use this information for the List It activity. Allow them to work in small groups to come up with examples for each strategy.

Integrating Test-Taking Skills

Encourage students to take practice tests on the computer before taking actual computerized tests. This will help them get comfortable with basic test-taking procedures. Many test preparation books come with CD-ROMs that contain sample tests. These can usually be found in libraries and bookstores.

Step-by-Step Teaching Guide

Analyzing Errors in Writing

Teaching Resources: Standardized Test Preparation Workbook, pp. 27–28

1. Read and discuss the list of suggestions for recognizing errors in spelling, punctuation, and capitalization. Can students think of any other helpful hints to add to the list? (Example: Be aware of the use of punctuation in conjunction with quotation marks.)

2. Explain to students that, on the type of test question explored here, they will be required to identify errors, but not to correct them. If they think something looks wrong, then it probably is. They don't have to explain exactly what is wrong, and why.

3. Have students complete the practice items on page 320. When they finish, review their answers and address any questions they might have.

4. For each question, make sure students can correct the error. Even though they don't need this skill for this type of test, they will encounter tests and essays in which making corrections is required.

Standardized Test Preparation Workshop

Analyzing Errors in Writing

When answering essay-test questions or other forms of assessment, pay close attention to the grammar, usage, and mechanics of your responses. Standardized tests frequently measure your ability to recognize errors in your writing. Following are some methods that will help you address some problems in spelling, punctuation, and capitalization:

- Reread sentences to check punctuation.

- When writing on a computer, use the spell-check feature.

- When a dictionary is available, look up any words that might be misspelled.

- Check for homophones—words that sound like the word you need to use but are spelled differently.

The following sample test items will give you practice with errors in writing.

Test Tip

Look over each sentence carefully. If something looks strange to you when you first glance at the sentence, chances are good that it is incorrect in some form.

Sample Test Items	Answers and Explanations

Directions: Read the following passages, and decide which type of errors, if any, appear in the underlined sections. Mark the letters for your answer.
 	
We had to go to the grocery store. <u>Mom</u>
(1)
<u>wanted us to pick up tomatoes lettuce and</u>
 	
<u>salsa for the burritos.</u>
 	
1 A Spelling error
  B Capitalization error
  C Punctuation error
  D No error
	The correct answer is C. A comma is needed after both *tomatoes* and *lettuce* in order to punctuate the series correctly.

The burritos were done and ready to eat. <u>All</u>
(2)
<u>they needed now was a dab of sour creme.</u>
 	
2 F Spelling error
  G Capitalization error
  H Punctuation error
  J No error
	The correct answer is F. The word *cream* is spelled incorrectly in the passage.

320 • Writing for Assessment

✎ TEST-TAKING TIP

Students might find it helpful to jot down test sentences in their correct form. This might make it easier for them to determine exactly where the error is located, and what type of error it is.

Students might also find it helpful to read the sentences aloud to themselves. Often, the presence of an error will cause a reader to stumble slightly. Encourage them to pay attention to specific parts of the passage that cause them trouble.

▶ **Practice 1** **Directions:** Read the following passages, and decide which type of error, if any, appears in the underlined sections. Mark the letters for your answer.

It was an easy two-pointer. <u>"Give me the (1) ball!" screamed Mark again, I'm open!"</u>

<u>But they continued to ignore him.</u> Here he (2) was, three feet away from the basket with no one guarding him, and his teammates acted as though he didn't exist.

<u>Mark, insensed, couldn't figure it out.</u> (3) What had he done this time to deserve such treatment?

During the next time out, the coach, (4) <u>Mr. anderson, called them all over.</u> "Okay, gentlemen, would someone like to explain to me what is going on here?"

<u>His question was met with dead silence</u> (5) The players looked down at the floor.

<u>"I'm going to get to the bottom of this,</u> (6) <u>weather you like it or not.</u> After all, you are grown men, not little boys, although you can't tell from the way you are behaving!"

1 A Spelling error
 B Capitalization error
 C Punctuation error
 D No error

2 F Spelling error
 G Capitalization error
 H Punctuation error
 J No error

3 A Spelling error
 B Capitalization error
 C Punctuation error
 D No error

4 F Spelling error
 G Capitalization error
 H Punctuation error
 J No error

5 A Spelling error
 B Capitalization error
 C Punctuation error
 D No error

6 F Spelling error
 G Capitalization error
 H Punctuation error
 J No error

Customize for
ESL Students

Encourage students to keep a list of the words that are misspelled on standardized tests, and to add these words to their vocabulary notebooks. Remind them to study these lists often so they become familiar with common spelling patterns. This will make it easier for them to spot spelling errors on standardized tests.

Customize for
More Advanced Students

Have students write two paragraphs that continue the story about Mark and his basketball team. In it, they should place five spelling, punctuation, or capitalization errors. Have students exchange papers and find the errors in one another's papers. In addition, have them compare and contrast their versions of the story.

In-Depth Lesson Plan

	LESSON FOCUS	PRINT AND MEDIA RESOURCES
DAY 1	**Introduction to Workplace Writing; Business Letter** Students learn about the purpose, characteristics, and kinds of workplace writing; students learn to compose a business letter. (pp. 322–325/H204–207)	*Writers at Work* DVD, Practical and Technical Writing **Teaching Resources** *Writing Support Transparencies,* 15-A *Writing and Grammar* Interactive Text, Ch. 15, Introduction through Section 15.1
DAY 2	**Meeting Minutes** Students learn how to structure and write meeting minutes. (pp. 326–327/H208–209)	**Teaching Resources** *Writing Support Transparencies,* 15-B *Writing and Grammar* Interactive Text, Section 15.2
DAY 3	**Forms and Applications** Students learn to carefully read and complete business forms. Students review the concepts presented in the chapter. (pp. 328–329/H210–211)	**Teaching Resources** *Writing Support Transparencies,* 15-C–D; *Writing Support Activity Book,* 15-1–2; *Writing Assessment and Portfolio Management; Formal Assessment,* Ch. 15 *Writing and Grammar* Interactive Text, Section 15.3

Accelerated Lesson Plan

	LESSON FOCUS	PRINT AND MEDIA RESOURCES
DAY 1	**Introduction to Workplace Writing; Business Letter** Students learn about the purpose, characteristics, and kinds of workplace writing; students learn to compose a business letter. (pp. 322–325/H204–207)	*Writers at Work* DVD, Practical and Technical Writing **Teaching Resources** *Writing Support Transparencies,* 15-A *Writing and Grammar* Interactive Text, Ch. 15, Introduction through Section 15.1
DAY 2	**Meeting Minutes; Forms and Applications** Students learn to structure and write meeting minutes and carefully complete business forms. (pp. 326–329/H208–211)	**Teaching Resources** *Writing Support Transparencies,* 15-B–D; *Writing Support Activity Book,* 15-1–2; *Writing Assessment and Portfolio Management; Formal Assessment,* Ch. 15 *Writing and Grammar* Interactive Text, Sections 15.2–3

Options for Adapting Lesson Plans

HOMEWORK

Have students complete any stage of the lesson for homework.

FEATURES

Extend coverage with Connected Assignment (p. 330), Spotlight on the Humanities (p. 332), Media and Technology Skills (p. 333), and the Standardized Test Preparation Workshop (p. 334).

TECHNOLOGY

Students can complete any stage of the lesson on the computer, using *Writing and Grammar* Interactive Text or a word-processing program. Have them print out their completed work.

Writing and Grammar Handbook Alignment

Page numbers in Step-by-Step Teaching Guides in this Teacher's Edition refer to pages from the full student text. Handbook page references, indicated with this icon ⊞, are provided in Time and Resource Manager boxes and at the bottom of each Teacher's Edition page.

INTEGRATED SKILLS COVERAGE

Vocabulary Skills
ATE p. 324

Workplace Skills
Meeting Minutes and Agendas, ATE p. 326
Job Applications, ATE p. 329

Viewing and Representing
Critical Viewing, SE pp. 322, 330, 332/⊞204
Understanding Connections Between Art Forms, SE p. 332
Designing a Fax Form, ATE p. 328

Technology Skills
Utilizing Business Technology, SE p. 333
ATE p. 331

Speaking and Listening Skills
ATE p. 331

Real-World Connection
ATE p. 326

ASSESSMENT SUPPORT

Standardized Test Preparation Workshop SE p. 334; ATE p. 324
Standardized Test Preparation Workbook, pp. 29–30
Formal Assessment, Ch. 15

MEETING INDIVIDUAL NEEDS

More Advanced Students ATE pp. 323, 335
Less Advanced Students ATE p. 333. See also Ongoing Assessments ATE pp. 325, 327, 329.
ESL Students ATE pp. 325, 327

BLOCK SCHEDULING

Pacing Suggestions
For 90-minute Blocks
• Have students select a type of workplace writing to work on and complete the Prewriting and Drafting stages in a single period.
• Focus one class period on revising, editing, and proofreading a piece of workplace writing and preparing it for presentation. Allow at least 30 minutes for peer revision.

Resources for Varying Instruction
• *Writing and Grammar* Interactive Text A 90-minute block provides an ideal opportunity for students to work on the computer.
• *Writers at Work* DVD Show the Practical and Technical Writing segment in class.

Professional Development Support
• *How to Manage Instruction in the Block* This teaching resource provides management and activity suggestions.

MEDIA AND TECHNOLOGY

For the Student
• *Writing and Grammar* Interactive Text, Ch. 15

For the Teacher
• *Writers at Work* DVD, Practical and Technical Writing
• **TeacherEXPRESS** CD-ROM

WRITING AND GRAMMAR ON-LINE

Interactive Text (On-line or on CD-ROM)
• Easily navigable instruction with interactive Revision Checkers
• Full use of e-rater™, the essay-scoring system (on-line only)

Companion Web Site PHSchool.com
• Scoring rubrics with models (use Web Code eek-1001)

See the Go On-line! feature, SE p. iii.

Lesson Objectives

1. To write in various forms with particular emphasis on workplace writing, such as business letters, meeting minutes, and various business forms

2. To write in a voice and style appropriate to audience and purpose

3. To use prewriting strategies to generate ideas, develop voice, and plan

4. To compile ideas and representations into reports and summaries

5. To organize ideas in writing to ensure coherence, logical progression, and support

6. To develop and revise drafts in terms of structure, paragraphs, sentences, and word choice

7. To edit and proofread to ensure standard English usage and grammar

8. To evaluate writing for both mechanics and content

9. To refine selected work for publication

Critical Viewing

Analyze Students should note that every person in the photograph is working in some way with a written document. These documents might be job applications, interoffice memos, publicity letters, employee announcements, company newsletters, or business reports.

Chapter 15 Workplace Writing

▲ Critical Viewing
What clues in this photograph indicate that writing is an important workplace skill? **[Analyze]**

Workplace Writing in Everyday Life

When you complete a deposit slip at the bank or write a letter proposing your school as a site for a county competition, you are using workplace writing skills. Workplace writing helps people communicate with their classmates, co-workers, customers, or club members. It also carries messages from business to business and government to government. Effective workplace writing can inform consumers about their purchases, advise employees of changes in company policy, move time-linked information quickly, and even communicate important messages from one world leader to another.

322 • Workplace Writing

⏱ TIME AND RESOURCE MANAGER

Resources
Print: *Writing Support Transparencies*, 15-A
Technology: *Writers at Work* DVD,
Practical and Technical Writing; *Writing and Grammar* Interactive Text, Ch. 15

Using the Full Student Edition	Using the Handbook 🄷
• Cover pp. 322–323 in class; discuss the types of workplace writing. • Read and identify in class the elements of the business letter on p. 324. • Review the Topic Bank on p. 325 and make sure each student has a topic. • Review the steps in the writing process.	• Cover pp. 204–205 in class; discuss the types of workplace writing. • Read and identify in class the elements of the business letter on p. 206. • Review the Topic Bank on p. 207 and make sure each student has a topic. • Review the steps in the writing process.

What Is Workplace Writing?

Workplace writing includes many different written products, all of which are fact-based and geared to communicate specific information in recognizable formats. Most pieces of workplace writing are informative or persuasive in nature. The ways we publish workplace writing are changing rapidly and now include the postal service, messengers, e-mail, interoffice memos, electronic bulletin boards, and more. Effective workplace writing

- gets a message across as clearly, directly, and briefly as possible within the chosen format.
- anticipates and answers any questions the readers might have.
- addresses manageable topics and stays focused on those topics.
- is neatly formatted and effectively organized.
- contains accurate information.

Types of Workplace Writing

There are several basic forms of workplace writing that you may encounter over the next few years. Others you'll get to know when you enter the work force full time. Each type of workplace writing has its own purpose and audience:

- **Business letters** are written to communicate information on business topics of interest to the writer and recipients.
- **Meeting minutes** provide a written record of the issues, facts, and opinions addressed at a meeting for the benefit of those present and other interested parties.
- **Forms and applications** must be completed in many different situations in order to provide specific factual information requested by a business or corporation.

PREVIEW
Chapter Contents

In this chapter, you will become familiar with several examples of workplace writing, including a business letter, minutes of a meeting, and forms and applications. Writing techniques accompany the examples to guide you as you practice workplace writing.

Writers in ACTION

As you move into adult life and use workplace writing more and more frequently, remember these words spoken long ago by British author and dictionary writer Samuel Johnson:

"Knowledge is of two kinds. We know a subject ourselves, or we know where we can find information upon it."

There are many rules and conventions governing workplace writing. When you don't understand them or find them unfamiliar, ask!

Interest GRABBER Divide the class into small groups. Have students brainstorm for every kinds of workplace writing they can think of in three minutes. Have each group share their ideas. How many of the examples are forms with which students have had personal experience?

Activate Prior Knowledge

Ask students to recall the last thing they wrote outside of school. Remind them that notes, letters, invitations, and e-mails are all writing. How might their example be compared to writing in a business environment? (Examples: a "For Sale" sign compares to an advertisement; a team note to an interoffice memo.)

More About the Writer

Samuel Johnson (1709–1784) spent his childhood in poverty. However, as a bookseller's son he was surrounded by literature. He became a teacher and eventually one of the most important English literary figures of the eighteenth century. He is perhaps most famous for his *A Dictionary of the English Language*, a colossal achievement known for its thorough and often amusing definitions.

Customize for
More Advanced Students

Have each student write an occupation on a note card. Collect the cards, mix them up, and redistribute them. Ask each student to note all the types of workplace writing that might apply to that occupation. (Example: doctor—research papers, medical records, prescription forms, memos, grant applications.)

Business Letter

Teaching Resources: Writing Support Transparencies, 15-A

1. Tell students that workplace writing has a specific audience and purpose, and these must be kept in mind.

2. Explain that it is wise to always use a formal writing style.

3. Display Transparency 15-A and review with students each part of the letter. Ask which elements are similar to other types of letters they've written, and which are different.

4. Point out that, in the salutation, the colon is used in a formal letter. In a letter to a friend, a comma is appropriate.

5. Ask students to describe the style and language used by Sam in his letter. (Students may cite the formal but friendly language, polite yet confident tone, clear focus and purpose, correct use of grammar, and precise use of words.)

Integrating Vocabulary Skills

Tone Explain that using appropriate words creates the desired tone in a letter. Have the class identify the positive adjectives, nouns, and verbs that help give Sam's letter its enthusiastic tone, and list them on the board. (Students may cite *interested, great time, eager, hope, love,* and *appreciate.*)

15.1 Business Letter

What Is a Business Letter?

Business letters address every type of business issue in all fields and professions, from a letter of complaint to a letter congratulating a team of employees for a job well done. An effective business letter

- includes six parts: the heading, the inside address, the salutation, the body, the closing, and the signature.

- follows one of several acceptable forms: Each part of the letter begins at the left margin when you use a *block format*. In a *modified block format*, the heading, the closing, and the signature are indented to the center of the page.

- contains formal, polite language, regardless of its content.

*In the **heading,** include your own address and the date on which the letter is sent. Including a phone number or e-mail address is optional.*

Model Business Letter

In this business letter, Sam Kendra inquires about counselor jobs at a local camp.

*In the **inside address,** include the name and title of the addressee, as well as the company or organization name.*

*In the **salutation,** use the addressee's work title. If you do not have the name of a specific person within the company, use "To whom it may concern:"*

*In the **body** of the letter, state your purpose and include important details.*

*Depending on whom you are addressing and your purpose, decide on an appropriate **closing.** Options include "Sincerely," "Respectfully," "Regards," and "With regret."*

3599 Parkview Drive
Marietta, GA 30060
(001) 376-5983

March 14, 20–

Jackson Ramirez, Director
Marietta Department of Parks and Recreation
800 Turner Road
Marietta, GA 30066

Dear Mr. Ramirez:

I am interested in working as a counselor in your summer camp program. I attended the camp myself as a young child and had a great time. My experiences at the camp taught me important lessons that I'd like to help other youngsters learn.

Please send me some information about becoming a Parks and Recreation counselor. What are the dates and hours that the camp will run? How many counselors will you be hiring, and when do you plan to begin the process?

I'm eager to work as a counselor and hope you will consider me for the job. Although I've never been a counselor, I have three younger brothers and sisters, so I'm used to organizing activities for young children. I love sports and nature.

I appreciate the time you will take to answer my questions and look forward to meeting you soon.

Sincerely,

Sam Kendra

Sam Kendra

324 • Workplace Writing

Standardized test questions may require students to analyze the persuasive techniques of media messages.

Which of the answers below best describes the statement?

All teenagers want to drive before they have reached the legal driving age.

This statement is an example of

A loaded language

B circular reasoning

C overgeneralization

D either-or argument

Students should recognize that the correct answer is **C**. The statement makes a generalization about all teenagers based on what might be true about only some of them.

TOPIC BANK

To write a business letter that communicates successfully, choose a situation with which you are familiar. If you're having trouble coming up with your own topic, consider these possibilities:

1. **Letter About a Pet** Suppose you've just gotten a pet—an animal that you never had before. Write a letter to a local pet store, pet owners' association, or veterinarian asking for information about how to care for your pet.

2. **Letter About Computers** Many schools are changing their technology systems to include more or different kinds of computers. To help them make successful choices, they may ask for student input. Write a letter to your local school board in which you identify ways that you use computers. Make at least one suggestion about the features school computers should have.

Prewriting Identify to whom you will be writing, and jot down his or her address, company name, business title, and business address. Then, take a few moments to think about why you are writing—what you hope to achieve by writing the letter. Also, take notes on the questions you have and how you would like the recipient of the letter to respond.

Drafting As you draft, follow the format—block or modified block—that you have chosen. Provide necessary details that clearly explain why you are writing. Remember to keep a positive and appreciative tone in letters that request something, but always remain polite even in letters of complaint.

Revising Carefully review your letter. Check to be sure that you clearly state your purpose in the opening lines. The paragraphs that follow should contain only necessary information; delete details that stray from your main point. Also, review your language to be sure that you have chosen formal language.

Editing and Proofreading Begin by checking your letter's format for correctness and consistency. Then, check to be sure that you have spelled names, addresses, titles, and phone numbers correctly.

Publishing Write, type, or word-process your letter on 8 1/2 x 11 inch paper. Keep the appearance of your letter conservative to focus the reader's attention on the content. Always sign a business letter to show that you stand behind its words. Mail your neatly folded letter in a properly addressed and stamped matching envelope.

Business Letter • 325

Choosing a Topic

1. Have students brainstorm for ideas about the sort of people to whom they might write business letters. Suggest that they think about local service providers, magazines and newspapers, and stores or other businesses with which they interact.

2. Discuss the reasons people write business letters (to complain, ask questions, get information, express opinions, and deliver information or tell others what needs to be done).

3. Suggest that students choose an audience for their letters from the list they made in step 1 above, and a purpose from the list they made in step 2. Or, they can choose one of the ideas from the Topic Bank.

Customize for
ESL Students

Suggest that students choose a topic with which they are very familiar, so that their focus is on language and style, not on worrying about details. They might consider a letter to the maker of a daily-use item or a food product, a company for which a friend or parent works, or an employer for whom they would like to work.

Prewriting, Drafting, Revising

1. Suggest that students take a few minutes to think about how they will address their audience and accomplish their purpose.

2. Recommend that students find the appropriate person to address a letter to by using the library, the Internet, or a company's customer service department.

3. Encourage students to decide on a format before drafting. Suggest that, as they draft, they focus on language and tone.

4. As students revise, suggest that they give each paragraph a specific focus. They can look again at the model on page 324 for well-focused paragraphs.

☑ ONGOING ASSESSMENT: Monitor and Reinforce

If students have difficulty completing any of the writing assignments in this chapter, try one of the following options.

Option 1 Suggest that students imitate the models fairly closely, changing only the names of the recipients, the name of the company, and perhaps one other element in each piece.	**Option 2** Suggest that students freewrite about a product they have used that they either loved or disliked. Then, have them use the freewriting to create a letter to the manufacturer.

Meeting Minutes

Teaching Resources: Writing Support Transparencies, 15-B

1. Ask whether any students have ever taken meeting minutes or attended a meeting at which someone else took minutes. Have them describe the minutes and explain why they were needed.

2. Ask students for examples of situations or organizations in which meeting minutes are taken (businesses, clubs, committees).

3. Display Transparency 15-B and point out the elements of standard minutes format and content.

4. Remind students that the language in meeting minutes is formal and impersonal. The writer's job is to record actions, decisions, and people's comments without giving an opinion.

Real-World Connection

Meeting minutes are vital business documents. The minutes of business meetings, budget meetings, and corporate shareholder meetings, for example, allow individuals who are unable to attend to know what transpired. Hence, those individuals can have access to information that might affect them or their jobs.

Integrating Workplace Skills

Meeting Minutes and Agendas
Many organizations distribute copies of their previous meeting minutes prior to the next meeting. Some distribute meeting agendas. This gives attendees a sense of what the meeting will cover and how it will relate to previous events and meetings.

15.2 Meeting Minutes

What Are Meeting Minutes?

Meeting minutes are a written record of a meeting—of the issues discussed, the opinions expressed, and any votes taken concerning group actions. Effective meeting minutes

* note the meeting's attendees, absentees, and date and time of the meeting.
* list and summarize issues discussed at the meeting and note action items—steps to take to resolve issues.
* contain factual information only.

Model Meeting Minutes

Tracy Mueller published the following minutes of a meeting that she attended for her school newspaper.

> Meetings usually begin with ongoing, or "old" business such as reviewing the minutes of the previous meeting.

> Title each topic, briefly summarize the discussion and opinions presented, and then describe the action items and tell who is assigned to each.

> Use features such as bulleted lists, boldface, and underlining to help readers quickly find the information they need.

> Sign meeting minutes so that group members know whom to contact to have information clarified or corrected.

> In the heading, identify the group members, the reason for the meeting, and the date of the meeting.

Monthly Editorial Meeting: November 8, 20--

Attended: Tuong Tran, John Applebee, Doreen Rigoletti, T. J. Bairos, Paul Nathan, Suzanne Wood, Tracy Mueller
Absent: Jennie Wu

Old Business
* October Meeting Minutes: Minutes of last month's meeting were read. Tuong corrected the chart of closing dates, noting that February's closing date is unusual because of President's Day.

* New Camera Fund: We need $50 more to buy a camera. T. J. suggested that we ask the school board to fund the remaining money. A motion was made and unanimously approved to make the request at the December board meeting. John will make the presentation.

Action Item: Prepare written presentation to board. (Paul and Doreen) Present proposal to board. (John)

New Business
* December Issue: Staff members discussed articles planned for December in order to choose a lead story. Tracy suggested the article on vacation activities for the lead. Tuong felt we should lead with the article on ways to help others during the holidays. Everyone agreed, including Tracy, that this was the best lead.

Action Item: Write and lay out lead story. (Doreen)

Next Meeting: December 2, 20-- (Remember that this meeting will be before school, due to after-school rehearsals for holiday events.)

Respectfully submitted,
Tracy Mueller

326 • Workplace Writing

⏲ TIME AND RESOURCE MANAGER

Resources
Print: *Writing Support Transparencies,* 15–B
Technology: *Writing and Grammar,* Interactive Text, Section 15.2

Using the Full Student Edition	Using the Handbook Ⓗ
• Review pp. 326–327 in class. • Ask students to compare and contrast meeting minutes with business letters. • Have students select a topic for writing meeting minutes. • Review the steps in the writing process and have students apply each step while writing their meeting minutes.	• Review pp. 208–209 in class. • Ask students to compare and contrast meeting minutes with business letters. • Have students select a topic for writing meeting minutes. • Review the steps in the writing process and have students apply each step while writing their meeting minutes.

TOPIC BANK

When taking minutes of a meeting, come prepared with notepaper, some pens, and your attention. If you'd like to practice writing meeting notes and need some help getting started, consider these possibilities:

1. **Minutes of the Club Meeting** People form clubs to enjoy common interests, such as gardening or skiing. Attend the meeting of a club you belong to, or ask permission to visit the meeting of one you don't belong to. Record and write up minutes of the meeting.

2. **Minutes of a Family or Neighborhood Meeting** Discussions by family members and neighbors about how to handle common issues such as garbage collection or late-night noise are meetings, even if they are not formally labeled this way. Get permission to record meeting minutes at one of these gatherings.

Prewriting Gather and scan handouts offered at the meeting. Then, write down the names of people present. Use short sentences or phrases to jot down the issues addressed and the views expressed. List actions agreed to, and note the people to whom they are assigned. Organize your notes in a consistent way—using people's initials to indicate various speakers, for example. Keep any handouts after the meeting for later reference.

Drafting Prepare the minutes as soon as you can after the meeting. That way, your memory will be fresh. If there was a meeting agenda, follow its organization; if not, organize your notes chronologically. As you draft, use headings, boldface, or other type features to make your organization clear.

Revising First, reread your original notes against your draft to be sure that you have left nothing out. Then, review your draft for clarity. Delete cluttering details and revise emotionally biased words to reflect a neutral tone. Add or change organizational features, such as numbered lists and bulleting, to help readers locate information easily.

Editing and Proofreading Review the minutes, and correct any spelling and grammar errors you have made. If there are any inconsistencies in your formatting, correct them now.

Publishing Print out and distribute your meeting minutes before your group has its next meeting. If group members are on-line, you may prefer to send the meeting notes to group members via e-mail.

Meeting Minutes • **327**

Choosing a Topic

1. Ask students to list all of the clubs, organizations, teams, and groups they belong to that hold meetings. Ask for suggestions and write them on the board (this may help trigger ideas for other students).

2. Once students have chosen their topics, ask them to note the audience and purpose for the meeting.

3. It is likely that some students will not have a meeting to attend. In this case, you might invite them to a meeting you know about, such as a student government meeting or an open forum available at your school. Perhaps one of the school clubs would be willing to have visitors for this assignment.

4. Remind students to use each step in the writing process when writing their meeting minutes.

Customize for
ESL Students

Students may find it challenging to pick out the important statements in spoken conversation. Suggest they try tape-recording a meeting, while taking notes at the same time. Then, they can review the tape, alone or in a group, to add any points they missed to their notes or to stop and look up words.

✓ **ONGOING ASSESSMENT: Monitor and Reinforce**

If a number of students have difficulty selecting a topic and completing the assignment, try one of the following options.

Option 1 As a class, select several places where meeting minutes might be taken. Arrange students into small groups, and have them attend the meetings together. In cases where note-taking skills are limited, allow students to combine notes to create one set of meeting minutes.	**Option 2** Have the entire class attend and take meeting minutes at the same event. This will enable you to focus more on issues of drafting, formatting, and revising.

 TIME SAVERS!

 Writing Support Transparencies
Use the transparencies for Chapter 15 to facilitate teaching of various forms of workplace writing.

Fax Cover Sheet

Teaching Resources: Writing Support Transparencies, 15-C; Writing Support Activity Book, 15-1

1. Ask how many students have sent or received a fax. What did they think were the advantages (speed) and disadvantages (image quality) of faxing.

2. As students review the bulleted points, ask them to explain why each point is important. (Missing information delays the process and makes a bad impression. Inaccurate information may cause problems. Blue or black ink is easier for people to read; a fax machine might not pick up and transmit lighter inks or pencil.)

3. Display Transparency 15-C and review each point on the fax cover sheet.

4. Explain that a fax needs a cover sheet because, unlike e-mail messages, most faxes do not identify the sender, and there is no "reply" button. If someone doesn't know who sent a fax, or doesn't know the fax number of the sender, it may be impossible to respond.

5. Remind students to consider purpose and audience when filling out a fax cover sheet. This can affect language and style.

Integrating Viewing and Representing Skills

Have students glance at the fax model for only a few seconds. Ask what element of the form's appearance stands out most in their minds. Was it "Fax" in bold? The company name aligned with the right margin? In business, forms are designed so that important elements stand out. Encourage students to design their own fax forms so that the important information is easy to see, even at a glance.

15.3 Forms and Applications

What Are Business Forms?

Forms are preprinted documents with spaces for the user to enter specific information. Some contain directions; others assume that users will follow the labels and common conventions. Two common forms in the workplace are *fax cover sheets* and *applications*. An effectively completed form

- is accurately and completely filled out.
- is written in blue or black ink.
- contains only information that is requested on the form.

> Using letterhead or otherwise heading the page with the sender's name immediately tells readers who is sending the fax.

Model Fax Cover Sheet

A fax (short for facsimile) is a document that is electronically transmitted. Cover sheets tell whom the fax is for, whom it is from, and how long it is. The cover sheet should also list a phone number for the transmitter, in case the recipient has difficulty receiving or reading the fax.

> A fax should contain the recipient's full name and title or the name of the company, to ensure that it gets delivered.

> Note the total page count (including the cover sheet) so that recipients can tell whether all the pages have been transmitted.

> Cover sheets are usually completed by hand. Neat handwriting is a must, especially as some clarity can be lost in transmission.

YOUNGS PRINTING
45 Hook Street • Utica, NY 11581
phone 315.555.3166 • fax 315.555.2244 e-mail: young@nynet.com

Fax

FACSIMILE COVER SHEET

DATE: *10/25/20--*

TO: *Marci Conroy — c/o Hale High School*

FAX NUMBER: *315-555-5983*

FAX SOURCE TRANSMISSION NUMBER: *315-555-2244*

FROM: *Peter Dabbs*

TOTAL NUMBER OF PAGES (including this cover sheet): *2*

REMARKS:

We'll be ready to print your newspaper by next Tuesday. I need to know how many copies you want so I can order the necessary paper stock. I've attached prices for different quantities. Call, fax, or e-mail me when you've settled on a number. Talk to you soon.

Thanks! Peter

328 • Workplace Writing

⏱ TIME AND RESOURCE MANAGER

Resources
Print: *Writing Support Transparencies* 15-C–D; *Writing Support Activity Book,* 15-1–2; *Formal Assessment,* Ch. 15
Technology: *Writing Lab* CD-ROM, Practical and Technical Writing; *Writing and Grammar* Interactive Text, Section 15.3

Using the Full Student Edition	Using the Handbook Ⓗ
• Read through pp. 328–329 with the class.	• Read through pp. 210–211 with the class.
• Using the models, point out the elements of a fax cover sheet and an application.	• Using the models, point out the elements of a fax cover sheet and an application.
• Review the writing process and discuss ways of applying each step to forms and applications.	• Review the writing process and discuss ways of applying each step to forms and applications.

Model Application

Many young people work part-time jobs to make money for school expenses or other needs. Often, potential employers will use a standard form like this one to gather basic information about job applicants.

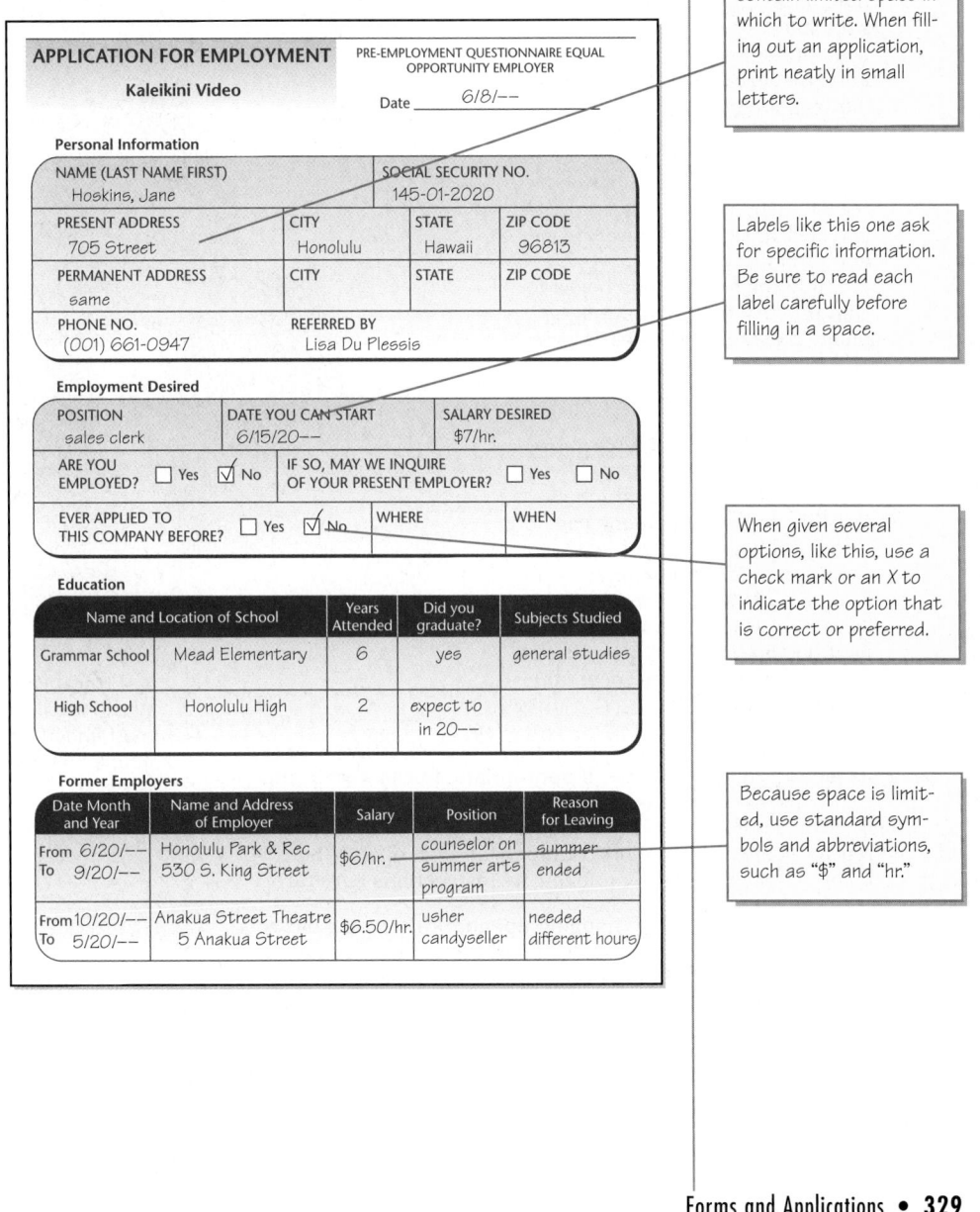

Forms such as this one contain limited space in which to write. When filling out an application, print neatly in small letters.

Labels like this one ask for specific information. Be sure to read each label carefully before filling in a space.

When given several options, like this, use a check mark or an X to indicate the option that is correct or preferred.

Because space is limited, use standard symbols and abbreviations, such as "$" and "hr."

Forms and Applications • **329**

Applications

Teaching Resources: Writing Support Transparencies, 15-D; Writing Support Activity Book, 15-2

1. Display Transparency 15-D and review each section of the application form.

2. Advise students that it is always a good idea to look over a form completely before writing.

3. Explain that it is helpful to read directions and determine not only what information is needed, but how it should appear.

4. Advise students to be aware of where to write the information. Are they supposed to write above or below the line? Are check-off boxes located to the left or right of the answers?

5. Encourage students to find out ahead of time what information is needed. Sometimes, they will need information that they don't always carry with them, such as a birth certificate or passport.

6. For important applications, suggest that students photocopy the form and do a draft. This will allow them to revise and edit without having to hand in a messy form.

7. Encourage students always to proofread applications for accurate and complete answers.

Integrating Workplace Skills

Job Applications How you fill out a job application can be just as important as what you write on it. Remind students that neatness, concise answers, and truthful statements are essential on any application. Remind them that their signature at the bottom asserts that all of their statements are true.

☑ ONGOING ASSESSMENT: Monitor and Reinforce

Some students may have difficulty filling out forms or understanding their importance. Try one of the following options

Option 1 Using form 15-2 in the *Writing Support Activity Book*, go through the form step by step as a class. Have students compare their answers and discuss which ones are best suited to the application's audience.	**Option 2** Bring copies of a sample job application to class, and have students fill them out. Have students exchange applications with partners and discuss the answers that might have a positive or negative effect on an employer.

Lesson Objectives

1. To take and leave thorough and accurate phone messages

2. To focus attention, interpret, respond, and evaluate speaker's message

3. To use informal, standard, and technical language effectively to meet the needs of purpose, audience, occasion, and task

Connected Assignment
Phone Messages

If you're like most people, you hate missing phone calls. In the workplace, phone calls are often a key link between service providers and customers, workers and home offices, laboratories and physicians, and so on. Thus, creating phone messages—whether you compose them as the caller or record them as a message-taker— is a critical skill in the workplace and at home.

Study the suggestions below to gain practice leaving and taking phone messages. Start with leaving phone messages.

▲ **Critical Viewing**
What information is most important in a phone message? **[Assess]**

Leaving Phone Messages

Before the Call As much as possible, focus your phone calls on recognizable goals. If you wish, jot down reminders of the topics you wish to address. Be prepared to leave a message by gathering pertinent documents, such as a disputed bill or other records, near your phoning station.

Leaving the Message Introduce yourself, using your full name and company name, if appropriate. Speak slowly and clearly as you state the reason for your call and how you can be reached. Highlight any unusual contact information by repeating special telephone numbers at least once. When using a voice-mail system, follow its instructions carefully.

Following Up Before hanging up, check that your message has been accurately received. Prompt a voice-mail system to replay your message, or ask your message-taker to read back the message.

Taking Phone Messages

Before the Call Create a space near your telephone for message-taking. Keep paper and writing tools handy, perhaps using preprinted message log forms to save writing time. At home, consider posting a chalkboard or dry-erase board. If you're expecting an important call, create an optimum environment by turning off music or the television.

During the Call Be absolutely certain that you get the facts straight by listening carefully and asking the caller to repeat any confusing information. If the caller's name or company affiliation has an unusual spelling, read it back to verify accuracy. If you're using a preprinted form, check off appropriate boxes to speed your writing. Always read back the message, and ask for any necessary clarification before hanging up.

After the Call Check your message for legibility and, if necessary, rewrite it. (Make sure that you transfer information such as names, addresses, and phone numbers accurately.) Note the time of the call, and sign your name so that the phone-call recipient can ask clarifying questions.

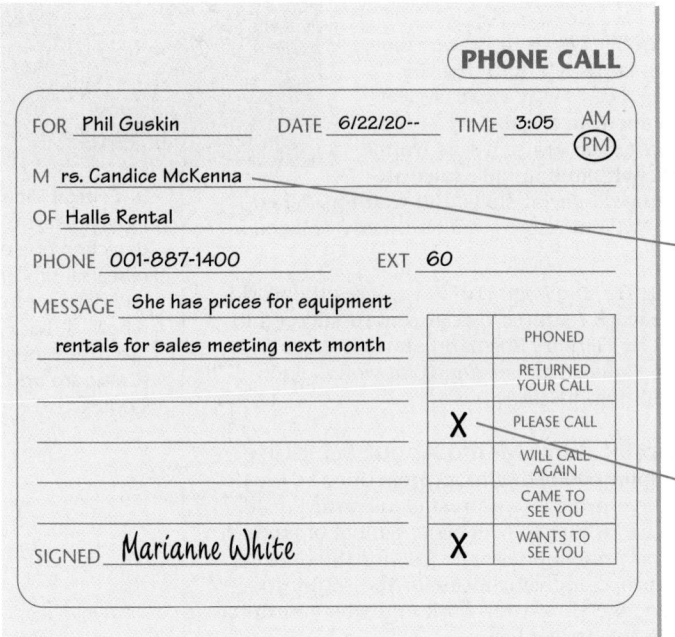

Message-takers should make every effort to be accurate. Here, the caller's name had an unusual spelling requiring careful notation.

When possible, checking off boxes limits the amount of writing necessary. Message-takers should always sign their names so that phone-call recipients can ask clarifying questions about the call.

Integrating Speaking and Listening Skills

Some students might be reluctant to ask someone to repeat confusing information or spell unfamiliar names. Reassure students that this is a completely acceptable practice. Asking a lot of questions is much more acceptable than delivering erroneous information.

Integrating Technology Skills

Encourage students to familiarize themselves with all of the features of their telephone. For example, they should know how to use "hold" and how to transfer calls. This way, they are less likely to cause confusion during important calls.

Understanding Connections Between Art Forms

1. If possible, bring in reproductions of some of Degas's paintings, or assign students to look for reproductions in the library or on the Internet. Discuss some of the repeated elements in his work, focusing on his paintings of dancers.

2. Have interested students conduct research on Degas's life and work. As an alternative, students might research the Impressionist movement or another painter of the period and share their findings with the class.

3. Students who are interested in dance might rent the film *The Turning Point.* Or, they might research the history of ballet and how it spread from France to other countries. Have them share their findings with the class

Viewing and Representing

Activity For the writing application, suggest that students look in the library for books on ballet. The photographs might give them ideas for their sculpture proposals. When they finish, have students display their sketches in the classroom.

Critical Viewing

Compare and Contrast Students might note that the excitement and anxiety in the room might occur at a dance rehearsal at any time or place.

Spotlight on the Humanities

Understanding Connections Between Art Forms

Focus on Art: Edgar Degas

Often, famous artists and sculptors are commissioned to create works of art for companies, collectors, or museums. French artist Edgar Degas (1834–1917) was part of the Impressionist movement of painters, but his emphasis on movement and the human form set him apart from his contemporaries. During the 1870's, one of his favorite themes was the female ballet dancer. Sketching a live ballet dancer as a model in his studio, he then created a series of paintings of ballet dancers onstage, in rehearsal, or offstage awaiting performance. His works, which hang in museums around the world, are favorites of both critics and the general public.

Dance Connection Ballet began in France more than 300 years ago. King Louis XIV founded the first dancing academy in 1661. Many experts view this act as a defining moment in the history of ballet. As ballet developed over the years, it was transformed from a courtly activity into a more intricate form of artistry that required special skills and training. When Edgar Degas painted his ballet dancers, ballet already enjoyed a rich heritage.

Film Connection *The Turning Point* (1977) explores the world of ballet and the intense work required by dancers to succeed in a dance career. Directed by Herbert Ross and starring Anne Bancroft and Shirley MacLaine, *The Turning Point* won Golden Globe Awards for Best Film and Best Director.

Workplace Writing Application: Memo About Sculpture
Suppose you were a sculptor competing in a competition to create a work of art to adorn the entrance to a prestigious dance academy. The winning sculpture is sure to become a symbol of modern dance and will be used on promotional materials for the dance company. Write a letter proposing your ideas for the sculpture, including an introductory sketch of your work and why you think your creation should win the art contest.

Ballet Class, Edgar Degas

▲ **Critical Viewing**
In what ways is this depiction of a dance rehearsal similar to and different from a rehearsal that might take place today? **[Compare and Contrast]**

Media and Technology Skills

Utilizing Business Technology
Activity: Compile a Help Tutorial

When you first start to use a new software program, you might be baffled by its many options and features. Once you are familiar with a program, however, using these functions becomes second nature. Prepare a help tutorial to share your knowledge with other students, highlighting features that you find particularly useful.

Think About It Choose a software program with which you are familiar or one that you would like to learn. Word-processing and page-layout programs are particularly helpful for workplace writing. You might also evaluate graphics utilities or database software.

Review It Use the software's on-screen Help function as well as the manual to learn or review the software's basic features. If you are using word-processing software, look for and practice these features:

- **Cut, copy, and paste:** These editing functions allow you to change written material quickly. Cut and paste allows you to move a selected item. Copy and paste allows you to place an exact copy without removing the original text.

- **Spelling check:** Many programs offer utilities to check the spelling of your text. Review how the tool works, and identify its limitations.

- **Thesaurus:** Use a thesaurus tool to identify alternative words or phrases.

- **Toolbar**: The toolbar feature, like the own shown below, makes the most common functions available at the click of a mouse.

| File   Edit   View   Insert   Format   Font   Tools   Table   Window   Work   Help | 10:34:51 AM |

Teach It After you have learned the basic software functions, brainstorm for a list of hints and suggestions you would like to share with other students. Choose your best tips, and compile them in a Help Tutorial. Organize your ideas by topic so that readers can find the information they need quickly. Publish your tutorial as a pamphlet or brochure for your class or school computer center.

Media and Technology Skills • **333**

Saving and Backing Up Files

Save your work frequently in case of computer or power failures. Some programs allow automatic saving at desired intervals, such as every five or ten minutes. Check the Preferences, Options, or Help menu to see if this function is available.

Always remember to back up your work files carefully. Store backup disks away from heat and magnetic sources.

▶ **Lesson Objectives**

1. To use technology for aspects of creating, revising, editing, and publishing texts
2. To use writing to discover, organize, support, and communicate what is known about a topic
3. To compile written ideas and representations into reports, summaries, or other formats

Step-by-Step Teaching Guide

Utilizing Business Technology

1. Encourage students to begin listing technological terms that they recall learning in recent years, and especially any that are still unfamiliar.

2. Suggest that students consider the projected audience for their glossary, and remind them that people both younger and older than they are likely to share the same lack of familiarity with many technological terms. Urge them to write is such a way that both groups can use their glossaries to build confidence.

3. Have students trade papers with someone who is unfamiliar with the technologies that they are writing about. These students can help them determine which of their glossary definitions need to be clearer.

4. Finally, have students use a word processing program to publish their glossaries.

Customize for
Less Advanced Students

It can be very difficult to write clear explanations of complex computer features. Allow students to focus on two or three features, rather than five to ten. Help them create a list of specific verbs that are commonly used to describe computer functions.

Step-by-Step Teaching Guide

Applying Usage Rules to Writing

Teaching Resources: Standardized Test Preparation Workbook, pp. 29–30

1. Review subject-and-verb agreement with students. Remind them that singular subjects take singular verbs and plural subjects take plural verbs. Compound subjects joined by *and* generally take plural verbs.

2. Review pronoun case with students. Remind them that *who* can be the subject of a verb or a predicate nominative. *Whom* can be a direct object or the object of a preposition.

Standardized Test Preparation Workshop

Applying Usage Rules to Writing

Writing in the workplace should be error-free and should follow the rules of grammar, usage, and mechanics. These workplace criteria are often assessed on standardized tests, which measure your ability to recognize errors in grammar, spelling, or punctuation. Use the following strategies to ensure that you avoid errors in usage:

- Check verbs to make sure that they agree with their subjects.
- Make sure that verb tense is consistent.
- Look for homophones—words that sound alike but are spelled differently.
- Fix double negatives.
- Check pronoun case to make sure that it agrees with its antecedent.

Answer the following sample test item to practice identifying usage problems.

Sample Test Item	Answer and Explanation
Directions: Read this passage, and decide which type of error, if any, appears in the underlined section. Choose the appropriate letter for your answer. The work-study members <u>are forming a com-</u> (1) <u>mitee that will elect leaders</u>.	

1 **A** Spelling error
 	
    B Capitalization error
 	
    C Punctuation error
 	
    D No error
	The correct answer is *A.* The word *committee* is spelled incorrectly.

334 • Workplace Writing

⚓ TEST-TAKING TIP

Encourage students to answer fill-in questions on their own before looking at the answer choices. If necessary, they can write the answer on the blank line in the test booklet. Then, they should check to see whether that answer is one of the choices. If so, it is probably correct.

Have students focus on the sample test item on this page. Explain that spelling errors are often a matter of just one incorrect letter, so they can be easy to miss. Encourage students to reread a sentence carefully before choosing "No error."

> **Practice 1** **Directions:** Read the passage, and choose the word or group of words that belongs in each space. Choose the appropriate letter for your answer.

My job interview for computer inputter went well. After ___(1)___ our common interest in sports, the job interviewer ___(2)___ to ask me questions about my skills. I ___(3)___ well in keyboarding class and was also familiar with many programs. I also told her that I will soon have extra time after school because I ___(4)___ the work study program. I ___(5)___ the job next week!

1 **A** discussed
   B will be discussing
   C discuss
   D discussing

2 **F** begins
   G began
   H was beginning
   J have begun

3 **A** will be doing
   B done
   C will do
   D had done

4 **F** join
   G will be joining
   H is joining
   J have been joining

5 **A** started
   B start
   C have started
   D is starting

> **Practice 2** **Directions:** Read the passage, and decide which type of error, if any, appears in each underlined section. Choose the appropriate letter for your answer.

Amy and Nick were elected Co-Leaders of
(1)
the school Literary Magazine. Working
(2)   (3)
together closely, their coming up with
                        (4)
interesting ways to layout the magazine.

This issue promises to be the best literary
                                    (5)
magazine, the school has ever produced.

1 **A** Spelling error
   B Capitalization error
   C Punctuation error
   D No error

2 **F** Spelling error
   G Capitalization error
   H Punctuation error
   J No error

3 **A** Spelling error
   B Capitalization error
   C Punctuation error
   D No error

4 **F** Spelling error
   G Capitalization error
   H Punctuation error
   J No error

5 **A** Spelling error
   B Capitalization error
   C Punctuation error
   D No error

Answer Key

> **Practice 1**
1. D
2. G
3. D
4. G
5. B

> **Practice 2**
1. B
2. G
3. D
4. F
5. C

Customize for
More Advanced Students

In addition to answering the questions in Practice 2, have students compose a short written explanation for each answer. Then, have them lead a class discussion about the explanations.

Objectives

1. To understand parts of speech and basic sentence patterns and to apply relevant concepts to one's own writing

2. To learn and apply key concepts governing usage of verbs

3. To understand concepts of agreement relating to subjects and verbs and pronouns and antecedents, and to apply this understanding to one's own writing

4. To compose sentences of increasing sophistication and appropriateness

5. To analyze works of literature as models of appropriate and effective English usage

6. To recognize appropriate English usage in one's own reading and writing

7. To use "hands-on" strategies to reinforce understanding of grammar and usage concepts

8. To master the conventions of capitalization, punctuation, and spelling, and to apply them accurately to one's own writing

PART 2

Grammar, Usage, and Mechanics

Delta, 1990, Paul Giovanopoulos, Louis K. Meisel Gallery, New York

Grammar, Usage, and Mechanics • 337

Step-by-Step Teaching Guide

Responding to Fine Art
Delta by **Paul Giovanopoulos**

Use this work of art to start a discussion about the functions of grammar, usage, and mechanics.

1. Have students examine the painting on pages 336–337. You might use the following questions to prompt discussion:

    How many different variations of the same shape can students see? What details make these shapes differ from one another? Which stand out the most? What might each stand for in the artist's mind?

    Are there patterns in the painting, or are the shapes arranged arbitrarily? Do any of the shapes resemble real-world objects, or do you feel they are purely abstract?

2. At first glance, the shapes in the painting seem almost alike, as though each was indeed a *delta* (a letter in the Greek alphabet). Ask students to relate this idea to the structure of English grammar. For example, how do parts of speech, both similar to and different from each other, help a writer make subtle distinctions among thoughts? How can good grammar make ideas more distinct and clear?

About the Artist

Though born in Greece in 1939, Paul Giovanopoulos became a citizen of the United States in 1961. His paintings are frequently, as in *Delta*, made up of repeated images of the same subject, laid out on a grid, each image differing slightly from the next. Rather than being repetitive, however, the effect of the paintings is rhythmic, at once soothing and exciting the eye. Because Giovanopoulos is interested in groups and transformations of all kinds, some of his paintings are group portraits of famous persons both living and dead. *Players*, for example, shows a group of poker players that includes Mahatma Gandhi, George Washington, and Leonardo Da Vinci. Another, *Your Secret Self*, is a scene crowded with human figures who are fitted with frogs' heads, birds' wings, horns, or extra eyes.

213 H • **337**

LESSON FOCUS	PRINT AND MEDIA RESOURCES
DAY 1 — **Nouns** Students learn and apply concepts relating to different types of nouns, such as proper and collective nouns. (pp. 338–343/Ⓗ214–219)	**Writing and Grammar** Interactive Text, Section 16.1; **On-line Exercise Bank,** Section 16.1 **Teaching Resources** *Grammar Exercise Workbook,* pp. 1–4; *Grammar Exercises Answers on Transparencies,* Ch. 16
DAY 2 — **Pronouns** Students learn and apply concepts relating to pronouns and antecedents, as well as types of pronouns, such as relative and indefinite. (pp. 344–351/Ⓗ220–227)	**Writing and Grammar** Interactive Text, Section 16.2; **On-line Exercise Bank,** Section 16.2 **Teaching Resources** *Grammar Exercise Workbook,* pp. 5–12
DAY 3 — **Action Verbs and Linking Verbs** Students learn and apply concepts relating to verbs and do the Hands-on Grammar activity. (pp. 352–359/Ⓗ228–235)	**Writing and Grammar** Interactive Text, Section 16.3; **On-line Exercise Bank,** Section 16.3 **Teaching Resources** *Grammar Exercise Workbook,* pp. 13–18; *Hands-on Grammar Activity Book,* Ch. 16
DAY 4 — **Verb Phrases** Students learn and apply concepts relating to verb phrases and helping verbs. (pp. 360–363/Ⓗ236–239)	**Writing and Grammar** Interactive Text, Section 16.4; **On-line Exercise Bank,** Section 16.4 **Teaching Resources** *Grammar Exercise Workbook,* pp. 19–20
DAY 5 — **Review and Assess** Students review the chapter and demonstrate mastery of concepts. (pp. 364–366)	**Writing and Grammar** Interactive Text, Ch. 16, Chapter Review **Teaching Resources** *Formal Assessment,* Ch. 16

Accelerated Lesson Plan

LESSON FOCUS	PRINT AND MEDIA RESOURCES
DAY 1 — **Nouns and Pronouns** Students learn and apply concepts relating to nouns and pronouns. (pp. 338–351/Ⓗ214–227)	**Writing and Grammar** Interactive Text, Sections 16.1–2; **On-line Exercise Bank,** Sections 16.1–2 **Teaching Resources** *Grammar Exercise Workbook,* pp. 21–26; *Grammar Exercises Answers on Transparencies,* Ch. 16
DAY 2 — **Verbs and Verb Phrases** Students learn and apply concepts relating to verbs, verb phrases, and helping verbs. (pp. 352–363/Ⓗ228–239)	**Writing and Grammar** Interactive Text, Sections 16.3–4; **On-line Exercise Bank,** Sections 16.3–4 **Teaching Resources** *Grammar Exercise Workbook,* pp. 27–30
DAY 3 — **Review and Assess** Students review the chapter and demonstrate mastery of parts of speech. (pp. 364–366)	**Writing and Grammar** Interactive Text, Ch. 16, Chapter Review **Teaching Resources** *Formal Assessment,* Ch. 16

Options for Adapting Lesson Plans

FEATURES

Extend coverage with the Grammar in Literature features (pp. 341, 347, 352/Ⓗ217, 223, 228), the Hands-on Grammar activity (p. 358/Ⓗ234), and the Standardized Test Preparation Workshop (p. 367).

TECHNOLOGY

Students can use *Writing and Grammar* Interactive Text to complete the exercises interactively on computer. They can complete additional exercises in the *On-line Exercise Bank:* The Auto Check feature will grade their work. Go on-line: PHSchool.com Use Web Code: eek-1002

Writing and Grammar Handbook Alignment

Page numbers in Step-by-Step Teaching Guides in this Teacher's Edition refer to pages from the full student text. Handbook page references, indicated with this icon **H**, are provided in Time and Resource Manager boxes and at the bottom of each Teacher's Edition page.

INTEGRATED SKILLS COVERAGE

Grammar in Literature
SE pp. 341, 347, 352/**H**217, 223, 228

Writing
Find It in Your Writing SE pp. 343, 351, 359, 363/**H**219, 227, 235, 239
Writing Application SE pp. 343, 351, 359, 363, 366/**H**219, 227, 235, 239

Spelling
SE pp. 342, 349/**H**218, 225

Viewing and Representing
Critical Viewing SE pp. 338, 341, 342, 345, 347, 352, 354, 357, 361, 362/**H**214, 217, 218, 221, 223, 228, 230, 233, 237, 238

Real-World Connection
ATE p. 354

ASSESSMENT SUPPORT

Standardized Test Preparation Workshop SE p. 367;
ATE pp. 346, 355

Standardized Test Preparation Workbook, pp. 33–34

Formal Assessment, Ch. 16

MEETING INDIVIDUAL NEEDS

Less Advanced Students ATE pp. 340, 349, 355, 367. See also Ongoing Assessments ATE pp. 341, 345, 347, 349, 350, 353, 354, 356, 357, 361, 362.

ESL Students ATE pp. 346, 354

More Advanced Students ATE pp. 342, 345, 362, 367

Bodily/Kinesthetic Learners ATE p. 354

Spatial Learners ATE p. 356

BLOCK SCHEDULING

Pacing Suggestions
For 90-minute Blocks
• Administer the Diagnostic Test to students to determine instructional coverage.
• Have students complete the necessary exercises in class. Use the Hands-on Grammar activity to provide a change of pace.

Resources for Varying Instruction
• *Writing and Grammar* Interactive Text A 90-minute block provides an ideal opportunity for students to work on the computer.

Professional Development Support
• *How to Manage Instruction in the Block* This teaching resource provides management and activity suggestions.

MEDIA AND TECHNOLOGY

For the Student
• *Writing and Grammar* Interactive Text, Ch. 16
• *On-line Exercise Bank,* Sections 16.1–4

For the Teacher
• Teacher**EXPRESS** CD-ROM

WRITING AND GRAMMAR ON-LINE

Interactive Text (On-line or on CD-ROM)
• Easily navigable instruction with on-line supporting resources
• Self-scoring exercises and diagnostic tests

Companion Web Site PHSchool.com
• On-line Exercise Bank (use Web Code eek-1002)

See the Go On-line! **feature, SE p. iii.**

LITERATURE CONNECTIONS

Grammar in Literature selections from *Prentice Hall Literature, Penguin Edition,* Grade 10:

from *Swimming to Antarctica,* Lynne Cox, SE p. 341/**H**217
from "Games at Twilight," Anita Desai, SE p. 347/**H**223
from "How Much Land Does a Man Need?" Leo Tolstoy, SE p. 352

Lesson Objectives

1. To identify and distinguish among various types of nouns
2. To identify and distinguish among various types of pronouns and to recognize their antecedents
3. To recognize action verbs and to distinguish between transitive and intransitive action verbs
4. To recognize forms of *be* and other verbs as linking verbs
5. To recognize and use verb phrases
6. To demonstrate control over grammatical elements such as nouns, pronouns, and verb forms
7. To evaluate writing for both mechanics and content

Critical Viewing

Identify, Relate Nouns may include *soldiers, woods, forest, battlefield, trees, smoke, uniforms,* and proper nouns such as *France* and *World War I.*

Chapter 16 Nouns, Pronouns, and Verbs

▲ Critical Viewing
What nouns can you use to name the people, places, and things in this photo? **[Identify, Relate]**

Every word you use can be classified as one of the eight *parts of speech*: nouns, pronouns, verbs, adjectives, adverbs, prepositions, conjunctions, and interjections.

Nouns, pronouns, and verbs form the heart of a sentence. Nouns are words that name people, places, and things. In writing about World War I, for instance, you might use nouns to name ships, planes, generals, countries, and so forth. Pronouns act as stand-ins for nouns. Instead of repeating the name each time, you may use the pronouns *he, she,* or *they.* Verbs tell something about nouns and pronouns, often by expressing some kind of action. For instance, you might write *Planes landed, and troops moved.* The words *landed* and *moved* are verbs.

The next three sections will explain these three important parts of speech.

338 • Nouns, Pronouns, and Verbs

✓ ONGOING ASSESSMENT: Diagnose

If students miss more than one item in any category, direct them to the relevant pages of the textbook and assign exercises for practice and review.

Nouns, Pronouns, and Verbs	Diagnostic Test Items	Teach	Practice	Section Reviews	Chapter Review
Skill Check A					
Nouns	A 1–5	pp. 340–342/ Ⓗ216–218	Ex. 1–4	Ex. 5–6	Ex. 46
Skill Check B					
Pronouns and Antecedents	A 6–10	pp. 344–350/ Ⓗ220–226	Ex. 10–15	Ex. 16–19	Ex. 47–50

Diagnostic Test

Directions: Write all answers on a separate sheet of paper.

Skill Check A. Identify the nouns in the following sentences. Label each *common* or *proper* and *concrete* or *abstract*. Circle any compound nouns.

1. World War I began as a local conflict between Austria-Hungary and Serbia.
2. The conflict escalated when war was declared on Russia.
3. Tension created by strong nationalism drew in other groups.
4. World War I eventually involved thirty-two nations.
5. On one side were the Allies; on the other side, the Central Powers.

Skill Check B. Identify each pronoun. Label it *personal*, *indefinite*, *reflexive*, *intensive*, *relative*, or *demonstrative*.

6. Many nations found themselves at war because of alliances they had made with other countries.
7. The war was precipitated by the assassination of Archduke Francis Ferdinand, who was heir to the Austrian throne.
8. Nationalism was one of the main factors in the war.
9. Germany, one of the primary aggressors, was itself once divided into many small principalities and kingdoms.
10. Those, however, had been united into one empire in 1871.

Skill Check C. Identify the verbs in the following sentences, and label them *action* or *linking*, *transitive* or *intransitive*.

11. Germany declared war on Russia on August 1, 1914.
12. The French mobilized on the same day.
13. A large-scale war appeared inevitable in Europe.
14. Concern in the United States grew as Germany employed submarine warfare.
15. American forces landed in France in 1917.

Skill Check D. Write the verb phrases in the following sentences, and underline each helping verb.

16. There had been many threats of war in Europe prior to World War I.
17. In one crisis, Germany had supported Morocco when it was agitating for independence from France.
18. This crisis was eventually settled by international conferences.
19. Austria-Hungary had annexed Bosnia and Herzegovina, and the Serbs had threatened to declare war.
20. Several diplomatic efforts had been made after the archduke was assassinated, but they had failed.

Nouns, Pronouns, and Verbs • **339**

Activate Prior Knowledge

Discuss the human drive to give names to things and experiences. Elicit the names of concrete objects (desk, window, book), of individuals (teacher, Mary, boy), and of intangibles (joy, sadness, freedom).

TEACH

Step-by-Step Teaching Guide

Concrete and Abstract Nouns

1. Point out that some nouns name things that are apparent to our senses (objects, people, places) and some name things that are not (concepts, qualities).

2. Ask students to write down one more example for each of the categories in the chart.

Step-by-Step Teaching Guide

Collective Nouns

1. Tell students that a word referring to a group of people or things is a collective noun.

2. Ask students to add to the collective nouns on this page. (Examples: committee, class, troop, family)

Customize for
Less Advanced Students

Students may be confused that collective nouns can be singular despite naming groups. Provide extra practice.

Critical Viewing

Connect, Respond Abstract nouns might include *nature, beauty, peace.*

Section 16.1 Nouns

The names people give to themselves and others, to the places where they live, and to the things that surround them are called *nouns.*

▶ **KEY CONCEPT** A **noun** is a word that names a person, place, thing, or idea. ■

Concrete and Abstract Nouns

Some nouns name things that can be perceived with the senses. Other nouns name qualities, characteristics, or ideas that are not known through the senses.

▶ **KEY CONCEPT** **Nouns** name things that can be seen and touched as well as those things that exist as concepts: ideas, qualities, and conditions. ■

The chart below shows examples of a variety of types of nouns.

CATEGORIES OF NOUNS			
People	Wilhelm	citizen	Aunt Jo
Places	beach	battlefield	Europe
Visible Things	hand	tree	lightning
Ideas	freedom	religion	friendship
Actions	decision	treatment	punishment
Conditions	health	dismay	happiness
Qualities	wisdom	strength	courage

Nouns that name people, places, or things that can be seen or recognized through any of the five senses are called *concrete nouns.* Nouns that name other things—such as ideas, actions, conditions, and qualities—are called *abstract nouns.*

Collective Nouns

Another special type of noun is used to name *groups* of people or things. Nouns of this type are called *collective nouns.*

COLLECTIVE NOUNS: community   army   team   flock
                    class   family club   committee

Do not confuse collective nouns—nouns that name a collection of people or things acting as a unit—with plural nouns.

340 • Nouns, Pronouns, and Verbs

Theme: World War I

In this section, you will learn about nouns. The examples and exercises in this section are about World War I.

Cross-Curricular Connection: Social Studies

⏱ TIME AND RESOURCE MANAGER

Resources
Print: *Grammar Exercise Workbook,* pp. 1–4; *Grammar Exercises Answers on Transparencies,* Ch. 16
Technology: *Writing and Grammar* Interactive Text, Section 16.1; *On-Line Exercise Bank,* Section 16.1

Using the Full Student Edition	Using the HandbookⒽ
• Work through all key concepts, pp. 340–342.	• Work through all key concepts, pp. 216–218.
• Assign and review Exercises 1–4.	• Assign and review Exercises 1–4.
• Read and discuss Grammar in Literature, p. 341.	• Read and discuss Grammar in Literature, p. 217.

GRAMMAR IN LITERATURE

from **Swimming to Antarctica**
Lynne Cox

Notice the concrete nouns in the following excerpt.

I stared out the *window* at the brown crescent-shaped *beach*. There were snow-covered *hills* directly above the *beach*, and massive *glaciers* on either side.

▲ Critical Viewing
What abstract nouns does this field of flowers bring to mind?
[Connect, Respond]

Compound Nouns

Some nouns—such as *Private Jones*, *son-in-law*, and *baseball*—consist of two or more words acting as a unit.

▶ **KEY CONCEPT** A **compound noun** is a noun that is made up of more than one word. ■

Notice the three ways in which compound nouns are formed:

TYPES OF COMPOUND NOUNS		
Separated	Hyphenated	Combined
fire engine	rock-and-roll	toothbrush
soap opera	jack-of-all-trades	dishwasher

▶ **Exercise 1** Classifying Nouns Identify the nouns in the following sentences, labeling each *concrete* or *abstract*. Circle each compound noun. Underline each collective noun.
1. Prewar Europe was permeated by nationalism.
2. Political and economic rivalries existed between countries.
3. My class learned that European economic expansion was chiefly centered in Africa.
4. Feeling a military threat, each nation maintained a large army even in peacetime.
5. Archduke Ferdinand was the heir-presumptive to the Austro-Hungarian throne.

▶ **Exercise 2** Writing With Nouns Write a paragraph using each of the following nouns: *soldiers*, *team*, *fund-raiser*, *general*, *bravery*, *victory*, *battlefield*.

▶ **More Practice**

Grammar Exercise Workbook
• pp. 1–4

On-line Exercise Bank
• Section 16.1

Go on-line:
PHSchool.com
Enter Web Code:
eek-1002

Nouns • 341

☑ ONGOING ASSESSMENT: Monitor and Reinforce

If students have difficulty with Exercise 1, 2, 3, or 4, refer them to the following for additional practice.

In the Textbook	Print Resources	Technology
Section Review, Ex. 5–6, Section 16.1	*Grammar Exercise Workbook*, pp. 1–2	*On-Line Exercise Bank*, Section 16.1

Step-by-Step Teaching Guide

Grammar in Literature

1. Explain that these lines are from a poem that describes a World War I cemetery.
2. Why are the highlighted nouns concrete? (they name visible things)

More About the Writer

Lynne Cox (b. 1957) began breaking swimming records at age fifteen when she broke the men's and the women's records for swimming the English Channel. Her high percentage of body fat, evenly distributed around her body, helps her float and provides insulation. She is the most successful cold-water long-distance swimmer ever.

Connections With Literature

A longer excerpt from *Swimming to Antarctica* is found in *Prentice Hall Literature, Penguin Edition,* Grade 10.

Step-by-Step Teaching Guide

Compound Nouns

1. Add more examples of each formation of compound noun.
2. Emphasize that dictionaries can confirm correct forms.

Answer Key

▶ **Exercise 1**

1. Europe–concrete; nationalism–abstract
2. rivalries–abstract; countries–concrete
3. class–concrete; expansion–abstract; Africa–concrete
4. threat–abstract; nation–concrete; army–concrete, collective; peacetime–abstract, compound
5. Archduke Ferdinand–concrete, compound; heir-presumptive–concrete, compound; throne–abstract

▶ **Exercise 2**

Answers will vary. Encourage students to include some proper nouns in their paragraphs. Have students exchange papers and check for appropriate grammar and usage.

Step-by-Step Teaching Guide

Common and Proper Nouns

1. Emphasize that common nouns are general terms for people, places, and things and are thus not capitalized.

2. Have students suggest more examples in both categories.

3. Ask for a volunteer to explain the difference between the use of "uncle" in the two sentences. Explain that a situation involving direct address of an individual makes that address a proper noun.

Customize for
More Advanced Students

Most students are familiar with the names of certain groups of animals such as *school* of fish or *flock* of birds. Ask students to learn the group names of the following:

bees (hive)	snakes (bed)
ants (colony)	geese (gaggle)
monkeys (troop)	elk (gang)

Have them use these in sentences. (Example: A gaggle of geese flew overhead.) Suggest that students research the names of additional animal groups.

Critical Viewing

Speculate Proper nouns might include *Belgium, France, Europe, Western Front, World War I.*

Answer Key

Exercise 3

Answers will vary; samples are given.

1. common–Chicago
2. common–World War II
3. common–Asia
4. proper–ruler
5. proper–alliance
6. proper–country
7. common–United States
8. common–General Pershing
9. common–Battle of Verdun
10. proper–month

Exercise 4

Answers will vary. If students have trouble getting started, brainstorm for proper nouns of each category and write them on the board.

Common and Proper Nouns

All nouns are either *common nouns* or *proper nouns.*

▶ **KEY CONCEPTS** A **common noun** names any one of a class of people, places, or things. A **proper noun** names a specific person, place, or thing. ■

Proper nouns always begin with capital letters.

Common Nouns	Proper Nouns
novelist	Willa Cather, Erich Remarque
continent	North America, Africa
city	Paris, Berlin
planet	Mercury, Venus

Note About *Names of Family Members:* A noun used to describe a person's role in a family may be either common or proper, depending on how it is used. A name used simply to indicate a person's role is a common noun. A name used as a title before a personal name or as a name in direct address should be capitalized as a proper noun.

COMMON: My favorite person is my *uncle.*
PROPER: My favorite person is *Uncle* Barry.
DIRECT ADDRESS: Please, *Dad*, may I go out tonight?

▶ **Exercise 3** Distinguishing Between Common and Proper Nouns Identify each noun as *common* or *proper.* Supply a proper noun of the same category for each common noun. Supply a common noun of the same category for each proper noun.

1. town
2. war
3. continent
4. Wilhelm
5. League of Nations
6. England
7. country
8. general
9. battle
10. June

▶ **Exercise 4** Writing With Common and Proper Nouns Write a sentence using each of these words as a common noun. Then, write a sentence using each as part of a proper noun: *aunt, president, river, war, mountains.*

342 • Nouns, Pronouns, and Verbs

🔆 Spelling Tip

Every proper noun begins with a capital letter. Consult a dictionary if you are unsure whether a noun is common or proper.

▼ Critical Viewing
Think of some proper nouns to explain where these soldiers might be. **[Speculate]**

☑ **ONGOING ASSESSMENT: Assess Mastery**

Use the following resources to assess student mastery of nouns.

In the Textbook	Technology
Chapter Review, Ex. 46	*Writing and Grammar* Interactive Text, Section 16.1, Section Review; *On-Line Exercise Bank,* Section 16.1

Section Review

GRAMMAR EXERCISES 5–9

Exercise 5 Identifying Nouns

Identify the nouns in each sentence, and label them *concrete* or *abstract*.

1. The assassination of the Austrian archduke was a result of extreme nationalism.
2. Austria issued a declaration of war against the Serbs.
3. Soon, every major power in Europe was involved in the conflict.
4. To the east, the Russians achieved several victories against the Germans.
5. The reinforcement of the German Army enabled it to drive the enemy back to Russia by 1915.
6. No decision was achieved in the east, but Russia lost many men and supplies.
7. In December 1914, the Turks began an invasion of the Russian Caucasus region.
8. Russia sought the aid of the Allies to remove some of the Turkish pressure.
9. The Allied landings at Gallipoli were failures.
10. The United States maintained its neutrality until 1917.

Exercise 6 Recognizing Kinds of Nouns Identify the nouns in each sentence, labeling each *common* or *proper*. Also, indicate whether a noun is *collective* or *compound*.

1. In 1917, the Allies began an invasion of Greece and pressured the king to abdicate.
2. After King Constantine abdicated, the government of Greece declared war on the Central Powers.
3. Besides Greece, battles took place in other areas of the Balkans, in Italy, and in the Middle East.
4. After Russia and Romania made peace with the Central Powers, the outlook seemed ominous for the rest of the European community.
5. Allied progress in the Balkans led to the defeat of Bulgaria.
6. The Allied campaign in the Middle East also came to a successful conclusion in 1918.
7. The success of the Allied army led to the breakup of the Austro-Hungarian Empire.
8. The Czechs and the Slovaks formed a democratic state, the emperor abdicated, and an armistice was concluded.
9. The treaty of Versailles and other treaties changed the face of Europe.
10. People put their trust in the League of Nations to maintain peace.

Exercise 7 Find It in Your Reading

Read through a section of a history book about World War I. Find two examples of each of the following types of nouns: *abstract, concrete, common, proper, collective,* and *compound.*

Exercise 8 Find It in Your Writing

In a sample of your own writing, find five common nouns, one collective noun, and one compound noun. Name a proper noun that could replace each common noun. Explain whether replacing each common noun would or would not make your writing more clear.

Exercise 9 Writing Application

Write a brief account of an event that changed history in some way. Include at least two proper nouns, one compound noun, and one collective noun.

Section Review • **343**

ASSESS

Section Review

Each of these exercises correlates to the instruction on nouns, pages 342–344. These exercises may be used for more practice, for reteaching, or for review of the key concepts presented.

Answer Key

Exercise 5

Students may disagree about whether some nouns are concrete or abstract.

1. assassination, archduke–concrete; result, nationalism–abstract
2. Austria, war, Serbs–concrete; declaration–abstract
3. Europe, conflict–concrete; power–abstract
4. east, Russians, victories, Germans–concrete
5. Army, enemy, Russia–concrete; reinforcement–abstract
6. east, Russia, men, supplies–concrete; decision–abstract
7. December, 1914, Turks, region–concrete; invasion–abstract
8. Russia, Allies–concrete; aid, pressure–abstract
9. landings, Gallipoli–concrete; failures–abstract
10. United States, 1917–concrete; neutrality–abstract

Exercise 6

1. 1917, invasion, king–common; Allies, Greece–proper
2. King Constantine, Central Powers–proper, compound; Greece–proper; government, war–common
3. Greece, Balkans, Italy–proper; battles, areas–common; Middle East–compound, proper
4. Russia, Romania–proper; peace, outlook, rest–common; Central Powers–compound, proper; community–common collective
5. Balkans, Bulgaria–proper; progress, defeat–common
6. Middle East–compound, proper; campaign, conclusion, 1918–common
7. Empire–proper; success, army, breakup–common; army–collective
8. Czechs, Slovaks–proper; state, emperor, armistice–common
9. Versailles, Europe–proper; treaty, face, treaties–common
10. League of Nations–proper, compound; people, trust, peace–common

continued

Answer key continued

Exercise 7

Find It in Your Reading

Answers will vary. If students do not have access to world history books, encourage them to search for the nouns in another book.

Exercise 8

Find It in Your Writing

If students cannot find examples of each type of noun, urge them to add these to their writing. Students who have difficulty substituting proper nouns for common nouns may form groups and brainstorm for them.

Exercise 9

Writing Application

Check students' work to make sure they have included proper, collective, and compound nouns correctly. Point out to students that the name of their historical event (the Vietnam War, the march to Selma) is likely to consist of or contain at least one proper noun.

PREPARE and ENGAGE

Interest GRABBER Write the following on the board:

Katy reassured Katy that Katy shouldn't worry about Katy's grades because Katy had studied very hard.

Ask students to reword this awkward sentence using correctly substituted words *(herself, she, her, she)*. Point out that these are different types of pronouns: *herself* is reflexive, *she* and *her* are personal, and *her* shows possession.

Activate Prior Knowledge

Review the concept of point of view with the class. Point out that narrative point of view is determined by the writer's use of pronouns. Ask volunteers to read examples of different points of view from their writing portfolios, and have students list the pronouns they hear.

TEACH

Step-by-Step Teaching Guide

Antecedents of Pronouns

1. Offer additional examples and ask students to identify pronouns, antecedents, and location of antecedent in relation to its pronoun:

   Each of the puppies has spots on its fur. (Each, before)

   Jason couldn't believe his ears. (Jason, before)

2. Point out that pronouns in some sentences will have no antecedents. Example:

   When you visit, you must stay with us. (no antecedents)

Answer Key

Exercise 10

1. its–Taos
2. who–artists; its–area
3. they–Spaniards; it–town
4. their–Native Americans, Spaniards
5. his–D. H. Lawrence

Pronouns

Repeating the same noun over and over in writing or speaking results in awkward, choppy sentences. You can avoid repeating the same noun by using substitutes called *pronouns.*

KEY CONCEPT **Pronouns** are words that act as stand-ins for nouns or for words that take the place of nouns. ■

Antecedents of Pronouns

Pronouns get their meaning from the words they stand for. These words are called *antecedents.*

KEY CONCEPT **Antecedents** are nouns (or words that take the place of nouns) for which pronouns stand. ■

In the following examples, the arrows point from the pronouns to their antecedents. In the first sentence, the pronouns *you* and *your* stand for the noun *Tom.* In the second sentence, the pronoun *it* stands for a group of words that takes the place of a noun, *Making chili for dinner.*

EXAMPLES: Tom, did *you* submit *your* article on New Mexico?

Making chili for dinner was easy, and *it* was fun.

Antecedents usually come before their pronouns, as in the examples above. Sometimes, however, this pattern is reversed:

EXAMPLE: *That* is the best book I have ever read.

Exercise 10 Identifying Pronouns and Antecedents
Identify each pronoun and its antecedent.
(1) Taos in New Mexico is famous for its art colonies. (2) The area attracts artists who are drawn to its beauty. (3) The town was settled by Spaniards in the early seventeenth century, and they called it Don Fernando de Taos. (4) Native Americans and Spaniards traded their goods in town. (5) Author D. H. Lawrence did some of his writing there in the 1920's.

Theme: Tourist Attractions

In this section, you will learn about pronouns. Examples and exercises in this section are about tourist attractions in various states.

Cross-Curricular Connection: Social Studies

Get instant feedback! Exercise 10 is available on-line or on CD-ROM.

More Practice

Grammar Exercise Workbook
• pp. 5–8
On-line Exercise Bank
• Section 16.2
Go on-line:
PHSchool.com
Enter Web Code:
eek-1002

⏱ TIME AND RESOURCE MANAGER

Resources
Print: *Grammar Exercise Workbook,* pp. 5–12; *Grammar Exercises Answers on Transparencies,* Ch. 16
Technology: *Writing and Grammar* Interactive Text, Section 16.2; *On-Line Exercise Bank,* Section 16.2

Using the Full Student Edition	Using the Handbook⒣
• Work through all key concepts, pp. 344–350. • Assign and review Exercises 10–15. • Read and discuss Grammar in Literature, p. 347.	• Work through all key concepts, pp. 220–226. • Assign and review Exercises 10–15. • Read and discuss Grammar in Literature, p. 223.

Personal, Reflexive, and Intensive Pronouns

The pronouns that you use most often to refer to yourself, to other people, and to things are called *personal pronouns.* *Reflexive* and *intensive pronouns* are formed by adding *-self* or *-selves* to some of the personal pronouns.

Personal Pronouns

Personal pronouns are used more often than any other type of pronoun.

▶ **KEY CONCEPT** **Personal pronouns** refer to (1) the person speaking, (2) the person spoken to, or (3) the person, place, or thing spoken about. ■

First-person pronouns refer to the person who is speaking. *Second-person pronouns* refer to the person spoken to. *Third-person pronouns* refer to the person, place, or thing spoken about.

◀ Critical Viewing
What might you assume about the people who made this pottery? [Infer, Support]

PERSONAL PRONOUNS		
	Singular	Plural
First Person	I, me, my, mine	we, us, our, ours
Second Person	you, your, yours	you, your, yours
Third Person	he, him, his, she, her, hers, it, its	they, them, their, theirs

In the first example below, the antecedent of the personal pronoun is the person speaking. In the second, the antecedent of the personal pronoun is the person being spoken to. In the last example, the antecedent of the personal pronoun is the thing spoken about.

FIRST PERSON: *My* name is not George.

SECOND PERSON: When *you* left for camp, *you* forgot *your* raincoat.

THIRD PERSON: Don't judge a book by *its* cover.

Reflexive and Intensive Pronouns

1. Using the chart, ask students to offer sentences using these pronouns. (Example: *Jack gave himself a break.*) Show students that the sentence would make sense if the noun were inserted. (*Jack gave Jack a break.*)

2. Then ask students to use these same pronouns as intensives. (Example: *Jack himself is arriving.*) Show students that a noun cannot logically replace the intensive. (*Jack Jack is arriving* would make no sense.)

3. To summarize intensive pronouns, ask students what words sound like *intensive (intensity, intensify)* and use them to help students remember the function of intensive pronouns: the pronoun intensifies or emphasizes the meaning of the word it renames.

Customize for
ESL Students

Have students work in pairs. One student should recount a recent event in a brief two or three sentence story (for example: a trip to the store, a homework project, a sports game), while the other listens to this story and writes it down. Then, the second student tells a story to the first student, who writes it down. Have students exchange papers and underline each other's pronouns and identify the person and number of each. Students may use the charts on this page and the preceding page for help.

Language Highlight

Romance languages use pronouns as parts of certain verbs. Instead of using a possessive pronoun and a noun to say "*My name is . . .*," as we do in English, speakers of French, Spanish, and Italian use the pronoun reflexively to say "I call myself . . . ." (*Je m'appelle. . . ; Me llamo. . . ; Mi chiamo. . . .*)

16.2

Reflexive and Intensive Pronouns

Pronouns that end in *-self* or *-selves* are either reflexive pronouns or intensive pronouns.

▶ **KEY CONCEPTS** A **reflexive pronoun** ends in *-self* or *-selves* and adds information to a sentence by pointing back to a noun or pronoun earlier in the sentence. An **intensive pronoun** ends in *-self* or *-selves* and simply adds emphasis to a noun or pronoun in the same sentence. ■

The reflexive and intensive pronouns are shown in the following chart.

REFLEXIVE AND INTENSIVE PRONOUNS		
	Singular	**Plural**
First Person	myself	ourselves
Second Person	yourself	yourselves
Third Person	himself, herself, itself	themselves

A reflexive pronoun always adds information to a sentence. It cannot be left out without changing the meaning. In the first example, *himself* tells whom Michael taught. In the second, *herself* tells for whom the jeans were bought.

REFLEXIVE: Michael taught *himself* to play the guitar.

Gloria bought *herself* a new pair of jeans.

An intensive pronoun emphasizes its antecedent but does not add information to a sentence. If an intensive pronoun is removed, a sentence will still have the same meaning.

Usually, an intensive pronoun immediately follows its antecedent, as shown in the first of the following examples. Sometimes, however, an intensive pronoun is located in another part of the sentence, as shown in the second example.

INTENSIVE: The President *himself* attended the gala opening.

We spliced the cable *ourselves*.

▶ **More Practice**

Grammar Exercise Workbook
• pp. 7–8
On-line Exercise Bank
• Section 16.2
Go on-line:
PHSchool.com
Enter Web Code:
eek-1002

⟨ STANDARDIZED TEST PREPARATION WORKSHOP

Grammar and Usage Many standardized tests require students to use their knowledge of nouns to respond correctly. Use the following example to demonstrate:

After only two short years, she had become the chief-executive-officer of the company.

How should <u>chief-executive-officer</u> be written in this sentence?

A Chief-Executive-Officer

B chief executive officer

C Chief-Executive Officer

D Correct as is

The correct answer is **B**. The compound noun is not spelled with hyphens, and it is not capitalized because it is not a proper noun: It does not formally name a specific person.

GRAMMAR IN LITERATURE

from **Games at Twilight**
Anita Desai

The personal pronouns in this passage are highlighted in blue italics.

But Ravi would not let *them*. *He* tore himself out of *his* mother's grasp and pounded across the lawn into *their* midst, charging at *them* with *his* head lowered so that *they* scattered in surprise. "*I* won, *I* won, *I* won," he bawled, shaking *his* head so that the big tears flew. "Raghu didn't find *me*. . . ."

> **Exercise 11** Identifying Personal, Reflexive, and Intensive Pronouns
> Identify each pronoun and label it *personal, reflexive,* or *intensive.*
> 1. Have you ever been to Houston?
> 2. Is Daniel himself making the plans?
> 3. Houston is a large city, but it is not the state's capital.
> 4. The city was named after Samuel Houston; he was the first president of Texas when it became independent.
> 5. Independence itself lasted less than ten years.
> 6. During Texas's time as a republic, Houston was its capital.
> 7. The city found itself growing rapidly.
> 8. Not only was Samuel Houston president of the Republic of Texas, he was among the first to represent the state when it was admitted to the Union.
> 9. The citizens of Houston are proud of their city, its symphony, and its Museum of Fine Arts.
> 10. Houston has many parks, among them Hermann Park.

> **Exercise 12** Revising to Use Pronouns to Avoid Repetition
> Revise this paragraph, replacing nouns with pronouns to avoid repetition. You might also combine some of the sentences.
>
> Paul and Robert visited Houston last spring. Paul and Robert loved spending time in Houston. Paul's uncle Richard lives in Houston. The two boys stayed at Uncle Richard's house. Uncle Richard invited Paul and Robert to come back for another visit. Paul and Robert told Uncle Richard that next winter would be an ideal time.

❓ Learn More

To learn more about how to use pronouns correctly, see Chapter 23, "Pronoun Usage."

▲ **Critical Viewing** How would you describe this scene in one sentence? What pronouns can replace the nouns you used? **[Assess]**

Pronouns • 347

Step-by-Step Teaching Guide

Demonstrative Pronouns

1. Help students avoid confusing demonstrative pronouns with demonstrative adjectives. Use this example: *This is the top for that box.* Point out that *This* is a demonstrative pronoun and *that* is a demonstrative adjective because it modifies *box.*

2. Ask students to write sentences for each of the demonstrative pronouns in the chart and to identify the antecedent of each. Make sure students note that the antecedent does not always appear in the same sentence.

3. Caution students that a demonstrative pronoun will not always be followed directly by a noun but rather might be followed directly by a verb (*That is . . .*) or by a phrase (*those in the back.*)

Step-by-Step Teaching Guide

Relative Pronouns

1. Demonstrate complex sentences with adjective clauses. Use these examples, pointing out the subordinate clause in each:

    Here is the paper <u>that you asked for</u>.

    The man <u>who called earlier</u> didn't leave a message.

    Gene is the one <u>whose car was damaged</u>.

2. Have students identify each relative pronoun (that, who, whose) and indicate its antecedent (paper, man, one).

3. Be sure they recognize that English has only five relative pronouns (see chart) and discuss the examples.

4. Have students write complex sentences using each of the pronouns.

5. For additional practice, use these sentences:

    The student who wins the prize must excel in physical science.

    She bought shoes that matched her dress.

    A person whom I will never forget is my grandfather.

    Have students identify each subordinate clause, relative pronoun, and antecedent.

16.2

Demonstrative, Relative, and Interrogative Pronouns

Three other kinds of pronouns—called *demonstrative, relative,* and *interrogative* pronouns—have very special uses.

KEY CONCEPT **Demonstrative pronouns** direct attention to specific people, places, or things. ■

The following chart shows the four demonstrative pronouns.

DEMONSTRATIVE PRONOUNS	
Singular	Plural
this, that	these, those

Demonstrative pronouns may come before or after their antecedents:

BEFORE: *That* is the ranch I would like to own.

AFTER: I hope to visit Butte and Helena. *Those* are my first choices.

One of the demonstrative pronouns, *that*, can also be used as a *relative pronoun*.

KEY CONCEPT A **relative pronoun** begins a subordinate clause and connects it to the rest of the sentence. ■

RELATIVE PRONOUNS				
that	which	who	whom	whose

In the following sentences, relative pronouns connect a subordinate clause (shown in blue) to a word (shown in red).

EXAMPLE: He found the cattle *that* he had lost.

Carl, *whom* we all admire, rides well.

All relative pronouns except *that* can also be interrogative pronouns.

▶ **KEY CONCEPT** An **interrogative pronoun** is used to begin a question. ■

The following chart shows the five interrogative pronouns.

INTERROGATIVE PRONOUNS
what   which   who   whom   whose

In the following examples, notice that interrogative pronouns do not always have specific antecedents.

EXAMPLES: *What* did you say?

Which of the answers is best?
With *whom* did you wish to speak?
Mine is blue. *Whose* is red?

▶ **Exercise 13** Recognizing Demonstrative, Relative, and Interrogative Pronouns Identify the pronoun in each of the following sentences. Then, label each *demonstrative, relative,* or *interrogative*.

1. Butte, whose full name is Butte-Silver Bow, is in south-western Montana.
2. The city is situated in an area that is rich in minerals.
3. What is the history of Butte?
4. Butte was settled by prospectors, who came to mine gold in the 1860's.
5. That was an activity later replaced by silver mining.
6. Was this later replaced by copper mining?
7. Gold, silver, and copper were the metals mined there; those brought prosperity to the area.
8. Which is more interesting: Butte's historic district or the Copper King Mansion?
9. The community, which was named after a nearby butte, was incorporated in 1897.
10. We learned about energy research, tourism, medicine, and mining; these have been most important to Butte's economy.

▶ **Exercise 14** Writing With Demonstrative, Relative, and Interrogative Pronouns Write an imaginary dialogue between you and a friend, discussing an interesting place that one of you has visited. Use at least four demonstrative pronouns, three relative pronouns, and three interrogative pronouns.

✔ Spelling Tip

Do not confuse *who's* and *whose. Who's* is always a contraction of *who is* and should never be used as a pronoun.

▶ **More Practice**

Grammar Exercise Workbook
• pp. 9–10
On-line Exercise Bank
• Section 16.2
Go on-line:
PHSchool.com
Enter Web Code:
eek-1002

Interactive Textbook

Complete the exercises on-line! Exercises 13 and 14 are available on-line or on CD-ROM.

✔ ONGOING ASSESSMENT: Monitor and Reinforce

If students have difficulty with Exercise 13 or 14, refer them to the following for additional practice.

In the Textbook	Print Resources	Technology
Section Review, Ex. 18, Section 16.2	*Grammar Exercise Workbook,* pp. 9–10	*On-Line Exercise Bank,* Section 16.2

Interrogative Pronouns

1. Ask students which words can be both relative and interrogative pronouns *(which, who, whom, whose)*. Ask students to identify the differences between them:
   • Interrogative pronouns ask questions and often begin sentences.
   • Relative pronouns begin subordinate clauses and connect them.
2. As students examine the examples beneath the chart, point out that only one *(Which)* has an antecedent.
3. Ask students to write two sentences with each of the interrogative pronouns, one with an antecedent and one without.

Customize for
Less Advanced Students

Students may have difficulty distinguishing between the use of *who* and *whom*. Point out that *who* is a subject or predicate nominative and *whom* is an object. Emphasize that this distinction is true for both relative and interrogative pronouns. Give students practice using these two pronouns correctly:

___ owns that car? (Who, subject)
The car is owned by ___? (whom, object of a preposition)
The grand prize winner is ___? (who, predicate nominative)

Answer Key

▶ **Exercise 13**

1. whose–relative
2. that–relative
3. What–interrogative
4. who–relative
5. That–demonstrative
6. this–demonstrative
7. those–demonstrative
8. Which–interrogative
9. which–relative
10. We–personal; these–demonstrative

▶ **Exercise 14**

Answers will vary. Have students exchange papers and search for the demonstrative, relative, and interrogative pronouns in their partners' dialogues.

Indefinite Pronouns

1. Warn students that, though indefinite pronouns refer to people, places, or things, they do not always specify which and will often appear without antecedents.

2. Caution students not to confuse indefinite pronouns with indefinite adjectives. Give them this example:

   Many in the class made *many* mistakes on the test.

   (The first *Many* is an indefinite pronoun; the second is an adjective.)

3. Have students practice by writing two sentences for any five indefinite pronouns in the chart—once with no antecedent and once with.

Answer Key

▶ **Exercise 15**

1. several
2. Everybody
3. most
4. Something
5. Anyone
6. Many
7. everyone
8. some
9. More
10. each

16.2

Indefinite Pronouns

Indefinite pronouns also often lack specific antecedents.

▶ **KEY CONCEPT** **Indefinite pronouns** refer to people, places, or things, often without specifying which ones. ■

INDEFINITE PRONOUNS			
Singular		**Plural**	**Singular or Plural**
another	much	both	all
anybody	neither	few	any
anyone	nobody	many	more
anything	no one	others	most
each	nothing	several	none
either	one		some
everybody	other		
everyone	somebody		
everything	someone		
little	something		

SPECIFIC ANTECEDENT: *Several* of the guests were late.
NO SPECIFIC ANTECEDENTS: *Everyone* ate *everything* offered.

In addition to functioning as pronouns, indefinite pronouns can also function as adjectives.

PRONOUN: *Few* are as famous as the Cleveland Orchestra.
ADJECTIVE: *Few* orchestras are as famous as this one.

▶ **Exercise 15** Recognizing Indefinite Pronouns Identify the indefinite pronouns in the following paragraph.

EXAMPLE: Did you eat any?
ANSWER: any

(1) Cleveland has several ways to attract visitors. (2) Everybody will enjoy the Rock and Roll Hall of Fame and Museum. (3) The museum is open for most of the year. (4) Something to remember is that admission is free on Wednesday evenings in the summer. (5) Anyone joining the museum receives unlimited free admission. (6) Many of the artists with exhibits at the museum do not allow their items to be photographed. (7) Not everyone likes rock-and-roll. (8) The Cleveland Ballet is popular with some. (9) More of the city's cultural institutions are found in University Circle. (10) Here are Cleveland's museums of art and natural history; each is worth a visit.

▶ **More Practice**

Grammar Exercise Workbook
• pp. 11–12
On-line Exercise Bank
• Section 16.2
Go on-line:
PHSchool.com
Enter Web Code:
eek-1002

Get instant feedback! Exercise 15 is available on-line or on CD-ROM.

☑ **ONGOING ASSESSMENT: Monitor and Reinforce**

If students miss more than two items in Exercise 15, refer them to the following for additional practice.

In the Textbook	Print Resources	Technology
Section Review, Ex. 19, Section 16.2	*Grammar Exercise Workbook,* pp. 11–12	*On-Line Exercise Bank,* Section 16.2

Section 16.2 Section Review

GRAMMAR EXERCISES 16–22

▶ **Exercise 16** Identifying Pronouns and Antecedents Identify the pronoun and antecedent in each sentence. If a pronoun has no antecedent, write *none*.

1. Ithaca, which is in southcentral New York, is located on Cayuga Lake.
2. It was settled in 1789.
3. De Witt Clinton, the American statesman, made his home in Ithaca.
4. Residents of Ithaca find themselves surrounded by great natural beauty.
5. There are many cliffs and deep ravines, and their beauty is overwhelming.

▶ **Exercise 17** Identifying Personal, Reflexive, and Intensive Pronouns Identify the pronouns, and label each *personal*, *reflexive*, or *intensive*.

1. Taos, New Mexico, sits in the hills near its neighbor, Santa Fe.
2. The city itself has long been attractive to visitors from other states and countries.
3. They enjoy the beauty of the land and the spirit of the residents there.
4. At the Kit Carson Home and Museum, you can look at objects owned by Carson himself.
5. Literary buffs can occupy themselves at the D. H. Lawrence Ranch and Shrine.

▶ **Exercise 18** Recognizing Demonstrative, Relative, and Interrogative Pronouns Identify the pronouns in each sentence, and label them *demonstrative*, *relative*, or *interrogative*.

1. Visitors who come to Houston find a thriving city in southeast Texas.
2. These are often people interested in the history and culture of the area.
3. Which would you like to see: the ballet or the opera?

4. The Houston Grand Opera, whose home is in the Civic Center Complex, performs at the Gus Wortham Theater Center.
5. That is the theater of the Houston Ballet.

▶ **Exercise 19** Supplying Indefinite Pronouns Complete each sentence by adding an indefinite pronoun.

1. Has __?__ here visited Cleveland, Ohio?
2. __?__ of the attractions in Cleveland's park system include a zoo and an aquarium.
3. The Metropolitan Park System gives __?__ a chance to enjoy nature.
4. A __?__ of Cleveland's roads lead to Lake Erie.
5. Not __?__ can name __?__ of the Great Lakes.

▶ **Exercise 20** Find It in Your Reading Identify the reflexive pronoun in the excerpt from "Games at Twilight" on page 347. Then, find an example of this type of pronoun in another piece of literature.

▶ **Exercise 21** Find It in Your Writing In your own writing, find at least one example of each of these kinds of pronouns: *personal*, *demonstrative*, *relative*, *interrogative*, and *indefinite*. Then, replace at least two nouns with pronouns.

▶ **Exercise 22** Writing Application Write a short description of a city you would like to visit. Use at least two of each type of pronoun.

Section Review • 351

ASSESS

Section Review

Each of these exercises correlates to the instruction on pronouns, pages 344–350. These exercises may be used for more practice, for reteaching, or for review of the key concepts presented.

Answer Key

▶ **Exercise 16**

1. which–Ithaca
2. It–Ithaca
3. his–DeWitt Clinton
4. themselves–Residents
5. their–cliffs, ravines

▶ **Exercise 17**

1. its–personal
2. itself–intensive
3. They–personal
4. you–personal; himself–intensive
5. themselves–reflexive

▶ **Exercise 18**

1. who–relative
2. These–demonstrative
3. Which–interrogative; you–personal
4. whose–relative
5. That–demonstrative

▶ **Exercise 19**

Answers may vary. Possible answers:

1. anyone
2. Some
3. anyone
4. few
5. everyone; all

▶ **Exercise 20**

Find It in Your Reading
himself, answers will vary

▶ **Exercise 21**

Find It in Your Writing
If students cannot locate at least one example of each kind of pronoun, make sure they add them to their writing.

▶ **Exercise 22**

Writing Application
Remind students that some cities are often referred to with feminine personal or possessive pronouns; "she" or "her" in the case of Paris, for example.

Interest GRABBER Write these words on the board:

Hazard	Harness
Effect	Love
March	Pantomime

Have students define each as a noun. (Examples: *A hazard is something dangerous. A harness is something attached to a draft animal.*)

Then have students define each as a verb. (Examples: *To hazard* means *to risk. To harness* means *to employ* or *to put to use.*) Finally, have students write these words as verbs in sentences.

Activate Prior Knowledge

Ask students, one at a time, to offer two statements: one describing dramatic action and one describing something they thought or felt. As you hear each answer, write the statement. When you have about ten sentences on the board, ask students to identify each verb as describing *visible action, mental action,* or *condition.*

Step-by-Step Teaching Guide

Action Verbs

1. Remind students that verbs change form to show differences in time and that most verbs have subjects that precede them in sentences: The dog *chased* the cat.

2. List on the board Visible Action and Mental Action. Ask students for examples.

Step-by-Step Teaching Guide

Grammar in Literature

1. Read the passage aloud and have students write down the verbs. (All verbs are visible actions).

continued

Critical Viewing

Describe Possible answers: sparkle, swirl, burn, explode, shine.

Section 16.3

Action Verbs and Linking Verbs

Nouns are necessary to name all people, places, and things. To tell something about the nouns, *verbs* are also necessary.

▶ **KEY CONCEPT** A **verb** is a word that expresses time while showing an action, a condition, or the fact that something exists. ■

Action Verbs

▶ **KEY CONCEPT** An **action verb** is a verb that tells what action someone or something is performing, has performed, or will perform. ■

In the following examples, the verbs tell what actions have been or are being performed by Hank and the horse.

ACTION VERBS: Hank *painted* the toolshed.
The horse *waited* patiently.

GRAMMAR IN LITERATURE

from **How Much Land Does a Man Need?**
Leo Tolstoy
Translated by Louise and Aylmer Maude

The action verbs in this passage are highlighted in blue italics.

He *unfastened* his girdle and *tied* it tight below his stomach, *put* a little bag of bread into the breast of his coat, and, tying a flask of water to his girdle, he *drew* up the tops of his boots, *took* the spade from his man, and *stood* ready to start.

352 • Nouns, Pronouns, and Verbs

Theme: New Mexico

In this section, you will learn about verbs. The examples and exercises in this section are about New Mexico.

Cross-Curricular Connection: Social Studies

▼ **Critical Viewing** What action verbs could you use in describing this picture? **[Describe]**

⏱ TIME AND RESOURCE MANAGER

Resources
Print: *Grammar Exercise Workbook,* pp. 13–18; *Grammar Exercises Answers on Transparencies,* Ch. 16; *Hands-on Grammar Activity Book,* Ch. 16
Technology: *Writing and Grammar* Interactive Text, Section 16.3; *On-Line Exercise Bank,* Section 16.3

Using the Full Student Edition	Using the Handbook🄷
• Work through all key concepts, pp. 352–357.	• Work through all key concepts, pp. 228–233.
• Assign and review Exercises 23–29.	• Assign and review Exercises 23–29.
• Read and discuss Grammar in Literature, p. 352.	• Read and discuss Grammar in Literature, p. 228.
• Do the Hands-on Grammar activity, p. 358.	• Do the Hands-on Grammar activity, p. 234.

> **Exercise 23** Identifying Action Verbs Identify the action verb in each of the following sentences.

1. The earliest known inhabitants of New Mexico arrived around ten thousand years ago.
2. The Pueblo people inhabited adobe dwellings.
3. Nomadic Navajo and Apache peoples settled in New Mexico in the fifteenth century.
4. They attacked the Pueblo peoples, leading to four centuries of warfare.
5. Europeans learned about New Mexico in the late 1500's.

> **Exercise 24** Supplying Action Verbs On a separate sheet of paper, complete each sentence by supplying an action verb.

1. Spanish conquerers ___?___ control of the land from the Native Americans.
2. The United States Army ___?___ New Mexico in 1846 and claimed it for the United States.
3. The United States government ___?___ the Arizona Territory from western New Mexico.
4. In 1863, the government ___?___ the boundaries of New Mexico to their present position.
5. When people ___?___ gold and silver, mining became a major industry.

Transitive and Intransitive Verbs

An action verb can be *transitive* or *intransitive*, depending on whether or not it transfers its action to another word in the sentence.

> **KEY CONCEPTS** A **transitive verb** takes an object. An **intransitive verb** does not direct its action to an object. ■

The word that receives the action of a transitive verb is called the *object* of the verb. The object is often a noun or pronoun.

Intransitive verbs do not have objects. The action is not directed toward any noun or pronoun in the sentence.

To find out whether a verb in a sentence is transitive or intransitive, ask *Whom?* or *What?* after the verb. If you can find an answer in the sentence, the verb is transitive. If there is no answer, the verb is intransitive

TRANSITIVE: Robert *polished* his saddle.
                Polished *what?* (saddle)

INTRANSITIVE: Linda *waited* for the wagon.
                Waited *what?* (*no answer*)

> **More Practice**

Grammar Exercise Workbook
• pp. 13–14
On-line Exercise Bank
• Section 16.3
  Go on-line:
  PHSchool.com
  Enter Web Code:
  eek-1002

Complete the exercises on-line! Exercises 23 and 24 are available on-line or on CD-ROM.

Action Verbs and Linking Verbs • **353**

☑ **ONGOING ASSESSMENT: Monitor and Reinforce**

If students miss more than one item in Exercise 23 or 24, refer them to the following for additional practice.

In the Textbook	Print Resources	Technology
Section Review, Ex. 31, Section 16.3	*Grammar Exercise Workbook,* pp. 13–14	*On-Line Exercise Bank,* Section 16.3

Step-by-Step Teaching Guide continued

2. Ask students to write an original sentence for each verb.
3. If possible, have students write two additional sentences for each verb: one in present time and one in future. (*unfastens, will unfasten; ties, will tie; puts, will put; draws, will draw; takes, will take; stands, will stand*)

More About the Writer

Leo Tolstoy (1828–1910) inherited his family estate at age nineteen. After publishing two masterpieces, the novels *War and Peace* and *Anna Karenina*, Tolstoy became depressed. He began to follow a mystical spirituality, giving up luxuries and working in his fields. Tolstoy's beliefs about overcoming evil inspired later activists such as Dr. Martin Luther King, Jr.

Connections With Literature

"How Much Land Does a Man Need?" can be found in *Prentice Hall Literature, Penguin Edition*, Grade 10.

Answer Key

> **Exercise 23**

1. arrived	4. attacked
2. inhabited	5. learned
3. settled	

> **Exercise 24**

Answers may vary. Possible answers:

1. took	4. changed
2. invaded	5. discovered
3. ruled	

> *Step-by-Step Teaching Guide*

Transitive and Intransitive Verbs

1. Remind students that linking verbs are always intransitive.
2. Suggest that students look for a direct object to determine the status of the verb. Remind them of the distinction between a direct object and a predicate nominative (The latter follows a linking verb).
3. Ask students to use the following words in sentences as both transitive and intransitive verbs.

  wrote   *watch*
  believe   *danced*

Real-World Connection

Verbs are used widely to provide information. Many street signs use verbs to convey critical information: *(Stop! Yield. Merge.)* Many packages and pamphlets use verbs to tell users how to assemble toys or program appliances. Have students list verbs they find in the real world.

Customize for
ESL Students

Have students divide their papers in half, labeling the left half *Visible Action* and the right half *Mental Action*. Have them write a sentence for each of these verbs, placing it in the appropriate column.

think	*write*
throw	*eat*
believe	*sail*

Once they have written their sentences, have them underline subjects, double underline verbs, and circle any words that complete the actions of verbs.

Customize for
Bodily/Kinesthetic Learners

Write each of the following verbs on a separate index card and distribute them among students. Ask each student to act out or pantomime the verb so that the rest of the group can guess the word.

eat	*fly*
worry	*throw*
spin	*swim*
hear	*lean*
jump	*think*

As students guess a word, ask whether it shows visible or mental action.

Answer Key

Exercise 25

1. call–transitive–New Mexico
2. flock–intransitive
3. enjoy–transitive–culture
4. comprises–transitive–regions
5. extend–intransitive
6. contains–transitive–part
7. lies–intransitive
8. consists–intransitive
9. flows–intransitive
10. crosses–transitive–state

Critical Viewing

Analyze, Identify Possible answers: wild, wide-open, rocky, desolate, beautiful, spectacular.

Most action verbs can be transitive or intransitive, depending on their use in the sentence. Some action verbs, however, can only be transitive, and others can only be intransitive.

TRANSITIVE OR INTRANSITIVE:	I *wrote* a letter from New Mexico. The secretary *wrote* quickly.
ALWAYS TRANSITIVE:	California grapes *rival* those of France.
ALWAYS INTRANSITIVE:	She *winced* at the sound of his voice.

Consult a dictionary if you are uncertain about whether an action verb should have an object.

▶ **Exercise 25** Distinguishing Between Transitive and Intransitive Verbs Write the verb in each sentence. Then, label each *transitive* or *intransitive*. Finally, write the object of each transitive verb.

1. People call New Mexico the Land of Enchantment.
2. Tourists flock there for the beautiful scenery.
3. They also enjoy the state's unique culture.
4. The New Mexican landscape comprises four regions.
5. The Rocky Mountains extend southward into the state.
6. Western New Mexico contains part of the Colorado Plateau, a land of cliffs, canyons, and flat-topped hills.
7. Part of the Great Plains lies in the eastern part of the state's high peaks.
8. The basin and range region consists of wide valleys and high peaks.
9. The Rio Grande flows through New Mexico.
10. The Continental Divide crosses the state from north to south.

▶ **Critical Viewing** How would you describe this landscape? **[Analyze, Identify]**

✓ ONGOING ASSESSMENT: Monitor and Reinforce

If students miss more than two items in Exercise 25, refer them to the following for additional practice.

In the Textbook	Print Resources	Technology
Section Review, Ex. 30–31, Section 16.3	*Grammar Exercise Workbook,* pp. 13–14	*On-Line Exercise Bank,* Section 16.3

Linking Verbs

Linking verbs link, or join, two or more words in a sentence.

> **KEY CONCEPT** A **linking verb** is a verb that connects a word or words at or near the beginning of a sentence with a word or words at or near the end. ■

In the following examples, *was* connects the subject *Sam Houston* with the word *president,* and *is* connects the subject *calf* with the words *miserable and scared.* The verbs allow *president* and *miserable and scared* to help identify or describe the subjects.

LINKING VERBS: Sam Houston *was* president of Texas from 1841 to 1844.

The feverish calf *is* miserable and scared.

The above examples both use verbs that are forms of *be,* the most common linking verb. *Be* has many different forms, as shown in the following chart.

THE FORMS OF *BE*			
am	am being	can be	have been
are	are being	could be	has been
is	is being	may be	had been
was	was being	might be	could have been
were	were being	must be	may have been
		shall be	might have been
		should be	must have been
		will be	shall have been
		would be	should have been
			will have been
			would have been

Note About *Verbs Expressing Existence:* The forms of *be* do not always function as linking verbs. Instead, they express existence, usually by showing where something is located. The following examples show forms of *be* expressing existence.

EXAMPLES: Your shirt *is* in the closet.
Your *are* several mistakes in that article.

Twelve other verbs may also act as linking verbs. The verbs are shown in the chart on the next page.

▶ **More Practice**

Grammar Exercise Workbook
• pp. 15–16
On-line Exercise Bank
• Section 16.3
Go on-line:
PHSchool.com
Enter Web Code:
eek-1002

Linking Verbs

1. The key concept can be demonstrated with a simple diagram to show how a linking verb balances two ideas—a subject and its complement—to directly associate them. Write this on the board, explaining that the two-sided arrow represents a linking verb:

   Subject ◄──► *Complement*

2. Explain that a linking verb usually connects the subject of its sentence with another word that describes it.

3. Use the Note on this page to explain the exception to linking verbs connecting the subject and a complement. In the examples, show that the linking verb connects the subject with a prepositional phrase and an adverb to express the existence of something.

Customize for
Less Advanced Students

Have students bring an interesting newspaper or magazine article to class. Ask students to underline the first ten verbs they find in their articles, including any helping verbs. Next tell them to find and circle the word, if any, that is the object or complement of each verb. Have volunteers offer their answers so that all can check the accuracy of their choices, and then ask students to label each verb *action* or *linking.* Then have students label their action verbs *transitive* or *intransitive.*

✎ STANDARDIZED TEST PREPARATION WORKSHOP

Grammar and Usage Many standardized tests require students to use their knowledge of verbs to respond correctly to test questions. Use the following example:

Read the passage and choose the word or group of words that belongs in the blank.

> *Bucharest, the capital of Romania, has a charm that is unique in Eastern Europe. There still ___ many old, elaborately decorated buildings that survived the bombing of World War II.*

A exist

B did exist

C existed

D had existed

The answer is **A.** Because the verb *has* in the first sentence and the adverb *still* in the second establish present time, the verb must remain consistent.

Answer Key

Customize for
Spatial Learners

To help students recognize linking verbs and understand their function in sentences, have students draw multiple copies of two boxes with an equal sign between them. Have students take each sentence from the exercises on this page and sort the words this way: Place the linking verb over the equal sign, place the subject and any of its modifiers in the left box, and place the complements and modifiers in the right box. In the first sentence of Exercise 26, students would write *was* over the equal sign and then write *New Mexico* inside the left box and *physically larger* inside the right box.

16.3

OTHER LINKING VERBS

appear	feel	look	seem	sound	taste
become	grow	remain	smell	stay	turn

These verbs also allow another word in the sentence to name or describe the subject of the sentence.

EXAMPLES: He *remained* a hermit for many years.

The music *sounded* tuneless to her.

▶ **Exercise 26** Recognizing Forms of *Be* Used as Linking Verbs Write each sentence, underlining the linking verb. Then, draw an arrow to show which words are linked by the verb. If the verb does not function as a linking verb, write *none*.

EXAMPLE: New Mexico <u>could have been</u> our home.

1. New Mexico was physically larger in the last century.
2. It is a land of magnificent and varied scenery.
3. The deserts have been there for thousands of years.
4. Irrigation would be impossible without reservoirs.
5. The landscape must have been very unfamiliar to European settlers.
6. Most rainfalls in New Mexico are brief and heavy.
7. The winters are drier than the summers.
8. The state is home to a wide variety of animal life.
9. Human impact has been a negative influence on some species.
10. The state will be the subject of interest long into future decades.

▶ **Exercise 27** Identifying Other Linking Verbs Write each sentence, underlining the linking verb. Then, draw an arrow to show which words are linked by the verb.

1. Despite the dry climate, agriculture remains economically important in the state.
2. Ranching seems more profitable than farming.
3. Overgrazing appeared ruinous to the grasslands.
4. As a result, the number of cattle became smaller.
5. With improved grazing practices, the outcome looks promising.

356 • Nouns, Pronouns, and Verbs

▶ More Practice

Grammar Exercise Workbook
• pp. 17–18
On-line Exercise Bank
• Section 16.3
Go on-line:
PHSchool.com
Enter Web Code:
eek-1002

Get instant feedback!
Exercises 26, 27, 28, and 29 are available on-line or on CD-ROM.

☑ ONGOING ASSESSMENT: Monitor and Reinforce

If students have difficulty with Exercise 26 or 27, refer them to the following for additional practice.

In the Textbook	Print Resources	Technology
Section Review, Ex. 32, Section 16.3	*Grammar Exercise Workbook*, pp. 15–16	*On-Line Exercise Bank*, Section 16.3

Linking Verb or Action Verb?

Most of the verbs in the chart on page 356 can be either linking verbs or action verbs. To see whether a verb is a linking verb, substitute *am, are,* or *is* for the verb. If the substitution makes sense and connects two words, then the original is a linking verb. Otherwise, the original is an action verb.

KEY CONCEPT *Am, are,* or *is* will make sense when substituted for another linking verb in a sentence. ■

Notice how each of the verbs in these examples has been tested to see whether it is an action verb or a linking verb.

EXAMPLES: The breeze *felt* cool.
The breeze *is* cool? (linking)
Henry *felt* the sand.
Henry *is* the sand? (action)

Exercise 28 Distinguishing Between Linking Verbs and Action Verbs Identify each verb as either an action verb or a linking verb.
1. Reminders of the advanced cultures in New Mexico thousands of years ago remained today.
2. The Santa Fe Trail remained popular as a trading route between St. Louis and Santa Fe in the early 1880's.
3. Railroads appeared rapidly in New Mexico after the 1880's.
4. New Mexico sounds ideal for outdoor enthusiasts.
5. Chili peppers, which taste hot, are an important New Mexican crop.

Exercise 29 Supplying Linking Verbs and Action Verbs Complete each sentence with a form of one of the following verbs: *remain, feel, grow, look, sound, appear,* or *taste.* Label each verb *linking* or *action.*
1. New Mexicans ___?___ proud of their blend of cultures.
2. At Carlsbad Caverns National Park, tourists can ___?___ at the largest underground cave system in North America.
3. The echoes in the caves ___?___ eerie.
4. The New Mexican desert ___?___ beautiful at sunrise.
5. Have you ever ___?___ chili?

▼ Critical Viewing
What actions might the inhabitants of these dwellings perform? [Infer, Interpret]

Action Verbs and Linking Verbs • 357

ONGOING ASSESSMENT: Monitor and Reinforce

If students miss more than one item in Exercise 28 or 29, refer them to the following for additional practice.

In the Textbook	Print Resources	Technology
Section Review, Ex. 33, Section 16.3	*Grammar Exercise Workbook,* pp. 17–18	*On-Line Exercise Bank,* Section 16.3

Hands-on Grammar

Teaching Resources: Hands-on Grammar Activity Book, Ch. 16

1. If you wish to do this activity in class, be prepared with paper for the students. Give each student a copy of the Hands-on Grammar activity sheet.

2. Have students follow the directions to prepare their intransitive verb translators.

3. If students have difficulty getting started, brainstorm for subjects and objects to fit the verbs.

4. Students should notice that *waited* is always intransitive and that *wandered* can be transitive only in constructions like "He wandered the countryside"; *wander* is usually intransitive.

Find It in Your Reading

Students should take only the subject, verb, and object from sentences they find. Remind them that they can take the elements they need from long or complex sentences.

Find It in Your Writing

Encourage students to develop an eye for verbs that can be transitive or intransitive. If students choose examples that use linking verbs, use the opportunity to emphasize the difference between action verbs and linking verbs.

16.3

Hands-on Grammar

Intransitive Verb Translator

Divide a sheet of paper into three columns. Label the first column *Subject*, the second column *Action Verb*, and the third column *What?* Then, fold the paper so the third column does not show. In the *Action Verb* column, list the following verbs: *traveled, blew, called, visited, wandered, waited, believed, asked,* and *helped.* In the *Subject* column, write a subject that makes sense with the verb. Read the sentence you have constructed.

Unfold the paper so that the third column shows. Add an object to each subject-verb combination. Before you add an object, the verb is intransitive. When you add an object, the verb becomes transitive. You may notice, however, that you cannot add an object to some of your subject-verb combinations because some verbs are always intransitive.

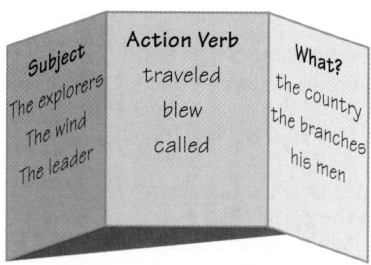

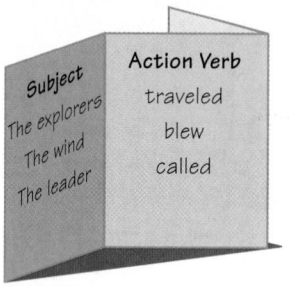

Find It in Your Reading Try this activity out with subject-verb combinations from an interesting piece of nonfiction that you read recently.

Find It in Your Writing Try the activity with subjects and verbs from a piece of your own writing.

⏱ TIME SAVERS!

✋ **Hands-on Grammar**
Use the Hands-on Grammar activity sheet for Chapter 16 to facilitate this activity.

☑ ONGOING ASSESSMENT: Assess Mastery

Use the following resources to assess student mastery of action verbs and linking verbs.

In the Textbook	Technology
Chapter Review, Ex. 51–53	*Writing and Grammar* Interactive Text, Section 16.3, Section Review; *On-Line Exercise Bank,* Section 16.3

Section Review

GRAMMAR EXERCISES 30–36

▶ **Exercise 30** Identifying Transitive
and Intransitive Action Verbs Identify
the action verb in each sentence, and label
it *transitive* or *intransitive*.

1. People often imagine New Mexico as a
faraway, quiet place.
2. In fact, New Mexico has developed into
a vital, vibrant, and diverse state.
3. Many interesting and unusual events
have occurred in New Mexico.
4. For instance, the federal government
selected Los Alamos as a site for
nuclear research in 1942.
5. Some people wonder about supposed
extraterrestrial landings in Roswell.

▶ **Exercise 31** Supplying Action
Verbs Complete each sentence by supplying an action verb. Label the verb *transitive* or *intransitive*.

1. Taos, a small town, ___?___ national
fame as an art center.
2. The Santa Fe Opera ___?___ outdoors
during the summer.
3. Billy the Kid ___?___ from the Old
Lincoln County Courthouse in 1881.
4. Sheriff Pat Garrett ___?___ Billy in
Fort Summer, New Mexico.
5. To this day, many visitors ___?___ in
the state's lakes and reservoirs.

▶ **Exercise 32** Recognizing Linking
Verbs Write each sentence, underlining
the linking verb. Draw an arrow showing
which words are linked by the verb.

1. Santa Fe is the second-oldest city in
the United States.
2. The Palace of the Governors is now the
home of major museums.
3. This building had been the seat of government during the Spanish and

Mexican occupations.
4. Native American and Hispanic cultures
remain influential in New Mexico.
5. Native Americans seem eager to contribute to the social and economic
affairs of the state.

▶ **Exercise 33** Distinguishing
Between Linking Verbs and Action
Verbs Complete each sentence with a form
of one of the following verbs: *feel, grow,
look, sound, taste, appear*. Then, label the
verb *linking* or *action*.

1. Even a hot day in New Mexico ___?___
comfortable because the air is so dry.
2. Farmers in New Mexico ___?___ chili
peppers, onions, and potatoes.
3. This chili ___?___ very hot and spicy.
4. When I ___?___ something spicy, I
drink a big glass of water after it.
5. When the sun first ___?___, it shows
off the colors of the landscape.

▶ **Exercise 34** Find It in Your
Reading Choose ten verbs in a short
story from your literature book. Label each
action verb *transitive* or *intransitive*. Then,
identify any linking verbs.

▶ **Exercise 35** Find It in Your
Writing In your writing, find five examples of action verbs and five examples of
linking verbs. Identify the words that are
connected by the linking verbs.

▶ **Exercise 36** Writing Application
Write ten sentences using these verbs,
both as linking verbs and as action verbs.

taste, remain, stay, turn, become

Section Review • **359**

Section Review

Each of these exercises correlates to
the instruction on action verbs and
linking verbs, pages 352–357. These
exercises may be used for more
practice, for reteaching, or for review
of the key concepts presented.

Answer Key

▶ **Exercise 30**

1. imagine–transitive
2. has developed–intransitive
3. have occurred–intransitive
4. selected–transitive
5. wonder–intransitive

▶ **Exercise 31**

Answers may vary. Possible answers:

1. gained–transitive
2. performs–intransitive
3. escaped–intransitive
4. caught–transitive
5. fish–intransitive

▶ **Exercise 32**

1. *is* links *Santa Fe* to *city*
2. *is* links *Palace of the Governors* to
home
3. *had been* links *building* to *seat*
4. *remain* links *cultures* to *influential*
5. *seem* links *Native Americans* to
eager

▶ **Exercise 33**

Answers may vary. Possible answers:

1. feels–linking
2. grow–action
3. tastes–linking
4. taste–action
5. appears–action

▶ **Exercise 34**

Find It in Your Reading
Answers will vary. Encourage students
to choose passages that will
challenge them.

▶ **Exercise 35**

Find It in Your Writing
Students might rewrite their
sentences using linking verbs in place
of action verbs and vice versa.

▶ **Exercise 36**

Writing Application
Have students read aloud the
sentences containing forms of *taste,
remain, stay, turn,* and *become* used as
action and linking verbs.

Ask students to think of single verbs that could logically complete this sentence:

Our choir ___ perform a solo with the band.

(Possible answers: *should, will, could, did, might, should, may, can.*)

List these words on the board and test student understanding by writing this on the board:

We will have been sleeping for three hours.

Ask students to identify the helpers (*will, have, been*) and point out that the longest verb phrases are four words long.

Activate Prior Knowledge

Place this list on the board and ask students for examples of public places where they have seen these verbs used:

does	*will*	*might*
did	*would*	*must*
shall	*could*	*can*
should	*may*	*do*

Example: "Hardhats <u>must</u> be worn in this area" might be seen on signs at construction sights. As students suggest phrases or sentences with these verbs, write some on the board and ask students to identify the main verb and all helpers.

TEACH

Step-by-Step Teaching Guide

Verb Phrases

1. Emphasize that main verbs indicate action or condition, but that helping verbs clarify such things as time and number.

2. Using the sentences from the chart, ask students to substitute another verb for *returned* (e.g., *read, bought, enjoyed*) and to form three verb phrases similar to the model.

   Give students the following verb phrases and ask them to suggest adverbs that might interrupt them:
   is talking   (*always, not*)
   should have flown   (*not, never*)
   was sleeping   (*finally, quietly*)

continued

Section 16.4 — Verb Phrases

One verb may consist of as many as four words. Acting as a unit, these words form a *verb phrase.*

KEY CONCEPTS A **verb phrase** is made up of a main verb and one or more helping verbs. Any of the many forms of *be* as well as some other verbs can be used as helping verbs. ■

Below are other verbs besides *be* that can be used as helping verbs.

HELPING VERBS OTHER THAN *BE*

do	have	shall	can
does	has	should	could
did	had	will	may
		would	might
			must

Remember that the verb *be* can also be the main verb in a sentence. Many of the helping verbs above can be used with *be*.

Helping verbs are sometimes called *auxiliary verbs* or *auxiliaries* because they help add meaning to other verbs. Notice how helping verbs change the meaning of the sentences in the following chart.

Without Helping Verbs	With Helping Verbs
I *talk* on the telephone.	I *will talk* on the telephone.
He *returned* that book.	He *should have returned* that book.

A verb and its helping verbs are sometimes interrupted by other words, especially in questions.

UNINTERRUPTED VERB PHRASE: The groundhog *will see* its shadow.

INTERRUPTED VERB PHRASES: The groundhog *will* probably not *see* its shadow.

Will the groundhog *see* its shadow?

Theme: Alcatraz Island

In this section, you will learn about verb phrases. The examples and exercises in this section are about the history of Alcatraz Island.

Cross-Curricular Connection: Social Studies

⏱ TIME AND RESOURCE MANAGER

Resources
Print: *Grammar Exercise Workbook,* pp. 19–20; *Grammar Exercises Answers on Transparencies,* Ch. 16
Technology: *Writing and Grammar* Interactive Text, Section 16.4; *On-Line Exercise Bank,* Section 16.4

Using the Full Student Edition	Using the Handbook Ⓗ
• Work through all key concepts, p. 360.	• Work through all key concepts, p. 236.
• Assign and review Exercises 37–40.	• Assign and review Exercises 37–40.

◄ Critical Viewing Why would Alcatraz Island (shown here) make an ideal spot for a prison? [Analyze]

Exercise 37 Recognizing Verb Phrases Identify the verb phrase or phrases in each sentence. Do not include any words that come between the helping verb and the main verb. Indicate which verb in each phrase is the helping verb.

1. During the Civil War, the Confederacy hoped that Colonel Johnston would somehow help them bring California into the Confederacy.
2. Confederate sympathizers could not have been more wrong about Colonel Johnston.
3. He had, in fact, been born in the South.
4. However, Johnston would still do what he felt to be his duty.
5. During the Civil War, Alcatraz Island was considered the chief Union defense post of San Francisco Bay.
6. Though Johnston had been arming it for defense, no one attacked the island.
7. A group of Confederates had planned to attack the island, but the scheme was ruined after one of them had foolishly bragged of the plan in a public place.
8. How might the success of this plan have affected the outcome of the Civil War?
9. The island's weapons were never used, and by the end of the war, they had become obsolete.
10. The island was then turned into a military prison, and many Confederate sympathizers were incarcerated there.

 **More Practice**

Grammar Exercise Workbook
• pp. 19–20
On-line Exercise Bank
• Section 16.4
Go on-line:
PHSchool.com
Enter Web Code:
eek-1002

Interactive Textbook

Get instant feedback! Exercise 37 is available on-line or on CD-ROM.

Verb Phrases • 361

Step-by-Step Teaching Guide continued

3. Ask students to use the helping verbs in the chart on page 360 to write original sentences. In each, have them use at least one helping verb and add an adverb to the verb phrase.

Critical Viewing

Analyze Possible answer: The distance from other land, the strong currents, and the cold water make Alcatraz Island difficult to escape from.

Answer Key

Exercise 37

Helping verbs are underlined.

1. <u>would</u> help
2. <u>could have</u> been
3. <u>had been</u> born
4. <u>would</u> do
5. <u>was</u> considered
6. <u>had been</u> arming
7. <u>had</u> planned, <u>was</u> ruined, <u>had</u> bragged
8. <u>might have</u> affected
9. <u>were</u> used, <u>had</u> become
10. <u>was</u> turned, <u>were</u> incarcerated

☑ **ONGOING ASSESSMENT: Monitor and Reinforce**

If students miss more than two items in Exercise 37, refer them to the following for additional practice.

In the Textbook	Print Resources	Technology
Section Review, Ex. 42, Section 16.4	Grammar Exercise Workbook, pp. 19–20	On-Line Exercise Bank, Section 16.4

⏱ **TIME SAVERS!**

Answers on Transparencies Use the *Grammar Exercises Answers on Transparencies* for Chapter 16 to facilitate correction by students.

On-Line Exercise Bank Have students complete the exercises on computer. The Auto Check feature will grade their work for you!

16.4

> **Exercise 38** Supplying Helping Verbs Add a helping verb to complete each sentence.
> 1. Alcatraz Island __?__ become home to numerous colonies of birds.
> 2. The island's natural and manmade features __?__ preserved by the National Park Service.
> 3. The name of the island __?__ attributed to a Spanish explorer.
> 4. He might __?__ called it *Isla de los Alcatraces* (Island of the Pelicans) because the birds were plentiful there.
> 5. *Alcatraz* __?__ become the anglicized form of the original name.

> **Exercise 39** Writing Sentences With Verb Phrases Write a sentence in which you use each of the following verbs as the main verb in a verb phrase.
> 1. captured
> 2. imprisoned
> 3. isolated
> 4. preserved
> 5. visited

> **Exercise 40** Revising to Add Verb Phrases Revise the following paragraph so that each sentence contains a verb phrase.
> (1) Alcatraz Island is in the middle of San Francisco Bay. (2) In 1933, the federal government built a maximum security prison there. (3) Today, the prison is a tourist attraction. (4) The west coast's oldest operating lighthouse is also on the island. (5) Another feature of the island is the beautiful views of the bay that it provides.

▶ **Critical Viewing** What verb phrases might you use to describe what it was like to be imprisoned in these quarters in Alcatraz? **[Describe]**

362 • Nouns, Pronouns, and Verbs

✓ **ONGOING ASSESSMENT: Monitor and Reinforce**

If students miss more than one item in Exercise 38, 39, or 40, refer them to the following for additional practice.

In the Textbook	Print Resources	Technology
Section Review, Ex. 41–43, Section 16.4	*Grammar Exercise Workbook*, pp. 19–20	*On-Line Exercise Bank*, Section 16.4

Section 16.4 Section Review

GRAMMAR EXERCISES 41–45

Exercise 41 Supplying Helping Verbs Complete each sentence by adding a helping verb to fill each blank.

1. The army __?__ not anticipated the problems that the isolation of the island __?__ cause.
2. Prisoners __?__ work on the island, but the cost of transporting supplies __?__ becoming increasingly expensive.
3. The Great Depression __?__ contribute to the army's decision to close Alcatraz.
4. Most of the prisoners __?__ transferred to Fort Leavenworth or Fort Jay.
5. Tourists __?__ able to see the remains of Fortress Alcatraz and the disciplinary barracks.
6. The National Park Service __?__ working to make the island more accessible to tourists.
7. Visitors __?__ advised to purchase tickets well in advance.
8. The weather on the island __?__ change suddenly.
9. Tours to the island __?__ not begin until 9:30 A.M.
10. Sometimes the island __?__ closed because of adverse weather conditions.

Exercise 42 Identifying Verb Phrases Identify the verb phrase or phrases in each sentence. Do not include any words that interrupt the verb phrases.

1. Some visitors may find the quarter-mile walk from the dock to the cellhouse difficult.
2. They can certainly ride the electric shuttle.
3. Eating and drinking are permitted only on the dock; bottled water may also be purchased there.
4. Visitors should know that tours may be sold out up to a week in advance.

5. Alcatraz has been part of the Golden Gate National Recreation Area since 1972 and has now become one of its most popular destinations.

Exercise 43 Find It in Your Reading Read the following excerpt from "Diamond Island: Alcatraz," by Darryl Babe Wilson. On a separate sheet of paper, write each verb phrase. Underline the helping verb(s) in each phrase.

There was a single letter in the mailbox. Somehow it seemed urgent. The address, although it was labored over, could hardly be deciphered—square childlike print that did not complete the almost individual letters. . . . Each word pressed heavily into the paper. I could not read it but I could feel the message. "Al traz" was in the first paragraph, broken and scattered, but there. At the very bottom of the final page—running out of space—he scrawled his name. The last letter of his name, *n*, did not fit: *Gibso.*

Exercise 44 Find It in Your Writing Identify the verb phrases in a piece of your own writing. Underline the helping verb(s) in each verb phrase.

Exercise 45 Writing Application Imagine that you had to stay on an isolated island by yourself for a week. Write a description of the things that you would like to take with you. Use at least five verb phrases in your writing. Underline the helping verbs.

ASSESS and CLOSE

Section Review

Each of these exercises correlates to the instruction on verb phrases, pages 360–362. These exercises may be used for more practice, for reteaching, or for review of the key concepts presented.

Answer Key

Exercise 41

Answers may vary. Possible answers:

1. had, would
2. would, was
3. did
4. were
5. are
6. is
7. are
8. can
9. do
10. is

Exercise 42

1. may find
2. can ride
3. are permitted, may be purchased
4. should know, may be sold
5. has been, has become

Exercise 43

Find It in Your Reading

<u>was</u> labored
<u>could be</u> deciphered
<u>did</u> complete
<u>could</u> read
<u>could</u> feel
<u>did</u> fit

Exercise 44

Find It in Your Writing

Suggest that students rewrite a paragraph from their writing to include more verb phrases.

Exercise 45

Writing Application

Ask students to add a paragraph to their description in which they use verb phrases to describe what actions they would take on the island.

CHAPTER REVIEW

Each of these exercises correlates to a section of the chapter on nouns, pronouns, and verbs, pages 338–363.

Answer Key

▶ **Exercise 46**

1. Alcatraz Island–concrete, proper, compound; California–concrete, proper; aspects, history–common, abstract
2. Pacific Ocean–concrete, proper, compound; state–common, concrete
3. resources, economy–common, abstract
4. gold, 1848, <u>people</u>–common, concrete; imaginations–common, abstract
5. discovery, role, admission– common, abstract; Union–proper, concrete
6. Gold, sawmill–common, concrete; Sacramento–proper, concrete
7. Gold Rush–proper, abstract, compound; prospectors, world–common, concrete
8. <u>people</u>–common, concrete; Forty-niners–proper, concrete, compound
9. arrival, railroad–common, concrete; group–common, concrete, collective; growth, expansion–common, abstract
10. nickname–common, concrete; California–proper, concrete; Golden State–proper, concrete, compound

▶ **Exercise 47**

1. That–novel
2. its–state
3. who–William Randolph Hearst; that–castle; he–Hearst
4. much–California; It–San Andreas Fault; many–earthquakes
5. who–people

▶ **Exercise 48**

1. themselves–intensive
2. themselves–reflexive; their–personal
3. it–personal
4. they–personal
5. itself–reflexive; it–personal

▶ **Exercise 49**

1. that–relative
2. which–relative
3. That–demonstrative
4. What–interrogative
5. these–demonstrative
6. All–indefinite; who–relative; it–personal

continued

364

GRAMMAR EXERCISES 46–57

▶ **Exercise 46** Identifying Types of Nouns Identify the nouns in each sentence, and label them *concrete* or *abstract* and *common* or *proper*. Circle compound nouns, and underline collective nouns.

1. Alcatraz Island reflects various aspects of the history of California.
2. The state, which borders the Pacific Ocean, is our third largest state.
3. Its many natural resources are important to the state's economy.
4. When gold was found in 1848, it fired the imaginations of many people.
5. The discovery played an important role in the state's admission to the Union.
6. Gold was found near a sawmill outside Sacramento.
7. The ensuing Gold Rush drew prospectors from all over the world.
8. These people later became known as the Forty-niners.
9. The arrival of this group stimulated economic growth and the expansion of the railroad.
10. The nickname of California is the Golden State.

▶ **Exercise 47** Recognizing Pronouns and Antecedents Identify each pronoun and its antecedent.

1. A Spanish novel written a long time ago describes a fictional place called California. <u>That</u> may be the source of California's name.
2. The variety of climates in the state result from <u>its</u> size and location.
3. William Randolph Hearst, <u>who</u> was a journalist and publisher, lived in a lavish castle <u>that</u> <u>he</u> called San Simeon.
4. The San Andreas Fault runs through much of California. <u>It</u> causes many of the state's earthquakes.

5. California includes people who come from many cultural heritages.

▶ **Exercise 48** Identifying Personal, Reflexive, and Intensive Pronouns Write the pronouns in each sentence, and label them *personal*, *reflexive*, or *intensive*.

1. Major earthquakes themselves are rare, but minor tremors, landslides, and the like occur frequently.
2. Californians pride themselves on their ability to endure life on the fault.
3. Mount Whitney is located in California; it is the highest peak in the United States outside of Alaska.
4. When James W. Marshall and John A. Sutter found gold, they did not realize the impact their discovery would have.
5. The Gold Rush wore itself out almost as quickly as it began.

▶ **Exercise 49** Identifying Demonstrative, Relative, Interrogative, and Indefinite Pronouns Identify all of the pronouns. Label each *demonstrative*, *relative*, *interrogative*, or *indefinite*.

1. California has national parks that are among the most visited in the nation.
2. The General Sherman giant sequoia, which is considered the most massive tree in the world, is found in Sequoia National Park.
3. That tree has a circumference of eighty-three feet.
4. What grows in California to nearly one hundred feet high?
5. Many trees can be found in Redwood National Park; these are some of the tallest in the world.
6. All who go to California enjoy it.
7. Which does Mike prefer: the beach or

☑ **ONGOING ASSESSMENT: Assess Mastery**

Use the following resources to assess student mastery of nouns, pronouns, and verbs.

In the Textbook	Print Resources	Technology
Chapter Review, Ex. 52–56	*Formal Assessment*, Ch. 16	*Writing and Grammar* Interactive Text, Ch. 16, Chapter Review; *On-Line Exercise Bank*, Section 16.4

the mountains?
8 California has both of those.
9. Each of the travel agents recommends visiting the zoo in San Diego.
10. Who can go to California without visiting a movie studio?

Exercise 50 Supplying Nouns and Pronouns

Complete the following paragraph by supplying a noun or pronoun to fill in each blank. Avoid unnecessarily repeating the same noun.

(1) Joe and __?__ want to go to California. (2) __?__ of us has ever been to __?__. (3)__?__ would probably fly into Los Angeles. (4) After visiting Hollywood and Beverly Hills, __?__ would rent a car and drive up the coast to San Francisco. (5) __?__ of our friends who have been to __?__ recommend the drive. (6) __?__ tell us that the coastal section known as Big Sur is breathtaking. (7) Huge cliffs drop suddenly into the bright blue sea, and the __?__ pounds steadily onto the rocky shore. (8) __?__ have heard that we have to drive carefully as we head up the coast, because the __?__ are windy and at times __?__. (9) Once we reached San Francisco, Joe and __?__ would visit the Golden Gate Bridge and walk throughout the __?__, admiring the architecture of __?__ buildings. (10) We would also probably take a boat out to Alcatraz. __?__ of __?__ friends who have visited the island say that the prison tour was one of the most memorable parts of __?__ trip to __?__.

Exercise 51 Supplying Action Verbs

Complete each sentence by adding an action verb. Label it *visible* or *mental* and *transitive* or *intransitive*.

1. Many professional sports teams __?__ in California.

2. Do you __?__ their names?
3. Should we __?__ the game tonight?
4. We __?__ Redwood National Park.
5. I never __?__ such tall trees.
6. James W. Marshall __?__ gold in 1848.
7. The Gold Rush __?__ the following year.
8. The San Andreas Fault __?__ California's earthquakes.
9. Did you __?__ Death Valley?
10. Nothing much __?__ in such heat.

Exercise 52 Identify Linking Verbs, Helping Verbs, and Verb Phrases

Identify the linking verbs and verb phrases in these sentences. List the words that each linking verb connects. Then, identify the helping verb in each verb phrase.

1. California has been a state since 1850.
2. Death Valley is the lowest point in the country.
3. Parts of Death Valley look bleak.
4. The heat can feel oppressive.
5. The temperature could not have been hotter there.
6. California's pleasant climate has been an important factor in its popularity.
7. The desert turns cold at night.
8. Despite the threat of earthquakes, California remains a popular tourist destination.
9. Can you smell the sea air?
10. California's population has grown.

Exercise 53 Classifying Verbs

Identify the verbs and verb phrases in these sentences. Label each *action verb*, *linking verb*, or *verb phrase*.

1. California's pleasant climate draws people there.
2. Parts of the Pacific Ocean have been preserved as a habitat for blue whales.
3. Without protection, the blue whale could become extinct.
4. It is the largest mammal on Earth.

Chapter Review • 365

Exercise 49

7. Which–interrogative
8. both–indefinite; those–demonstrative
9. Each–indefinite
10. Who–interrogative

Exercise 50

Answers will vary. Possible answers:

1. I
2. Neither, that state
3. We
4. we
5. Some, California
6. They
7. surf
8. We, roads, frightening
9. I, city, its
10. Many, our, their, California

Exercise 51

Answers may vary. Possible answers:

1. play–visible, intransitive
2. know–mental, transitive
3. attend–visible, transitive
4. toured–visible, transitive
5. imagined–mental, transitive
6. found–visible, transitive
7. started–mental, intransitive
8. causes–mental, transitive
9. visit–visible, transitive
10. grows–visible, intransitive

Exercise 52

Helping verbs are underlined.

1. has been–California, state
2. is–Death Valley, point
3. look–parts, bleak
4. can feel–heat, oppressive
5. could have been–temperature, hotter
6. has been –climate, factor
7. turns–desert, cold
8. remains–California, destination
9. Can smell [action]
10. has grown [action]

Exercise 53

1. draws–action
2. have been preserved–action, phrase
3. could become–linking, phrase
4. is–linking

continued

Exercise 53

5. <u>would</u> be–linking, phrase
6. <u>are</u> constructing–action, phrase
7. prepare–action
8. <u>Have</u> learned–action, phrase
9. has–action; feel–action;
   is–action/existence
10. <u>should</u> take–action, phrase

Exercise 54

Answers will vary. Possible answers:

1. California's pleasant climate has drawn people there for years.
2. Governments preserve parts of the Pacific Ocean as habitat for blue whales.
3. What if blue whales became extinct?
4. It has been recognized as the largest mammal on earth.
5. Such an animal's extinction causes a great loss to the planet.

Exercise 55

Answers will vary. Possible answers:

1. Many–adjective; people–noun
2. Some–pronoun; others–pronoun
3. learn–verb; study–verb
4. event–noun; went–verb; their–pronoun
5. is–verb; its–pronoun

Exercise 56

Answers will vary. Sample answer:

(1) California's cities each <u>offer</u> their own distinctive features and attractions. (2) California's capital, Sacramento, <u>displays</u> a re-creation of what <u>it</u> was like a century ago. (3) This old city is a popular destination for people visiting <u>the capital</u>. (4) San Francisco is <u>famed</u> for attractions such as the Golden Gate Bridge and Chinatown, and <u>it</u> features many hills and a stunningly beautiful bay. (5) <u>The city</u> is also remembered by some people who visit <u>it</u> for <u>its</u> cool, breezy days. (6) Los Angeles has warmer temperatures than San Francisco, and <u>it</u> is also larger. (7) <u>Los Angeles</u> is known, among other things, as the <u>heart</u> of the movie industry. (8) Many of the <u>stars</u> who perform in the movies and on television live in Los Angeles. (9) <u>Visitors</u> often take a tour of the <u>neighborhoods</u> where many of the movie stars live. (10) Another <u>tourist</u> attraction is <u>Rodeo Drive</u> in Beverly Hills.

Chapter Review Exercises cont'd.

5. Such an animal's extinction would be a great loss to the planet.
6. Californians are now constructing buildings to withstand earthquakes.
7. They prepare for the threat of earthquakes.
8. Have Californians learned to live with that concern?
9. Because the state has many attractions, natural beauty, and a great climate, residents feel it is worth living with the threat of earthquakes.
10. Everyone should take precautions, however.

Exercise 54 Revising the Use of Verbs Revise five of the sentences in the previous exercise to change the type of verb that is used. For example, you might rework a sentence containing an action verb so that it contains a verb phrase.

Exercise 55 Supplying Nouns, Pronouns, and Verbs Add nouns, pronouns, and verbs to the following sentences to complete them. Label the part of speech of each word you add.

1. ___?___ famous and ordinary ___?___ have lived in California.
2. ___?___ have come from other states; ___?___ have also come from foreign countries.
3. Many people ___?___ about the famous Gold Rush when they ___?___ California history.
4. This ___?___ played an important role in California's history, because many people ___?___ west to make ___?___ fortunes.
5. Today California ___?___ known as "The Golden State" based on ___?___ history.

Exercise 56 Revision Practice: Focusing on the Use of Nouns, Pronouns, and Verbs Revise this paragraph. (1) Replace general nouns with more specific ones. (2) Replace common nouns with proper nouns where appropriate. (3) Replace proper nouns with common nouns to avoid repetition. (4) Replace nouns with pronouns where appropriate to reduce repetition. (5) Replace general verbs with more specific ones wherever possible. (6) Rework sentences where you can to replace linking verbs with action verbs.

(1) California's cities each have their own distinctive features and attractions. (2) California's capital, Sacramento, has a re-creation of what Sacramento was like a century ago. (3) This old city is a popular destination for people visiting Sacramento. (4) San Francisco is known for attractions such as the Golden Gate Bridge and Chinatown, and San Francisco also features many hills and a stunningly beautiful bay. (5) San Francisco is also remembered by some people who visit San Francisco for the city's cool, breezy days. (6) Los Angeles has warmer temperatures than San Francisco, and Los Angeles is also larger than San Francisco. (7) The city is known, among other things, as the home of the movie industry. (8) Many of the people who perform in the movies and on television live in Los Angeles. (9) People who visit Los Angeles often take a tour of the places where many of the movie stars live. (10) Another popular attraction is the shopping district in Beverly Hills.

Exercise 57 Writing Application Write an essay persuading people to visit your state. Include proper nouns to name specific places or things. Also include three action verbs, three linking verbs, and three verb phrases.

Exercise 57

Students' essays should contain the required grammatical elements as well as use persuasive structure and word choice.

Standardized Test Preparation Workshop

Analogies

Analogy questions test your ability to determine a relationship between a given pair of words and to identify a similar relationship between the words in the second pair. Common relationships used in analogies are

Antonyms, such as fast : slow
Part-Whole or *Whole-Part,* such as buttons : sweater
Definitional/Synonyms, such as joke : humorous
Cause-Effect or *Effect-Cause,* such as rain : floods
Functional Relationship, such as artist : painting
Relationship of Degrees, such as smart : brilliant

When responding to analogies, determine the relationship between the first pair of words. Then, choose the pair that most closely reflects that relationship.

Sample Test Item

Directions: Each question below consists of a related pair of words followed by five pairs of words labeled *A* through *E.* Select the pair that *best* expresses a relationship similar to that expressed in the original pair.

LOCOMOTIVE : TRAIN ::

(A) horse : saddle

(B) tractor : plough

(C) rudder : rowboat

(D) camel : desert

(E) gasoline : automobile

Answer and Explanations

The correct answer is *E.* The relationship is functional: *A* locomotive powers a train; gasoline powers an automobile.

▶ **Practice** **Directions:** Each question below consists of a related pair of words or phrases, followed by five pairs of word or phrases labeled *A* through *E.* Select the pair that best expresses a relationship similar to that expressed in the original pair.

1 ABRIDGE : NOVEL ::

(A) interrupt : conversation

(B) rehearse : play

(C) terminate : ending

(D) punctuate : sentence

(E) abbreviate : word

2 AUDIENCE : THEATER ::

(A) crew : ship

(B) scholars : library

(C) group : society

(D) spectators : arena

(E) actors : stage

▶ **Lesson Objectives**

1. To discriminate between connotative and denotative meanings
2. To read and understand analogies

Step-by-Step Teaching Guide

Analogies

Teaching Resources: Standardized Test Preparation Workbook, pp. 31–32

1. Emphasize to students that analogies focus on relationships between words and pairs of words.

2. Ask volunteers to offer examples of analogies. You might give students a list of analogies to discuss and identify, working in small groups.

3. Tell students that in a test situation, they should read the first word pair and identify the type of relationship between the words. As they read the possible responses, students should quickly eliminate any word pairs whose relationship does not match that of the first pair.

4. Point out that the correct response usually contains words that are the same parts of speech as the original pair. Remind students that prefixes and suffixes can provide clues to a word's part of speech.

Answer Key

▶ **Practice**

1. E   2. D

Customize for
Less Advanced Students

Have students practice identifying simple parts of speech. This should help them identify word pair relationships that will most likely match the first word pair.

Customize for
More Advanced Students

Have students work in groups to discuss the nuances of relationships among practice word pairs.

⬥ **TEST-TAKING TIP**

Tell students that they should avoid focusing on the definitions of the words in the pairs; they should focus instead on their relationship. Use the following sample item to illustrate this point:

needle : thread ::

A hammer : nail

B thimble : finger

Explain that the answer is **A** because both word pairs describe the function of a tool in attaching one thing to another. Although Answer B relates to sewing, the words do not describe a similar function.

Chapter 17 Time and Resource Manager

In-Depth Lesson Plan

	LESSON FOCUS	PRINT AND MEDIA RESOURCES
DAY 1	**Adjectives** Students learn and apply concepts relating to adjectives, nouns used as adjectives, and proper and compound adjectives. (pp. 370–374/H242–246)	*Writing and Grammar* Interactive Text, Section 17.1; *On-line Exercise Bank,* Section 17.1 **Teaching Resources** *Grammar Exercise Workbook,* pp. 21–24; *Grammar Exercises Answers on Transparencies,* Ch. 17
DAY 2	**Adjectives** *continued* Students learn and apply concepts relating to pronouns and verbs used as adjectives and do the Hands-on Grammar activity. (pp. 375–379/H247–251)	**Teaching Resources** *Grammar Exercise Workbook,* pp. 25–26; *Hands-on Grammar Activity Book,* Ch. 17
DAY 3	**Adverbs** Students learn and apply concepts relating to adverbs, including nouns used as adverbs, and learn to distinguish between adjectives and adverbs. (pp. 380–385/H252–257)	*Writing and Grammar* Interactive Text, Section 17.2; *On-line Exercise Bank,* Section 17.2 **Teaching Resources** *Grammar Exercise Workbook,* pp. 27–30
DAY 4	**Review and Assess** Students review the chapter and demonstrate mastery of concepts. (pp. 386–389)	*Writing and Grammar* Interactive Text, Ch. 17, Chapter Review **Teaching Resources** *Formal Assessment,* Ch. 17

Accelerated Lesson Plan

	LESSON FOCUS	PRINT AND MEDIA RESOURCES
DAY 1	**Adjectives** Students learn and apply concepts relating to adjectives. (pp. 370–379/H242–251)	*Writing and Grammar* Interactive Text, Section 17.1; *On-line Exercise Bank,* Section 17.1 **Teaching Resources** *Grammar Exercise Workbook,* pp. 21–26; *Grammar Exercises Answers on Transparencies,* Ch. 17
DAY 2	**Adverbs** Students learn and apply concepts relating to adverbs. (pp. 380–385/H252–257)	*Writing and Grammar* Interactive Text, Section 17.2; *On-line Exercise Bank,* Section 17.2 **Teaching Resources** *Grammar Exercise Workbook,* pp. 27–30
DAY 3	**Review and Assess** Students review the chapter and demonstrate mastery of parts of speech. (pp. 386–389)	*Writing and Grammar* Interactive Text, Ch. 17, Chapter Review **Teaching Resources** *Formal Assessment,* Ch. 17

Options for Adapting Lesson Plans

HOMEWORK

Have students complete any stage of the lesson for homework.

FEATURES

Extend coverage with the Grammar in Literature features (pp. 373, 382/H245, 254), the Hands-on Grammar activity (p. 378/H250), and the Standardized Test Preparation Workshop (p. 388).

TECHNOLOGY

Students can use *Writing and Grammar* Interactive Text to complete the exercises interactively on computer. They can complete additional exercises in the *On-line Exercise Bank:* The Auto Check feature will grade their work. Go on-line: PHSchool.com Use Web Code: eek-1002

Writing and Grammar Handbook Alignment

Page numbers in Step-by-Step Teaching Guides in this Teacher's Edition refer to pages from the full student text. Handbook page references, indicated with this icon ⊞, are provided in Time and Resource Manager boxes and at the bottom of each Teacher's Edition page.

INTEGRATED SKILLS COVERAGE

Grammar in Literature
SE pp. 373, 382/⊞245, 254

Writing
Find It in Your Writing SE pp. 378, 379, 385/⊞250, 251, 257
Writing Application SE pp. 379, 385, 387/⊞251, 257
Grammar and Style Tip SE pp. 374, 383/⊞246, 255

Spelling
SE pp. 370, 382/⊞242, 254
ATE p. 373

Vocabulary
ATE pp. 371, 377

Viewing and Representing
Critical Viewing SE pp. 368, 371, 372, 377, 381, 383, 384/
⊞240, 243, 244, 249, 253, 255, 256

Real-World Connection
ATE p. 384

ASSESSMENT SUPPORT

Standardized Test Preparation Workshop SE p. 388; ATE p. 375
Standardized Test Preparation Workbook, pp. 33–34
Formal Assessment, Ch. 17

MEETING INDIVIDUAL NEEDS

Less Advanced Students ATE pp. 375, 389. See also Ongoing Assessments, ATE pp. 371, 372, 374, 377, 381, 382.
ESL Students ATE pp. 374, 383
More Advanced Students ATE pp. 381, 389
Linguistic Learners ATE p. 370

BLOCK SCHEDULING

Pacing Suggestions
For 90-minute Blocks
• Administer the Diagnostic Test to students to determine instructional coverage.
• Have students complete the necessary exercises in class. Use the Hands-on Grammar activity to provide a change of pace.

Resources for Varying Instruction
• Writing and Grammar Interactive Text A 90-minute block provides an ideal opportunity for students to work on the computer.

Professional Development Support
• How to Manage Instruction in the Block This teaching resource provides management and activity suggestions.

MEDIA AND TECHNOLOGY

For the Student
• Writing and Grammar Interactive Text, Ch. 17
• On-line Exercise Bank, Sections 17.1–2

For the Teacher
• TeacherEXPRESS™ CD-ROM

WRITING AND GRAMMAR ON-LINE

Interactive Text (On-line or on CD-ROM)
• Easily navigable instruction with on-line supporting resources
• Self-scoring exercises and diagnostic tests

Companion Web Site PHSchool.com
• On-line Exercise Bank (use Web Code eek-1002)

See the Go On-line! feature, SE p. iii.

LITERATURE CONNECTIONS

Grammar in Literature selection from Prentice Hall Literature, Penguin Edition, Grade 10:

from What Makes a Degas a Degas? Richard Mühlberger, SE p. 373/⊞245

▶ **Lesson Objectives**

1. To identify adjectives as modifiers of nouns and pronouns
2. To distinguish between definite and indefinite articles
3. To identify nouns, pronouns, and verbs used as adjectives
4. To recognize proper and compound adjectives
5. To recognize adverbs and the functions they serve in sentences
6. To distinguish adverbs from adjectives
7. To demonstrate contol over grammatical elements such as parts of speech
8. To evaluate writing for both mechanics and content
9. To analyze the characteristics of clearly written texts, including the patterns of organization, syntax, and word choice

Critical Viewing

Analyze Adjectives to describe the mother bird might include *red, patient, protective.* The baby birds might be crying *loudly* and *incessantly.*

Language Highlight

The origin of the adjective *cardinal* begins with the Latin word *cardinalis,* meaning "a hinge." The word was first applied to the *cardinal virtues*—justice, prudence, temperance, and fortitude—upon which all of human nature was believed to hinge. The Catholic Church, for instance, depends fundamentally upon its *cardinals,* the princes of the church who elect the popes. Their hats, always a deep scarlet color, are replicated in the crest of head feathers on the red American finch, now known as the *cardinal-bird.*

Chapter 17 Adjectives and Adverbs

▲ **Critical Viewing**
Name three adjectives to describe the mother bird and two adverbs to describe how the baby birds are crying. **[Analyze]**

Nouns, pronouns, and verbs make simple communication possible. These three parts of speech can express essential ideas, such as *I need food.* For more descriptive and detailed communication, however, two other parts of speech are necessary: *adjectives* and *adverbs.*

Consider, for example, the incredible variety of birds that live in the world. Each species has unique features, abilities, and habits that make it different from every other species. Adjectives and adverbs give writers the ability to communicate these differences. In the sentence *Two majestic red-tailed hawks flew gracefully,* the adjectives *two, majestic,* and *red-tailed* provide important details about the hawks, while the adverb *gracefully* describes their action.

These two parts of speech that add description and detail to your written and spoken words are called *modifiers.* In this chapter, you will examine the ways adjectives and adverbs modify other words.

☑ ONGOING ASSESSMENT: Diagnose

If students miss more than one item in any category, direct them to the relevant pages of the textbook and assign exercises for practice and review.

Adjectives and Adverbs	Diagnostic Test Items	Teach	Practice	Section Review	Chapter Review
Skill Check A					
Adjectives, Including Articles	A 1–5	pp. 370–371/🄷242–243	Ex. 1	Ex. 6	Ex. 21
Skill Check B					
Proper and Compound Adjectives	B 6–10	pp. 373–374/🄷245–246	Ex. 3	Ex. 7	Ex. 22
Skill Check C					
Nouns Used as Adjectives	C 14–15	p. 372/🄷244	Ex. 2	Ex. 8	Ex. 23

Diagnostic Test

Directions: Write all answers on a separate sheet of paper.

Skill Check A. Identify all adjectives, including articles, in each of the following sentences.

1. Ostriches are the largest birds in the world.
2. Mature males may attain a height of 8 feet.
3. The birds are characterized by long, thin necks and strong legs.
4. Ostriches also have short, stubby wings, but they cannot fly.
5. The soft, fluffy feathers of the male are black and white.

Skill Check B. List the proper and compound adjectives in the following sentences, and label each one *proper* or *compound.*

6. Ostriches live on the African continent.
7. They can be found in grassland areas below the Sahara.
8. Most American students have seen ostriches only in a zoo.
9. Ostriches are the fastest two-legged animals on the planet.
10. These overgrown birds can maintain speeds of 40 miles per hour for up to 30 minutes.

Skill Check C. Identify any nouns, pronouns, or verbs used as adjectives in the following sentences. Label each appropriately.

11. Foraging ostriches eat a variety of grasses and crawling insects.
12. Like other birds, ostriches do not have any teeth.
13. They swallow most selected foods whole.
14. Ostriches consume small stones to help them digest their stomach contents.
15. These birds must also remain near a water source, as they require two gallons of water per day.

Skill Check D. In each of the following sentences, identify the adverbs and the word each adverb modifies.

16. The zoologist held an ostrich egg gently in her hands.
17. The incredibly heavy egg weighed nearly 3 pounds.
18. Female ostriches normally lay ten perfectly white eggs each season.
19. Approximately fifty eggs may be concentrated into one centrally located nest.
20. The dominant male incubates the eggs nightly, and the females incubate them daily.

Skill Check E. Identify each underlined word below as either an *adjective* or an *adverb.*

21. The ostriches stood <u>close</u> to the nest to protect their eggs.
22. Incubation is a <u>daily</u> task for the ostriches.
23. The eggs will not hatch <u>early</u>.
24. The <u>ungainly</u> birds try to chase away predators.
25. The birds are formidable because they run so <u>fast</u>.

Adjectives and Adverbs • 369

✓ ONGOING ASSESSMENT: Diagnose *continued*

Adjectives and Adverbs	Diagnostic Test Items	Teach	Practice	Section Review	Chapter Review
Pronouns Used as Adjectives	C 12, 14–15	pp. 375–376/Ⓗ247–248	Ex. 4	Ex. 8	Ex. 23
Verbs Used as Adjectives	C 11, 13	p. 377/Ⓗ249	Ex. 5	Ex. 8	Ex. 23
Skill Check D					
Identifying Adverbs	D 16–20	pp. 380–381/Ⓗ252–253	Ex. 12–13	Ex. 15–16	Ex. 25–26
Skill Check E					
Adverb or Adjective?	E 21–25	p. 383/Ⓗ255	Ex. 14	Ex. 17	Ex. 21, 24
Cumulative Reviews and Applications				Ex. 9–11, 18–20	Ex. 27

Interest GRABBER Give students a few minutes to write a description of an animal without naming it. Read some of the descriptions aloud and have other students guess the identity of each animal. On the board, write some of the adjectives that were used. Point out that adjectives make nouns or pronouns more specific.

Activate Prior Knowledge

Ask students to write a description of a place where they have met someone. Have them underline the words that describe this place. Then have the students explain why each adjective was important in their descriptions.

TEACH

Step-by-Step Teaching Guide

Functions of Adjectives

1. Once the students have read the key concept about modification, refer them to the chart on page 370.

2. Explain that an adjective may come before or after the noun it modifies. Provide these examples, then have students write their own sentences using adjectives before and after nouns.

   The happy child was eating ice cream.

   The child eating ice cream was happy.

3. Have students tell what questions the adjectives in their examples answer.

Customize for
Linguistic Learners

Have students write one sentence using many similar adjectives. Provide the following as an example.

Several short, stubby, under-grown, chunky mushrooms grew under the stairs in the cellar.

Have students discuss whether using this many adjectives makes a sentence effective or confusing.

Section 17.1 # Adjectives

Whenever you want to create a clearer picture of a person, place, or thing, you are likely to use an *adjective*.

▶ **KEY CONCEPT** An **adjective** is a word used to describe a noun or pronoun or to give a noun or pronoun a more specific meaning. ■

The way an adjective describes a word or makes it more specific is called *modification*. Modification is the act of changing something slightly. An adjective modifies a noun or pronoun by adding information that answers any of four questions about the noun or pronoun:

▶ **KEY CONCEPT** Adjectives answer the question *What kind? Which one? How many?* or *How much?* about the nouns and pronouns they modify. ■

In the following chart, the examples show adjectives that answer the four questions noted about nouns or pronouns.

QUESTIONS THAT ADJECTIVES ANSWER	
What Kind?	
large hawk	*lost* boy
metallic gleam	*purple* feather
Which One?	
that bird	*any* number
other door	*last* opportunity
How Many?	
both swans	*some* falcons
five dollars	*frequent* interruptions
How Much?	
enough birdseed	*more* fun
less effort	*adequate* space

When an adjective modifies a noun, it usually comes before the noun. Occasionally, though, the adjective may follow the noun.

Theme: Birds

In this section, you will learn how adjectives are used to modify nouns and pronouns. The examples and exercises are about different species of birds.

Cross-Curricular Connection: Science

Spelling Tip

Suffixes such as *-ive, -ible,* and *-able* are often used to transform nouns into adjectives. For example, *response* becomes *responsive* or *responsible* and *reason* becomes *reasonable.*

⏱ TIME AND RESOURCE MANAGER	
Resources	

Print: *Grammar Exercise Workbook,* pp. 21–26; *Grammar Exercises Answers on Transparencies,* Ch. 17; *Hands-on Grammar Activity Book,* Ch. 17
Technology: *Writing and Grammar* Interactive Text, Section 17.1; *On-Line Exercise Bank,* Section 17.1

Using the Full Student Edition	Using the Handbook🄷
• Work through all key concepts, pp. 370–377.	• Work through all key concepts, pp. 242–249.
• Assign and review Exercises 1–5.	• Assign and review Exercises 1–5.
• Read and discuss Grammar in Literature, p. 373.	• Read and discuss Grammar in Literature, p. 245.
• Do the Hands-on Grammar activity, p. 378.	• Do the Hands-on Grammar activity, p. 250.

▶ **KEY CONCEPT** An adjective may come before or after the noun it modifies. ■

BEFORE: The *large* condor is at the zoo.

AFTER: The condor at the zoo is *large*.

▶ **KEY CONCEPT** Two or more adjectives can modify one word. ■

EXAMPLE: *Several small, fuzzy* chicks were running around the farm.

Note About *a, an,* and *the*: Three adjectives—*a, an,* and *the*—are called *articles*. *The* is called a *definite article* because it refers to a specific noun. *A* and *an* are called *indefinite articles* because they refer to any one of a class of nouns. In the examples below, *the* refers to a specific zoo, while *an* refers to any apple.

DEFINITE: We will go to *the* zoo.

INDEFINITE: The parrot ate *an* apple.

▶ **Exercise 1** Recognizing Adjectives Write the adjectives, including articles, in each sentence below.

EXAMPLE: The swift parrot chased a small lizard.
ANSWER: The, swift, a, small

1. Parrots are found in the warm tropical areas of the planet.
2. A small number of species inhabit the cooler temperate regions.
3. The colorful birds have red, green, blue, and yellow plumage.
4. Parrots eat a wide variety of hearty seeds and nutritious fruits.
5. Parrots are monogamous, often remaining with a single mate for life.

▼ **Critical Viewing** Name three adjectives to describe either of the parakeets in this picture. What question does each adjective answer about the parakeet? **[Analyze, Connect]**

▶ **More Practice**

Grammar Exercise Workbook
• pp. 21–22
On-line Exercise Bank
• Section 17.1
  Go on-line:
  PHSchool.com
  Enter Web Code:
  eek-1002

Adjectives • 371

☑ **ONGOING ASSESSMENT: Monitor and Reinforce**

If students miss more than one item in Exercise 1, refer them to the following for additional practice.

In the Textbook	Print Resources	Technology
Section Review, Ex. 6, Section 17.1	*Grammar Exercise Workbook,* pp. 21–22	*On-Line Exercise Bank,* Section 17.1

Nouns Used as Adjectives

1. Point out that a noun used as an adjective will answer the question *What kind?* or *Which one?*

2. Ask students to suggest more examples of nouns modifying other nouns (e.g.,*coffee* mug, *hockey* rink, *baseball* game).

Answer Key

Exercise 2

1. parrot
2. canyon
3. nest
4. food
5. tree
6. forest
7. winter
8. macaw
9. Cattle
10. wildlife

Critical Viewing

Speculate, Identify Sample responses: <u>wing</u> feathers, <u>neck</u> ruff, <u>beak</u> opening.

Customize for
Less Advanced Students

Have students play "Categories" by drawing a chart with five columns and four rows. Label the columns *Animals, Food, Cars, Flowers*, and *Houses*. Label the rows *S, T, M,* and *F.* Tell students to find adjectives that modify the categories in each column and begin with each of the letters of each row. After completing the grid, have students choose new categories that require nouns used as adjectives as well as proper and compound adjectives. Set a ten-minute time limit for the completion of each grid. Have students compare their answers to see who thought of the same adjectives and who had different adjectives.

17.1

Nouns Used as Adjectives

Many nouns can be used as adjectives. They become adjectives when they modify other nouns and answer one of two questions about the nouns they are modifying.

▶ **KEY CONCEPT** A noun used as an adjective answers the question *What kind?* or *Which one?* about a noun that follows it. ■

Noun	Adjective
pineapple	*pineapple* juice (*What kind* of juice?)
summer	*summer* habitat (*Which* habitat?)

▶ **Exercise 2** Identifying Nouns Used as Adjectives Write the noun used as an adjective in each sentence below.

EXAMPLE: The macaw perched on the top of the rock ledge.
ANSWER: rock

1. Macaws are large, noisy members of the parrot family.
2. The colorful macaws live in large flocks and roost along steep canyon walls.
3. They dig small nest holes in the relatively soft sandstone.
4. Major food sources for macaws are fruits and nuts.
5. Macaws perch among the tree branches while they eat.
6. Occasionally, they will also search the forest floor for food.
7. Because they live in the warm tropics of South America, the birds do not migrate to a winter territory.
8. Unfortunately, the macaw population is dwindling because of the actions of humans.
9. Cattle ranches are the biggest threat to the remaining habitat of the macaw.
10. The birds are also threatened by wildlife poachers.

▶ Critical Viewing Each part of this parrot can be named by a noun. Can any of these nouns also act as adjectives to modify another noun? Give an example. **[Speculate, Identify]**

372 • Adjectives and Adverbs

*i*nteractive Textbook

Get instant feedback! Exercise 2 is available on-line or on CD-ROM.

▶ **More Practice**

Grammar Exercise Workbook
• pp. 23–24
On-line Exercise Bank
• Section 17.1
  Go on-line:
  PHSchool.com
  Enter Web Code:
  eek-1002

☑ **ONGOING ASSESSMENT: Monitor and Reinforce**

If students miss more than two items in Exercise 2, refer them to the following for additional practice.

In the Textbook	Print Resources	Technology
Section Review, Ex. 8, Section 17.1	*Grammar Exercise Workbook,* pp. 23–24	*On-Line Exercise Bank,* Section 17.1

GRAMMAR IN LITERATURE

from What Makes a Degas a Degas?

Richard Mühlberger

Notice the different types of adjectives, including proper and compound, highlighted in blue italics in the following excerpt.

Degas placed a *cream-colored* umbrella in the middle of the painting above some of the figures in the carriage. Near it, balanced on the back of the driver's seat, is a *black* bulldog. . . .

. . . Throughout his life, the artist drew inspiration from the masterpieces in the Louvre in Paris, one of the *greatest* museums in the world. He also found ideas in *Japanese* prints.

Proper and Compound Adjectives

Two other types of adjectives are *proper adjectives* and *compound adjectives.*

Proper Adjectives Sometimes, proper nouns are used as adjectives or changed in form to become adjectives.

KEY CONCEPT A **proper adjective** is a proper noun used as an adjective or an adjective formed from a proper noun. ■

Notice in the following chart that proper adjectives modify nouns by answering the questions *What kind?* or *Which one?*

Proper Nouns	Proper Adjectives
Vermont	*Vermont* cheddar (*What kind* of cheddar?)
Brahms	the *Brahms* symphony (*Which* symphony?)

Sometimes, proper nouns change their form when they are used as proper adjectives.

Proper Nouns	Proper Adjectives
Shakespeare	*Shakespearean* play (*What kind* of play?)
Germany	*German* tribes (*Which* tribes?)

Proper adjectives generally begin with a capital letter.

Step-by-Step Teaching Guide

Grammar in Literature

1. Ask students to match each adjective in the excerpt with the question it answers (*cream-colored, black, Japanese*—What kind?; *greatest*—Which one?).
2. Ask a student to read the paragraph without the adjectives. Discuss the effect this has on the paragraph.

More About the Writer

Richard Mühlberger (b. 1938) is an art critic and museum administrator. While working at the Metropolitan Museum of Art in New York City, he began producing a series of books that make the works of famous artists accessible to the average viewer. The series includes books about Degas, Van Gogh, Monet, and others.

Connections With Literature

What Makes a Degas a Degas? can be found in *Prentice Hall Literature, Penguin Edition,* Grade 10. Encourage students to choose a passage and copy the adjectives that appear in that excerpt.

Step-by-Step Teaching Guide

Proper Adjectives

1. Remind students that proper nouns used as adjectives are called *proper adjectives* and usually begin with capital letters.
2. After reading the charts on this page, have students write additional examples (*Wisconsin* lakes, *Elizabethan* theater).

ONGOING ASSESSMENT: Prerequisite Skills

If students have difficulty with proper and compound adjectives, you may find it necessary to review the following to ensure coverage of prerequisite knowledge.

In the Textbook	Print Resources	Technology
Compound Nouns, Section 16.1 Proper Nouns, Section 16.1	*Grammar Exercise Workbook,* pp. 1–4	*Writing and Grammar* Interactive Text, Section 16.1; *On-Line Exercise Bank,* Section 16.1

Integrating Spelling Skills

Proper Adjectives Read the names of the six inhabited continents aloud. Ask students to listen and write the names of their inhabitants on their papers. Now ask students to use these words as adjectives in sentences. (*The South American parrot is large.*) Have them check the spelling of their proper adjectives.

Compound Adjectives

1. Tell students that some adjectives are compound and can be written as hyphenated words, combined words, or separate words.

2. Explain that separate-word adjectives preceding nouns are nearly always proper adjectives, such as *Near Eastern*.

3. Remind students to check a dictionary if they are uncertain about the spelling of a compound adjective.

Customize for
ESL Students

Because many languages, including Spanish, do not use compound adjectives, students will benefit from additional practice. Supply (or have each student bring in) magazines or newspapers. Have students skim articles, looking for compound adjectives. Discuss the meaning of each compound adjective and construct sentences using some of them.

Answer Key

▶ **Exercise 3**

1. long-legged: compound
2. multicolored: compound
3. African: proper; South American: proper and compound
4. downward-turned: compound; underwater: compound
5. Caribbean: proper
6. Chilean: proper; lowland: compound; South American: proper and compound
7. worldwide: compound
8. cone-shaped: compound; off-white: compound
9. newborn: compound; self-sufficient: compound
10. North American: proper and compound; saltwater: compound; freshwater: compound

---

17.1

▶ **KEY CONCEPT** A **compound adjective** is an adjective that is made up of more than one word. ■

Most compound adjectives are hyphenated, but some are written as combined words.

Hyphenated	Combined
freeze-dried coffee	*farsighted* planner
heavy-duty boots	*underpaid* staff

If you are uncertain about the spelling of a compound adjective, consult a dictionary.

▶ **Exercise 3** Recognizing Proper and Compound Adjectives
Write only the proper and compound adjectives in each sentence below, and label each. (Note: Some may be compound proper adjectives.)

EXAMPLE: Flamingos can be found in the Brazilian forests.
ANSWER: Brazilian

1. The flamingo is the name for a family of long-legged birds.
2. Scientists are fascinated by these multicolored birds.
3. Flamingos are common throughout the world, and they can be found from the African savannas to the South American mountains.
4. They are characterized by a downward-turned bill, which is used to filter underwater organisms and vegetation.
5. The largest species, called the greater flamingo, inhabits the Caribbean region.
6. The Chilean flamingo is a variety that may be found in the lowland areas of Chile and Argentina on the South American mainland.
7. The lesser flamingo is the most common type, with a worldwide population of 4 million.
8. Flamingos fashion cone-shaped nests from mud, and they generally lay one off-white egg.
9. The newborn chicks are fed by the parents for months; however, they are self-sufficient after 30 days.
10. Flamingos make their North American homes in saltwater marshes and shallow freshwater ponds.

● Grammar
and Style Tip

Adjectives are an essential tool for writers because they add important details. However, writers should avoid using long strings of adjectives to describe every noun. The excessive use of adjectives may complicate your message or confuse your reader.

☑ **ONGOING ASSESSMENT: Monitor and Reinforce**

If students miss more than two items in Exercise 3, refer them to the following for additional practice.

In the Textbook	Print Resources	Technology
Section Review, Ex. 7, Section 17.1	*Grammar Exercise Workbook,* pp. 23–24	*On-Line Exercise Bank,* Section 17.1

Pronouns Used as Adjectives

Just as nouns can be used as adjectives, so can certain pronouns. In fact, some personal pronouns, known as *possessive pronouns* or *possessive adjectives*, act as both pronouns *and* adjectives. Others act as either pronouns *or* adjectives.

KEY CONCEPT A pronoun functions as an adjective if it modifies a noun. ■

Possessive Pronouns or Adjectives Seven personal pronouns are known as *possessive pronouns* or *possessive adjectives*. They are pronouns because they have antecedents. They are adjectives because they modify nouns and answer the question *Which one?*

POSSESSIVE PRONOUNS OR ADJECTIVES
my   your   his   he   its   our   their
ANTECEDENT   WORD MODIFIED
The *flock* reached *its* winter feeding *grounds*.

Demonstrative Adjectives All four of the demonstrative pronouns can be used as adjectives. Unlike the personal pronouns above, they become demonstrative adjectives *instead of* pronouns. When they function as adjectives, they always come before the nouns they modify and never directly before a verb.

DEMONSTRATIVE ADJECTIVES	
this that these those	
Demonstrative Pronouns	**Demonstrative Adjectives**
Did the bird drop *this?*	Did the bird drop *this* feather?
Those are pretty birds.	*Those* birds are pretty.

Interrogative Adjectives Three of the interrogative pronouns become *interrogative adjectives* when they modify a noun.

INTERROGATIVE ADJECTIVES	
which what whose	
Interrogative Pronouns	**Interrogative Adjectives**
What happened?	*What* color is the egg?
Whose is that?	*Whose* pet is the canary?

Adjectives • **375**

Step-by-Step Teaching Guide

Pronouns Used as Adjectives

1. Discuss with students the four types of pronouns that can be used as adjectives.

2. Remind students that possessive pronouns are adjectives when they tell who possesses the noun.

   Mary did her homework.

   (*her* modifies homework—adjective; her *refers to* Mary—pronoun)

3. Help students grasp the difference between demonstrative and interrogative pronouns and their adjective forms. As adjectives, they come before the nouns they modify. As pronouns, they stand alone.

   Bob enjoyed that program. (that modifies program—adjective)

   Bob enjoyed that. (that stands alone—pronoun)

Customize for
Less Advanced Students

To clarify the idea that a possessive pronoun can also be a possessive adjective, have students write a simple sentence for each of these pronouns: *my, your* or *yours, his, her* or *hers, its, our* or *ours, their* or *theirs*. Ask students to underline the possessive word in each sentence, double underline the word it is modifying (used as adjective), and circle the word to which it refers, or its antecedent (used as pronoun).

John left his keys on the desk.

STANDARDIZED TEST PREPARATION WORKSHOP

Grammar and Usage Many standardized tests require an understanding of modifiers to answer questions about reading comprehension.

She took the book into her room, that place where she most enjoyed reading.

To what does the underlined word refer?

A It tells who owns the book.
B It tells which place.
C It means the same as *room.*
D It serves no function in the passage.

The answer is **B**. The word *that* modifies the noun *place*. If the sentence had read *That was where she enjoyed reading*, then *That* would have been a demonstrative pronoun referring to *room.*

TIME SAVERS!

Answers on Transparencies
Use the *Grammar Exercises Answers on Transparencies* for Chapter 17 to facilitate correction by students.

On-Line Exercise Bank
Have students complete the exercises on computer. The Auto Check feature will grade their work for you!

Indefinite Adjectives

1. Tell students that an indefinite pronoun becomes an indefinite adjective when it is used to modify a noun.

2. Remind them that the indefinite word is being used as a pronoun if the noun is missing.

3. Ask student to use the singular or plural words in the chart on this page to write sentences illustrating their use both as pronouns and adjectives. You might start with these examples.

   Do you want another?
   (pronoun)

   Do you want another chocolate?
   (adjective)

   How many do you have?
   (pronoun)

   How many candles do you have?
   (adjective)

Answer Key

> **Exercise 4**

1. my: adjective modifying *friends*
2. Those: pronoun; their: adjective modifying *beaks*
3. That: adjective modifying *beak*; its: adjective modifying *length*
4. Our: adjective modifying *guide*; some: adjective modifying *toucans*
5. These: adjective modifying *birds*
6. one: adjective modifying *species*
7. all: adjective modifying *toucans*
8. few: adjective modifying *people*; what: adjective modifying *foods*
9. most: adjective modifying *toucans*; several: pronoun
10. which: pronoun; many: adjective modifying *birds*; his: adjective modifying *favorite*

17.1

Indefinite Adjectives Many indefinite pronouns become *indefinite adjectives* when they modify nouns. The charts below show whether they modify singular or plural nouns.

INDEFINITE ADJECTIVES		
Singular	**Plural**	**Singular or Plural**
another much	both	all other
each neither	few	any some
either one	many	more
little	several	most

Indefinite Pronouns	Indefinite Adjectives
The parakeet ate *one*.	The parakeet ate *one* nut.
Few live in the Arctic.	*Few* birds live in the Arctic.
We saw *some* at the lake.	We saw *some* ducks at the lake.

> **Exercise 4** Distinguishing Between Pronouns and Adjectives Identify whether the underlined word in each sentence below functions as a *pronoun* or as an *adjective*. If it functions as an adjective, tell which word it modifies.

EXAMPLE: We watched <u>that</u> toucan fly from the perch.
ANSWER: adjective (modifies toucan)

1. On a recent trip to the zoo, <u>my</u> friends and I learned about toucans.
2. <u>Those</u> are brightly colored birds known for <u>their</u> large beaks.
3. <u>That</u> toucan's beak measures more than half of <u>its</u> body length.
4. <u>Our</u> tour guide said <u>some</u> toucans may grow to be 25 inches long.
5. <u>These</u> interesting birds inhabit the tropical forests of Central and South America.
6. Only <u>one</u> species, the toucanet, lives in the mountains.
7. <u>All</u> toucans have two forward-facing toes and two backward-facing toes.
8. A <u>few</u> people in the group asked <u>what</u> foods were eaten by toucans.
9. The tour guide said <u>most</u> toucans eat small fruits and berries, but <u>several</u> eat insects and small lizards.
10. We asked <u>which</u> of the zoo's <u>many</u> birds was <u>his</u> favorite.

> **More Practice**

Grammar Exercise Workbook
• pp. 25–26
On-line Exercise Bank
• Section 17.1
  Go on-line:
  PHSchool.com
  Enter Web Code:
  eek-1002

Get instant feedback! Exercises 4 and 5 are available on-line or on CD-ROM.

Verbs Used as Adjectives

Many words that look like verbs can function as adjectives in sentences.

KEY CONCEPT Some verb forms, especially those ending in *-ing* and *-ed*, function as adjectives when they modify a noun. ■

Below are verbs used first as verbs and then as adjectives.

Verbs	Adjectives
The owl *was sitting* still.	The *sitting* owl was still.
The ice *melted* in the sun.	The *melted* ice was in the sun.

Exercise 5 Distinguishing Between Verbs and Adjectives
Identify whether the underlined word in each sentence below functions as a *verb* or as an *adjective*. If it functions as an adjective, tell which word it modifies.

EXAMPLE: A <u>startled</u> peacock will make a lot of noise.
ANSWER: adjective (modifies peacock)

1. The peacock, a member of the pheasant family, is known for its brilliantly <u>colored</u> feathers.
2. Only the males are <u>endowed</u> with colorful blue, gold, and green plumage.
3. The <u>camouflaged</u> females, called peahens, have drab brown-and-green feathers.
4. <u>Competing</u> males display their ornate feathers to attract mates.
5. At night, peacocks usually <u>sleep</u> in high tree branches.
6. <u>Consuming</u> small snakes and lizards, they spend their days on the ground.
7. Until recently, scientists thought that these birds <u>inhabited</u> only the forests of Southeast Asia and India.
8. The Congo peacock is a rare species that occupies a very <u>confined</u> area in central Africa.
9. Because it had eluded scientists until 1936, this bird was considered a <u>living</u> mystery when it was discovered.
10. Today, the Congo peacock is a <u>protected</u> species.

▼ Critical Viewing
Use *singing* as a verb and then as an adjective in sentences about this bird.
[Connect]

Adjectives • 377

Step-by-Step Teaching Guide

Verbs Used as Adjectives

1. Tell students that verbs can act as adjectives in a sentence; they do this when they modify nouns.
2. Refer to the word *melted* in the chart. As a verb, it describes the *action* that the *ice* performed; as an adjective, it tells what kind of *ice*.
3. Ask students to write pairs of sentences using *growing, laughing, sailing,* and *listening* both as verbs and as adjectives.

Integrating Vocabulary Skills

Verbs as Adjectives Have students make a list of verbs that describe the actions of birds (*to fly, to flock, to nest, to chirp, to live,* etc). Tell students to change the verbs into adjectives and use them in sentences. (*The flying bird zoomed across the sky.*) Students can increase their adjective vocabulary by using other parts of speech as adjectives.

Answer Key

Exercise 5

1. adjective modifying *feathers*
2. verb
3. adjective modifying *females*
4. adjective modifying *males*
5. verb
6. adjective modifying *they*
7. verb
8. adjective modifying *area*
9. adjective modifying *mystery*
10. adjective modifying *species*

Critical Viewing

Connect Sample response: The canary is <u>singing</u> to us; <u>singing</u> birds, such as canaries, are popular pets.

✓ ONGOING ASSESSMENT: Monitor and Reinforce

If students miss more than two items in Exercise 4 or 5, refer them to the following for additional practice.

In the Textbook	Print Resources	Technology
Section Review, Ex. 8, Section 17.1	*Grammar Exercise Workbook,* pp. 25–26	*On-Line Exercise Bank,* Section 17.1

⏱ TIME SAVERS!

Answers on Transparencies Use the *Grammar Exercises Answers on Transparencies* for Chapter 17 to facilitate correction by students.

On-Line Exercise Bank Have students complete the exercises on computer. The Auto Check feature will grade their work for you!

Hands-on Grammar

Teaching Resources: Hands-on Grammar Activity Book, Ch. 17

1. If you wish to do this activity in class, be prepared with scissors, index cards, and construction paper. Have students work in pairs, and give each pair the needed materials.

2. Go through the directions and diagrams with students so that they understand how to cut the windows and tape the index cards onto the paper.

3. As a class, work through the examples suggested in the text. Then have student pairs come up with their own words and phrases.

Find It in Your Reading

You might wish to have students peruse a literature selection or unit they have recently studied to find verb forms in introductory adjective phrases.

Find It in Your Writing

Students could work with their partners to see if they have correctly converted verbs into adjectives.

17.1

Hands-on Grammar

Turning Verbs Into Adjectives

To practice converting verb forms into adjectives, try this activity. Take several index cards, and cut out a long opening in each to create a box with two "wings," as in the model below. On one side of the card, write a verb phrase, such as *is crying, was shouting, has been forgotten,* or *was protected.* Flip the card over, and write just the participle form on the other side: *crying, shouting, forgotten, protected.*

Tape the edges of the wings of a card onto a piece of paper. In the opening, write an article and a noun spaced apart, so that a sentence such as *The child is crying* would appear. Now, bend the card to place *crying* between *the* and *child* to create the phrase *The crying child.* Create additional verb/adjective conversions. Then, extend the activity by writing a phrase after the verb form on both sides of the card. For example: Write *was shouting at his friend* on one side of a card and *shouting at his friend* on the flip side. This time, put the article and noun close together. Connecting this new card to *The child,* you can create an introductory adjective phrase such as *Shouting at his friend* to add to a longer sentence about the child.

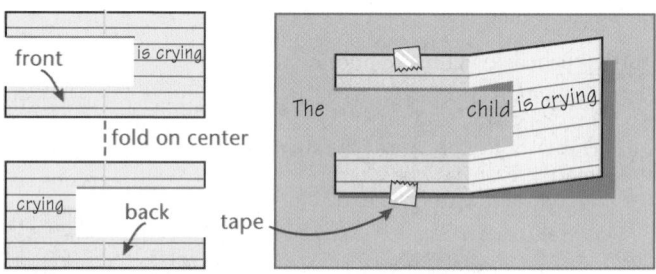

Find It in Your Reading In your reading, find examples of sentences that contain verb forms used in introductory adjective phrases. Write the sentences on your paper, and underline the verb form acting as an adjective and the noun being modified.

Find It in Your Writing Look through samples of your own writing to find sentences in which you have used *-ing* and *-ed* forms of verbs. Rewrite the sentences, changing the verbs to adjectives and expanding the sentences.

✋ **Hands-on Grammar**
Use the Hands-on Grammar activity sheet for Chapter 17 to facilitate this activity.

☑ **ONGOING ASSESSMENT: Assess Mastery**

Use the following resources to assess student mastery of adjectives.

In the Textbook	Technology
Chapter Review, Ex. 21–23	*On-Line Exercise Bank,* Section 17.1

Section 17.1 Section Review

GRAMMAR EXERCISES 6–11

> **Exercise 6** Recognizing Types of Adjectives Identify each underlined adjective below as *article*, *proper adjective*, *compound adjective*, *possessive adjective*, *indefinite adjective*, or *demonstrative adjective*.

1. The kiwi is a strange-looking bird that can be found only in some areas of New Zealand.
2. While kiwis are defenseless, their survival has been made possible because they have no natural predators on this South Pacific island.
3. Although New Zealand kiwis have small, stubby wings, they are earth-bound birds that cannot fly.
4. Long, hairlike feathers are another feature of a kiwi.
5. It is also the only Asian bird that locates food by its sense of smell.

> **Exercise 7** Recognizing Other Parts of Speech Used as Adjectives Identify any nouns, pronouns, or verbs used as adjectives in the following sentences. Write them on your paper, and label each. If none are used, write *none*.

1. The owl is a bird variety that is characterized by a large head, forward-facing eyes, and sharp claws.
2. The barn owl is the most common species in the United States.
3. The smallest species resides in the deserts of the Southwest.
4. In which places besides trees and abandoned buildings do owls make their homes?
5. The burrowing owl, for instance, may make its home in old rabbit holes.
6. Most owls are active after the evening stars have emerged.
7. They are the only birds whose eyes are located on the front of the face.
8. All owls also have excellent hearing abilities to assist their hunting efforts.
9. Rain deters hunting owls, since they cannot fly quietly with wet wing feathers.
10. Though many people dislike owls, these birds are our allies against rodents.

> **Exercise 8** Supplying Adjectives to Add Details Rewrite the paragraph below on your paper, supplying an adjective in each blank.

(1) The wild turkey is among the ___?___ birds in North America, much bigger than most other fowl. (2) Wild turkeys are found in ___?___ areas deep among the trees. (3) Males are ___?___ and ___?___ than females and are also more ___?___ . (4) The males can also be distinguished by the wattle, a ___?___ piece of ___?___ skin that hangs from the beak. (5) The skin of the head and neck of a wild turkey is usually ___?___ in color, but it may also be a brighter shade of ___?___ or ___?___ .

> **Exercise 9** Find It in Your Reading In the excerpt from "What Makes a Degas a Degas?" on page 373, identify the *compound adjective* and the *proper adjective*.

> **Exercise 10** Find It in Your Writing In your own writing, find at least one example of each of the following kinds of adjectives: *proper*, *compound*, *possessive*, and *demonstrative*. Copy the sentences, and label each type of adjective.

> **Exercise 11** Writing Application Write a description of your favorite bird. Be sure to use precise adjectives to bring the bird to life for your readers.

Answer Key

> **Exercise 6**

1. The, article; strange-looking, compound adjective; some, indefinite adjective
2. defenseless, compound adjective; their, possessive adjective; this, demonstrative adjective; South Pacific, proper and compound adjective
3. New Zealand, proper and compound adjective; earthbound, compound adjective
4. hairlike, compound adjective; another, indefinite adjective; a, article
5. Asian, proper adjective; its, possessive adjective

> **Exercise 7**

1. bird: noun; forward-facing: verb
2. barn: noun
3. none
4. which: pronoun; abandoned: verb; their: pronoun
5. burrowing: verb; its: pronoun; rabbit: noun
6. Most: pronoun; evening: noun
7. whose: pronoun
8. All: pronoun; hearing: verb; their: pronoun; hunting: verb
9. hunting: verb; wing: noun
10. many: pronoun; these: pronoun; our: pronoun

continued

Answer Key continued

> **Exercise 8**

Answers will vary. Possible answers:

1. largest
2. forested
3. bigger, heavier, colorful
4. long, loose
5. pale, red, blue

> **Exercise 9**

Find It in Your Reading
Compound adjective: cream-colored
Proper adjective: Japanese

> **Exercise 10**

Find It in Your Writing
If students have difficulty finding adjectives in their writing, encourage them to revise a piece of their writing to include the requested kinds.

> **Exercise 11**

Writing Application
When students have finished, have volunteers read their descriptions aloud. Have others in the class comment on the use of adjectives.

Interest GRABBER Write the following words on the board: *quickly, carefully, skillfully,* and *never.* Then write this incomplete sentence: *Carl ___ reported the accident to the police.* Have a student read the sentence aloud, filling in the blank with one of the words on the board. Ask students how each word alters the meaning of the sentence. (The words describe different ways of reporting.) Tell students that words that modify verbs are *adverbs* and that adverbs have other uses as well.

Activate Prior Knowledge

Ask students to use the word *almost* in sentences. Provide examples such as the following, one of which uses *almost* to modify a verb and one that uses *almost* to modify an adjective.

*Our team almost won the championship. (*modifying the verb *won)*

*Our almost perfect season put us in the playoffs. (*modifying the adjective *perfect)*

Explain that adverbs can modify verbs, adjectives, and other adverbs.

TEACH

Step-by-Step Teaching Guide

Adverbs

1. Ask students to use the adverbs *nearly, happily, late,* and *away* in original sentences as verb modifiers. Ask what questions the adverbs answer.

2. Ask students to use the adverbs in the chart to modify adjectives or other adverbs.

Section 17.2 *Adverbs*

Like adjectives, *adverbs* are used to describe or add information about other words.

▶ **KEY CONCEPT** An **adverb** is a word that modifies a verb, an adjective, or another adverb. ■

Just as adjectives answer questions about nouns and pronouns, adverbs answer questions about words they modify.

▶ **KEY CONCEPT** An adverb answers one of four questions about the word it modifies: *Where? When? In what way?* or *To what extent?* ■

An adverb modifying a verb can answer any of the four questions. An adverb modifying an adjective or another adverb, however, will answer only one question: *To what extent?*

The chart below shows adverbs answering each of the four questions. Notice the positions of the adverbs. When an adverb modifies a verb or verb phrase, it may come *before* or *after* the verb or verb phrase. Frequently, it comes *within* the verb phrase. If an adverb modifies an adjective or another adverb, it generally comes *immediately before* the adjective or adverb.

Verbs	Adjectives
Where?	**When?**
slide *under* move *near* sit *there* slipped *between*	*often* asks sails *daily* should have answered *promptly* *soon* will depart
In What Way?	**To What Extent?**
reacted *positively* *silently* nodded left *quickly* *rudely* laughed was *cheerfully* humming	*widely* read *barely* walks researched *further* had *just* started must *not* have finished
Adverbs Modifying Adjectives	**Adverbs Modifying Adverbs**
To What Extent?	**To What Extent?**
very tall *somewhat* satisfied *frequently* absent *not* sad	*very* thoroughly *not* exactly *more* quickly *quite* definitely

380 • Adjectives and Adverbs

Theme: Seashells

In this section, you will learn how adverbs are used to modify verbs, adjectives, and other adverbs. The examples and exercises are about different kinds of seashells.

Cross-Curricular Connection: Science

⏱ **TIME AND RESOURCE MANAGER**

Resources
Print: *Grammar Exercise Workbook,* pp. 27–30; *Grammar Exercises Answers on Transparencies,* Ch. 17
Technology: *Writing and Grammar* Interactive Text, Section 17.2; *On-Line Exercise Bank,* Section 17.2

Using the Full Student Edition	Using the Handbook Ⓗ
• Work through all key concepts, pp. 380–383. • Assign and review Exercises 12–14. • Read and discuss Grammar in Literature, p. 382.	• Work through all key concepts, pp. 252–255. • Assign and review Exercises 12–14. • Read and discuss Grammar in Literature, p. 254.

◀ Critical Viewing
Using this photo and the information in Exercise 12, describe these cowries with phrases containing adverbs that answer each of the four questions on page 380. **[Analyze]**

Exercise 12 Recognizing Adverbs Identify the adverbs in each sentence below. Then, tell which word each adverb modifies.

EXAMPLE: The porpoise swam very rapidly.
ANSWER: very (modifies rapidly), rapidly (modifies swam)

1. Cowries are a very common variety of sea snails that are generally found in warm tropical waters.
2. They are mostly nocturnal animals, and they usually feed on algae.
3. A few species crawl slowly among corals and feed hungrily upon them.
4. These small creatures often have brilliantly colored shells.
5. For many years, cowry shells were used quite frequently by people in Africa, Asia, and Melanesia as a form of currency.

Nouns Used as Adverbs

A few words that are usually nouns can also act as adverbs.

▶ **KEY CONCEPT** Nouns used as adverbs answer the question *Where?* or *When?* about a verb. ■

Some of the nouns that can be used as adverbs are *home*, *yesterday*, and *today*.

Nouns	Adverbs
The crab's *home* is under that rock.	The crab crawled *home*. (crawled *where?*)
The warm, summer *nights* cause the jellyfish to rise to the water's surface.	The jellyfish are active *nights*. (are active *when?*)

More Practice
Grammar Exercise Workbook
• pp. 27–28
On-line Exercise Bank
• Section 17.2
Go on-line:
PHSchool.com
Enter Web Code:
eek-1002

Interactive Textbook

Get instant feedback! Exercise 12 is available on-line or on CD-ROM.

Adverbs • 381

Grammar in Literature

On a piece of paper, have students write the question that each adverb in the excerpt answers. (*suddenly*—When?; *too*—To what extent?)

More About the Writer

Israeli poet Dahlia Ravikovitch (b. 1936) was born near Tel Aviv and raised in a cooperative settlement called a kibbutz. Her father's death when she was six years old greatly influenced her. She writes intensely personal poems charged with images from nature, history, and religion.

Answer Key

▶ Exercise 13

1. (Weekends), relatively
2. carefully, some (mornings)
3. Most (days), seldom
4. (Today), nearby
5. always, (home)
6. (Afternoons), thoroughly
7. eagerly, (tomorrow)
8. (Sundays), generally
9. fully, (outside)
10. Unfortunately, (weekdays)

17.2

GRAMMAR IN LITERATURE

from **Pride**
Dahlia Ravikovitch

The adverbs in this excerpt are printed in blue italics.

And *suddenly* the rock has an open wound.
I told you, when rocks break, it happens by surprise.
And people, *too*.

▶ **Exercise 13** Recognizing Nouns Used as Adverbs Identify two adverbs in each sentence below, and write them on your paper. Then, circle each noun used as an adverb.

EXAMPLE: Yesterday, I casually walked to the beach and collected seashells.

ANSWER: (Yesterday,) casually

1. Weekends, I like to take my little brother to a relatively unknown stretch of seashore.
2. We carefully search the beach for shells some mornings.
3. Most days, we are seldom disappointed.
4. Today, for example, we found a dozen shells nearby.
5. My brother always races home to show our parents the assortment of cowry, cone, and conch shells that we have found.
6. Afternoons, he thoroughly cleans any sand or other debris from the shells.
7. Both of us are eagerly awaiting our trip tomorrow.
8. Sundays, we generally have the whole beach to ourselves.
9. I fully enjoy being outside in the warm sea air.
10. Unfortunately, I have to work weekdays.

💡 Spelling Tip

To form adverbs from many words ending in *y*, change the *y* to *i* and then add the suffix *-ly*. For example, *happy* becomes *happily* and *lazy* becomes *lazily*.

⏱ TIME SAVERS!

📖 **Answers on Transparencies**
Use the *Grammar Exercises Answers on Transparencies* for Chapter 17 to facilitate correction by students.

💻 **On-Line Exercise Bank**
Have students complete the exercises on computer. The Auto Check feature will grade their work for you!

☑ ONGOING ASSESSMENT: Monitor and Reinforce

If students miss more than two items in Exercise 13, refer them to the following for additional practice.

In the Textbook	Print Resources	Technology
Section Review, Ex. 16, Section 17.2	*Grammar Exercise Workbook*, pp. 27–28	*On-Line Exercise Bank*, Section 17.2

Adverb or Adjective?

Sometimes, the same word can be either an adverb or an adjective, depending upon how it is used in a sentence.

KEY CONCEPT Remember that an adverb modifies a verb, an adjective, or another adverb; an adjective modifies a noun or a pronoun. ■

Notice in the following examples that the adverb modifies a verb. The same word used as an adjective, on the other hand, modifies a noun.

ADVERB: The fish swam *straight* through the channel.

ADJECTIVE: The path was *straight*.

Generally, adverbs and adjectives have different forms. Many adverbs, in fact, are formed by adding *-ly* to an adjective.

Adjectives	Adverbs With *-ly* Endings
honest response	responded *honestly*
awkward movement	moved *awkwardly*

A few words ending in *-ly*, however, are adjectives.

ADJECTIVE: We found a *lovely* shell with *curly* edges.

▲ **Critical Viewing** If you used *lovely, hard,* and *underwater* in sentences about this turtle cone shell, would those words be adjectives or adverbs? Can any of them be both? **[Distinguish]**

⚙ **Grammar and Style Tip**

When using a word ending in *-ly* directly before a noun, check to make sure that it is an adjective.

Adverbs • 383

Critical Viewing

Distinguish *Hard* and *underwater* might be used as either adjectives or adverbs, depending on the context. *Lovely* could be used only as an adjective.

Step-by-Step Teaching Guide

Adverb or Adjective?

1. Tell students that the same word can act as an adjective or an adverb. (The *early* morning. [adjective] We should start *early*. [adverb])

2. Note that many adverbs are formed by adding *-ly* to adjectives. Refer to the chart.

3. Ask students to give additional examples of adjectives that form adverbs by the addition of *-ly*. (*bright, kind, smart*)

4. Remind students that some words that end in *-ly* can be adjectives. (*early, daily, kindly*)

Customize for
ESL Students

Put the following in two columns on the board.

Adjectives: happy, loud, quiet, quick

Adverbs: happily, loudly, quietly, quickly

Ask students to write a sentence for each of the words in the pair. Emphasize that in English, unlike Spanish and some other languages, a descriptive adjective usually comes before the noun it modifies. Have students switch papers and underline the adjective or adverb in each sentence and circle the word that it modifies. Use this example to demonstrate.

The noisy ⟨train⟩ pulled into the station.

The train ⟨moved⟩ slowly into the station.

⬦ **STANDARDIZED TEST PREPARATION WORKSHOP**

Grammar and Usage Many standardized tests require students to recognize and solve common usage problems. Use the following example to demonstrate.

A Martin's examination grades were good.

B Susan's examination also went good.

C Sam did well on his final exams.

D We all want good results when we study hard.

Which of the preceding sentences contains an error?

The answer is **B.** The word *good* is an adjective and cannot modify a verb. The adverb *well* should be used to modify the verb *went*.

Critical Viewing

Connect, Analyze Responses will vary. In a sentence beginning *The shell I like best . . .* , *best* is an adverb. However, *best* could also function as an adjective: *The best shell . . .*

Answer Key

Real-World Connection

Adjectives and adverbs are invaluable in descriptions of all kinds. Law enforcement agents rely on description to understand a crime and to catch the criminal. When questioning eyewitnesses, they ask for adjectives describing the appearance of the perpetrator. This will help them catch the right person. Adverbs help investigators establish the scene and events of the crime.

Integrating Speaking and Listening Skills

Adverb or Adjective? Read aloud these two sentences.

I read the daily newspaper.

I read the newspaper daily.

Ask students to identify which sentence uses the word as an adjective and which uses it as an adverb. Then, have a student write the two sentences on the board, underline the modifiers, and draw an arrow from each modifier to the word it modifies.

17.2

▲ **Critical Viewing**
Write a sentence containing *best*, in which you reveal your favorite type of shell. In your sentence, is *best* functioning as an adjective or an adverb? **[Connect, Analyze]**

▶ **Exercise 14** Distinguishing Between Adverbs and Adjectives Identify each underlined word below as an *adverb* or *adjective*.

EXAMPLE: The small fish eggs were <u>barely</u> visible.
ANSWER: adverb

1. Cone snails are an unusual variety of sea snails that have <u>hard</u>, elaborately colored shells.
2. These snails are <u>quite</u> effective hunters.
3. They may feed <u>daily</u> on live or dead fish.
4. They attack their prey with <u>deadly</u> accuracy.
5. Cone snails shoot poison-tipped darts <u>straight</u> at any fish that swims within range.
6. The unwitting fish may work <u>hard</u> to escape before the snail's venom immobilizes it.
7. These <u>lovely</u> mollusks live in the warm tropical waters between Australia and India.
8. Occasionally, their empty shells are found among the <u>stately</u> palms on South Pacific islands.
9. Some of the most visually stunning varieties are spotted <u>only</u> occasionally by lucky searchers.
10. This rare shell is the <u>only</u> shell of its kind at the auction.

▶ **More Practice**

Grammar Exercise Workbook
• pp. 29–30
On-line Exercise Bank
• Section 17.2
Go on-line:
PHSchool.com
Enter Web Code:
eek-1002

384 • Adjectives and Adverbs

☑ ONGOING ASSESSMENT: Assess Mastery

Use the following resources to assess student mastery of adverbs.

In the Textbook	Technology
Chapter Review, Ex. 21, 24–26	*Writing and Grammar* Interactive Text, Section 17.2, Section Review; *On-Line Exercise Bank*, Section 17.2

Section 17.2 Section Review

GRAMMAR EXERCISES 15–20

> **Exercise 15** Recognizing Adverbs

List the adverbs you find in each sentence below and the word each modifies.

1. The rarely studied nautilus is an extremely odd mollusk.
2. It is related most closely to squids and octopuses, but it really bears little resemblance to its relatives.
3. This unusual shellfish is entirely enclosed in a perfectly spiraled shell.
4. The nautilus also has approximately ninety tentacles that extend ominously from the opening of its shell.
5. During the day, these odd-looking shellfish usually hide quietly among the rocks on the ocean floor.
6. Nautiluses cautiously emerge after the sun has set.
7. They gradually begin to swim toward the surface and eventually reach the shallow waters of a coral reef.
8. Nautiluses feed ravenously upon crabs, which they capture easily.
9. At first light, they rapidly retreat to the relatively safe ocean floor.
10. The nautiluses' uniquely designed shells are highly prized by collectors.

> **Exercise 16** Supplying Nouns

Used as Adverbs Rewrite the sentences below on your paper, supplying a noun used as an adverb to fill each blank.

1. ___?___, I regularly dive along the coral reefs.
2. ___?___, I saw a very interesting mollusk called a giant clam.
3. The 4-foot-wide creature is active ___?___ and night.
4. The incredibly heavy shell was far too big to bring ___?___.
5. ___?___, I plan to dive down to the giant clam again to show it to my cousin.

> **Exercise 17** Distinguishing

Between Adverbs and Adjectives Label each underlined word below adverb or adjective.

1. Hermit crabs are <u>most</u> often found along the Atlantic coast of the United States.
2. Despite its name, many consider the hermit crab a <u>friendly</u> pet.
3. Because it lacks a <u>hard</u> shell, the young hermit crab is vulnerable to predators.
4. It works <u>hard</u> to insert its body into a discarded seashell, and then it carries the shell with it wherever it goes.
5. The crab cannot keep the same shell <u>long</u>, since it must move to a larger shell as it grows.

> **Exercise 18** Find It in Your

Reading In the excerpt from "Pride," on page 382, identify the words that the highlighted adverbs modify, and indicate whether each modified word is a verb, an adjective, or an adverb.

> **Exercise 19** Find It in Your

Writing Choose a piece of writing from your portfolio, and identify five adverbs. Are there places where you can add adverbs to create a clearer picture of the action for your readers?

> **Exercise 20** Writing Application

Write a short essay about something you collect or would like to collect. Include adverbs to add details to verbs, adjectives, and other adverbs.

Section Review • 385

ASSESS and CLOSE

Section Review

Each of these exercises correlates to the instruction on adverbs, pages 380–383. The exercises may be used for more practice, for reteaching, or for review of the key concepts presented. Answers are available in *Grammar Exercises Answers on Transparencies* in your Teaching Resources.

Answer Key

> **Exercise 15**

1. rarely, studied; extremely, odd
2. most, closely; closely, related; really, bears
3. entirely, enclosed; perfectly, spiraled
4. also, has; approximately, ninety; ominously, extend
5. usually, hide; quietly, hide
6. cautiously, emerge
7. gradually, begin; eventually, reach
8. ravenously, feed; easily, capture
9. rapidly, retreat; relatively, safe
10. uniquely, designed; highly, are prized

> **Exercise 16**

Answers will vary; samples are given.

1. Saturdays
2. Yesterday
3. day
4. home
5. Tomorrow

> **Exercise 17**

1. most, adverb
2. friendly, adjective
3. hard, adjective
4. hard, adverb
5. long, adverb

continued

Answer Key continued

> **Exercise 18**

Find It in Your Reading
suddenly modifies *has,* a verb
too modifies *break* (understood), a verb

> **Exercise 19**

Find It in Your Writing
If students have difficulty locating adverbs in their writing, encourage them to revise to add effective adverbs.

> **Exercise 20**

Writing Application
Answers will vary. Ask students to underline the adverbs they use and circle the words that those adverbs modify.

> ⏱ **TIME SAVERS!**

Answers on Transparencies Use the *Grammar Exercises Answers on Transparencies* for Chapter 17 to facilitate correction by students.

On-Line Exercise Bank Have students complete the exercises on computer. The Auto Check feature will grade their work for you!

Each of these exercises correlates to a section of the chapter on adjectives and adverbs, pages 368–385. The exercises may be used for more practice, for reteaching, or for review of the key concepts presented.

Answer Key

▶ Exercise 21

1. unusual, adjective; often, adverb; rocky, adjective
2. average, adjective; five, adjective; sometimes, adverb; even, adverb
3. generally, adverb; chewy, adjective; crunchy, adjective
4. easily, adverb; apart, adverb; hard, adjective
5. seldom, adverb; nutritious, adjective

▶ Exercise 22

1. underwater, compound
2. Their, possessive; worldwide, compound
3. Its, possessive; spine-covered, compound; purple-colored, compound
4. Florida, proper
5. their, possessive; beaklike, compound; Atlantic Ocean, proper and compound
6. worn-down, compound
7. offshore, compound
8. California, proper
9. once-occupied, compound; American, proper
10. Atlantic, proper; Pacific, proper

▶ Exercise 23

1. yesterday, noun; this, pronoun
2. none
3. home, noun as adverb; sea, noun; coral, noun; river, noun
4. extended, verb; grasping, verb
5. swimming, verb; its, pronoun
6. foraging, verb; fish, noun
7. Another, pronoun; male, noun; fertilized, verb
8. Baby, noun; many, pronoun
9. Few, pronoun; adult, noun; its, pronoun
10. threatened, verb; species, noun; today, noun as adverb

▶ Exercise 24

1. hard, adjective
2. close, adverb

continued

GRAMMAR EXERCISES 21–28

▶ **Exercise 21** Identifying Adjectives and Adverbs Identify each underlined word below as an *adjective* or *adverb*.

1. Starfish are <u>unusual</u> creatures that can <u>often</u> be found on the <u>rocky</u> floor of the ocean.
2. The <u>average</u> starfish has <u>five</u> arms, but species have <u>sometimes</u> been found that have <u>even</u> more arms.
3. Starfish eat many small animals, but they <u>generally</u> prefer soft mollusks, <u>chewy</u> sponges, and <u>crunchy</u> corals.
4. The strong arms of a starfish can <u>easily</u> pull <u>apart</u> the <u>hard</u> shell of a clam.
5. Animals <u>seldom</u> eat starfish because they are neither <u>nutritious</u> nor tasty.

▶ **Exercise 22** Recognizing Proper, Compound, and Possessive Adjectives List any proper, compound, and possessive adjectives in the following sentences, and label each.

1. Sea urchins are underwater animals that are related to the starfish.
2. Their range is worldwide, and they can be found in most marine environments.
3. Its round, spine-covered body may be purple-colored or red.
4. With the exception of a species that lives near the Florida coast, sea urchins are basically harmless to people.
5. They use their beaklike mouths to scrape algae from rocks on the Atlantic Ocean bed.
6. Constant scraping against the rocks ruins the teeth of the sea urchin, but worn-down teeth are quickly replaced.
7. Sea urchins prefer colder offshore waters, but they also live near land.
8. California sea otters are members of the small group of animals that prey upon the sea urchin.

386 • Adjectives and Adverbs

9. The once-occupied shells of sea urchins often litter American beaches.
10. If you visit the Atlantic or Pacific coast, you may see these empty shells.

▶ **Exercise 23** Recognizing Other Parts of Speech Used as Adjectives or Adverbs List and label nouns, pronouns, or verbs used as adjectives, as well as nouns used as adverbs, in the sentences below.

1. I saw a seahorse yesterday at an aquarium and decided to learn more about this unusual fish.
2. Here are all the facts I learned.
3. When a seahorse heads home, it swims to sea grasses near coral reefs and river estuaries.
4. The seahorse is characterized by an extended snout and a grasping tail.
5. A swimming seahorse moves by fanning its tiny fin.
6. Because they have no teeth, foraging seahorses swallow fish larvae whole.
7. Another unusual characteristic is that the male seahorse, not the female, carries the fertilized eggs.
8. Baby seahorses resemble adults at birth but take many months to mature.
9. Few animals prey upon the adult seahorse because of its hard skin.
10. Nevertheless, certain types of seahorses are on the threatened species list today because of overfishing.

▶ **Exercise 24** Distinguishing Adverbs From Adjectives Identify each underlined word in the items that follow as an *adjective* or *adverb*.

1. An ordinary lobster has a <u>hard</u>, segmented shell and two large claws.

☑ **ONGOING ASSESSMENT: Assess Mastery**

Use the following resources to assess student mastery of adjectives and adverbs.

In the Textbook	Print Resources	Technology
Section Review, Ex. 21–26 Standardized Test Preparation Workshop	*Formal Assessment*, Ch. 17	*Writing and Grammar* Interactive Text, Ch. 17, Chapter Review; *On-Line Exercise Bank*, Sections 17.1–2

2. Do not put your hands <u>close</u> to those powerful claws!
3. That diver had a <u>close</u> call when a lobster aggressively defended its territory.
4. In the <u>early</u> part of the day, most lobsters remain hidden among the rocks.
5. They usually emerge from their hiding places <u>late</u> at night.

Exercise 25 Supplying Adjectives and Adverbs in Sentences Rewrite the sentences below on your paper, supplying an adjective or adverb to fill each blank. Underline each adjective you add and circle each adverb.

1. ___?___ , I learned about the ___?___ odd horseshoe crab.
2. Despite ___?___ name, the horseshoe crab is not ___?___ a true crab.
3. It is actually a ___?___ relative of spiders and scorpions.
4. Horseshoe crabs are ___?___ found along ___?___ shores, but ___?___ species live ___?___ near the Pacific.
5. One very ___?___ reason for the horseshoe crab's durability is that it can live for a ___?___ year without eating!
6. The crabs can also endure ___?___ dramatic changes in ___?___ temperature.
7. Horseshoe crabs ___?___ feed nights.
8. However, some have been known to conduct their food search ___?___ , too.
9. They ___?___ hunt clams, oysters, and other ___?___ mollusks.
10. At the beach ___?___ , I will ___?___ see ___?___ of these ___?___ animals.

Exercise 26 Revising Dull Writing by Adding Adjectives and Adverbs Revise this dull paragraph by adding adjectives and adverbs where appropriate.

(1) Oysters are valuable both as a food and as a source of pearls. (2) Pearls start out as a piece of shell or a parasite that enters an oyster's shell. (3) The oyster spreads a substance called *nacre* in layers over the invader. (4) The process happens. (5) The invader becomes enclosed in the substance, forming a pearl.

Exercise 27 Writing Application
Imagine that you are exploring the ocean in a diving vessel. Write an account of your trip. Describe the things you might find, such as marine life or sunken treasure. Include adjectives and adverbs to make your description more interesting.

Exercise 28 CUMULATIVE REVIEW
Parts of Speech Identify the underlined words in the following sentences as *nouns*, *pronouns*, *verbs*, *adjectives*, or *adverbs*.
1. Corals are tiny <u>shelled</u> creatures <u>that</u> play a <u>particularly</u> <u>vital</u> <u>role</u> in the ocean's ecology.
2. <u>Many</u> people <u>think</u> that corals are simply <u>underwater</u> plants, but <u>they</u> are actually animals.
3. <u>Each</u> has a tube-shaped body, which <u>is surrounded</u> at the top by a mass of <u>gently</u> <u>waving</u> tentacles.
4. The coral uses its tentacles to gather <u>minute</u> <u>particles</u> of food that <u>randomly</u> <u>drift</u> with the <u>ocean</u> current.
5. A young <u>free-floating</u> coral will attach <u>itself</u> <u>securely</u> to a rock and immediately <u>begin</u> creating a <u>hard</u> shell.
6. <u>Eventually</u>, small corals of the same species <u>form</u> a colony, which is <u>commonly</u> mistaken for <u>one</u> large organism.
7. <u>These</u> types of corals <u>often</u> contain <u>red</u>, blue, yellow, or green pigments.
8. In time, many different <u>colonies</u> of coral may create a coral reef, which serves as a <u>home</u> for thousands of <u>marine</u> animals.
9. <u>Certain</u> sea stars and <u>several</u> varieties of fish eat hard corals.
10. One <u>incredibly</u> destructive parrotfish <u>may</u> <u>consume</u> <u>five</u> tons of coral in a single <u>year</u>!

387

Lesson Objectives

1. To demonstrate correct use of modifiers
2. To demonstrate control over grammatical elements

Using Adjectives and Adverbs

Teaching Resources: Standardized Test Preparation Workbook, pp. 33–34

1. Remind students that adjectives and adverbs are called modifiers; they give more specific information about other words in a sentence.

2. You might want to review adjectives and adverbs more specifically, depending on the needs of the class. Using sample sentences, have students locate the adjectives and adverbs, as well as the particular nouns, pronouns, adjectives, verbs, or other adverbs they modify.

3. Discuss the importance of paying close attention to content when choosing a test response. For example, in Practice 1, Item 1, it would only be startling for an animal to be speedy if it were large; given the context, the word *enormous* is most logical.

Standardized Test Preparation Workshop

Using Adjectives and Adverbs

Standardized tests often measure your understanding of grammar and usage. One way to measure this is to evaluate your understanding of modifiers. These types of questions will ask you to read a passage and choose which modifier, adjective, or adverb completes the sentence in a correct and logical way. Use the following steps when answering a question that tests these skills:

- Read the entire passage first.

- Ask yourself what type of description is needed—an adjective will tell *what kind, which one, how much,* and *how many,* and an adverb will tell *when, where, in what way,* or *to what extent* about a word in the sentence.

- Choose the modifier that will add that information and also fit the meaning of the passage.

The following sample test item will give you practice with questions that test your ability to choose the correct modifier.

Test Tips

- If you are unsure of an answer, try filling in the blank with your own word, then identify the part of speech and meaning of your word. Select the answer most similar to your word.
- After you make your choices, reread the passage with the words in the blanks to be sure the passage makes sense.

Sample Test Item	Answers and Explanations
Directions: Read the passage, and choose the letter of the word or group of words that belongs in each space. Whether grown in the mounding or trailing form, the nasturtium flower, with its strong, __(1)__ flavor, is __(2)__ used as a tasty and attractive salad garnish.	
1 A unpleasant B unpleasantly C pungent D pungently	The correct choice for the first blank is *C.* An adjective is needed to modify the noun *flavor.* Since the sentence indicates that the flower is edible, it is unlikely that the answer would be *unpleasant.* So the best choice is the adjective *pungent.*
2 F frequently G frequent H rarely J rare	The correct choice for the second blank is *F.* An adverb is needed to modify the verb *is used.* Since the sentence describes positive qualities of the nasturtium flower, the adverb *rarely* is an illogical choice. So the best choice is the adverb *frequently.*

388 • Adjectives and Adverbs

✎ TEST-TAKING TIP

Reinforce the importance of context when choosing modifiers. Tell students to be sure to read the entire passage before choosing any responses. This will help clarify the subject of the passage and a general point of view about the subject. Filling in the blanks with possible words will provide clues about the correct response.

Practice 1 **Directions:** Read the passage, and choose the letter of the word or group of words that belongs in each space.

Startlingly speedy for his size, the __(1)__ alligator climbed up the __(2)__ bank at the edge of the everglade. He bellowed __(3)__, as if to announce his presence to any marsh trespassers. A __(4)__ ibis escaped into the __(5)__ sky.

1 A enormously
  B enormous
  C dainty
  D daintily

2 F clear
  G clearly
  H clean
  J muddy

3 A softly
  B softer
  C loud
  D loudly

4 F calm
  G calmly
  H startled
  J startling

5 A clear
  B clearly
  C spry
  D spryly

Practice 2 **Directions:** Read the passage, and choose the letter of the word or group of words that belongs in each space.

Fresh-baked bread __(1)__ tops Isaac's list of __(2)__ foods. He loves stirring the dough __(3)__ and kneading it with his __(4)__ hands. __(5)__ week he bakes two loaves for his volunteer work at the nursing home.

1 A always
  B rarely
  C happy
  D happily

2 F badly
  G bad
  H lovingly
  J favorite

3 A softly
  B soft
  C briskly
  D brisk

4 F weak
  G weakly
  H powerful
  J gently

5 A Each
  B Last
  C Next
  D One

Answer Key

Practice 1
1. B
2. J
3. D
4. H
5. A

Practice 2
1. A
2. J
3. C
4. H
5. A

Customize for
Less Advanced Students

Tell students to read each sentence silently, inserting the possible responses. It is always helpful to listen to how a word sounds in a sentence before making a final choice.

Customize for
More Advanced Students

Tell students to check any answer of which they are unsure by identifying its part of speech and the word it modifies in the sentence.

In-Depth Lesson Plan

	LESSON FOCUS	PRINT AND MEDIA RESOURCES
DAY 1	**Prepositions** Students learn and apply concepts relating to prepositions, prepositional phrases, and how to distinguish between prepositions and adverbs. (pp. 390–396/Ⓗ258–264)	*Writing and Grammar* Interactive Text, Section 18.1; *On-line Exercise Bank,* Section 18.1 **Teaching Resources** *Grammar Exercise Workbook,* pp. 31–34; *Grammar Exercises Answers on Transparencies,* Ch. 18
DAY 2	**Conjunctions** Students learn and apply concepts relating to conjunctions. (pp. 397–401/Ⓗ265–269)	*Writing and Grammar* Interactive Text, Section 18.2; *On-line Exercise Bank,* Section 18.2 **Teaching Resources** *Grammar Exercise Workbook,* pp. 35–38
DAY 3	**Interjections** Students learn and apply concepts relating to interjections and do the Hands-on Grammar activity. (pp. 401–403/Ⓗ269–271)	**Teaching Resources** *Grammar Exercise Workbook,* pp. 39–40; *Hands-on Grammar Activity Book,* Ch. 18
DAY 4	**Review and Assess** Students review the chapter and demonstrate mastery of concepts. (pp. 404–405)	*Writing and Grammar* Interactive Text, Ch. 18, Chapter Review **Teaching Resources** *Formal Assessment,* Ch. 18

Accelerated Lesson Plan

	LESSON FOCUS	PRINT AND MEDIA RESOURCES
DAY 1	**Prepositions** Students cover prepositions as determined by their performance on the Diagnostic Test. (pp. 390–396/Ⓗ258–264)	*Writing and Grammar* Interactive Text, Section 18.1; *On-line Exercise Bank,* Section 18.1 **Teaching Resources** *Grammar Exercise Workbook,* pp. 31–34; *Grammar Exercises Answers on Transparencies,* Ch. 18
DAY 2	**Conjunctions and Interjections** Students cover conjunctions and interjections as determined by the Diagnostic Test. (pp. 397–403/Ⓗ265–271)	*Writing and Grammar* Interactive Text, Section 18.2; *On-line Exercise Bank,* Section 18.2 **Teaching Resources** *Grammar Exercise Workbook,* pp. 35–40
DAY 3	**Review and Assess** Students review the chapter and demonstrate mastery of concepts. (pp. 404–405)	*Writing and Grammar* Interactive Text, Ch. 18, Chapter Review **Teaching Resources** *Formal Assessment,* Ch. 18

Options for Adapting Lesson Plans

HOMEWORK

Have students complete any section of the chapter for homework.

FEATURES

Extend coverage with the Grammar in Literature features (pp. 393, 399/Ⓗ261,267) and the Standardized Test Preparation Workshop (p. 406).

TECHNOLOGY

Students can use *Writing and Grammar* Interactive Text to complete the exercises interactively on computer. They can complete additional exercises in the *On-line Exercise Bank:* The Auto Check feature will grade their work. Go on-line: PHSchool.com Use Web Code: eek-1002

Writing and Grammar Handbook Alignment

Page numbers in Step-by-Step Teaching Guides in this Teacher's Edition refer to pages from the full student text. Handbook page references, indicated with this icon Ⓗ, are provided in Time and Resource Manager boxes and at the bottom of each Teacher's Edition page.

INTEGRATED SKILLS COVERAGE

Grammar in Literature
SE pp. 393, 399/Ⓗ261, 267

Writing
Find It in Your Writing SE pp. 396, 402, 403/Ⓗ264, 270, 271; ATE pp. 396, 402, 403
Writing Application SE pp. 396, 402, 405, 409/Ⓗ264, 270; ATE pp. 402, 409
Grammar and Style SE pp. 393, 401, 403/Ⓗ261, 269, 271

Vocabulary
ATE p. 397

Spelling
ATE p. 401

Viewing and Representing
Critical Viewing SE pp. 390, 393, 398, 399/Ⓗ258, 261, 266, 267; ATE pp. 390, 393, 394, 398, 399

Real-World Connection ATE p. 398

Workplace ATE p. 394

ASSESSMENT SUPPORT

Standardized Test Preparation Workshop SE p. 406; ATE pp. 399, 403

Standardized Test Preparation Workbook, pp. 35–36

Formal Assessment, Ch. 18

MEETING INDIVIDUAL NEEDS

Less Advanced Students ATE pp. 395, 407. See also Ongoing Assessments ATE pp. 394, 395, 398, 400, 401.
More Advanced Students ATE pp. 399, 407
ESL Students ATE pp. 392, 400
Bodily/Kinesthetic Learners ATE p. 401

BLOCK SCHEDULING

Pacing Suggestions
For 90-minute Blocks
- Administer the Diagnostic Test to students to determine instructional coverage.
- Have students complete the necessary exercises in class. Use the Hands-on Grammar activity to provide a change of pace.

Resources for Varying Instruction
- *Writing and Grammar* Interactive Text A 90-minute block provides an ideal opportunity for students to work on the computer.

Professional Development Support
- *How to Manage Instruction in the Block* This teaching resource provides management and activity suggestions.

MEDIA AND TECHNOLOGY

For the Student
- *Writing and Grammar* Interactive Text, Ch. 18
- *On-line Exercise Bank,* Sections 18.1–2

For the Teacher
- TeacherEXPRESS™ CD-ROM

WRITING AND GRAMMAR ON-LINE

Interactive Text (On-line or on CD-ROM)
- Easily navigable instruction with on-line supporting resources
- Self-scoring exercises and diagnostic tests

Companion Web Site PHSchool.com
- On-line Exercise Bank (use Web Code eek-1002)

See the Go On-line! feature, SE p. iii.

▶ **Lesson Objectives**

1. To recognize one-word and compound prepositions and use them in sentences
2. To identify prepositional phrases and objects of prepositions
3. To distinguish between prepositions and adverbs in sentences
4. To identify and distinguish among coordinating, correlative, and subordinating conjunctions
5. To identify words as conjunctions, prepositions, or adverbs
6. To relate ideas by using conjunctive adverbs
7. To use appropriate interjections in sentences
8. To evaluate writing for both mechanics and content
9. To demonstrate control over grammatical elements such as parts of speech

Critical Viewing

Compare Sample response: Central Park has a place <u>for boating within its boundaries</u>. A walking bridge stretches <u>over that waterway</u>.

Chapter 18 Prepositions, Conjunctions, and Interjections

Prepositions, conjunctions, and *interjections* add meaning to sentences. Prepositions and conjunctions make connections and show special relationships between words. *Interjections* add emotion and expression to a sentence.

Whether you describe places, such as famous parks, or people, such as the Navajo, you will depend on these parts of speech to help you convey meaning effectively.

Learn how to use prepositions, conjunctions, and interjections correctly while exploring this chapter.

▲ **Critical Viewing**
Based on this photograph, how would you compare Central Park in New York City to other parks you've visited? What prepositions and conjunctions would you use in making these comparisons? **[Compare]**

390 • Prepositions, Conjunctions, and Interjections

☑ **ONGOING ASSESSMENT: Diagnose**

If students miss more than one item in any category, direct them to the relevant pages of the textbook and assign exercises for practice and review.

Prepositions, Conjunctions, and Interjections	Diagnostic Test Items	Teach	Practice	Section Review	Chapter
Skill Check A					
Identify Prepositions	A 1–5	pp. 392–93/Ⓗ260–261	Ex. 1–2	Ex. 7–8	Ex. 24–25
Skill Check B					
Identify Prepositional Phrases	B 6–10	p. 394/Ⓗ262	Ex. 3–4	Ex. 7–8	Ex. 24
Skill Check C					
Preposition or Adverb?	C 11–15	p. 395/Ⓗ263	Ex. 5–6	Ex. 9	Ex. 27

Diagnostic Test

Directions: Write all answers on a separate sheet of paper.

Skill Check A. Write the prepositions in the following sentences.
1. Mr. Lee's favorite park in New York City is Van Cortlandt Park.
2. This 1,100-acre Bronx park is located next to Riverdale.
3. Miles of wooded trails wind within its boundaries.
4. Apart from the woods, visitors can play baseball, cricket, or golf or relax upon its rolling green fields.
5. Many enjoy the playgrounds instead of the hiking trails.

Skill Check B. Write the complete prepositional phrases. Underline the object or objects of each preposition.
6. The Wiechquaeskeck people once lived in the area of Van Cortlandt Park.
7. According to scientists, they built their permanent settlements there about 1,000 years ago.
8. They fished along the banks of Tibbets Brook.
9. Their crops were planted upon the present-day sites of the Parade Ground and Indian Field.
10. The park's lake didn't exist when Europeans arrived in America.

Skill Check C. Label underlined words *prepositions* or *adverbs*.
11. In 1639, the Dutch West India Company purchased much of the land <u>along</u> the lower Hudson Valley from Native Americans.
12. Travel <u>through</u> it was difficult, due to unrest in the area.
13. Jacobus Van Cortlandt bought the land in the 1690's, but the wealthy Philipse family had owned it <u>before</u>.
14. He looked <u>around</u> and decided to grow crops on his land.
15. Van Cortlandt began to grow grain and to mill <u>on</u> his property.

Skill Check D. Write the conjunctions, conjunctive adverbs, and interjections in the following sentences. If the word is a conjunction, label it *coordinating, correlative,* or *subordinating.*
16. The Van Cortlandts owned the land; subsequently, they built a home and dammed Tibbets Brook.
17. Yes, you can explore both the house and the man-made lake.
18. Say, let's go to the park today, or you may prefer the museum.
19. Because it was built in 1748, it's the oldest house in the Bronx.
20. Unless I'm mistaken, their estate became parkland in 1888.

Skill Check E. Label each underlined word *subordinating conjunction, preposition,* or *adverb.*
21. Have you explored Vault Hill <u>before</u>?
22. Frederick Van Cortlandt was buried here, and this has been the family burial ground ever <u>since</u>.
23. <u>When</u> the American Revolution began, City Clerk Augustus Van Cortlandt hid New York City records from the British here.
24. <u>After</u> a time, family remains were moved to Woodlawn Cemetery.
25. <u>After</u> we explore Vault Hill, let's visit an even older burial ground.

Prepositions, Conjunctions, and Interjections • 391

Diagnostic Test

Each item in the Diagnostic Test corresponds to a specific section in the prepositions, conjunctions, and interjections chapter. This will enable you to tailor instruction to the particular needs of your students. See "Ongoing Assessment: Diagnose" below for further details.

Skill Check A

1. in
2. next to
3. of, within
4. Apart from, upon
5. instead of

Skill Check B

6. in the <u>area</u>, of <u>Van Cortlandt Park</u>
7. According to <u>scientists</u>, about 1,000 <u>years</u> ago
8. along the <u>banks</u>, of <u>Tibbets Brook</u>
9. upon the present-day <u>sites</u>, of the <u>Parade Ground</u> and <u>Indian Field</u>
10. in <u>America</u>

Skill Check C

11. preposition
12. preposition
13. adverb
14. adverb
15. preposition

Skill Check D

16. subsequently–conjunctive adverb; and–coordinating conjunction
17. Yes–interjection; both . . . and–correlative conjunction
18. Say–interjection; or–coordinating conjunction
19. Because–subordinating conjunction
20. Unless–subordinating conjunction

Skill Check E

21. adverb
22. adverb
23. subordinating conjunction
24. preposition
25. subordinating conjunction

☑ ONGOING ASSESSMENT: Diagnose *continued*					
Prepositions, Conjunctions, and Interjections	Diagnostic Test Items	Teach	Practice	Section Review	Chapter Review
Skill Check D					
Identify Conjunctions, Conjunctive Adverbs, Interjections	D 16–20	pp. 397–401/ⓗ265–269	Ex. 13–17	Ex. 18–20	Ex. 26, 28–31
Skill Check E					
Identify Subordinating Conjunctions, Prepositions, Adverbs	E 21–25	p. 399/ⓗ267	Ex. 14–15	Ex. 19	Ex. 27
Cumulative Reviews and Applications				Ex. 10–12, 21–23	Ex. 32

Write these words on the board:

above	behind	on
across	below	opposite
against	beside	outside
along	near	upon

Ask students to copy the following:

Two men sat ___ a park bench ___ the street and ___ a tree.

Ask them to fill in the blanks, using any of the words from the list. Have students read aloud some of their sentences. Then have each student write two different versions of the sentence by using other prepositions.

Activate Prior Knowledge

Ask a student volunteer to pantomime in slow motion an action that they perform as part of their daily chores, such as cleaning up their rooms. Have the class list the steps they think are being performed. As they tell you what they wrote, write these on the board, circling the prepositions. Ask what function these words serve in the sentence.

TEACH

Step-by-Step Teaching Guide

Words Used as Prepositions

1. Point out that a preposition is usually one word, but a compound preposition contains more than one word.

2. Ask students to think of original sentences using prepositions from the two charts on this page.

Customize for
ESL Students

Prepare flashcards showing prepositions of location and direction such as *above, behind, into*. Have a student sit on a chair, and ask another student to hold the card in the proper position relative to the seated student. For example, hold the "above" card above the seated student's head. Have the students say the word aloud as this is done and then to suggest sentences or phrases using the preposition. Repeat using other prepositions.

Section 18.1

Prepositions

Prepositions add meaning to a sentence by showing the relationship between words.

▶ **KEY CONCEPT** A **preposition** is a word that relates a noun or pronoun that appears with it to another word in the sentence. ■

Words Used as Prepositions

A preposition can affect the entire meaning of a sentence.

▶ **KEY CONCEPT** The choice of preposition affects the way the other words in a sentence relate to each other. ■

Sixty of the words most often used as prepositions are listed in the following chart.

FREQUENTLY USED PREPOSITIONS				
aboard	before	despite	off	throughout
about	behind	down	on	till
above	below	during	onto	to
across	beneath	except	opposite	toward
after	beside	for	out	under
against	besides	from	outside	underneath
along	between	in	over	until
amid	beyond	inside	past	up
among	but	into	regarding	upon
around	by	like	round	with
at	concerning	near	since	within
barring	considering	of	through	without

Some prepositions consist of more than one word and are called *compound prepositions*.

COMPOUND PREPOSITIONS			
according to	because of	in place of	next to
ahead of	by means of	in regard to	on account of
apart from	in addition to	in spite of	out of
aside from	in back of	instead of	owing to
as of	in front of	in view of	prior to

Theme: City Parks

In this section, you will learn about prepositions. The examples and exercises in this section are about city parks.

Cross-Curricular Connection: Social Studies

▶ **More Practice**

Grammar Exercise Workbook
• pp. 31–32
On-line Exercise Bank
• Section 18.1
  Go on-line:
  PHSchool.com
  Enter Web Code:
  eek-1002

⏱ **TIME AND RESOURCE MANAGER**

Resources
Print: *Grammar Exercise Workbook*, pp. 31–34; *Grammar Exercises Answers on Transparencies*, Ch. 18
Technology: *Writing and Grammar* Interactive Text, Section 18.1; *On-Line Exercise Bank*, Section 18.1

Using the Full Student Edition	Using the Handbook Ⓗ
• Work through all key concepts, pp. 392–395.	• Work through all key concepts, pp. 260–263.
• Assign and review Exercises 1–6.	• Assign and review Exercises 1–6.
• Read and discuss Grammar in Literature, p. 393.	• Read and discuss Grammar in Literature, p. 261.

GRAMMAR IN LITERATURE

from Mowing
Robert Frost

The prepositions in this excerpt from a poem by Robert Frost are highlighted in blue italics.

There was never a sound *beside* the wood *but* one,
And that was my long scythe whispering *to* the ground.
What was it it whispered? I knew not well myself;
Perhaps it was something *about* the heat *of* the sun,
Something, perhaps, *about* the lack *of* sound—
And that was why it whispered and did not speak.

▲ **Critical Viewing**
What prepositions might you use in describing these two men? Why? **[Describe]**

Notice how choosing different prepositions affects the relationship between words and gives each sentence a different meaning.

EXAMPLE:

We saw a squirrel $\begin{Bmatrix} \text{inside} \\ \text{near} \\ \text{within} \\ \text{next to} \end{Bmatrix}$ the *park*.

> **Exercise 1** **Identifying Prepositions** Identify the prepositions and compound prepositions in this paragraph.
> (1) Central Park, one of America's first landscaped parks, was designed by Frederick Law Olmsted and Calvert Vaux. (2) Poor Irish and German immigrants occupied the land prior to the park's creation. (3) There was also a thriving African American community, Seneca Village, at Eighth Avenue and 82nd Street. (4) The park has been open since the late 1850's. (5) It remains extremely popular, owing to its wooded paths, baseball diamonds, green lawns, and, of course, the animals in its famous zoo.

> **Exercise 2** **Revising to See How Prepositions Affect Meaning** Revise the paragraph above, replacing the prepositions with other ones from the two facing lists. Explain how the changes in prepositions alter meaning.

⚙ Grammar and Style Tip

In your writing, use the correct preposition to clarify a relationship between separate things, such as location, direction, cause, or possession.

Prepositions • **393**

☑ **ONGOING ASSESSMENT: Monitor and Reinforce**

If students have difficulty with Exercise 1 or 2, refer them to the following for additional practice.

In the Textbook	Print Resources	Technology
Section Review, Ex. 7, Section 18.1	*Grammar Exercise Workbook,* pp. 31–32	*On-Line Exercise Bank,* Section 18.1

Prepositional Phrases

1. Remind students that a preposition never stands alone in a sentence; it is always used with a noun or pronoun.

2. Point out the two parts of a prepositional phrase: the *preposition* and the *object*.

3. Have students think of a preposition and write a sentence, underlining the prepositional phrase and circling the object. Provide this sample:

   I found my homework among the papers.

Answer Key

> **Exercise 3**

1. In 1868; of the Golden Gate Park
2. by this selection; because of its windy landscape
3. in 1890; from neglect and overuse
4. Under his supervision; during 1894; from it; except the Japanese Tea Garden and a museum
5. for a variety of gatherings

> **Exercise 4**

Answers will vary; samples are given.

1. The cables arch over the roadway.
2. The support pillars seem to tower to the sky.
3. Rolling hills lie beyond the bridge.
4. More hills rise in the distance.
5. The Pacific Ocean surges under the bridge.

Critical Viewing

Apply Possible answers: The bridge crosses the entrance to San Francisco Bay. It spans the bay between San Francisco and northern California.

Integrating Workplace Skills

Prepositional Phrases Tell students that it is important to place a prepositional phrase close to the word or words it modifies; otherwise, the meaning of the sentence will not be clear. Point out that this is especially important in the workplace, where misplaced prepositional phrases can cause costly confusion.

18.1

Prepositional Phrases

> **KEY CONCEPT** A **prepositional phrase** is a group of words that includes a preposition and a noun or pronoun, called the object of the preposition. ■

EXAMPLE: We had a picnic in the park.

In the preceding example, *park* is the object of the preposition *in*.

PREPOSITIONAL PHRASES	
Prepositions	Objects of the Prepositions
for	*you*
throughout	the *school*
between	*you* and *me*

> **Exercise 3** Identifying Prepositional Phrases In each sentence, identify the prepositional phrase or phrases. Write each on a piece of paper, underline the preposition, and circle its object.

1. In 1868, San Francisco selected the roughly 1,000 acres of the Golden Gate Park.
2. Few were pleased by this selection because of its windy landscape.
3. When John McLaren became superintendent in 1890, the site was suffering from neglect and overuse.
4. Under his supervision, an international exposition was held during 1894; nothing was preserved from it except the Japanese Tea Garden and a museum.
5. It has been a popular setting for a variety of gatherings.

> **Exercise 4** Writing Sentences With Prepositional Phrases Use each phrase in a sentence about the picture.

1. over the roadway
2. to the sky
3. beyond the bridge
4. in the distance
5. under the bridge

394 • Prepositions, Conjunctions, and Interjections

More Practice

Grammar Exercise Workbook
• pp. 33–34
On-line Exercise Bank
• Section 18.1
  Go on-line:
  PHSchool.com
  Enter Web Code:
  eek-1002

▼ **Critical Viewing** The Golden Gate Bridge is in California. What other prepositional phrases can you use in sentences about this bridge? **[Apply]**

✓ ONGOING ASSESSMENT: Monitor and Reinforce

If students miss more than one item in Exercise 3 or 4, refer them to the following for additional practice.

In the Textbook	Print Resources	Technology
Section Review, Ex. 7–8, Section 18.1	*Grammar Exercise Workbook,* pp. 31–32	*On-Line Exercise Bank,* Section 18.1

Preposition or Adverb?

Many of the words listed as prepositions in the charts on page 392 can also be adverbs.

KEY CONCEPT Prepositions always have objects; adverbs do not. ■

If a word that can be used either as a preposition or as an adverb has an object, the word is acting as a preposition.

Prepositions	Adverbs
The smoke drifted *up* the chimney.	The dark, ugly smoke drifted *up*.
Flowers grew *along* the path.	Won't you come *along* with us?
The park is *near* our house.	We knew a park was *near*.

For a word to act as a preposition, it must have an object and be part of a prepositional phrase. In the preceding examples, notice that the adverb examples are not followed by nouns. They do not have objects.

EXAMPLE: People wandered through.
ANSWER: through (adverb)

Exercise 5 Distinguishing Between Prepositions and Adverbs Label underlined words *prepositions* or *adverbs*.
1. Hyde Park is located <u>near</u> Kensington Gardens in England.
2. Walk <u>in</u> and find a natural respite from urban London.
3. You will see horse riders trotting <u>around</u>.
4. <u>In</u> the past, the park was the hunting grounds of royalty.
5. Is the Achilles statue located <u>around</u> the park's center?

Exercise 6 Revising Sentences by Adding Objects Revise each sentence by adding an object to change the adverb to a preposition.
1. The park is near.
2. Will you walk in?
3. Stroll around and enjoy the scenery.
4. However, don't wander off.
5. The sign says "Keep off."

Step-by-Step Teaching Guide

Preposition or Adverb

1. Point out that some words can be used as adverbs or as prepositions and that prepositions always have objects but adverbs do not.
2. Read each example in the chart aloud with the class, emphasizing the object of each preposition.
3. Ask students to give additional examples of words that can be used as either a preposition or an adverb (Examples: *outside, beyond, down*).

Customize for
Less Advanced Students

Ask students to write three sentences using the words *in, around,* and *after* as prepositions. Have them switch papers, underline the prepositional phrases, and circle the objects. Then, on that same piece of paper, have the students write three sentences using *in, around,* and *after* as adverbs. Have them hand the papers back to the original writer, who will check for an object to see if the word is now being used as an adverb.

Answer Key

▶ **Exercise 5**
1. preposition
2. adverb
3. adverb
4. preposition
5 preposition

▶ **Exercise 6**
Answers will vary; samples are given.
1. The park is near my house.
2. Will you walk in the mud?
3. Stroll around the outside path . . .
4. . . . off the paved section.
5. . . . "Keep off the grass."

ONGOING ASSESSMENT: Monitor and Reinforce

If students miss more than one item in Exercise 5 or 6, refer them to the following for additional practice.

In the Textbook	Print Resources	Technology
Section Review, Ex. 9, Section 18.1	*Grammar Exercise Workbook,* pp. 33–34	*On-Line Exercise Bank,* Section 18.1

Section Review

Each of these exercises correlates to the instruction on prepositions, pages 392–395. These exercises may be used for more practice, for reteaching, or for review of the key concepts presented.

Answer Key

> **Exercise 7**

1. <u>on</u> the western (edge); <u>of</u> (Paris)
2. <u>during</u> the (reign); <u>of</u> (Napoleon III)
3. <u>by</u> (Baron Georges-Eugène Haussmann)
4. <u>According to</u> many (people); <u>such as</u> (Hyde Park) and (Regents Park)
5. <u>for</u> (Parisians)

> **Exercise 8**

Answers will vary; samples are given. Item 3 involves an adverb, not a preposition.

1. through another famous park
2. in the United States
3. aside
4. as a military training ground and a cattle pasture
5. in 1725
6. for executions
7. during the Revolution
8. Around the park
9. along its borders
10. on the famous Freedom Trail

> **Exercise 9**

1. preposition
2. preposition
3. preposition
4. adverb
5. adverb

> **Exercise 10**

Find It in Your Reading
Students' rewrites will vary. The prepositions in the verse are as follows: in; for; of; through; like; on; of.

> **Exercise 11**

Find It in Your Writing
After students complete this process, have them exchange papers with a writing partner for a review of prepositions.

> **Exercise 12**

Writing Application
After students finish, have them discuss how the prepositional phrases made their descriptions more precise.

Section 18.1 Section Review

GRAMMAR EXERCISES 7–12

> **Exercise 7** Identifying Prepositions and Prepositional Phrases Write each prepositional phrase. Then, underline each preposition and circle each object.

1. The famous Bois de Boulogne is located on the western edge of Paris.
2. It was created during the reign of Napoleon III.
3. The park was designed by Baron Georges-Eugène Haussmann.
4. According to many people, he greatly admired the large London parks, such as Hyde Park and Regents Park.
5. Napoleon wanted similar large parks for Parisians.

> **Exercise 8** Revising Prepositions and Prepositional Phrases Revise the following paragraph by replacing prepositions and prepositional phrases with ones that better convey the intended meaning.

(1) Have you strolled over another famous park, Boston Common? (2) It is the oldest public park from the United States. (3) The parkland was set outside in 1634. (4) It was first used for a military training ground and a cattle pasture. (5) Boston Common was enclosed on 1725, and its grounds were designed by famed architect Charles Bulfinch. (6) In the past, it was used in executions of pirates and other criminals. (7) In addition to this, the British Army camped there within the Revolution. (8) Under the park, you will see many magnificent statues and fountains. (9) A bandstand, tennis courts, and a cemetery are found among its borders. (10) In view of its historical significance, Boston Common is a fitting first stop at the famous Freedom Trail.

> **Exercise 9** Distinguishing Between Prepositions and Adverbs Identify each underlined word as *preposition* or *adverb*.

(1) Have you had a chance to walk <u>around</u> the Tuileries garden in Paris? (2) It is located <u>near</u> the center of the French capital. (3) The park stretches <u>on</u> a straight line from the Place de la Concorde to the Louvre. (4) Look <u>around</u> and you will see throngs of people admiring the toy boats in the square's fountain. (5) Hold <u>on</u>, I want to eat at one of the cafes within the Tuileries.

> **Exercise 10** Find It in Your Reading Identify the prepositions in this verse by Paul Simon. Then, rewrite the verse, replacing each preposition with a different one. Explain how the changes affect meaning.

Lost in their overcoats,
Waiting for the sunset.
The sounds of the city
Sifting through the trees,
Settle like dust
On the shoulders
Of the old friends.

> **Exercise 11** Find It in Your Writing Identify at least ten prepositions in a piece of your own writing. Experiment with changing the prepositions. See if any of the changes would convey your intended meaning more clearly.

> **Exercise 12** Writing Application Imagine spending an afternoon boating in Central Park, as pictured on page 390. Write a description of your adventure using at least five prepositional phrases.

☑ ONGOING ASSESSMENT: Assess Mastery

Use the following resources to assess student mastery of prepositions and prepositional phrases.

In the Textbook	Technology
Chapter Review, Ex. 24–25	*Writing and Grammar* Interactive Text, Section 18.1, Section Review; *On-Line Exercise Bank*, Section 18.1

Section 18.2 Conjunctions and Interjections

The last two parts of speech you will learn about are *conjunctions* and *interjections*. You will use conjunctions more often than you will use interjections.

Different Kinds of Conjunctions

Unlike prepositions, which show relationships between words, conjunctions make direct connections between words.

▶ **KEY CONCEPT** A **conjunction** is a word used to connect other words or groups of words. ■

Three main kinds of conjunctions connect words: *coordinating conjunctions*, *correlative conjunctions*, and *subordinating conjunctions*.

Coordinating Conjunctions The seven *coordinating conjunctions* connect similar words or groups of words.

COORDINATING CONJUNCTIONS						
and	but	for	nor	or	so	yet

EXAMPLES: Joaquin *and* I studied Navajo weaving and cloth making.

The loom broke, *yet* the weaver continued her work.

She hung the Navajo blanket on the wall *and* then stepped back to admire it.

She wrapped herself in the blanket, *for* it had become very cold in her room.

Correlative Conjunctions *Correlative conjunctions* are similar to coordinating conjunctions. They differ only in that correlative conjunctions are always used in pairs.

CORRELATIVE CONJUNCTIONS		
both . . . and	neither . . . nor	whether . . . or
either . . . or	not only . . . but also	

EXAMPLES: He made *neither* that blanket *nor* that rug.
Both gold *and* silver bracelets were considered.
Brenda purchased *either* a Navajo bracelet *or* a Navajo blanket.

Theme: Native Americans

In this section, you will learn about conjunctions and interjections. The examples and exercises in this section are about Native American culture and history.

Cross-Curricular Connection: Social Studies

▶ **More Practice**

Grammar Exercise Workbook
• pp. 35–36
On-line Exercise Bank
• Section 18.2
 Go on-line:
 PHSchool.com
 Enter Web Code:
 eek-1002

Conjunctions and Interjections • **397**

⏱ **TIME AND RESOURCE MANAGER**

Resources
Print: *Grammar Exercise Workbook*, pp. 35–40; *Grammar Exercises Answers on Transparencies*, Ch. 18; *Hands-on Grammar Activity Book*, Ch. 18
Technology: *Writing and Grammar* Interactive Text Section 18.2; *On-Line Exercise Bank*, Section 18.2

Using the Full Student Edition	Using the Handbook 🄷
• Work through all key concepts, pp. 397–401.	• Work through all key concepts, pp. 265–269.
• Assign and review Exercises 13–17.	• Assign and review Exercises 13–17.
• Read and discuss Grammar in Literature, p. 399.	• Read and discuss Grammar in Literature, p. 267.
• Do the Hands-on Grammar activity, p. 403.	• Do the Hands-on Grammar activity, p. 271.

Step-by-Step Teaching Guide

Subordinating Conjunctions

1. Point out that the only type of conjunction that does not join ideas of equal importance is the subordinating conjunction.

2. Have students write one sentence for any five of the subordinating conjunctions in the chart. Caution them to have two pairs of subjects and verbs in their sentences to achieve two ideas. As students read their examples, ask which is the main idea and which idea is less important.

Real-World Connection

The three different kinds of conjunctions are important in forming lists, especially directional lists like recipes. A recipe may read "*Before* you add the salt, combine the flour *and* the butter." The subordinating conjunction *before* places the adding of the salt after the combining of the flour and butter, which are made equal to each other with the coordinating conjunction *and*. Discuss the problems that could occur should inappropriate conjunctions be used (*After* adding the salt, combine the flour and the butter.). Ask students to discuss other situations that rely on conjunctions (driving directions, assembly instructions, etc.).

Answer Key

▶ **Exercise 13**

1. while–subordinating
2. and–coordinating
3. Even though–subordinating
4. before–subordinating
5. for–coordinating
6. so–coordinating
7. not only . . . but also–correlative
8. Whether . . . or–correlative
9. While–subordinating
10. Neither . . . nor–correlative

Critical Viewing

Describe Sample response: bold <u>and</u> symmetrical

Subordinating Conjunctions *Subordinating conjunctions* connect two complete ideas by making one of the ideas subordinate to, or less important than, the other.

FREQUENTLY USED SUBORDINATING CONJUNCTIONS			
after	because	now that	until
although	before	since	when
as	even if	so that	whenever
as if	even though	than	where
as long as	if	though	wherever
as soon as	in order that	till	while
as though	lest	unless	

The following example shows how a subordinating conjunction is used to connect related ideas.

EXAMPLE: subord. idea   main idea
Because Carol practices, she is a good artist.

▶ **Exercise 13** **Identifying Conjunctions** Write the conjunction in each sentence. Then, label each *coordinating, correlative,* or *subordinating*.

1. Traditionally, Navajo men work as silversmiths, while the women are weavers.
2. Navajo silversmiths are among the most talented and creative in the world.
3. Even though they are immensely skilled in working silver, they are relatively new to the craft.
4. The Navajos had learned silversmithing from neighboring Mexicans before they were relocated by the government in 1864–1866, an event known as "The Long Walk."
5. In the late nineteenth century, Navajo fortunes improved, for traders recognized the market for the jewelry.
6. Trader Lorenzo Hubbell brought Mexican silversmiths to the reservation so even more Navajo men learned the craft.
7. These craftsmen would use not only Mexican but also United States coins for their raw material.
8. Whether it was a belt buckle, ring, necklace, or earring, the silversmiths' works were uniquely intricate.
9. While their silver work was already expert, the Navajos began adding their distinctive turquoise settings to jewelry in the late 1890's.
10. Neither the Navajo silversmiths nor the traders foresaw the great popularity of this jewelry.

398 • Prepositions, Conjunctions, and Interjections

▼ **Critical Viewing** What are two words you would use to describe this vase, and what conjunction would you use to connect the words? **[Describe]**

☑ ONGOING ASSESSMENT: Monitor and Reinforce

If students miss more than two items in Exercise 13, refer them to the following for additional practice.

In the Textbook	Print Resources	Technology
Section Review, Ex. 18, Section 18.2	*Grammar Exercise Workbook,* pp. 35–36	*On-Line Exercise Bank,* Section 18.2

GRAMMAR IN LITERATURE

from A Raisin in the Sun, Act I, Scene II
Lorraine Hansberry

The conjunctions in the following excerpt are highlighted in blue italics.

MAMA. . . . In my time we was worried about not being lynched *and* getting to the North if we could *and* how to stay alive *and* still have a pinch of dignity too . . . Now here come you *and* Beneatha—talking 'bout things we ain't never even thought about hardly, me *and* your daddy. You ain't satisfied *or* proud of nothing we done.

Conjunction, Preposition, or Adverb?

After, before, since, till, and *until* can be subordinating conjunctions or prepositions. *After, before,* and *since* can also be adverbs. *When* and *where* can be subordinating conjunctions or adverbs. The part of speech of these words depends on their use within a sentence.

▶ **KEY CONCEPT** **Subordinating conjunctions** connect complete ideas. ■

The following examples show the word *before* used in three different ways.

SUBORDINATING CONJUNCTION:	She started to weave *before* she turned ten.
PREPOSITION:	The weaver starts work *before* sunrise.
ADVERB:	Have you ever watched a weaver make a blanket *before*?

▼ **Critical Viewing** How does this picture connect to the examples shown on the left? **[Connect]**

Conjunctions and Interjections • 399

STANDARDIZED TEST PREPARATION WORKSHOP

Sentence Style Many standardized tests require students to revise written work correctly. Use the following example to demonstrate.

Very little is known to writers living today of Shakespeare's early life.

Choose the best way to write the above sentence.

A Correct as is.

B Very little to writers living today is known of Shakespeare's early life.

C Very little of Shakespeare's early life is known to writers living today.

D Of Shakespeare's early life to writers living today, very little is known.

The correct answer is **C**, because the prepositional phrase "of Shakespeare's early life" should be placed as close as possible to the word it modifies *(little)*.

Answer Key

Step-by-Step Teaching Guide

Conjunctive Adverbs

1. Point out that the words in the chart on this page are frequently used to link ideas in the same sentence or in two different sentences.
2. Read the examples beneath the chart and show that a conjunctive adverb preceded by a period or semicolon is followed by a comma.

Language Highlight

Present-day English has borrowed many words from Native Americans. The word *moose* is of Algonquian origin. *Moose* and other words such as *hickory, pecan*, and *raccoon* refer to plants and animals that were unknown to early European settlers. The meanings of some Native American words have undergone changes over the years. *Powwow* originally meant a priest or medicine man; later, it referred to a ceremony in which feasting, dancing, and magic were parts. Today, *powwow* is used to describe a Native American council or a get-together of any kind.

Customize for
ESL Students

Some students may not pick up the slight pause that normally precedes and follows the use of a conjunctive adverb and helps distinguish it from a coordinating conjunction. Read the second example sentence as if it had a coordinating conjunction (". . . during their visit, *and* the outdoor . . ."), and then read it again with *accordingly, therefore*, and *thus*. Have ESL students note the pauses in each case, which were not there in the version with the coordinating conjunction *and*.

Exercise 14 Identifying Words as Conjunctions, Prepositions, or Adverbs Label each underlined word *subordinating conjunction, preposition,* or *adverb.*

1. Navajo women have practiced the art of weaving <u>since</u> they learned the skill from Pueblo Indians in the 1800's.
2. As with silver, traders saw the potential value of Navajo-made cloth <u>when</u> setting up shops near the reservation.
3. Navajo cloths—such as blankets, belts, rugs, and bags—have been highly prized ever <u>since</u>.
4. The Navajos used pigments collected from local vegetation <u>until</u> they started weaving for a wider audience.
5. <u>Since</u> that time, they have begun to use commercially made dyes.

Exercise 15 Writing With Conjunctions, Prepositions, and Adverbs Write three sets of three sentences using *after, before,* and *until* as conjunctions, prepositions, and adverbs.

Conjunctive Adverbs

Some words act as both conjunctions and adverbs at the same time. These words are called *conjunctive adverbs.*

KEY CONCEPT A **conjunctive adverb** is an adverb that acts as a conjunction to connect complete ideas. ■

FREQUENTLY USED CONJUNCTIVE ADVERBS

accordingly	finally	nevertheless
again	furthermore	otherwise
also	however	then
besides	indeed	therefore
consequently	moreover	thus

Conjunctive adverbs are often used as transitions—words that serve as links between different ideas. In the following example, notice how conjunctive adverbs work to make transitions between related ideas.

EXAMPLES: They had never been on a reservation before. *Indeed*, they had never been far away from home.

It had rained during their visit; *consequently*, the outdoor Navajo art exhibit was canceled.

The conjunctive adverb is followed by a comma.

More Practice

Grammar Exercise Workbook
• pp. 37–38
On-line Exercise Bank
• Section 18.2
Go on-line:
PHSchool.com
Enter Web Code:
eek-1002

Complete the exercises on-line! Exercises 14, 15, 16, and 17 are available on-line or on CD-ROM.

▽ ONGOING ASSESSMENT: Monitor and Reinforce		
If students have difficulty with Exercise 14 or 15, refer them to the following for additional practice.		
In the Textbook	**Print Resources**	**Technology**
Section Review, Ex. 18, 21, Section 18.2	*Grammar Exercise Workbook,* pp. 37–38	*On-Line Exercise Bank,* Section 18.2

▶ **Exercise 16** Revising With Conjunctive Adverbs Revise this paragraph, adding conjunctive adverbs to connect ideas.

(1) The Navajos live in a southwestern desert country of mesas, cliffs, and canyons. This is reflected in the geometric patterns they choose for their blankets and rugs. (2) They changed their weaving styles after acquiring non-Navajo customers in the late nineteenth century. The years 1850 to 1880 are considered the "Classic Period" of weaving. (3) From the 1880's on, the Navajos adapted their weaving techniques and traditions to satisfy tourist demands. These years are referred to as the "Transitional Period." (4) Tourists preferred brighter colors. Weavers began using commercial dyes in their works. (5) Tourists also preferred rugs to blankets. Navajos began producing more rugs.

Interjections

Interjections are used mainly in speaking, not in writing.

▶ **KEY CONCEPT** An **interjection** is a word that expresses feeling or emotion and functions independently of a sentence. ■

Many feelings can be expressed by interjections, such as *ah, hey, oh, ouch, uh, well,* or *wow.* These examples show other interjections used to express different emotions.

JOY:	*Hurray!* We won!	EXHAUSTION:	*Whew!* That was hard.
SURPRISE:	*Aha!* I found the sandpainting.	SORROW:	She knew, *alas,* the truth.

Since interjections are independent from other words, they are set off by exclamation marks or commas.

▶ **Exercise 17** Supplying Interjections For each sentence, supply an interjection that suggests the specified emotion.

EXAMPLE: You spilled your milk on the rug. [dismay]
ANSWER: Oh, no! You spilled your milk on the rug.

1. I bought a Navajo blanket. [pleasure]
2. It was an imitation of a Navajo blanket. [anger]
3. Should I return it to the store? [hesitation]
4. The owner was a very large and threatening man. [fear]
5. He told me he would accept no returns. [acceptance]

More Practice

Grammar Exercise Workbook
• pp. 39–40
On-line Exercise Bank
• Section 18.2
Go on-line:
PHSchool.com
Enter Web Code:
eek-1002

Grammar and Style Tip

Avoid interjections in your formal writing except in a special situation such as a direct quote.

Conjunctions and Interjections • 401

☑ **ONGOING ASSESSMENT: Monitor and Reinforce**

If students miss more than one item in Exercise 16 or 17, refer them to the following for additional practice.

In the Textbook	Print Resources	Technology
Section Review, Ex. 19–20, 23	*Grammar Exercise Workbook,* pp. 39–40	*On-Line Exercise Bank,* Section 18.2

Section Review

Each of these exercises correlates to the instruction on conjunctions and interjections, pages 397–401. These exercises may be used for more practice, for reteaching, or for review of the key concepts presented.

Answer Key

Exercise 18

1. or–coordinating
2. Even though–subordinating
3. and–coordinating
4. Because–subordinating
5. both . . . and–correlative

Exercise 19

1. conjunction	6. conjunction
2. interjection	7. conjunction
3. conjunction	8. preposition
4. adverb	9. conj. adverb
5. conj. adverb	10. interjection

Exercise 20

Choices will vary; samples are given.

1. however	4. then
2. nevertheless	5. also
3. therefore	

Exercise 21

Find It in Your Reading
and—coordinating
and—coordinating
and—coordinating
and—coordinating
and—coordinating
or—coordinating

Exercise 22

Find It in Your Writing
When they finish, have students exchange papers with a partner and check that conjunctions link related ideas.

Exercise 23

Writing Appplication
Answers will vary. Sample answers:

1. Hey! Quit that and get to work!
2. Oh, I'm sorry, but I forgot.
3. Tsk! Tsk! When you left early, you should have known better.
4. Darn, I can remember neither his address nor his phone number.
5. Whew! I passed the test, even though I didn't study hard.

Section Review

GRAMMAR EXERCISES 18–23

> **Exercise 18** Identifying **Conjunctions** Write the conjunctions in the following sentences. Then, label each *coordinating*, *correlative*, or *subordinating*.

1. Are you familiar with the Navajo art of sandpainting or drypainting?
2. Even though it has its roots in Navajo ceremonies, sandpainting is also a commercial art form.
3. Most scholars agree that the Navajos borrowed the idea of sandpainting and changed it to fit with their own ideas.
4. Because early sandpaintings were not permanent, there is little evidence to prove how this process occurred.
5. This sandpainting is both permanent and colorful.

> **Exercise 19** Identifying Different **Parts of Speech** Label the underlined words *conjunction*, *adverb*, *conjunctive adverb*, *preposition*, or *interjection*.

The first permanent sandpaintings were made in the late nineteenth century (1) <u>in order that</u> Navajo culture would be preserved. (2) <u>Wow</u>, did many Navajos object to this, but they were created anyway? (3) <u>When</u> they were published, interest in sandpaintings grew greater than (4) <u>before</u>. In 1915, Franc J. Newcomb, a trader's wife, befriended Hosteen Klah, a famous medicine man; (5) <u>consequently</u>, Newcomb amassed a large collection of sandpaintings drawn (6) <u>both</u> by her <u>and</u> by Navajos. (7) <u>Now that</u> it was filtering into non-Navajo land, artists began to use sandpainting motifs in permanent works. (8) <u>Before</u> this commercial use, however, the Navajos were careful to remove or alter certain designs. (9) <u>However</u>, despite their precautions, the acceptance of drypaintings as commercial art is still somewhat controversial, and (10) <u>yes</u>, many Navajos still do not approve.

> **Exercise 20** Revising With **Conjunctive Adverbs** Revise the following sentences using conjunctive adverbs.

1. The sandpainting is supervised by one person. Its construction is left to the most artistic.
2. Sandpaintings are difficult. Three to six men create one in about four hours.
3. It is made with colored pigments from rocks. The rocks must be collected and ground.
4. The paintings are made by sprinkling crushed rock over a floor of sand. Paintings for ceremonies are later destroyed.
5. Sandpaintings were created in Japan in the seventh century. They were created in England in the 1700's and 1800's.

> **Exercise 21** Find It in Your **Reading** Read the excerpt from *A Raisin in the Sun* on page 399. List the conjunctions, and label them by type.

> **Exercise 22** Find It in Your **Writing** Choose a writing sample from your portfolio. Find any conjunctions you have used. Challenge yourself to combine three to five sentences with similar ideas by connecting them using conjunctions.

> **Exercise 23** Writing Application Write five sentences based on the following emotions, each using an interjection and a conjunction.

1. outrage
2. sadness
3. disapproval
4. frustration
5. relief

☑ ONGOING ASSESSMENT: Assess Mastery

Use the following resources to assess student mastery of conjunctions and interjections.

In the Textbook	Technology
Chapter Review, Ex. 26–29	*On-Line Exercise Bank*, Section 18.2

Hands-on Grammar

Fill In the Blanks

Cut several pieces of construction paper into strips, each about an inch wide. Then, from a different-colored sheet of construction paper, cut several dozen squares about one inch by one inch. Next, write a sentence on each of the strips. Construct the sentences so that each contains one or more prepositions or conjunctions. Then, paste the squares over all of the prepositions and conjunctions.

Write prepositions and conjunctions on all of the remaining squares. Then, with a group of classmates, experiment with placing different squares in the various sentences. Discuss how the changes in the prepositions and conjunctions affect the meaning of the sentences.

When you've finished, write a few paragraphs summing up what you learned from the activity.

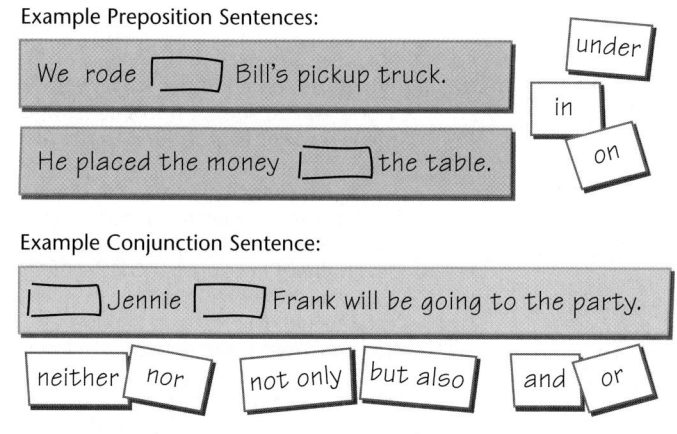

Example Preposition Sentences:

We rode [ ] Bill's pickup truck.

He placed the money [ ] the table.

under

in

on

Example Conjunction Sentence:

[ ] Jennie [ ] Frank will be going to the party.

neither | nor | not only | but also | and | or

Find It in Your Reading Try this activity with sentences from a nonfiction article that you have read recently.

Find It in Your Writing Try this activity with sentences from a piece of your own writing.

Hands-on Grammar

Teaching Resources: Hands-on Grammar Activity Book, Ch. 18

1. If you wish to do this activity in class, be prepared with scissors, construction paper, and, optionally, paper clips. Have students work in groups, and give each group the needed materials.

2. Go through the directions and the samples with the whole class. Have them supply appropriate prepositions or conjunctions for each sentence (for example, *in Bill's pickup truck*, *on the table*, *Neither Jennie nor Frank*).

3. Now have students make their own squares with prepositions and conjunctions and apply them to the original sentences that they write.

4. After students have finished and written summaries of the activity, have some of them share their thoughts with the class.

Find It in Your Reading

Students may either find their own nonfiction articles or work with some from their literature texts.

Find It in Your Writing

Have students work individually with sentences from their own writing. They can then share the results within their groups.

✦ STANDARDIZED TEST PREPARATION WORKSHOP

Grammar and Usage Many standardized tests require students to revise compositions. Use the following example to demonstrate.

(1) The average daytime temperature on the moon is 210 degrees <u>Fahrenheit.</u>
(2) <u>Life on the moon</u> may be impossible.

Which is the BEST way to write the underlined portion?

A Best as is
B Fahrenheit; as a result, life on the moon
C Fahrenheit, however, life on the moon
D Fahrenheit. In addition, life on the moon

The correct answer is **B** because the conjunctive adverb *as a result* indicates a conclusion based on the data given in sentence one.

⏱ TIME SAVERS!

Hands-on Grammar
Use the Hands-on Grammar activity sheet for Chapter 18 to facilitate this activity.

CHAPTER REVIEW

Each of these exercises correlates to a section of the chapter on prepositions, conjunctions, and interjections, pages 392–403. The exercises may be used for more practice, for reteaching, or for review of the key concepts presented.

Answer Key

Exercise 24

Prepositions are underlined; objects of prepositions are circled.

1. in side (North America)
2. of the Athabascan (family)
3. in (Canada)
4. from (Canada); between (900) and (1200)
5. in the (Southwest); under Pueblo (influences)

Exercise 25

Answers will vary; samples are given.

1. about herding
2. between the two tribes
3. During the eighteenth century
4. because of drought and famine
5. On account of their extended visit and compatibility

Exercise 26

1. *where*–subordinating
2. *neither . . . nor*–correlative
3. *Although*–subordinating
4. *but*–coordinating
5. *yet*–coordinating

Exercise 27

1. conjunction
2. preposition
3. conjunction
4. conjunction
5. conjunction

404

▶ **Exercise 24** Identifying **Prepositional Phrases** Identify each prepositional phrase in these sentences. Indicate the prepositions and the object.

1. Today, the Navajos are the largest Native American tribe inside North America.
2. The Navajos speak Apachean, a language of the Athabascan family.
3. This language has its roots in Canada.
4. The Navajos probably migrated from Canada between 900 and 1200.
5. Since their arrival in the Southwest, the Navajos have come under Pueblo influences.

▶ **Exercise 25** Revising **Prepositions and Prepositional Phrases** Revise the following paragraph by replacing prepositions and prepositional phrases with ones that better convey the intended meaning.

1. In addition to farming, the Pueblos taught them herding.
2. Contact around the two tribes was recorded around the seventeenth century.
3. Within the eighteenth century, the Hopi lived with the Navajo.
4. The Hopi left their former dwellings despite drought and famine.
5. In spite of their extended visit and compatibility, the Pueblos influenced the Navajos in many ways.

▶ **Exercise 26** Classifying **Conjunctions** Write the conjunctions in the sentences below, and label them *coordinating*, *correlative*, or *subordinating*.

1. The Navajo Reservation is now the area where many Navajos reside.

2. The Navajo lands are neither well irrigated nor large enough to provide a livelihood for everyone.
3. Although many live on the reservation, thousands earn their living outside of it.
4. Travel to an outside job may be the answer for some Navajos, but many have chosen to relocate.
5. Settling on irrigated lands, yet being culturally removed from the reservation, presents a difficult choice.

▶ **Exercise 27** Distinguishing **Between Conjunctions, Prepositions, or Adverbs** Label each underlined word *conjunction*, *preposition*, or *adverb*.

1. <u>When</u> the United States was involved in World War II, several hundred Navajos made a major contribution to the Allied victory.
2. <u>Before</u> receiving help from the Navajos, the military had been worried about enemies intercepting information.
3. The military developed a code system that was foolproof, and <u>after</u> that was established, the Navajos took over.
4. This was not a code <u>in which</u> artificial words and signals were used, but simply the Navajo language.
5. <u>Since</u> the Navajo language is difficult to learn, still unwritten, and few speak it, the language was the perfect code.

▶ **Exercise 28** Revising to Add **Conjunctions and Prepositions to Connect Ideas** Revise the following paragraphs. Combine sentences and add conjunctions and prepositions where appropriate to better connect the ideas.

(1) Using the Navajo language made Allied communication extremely secure. It

was more secure than communication had ever been during wartime. (2) The Navajo code talkers were able to perform in complete secrecy. The secrecy was maintained throughout the war. (3) The code talkers were trained in the Pacific. They were prepared to begin work.

(4) The Navajo language has survived to this day. There were pressures on the Navajo people to communicate only in English. (5) Maintaining traditional languages is important. Maintaining cultural values is also important.

Exercise 29 Revising Sentences With Conjunctive Adverbs Use conjunctive adverbs to make transitions between or combine the following groups of sentences.

1. The Navajo code talkers translated messages. They transmitted messages.
2. They assigned the names of birds to military terms. They translated them into Navajo.
3. The code talkers transmitted the messages. The last step was for a member of the team on the other end to translate them into English.
4. Navajo code talkers often worked in noisy command posts or combat zones. They were hunched over radio sets.
5. The Navajo code talkers' contribution was invaluable. Many believe they are greatly responsible for the victory over Japan.

Exercise 30 Classifying Prepositions, Conjunctions, and Interjections Label each underlined word preposition, conjunction, or interjection. If the word is a conjunction, identify it as coordinating, correlative, or subordinating. If it is a preposition, write its object.

The ancient Navajo myths and legends date back thousands of years (1) but still reflect the tribe's association with their surrounding environment. (2) According to many scholars, the story of the movement through four worlds may reflect the early history of the Navajos, (3) when they eventually migrated to their present location. (4) Although the settlement (5) of the Americas is still (6) under debate, many believe the continents were settled thousands of years ago (7) as bands of nomads migrated south. (8) Whether the Navajos first settled elsewhere or came directly to the Southwest is rarely debated, (9) for most archaeologists agree they probably first settled (10) in the Far North.

Exercise 31 Revising With Prepositions, Conjunctions, and Interjections Revise this paragraph, adding or replacing prepositions, conjunctions, and interjections where appropriate.

The Navajos probably first migrated on the Southwest hundreds of years ago. The new region presented a radical climate change. The early Navajo nomads probably had to alter much of their way of life. Their clothing and their dwellings were not suitable for the new environment. The fish and game were very different. New ways of finding food were needed. The greatest change that took place was in their system of beliefs. The Navajos had to adjust their cultural beliefs to reflect their new land. They also had to adjust their religious beliefs. They did this. It occurred over time. The Navajos assimilated to their new home. Their lives were changed.

Exercise 32 Writing Application Write a narrative about a custom or tradition that you enjoy or one that you would like to begin in your home, school, or community. Include one sentence containing two prepositions, one sentence containing two subordinating conjunctions, one sentence containing one coordinating conjunction, and one sentence containing one subordinating conjunction.

Chapter Review • 405

Answer Key

Exercise 28

Answers will vary; samples are given.

1. Using the Navajo language not only made Allied communication secure, it also made it more secure than it had ever been during wartime.
2. The Navajo code talkers were able to perform in complete secrecy and maintain that secrecy . . .
3. After the code talkers were trained in the Pacific, they were prepared to . . .
4. The Navajo language has survived to this day, though there were pressures on the . . .
5. Maintaining traditional languages and cultural values is . . .

Exercise 29

Choices will vary; samples are given.

1. furthermore   4. consequently
2. then   5. indeed
3. finally

Exercise 30

1. coordinating conjunction
2. preposition–scholars
3. subordinating conjunction
4. subordinating conjunction
5. preposition–Americas
6. preposition–debate
7. subordinating conjunction
8. correlative conjunction
9. coordinating conjunction
10. preposition–North

Exercise 31

Answers will vary; a sample is given.

When Navajos first migrated to the Southwest, probably hundreds of years ago, the new region presented a radical climate change. The early Navajo nomads probably had to alter much of their way of life, since their clothes and their dwellings were not suitable for the new environment. The fish and game were very different, and new ways of finding food were needed. However, the greatest change that took place was in their system of beliefs. The Navajos had to adjust their cultural and religious beliefs to reflect their new land. Yes, they did all this. Over time, the Navajos assimilated into their new homes and changed their lives.

Exercise 32

Have students work in pairs and read each other's paragraphs to check for examples of the four kinds of assigned sentences.

☑ **ONGOING ASSESSMENT: Assess Mastery**

Use the following resources to assess student mastery of prepositions, conjunctions, and interjections.

In the Textbook	Print Resources	Technology
Chapter Review, Ex. 24–32 Standardized Test Preparation Workshop	Formal Assessment, Ch. 18	Writing and Grammar Interactive Text, Ch. 18, Chapter Review; On-Line Exercise Bank, Sections 18.1–2

Step-by-Step Teaching Guide

Revising and Editing

Teaching Resources: Standardized Test Preparation Workbook pp. 35–36

1. Discuss with students, using examples from the Sample Test Item and the Practices, the reasons for revising some writing. Point out choppy sentences, sentence fragments, and awkward phrasing.

2. Review some common conjunctions and prepositions. Tell students that a conjunction is a word that is used to join words or groups of words, such as *and, but, or, nor,* and *for.* Remind them that prepositions are words that show how a noun or pronoun relates to another word, such as *above, below, during, from, by,* and *in.* Go over examples of sentences that include conjunctions and prepositions.

3. Point out that when several details are used to describe one item, the details usually can be combined in a series.

Standardized Test Preparation Workshop

Revising and Editing

Standardized tests often test your ability to connect ideas using prepositional phrases and conjunctions. Often, you will be asked to identify the best revision of a sentence or passage from among several choices. The best revision may or may not use prepositions and conjunctions to join ideas. When you approach items that require the best revision, keep the following points in mind.

- The first choice that combines ideas with a conjunction is not necessarily the best choice.
- Different conjunctions and prepositions have different meanings. Make sure you choose the revision that reflects the meaning of the original sentence or passage.

The following sample test items illustrate one of the formats used to test your ability to use prepositions and conjunctions.

Test Tip

If two choices appear to be the same, look for the small difference that distinguishes them. One of the choices is a distractor.

Sample Test Item	Answer and Explanation
Directions: Read the passage, and choose the best way to revise each underlined section. Many African cultures created music. (1) Drums and rhythms are the basis of this music. **A** Many African cultures created music, and drums and rhythms are the basis of this music. **B** Many African cultures created music based on drums and rhythms. **C** Many African cultures created rhythms. **D** Drums and rhythms are the basis of this music, but many African cultures created music.	The best answer is *B*. Since both sentences are about African music, it is logical to combine information with the prepositional phrase *on drums and rhythms.*

TEST-TAKING TIP

Tell students to read carefully only the sentences they are considering for revision. They should ask themselves: Are the sentences short and choppy? Are there any sentence fragments? Do the sentences describe one topic? With these questions answered, students will be able to revise the sentences more efficiently. Remind them to find the main idea in the group of sentences and to make sure this idea is clear in the revision.

> **Practice 1** **Directions:** Read the passage, and choose the best way to rewrite the underlined sections.

Different tones are produced. Different
(1)
drum sizes and shapes as well as hand

positions produce these tones. The
                                    (2)
music can be quite complex. It is not

uncommon for six or seven drummers to

play in different signatures.

1 **A** Different tones are produced, and different drum sizes and shapes as well as hand positions produce these tones.
  B Different tones are produced by a variety of different drum sizes and shapes as well as hand positions.
  C Different tones are produced on different drum sizes and shapes as well as hand positions which produce these tones.
  D Different tones are produced, but different drum sizes and shapes as well as hand positions produce the different tones.
2 **F** The music can be quite complex, and it is not uncommon for six or seven drummers to play in different signatures.
  G The music can be quite complex with many different signatures.
  H The music can be quite complex, but it is not uncommon for six or seven drummers to play in different signatures.
  J The music of six or seven drummers can be quite complex.

> **Practice 2** **Directions:** Read the passage, and choose the best way to rewrite the underlined sections.

The drum is one of the oldest musical
(1)
instruments. And one of the most popular.

It is an instrument that is played.
(2)
By striking it with the hand,

sticks, or other objects.

1 **A** The drum is one of the oldest musical instruments and one of the most popular.
  B The drum is not only one of the oldest musical instruments, but also one of the most popular.
  C The drum is either the oldest musical instrument or the most popular.
  D The drum is the oldest yet most popular instrument.
2 **F** It is an instrument that is played by striking it with the hand or with sticks or with other objects.
  G It is an instrument that is played by striking it with the hand and with sticks or with other objects.
  H It is an instrument that is played by striking it with the hand, sticks, or other objects.
  J With the hand, it is an instrument that is played by striking it with sticks or other objects.

Answer Key

> **Practice 1**
1. B
2. F

> **Practice 2**
1. B
2. H

Customize for
Less Advanced Students

Help students use coordinating conjunctions to practice combining several short sentences. You might review run-on sentences so that students avoid creating run-ons as they combine shorter sentences.

Customize for
More Advanced Students

Show students that a certain kind of conjunction, called a subordinating conjunction, can be used to combine two or more short sentences. For example:

I waited for the doctor.

I read a book.

While I waited for the doctor, I read a book.

Answer Key

> **Exercise A**

Nouns

Answers use these abbreviations:

Cd = compound
S = singular
Pl = plural
A = abstract
Cc = concrete
Cm = common
Pr = proper

1. **Arctic**–S, Pr, Cc; **area**–S, Cm, Cc; **North Pole**–Cd, S, Pr, Cc
2. **area**–S, Cm, Cc; **Arctic Ocean**–Cd, S, Pr, Cc; **islands**–Pl, Cm, Cc; **parts**–Pl, Cm, Cc; **North America**–Cd, S, Pr, Cc; **Asia**–S, Pr, Cc; **Europe**–S, Pr, Cc
3. **areas**–Pl, Cm, Cc; **Canada**–S, Pr, Cc; **Russia**–S, Pr, Cc; **Greenland**–S, Pr, Cc
4. **location**–S, Cm, A; **Arctic Circle**–S, Pr, Cc; **name**–S, Cm, Cc
5. **Arctic**–S, Pr, Cc; **plateau**–S, Cm, Cc; **Antarctica**–S, Pr, Cc; **ocean**–S, Cm, Cc; **land**–S, Cm, Cc
6. **landmasses**–Cd, Pl, Cm, Cc; **types**–Pl, Cm, A; **granite**–S, Cm, Cc; **gneiss**–S, Cm, Cc
7. **rivers**–Pl, Cm, Cc; **Arctic**–S, Pr, Cc
8. **Mackenzie**–S, Pr, Cc; **Yukon**–S, Pr, Cc; **Arctic**–S, Pr, Cc
9. **North Pole**–S, Pr, Cc; **spot**–S, Cm, Cc; **Arctic**–S, Pr, Cc; **ocean**–S, Cm, Cc
10. **Oymyakon, Siberia**–S, Pr, Cc; **temperature**–S, Cm, Cc

Pronouns

1. it–personal, *Arctic*
4. its, it, its–personal, *Arctic*
5. that–relative, *plateau*
6. which–relative, *landmasses*
7. What–interrogative, no clear antecedent; some–indefinite, *rivers*
8. others–indefinite, *rivers* (item 7)
9. it–personal, *North Pole*

> **Exercise B**

1. <u>had</u> migrated–visible, intransitive
2. reached–visible, transitive; lived–visible, intransitive
3. are–linking
4. inhabit–visible, transitive; occupy–visible, transitive
5. like–mental, transitive

Cumulative Review

PARTS OF SPEECH

> **Exercise A** Identifying Nouns and Pronouns List the nouns in the following sentences, labeling each *compound*, *singular* or *plural*, *abstract* or *concrete*, and *common* or *proper*. Then, list the pronouns and label each *personal*, *demonstrative*, *interrogative*, *reflexive*, *intensive*, *relative*, or *indefinite*. Identify the antecedent of each pronoun.

1. The Arctic is the area near the North Pole, but it is not clearly defined.
2. The area includes the Arctic Ocean, several islands, and parts of North America, Asia, and Europe.
3. The largest areas are in Canada, Russia, and Greenland.
4. Its location, north of the Arctic Circle, gives it its name.
5. The Arctic, unlike the ice-covered plateau that is Antarctica, has a central ocean almost enclosed by land.
6. There are three landmasses, which are composed of the rock types granite and gneiss.
7. What are some rivers in the Arctic?
8. There are the Mackenzie and Yukon as well as others in the Russian Arctic.
9. The North Pole is not the coldest spot in the Arctic because the ocean warms it.
10. Oymyakon, Siberia, holds the record low temperature in the Arctic.

> **Exercise B** Identifying Verbs Write the verbs in the following sentences. Label the action verbs *visible* or *mental action* and *transitive* or *intransitive*. Then, label the *linking verbs*. Next, indicate any *verb phrases* and, underline *helping verbs*.

1. Ethnic groups had migrated from Asia to various parts of the Arctic.
2. The Inuit reached the Atlantic Ocean

in Greenland, and the Saami lived in Norway.
3. In North America, the three main groups are the Aleuts, Native Americans, and Inuit.
4. The Aleuts inhabit the area around the Bering Sea, while Native Americans occupy the grasslands.
5. The Inuit like the areas in northern Alaska, northern Canada, and some of Greenland.

> **Exercise C** Revising Verbs Revise the following sentences, replacing linking verbs and verb phrases with action verbs where possible.

1. Natural materials are used by some indigenous residents for clothing, tools, and shelters.
2. Hunting and fishing are what they frequently do to gather food.
3. The time of settlement among Norse in the Arctic was in the ninth century A.D.
4. The average population of Arctic cities in North America is less than 10,000.
5. Communities of scientists have been established in Arctic regions.

> **Exercise D** Identifying Adjectives and Adverbs Identify the underlined words in these sentences as *adjectives* or *adverbs* and write the word each modifies.

1. Robert Edwin Peary is generally credited with leading the <u>first</u> party to the North Pole.
2. Before becoming an explorer, he <u>first</u> was a civil engineer.
3. Peary participated in the Nicaragua Canal Survey and <u>several</u> polar explorations.
4. He <u>finally</u> proved that Greenland was not a continent but an island.

> **Exercise C**

1. All indigenous residents use natural materials for clothing . . .
2. They hunt and fish to gather food.
3. The Norse settled the Arctic . . .
4. Fewer than 10,000 people live in the average Arctic city in . . .
5. Scientists have established communities . . .

> **Exercise D**

1. first, adjective modifying *party*
2. first, adverb modifying *was*
3. several, adjective modifying *explorations*
4. finally, adverb modifying *proved*
5. unsuccessful, adjective modifying *attempts*

5. In 1902, 1905, and 1906, Peary made <u>unsuccessful</u> attempts to reach the North Pole.

Exercise E Recognizing Prepositions, Conjunctions, and Interjections
Write and label each *preposition*, *conjunction*, and *interjection*. Then, identify each conjunction as *coordinating*, *correlative*, *subordinating*, or as a *conjunctive adverb*.

1. Wow! Matthew Henson was an adventurous and brave person.
2. After running away from home at age 12, he traveled on a merchant ship.
3. He worked both on that ship and in a Washington, D.C., hat store.
4. Robert Peary hired him to be his valet; consequently, Henson became his translator and navigator.
5. Yes, Henson was also responsible for breaking the trail.

Exercise F Revising With Prepositions, Conjunctions, and Interjections
Revise these sentences, adding and replacing prepositions, conjunctions, and interjections to precisely convey the relationships among ideas. Also, combine sentences where appropriate.

1. Henson walked ahead of Peary and the four Inuit. He may have reached the North Pole up to forty-five minutes under the rest of the party.
2. President Taft recommended Henson to a job in New York City. He wanted to recognize his work in the Arctic.
3. Was he really given a medal in the United States Congress?
4. President Eisenhower recognized Henson's achievements. He was soon forgotten.
5. In 1988, Henson was reburied on Arlington National Cemetery with full honors.

Exercise G Identifying All Parts of Speech
Write this paragraph on a separate sheet of paper. Then, label each word according to its part of speech.

Before the Vikings explored the Arctic regions, the Greeks of the fourth century were aware of these regions. Some Norsemen reached Iceland, which already had a colony of Irish monks. Their voyages did not lead to the discovery of Greenland until Eric the Red landed there A.D. 982.
On April 6, 1909, Robert Edwin Peary and a small group either reached the North Pole or came very close to it. Peary made the official announcement on September 6, but Frederick Cook had announced it five days before. Experts then determined that Cook's claim was false. Peary's records were accepted, and he was given the rank of rear admiral. Scientists still debate whether Peary reached the exact location of the North Pole.

Exercise H Revising: Using Precise Language
Revise the following paragraph, adding and revising words to make the paragraph more vivid and precise.

From the boat, I watched the sun set over the mountains of Alaska. The sunset was pretty, filling the sky with colors. The colors could be seen on the sea. Birds flew around the boat as the sky grew darker. The scene surrounding me made me feel good that I had decided to come on the trip.

Exercise I WRITING APPLICATION
Write a brief description of a place that you would like to visit or explore. When you have finished, go through your work and identify each part of speech you have used.

Answer Key

Exercise E
1. Wow–interjection; and–coordinating conjunction
2. After–subordinating conjunction; from–preposition; at–preposition; on–preposition
3. both . . . and–correlative conjunction; on–preposition; in–preposition
4. consequently–conjunctive adverb; and–coordinating conjunction
5. Yes–interjection; for–preposition

Exercise F
Answers will vary; samples are given.

1. Because Henson walked ahead . . . he may have reached the North Pole up to forty-five minutes before . . .
2. President Taft recommended Henson for a job in New York City because Taft wanted to recognize Henson's . . .
3. Was he really given a medal by . . .
4. President Eisenhower recognized Henson's achievements, but Henson was . . .
5. In 1988, Henson was reburied in . . .

Exercise G
Before–conjunction (C); the–adjective (Adj); Vikings–noun (N); explored–verb (V); the–Adj; Arctic–Adj; regions–N; the–Adj; Greeks–N; of–preposition (Prep); the–Adj; fourth–Adj; century–N; were–V; aware–Adj; of–Pr; these–Adj; regions–N; Some–Adj; Norsemen–N; reached–V; Iceland–N; which–pronoun (Pn); already–Adv; had–V; a–Adj; colony–N; of–Pr; Irish–Adj; monks–N; Their–Adj; voyages–N; did–V; not–Adv; lead–V; to–Pr; the–Adj; discovery–N; of–Pr; Greenland–N; until–C; Eric the Red–N; landed–V; there–Adv; A.D. 982–N.

On–Pr; April 6 1909–N; Robert Edwin Peary–N; and–C; a–Adj; small–Adj; group–N; either–C; reached–V; the–Adj; North Pole–N; or–C; came–V; very–Adv; close–Adv; to–Pr; it–Pn; Peary–N; made–V; the–Adj; official–Adj; announcement–N; on–Pr; September 6–N; but–C; Frederick Cook–N; had announced–V; it–Pn; five–Adj; days–N; before–Adv; Experts–N; then–Adv; determined–V; that–C; Cook's–Adj; claim–N; was–V; false–Adj;

continued

Answer Key continued

Exercise G
Peary's–Adj; records–N; were accepted–V; and–C; he–Pn; was–V; given–V; the–Adj; rank–N; of–Pr; rear–Adj; admiral–N; Scientists–N; still–Adv; debate–V; whether–C; Peary–N; reached–V; the–Adj; exact–Adj; location–N; of–Pr; the–adjective; North Pole–N

Exercise H
Responses will vary. If students have difficulty, have the class brainstorm for vague and imprecise words in the passage.

Exercise I
Writing Application
When students have finished, have them critique each other's writing.

In-Depth Lesson Plan

	LESSON FOCUS	PRINT AND MEDIA RESOURCES
DAY 1	**Subjects and Predicates** Students learn and apply concepts relating to simple and compound subjects and predicates. (pp. 412–417/H274–279)	*Writing and Grammar* **Interactive Text,** Section 19.1; *On-line Exercise Bank,* Section 19.1 **Teaching Resources** *Grammar Exercise Workbook,* pp. 41–48; *Grammar Exercises Answers on Transparencies,* Ch. 19
DAY 2	**Hard-to-Find Subjects** Students learn and apply concepts relating to hard-to-find subjects and do the Hands-on Grammar activity. (pp. 418–424/H280–286)	*Writing and Grammar* **Interactive Text,** Section 19.2; *On-line Exercise Bank,* Section 19.2 **Teaching Resources** *Grammar Exercise Workbook,* pp. 29–50; *Hands-on Grammar Activity Book,* Ch. 19
DAY 3	**Objects and Complements** Students learn and apply concepts relating to direct and indirect objects and objective and subject complements. (pp. 425–435/H287–297)	*Writing and Grammar* **Interactive Text,** Sections 19.3–4; *On-line Exercise Bank,* Sections 19.3–4 **Teaching Resources** *Grammar Exercise Workbook,* pp. 51–56
DAY 4	**Review and Assess** Students review the chapter and demonstrate mastery of basic sentence parts. (pp. 436–439)	*Writing and Grammar* **Interactive Text,** Ch. 19, Chapter Review **Teaching Resources** *Formal Assessment,* Ch. 19

Accelerated Lesson Plan

	LESSON FOCUS	PRINT AND MEDIA RESOURCES
DAY 1	**Subjects and Predicates; Hard-to-Find Subjects** Students cover subjects, predicates, and hard-to-find subjects as determined by the Diagnostic Test. (pp. 412–423/H274–285)	*Writing and Grammar* **Interactive Text,** Sections 19.1–2; *On-line Exercise Bank,* Sections 19.1–2 **Teaching Resources** *Grammar Exercise Workbook,* pp. 23–28; *Grammar Exercises Answers on Transparencies,* Ch. 18
DAY 2	**Objects and Complements** Students cover direct and indirect objects and objective and subject complements as determined by the Diagnostic Test. (pp. 425–434/H287–296)	*Writing and Grammar* **Interactive Text,** Sections 19.3–4; *On-line Exercise Bank,* Sections 19.3–4 **Teaching Resources** *Grammar Exercise Workbook,* pp. 29–32
DAY 3	**Review and Assess** Students review the chapter and demonstrate mastery of the concepts. (pp. 436–439)	*Writing and Grammar* **Interactive Text,** Ch. 19, Chapter Review **Teaching Resources** *Formal Assessment,* Ch. 19

Options for Adapting Lesson Plans

HOMEWORK

Have students complete any section of the chapter for homework.

FEATURES

Extend coverage with the Grammar in Literature features (pp. 415, 421, 433/H277, 283, 295) and the Standardized Test Preparation Workshop (p. 438).

TECHNOLOGY

Students can use *Writing and Grammar* Interactive Text to complete the exercises interactively on computer. They can complete additional exercises in the *On-line Exercise Bank:* The Auto Check feature will grade their work. Go on-line: PHSchool.com Use Web Code: eek-1002

Writing and Grammar Handbook Alignment

Page numbers in Step-by-Step Teaching Guides in this Teacher's Edition refer to pages from the full student text. Handbook page references, indicated with this icon 🄷, are provided in Time and Resource Manager boxes and at the bottom of each Teacher's Edition page.

INTEGRATED SKILLS COVERAGE

Grammar in Literature
SE pp. 415, 421, 433/🄷277, 283, 295

Writing
Find It in Your Writing SE pp. 417, 423, 424, 431, 435/🄷279, 285, 286, 293, 297

Writing Application SE pp. 417, 424, 431, 435, 437/🄷279, 286, 293, 297

Grammar and Style SE p. 414/🄷276

Integrating Writing Skills ATE p. 439

Spelling Skills SE pp. 419, 430/🄷281, 292

Viewing and Representing Skills
Critical Viewing SE pp. 410, 414, 420, 422, 427, 429, 433, 434/🄷272, 276, 282, 284, 289, 291, 295, 296

Real-World Connection ATE p. 421

Workplace Skills ATE. p. 418

Vocabulary Skills ATE p. 434

ASSESSMENT SUPPORT

Standardized Test Preparation Workshop SE p. 438; ATE pp. 420, 438

Standardized Test Preparation Workbook, pp. 37–38

Formal Assessment, Ch. 19

MEETING INDIVIDUAL NEEDS

Less Advanced Students ATE pp. 412, 414, 428. See also Ongoing Assessments ATE pp. 414, 419, 422, 427, 428, 430, 434.

More Advanced Students ATE pp. 419, 428, 439

ESL Students ATE pp. 413, 420

BLOCK SCHEDULING

Pacing Suggestions
For 90-minute Blocks
• Administer the Diagnostic Test to students to determine instructional coverage.
• Have students complete the necessary exercises in class. Use the Hands-on Grammar activity to provide a change of pace.

Resources for Varying Instruction
• *Writing and Grammar* **Interactive Text** A 90-minute block provides an ideal opportunity for students to work on the computer.

Professional Development Support
• *How to Manage Instruction in the Block* This teaching resource provides management and activity suggestions.

MEDIA AND TECHNOLOGY

For the Student
• *Writing and Grammar* **Interactive Text,** Ch. 19
• *On-line Exercise Bank,* Sections 19.1–4

For the Teacher
• Teacher**EXPRESS** CD-ROM

WRITING AND GRAMMAR ON-LINE

Interactive Text (On-line or on CD-ROM)
• Easily navigable instruction with on-line supporting resources
• Self-scoring exercises and diagnostic tests

Companion Web Site PHSchool.com
• On-line Exercise Bank (use Web Code eek-1002)

See the Go On-line! feature, SE p. iii.

LITERATURE CONNECTIONS

Grammar in Literature selections from *Prentice Hall Literature, Penguin Edition,* Grade 10

from "The Dog That Bit People," James Thurber, SE p. 415/🄷277

from "Damon and Pythias," William F. Russell, SE p. 421/🄷283

from "In Commemoration: One Million Volumes," Rudolfo Anaya, SE p. 433/🄷295

1. To locate and identify complete and simple subjects and predicates
2. To locate and identify compound subjects and verbs
3. To locate and identify subjects in sentences giving orders and directions and in various kinds of inverted sentences
4. To locate and identify subject complements in sentences
5. To demonstrate control over grammatical elements
6. To evaluate writing for both mechanics and content

Critical Viewing

Analyze Sample response: The Ferris wheel is turning.

Chapter 19 Basic Sentence Parts

◀ **Critical Viewing**
Who or what is doing an action in this photo? What is the action? Combine your answers into a sentence. **[Analyze]**

The Ferris wheel is a popular attraction at carnivals. Its simple rotating motion hides the fact that many gears and other essential moving parts keep the wheel going around. Similarly, you use sentences every time you speak or write, yet you may not always think about their essential parts.

Like a Ferris wheel or any other device, a good sentence functions well when its parts work together correctly. Knowing how the parts of sentences work together will give you a better understanding of how to communicate your ideas effectively.

410 • Basic Sentence Parts

☑ ONGOING ASSESSMENT: Diagnose

If students miss more than one item in any category, direct them to the relevant pages of the textbook and assign exercises for practice and review.

Basic Sentence Parts	Diagnostic Test Items	Teach	Practice	Section Review	Chapter Review
Skill Check A					
Complete Subjects and Predicates	A 1–5	p. 412/Ⓗ274	Ex. 1	Ex. 5	Ex. 41
Simple Subjects and Predicates	A 1–5	p. 413/Ⓗ275	Ex. 2	Ex. 5, 6	Ex. 41
Compound Subjects and Verbs	A 2	p. 414/Ⓗ276	Ex. 3–4	Ex. 6, 7	Ex. 41
Skill Check B					
Subjects in Orders and Directions	B 8	p. 418/Ⓗ280	Ex. 11	Ex. 16, 18	Ex. 42
Subjects in Inverted Order	B 6–7, 9–10	pp. 418–421/Ⓗ280–283	Ex. 12–15	Ex. 17–18	Ex. 42

Diagnostic Test

Directions: Write all answers on a separate sheet of paper.

Skill Check A. Write the complete subject and complete predicate in each sentence. Underline the simple subject once and the verb twice.

1. Fairs were an important part of commerce in the Middle Ages.
2. Buyers and sellers would trade commodities and merchandise.
3. Fairs improved and increased trade all over Europe.
4. Fairs for pleasure and commerce were often held together.
5. The largest fairs drew people from miles around.

Skill Check B. Write the subject of each sentence.

6. There are many fairs around the world.
7. When were these fairs established?
8. Take your brother to the fair.
9. Will Nancy be going with you?
10. Over the bridge lay the fairgrounds.

Skill Check C. Write each complement, and label it *direct object*, *indirect object*, or *objective complement*.

11. American engineer George Washington Gale Ferris invented the Ferris wheel.
12. After college, Ferris built bridges, railroads, and tunnels.
13. He eventually founded his own company.
14. He named it G.W.G. Ferris and Company.
15. Ferris showed the organizers of an 1893 exposition his plans for a 250-foot, steel-framed wheel ride.
16. The exposition organizers found his plans impressive.
17. They accepted Ferris's design.
18. Ferris promised them timely construction.
19. By selling stock in the project, he earned a profit of more than a million dollars.
20. The public considered Ferris's wheel a success.

Skill Check D. Write each complement, and label it *predicate nominative* or *predicate adjective*.

21. The most common type of fair in the United States was the agricultural fair.
22. The first United States fair, held in Massachusetts, was successful.
23. Some of the products on display were livestock, produce, and preserves.
24. The fair was quite profitable and popular among the local farmers.
25. Danbury, Connecticut, was the site of another famous fair.

Basic Sentence Parts • 411

Diagnostic Test

Each item in the Diagnostic Test corresponds to a specific section in the basic sentence parts chapter. This will enable you to tailor instruction to the particular needs of your students. See "Ongoing Assessment: Diagnose" below for further details.

Skill Check A

1. <u>Fairs</u>/<u>were</u> an important part of commerce in the Middle Ages.
2. <u>Buyers</u> and <u>sellers</u>/<u>would</u> <u>trade</u> commodities and merchandise.
3. <u>Fairs</u>/<u>improved</u> and <u>increased</u> trade all over Europe.
4. <u>Fairs</u> for pleasure and commerce/<u>were</u> often <u>held</u> together.
5. The largest <u>fairs</u>/<u>drew</u> people from miles around.

Skill Check B

6. fairs
7. fairs
8. [You]
9. Nancy
10. fairgrounds

Skill Check C

11. Ferris wheel—direct object
12. bridges, railroads, tunnels—direct objects
13. company—direct object
14. it—direct object; G.W.G. Ferris and Company—objective complement
15. organizers—indirect object; plans—direct object
16. plans—direct object; impressive—objective complement
17. design—direct object
18. them—indirect object; construction—direct object
19. profit—direct object
20. wheel—direct object; success—objective complement

Skill Check D

21. fair—predicate nominative
22. successful—predicate adjective
23. livestock, produce, preserves—predicate nominatives
24. profitable, popular—predicate adjectives
25. site—predicate nominative

✓ **ONGOING ASSESSMENT: Diagnose** *continued*

Basic Sentence Parts	Diagnostic Test Items	Teach	Practice	Section Review	Chapter Review
Skill Check C					
Direct and Indirect Objects	C 11–20	pp. 425–29/Ⓗ287–291	Ex. 22–25	Ex. 27–29	Ex. 43–44, 46
Objective Complements	C 14, 16, 20	p. 430/Ⓗ292	Ex. 26	Ex. 28–29	Ex. 45–46
Skill Check D					
Predicate Nominatives and Adjectives	D 21–25	pp. 432–434/Ⓗ294–296	Ex. 33–34	Ex. 35–37	Ex. 43–44, 46
Cumulative Reviews and Applications				Ex. 8–10, 19–21, 30–32, 38–40	Ex. 47

PREPARE and ENGAGE

Interest GRABBER Write the following on the board:

my uncle	*fell on the house*
a large tree	*jumped in the water*
the beagle	*arrived at the scene*

Ask students to combine various words from the left list with those in the right to form complete sentences.

Activate Prior Knowledge

Ask students to write a brief statement that tells what a favorite television commercial is about. As they read some sentences aloud, choose sentences that contain compound subjects and verbs and write them on the board. Underline the compound subjects and double underline the compound verbs.

TEACH

Step-by-Step Teaching Guide

Complete Subjects and Predicates

1. Have students read the key concept aloud; ask what they think "complete thought" means. (The idea must make sense.)

2. Have them read the two examples. Emphasize that both the complete subject and complete predicate may be one word or several.

Customize for
Less Advanced Students

If students are having difficulty recognizing complete sentences, present the phrases below. For each, ask the class why it is not a complete thought.

> *opened the umbrella unnecessarily*
>
> *Abby and her best friend*

Answer Key

▶ Exercise 1

1. Mardi Gras—is celebrated . . .
2. The grand carnival—marks . . .
3. Many Christians—fast during Lent.
4. They—indulge . . .
5. Food and drink—are . . .

Section 19.1

Subjects and Predicates

Theme: Carnivals

In this section, you will learn about the two main parts of sentences, subjects and predicates. The examples and exercises are about carnivals and celebrations.

Cross-Curricular Connection: Social Studies

When you are speaking to your friends, you may speak in partial sentences and still be understood. When you are writing, however, you should use complete sentences to express complete thoughts. Recognizing that every sentence must have two key parts will help you write clear, complete sentences.

Complete Subjects and Predicates

Every *sentence* that is grammatically correct consists of two parts: a *complete subject* and a *complete predicate.*

▶ **KEY CONCEPT** A **sentence** is a group of words with two main parts: a complete subject and a complete predicate. Together, these parts express a complete thought. ■

The complete subject includes a noun or pronoun that names the person, place, or thing that the sentence is about. The complete predicate includes a verb or verb phrase that tells something about the complete subject. The examples show that a complete subject or complete predicate may consist of only a single essential word (a noun or pronoun for the complete subject and a verb for the complete predicate). Often, however, a complete subject or complete predicate includes many other words that modify the essential words.

EXAMPLES:

They	were celebrating in the streets.
COMPLETE SUBJECT	COMPLETE PREDICATE

The three clowns in the ring	tumbled.
COMPLETE SUBJECT	COMPLETE PREDICATE

▶ **Exercise 1** Recognizing Complete Subjects and Complete Predicates Make two columns as shown in the example. Then, write each complete subject in the first column and each complete predicate in the second column.

EXAMPLE: The fluffy squirrel chattered at us.

ANSWER:

Complete Subject	Complete Predicate
The fluffy squirrel	chattered at us.

1. Mardi Gras is celebrated in many countries.
2. The grand carnival marks the beginning of Lent.
3. Many Christians fast during Lent.
4. They indulge in merrymaking before this solemn time.
5. Food and drink are plentiful during Mardi Gras.

412 • Basic Sentence Parts

▶ **More Practice**

Grammar Exercise Workbook
• pp. 41–42
On-line Exercise Bank
• Section 19.1
Go on-line:
PHSchool.com
Enter Web Code:
eek-1002

Interactive Textbook

Get instant feedback! Exercise 1 is available on-line or on CD-ROM.

 **TIME AND RESOURCE MANAGER**

Resources
Print: *Grammar Exercise Workbook,* pp. 41–48; *Grammar Exercises Answers on Transparencies,* Ch. 19
Technology: *Writing and Grammar* Interactive Text, Section 19.1; *On-Line Exercise Bank,* Section 19.1

Using the Full Student Edition	Using the Handbook ⊞
• Work through all key concepts, pp. 412–415.	• Work through all key concepts, pp. 274–277.
• Assign and review Exercises 1–4.	• Assign and review Exercises 1–4.
• Read and discuss Grammar in Literature, p. 415.	• Read and discuss Grammar in Literature, p. 277.

Simple Subjects and Predicates

Every complete subject and complete predicate contains a word or group of words that is essential to the sentence.

KEY CONCEPTS The **simple subject** is the essential noun, pronoun, or group of words acting as a noun that cannot be left out of the complete subject. The **simple predicate** is the essential verb or verb phrase that cannot be left out of the complete predicate. ■

In the following examples, notice that all the other words in the complete subject modify or add information to the *simple subject*. In the same way, all the other words in the complete predicate either modify the *simple predicate* or help it complete the meaning of the sentence.

EXAMPLES:

SIMPLE SUBJECT	SIMPLE PREDICATE
Jugs of sweet cider	*covered* the table.
COMPLETE SUBJECT	COMPLETE PREDICATE

SIMPLE SUBJECT	SIMPLE PREDICATE
Some *people*	*do* not *like* cider.
COMPLETE SUBJECT	COMPLETE PREDICATE

Notice in the first example that the simple subject of the sentence is *jugs*, not *cider*. The object of a preposition can never be a simple subject. Notice also that in the next example, the verb phrase *do like* is split by an adverb, *not*.

Note About the Terms *Subject* and *Verb*: From this point on in this book, the word *subject* will refer to the simple subject and the word *verb* will refer to the simple predicate.

To find the subject of a sentence before the verb, ask, "What word is the sentence about?" Then, ask yourself, "What did the subject *do*?" The answer will be an action verb. If there is no answer to the second question, look for a linking verb.

EXAMPLE: The revelers marched happily through the park.
Subject: revelers *Question:* What did the revelers do? *Answer:* marched

If you find it easier to locate the verb before locating the subject, first look for an action verb or a linking verb. Then, ask *Who?* or *What?* before the verb. The answer will be the subject.

EXAMPLE: A colorful flag was hanging above the porch.
Verb: was hanging *Question:* What was hanging? *Answer:* flag

Subjects and Predicates • 413

Simple Subjects and Predicates

1. To clarify the meaning of simple subject, quickly review nouns and adjectives. Give an example: *the bright sun.* Ask for the noun (*sun*) and adjectives (*the, bright*). Point out that these words might be used as a complete subject but the noun alone is the basic performer of the action in a complete idea and is considered the simple subject.

2. Then read the first example and point out that one cannot just look for a noun to identify the simple subject. *Jugs of sweet cider* contains two nouns. Ask which is the simple subject (*Jugs*) and ask why. (It was jugs, not cider, that performed the action of covering the table; the phrase *of sweet cider* describes the jugs.)

3. Explain that a complete predicate may also contain modifiers and other words, but the verb alone forms the simple predicate.

Language Highlight

Many of the words we use to describe festivals and celebrations come from the Anglo-Saxons of the early Middle Ages. They were agricultural people, and words like *ox, sheep, swine, dog, plough, field,* and *work* come from their language, Old English. They also liked to celebrate: words like *merry, laughter, glee, glad,* and *play* all come to us from Old English.

Customize for
ESL Students

Many students rely on their listening skills to expand their facility with English. Use the distinction between subject and predicate to help them listen for meaning in English sentences. Tell students to make ten observations by writing ten complete thoughts (sentences) during the course of a day. Then, have them draw lines in their sentences to distinguish the complete subjects from the complete predicates. Finally, have students explain orally the meanings in some of their sentences.

☑ ONGOING ASSESSMENT: Monitor and Reinforce

If students miss more than one item in Exercise 1, refer them to the following for additional practice.

In the Textbook	Print Resources	Technology
Section Review, Ex. 5, Section 19.1	*Grammar Exercise Workbook,* pp. 41–42	*On-Line Exercise Bank,* Section 19.1

Exercise 2

1. costumes—abound
2. celebrations—last
3. *Mardi Gras*—means
4. city—is
5. fireworks—end

Step-by-Step Teaching Guide

Compound Subjects

1. After students read the key concept, remind them that subjects are nouns or pronouns. Point out that their modifiers may be part of the complete subject, but a compound subject contains two or more nouns or pronouns.

2. Have a student read the example aloud without the word *Clowns* and ask if the subject would still be compound. (It would.) Then, read the example without *Clowns* and *balloons* and ask again. (It is still compound.)

Customize for
Less Advanced Students

Because they take the same plural verb, compound subjects and a simple subject made up of a plural word may be confusing to some students. Tell them that if the key concept example sentence had read "Balloons were offered at the carnival," the sentence would have merely a simple subject, not a compound subject, even though the verb is plural.

Critical Viewing

Connect Sample response: The jester jumped, twirled, and danced.

19.1

Exercise 2 Recognizing Simple Subjects and Simple Verbs

Write the simple subject and simple verb in each sentence. Underline the subject once and the verb twice.

EXAMPLE: Ancient legends still fascinate us today.
ANSWER: legends   fascinate

1. Elaborate costumes abound at Mardi Gras celebrations.
2. Traditional celebrations of Mardi Gras last a full week.
3. *Mardi Gras* means "Fat Tuesday" in French.
4. The city of New Orleans is especially famous for its Mardi Gras festivities.
5. Spectacular fireworks end the carnival.

Compound Subjects and Verbs

The word *compound* describes a noun, adjective, or preposition with more than one part. *Airport*, for example, is a compound noun. *Compound* also describes subjects or verbs connected by conjunctions.

Compound Subjects The complete subject of a sentence may contain two or more subjects.

KEY CONCEPT A **compound subject** is two or more subjects that have the same verb and are joined by a conjunction such as *and* or *or*. ■

In the next example, the parts of the *compound subject* are underlined once, and the verb is underlined twice.

EXAMPLE: Clowns, balloons, pony rides, and face-painting *were offered* at the carnival.

414 • Basic Sentence Parts

More Practice

Grammar Exercise Workbook
• pp. 45–46
On-line Exercise Bank
• Section 19.1
Go on-line:
PHSchool.com
Enter Web Code:
eek-1002

Grammar and Style Tip

Compound subjects joined with *and* take the plural form of a verb. Compound subjects joined with *or* take the form of the verb that agrees with the subject closest to the verb.

◄ **Critical Viewing**
Think of a series of actions a jester might do, and include them as compound verbs in a sentence.
[Connect]

TIME SAVERS!

Answers on Transparencies
Use the *Grammar Exercises Answers on Transparencies* for Chapter 19 to facilitate correction by students.

On-Line Exercise Bank
Have students complete the exercises on computer. The Auto Check feature will grade their work for you!

✓ ONGOING ASSESSMENT: Monitor and Reinforce

If students miss more than one item in Exercise 2, refer them to the following for additional practice.

In the Textbook	Print Resources	Technology
Section Review, Ex. 5–6, Section 19.1	*Grammar Exercise Workbook,* pp. 45–46	*On-Line Exercise Bank,* Section 19.1

GRAMMAR IN LITERATURE

from **The Dog That Bit People**
James Thurber

The compound verbs in the first sentence of this excerpt are highlighted in blue italics.

One morning when Muggs bit me slightly, more or less in passing, I *reached* down and *grabbed* his short stumpy tail and *hoisted* him into the air. It was a foolhardy thing to do and the last time I saw my mother, about six months ago, she said she didn't know what possessed me.

Compound Verbs Sentences may also contain two or more verbs in the complete predicate.

> ▶ **KEY CONCEPT** A **compound verb** is two or more verbs that have the same subject and are joined by a conjunction such as *and* or *or*. ■

In the following example, the compound verb has three parts.

EXAMPLE: The <u>star</u> <u>signed</u> autograph books, <u>smiled</u> at her fans, and then <u>departed</u> in a limousine.

Sentences may also have both compound subjects and compound verbs.

EXAMPLE: <u>Megan</u> and her <u>friends</u> <u>cheered</u> and <u>shouted</u>.

Note About *Compound Verbs:* When a compound verb consists of two or more verb phrases with the same helping verb, the helping verb is often used only with the first verb.

AWKWARD
REPETITION: The banjo <u>player</u> <u>was strumming</u> his banjo, <u>was stomping</u> his feet, and <u>was singing</u> enthusiastically.

HELPING VERB
NOT REPEATED: The banjo <u>player</u> <u>was strumming</u> his banjo, <u>stomping</u> his feet, and <u>singing</u> enthusiastically.

Subjects and Predicates • 415

Step-by-Step Teaching Guide

Grammar in Literature

1. After students read the passage, have a volunteer reread the first sentence aloud.

2. Ask students to identify the three verbs that comprise the compound verbs (*reached, grabbed, hoisted*).

More About the Author

James Thurber (1894–1961) was a humorist known for his essays and cartoons in *The New Yorker* magazine. He won fame for his whimsical depictions of human (and animal) silliness. When his eyesight failed, he continued to write stories and articles for the magazine. His collections, including *The Thurber Carnival*, are considered classics of humor writing.

Connections With Literature

"The Dog That Bit People" can be found in *Prentice Hall Literature, Penguin Edition*, Grade 10.

Step-by-Step Teaching Guide

Compound Verbs

1. Have students read the key concept; point out that compound verbs can be joined by certain coordinating conjunctions as well as correlative conjunctions such as *neither . . . nor, either . . . or, both . . . and.*

2. Then have students substitute appropriate correlative conjunctions in the second example sentence and read the variations aloud:

   Example: Megan and her friends *both cheered and shouted.*

Answer Key

▶ **Exercise 3** Recognizing Compound Subjects and Compound Verbs Write the sentence. Then, underline the words that make up each compound subject once and each compound verb twice.

EXAMPLE: Harvest <u>festivals</u> <u>exist</u> in many cultures and <u>appear</u> in many varieties.

1. Flowers, fruits, and vegetables are often used to decorate homes.
2. Harvest festivals center around a happy event, feature a special crop, or honor heroes.
3. Families and friends gather together and celebrate with traditional foods and rituals.
4. New England colonists and neighboring Native Americans celebrated the first Thanksgiving Day and shared the bountiful harvest.
5. Community events and family observances provide an opportunity for reflection, celebrate heritage, and enrich culture.

▶ **Exercise 4** Revising Sentences by Forming Compound Subjects and Compound Predicates Revise each pair of sentences by combining information to form compound subjects or verbs.

EXAMPLE: After school, the band met. Then it practiced
REVISION: After school the band met and practiced.

1. Solar calendars determine the timing of some seasonal festivals. Lunar calendars determine the timing of other seasonal festivals.
2. Chinese New Year is set by the lunar calendar. It is celebrated for a whole month.
3. Boisterous parades and colorful costumes mark the celebration of Chinese New Year. Theatrical performances mark the celebration of Chinese New Year, too.
4. A Swiss festival celebrates the end of winter. At the same time, it welcomes the advent of spring.
5. The Swiss people burn straw dummies during Homstrom. They are saying goodbye to Old Man Winter.

▶ **More Practice**

Grammar Exercise Workbook
• pp. 47–48
On-line Exercise Bank
• Section 19.1
Go on-line:
PHSchool.com
Enter Web Code:
eek-1002

Get instant feedback! Exercises 3 and 4 are available on-line or on CD-ROM.

✓ ONGOING ASSESSMENT: Assess Mastery

Use the following resources to assess student mastery of subjects and predicates.

In the Textbook	Technology
Chapter Review, Ex. 41	*Writing and Grammar* Interactive Text, Section 19.1, Section Review; *On-Line Exercise Bank*, Section 19.1

Section 19.1 Section Review

GRAMMAR EXERCISES 5–10

Exercise 5 Identifying Complete and Simple Subjects and Predicates
Make two columns. Write each complete subject in the first column and each complete predicate in the second. Underline the simple subject once and the verb twice.

1. Important festivals of respect in many countries honor the dead.
2. Such festivals have long been observed.
3. Today, people continue age-old customs honoring national heroes.
4. In the Far East, festivals of the dead include family reunions and ceremonial meals at ancestral tombs.
5. Mexicans observe *El Dia de Los Muertos* (The Day of the Dead) with offerings of flowers, pottery, food, and toys.

Exercise 6 Recognizing Subjects and Predicates Write the subject and verb in each sentence, underlining the subjects once and the verbs twice. Some may be compound.

1. The most famous annual festival in Wales is the Royal National Eisteddfod.
2. The Eisteddfod honors the finest talent in Welsh literature and music.
3. Welsh language, literature, music, and culture are promoted at the festival.
4. The history of the Eisteddfod predates the Christian era.
5. The week-long ceremony revives ancient Welsh customs, offers cultural competitions, and gives Welsh poets and musicians an opportunity to perform.

Exercise 7 Revising Sentences by Creating Compound Subjects and Compound Predicates Revise each pair of sentences by combining information to form compound subjects or verbs.

1. Cultural festivals are popular all over the world. Commemorative days are also popular all over the world.
2. Kalevala Day in Finland honors the Finnish national epic, the *Kalevala*. It also recognizes the achievements of Finnish scholar Elias Lönnrot.
3. The Salzburg Music Festival is held in Austria each year. The festival celebrates the rich legacy of some of the world's finest composers.
4. Great food is a highlight of Hawaii's annual Aloha Festival. Native entertainment is also featured.
5. Film festivals, dance celebrations, and children's carnivals crowd the calendars of many nations. They attract tourists from around the world.

Exercise 8 Find It in Your Reading
Identify the simple subject and predicate of each sentence in this excerpt from "The Masque of the Red Death."

> . . . [I]n this chamber only, the color of the windows failed to correspond with the decorations. The panes here were scarlet—a deep blood color.

Exercise 9 Find It in Your Writing
Look through your writing portfolio. Find examples of sentences with a compound subject or compound verb. Identify the complete subject and predicate in each sentence.

Exercise 10 Writing Application
Write a description of your favorite holiday or feast day. Tell how you celebrate the day, what food you eat, and what activities you enjoy. In each of your sentences, underline the simple subject once and the verb twice.

Section Review • 417

ASSESS

Section Review

Each of these exercises correlates to the instruction on subjects and predicates, pages 412–415. These exercises may be used for more practice, for reteaching, or for review of the key concepts presented.

Answer Key

Exercise 5

1. Important <u>festivals</u> of respect in many countries/<u>honor</u> the dead.
2. Such <u>festivals</u>/<u>have</u> long <u>been</u> <u>observed</u>.
3. Today, <u>people</u>/<u>continue</u> age-old customs honoring national heroes.
4. In the Far East, <u>festivals</u> of the dead/<u>include</u> family reunions and ceremonial meals at ancestral tombs.
5. <u>Mexicans</u>/<u>observe</u> *El Día de Los Muertos* (The Day of the Dead) with offerings of flowers, pottery, food, and toys.

Exercise 6

1. <u>festival</u>—<u>is</u>
2. <u>Eisteddfod</u>—<u>honors</u>
3. <u>language, literature, music, culture</u>—<u>are promoted</u>
4. <u>history</u>—<u>predates</u>
5. <u>ceremony</u>—<u>revives</u>, <u>offers</u>, <u>gives</u>

Exercise 7

Answers will vary; samples are given.

1. Cultural festivals and commemorative days are popular all over the world.
2. Kalevala Day in Finland honors the Finnish national epic, the Kalevala, and recognizes . . .
3. The Salzburg Music Festival is held in Austria each year and celebrates the rich legacy . . .

continued

Answer Key continued

Exercise 7

4. Great food and native entertainment are highlights . .
5. Film festivals . . . carnivals crowd the calendars of many nations and attract tourists . . .

Exercise 8

Find It in Your Reading
color, failed; panes, were

Exercise 9

Find It in Your Writing
After students complete this process with samples from their portfolios, have them exchange papers with a writing partner for a review of subjects and predicates.

Exercise 10

Writing Application
Students who celebrate holidays generally unfamiliar to the class should be encouraged to read their descriptions aloud.

⏱ **TIME SAVERS!**

📄 **Answers on Transparencies**
Use the *Grammar Exercises Answers on Transparencies* for Chapter 19 to facilitate correction by students.

💻 **On-Line Exercise Bank**
Have students complete the exercises on computer. The Auto Check feature will grade their work for you!

Present these sentences and have students find the subjects:

Tell me more.

Here comes our captain.

Are you coming with us?

Not far away was a radio.

As they offer answers, remind them that subjects can be difficult to find. Suggest that they try to reorder each sentence's words.

Activate Prior Knowledge

Ask students to imagine that they are at a construction site. Ask them to tell some of the work-related questions and orders they might hear. Write these samples: *Where are the two-by-fours? Cover those tubs of joint compound, Frankie.* Ask students to identify the subject of each.

TEACH

Step-by-Step Teaching Guide

Subjects in Orders and Directions

1. Use the chart to help students visualize the location and function of an understood subject.

2. Point out in the second example that *Kim* is the person spoken to, but the subject is still understood, not stated. *Kim* is not a basic part of the sentence; it is parenthetical—a noun of direct address. In the sentence *Kim gave me an apple, Kim* is the subject.

Integrating Workplace Skills

Imperatives Store owners and sign makers frequently look for economies of space by omitting or implying subjects in their ads, banners, signs, posters, etc. Imperatives such as *Stop & Browse*; *Save 50%*; and *Buy now, pay later* stress the actions they desire from customers.

Answer Key

▶ **Exercise 11**

Answers will vary. Have volunteers read their sentences aloud.

Hard-to-Find Subjects

In most English sentences, a subject is followed by a verb. This section will present sentences with subjects that are not so easily found.

Subjects in Orders and Directions

▶ **KEY CONCEPT** In sentences that give orders or directions, the subject is often understood to be *you.* ■

The following chart contrasts sentences with and without the understood *you.* The subjects are underlined once and the verbs twice. Notice in the last sentence that even when a person is addressed, the subject is still understood to be *you.*

Orders or Directions	With Understood *You* Added
Dust the furniture and then wax the floor.	[You] dust the furniture and then wax the floor.
Kim, give me an apple.	Kim, [you] give me an apple.

▶ **Exercise 11** **Creating Sentences With Understood Subjects** Use each verb in a sentence that gives an order or a direction. Add the understood subject in parentheses in each.

1. give
2. call
3. proofread
4. ask
5. train
6. ride
7. order
8. protect
9. tie
10. offer

Subjects in Inverted Sentences

In some sentences, the usual subject-verb order is *inverted*—that is, reversed. Sentences that may be inverted in English include questions and sentences beginning with *there* or *here.* In addition, some sentences are inverted for emphasis.

Subjects in Questions Questions are often inverted.

▶ **KEY CONCEPT** In questions, the subject often follows the verb. ■

An inverted question can begin with a verb, a helping verb, or one of the following words: *how, what, when, where, who, whose,* or *why.*

To find the subject in an inverted question, rephrase the question mentally as a statement. Then, the subject and verb will fall into the usual order.

418 • Basic Sentence Parts

Theme: Knights and Castles

In this section, you will learn how to locate hard-to-find subjects in sentences. The examples and exercises are about knights and castles.

Cross-Curricular Connection: Social Studies

⏱ **TIME AND RESOURCE MANAGER**

Resources

Print: *Grammar Exercise Workbook,* pp. 49–50; *Grammar Exercises Answers on Transparencies,* Ch. 19; *Hands-on Grammar Activity Book,* Ch. 19

Technology: *Writing and Grammar* Interactive Text, Section 19.2; *On-Line Exercise Bank,* Section 19.2

Using the Full Student Edition	Using the Handbook🄗
• Work through all key concepts, pp. 418–421. • Assign and review Exercises 11–15. • Read and discuss Grammar in Literature, p. 421. • Do the Hands-on Grammar activity, p. 423.	• Work through all key concepts, pp. 280–283. • Assign and review Exercises 11–15. • Read and discuss Grammar in Literature, p. 283. • Do the Hands-on Grammar activity, p. 285.

Questions	Reworded as Statements
Are we ready?	We are ready.
Do you like castles?	You do like castles.
Where was the car parked?	The car was parked where.

Note About *Questions*: Some questions are not inverted. Those beginning with an interrogative adjective or pronoun may be in the usual subject-verb order.

EXAMPLES: Which troubadour won the prize this year?
Who cares about such nonsense?

Exercise 12 Finding Subjects in Questions Write each sentence, underlining the subject once and the verb twice.

EXAMPLE: Where was the castle located?

1. Who trained knights during the age of chivalry?
2. Where were the knights trained?
3. What were the requirements for knighthood?
4. Do knights still exist?
5. Was armor worn by all knights?
6. Which countries had a feudal system?
7. What are the dates of the Middle Ages?
8. Did you read about the Crusades?
9. How did gunpowder change knighthood?
10. Do knights fight in wars anymore?

Sentences Beginning With *There* or *Here* Two words that are often used to begin inverted sentences are *there* and *here*.

KEY CONCEPT The subject of a sentence is never *there* or *here*. ∎

When *there* or *here* begins a sentence, the subject usually follows the verb. As with inverted questions, mentally rephrase the sentence to find the subject.

Note About *Sentences Beginning With There or Here*: Some sentences beginning with *there* or *here* are not in inverted order, however. In such cases, the words *there* or *here* usually point out a specific location

EXAMPLES: There you are!
Here the castle stands.

More Practice

Grammar Exercise Workbook
• pp. 49–50
On-line Exercise Bank
• Section 19.2
Go on-line:
PHSchool.com
Enter Web Code:
eek-1002

Spelling Tip

Because English includes words borrowed from other languages, proper spelling is often a challenge. *Chivalry,* for instance, comes from the Old French word *chevalier,* which means "knight." When in doubt, look in a dictionary for the correct spelling of tricky words.

Subjects in Inverted Sentences

1. Read the explanation on the bottom of page 418 and then offer this example of a question written in inverted order:

   Did the troubadour win the prize?

2. Ask students to identify the subject and the verb. Point out that part of a verb phrase in a question often precedes the subject.

3. Next use the examples on the top of page 419, pointing out that these are exceptions because these do not invert the normal order of subject and verb.

4. Tell students that the same mental rephrasing for sentences in question form can be applied to sentences beginning with *there* and *here*.

Answer Key

Exercise 12

1. Who trained knights during the age of chivalry?
2. Where were the knights trained?
3. What were the requirements for knighthood?
4. Do knights still exist?
5. Was armor worn by all knights?
6. Which countries had a feudal system?
7. What are the dates of the Middle Ages?
8. Did you read about the Crusades?
9. How did gunpowder change knighthood?
10. Do knights fight in wars anymore?

Customize for
More Advanced Students

Ask students to bring in examples of inverted order sentences from magazines, books, or newspapers. When they bring these to class, ask them to read each sentence and its surrounding sentences aloud. Ask the class to identify the subjects in these sentences. Discuss why the writer or author chose to use an inverted order.

☑ ONGOING ASSESSMENT: Monitor and Reinforce

If students miss more than two items in Exercise 11 or 12, refer them to the following for additional practice.

In the Textbook	Print Resources	Technology
Section Review, Ex. 16–18, Section 19.2	*Grammar Exercise Workbook,* pp. 49–50	*On-Line Exercise Bank,* Section 19.2

Answer Key

19.2

Sentences Beginning With *There* or *Here*	Reworded With Subjects Before Verbs
There <u>is</u> my old, battered <u>suitcase.</u>	My old, battered <u>suitcase</u> <u>is</u> there.
Here <u>is</u> the <u>museum</u>!	The <u>museum</u> <u>is</u> here.

In the sentences in the chart above, *there* and *here* are adverbs; they modify the verbs and tell *where.* Occasionally, *there* is merely used to help the sentence get started and does not modify the verb. When *there* is used in this way, it is not an adverb but an *expletive.*

EXAMPLES: There <u>is</u> no <u>bridge</u> across this river.
                    There <u>will be</u> a drastic <u>change</u> in the weather.

In sentences where *there* is an expletive, rephrasing to find the subject may not work. To find the subject in this situation, mentally drop *there* and ask *Who?* or *What?* before the verb.

Sentences With Expletive *There*	Questions for Finding Subjects
There <u>are</u> many <u>castles</u> in England.	*Question: What* are? *Answer:* castles
There <u>may</u> not <u>be</u> any logical <u>answer</u> to that question.	*Question: What* may be? *Answer:* answer

> **Exercise 13** Finding Subjects in Sentences Beginning With *There* or *Here* Write each sentence on your paper, underlining the subject once and the verb twice.

EXAMPLE: Here <u>is</u> my <u>book</u> about castles!

1. There are the turrets at the top.
2. Here is my favorite book on King Arthur.
3. There are many versions of the King Arthur legend.
4. There is no way of knowing the truth behind the legend.
5. There on the dresser is my copy of *Le Morte d'Arthur.*

▼ **Critical Viewing** Write three statements a tour guide might make about this castle. Start each with *there* or *here.* Underline each simple subject and verb. **[Analyze]**

420 • Basic Sentence Parts

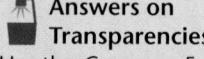
✎ **STANDARDIZED TEST PREPARATION WORKSHOP**

Grammar and Usage Many standardized tests require students to recognize and use sentence parts correctly. Use the following example to demonstrate.

On a raft floating down the river was their treasured belongings.

What is the BEST way to change this sentence?

A Floating down the river on a raft was their treasured belongings.

B Their treasured belongings on a raft floating down the river.

C On a raft floating down the river were their treasured belongings.

D No change is necessary.

The correct answer is **C.** The subject of this inverted order sentence is *belongings,* which is a plural noun. The verb must also be plural and should be *were.*

GRAMMAR IN
LITERATURE

from **Damon and Pythias**
Retold by William F. Russell

In the following excerpt, the subject-verb order is inverted both to supply emphasis and to recreate the style of older language.

Thus <u>did</u> <u>the two friends</u> of Syracuse, by the faithful love they bore to each other, <u>conquer</u> the hard heart of a tyrant king, and in the annals of true friendship there <u>are</u> no more honored <u>names</u> than those of Damon and Pythias—for no person can do more than be willing to lay down his life for the sake of his friend.

Inverted Order for Emphasis Sometimes, the subject-verb order is deliberately inverted to emphasize the word or words at the end of the sentence.

▶ **KEY CONCEPT** In some sentences, the subject is placed after the verb in order to receive greater emphasis. ■

Inverted subject-verb order directs attention to the subject at the end of the sentence and adds a sense of drama or surprise to the sentence. Rephrased in normal subject-verb order, the sentence is less dramatic.

Notice the different dramatic impact the sentence in the chart below makes when presented in inverted order instead of in normal subject-verb order.

Inverted Word Order for Emphasis	Reworded With Subject Before Verbs
Beneath the ruined temple <u>waited</u> the deadly <u>cobra</u>.	The deadly <u>cobra</u> <u>waited</u> beneath the ruined temple.

Grammar in Literature

1. Ask volunteers to read aloud the segments of this passage using inverted word order. Then, ask students to reorder the words in these lines.

2. Ask how the inverted order changes the tone of the passage (possible answer: it makes the tone more formal.)

More About the Author

Over the centuries, the legend of Damon and Pythias has been retold and adapted in many forms, including plays. William F. Russell, a recent reteller of this and many other myths and legends, is also the author of a widely read newspaper column on education.

Connections With Literature

A retelling of "Damon and Pythias" can be found in *Prentice Hall Literature, Penguin Edition,* Grade 10.

Step-by-Step Teaching Guide

Inverted Order for Emphasis

1. Emphasize that writers will use inverted order to achieve an effect.

2. Have them decide which of these sentences would be more effective in a mystery:

   Out of the swirling fog emerged a hooded figure.

   A hooded figure emerged out of the swirling fog.

Real-World Connection

Tour guides often use inverted order to direct one's attention before pointing out something interesting. (Examples: *On your left <u>sits</u> the oldest <u>building</u> in town! Up ahead <u>is</u> the <u>museum!</u>*)

Answer Key

Exercise 14

1. squire
2. enemy
3. safety
4. castle
5. arrows
6. monarch
7. life
8. guards
9. flags
10. king

Exercise 15

Allow slight variation in wording.

1. Three mounted knights waited in the clearing near the ancient castle.
2. Atop a majestic steed sat one of the knights.
3. Toward the castle at breakneck speed raced the armed knights.
4. Standing guard at the castle wall was a young, inexperienced squire.
5. Above the castle shone a bright moon.
6. The squire's face was highlighted by the light of the full moon.
7. A look of total fear was filling his eyes.
8. A drawbridge was serving as a barrier between the attackers and the castle.
9. Near the squire's hand was the crank that operated the drawbridge.
10. Outside the castle walls there were three frustrated knights.

Critical Viewing

Analyze Sample response: How heavy is your armor? Are you ever nervous during a fight? How often are you knocked from your horse?

19.2

▶ **Exercise 14** Finding Subjects in Sentences Inverted for **Emphasis** Write the subject of each sentence.

EXAMPLE: Behind the bookcase was hidden a secret door.
ANSWER: door

1. At his master's side rode the brave young squire.
2. Outside the castle lurked the enemy.
3. Across the moat lay safety.
4. Atop the steep hillside stood the majestic castle.
5. Through the battlements came dangerous arrows.
6. From the castle ruled the noble monarch.
7. Uncomfortable was life in the castle.
8. Along the tops of the walls and towers walked the guards.
9. Above the castle flew the colorful flags.
10. With fairness governed the beloved king.

▶ **Exercise 15** Revising Sentences by Changing Subject-**Verb Order** Revise the following sentences, changing them from subject-verb order to inverted order or from inverted order to subject-verb order.

EXAMPLE: A trapdoor was hidden in the floor
REVISION: Hidden in the floor was a trapdoor.

1. In the clearing near the ancient castle waited three mounted knights.
2. One of the knights sat atop a majestic steed.
3. The armed knights raced toward the castle at break-neck speed.
4. A young, inexperienced squire was standing guard at the castle wall.
5. A bright moon shone above the castle.
6. Highlighted by the light of the full moon was the squire's face.
7. Filling his eyes was a look of total fear.
8. Serving as a barrier between the attackers and the castle was a drawbridge.
9. The crank that operated the drawbridge was near the squire's hand.
10. Three frustrated knights were there outside the castle walls.

▶ **Critical Viewing** Write three questions you might ask this knight about jousting. Identify the simple subject and verb in each question. [Analyze]

More Practice

Grammar Exercise Workbook
• pp. 49–50
On-line Exercise Bank
• Section 19.2
Go on-line:
PHSchool.com
Enter Web Code:
eek-1002

interactive **Textbook**

Get instant feedback! Exercises 14 and 15 are available on-line or on CD-ROM.

422 • Basic Sentence Parts

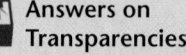 **TIME SAVERS!**

Answers on Transparencies
Use the *Grammar Exercises Answers on Transparencies* for Chapter 19 to facilitate correction by students.

On-Line Exercise Bank
Have students complete the exercises on computer. The Auto Check feature will grade their work for you!

✓ **ONGOING ASSESSMENT: Monitor and Reinforce**

If students miss more than two items in Exercise 14 or 15, refer them to the following for additional practice.

In the Textbook	Print Resources	Technology
Section Review, Ex. 17–18, Section 19.2	*Grammar Exercise Workbook;* pp. 49–50	*On-Line Exercise Bank,* Section 19.2

Hands-on Grammar

Inverted-Sentence Cards

In most sentences, the subject comes before the verb. Sentences can be inverted, however, to show emphasis or for dramatic effect. Explore the effect of subject-verb placement with the following activity.

On each of four index cards, write *subject*. On the reverse of each card, write one of these article/noun combinations: *the king, the queen, the knight, the squire.* Next, make four cards that say *verb* on one side and have a verb on the reverse. Use these verbs: *waits, stood, spoke, reads.* Finally, make a set of cards for the adverbs and adverb phrases: *impatiently, proudly, in the castle, at the door.*

Place each set of cards in a pile so that you can read the part of speech. Choose one card from each pile and line them up in the following order: *subject, verb, adverb (or adverb phrase),* Turn the cards over to read the sentence you have created. Then, turn the cards over again to read the part of speech. While the cards are still showing the part of speech, arrange them in the following order: *adverb (or adverb phrase), verb, subject.* Flip the cards to read the new sentence. Complete these steps with the rest of the cards in each pile. (Because the first word of the sentence depends on the arrangement of cards, none of the words on your cards are capitalized. Remember that if you were writing these sentences, you would capitalize the first word of each sentence.)

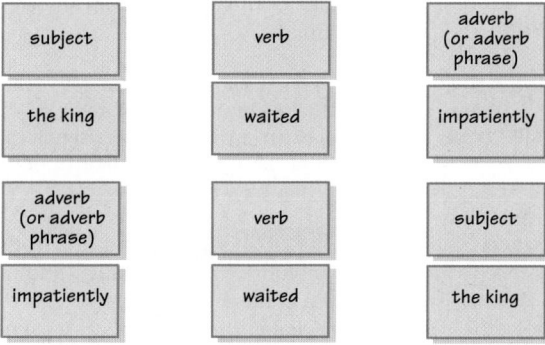

When you are finished, create a new set of cards and work with a partner to challenge each other to identify the subject in inverted sentences. Turn the cards over to check your answers. Create some inverted sentences that contain both adverbs and adverb phrases.

Find It in Your Reading Find an inverted sentences in a folk tale or a poem. Identify each part of the inverted sentence.

Find It in Your Writing Look through your portfolio to find a sentence that could be inverted for emphasis or effect. Identify the subject of the revised sentence.

Hard-to-Find Subjects • 423

Step-by-Step Teaching Guide

Hands-on Grammar

Teaching Resources: Hands-on Grammar Activity Book, Ch. 19

1. If you wish to do this activity in class, be prepared with scissors and index cards. Have students work in pairs, and give each pair the needed materials.

2. Have each pair of students come up with their own two sentences that can be inverted. Encourage them to spend time so that their sentences sound natural rather than awkward.

3. Go through the directions and diagrams with students so that they understand how to make the paddlewheel. Then have them proceed on their own.

Find It in Your Reading

You might ask students to evaluate the inverted sentences they find. Would any sound better in natural order?

Find It in Your Writing

Have students discuss their new inverted sentences with their partners.

⏱ TIME SAVERS!

 Hands-on Grammar
Use the Hands-on Grammar activity sheet for Chapter 19 to facilitate this activity.

Section Review

Each of these exercises correlates to the instruction on hard-to-find subjects, pages 418–421. These exercises may be used for more practice, for reteaching, or for review of the key concepts presented.

Answer Key

Exercise 16

1. you—Do know
2. hundreds—were built
3. some—are standing
4. castle—was built
5. construction—was completed
6. you—can name
7. article—is
8. information—may be
9. you—Are going
10. we—go
11. (you)—look
12. swords—hung
13. squires—wait
14. knights—strode
15. crests—appeared

Exercise 17

1. A moat does surround the castle.
2. Our enemies will use ladders to scale the walls of the castle.
3. The lowest wall of the castle is there.
4. Several deadly fish swim within the moat.
5. We will establish our best defense of the castle here.

Exercise 18

Students' sentences will vary. Have volunteers read their sentences aloud, and have other students identify their subjects.

Exercise 19

Find It in Your Reading
King Arthur, I, this, (you), it

Exercise 20

Find It in Your Writing
After students complete this process with samples from their portfolios, have them exchange papers with a writing partner for a review of hard-to-find subjects.

Exercise 21

Writing Application
When students finish this activity, have them exchange papers with a partner and check one another's agreement.

Section 19.2 Section Review

GRAMMAR EXERCISES 16–21

Exercise 16 Identifying Hard-to-Find Subjects Write the subject and verb in each sentence, underlining the subject once and the verb twice. If the subject is understood, write (you).

1. Do you know much about castles?
2. There were hundreds of castles built in Europe.
3. There are some still standing.
4. Where was the first castle built?
5. When was its construction completed?
6. Can you name all of the castles in Ireland?
7. Here is the article about feudalism.
8. There may not be enough information on-line.
9. Are you going to visit any castles?
10. Here we go!
11. Look at this painting of a medieval castle.
12. On the wall hung the knights' swords.
13. In the background wait the loyal squires.
14. Beneath the flapping flags strode the valiant knights.
15. On their shields appeared their crests.

Exercise 17 Rewriting Inverted Sentences to Locate Their Subjects Rewrite the following inverted sentences to put the subject before the verb. Then, underline the subject once and the verb twice.

1. Does a moat surround the castle?
2. Will our enemies use ladders to scale the walls of the castle?
3. There is the lowest wall of the castle.
4. Within the moat swim several deadly fish.
5. Here will we establish our best defense of the castle.

Exercise 18 Writing Orders, Directions, and Inverted Sentences Follow these instructions to write five sentences of your own. Underline the subject of each sentence. If the subject is understood, write (you).

1. Write a sentence addressing someone and giving the person an order.
2. Write a sentence that directs someone to do two things, one after the other.
3. Write a sentence that begins with here.
4. Write the first sentence of directions for building or cooking something.
5. Write a sentence with the order inverted for emphasis.

Exercise 19 Find It in Your Reading Identify the subject in each clause of this excerpt from "Morte d' Arthur."

Then spoke King Arthur, drawing thicker breath:/"Now see I by thine eyes that this is done./Speak out: What is it thou hast heard, or seen?"

Exercise 20 Find It in Your Writing In your writing portfolio, find a question and a sentence that begins with there or here. Label the subjects of the sentences. Also, challenge yourself to rewrite one of your sentences in inverted order.

Exercise 21 Writing Application Imagine that you are a knight. Write an advertisement seeking a squire to assist you. Include one sentence that gives directions, one that asks a question, and one that begins with there or here. Identify the subjects in your sentences.

✓ ONGOING ASSESSMENT: Assess Mastery

Use the following resources to assess student mastery of hard-to-find subjects.

In the Textbook	Technology
Chapter Review, Ex. 42	On-Line Exercise Bank, Section 19.2

Section 19.3

Direct Objects, Indirect Objects, and Objective Complements

In addition to a verb, a complete predicate may also have one or more *complements*.

> ◣ **KEY CONCEPT** A **complement** is a word or group of words that completes the meaning of the predicate of a sentence. ■

This section presents three different kinds of complements used in sentences with action verbs: *direct objects*, *indirect objects*, and *objective complements*.

The Direct Object

Direct objects usually follow action verbs.

> ◣ **KEY CONCEPT** A **direct object** is a noun or pronoun that receives the action of a transitive action verb. ■

To find a direct object, ask *Whom?* or *What?* after an action verb. In the following examples, subjects are underlined once, action verbs twice, and direct objects are boxed and labeled. Notice how the direct objects answer the questions *Whom?* and *What?*

EXAMPLES: A <u>blanket</u> of snow <u><u>covered</u></u> the [pagoda]. ^{DO}
Covered *what? Answer:* pagoda

The <u>woman</u> <u><u>is watching</u></u> the [children]. ^{DO}
Watching *whom? Answer:* children

Only transitive action verbs direct their action toward someone or something—the direct object. Intransitive verbs have no direct objects.

TRANSITIVE: The tidal <u>wave</u> <u><u>sank</u></u> the [ship]. ^{DO}
Sank *what? Answer:* ship

INTRANSITIVE: The <u>wheels</u> <u><u>sank</u></u> into the mud.
Sank *what? Answer:* none

Theme: Japan

In this section, you will learn to recognize direct objects, indirect objects, and objective complements. The examples and exercises are about Japan and its culture.

Cross-Curricular Connection: Social Studies

Direct Objects, Indirect Objects, and Objective Complements • 425

⏱ TIME AND RESOURCE MANAGER

Resources
Print: *Grammar Exercise Workbook,* pp. 51–54; *Grammar Exercises Answers on Transparencies,* Ch. 19
Technology: *Writing and Grammar* Interactive Text, Section 19.3; *On-Line Exercise Bank,* Section 19.3

Using the Full Student Edition	Using the Handbook🄷
• Work through all key concepts, pp. 425–430. • Assign and review Exercises 22–26.	• Work through all key concepts, pp. 287–292. • Assign and review Exercises 22–26.

Direct Objects in Questions When a question follows the normal subject-verb order, you can still find the direct object by asking *Whom?* or *What?* after an action verb.

EXAMPLE: Who wrote that $\boxed{\text{story}}$?

When a question is inverted, however, the direct object will sometimes appear near the beginning, before the verb. To find the direct object, reword the question as a statement in normal word order, as shown in the following examples.

INVERTED QUESTION: Which book did you read?

REWORDED AS   You <u>did read</u> which $\boxed{\text{book}}$.
A STATEMENT:

Compound Direct Objects When an action verb directs action toward more than one direct object, the result is a compound direct object. If there is a compound direct object in a sentence, asking *Whom?* or *What?* after the verb will give you two or more answers.

EXAMPLE: The tourists visited Japanese $\boxed{\text{temples}}$ and $\boxed{\text{shrines}}$.

> **Exercise 22** Identifying Direct Objects in Statements and Questions List the direct object or compound direct object in each sentence below.

EXAMPLE: Japanese workers spend long hours on the job.
ANSWER: hours

1. Japan owes much of its economic success to its workers.
2. Japanese workers often express loyalty and respect toward their companies.
3. They take great pride in their companies' success.
4. They work longer hours and take fewer vacations than Western workers.
5. How do Japanese companies treat their employees?
6. Large companies often offer incentives to attract and keep workers.
7. Which benefits do workers appreciate most?
8. Many workers receive free housing or medical care.
9. These benefits keep the workers happy.
10. As a result, Japanese workers produce more goods than workers in most other countries do.

> **More Practice**

Grammar Exercise Workbook
• pp. 51–54
On-line Exercise Bank
• Section 19.3
  Go on-line:
  PHSchool.com
  Enter Web Code:
  eek-1002

Get instant feedback! Exercises 22 and 23 are available on-line or on CD-ROM.

Direct Object or Object of a Preposition? A direct object is never the noun or pronoun at the end of a prepositional phrase. Do not confuse these two sentence parts.

EXAMPLES:

                            DO   PREP PHRASE
I photographed the [woman] with the children.
Photographed *whom? Answer*: woman

              PREP PHRASE   PREP PHRASE
We walked with the children through the zoo.
Walked *what? Answer*: none

Exercise 23 **Identifying Direct Objects and Objects of Prepositions** On your paper, indicate whether the underlined word in each sentence is a *direct object* or *object of a preposition.*

EXAMPLE: A group of tourists stood outside the pagoda.

ANSWER: object of a preposition

1. Many Japanese pagodas are made of wood.
2. They are very vulnerable to fire.
3. Yet these pagodas can withstand earthquakes and typhoons.
4. Their interlocking construction makes them so strong.
5. A 1,300-year-old pagoda in Nara still shows no sign of weakness in its structure.

▼ **Critical Viewing** Add a compound direct object to complete this sentence: *When I look at this pagoda, I see . . .* **[Identify]**

Direct Objects, Indirect Objects, and Objective Complements • **427**

☑ ONGOING ASSESSMENT: Monitor and Reinforce

If students have difficulty with Exercise 22 or 23, refer them to the following for additional practice.

In the Textbook	Print Resources	Technology
Section Review, Ex. 27, Section 19.3	*Grammar Exercise Workbook;* pp. 51–52	*On-Line Exercise Bank,* Section 19.3

Exercise 24

Allow slight variation in wording.

1. At first, the Japanese educated only the <u>members</u> of the aristocracy.
2. Buddhist priests later assumed the <u>responsibility</u> for education.
3. This change made <u>education</u> available to a larger portion of society.
4. The Japanese maintained this <u>system</u> until the 1800's.
5. The Japanese first adopted a universal <u>code</u> for education under Emperor Meiji in the late 1800's.

Step-by-Step Teaching Guide

The Indirect Object

1. Have students read the key concept aloud; add that the indirect object is usually the receiver of the direct object.
2. Use the first example to demonstrate. Point out that *sister* (IO) receives the promise of the *book* (DO).
3. Use the last example on the page to demonstrate compound indirect objects. Ask who receives the promise of a book (*sister* and *brother*).

Customize for
Less Advanced Students

Give students practice changing objects of prepositions into indirect objects. This will help them become familiar with indirect objects. Begin by giving them these sentences to rewrite with indirect objects:

We gave a bouquet of flowers to her.

Jim's father gave a new watch to him.

Customize for
More Advanced Students

Tell students that certain verbs often lead to indirect objects. Have students identify the verbs in the examples on these two pages (*promise, give, handed, told*). Then have students think of other verbs that may have indirect objects (*send, draw, buy, play, show,* etc.) and to use them in original sentences containing indirect objects.

19.3

> **Exercise 24** Revising by Using Direct Objects Revise each question and answer below to form a sentence that includes a direct object or compound direct object. Underline the direct object(s).

EXAMPLE: What does Japan have? A long coastline and mountainous terrain.

ANSWER: Japan has a long <u>coastline</u> and mountainous <u>terrain</u>.

1. Who did the Japanese educate at first? Only the members of the aristocracy
2. Who later assumed the responsibility for education? Buddhist priests
3. How did this change affect education? It made it available to a larger portion of society.
4. How long did the Japanese maintain this system? Until the 1800's
5. What happened under Emperor Meiji in the late 1800's? A universal code for education was first adopted by the Japanese.

The Indirect Object

Sentences with direct objects may have *indirect objects*, too.

> **KEY CONCEPT** An **indirect object** is a noun or pronoun that appears with a direct object and names the person or thing that something is given to or done for. ■

To find an indirect object, first be certain that the sentence has a direct object. Then, having found the direct object, ask *To or for whom?* or *To or for what?* after the action verb.

EXAMPLES:
Liz promised her [sister] a [book] about Japan. (IO / DO)
Promised *to whom?* *Answer:* sister

We should give Fred's [idea] a [chance]. (IO / DO)
Should give *to what?* *Answer:* idea

Compound Indirect Objects When there is a compound indirect object in a sentence, asking *To or for whom?* or *To or for what?* after the verb will lead to two or more answers.

EXAMPLE:
Liz promised her [sister] and [brother] a book. (IO / IO)
Promised *to whom? Answer:* sister and brother

> **More Practice**

Grammar Exercise Workbook
• pp. 51–54
On-line Exercise Bank
• Section 19.3
Go on-line:
PHSchool.com
Enter Web Code:
eek-1002

Complete the exercises on-line! Exercises 24 and 25 are available on-line or on CD-ROM.

☑ **ONGOING ASSESSMENT: Monitor and Reinforce**

If students miss more than one item in Exercise 24, refer them to the following for additional practice.

In the Textbook	Print Resources	Technology
Section Review, Ex. 27, Section 19.3	*Grammar Exercise Workbook;* pp. 51–52	*On-Line Exercise Bank,* Section 19.3

Indirect Object or Direct Object? To avoid confusing an indirect object with a direct object, remember that an indirect object almost always comes between the verb and the direct object. In a sentence in normal subject-verb order, the pattern is always verb-indirect object-direct object.

EXAMPLE: Uncle Charlie handed the <u>bellhop</u> a <u>tip</u>.
                                                              IO   DO

Asking the questions for direct and indirect objects will also help you distinguish between the two kinds of complements. In the above example, the question for direct objects—handed *what?*—gives the answer *tip*. The question for indirect objects—handed *to whom?*—leads to the indirect object *bellhop*.

Indirect Object or Object of a Preposition? Do not confuse an indirect object with an object of a preposition. An indirect object is never preceded by the word *to* or *for*. Moreover, it almost never follows the direct object. In the first example below, *friends* is the object of a preposition and is located after the direct object. In the second, there is no preposition and *friends* comes before the direct object.

EXAMPLES: Angela told the <u>news</u> to her friends.
                                               DO   PREP PHRASE

                    Angela told her <u>friends</u> the <u>news</u>.
                                           IO   DO

▲ **Critical Viewing**
Write a sentence about this performer using the word *audience* as an indirect object. What is the direct object of your sentence? **[Analyze]**

> **Exercise 25** **Recognizing Indirect Objects** Write each indirect object, including any compound indirect objects. If a sentence has no indirect object, write *none*.

EXAMPLE: They sent Mark and Elizabeth travel brochures.
ANSWER: Mark, Elizabeth

1. Mark's parents bought him plane tickets to Tokyo for his birthday.
2. He asked his boss for a leave of absence.
3. The company granted Mark eight weeks.
4. His friend lent him a suitcase large enough for his long journey.
5. As his plane lifted off, Mark felt a rush of excitement and nervousness.
6. While away, Mark wrote his parents a letter every week.
7. He told them about the culture and people of Japan.
8. A guide gave him a complete tour of the city.
9. Mark visited Tokyo's financial and commercial centers.
10. When Mark returned, he showed his friends pictures of Tokyo.

Direct Objects, Indirect Objects, and Objective Complements • 429

Step-by-Step Teaching Guide

Indirect Object or Direct Object?

1. Ask students what direct and indirect objects have in common. (They both complete the action of a verb.)
2. Then ask how they differ. (The direct object receives the action; the indirect object receives the direct object.)
3. If necessary to demonstrate syntax, place the example on the board and draw an arrow from *handed* to *tip* and another arrow from *tip* to *bellhop*.

Step-by-Step Teaching Guide

Indirect Object or Object of a Preposition?

1. Use the example to show how the same word (*friends*) can be structured as either an indirect object or an object of a preposition.
2. If necessary, give students additional examples. For each, have them identify the underlined structure and then rewrite the sentence as the alternate structure.

   Won't anyone give <u>me</u> a ride?

   I wrote a letter <u>to</u> <u>my</u> <u>pen</u> pal.

   Mr. Smith gave A's <u>to</u> <u>everybody</u>.

Answer Key

> **Exercise 25**

1. him   6. parents
2. none   7. none
3. Mark   8. him
4. him   9. none
5. none   10. friends

Critical Viewing

Analyze Sample response: *This performer offers her audience an interesting show.* The direct object is *show.*

Step-by-Step Teaching Guide

The Objective Complement

1. Read the key concept aloud and point out that an objective complement normally appears directly after a direct object. Point out that it is never a prepositional phrase, but a noun that renames the direct object or an adjective that describes it.

2. Use the examples. In the first, ask what kind of information the objective complement adds (it renames *dog*). In the second, ask what kind of information this objective complement adds (it describes *hair*).

3. Ask students to think of an original sentence with a compound objective complement that renames the direct object. (Example: *He considered the man his guide and his friend.*)

Answer Key

Exercise 26

1. symbol
2. sacred, inviolable
3. ceremonial
4. head
5. emperor
6. symbolic
7. populated
8. difficult
9. paradise
10. "land of the rising sun"

The Objective Complement

A third kind of complement, one that generally comes after a direct object, is called an *objective complement.*

▶ **KEY CONCEPT** An **objective complement** is an adjective or noun that appears with a direct object and describes or renames it. ∎

Objective complements do not occur often. They are used only with verbs such as *appoint, name, make, think,* or *call.*

An objective complement can be found only in a sentence that has a direct object. To determine whether a word is an objective complement, say the verb and the direct object and then ask *What?* The following examples illustrate the method you should use to locate objective complements.

EXAMPLES: Ben called his <u>dog</u> <u>Rover</u>.
                          Called dog *what? Answer:* Rover

                          The beautician made Ann's <u>hair</u> <u>short</u> and <u>curly</u>.
                          Made hair *what? Answer:* short and curly

The objective complement in the last example is compound.

▶ **Exercise 26** Recognizing Objective Complements Write the objective complement in each sentence, including all parts of any compound objective complements.

EXAMPLE: Mr. Matsuto made his reply very short.
ANSWER: short

1. The Japanese consider the emperor the symbol of their nation.
2. They once thought their emperor sacred and inviolable.
3. Japan's 1947 constitution declared the emperor's position ceremonial.
4. The constitution named the prime minister head of state.
5. In 1989, Japan declared Akihito emperor.
6. The people considered his marriage to a commoner symbolic of Japan's democracy.
7. Japan's limited land and large population make the country densely populated.
8. Limited space makes housing development difficult.
9. In spite of the overcrowding, the Japanese find their homeland a paradise.
10. The Japanese call their country the "land of the rising sun."

💡 Spelling Tip

Note the difference between *complement* and *compliment:* A *complement* is something that completes or brings to perfection. A *compliment* is an expression of courtesy or praise.

⏱ TIME SAVERS!

🛒 **Answers on Transparencies**
Use the *Grammar Exercises Answers on Transparencies* for Chapter 19 to facilitate correction by students.

🖥 **On-Line Exercise Bank**
Have students complete the exercises on computer. The Auto Check feature will grade their work for you!

☑ ONGOING ASSESSMENT: Monitor and Reinforce

If students miss more than two items in Exercise 25 or 26, refer them to the following for additional practice.

In the Textbook	Print Resources	Technology
Section Review, Ex. 28–29, Section 19.3	*Grammar Exercise Workbook,* pp. 53–54	*On-Line Exercise Bank,* Section 19.3

Section Review

GRAMMAR EXERCISES 27–32

Exercise 27 Recognizing Direct Objects Write the direct object in each sentence, including all parts of any compound direct objects.

(1) Japanese comprise 99 percent of the population of Japan. (2) The small remainder includes Koreans, Chinese, and Ainu. (3) The Ainu represent the aborigines of Japan. (4) They once inhabited the northernmost islands of Japan. (5) They possessed distinct biological characteristics. (6) After World War II, however, Japanese culture almost fully assimilated the Ainu. (7) Metropolitan areas now dominate the Japanese landscape. (8) Its people have created an industrialized urban society with relatively few resources. (9) Nearly all citizens speak Japanese. (10) In addition to speaking the official language, many Japanese also know some English.

Exercise 28 Recognizing Complements Used With Action Verbs Write and label each *direct object, indirect object,* and *objective complement.*

1. The Japanese named their country *Dia Nihon,* which means "origin of the sun."
2. The Treaty of Versailles made the Caroline Islands a part of Japan.
3. I showed my father the cities of Yokohama and Osaka on the map.
4. The rugged mountains and rocky soil of Japan make farming difficult.
5. Kirisawa wrote some of the Japanese ideogrammatic alphabet on the chalkboard for the class.
6. The University of Tokyo granted the foreign students a scholarship.
7. Our hosts offered us sushi for lunch.
8. At the Japanese festival, I ate blowfish.
9. The prime minister of Japan appoints legislators and cabinet members.

10. Frank sent me his book of Japanese architecture.

Exercise 29 Writing Sentences With Complements Complete each sentence by adding the complement(s) indicated in parentheses, plus needed modifiers.

1. Frances painted ___?___. (direct object)
2. The Japanese musician played ___?___. (compound direct object)
3. Anna's friend wrote ___?___. (indirect object and direct object)
4. Charlie bought ___?___. (compound indirect object and direct object)
5. Andrew considered ___?___. (direct object and objective complement)

Exercise 30 Find It in Your Reading In a newspaper, find an article about another country. Label any *direct objects, indirect objects,* and *objective complements* in the article.

Exercise 31 Find It in Your Writing In your own writing, find five direct objects and two indirect objects. Also, note whether you have used objective complements in any of your compositions.

Exercise 32 Writing Application Japan exports many products, such as automobiles and electronics, to the United States. Write a description of an item in your home that may have been imported from another country, and discuss how it works. Include and label two *direct objects,* one *indirect object,* and one *objective complement* in your description.

Section Review • 431

ASSESS

Section Review

Each of these exercises correlates to the instruction on direct objects, indirect objects, and objective complements, pages 425–430. These exercises may be used for more practice, for reteaching, or for review of the key concepts presented.

Answer Key

Exercise 27

(1) percent; (2) Koreans, Chinese, Ainu; (3) aborigines; (4) islands; (5) characteristics; (6) Ainu; (7) landscape; (8) society; (9) Japanese; (10) English

Exercise 28

1. country—DO; *Dia Nihon*—OC
2. Caroline Islands—DO; part—OC
3. father—IO; cities—DO
4. farming—DO; difficult—OC
5. some—DO
6. students—IO; scholarship—DO
7. us—IO; sushi—DO
8. blowfish—DO
9. legislators, members—DO
10. me—IO; book—DO

Exercise 29

Answers will vary; samples are given.

1. a beautiful picture
2. the flute and the piano
3. her a nasty letter
4. his mother and father a table
5. us his friends

Exercise 30

Find It in Your Reading
Tell students to search through features as well as news stories.

Exercise 31

Find It in Your Writing
When students finish this activity, have them exchange papers with a partner and check the direct and indirect objects each found.

Exercise 32

Writing Application
Have students work in pairs to read each other's descriptions to check for the correct identification of the objects and objective complement.

Draw this graphic on the board:

| X | is | X |

Ask students what they think it represents (a sentence). Ask for the part of speech of *is* (linking verb) and then ask for real words to replace the X's. Write some of these words beneath each X, asking volunteers to choose either location. Ask students to identify the part of speech represented by most words beneath the first X (nouns or pronouns) and point out that these may be subjects. Then ask for the parts of speech of those beneath the second X (nouns, pronouns, and adjectives). Point out that these are not direct objects.

Activate Prior Knowledge

Write the following words on the board: *Harry S. Truman, New Orleans, Spanish.* Ask what categories these words belong to (American presidents, cities, languages). Ask students to give other examples in these categories and to use both the examples and categories in sentences, beginning with examples as in the following.

Spanish is my native language.

Remind students that *is* is a linking verb and then explain to them what subject complements are.

TEACH

Step-by-Step Teaching Guide

The Predicate Nominative

1. Read the Key Concept and add that a predicate nominative answers the question *Who?* or *What?* after a linking verb but is not a direct object.

2. Make an equation to explain the structure of the first example. Write on the board *painting = masterpiece.* Explain that by explaining (or renaming or identifying), a predicate nominative sets up an equation.

Section 19.4 — Subject Complements

In this section, you will see linking verbs followed by other kinds of complements, called *subject complements.*

▶ **KEY CONCEPT** A **subject complement** is a noun, pronoun, or adjective that appears with a linking verb and tells something about the subject of the sentence. ■

A subject complement will almost always be found *after* a linking verb. The two kinds of subject complements are known as *predicate nominatives* and *predicate adjectives.*

The Predicate Nominative

The word *nominative* comes from the Latin word *nomen* meaning "name." The words *noun* and *pronoun* are also derived from *nomen.* A *predicate nominative* names or identifies the subject of a sentence.

▶ **KEY CONCEPT** A **predicate nominative** is a noun or pronoun that appears with a linking verb and renames, identifies, or explains the subject of the sentence. ■

A subject and a predicate nominative are two different words for the same person, place, or thing. Acting as an equal sign, the linking verb joins these two parts and equates them.

In the examples, subjects are underlined once, linking verbs twice, and predicate nominatives are boxed and labeled.

EXAMPLES: That <u>painting</u> of the shoreline <u>is</u> a [masterpiece]. (*Masterpiece* explains *painting.*)

The new <u>lifeguard</u> at the pool <u>will be</u> [Sue]. (*Sue* renames *lifeguard.*)

Their first <u>choice</u> <u>was</u> [you]. (*You* identifies *choice.*)

Like other sentence parts, predicate nominatives may be compound.

EXAMPLES: Most <u>people</u> at the beach <u>were</u> [sunbathers] or [surfers]. (*Sunbathers* and *surfers* name *people.*)

The new <u>lifeguard</u> <u>may be</u> either [Sue] or [Celia]. (*Sue* or *Celia* renames *lifeguard.*)

432 • Basic Sentence Parts

Theme: Beaches and Tides

In this section, you will learn about predicate nominatives and predicate adjectives. The examples and exercises are about beaches and tides.

Cross-Curricular Connection: Science

▶ **More Practice**

Grammar Exercise Workbook
• pp. 55–56
On-line Exercise Bank
• Section 19.4
Go on-line:
PHSchool.com
Enter Web Code:
eek-1002

⏱ TIME AND RESOURCE MANAGER

Resources
Print: *Grammar Exercise Workbook,* pp. 55–56; *Grammar Exercises Answers on Transparencies,* Ch. 19
Technology: *Writing and Grammar* Interactive Text, Section 19.4; *On-Line Exercise Bank,* Section 19.4

Using the Full Student Edition	Using the Handbook 🄷
• Work through all key concepts, pp. 432–434. • Assign and review Exercises 33–34. • Read and discuss Grammar in Literature, p. 433.	• Work through all key concepts, pp. 294–296. • Assign and review Exercises 33–34. • Read and discuss Grammar in Literature, p. 295.

GRAMMAR IN LITERATURE

from **In Commemoration: One Million Volumes**

Rudolfo A. Anaya

In the following excerpt, the predicate nominatives are shown in blue italics.

I was a librarian's *dream*. My tattered library card was my *ticket* into the same worlds my grandfather had known, worlds of magic that fed the imagination.

▶ **Exercise 33** Recognizing Predicate Nominatives Write the predicate nominative in each sentence, including all parts of any compound predicate nominatives.

EXAMPLE: This beach is a good site for fishing and an excellent place for diving.

ANSWER: site place

1. Beaches are strips of land bordering an ocean or another body of water.
2. Some of our favorite beaches are barrier beaches.
3. Barrier beaches are generally elongated islands or sandbars.
4. The beach at Coney Island, in New York, is a barrier beach.
5. Beaches along the islands of Hawaii are the main attraction for tourists.
6. Waves, tides, and the wind will always be a beach's worst enemy.
7. These elements are the primary cause of erosion.
8. Sand dunes are one result of winds and tides.
9. White sand on a beach is the product of coral and limestone deposits.
10. High tides and storms are cause for alarm for beach residents.

▼ **Critical Viewing** Complete this sentence: *This rocky coastline would be a great . . .* What is the predicate nominative in your sentence? **[Analyze]**

Subject Complements • **433**

Grammar in Literature

1. Have students read the passage aloud and point out that each sentence contains a linking verb. Ask students to identify each linking verb (*was, was*).

2. Have them identify the nouns or pronouns linked by each verb (*I, dream; card, ticket*).

More About the Author

Rudolfo Anaya is a contemporary American novelist and short-story writer. Born in New Mexico, Anaya absorbed the traditions of Hispanic farming and ranching and used them in his writing. His most famous novel, *Bless Me, Ultima,* explores farming and ranching as two different ways of relating to nature.

Connections With Literature

A longer excerpt from "In Commemoration: One Million Volumes" can be found in *Prentice Hall Literature, Penguin Edition,* Grade 10.

Answer Key

▶ **Exercise 33**

1. strips
2. (predicate) beaches
3. islands, sandbars
4. (predicate) beach
5. attraction
6. enemy
7. cause
8. result
9. product
10. cause

Critical Viewing

Analyze Possible answer: This rocky coastline would be a great place to enjoy the scenery. *Place* is the predicate nominative.

The Predicate Adjective

1. Read the key concept and explain that a predicate adjective works in much the same way grammatically as a predicate nominative.

2. Use the first example to show that *fun*, an adjective, describes the subject, *trip*. Have students suggest a noun phrase to replace *fun* (a big event, an ordeal) and remind them that a noun in this position is a predicate nominative.

3. Again show an equation that represents an example on the page: *trip = fun*. Explain that in this case the complement doesn't rename the subject; it describes it.

Answer Key

▶ **Exercise 34**

1. luminous
2. closer
3. stronger
4. responsive
5. great, constant
6. higher
7. plentiful
8. hardy, adaptable
9. smooth, gleaming
10. unreal

Critical Viewing

Analyze Sample response: The beach was <u>calm</u> and <u>quiet.</u> The sunset was <u>beautiful.</u>

Integrating Vocabulary Skills

Latin Roots Have students look up the words *predicate* and *adjective* (*predicate* is from the Latin *predicatus,* "to proclaim or announce"; *adjective* is from the Latin *adjicere,* "to add to"). Ask how these word origins help explain the functions of predicates, predicate nominatives, and predicate adjectives in sentences. (*Predicate* proclaims what is said about the subject in the sentence; *predicate nominative* occurs with a linking verb to rename the subject; *predicate adjective* follows a linking verb and adds a quality to the subject.)

19.4

The Predicate Adjective

The other kind of subject complement is called a *predicate adjective*. With a linking verb, it describes the subject.

▶ **KEY CONCEPT** A **predicate adjective** is an adjective that appears with a linking verb and describes the subject of the sentence. ■

In each of the following examples, you can see that the linking verb joins the subject to a word that describes the subject. These descriptive words are predicate adjectives.

EXAMPLES: A trip to the beach <u>will be</u> fun.   P.A.

My sunburn <u>feels</u> hot and painful.   P.A.

▶ **Exercise 34**   Recognizing Predicate Adjectives   Write the predicate adjective in each sentence, including all parts of any compound predicate adjectives.

1. In the cloudless sky, the moon appeared luminous.
2. The moon is closer to the Earth than the sun is.
3. Its gravitational pull on the Earth is stronger.
4. The Earth's oceans are responsive to the pull of the moon.
5. The gravitational pull of the moon is great and constant
6. Tides are higher at certain times of the day because of the moon's pull.
7. Marine life is plentiful at the edge of the sea.
8. These forms of life must be hardy and adaptable.
9. The fronds of seaweed were smooth and gleaming.
10. The delicate shells on the shore looked unreal.

▶ Critical Viewing Write two sentences containing predicate adjectives to describe the beach and the sunset in this photograph. [Analyze]

434 • Basic Sentence Parts

Get instant feedback! Exercise 34 is available on-line or on CD-ROM.

▶ **More Practice**

Grammar Exercise Workbook
• pp. 55–56
On-line Exercise Bank
• Section 19.4
Go on-line:
PHSchool.com
Enter Web Code:
eek-1002

☑ **ONGOING ASSESSMENT: Monitor and Reinforce**

If students miss more than two items in Exercise 33 or 34, refer them to the following for additional practice.

In the Textbook	Print Resources	Technology
Section Review, Ex. 35–37, Section 19.4	*Grammar Exercise Workbook;* pp. 55–56	*On-Line Exercise Bank,* Section 19.4

Section 19.4 Section Review

ASSESS and CLOSE

Section Review

Each of these exercises correlates to the instruction on subject complements, pages 432–434. These exercises may be used for more practice, for reteaching, or for review of the key concepts presented.

Answer Key

> **Exercise 35**

1. home: PN
2. unique, delicate: PA
3. source: PN
4. basins: PN
5. adaptable: PA
6. forms: PN
7. dangerous: PA
8. protections: PN
9. host: PN
10. resilient: PA

> **Exercise 36**

Answers will vary; samples are given.

1. ominous
2. wet, squishy
3. ball
4. source
5. means
6. expensive
7. highest
8. numerous, noisy
9. spot
10. life jacket

> **Exercise 37**

Answers will vary; samples are given.

1. Our morning walk along the beach was refreshing.
2. The shoreline was rocky and craggy.
3. A distant boat was a tiny speck on the horizon.
4. Fresh fish and vegetables were our dinner.
5. The beach at night seems mysterious.

> **Exercise 38**

Find It in Your Reading
pallid (PA); disc (PN)

> **Exercise 39**

Find It in Your Writing
After students finish this activity with examples from their portfolios, have them exchange papers with a writing partner for a review of predicate nominatives.

> **Exercise 40**

Writing Application
After students finish this activity, have them exchange papers with a partner and check one another's examples of predicate nominatives and adjectives.

GRAMMAR EXERCISES 35–40

> **Exercise 35** Recognizing Subject Complements Write and label the predicate nominatives or predicate adjectives in each sentence.

1. Shorelines are home to tidal pools.
2. The environments of tidal pools are unique and delicate.
3. The current is the source of a rich supply of nutrients along beaches.
4. Tidal pools are natural basins in sand.
5. Creatures in tidal pools are adaptable.
6. They are strange and beautiful forms of life.
7. Buffeting waves and frequent submersion are dangerous to them.
8. Suction-cup feet are the only protections of a starfish.
9. Rocks and boats are often host to marine animals like barnacles.
10. Seaweed is quite resilient.

> **Exercise 36** Supplying Subject Complements in Sentences Write a subject complement or compound subject complement to complete each sentence.

1. The waves that crashed on the shore were ___?___ .
2. The foam felt ___?___ and ___?___ .
3. The sun was a giant orange ___?___ in the sky.
4. Tides are a good ___?___ of energy.
5. A dam can be an essential ___?___ for capturing this energy.
6. Dams can be ___?___ , but they are worth the money.
7. The 50-foot tides in the Bay of Fundy in Canada are the ___?___ in the world.
8. Birds flying over the bay were ___?___ and ___?___ .
9. The beach is a good ___?___ to play or relax.
10. The most unusual thing I saw in the water was a ___?___ .

> **Exercise 37** Revising Sentences by Using Subject Complements Revise each sentence below so that it includes a predicate nominative or predicate adjective.

1. We took a refreshing morning walk along the beach.
2. We saw a rocky and craggy shoreline.
3. A distant boat seemed to be a tiny speck on the horizon.
4. Our dinner consisted of fresh fish and vegetables.
5. The beach at night has a mysterious quality.

> **Exercise 38** Find It in Your Reading Identify the predicate nominative and predicate adjective in this excerpt from *The Marginal World* by Rachel Carson.

. . . Water and air were pallid. Across the bay the moon was a luminous disc in the western sky, suspended above the dim line of the distant shore. . . .

> **Exercise 39** Find It in Your Writing Look through your writing portfolio. Find two examples of predicate nominatives and two examples of predicate adjectives. Label the complements, and underline the subject once and the linking verb twice in each sentence.

> **Exercise 40** Writing Application Write a description of a day at a beach or park. Include a predicate nominative, a compound predicate nominative, and two predicate adjectives in your description.

Section Review • 435

☑ **ONGOING ASSESSMENT: Assess Mastery**

Use the following resources to assess student mastery of basic sentence parts.

In the Textbook	Print Resources	Technology
Chapter Review, Ex. 43–46 Standardized Test Preparation Workshop	*Formal Assessment,* Chapter 19	*On-Line Exercise Bank,* Chapter 19

Answer Key

► Exercise 41 Identifying Basic
Sentence Parts Write each of the following sentences on your paper. Draw a vertical line separating the complete subject from the complete predicate. Underline each simple subject once and each verb twice. Then, identify the function of any italicized complement.

1. Surfing became a popular water *sport* in the 1960's.
2. The sport is *popular* today in the United States, Australia, and Japan.
3. A person participating in this sport rides *waves* in the ocean.
4. The surfer lies, kneels, or stands on a surfboard.
5. People in Hawaii gave *surfing* its start hundreds of years ago.
6. They made *themselves* wooden boards.
7. Today's boards are *compositions* of polyurethane wrapped in fiberglass.
8. Surfers call boards under 8 feet in length *short boards*.
9. The beaches of Hawaii are the most famous surfing *locations* in the world.
10. All forms of surfing require exact *timing* and quick *reflexes*.
11. The most popular form of surfing is *stand-up*.
12. The surfer paddles the *board* out beyond the breaking waves.
13. He or she stands and rides a *wave* toward the shore.
14. Annual surfing competitions in Hawaii, California, and Australia are *exciting*.
15. Bodysurfing and windsurfing are other aquatic *sports*.

► Exercise 42 Identifying Hard-to-
Find Subjects On your paper, write the following sentences. Underline each subject once and each verb twice. If a subject is understood, write (*you*).

1. Do you play beach volleyball?
2. Here is the only available volleyball net on the beach.
3. Are there enough players for a game?
4. Where are the rest of your friends?
5. Gather your friends to form a team.
6. There are no open spots left on the beach.
7. Here is my favorite place to play volleyball.
8. There are never enough people with whom to play.
9. Would you like to play against us?
10. Which ball would you prefer to use?
11. On the beach are some annoying insects.
12. Along the Atlantic coast from Canada to Argentina is found the common sand flea.
13. Avoid this freaky critter.
14. With a sudden leap comes the sand flea.
15. On almost any kind of decaying vegetable or animal matter feast these tiny creatures.

► Exercise 43 Identifying
Complements Write and label any direct objects, indirect objects, objective complements, predicate nominatives, or predicate adjectives you find in the following sentences.

1. Carol spent her childhood at the beach.
2. Studying marine life is her passion.
3. As a high-school student, she studied biology avidly.
4. In college, Carol focused her studies on marine biology.
5. Now, Carol supervises marine biologists and researchers in the navy.
6. She recently bought herself a small cottage at the shore.
7. She proudly showed her mother and father the place.

continued

8. They gave her a housewarming present during their visit.
9. They considered the cottage lovely.
10. Carol felt thrilled by their response.
11. Next to the cottage, she has planted some flowers.
12. She gives the flowers water every day in the summer.
13. She has outlined the flower bed with many different kinds of shells.
14. Friends gave her their nicest shells.
15. She calls her garden "my cozy posies."

Exercise 44 Adding Basic Parts to Complete Sentences Complete each sentence with a noun, pronoun, or adjective. Identify the use of the word in the sentence as a *subject, direct object, indirect object, predicate nominative,* or *predicate adjective.*

1. My favorite summer ___?___ is swimming.
2. Jen bought ___?___ a new swimsuit.
3. The sky looks ___?___ and ___?___ this morning.
4. Bring your ___?___ to the beach.
5. This is a good ___?___ for sailing.
6. My father and ___?___ rented a ___?___ for the day.
7. My father's ___?___ taught ___?___ sailing.
8. His sailing skills were ___?___.
9. We still had ___?___, however.
10. The lake water felt ___?___ and ___?___.

Exercise 45 Writing Sentences With Objective Complements Add an objective complement of the type indicated to each of the following sentences.

1. We named our pet starfish (noun).
2. The dock master considered his staff (adjective).
3. Unanimously, the beach club members appointed me (noun).

4. The hurricane left the shoreline (adjective) and (adjective).
5. I called Dave a powerful (noun) and a fine (noun).

Exercise 46 Revising Sentences by Adding Complements Revise the following sentences by following the directions in parentheses.

1. Jacques bought a goldfish. (Add an indirect object.)
2. The fish was bright orange. (Add another predicate adjective.)
3. They bought for the goldfish (Add a direct object.)
4. The most interesting thing in the bowl was (Add a predicate nominative.)
5. The goldfish gave a lot of pleasure. (Add an indirect object.)
6. We named the fish. (Add an objective complement.)
7. In the last few weeks, Jacques has bought many for his aquarium. (Add a compound direct object.)
8. Keeping fish has become a favorite of his. (Add a predicate nominative.)
9. Keeping fish can be very (Add a compound predicate adjective.)
10. All of Jacques friends consider him (Add an objective complement.)

Exercise 47 Writing Application Write a description of a marine animal that you have seen at the beach, at an aquarium, or on film. Underline the subject of each sentence once, the verb twice, and circle each complement. Include at least one sentence in inverted order.

Lesson Objectives

1. To demonstrate control over grammatical elements such as sentence construction
2. To recognize appropriate English usage within a written passage

Step-by-Step Teaching Guide

Recognizing Appropriate Sentence Construction

Teaching Resources: Standardized Test Preparation Workbook, pp. 37–38

1. Review with students what they have learned in this chapter about subjects and predicates, hard-to-find subjects, and the various kinds of complements. Tell them that this workshop gives them a chance to apply that knowledge and to practice taking standardized tests.

2. Have students answer the sample test item on this page. Ask them why the sentence is not correct as it is. (The second part, "By Nicholas Cugnot," is a fragment. It is a prepositional phrase.)

3. Challenge students to come up with another clear way to rewrite the sentence. (Possible answer: In 1769, the first automobile was built by Nicholas Cugnot, a French military officer.)

4. Have students complete the practice tests on page 439. Discuss their answers, making sure they can explain why each incorrect choice is incorrect.

Standardized Test Preparation Workshop

Recognizing Appropriate Sentence Construction

Knowing how to use the basic parts of a sentence correctly is the foundation for good writing. Every sentence must contain a subject (the *who* or *what* that performs the action) and a verb (the action the subject is performing) and express a complete thought. If one of these parts is missing, it is an incomplete sentence.

Standardized tests measure your ability to identify complete sentences. When answering these test questions, check each group of words for a subject and a verb, and then determine whether it expresses a complete thought. Also, make sure that the sentence is not really two sentences placed together incorrectly.

The following question will give you practice with the format used for testing your knowledge of basic sentence parts.

Test Tips

- Remember that a verb can either follow or come before its subject. Also, a form of *be* can act as the main verb of a sentence.
- Watch out for answer choices that are really two sentences run together with no punctuation or with just a comma separating them.

Sample Test Item	Answer and Explanation
Directions: Choose the letter of the best way to rewrite each underlined section. If the underlined section needs no change, choose "Correct as is." <u>In 1769, the first automobile was built.</u> (1) <u>By Nicholas Cugnot. He was a French</u> <u>military officer.</u> **A** In 1769, the first automobile was built by a French military officer. Nicholas Cugnot. **B** In 1769, Nicholas Cugnot, a French military officer, built the first automobile. **C** In 1769, Nicholas Cugnot built the first automobile, he was a French military officer. **D** Correct as is	The correct answer is *B*. The sentence provides all of the information from the original without introducing either an incomplete sentence (as in *A*) or incorrectly running together two sentences (as in *C*).

438 • Basic Sentence Parts

◇ TEST-TAKING TIP

For students who tend to get stuck on questions, suggest that they move on to the next question and return to a difficult one later if time permits. If the test does not deduct points for incorrect answers, tell students to make sure they fill in an answer for every question.

You may wish to provide students with standardized test answer sheets so they can get used to filling in their answers. Remind them to make their marks neat and dark. If students have time, encourage them to make sure their answers are marked in the right places. Inadvertently skipping one question can throw off an entire answer sheet.

▶ **Practice 1** **Directions:** Choose the letter of the best way to write each underlined section. If the underlined section needs no change, choose "Correct as is."

In a head-on crash. A car's driver and
(1)
passengers can be thrown forward. And

seriously injured. To protect those inside
(2)
most new cars have airbags. Airbags pop
(3)
out of the steering wheel. Or the dashboard.

They inflate instantly with nitrogen gas.

1 **A** In a head-on crash, a car's driver and passengers can be thrown forward. And seriously injured.

B In a head-on crash. A car's driver and passengers can be thrown forward they can be seriously injured.

C In a head-on crash, a car's driver and passengers can be thrown forward and seriously injured.

D Correct as is

2 **F** To protect those inside. Most new cars have airbags.

G Most new cars have airbags. This is to protect those inside.

H Most new cars have airbags, this is to protect those inside.

J Correct as is

3 **A** Airbags pop out of the steering wheel or dashboard. They inflate instantly. With nitrogen gas.

B Airbags pop out of the steering wheel or dashboard and inflate instantly with nitrogen gas.

C Airbags inflate instantly with nitrogen gas and they pop out of the steering wheel or dashboard.

D Correct as is

▶ **Practice 2** **Directions:** Choose the letter of the best way to write each underlined section. If the underlined section needs no change, choose "Correct as is."

An airbag system contains three things.
(1)
Electronic sensors, an inflator, and the bag

itself. The sensors in the system are set. To
(2)
ignore collisions. When the cars are going

less than ten to fourteen miles per hour.

In a crash, the bag becomes fully inflated.
(3)
In one twentieth of a second.

1 **A** An airbag system contains electronic sensors, an inflator, and the bag itself.

B An airbag system contains three things. The three things are electronic sensors, an inflator, and the bag itself.

C An airbag system contains. Electronic sensors, an inflator, and the bag itself.

D Correct as is

2 **F** The sensors are set to ignore collisions. When the cars are going less than ten to fourteen miles per hour.

G The sensors are set to ignore collisions. The cars are going less than ten to fourteen miles per hour.

H The sensors are set to ignore collisions when the cars are going less than ten to fourteen miles per hour.

J Correct as is

3 **A** In a crash. The bag becomes fully inflated in one twentieth of a second.

B In a crash, the bag becomes fully inflated in one twentieth of a second.

C The bag becomes fully inflated in a crash.

D Correct as is

▶ **Practice 1**
1. C
2. J
3. B

▶ **Practice 2**
1. A
2. H
3. B

Customize for *More Advanced Students*

Challenge students to rewrite question 1 in Practice 2 by using a colon. *(An airbag system contains three things: electronic sensors, an inflator, and the bag itself.)* Remind them that colons can be used to introduce a list of items following an independent clause. The colon should not immediately follow a verb.

Integrating Writing Skills

Have interested students do some research on the way an airbag functions. Have them write two paragraphs that might follow those on this page. Make sure they use appropriate sentence construction in their writing. When they finish, have them share their findings with the class.

In-Depth Lesson Plan

	LESSON FOCUS	PRINT AND MEDIA RESOURCES
DAY 1	**Prepositional Phrases and Appositive Phrases** Students learn and apply concepts relating to prepositional phrases used as adjective or adverb phrases and to appositives and appositive phrases. (pp. 440–448/⊞298–306)	*Writing and Grammar* **Interactive Text**, Section 20.1; *On-line Exercise Bank,* Section 20.1 **Teaching Resources** *Grammar Exercise Workbook*, pp. 57–60; *Grammar Exercises Answers on Transparencies*, Ch. 20
DAY 2	**Verbal Phrases** Students learn and apply concepts relating to participles, gerunds, infinitives, and their respective phrases. (pp. 449–463/⊞307–321)	**Teaching Resources** *Grammar Exercise Workbook*, pp. 61–74; *Grammar Exercises Answers on Transparencies*, Ch. 20
DAY 3	**Clauses** Students learn and apply concepts relating to independent, subordinate, and adjective clauses. (pp. 464–470/⊞322–328)	*Writing and Grammar* **Interactive Text**, Section 20.2; *On-line Exercise Bank,* Section 20.2 **Teaching Resources** *Grammar Exercise Workbook*, pp. 75–78
DAY 4	**Clauses** *continued* Students learn and apply concepts relating to adverb and noun clauses and do the Hands-on Grammar activity. (pp. 470–479/⊞328–337)	**Teaching Resources** *Grammar Exercise Workbook*, pp. 79–80; *Hands-on Grammar Activity Book*, Ch. 20
DAY 5	**Review and Assess** Students review the chapter and demonstrate mastery of the concepts. (pp. 480–481)	*Writing and Grammar* **Interactive Text**, Ch. 20, Chapter Review **Teaching Resources** *Formal Assessment,* Ch. 20

Accelerated Lesson Plan

	LESSON FOCUS	PRINT AND MEDIA RESOURCES
DAY 1	**Phrases** Students cover types of phrases as determined by their performance on the Diagnostic Test. (pp. 440–463/⊞298–321)	*Writing and Grammar* **Interactive Text**, Section 20.1; *On-line Exercise Bank,* Section 20.1 **Teaching Resources** *Grammar Exercise Workbook*, pp. 57–74; *Grammar Exercises Answers on Transparencies*, Ch. 20
DAY 2	**Clauses** Students cover types of clauses as determined by the Diagnostic Test. (pp. 464–479/⊞322–337)	*Writing and Grammar* **Interactive Text**, Section 20.2; *On-line Exercise Bank,* Section 20.2 **Teaching Resources** *Grammar Exercise Workbook*, pp. 75–80; *Grammar Exercises Answers on Transparencies*, Ch. 20
DAY 3	**Review and Assess** Students review the chapter and demonstrate mastery of the concepts. (pp. 480–481)	*Writing and Grammar* **Interactive Text**, Ch. 20, Chapter Review **Teaching Resources** *Formal Assessment,* Ch. 20

Options for Adapting Lesson Plans

FEATURES

Extend coverage with the Grammar in Literature features (pp. 450, 474/⊞308, 332) and the Standardized Test Preparation Workshop (p. 482).

TECHNOLOGY

Students can use *Writing and Grammar* Interactive Text to complete the exercises interactively on computer. They can complete additional exercises in the *On-line Exercise Bank:* The Auto Check feature will grade their work. Go on-line: PHSchool.com Use Web Code: eek-1002

Writing and Grammar Handbook Alignment

Page numbers in Step-by-Step Teaching Guides in this Teacher's Edition refer to pages from the full student text. Handbook page references, indicated with this icon 🄷, are provided in Time and Resource Manager boxes and at the bottom of each Teacher's Edition page.

INTEGRATED SKILLS COVERAGE

Grammar in Literature SE pp. 450, 474/🄷308, 332; ATE pp. 450, 474

Writing
Find It in Your Writing SE pp. 463, 477, 479; ATE p. 477/🄷321, 335, 337
Writing Application SE pp. 463, 479, 481/🄷321, 337
Grammar and Style SE pp. 447, 468/🄷305, 326

Punctuation ATE p. 465

Vocabulary ATE p. 459

Spelling SE p. 452/🄷310

Viewing and Representing Critical Viewing SE pp. 440, 445, 448, 451, 453, 454, 457, 459, 465, 466, 469, 471, 476/🄷298, 303, 306, 309, 311, 312, 315, 317, 323, 324, 327, 329, 334; ATE pp. 440, 445, 448, 451, 454, 457, 465, 466, 469, 471, 476

Real-World Connection ATE p. 467

Workplace Skills ATE p. 457

Research Skills SE p. 472/🄷330

Speaking and Listening SE p. 444/🄷302; ATE pp. 447, 466

ASSESSMENT SUPPORT

Standardized Test Preparation Workshop SE p. 482; ATE p. 452

Standardized Test Preparation Workbook, pp. 39–40

Formal Assessment, Ch. 20

MEETING INDIVIDUAL NEEDS

Less Advanced Students ATE pp. 443, 454, 483. See also Ongoing Assessments ATE pp. 443, 445, 447, 448, 451, 453, 455, 457, 459, 465, 467, 469, 473, 475, 483.

More Advanced Students ATE pp. 474, 483

ESL Students ATE pp. 455, 466

Gifted and Talented Students ATE p. 476

Logical/Mathematical Learners ATE p. 472

Linguistic Learners ATE p. 446

Spatial Learners ATE p. 475

BLOCK SCHEDULING

Pacing Suggestions
For 90-minute Blocks
- Administer the Diagnostic Test to students to determine instructional coverage needed.
- Have students complete the necessary exercises in class. Use the Hands-on Grammar activity.

Resources for Varying Instruction
- *Writing and Grammar* Interactive Text A 90-minute block provides an ideal opportunity for students to work on the computer.

Professional Development Support
- *How to Manage Instruction in the Block* This teaching resource provides management and activity suggestions.

MEDIA AND TECHNOLOGY

For the Student
- *Writing and Grammar* Interactive Text, Ch. 20
- *On-line Exercise Bank,* Sections 20.1–2

For the Teacher
- Teacher**EXPRESS** CD-ROM

WRITING AND GRAMMAR ON-LINE

Interactive Text (On-line or on CD-ROM)
- Easily navigable instruction with on-line supporting resources
- Self-scoring exercises and diagnostic tests

Companion Web Site PHSchool.com
- On-line Exercise Bank (use Web Code eek-1002)

See the Go On-line! feature, SE p. iii.

LITERATURE CONNECTIONS

Grammar in Literature selections from *Prentice Hall Literature, Penguin Edition,* Grade 10:

from *Antigone,* Sophocles, SE p. 450/🄷308

from *The Tragedy of Julius Caesar,* William Shakespeare, SE p. 474/🄷332

▶ *Lesson Objectives*

1. To recognize and use prepositional phrases as adjective and adverb phrases
2. To recognize and use appositives and appositive phrases
3. To identify and use participles and participial phrases
4. To identify and use gerunds and gerund phrases and understand their functions in sentences
5. To identify and use infinitives and infinitive phrases and understand their functions in sentences
6. To compose increasingly more involved sentences that contain gerunds, participles, and infinitives
7. To distinguish between independent and subordinate clauses
8. To identify and write subordinate clauses as adjective, adverb, and noun clauses
9. To demonstrate control over grammatical elements

Critical Viewing

Analyze Students will point out that the modern glass-and-steel construction creates a sharp contrast with the greatly older surrounding building.

Chapter 20 Phrases and Clauses

Louvre Museum, Paris, France

▲ Critical Viewing
The glass pyramid became part of the Louvre in 1988. What is its effect placed in front of the museum's original buildings? [Analyze]

The preceding chapters have described the simple building blocks of grammar, including the various parts of speech and the basic sentence parts. This chapter will focus on two additional elements—phrases and clauses—that function in specific ways in sentences.

A **phrase** is a group of words, without a subject and verb, that functions in a sentence as one part of speech. A **clause** is a group of words with its own subject and verb. Some clauses can stand by themselves as complete sentences; others can function only as parts of sentences.

Phrases and clauses add important pieces of information to your writing. In a composition about France, for instance, your phrases and clauses might add information about the culture, social groups, politics, and economics of the country.

As you have seen in previous chapters, sentences are a mixture of subjects, verbs, and modifiers that work together to communicate an idea. In this chapter, you will learn how various phrases and clauses can be incorporated into sentences to enrich the quality of your writing.

440 • Phrases and Clauses

☑ **ONGOING ASSESSMENT: Diagnose**

If students miss more than one item in any category, direct them to the relevant pages of the textbook and assign exercises for practice and review.

Phrases and Clauses	Diagnostic Test Items	Teach	Practice	Section Reviews	Chapter Review
Skill Check A					
Prepositional Phrases	A 2, 4–5	pp. 442–444/Ⓗ300–302	Ex. 1–2	Ex. 18	Ex. 46
Appositives	A 1, 3	pp. 445–447/Ⓗ303–305	Ex. 3–4	Ex. 19	Ex. 46
Skill Check B					
Verbals and Verbal Phrases	B 6–10	pp. 449–461/Ⓗ307–319	Ex. 5–17	Ex. 20–24	Ex. 47–48

Diagnostic Test

Directions: Write all answers on a separate sheet of paper.

Skill Check A. List the prepositional phrases, appositives, and appositive phrases in the following sentences, and label each. For each item that you list, identify the word it modifies or renames.

1. The Eiffel Tower, France's most recognizable structure, is a Paris landmark.
2. The tower was built for the Paris World's Fair of 1889.
3. Alexandre Gustave Eiffel, an engineer, was the tower's designer.
4. The tower is made of wrought iron and exceeds 984 feet in height.
5. The Eiffel Tower attracts thousands of visitors each year.

Skill Check B. Identify and label the infinitive phrase, gerund phrase, or participial phrase in each sentence. Identify the word modified by each participial phrase, and identify the function of each gerund and infinitive phrase.

6. Fontainebleau is a large chateau located southeast of Paris.
7. Constructing the chateau was the idea of King Francis I.
8. Many well-known artists were hired to decorate the ornate interior of the building.
9. Fontainebleau was looted during the French Revolution, but Napoleon managed to restore the palace to its former glory.
10. The republican government, assuming control of the chateau in 1871, made it a national monument.

Skill Check C. Write the subordinate clause in each sentence, and then tell whether it is an adjective, an adverb, or a noun clause. If a clause is elliptical, write the missing word or words.

11. Versailles is more famous than any other palace in Europe.
12. The enormous building, which has 1,300 rooms, was constructed on the site of a small hunting lodge.
13. Although more than 30,000 craftsmen labored on the palace, it still took longer than forty years to complete.
14. King Louis XIV, who ruled France for much of the seventeenth century, moved the royal court to Versailles in 1682.
15. Whoever visits the palace will be overwhelmed by the sheer size and beauty of the building.

Skill Check D. 16–20 For each adjective and adverb clause in Skill Check C, identify the word it modifies. Tell how each noun clause functions in its sentence.

Each item in the Diagnostic Test corresponds to a specific section in the phrases and clauses chapter. This will enable you to tailor instruction to the particular needs of your students. See "Ongoing Assessment: Diagnose" below for further details.

Skill Check A

1. France's most recognizable structure-appositive phrase-*Eiffel Tower*
2. for the Paris World's Fair-prepositional phrase-*was built;* of 1889-prepositional phrase-*Paris World's Fair*
3. an engineer-appositive-*Alexandre Gustave Eiffel*
4. of wrought iron-prepositional phrase-*made;* in height-prepositional phrase-*feet*
5. of visitors-prepositional phrase-*thousands*

Skill Check B

6. located southeast of Paris-participial phrase-*chateau*
7. Constructing the chateau-gerund phrase-subject
8. to decorate the ornate interior of the building-infinitive phrase-adverb modifying *hired*
9. to restore the palace to its former glory-infinitive phrase-noun as direct object of *managed*
10. assuming control of the chateau in 1871-participial phrase-*government*

Skill Check C

11. than any other palace in Europe-elliptical adverb clause-*is famous*
12. which has 1,300 rooms-adjective clause
13. Although more than 30,000 craftsmen labored on the palace-adverb clause
14. who ruled France for much of the seventeenth century-adjective clause
15. Whoever visits the palace-noun clause

Skill Check D

16. *famous*
17. *building*
18. *took*
19. *King Louis XIV*
20. subject

✓ ONGOING ASSESSMENT: Diagnose *continued*

Phrases and Clauses	Diagnostic Test Items	Teach	Practice	Section Reviews	Chapter Review
Skill Check C					
Identifying Adjective Clauses	C 12, 14	pp. 464–469/ 322–327	Ex. 28–31	Ex. 38–39, 41	Ex. 49–50
Identifying Adverb Clauses	C 11, 13	pp. 470–472/ 328–330	Ex. 32–35	Ex. 42	Ex. 49–50
Identifying Noun Clauses	C 15	pp. 474–476/ 332–334	Ex. 36–37	Ex. 40	Ex. 49–50
Cumulative Reviews and Applications				Ex. 25–27, 43–45	Ex. 51–52

PREPARE and ENGAGE

Interest GRABBER Have students participate in a pantomime in which they must guess the directions or locations you indicate by using prepositional phrases only. Write PREPOSITIONAL PHRASE on the chalkboard. To begin the pantomime, walk toward the door and look to students to supply phrases. Some may say "You're walking over to the door!" Point emphatically to the word PHRASE on the chalkboard until students respond with "to the door." Write this on the board. Next, lay a book on the floor and when students say "on the floor," write this on the chalkboard. Gather as many examples as are needed.

Activate Prior Knowledge

Review prepositions and objects of prepositions. Then, challenge students to write a description of any object they see around them, using phrases beginning with prepositions. Example:

> A poster _of England_ hangs _on the wall_.

Have students write their descriptions on the chalkboard and underline the phrases that begin with prepositions. Have them identify the parts of speech of the words described and point out why each phrase functions as an adjective or adverb.

TEACH

Step-by-Step Teaching Guide

Adjective Phrases

1. Ask students to recall common prepositions and remind them that these words initiate prepositional phrases.

2. Write a prepositional phrase on the chalkboard (_over the house_) and ask students to identify the preposition and its object.

3. Use the chart, and then point out the questions underneath it answered by adjective phrases.

4. Use the top of the right page to demonstrate adjective phrases at work in sentences. Have students explain what the arrows mean.

Section 20.1 Phrases

There are several kinds of _phrases_, among them prepositional phrases, appositive phrases, participial phrases, gerund phrases, and infinitive phrases. In this section, you will learn how phrases can be used to add meaning and variety to your sentences.

Prepositional Phrases

A **prepositional phrase** is a group of words made up of a preposition and a noun or pronoun, called the object of the preposition. _Over their heads, until dark,_ and _after the baseball game_ are all examples of prepositional phrases. Sometimes, a single prepositional phrase may have two or more objects joined by a conjunction. _Between the window and the wall_ and _with the wind and freezing rain_ are examples of prepositions followed by compound objects. (See Chapter 18 to review prepositions.)

In this section, you will learn how prepositional phrases modify other words by functioning either as adjectives or as adverbs within sentences.

Adjective Phrases

A prepositional phrase that acts as an adjective is called an _adjective phrase._

> **KEY CONCEPT** An **adjective phrase** is a prepositional phrase that modifies a noun or pronoun by telling _what kind_ or _which one_. ■

The following chart contrasts adjectives with adjective phrases.

Adjectives	Adjective Phrases
A _beautiful_ French painting hung in the palace.	A French painting _of great beauty_ hung in the palace.
Mary took a _boxed_ lunch.	Mary took lunch _in a box_.

A prepositional phrase that answers the question _What kind?_ or _Which one?_ will be an adjective phrase. In the first sentence on the right in the chart, for example, the question _What kind of painting?_ is answered by _of great beauty._

Adjective phrases usually modify nouns functioning as subjects, direct objects, indirect objects, or predicate nominatives.

442 • Phrases and Clauses

Theme: France

In this section, you will learn to use prepositional, appositive, and verbal phrases. The examples and exercises in this section are about France.

Cross-Curricular Connection: Social Studies

Learn More

To review basic information about prepositions, turn to Chapter 18.

⏱ TIME AND RESOURCE MANAGER

Resources

Print: _Grammar Exercise Workbook,_ pp. 57–74; _Grammar Exercises Answers on Transparencies,_ Ch. 20

Technology: _Writing and Grammar_ Interactive Text, Section 20.1; _On-Line Exercise Bank,_ Section 20.1

Using the Full Student Edition	Using the Handbook🄷
• Work through all key concepts, pp. 442–461.	• Work through all key concepts, pp. 300–319.
• Assign and review Exercises 1–17.	• Assign and review Exercises 1–17.
• Read and discuss Grammar in Literature, p. 450.	• Read and discuss Grammar in Literature, p. 308.

MODIFYING A SUBJECT: The mansion *across the road* has been abandoned.

MODIFYING A
DIRECT OBJECT: Let's take a picture *of the Eiffel Tower.*

MODIFYING AN
INDIRECT OBJECT: They gave the students *on the bus* a tour.

MODIFYING A
PREDICATE NOMINATIVE: France is a country *with many charms.*

A sentence may often have a series of two or more adjective phrases. When this happens, each succeeding phrase may modify the object of the preceding phrase.

EXAMPLE: We bought tickets *for the trip to Paris.*

The adjective phrase *for the trip* describes *tickets.* The adjective phrase *to Paris* modifies *trip.*
More than one adjective phrase may describe the same noun.

EXAMPLE: The painting *of the palace in the museum* is old.

▶ **Exercise 1** Identifying Adjective Phrases Write each sentence, underlining the adjective phrase or phrases in each. Then, draw an arrow from each phrase to the word it modifies.

EXAMPLE: France has miles of coastline.

ANSWER: France has miles <u>of coastline</u>.

1. France is the second-largest country in Europe.
2. The capital city of France is Paris.
3. Lyon, Toulouse, and Marseille are three other major cities in France.
4. The nickname of France is *L'Hexagone.*
5. The country borders two major bodies of water: the Atlantic Ocean and the Mediterranean Sea.
6. The Pyrenees Mountains along the southern border separate France and Spain.
7. One border country to the east of France is Switzerland.
8. North of France is the tiny principality of Luxembourg.
9. France controls a group of islands in the Pacific.
10. A rough estimate of the country's population is sixty million.

▶ **More Practice**

Grammar Exercise Workbook
• pp. 57–58
On-line Exercise Bank
• Section 20.1
Go on-line:
PHSchool.com
Enter Web Code:
eek-1002

Interactive Textbook

Get instant feedback! Exercise 1 is available on-line or on CD-ROM.

Phrases • 443

Adverb Phrases

1. Read the key concept aloud and point out that adverb phrases act just as single-word adverbs do: they modify verbs, adjectives, and other adverbs.

2. Use the chart to demonstrate how adverb words and phrases answer similar questions. In the first pair, ask students which question the italicized words answer (how?), and then point out that both the single-word adverb as well as the adverb phrase add the same information by answering the same question.

3. Review the questions answered by adverbs, and then direct students to the examples at the bottom of the page.

4. Have a student read each example aloud and explain the purpose of the arrow. (It points to the word that the phrase modifies.)

5. Be sure students recognize that an adverb phrase may sometimes appear *before* the word it modifies.

6. Use the final example on the preceding page to illustrate how two adverb phrases may modify the same word.

Language Highlight

Many clichés in the English language are recognizable prepositional phrases. Such phrases as *on the spot, in hot water,* and *out of the blue* are familiar examples. The origins of these expressions can be interesting. The phrase *on the spot* is used to describe people under pressure to explain their actions or to perform some activity that will meet expectations. Its original meaning came from early seagoing pirates. It meant "to be marked for execution." The "spot" was a black mark on a card which pirates gave to traitors to show that they were to be executed. By the early twentieth century, its meaning was less severe. Have students find the origins of other prepositional phrases used as clichés.

Adverb Phrases

A prepositional phrase can also act as an adverb.

KEY CONCEPT An **adverb phrase** is a prepositional phrase that modifies a verb, an adjective, or an adverb by pointing out *where, when, in what way,* or *to what extent.* ∎

The following chart shows that adverb phrases function in a similar way to single-word adverbs.

Adverbs	Adverb Phrases
She ran *swiftly*.	She ran *with speed*.
They were happy *there*.	They were happy *at the French cafe*.

If a prepositional phrase is an adverb phrase, it will answer the question: *Where? When? In what way?* or *To what extent?* In the first example on the right in the chart, the question *Ran in what way?* is answered by *with speed*, an adverb phrase.

Unlike an adjective phrase, which almost always follows the word it modifies, an adverb phrase may either follow the word it modifies or be located elsewhere in the sentence.

EXAMPLES: An alpine village vanished *during the avalanche*.

During the avalanche, an alpine village vanished.

Like single-word adverbs, adverb phrases can modify verbs, adjectives, or adverbs.

MODIFYING
A VERB: The runner dashed *past the spectators*.

MODIFYING
AN ADJECTIVE: The Loire Valley is rich *in historical buildings*.

MODIFYING
AN ADVERB: The French exchange student arrived late *for class*.

Like adjective phrases, two or more adverb phrases may modify the same word.

EXAMPLE: *In the afternoon*, we walked *to Notre Dame*.

Speaking and Listening Tip

Many of the examples and exercises in this section contain names of French places and people, which may be unfamiliar or seem difficult to pronounce. Get together with a classmate who is studying French, and let him or her help you practice French pronunciation.

▶ **Exercise 2** Identifying Adverb Phrases Write each sentence, underlining the adverb phrase or phrases in each. Then, draw an arrow from each phrase to the word it modifies.

EXAMPLE: France is situated above the Iberian Peninsula.

ANSWER: France is situated <u>above the Iberian Peninsula</u>.

1. France's geography is marked by various natural formations.
2. Several large rivers cut across the country.
3. Without a doubt, the Seine River is the most important French river.
4. It flows through Paris and empties into the English Channel.
5. The Rhone, Loire, and Rhine rivers are also important to France.
6. Two impressive mountain ranges exist within French territory.
7. The French Alps rise majestically near France's southwestern boundary.
8. Europe's second-highest peak is located within this mountain range.
9. Cable cars carry skiers high up the mountain.
10. The Pyrenees Mountains stretch along the Spanish border.

▶ **More Practice**

Grammar Exercise Workbook
• pp. 57–58
On-line Exercise Bank
• Section 20.1
Go on-line:
PHSchool.com
Enter Web Code:
eek-1002

▲ Critical Viewing In what ways might a winter-sports enthusiast react to skiing on Mont Blanc, the highest peak in the Alps? Use a prepositional phrase in your answer. [Infer]

Appositives and Appositive Phrases

The term *appositive* comes from a Latin verb meaning "to put near or next to."

Appositives

Using **appositives** in your writing is an easy way to give additional meaning to nouns and pronouns.

▶ **KEY CONCEPT** An **appositive** is a noun or pronoun placed next to another noun or pronoun to identify, rename, or explain it. ■

As the next chart shows, appositives generally follow immediately after the words they identify, rename, or explain.

Phrases • 445

☑ **ONGOING ASSESSMENT: Monitor and Reinforce**

If students miss more than two items in Exercise 1 or 2, refer them to the following for additional practice.

In the Textbook	Print Resources	Technology
Section Review, Ex. 18, Section 20.1	*Grammar Exercise Workbook,* pp. 57–58	*On-Line Exercise Bank,* Section 20.1

Step-by-Step Teaching Guide

Appositive Phrases

1. Explain that this key concept and the one preceding it both define appositives; appositives can be single words or phrases.

2. On the next page are the chart and the examples that demonstrate appositive phrases. Work through these in sequence.

3. First, use the chart to explain that appositive phrases may contain several words. Ask students to locate the simple appositive in each, and then to identify the words that describe it.

4. Then, remind students that an appositive can rename a noun that functions as any of the basic sentence parts.

5. For each example, have students identify all basic sentence parts.

6. Finally, use the last two examples to show students how to use appositives to combine sentences.

Customize for
Linguistic Learners

Ask students to rewrite the first two sentences in Section Review Exercise 18 to create a new sentence with an appositive phrase. For example, the sentences could be combined to read "Charlemagne, the first true ruler of France, was an influential figure in French history." Tell them to try combining any other two sentences to form one sentence with an appositive phrase. Check their work as they write to ensure that both sentence structure and meaning are intact. Finally, have students read their sentence combinations to the class and have others listen for and identify the appositives formed.

20.1

> ### APPOSITIVES
>
> Some French villagers, the *old-timers*, prefer to travel the dirt roads.
>
> Her greatest attribute, *charm*, was not enough.

Notice that commas are used because these appositives are *nonessential*. In other words, they could be omitted from the sentences without altering the basic meanings of the sentences.

Some appositives, however, are not set off by any punctuation because they are *essential* to the meaning of the sentence.

EXAMPLE: The artist *Monet* was a great French painter.

Note About Terms: Sometimes, the terms *nonrestrictive* and *restrictive* are used in place of *nonessential* and *essential*.

> **Exercise 3** Identifying Appositives Write the appositive in each sentence. Then, write the word each appositive renames.

EXAMPLE: Jacques, our guide, told us about French people.
ANSWER: guide (Jacques)

1. Sixty million people, France's population, are dispersed throughout the country.
2. Many rural people, farmers, are moving to urban areas.
3. Today, nearly one sixth of the population is located near Paris, the capital.
4. The most mountainous area, the southeast, has experienced a large decline in population in recent years.
5. France has a lower population growth rate than its neighbor Germany.

Appositive Phrases

When an appositive is accompanied by its own modifiers, it is called an *appositive phrase*.

> **KEY CONCEPT** An **appositive phrase** is a noun or pronoun with modifiers, placed next to a noun or pronoun to add information and details. ■

The modifiers within an appositive phrase can be adjectives, adjective phrases, or other groups of words functioning as adjectives.

> **More Practice**

Grammar Exercise Workbook
• pp. 59–60
On-line Exercise Bank
• Section 20.1
  Go on-line:
  PHSchool.com
  Enter Web Code:
  eek-1002

Get instant feedback! Exercise 3 is available on-line or on CD-ROM.

446 • Phrases and Clauses

APPOSITIVE PHRASES

France was invaded during World War II, *the most terrible war the world has known.*

Amethyst, *a purple birthstone*, is the gem for February.

Fred explained numismatics, *the hobby of coin collecting.*

Appositives and appositive phrases may follow nouns or pronouns used in almost any role within a sentence.

WITH A SUBJECT:	Ernest Hemingway, *a famous author*, wrote in a terse style.
WITH A DIRECT OBJECT:	The chef prepared *escargots, a snail dish.*
WITH AN INDIRECT OBJECT:	I brought my brother, *a boy of six*, a souvenir from the Louvre.
WITH AN OBJECTIVE COMPLEMENT:	I chose the color purple, *an unusual color for a house.*
WITH A PREDICATE NOMINATIVE:	My favorite food was cassoulet, *a hearty stew.*
WITH THE OBJECT OF A PREPOSITION:	Store the onions in the cellar, *a cool, dry place.*

Appositives and appositive phrases may also be compound.

EXAMPLE:	Armand, both *his schoolmate* and *his confidant*, was always welcome in the house.

When appositives or appositive phrases are used to combine sentences, they help to eliminate unnecessary words. The following examples show how two sentences may be joined.

TWO SENTENCES:	Marseille is located on the Mediterranean Sea. The city is an important French seaport.
COMBINED:	Marseille, *an important French seaport*, is located on the Mediterranean Sea.

⚙ Grammar and Style Tip

One good way to streamline your writing is to combine sentences using an appositive phrase. For instance, in the second example, the sentence could have started as two choppy sentences: The chef prepared *escargots. Escargots* is a snail dish.

Integrating Speaking and Listening Skills

Appositives Have students write the numbers one through five on their papers, and listen closely as you read aloud several sentences containing essential and nonessential appositives. Ask students to state whether the appositive in each sentence is essential or nonessential. Then, write the five sentences on the board. Have students check their answers by looking for appositive phrases set off with commas and those not set off by any punctuation. Explain to students that certain spoken clues (pauses) and written clues (the noun renamed by the appositive) will help them decide whether a phrase is essential or nonessential.

✓ ONGOING ASSESSMENT: Monitor and Reinforce

If students miss more than one item in Exercise 3, refer them to the following for additional practice.

In the Textbook	Print Resources	Technology
Section Review, Ex. 19, Section 20.1	*Grammar Exercise Workbook,* pp. 59–60	*On-Line Exercise Bank,* Section 20.1

⏱ TIME SAVERS!

Answers on Transparencies Use the *Grammar Exercises Answers on Transparencies* for Chapter 20 to facilitate correction by students.

On-Line Exercise Bank Have students complete the exercises on computer. The Auto Check feature will grade their work for you!

Exercise 4

Answers may vary. Examples are given.

1. France's educational system, subsidized by the government, is one of Europe's best.
2. Children are required to attend school until they reach early adulthood, generally sixteen years of age.
3. *Écoles*, French primary schools, educate children six through ten years old.
4. *Lycées*, French secondary schools, are attended by students between the ages of eleven and eighteen.
5. Jean-Luc, a tenth grader, attends a religious school, as do nearly one fifth of the students in France.
6. A large number of French students take the *baccalauréat*, a difficult college-entrance exam.
7. After passing the test, students are eligible to attend college for free for one year, their freshman year.
8. Students are given licenses, degrees similar to a bachelor's degree, after three years of study.
9. Some students choose alternative post-high-school paths, perhaps technical schools or trade schools.
10. France also offers its most ambitious students, mainly business, science, and engineering majors, the option to attend specialized institutions called *grandes écoles*.

Critical Viewing

Relate Answers will vary, but should contain correctly used and punctuated appositive phrases.

20.1

Exercise 4 Combining Sentences With Appositive Phrases
Combine each pair of sentences by turning one of them into an appositive phrase.

EXAMPLE: Marie is a Sorbonne student. She is well educated.
ANSWER: Marie, a Sorbonne student, is well educated.

1. France's educational system is one of Europe's best. It is subsidized by the government.
2. Children are required to attend school until they reach early adulthood. That is generally sixteen years of age.
3. *Écoles* educate children six through ten years old. *Écoles* are French primary schools.
4. *Lycées* are attended by students between the ages of eleven and eighteen. *Lycées* are French secondary schools.
5. Jean-Luc attends a religious school, as do nearly one fifth of the students in France. Jean-Luc is a tenth grader.
6. A large number of French students take the *baccalauréat*. It is a difficult college-entrance exam.
7. After passing the test, students are eligible to attend college for free for one year. The year is their freshman year.
8. Students are given licenses after three years of study. The licenses are degrees similar to a bachelor's degree.
9. Some students choose alternative post-high-school paths. The paths may be technical schools or trade schools.
10. France also offers its most ambitious students the option to attend specialized institutions called *grandes écoles*. Those students are mainly business, science, and engineering majors.

The Panthéon, Paris

◀ **Critical Viewing**
The Panthéon contains the remains of illustrious French citizens—among them, writer Victor Hugo and scientist Marie Curie. How might this building serve to inspire the university students who pass by each day? Answer using an appositive phrase. **[Relate]**

✓ ONGOING ASSESSMENT: Monitor and Reinforce

If students miss more than two items in Exercise 4, refer them to the following for additional practice.

In the Textbook	Print Resources	Technology
Section Review, Exercise 19, Section 20.1	*Grammar Exercise Workbook*, pp. 59–60	*On-Line Exercise Bank,* Section 20.1

Verbal Phrases

When a verb is used as a noun, an adjective, or an adverb, it is called a *verbal*. Although a verbal does not function as a verb, it still retains two characteristics of verbs: It can be modified in different ways, and it can have one or more complements. A verbal with modifiers or a complement is a *verbal phrase*.

Participles

Many of the adjectives you use are actually verbals known as *participles*.

> **KEY CONCEPT** A **participle** is a form of a verb that can act as an adjective. ∎

The most common kinds of participles are *present participles* and *past participles*. These two kinds of participles can be distinguished from each other by their endings. Present participles end in *-ing* (*frightening, entertaining*). Past participles usually end in *-ed* (*frightened, entertained*), but many have irregular endings such as *-t* or *-en* (*burst, written*).

The following chart shows participles modifying nouns within sentences.

Present Participles	Past Participles
Limping, the hiker favored his *aching* ankle.	*Confused*, Nan returned to her *interrupted* work.

Notice that participles answer the adjective question *What kind?* or *Which one?* about the nouns or pronouns that they modify.

EXAMPLES: Irma's *shining* eyes betrayed her excitement.
What kind of eyes? *Answer: shining* eyes
The *shattered* window needs replacement.
Which window? Answer: the *shattered* window

Note About *Being* and *Having*: Participles also have a present perfect form.

EXAMPLE: *Having decided*, Madeleine acted quickly.
Being greeted by his friends, François shakes hands all around.

⟳ Learn More

For information about irregular verb endings, turn to Chapter 22.

Step-by-Step Teaching Guide

Participles

1. Write any *-ing* word on the board (*singing*) and ask a student to use it as the verb in a sentence (The bird was singing happily.) Then ask another student to use the same *-ing* word to describe another word (*the singing bird*). Explain the difference between the *verb* in a sentence (it expresses the action of the subject) and a *verbal* (it describes a noun or pronoun).

2. Use the examples in the chart to illustrate the difference between a *verb* and a *verbal* (participle). Point out that the first example has a verb (*favored*) and that the participles *Limping* and *aching* describe nouns in the sentence.

3. Use the other example to explain that past participles also can act as verbs or verbals. Explain that *returned* is the verb in the sentence and *Confused* and *interrupted* describe nouns.

4. Finally, have students read the examples beneath the chart and identify all verbs and participles.

⏱ TIME SAVERS!

▣ Answers on Transparencies
Use the *Grammar Exercises Answers on Transparencies* for Chapter 20 to facilitate correction by students.

▢ On-Line Exercise Bank
Have students complete the exercises on computer. The Auto Check feature will grade their work for you!

Grammar in Literature

1. Ask students whether highlighted words are used as verbs or verbals and how they function in their sentences (as verbals: they are adjectives modifying nouns).

2. If students don't easily recognize these participles as adjectives, have them identify the verb in each of these sentences (*is, go*).

More About the Writer

Born near Athens, the Greek dramatist Sophocles wrote 123 plays, of which only seven still exist. His most famous plays, including *Antigone,* chronicle the lives of Oedipus and his children. He won the prize for tragedy at the Greek dramatic competitions twenty-four times. Sophocles was the first to add a third actor on stage during dramatic performances, an innovation that significantly changed the genre.

Connections With Literature

Sophocles' *Antigone* can be found in *Prentice Hall Literature, Penguin Edition,* Grade 10.

Answer Key

> **Exercise 5**

1. established (past)
2. adopted (past)
3. governing (present)
4. proposed (past)
5. elected (past)

> **Exercise 6**

1. voting
2. Staggered
3. designated
4. taxing
5. armed

20.1

GRAMMAR IN LITERATURE

from Antigone

Sophocles
Translated by Dudley Fitts and Robert Fitzgerald

Notice the highlighted past participles in this selection.

There's nothing in the world so demoralizing as money.
Down go your cities,
Homes *gone*, men *gone*, honest hearts *corrupted*,
Crookedness of all kinds, and all for money!

▶ **Exercise 5** **Identifying Present and Past Participles** Write the participle in each sentence. Then, label it *present* or *past.*
1. The established form of government in France is democracy.
2. The last adopted constitution of France was written in 1958.
3. According to the constitution, the people are represented by two large governing bodies.
4. The 577-member National Assembly is responsible for all proposed legislation.
5. The smaller group of elected officials, the Senate, must either ratify or veto the Assembly's legislation.

▶ **Exercise 6** **Supplying Participles** Complete each sentence by supplying the *present* or *past participle,* as indicated, of each word in parentheses.
1. The ___?___ Public elects a president to a seven-year term. (vote—present)
2. ___?___ elections determine the new members of the Assembly and the Senate. (stagger—past)
3. The ___?___ president must also select a Council of Ministers. (designate—past)
4. The prime minister holds one of the most ___?___ posts in the government. (tax—present)
5. The French president serves as the commander in chief of the country's ___?___ forces. (arm—past)

▶ **More Practice**

Grammar Exercise Workbook
• pp. 61–66
On-line Exercise Bank
• Section 20.1
Go on-line:
PHSchool.com
Enter Web Code:
eek-1002

Get instant feedback! Exercises 5, 6, and 7 are available on-line or on CD-ROM.

Verb or Participle?

It is easy to confuse a participle acting as part of a verb phrase with a participle acting as an adjective because they share the endings -*ing* and -*ed*.

▶ **KEY CONCEPTS** A **verb** shows an action, a condition, or the fact that something exists. A **participle** acting as an adjective modifies a noun or a pronoun. ■

The following chart shows verbs and then participles as adjectives. Notice that as verbs, the words tell what someone or something does or did. The participles, however, describe someone or something.

Verbs	Participles
The dog is *snarling* at the plumber. (What is the dog doing?)	The *snarling* dog attacked the plumber. (*Which* dog?)
The mimes *delighted* their audience. (What did the mimes *do*?).	*Delighted*, the audience applauded. (*What kind* of audience?)

▶ **Exercise 7** **Distinguishing Between Verbs and Participles**
Identify each underlined word as a *verb* or *participle*. If it is a participle, write the word it modifies.

EXAMPLE: The French people have experienced <u>increasing</u> prosperity since the 1940's.

ANSWER: participle (prosperity)

1. Until World War II, France <u>based</u> its economy mainly on agriculture.
2. Today, the country has a very <u>diversified</u> economy.
3. France is a <u>leading</u> industrial power in the world.
4. It is a major producer of <u>advanced</u> electronics and other high-tech devices.
5. The government is <u>playing</u> an important role in the European Union.

▼ Critical Viewing
Use a participle as an adjective in a sentence describing two features of the French countryside depicted in this photograph. **[Describe]**

Phrases • 451

Verb or Participle?

1. Have a student read the key concepts aloud, and then turn this information into questions that test whether a word is a verb or a participle. Write this on the board:

   Does it show action, condition, or existence? (verb)

   Does it modify a noun or a pronoun? (verbal—participle)

2. Explain that the same word can act either as a verb or as a participle. Use the words *snarling* and *delighted* in the chart to illustrate.

3. Supply students with additional present and past participles and have volunteers use each both as verbs and verbals (participles). Use these: *running, dripping, frozen,* and *singing.*

Answer Key

▶ **Exercise 7**

1. verb
2. participle-economy
3. participle-power
4. participle-electronics
5. verb

Critical Viewing

Describe Answers will vary, but answers should contain correctly-used participles.

☑ **ONGOING ASSESSMENT: Monitor and Reinforce**

If students miss more than one item in Exercise 5, 6, or 7, refer them to the following for additional practice.

In the Textbook	Print Resources	Technology
Section Review, Ex. 20, 22, Section 20.1	*Grammar Exercise Workbook,* pp. 61–62	*On-Line Exercise Bank,* Section 20.1

Participial Phrases

1. Have students read the key concept aloud and use it to analyze the three examples beneath it.

2. Point out that the first example is a participle with an adverb, the second a participle with a prepositional phrase acting as an adverb, and the third is a participle with a complement.

3. To help students understand each example, ask them to substitute a prepositional phrase in place of the participial phrase (for the first example: *On our trip*) and then to explain the difference.

4. Use the chart on this page to illustrate nonessential and essential phrases. Remind students of appositives and explain that these function similarly.

5. Finally, use the examples on the right page to illustrate sentence combining.

20.1

Participial Phrases

Participles may be parts of *participial phrases*.

▶ **KEY CONCEPT** A **participial phrase** is a participle modified by an adverb or adverb phrase or accompanied by a complement. The entire phrase acts as an adjective. ■

The following examples show different ways that participles may be expanded into phrases.

EXAMPLES: *Traveling quickly*, we saw much of the French countryside.

The tourist, *confused by the signs*, got lost.

Scanning the French dictionary, Ann found the words for "entrance" and "exit"—*entrée* and *sortie*.

Participial phrases are punctuated according to their use within a sentence. The following chart contrasts nonessential and essential participial phrases. In the sentences on the left, the participial phrases could be removed without altering the basic meaning of the sentence. However, if you remove the participial phrases from the sentences on the right, the meaning of the sentences will not be the same.

Nonessential Phrases	Essential Phrases
There is Craig, *standing by the bus stop.*	The boy *standing by the bus stop* is Craig.
Painted in 1497, the mural is Leonardo's masterpiece.	The mural *painted in 1497* is almost beyond repair.

In the first sentence on the left in the chart, *standing by the bus stop* merely adds information about *Craig*, who has already been identified. In a similar sentence on the right, however, the same phrase is essential for the identification of *boy*, because there could be many different boys in view. In the second sentence on the left, *painted in 1497* is an additional description of *mural*. In the sentence on the right, the phrase is essential. It identifies the mural that is being discussed.

✐ Spelling Tip

Notice that many French words—even some commonly used in English—have accent marks. Watch for accents on words such as *résumé, café,* and *entrée* and on names such as *André* and *Renée.*

🎸 STANDARDIZED TEST PREPARATION WORKSHOP

Grammar and Usage Many standardized tests require students to use their knowledge of essential and nonessential phrases to respond correctly. Use the following example to demonstrate.

Read the sentence below and answer the question.

The desk now standing next to me is the one on which the Declaration of Independence was signed.

What revision, if any, is needed to this sentence?

A Place a comma after *desk.*

B Place a comma after *me.*

C Place a comma after *desk* and *me.*

D No correction is needed.

The correct answer is **D**. The phrase *now standing next to me* identifies which *desk* the speaker, possibly a tour guide, is discussing; it is an essential participial phrase that should not be set apart from the rest of the sentence.

▶ **KEY CONCEPT** Participial phrases can often be used to combine information from two sentences into one. ■

TWO
SENTENCES: We were exhausted by the climb up Mont Blanc.
              We rested by the side of the trail.

COMBINED: Exhausted by the climb up Mont Blanc, we rested by the side of the trail.

▶ **Exercise 8** Recognizing Participial Phrases Write the participial phrase in each sentence. Then, write the word the participial phrase modifies. Finally, label the phrase *essential* or *nonessential*.
1. Pioneering in different fields, the French have been leaders in the scientific world.
2. The French government, having supported scientific research for more than 350 years, has made many advances possible.
3. In 1635, the Royal Garden became one of the first scientific research centers sponsored by a government.
4. King Louis XIV, known as the Sun King, founded the Royal Academy of Science.
5. Revered as the father of modern chemistry, Antoine Lavoisier gave much to science.

▶ **Exercise 9** Combining
Sentences With Participial Phrases
Combine each pair of sentences by turning one into a participial phrase.
1. Marie Curie helped found the field of nuclear chemistry. She did so studying radioactive elements.
2. French researchers have also achieved numerous medical breakthroughs. They have been striving to improve the quality of life.
3. During the eighteenth century, Marie François Xavier Bichat conducted research. It focused on the study of human anatomy.
4. Another French researcher, Louis Pasteur, invented several vaccines. He invented them for a world plagued by disease.
5. Pasteur devoted his life to scientific study. He made many other crucial discoveries.

▶ **More Practice**
Grammar Exercise Workbook
• pp. 61–66
On-line Exercise Bank
• Section 20.1
Go on-line:
PHSchool.com
Enter Web Code:
eek-1002

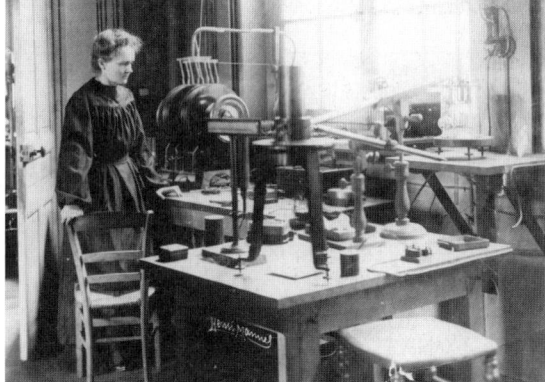

▲ **Critical Viewing**
Use a participial phrase in a sentence comparing one aspect of Marie Curie's laboratory with an aspect of a modern one.
[**Compare and Contrast**]

Phrases • 453

☑ **ONGOING ASSESSMENT: Monitor and Reinforce**

If students miss more than one item in Exercise 8 or 9, refer them to the following for additional practice.

In the Textbook	Print Resources	Technology
Section Review, Ex. 20, Section 20.1	*Grammar Exercise Workbook,* pp. 63–64	*On-Line Exercise Bank,* Section 20.1

Gerunds and Gerund Phrases

1. Explain that gerunds always are *-ing* forms and that they can occupy any noun position in a sentence.

2. Use the chart on this page to illustrate. First, have students read the functions that gerunds can perform (subject, direct object, etc.), and then analyze each example sentence.

Customize for
Less Advanced Students

Gerunds following forms of the verb *to be* can be confusing for students. Put these sentences on the board:

My favorite uncle is fishing.

My favorite sport is fishing.

Point out that these sentences seem superficially the same. What makes them different is their sense. In the first sentence, a person is performing the action of fishing. *Fishing* is part of the verb. In the second sentence, it is nonsensical to imagine that a sport is fishing. Therefore, the action of fishing is not being performed. Instead, it is used as an idea, as a gerund serving as a predicate nominative identifying which sport is the speaker's favorite. Encourage students to apply this thought process when looking for gerunds in sentences with *-ing* words following forms of the verb *to be*.

Critical Viewing

Relate Answers will vary, but descriptions should include a gerund or gerund phrase.

Answer Key

Exercise 10

1. training (object of a preposition)
2. learning (object of a preposition)
3. Jogging, running, walking (subjects)
4. climbing, hiking (appositives)
5. Skiing (subject)

Gerunds

Many nouns ending in *-ing* are actually verbals known as *gerunds*. Gerunds are not difficult to recognize once you realize that they always end in *-ing* and always function as nouns.

▶ **KEY CONCEPT** A **gerund** is a form of a verb that acts as a noun. ■

The following examples show some of the ways gerunds may be used as nouns.

GERUNDS	
Subject	*Eating* is my favorite pastime in France.
Direct Object	The French people make *visiting* a pleasure.
Indirect Object	Mr. Mendoza's lecture gave *traveling* a new dimension.
Predicate Nominative	One Frenchman's favorite activity is *debating*.
Object of a Preposition	Their well-behaved dog showed signs of careful *training*.
Appositive	Brady's profession, *advertising*, is very competitive.

▶ **Exercise 10** Identifying Gerunds Write the gerund in each sentence. Label each one *subject, direct object, indirect object, predicate nominative, object of a preposition,* or *appositive*.

EXAMPLE: She gave fencing her best effort.
ANSWER: fencing (indirect object)

1. Nearly one third of the French population is involved in some type of athletic training.
2. This is remarkable, because the schools focus mainly on learning.
3. Jogging, running, and walking are practiced by hundreds of thousands of French people every day.
4. Rugged individual sports—climbing and hiking—are popular all over France.
5. Skiing is another widely enjoyed individual sport.

▼ **Critical Viewing** Describe a structure in the United States that is as recognizable as the Eiffel Tower to people around the world. Use a gerund in your response. **[Relate]**

Verb, Participle, or Gerund?

Words ending in -*ing* may be either parts of verb phrases, participles acting as adjectives, or gerunds.

> **KEY CONCEPT** Words ending in -*ing* that act as nouns are gerunds. They do not have helping verbs like verbs ending in -*ing*, nor do they act as adjectives, as participles do. ■

The following chart shows the same word functioning in sentences as a verb, a participle, and a gerund.

Verb	Participle	Gerund
Kevin is yawning at his desk.	The yawning boy was very tired.	Yawning is contagious.

> **Exercise 11** Distinguishing Between Verbs, Participles, and Gerunds Identify each underlined word as a *verb*, *participle*, or *gerund*.

EXAMPLE: The French have been <u>increasing</u> the national literacy rate for the last fifty years.

ANSWER: verb

1. <u>Reading</u> is a popular pastime throughout France.
2. <u>Reading</u> newspapers and magazines, the commuter waited for the metro.
3. French people are <u>reading</u> more periodicals than ever.
4. Articles written in both English and French are strong <u>selling</u> points for many magazines.
5. <u>Selling</u> magazines is a difficult task in the competitive French market.
6. One of France's oldest newsmagazines, *L'Express* is <u>selling</u> well after many years of publication.
7. The <u>leading</u> daily newspapers include *Le Monde, Le Parisien,* and *Le Figaro.*
8. *The New York Times* and *The Washington Post* are <u>leading</u> the way for other English-language papers in France.
9. <u>Publishing</u> books is an ever-expanding industry in France.
10. Ironically, authors are <u>publishing</u> more comic books today than many other types of books.

> **More Practice**
>
> Grammar Exercise Workbook
> • pp. 67–68
> On-line Exercise Bank
> • Section 20.1
> Go on-line:
> PHSchool.com
> Enter Web Code:
> eek-1002

Interactive Textbook

Get instant feedback! Exercises 10 and 11 are available on-line or on CD-ROM.

Verb, Participle, or Gerund?

1. Remind students that the past participle form of a verb (the form usually ending -*ed, -n,* or -*t*) can act as an adjective but point out that the present participle (the form ending -*ing*) can act as an adjective or a noun.

2. Review the definitions of verbals (participle = adjective; gerund = noun).

3. Use the chart to illustrate how one verb form (*yawning*) can be used in three ways: as a verb, participle, or gerund. Give students another present participle (*shivering*) and ask students to use it all three ways.

Customize for ESL Students

ESL students may assume that "Words ending in -*ing* . . ." at the top of the page means *all* words that they read or hear ending that way. Be certain that they understand that this means only words ending with the suffix, the word part, of -*ing*. Words such as *bring, sing, wing* and so forth are not in that category. The -*ing* ending must be part of a word that makes sense when -*ing* is removed.

Answer Key

> **Exercise 11**

1. gerund
2. participle
3. verb
4. participle
5. gerund
6. verb
7. participle
8. verb
9. gerund
10. verb

> ☑ **ONGOING ASSESSMENT: Monitor and Reinforce**
>
> If students have difficulty with Exercise 10 or 11, refer them to the following for additional practice.

In the Textbook	Print Resources	Technology
Section Review, Ex. 21–22, Section 20.1	*Grammar Exercise Workbook,* pp. 67–68	*On-Line Exercise Bank,* Section 20.1

Gerund Phrases

1. After you read the key concept, ask students to identify the kinds of modifiers and complements that may help create gerund phrases. (These are listed in the chart.)

2. Then, use each example in the chart to analyze how gerund phrases are formed.

3. If necessary for practice, reuse the examples in the chart on the preceding left page by having students suggest modifiers and complements to add to each gerund. (Examples: Eating green grapes, visiting their country.)

4. Point out that pronouns can show ownership of gerunds just like any other nouns. Use the example beneath the chart to illustrate.

Answer Key

Exercise 12

1. Making movies (subject)
2. producing roughly 150 movies (direct object)
3. making more movies than France (object of a preposition)
4. Viewing American movies—promoting their own films (subject—direct object)
5. the showing of American films (direct object)

20.1

Gerund Phrases

Like participles, gerunds may be joined by other words to make *gerund phrases.*

▶ **KEY CONCEPT** A **gerund phrase** is a gerund with modifiers or a complement, all acting together as a noun. ■

The following examples show just a few of the ways that gerunds may be expanded into gerund phrases.

GERUND PHRASES	
With adjectives:	*His constant, angry ranting* made Napoleon difficult to tolerate.
With an adjective phrase:	*Arguing about grades* will get you nowhere.
With an adverb:	*Answering quickly* is not always a good idea.
With a prepositional phrase:	Many places in France prohibit *walking on the grass.*
With an object of a preposition:	Pierre was incapable of *reciting the poem.*
With indirect and direct objects:	The French teacher tried *giving her students praise.*

Note About *Gerunds* and *Possessive Pronouns:* Always use the possessive form of a personal pronoun in front of a gerund.

INCORRECT: We never listen to *him boasting.*

CORRECT: We never listen to *his boasting.*

▶ **Exercise 12** Identifying Gerund Phrases Write the gerund phrase or phrases in each sentence. Label each one *subject, direct object,* or *object of a preposition.*
1. Making movies is a big business in France.
2. An average year for the French film industry entails producing roughly 150 movies.
3. Only India and the United States are known for making more movies than France.
4. Viewing American movies is a popular French pastime, but the French try promoting their own films.
5. Government restrictions limit the showing of American films to one third of the nation's theaters.

Get instant feedback! Exercises 12 and 13 are available on-line or on CD-ROM.

▶ **More Practice**

Grammar Exercise Workbook
• pp. 60–70
On-line Exercise Bank
• Section 20.1
Go on-line:
PHSchool.com
Enter Web Code:
eek-1002

◀ **Critical Viewing**
What might be some of the reasons for the popularity of Notre Dame, the Gothic cathedral in the middle of Paris? Use at least one gerund phrase in your response. **[Speculate]**

▶ **Exercise 13** **Revising to Form Gerund Phrases** Revise each sentence, changing the underlined words to a gerund phrase. You may have to add or change words to keep the meaning of the sentence.

EXAMPLE: Construction of *Notre Dame de Paris* began in 1163 <u>when the cornerstone was laid</u>.

ANSWER: Construction of *Notre Dame de Paris* began in 1163 with the laying of the cornerstone.

1. <u>To complete the cathedral</u> was no small task
2. <u>To gaze at Gothic architecture</u> makes our thoughts ascend.
3. Gothic architects and artisans worked <u>to craft</u> the rose windows of stained glass.
4. <u>To build it</u> took teams of workers eighty-seven years.
5. No expense was spared <u>to erect</u> a church that would reflect the prestige of Paris.

Phrases • 457

Integrating Workplace Skills

Phrases: Professional writers of dialogue sometimes try to simulate familiar speech patterns by writing incomplete sentences. Read this aloud and ask students to identify the kinds of phrases used:

Lisa: *Where did the accident happen?*

Joy: *At the corner of Main and Oak.* (two prepositional phrases)

Lisa : *About your car?* (prepositional phrase)

Joy: *Smashed beyond recognition!* (participial phrase)

Lisa: *What's your next move?*

Joy: *Suing for damages.* (gerund phrase)

For practice, have students create original dialogue, identifying the kinds of phrases they use.

Answer Key

▶ **Exercise 13**

1. Completing the cathedral was no small task.
2. Gazing at Gothic architecture makes our thoughts ascend.
3. Gothic architects and artisans worked crafting the rose windows of stained glass.
4. Building Notre Dame took teams of workers eighty-seven years.
5. No expense was spared erecting a church that would reflect the prestige of Paris.

Critical Viewing

Speculate Possible answer: People enjoy gazing at the beautiful windows.

☑ **ONGOING ASSESSMENT: Monitor and Reinforce**

If students miss more than one item in Exercise 12 or 13, refer them to the following for additional practice.

In the Textbook	Print Resources	Technology
Section Review, Exercise 21, Section 20.1	*Grammar Exercise Workbook,* pp. 69–70	*On-Line Exercise Bank,* Section 20.1

⏱ **TIME SAVERS!**

🔖 **Answers on Transparencies** Use the *Grammar Exercises Answers on Transparencies* for Chapter 20 to facilitate correction by students.

🖥 **On-Line Exercise Bank** Have students complete the exercises on computer. The Auto Check feature will grade their work for you!

Infinitives

1. As students read the key concept, write these two sentences:

   The traveler went to Paris.

   The traveler went to explore Paris.

   Ask students to explain the difference between the underlined phrases modifying *went*. (The first is a preposition followed by its object; the second looks like a preposition followed by a verb and its direct object.)

2. Tell students that the second *to* is not a preposition because the word is followed by a verb. Explain that the word *to* signals one of two things: the start of a prepositional phrase or, as in the case of the second sentence, the beginning of an infinitive or infinitive phrase. As a preposition, *to* is followed by a noun or pronoun. As an infinitive, *to* is followed immediately by a verb.

3. Use the charts on this page to illustrate the functions of infinitives in sentences.

4. Have students locate each infinitive in the first chart and identify the basic sentence parts.

5. In the second chart, have students explain the purpose of each arrow. (They point to the words modified by an infinitive.)

Answer Key

Exercise 14

1. I have not been able <u>to visit</u> Paris for three years.
2. <u>To watch</u> people stroll the boulevards is a day's entertainment.
3. My family was about <u>to ride</u> the river boats, but we arrived late.
4. My dream is <u>to eat</u> chocolate crepes all day.
5. About Paris I have one wish, <u>to return.</u>

20.1

Infinitives

The third and last kind of verbal is the *infinitive.*

▶ **KEY CONCEPT** An **infinitive** is a form of a verb that generally appears with the word *to* and acts as a noun, an adjective, or an adverb. ■

The next chart shows examples of infinitives acting as nouns. When infinitives function as nouns in sentences, they can be used in almost as many ways as gerunds are.

INFINITIVES USED AS NOUNS	
Subject	To understand requires maturity and acceptance.
Direct Object	The peasants of France decided to rebel.
Predicate Nominative	The French soldier's only hope was to surrender.
Object of a Preposition	Our flight from Paris was about to leave.
Appositive	You have only one choice, to stay.

Unlike gerunds, infinitives can also act as adjectives and adverbs.

INFINITIVES USED AS MODIFIERS	
Adjective	The children showed a willingness *to cooperate.*
Adverb	During the war, the French people struggled *to resist.* Some people were unable *to fight.*

▶ **Exercise 14** Writing Sentences With Infinitives Write sentences on the subject of another country, using infinitives according to the instructions given.

1. Use *to visit* as an adverb.
2. Use *to watch* as a subject.
3. Use *to ride* as the object of a preposition.
4. Use *to eat* as a predicate nominative.
5. Use *to return* as an appositive.

▶ **More Practice**

Grammar Exercise Workbook
• pp. 71–72
On-line Exercise Bank
• Section 20.1
Go on-line:
PHSchool.com
Enter Web Code:
eek-1002

> **Exercise 15** Identifying Infinitives Write the infinitive in each sentence. Then, label each *subject, direct object, predicate nominative, object of a preposition, appositive, adjective,* or *adverb.*

EXAMPLE: Museums are my favorite places to visit.

ANSWER: to visit (adjective)

1. France has a large number of interesting museums to visit.
2. Almost every museum contains numerous priceless works of art for the visitor to admire.
3. Since many museums were in disrepair, the government decided in 1956 to renovate them.
4. To modernize was the ultimate goal of the government program.
5. Constructed originally as a fortress by King Philippe August, the Louvre was intended to defend Paris from its enemies.
6. To explore France's most important museum requires several full days.
7. Massive crowds during the 1980's left the museum with only one option, to expand.
8. American architect I. M. Pei was hired to design a new entrance.
9. To enter the Louvre through the enormous glass pyramid is a most awesome experience.
10. To economize, visitors can buy a three-day pass for the Louvre and other French museums.

Internet Tip

To learn more about the Louvre's history and collections, go to its official Web site at **http://www.louvre.fr/** Choose the **English** option.

◄ Critical Viewing What features of this Louvre gallery make viewing its art an enjoyable experience for visitors? Use an infinitive phrase in your response. [Evaluate]

Phrases • **459**

> **Exercise 15**

1. to visit (adjective)
2. to admire (adjective)
3. to renovate (direct object)
4. To modernize (subject)
5. to defend (direct object)
6. To explore (subject)
7. to expand (appositive)
8. to design (direct object)
9. to enter (subject)
10. To economize (adverb)

Integrating Vocabulary Skills

Homophones To, Too, Two Point out to students that, in English, the word *to* and its homophones are used frequently and are frequently confused. *To* is a common preposition when followed by a noun or pronoun. *To* also begins the infinitive form of verbs. Explain further that *to* should not be confused with the number *two* or the adverb *too. Too* means "as well" or "in addition." The spelling of *too* has developed from an emphasized form of *to* and is not connected to the root word for the number *two.*

Critical Viewing

Evaluate Possible answer: The spacious gallery allows visitors to admire the paintings from a distance or from close up.

☑ ONGOING ASSESSMENT: Monitor and Reinforce

If students have difficulty with Exercise 14 or 15, refer them to the following for additional practice.

In the Textbook	Print Resources	Technology
Section Review, Ex. 23–24, Section 20.1	*Grammar Exercise Workbook,* pp. 71–72	*On-Line Exercise Bank,* Section 20.1

⏱ TIME SAVERS!

Answers on Transparencies Use the *Grammar Exercises Answers on Transparencies* for Chapter 20 to facilitate correction by students.

On-Line Exercise Bank Have students complete the exercises on computer. The Auto Check feature will grade their work for you!

Prepositional Phrase or Infinitive?

1. Revisit the word *to* and ask students how this word is used in sentences (at the beginning of a prepositional phrase or to start an infinitive).

2. Read the key concept aloud, and then the examples in the chart.

3. Ask students how the word *command* is used differently in the two examples. (In the prepositional phrase, it is a noun; in the infinitive, it is a verb.)

Answer Key

▶ **Exercise 16**

1. To travel (infinitive)
2. to tour (infinitive)
3. to start (infinitive)
4. to every part (prepositional phrase)
5. to the Latin Quarter (prepositional phrase)
6. to buy (infinitive)
7. to cities (prepositional phrase)
8. to speeds (prepositional phrase)
9. to take (infinitive)
10. to most European cities (prepositional phrase)

20.1

Prepositional Phrase or Infinitive?

The difference between a prepositional phrase and an infinitive is easy to recognize once you are aware of it.

▶ **KEY CONCEPTS** A prepositional phrase always ends with a noun or pronoun. An infinitive always ends with a verb. ■

Notice the difference between the prepositional phrase and the infinitive in the following chart.

Prepositional Phrase	Infinitive
The French soldier listened *to the command.*	A general's purpose in the army is *to command.*

Note About *Infinitives Without* To: Sometimes infinitives do not include the word *to.* When an infinitive follows one of the eight verbs listed here, the *to* is generally omitted.

dare	help	make	see
hear	let	please	watch

EXAMPLES: She doesn't dare *go* without permission.
Did you hear the French vocalist Edith Piaf *sing* on that old recording?

▶ **Exercise 16** Distinguishing Between Prepositional Phrases and Infinitives Write the infinitive or the prepositional phrase beginning with *to* in each sentence. Then, label each *prepositional phrase* or *infinitive*.

EXAMPLE: When I am in Paris, I like to drive.
ANSWER: to drive (infinitive)

1. To travel is very easy in France.
2. There are many different ways to tour.
3. In Paris, the subway is a good place to start.
4. The subway will take you to every part of the city.
5. You can travel easily from the fancy Sixteenth District to the Latin Quarter, where students hang out.
6. You will want to buy a book of tickets good for ten rides.
7. Outside of Paris, high-speed trains can take travelers to cities in several parts of the country.
8. These trains can accelerate to speeds of more than 200 miles per hour.
9. Travelers are also able to take high-speed trains as far as Amsterdam, Holland.
10. Trains to most European cities leave Paris often.

460 • Phrases and Clauses

📙 **Journal Tip**

This section has provided information on France and French culture. Go back and take notes in your journal on some topics that have interested you. You can review them later to find a subject for a report or research paper.

✓ **ONGOING ASSESSMENT: Monitor and Reinforce**

If students miss more than two items in Exercise 16 or 17, refer them to the following for additional practice.

In the Textbook	Print Resources	Technology
Section Review, Ex. 24, Section 20.1	*Grammar Exercise Workbook,* pp. 71–74	*On-Line Exercise Bank,* Section 20.1

Infinitive Phrases

Infinitives also can be joined with other words to form phrases.

▶ **KEY CONCEPT** An **infinitive phrase** is an infinitive with modifiers, complements, or a subject, all acting together as a single part of speech. ■

INFINITIVE PHRASES	
With an adverb:	Jeffrey's entire family likes *to rise early.*
With adverb phrases:	*To skate on the ice* without falling was not easy for him.
With a direct object:	He hated *to leave the city of Lyon.*
With indirect and direct objects:	They promised *to show us the slides* from their trip to France.
With subject and complement:	I would like her *to determine her own goals.*

▶ **Exercise 17** Revising Sentences to Change Participles and Gerunds to Infinitives Rewrite each sentence, changing the participles and gerunds to infinitives.

EXAMPLE: One of my favorite activities is watching the French cooking show on Channel four.

ANSWER: One of my favorite activities is to watch the French cooking show on Channel four.

1. Eating in France is eating well.
2. Many French people prefer dining at home.
3. They browse among the small shops and markets, looking for the freshest ingredients.
4. Many French people learn cooking with herbs and spices.
5. Making a delicious meal with little money is a notable ability of French people.
6. Tempting travelers, each part of the country offers regional specialties.
7. Choosing among the wide variety of cooking styles in France is a difficult task.
8. The object of one style, *haute cuisine,* is preparing rich, elaborately presented meals.
9. The object of the style known as *nouvelle cuisine* is making light dishes without the heavy cream of *haute cuisine.*
10. The aim of all French cuisine is preparing food that is not only delectable but also attractively served.

▶ **More Practice**

Grammar Exercise Workbook
• pp. 71–74
On-line Exercise Bank
• Section 20.1
Go on-line:
PHSchool.com
Enter Web Code:
eek-1002

Interactive Textbook

Get instant feedback! Exercises 16 and 17 are available on-line or on CD-ROM.

Phrases • 461

☑ **ONGOING ASSESSMENT: Assess Mastery**	
Use the following resources to assess student mastery of phrases.	
In the Textbook	**Technology**
Chapter Review, Exercises 46–48	*On-Line Exercise Bank,* Section 20.1

Section Review

Each of these exercises correlates to the instruction on phrases, pages 442–461. These exercises may be used for more practice, for reteaching, or for review of the key concepts presented.

Answer Key

▶ **Exercise 18**

1. Charlemagne was an influential figure <u>in French history</u>. (adjective phrase)
2. <u>During the Middle Ages</u>, he became the first true ruler <u>of France</u>. (adverb, adjective)
3. <u>In 771</u>, Charlemagne inherited the territory <u>of his father and brother</u>. (adverb, adjective)
4. He soon initiated a long series <u>of wars</u> <u>against rival factions</u> <u>throughout western Europe</u>. (adjective, adjective, adverb)
5. <u>Around this time</u>, he also provided military aid <u>to the Pope</u> <u>in Rome</u>. (adverb, adjective, adjective)
6. <u>For a reward</u>, the Pope gave Charlemagne the title <u>of Holy Roman Emperor</u>. (adverb, adjective)
7. <u>By the year 800</u>, Charlemagne ruled <u>over the majority</u> <u>of western Europe</u>. (adverb, adverb, adjective)
8. He founded his permanent capital <u>of Aix-la-Chapelle</u> <u>in present-day western Germany</u>. (adjective, adverb)
9. Charlemagne imposed <u>upon his subjects</u> an intelligent system <u>of laws and government</u>. (adverb, adjective)
10. He also established a number <u>of crude educational centers</u> <u>among the monasteries</u> <u>under his control</u>. (adjective, adverb, adjective)

▶ **Exercise 19**

Answers will vary; a sample is given.

Joan of Arc, the national heroine of France, saved the country from English rule during the Hundred Years' War. She was born in Domremy, a small town in northeastern France, in 1412. Joan believed she had a divine mission, the liberation of France. Charles VII, the French king, allowed her to lead his soldiers into battle against the English. After several important victories, Joan was captured by England's allies, the Burgundians.

GRAMMAR EXERCISES 18–27

▶ **Exercise 18** Identifying Adjective and Adverb Phrases Write the sentences, underlining each prepositional phrase. Identify each as either an *adjective phrase* or an *adverb phrase*.

1. Charlemagne was an influential figure in French history.
2. During the Middle Ages, he became the first true ruler of France.
3. In 771, Charlemagne inherited the territory of his father and brother.
4. He soon initiated a long series of wars against rival factions throughout western Europe.
5. Around this time, he also provided military aid to the Pope in Rome.
6. For a reward, the Pope gave Charlemagne the title of Holy Roman Emperor.
7. By the year 800, Charlemagne ruled over the majority of western Europe.
8. He founded his permanent capital of Aix-la-Chapelle in present-day western Germany.
9. Charlemagne imposed upon his subjects an intelligent system of laws and government.
10. He also established a number of crude educational centers among the monasteries under his control.

▶ **Exercise 19** Revising a Paragraph to Combine Sentences Using Appositives and Appositive Phrases Revise this paragraph, combining short sentences by using appositives and appositive phrases.

Joan of Arc was the national heroine of France. She saved the country from English rule during the Hundred Years' War. She was born in Domremy in 1412. Domremy was a small town in northeastern France. Joan believed she had a divine mission.

462 • Phrases and Clauses

The mission was the liberation of France. Charles VII allowed her to lead his soldiers into battle against the English. Charles VII was the French king. After several important victories, Joan was captured by the Burgundians. The Burgundians were England's allies. The English executed Joan for the act of opposing the laws of the church. Such an act is called heresy.

▶ **Exercise 20** Supplying Participles Depending on the context of the sentence, supply either the present or past participle of the verb in parentheses. Then, label each participial phrase *essential* or *nonessential*.

1. The French author Voltaire is one of the most (admire) writers of the eighteenth century.
2. He was born with the (give) name François Marie Arouet in Paris in 1694.
3. (Serve) time in prison at age twenty-four, Arouet changed his name to Voltaire.
4. The young man was already a (respect) writer by this time.
5. (Achieve) popular and critical acclaim in 1718, the drama *Oedipe* is regarded as Voltaire's first major success.
6. In addition to being a writer, Voltaire was also an (aspire) philosopher.
7. (Rebel) against intolerance, censorship, and injustice, he founded a reformist group (call) the *Philosophes*.
8. This group of intellectuals attempted to change society by presenting (oppose) views of (accept) theories.
9. In all of his work, Voltaire offers his readers material (distinguish) by wit and intelligence.
10. The author of countless letters, plays, poems, and essays, he was clearly a master of the (write) word.

The English executed Joan for heresy, the act of opposing the laws of the church.

▶ **Exercise 20**

1. admired (essential)
2. given (essential)
3. Serving time in prison at age twenty-four (nonessential)
4. respected (essential)
5. Achieving popular and critical acclaim in 1718 (nonessential)
6. aspiring (essential)
7. Rebelling against intolerance, censorship and injustice (nonessential); called (essential)
8. opposing (essential); accepted (essential)
9. distinguished by wit and intelligence (essential)
10. written (essential)

Exercise 21 Identifying Gerunds and Gerund Phrases Write the gerund or gerund phrase in each sentence. Identify the function of each as *subject, direct object, indirect object, predicate nominative, object of a preposition,* or *appositive.*

1. In 1642, the French king Louis XIV began the difficult task of ruling.
2. As he was only four years old, the running of France was left to his mother and her counselor until Louis was older.
3. After the death of his mother's counselor, Louis instituted a new policy: governing without a prime minister.
4. One of Louis's obsessions was expanding the power and influence of France.
5. Louis made conquering the Netherlands and defeating the English his priorities.

Exercise 22 Distinguishing Between Verbs, Participles, and Gerunds Identify each underlined word as *verb, participle,* or *gerund.*

1. <u>Conquering</u> Europe was the goal of French emperor Napoleon Bonaparte.
2. His <u>conquering</u> armies defeated the united forces of Europe in many battles.
3. French soldiers were <u>conquering</u> enemy armies for more than fifteen years.
4. After <u>attacking</u> Russia in 1812, Napoleon's army was forced to retreat.
5. In less than a year, France and allied European forces were <u>fighting</u> again.

Exercise 23 Writing Sentences With Verbal Phrases Write sentences about a political or military leader, using verbal phrases as instructed.

1. Use *leading* as a subject.
2. Use *inspired* as a predicate adjective.
3 Use *to continue* as a direct object.
4. Use *forgetting* as the object of the preposition *without.*
5. Use *to remember* as a subject.

Exercise 24 Identifying Infinitives and Infinitive Phrases Write the infinitive or infinitive phrase in each of the following sentences. Label each *subject, direct object, predicate nominative, object of a preposition, appositive, adjective,* or *adverb.*

1. Charles de Gaulle was to lead France through World War II and the difficult post-war years.
2. In the 1930's, De Gaulle thought the French army was unprepared for the war it was about to fight.
3. After the French government surrendered in 1940, De Gaulle felt he had but one choice, to escape.
4. He resolved to form a new French government in England.
5. For the remainder of the war, he continued to command the resistance groups and the Free French army.

Exercise 25 Find It in Your Reading In the excerpt from *Antigone* on page 450, name the word that each participle modifies.

Exercise 26 Find It in Your Writing In the compositions in your portfolio, find an example of an adjective and adverb phrase, an appositive, a participle, a gerund, and an infinitive. If you cannot find an item, challenge yourself to add it in an appropriate place in your writing.

Exercise 27 Writing Application Imagine that you are going to host a French exchange student. Write a brief letter telling the student about your school and town and what to bring to this country for the visit.

Section Review • 463

Exercise 21

1. ruling (object of a preposition)
2. the running of France (subject)
3. governing without a prime minister (appositive)
4. expanding the power and influence of France (predicate nominative)
5. conquering the Netherlands and defeating the English (indirect object, indirect object)

Exercise 22

1. gerund
2. participle
3. verb
4. gerund
5. verb

Exercise 23

Answers will vary. Samples are given.

1. Leading the country has always been the responsibility of the President of the United States.
2. If a president is fortunate, his or her policies will seem inspired.
3. A successful first term makes any president want to continue.
4. Without forgetting, a president must deliver lengthy speeches.
5. To remember constituents is a president's chief task.

Exercise 24

1. to lead France through World War II and the difficult post-war years (predicate nominative)
2. to fight (object of a preposition)
3. to escape (appositive)
4. to form a new French government in England (direct object)
5. to command the resistance groups and the Free French army. (direct object)

continued

Answer Key continued

Exercise 25

Find It in Your Reading

demoralizing (present participle)—nothing; gone (past participle)—Homes; gone (past participle)—men; corrupted (past participle)—hearts

Exercise 26

Find It in Your Writing

After students complete this process with samples from their portfolios, have them

exchange papers with a writing partner for a review of phrases.

Exercise 27

Writing Application

When students have finished this writing assignment, have them exchange papers with a partner and check for examples of phrases.

TIME SAVERS!

Answers on Transparencies Use the *Grammar Exercises Answers on Transparencies* for Chapter 20 to facilitate correction by students.

On-Line Exercise Bank Have students complete the exercises on computer. The Auto Check feature will grade their work for you!

 **Interest GRABBER** Ask students whether this sentence is complete:

Our dog went to the vet because.

Ask what seems incomplete about it. (It indicates that there is a reason that the dog was taken to the vet but does not state what it is.) Have students offer words to complete the idea, such as "it was limping." Point out that their suggestions contain subjects and verbs and that they are clauses. Place their suggestions on the chalkboard and point out the two clauses at work in each.

Activate Prior Knowledge

Have students recall as many subordinating conjunctions as they can. Then explain that these begin clauses that contain subjects and verbs. Give the class a complex sentence that might begin a scary story. (Example: "As we got closer to the woods, we heard strange sounds.") Then have students continue the story by adding sentences with a subordinating conjunction and a subordinate clause. (As prepositional phrases crop up, point them out.)

TEACH

Step-by-Step Teaching Guide

Independent and Subordinate Clauses

1. Be sure students can distinguish phrases from clauses.

2. After they read the descriptions of clauses, give students more examples to study. Have them begin by locating the number and types of clauses in these:

    We want to visit the Rockies, but we will wait until summer. (2 independent clauses)

    After we visit the Rockies, we plan to drive south. (1 subordinate, 1 independent)

    We will then drive through Arizona and other southwestern states. (1 independent clause)

Section 20.2 *Clauses*

Every clause contains a subject and a verb. However, not every clause can stand by itself as a complete thought.

▶ **KEY CONCEPT** A **clause** is a group of words with its own subject and verb. ■

Independent and Subordinate Clauses

The two basic kinds of clauses are the *independent clause* and the *subordinate clause.*

▶ **KEY CONCEPT** An **independent clause** can stand by itself as a complete sentence. ■

Independent clauses are used in several different ways.

STANDING ALONE:	That woman teaches Latin.
WITH ANOTHER INDEPENDENT CLAUSE:	Mudslides will engulf these hillside villas, *and some will be ruined.*
WITH A SUBORDINATE CLAUSE:	Brian asked to be excused from studying *because he was ill.*

▶ **KEY CONCEPT** A **subordinate clause,** although it has a subject and verb, cannot stand by itself as a complete sentence; it can only be part of a sentence. ■

EXAMPLE: The woman *to whom I introduced you* teaches Latin.

This sentence contains the subordinate clause *to whom I introduced you,* which appears in the middle of an independent clause.

EXAMPLE: *Unless the rain stops soon,* mudslides will engulf these hillside villas.

In this sentence, the subordinate clause, *unless the rain stops soon,* precedes the independent clause.

EXAMPLE: Brian asked *that he be excused.*

Here, the subordinate clause follows the independent clause.

Like phrases, subordinate clauses can function as adjectives, adverbs, and nouns in sentences.

Theme: Ancient Rome

In this section, you will learn about adjective, adverb, and noun clauses. The examples and exercises in this section are about Ancient Rome.

Cross-Curricular Connection: Social Studies

 **Learn More**

To find out how different combinations of clauses determine different types of sentences, see Chapter 21.

⏱ TIME AND RESOURCE MANAGER

Resources
Print: *Grammar Exercise Workbook,* pp. 75–80; *Grammar Exercises Answers on Transparencies,* Ch. 20; *Hands-on Grammar Activity Book,* Ch. 20
Technology: *Writing and Grammar* Interactive Text, Section 20.2; *On-Line Exercise Bank,* Section 20.2

Using the Full Student Edition	Using the Handbook🄷
• Work through all key concepts, pp. 464–476.	• Work through all key concepts, pp. 322–334.
• Assign and review Exercises 28–37.	• Assign and review Exercises 28–37.
• Read and discuss Grammar in Literature, p. 474.	• Read and discuss Grammar in Literature, p. 332.
• Do the Hands-on Grammar activity, p. 477.	• Do the Hands-on Grammar activity, p. 335.

▶ **Exercise 28** Recognizing **Independent and Subordinate Clauses** Write and label the independent and subordinate clauses in these sentences.

1. The luxury of baths, which we have come to associate with Rome, was imported from the East.
2. The earliest Roman literature, which contained translations from Greek classics, was based on Greek models.
3. Roman boys, who received better training than the girls did, were taught the Greek classics.
4. The Greeks were conquered by Rome, but culturally the Greeks were the conquerors.
5. Romans were proud of their civilization, although much of it was Greek in origin.

▲ **Critical Viewing** What might some of the figures on these ancient coins represent? Answer using a sentence with a subordinate clause. **[Speculate]**

Adjective Clauses

One way to add description and detail to a sentence is by using an *adjective clause.*

▶ **KEY CONCEPT** An **adjective clause** is a subordinate clause that modifies a noun or pronoun by telling *what kind* or *which one.* ■

Most often, adjective clauses begin with one of the relative pronouns: *that, which, who, whom,* or *whose.* Sometimes, however, adjective clauses may begin with a *relative adverb,* such as *before, since, when, where,* or *why.* All of these words relate the clause to the word it modifies.

▶ **KEY CONCEPT** An adjective clause begins with a relative pronoun or a relative adverb. ■

In the chart on the next page, the adjective clauses are italicized. Arrows indicate the noun or pronoun modified by each clause. These are adjective clauses because they answer the questions *What kind?* and *Which one?* Notice also that the first three clauses begin with relative pronouns and the last two begin with relative adverbs.

Clauses • 465

☑ **ONGOING ASSESSMENT: Monitor and Reinforce**

If students miss more than one item in Exercise 28, refer them to the following for additional practice.

In the Textbook	Print Resources	Technology
Section Review, Ex. 38, Section 20.2	*Grammar Exercise Workbook,* pp. 75–76	*On-Line Exercise Bank,* Section 20.2

Answer Key

▶ **Exercise 28**

1. The luxury of baths was imported from the East (ind.); which we have come to associate with Rome (sub.)
2. The earliest Roman literature was based on Greek models (ind.); which contained translations from Greek classics (sub.)
3. Roman boys were taught the Greek classics (ind.); who received better training than girls did (sub.)
4. The Greeks were conquered by Rome (ind.); but culturally the Greeks were the conquerors (ind.)
5. Romans were proud of their civilization (ind.); although much of it was Greek in origin (sub.)

Step-by-Step Teaching Guide

Adjective Clauses

1. Explain that every subordinate clause adds information to the rest of its sentence.
2. Compare clauses to phrases and explain that clauses, too, can act as modifiers (adjectives and adverbs) as well as nouns. Remind students that clauses contain their own subjects and verbs while phrases do not.

Integrating Punctuation Skills

Clauses Explain to students that the point where independent and dependent clauses meet provides graceful opportunities for writers to break line of dialogue. Use this example:

"After you leave the building," she warned, "a car may follow you."

Critical Viewing

Speculate Possible answer: Athena, who is pictured on this coin, was the goddess of wisdom.

Adjective Clauses

1. Explain that some adjective clauses are set off by commas because they are not essential to the meaning of a sentence.

2. Revisit the chart and ask why only the third sentence contains commas.

Critical Viewing

Analyze Possible answer: The armor that the statue is wearing shows that it is of a soldier.

Integrating Speaking and Listening Skills

Subordinate Clauses Have students listen carefully as you read four or five complex sentences, each consisting of one independent clause and one or more subordinate clauses. Ask students to write on their papers only the main clause they hear in each sentence. Then, write all of the subordinate clauses on the board and ask students to attach them to the independent clauses on their papers, underlining the subordinate clauses and drawing arrows to the words they modify.

Customize for
ESL Students

Students may find it hard to understand how an entire clause with a subject and verb can modify a word. Write some simple sentences on the board: "A barking dog ran down the street." Read them aloud with the students. Help students change the single adjective into a clause: "A dog that was barking ran down the street." Point out that both the single word *barking* and the clause *that was barking* serve the same function in the sentence. Have students practice expanding modifiers into clauses.

20.2

ADJECTIVE CLAUSES

Anyone *who reads about ancient Rome* will find it very interesting.

I finished reading the book *that you loaned me.*

We gave the story, *which we found fascinating,* a second read.

Spring is the time *when peepers make their shrill evening sound.*

Our trip to Italy ended with a visit to the town *where my parents were born.*

Like appositives and participial phrases, adjective clauses can often be used to combine information from two sentences into one. Using adjective clauses to combine sentences can indicate the relationship between ideas as well as add detail to a sentence.

TWO SENTENCES: This statue represents a Roman soldier. He is dressed for battle.

COMBINED: This statue represents a Roman soldier who is dressed for battle.

Adjective clauses, like appositive and participial phrases, are set off by punctuation only when they are not essential to the meaning of a sentence. The chart on the following page contrasts nonessential and essential adjective clauses.

Notice that in the sentences on the left, omitting the adjective clauses would not change the basic message. However, if you were to take away the adjective clauses on the right, the message would not be complete. (See Chapter 28 for more about punctuating adjective clauses.)

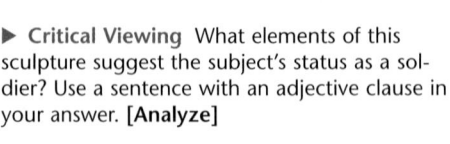

▶ **Critical Viewing** What elements of this sculpture suggest the subject's status as a soldier? Use a sentence with an adjective clause in your answer. [**Analyze**]

466 • Phrases and Clauses

Nonessential Clauses	Essential Clauses
One of Dickens's best characters is Charles Darnay, *who appears in Dickens's novel about the French Revolution.*	The novel *that everyone must read by Monday afternoon* promises to be very exciting.
Jean McCurdy, *who studied three hours every evening for a month,* won the statewide competition.	A student *who studies regularly* usually finds test-taking easy.

In the sentences on the left, the commas indicate that the clauses give additional information. In the sentences on the right, the lack of commas shows that the clauses are needed to identify the words they modify. Read the contrasting sentences aloud. Notice that you naturally pause before and after the nonessential clauses and that your voice drops as you read them. Realizing this should help you recognize clauses in your own writing that need to be set off with commas.

▶ **Exercise 29** Identifying Adjective Clauses and the Words They Modify Write the adjective clause in each sentence. Then, write the word or words the adjective clause modifies. Finally, label the clause *nonessential* or *essential.*

EXAMPLE: The Roman Empire, which achieved greatness, had humble beginnings.

ANSWER: which achieved greatness; The Roman Empire (nonessential)

1. The Punic Wars, a name derived from the Latin word for *Phoenician,* were fought between Rome and Carthage.
2. The first war, which made Rome a naval power, ended in 241 B.C.
3. A second war that was fought between the two powers began in 218 B.C.
4. The Carthaginians, who were led by Hannibal, marched on Italy but failed to completely conquer the Romans.
5. The third Punic War, which resulted in ruin for Carthage, removed any serious threat to Rome's supremacy.
6. Slaves and gold that reached Rome from the new territories kindled the idea that conquest was profitable.
7. The city that began as a republic was becoming an empire.
8. The Romans conquered Gaul, now known as France.
9. The Greeks, who looked on the Romans as barbarians, were instrumental in shaping Roman culture.
10. The period of relative stability that Roman rule brought to its conquered territories was known as *pax romana* (Roman peace).

▶ **More Practice**

Grammar Exercise Workbook
• pp. 75–76
On-line Exercise Bank
• Section 20.2
  Go on-line:
  PHSchool.com
  Enter Web Code:
  eek-1002

Interactive Textbook

Get instant feedback! Exercise 29 is available on-line or on CD-ROM.

Clauses • 467

Essential and Nonessential Clauses

1. Use the chart on this page to demonstrate uses of commas with adjective clauses.
2. Ask students to explain why each clause in the chart is nonessential or essential.

Real-World Connection

People who write book reviews depend on descriptive phrases and clauses in their writing. They must read each book, form an opinion about it, and write a clear concise report on it. Have students bring in copies of book reviews and have them pick out the descriptive phrases and clauses (adjective and adverb) they think are most effective and explain why.

Answer Key

▶ **Exercise 29**

1. a name derived from the Latin for *Phoenician*—Punic Wars (non.)
2. which made Rome a naval power—war (non.)
3. that was fought between the two powers—war (ess.)
4. who were led by Hannibal—Carthaginians (non.)
5. which resulted in ruin for Carthage—Punic War (non.)
6. that reached Rome from the new territories—slaves, gold (ess.)
7. that began as a republic—city (ess.)
8. now known as France—Gaul (non.)
9. who looked on the Romans as barbarians—Greeks (non.)
10. that Roman rule brought to its conquered territories—period (ess.)

☑ **ONGOING ASSESSMENT: Monitor and Reinforce**

If students miss more than two items in Exercise 29, refer them to the following for additional practice.

In the Textbook	Print Resources	Technology
Section Review, Exercise 39, Section 20.2	*Grammar Exercise Workbook,* pp. 75–76	*On-Line Exercise Bank,* Section 20.2

🕐 **TIME SAVERS!**

Answers on Transparencies Use the *Grammar Exercises Answers on Transparencies* for Chapter 20 to facilitate correction by students.

On-Line Exercise Bank Have students complete the exercises on computer. The Auto Check feature will grade their work for you!

Relative Pronouns in Adjective Clauses

1. Have a student read the key concept aloud. Ask students to recall relative pronouns *(who, whom, whose, that, which)* and explain that these are usually the first words in adjective clauses.

2. Point out the subheads in the chart and explain that these are the functions of relative pronouns within adjective clauses.

3. Have a student read each example and explanation aloud. Then ask for the word modified by each clause *(structure, brother-in-law, book, senator).*

4. Point out that the relative pronoun is the second word in the third example. Ask why (it is the object of a preposition within the clause).

Understood Words With Adjective Clauses

1. Use the first example to illustrate a missing (elliptical) relative pronoun.

2. Offer a few more examples aloud and ask students to supply the missing words:

   He is someone I respect. (whom)

   The moon is a place I don't expect to visit. (that)

   The book you requested has arrived. (that)

20.2

Relative Pronouns

Relative pronouns function in two ways.

▶ **KEY CONCEPT** **Relative pronouns** connect adjective clauses to the words they modify and act as subjects, direct objects, objects of prepositions, or adjectives in the clauses. ■

To tell how a relative pronoun is used within a clause, separate the clause from the rest of the sentence, and find the subject and verb in the clause.

THE USES OF RELATIVE PRONOUNS WITHIN CLAUSES
As a Subject

A structure *that is built on a good foundation* is built to last.
    Clause: that is built on a good foundation.
    Subject: that   *Verb:* is built
    Use of relative pronoun: subject

As a Direct Object

My brother-in-law, *whom my sister met at college,* is a poet.
    Clause: whom my sister met at college
    Reworded clause: my sister met whom at college
    Subject: sister   *Verb:* met
    Use of relative pronoun: direct object

As an Object of a Preposition

This is the book *about which I read enthusiastic reviews.*
    Clause: about which I read enthusiastic reviews.
    Reworded clause: I read enthusiastic reviews about which
    Subject: I   *Verb:* read
    Use of relative pronoun: object of a preposition

As an Adjective

The senator *whose opinion was in question* spoke to the press.
    Clause: whose opinion was in question
    Subject: opinion   *Verb:* was
    Use of relative pronoun: adjective

Note About *Understood Words:* Sometimes in writing and in speech, a relative pronoun is left out of an adjective clause. The missing word, though simply understood, still functions in the sentence.

EXAMPLES: The legendary heroes [*whom*] *we studied* were great men and women.
    The suggestions [*that*] *they made* were ignored.

⚙ Grammar and Style Tip

Although adding adjective and adverb clauses to your sentences can make your writing more interesting, be careful not to make your sentences too long. Too many long sentences can be just as distracting as too many short, choppy ones.

Relative Adverbs

Unlike a relative pronoun, a relative adverb has only one use within a clause.

▶ **KEY CONCEPT** **Relative adverbs** connect adjective clauses to the words they modify and act as adverbs in the clauses. ■

The following chart shows an adjective clause introduced by a relative adverb.

THE USE OF RELATIVE ADVERBS WITHIN CLAUSES

Pat yearned for the day *when she could walk without crutches*.
    Clause: when she could walk without crutches
    Reworded clause: she could walk when without crutches
    Subject: she   *Verb:* could walk
    Use of relative adverb: adverb

▶ **Exercise 30** **Recognizing the Uses of Relative Pronouns and Relative Adverbs** Write the adjective clause in each sentence, circling the relative pronoun or relative adverb. Then, label the use of the relative pronoun within the clause *subject, direct object, object of a preposition, adjective,* or *adverb.*

EXAMPLE: The first great ruler (that) we learned about was Julius Caesar.

ANSWER: that we learned about (object of a preposition)

1. Julius Caesar, about whom Shakespeare later wrote a play, was renowned as the conqueror of Gaul.
2. Rome, which was expanding quite rapidly, was undergoing a great deal of turmoil at home.
3. Julius Caesar, whose seven years in Gaul removed him from much of the intrigue, was a talented politician.
4. The army, which Caesar commanded ably, was devoted to him.
5. Julius Caesar claimed to be defending the republic at the moment when he and his army marched on Rome in 49 B.C.

More Practice

Grammar Exercise Workbook
• pp. 75–76
On-line Exercise Bank
• Section 20.2
Go on-line:
PHSchool.com
Enter Web Code:
eek-1002

▲ Critical Viewing
How well do you think this sculpture represents real human qualities? Answer using an adjective clause. [Evaluate]

Clauses • 469

Relative Adverbs

1. Remind students that adjective clauses begin with relative pronouns and relative adverbs.

2. Explain to students that locating the relative adverb will cue them to the beginning of an adjective clause that modifies other words in the sentence.

3. To illustrate the function of relative adverbs in sentences, write the following sentences on the chalkboard. Write the relative adverb in capital letters, bracket the words the relative adverb modifies, and underline the whole of the adjective clause:

In the week <u>SINCE the report [was given]</u>, many facts have changed.

Weddings are times <u>WHEN many people [cry]</u>.

Critical Viewing

Evaluate Possible answer: The sculpture shows lines and folds that a real human face would have.

Answer Key

▶ **Exercise 30**

1. about (whom) Shakespeare later wrote a play (object of a preposition)
2. (which) was expanding quite rapidly (subject)
3. (whose) seven years in Gaul removed him from much of the intrigue (adjective)
4. (which) Caesar commanded ably (direct object)
5. (when) he and his army marched on Rome in 49 B.C. (adverb)

☑ **ONGOING ASSESSMENT: Monitor and Reinforce**

If students miss more than one item in Exercise 30, refer them to the following for additional practice.

In the Textbook	Print Resources	Technology
Section Review, Ex. 39, Section 20.2	*Grammar Exercise Workbook,* pp. 75–76	*On-Line Exercise Bank,* Section 20.2

Answers may vary; samples are given.

1. Caesar fought a civil war, <u>in which he challenged those who might oppose him</u>, for four years after his march on Rome. (arrow from "which" back to "war".)
2. Julius Caesar, <u>who made friends with his former enemies</u>, was not a vicious conqueror. (arrow from "who" back to "Caesar".)
3. He was made dictator for life, <u>which would be a position similar to a monarch.</u> (arrow from "which" back to "dictator".)
4. Romans, <u>who placed a high value on tradition</u>, felt a monarchy would violate their ideals. (arrow from "who" back to "Romans".)
5. His enemies, <u>who united against him</u>, assassinated him in 44 B.C. (arrow from "who" back to "enemies".)

Step-by-Step Teaching Guide

Adverb Clauses

1. Read the first key concept and explain that adverb clauses, like adjective clauses, modify words in the independent clauses.

2. Read the second key concept and explain that adverb clauses contain subjects and verbs, just like adjective clauses, but that they begin instead with subordinating conjunctions.

3. Use the chart on this page to build students' recognition of subordinating conjunctions. Ask volunteers to offer original clauses—each with a subject and verb—for words in the chart.

4. If necessary, demonstrate the difference between an adverb prepositional phrase and an adverb clause, each beginning with the same word, as follows:

   After the game, we walked home. (prepositional phrase, adverb)

   After we watched the game, we walked home. (adverb clause)

20.2

▶ **Exercise 31** Combining Sentences With Adjective Clauses
Turn each pair of sentences into a single sentence with an adjective clause. Then, underline each adjective clause, and draw an arrow from it to the word or words it modifies.
1. Caesar fought a civil war for four years after his march on Rome. He challenged those who might oppose him.
2. Julius Caesar was not a vicious conqueror. He made friends with his former enemies.
3. He was made dictator for life. This would be a position similar to that of a monarch.
4. Romans felt a monarchy would violate their ideals. They placed a high value on tradition.
5. Caesar's enemies united against him. They assassinated him in 44 B.C.

Adverb Clauses

Subordinate clauses can also act as adverbs.

▶ **KEY CONCEPT** **Subordinate adverb clauses** modify verbs, adjectives, adverbs, or verbals by telling *where, when, in what way, to what extent, under what condition,* or *why.* ■

▶ **KEY CONCEPT** All adverb clauses begin with subordinating conjunctions. ■

The following chart shows some of the most common subordinating conjunctions.

SUBORDINATING CONJUNCTIONS		
after	even though	unless
although	if	until
as	in order that	when
as if	since	whenever
as long as	so that	where
because	than	wherever
before	though	while

Recognizing these subordinating conjunctions will help you identify adverb clauses. In the next chart, the adverb clauses are italicized. Arrows point to the words modified by each clause. The first answers the question *When?*, the second adverb clause answers the question *Where?*, and so on. The last two adverb clauses are different because they provide information that a single adverb cannot. The next-to-last adverb clause answers the question *Under what condition?* The question *Why?* is answered by the last adverb clause in the chart.

Grammar Exercise Workbook
• pp. 75–76
On-line Exercise Bank
• Section 20.2
Go on-line:
PHSchool.com
Enter Web Code:
eek-1002

interactive Textbook

Complete the exercise on-line! Exercise 31 is available on-line or on CD-ROM.

Adverb Clauses

1. Use the chart on this page to explain and demonstrate how adverb clauses function in sentences.

2. Begin with the subheading above each example and ask students to explain the purpose of the arrow in each. (It points to the word modified by the clause.)

3. If necessary, have students parse each example and label each sentence part.

4. Use the examples beneath the chart to show that adverb clauses can appear at the beginning, at the end, or in the middle of complex sentences.

5. Use the last example to illustrate combining sentences using adverb clauses.

ADVERB CLAUSES
Modifying a Verb
When you finish your book about Rome, you should then begin your report.
Modifying an Adjective
Tricia seemed happy *wherever she was.*
Modifying an Adverb
Faster *than the eye could follow*, the race car sped away.
Modifying a Participle
Laughing *until he gasped for breath*, Fred could not speak.
Modifying a Gerund
Driving a car *if you do not have a license* is illegal.
Modifying an Infinitive
We decided to remain in our seats *so that we could watch the movie again.*

Whether an adverb clause appears at the beginning, middle, or end of a sentence can sometimes affect the meaning.

EXAMPLES: *Before the year was over,* Caesar made plans to march into Rome.

Caesar made plans to march into Rome *before the year was over.*

Like adjective clauses, adverb clauses can be used to combine the information from two sentences into one. The combined sentence shows a close relationship between the ideas.

TWO SENTENCES: It was storming. They did not launch the attack.

COMBINED: *Because it was storming,* they did not launch the attack.

▼ Critical Viewing Using an adverb clause, describe characteristics of this sculpture that are not unlike men's features today. **[Compare]**

Critical Viewing

Compare Possible answer: The sculpture has features like people's today because the artist created a realistic image.

Clauses • 471

☑ ONGOING ASSESSMENT: Monitor and Reinforce

If students miss more than one item in Exercise 31, refer them to the following for additional practice.

In the Textbook	Print Resources	Technology
Section Review, Exercise 41, Section 20.2	*Grammar Exercise Workbook,* pp. 75–76	*On-Line Exercise Bank,* Section 20.2

 **TIME SAVERS!**

Answers on Transparencies
Use the *Grammar Exercises Answers on Transparencies* for Chapter 20 to facilitate correction by students.

On-Line Exercise Bank
Have students complete the exercises on computer. The Auto Check feature will grade their work for you!

Exercise 32

1. Because he was Caesar's nephew (hunted)

2. After he fought in Egypt and returned to Rome (became)

3. that the army had supported him (fortunate)

4. as if he himself were emperor (Acting)

5. Since he was given the honorary title of Augustus (has been known)

Step-by-Step Teaching Guide

Elliptical Adverb Clauses

1. After students read the key concept, explain that the key to understanding an ellipsis is to recognize words that have been omitted.

2. Use the examples on this page and then provide additional examples. For each, ask students to supply the missing words:

   My little brother is now as tall as I. (am)

   The story appealed to me more than them. (it appealed to)

   The tour was more exhausting than informative. (it was)

3. Be sure students can locate the entire adverb clause (*as I am, than it appealed to them,* and so on).

Customizing for
Logical/Mathematical Learners

As students study elliptical clauses, explain that the word *ellipsis* refers to something omitted. Ask students to investigate the meaning of *elliptical* in mathematics and to explain an *ellipsis* (a geometric shape) or something *elliptical* (a planetary orbit) in mathematical or geometrical terms.

20.2

> **Exercise 32** Identifying Adverb Clauses and the Words They Modify Write the adverb clause in each sentence. Then, write the word or words each adverb clause modifies.

EXAMPLE: After Caesar was killed, his nephew Octavius gained power.

ANSWER: After Caesar was killed (gained)

1. Because he was Caesar's nephew, Octavius hunted Caesar's assassins after his death.
2. After he fought in Egypt and returned to Rome, he became emperor in all but name.
3. He was fortunate that the army had supported him.
4. Acting as if he himself were emperor, he was treated as one.
5. Since he was given the honorary title of Augustus, he has been known as Caesar Augustus.

Elliptical Adverb Clauses

Sometimes, words are omitted in adverb clauses, especially in those clauses that begin with *as* or *than* and are used to express comparisons. Such clauses are said to be *elliptical.*

> **KEY CONCEPT** An **elliptical clause** is a clause in which the verb or subject and verb are understood but not actually stated. ■

Even though the subject or the subject and the verb have been left out of an elliptical clause, they still function to make the clause express a complete thought. In the following examples, the understood words have been added in brackets. The sentences are alike except for the words *he* and *him.* In the first sentence, *he* is a subject. In the second sentence, *him* functions as a direct object. The use of each word is easy to see when the omitted words are noted.

VERB UNDERSTOOD: She resembles their father more *than he* [*does*].

SUBJECT AND VERB UNDERSTOOD: She resembles their father more *than* [*she resembles*] *him.*

When you read or write elliptical clauses, mentally include the omitted words. Doing this should help clarify the meaning you intend.

🔒 **Research Tip**

Look for information about Roman emperors under "Ancient Rome" or under the names of particular rulers: "Julius Caesar," "Caesar Augustus," "Tiberius," "Nero," "Marcus Aurelius," and so on.

Exercise 33 Recognizing Elliptical Adverb Clauses Write each sentence, adding the missing words in any elliptical clause. Then, underline the complete adverb clause in each sentence, and circle the words you have added.

EXAMPLE: Roman emperors were treated more like gods than men.

ANSWER: Roman emperors were treated more like gods than (they were treated like) men.

1. Caesar Augustus was considered as divine as his uncle.
2. Rome's territories increased more under Augustus' rule than under his uncle's.
3. His successors expanded the empire even farther than he.
4. They depended on the army as much as Caesar Augustus.
5. The empire as we know it owes as much to his successors as to Caesar Augustus.

Exercise 34 Combining Sentences With Adverb Clauses
Turn each pair of sentences into a single sentence with an adverb clause. Then, underline each adverb clause.

EXAMPLE: Rome was hard to rule. It was a large bureaucracy.

ANSWER: Rome was hard to rule because it was a large bureaucracy.

1. The nature and government of Rome resulted from Caesar Augustus. They evolved gradually.
2. Many emperors appointed their heirs. Control of the empire would be hereditary.
3. There were twelve emperors in the century following Augustus' death. Only four were related to him.
4. Augustus' line ended in A.D. 68. Nero, the last emperor related to him, died in A.D. 68.
5. The Senate might endorse or appoint a successor. Real power remained with the army.

Exercise 35 Writing Sentences With Adverb Clauses
Write sentences about a historical era using adverb clauses, as indicated below.
1. Use *although* in a clause modifying a verb.
2. Use *if* in a clause modifying a gerund.
3. Use *as much as* in an elliptical clause.
4. Use *whenever* in a clause modifying an adjective.
5. Use *while* in a clause modifying a participle.

More Practice

Grammar Exercise Workbook
• pp. 77–78
On-line Exercise Bank
• Section 20.2
Go on-line:
PHSchool.com
Enter Web Code:
eek-1002

Interactive Textbook

Get instant feedback! Exercises 32, 33, 34, and 35 are available on-line or on CD-ROM.

Clauses • **473**

Answer Key

Exercise 33

1. Caesar Augustus was considered <u>as divine as his uncle (was)</u>.
2. Rome's territories increased more under Augustus' rule <u>than (they did) under his uncle's</u>.
3. His successors expanded the empire even further <u>than he (had)</u>.
4. They depended on the army <u>as much as Caesar Augustus (had done)</u>.
5. The empire as we know it owes as much to his successors <u>as (it does) to Caesar Augustus</u>.

Exercise 34

Answers may vary; samples are given.

1. <u>Although they evolved gradually,</u> the nature and government of Rome resulted from Caesar Augustus.
2. Many emperors appointed heirs <u>so that control of the empire would be hereditary</u>.
3. There were twelve emperors in the century following Augustus' death, <u>although only four were related to him</u>.
4. Augustus' line ended in A.D. 68 <u>when Nero, the last emperor related to him, died</u>.
5. The Senate might endorse or appoint a successor <u>although real power remained with the army</u>.

Exercise 35

Answers may vary; samples are given.

1. Although you haven't been to Rome, you can read about it.
2. Reading about Rome if you haven't been there is a start.
3. I admire the Romans as much as anyone else.
4. The subject of Rome is interesting whenever I study it.
5. Fiddling while the city burned, Nero displayed contempt for Rome.

ONGOING ASSESSMENT: Monitor and Reinforce

If students miss more than one item in Exercise 33, 34, or 35, refer them to the following for additional practice.

In the Textbook	Print Resources	Technology
Section Review, Ex. 42, Section 20.2	*Grammar Exercise Workbook,* pp. 77–78	*On-Line Exercise Bank,* Section 20.2

Step-by-Step Teaching Guide

Noun Clauses

1. Explain that noun clauses contain their own subjects and verbs, but they do not modify words in the independent clauses.

2. To help students identify noun clauses, point out that if the clause can be replaced by a single noun, it probably is a noun clause.

Step-by-Step Teaching Guide

Grammar in Literature

1. Point out that many lines reflect an independent or subordinate idea.

2. Have students identify as many phrase and clause structures as they can. Point out that lines 1 and 8 have noun clauses and that line 5 contains an adverb clause.

3. Give students help with Elizabethan vocabulary: *meet* (fitting); *nice* (trivial); *mart your offices* (peddle influence)

More About the Writer

Shakespeare wrote *The Tragedy of Julius Caesar* around 1599. It is a tragedy of political rivalries and differs greatly from his other famous tragedy of this period, *Romeo and Juliet*.

Connections With Literature

Shakespeare's *The Tragedy of Julius Caesar* can be found in *Prentice Hall Literature, Penguin Edition*, Grade 10.

Customize for
More Advanced Students

Have students familiarize themselves with the introductory words of noun clauses (*that, which, whichever, what, whatever, who, whoever,* and so on). Ask them to write at least five original sentences with noun clauses, each performing a different function and each using a different introductory word. Example:

He would pay whatever it cost to repair his car. (direct object)

Noun Clauses

Subordinate clauses can also act as nouns.

▶ **KEY CONCEPT** A **noun clause** is a subordinate clause that acts as a noun. ■

A *noun clause* acts in almost the same way as a single-word noun does in a sentence.

▶ **KEY CONCEPT** In a sentence, a noun clause may act as a subject, direct object, indirect object, predicate nominative, object of a preposition, or appositive. ■

The chart on the following page contains examples of the various functions of noun clauses.

⟳ Learn More

To review basic sentence parts, turn to Chapter 19.

GRAMMAR IN
LITERATURE

from Julius Caesar
William Shakespeare

Act IV, Scene iii, Brutus' tent

In these lines, the noun clauses are highlighted in blue. In Brutus' last speech, notice that the word that, *introducing the noun clause, is understood.*

CASSIUS. *That you have wronged me* doth appear in this:
You have condemned and noted Lucius Pella
For taking bribes here of the Sardians;
Wherein my letters, praying on his side,
Because I knew the man, was slighted off.

BRUTUS. You wrong yourself to write in such a case.

CASSIUS. In such a time as this it is not meet
That every nice offense should bear his comment.

BRUTUS. Let me tell you, Cassius, *you yourself
Are much condemned to have an itching palm,
To sell and mart your offices for gold
To undeservers.*

Introductory Words

Noun clauses frequently begin with the words *that, which, who, whom,* or *whose,* the same words that are used to begin adjective clauses. *Whichever, whoever,* or *whomever* may also be used as introductory words in noun clauses. Other noun clauses begin with the words *how, if, what, whatever, where, when, whether,* or *why.*

KEY CONCEPT Introductory words may act as subjects, direct objects, objects of prepositions, adjectives, or adverbs in noun clauses, or they may simply introduce the clauses. ■

Note in this chart that the introductory word *that* in the last example has no function except to introduce the clause.

NOUN CLAUSES	
Subject	*Whoever is last* must pay a penalty.
Direct Object	Please invite *whomever you want.*
Indirect Object	His manner gave *whoever met him* a shock.
Predicate Nominative	Our problem is *whether we should stay here or leave.*
Object of a Preposition	Use the money for *whatever purpose you choose.*
Appositive	The occupied country rejected our plea *that orphans be cared for by the Red Cross.*

Exercise 36 Identifying Noun Clauses Write the noun clause in each sentence. Then, label the clause *subject, direct object, indirect object, predicate nominative, object of a preposition,* or *appositive.*

EXAMPLE: Whoever was Roman felt it a great honor.

ANSWER: Whoever was Roman (subject)

1. In the beginning, a Roman citizen was whoever was born in Rome.
2. Later, what was necessary was to be born in Roman territory.
3. Citizenship was available only to whoever was free-born.
4. Romans often made whomever they conquered slaves.
5. Romans often let conquered peoples do whatever they wanted as long as taxes were paid.

More Practice

Grammar Exercise Workbook
• pp. 78–79
On-line Exercise Bank
• Section 20.2
Go on-line:
PHSchool.com
Enter Web Code:
eek-1002

Interactive Textbook

Get instant feedback! Exercise 36 is available on-line or on CD-ROM.

Clauses • 475

Step-by-Step Teaching Guide

Introductory Words

1. Have students list the words that can begin noun clauses; then read the key concept aloud.

2. Use the chart to practice recognizing noun clauses, their introductory words, and the function of each in a sentence.

Answer Key

Exercise 36

1. whoever was born in Rome (predicate nominative)
2. what was necessary (subject)
3. whoever was free-born (object of a preposition)
4. whomever they conquered (indirect object)
5. whatever they wanted (direct object)

Customize for *Spatial Learners*

Help students visualize complex sentences by representing subordinate clauses with boxes and their functions with arrows. Place this on the board:

They told us where they live.
S   V IO   DO

Have students put sentences from the exercises into similar graphics.

☑ **ONGOING ASSESSMENT: Monitor and Reinforce**

If students miss more than one item in Exercise 36, refer them to the following for additional practice.

In the Textbook	Print Resources	Technology
Section Review, Ex. 40, Section 20.2	*Grammar Exercise Workbook,* pp. 79–80	*On-Line Exercise Bank,* Section 20.2

Noun Clauses

1. Point out that certain introductory words can begin adjective or adverb clauses as well as noun clauses.

2. Use the final Note to illustrate elliptical noun clauses.

Customize for
Gifted and Talented Students

Have students analyze sentences from a newspaper or magazine so that they each generate a list of twenty adjective, adverb, and noun clauses. Tell them to label each clause. Allow them to share some of their clauses and labels with the class before having them exchange lists. Then, have each student write a brief passage incorporating any five of the clauses they find on their new lists. (Allow them to alter some words for clarity.) Tell them to underline each clause they use, to label its type, and to draw an arrow to the word it modifies. For noun clauses, have students label its function in its sentence.

Critical Viewing

Relate Possible answer: Like the Colosseum, modern stadiums have seats arranged so that whoever sits in any seat has a clear view.

Answer Key

Exercise 37

1. whoever (subject)
2. what (subject)
3. whoever (subject)
4. whomever (direct object)
5. whatever (direct object)

NOUN CLAUSES	
Direct object:	*Whatever he accomplished* would be satisfactory.
Adjective:	The little girl could not decide *which flavor of ice cream she would like.*
No function in clause:	The officials determined *that the polls had been rigged.*

Most words that begin noun clauses may also introduce adjective or adverb clauses. To decide whether a clause acts as a noun, look at the role of the clause in the sentence. In the following examples, all three subordinating clauses begin with *where,* but only the first is a noun clause because it functions in the sentence as a direct object.

NOUN CLAUSE: Caesar told his soldiers *where they would gather for battle.*

ADJECTIVE CLAUSE: They took the soldier to a tent *where a doctor examined his wound.*

ADVERB CLAUSE: She lives *where the weather is warm all year.*

Note About *Introductory Words:* The introductory word *that* is often omitted from a noun clause. In the following example, the understood word *that* is in brackets.

EXAMPLE: The secretary suggested [*that*] *you leave your name.*

▶ **Exercise 37**   Recognizing the Uses of Introductory Words
Write the introductory word from each noun clause in Exercise 36. Then, label the use of each within the clause *subject, direct object, object of a preposition, adjective, adverb,* or *a word with no function.*

EXAMPLE: Whoever was Roman felt it to be a great honor.
ANSWER: Whoever (subject)

▲ Critical Viewing
Many aspects of present-day stadiums resemble the Roman Colosseum. Using a noun clause, describe one or two of them. **[Relate]**

Hands-on Grammar

Noun Clause Flip-and-Folds

Practice with a Noun Clause Flip-and-Folds to learn how to vary your sentences by using noun clauses in various positions. Begin with several narrow strips of paper about 4" long. On one strip, print WAS THAT WE WON THE CONTEST. On another strip, print IT WAS GOOD NEWS. On a third strip, print WE HEARD THE. Now begin making sentences. Put the first two strips together, beginning with IT WAS . . . ; cover up the WAS at the beginning of the second strip. You will have a sentence in which THAT WE WON THE CONTEST is an appositive.

| IT WAS GOOD NEWS | THAT WE WON THE CONTEST |

Next, fold under IT WAS on the first strip, uncover WAS on the second strip, and use THE from the third strip. The noun clause is now a predicate noun.

| THE | GOOD NEWS | WAS THAT WE WON THE CONTEST |

Next, add WE HEARD THE to form these variations—one making the clause a direct object, and the other, again, an appositive:

| WE HEARD | THAT WE WON THE CONTEST |

| WE HEARD THE | GOOD NEWS | THAT WE WON THE CONTEST |

Now, flip the two strips, fold under WAS on the noun clause strip, and fold under IT on the other strip. Note that the noun clause becomes the subject of the sentence.

| THAT WE WON THE CONTEST | WAS GOOD NEWS |

When you have finished, make other strips to flip and fold. Try these sentence parts: WE KNOW / WE TALK ABOUT / WHO WON THE CONTEST / IT WAS OUR FRIEND / WHEN WE WON THE CONTEST. Add other sentence parts that you can flip and fold to make noun clauses. Be on the lookout for some constructions that may actually be adjective clauses.

Find It in Your Reading Find examples of noun clauses in a story or article. For each one, identify its function in the sentence.

Find It in Your Writing Review a piece of writing from your portfolio. Combine two pairs of sentences using noun clauses.

Clauses • 477

Step-by-Step Teaching Guide

Hands-on Grammar

Teaching Resources: Hands-on Grammar Activity Book, Ch. 20

1. If you wish to have students do this activity in class, you may wish to have scissors, heavy paper, and marker pens available.

2. Have students follow directions to construct their flip-and-folds.

3. Use the sample sentences in the textbook to get students started on the activity. Lead students to recognize how revising sentence structure can add variety to their writing.

Find It in Your Reading

You might have students work with a story they have been assigned in class. Have students compete to see who can find the first noun clause, and then the most noun clauses.

Find It in Your Writing

Suggest that students make flip-and-folds for the sentences they find in the Find It in Your Reading activity and combine the noun clauses with new sentence parts that they write themselves. When students have finished the activity, have them read their new sentences aloud.

☑ ONGOING ASSESSMENT: Assess Mastery

Use the following resources to assess student mastery of phrases and clauses.

In the Textbook	Print Resources	Technology
Chapter Review, Ex. 49–50 Standardized Test Preparation Workshop	*Formal Assessment,* Chapter 20	*On-Line Exercise Bank,* Chapter 20

⏱ TIME SAVERS!

✋ **Hands-on Grammar**
Use the Hands-on Grammar activity sheet for Chapter 20 to facilitate this activity.

Each of these exercises correlates to the instruction on clauses, pages 464–476. These exercises may be used for more practice, for reteaching, or for review of the key concepts presented. Answers for all chapter exercises are available in *Grammar Exercises Answers on Transparencies* in your Teaching Resources.

Answer Key

▶ **Exercise 38**

1. The ruins of many of the Romans' great buildings are still standing. (ind.)
2. Later civilizations used stones from the Roman ruins (ind.); when they wanted to build (sub.)
3. This scavenging has reduced the available information about the Romans (ind.); which occurred in many countries (sub.)
4. The ruins of the city itself are most amazing (ind.); which are dotted throughout present-day Rome (sub.)
5. Ruins can also be found in other European cities (ind.); that were once a part of the Roman Empire (sub.)

▶ **Exercise 39**

1. (which) had a million inhabitants at its zenith (Rome) (*which* = subject) (nonessential)
2. (that) was built in Spain— (aqueduct) (*that* = subject) (essential)
3. (whose) concerns were uniformity and tradition (Romans) (*whose* = adjective) (nonessential)
4. (which) served as a meeting place (forum) (*which* = subject) (nonessential)
5. (who) were fond of their comforts (Romans) (*who* = subject) (nonessential)
6. (that) wealthy Romans took for granted (things) (*that* = direct object) (essential)
7. (whom) later cultures respected (Virgil) (*whom* = direct object) (nonessential)
8. about (whom) much has been said in praise (writer) (*whom* = object of a preposition) (essential)
9. (when) his father's farm was confiscated (moved) (*when* = adverb) (essential)

GRAMMAR EXERCISES 38–45

▶ **Exercise 38** Recognizing Independent and Subordinate Clauses
Identify the independent and subordinate clause in each sentence.

1. The ruins of many of the Romans' great buildings are still standing.
2. Later civilizations used stones from the Roman ruins when they wanted to build.
3. This scavenging, which occurred in many countries, has reduced the available information about the Romans.
4. The ruins of the city itself, which are dotted throughout present-day Rome, are most amazing.
5. Ruins can also be found in other European cities that were once a part of the Roman Empire.

▶ **Exercise 39** Identifying Adjective Clauses, the Words They Modify, and Introductory Words Write the adjective clause in each sentence and the word the clause modifies. Circle each relative pronoun or adverb, and label its use *subject, direct object, object of a preposition, adjective,* or *adverb.* Finally, label the clause *essential* or *nonessential.*

1. Ancient Rome, which had a million inhabitants at its zenith, was the supreme city of the empire.
2. A Roman aqueduct that was built in Spain still carries water to the city of Segovia.
3. Romans, whose concerns were uniformity and tradition, built or added on to cities.
4. Each city had temples, baths, theaters, and a forum, which served as a meeting place.
5. The Romans, who were fond of their comforts, had indoor heating and plumbing.

478 • Phrases and Clauses

6. The things that wealthy Romans took for granted fell into disuse for many centuries after the Romans' fall.
7. Virgil, whom later cultures respected, was perhaps the most famous Roman writer.
8. He is a writer about whom much has been said in praise.
9. Virgil moved to Rome when his father's farm was confiscated.
10. The poet, whose greatest work was the *Aeneid,* died before he could give it the final revision.

▶ **Exercise 40** Identifying Noun Clauses Write the noun clause in each sentence. Label the clause *subject, direct object, indirect object, predicate nominative, object of a preposition,* or *appositive.*

1. Historians observe that the Roman Empire was attacked by many tribes.
2. The British Isles were the site where invading barbarians wiped out most traces of the Romans.
3. One fact became clear: that the Roman bureaucracy could no longer support the empire.
4. Whoever wanted to avoid paying taxes moved to the country.
5. Whatever group invaded a particular area often assumed Roman administrative duties.
6. Roman armies often consisted of soldiers from whatever groups were living in a particular region.
7. Romans maintained whatever traditions they could.
8. Many people believed that the empire was still an entity.
9. Today's civilization owes whoever promoted Roman ideals a great debt.
10. We should remember one fact: that much of our language and culture comes from the Romans.

10. (whose) greatest work was the *Aeneid* (poet) (*whose* = adjective) (nonessential)

▶ **Exercise 40**

1. that the Roman Empire was attacked by many tribes (direct object)
2. where invading barbarians wiped out most traces of the Romans (predicate nominative)
3. that the Roman bureaucracy could no longer support the empire (appositive)
4. Whoever wanted to avoid paying taxes (subject)
5. Whatever group invaded a particular area (subject)

6. whatever groups were living in a particular region (object of a preposition)
7. whatever traditions they could (direct object)
8. that the empire was still an entity (direct object)
9. whoever promoted Roman ideals (indirect object)
10. that much of our language and culture comes from the Romans (appositive)

> **Exercise 41** Supplying Relative
Adverbs Supply a logical relative
adverb to complete each sentence. Then,
write the word or words it modifies.
Finally, add the missing words in the elliptical clauses.

1. In the third century A.D., the Romans
   encountered trouble __?__ they turned.
2. Barbarian tribes wanted to cross the
   frontier __?__ they could settle in
   Roman lands.
3. Trying appeasement __?__ they resort-
   ed to war, the Romans hoped to avoid
   fighting.
4. Refortifying towns __?__ they could be
   protected against raids was common.
5. Taxes had to be raised __?__ these
   defenses could be built.
6. Economic recession was soon widespread __?__ were the crushing taxes.
7. The Goths crossed into Roman territory earlier __?__ the Franks.
8. To repel the invaders, Romans collected more taxes __?__ before.
9. As a ruler, the emperor Aurelian was
   better __?__ others.
10. One of his successors, Diocletian,
    divided the empire so that it came to
    resemble two empires more __?__ one.

> **Exercise 42** Revising to Combine
Sentences Using Adjective and Adverb
Clauses Turn each pair of sentences into
one with an adjective or adverb clause.
Underline each clause, and indicate the
word or words it modifies.

1. Diocletian appointed a co-emperor.
   The co-emperor had the same powers
   as he did.
2. Diocletian laid more emphasis on the
   divine status of the emperor. He was
   less tolerant of Christianity.
3. Under Diocletian, the army increased
   in size. Conscription was reintroduced.

4. Later, Constantine gained control. He
   then reunited the divided empire
   under one ruler.
5. He ordered his soldiers to wear a
   Christian symbol on their shields. He
   wanted to see whether the God of the
   Christians would help him win a battle.
6. Tolerance of Christianity was promoted.
   Persecution was only a sporadic
   occurrence.
7. Christianity became officially protected. It was able to grow and develop
   within the empire.
8. Constantine built a new city called
   Constantinople. It then remained an
   imperial capital for a thousand years.
9. In A.D. 380, the emperor Theodosius
   came to power. He then forbade
   worship of the old pagan gods.
10. Constantinople and the East were
    progressing. The West was declining.

> **Exercise 43** Find It in Your
Reading In the excerpt from *Julius
Caesar* on page 474, identify the function
of the highlighted noun clause in each
sentence.

> **Exercise 44** Find It in Your
Writing Look through your writing
portfolio. Find an example of each of the
three types of subordinate clauses—adjective, adverb, and noun. If you cannot find
an example of a particular type of clause,
find a place where you can add such a
clause to a piece of writing.

> **Exercise 45** Writing Application
Choose a period in ancient history that
you would like to visit. Write a description
of what you think life would be like for you
in that time. Include at least one adjective
clause, one adverb clause, and one noun
clause.

Section Review • 479

Answer Key continued

> **Exercise 44**

Find It in Your Writing

After students finish this activity with examples
from their portfolios, have them exchange
papers with a writing partner and review
subordinate clauses.

> **Exercise 45**

Writing Application

After students finish this activity, have them
exchange papers with a partner and check one
another's examples of clauses.

Answer Key

> **Exercise 41**

1. wherever (encountered)
2. so that (wanted)
3. before (Trying)
4. so that (Refortifying)
5. so that (had to be raised)
6. as (widespread)
7. than [did] the Franks (earlier)
8. than [they did] before (collected)
9. than [were] others (better)
10. than [it resembled] one (more)

> **Exercise 42**

Sentences will vary. Samples are
provided.

1. Diocletian appointed a co-
   emperor who had the same
   powers as he did. (co-emperor)
2. Diocletian, who was less tolerant
   of Christianity, laid more
   emphasis on the divine status of
   the emperor. (Diocletian)
3. Under Diocletian, the army
   increased in size because
   conscription was reintroduced.
   (increased)
4. Later, Constantine gained
   control, after which he united
   the divided empire under one
   ruler. (gained)
5. He ordered his soldiers to wear a
   Christian symbol on their shields
   because he wanted to see
   whether the God of the
   Christians would help him win a
   battle. (ordered)
6. Tolerance of Christianity was
   promoted although persecution
   was a sporadic occurrence. (was
   promoted)
7. Because Christianity became
   officially protected, it was able
   to grow and develop within the
   empire. (was able)
8. Constantine built a new city
   called Constantinople, which
   remained an imperial capital
   for a thousand years.
   (Constantinople)
9. In A.D. 380, after the emperor
   Theodosius came to power, he
   forbade the worship of the old
   pagan gods. (forbade)
10. While Constantinople and the
    East were progressing, the West
    was declining. (was declining)

> **Exercise 43**

Find It in Your Reading

That you have wronged me (subject)
You yourself are much condemned
(direct object)

continued

Answer Key

Exercise 46

1. of great renown—writers, scholars (adjective)
2. after the decline—was felt (adverb); of the Roman Empire—decline (adjective)
3. to Roman learning—indebted (adverb)
4. During the Middle Ages—were considered (adverb); for other universities—models (adjective)
5. for the training—were intended (adverb); of clergy and administrators—training (adjective)
6. the Romans' language—Latin (appositive); of the universities—language (adjective)
7. of a great change—center (adjective); in education and culture—change (adjective)
8. a flowering of art and culture—Renaissance (appositive); of art and culture—flowering (adjective); by classical antiquity—was inspired (adverb)
9. by the Italian artists—justified (adverb); Michelangelo, Raphael, Leonardo da Vinci—artists (appositive)
10. in several areas—excellence (adjective); painting, sculpture, architecture—areas (appositive); to the end—led (adverb); of religious domination—end (adjective); of culture—domination (adjective)

Exercise 47

1. struggling (verb)
2. Desiring—country (present participle)
3. winning—side (present participle); siding (gerund)
4. voting (gerund); favored (verb)
5. reigning—king (present participle); leaving—king (present participle)

Exercise 48

1. (participial)—*tourists*
2. (gerund)—subject
3. (gerund)—object of a preposition
4. (participial)—*Colosseum*

5. (gerund)—subject; (gerund)—object of a preposition
6. (gerund)—subject
7. (infinitive)—*walk*
8. (infinitive)—*easier;* (infinitive)—*is*
9. (infinitive)—subject
10. (infinitive)—direct object

GRAMMAR EXERCISES 46–52

▶ **Exercise 46** Identifying Adjective, Adverb, and Appositive Phrases Write and label each adverb and adjective phrase. Identify the word or words it modifies. Write each appositive phrase and the word or words it renames.

1. Ancient Rome produced many writers and scholars of great renown.
2. Their influence was felt long after the decline of the Roman Empire.
3. Italian culture is indebted to Roman learning.
4. During the Middle Ages, Italian universities were considered models for other universities.
5. The earliest universities were intended for the training of clergy and administrators.
6. Latin, the Romans' language, was the language of the universities.
7. Italy was the center of a great change in education and culture.
8. The Renaissance, a flowering of art and culture, was inspired by classical antiquity.
9. The belief seemed justified by the Italian artists, Michelangelo, Raphael, and Leonardo da Vinci.
10. Their excellence in several areas—painting, sculpture, and architecture—led to the end of religious domination of culture.

▶ **Exercise 47** Distinguishing Between Participles, Verbs, and Gerunds Identify each underlined word in the following sentences as a *participle*, *verb*, or *gerund*. For each participle, tell whether it is *past* or *present*, and write the word or words it modifies.

1. In the first half of the twentieth century, Italy was <u>struggling</u> for power in Europe.
2. <u>Desiring</u> recognition, the country fought in both world wars.
3. In the first war, Italy was on the <u>winning</u> side, but <u>siding</u> with the losers in the second war led to much turmoil.
4. After World War II, <u>voting</u> in general elections revealed that a majority <u>favored</u> the formation of a republic.
5. The <u>reigning</u> king, Humbert, abdicated, <u>leaving</u> the country.

▶ **Exercise 48** Identifying Gerund, Participial, and Infinitive Phrases Identify each underlined phrase as either *gerund*, *participial*, or *infinitive*. If participial or infinitive, write the word or words it modifies. If gerund or infinitive, tell how it functions in the sentence.

1. <u>Deciding to start in the country's capital</u>, many tourists begin their trip to Italy in Rome.
2. <u>Careful planning</u> is necessary when visiting Rome.
3. Everyone looks forward to <u>visiting the former center of civilization</u>.
4. <u>Having room for fifty thousand people</u>, the Colosseum was the arena where Romans went to be entertained.
5. <u>Being able to look at an ancient Roman interior</u> is a good incentive for <u>going to the Pantheon</u>.
6. <u>Looking almost anywhere in Rome</u> reveals how the modern city is built on the ruins of Rome.
7. <u>To visit some of the oldest ruins in Rome</u>, walk two blocks from the Pantheon.
8. It is easier <u>to travel in the Vatican City by shuttle bus</u> than it is <u>to walk</u>.

9. To call St. Peter's Cathedral impressive is an understatement.
10. No modern Roman building is allowed to be taller than St. Peter's.

Exercise 49 Identifying Adjective, Adverb, and Noun Clauses

Write the subordinate clause in each sentence, and identify it as *adjective*, *adverb*, or *noun*. For each adjective or adverb clause, name the word or words it modifies.

1. Florence, which was the birthplace of the Renaissance, has the best collection of Renaissance art in Europe.
2. Michelangelo, whose work includes the magnificent statue *David*, lived and worked for a time in Florence.
3. The people whom he lived with, the Medicis, were rulers of Florence.
4. Florence was the city that commissioned *David* from Michelangelo.
5. The Uffizi Gallery, where the best paintings in Italy are found, is in Florence.
6. Siena enjoyed status as a major military power until Florence defeated it.
7. As a result, the town has more Gothic art than it has Renaissance art.
8. The National Picture Gallery offers prime examples of Gothic Sienese art, even though most tourists prefer to see Renaissance art.
9. Milan's art is not as grand as that of other Roman cities, although its church is the third largest in Europe.
10. Before the day is over, we must look at Da Vinci's *Last Supper*.

Exercise 50 Revising a Paragraph to Combine Sentences Using Clauses

Revise this paragraph, using clauses to combine short sentences. Underline your new clause, and label it.

Siena is convenient to Florence. It does not have any major attractions. The cathedral in Florence has a magnificent dome.

It is not as large as the one in St. Peter's Basilica. Michelangelo planned St. Peter's dome. He admitted it could never be as fine as the dome in Florence. The Palazzo Vecchio is a Florentine landmark. It was once the home of the Medicis. The Uffizi Gallery has the greatest collection of Italian paintings anywhere. There are works by Da Vinci, Raphael, Botticelli, and Michelangelo there.

Exercise 51 Writing Application

Write a short essay about a place or an attraction in Italy that you would like to see. Tell why this place interests you. Include adjective, adverb, participial, and gerund phrases to add details. Also, include one adjective and one adverb clause. Label each of these items.

Exercise 52 CUMULATIVE REVIEW Parts of Speech and Basic Sentence Parts

Identify each underlined item as a *subject*, *verb*, *direct object*, *indirect object*, *predicate nominative*, or *predicate adjective*.

1. We found Milan less magnificent than Rome or Florence.
2. Do people in Milan care more about soccer than about art?
3. Locals give their team the greatest support.
4. Milan is an industrial city.
5. It is more famous for fashion than for antiquities.
6. The City Tower of Siena offers tourists a three-hundred-step climb.
7. From the top is one of the best views in Italy.
8. The Uffizi Gallery is not a very large museum.
9. The square contains statues of great Italians.
10. Would you like to visit Fiesole?

Answer Key

Exercise 49

1. which was the birthplace of the Renaissance (adjective)—Florence
2. whose work includes the magnificent statue *David* (adjective)—Michelangelo
3. whom he lived with (adjective)—people
4. that commissioned *David* from Michelangelo (adjective)—city
5. where the best paintings in Italy are found (adjective)—Uffizi Gallery
6. until Florence defeated it (adverb)—enjoyed
7. than it has Renaissance art (adverb)—more
8. even though most tourists prefer to see Renaissance art (adverb)—offers
9. although its church is the third largest in Europe (adverb)—is
10. Before the day is over (adverb)—look

Exercise 50

Answers may vary; samples are given.

1. Siena is convenient to Florence although it does not have any major attractions. (adverb clause)
2. The cathedral in Florence has a magnificent dome, which is not as large as the one in St. Peter's Basilica. (adjective clause)
3. Michelangelo planned St. Peter's dome even though he admitted it could never be as fine as the dome in Florence. (adverb clause)
4. The Palazzo Vecchio is a Florentine landmark that was once the home of the Medicis. (adjective clause)
5. The Uffizi Gallery has the greatest collection of Italian paintings anywhere because there are works by Da Vinci, Raphael, Botticelli, and Michelangelo. (adverb clause)

Exercise 51

Writing Application

Have students work in pairs and read each other's essays, looking for the labeled four kinds of phrases and two clauses.

continued

Exercise 52

Cumulative Review

1. direct object
2. verb
3. indirect object
4. predicate nominative
5. predicate adjective
6. direct object
7. subject
8. predicate nominative
9. verb
10. subject

Step-by-Step Teaching Guide

Recognizing Appropriate Sentence Construction

Teaching Resources: Standardized Test Preparation Workbook, pp. 39–40

1. Remind students that a clause is a group of words that has a subject and verb and is used as part of a sentence. A phrase is a group of words without a subject and verb. (*Gesturing wildly*, the driver tried to attract attention.)

2. Emphasize that this practice test measures students' understanding of basic sentence structure.

3. Go over the sample test item and the answer.

4. Explain why answers A, B, and C are incorrect (in A and C the word *this* has no clear antecedent, and sentences in B have not been combined).

5. Assign the two practice items, and go over the answers with students.

Standardized Test Preparation Workshop

Recognizing Appropriate Sentence Construction

On standardized tests, questions that measure your ability to use phrases and clauses reveal your understanding of basic sentence construction and style. A phrase is a group of words that acts as a unit without a subject and a verb; a clause is a group of words that contains a subject and verb. When faced with these types of questions, first read the entire passage to get an idea of the author's purpose. Focus on the underlined group of words, and note any ways they might be combined without changing the meaning. Then, choose a revision that uses a phrase or clause to combine like ideas without changing the meaning or author's message. The following test items will give you practice with these types of questions.

Test Tip

Watch for repetition in consecutive sentences. Often, the correct answer eliminates the repetition by combining the sentences with a phrase or clause or by forming a compound subject or verb while maintaining the sense of the original sentences.

Sample Test Item	Answer and Explanation
Directions: Read the passage, and choose the letter of the best way to rewrite the underlined sentences. Ian bought a flexible airline ticket for his (1) upcoming vacation. Its flexibility means that he will be able to stop in several places.	
1 A Ian just bought a flexible airline ticket for his upcoming vacation, and this means he can stop in several places. **B** Ian bought an airline ticket for his upcoming vacation. He will stop in more than one place because it is flexible. **C** For his upcoming vacation, Ian bought a flexible airline ticket, and this means he can stop in several places. **D** For his upcoming vacation, Ian bought a flexible airline ticket, which will let him stop in several places.	The correct answer is *D*. This revision combines the two sentences, successfully eliminating extra words and repetition while keeping the sense of the original. Choices *A* and *C* are awkward because there is no clear antecedent for the word *this*. Choice *B* moves words around without actually combining the sentences. It also leaves *it* without a clear antecedent.

482 • Phrases and Clauses

🔧 TEST-TAKING TIP

Tell students that on an exam testing appropriate sentence construction, they should keep the following points in mind.

1. When reading rewritten sentences, avoid choosing a sentence with a dangling or misplaced modifier. (*Barking up a tree, he found the beagle.*)

2. Though an answer may make sense, it may omit words from the original passage, as in choice 3B of Practice 2.

3. Avoid choosing an answer that seems wordier than the original sentences, as in choices 2G and 3C in Practice 1.

▶ **Practice 1** **Directions:** Read the passage, and choose the letter of the best way to rewrite the underlined sentences.

There are two places Ian wants to visit.
(1)
The places are Hong Kong and New

Zealand. The flight leaves from New York.
              (2)
There is a one-day stopover in Alaska. From
                                      (3)
Alaska, the flight continues to Hong Kong.

In Hong Kong, Ian will spend a week.

1 A Hong Kong and New Zealand are two of the places Ian wants to visit.

 B Two places Ian wants to visit are Hong Kong and New Zealand.

 C There are two places, Hong Kong and New Zealand, that Ian wants to visit.

 D Ian wants to visit two places, and they are Hong Kong and New Zealand.

2 F The flight leaves from New York and has a one-day stopover in Alaska.

 G The flight leaves from New York, and there is a one-day stopover in Alaska.

 H The flight leaves New York, and then it stops over in Alaska for one day.

 J The flight leaves New York and has a stopover of one day in Alaska.

3 A From Alaska, the flight continues to Hong Kong, and Ian will spend a week there.

 B Ian will spend a week in Hong Kong after arriving there from Alaska.

 C From Alaska, the flight continues to Hong Kong, where Ian will spend a week.

 D The flight continues to Hong Kong; Ian will spend a week in Hong Kong.

▶ **Practice 2** **Directions:** Read the passage, and choose the letter of the best way to rewrite the underlined sentences.

After a week in Hong Kong, Ian will be
(1)
ready to move on. New Zealand is his next

stop. He is interested in the Maoris. The
                                      (2)
Maoris were the first known people in New

Zealand. It will be quite a journey. It will
                              (3)
be one that Ian most likely will never forget.

1 A After Hong Kong, Ian will be ready to move on to his next stop, and that will be New Zealand.

 B Once Ian has spent a week in Hong Kong, he'll be ready to move on to New Zealand.

 C After Hong Kong, Ian will be ready for New Zealand—the next stop.

 D After a week in Hong Kong, Ian will be ready to move on to New Zealand.

2 F Ian is interested in the Maoris, who were the first known people in New Zealand.

 G Called the Maoris, New Zealand's first people are of interest to Ian.

 H Ian is interested in the Maoris because they were the first known people in New Zealand.

 J Ian is interested in the Maoris, and they were New Zealand's first people.

3 A It will most likely be quite a journey that Ian will never forget.

 B Ian will most likely never forget the journey.

 C It will be quite a journey, and Ian will never forget it most likely.

 D It will be quite a journey, one that Ian most likely will never forget.

▶ **Practice 1**

1. B
2. F
3. C

▶ **Practice 2**

1. D
2. F
3. D

Customize for
Less Advanced Students

Go over the answer choices on the practice tests, and explain why the "wrong" answers in each case should not have been chosen.

Customize for
More Advanced Students

Urge students to be on the lookout for and avoid choosing run-on sentences as correct answers.

Chapter 21 Time and Resource Manager

In-Depth Lesson Plan

	LESSON FOCUS	PRINT AND MEDIA RESOURCES
DAY 1	**The Four Functions of a Sentence; Sentence Combining** Students learn and classify the four functions of a sentence, combine sentences for sentence variety, and do the Hands-on Grammar activity. (pp. 484–495/⊞338–349)	*Writing and Grammar* Interactive Text, Sections 21.1–2; *On-line Exercise Bank,* Sections 21.1–2 **Teaching Resources** *Grammar Exercise Workbook,* pp. 81–86; *Grammar Exercises Answers on Transparencies,* Ch. 21; *Hands-on Grammar Activity Book,* Ch. 21
DAY 2	**Varying Sentences** Students learn to vary sentences by adjusting lengths and beginnings. (pp. 496–499/⊞350–353)	*Writing and Grammar* Interactive Text, Section 21.3; *On-line Exercise Bank,* Section 21.3 **Teaching Resources** *Grammar Exercise Workbook,* pp. 87–92
DAY 3	**Avoiding Fragments and Run-ons** Students learn to recognize and correct sentence fragments and run-ons. (pp. 500–506/⊞354–360)	*On-line Exercise Bank,* Section 21.4 **Teaching Resources** *Grammar Exercise Workbook,* pp. 93–96
DAY 4	**Misplaced and Dangling Modifiers** Students learn to recognize and correct modifier errors. (pp. 507–511/⊞361–365)	**Teaching Resources** *Grammar Exercise Workbook,* pp. 97–102
DAY 5	**Review and Assess** Students review the chapter and demonstrate mastery of basic sentence functions and structures. (pp. 512–515)	*Writing and Grammar* Interactive Text, Ch. 21, Chapter Review **Teaching Resources** *Formal Assessment,* Ch. 21

Accelerated Lesson Plan

	LESSON FOCUS	PRINT AND MEDIA RESOURCES
DAY 1	**The Four Functions of a Sentence; Sentence Combining** Students cover four functions of a sentence, combine sentences for sentence variety, and learn to vary sentence length and sentence beginnings. (pp. 484–499/⊞338–353)	*Writing and Grammar* Interactive Text, Sections 21.1–3; *On-line Exercise Bank,* Sections 21.1–3 **Teaching Resources** *Grammar Exercise Workbook,* pp. 81–92; *Grammar Exercises Answers on Transparencies,* Ch. 21
DAY 2	**Avoiding Fragments and Run-ons; Misplaced and Dangling Modifiers** Students cover correcting sentence fragments, run-ons, and modifier errors. (pp. 500–511/⊞354–365)	*Writing and Grammar* Interactive Text, Section 21.4; *On-line Exercise Bank,* Section 21.4 **Teaching Resources** *Grammar Exercise Workbook,* pp. 93–102
DAY 3	**Review and Assess** Students review the chapter and demonstrate mastery of the concepts. (pp. 512–515)	*Writing and Grammar* Interactive Text, Ch. 21, Chapter Review **Teaching Resources** *Formal Assessment,* Ch. 21

Options for Adapting Lesson Plans

FEATURES

Extend coverage with the Grammar in Literature feature (p. 497/⊞351) and the Standardized Test Preparation Workshop (p. 514).

TECHNOLOGY

Students can use *Writing and Grammar* Interactive Text to complete the exercises interactively on computer. They can complete additional exercises in the *On-line Exercise Bank:* The Auto Check feature will grade their work. Go on-line: PHSchool.com Use Web Code: eek-1002

Writing and Grammar Handbook Alignment

Page numbers in Step-by-Step Teaching Guides in this Teacher's Edition refer to pages from the full student text. Handbook page references, indicated with this icon 🄷, are provided in Time and Resource Manager boxes and at the bottom of each Teacher's Edition page.

INTEGRATED SKILLS COVERAGE

Grammar in Literature
SE p. 497/🄷351

Writing
Find It in Your Writing SE pp. 488, 494, 495, 499, 511/🄷342, 348, 349, 353, 365
Writing Application SE pp. 495, 499, 511, 513, 517/🄷349, 353, 365
Grammar and Style SE p. 497/🄷351

Viewing and Representing
Critical Viewing SE pp. 484, 486, 489, 491, 493, 497, 500, 503, 505, 506, 508, 510/🄷338, 340, 343, 345, 347, 351, 354, 357, 359, 360, 362, 364

Vocabulary Skills
ATE pp. 487, 501

Spelling Skills
SE p. 502/🄷356

ASSESSMENT SUPPORT

Standardized Test Preparation Workshop SE p. 514; ATE pp. 504, 506
Standardized Test Preparation Workbook, pp. 41–42
Formal Assessment, Ch. 21

MEETING INDIVIDUAL NEEDS

Less Advanced Students ATE p. 515. See also Ongoing Assessments ATE pp. 487, 490, 491, 492, 493, 497, 501, 503, 505, 508.
More Advanced Students ATE p. 505
ESL Students ATE pp. 491, 507
Spatial Learners ATE p. 501

BLOCK SCHEDULING

Pacing Suggestions
For 90-minute Blocks
- Administer the Diagnostic Test to students to determine instructional coverage needed.
- Have students complete the necessary exercises in class. Use the Hands-on Grammar activity to provide a change of pace.

Resources for Varying Instruction
- *Writing and Grammar* Interactive Text A 90-minute block provides an ideal opportunity for students to work on the computer.

Professional Development Support
- *How to Manage Instruction in the Block* This teaching resource provides management and activity suggestions.

MEDIA AND TECHNOLOGY

For the Student
- *Writing and Grammar* Interactive Text, Ch. 21
- *On-line Exercise Bank,* Sections 21.1–4

For the Teacher
- Teacher**EXPRESS** CD-ROM

WRITING AND GRAMMAR ON-LINE

Interactive Text (On-line or on CD-ROM)
- Easily navigable instruction with on-line supporting resources
- Self-scoring exercises and diagnostic tests

Companion Web Site PHSchool.com
- On-line Exercise Bank (use Web Code eek-1002)

See the Go On-line! feature, SE p. iii.

LITERATURE CONNECTIONS

Grammar in Literature selection from *Prentice Hall Literature, Penguin Edition,* Grade 10:
from "The Bean Eaters," Gwendolyn Brooks, SE p. 497/🄷351

▶ **Lesson Objectives**

1. To understand the four functions of sentences

2. To use varied sentence structure to express meanings

3. To analyze the characteristics of clearly written texts, including patterns of organization, syntax, and word choice

4. To evaluate writing for both mechanics and content

5. To proofread writing for appropriateness of organization, content, style, and conventions

6. To demonstrate control over grammatical elements

7. To recognize and avoid phrase and clause fragments in written compositions

8. To recognize and correct run-on sentences

9. To recognize and correct misplaced modifiers

Critical Viewing

Contrast Possible answers: Are hundreds of penguins walking upright on the shore? People on the cruise ship probably are entranced by us.

Chapter 21 Effective Sentences

When we first learn to talk, we start by speaking single words. Then, we begin grouping words together to form sentences. It is at this point that we are able to start communicating in a meaningful way. Putting words together into sentences—nouns or pronouns accompanied by verbs to express complete thoughts—is the first step toward being an effective communicator, both as a speaker and as a writer. In this chapter, you will learn basic sentence functions and structures—ways in which you can vary sentence structures to make your writing more clear and interesting—and some of the types of errors that can occur in your sentences.

▲ **Critical Viewing**
Write two sentences about this scene, one from the point of view of a passenger on the ship and one from the point of view of a penguin. **[Contrast]**

484 • Effective Sentences

☑ **ONGOING ASSESSMENT: Diagnose**

If students miss more than one item in any category, direct them to the relevant pages of the textbook and assign exercises for practice and review.

Effective Sentences	Diagnostic Test Items	Teach	Practice	Section Reviews	Chapter Review
Skill Check A					
The Four Functions of a Sentence	A 1–5	pp. 486–487/ 🖥340–341	Ex. 1–3	Ex. 4–6	Ex. 45
Skill Check B					
Sentence Combining	B 6–10	pp. 489–493/ 🖥343–347	Ex. 10–14	Ex. 15–17	Ex. 46

Diagnostic Test

Directions: Write all answers on a separate sheet of paper.

Skill Check A. Label each sentence *declarative, interrogative, imperative,* or *exclamatory.*

1. Have you ever wanted to visit Antarctica?
2. Make sure to dress as warmly as you can for that adventure.
3. What an amazing animal a penguin is!
4. How can the penguin survive in such a frigid environment?
5. Their bodies are well adapted to life in subfreezing temperatures.

Skill Check B. Combine these sentences using the method indicated.

6. Antarctica was not discovered until the early 1800's. This was mostly because of its remoteness. (turn a sentence into a phrase)
7. Captain James Cook was the first explorer to cross the Antarctic Circle. He was on a mission from the British navy. (join with a relative pronoun)
8. Cook circumnavigated Antarctica. He never actually sighted the continent. (join with a comma and a coordinating conjunction)
9. Cook studied deposits of rocks in icebergs at sea. Cook concluded that a barren southern continent existed. (use a compound verb)
10. Cook reported his findings. Explorers from several other countries began their own search for the southern continent. (join with subordinating conjunction)

Skill Check C. Rewrite the following sentences to be more direct or to vary their beginnings as indicated in parentheses.

11. A Russian expedition sailed around Antarctica and discovered some offshore islands in 1821. (prepositional phrase)
12. The first known landing on Antarctica was by John Davis, who was an American explorer and whose main interest was commerce. (appositive)
13. James Weddell, traveling farther south than any other explorer, discovered the sea that bears his name. (participial phrase)
14. It was in the 1840's, at which time Antarctica's status as a continent was finally established. (Be more direct.)
15. One determined explorer, James Ross, was an explorer from Britain who sailed into a gulf that is now called the Ross Sea. (Be more direct.)

Skill Check D. Label each of the following items *fragment, run-on,* or *misplaced modifier.* Then, rewrite the item so that it is correct.

16. Many expeditions in the late 1800's and early 1900's.
17. One scientific expedition became caught on the ice, its members spent the winter of 1897–1898 stranded there.
18. Ernest Shackleton led a British expedition before turning back because of exhausted supplies to within 97 miles of the South Pole.
19. The Norwegian Roald Amundsen and a party of four reached the South Pole using dogs to pull their sleds on December 14, 1911.
20. Arrived five weeks before a British expedition led by Robert Scott.

Effective Sentences • **485**

Skill Check A

1. interrogative   4. interrogative
2. imperative   5. declarative
3. exclamatory

Skill Check B

Answers will vary; samples are given.

6. Antarctica was not discovered until the early 1800's, mostly because of its remoteness.
7. Captain James Cook, who was the first explorer to cross the Antarctic Circle, was on a mission from the British navy.
8. Cook circumnavigated Antarctica, but he never actually sighted the continent.
9. Cook studied deposits of rocks in icebergs at sea and concluded that . . .
10. When Cook reported his findings, explorers . . .

Skill Check C

Answers will vary; samples are given.

11. In 1821, a Russian expedition . . . offshore islands.
12. John Davis, an American explorer whose main interest was commerce, made the first known landing on Antarctica.
13. Traveling farther south than any other explorer, James Weddell discovered the sea that bears his name.
14. Antarctica's status as a continent was finally established in the 1840s.
15. James Ross, a determined British explorer, sailed . . . Ross Sea.

Skill Check D

Answers will vary; samples are given.

16. (fragment) Many expeditions in the late 1800's and early 1900's failed.
17. (run-on) One scientific . . . ice, and its members . . . there.
18. (misplaced modifier) Before turning back because of exhausted supplies, Ernest Shackleton led a British expedition to within 97 miles of the South Pole.
19. (misplaced modifier) Using dogs to pull their sleds, Norwegian . . . South Pole on December 14, 1911.
20. (fragment) The Norwegians arrived five weeks before . . .

✓ ONGOING ASSESSMENT: Diagnose *continued*

Effective Sentences	Diagnostic Test Items	Teach	Practice	Section Reviews	Chapter Review
Skill Check C					
Varying Sentences	C 11–15	pp. 496–498/ Ⓗ350–352	Ex. 21–24	Ex. 25–28	Ex. 47
Skill Check D					
Avoiding Sentence Problems	D 16–20	pp. 500–509/ Ⓗ354–363	Ex. 32–38	Ex. 39–41	Ex. 48
Cumulative Reviews and Applications				Ex. 7–9, 18–20, 29–31, 42–44	Ex. 49–50, A–F

The Four Functions of a Sentence

Sentences can be classified according to what they do. The four types of sentences in English are *declarative, interrogative, imperative,* and *exclamatory.*

Declarative sentences are the most common type. They are used to "declare," or state facts.

 **KEY CONCEPT** A **declarative sentence** states an idea and ends with a period. ∎

DECLARATIVE: Hot-air balloons are flown mainly for recreation. Recently, adventurers succeeded in flying around the world in a hot-air balloon.

Interrogative means "asking." An *interrogative sentence* is a question.

KEY CONCEPT An **interrogative sentence** asks a question and ends with a question mark. ∎

INTERROGATIVE: Have you ever flown in a hot-air balloon? Do you think you would enjoy the experience?

Exercise 1 Identifying Declarative and Interrogative Sentences Write each of the following sentences on your paper. Identify each as declarative or interrogative, and punctuate it correctly.

1. Have you ever been to a balloon festival
2. We went to one in Albuquerque last year
3. Although I had heard about such festivals, I wondered what I would see there
4. When we arrived, the balloons were still on the ground
5. Next year, do you think you might go

▶ Critical Viewing Write a sentence comparing these festive balloons to the kinds of balloons used in a balloon festival. **[Compare and Contrast]**

486 • Effective Sentences

The word *imperative* is related to the word *emperor*, a person who gives commands. *Imperative sentences* are like emperors: They give commands.

> **KEY CONCEPT** An **imperative sentence** gives an order or a direction and ends with either a period or an exclamation mark. ■

Most imperative sentences start with a verb. In this type of imperative sentence, the subject is understood to be *you*.

IMPERATIVE: Follow the directions carefully.
Wait for me!

Notice the punctuation at the end of these examples. In the first sentence, the period suggests that a mild command is being given in an ordinary tone of voice. The exclamation mark at the end of the second sentence suggests a strong command, one given in a loud voice.

To *exclaim* means to "shout out." *Exclamatory sentences* are used to "shout out" emotions, such as happiness, fear, delight, and anger.

> **KEY CONCEPT** An **exclamatory sentence** conveys strong emotion and ends with an exclamation mark. ■

EXCLAMATORY: She's not going to make that balloon trip without me!
I have been waiting for the opportunity all my life!

> **Exercise 2** Identifying Imperative and Exclamatory Sentences Write each of the following sentences on your paper. Add the correct punctuation to the end of each sentence. Label imperative sentences *I* and exclamatory sentences *E*.
> 1. Tell me about the festival
> 2. What an amazing sight it was
> 3. I have never seen so many balloons
> 4. Wait until next year
> 5. Come with us, and you'll see what I mean

> **Exercise 3** Writing the Four Types of Sentences Write a paragraph to one of your friends encouraging him or her to participate in some type of adventure with you. Use each of the four types of sentences at least once. Identify each type you have used.

> **More Practice**
> **Grammar Exercise Workbook**
> • pp. 81–84
> **On-line Exercise Bank**
> • Section 21.1
>   *Go on-line:*
>   PHSchool.com
>   *Enter Web Code:*
>   eek-1002

> Complete the exercises on-line! Exercises 1, 2, and 3 are available on-line or on CD-ROM.

The Four Functions of a Sentence • 487

Imperative and Exclamatory Sentences

1. Point out that both imperative and exclamatory sentences use exclamation marks, but that an imperative sentence can end with a period if the order is not intended to sound urgent.

2. Have students make decisions about ending imperative sentences with periods or exclamation marks. Give examples and have them supply the most likely punctuation:

   Wash up before you eat (period)
   Watch out (exclamation mark)
   Please sit near me (period)
   Run and hide (exclamation mark)
   Run for daily exercise (period)
   Save him (exclamation mark)

3. Explain that imperative sentences have understood subjects: *you.*

4. Remind students that exclamatory sentences convey strong emotion.

Integrating Vocabulary Skills

Conversational Tags Explain that conversational tags in written dialogue (such as "he said" or "she exclaimed") along with an end mark can tell a reader what type of sentence is being spoken. Have students practice writing conversational tags for the different sentence functions. If necessary, have students use the dictionary or thesaurus to find words to use instead of *said* or *asked.*

Answer Key

> **Exercise 2**

1. . I
2. . or ! E
3. . or ! E
4. . or ! I
5. . or ! I

> **Exercise 3**

Answers will vary; samples are given.

1. Have you heard about our plans to go hiking? (interrogative)
2. Start packing! (imperative)
3. We have been planning this for weeks. (declarative)
4. What fun it will be! (exclamatory)

☑ **ONGOING ASSESSMENT: Monitor and Reinforce**

If students have difficulty with Exercise 1, 2, or 3, refer them to the following for additional practice.

In the Textbook	Print Resources	Technology
Section Review, Ex. 4–6, Section 21.1	*Grammar Exercise Workbook,* pp. 81–84	*On-Line Exercise Bank,* Section 21.1

Section Review

Each of these exercises correlates with the instruction on the four functions of a sentence, pages 486–487. The exercises may be used for more practice, for reteaching, or for review of the key concepts presented. Answers for all chapter exercises are available in *Grammar Exercises Answers on Transparencies* in your Teaching Resources.

Answer Key

Exercise 4

1. Interrogative
2. Declarative
3. Exclamatory
4. Interrogative
5. Imperative
6. Interrogative
7. Declarative
8. Exclamatory
9. Imperative
10. Declarative

Exercise 5

1. .
2. .
3. ?
4. .
5. .
6. !
7. .
8. ?
9. .
10. !

Exercise 6

Answers may vary; samples are given.

1. The Montgolfier brothers first experimented with hot-air balloons.
2. That is the most amazing thing I have ever heard!
3. How can I learn more about ballooning?
4. Did Jacques Alexandre Charles and the Roberts brothers launch the first hydrogen balloon?
5. Tell me more.

Exercise 7

Find It in Your Reading
You may want to bring in travel magazines or brochures for your students to search.

Exercise 8

Find It in Your Writing
If students find an excess of a particular kind of sentence, encourage them to make revisions.

Exercise 9

Writing Application
Encourage students to present their narratives to the class.

Section 21.1 Section Review

GRAMMAR EXERCISES 4–9

Exercise 4 Classifying Sentences by Function Label each sentence *declarative, interrogative, imperative,* or *exclamatory.*

1. Did you know that the Four Corners Hot-Air Balloon Fiesta is held in late May?
2. What I didn't know is that the International Balloon Fiesta is held in October.
3. Last year's festival was fantastic!
4. Which festival did you attend?
5. When you go to next year's festival, take lots of pictures.
6. Have you ever gone up in a balloon?
7. Miranda said it was the most exciting experience she's ever had.
8. What a thrill that would be!
9. Let me know if you decide to do it.
10. Maybe I'll try it, too.

Exercise 5 Supplying Appropriate Punctuation for Sentences Punctuate each sentence according to its function.

1. The Montgolfier brothers were the first to experiment with hot-air balloons
2. When they began experimenting in the 1700's, no one else had yet been successful
3. Who do you think their first passengers were
4. Even if you don't know, take a guess
5. A duck, a rooster, and a sheep were the first passengers
6. That's crazy
7. Balloon flights soon became a fad in Europe
8. Which was more popular, the hot-air balloon or the hydrogen-gas balloon
9. Look at this picture of the Montgolfier brothers
10. How daring they were

488 • Effective Sentences

Exercise 6 Writing Sentences to Fit Functions Write a sentence that revises or answers each of the sentences below. The sentence you write should have the function indicated in parentheses.

1. Who first experimented with hot-air balloons? (declarative)
2. Is that the most amazing thing you've ever heard? (exclamatory)
3. I hope to learn more about ballooning. (interrogative)
4. Jacques Alexandre Charles and the Roberts brothers launched the first hydrogen balloon. (interrogative)
5. Will you tell me more? (imperative)

Exercise 7 Find It in Your Reading
Skim through a travel magazine to find at least two examples of each of the four types of sentences. You can find your examples in advertisements and in articles.

Exercise 8 Find It in Your Writing
Review a short story or a piece of autobiographical writing from your portfolio. Find at least one example of each type of sentence. Check to see that you have punctuated each correctly.

Exercise 9 Writing Application
Write a brief narrative about a group of people your age who take part in an unusual adventure, such as a ballooning expedition. You can include dialogue. Try to use each type of sentence at least twice in your story.

☑ ONGOING ASSESSMENT: Assess Mastery

Use the following resources to assess student mastery of the four functions of a sentence.

In the Textbook	Technology
Chapter Review, Ex. 45	*On-Line Exercise Bank,* Section 21.1

Sentence Combining

Books written for very young readers present information in short, direct sentences. While this makes the book easy to read, it doesn't make it enjoyable or interesting to mature readers. Writing that is to be read by mature readers should include sentences of varying lengths and complexity to create a flow of ideas. One way to achieve sentence variety is to combine sentences—to express two or more related ideas or pieces of information in a single sentence.

EXAMPLE: We went to the South Pole.
             We met scientists.

             We went to the South Pole and met scientists.
             We met scientists at the South Pole.
             We met scientists when we went to the South Pole.

▶ **KEY CONCEPT** Sentences can be combined by using a compound subject, a compound verb, or a compound object. ■

EXAMPLE: Moira enjoyed learning about Antarctic exploration.
                     Tom enjoyed learning about Antarctic exploration.

COMPOUND SUBJECT: Moira and Tom enjoyed learning about Antarctic exploration.

EXAMPLE: Lisa raced her dog sled.
                     Lisa won a prize.

COMPOUND VERB: Lisa raced her dog sled and won a prize.

EXAMPLE: Scott rode the icebreaker.
                     Scott rode the snowmobile.

COMPOUND OBJECT: Scott rode the icebreaker and the snowmobile.

Theme: Antarctica

In this section, you will learn ways to combine sentences. The examples and exercises are about Antarctica and the South Pole.

Cross-Curricular Connection: Social Studies

◀ Critical Viewing Write a series of sentences describing this picture. Then, combine two sentences following one of the examples above. [Describe]

Sentence Combining • 489

⏱ TIME AND RESOURCE MANAGER

Resources
Print: *Grammar Exercise Workbook,* pp. 85–86; *Grammar Exercises Answers on Transparencies,* Ch. 21; *Hands-on Grammar Activity Book,* Ch. 21
Technology: *Writing and Grammar* Interactive Text, Section 21.2; *On-Line Exercise Bank,* Section 21.2

Using the Full Student Edition	Using the Handbook🄷
• Work through all key concepts, pp. 489–493.	• Work through all key concepts, pp. 343–347.
• Assign and review Exercises 10–14.	• Assign and review Exercises 10–14.
• Do the Hands-on Grammar activity, p. 494.	• Do the Hands-on Grammar activity, p. 348.

PREPARE and ENGAGE

Interest GRABBER Write these three sentences on the board: *I need to buy toothpaste. I need to buy oranges. I also need to buy the newspaper.* Ask what is wrong with the style of this passage (repetitious words and structures), and ask a volunteer for the best way to revise it (combine into one sentence with a compound object of the infinitive *to buy*).

Activate Prior Knowledge

Ask students to bring to class passages that contain short, simple sentences (simple directions for assembling a model, pages from a children's story). Ask them to note what most of these sentences lack (subordinate clauses, verbal phrases, items in series), and then explain that good writers use complex constructions among their sentences. Then, have students experiment with rewriting the passages they have brought to class by combining some of the short sentences into longer ones.

TEACH

Step-by-Step Teaching Guide

Combining Sentences by Forming Compounds

1. If necessary, review compound subjects, compound verbs, and compound objects. Start with the examples beneath the Key Concept. Parse each example so that students can practice identifying the subject, verb, and complement in each one.

2. Caution students against adding commas in compound structures. Frequently, students will misidentify a compound verb phrase for a compound sentence. Show them the difference.

3. As you work with each example, point out that the combination is more efficient than the uncombined sentences. Have students tell you which words have been eliminated.

Critical Viewing

Describe Possible answer: Sled dogs are pulling a man in a sled. They are pulling him over the ice. (Sled dogs are pulling a man in a sled over the ice.)

Answer Key

Exercise 10

1. Sir Edmund Winterbottom and his son, Cecil, were explorers. (compound subject)
2. They wanted to go on an adventure together and decided to visit the South Pole. (compound verb)
3. Their trip took months of preparation and detailed planning. (compound direct object)
4. Long underwear and warm coats had to be purchased. (compound subject)
5. They would travel to the southern tip of South America and fly from there to the American Antarctic outpost. (compound verb)
6. The Winterbottoms also needed a guide and transport across the ice. (compound direct object)
7. Following months of preparation, they were excited and ready to go. (compound complement—predicate adjectives)
8. Sir Edmund and Cecil packed large bags. (compound subject)
9. Their guide met them at the outpost with provisions and his dog-sled team. (compound object of preposition)
10. Within minutes, they had their equipment packed and were off! (compound verb)

Step-by-Step Teaching Guide

Joining Independent Clauses

1. Review the concept of *clause* (structure containing its own subject and verb) and differentiate between independent and subordinate clauses. Then, focus on independent clauses and review the coordinating conjunctions that can be used to connect them (*and, but, nor, or, for, yet*).
2. Be sure students understand that both a comma and a coordinating conjunction are used to connect related independent clauses.
3. Tell students that they have the option of using a semicolon in place of the comma-and-conjunction method of combining independent clauses.

21.2

Exercise 10 Combining Sentences Using Compound Verbs, Subjects, and Objects Combine each pair of sentences in the way that makes the most sense. Identify what you have done to combine them.

EXAMPLE: Milly chopped ice with a pick. She also used an axe.

ANSWER: Milly chopped ice with a pick and an axe. (compound objects)

1. Sir Edmund Winterbottom was an explorer. So was his son, Cecil.
2. They wanted to go on an adventure together. They decided to visit the South Pole.
3. Their trip took months of preparation. Their trip took detailed planning.
4. Long underwear had to be purchased. Then, warm coats had to be bought.
5. They would travel to the southern tip of South America. They would fly from there to the American Antarctic outpost.
6. The Winterbottoms also needed a guide. They required transport across the ice.
7. Following months of preparation, they were ready to go. They were excited.
8. Sir Edmund packed a large bag. Cecil did, too.
9. Their guide met them at the outpost with provisions. He also met them with his dog-sled team.
10. Within minutes, they had their equipment packed. They were off!

KEY CONCEPT Sentences can be combined by joining two independent clauses to form a compound sentence. ■

Use a compound sentence when combining ideas that are related but independent. Compound sentences are formed by joining two independent clauses either with a comma and a conjunction or with a semicolon.

EXAMPLE: The wind chilled the tundra. The snow battered my face.

COMPOUND SENTENCE: The wind chilled the tundra, and the snow battered my face.

EXAMPLE: The snowstorm lasted for hours. The wind and the snow mingled with the air.

COMPOUND SENTENCE: The snowstorm lasted for hours; the wind and the snow mingled with the air.

490 • Effective Sentences

More Practice

Grammar Exercise Workbook
• pp. 85–86
On-line Exercise Bank
• Section 21.2
Go on-line:
PHSchool.com
Enter Web Code:
eek-1002

Complete the exercises on-line! Exercises 10 and 11 are available on-line or on CD-ROM.

ONGOING ASSESSMENT: Monitor and Reinforce

If students miss more than two items in Exercise 10, refer them to the following for additional practice.

In the Textbook	Print Resources	Technology
Section Review, Ex. 15, Section 21.2	*Grammar Exercise Workbook*, pp. 85–86	*On-Line Exercise Bank*, Section 21.2

Exercise 11 Forming Compound Sentences by Joining Independent Clauses Combine the following sentences using the method given in parentheses.

EXAMPLE: (semicolon) The South Pole is very cold. Ice is everywhere.

ANSWER: The South Pole is very cold; ice is everywhere.

1. (semicolon) The South Pole is a point at the southern end of the Earth's axis. It rests in central Antarctica.
2. (comma and conjunction) It is often associated with the magnetic South Pole. They are 1,600 miles apart.
3. (comma and conjunction) The magnetic poles change location with time, a phenomenon known as polar wandering. The direction of wandering has been observed to reverse.
4. (semicolon) Compasses do not work at the magnetic poles. The magnetic field at these poles is vertical.
5. (comma and conjunction) As for the South Pole, a Norwegian explorer named Roald Amundsen reached it first. He did so on December 14, 1911.
6. (comma and conjunction) Today, people actually live at the South Pole part of the year doing scientific research. Amundsen's feat was herculean for its day.
7. (semicolon) Antarctica is the coldest continent on Earth. It holds the record for the lowest temperature ever recorded: –128.6° F.
8. (semicolon) The interior of Antarctica is a windy polar desert. Average precipitation is less than two inches each year.
9. (comma and conjunction) Coastal areas of the Antarctic are milder. Precipitation in those regions averages up to eight inches per year.
10. (comma and conjunction) The precipitation that falls on the South Pole is always in the form of snow. It usually is the byproduct of cyclones.

KEY CONCEPT Sentences can be combined by changing one of them into a subordinate clause. ■

Use a compound sentence when you are combining sentences to show the relationship between ideas. The subordinating conjunction will help readers understand the relationship.

EXAMPLE: We were frightened. We thought there might be an avalanche.

COMBINED WITH A SUBORDINATE CLAUSE: We were frightened because we thought there might be an avalanche.

▲ Critical Viewing Write two separate sentences describing this penguin. Then, combine the sentences to form a compound sentence. [Describe]

Sentence Combining • 491

Step-by-Step Teaching Guide

Creating Subordinate Clauses

1. Review the concept of *subordinate clauses* and ask students to recall the subordinating conjunctions that are most frequently used (while, since, as, because, although, etc.). Have students explain the meanings that each subordinating conjunction can add to a sentence (e.g., *while* tells that one thing is happening at the same time as another).

2. Read the example aloud and ask students why *because* is a good choice of subordinating conjunction (it helps establish a reason "we were frightened").

Customize for ESL Students

Give ESL students a passage containing short, fairly simple sentences for them to read, reread if necessary, and comprehend—perhaps even discuss. (Use an appropriate passage from any of their textbooks or one that you locate for this activity.) Once students have digested the series of sentences several times, they will be better positioned for combining the ideas. Begin by having them circle any two sentences (or by having them copy two sentences onto their paper). Then, give them a list of conjunctions and have them use any of these to combine the ideas. Allow them to practice by making several different combinations for each sentence pair.

Critical Viewing

Describe Possible answer: This penguin lives in Antarctica. The penguin rests on the rocks. (This penguin lives in Antarctica; it rests on the rocks.)

ONGOING ASSESSMENT: Monitor and Reinforce

If students miss more than two items in Exercise 11, refer them to the following for additional practice.

In the Textbook	Print Resources	Technology
Section Review, Ex. 16, Selection 21.2	*Grammar Exercise Workbook,* pp. 85–86	*On-Line Exercise Bank,* Section 21.2

Answer Key

▶ **Exercise 12**

1. . . . square miles, although it does not always stay . . .
2. . . . doubles in size because a large amount . . .
3. . . . Antarctic Convergence, which is a sharply defined zone . . .
4. . . . warmer waters moving south, where the convergence . . .
5. Because a measurable physical difference in the ocean occurs at this point, the water surrounding . . .
6. Even though Antarctica has no native population, scientific and support staffs reside there . . .
7. . . . Emilio Palma, whose father was an Argentine . . .
8. Ninety-five percent of the surface of Antarctica, which contains 70 percent of the Earth's freshwater supply, is covered by ice.
9. Since it has a thick ice cover, it has the highest average . . .
10. Although lower points may exist, the lowest point . . .

▶ **Exercise 13**

Answers may vary; samples are given.

1. Even though the continent was uninhabited, seven nations— Argentina, Australia, Chile, France, Great Britain, New Zealand, and Norway—once declared territorial claims to parts of the Antarctic.
2. Since the Antarctic Treaty was signed in 1961, their claims have been renounced in the interest of international cooperation and scientific research.
3. Future economic development of the Antarctic landmass is unlikely because it is so icebound.
4. Extensive resources have yet to be harvested from the continental shelf, although the technology is in development.
5. However, marine life, which is plentiful in the Antarctic waters, is being economically developed.

21.2

▶ **Exercise 12** Combining Sentences Using Subordinating Clauses Using the subordinating conjunction or relative pronoun in parentheses, combine these pairs of sentences.

1. (although) Antarctica's total area in summer is about 5.5 million square miles. It does not always stay the same size.
2. (because) During the winter, Antarctica nearly doubles in size. A large amount of sea ice forms at its periphery.
3. (which) The true boundary of Antarctica is not the coastline of the continent but the Antarctic Convergence. It is a sharply defined zone at the southern ends of the Atlantic, Indian, and Pacific oceans.
4. (where) Colder waters flowing north from Antarctica mix with warmer waters moving south. The convergence is defined.
5. (because) A measurable physical difference in the ocean occurs at this point. The water surrounding the Antarctic continent is considered an ocean unto itself.
6. (even though) Antarctica has no native population. Scientific and support staffs reside there usually for no more than one year at a time.
7. (whose) The first person born in Antarctica was Emilio Palma. His father was an Argentine naval officer.
8. (which) Ninety-five percent of the surface of Antarctica is covered by ice. Antarctica contains 70 percent of Earth's freshwater supply.
9. (since) It has a thick ice cover. It has the highest average elevation of all the continents.
10. (although) The lowest point on the continent appears to be the Bentley Subglacial Trench, which is 8,200 feet below sea level and is covered by 9,840 feet of ice. Lower points may exist.

▶ **Exercise 13** Combining Sentences Using Subordinating Conjunctions or Relative Pronouns Using a subordinating conjunction or relative pronoun of your choice, combine the following pairs of sentences.

1. Seven nations—Argentina, Australia, Chile, France, Great Britain, New Zealand, and Norway—once declared territorial claims to parts of the Antarctic. The continent was uninhabited.
2. The Antarctic Treaty was signed in 1961. Their claims were renounced in the interests of international cooperation and scientific research.
3. Future economic development of the Antarctic landmass is unlikely. It is so icebound.
4. Extensive resources have yet to be harvested from the continental shelf. The technology is in development.
5. However, marine life in the Antarctic waters is being economically developed. It is plentiful.

492 • Effective Sentences

▶ **More Practice**

Grammar Exercise Workbook
• pp. 85–86
On-line Exercise Bank
• Section 21.2
Go on-line:
PHSchool.com
Enter Web Code:
eek-1002

Get instant feedback! Exercises 12, 13, and 14 are available on-line or on CD-ROM.

☑ **ONGOING ASSESSMENT: Monitor and Reinforce**

If students have difficulty with Exercise 12 or 13, refer them to the following for additional practice.

In the Textbook	Print Resources	Technology
Section Review, Exercise 16, Section 21.2	*Grammar Exercise Workbook,* pp. 85–86	*On-Line Exercise Bank,* Section 21.2

KEY CONCEPT Sentences can be combined by changing one of them into a phrase. ■

Change a sentence into a phrase when you are combining sentences in which one of the sentences just adds detail.

EXAMPLES: My dog-sled team races tomorrow. We race on the tundra of the Antarctic.
My dog-sled team races tomorrow on the tundra of the Antarctic.

My dog-sled team races tomorrow on the tundra of the Antarctic. The Antarctic is one of the most inhospitable places on Earth.
My dog-sled team races tomorrow on the tundra of the Antarctic, one of the most inhospitable places on Earth.

Exercise 14 Combining Sentences With Phrases Combine the following pairs of sentences by changing one to a phrase.
1. Antarctica was once a central, tropical region of Gondwanaland. Gondwanaland was an ancient supercontinent on Earth.
2. Gondwanaland broke apart many years ago. It broke from the force of shifts in the Earth's plates.
3. The supercontinent split to form the separate continents in the current Southern Hemisphere. It split during the late Mesozoic era.
4. Antarctica consists of two main geologic areas. These areas are East Antarctica and West Antarctica.
5. East Antarctica is covered by massive layers of ice. The ice is thousands of meters thick.
6. West Antarctica appears to be a continuation of the Andes Mountains. The Andes are in South America.
7. Glaciologists and geologists speculate that without its ice cover, West Antarctica would be an island archipelago. An island archipelago is a sea containing a large group of islands.
8. Despite its frozen landscape, West Antarctica is home to Mount Erebus. Erebus is a 12,448-foot volcano.
9. The two areas are separated by the Transantarctic Mountains. The mountain range is running across the entire continent.
10. Within these mountains are many coal deposits and fossil remains. The remains come from the time that Antarctica had a tropical climate.

▼ Critical Viewing
Write a sentence about this photo in which you include the phrase *rising above the thick ice.* **[Describe]**

Sentence Combining • 493

Creating Phrases

1. Identify for students the kinds of phrases that they might write in their sentences (prepositional, participial, gerund, infinitive, appositive) and review their typical syntactic relationships (participial phrases modify nouns or pronouns, gerund phrases function as nouns, and so on).

2. As students read the examples, have them identify the words that were eliminated in order to combine the structures.

3. Then, have students identify the kinds of phrases that remained (prepositional, appositive).

4. If students need practice recognizing movable structures, have them find additional combinations for the examples (*Tomorrow, on the tundra of the Antarctic, my dog-sled team races.*).

Answer Key

▶ **Exercise 14**

Answers may vary; samples are given.
1. . . . Gondwanaland, an ancient . . .
2. . . . years ago from the force of shifts. . .
3. The supercontinent split during the late Mesozoic era to form the separate continents in the current Southern Hemisphere.
4. . . . geologic areas, East Antarctica and West Antarctica.
5. East Antarctica is covered by thousands of meters of ice.
6. West Antarctica appears to be a continuation of the Andes Mountains of South America.
7. . . . an island archipelago, a sea containing a large group of islands.
8. . . . home to Mount Erebus, a 12,448-foot volcano.
9. The two areas are separated across the entire continent by the Transantarctic Mountains.
10. . . . coal deposits and fossil remains from Antarctica's early tropical climate.

Critical Viewing

Describe Sample answer: Rising above the thick ice, rocky outcroppings can be seen.

☑ **ONGOING ASSESSMENT: Monitor and Reinforce**

If students miss more than two items in Exercise 14, refer them to the following for additional practice.

In the Textbook	Print Resources	Technology
Section Review, Ex. 17, Section 21.2	*Grammar Exercise Workbook,* pp. 85–86	*On-Line Exercise Bank,* Section 21.2

Hands-on Grammar

Teaching Resources: Hands-on Grammar Activity Book, Ch. 21

1. If you wish to do this activity in class, provide scissors and sheets of colored paper for the class. Give each student a copy of the Hands-on Grammar activity sheet.

2. Have students follow the directions to prepare the strips.

3. You may wish to expand this activity by having students use this method to combine sentences with phrases from one of the exercises on the previous pages.

Find It in Your Reading

If students have difficulty finding appropriate sentences in their textbooks, encourage them to search in popular magazines and newspapers.

Find It in Your Writing

Have students exchange papers from their portfolios and look for sentences to combine in their partners' writing.

21.2

Hands-on Grammar

Folding in Phrases

You can practice what you have learned about combining sentences with phrases by doing the following activity.

Cut out several long, narrow strips from a legal size (8 1/2" by 14") piece of paper. On each strip, write one of the following pairs of related sentences:

Antarctica is a cold, white continent. It is covered almost entirely by ice and snow.

One animal that thrives in Antarctica is the southern elephant seal. It is the largest seal in the world.

Mount Erebus is Antarctica's most active volcano. It occasionally spurts volcanic rock over the island on which it sits.

In 1911, Norwegian explorer Roald Amundsen won the race to the South Pole. His victory was by a five-week margin.

Now combine the sentence pairs by folding over the paper to cover up the first few words of the second sentence that come before the phrase you want to connect to the first sentence. For example, by covering up *It is* on the second sentence of the first pair, you would be able to read: *Antarctica is a cold, white continent covered almost entirely by ice and snow.*

Read your combined sentences aloud to be sure they make sense. Then, write some new pairs of sentences of your own on additional strips of paper, and test your classmates' ability to combine them.

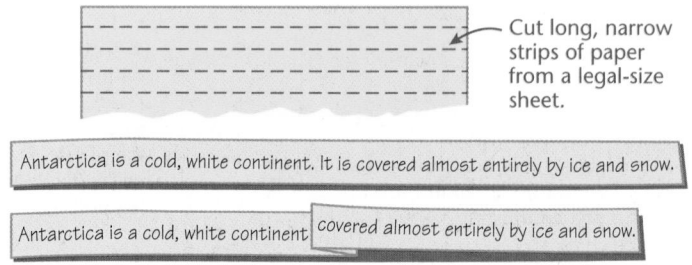

Cut long, narrow strips of paper from a legal-size sheet.

Antarctica is a cold, white continent. It is covered almost entirely by ice and snow.

Antarctica is a cold, white continent covered almost entirely by ice and snow.

Find It in Your Reading Select a long sentence from one of your textbooks. Split it into several shorter sentences that the writer may have combined.

Find It in Your Writing Look through your portfolio for paragraphs that contain several short sentences in a row. Combine the sentences using one of the ways you have learned in this chapter.

494 • Effective Sentences

⏱ **TIME SAVERS!**

✋ **Hands-on Grammar**
Use the Hands-on Grammar activity sheet for Chapter 21 to facilitate this activity.

☑ **ONGOING ASSESSMENT: Assess Mastery**

Use the following resources to assess student mastery of sentence combining.

In the Textbook	Technology
Chapter Review, Ex. 46	*Writing and Grammar* Interactive Text, Section 21.2, Section Review; *On-Line Exercise Bank,* Section 21.2

Section Review

GRAMMAR EXERCISES 15–20

Exercise 15 Combining Sentences Using Compound Parts Combine each pair of sentences by creating a compound subject, verb, or object.

1. I watched a program about the South Pole. My dad saw it with me.
2. The show focused on exploration. It also highlighted elements of the climate.
3. The geography of Antarctica was mentioned. Also, its wildlife was discussed.
4. The program started on Monday. It concluded on Tuesday.
5. We found the program interesting. It was also intellectually stimulating.

Exercise 16 Combining Clauses and Phrases Combine each pair of sentences by creating a compound sentence, forming a complex sentence, or changing one sentence into a phrase.

1. The soil in the interior of Antarctica is very dry. The area receives only two inches of snow each year.
2. The soil is so dry. Some geologists call it a "polar desert."
3. Rainfall and snowfall are heavier in some areas. These areas are along the coasts.
4. Icy winds make the continent seem even colder. They blow across Antarctica throughout the year.
5. The largest ice shelf in Antarctica is the Ross Ice Shelf. It is the size of Texas.
6. Antarctica is isolated from the rest of the world. It has avoided problems found on other continents.
7. The ice there is the purest in the world. It is untainted by industrial pollution.
8. Residents obtain the water they need. They do this by melting ice and snow.
9. The climate is so cold. Few insects live on the mainland of Antarctica.
10. Few animals live on the mainland. The Antarctic Ocean abounds with wildlife.

Exercise 17 Revising a Paragraph by Combining Sentences Using phrases, combine pairs of sentences in the following passage.

Antarctica was not discovered until the early 1800's. This delay occurred because of its remoteness. The ancient Greeks first theorized about the existence of Antarctica. They were advanced in geography. They believed that the Southern Hemisphere must have large continents. These continents existed to balance those in the Northern Hemisphere. In 1772, British explorer James Cook sailed as far south as he could. Cook searched for the southern continent. Huge ice blocks prevented him from reaching Antarctica. He did spot many whales and seals. Groups of hunters arrived in the area. They arrived soon after Cook's voyage. Several hunters reached the continent. This occurred a few years later.

Exercise 18 Find It in Your Reading Select a long sentence from a story or textbook. Determine what ideas the writer has combined in the sentence and what method was used to combine ideas.

Exercise 19 Find It in Your Writing Revise a piece of writing from your portfolio. Combine at least five pairs of sentences, using different techniques.

Exercise 20 Writing Application Imagine that you were an early explorer of Antarctica. Write several short sentences from the journal you kept. Then, combine some of the sentences.

Section Review • 495

List these sentences on the board, on the overhead, or on a handout:

John likes baseball.
He likes batting.

It is his favorite sport.
He likes batting better than fielding.

He plays every day.
He is not interested in other sports.

Challenge students to combine this information into three sentences, none of which starts with the same construction as any other.

Activate Prior Knowledge

Have students bring to class papers they have written that they are proud of. Tell students that most of their sentences probably begin with a subject and verb, and then ask students to think of the different kinds of structures (words, phrases, and clauses) that can begin sentences.

TEACH

Step-by-Step Teaching Guide

Vary Sentence Length

1. Remind students that combining shorter sentences to make one longer sentence is one way to make writing more interesting.

2. Ask students to explain the effect of the last example sentence, the shortest. Explain that a short sentence following a series of longer sentences catches readers' attention because it stands out—it is short and to the point.

Answer Key

Answers may vary; samples are given.

1. Plucked lutes . . . *oud*. The name . . . *oud*.
2. The neck . . . *pipa*. It may also . . . body.
3. Frequently, . . . a fingerboard. This fingerboard . . . sound.
4. The technique . . . plucking. Fiddles, or bowed lutes . . . Middle Ages.
5. The violin . . . sedate viol. The violin and its relatives became dominant during the 1700's.

Section 21.3

Varying Sentences

Vary your sentences to produce a rhythm, to achieve an effect, or to emphasize key points or connections among ideas. There are many ways that you can achieve sentence variety.

Vary Sentence Length

You have already learned that you can combine several short, choppy sentences to form a longer sentence. However, having too many long sentences in a row is as uninteresting as having too many short ones. When you want to emphasize a point or surprise a reader, insert a short, direct sentence to interrupt the flow of long sentences. Look at this example:

The viola, which evolved from medieval fiddles, is first depicted in early sixteenth-century drawings and literature. Like most instruments of the Renaissance, it was built in a range of sizes. Played standing up, the largest violas were the specialties of Italian masters. <u>One such master was Antonio Stradivari.</u>

Some sentences contain only one idea and cannot be broken up. It may be possible, however, to state the idea in a shorter sentence. Other sentences contain two or more ideas and might be shortened by breaking up the ideas.

▶ **Exercise 21** Making Simpler Sentences In the following items, break up long sentences into two or more sentences or restate long sentences in a simpler, more direct way.
1. Plucked lutes include the banjo and guitar as well as the Arabic *oud*, from which the name of the European lute is derived.
2. The neck of a lute may be a short elongation of the body, as in the Chinese *pipa*, or it may be a separate element fastened to or piercing the body.
3. Frequently, the neck incorporates a fingerboard, which may have frets, against which the strings can be pressed to alter their sound.
4. The technique of bowing is not as old as that of plucking, and fiddles, or bowed lutes, such as the violin or viol, arrived in Europe from Asia only in the Middle Ages.
5. The violin and its relatives, at first associated with country dance music and considered inferior to the quieter, more sedate viol, became dominant during the 1700's.

Theme: Musical Instruments

In this section, you will learn ways to vary sentence lengths and beginnings to make your writing more interesting. The examples and exercises are about different musical instruments.

Cross-Curricular Connection: Music

▶ **More Practice**

Grammar Exercise Workbook
• pp. 87–88
On-line Exercise Bank
• Section 21.3
Go on-line:
PHSchool.com
Enter Web Code:
eek-1002

Interactive Textbook

Complete the exercises on-line! Exercises 21 and 22 are available on-line or on CD-ROM.

🕐 **TIME AND RESOURCE MANAGER**

Resources
Print: *Grammar Exercise Workbook*, pp. 87–92; *Grammar Exercises Answers on Transparencies*, Ch. 21
Technology: *Writing and Grammar* Interactive Text, Section 21.3; *On-Line Exercise Bank*, Section 21.3

Using the Full Student Edition	Using the Handbook Ⓗ
• Work through all key concepts, pp. 496–498. • Assign and review Exercises 21–24. • Read and discuss Grammar in Literature, p. 497.	• Work through all key concepts, pp. 350–352. • Assign and review Exercises 21–24. • Read and discuss Grammar in Literature, p. 351.

GRAMMAR IN LITERATURE

from **The Bean Eaters**
Gwendolyn Brooks

The poet gives plain words an eloquent rhythm by varying the length of her sentences.

They eat beans mostly, this old yellow pair.
Dinner is a casual affair.
Plain chipware on a plain and creaking wood,
Tin flatware.

Two who are Mostly Good.
Two who have lived their day,
But keep on putting on their clothes
And putting things away.

▼ **Critical Viewing**
Write two sentences, one long and one short, to compare the sound of a violin to that of a guitar or a bass. [**Compare**]

▶ **Exercise 22** Revising a Paragraph to Improve Sentence Variety Rewrite this paragraph, breaking up long sentences into two or more simple sentences or restating long sentences more simply.

Just as mechanical inventions served European music when the fully developed keyboard arose in the Middle Ages, so electrical engineers have offered twentieth-century musicians innovative ways of producing and controlling sounds. Since the 1930's, electric amplification has altered the technique of popular singers and instrumentalists. Electric organs have mostly influenced popular music, but since the mid-1960's, synthesizers have been important tools of composers of many music styles. Except in the manipulations of sound used in rock music, however, amplification, like broadcasting and recording, serves chiefly to disseminate music rather than to create it. With the electric guitar, such amplification replaced the sound box and stimulated new musical effects; the long-term implications of sound production cannot yet be predicted.

🕸 Grammar and Style Tip

One way to test how smoothly your sentences flow is to read them aloud. By reading your work aloud in a lively way, you will be able to identify when your sentence structure falls flat, grows boring, or does not provide the necessary interest for the subject matter. Reading your work aloud also helps you catch some of the common sentence errors discussed later in this chapter.

Varying Sentences • 497

☑ ONGOING ASSESSMENT: Monitor and Reinforce

If students have difficulty with Exercise 21 or 22, refer them to the following for additional practice.

In the Textbook	Print Resources	Technology
Section Review, Ex. 25, Section 21.3	*Grammar Exercise Workbook,* pp. 87–88	*On-Line Exercise Bank,* Section 21.3

Vary Sentence Openers and Structures

1. Ask students if they can think of ways to vary sentences other than length (the way sentences begin, the way they are structured internally, the number of phrases and clauses they contain).

2. As you review the different sentence openers on this page, point out that the first—noun—is the way most sentences begin: normal subject-verb order. As you examine each sentence opener, have students suggest additional examples. Place some of them on the board or on an overhead and explain the syntactic relationship of each opener with the rest of the sentence.

3. Tell students that adverb clauses also can begin sentences and provide an example:

   When the conductor walked onto the stage, everyone stood and applauded.

Answer Key

> **Exercise 23**

Answers may vary; samples are given.

1. Separately, all drums are classified . . .
2. For sound resonance, a drum has . . .
3. Stretched across a frame, the heads of a drum . . .
4. From huge basses to shallow snares, cylindrical drums vary . . .
5. Surprisingly, the snare's intense . . .

> **Exercise 24**

Answers may vary; samples are given.

1. From backstage enters the orchestra.
2. Here is the conductor.
3. In the auditorium is held the rehearsal.
4. Before the concert, silent remained the instruments.
5. Beautiful is the sound of a violin.

21.3

Varying Sentence Openers and Structures

Another way to produce sentence variety is to avoid starting each sentence in the same way. Consider these options:

START WITH A NOUN: The piano is a difficult instrument to learn.

START WITH AN ADVERB: Surprisingly, the piano is a difficult instrument to learn.

START WITH A PARTICIPLE: Having played the piano, I know it is a difficult instrument to learn.

START WITH A PREPOSITIONAL PHRASE: For many young musicians, the piano is difficult to learn.

You can also vary sentence beginnings by reversing the traditional subject-verb order.

EXAMPLES:

        S   LV COMP
The pipers are here.

COMP LV   S
Here are the pipers.

      S   V   ADV. PHRASE
The parade came around the corner.

  ADV. PHRASE   V   S
Around the corner came the parade.

> **Exercise 23** Revising to Vary Sentence Openers Follow the instructions in parentheses to revise each sentence.
> 1. (Start with an adverb.) All drums are separately classified as part of the membranophone family of instruments.
> 2. (Start with a prepositional phrase.) A drum has one or two heads for sound resonance.
> 3. (Start with a participle.) The heads of a drum stretched across a frame are usually made of plastic or animal skin.
> 4. (Start with a prepositional phrase.) Cylindrical drums vary in size from huge basses to shallow snares.
> 5. (Start with an adverb.) The snare's intense, crisp sound surprisingly makes up for its lack in size.

> **Exercise 24** Revising to Invert Sentences Rewrite each sentence, reversing the traditional subject-verb order.
> 1. The orchestra enters from backstage.
> 2. The conductor is here.
> 3. Rehearsal is held in the auditorium.
> 4. The instruments remained silent before the concert.
> 5. The sound of a violin is beautiful.

> **More Practice**
>
> **Grammar Exercise Workbook**
> • pp. 89–92
> **On-line Exercise Bank**
> • Section 21.3
> *Go on-line:*
> PHSchool.com
> *Enter Web Code:*
> eek-1002

Complete the exercises on-line! Exercises 23 and 24 are available on-line or on CD-ROM.

✓ **ONGOING ASSESSMENT: Assess Mastery**

Use the following resources to assess student mastery of sentence variety.

In the Textbook	Technology
Chapter Review, Ex. 47	*Writing and Grammar* Interactive Text, Section 21.3, Section Review; *On-Line Exercise Bank*, Section 21.3

Section Review

GRAMMAR EXERCISES 25–31

▶ **Exercise 25** Revising to Simplify Long Sentences In these items, break up long sentences into simple sentences or restate them more simply.

1. The xylophone, whose name comes from the Greek *xylon*, meaning "wood," is a percussion instrument consisting of a series of wooden bars that are struck with mallets to produce sounds.
2. Xylophones were developed in Southeast Asia by the fourteenth century, and they arrived and took root as folk instruments in Central Europe about 1500.
3. In Africa, where the xylophone was imported from Madagascar, its use spread throughout the continent; the xylophone became a prominent instrument in African music.
4. Africans who had been enslaved introduced the xylophone to Latin America, where it is known as a *marimba*.
5. By the nineteenth century, performers had popularized the xylophone in western Europe, and its first orchestral use was in *Danse Macabre* (1874) by the French composer Camille Saint-Saëns.

▶ **Exercise 26** Varying Sentence Openers Rewrite this sentence five times, each time beginning with one of the sentence parts listed below: *The members of the orchestra tuned their instruments.* (1) an adverb; (2) a prepositional phrase; (3) a participial phrase; (4) a different prepositional phrase; (5) a different adverb

▶ **Exercise 27** Revising Sentences by Inverting Subject-Verb Order Revise each sentence using an inverted structure.

1. The parade marches down the street.

2. The people along the curb are smiling and waving.
3. The brass instruments shine in the sun.
4. The shofar sounded low and mournful.
5. The orchestra is here.

▶ **Exercise 28** Revising Sentences in Several Ways Revise the paragraph below by varying sentence length, sentence beginnings, or word order.

A glass harmonica was invented by Benjamin Franklin. It is known as the Franklin harmonica and consists of a set of glass bowls, graduated in size to produce distinct pitches, and the bowls are fine-tuned by filling them with different amounts of water. The Franklin harmonica was popular in the early 1800's. Mozart and Beethoven were intrigued by the instrument. The pieces they wrote for the instrument are still performed occasionally.

▶ **Exercise 29** Find It in Your Reading Find a paragraph in a magazine article that illustrates strong sentence variety. Present your example to the class.

▶ **Exercise 30** Find It in Your Writing Make at least five revisions in a piece of your own writing to improve sentence variety.

▶ **Exercise 31** Writing Application Write a review of a concert by the school band or by your favorite band. Use sentences of different lengths, and vary the way your sentences begin or their subject-verb order to provide more interesting reading.

Section Review • **499**

Bring in a piece of string at least four feet long. Ask your students what it would be like to have to lace their shoes using such a long string. Students will note, of course, that the excess of string causes complications; point out that excess words, phrases, and clauses in sentences can cause similar complications—as well as confusion for readers.

Activate Prior Knowledge

Ask students what they find frustrating about the following:

When it isn't too loud.

Students will point out that the identity of *it* is unclear; important information has been omitted, and it seems like only part of an idea. Explain that this is a "fragment" and that such incomplete structures must be reworked.

TEACH

Step-by-Step Teaching Guide

Recognizing Fragments

1. Review the basic parts of sentences: subject, verb, and complement, as well as phrases and clauses.

2. Explain why people sometimes confuse fragments for complete sentences (a phrase may look complete because it contains a verb).

3. Compare the fragments and completed sentences in the charts on the right page. Read the first fragment, then read the first sentence. Ask students to explain what the fragment needed to make it a complete sentence (subject and verb). Continue this process with all five examples.

Critical Viewing

Compare Possible answer: Neither a sentence fragment nor an incomplete orchestra can express the complete thoughts of their composers.

Section 21.4

Avoiding Sentence Problems

Fragments, run-on sentences, and misplaced modifiers can all make your writing confusing. Being able to recognize the parts of sentences and different kinds of clauses and phrases can help you avoid certain errors in your writing.

Recognizing Fragments

Some groups of words, even though they have a capital at the beginning and a period at the end, are not complete sentences. They are *fragments*.

> **KEY CONCEPT** A **fragment** is a group of words that does not express a complete thought but is punctuated as if it were a sentence. ∎

A fragment is only *part* of a sentence, but a sentence always has a subject *and* a verb. A fragment does not always have both parts. It can be a group of words with no subject. It can be a group of words that includes a possible subject but no verb. It can be a group of words with a possible subject and only part of a possible verb. It can even be a subordinate clause standing alone.

Theme: Instruments of the Orchestra

In this section, you will learn how to recognize and correct fragments, run-on sentences, and misplaced modifiers. The examples and exercises are about instruments in an orchestra.

Cross-Curricular Connection: Music

▼ **Critical Viewing** What happens if only part of an orchestra arrives for a concert? How does that compare to a sentence fragment? **[Compare]**

500 • Effective Sentences

⏱ TIME AND RESOURCE MANAGER

Resources
Print: *Grammar Exercise Workbook,* pp. 93–106; *Grammar Exercises Answers on Transparencies,* Ch. 21
Technology: *Writing and Grammar* Interactive Text, Section 21.4; *On-Line Exercise Bank,* Section 21.4

Using the Full Student Edition	Using the Handbook 🅗
• Work through all key concepts, pp. 500–510. • Assign and review Exercises 32–38.	• Work through all key concepts, pp. 354–364. • Assign and review Exercises 32–38.

FRAGMENTS

To hear the orchestra play.
Listened carefully and happily.
The tuba in the marching band.
The parade coming around the bend.
When the band played.

You will usually be able to tell whether a group of words expresses a complete thought. One trick is to read the words aloud. This will help you hear whether or not some part is missing.

In the chart below, words have been added to the preceding fragments to make complete sentences. Read each italicized fragment; then read the sentence. Can you hear the difference? What part is missing in the fragment?

COMPLETED SENTENCES

We went *to hear the orchestra play.*
We *listened carefully and happily.*
I play *the tuba in the marching band.*
The parade was *coming around the bend.*
When the band played, I didn't recognize the song.

Each of the preceding examples needed one or more new parts. The first needed both a subject and a verb. The second needed only a subject. The third became complete when a subject and a verb were added. The fourth became complete when a helping verb was added. The final example needed a complete independent clause to go with the subordinate clause.

▶ **Exercise 32** Recognizing Sentence Fragments Write *F* for each item that is a fragment and *S* for complete sentences.
1. Consists of woodwind, brass, and percussion instruments.
2. Originally a section in ancient Greek theaters.
3. Located between the stage and the audience.
4. Dancers and instrumentalists used this area.
5. In a modern theater.
6. The part reserved for musicians called the orchestra pit.
7. The term *orchestra* now designates an area of seating in an auditorium.
8. The string section in four parts.
9. The double basses often duplicate the cello part an octave lower.
10. The number of instruments can vary.

Get instant feedback!
Exercise 32 is available on-line or on CD-ROM.

▶ **More Practice**

Grammar Exercise Workbook
• pp. 93–94
On-line Exercise Bank
• Section 21.4
  Go on-line:
  PHSchool.com
  Enter Web Code:
  eek-1002

Avoiding Sentence Problems • **501**

☑ ONGOING ASSESSMENT: Monitor and Reinforce

If students miss more than two items in Exercise 32, refer them to the following for additional practice.

In the Textbook	Print Resources	Technology
Section Review, Ex. 39, Section 21.4	*Grammar Exercise Workbook,* pp. 93–94	*On-Line Exercise Bank,* Section 21.4

Correcting Phrase Fragments

1. Point out that a phrase, when standing on a page by itself, is a type of fragment. Review with students the types of phrases (prepositional, participial, gerund, and infinitive) and demonstrate how these are used as modifiers of other words in their sentences. Point out that phrases are commonly mistaken for sentences.

2. Have a volunteer read aloud the first example. Explain that phrase fragments most often can be corrected by adding them to a nearby sentence that contains a word the phrase modifies. Warn students that if this is not possible (for instance, a word it could modify does not appear), then they must add words that will turn the fragment into a sentence.

3. Use the examples on this page to show students that they have options for placing phrases in relation to the words they modify. (Example: *On the stage* the musicians took their places.)

21.4

Correcting Phrase Fragments

A phrase by itself is a fragment. It cannot stand alone because it does not have both a subject and a verb.

▶ **KEY CONCEPT** A phrase should not be capitalized and punctuated as if it were a sentence. ■

Three types of phrases—prepositional, participial, and infinitive—are often mistaken for sentences. A *phrase fragment* can be changed into a sentence in either of two ways. The first way is to add the phrase fragment to a nearby sentence. This example shows a prepositional phrase following a sentence.

FRAGMENT: The musicians took their places. *On the stage.*

You can correct this fragment simply by attaching the phrase to the preceding sentence.

ADDED TO   The musicians took their places
NEARBY SENTENCE: *on the stage.*

You can correct other fragments simply by attaching them to the beginning of a sentence. The participial phrase fragment in the next example can easily be corrected in this way.

FRAGMENT: *Waiting for silence.* The conductor held his baton in the air.

ADDED TO   *Waiting for silence,* the conductor held
NEARBY SENTENCE: his baton in the air.

Sometimes, however, you may not be able to correct a phrase fragment by adding it to a nearby sentence. Then, you will need to use the second way to change a phrase fragment into a sentence: Correct the fragment by adding to the phrase whatever is needed to make it a complete sentence. Often this method requires adding a subject or a verb.

CHANGING PHRASE FRAGMENTS INTO SENTENCES	
Phrase Fragments	**Complete Sentences**
By the conductor.	The seating of an orchestra is determined *by the conductor.*
Listening to the opera.	*Listening to the opera,* I found myself swept away.
To play an instrument.	I would like *to play an instrument.*

502 • Effective Sentences

Spelling Tip

The common and similar suffixes *-er* and *-or* are often mistaken for each other. For instance, the word *conductor* is sometimes misspelled as *conducter.* When you encounter such a word and are unsure which ending to use, look it up in a dictionary.

◄ **Critical Viewing**
The timpani is sometimes called a kettledrum. Explain why in a complete sentence. [**Make a Judgment**]

> **Exercise 33** Revising to Change Phrase Fragments Into Sentences Use each of the following phrase fragments in a sentence. You may use the phrase at the beginning, at the end, or in any other position in the sentence. Check to see that each of your sentences contains a subject and a verb.

EXAMPLE: Arriving at the music hall.

ANSWER: Arriving at the music hall, the performers tuned their instruments.

1. Accompanied by other musicians.
2. Into the night air.
3. To the left of the conductor.
4. Behind the strings section.
5. Playing the kettledrum.
6. Hearing the glockenspiel.
7. With a harp or piano.
8. Feeling the pounding of the bass drum.
9. Without brass instruments.
10. Reserving two orchestra seats.

> **More Practice**

Grammar Exercise Workbook
• pp. 93–94
On-line Exercise Bank
• Section 21.4
   Go on-line:
   PHSchool.com
   Enter Web Code:
   eek-1002

Complete the exercise on-line! Exercise 33 is available on-line or on CD-ROM.

Answer Key

> **Exercise 33**

Answers will vary; samples are given.

1. Accompanied by other musicians, the piano sounded beautiful.
2. The concert's notes followed us into the night air.
3. The first and second violins are to the left of the conductor.
4. The woodwinds and brass are behind the strings section.
5. Playing the kettledrum well is no easy feat.
6. Hearing the glockenspiel reminds me of my uncle.
7. Some orchestras supplement their ensemble with a harp or piano.
8. I left the hall still feeling the pounding of the bass drum.
9. It is hard to imagine a parade without brass instruments.
10. Reserving two orchestra seats, I made plans to go to the concert.

Critical Viewing

Make a Judgment Sample answer: The timpani is sometimes called a kettledrum because of its shape and appearance, like that of a large kettle.

☑ **ONGOING ASSESSMENT: Monitor and Reinforce**

If students miss more than two items in Exercise 33, refer them to the following for additional practice.

In the Textbook	Print Resources	Technology
Section Review, Ex. 39, Section 21.4	*Grammar Exercise Workbook,* pp. 93–94	*On-Line Exercise Bank,* Section 21.4

⏱ **TIME SAVERS!**

🎨 **Answers on Transparencies**
Use the *Grammar Exercises Answers on Transparencies* for Chapter 21 to facilitate corrections by students.

🖥 **On-Line Exercise Bank**
Have students complete the exercises on computer. The Auto Check feature will grade their work for you!

Correcting Clause Fragments

1. Review different types of clauses: adjective, adverb, and noun. Point out that, though clauses contain subjects and verbs, they cannot sustain themselves independently as sentences do because they do not contain complete thoughts.

2. Read the key concept aloud and add that a subordinate clause *can* be capitalized if it is at the beginning of a sentence that also contains an independent clause. Give an example and point out that an introductory adverb clause usually is set off by a comma:

   > *Before the concert started*, we peeked backstage.

3. Ask students to recall the methods for correcting phrase fragments. Can they apply any of these methods to correcting clause fragments? (Yes. If they cannot join the clause to a nearby sentence, they can add an independent clause to it.) Remind students that a clause may be placed at the beginning, middle, or end of the sentence.

Answer Key

> **Exercise 34**

Answers may vary; samples are given.

1. The conductor directed the orchestra.
2. I was sorry to miss the concert that was performed last week.
3. The *Titanic* sank as the band played on.
4. The song that you like to hear is on the radio.
5. There are some tones that can be pleasing.
6. I left when the trombone player began.
7. I am not familiar with the music that she described.
8. After we played a concert last week, we went on tour.
9. The teacher who told me about the concert is a musician.
10. The conductor was speaking while the musicians tuned their instruments.

21.4

Correcting Clause Fragments

All clauses have subjects and verbs, but some cannot stand alone as sentences.

▶ **KEY CONCEPT** A subordinate clause should not be capitalized and punctuated as if it were a sentence. ■

Subordinate clauses do not express complete thoughts. Although a subordinate adjective or adverb clause has a subject and a verb, it cannot stand by itself as a sentence. Like phrase fragments, *clause fragments* can usually be corrected in either of two ways:

1. Attach the fragment to a nearby sentence.

FRAGMENT:	The class enjoyed the concert. *That was held in the auditorium.*
ADDED TO A NEARBY SENTENCE:	The class enjoyed the concert *that was held in the auditorium.*

2. Add an independent clause to the fragment.

CHANGING CLAUSE FRAGMENTS INTO SENTENCES	
Clause Fragments	**Complete Sentences**
That we heard.	I bought a recording of the music *that we heard.*
	The music *that we heard* is now on CD.
When the orchestra played.	People got up to dance *when the orchestra played.*
	When the orchestra played, people got up to dance.

▶ **Exercise 34** Revising Clause Fragments to Form Sentences

Rewrite each fragment to make it a complete sentence.

1. Who directed the orchestra.
2. That was performed last week.
3. As the band played on.
4. That you like to hear.
5. That can be pleasing.
6. When the trombone player began.
7. That she described.
8. After we played a concert last week.
9. Who told me about the concert.
10. While the musicians tuned their instruments.

504 • Effective Sentences

✎ STANDARDIZED TEST PREPARATION WORKSHOP

Grammar and Usage Many standardized tests require students to revise errors in a composition. Write the following passage on the board.

(1) The storm suddenly came upon them. (2) Surprising the two boys and catching them unprepared. (3) They hurried back to the cabin as winds seemed to push furiously against them.

What is the best way to rewrite sentence 2?

A Add it to the previous sentence.

B Place a comma after *boys*.

C Add a subject.

D No change is needed.

The correct answer is **A**. Item 2 is a phrase fragment containing two participial phrases. Because the phrases describe the storm, they can easily be added to sentence 1.

Correcting Run-on Sentences

Unlike a fragment, a *run-on sentence* is an overcrowded sentence—one that has too much information.

KEY CONCEPT A **run-on** is two or more complete sentences that are not properly joined or separated. ■

Two Kinds of Run-on Sentences

There are two kinds of run-on sentences. One kind is made up of two sentences run together without any punctuation between them. This type of run-on is called a *fused sentence*. The other consists of two or more sentences separated only by a comma. This is called a *comma splice*.

RUN-ONS	
With No Punctuation	**With Only a Comma**
I go to concerts often Mozart is my favorite composer.	A clarinet has an almost cylindrical tube, an oboe has a conical pipe.

▼ **Critical Viewing** Write a sentence comparing the appearance or sound of these three instruments. Make sure your sentence is not a run-on. **[Compare]**

Exercise 35 Recognizing Run-on Sentences
On your paper write *S* if the item is a sentence and *RO* if the item is a run-on.

EXAMPLE: Bells vibrate at their rim gongs vibrate at their center. (RO)

1. Musical instruments around the world vary in purpose and design they can be made from natural or human-made materials.
2. Any tool that can expand the scope of musical sounds—such as clapping, stamping, whistling, and singing—is a musical instrument.
3. Sound arises from vibrations transmitted by waves to the ear, some vibrations are simply noise.
4. Regular vibrations produce tones that can be pleasing to the ear, the faster the vibrations, the higher the pitch that is perceived.
5. Some pipe organs encompass the full audible range of pitch, more than ten octaves most instruments have a much more limited range.

Avoiding Sentence Problems • 505

☑ **ONGOING ASSESSMENT: Monitor and Reinforce**

If students miss more than two items in Exercises 34 or 35, refer them to the following for additional practice.

In the Textbook	Print Resources	Technology
Section Review, Ex. 39–40, Section 21.4	*Grammar Exercise Workbook*, pp. 93–96	*On-Line Exercise Bank*, Section 21.4

Step-by-Step Teaching Guide

Correcting Run-on Sentences

1. After students read the key concept, ask them why a run-on sentence may pose a problem for a reader (different ideas may become confused; the words in one idea may seem to connect incorrectly to words in another).

2. Focus on the two kinds of run-ons (chart) and point out that writers sometimes incorrectly use a comma without a conjunction to connect two independent clauses. Explain that this is called a *comma splice* and that the lack of a connecting element (conjunction or semicolon) can confuse readers.

3. Explain that the term *run-on* does not mean a sentence that is too long; instead, it means two complete ideas have collided without a proper connection.

Customize for
More Advanced Students

As students practice correcting clause fragments, review the characteristics of noun clauses. Because a noun clause functions as a basic part of a sentence (subject, complement, object of a preposition), the independent clause syntactically contains the noun clause. Give students a schematic for a sentence containing a noun clause:
What we wanted was a ticket to the concert.

subject – noun clause	verb	pred.

nom.	prep. phrase

Have students graphically represent the noun clauses they find in Exercise 35 as well as others you supply.

Critical Viewing

Compare Answers will vary. Possible answer: These instruments produce various pitches in different ways: the trumpet uses valves; the trombone, a slide; and the saxophone, keys.

Answer Key

Exercise 35

1. RO	4. RO
2. S	5. RO
3. RO	

Three Ways to Correct Run-ons

1. Review end marks with students (. ! ?) and ask them to recall the purposes of each. Inform students that separating a run-on into two separate sentences is advisable when the two independent clauses express very different ideas.

2. Then, have students recall the methods they used for forming compound sentences (joining independent clauses with commas and coordinating conjunctions or semicolons). Ask students in what circumstances they would use each conjunction (*and* will connect related ideas; *but* will connect contrasting ideas).

3. As you discuss the third method, ask students why semicolons are sometimes good choices over conjunctions (to effectively connect especially close, related ideas). Remind students that the first word following the semicolon is not capitalized unless it is a proper noun or the pronoun *I*.

Critical Viewing

Describe Answers will vary. Possible answer: The tuba's sound is deep. It sounds throaty. (The tuba sounds deep and throaty.)

Correcting Run-on Sentences

Using End Marks Properly used, an end mark splits a run-on into two shorter but complete sentences. Which end mark you use depends upon the function of the sentence.

RUN-ON:	Many instruments were improved in the nineteenth century the piano was made with a cast-iron frame, which allowed a greater range of sounds.
CORRECTED SENTENCES:	Many instruments were improved in the nineteenth century. The piano was made with a cast-iron frame, which allowed a greater range of sounds.
RUN-ON:	Have you heard the new song, I heard it yesterday.
CORRECTED SENTENCES:	Have you heard the new song? I heard it yesterday.

Using Commas and Coordinating Conjunctions
Sometimes, the two parts of a run-on are related and should stay in the same sentence. In that case, the run-on can be changed into a compound sentence. Use a comma and a coordinating conjunction to combine two independent clauses into a compound sentence. To separate the two clauses properly, it is necessary to use both a comma and a coordinating conjunction. A comma by itself is not enough.

RUN-ON:	The oldest instrument family consists of idiophones, they are also the most widespread of instruments.
CORRECTED SENTENCE:	The oldest instrument family consists of idiophones, and they are also the most widespread of instruments.
RUN-ON:	I would like to play an instrument, I do not have musical ability.
CORRECTED SENTENCE:	I would like to play an instrument, but I do not have musical ability.

Using Semicolons You can sometimes use a semicolon to punctuate the two parts of a run-on when the ideas expressed in the two parts are closely related.

RUN-ON:	Idiophones range in complexity from hollowed logs to cast-bronze bells, the family dates back to the Stone Age.
CORRECTED SENTENCE:	Idiophones range in complexity from hollowed logs to cast-bronze bells; the family dates back to the Stone Age.

▲ **Critical Viewing**
Write two sentences about the sound of this instrument. Then, combine your sentences without forming a run-on. **[Describe]**

506 • Effective Sentences

⬥ STANDARDIZED TEST PREPARATION WORKSHOP

Grammar and Usage Many standardized tests require students to revise errors in a composition. Write the following passage on the board.

(1) Gloria Leavitt, the architect of Leavitt Hills, became famous for the open spaces she created in the single-family dwellings she designed. (2) Priced well above average, buyers were attracted in droves to see her houses. (3) Within months, all homes in Leavitt Hills had sold out.

What revision is necessary in this passage?

A Remove the comma after *Leavitt* in sentence 1.

B Combine sentences 2 and 3 to form a compound.

C Revise sentence 2 to correct a dangling modifier.

D Revise sentence 3 to correct a dangling modifier.

The correct answer is **C**. Sentence 2 contains a dangling modifier (the participial phrase incorrectly modifies *buyers*). An accurate revision: *Priced well above average, her houses attracted buyers in droves.*

▶ **Exercise 36** Revising to Correct Run-ons Rewrite each of the following run-ons using any of the three methods described in this section.

1. Some instruments produce a tone with no identifiable pitch the triangle is one such instrument.
2. The greater the power of audio waves, the louder their sound, some electronically amplified music can reach a painful, ear-damaging intensity.
3. The tone color of the sound is influenced by the presence of the overtones in the sound wave, the perception of timbre is affected by the duration and location of the sound.
4. Musical sounds are caused by three components, the first component is the vibrating substance, such as a violin string, set into motion by bowing or striking.
5. The second component is the reflector, amplifier, or resonator connected to the vibrating substance, the third is the device that alters or varies the sound, such as a key, valve, or fret.

▶ **More Practice**

Grammar Exercise Workbook
• pp. 95–96
On-line Exercise Bank
• Section 21.4
  Go on-line:
  PHSchool.com
  Enter Web Code:
  eek-1002

Answers may vary; samples are given.

1. pitch; the triangle
2. sound, yet some
3. sound wave. The perception
4. components. The first
5. substance; the third

Recognizing Misplaced Modifiers

Recognizing Misplaced Modifiers

Misplaced Modifiers A phrase or clause that acts as an adjective or adverb should be placed close to the word it modifies. Otherwise, the meaning of the sentence may be unclear. A modifier placed too far away from the word it modifies is called a *misplaced modifier.* Because they are misplaced, such phrases and clauses seem to modify the wrong word in a sentence.

1. Remind students that phrases and clauses can be used as adjectives and adverbs. Note that the examples on this page demonstrate a prepositional phrase and a participial phrase. Explain that these are best placed as close as possible to the words they modify.

MISPLACED MODIFIER:	Nancy marched in the parade *with a smile* on her face.

The misplaced modifier is the phrase *with a smile.* It sounds as though the parade has a smile. The sentence needs to be reworded to put the modifier closer to *Nancy.*

CORRECTED SENTENCE:	*With a smile* on her face, Nancy marched in the parade.

2. Explain that the first example requires merely moving the phrase into the correct position (to modify *parade*), while in the second example, the noun intended to be modified by *Playing the trumpet* does not appear and must be added.

MISPLACED MODIFIER:	*Playing the trumpet,* the parade was enjoyable.

In this sentence, *playing the trumpet* should modify a person. Instead, it incorrectly modifies *parade.* The sentence needs to be rewritten to include the name of the musician.

CORRECTED SENTENCE:	*Playing the trumpet,* Elizabeth enjoyed the parade.

3. Summarize by asking students to define the term *misplaced modifier* (a word or phrase placed too far from the word it modifies). Explain that when a modifier has no word it can accurately modify, the modifier is "dangling" and will incorrectly add meaning to the wrong word.

Customize for
ESL Students

Because the syntax of their first languages may not be similar to that of English, some students may not understand why a modifier is misplaced. Help them see the different meanings created by placement of word and phrase modifiers.

Avoiding Sentence Problems • **507**

☑ **ONGOING ASSESSMENT: Monitor and Reinforce**

If students miss more than one item in Exercise 36, refer them to the following for additional practice.

In the Textbook	Print Resources	Technology
Section Review, Ex. 40, Section 21.4	*Grammar Exercise Workbook,* pp. 95–96	*On-Line Exercise Bank,* Section 21.4

21.4

▶ **Exercise 37** **Recognizing Misplaced Modifiers** Some of the sentences in the following exercise are correct, but most of them contain a misplaced modifier. Read each sentence carefully, and check the placement of the modifiers. If the sentence is correct, write *C* on your paper. If the sentence contains a misplaced modifier, write *MM*.

EXAMPLE: Touring extensively around the world, people love the Vienna Philharmonic Orchestra. (MM)

1. Zubin Mehta was born in Bombay, India, into a musical family.
2. His father from 1955 to 1959 served as associate concertmaster of the Halle Orchestra in Manchester, England.
3. As a child, Mehta studied piano and violin.
4. In Vienna, Austria, Mehta left India and medical studies at age eighteen to study conducting.
5. At his musical studio in Vienna, Mehta studied with Hans Swarowsky.
6. Organized by the Royal Liverpool Orchestra, Mehta won the first conductor's competition.
7. Including a one-year engagement as assistant to the resident maestro, Mehta benefited from the prizes of the competition.
8. Working for a number of prominent orchestras, his career soon expanded.
9. Appointed music director for the Los Angeles Philharmonic and the Montreal Symphony, Mehta became the first conductor to head two major North American orchestras simultaneously.
10. Mehta replaced Pierre Boulez as music director of the New York Philharmonic, receiving much critical acclaim.

▲ **Critical Viewing**
Use the phrase *looking up from their music* in a sentence about this picture. Make sure that the modifier is not misplaced. [Connect]

▶ **More Practice**

Grammar Exercise Workbook
• pp. 97–98
On-line Exercise Bank
• Section 21.4
Go on-line:
PHSchool.com
Enter Web Code:
eek-1002

Get instant feedback!
Exercise 37 is available on-line or on CD-ROM.

☑ **ONGOING ASSESSMENT: Monitor and Reinforce**

If students miss more than two items in Exercise 37 or 38, refer them to the following for additional practice.

In the Textbook	Print Resources	Technology
Section Review, Ex. 41, Section 21.4	*Grammar Exercise Workbook,* pp. 97–102	*On-Line Exercise Bank,* Section 21.4

Revising Sentences With Misplaced Modifiers

Among the most common misplaced modifiers are prepositional phrases, participial phrases, and adjective clauses. All are corrected in the same way—by placing the modifier as close as possible to the word it modifies.

First, consider a misplaced prepositional phrase. This error usually occurs in a sentence with two or more prepositional phrases in a row.

MISPLACED: *With their new instruments* in the auditorium, the orchestra practiced.

The misplaced modifier should be moved closer to *orchestra.*

CORRECTED: *With their new instruments*, the orchestra practiced in the auditorium.

Participial phrases are sometimes used at the beginning of sentences. When such a phrase is used this way, it must be followed immediately by a word that it can logically modify.

MISPLACED: *Raising their bows*, the signal from the conductor was their cue.

Who or what is raising their bows? The sentence needs to be rewritten to put a word such as *violinists* next to the modifier.

CORRECTED: *Raising their bows*, the violinists waited for the signal from the conductor.

A misplaced adjective clause should also be moved closer to the word it modifies. In the following sentence, the clause is so far away from *music* that it seems to modify *weeks* or *searching*. The sentence needs to be rearranged.

MISPLACED: I found the music after several weeks of searching *that the conductor recommended.*

CORRECTED: After several weeks of searching, I found the music *that the conductor recommended.*

Revising Sentences With Misplaced Modifiers

1. Train students to hear the error of misplaced modifiers. Have them look away from their books and read to them aloud each "misplaced" example on this page. For each, ask students to explain the *literal* (albeit incorrect) meaning of the sentence (the auditorium has new instruments, the signal raised their bows, the conductor recommended weeks of searching). Read each sentence a second or third time, as necessary, until students can identify the word each misplaced element should modify.

2. Then, have students look at the examples in the text to examine the corrected versions. See if they can suggest additional corrected versions (*With their new instruments, the orchestra practiced in the auditorium*).

3. For additional practice, give students these sentences to revise:

   Standing on one pink leg, we spotted a solitary flamingo.

   I ordered a steak and a salad cooked rare!

   She swam from the sinking ship gasping for breath.

Exercise 38

Answers may vary; samples are given.

1. <u>Living in the nineteenth century</u>, Gustav Mahler was an Austrian composer and conductor whose works influenced many twentieth-century composers. [arrow from *Living* to *Mahler*]

2. After studying at the Vienna Conservatory, <u>Mahler was named</u> the assistant conductor at Bad Hall in Austria. [arrow from *studying* to *Mahler*]

3. Mahler subsequently held posts <u>with opera companies</u> in several European cities. [arrow from *with* to *posts*]

4. Vienna became a great operatic center because of Mahler's <u>becoming artistic director of the Imperial Opera in Vienna</u>. [arrow from *becoming* to *Mahler*]

5. Mahler moved to New York City, <u>another city known for opera</u>, where he conducted the Metropolitan Opera and the New York Philharmonic. [arrow from *city* to *New York City*]

6. <u>After years of conducting</u>, Mahler composed four numbered symphonies that included solo voices with or without chorus. [arrow from *After* to *Mahler*]

7. <u>In his symphonies</u>, Mahler was the musical heir of Beethoven, Bruckner, and Wagner. [arrow from *symphonies* to *Mahler*]

8. <u>Achieving great fame</u>, Mahler had a great influence on twentieth-century music. [arrow from *achieving* to *Mahler*]

9. <u>Experimenting with the traditional system of keys and chords</u>, Mahler ended most of his symphonies in a key different from the initial key. [arrow from *Experimenting* to *Mahler*]

10. <u>Leaving an unfinished tenth symphony</u>, Mahler died in Vienna in 1911. [arrow from *Leaving* to *Mahler*]

Critical Viewing

Connect Sample answer: Holding a baton, the conductor stepped out to direct the orchestra.

21.4

▶ **Exercise 38** Revising Sentences to Correct Misplaced Modifiers Rewrite the sentences in the following exercise to eliminate the misplaced modifiers. In each rewritten sentence, underline the modifier that was misplaced in the original. Then, draw an arrow pointing from the modifier to the word it modifies.

EXAMPLE: Richard planned to meet Rachel before the concert at Radio City Music Hall at a restaurant.

ANSWER: Richard planned to meet Rachel <u>at a restaurant</u> before the concert at Radio City Music Hall.

1. Gustav Mahler was an Austrian composer and conductor whose works influenced many twentieth-century composers living in the nineteenth century.
2. After studying at the Vienna Conservatory, the assistant conductor at Bad Hall in Austria was named Mahler.
3. Mahler subsequently held posts in several European cities with opera companies.
4. Becoming artistic director of the Imperial Opera in Vienna, Vienna became a great operatic center because of Mahler.
5. Mahler moved to New York City, where he conducted the Metropolitan Opera and the New York Philharmonic, another city known for opera.
6. Mahler composed four numbered symphonies after years of conducting that included solo voices with or without chorus.
7. Mahler was the musical heir of Beethoven, Bruckner, and Wagner in his symphonies.
8. Achieving great fame, twentieth-century music was greatly influenced by Mahler.
9. Experimenting with the traditional system of keys and chords, most of his symphonies end in a key different from the initial key.
10. Leaving an unfinished tenth symphony, Mahler's death took place in Vienna in 1911.

▶ **Critical Viewing** Write a sentence about this picture that includes the participial phrase *holding a baton*. Make sure that the modifier is not misplaced. [Connect]

▶ **More Practice**

Grammar Exercise Workbook
• pp. 99–102
On-line Exercise Bank
• Section 21.4
Go on-line:
PHSchool.com
Enter Web Code:
eek-1002

Interactive Textbook

Complete the exercise on-line! Exercise 38 is available on-line or on CD-ROM.

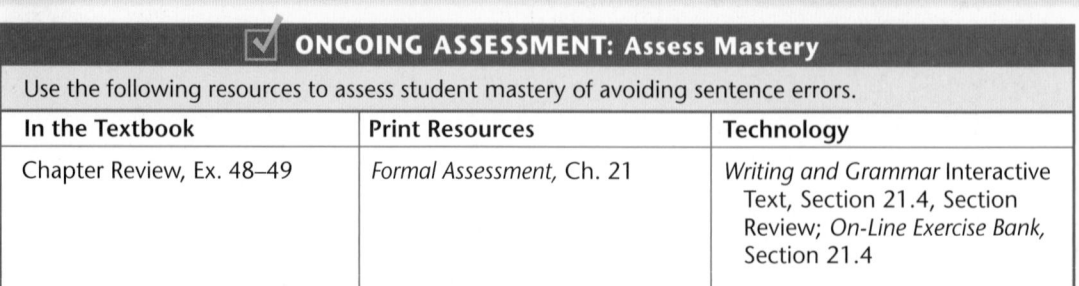

☑ **ONGOING ASSESSMENT: Assess Mastery**

Use the following resources to assess student mastery of avoiding sentence errors.

In the Textbook	Print Resources	Technology
Chapter Review, Ex. 48–49	*Formal Assessment,* Ch. 21	*Writing and Grammar* Interactive Text, Section 21.4, Section Review; *On-Line Exercise Bank,* Section 21.4

Section 21.4 Section Review

GRAMMAR EXERCISES 39–44

Exercise 39 Revising Fragments to Form Sentences Change each of the following fragments into a sentence. Check to see that each of your sentences contains an independent clause.

1. The marching band fun to watch.
2. Before the music started.
3. When the opera starts.
4. With a piano solo.
5. The musicians starting to play.
6. Bagpipes and loudly playing drums.
7. Marching down Main Street.
8. To buy a saxophone.
9. After the open-air concert.
10. Three friends singing with the chorus.

Exercise 40 Revising to Eliminate Run-on Sentences Identify and eliminate run-ons from the following items. If a sentence is correct, write *correct*.

1. The score is the musical notation for a multipart composition, the music that is to be performed by each voice or instrument is written on a separate staff.
2. A full score shows the music for all of the instruments all of the staves are aligned one above another.
3. The individual musicians are given separate parts these parts show only the music for their particular instrument.
4. Until the early thirteenth century, all European music was circulated in complete scores, and performers read from these scores.
5. The use of these scores was abandoned in the thirteenth century, this was done for reasons of space.

Exercise 41 Revising a Paragraph to Eliminate Sentence Errors Revise the following paragraph, correcting any fragments, run-ons, or misplaced modifiers.

The piano is a stringed keyboard musical instrument, it is sometimes called the pianoforte. Predecessors of the piano, keyboard players performed on clavicords or harpsicords prior to the eighteenth century. By varying the touch of the fingers, the sound of the piano can be intensified. Unlike with earlier keyboard instruments. A harpsichord maker of Florence, Italy, the first piano was built by Bartolomeo Cristofori. Little did he know. That his invention would have such an impact on both concert and popular music. Today, pianos sit in concert halls and homes all around the world, millions of children and adults take piano lessons every day.

Exercise 42 Find It in Your Reading In this sentence from "Like the Sun" by R. K. Narayan, identify how the writer has avoided creating a run-on sentence.

Sekhar paused for a moment outside the headmaster's room to button up his coat; that was another subject the headmaster always sermonized about.

Exercise 43 Find It in Your Writing Carefully review a piece of your own writing for fragments, run-ons, or misplaced modifiers. Correct any errors you find.

Exercise 44 Writing Application Pick a musical instrument, and write a description of how the instrument sounds. Proofread your description carefully to make sure it contains no fragments, run-ons, or misplaced modifiers.

Answer Key

Exercise 39

Answers will vary; samples are given.

1. The marching band was fun to watch.
2. Before the music started, we found our seats.
3. When the opera starts you should remain quiet.
4. The performance began with a piano solo.
5. The musicians were starting to play.
6. The festivities began with bagpipes and loudly playing drums.
7. Marching down Main Street, the pipers led the parade.
8. Lisa begged her parents to buy a saxophone for her.
9. After the open-air concert is over, let's get a sundae.
10. My sister and three friends will be singing with the chorus.

Exercise 40

Answers will vary; samples are given.

1. composition. The music
2. instruments; all
3. separate parts, which show only . . .
4. correct
5. century; this

Exercise 41

Answers will vary; a sample is given.

The piano is a stringed keyboard musical instrument, which is sometimes called the pianoforte. Prior to the eighteenth century, keyboard players performed on clavichords or harpsichords, the predecessors of the piano. Unlike with earlier keyboard instruments, varying the touch of the fingers can intensify the sound of the piano. Bartolomeo Cristofori, a
continued

Answer Key continued

Exercise 41

harpsichord maker of Florence, Italy, built the first piano. Little did he know that his invention would have such an impact on both concert and popular music. Today, pianos sit in concert halls and homes all around the world. Millions of children and adults take piano lessons every day.

Exercise 42

Find It in Your Reading
The writer inserted a semicolon after the word *coat.*

Exercise 43

Find It in Your Writing
Answers will vary. Encourage students to create more varied sentences as well as correcting errors.

Exercise 44

Writing Application
Answers will vary. If students have trouble getting started, have the class brainstorm for words that describe musical sounds. You might also model using a thesaurus to generate vivid words.

CHAPTER REVIEW

These exercises correlate with the concepts taught in this chapter on effective sentences, pp. 484–511. The exercises may be used for more practice, for reteaching, or for review of the key concepts presented.

Answer Key

Exercise 45

1. interrogative/?
2. declarative/.
3. imperative; declarative/.
4. interrogative/?
5. declarative/.
6. declarative/. or exclamatory/!
7. declarative/.
8. imperative/.
9. declarative/.
10. exclamatory/!

Exercise 46

Answers may vary; samples are given.

1. My sister plays the accordion and sings in a band.
2. I used to play the accordion; I was not very good.
3. I have always wanted to play a musical instrument well, but I have never taken lessons.
4. Our mother plays the harp and the lute.
5. My father does not play any instruments, although he appreciates people who have musical ability.
6. He has other talents, though, especially sketching.
7. When I went to a concert last weekend, I carefully studied the styles of different performers.
8. My sister would like to play professionally, and we are sure that she is good enough.
9. I will learn to play an instrument, the piano, this semester.
10. I cannot play soccer after school because I have piano practice.

Exercise 47

Answers may vary; samples are given.

1. Despite its name, the woodwind . . . instruments.
2. . . . flexible reed. When it is . . .
3. . . . pushing keys. This affects . . .
4. You can lengthen the column of air; doing so will make the tone lower.
5. Providing the deepest tones, the contrabassoon . . . orchestra.

Exercise 48

Answers may vary; a sample is given.

512

Exercise 45 Identifying and Punctuating the Four Functions of Sentences Identify each sentence as *declarative, interrogative, imperative,* or *exclamatory.* Then, write the end mark for each sentence.

1. Will you come to the concert with me
2. The school orchestra is performing
3. Bring your jacket; the concert is on the great lawn
4. Have you been to an outdoor concert before
5. This orchestra is quite good
6. I wish I could join
7. Your sister may want to come
8. Ask her if she is free Friday night
9. The weather should be clear
10. What fun it will be

Exercise 46 Combining Short Sentences Combine the pairs of sentences using the method indicated in parentheses.

1. My sister plays the accordion. She also sings in a band. (compound verb)
2. I used to play the accordion. I was not very good. (semicolon)
3. I have always wanted to play a musical instrument well. I have never taken lessons. (comma and coordinating conjunction)
4. Our mother plays the harp. She also plays the lute. (compound object)
5. My father does not play any instruments. He appreciates people who have musical ability. (form a subordinate clause)
6. He has other special talents, though. One of his talents is sketching. (phrase)
7. I went to a concert last weekend. I carefully studied the styles of different performers. (form a subordinate clause)

512 • Effective Sentences

8. My sister would like to play professionally. We are sure that she is good enough. (comma and coordinating conjunction)
9. I will learn to play an instrument this semester. I'll learn the piano. (phrase)
10. I cannot play soccer after school. I have piano practice. (form a subordinate clause)

Exercise 47 Varying Sentence Length and Beginnings Rewrite each sentence. Break the sentence into two sentences; rewrite it in a simpler, more direct way; or vary the beginning of the sentence.

1. The woodwind family of instruments contains both wood and metal instruments, despite its name.
2. The woodwind tube, which is long and narrow, is sometimes attached to a flexible reed, and, when it is played, the reed vibrates.
3. The air column vibrating within the instrument may be shortened or lengthened by covering finger holes or pushing keys, which affects the pitch of the tone that the instrument produces.
4. You can lengthen the column of air, and that action, if it is taken by a player, will make the tone lower.
5. The contrabassoon is the longest woodwind in the orchestra, and it is providing the deepest tones.

Exercise 48 Revising to Eliminate Sentence Errors Copy the following passage on a separate sheet of paper. Revise, eliminating any fragments, run-ons, or misplaced modifiers.

(1) Conductors gesture silently with their hands or a baton to direct the orchestra. (2) Generally, the right hand is used to indicate the tempo, while the left hand indicates both the entry of a different instrument and changes in volume. (3–4) The right hand moves in commonly recognized patterns for groups of two, three, four, or more beats per measure. These patterns have in common a downward movement on the first beat, sometimes called the downbeat. (5) Conductors of instrumental ensembles that contain many different performers generally use a baton. (6) The modern conductor, a professional responsible for total music interpretation, appeared only during the nineteenth century. (7) Correct. (8) Conductors of small choral ensembles that performed the polyphonic music of the Renaissance beat time with their hands or by tapping with a roll of paper or a rod. In the Baroque era, harmonies provided by a keyboard player were an essential feature of most music. (9) The conductor, who was often also the composer, kept the ensemble together with a steady background beat on the keyboard. (10) Correct.

Conductors gesture silently to direct the orchestra with their hands or a baton. Generally, the right hand is used to indicate the tempo the left hand indicates both the entry of a different instrument and changes in volume. The right hand moves in commonly recognized patterns for groups of two, three, four, or more beats per measure, these patterns have in common a downward movement on the first beat. Sometimes called the downbeat.

Conductors of instrumental ensembles generally use a baton that contains many different performers. The modern conductor appeared only during the nineteenth century. A professional responsible for total music interpretation. In earlier times, the conductor, often one of the performers, functioned mainly as the time beater. Conductors of small choral ensembles that performed the polyphonic music of the Renaissance beat time with their hands or by tapping with a roll of paper or a rod, in the Baroque Era, harmonies provided by a keyboard player were an essential feature of most music. The conductor kept the ensemble together with a steady background beat on the keyboard who was often also the composer. During the nineteenth century, conductors separated themselves from the ensemble, standing in front of it to direct; they also began using the baton.

Revision Practice: Writing Effective Sentences Copy the following passage on a separate sheet of paper. Revise, combining sentences or revising sentences as needed. Correct all errors in sentence structure.

The Vienna Philharmonic Orchestra, one of the most renowned classical music ensembles in the world. It was originally formed by musicians from the Vienna State Opera, the members of the opera joined together to establish a professional concert orchestra capable with the highest degree of competence of playing the most

difficult new works. They gave their first performance as the Vienna Philharmonic Orchestra on March 28, 1842, at the Grosser Redoutensaal. Then, Vienna's main concert hall. The conductor, German composer and conductor Otto Nicolai. At first, concerts took place sporadically they were further disrupted by Austria's Revolution of 1848. German pianist, violinist, and composer Carl Eckert conducted a few concerts during the 1850's, the orchestra did not play on a regular basis until 1860.

The Vienna Philharmonic moved to Karntnertortheater in 1860. It remained until the opening of the Musikverein in 1870. Its first permanent conductor was Austrian conductor Felix Dessoff. He was director of the orchestra from 1860 to 1875. He introduced the music of Hungarian-born composer Franz Lizst. He also introduced the work of German composers Richard Wagner and Johannes Brahms. Other early conductors of the Vienna Philharmonic include Austro-Hungarian conductor Hans Richter. Austrian composer and conductor Gustav Mahler. During Mahler's tenure as artistic director that the Vienna Philharmonic gained international prominence. There have been many notable conductors including the American Leonard Bernstein of the Vienna Philharmonic.

Writing Application Write a review of a concert or musical performance you have attended recently. Focus on varying the length and structure of your sentences, and proofread carefully to eliminate any fragments, run-on sentences, or misplaced modifiers.

Lesson Objectives

1. To demonstrate control over grammatical elements such as verb forms
2. To evaluate writing for both mechanics and content

Revising and Editing Sentences

Teaching Resources: Standardized Test Preparation Workbook, pp. 41–42

1. Work through the bulleted teaching points with the class. Emphasize that many of these ideas can help students to quickly eliminate incorrect answers when they are taking standardized tests.

2. Have students read the sample test items, and review with them the correct answers and explanations.

3. Encourage students to read test instructions carefully. Not all standardized tests are graded in the same way. Some tests do not penalize students for incorrect answers, so that they can increase their scores with a judicious guess.

4. Assign Practices 1 and 2. Check students' answers and go over any incorrect answers with the class.

5. You may wish to provide students with standardized test answer sheets to practice the mechanics of marking in answers.

Standardized Test Preparation Workshop

Revising and Editing Sentences

Whether writing an e-mail or an essay for a test, you must use sentences correctly and effectively to communicate logically. Because this skill is so important, it is often evaluated on standardized tests. When choosing the most effective sentence from the list of answer choices, use the following strategies:

- Avoid choosing run-on sentences in which two or more complete sentences are written as a single sentence.

- Identify and avoid any sentence fragments in your choices. Fragments do not express a complete thought.

- Determine whether you can combine several short sentences into one longer one.

- Be sure all modifiers are placed near the words they modify.

- Make sure your choice presents all of the important information without changing the meaning of the original.

Test Tip

Read each answer silently to yourself to help you pick out fragments or run-ons. Then, choose the sentence that best answers the question.

Sample Test Item	Answer and Explanation
Sandor has written an essay for chorus class. You have been asked to read the essay and offer suggestions for improving it. When you finish reading this passage, answer the multiple-choice question that follows. 1 Gioacchino Rossini produced several notable 2 operas. In the early 1800's. He was a 3 composer from Italy.	
1 What is the BEST way to combine the sentences in lines 1–3? (*"Gioacchino. . . Italy."*) **A** Gioacchino Rossini produced several notable Italian operas in the early 1800's. **B** In the early 1800's, Italian composer Gioacchino Rossini produced several notable operas. **C** Gioacchino Rossini, who was an Italian composer; created notable operas in the 1800's. **D** In Italy in the early 1800's. Gioacchino Rossini produced several notable operas.	The correct answer is *B.* Choice B correctly combines the important elements of all of the sentences and eliminates the fragment error.

514 • Effective Sentences

⬙ TEST-TAKING TIP

In a test situation, students may sometimes find it difficult to read sentences and/or sentence fragments that are numbered, underlined, and set in running text. Encourage students to quickly copy the test item on a separate sheet of paper before choosing the correct answer.

Students might rewrite the sentences correctly, and match their rewrite to one of the listed answer options. Make sure students inquire well before the test date whether or not they may use scrap paper in the testing site.

▶ **Practice 1** *Steven has written an essay for history class and has asked you to review it for him. When you finish reading the passage below, answer the multiple-choice questions that follow.*

1 The time was in the 1720's. Colonists
2 who were living in South Carolina.
3 Petitioned England. They wanted forts
4 built to their south. The forts were needed
5 to provide protection from the Spanish
6 in Florida, this was so the colonists.
7 could maintain their trade which was
8 active, and it was with the nearby Indians.

1 What is the BEST way to combine the sentences in lines 1–4? (*"The . . . south."*)

  A In the 1720's, colonists who were living in South Carolina. Petitioned England, They wanted forts built to their south.

  B In the 1720's in South Carolina, and colonists wanted forts built to their south, and they petitioned England.

  C In the 1720's, colonists living in South Carolina petitioned England to build forts to their south.

  D In the 1720's, colonists petitioned England, and they wanted forts built in South Carolina to their south.

2 What is the BEST way to rewrite the sentences in lines 4–8? (*"The . . . Indians."*)

  F The forts were needed to provide protection from the Spanish in Florida so the colonists could maintain their active trade with the nearby Indians.

  G The forts were needed to provide protection. From the Spanish in Florida. So the colonists could maintain their active trade with the nearby Indians.

  H The forts were needed to provide protection from the Spanish in Florida and from the nearby Indians.

  J The forts were providing protection from the Spanish in Florida, and the colonists were trading actively with the nearby Indians.

▶ **Practice 2** *Ashley has written a report for a social studies course. You have been asked to review it. When you finish reading the passage below, answer the multiple-choice questions that follow.*

1 Soon after the first real trains appeared.
2 Some began building ones that were
3 miniature in size who were engineers.
4 These trains were not toys, and they
5 were detailed models, and they were
6 built to try out ideas. For real trains.

1 What is the BEST way to combine the sentences in lines 1–3? (*"Soon . . . engineers."*)

  A Soon after the first real trains appeared, some engineers that were miniature in size began building ones.

  B Soon after the first real trains appeared, some engineers began building trains, and they were miniature in size.

  C Soon after the first real trains appeared. Ones that were miniature in size were built by some engineers

  D Soon after the first real trains appeared, some engineers began building miniature ones.

2 What is the BEST way to combine the sentences in lines 4–6? (*"These . . . trains."*)

  F These trains were not toys, they were detailed models, they were built to try out ideas for real trains.

  G These trains were not toys; they were detailed models built to try out ideas for real trains.

  H These trains were toys and detailed models, and they were built to try out ideas for real trains.

  J These trains were not toys. They were detailed models. They were built to try out ideas. The ideas were for real trains.

Standardized Test Preparation Workshop • **515**

Answer Key

▶ **Practice 1**

1. C
2. F

▶ **Practice 2**

1. D
2. G

Customize for
Less Advanced Students

Review the key concepts on sentence combining, pages 489–493. Alternatively, you may wish to use the *Grammar Exercise Workbook,* pages 85–86.

▶ **Exercise A**

Complements are set in boldface type.

1. Which <u>continent</u> <u>surrounds</u> the **South Pole**? (direct object, interrogative)
2. <u>Antarctica</u> <u>is</u> mostly **circular,** (predicate adjective) with one long arm reaching toward South America. (declarative)
3. <u>We</u> <u>call</u> the two large **indentations** (direct object) the Ross and Weddell **seas.** (objective complement, declarative)
4. The real <u>boundary</u> of Antarctica <u>is</u> the **Antarctic Convergence** (predicate nominative) beyond the end of the continent. (declarative)
5. There <u>is</u> <u>70 percent</u> of the world's fresh water in the ice. (declarative)

▶ **Exercise B**

Answers may vary; samples are given. Subject complements are set in boldface type.

1. <u>Whales</u> and shrimplike <u>animals</u> <u>live</u> in the waters around Antarctica.
2. Antarctica's two main geographic <u>areas</u> <u>are</u> **East Antarctica** and **West Antarctica**.
3. The <u>deposits</u> covering East Antarctica <u>are</u> **igneous** or **sedimentary**.
4. The <u>Transantarctic Mountains</u> <u>contain</u> coal **deposits** and **fossils**.
5. <u>Mount Erebus</u> <u>rises</u> above West Antarctica and <u>could erupt</u> some day.

▶ **Exercise C**

1. an American explorer, author, and aviator (appositive phrase), for his expeditions, to the Antarctic (prepositional phrases)
2. Making his first flight (gerund phrase), over the North Pole (prepositional phrase), which included a medal (adjective clause), from the government (prepositional phrase)
3. What Byrd did the next year (noun clause), to fly an airplane (infinitive phrase)
4. Assisted by Bernt Balchen, Bertrand Acosta, and George

516

Cumulative Review

PHRASES, CLAUSES, AND SENTENCES

▶ **Exercise A**   **Recognizing Basic Sentence Parts** Copy the following sentences, underlining each simple subject once and each simple predicate twice. Circle the complements and label each *direct object, indirect object, objective complement, predicate nominative,* or *predicate adjective.* Then, identify the function of each sentence as *declarative, imperative, interrogative,* or *exclamatory.*

1. Which continent surrounds the South Pole?
2. Antarctica is mostly circular, with one long arm reaching toward South America.
3. We call the two large indentations the Ross and Weddell seas.
4. The real boundary of Antarctica is the Atlantic Convergence, beyond the end of the continent.
5. There is 70 percent of the world's fresh water in the ice.

▶ **Exercise B**   **Revising to Combine Sentences** Rewrite the following sentences according to the directions in parentheses. In your new sentences, underline each simple subject once and each simple predicate twice. Circle each subject complement.

1. Whales live in the waters around Antarctica. There are also shrimplike animals in the water. (combine by forming a compound subject)
2. Antarctica has two main geographic areas; one is East Antarctica. West Antarctica is the other. (combine by forming a compound predicate nominative)
3. Some of the deposits covering East Antarctica are igneous. Other deposits

are sedimentary. (combine by forming a compound predicate adjective)
4. The Transantarctic Mountains contain coal deposits. There are fossils in the Transantarctic Mountains. (combine by forming a compound direct object)
5. Mount Erebus rises above West Antarctica. It could erupt some day. (combine by forming a compound verb)

▶ **Exercise C**   **Identifying Phrases and Clauses** Label each phrase in the following sentences *prepositional phrase, appositive phrase, participial phrase, gerund phrase,* or *infinitive phrase.* Label each clause *adjective clause, adverb clause,* or *noun clause.*

1. Richard Byrd, an American explorer, author, and aviator, is known for his expeditions to the Antarctic.
2. Making his first flight over the North Pole brought Byrd recognition, which included a medal from the government.
3. What Byrd did the next year was to fly an airplane.
4. Assisted by Bernt Balchen, Bertrand Acosta, and George Noville, Byrd flew from New York to France.
5. Byrd established Little America, a base on the Bay of Whales, when he made his first expedition to the Antarctic.
6. In 1929, he was the first to fly over the South Pole.
7. After he extensively mapped Antarctica, Byrd retired from the navy with the rank of rear admiral.
8. Researching in several fields, Byrd spent five months alone on Antarctica when he was on his second expedition.
9. There were four flights, which resulted in many discoveries, during the third expedition.

Noville (participial phrase), from New York, to France (prepositional phrases)
5. a base on the Bay of Whales (appositive phrase), on the Bay of Whales (prepositional phrase), when he made his first expedition (adverb clause), to the Antarctic (prepositional phrase)
6. In 1929 (prepositional phrase), to fly (infinitive phrase), over the South Pole (prepositional phrase)
7. After he extensively mapped Antarctica (adverb clause), from the Navy, with the rank, of rear admiral (prepositional phrases)
8. Researching in several fields (participial phrase), in several fields (prepositional

phrase), on Antarctica (prepositional phrase), when he was on his second expedition (adverb clause), on his second expedition (prepositional phrase)
9. which resulted in many discoveries (adjective clause), in many discoveries (prepositional phrase), during the third expedition (prepositional phrase)
10. to explore, to map more territory (infinitive phrases)

10. The fourth expedition was intended to explore and to map more territory.

Exercise D — Revising to Combine Sentences

Rewrite the following sentences according to the instructions in parentheses.

1. On December 14, 1911, Roald Amundsen reached the South Pole. He was the first person to do so. (combine by forming an adjective clause)
2. Amundsen lived in Antarctica for more than a year. He was a Norwegian explorer. (combine by forming an appositive phrase)
3. He was a success. The weather conditions were very favorable. (combine by forming an adverb clause)
4. Amundsen also had a great deal of knowledge. He was familiar with polar conditions. (combine by forming a prepositional phrase)
5. He had another ability. Amundsen could endure great physical stress. (combine by forming an infinitive phrase)
6. Robert Scott had set his goal. He hoped to be the first man to reach the South Pole. (combine by forming a gerund phrase)
7. He succeeded on January 18, 1912. He found Amundsen's tent and flag. (combine by forming a participial phrase)
8. His group of five people suffered on the return trip. They did not survive. (combine by forming an adjective clause)
9. Scott entered the Royal Navy at the age of 14. He commanded the National Antarctic Expedition. (combine by forming an appositive phrase)
10. He left England in 1901. Then, Scott established a base on McMurdo Sound in Antarctica. (combine by forming a participial phrase)

Exercise E — Revision Practice: Writing Effective Sentences

Revise the following passage, combining sentences or revising sentences as needed. Correct all errors in sentence structure.

Mount Erebus, an active volcano on the eastern coast of Ross Island. The mountain, who named it after one of his two vessels, was discovered by Sir James Ross. Sir Ernest Henry Shackleton established his winter quarters there and used it as a base. succeeded in climbing Mount Erebus. Shackleton joined the British merchant navy. In 1901 he sailed with Robert Scott. In 1908, he commanded the mission to reach the South Pole he came close to his goal. He attempted to cross the Antarctic continent. Shackleton wanted to travel from the Ross Sea to the Weddell Sea. Another explorer did this many years later. It was a 12-member British team called the Commonwealth Trans-Antarctic Expedition. The Ross Sea is actually an extension of the Pacific Ocean. It is free of ice in the summer; therefore, the shoreline serves as a departure site for expeditions.

Exercise F — Writing Application

Write a short description of a place you would like to see from the air. Make your writing interesting by varying your sentence lengths and structures. Avoid sentence errors. Underline each simple subject once and each simple verb twice. Then, circle at least three phrases and three clauses.

Answer Key

Exercise D

Answers may vary; samples are given.

1. On December 14, 1911, Roald Amundsen, who was the first person to do so, reached the South Pole.
2. Amundsen, a Norwegian explorer, lived in Antarctica for more than a year.
3. Because weather conditions were very favorable, he was a success.
4. Amundsen also had a great deal of knowledge of polar conditions.
5. Amundsen had another ability, to endure great physical stress.
6. Being the first man to reach the South Pole was Robert Scott's goal.
7. Finding Amundsen's tent and flag, he succeeded on January 18, 1912.
8. His group of five people, who suffered on the return trip, did not survive.
9. Scott, commander of the National Antarctic Expedition, entered the Royal Navy at the age of 14.
10. Leaving England in 1901, Scott established a base on McMurdo Sound in Antarctica.

Exercise E

Answers may vary; samples are given.

Mount Erebus is an active volcano on the eastern coast of Ross Island. Sir James Ross, who named it after one of his two vessels, discovered the mountain. Sir Ernest Henry Shackleton succeeded in climbing Mount Erebus, establishing his winter quarters there and using it as a base. Shackleton joined the British merchant navy, and, in 1901, sailed with Robert Scott. In 1908, Shackleton commanded the mission to reach the South Pole and came close to his goal of crossing the Antarctic continent. He wanted to travel from the Ross Sea to the Weddell Sea, as did a 12-member British team called the Commonwealth Trans-Antarctic Expedition many years later. Because the Ross Sea, actually an extension of the Pacific Ocean, is free of ice in the summer, it serves as a departure site for expeditions.

Exercise F

Answers will vary. Have students exchange papers and check one another's work.

In-Depth Lesson Plan

	LESSON FOCUS	PRINT AND MEDIA RESOURCES
DAY 1	**Verb Tenses** Students learn and apply concepts relating to the six tenses of the basic and progressive forms of verbs. (pp. 518–522/⊞366–370)	*Writing and Grammar* Interactive Text, Section 22.1; *On-line Exercise Bank,* Section 22.1 **Teaching Resources** *Grammar Exercise Workbook,* pp. 107–108; *Grammar Exercises Answers on Transparencies,* Ch. 22
DAY 2	**The Four Principal Parts of Verbs** Students learn that tenses are formed from principal parts and helping verbs and apply concepts relating to regular and irregular verbs. (pp. 523–527/⊞371–375)	**Teaching Resources** *Grammar Exercise Workbook,* pp. 109–110
DAY 3	**Conjugating the Tenses** Students learn to use verb tenses to express time in the basic and progressive forms and do the Hands-on Grammar activity. (pp. 528-533/⊞376–381)	**Teaching Resources** *Grammar Exercise Workbook,* pp. 111–120; *Hands-on Grammar Activity Book,* Ch. 22
DAY 4	**Active and Passive Voice** Students learn to distinguish between active and passive voice and use voice appropriately. Students review the chapter and demonstrate mastery of the concepts. (pp. 534–541/⊞382–385)	*Writing and Grammar* Interactive Text, Section 22.2; *On-line Exercise Bank,* Section 22.2 **Teaching Resources** *Grammar Exercise Workbook,* pp. 121–124

Accelerated Lesson Plan

	LESSON FOCUS	PRINT AND MEDIA RESOURCES
DAY 1	**Verb Tenses; The Four Principal Parts of Verbs** Students review verb tenses, with coverage determined by their performance on the Diagnostic Test. (pp. 518–527/⊞366–375)	*Writing and Grammar* Interactive Text, Section 22.1; *On-line Exercise Bank,* Section 22.1 **Teaching Resources** *Grammar Exercise Workbook,* pp. 107–118; *Grammar Exercises Answers on Transparencies,* Ch. 22
DAY 2	**Conjugating the Tenses; Active and Passive Voice** Students learn to use verb tenses and to distinguish between and use active and passive voice. They review the chapter and demonstrate mastery of the concepts. (pp. 528–541/⊞376–385)	*Writing and Grammar* Interactive Text, Section 22.2; *On-line Exercise Bank,* Section 22.2 **Teaching Resources** *Grammar Exercise Workbook,* pp. 119–124; *Grammar Exercises Answers on Transparencies,* Ch. 22; *Formal Assessment,* Ch. 22

Options for Adapting Lesson Plans

HOMEWORK

Have students complete any section of the chapter for homework.

FEATURES

Extend coverage with the Grammar in Literature feature (p. 536/⊞384) and the Standardized Test Preparation Workshop (p. 540).

TECHNOLOGY

Students can use *Writing and Grammar* Interactive Text to complete the exercises interactively on computer. They can complete additional exercises in the *On-line Exercise Bank:* The Auto Check feature will grade their work. Go on-line: PHSchool.com Use Web Code: eek-1002

Writing and Grammar Handbook Alignment

Page numbers in Step-by-Step Teaching Guides in this Teacher's Edition refer to pages from the full student text. Handbook page references, indicated with this icon **H**, are provided in Time and Resource Manager boxes and at the bottom of each Teacher's Edition page.

INTEGRATED SKILLS COVERAGE

Grammar in Literature
SE p. 536/H384

Writing
Find It in Your Writing SE pp. 531, 533, 537/H379, 381, 385
Writing Application SE pp. 533, 537, 539/H381, 385

Spelling
ATE p. 526

Viewing and Representing
Critical Viewing SE pp. 521, 522, 527, 530, 535/H369, 370, 375, 378, 383

Real-World Connection
ATE p. 536

Workplace Skills
ATE p. 535

ASSESSMENT SUPPORT

Standardized Test Preparation Workshop SE pp. 540–541; ATE pp. 525, 528

Standardized Test Preparation Workbook, pp. 43–44

Formal Assessment, Ch. 22

MEETING INDIVIDUAL NEEDS

Less Advanced Students ATE pp. 526, 541. See also Ongoing Assessments ATE pp. 521, 522, 524, 529, 535.

ESL Students ATE pp. 529, 534

Gifted and Talented Students ATE p. 525

Logical/Mathematical Learners ATE p. 525

BLOCK SCHEDULING

Pacing Suggestions
For 90-minute Blocks
• Administer the Diagnostic Test to students to determine instructional coverage.
• Have students complete the necessary exercises in class. Use the Hands-on Grammar activity to provide a change of pace.

Resources for Varying Instruction
• *Writing and Grammar* **Interactive Text** A 90-minute block provides an ideal opportunity for students to work on the computer.

Professional Development Support
• **How to Manage Instruction in the Block** This teaching resource provides management and activity suggestions.

MEDIA AND TECHNOLOGY

For the Student
• *Writing and Grammar* Interactive Text, Ch. 22
• *On-line Exercise Bank,* Sections 22.1–2

For the Teacher
• Teacher**EXPRESS** CD-ROM

WRITING AND GRAMMAR ON-LINE

Interactive Text (On-line or on CD-ROM)
• Easily navigable instruction with on-line supporting resources
• Self-scoring exercises and diagnostic tests

Companion Web Site PHSchool.com
• On-line Exercise Bank (use Web Code eek-1002)

See the Go On-line! feature, SE p. iii.

LITERATURE CONNECTIONS

Grammar in Literature selection from *Prentice Hall Literature, Penguin Edition,* Grade 10:

from "The Masque of the Red Death," Edgar Allan Poe, SE p. 536/H384

Lesson Objectives

1. To recognize and use correctly the various tenses of verbs
2. To identify and use the four principal parts of verbs
3. To distinguish between active voice and passive voice and to use these effectively in sentences
4. To demonstrate control over grammatical elements such as verb forms
5. To evaluate writing for both mechanics and content
6. To analyze the characteristics of clearly written texts, including the patterns of organization, syntax, and word choice

Critical Viewing

Connect, Contrast Students' responses might include such verbs as *spend* and *spent*, *save* and *saved*, *waste* and *wasted*, *borrow* and *borrowed*.

Chapter 22 Verb Usage

Having a good command of the English language requires a thorough understanding of how to use verbs. Verbs can help you explain when actions occur and how the time of one action relates to the time of another. Some verbs follow predictable rules to show a change in tense or form. Others follow irregular patterns that you must memorize.

Just as the nations of Europe now use a standard currency to facilitate the exchange of goods and services, the rules of verb usage facilitate the exchange of information. By following these rules, you can communicate more effectively.

This chapter shows how verbs are formed and how they are used to indicate the time when an action occurs. It also illustrates how verbs are used to indicate who is performing an action.

▲ **Critical Viewing** Think of the present and past tense forms of three verbs that describe actions you do with money. How do the two tenses vary in form? **[Connect, Contrast]**

518 • Verb Usage

☑ ONGOING ASSESSMENT: Diagnose

If students miss more than one item in each category, direct them to the relevant pages of the text and assign exercises for practice and review.

Verb Usage	Diagnostic Test Items	Teach	Practice	Section Reviews	Chapter Review
Skill Check A					
Identifying Verb Tense and Form	A 1–10	pp. 520–521/ ⊞368–369	Ex. 1–4	Ex. 12–14	Ex. 32
Skill Check B					
Writing the Four Principal Parts	B 11–15	pp. 523–526/ ⊞371–374	Ex. 5–8	Ex. 15–18	Ex. 33–34

Diagnostic Test

Directions: Write all answers on a separate sheet of paper.

Skill Check A. Identify the tense of each verb in italics. Then, tell whether the form is *basic* or *progressive*.

1. My aunt and uncle *are running* a financial planning business.
2. They *have taught* many people how to save and use money well.
3. They *used* their own savings to start their business.
4. Next month, they *will hold* a financial planning seminar for teens.
5. I *have been studying* economics in school and plan to attend their seminar.
6. My aunt thinks most people *are relying* too heavily on credit.
7. My aunt and uncle *had done* the same thing when they were young.
8. They *had been struggling,* but now they are helping other people with similar problems.
9. Because I have been following their advice, they expect that my investments *will be growing* in the future.
10. By the time I graduate from high school, I *will have been employing* their system for four years.

Skill Check B. Write the four principal parts of the following verbs.

11. save
12. deposit
13. cost
14. spend
15. grow

Skill Check C. Choose the correct form of the verb in parentheses.

16. People have long (striven, strove) to earn or raise money.
17. People have also (did, done) many unusual things to earn money.
18. In dance marathons in the 1930's, people danced to win cash prizes until they (grown, grew) weak.
19. Others have (swam, swum) or have (ran, run) great distances to win money.
20. Whenever people's bank accounts have (shrank, shrunk), they have (hit, hitted) upon new schemes to raise money.

Skill Check D. Identify the verb in each sentence below as *active* or *passive.*

21. Mexicans call their currency the *peso.*
22. The currency of China is known by the Chinese as the *yuan.*
23. Banks often exchange one form of currency for another.
24. The *euro* now serves as the currency of numerous European nations.
25. The U.S. dollar has been used for many years as the prevailing currency of international trade.

Verb Usage • 519

Answer Key

Diagnostic Test

Each item in the Diagnostic Test corresponds to a specific section in the verb usage chapter. This will enable you to tailor instruction to the needs of your students. See "Ongoing Assessment: Diagnose" below for further details. Answers for the Diagnostic Test and all chapter exercises are available in *Grammar Exercises Answers on Transparencies* in your Teaching Resources.

Skill Check A

1. present progressive
2. present perfect (basic)
3. past (basic)
4. future (basic)
5. present perfect progressive
6. present progressive
7. past perfect (basic)
8. past perfect progressive
9. future progressive
10. future perfect progressive

Skill Check B

11. save; saving; saved; (have) saved
12. deposit; depositing; deposited; (have) deposited
13. cost; costing; cost; (have) cost
14. spend; spending; spent; (have) spent
15. grow; growing; grew; (have) grown

Skill Check C

16. striven
17. done
18. grew
19. swum; run
20. shrunk; hit

Skill Check D

21. active
22. passive
23. active
24. active
25. passive

☑ **ONGOING ASSESSMENT: Diagnose** *continued*					
Verb Usage	**Diagnostic Test Items**	**Teach**	**Practice**	**Section Review**	**Chapter Review**
Skill Check C					
Using Correct Verb Forms	C 16–20	pp. 528–529/ Ⓗ376–377	Ex. 9–11	Ex. 19	Ex. 35–36
Skill Check D					
Identifying Passive and Active Voice	D 21–25	pp. 534–536/ Ⓗ382–384	Ex. 23–25	Ex. 26–28	Ex. 37–38
Cumulative Reviews and Applications				Ex. 20–22, Ex. 29–31	Ex. 39–40

Interest GRABBER Write the following paragraph on the board:

My parents brung home a mysterious package. I goes into their room for a peek when their closet door swang open and a puppy bursted into the room.

Ask volunteers to identify the errors (all verbs are incorrect). Have students suggest corrections *(brought, went, swung, burst)*. Point out that using incorrect verbs makes speech and writing difficult to follow.

Activate Prior Knowledge

Ask students what they know about verbs. (Verbs show action or state of being; can be simple or compound; have helpers). Then, ask whether verbs express time (most will agree they do). Ask students to suggest several verbs that show different times. Write these on the board and, for each, ask if the verb shows past, present, or future time. Explain that the verb forms that help express different times are called *tenses*.

TEACH

Step-by-Step Teaching Guide

The Six Tenses of Verbs

1. Review the forms and tenses of the verbs.

2. Explain that the basic forms of tenses express an action or state of being that has a fixed time— yesterday, today, or tomorrow— and then ends. *She is here. He was there.*

3. Point out that, because some actions or states are *ongoing*, a form is needed to indicate this. The progressive form shows ongoing or continuing states or actions.

4. Have students write sentences using the verb *save* in both forms of all six tenses. Ask volunteers to share sentences. Discuss how tense affects meaning.

Section 22.1 # *Verb Tenses*

In writing and speaking, the different *tenses* of verbs are used to express time.

▶ **KEY CONCEPT** A **tense** is a form of a verb that shows the time of an action or a condition. ■

The Six Tenses of Verbs

Verbs have six tenses, each of which can be expressed in two different forms—*basic* and *progressive*.

THE BASIC AND PROGRESSIVE FORMS OF THE SIX TENSES	
Present	She *writes* about U.S. currency for a living.
Past	She *wrote* an article about coin collecting last year.
Future	She *will write* a book about old coins next year.
Present Perfect	She *has written* for the best magazines.
Past Perfect	She *had written* her first article by the time she was eighteen.
Future Perfect	She *will have written* two books by July.
Present Progressive	She *is writing* a newsletter about rare coins now.
Past Progressive	She *was writing* her weekly column.
Future Progressive	She *will be writing* a new book soon.
Present Perfect Progressive	She *has been writing* for years.
Past Perfect Progressive	She *had been writing* speeches when her first book on coins was published.
Future Perfect Progressive	By the end of the year, she *will have been writing* about different forms of currency for a decade.

Theme: The Currency of the World

In this section, you will learn to recognize and use the six tenses of verbs in both their basic and progressive forms. The examples and exercises are about money around the world.

Cross-Curricular Connection: Social Studies

⏱ TIME AND RESOURCE MANAGER

Resources
Print: *Grammar Exercise Workbook,* pp. 107–120; *Grammar Exercises Answers on Transparencies,* Ch. 22; *Hands-on Grammar Activity Book,* Ch. 22
Technology: *Writing and Grammar* Interactive Text, Section 22.1; *On-Line Exercise Bank,* Section 22.1

Using the Full Student Edition	Using the Handbook Ⓗ
• Work through all key concepts, pp. 520–529. • Assign and review Exercises 1–11. • Work through the Hands-on Grammar activity, p. 531.	• Work through all key concepts, pp. 368–377. • Assign and review Exercises 1–11. • Work through the Hands-on Grammar activity, p. 379.

Exercise 1 Identifying Verb Tenses Using the chart on page 520, identify the tense of each verb in italics.

EXAMPLE: He *has been bartering* services for products.

ANSWER: present perfect progressive

1. Money *serves* as a convenient medium of exchange.
2. People *have used* money for many centuries.
3. Previously, people often *bartered* for goods and services.
4. This mode of exchange *had been serving* people for centuries when a simpler way of doing business was devised.
5. Soon, people *were using* shells and furs to make purchases.
6. Some cultures also *minted* coins from precious metals.
7. By the twentieth century, much of the world *had implemented* standard coins and paper money.
8. Today, we *are utilizing* a wide variety of means of exchange.
9. Imagine how we *will be buying* items in the year 3000.
10. By then, people *will have been conducting* business with one another for more than 4,000 years.

▲ **Critical Viewing** Write a series of sentences about the use of cash machines. Use three different verb tenses. **[Apply]**

EXPRESSING TIME THROUGH VERB TENSES		
Past	Existing or happening in the past	James collected old Spanish doubloons.
Past Perfect	Existing or happening before a specific time in the past	James had collected stamps until then.
Present	Existing or happening now	James now collects U.S. silver dollars.
Present Perfect	Existing or happening sometime before now	He has collected that particular coin for several years.
Future	Existing or happening in the future	He will collect coins for a long time.
Future Perfect	Existing or happening before a specific time in the future	By the time he is sixty years old, he will have collected coins for most of his life.

More Practice

Grammar Exercise Workbook
• pp. 107–112
On-line Exercise Bank
• Section 22.1
Go on-line:
PHSchool.com
Enter Web Code:
eek-1002

Interactive Textbook

Get instant feedback! Exercise 1 is available on-line or on CD-ROM.

Verb Tenses • 521

☑ **ONGOING ASSESSMENT: Monitor and Reinforce**

If students miss more than two items in Exercise 1, refer them to the following for additional practice.

In the Textbook	Print Resources	Technology
Section Review, Ex. 12, Section 22.1	*Grammar Exercise Workbook,* pp. 107–108	*On-Line Exercise Bank,* Section 22.1

Answer Key

▶ **Exercise 1**

1. present
2. present perfect
3. past
4. past perfect progressive
5. past progressive
6. past
7. past perfect
8. present progressive
9. future progressive
10. future perfect progressive

Critical Viewing

Apply Sample answers: In the past, people *withdrew* money at the bank. Today, we can *access* money almost anywhere. Banking *has become* much more convenient.

Step-by-Step Teaching Guide

Expressing Time Through Verb Tenses

1. Explain to students that there is often more to expressing time than just deciding on past, present, or future. There are also actions or states of being that may have been completed before another past, present, or future action or state of being. These verbs that come before are said to be "perfect," or completed.

2. Review the list of verb tenses, explanations of how they express time, and examples. Point out how the perfect tenses relate to the other tenses. (They are completed before the other tenses occur. For example: *I had been afraid* of water before last summer, when I *took* swimming lessons. Being afraid occurred in the past, but was completed before taking lessons began.)

3. Ask students to suggest sentences that show a sequence of events, using any of the tenses and the related perfect form. Have them use the examples in the chart as models.

22.1

▶ **Exercise 2** Identifying the Uses of Tense Identify the tense and time indicated by the italicized verb in each sentence.

EXAMPLE: People *have used* many metals to make coins.

ANSWER: present perfect; existing or happening some time before the present

1. American currency generally *has featured* pictures of past presidents.
2. George Washington's face *appears* on the quarter and the one-dollar bill.
3. The symbols and pictures that appear on coins and paper currency *have varied* from culture to culture.
4. The Greeks *were producing* coins with pictures of gods and goddesses on them in ancient times.
5. The ancient Romans *decorated* their coins with portraits of Roman emperors.

▶ **Exercise 3** Writing Sentences in Different Tenses Rewrite each sentence, supplying the verb in the tense indicated.

EXAMPLE: Massachusetts (become—past) the first American colony to mint coins.

ANSWER: Massachusetts became the first American colony to mint coins.

1. At first, the British (try—past progressive) to prevent the American colonies from printing their own money.
2. The British government (hope—past perfect progressive) to make the colonists trade exclusively with England.
3. Despite the restrictions, the colonists (manage—past perfect) to purchase goods from foreign traders.
4. By 1690, the colony of Massachusetts (issue—past progressive) its own coins and paper money.
5. Our class (examine—future) several colonial coins during a field trip to a museum next week.

▶ **Exercise 4** Revising Verb Tense Rewrite each sentence, correcting the tense of the italicized verb.
1. Until the twentieth century, coins used in the Islamic world *will contain* few pictures of people.
2. In the past, Islamic countries *adorn* their coins with inscriptions from the Koran, their holy book.
3. Today, in some countries, people *lobbied* to get new symbols and faces on their currency.
4. In the future, new faces *appear* on U.S. currency.
5. By 2300, people *had used* coins for nearly 3,000 years.

522 • Verb Usage

▼ **Critical Viewing** Which of the sentences in Exercise 2 do you think this coin illustrates? Why? **[Connect]**

Get instant feedback! Exercises 2, 3, and 4 are available on-line or on CD-ROM.

▶ **More Practice**

Grammar Exercise Workbook
• pp. 113–120
On-line Exercise Bank
• Section 22.1

Go on-line:
PHSchool.com
Enter Web Code:
eek-1002

☑ **ONGOING ASSESSMENT: Monitor and Reinforce**

If students miss more than one item in Exercise 2, 3, or 4, refer them to the following for additional practice.

In the Textbook	Print Resources	Technology
Section Review, Ex. 13–14, Section 22.1	*Grammar Exercise Workbook,* pp. 113–120	*On-Line Exercise Bank,* Section 22.1

The Four Principal Parts of Verbs

Tenses are formed from *principal parts* and helping verbs.

> **KEY CONCEPT** A verb has four principal parts: the present, the present participle, the past, and the past participle. ■

The chart below lists the principal parts of two verbs.

THE FOUR PRINCIPAL VERB PARTS			
Present	**Present Participle**	**Past**	**Past Participle**
walk	walking	walked	walked
run	running	ran	run

The first principal part is used to form the present and future tenses. To form the present, an -*s* or -*es* is added whenever the subject is *he, she, it,* or a singular noun (*he walks, Paul runs*). To form the future tense, the helping verb *will* is added (*he will walk, Paul will run*).

The second principal part is used with various helping verbs to produce all six of the progressive forms (*he is walking, Paul was walking,* and so on).

The third principal part is used to form the past tense (*he walked, Paul ran*).

The fourth principal part is used with helping verbs for the three perfect tenses (*he has walked, Paul had run,* and so on).

Regular Verbs

Most of the verbs in the English language, including the verb *walk,* are regular.

> **KEY CONCEPT** The past and past participle of a **regular verb** are formed by adding -*ed* or -*d* to the present form. ■

The past and past participle of regular verbs have the same form. In the chart at the top of the next page, *have* is in parentheses in front of the past participle to remind you that this verb form is a past participle only if it is used with a helping verb.

Notice that the final consonant is sometimes doubled to form the present participle (ski*pp*ing) as well as the past and the past participle (ski*pp*ed). Notice also that the final *e* may be dropped in forming the present participle (typing).

Step-by-Step Teaching Guide

The Four Principal Parts of Verbs

1. To help students memorize principal parts, draw a chart on the board with the following headings: *Present, Present Participle, Past,* and *Past Participle*. Fill in one column with a verb and have students supply the other principal parts of that verb.

2. Remind students that all verb tenses are constructed by using the four principal parts, often with "helper words" such as *will, have,* and *be.*

Step-by-Step Teaching Guide

Regular Verbs

1. Tell students that most verbs in English are regular: the past and past participle are formed by adding -*d* or -*ed*. For regular verbs that end in -*e*, one adds -*d* to the present (*change/changed*). For regular verbs that end in a consonant, one adds -*ed* to the present (*help/helped*).

2. Explain that when a verb ends in -*y* after a consonant, the -*y* changes to *i* before adding -*ed* (*carry* + *ed* = *carried,* not *carryed*). When the verb ends in a single consonant after a single short vowel, the final consonant is doubled before adding -*ed* (*stop* + *ed* = *stopped,* not *stoped*). Doubling the consonant applies to creating the present participle, as well (*stop, stopping*).

3. Have students think of five regular verbs and write down the past and past participle of each. Have students share some of the verbs they selected.

1. featured (past participle)
2. appears (present)
3. varied (past participle)
4. producing (present participle)
5. decorated (past)

Step-by-Step Teaching Guide

Irregular Verbs

1. Point out that students use irregular verbs all the time. They are among our most commonly used verbs.

2. Explain that what makes verbs irregular is how their past and past participle are formed. The present participle is formed the same as it is with regular verbs (adding -ing).

3. Point out that some verbs are irregular because the past and past participle are the same as the present—for example, bid, cost, let, cut, set, and shut. And read is almost in this category; it is spelled the same, but is pronounced differently in the past and past participle.

4. Have students select six irregular verbs and create sentences using the past and past participle. Then ask volunteers to share a few of their sentences.

5. Explain that the only way to master irregular verbs is to use them regularly. Eventually, for the more common verbs, the right form will begin to "sound" right.

6. Emphasize that the lists on pages 524–526 do not include all the irregular verbs, so students should consult a dictionary whenever they are unsure of the principal parts of a verb.

22.1

PRINCIPAL PARTS OF REGULAR VERBS

Present	Present Participle	Past	Past Participle
wash	(is) washing	washed	(have) washed
help	(is) helping	helped	(have) helped
type	(is) typing	typed	(have) typed
print	(is) printing	printed	(have) printed
issue	(is) issuing	issued	(have) issued
plot	(is) plotting	plotted	(have) plotted

Exercise 5 Identifying Principal Parts of Regular Verbs
Identify the principal part used to form each verb in Exercise 2 on page 522. The first one is done as an example below.

EXAMPLE: American currency generally *has featured* pictures of past presidents.

ANSWER: featured (past participle)

Irregular Verbs

Although most verbs are regular, a number of very common verbs, such as *run*, are irregular.

KEY CONCEPT The past and past participle of an **irregular verb** are not formed by adding -ed or -d to the present form. ■

The past and the past participle of irregular verbs are formed in various ways. Some common irregular verbs are shown in the charts that follow. Whenever you are in doubt about the principal parts of an irregular verb, use a dictionary to check them.

THE FOUR PRINCIPAL PARTS OF IRREGULAR VERBS

Present	Present Participle	Past	Past Participle
lay	laying	laid	(have) laid
bring	bringing	brought	(have) brought
begin	beginning	began	(have) begun
fly	flying	flew	(have) flown
cost	costing	cost	(have) cost
pay	paying	paid	(have) paid
lose	losing	lost	(have) lost
sell	selling	sold	(have) sold
spend	spending	spent	(have) spent

✓ ONGOING ASSESSMENT: Monitor and Reinforce

If students miss more than one item in Exercise 5, refer them to the following for additional practice.

In the Textbook	Print Resources	Technology
Section Review, Ex. 15, Section 22.1	*Grammar Exercise Workbook*, pp. 107–110	*On-Line Exercise Bank*, Section 22.1

IRREGULAR VERBS WITH THE SAME PRESENT, PAST, AND PAST PARTICIPLE

Present	Present Participle	Past	Past Participle
bid	bidding	bid	(have) bid
burst	bursting	burst	(have) burst
cost	costing	cost	(have) cost
cut	cutting	cut	(have) cut
hit	hitting	hit	(have) hit
hurt	hurting	hurt	(have) hurt
let	letting	let	(have) let
put	putting	put	(have) put
set	setting	set	(have) set
shut	shutting	shut	(have) shut
split	splitting	split	(have) split
spread	spreading	spread	(have) spread
thrust	thrusting	thrust	(have) thrust

IRREGULAR VERBS WITH THE SAME PAST AND PAST PARTICIPLE

Present	Present Participle	Past	Past Participle
bring	bringing	brought	(have) brought
build	building	built	(have) built
buy	buying	bought	(have) bought
catch	catching	caught	(have) caught
get	getting	got	(have) got or gotten
hang	hanging	hung	(have) hung
hold	holding	held	(have) held
keep	keeping	kept	(have) kept
lay	laying	laid	(have) laid
lead	leading	led	(have) led
leave	leaving	left	(have) left
lose	losing	lost	(have) lost
pay	paying	paid	(have) paid
sell	selling	sold	(have) sold
send	sending	sent	(have) sent
sit	sitting	sat	(have) sat
sleep	sleeping	slept	(have) slept
stand	standing	stood	(have) stood
stick	sticking	stuck	(have) stuck
strike	striking	struck	(have) struck
teach	teaching	taught	(have) taught
win	winning	won	(have) won
wring	wringing	wrung	(have) wrung

Technology Tip

The present participle can be used as a key word to locate information on the Internet. For instance, typing the word *flying* will lead you to Web sites that have information about flying airplanes and other related topics.

Verb Tenses • 525

Customize for *Gifted and Talented Students*

Have students review the charts to find past or past participle parts of irregular verbs that rhyme (*spoke/broke/woke*) and use them to create a few lines of verse about any topic they wish, possibly about irregular verbs (example: I must remember *woke* and *spoke*, and think that things aren't *breaked* but *broke*). Depending on the time available, this could be a few simple lines or a longer piece.

Customize for *Logical/Mathematical Learners*

Explain to students that in sentences containing more than one verb, the time sequence of verb tenses must be logical. Shifting tenses when describing a sequence of events can be confusing. If someone wrote, *He will be going to the store, then he came home*, it would be obvious that the writer got tenses confused. A reader would not know what was meant or when things occurred. Logic is the key here; make certain that a sentence is internally logical. Often, the tense and form remain the same: *I went to the store, then I came home* (both past tense). Remind students that the perfect tenses imply sequence because they represent actions or states of being that are complete before something else occurs or exists. So form changes, but logic is maintained: *I had been shopping all afternoon, but then I went home* (past perfect progressive and past).

STANDARDIZED TEST PREPARATION WORKSHOP

Grammar and Usage Many standardized tests require students to revise errors in compositions. Use the following passage to demonstrate.

Which sentence contains an error in usage?

A When the appeal for blood donors came, I sprang into my car and drove to the donation center.

B The technicians had just begun their day; everything was ready.

C I had chosen a chocolate bar for my snack.

D "After you've given blood, just lay there for about five minutes until the technician tells you to get up," I was told.

The correct answer is **D**. The verb *lay* means "to put (something down) or to place (something)" and is usually followed by a direct object. The verb *lie*, which means "to rest or recline," should be used in the sentence.

TIME SAVERS!

Answers on Transparencies
Use the *Grammar Exercises Answers on Transparencies* for Chapter 22 to facilitate correction by students.

On-Line Exercise Bank
Have students complete the exercises on computer. The Auto Check feature will grade their work for you!

Customize for
Less Advanced Students

Give students two irregular verbs: *break* and *rise*. Have them write down their best guesses about the four principal parts of these two verbs. Then, before sharing correct answers, have them check their own by consulting dictionaries. Once everyone agrees on the four principal parts of each, ask students to form two sentences for each verb: one with the past and one with the past participle. Finally, have students use four verbs of their own choosing, two each from the two charts of irregular verbs, to write pairs of original sentences.

Integrating Spelling Skills

Though irregular verbs have some odd forms, the present participle is formed consistently in all verbs, even the irregular ones: add *-ing*. However, in spelling this present participle, there are a few things to remember: if a verb ends in a single consonant, that consonant gets doubled (*cut/cutting, run/running, swim/swimming*); if the verb ends in an *-e*, remove it before adding *-ing* (*take/taking, shine/shining*). These are important steps to remember because there are verbs that differ only in that final *-e* (*bid/bide, shin/shine, sit/site*), and they differ in the present participle (*shinning/shining*) as well.

IRREGULAR VERBS THAT CHANGE IN OTHER WAYS

Present	Present Participle	Past	Past Participle
arise	arising	arose	(have) arisen
began	beginning	began	(have) begun
blow	blowing	blew	(have) blown
break	breaking	broke	(have) broken
choose	choosing	chose	(have) chosen
come	coming	came	(have) come
do	doing	did	(have) done
draw	drawing	drew	(have) drawn
drink	drinking	drank	(have) drunk
drive	driving	drove	(have) driven
eat	eating	ate	(have) eaten
fall	falling	fell	(have) fallen
fly	flying	flew	(have) flown
freeze	freezing	froze	(have) frozen
give	giving	gave	(have) given
go	going	went	(have) gone
grow	growing	grew	(have) grown
know	knowing	knew	(have) known
lie	lying	lay	(have) lain
ride	riding	rode	(have) ridden
ring	ringing	rang	(have) rung
rise	rising	rose	(have) risen
run	running	ran	(have) run
see	seeing	saw	(have) seen
shake	shaking	shook	(have) shaken
shrink	shrinking	shrank	(have) shrunk
sing	singing	sang	(have) sung
sink	sinking	sank	(have) sunk
slay	slaying	slew	(have) slain
speak	speaking	spoke	(have) spoken
spring	springing	sprang	(have) sprung
steal	stealing	stole	(have) stolen
stride	striding	strode	(have) stridden
strive	striving	strove	(have) striven
swear	swearing	swore	(have) sworn
swim	swimming	swam	(have) swum
take	taking	took	(have) taken
tear	tearing	tore	(have) torn
throw	throwing	threw	(have) thrown
wear	wearing	wore	(have) worn
write	writing	wrote	(have) written

More Practice

Grammar Exercise Workbook
• pp. 113–120
On-line Exercise Bank
• Section 22.1
Go on-line:
PHSchool.com
Enter Web Code:
eek-1002

▶ **Exercise 6** Using the Principal Parts of Irregular Verbs
Choose the correct form of the verb in parentheses.

1. The Chinese emperor Shi Huangdi (holded, held) the reigns of power in China around 220 B.C.
2. He (seeked, sought) ways to strengthen his country.
3. To protect China's northern border, Shi Huangdi had (drew, drawn) up plans for a huge stone wall.
4. Then, he had (put, putted) 300,000 workers to the task of constructing the wall.
5. Once the wall had been (build, built), Shi Huangdi turned to the country's economy.

▶ **Exercise 7** Supplying the Correct
Principal Parts of Irregular Verbs Rewrite each sentence, supplying the correct principal part of the verb given in parentheses.

1. He ___?___ out an order requiring all Chinese to use the same currency, a round coin with a square hole in the middle. (send)
2. A common currency ___?___ it easier for one region of China to trade goods with another. (make)
3. Eight hundred years later, the Chinese ___?___ the first people to use paper money. (become)
4. When Marco Polo visited in the 1200's, he ___?___ that the Chinese were using paper money instead of coins. (see)
5. Polo had ___?___ to European leaders about this practice after he had returned to Italy. (speak)

▶ **Exercise 8** Revising to Correct the Use of Irregular Verbs
Revise this paragraph, correcting any errors in the use of irregular verbs.

The Chinese begun issuing paper money around A.D. 600. Even after they had heard about Chinese paper money from Marco Polo, Europeans remained unconvinced. They keeped wondering how a piece of paper could have value. It wasn't until the 1600's that banks in Europe choosed to issue paper bills, called bank notes, to their customers. When depositors took bank notes to their banks, they could be given gold or silver coins in exchange. The idea of government-issued paper money had not catched on until the 1800's.

▲ Critical Viewing
Use two different irregular verbs in describing this photograph of the Great Wall of China. **[Describe]**

Verb Tenses • **527**

Answer Key

☑ **ONGOING ASSESSMENT: Monitor and Reinforce**

If students have difficulty with Exercise 6, 7, or 8, refer them to the following for additional practice.

In the Textbook	Print Resources	Technology
Section Review, Ex. 18, Section 22.1	*Grammar Exercise Workbook*, pp. 109–110	*On-Line Exercise Bank*, Section 22.1

Conjugating the Tenses

1. Explain that one way to learn all the forms of a verb is to conjugate it. A conjugation is a list of every singular and plural form in each person of a verb in a particular tense.

2. Before having students conjugate verb forms, ask a volunteer to review briefly the meaning of the terms *first person, second person,* and *third person (first person* is the person speaking, *second person* is spoken to, *third person* is spoken about).

3. After students feel comfortable with "person," ask them to conjugate one regular and one irregular verb in the basic forms (*walk* and *swim*). Have students refer to the chart on this page as they work or until they can conjugate the verbs without help.

4. You may then wish to select two other verbs and have students work through the progressive forms.

5. Point out that the verb *be* is more frequently used—as a verb and as a helper—than any other verb in English. It is also the most irregular verb, with three forms in the present tense (*am, is,* and *are*) and two forms in the past tense (*was* and *were*).

Language Highlight

Ask students whether the word *conjugate,* applied here to verbs, reminds them of another word (*conjunction*). Tell students that one meaning of the verb *to conjugate* is "to list the parts of a verb," but it also means "to unite or join together." *Conjunctions* are words that join other words. These two words are derived from the Latin *conjugare,* which means "to tie together."

22.1

Conjugating the Tenses

With the principal parts of verbs and helping verbs, you can form all the tenses.

▶ **KEY CONCEPT** A **conjugation** is a complete list of the singular and plural forms of a verb in a particular tense. ∎

For each tense, there are three singular forms and three plural forms that correspond to the first-, second-, and third-person forms of personal pronouns.

To conjugate the six tenses in their basic forms, you need only three of the principal parts: the present, the past, and the past participle. To conjugate the six tenses in their progressive forms, you need the present participle and a form of the verb *be.*

CONJUGATION OF THE BASIC FORMS OF *PAY*		
	Singular	**Plural**
Present		
First Person	I pay	we pay
Second Person	you pay	you pay
Third Person	he, she, it pays	they pay
Past		
First Person	I paid	we paid
Second Person	you paid	you paid
Third Person	he, she, it paid	they paid
Future		
First Person	I will pay	we will pay
Second Person	you will pay	you will pay
Third Person	he, she, it will pay	they will pay
Present Perfect		
First Person	I have paid	we have paid
Second Person	you have paid	you have paid
Third Person	he, she, it has paid	they have paid
Past Perfect		
First Person	I had paid	we had paid
Second Person	you had paid	you had paid
Third Person	he, she, it had paid	they had paid
Future Perfect		
First Person	I will have paid	we will have paid
Second Person	you will have paid	you will have paid
Third Person	he, she, it will have paid	they will have paid

528 • Verb Usage

 STANDARDIZED TEST PREPARATION WORKSHOP

Grammar and Usage Many standardized tests require students to use verb tenses correctly. Use the following example to demonstrate.

Which sentence contains an error in usage?

A *Susan was going to the library when she decided to visit some classmates.*

B *They had been talking about her when she comes in.*

C *Her classmates were embarrassed because they had not been expecting her.*

D *In the future, they will think twice before they talk about someone.*

The correct answer is **B.** *Had been talking* is the past perfect progressive tense and should not be used with the present tense verb *comes.* The shift in tense makes the sentence unclear. The correct form is *came.*

CONJUGATION OF THE PROGRESSIVE FORMS OF *PAY*

	Singular	Plural
Present Progressive		
First Person	I am paying	we are paying
Second Person	you are paying	you are paying
Third Person	he, she, it is paying	they are paying
Past Progressive		
First Person	I was paying	we were paying
Second Person	you were paying	you were paying
Third Person	he, she, it was paying	they were paying
Future Progressive		
First Person	I will be paying	we will be paying
Second Person	you will be paying	you will be paying
Third Person	he, she, it will be paying	they will be paying
Present Perfect Progressive		
First Person	I have been paying	we have been paying
Second Person	you have been paying	you have been paying
Third Person	he, she, it has been paying	they have been paying
Past Perfect Progressive		
First Person	I had been paying	we had been paying
Second Person	you had been paying	you had been paying
Third Person	he, she, it had been paying	they had been paying
Future Perfect Progressive		
First Person	I will have been paying	we will have been paying
Second Person	you will have been paying	you will have been paying
Third Person	he, she, it will have been paying	they will have been paying

Note About *Be:* The verb *be* is highly irregular. The following conjugation of the first two tenses lists the forms.

PRESENT:	I am	we are
	you are	you are
	he, she, it is	they are
PAST:	I was	we were
	you were	you were
	he, she, it was	they were

Verb Tenses • **529**

Customize for
ESL Students

An important verb for students to master is *to be*, and mastery requires that they train their ears to hear its forms in various contexts. To practice the conjugations of this verb, give your students a brief drill. Write on the board the present parts of the verb in any order *(am, are, is)*. Tell students that you will read aloud a sentence *(I am going to the store)*. Then, say another subject *(you, he, she, it, we,* or *they)* and have a student repeat the sentence with the new subject and the correct form of the verb *to be (You are going to the store; She is going to the store)*. Then, repeat the student's sentence, but only if it is correct; if it is not correct, assist him or her in determining the correct form. Once students are comfortable with the present tense, this same procedure can be used with the past tense and with other variations *(They were taking lessons; I was studying hard)*.

☑ ONGOING ASSESSMENT: Monitor and Reinforce

If students have difficulty with conjugating tenses of regular or irregular verbs, refer them to the following for additional practice.

In the Textbook	Print Resources	Technology
Section Review, Ex. 19, Section 22.1	*Grammar Exercise Workbook*, pp. 111–112	*On-Line Exercise Bank*, Section 22.1

1. Present: she stops
   Past: she stopped
   Future: she will stop
   Present Perfect: she has stopped
   Past Perfect: she had stopped
   Future Perfect: she will have stopped
2. Present: it costs
   Past: it cost
   Future: it will cost
   Present Perfect: it has cost
   Past Perfect: it had cost
   Future Perfect: it will have cost
3. Present: they collect
   Past: they collected
   Future: they will collect
   Present Perfect: they have collected
   Past Perfect: they had collected
   Future Perfect: they will have collected
4. Present: we sell
   Past: we sold
   Future: we will sell
   Present Perfect: we have sold
   Past Perfect: we had sold
   Future Perfect: we will have sold
5. Present: I choose
   Past: I chose
   Future: I will choose
   Present Perfect: I have chosen
   Past Perfect: I had chosen
   Future Perfect: I will have chosen

Exercise 10

1. Pres Prog: they are studying
   Past Prog: they were studying
   Fut Prog: they will be studying
   Pres Perf Prog: they have been studying
   Past Perf Prog: they had been studying
   Fut Perf Prog: they will have been studying
2. Pres Prog: he is putting
   Past Prog: he was putting
   Fut Prog: he will be putting
   Pres Perf Prog: he has been putting
   Past Perf Prog: he had been putting
   Fut Perf Prog: he will have been putting
3. Pres Prog: you are lending
   Past Prog: you were lending
   Fut Prog: you will be lending
   Pres Perf Prog: you have been lending
   Past Perf Prog: you had been lending
   Fut Perf Prog: you will have been lending

22.1

Exercise 9 Conjugating the Basic Forms of Verbs
Conjugate the basic forms of the five verbs below.

EXAMPLE: spend (conjugated with *we*)

ANSWER:
present: we spend   present perfect: we have spent
past: we spent   past perfect: we had spent
future: we will spend   future perfect: we will have spent

1. stop (conjugated with *she*)
2. cost (conjugated with *it*)
3. collect (conjugated with *they*)
4. sell (conjugated with *we*)
5. choose (conjugated with *I*)

Exercise 10 Conjugating the Progressive Forms of Verbs
Conjugate the progressive forms of the five verbs below.

EXAMPLE: spend (conjugated with *we*)

ANSWER: present progressive: we are spending
past progressive: we were spending
future progressive: we will be spending
present perfect progressive: we have been spending
past perfect progressive: we had been spending
future perfect progressive: we will have been spending

1. study (conjugated with *they*)   4. forget (conjugated with *I*)
2. put (conjugated with *he*)   5. strive (conjugated with *we*)
3. lend (conjugated with *you*)

Exercise 11 Supplying the Correct Tense of Verbs On your paper, write each sentence, using the indicated form for each verb in parentheses.

1. Until recently, most coins (contain) precious metals like gold or silver. (past perfect)
2. However, the number of coins in circulation today greatly (exceed) the world's supply of precious metals. (present)
3. Making gold coins (become) impractical. (present perfect)
4. It is likely that the value of old silver and gold coins (rise) in the future. (future)
5. For that reason, more people than ever (seek) to collect old coins. (future progressive)

530 • Verb Usage

▲ **Critical Viewing**
How does this coin compare with those we use today? What verb forms did you use in making your comparison? **[Compare]**

Interactive Textbook

Get instant feedback! Exercises 9, 10, and 11 are available on-line or on CD-ROM.

More Practice

Grammar Exercise Workbook
• pp. 113–120
On-line Exercise Bank
• Section 22.1
Go on-line:
PHSchool.com
Enter Web Code:
eek-1002

---

4. Pres Prog: I am forgetting
   Past Prog: I was forgetting
   Fut Prog: I will be forgetting
   Pres Perf Prog: I have been forgetting
   Past Perf Prog: I had been forgetting
   Fut Perf Prog: I will have been forgetting
5. Pres Prog: we are striving
   Past Prog: we were striving
   Fut Prog: we will be striving
   Pres Perf Prog: we have been striving
   Past Perf Prog: we had been striving
   Fut Perf Prog: we will have been striving

Exercise 11

1. had contained
2. exceeds
3. has become
4. will rise
5. will be seeking

Critical Viewing

Compare Answers will vary. Sample answer: This coin is made of gold whereas modern coins are not. (be)

Hands-on Grammar

Top-Ten List of Irregular Verbs

Complete the following activity to prepare a reference that you can use to remind you how to conjugate irregular verbs that you find especially troublesome.

Brainstorm with classmates to come up with a list of irregular verbs that have at times caused problems in your writing. One of you should record the verbs on the chalkboard or on a piece of paper.

Review the list of verbs, and choose the ten that you find most difficult to conjugate. Then, make a folding chart like the one below, in which you list the present, past, future, present perfect, past perfect, future perfect, present progressive, past progressive, future progressive, present perfect progressive, past perfect progressive, and future perfect progressive tenses of each verb.

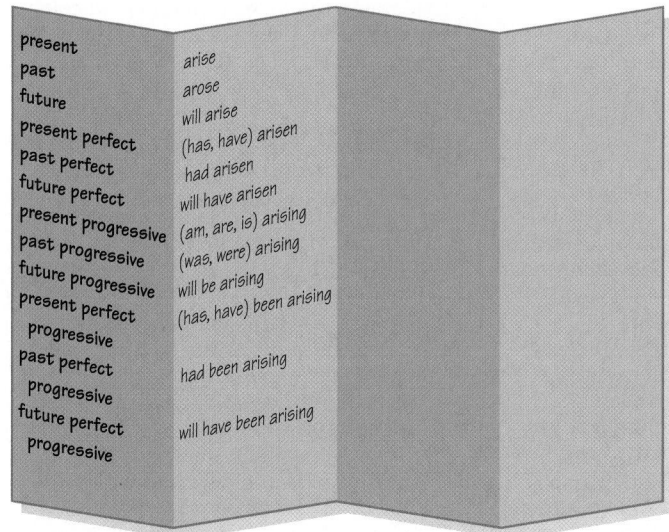

present	arise
past	arose
future	will arise
present perfect	(has, have) arisen
past perfect	had arisen
future perfect	will have arisen
present progressive	(am, are, is) arising
past progressive	(was, were) arising
future progressive	will be arising
present perfect progressive	(has, have) been arising
past perfect progressive	had been arising
future perfect progressive	will have been arising

Find It in Your Reading Scan through stories and essays you have read recently to help you come up with verbs to include on your list.

Find It in Your Writing Look through your portfolio to find examples of irregular verbs. Then, add them to your chart or, if necessary, compile a second chart.

Verb Tenses • 531

Hands-on Grammar

Teaching Resources: Hands-on Grammar Activity Book, Ch. 22

1. If you wish to do this activity in class, you might provide markers and paper of different colors that students can use to differentiate one verb from the next.

2. Suggest that students review the lists of irregular verbs on pages 524–526 and choose the verbs they find most difficult.

3. Encourage students to practice conjugating these verbs frequently. They can use their top ten lists to check their work for accuracy.

Find It in Your Reading

Have students make a list of all the verbs in the first few paragraphs of a short story. Then, they can list synonyms for each verb. This will give them a long list of verbs to choose from.

Find It in Your Writing

As they do this exercise, students might notice that they tend to overuse certain verbs. Encourage them to use fresh, vivid verbs in their next writing assignment.

☑ ONGOING ASSESSMENT: Assess Mastery

Use the following resources to assess student mastery of verb tenses.

In the Textbook	Technology
Chapter Review, Ex. 32–36	*Writing and Grammar* Interactive Text, Section 22.1, Section Review; *On-Line Exercise Bank*, Section 22.1

⏱ TIME SAVERS!

Hands-on Grammar
Use the Hands-on Grammar activity sheet for Chapter 22 to facilitate this activity.

Section Review

Each of these exercises correlates to the instruction on verb tenses, pages 520–529. The exercises may be used for more practice, for reteaching, or for review of the key concepts presented.

Answer Key

▶ Exercise 12

1. present perfect progressive
2. present basic
3. present perfect progressive
4. past perfect basic
5. present basic

▶ Exercise 13

1. present perfect: existing or happening sometime before now
2. past (passive): existing or happening in the past
3. present: existing or happening now
4. past perfect: existing or happening before a specific time in the past
5. present perfect: existing or happening sometime before now
6. past: existing or happening in the past
7. past perfect: existing or happening before a specific time in the past
8. present: existing or happening now
9. future: existing or happening in the future
10. future perfect: existing or happening before a specific time in the future.

▶ Exercise 14

sentence 2: changed: changes
sentence 3: [today] is [worth]: [today] was [worth]
sentence 4: [numismatists] establish: have established
sentence 5: has become: will have become

▶ Exercise 15

1. present
2. past
3. present participle
4. past participle
5. past participle

Section 22.1 Section Review

GRAMMAR EXERCISES 12–22

▶ **Exercise 12** Identifying Verb Tenses and Forms On your paper, label the tense and form of each verb in italics.

1. People *have been collecting* coins for hundreds of years.
2. People *call* coin collectors *numismatists*.
3. Coin collecting *has been rising* in popularity with the advent of the Internet.
4. Before being able to use the Internet, collectors often *had traveled* great distances to examine and buy coins.
5. Thanks to the Internet, numismatists can now *purchase* coins in faraway places with a click of a button.

▶ **Exercise 13** Identifying the Uses of Tense Label the tense and the time of the italicized verb in each sentence.

1. A second industry *has grown* alongside the development of national currencies.
2. Counterfeiting has been a major problem for banks and governments since the first coins and bills *were produced*.
3. Counterfeiters often *use* sophisticated methods to make fake money.
4. In some nations, counterfeit currency *had reduced* public confidence in the value of the country's currency.
5. By using new technology, the U.S. government *has thwarted* many recent attempts to counterfeit U.S. currency.
6. The government *changed* the design of the twenty-dollar bill to make it more difficult for counterfeiters to copy.
7. Many years ago, the U.S. government *had begun* to use special paper on which to print its money.
8. This unique paper *has* microscopic threads embedded in it.
9. It is certain that the world's governments *will use* new methods to deter counterfeiters in the future.

532 • Verb Usage

10. It is hoped that by the next millennium, governments *will have succeeded* in eradicating counterfeit currency.

▶ **Exercise 14** Revising to Correct Verb Tense Revise the following paragraph, correcting errors in verb tense.

A coin's condition influences its value. The value of coins changed with time. A rare penny that is worth thousands of dollars to collectors today is worth just one cent at one time. To help establish the value of a coin, numismatists establish five gradations to rank the condition of coins. It is possible that years from now, the change in your pocket has become valuable.

▶ **Exercise 15** Recognizing Principal Parts of Verbs Identify the principal part of each verb in italics.

1. Although most countries have their own currency, many *conduct* business using the U.S. dollar.
2. In the past, this situation *helped* to keep the value of the dollar stable.
3. At this very moment, people throughout the world *are making* business deals based on the U.S. dollar.
4. Improvements in international trade regulations and communication *have made* such transactions possible.
5. People *have bought* products from foreign businesses through the Internet without needing to convert currencies.

▶ **Exercise 16** Using the Principal Parts of Verbs Choose the principal part that is correct in each sentence on the next page.

▶ Exercise 16

1. written	6. seen
2. given	7. taken
3. known	8. shrunk
4. thrown	9. fallen
5. bought	10. grown

▶ Exercise 17

1. claimed
2. using
3. buy
4. has; been
5. made

▶ Exercise 18

1. happen: happens
2. payed: paid
3. will have became: will have become
4. will have saw: will have seen

1. Many books have been (wrote, written) on the value of money worldwide.
2. Writers have (gave, given) much thought to this topic.
3. Economists have long (knew, known) that the value of money fluctuates.
4. They have (threw, thrown) new light on that which gives money value.
5. For example, a dollar (buyed, bought) more in the 1920's than it does today.
6. Many of our grandparents have (saw, seen) prices double, triple, or even quadruple in their lifetimes.
7. Things that had (took, taken) five cents to purchase many years ago, now may cost several dollars.
8. In that sense, the value of a dollar has (shrank, shrunk) over the years.
9. As prices for goods have risen, the value of money has (fell, fallen).
10. All is not bad news, however. Along with rising prices, people's incomes have also (grew, grown).

> **Exercise 17** Supplying Correct Verb Forms Supply the correct principal part of the verb in parentheses.

1. Some economists have ___?___ that coins and bills will slowly be replaced by other forms of currency. (claim)
2. Indeed, fewer people than ever before are ___?___ cash today to purchase goods and services. (use)
3. These days, people routinely ___?___ goods and services with credit cards, debit cards, and checks. (buy)
4. This ___?___ not always ___?___ the case. (be)
5. Until recently, people had ___?___ most purchases with cash. (make)

> **Exercise 18** Revising to Correct the Use of Irregular Verbs Revise this passage, correcting errors in verb usage.

Today, many transactions occur without the exchange of coins or paper money.

This happen most often in wealthy countries when large amounts of money are involved. However, many employees are also payed by having funds deposited directly into their accounts. Experts speculate that in the future, very few people will be relying on cash to conduct business transactions. They speculate that once computer technology becomes common throughout the world, coins and paper money will have became obsolete. By 2010, we will have saw many changes.

> **Exercise 19** Conjugating the Basic and Progressive Forms of Verbs Conjugate the following verbs in both the basic and progressive forms.

1. earn (conjugate with *I*)
2. keep (conjugate with *you*)
3. go (conjugate with *they*)
4. tell (conjugate with *he*)
5. fly (conjugate with *we*)

> **Exercise 20** Find It in Your Reading Label the tense and form of each italicized verb in this excerpt from "Civil Peace" by Chinua Achebe.

. . . Jonathan *thought* he *heard* even more voices now than before and *groaned* heavily. His legs *were sagging* under him and his throat *felt* like sandpaper.

> **Exercise 21** Find It in Your Writing Choose a paragraph from one of your compositions. Circle each verb or verb phrase, and identify its tense and form.

> **Exercise 22** Writing Application In this section, you learned about the history of currency. Write about the history of something else that interests you. Use at least three different tenses. Circle each verb, and identify its tense.

Section Review • 533

Interest GRABBER Write on the board: *The boy flew a kite* and *A kite was flown by the boy.* Ask students to explain the differences between the two sentences. (In the first sentence, the boy seems more important; in the second, the kite. *Flew* sounds more dynamic than *was flown.*)

Activate Prior Knowledge

Ask students what the word *active* implies to them. Ask what the word *passive* implies. Tell them that active voice in grammar has similar connotations: It produces lively writing.

TEACH

Step-by-Step Teaching Guide

Differences Between Active and Passive Voice

1. Tell students that to distinguish between active and passive voice, they should ask who or what is performing the action. If the subject performs the action, then the verb is active. If the subject does not perform the action, then the verb is passive.

2. Explain that the passive voice is constructed using a form of the verb *be* and a past participle.

Customize for
ESL Students

Some students may feel that the active voice is too aggressive and that the passive voice is more polite. Be sensitive to cultural values, but reassure students that, in the United States, the active voice in and of itself is not seen as unpleasant.

Answer Key

Exercise 23

1. active	6. passive
2. passive	7. passive
3. passive	8. active
4. active	9. active
5. active	10. active

Section 22.2

Active and Passive Voice

In addition to using verbs to show the time that something happened, you can show whether the subject is performing or receiving the action. You can do this by changing the *voice* of a verb. You can show voice only with action verbs.

▶ **KEY CONCEPT** **Voice** is the form of a verb that shows whether the subject is performing the action. ■

There are two voices in English: *active* and *passive.*

▶ **KEY CONCEPTS** A verb is **active** if its subject performs the action. A verb is **passive** if its action is performed upon the subject. ■

Differences Between Active and Passive Voice

Any action verb, with or without a direct object, can be in the active voice. In these examples, the subject is doing the action.

ACTIVE VOICE: Ken *bought* a set of paints.
My sister *drives* to art school.

Most action verbs can also be used in the passive voice. A passive verb is made from a form of *be* and the past participle of a transitive verb (one that can have a direct object). In the first example below, Ken is still the performer; yet the word *Ken* is now the object of the preposition *by* and not the subject of the sentence. In the second example, *sister* is still the subject, but the person doing the action is not identified.

PASSIVE VOICE: A set of paints *was bought* by Ken.
My sister *was driven* to art school.

▶ **Exercise 23** Distinguishing Between the Active and Passive Voices Identify each verb or verb phrase as *active* or *passive.*
1. Many prominent nineteenth-century artists *lived* in France.
2. The Frenchman Auguste Rodin *is cherished* by art lovers.
3. Rodin's birthday, November 12, *is celebrated* by admirers.
4. Surprisingly, Rodin *did* not *grow* up in an artistic family.
5. His father *worked* as a police official.
6. Early success *was* not *experienced* by Rodin.
7. He *was denied* entrance to the finest art school in Paris.
8. Despite this setback, Rodin *persevered.*
9. He *pursued* sculpture on his own.
10. He also *worked* for other sculptors.

534 • Verb Usage

Theme: Artists

In this section, you will learn to recognize verbs in active or passive voice and practice rewriting sentences to use active voice verbs whenever possible. The examples and exercises are about artists and fine art.

Cross-Curricular Connection: Fine Art

Interactive Textbook

Get instant feedback! Exercises 23 and 24 are available on-line or on CD-ROM.

▶ **More Practice**

Grammar Exercise Workbook
• pp. 121–124
On-line Exercise Bank
• Section 22.2
  Go on-line:
  PHSchool.com
  Enter Web Code:
  eek-1002

⏱ TIME AND RESOURCE MANAGER

Resources
Print: *Grammar Exercise Workbook,* pp. 121–124; *Grammar Exercises Answers on Transparencies,* Ch. 22
Technology: *Writing and Grammar* Interactive Text, Section 22.2; *On-Line Exercise Bank,* Section 22.2

Using the Full Student Edition	Using the Handbook Ⓗ
• Work through all key concepts, pp. 534–535.	• Work through all key concepts, pp. 382–383.
• Assign and review Exercises 23–25.	• Assign and review Exercises 23–25.
• Read and discuss Grammar in Literature, p. 536.	• Read and discuss Grammar in Literature, p. 384.

Using Voice Correctly

To write well, you must know when to use the active voice and when to use the passive voice. There are no firm rules, but here are some suggestions:

> **KEY CONCEPT** Use the active voice whenever possible. ■

Good writing is crisp and direct. Sentences with active verbs are less wordy and more direct than those with passive verbs. Notice that both sentences below report the same information, but the sentence in the active voice is shorter and more direct.

ACTIVE VOICE: Esteban *sketched* the bowl of apples.

PASSIVE VOICE: The bowl of apples *was sketched* by Esteban.

There are, of course, times when it is more appropriate to use the passive voice. Use the passive voice to point out the receiver of an action whenever the performer is not important or not easily identified.

> **KEY CONCEPT** Use the passive voice to emphasize the receiver of an action rather than the performer of an action. ■

Placing a word at or near the beginning of a sentence helps emphasize its importance. When you want to stress the importance of the receiver of an action, then it is proper to use the passive voice.

PASSIVE VOICE: Maria *was given* an art award by a museum official.
                  The damaged statue *was placed* downstairs.

> **Exercise 24** Revising Sentences in the Passive Voice Rewrite each sentence below, changing it from passive to active voice.

1. The art exhibit was seen by our whole family.
2. A review of the exhibit had been read by us before we went.
3. Tickets for the exhibit were purchased by my mother.
4. The Internet was used by her to make the purchase.
5. Each work in the exhibit was painted by an Impressionist artist.

▼ Critical Viewing Think of two sentences concerning the creation of this painting, one in the active voice and one in the passive voice. Which sentence is shorter and more direct? [Connect, Contrast]

Tiberius and Agrippina, Peter Paul Rubens

Active and Passive Voice • 535

Step-by-Step Teaching Guide

Using Voice Correctly

1. Explain to students that the active voice makes writing more direct and lively. There is a place for the passive voice, but most sentences should be in the active voice to make the writing stronger and more dynamic.

2. Review the two main purposes for using passive voice: (1) to emphasize the receiver of an action rather than the performer of the action: *The winning run was driven in by the rookie*; and (2) if the actor is unknown or unimportant. Example: *The game was won in the bottom of the ninth inning.*

Integrating Workplace Skills

Use of passive voice in speaking or writing emphasizes the receiver of an action. Lawyers frequently speak about clients in passive voice. (*My client* was framed. *That evidence* was planted.) Ask students to think of other examples of passive voice and discuss why it is effective in certain situations (to redirect emphasis).

Critical Viewing

Connect, Contrast The woman *overshadows* the man. The man *is overshadowed* by the woman.

Answer Key

> **Exercise 24**

1. Our whole family saw the art exhibit.
2. We had read a review of the exhibit before we went.
3. My mother purchased tickets for the exhibit.
4. She used the Internet to make the purchase.
5. An Impressionist artist painted each work in the exhibit.

Grammar in Literature

1. Have students list the passive verb in the passage (*were quieted*).

2. Ask why Poe chose to use the passive voice in this passage (because the revelers are unknown; to emphasize their helplessness).

More About the Writer

Edgar Allan Poe was arguably the most important short-story writer of the nineteenth century. He is credited with inventing the detective story, and his many tales of terror and the supernatural continue to thrill readers and influence writers. His short story, "The Masque of the Red Death," concerns a medieval prince and a thousand noble friends secluded in his castle for months. They wrongfully assume that they remain immune to the Red Death, a hideous killer plague raging among the common people in the countryside.

Real-World Connection

When you type on a computer, you may find that your software will challenge the use of passive voice. Tell students that they must become confident with knowing when the passive voice is appropriate, so they can determine whether or not to heed the computer's warning.

Answer Key

▶ **Exercise 25**

Answers may vary; samples are given.

1. Many art scholars have heralded the mid-twentieth century . . .
2. active voice
3. Passive emphasizes receiver (audiences and critics)
4. active
5. Johns used thick layers of paint on his paintings.
6. This technique intensified the texture of his creations.
7. active
8. He attached objects like rulers and compasses to his paintings.
9. Passive emphasizes receiver (Johns)
10. Passive emphasizes receiver (many)

22.2

GRAMMAR IN LITERATURE

from The Masque of the Red Death

Edgar Allan Poe

This passage by Edgar Allan Poe artfully combines active voice verbs (in blue italics) and a passive voice verb (in red italics) to convey the helplessness of revelers in the grip of impending doom.

And then the music *ceased*, as I have *told*; and the evolutions of the waltzers *were quieted*; and there was an uneasy cessation of all things as before. But now there were twelve strokes to be sounded by the bell of the clock; and thus it *happened*, perhaps, that more of thought *crept*, with more of time, into the meditations of the thoughtful among those who *reveled*.

▶ **Exercise 25** Revising to Use the Active Voice On your paper, rewrite the following paragraph, changing at least four uses of the passive voice to the active voice. If you have chosen to leave any sentence in the passive voice, explain your reason.

EXAMPLE: The sculpture was honored with a blue ribbon.

ANSWER: Keep in passive voice because performer of action is unidentified.

(1) The mid-twentieth century has been heralded by many art scholars as an exciting era for innovative art. (2) Jasper Johns, one of the most interesting artists of that era, worked in the United States in the 1950's. (3) Audiences and critics were thrilled by Johns's bold paintings. (4) Exploring a new direction, he painted such ordinary objects as numerals and the letters of the alphabet. (5) Thick layers of paint were used by Johns on his paintings. (6) The texture of his creations was intensified by this technique. (7) In the late 1950's, he incorporated actual objects into his paintings. (8) Objects like rulers and compasses were attached by him to his paintings. (9) Johns is considered by many art scholars to be one of the most influential American artists of the twentieth century. (10) Many of his works are exhibited in prominent art museums and galleries around the world.

536 • Verb Usage

▶ **More Practice**

Grammar Exercise Workbook
• pp. 121–124
On-line Exercise Bank
• Section 22.2
Go on-line:
PHSchool.com
Enter Web Code:
eek-1002

Textbook

Complete the exercise on-line! Exercise 25 is available on-line or on CD-ROM.

☑ ONGOING ASSESSMENT: Assess Mastery

Use the following resources to assess student mastery of verb usage.

In the Textbook	Print Resources	Technology
Chapter Review, Ex. 37–39 Standardized Test Preparation Workshop	*Formal Assessment*, Ch. 22	*Writing and Grammar* Interactive Text, Section 22.2, Section Review; *On-Line Exercise Bank*, Section 22.2

Section Review

GRAMMAR EXERCISES 26–31

▶ **Exercise 26** Distinguishing Between the Active and Passive Voices
On your paper, identify the voice of the verb in each of the following sentences.

1. In the 1960's, Andy Warhol was noticed by the art world for his silk-screen prints of ordinary objects.
2. Common objects, such as soup cans and soft-drink bottles, were often depicted in these prints.
3. This seemingly defiant approach to art defined the Pop Art movement.
4. Warhol also made silk-screen prints of famous celebrities.
5. Warhol's reputation as an innovator was established by these prints.

▶ **Exercise 27** Using the Passive and Active Voices Identify the voice of the italicized verb in each sentence. Then, rewrite the sentence, changing the voice from active to passive or passive to active.

1. The works of Leonardo da Vinci *have inspired* viewers for hundreds of years.
2. Da Vinci *had been heralded* by his peers in Italy as a talented artist.
3. Modern critics *have praised* him as a superb painter, sculptor, architect, and scientist.
4. He *is remembered* best by art lovers for *The Last Supper* and the *Mona Lisa.*
5. *The Last Supper was painted* by Da Vinci on one wall of a dining hall of a monastery.
6. Many people *have described* the *Mona Lisa* as a masterpiece.
7. The work *depicts* a beautiful woman.
8. A sense of mystery *is captured* in the woman's smile.
9. The work also *displays* great technical mastery.
10. By the early 2000's, Da Vinci's works *will have been admired* by people for nearly five hundred years.

▶ **Exercise 28** Revising to Use the Active Voice Rewrite this paragraph, changing several uses of the passive voice to the active voice. Explain why you have left any sentence in the passive voice.

(1) The fourteenth and fifteenth centuries are described by art historians as a time of revival in European art and culture. (2) This period has often been called the Renaissance, or "rebirth." (3) Prior to the Renaissance, European art had been marked by a long period of inactivity. (4) The sculptor Donatello is considered by critics and historians to be one of the greatest Renaissance artists. (5) A golden era in sculpture was signaled by Donatello's completion of a statue of David in 1435.

▶ **Exercise 29** Find It in Your Reading Make a photocopy of a magazine article about one of the fine arts. Highlight all of the verbs in the active voice in one color and all of the verbs in the passive voice in another color.

▶ **Exercise 30** Find It in Your Writing In a piece of your own writing, find at least five sentences in the passive voice. Rewrite these sentences in the active voice.

▶ **Exercise 31** Writing Application Write a brief description of a work of art that you or one of your friends created. Use both active and passive voice verbs. Circle each verb, and identify its voice. Explain your use of the passive voice.

Section Review • 537

Answer Key

Exercise 32

1. present
2. present perfect
3. past perfect
4. past progressive
5. past; past
6. past perfect
7. past progressive
8. present progressive
9. future
10. future perfect

Exercise 33

1. been
2. caught
3. grew
4. sought
5. striving

Exercise 34

1. maked: made
2. taked: took
3. flinged: flung
4. become: became
5. [artists] do: did

Exercise 35

1. Present: I arrange
   Past: I arranged
   Future: I will arrange
   Present Perfect: I have arranged
   Past Perfect: I had arranged
   Future Perfect: I will have arranged
2. Present: it spreads
   Past: it spread
   Future: it will spread
   Present Perfect: it has spread
   Past Perfect: it had spread
   Future Perfect: it will have spread
3. Present: we draw
   Past: we drew
   Future: we will draw
   Present Perfect: we have drawn
   Past Perfect: we had drawn
   Future Perfect: we will have drawn
4. Present: you buy
   Past: you bought
   Future: you will buy
   Present Perfect: you have bought
   Past Perfect: you had bought
   Future Perfect: you will have bought

5. Present: they shake
   Past: they shook
   Future: they will shake
   Present Perfect: they have shaken
   Past Perfect: they had shaken
   Future Perfect: they will have shaken

Chapter 22 Chapter Review

GRAMMAR EXERCISES 32–40

Exercise 32 Identifying the Tenses of Verbs Identify the tense and form of each verb or verb phrase in italics.

1. Painters today *have* a great choice of subjects to depict.
2. Over the years, artists *have painted* various objects and people.
3. Before the 1600's, most European artists *had focused* on religious subjects.
4. Dutch artists in the 1600's *were experimenting* with new subject matter.
5. They *developed* genre painting, in which they *focused* on realistic depictions of scenes from ordinary life.
6. This shift in subject matter *had represented* a radical break from tradition.
7. For the first time, artists *were devoting* attention to the lives of ordinary people.
8. Even today, many artists *are working* in this tradition.
9. Artists *will paint* ordinary life as long as that subject matter continues to intrigue them.
10. By the year 2100, genre painting *will have aroused* the interest of painters and viewers for nearly 500 years.

Exercise 33 Supplying Principal Parts of Verbs Rewrite each sentence, supplying the correct principal part of the verb in parentheses.

1. One of the most important developments in twentieth-century painting has ___?___ Abstract Expressionism. (be)
2. Abstract Expressionism ___?___ the public's attention in the 1940's. (catch)
3. It ___?___ out of earlier artistic attempts to express emotions. (grow)
4. Until then, most artists had ___?___ ways to depict how objects really looked or seemed. (seek)

538 • Verb Usage

5. In contrast, Abstract Expressionist painters are ___?___ to express the emotional aspects of things. (strive)

Exercise 34 Revising the Usage of Irregular Verbs Revise this paragraph, correcting errors in verb usage.

Abstract Expressionists maked their creations by using bold colors and lines. Unlike painters from other schools who taked a lot of time to work over tiny details in their paintings, the Abstract Expressionists often flinged paints at a canvas as if they were in a frenzy. Jackson Pollock and Willem de Kooning were two Abstract Expressionists who become prominent artists. These artists do what few before them had dared to do.

Exercise 35 Conjugating the Basic and Progressive Forms of Verbs Conjugate the basic and progressive forms of the following verbs in the *present, past, future, present perfect, past perfect,* and *future perfect* tenses.

1. arrange (conjugate with *I*)
2. spread (conjugate with *it*)
3. draw (conjugate with *we*)
4. buy (conjugate with *you*)
5. shake (conjugate with *they*)

Exercise 36 Supplying the Correct Tenses of Verbs Write the indicated form for each verb in parentheses.

1. Present perfect—Artists (be) the subject of many feature films.
2. Past—In *The Agony and the Ecstasy,* Charlton Heston (portray) the Renaissance artist Michelangelo.

3. Present—The film (show) Michelangelo's total devotion to painting the ceiling of the Sistine Chapel.
4. Past perfect—The Dutch Impressionist painter Vincent van Gogh (serve) as a favorite subject of other popular films.
5. Present progressive—Today, many people (relate) painting to film.
6. Present perfect—Filmmakers often (view) the film frame as a canvas.
7. Present progressive—Many of today's films (feature) sophisticated effects.
8. Present perfect progressive—Promising young artists (create) these effects.
9. Future—Many future artists (express) their ideas with computer graphics.
10. Future progressive—By creating dazzling effects with computers, many young people (demonstrate) that art is not limited to canvas.

> **Exercise 37** Distinguishing Between Active and Passive Voices
Identify whether the verb in each sentence is in the *active* or *passive* voice.

(1) The earliest known paintings were created by cave dwellers thousands of years ago. (2) These cave dwellers lived in Europe. (3) Pictures of wild animals were drawn by them on cave walls. (4) The cave dwellers depicted deer, horses, and other animals in earth pigments. (5) Every year, thousands of visitors are drawn to a cave in Lascaux, France, to see these early paintings.

> **Exercise 38** Revising to Use the Active Voice Revise this paragraph, replacing passive voice verbs with active voice verbs where appropriate.

(1) Artists don't always start young. (2) Talent is shown by some artists after they have lived a full life. (3) Grandma Moses was noticed by art experts when she was in her seventies. (4) In the 1940's, her career was launched by art critics.

(5) Before then, she had lived a quiet life as a farmer's wife. (6) Rural scenes had been painted by her for her own pleasure. (7) Recognition from art experts quickly transformed her into a celebrity. (8) Her work was praised by experts for its simple depiction of rural life. (9) Many of her paintings have been purchased by museums and collectors. (10) Many amateur artists have been inspired by Grandma Moses' career.

> **Exercise 39** Revising to Improve Verb Usage Revise this passage, correcting verb usage and changing the passive voice into the active voice where appropriate.

Artists have seeked to make portraits and sculptures of people for thousands of years. The earliest known artistic representations of individuals are statues of ancient Egyptian rulers from around 2700 B.C. During the Middle Ages, portraits of rulers, nobles, and important church officials were generally drawed by artists. Later, they begin to focus on ordinary people. By the eighteenth century, portrait painting had became an established art form. Many artists, then and now, have make their living by painting portraits. The invention of photography has affected portrait painting. Today, an individual usually sit for a photograph, rather than a painting. Yet, a special impression is created by a portrait that has been did in oils. The art of portrait painting will continuing for many years to come.

> **Exercise 40** Writing Application
Write a real or made-up history of a painting or an artist. Use verbs in several different tenses and both voices in your paragraph.

Answer Key continued

> **Exercise 40**

Writing Application
Ask volunteers to read their paragraphs, noting first whether or not the history is real or made-up. Discuss how tense and voice contribute to the narrative.

Answer Key

> **Exercise 36**
1. have been
2. portrayed
3. shows
4. had served
5. are relating
6. have viewed
7. are featuring
8. have been creating
9. will express
10. will be demonstrating

> **Exercise 37**
1. were created: passive
2. lived: active
3. were drawn: passive
4. depicted: active
5. are drawn: passive

> **Exercise 38**
Answers may vary; samples are given.
1. Active
2. Passive. Some artists show talent after they have lived a full life.
3. Passive. Art experts noticed Grandma Moses . . .
4. Passive. Art critics launched her career in the 1940's.
5. Active
6. Passive. She had painted rural scenes for her own pleasure.
7. Active
8. Passive. Experts praised her work . . .
9. Passive. Museums and collectors have purchased . . . paintings.
10. Passive. Grandma Moses' career has inspired . . . artists.

> **Exercise 39**
Answers may vary; samples are given.
1. Artists have *sought* . . .
2. Correct
3. During the Middle Ages, artists generally *drew* portraits of . . .
4. Later, they *began* to focus on ordinary people.
5. By the 18th century, portrait painting had *become* . . .
6. Many artists, then and now, have *made* their living . . .
7. Correct
8. Today, an individual usually *sits* for a photograph . . .
9. Yet, a portrait *done* in oils creates a special impression.
10. The art of portrait painting will *continue* for many years to come.
continued

Standardized Test Preparation Workshop

Standard English Usage: Using Verbs

Many standardized tests assess your ability to apply the rules of verb usage. You may be given a passage that contains a series of blanks and asked to choose words to fill in the blanks. Often, the choice of words will involve selecting the correct form of a verb. When choosing a verb, first read the sentence silently to yourself, and determine when it is taking place. Then, choose a verb that indicates the same point in time or tense of the sentence.

The following test items will give you practice with the format of questions that test verb usage.

Sample Test Items	Answers and Explanations
Directions: Read the passage, and choose the letter of the word or group of words that belongs in each space. After serving as an ambulance driver during World War I, Ernest Hemingway __(1)__ time in Paris, along with many other writers, including Ezra Pound and F. Scott Fitzgerald. These writers __(2)__ known as the "Expatriates" because they had intentionally chosen to live outside the United States.	

1 A spend
  B had spent
  C spent
  D spended
	The correct answer is *C*. The passage is clearly set in the past, so the appropriate choice is the past tense of the verb *spend*. *Spend* is an irregular verb, and its past tense is *spent*, not *spended*.

2 F became
  G become
  H are
  J have been
	The correct answer is *F*. Again, because the passage describes events from the past, a past tense verb is called for. *Became* is the past tense of the verb *become*.

540 • Verb Usage

> **Practice 1** **Directions:** Read the passage, and choose the letter of the word or group of words that belongs in each space.

The United States __(1)__ from World War II as the most powerful nation on Earth. Proud of the part they __(2)__ in defeating the Axis, Americans now __(3)__ life to return to normal. Soldiers and sailors __(4)__ home, the rationing of scarce goods ended, and the nation __(5)__ .

1 A emerges
  B had emerged
  C emerged
  D will emerge

2 F had played
  G played
  H play
  J would have played

3 A want
  B wanted
  C had wanted
  D would want

4 F were coming
  G come
  H came
  J had come

5 A had prospered
  B would prosper
  C prospered
  D prospers

> **Practice 2** **Directions:** Read the passage, and choose the letter of the word or group of words that belongs in each space.

Real and lasting gains __(1)__ in civil rights after World War II. Those gains __(2)__ largely from the courageous actions of Martin Luther King, Jr., and other civil rights leaders of the 1950's and 1960's. One of the movement's major breakthroughs __(3)__ the passage of legislation that protected the voting rights of all Americans. Today, there __(4)__ many African Americans in political office. This situation would not __(5)__ without the efforts of Martin Luther King, Jr., and others.

1 A was made
  B were made
  C had been made
  D were maked

2 F were the result
  G resulting
  H had resulted
  J resulted

3 A is
  B were
  C was
  D are

4 F are
  G were
  H have been
  J will be

5 A be occurring
  B have occurred
  C occur
  D have occur

Answer Key

> **Practice 1**

1. C
2. F
3. B
4. H
5. C

> **Practice 2**

1. B
2. J
3. C
4. F
5. B

Customize for
Less Advanced Students

Often, when students read sentences several times to themselves, substituting one of the answer choices each time, all of the answers begin to sound plausible. To prevent this, advise students to determine the tense and form of the missing verb before looking at the answer choices. Then, they can choose the correct answer from the list.

Integrating Critical Thinking Skills

Explain to students that not all of the verbs in a passage will have precisely the same tense and form. For example, the past and the past perfect might be used in the same passage. This would signal that even though all the actions happened in the past, some happened before others.

Chapter 23 Time and Resource Manager

In-Depth Lesson Plan

	LESSON FOCUS	PRINT AND MEDIA RESOURCES
DAY 1	**Pronoun Case: Nominative and Objective** Students learn and apply concepts relating to the nominative and objective cases of pronouns. (pp. 544–549/H388–393)	***Writing and Grammar*** **Interactive Text,** Section 23.1; ***On-line Exercise Bank,*** Section 23.1 **Teaching Resources** *Grammar Exercise Workbook,* pp. 127–128; *Grammar Exercises Answers on Transparencies,* Ch. 23
DAY 2	**Pronoun Case: Possessive** Students learn and apply concepts relating to the possessive case of pronouns and do the Hands-on Grammar activity. (pp. 550–551/H394–395)	**Teaching Resources** *Grammar Exercise Workbook,* pp. 129–130; *Hands-on Grammar Activity Workbook,* Ch. 23
DAY 3	**Special Problems With Pronouns** Students learn and apply concepts relating to the use of *who* and *whom* and pronouns in elliptical clauses. (pp. 552–559/H396–403)	***Writing and Grammar*** **Interactive Text,** Section 23.2; ***On-line Exercise Bank,*** Section 23.2 **Teaching Resources** *Grammar Exercise Workbook,* pp. 131–132
DAY 4	**Review and Assess** Students review the chapter and demonstrate mastery of pronoun usage. (pp. 560–561)	***Writing and Grammar*** **Interactive Text,** Ch. 23, Chapter Review **Teaching Resources** *Formal Assessment,* Ch. 23

Accelerated Lesson Plan

	LESSON FOCUS	PRINT AND MEDIA RESOURCES
DAY 1	**Pronoun Case: Nominative, Objective, and Possessive** Students cover concepts of pronoun case as determined by the Diagnostic Test. (pp. 544–551/H388–395)	***Writing and Grammar*** **Interactive Text,** Section 23.1; ***On-line Exercise Bank,*** Section 23.1 **Teaching Resources** *Grammar Exercise Workbook,* pp. 127–130; *Grammar Exercises Answers on Transparencies,* Ch. 23
DAY 2	**Special Problems with Pronouns; Review and Assess** Students cover special problems with pronouns and then review the chapter and demonstrate mastery of the concepts. (pp. 552–561/H396–403)	***Writing and Grammar*** **Interactive Text,** Ch. 23, Section 23.2 through Chapter Review; ***On-line Exercise Bank,*** Section 23.2 **Teaching Resources** *Grammar Exercise Workbook,* pp. 131–132; *Formal Assessment,* Ch. 23

Options for Adapting Lesson Plans

HOMEWORK

Have students complete any section of the chapter for homework.

FEATURES

Extend coverage with the Grammar in Literature features (pp. 545, 555/ H389, 399) and the Standardized Test Preparation Workshop. (p. 562).

TECHNOLOGY

Students can use *Writing and Grammar* Interactive Text to complete the exercises interactively on computer. They can complete additional exercises in the *On-line Exercise Bank:* The Auto Check feature will grade their work. Go on-line: PHSchool.com Use Web Code: eek-1002

Writing and Grammar Handbook Alignment

Page numbers in Step-by-Step Teaching Guides in this Teacher's Edition refer to pages from the full student text. Handbook page references, indicated with this icon Ⓗ, are provided in Time and Resource Manager boxes and at the bottom of each Teacher's Edition page.

INTEGRATED SKILLS COVERAGE

Grammar in Literature
SE pp. 545, 555/Ⓗ389, 399

Writing
Find It in Your Writing SE pp. 551, 558/Ⓗ395, 402
Writing Application SE pp. 551, 559, 561/Ⓗ395, 403

Viewing and Representing
Critical Viewing SE pp. 542, 545, 547, 553, 555/Ⓗ386, 389, 391, 397, 399

Speaking and Listening
ATE p. 552

Vocabulary Skills
ATE p. 556

Real-World Connection
ATE p. 547

Technology Skills
SE pp. 549, 556/Ⓗ393, 400

Workplace Skills
ATE p. 553

ASSESSMENT SUPPORT

Standardized Test Preparation Workshop SE p. 562; ATE pp. 546, 556
Standardized Test Preparation Workbook, pp. 45–46
Formal Assessment, Ch. 23

MEETING INDIVIDUAL NEEDS

Less Advanced Students ATE pp. 550, 554. See also Ongoing Assessments ATE pp. 542, 543, 545, 547, 548, 549, 550, 553, 555, 557, 559.
ESL Students ATE pp. 546, 548
Gifted and Talented Students ATE p. 549
Linguistic Learners ATE p. 550
Logical/Mathematical Learners ATE p. 556

BLOCK SCHEDULING

Pacing Suggestions
For 90-minute Blocks
• Administer the Diagnostic Test to students to determine instructional coverage.
• Have students complete the necessary exercises in class. Use the Hands-on Grammar activity to provide a change of pace.

Resources for Varying Instruction
• *Writing and Grammar* Interactive Text A 90-minute block provides an ideal opportunity for students to work on the computer.

Professional Development Support
• *How to Manage Instruction in the Block* This teaching resource provides management and activity suggestions.

MEDIA AND TECHNOLOGY

For the Student
• *Writing and Grammar* Interactive Text, Ch. 23
• *On-line Exercise Bank,* Sections 23.1–2

For the Teacher
• Teacher**EXPRESS** CD-ROM

WRITING AND GRAMMAR ON-LINE

Interactive Text (On-line or on CD-ROM)
• Easily navigable instruction with on-line supporting resources
• Self-scoring exercises and diagnostic tests

Companion Web Site PHSchool.com
• On-line Exercise Bank (use Web Code eek-1002)

See the Go On-line! feature, SE p. iii.

LITERATURE CONNECTIONS

Grammar in Literature selection from *Prentice Hall Literature, Penguin Edition,* Grade 10:

from "Games at Twilight," Anita Desai, SE p. 545/Ⓗ389

► Lesson Objectives

1. To recognize the three cases of pronouns
2. To identify and use pronouns in the nominative case
3. To identify and use pronouns in the objective case
4. To recognize and avoid errors while using possessive pronouns
5. To use who and whom correctly in sentences
6. To determine case in subordinate clauses with parenthetical expressions
7. To identify and use pronouns correctly in elliptical clauses
8. To evaluate writing for both mechanics and content

Critical Viewing

Analyze Students may use singular pronouns such as *he, her,* and *his* to describe the positions and physical attitudes of each partner and plural pronouns to describe their movements together.

Chapter 23 Pronoun Usage

At one time in the history of the English language, the forms of both nouns and pronouns were changed to indicate how they were being used in a sentence. Today, nouns change form only to show possession: A noun is made possessive by adding an apostrophe and an *s* (a *woman's* dress) or just an apostrophe (the two *boys'* gloves).

Pronouns in modern English still have different forms depending on how they are used in a sentence. This chapter will explain the various forms of pronouns and their uses.

The rules of proper pronoun usage have developed over time to help us communicate more effectively and efficiently. Whether you are writing about modern times or about America in the "Roaring Twenties," you need to use pronouns correctly in order to communicate.

▲ **Critical Viewing** Describe the actions of both people in the picture, using such pronouns as *he, she, him, her, his, they,* and *their.* **[Analyze]**

542 • Pronoun Usage

☑ ONGOING ASSESSMENT: Diagnose

If students miss more than one item in any category, direct them to the relevant pages of the textbook and assign exercises for practice and review.

Pronoun Usage	Diagnostic Test Items	Teach	Practice	Section Reviews	Chapter Review
Skill Check A					
Recognizing Pronoun Case	A 1–5	p. 544/ 🖽388	Ex. 1	Ex. 8–10	Ex. 24
Skill Check B					
Recognizing Uses of Pronoun Case	B 6–10	pp. 546–550/ 🖽390–394	Ex. 2–6	Ex. 8–10	Ex. 25–26

Diagnostic Test

Directions: Write all answers on a separate sheet of paper.

Skill Check A. Write the pronouns in each sentence, and identify the case for each as *nominative*, *objective*, or *possessive*.

1. They danced a popular dance from the 1920's.
2. The author dedicated his book on the Jazz Age to her.
3. We saw pictures of fancy dresses worn in the 1920's.
4. Grandfather remembers his best friend from way back then.
5. "The happiest people were we children," he recalled.

Skill Check B. Identify the case of each underlined pronoun in the following sentences, and tell how it is used in the sentence.

6. <u>Her</u> grandmother lived during the 1920's.
7. <u>She</u> is extremely happy that we are interested in <u>her</u> stories.
8. She enjoys telling <u>me</u> her stories.
9. The two biggest fans of the 1920's are she and <u>I</u>.
10. Talking to her fascinates <u>me</u>.

Skill Check C. Indicate the correct pronoun to complete the following sentences.

11. One of (me, my) favorite heroes of the 1920's is Charles Lindbergh.
12. (His, His') adventures were followed by people from all over the world.
13. His quest was known for (it's, its) difficulty.
14. Do you know where (you're, your) ancestors were in the 1920's?
15. I am sure that (their, they're) experiences are very interesting.

Skill Check D. Choose the correct pronoun in parentheses, and identify its function in the sentence or clause.

16. I know (who, whom) gave her the article about 1920's fashion.
17. She is not sure (who, whom) they are featuring next.
18. To (who, whom) did she lend her book?
19. Do you know (who, whom) made the first solo flight across the Atlantic Ocean?
20. Give it to (whoever, whomever) wrote this report on famous aviators.

Skill Check E. Choose the correct pronoun in parentheses. Then, write any words or phrases that are understood to precede or follow the pronoun.

21. I know more about the fads of the 1920's than (she, her).
22. The speaker knows less about the 1920's than (I, me).
23. The films of the 1920's are as familiar to his grandmother as (he, him).
24. No living silent film star is as respected as (she, her).
25. This collection of photographs from the 1920's is more precious to me than (they, them).

Pronoun Usage • 543

Skill Check A

1. They–nominative
2. his–possessive; her–objective
3. We–nominative
4. his–possessive
5. we–nominative; he–nominative

Skill Check B

6. possessive–to show ownership
7. nominative–subject; possessive–to show ownership
8. objective–indirect object
9. nominative–predicate nominative
10. objective–direct object

Skill Check C

11. my	14. your
12. His	15. their
13. its	

Skill Check D

16. who (subject)
17. whom (object)
18. whom (indirect object)
19. who (subject)
20. whoever (subject)

Skill Check E

21. she (knows)
22. I (know)
23. (they are to) him
24. she (is respected)
25. (it is to) them

ONGOING ASSESSMENT: Diagnose *continued*

Pronoun Usage	Diagnostic Test Items	Teach	Practice	Section Reviews	Chapter Review
Skill Check C					
Using Possessive Pronouns	C 11–15	p. 550/Ⓗ394	Ex. 7	Ex. 9–10	Ex. 27
Skill Check D					
Using *Who* and *Whom* Correctly	D 16–19, 20	pp. 552–554/Ⓗ396–398	Ex. 14–15	Ex. 18–19	Ex. 28
Skill Check E					
Using Pronouns in Elliptical Clauses	E 21–25	p. 556/Ⓗ400	Ex. 16–17	Ex. 20	Ex. 29
Cumulative Reviews and Applications				Ex. 11–13, 21–23	Ex. 30–32

Interest GRABBER Have students think of a sports activity involving both boys and girls and write several sentences about it, using as many different pronouns as they can. (Examples: _He spiked the ball over the net right at me. I hit it back to their side, but she could not reach it._) When they finish, have them list all the pronouns they used.

Activate Prior Knowledge

Put these sentences on the board and have students replace the underlined nouns with pronouns. Then, ask them to identify the case of each pronoun. (Answers are in parentheses.)

Terence and Ceretha like antique cars. (_she_: nominative)

David told Terence and Ceretha about a car show that is coming to town. (_her_: objective)

Ceretha's mother may get tickets for the show. (_Her_: possessive)

TEACH

Step-by-Step Teaching Guide

The Three Cases

1. Make sure students understand that the reason pronouns change form has to do with their use in a sentence.

2. Using the two charts, have students give example sentences of common pronoun uses, such as subjects and direct objects.

3. Have students notice in the second chart the two pronouns with the same nominative and objective form (_you, it_).

Language Highlight

Explain that other words for _you_ and _your_ were used in the 1500's. _Thou_ was used to express the second-person singular; _thy_ and _thine_ were used to express the second-person singular possessive. _Thee_ is the objective form of _thou_. Point out that students may still encounter these archaic pronouns in their reading. Have them recall where they have seen these and other archaic forms.

Section 23.1 Case

Case is a term used to describe the different forms of nouns and pronouns.

▶ **KEY CONCEPT** **Case** is the form of a noun or a pronoun that indicates its use in a sentence. ■

The Three Cases

Both nouns and pronouns have three cases:

▶ **KEY CONCEPT** The three cases are the _nominative_, the _objective_, and the _possessive_. ■

The following chart shows the uses of each of these three cases.

Case	Use in Sentence
Nominative	Subject or Predicate Nominative
Objective	Direct Object, Indirect Object, Object of a Preposition, or Object of a Verbal
Possessive	To Show Ownership

Using the correct case of nouns is seldom a problem because the form changes only in the possessive case.

NOMINATIVE: The old _car_ would not start.
OBJECTIVE: We could not start the old _car_.
POSSESSIVE: The old _car's_ battery needed to be replaced.

In the first sentence, _car_ is the subject. In the second sentence, _car_ is the direct object. The form changes only in the _possessive_ case, by adding an apostrophe and an _s_.

In contrast to nouns, personal pronouns have different forms for all three cases.

Nominative	Objective	Possessive
I	me	my, mine
you	you	your, yours
he, she, it	him, her, it	his, her, hers, its
we	us	our, ours
they	them	their, theirs

544 • Pronoun Usage

⏱ TIME AND RESOURCE MANAGER

Resources
Print: _Grammar Exercise Workbook_, pp. 125–130; _Grammar Exercises Answers on Transparencies_, Ch. 23
Technology: _Writing and Grammar_ Interactive Text, Section 23.1; _On-Line Exercise Bank_, Section 23.1

Using the Full Student Edition	Using the Handbook Ⓗ
• Work through all key concepts, pp. 544–550.	• Work through all key concepts, pp. 388–394.
• Assign and review Exercises 1–7.	• Assign and review Exercises 1–7.
• Read and discuss Grammar in Literature, p. 545.	• Read and discuss Grammar in Literature, p. 389.

Theme: Roaring Twenties

In this section, you will learn about the three cases of pronouns and their uses and forms. The examples and exercises in this section are about the Roaring Twenties.

Cross-Curricular Connection: Social Studies

GRAMMAR IN LITERATURE

from **Games at Twilight**

Anita Desai

Notice the pronouns in the nominative case (in red italics) and in the objective case (in blue italics) in this excerpt. How is each pronoun used?

Ravi had a frightening glimpse of *them* as Raghu combed the hedge of crotons and hibiscus, trampling delicate ferns underfoot as *he* did so. Ravi looked about *him* desperately, swallowing a small ball of snot in his fear.

▲ **Critical Viewing**
Write three sentences describing both the man holding the horse and the women in the carriage. Use *he, him, she, her, they,* or *them* in your sentences. **[Analyze]**

> **Exercise 1** **Identifying Case** Write the case of each under-lined pronoun. Then, indicate its usage.

EXAMPLE: The reporter told the truth about <u>them</u>.
ANSWER: objective (object of a preposition)

1. <u>Our</u> ancestors lived through the 1920's, a remarkable period in history.
2. If <u>you</u> had been alive in the 1920's, you would have wit-nessed many exciting events.
3. The people of the 1920's saw <u>their</u> world change rapidly.
4. <u>They</u> enjoyed benefits brought about by advances in com-merce and technology.
5. Many of <u>them</u> heard the world's first radio broadcast.
6. Other innovations in science and business amazed and excited <u>them</u>.
7. These advances brought about great prosperity for many Americans and <u>their</u> descendants.
8. Such advances in technology gave <u>them</u> a sense of opti-mism for the future.
9. The beneficiaries of their optimism are <u>we</u>.
10. Reading about events of the 1920's and studying <u>them</u> can offer many insights into modern times.

> **More Practice**

Grammar Exercise Workbook
• pp. 125–126
On-line Exercise Bank
• Section 23.1
> Go on-line:
> PHSchool.com
> Enter Web Code:
> eek-1002

Case • 545

Grammar in Literature

1. Ask a student to read the selection aloud.
2. Have a volunteer identify the uses of each pronoun (object of preposition, subject, object of preposition).
3. Ask students to decide whether the antecedent of *he* is Ravi or Raghu (Raghu) and explain how they decided this.

More About the Writer

Anita Desai (b. 1937) is widely regarded as one of India's foremost novelists. Her stories are often about the relationships among family members. Desai has been praised for her ability to create vivid portraits of her characters and for her powerful images.

Connections With Literature

"Games at Twilight" by Anita Desai can be found in *Prentice Hall Literature, Penguin Edition,* Grade 10.

Critical Viewing

Analyze Sample response: This seems to be a formal portrait of a family in their carriage. He is standing in front of the horse, and she is sitting behind it with other women and a child in the carriage. The horse separates them.

Answer Key

> **Exercise 1**

1. possessive–to show ownership
2. nominative–subject
3. possessive–to show ownership
4. nominative–subject
5. objective–object of preposition
6. objective–direct object
7. possessive–to show ownership
8. objective–indirect object
9. nominative–predicate nominative
10. objective–object of a gerund

☑ **ONGOING ASSESSMENT: Monitor and Reinforce**

If students have difficulty with Exercise 1, refer them to the following for additional practice.

In the Textbook	Print Resources	Technology
Section Review, Exercise 8, Section 23.1	*Grammar Exercise Workbook,* pp.125–126	*On-Line Exercise Bank,* Section 23.1

The Nominative Case

1. Remind students that in compounds using the first-person singular pronoun (*I, me, my*), that pronoun is typically placed last.

2. Explain that in informal English, especially informal speech, students will often hear an objective pronoun used after a noun (*It's me; That was him*). Advise students to avoid this use in writing and in any speaking situations where they are not certain of their audience.

3. Tell students that, as with compounds, the correct pronoun form for appositives can be determined by dropping the appositive. To demonstrate, have volunteers read aloud the example sentences on page 546, dropping *musicians* and *sophomores*.

Customize for
ESL Students

In a directed activity, give students practice in supplying the correct nominative pronoun for each person, group of people, or object that you point to. For example, point to a man in a photograph and have students supply the pronoun that represents that person (*he*). Hold up an object like a pen and have students supply the appropriate pronoun (*it*). After you have used all or most personal pronouns, have students repeat the activity among themselves using photographs in their textbooks or in other works.

23.1

The Nominative Case

There are two major uses of pronouns in the nominative case:

▶ **KEY CONCEPT** Use the nominative case when a pronoun is used as the *subject* of a verb or as a *predicate nominative*. ■

The chart below illustrates these two uses.

NOMINATIVE PRONOUNS	
Subject	*She* is the conductor of the band. *I* want to learn more about the music of the 1920's. *They* danced the Charleston while we sat.
Predicate Nominative	The famous historian is *she*. It is *I*. Our closest friends have always been *they*.

Nominative Pronouns in Compounds When using a compound subject or a compound predicate nominative, check the case by mentally removing the other part of the compound or by mentally inverting the sentence.

COMPOUND SUBJECT:	Marie and *I* watched a film about the 1920's. (*I* watched a film about the 1920's.) Beth and *he* will learn more about that time from his grandmother. (*He* will learn more about that time from his grandmother.)
COMPOUND PREDICATE NOMINATIVE:	The winners were Tim and *she*. (Tim and *she* were the winners.) The best dancers are Kay and *I*. (Kay and *I* are the best dancers.)

Nominative Pronouns With Appositives Appositives sometimes follow a pronoun in order to rename it or identify it. If a pronoun used as a subject or predicate nominative is followed by an appositive, the nominative case is still used.

SUBJECT:	*We* musicians love music of the 1920's.
PREDICATE NOMINATIVE:	The ones with the most spirit are *we* sophomores.

▶ **More Practice**

Grammar Exercise Workbook
• pp. 127–128
On-line Exercise Bank
• Section 23.1
Go on-line:
PHSchool.com
Enter Web Code:
eek-1002

✎ STANDARDIZED TEST PREPARATION WORKSHOP

Grammar and Usage: Many standardized tests require students to draw upon their knowledge of pronoun usage to revise sentence errors. Use the following example to demonstrate.

The woman hoped to befriend the children in her new neighborhood. At first, they were afraid of her. But they soon realized that it was her who was their best friend.

How would you correct the underlined sentence in this passage?

A Change *her* to *she*.

B Remove *that* from the sentence.

C Change *their* to *they're*.

D Correct as is.

The correct answer is **A**. The construction "it was ___" requires a predicate nominative, and so the nominative form *she* must be used.

▶ **Exercise 2** Identifying Pronouns in the Nominative Case
Choose the nominative case pronoun that completes each sentence.
1. (We, Us) Americans have always enjoyed sports.
2. Fiercely devoted sports fans are (we, us).
3. My great-grandfather and (I, me) often talk about sports heroes from the 1920's.
4. My great-grandfather was obsessed with sports in the 1920's when (he, him) was a young boy.
5. (I, Me) have learned much about Babe Ruth and Red Grange from him.
6. His first heroes in baseball and football were (they, them).
7. My great-grandfather described a time when (he, him) saw Babe Ruth smack a home run.
8. His brother and (he, him) went to that game together.
9. He said that the most excited fans in the stadium were (they, them).
10. "(He, Him) and I almost caught that baseball," he recalled.

▶ **Exercise 3** Using Pronouns in the Nominative Case Write a nominative pronoun to complete each sentence. Then, identify how the pronoun is used in the sentence.
1. My friends and ___?___ have been learning about the Roaring Twenties.
2. Did ___?___ know that the Roaring Twenties closely followed World War I?
3. ___?___ Americans were excited by the return of peace and improvements in our economy.
4. Many Americans supported the Republican party, and ___?___ elected Warren G. Harding president in 1920.
5. It was ___?___ who became the twenty-ninth president of the United States.

▶ **Exercise 4** Revising to Correct Errors in Pronoun Usage
Revise the following sentences to correct errors in pronoun usage. If a sentence is correct, write *correct*.
1. I learned that him and his wife were from Ohio.
2. My friends and me are interested in learning more about Harding.
3. Harding appointed many friends to government positions. Some of they became involved in several scandals.
4. Harding served as president until August 1923, when he died of a heart attack in San Francisco, California.
5. Calvin Coolidge was vice president, so Harding's successor was he.

President
Warren G. Harding

Vice-President
Calvin Coolidge

▼ Critical Viewing
Describe your impression of these two political leaders. Use *I, he,* and *they* in your sentences. **[Describe]**

Case • 547

Real-World Connection

Explain to students that nominative case pronouns often are used with appositives when people take oaths or make solemn declarations. For instance, witnesses who are called to testify in court sometimes say, "I [full name] do hereby swear to tell the truth, the whole truth, and nothing but the truth." Ask students to think of other examples of formal writing (wills, contracts, deeds) and to speculate about the case forms of pronouns that might be used.

Answer Key

▶ **Exercise 2**
1. We
2. we
3. I
4. he
5. I
6. they
7. he
8. he
9. they
10. He

▶ **Exercise 3**
Allow some variation in response.
1. I–subject
2. you–subject
3. We–subject
4. they–subject
5. he–predicate nominative

▶ **Exercise 4**
1. . . . he and his wife . . .
2. My friends and I . . .
3. . . . Some of them . . .
4. correct
5. correct

Critical Viewing

Analyze Students may either react only to the art (*I think they appear serious and determined,* etc.) or base their sentences on information in Exercise 4 (*I wonder if Coolidge knew what he was getting into.*)

The Objective Case

1. If students need more review of verbals with objects, give these examples (objects are underlined).

   The flappers created a scandal wearing such short <u>skirts</u>.

   Imagining Mom's <u>great-aunt</u> dressed that way seems funny.

   But she did like to shock <u>Great Granddad</u> with her new clothes.

   Have students identify the object in each sentence and then replace each with an appropriate pronoun (*them, her, him*).

2. To further emphasize that the objective case follows *between*, have students replace *me* in the correct sentence at the bottom of this page with other objective pronouns (*her, him, us, them*).

Customize for
ESL Students

Give students practice using objective case pronouns in answers to simple questions. Place two or three key questions on paper or on the board. Examples:

Do you know ___? Yes, I know ___ .

Did you see ___? Yes, I saw ___.

Then, have students speak or write a noun to complete each question and a corresponding objective case pronoun to answer the question (Examples: *James, him; Helene, her.*) Make the questions increasingly complicated by adding compounds so that students must use *them* and *us*.

Critical Viewing

Analyze Sample response: A new song is playing in <u>her</u> favorite club. <u>She</u> is dancing to the music. People are watching <u>her</u>.

23.1

The Objective Case

The objective case is used with the objects of verbs and prepositions as well as with the objects of verbals.

▶ **KEY CONCEPT** Use the objective case when a pronoun is used as the object of any verb, preposition, or verbal. ■

The chart below illustrates the uses of objective pronouns.

OBJECTIVE PRONOUNS	
Use	**Examples**
Direct Object	I baked *them* yesterday. Our teacher praised *her.*
Indirect Object	Give *him* the good news. Alice gave *us* the poster from the 1920's.
Object of Preposition	Between *us*, there are no secrets. Walk beside *them.*
Object of Participle	Racing *her,* he crashed into an antique car. The girl chasing *them* was her sister.
Object of Gerund	Dad likes helping *me* with my homework. Warning *them* was my primary concern.
Object of Infinitive	To tell *them* clearly, he had to shout. He wants to ask *me* about my visit.

Objective Pronouns in Compounds Errors with objective case pronouns most often occur in compounds. To check yourself, mentally remove the other part of the compound.

EXAMPLES: Our history teacher praised John and *her.*
(Our history teacher praised *her.*)

The project was assigned to Charles and *him.*
(The project was assigned to *him.*)

Take special care to use the objective case after the preposition *between.*

INCORRECT: This matter is between *you* and *I.*

CORRECT: This matter is between *you* and *me.*

548 • Pronoun Usage

▶ **More Practice**

Grammar Exercise Workbook
• pp. 127–128
On-line Exercise Bank
• Section 23.1
Go on-line:
PHSchool.com
Enter Web Code:
eek-1002

▼ **Critical Viewing** Write three sentences about this flapper. Use a pronoun in a different case in each sentence. **[Analyze]**

☑ ONGOING ASSESSMENT: Prerequisite Skills

If students have difficulty with some of the constructions requiring the objective case, you may need to review the following to ensure coverage of prerequisite knowledge.

In the Textbook	Print Resources	Technology
Phrases, Section 20.1	*Grammar Exercise Workbook,* pp. 57–58, 63–64, 69–70, 73–74	*On-Line Exercise Bank,* Section 20.1

Objective Pronoun With Appositives

Objective Pronoun With Appositives If an appositive appears after a pronoun used as an object, make sure that you use an objective pronoun.

DIRECT OBJECT:	The musical entertained *us* girls.
INDIRECT OBJECT:	The club gave *us* leaders an award.
OBJECT OF A PREPOSITION:	All of *us* history students were nervous about the assignment.

> **Exercise 5** Identifying Pronouns in the Objective Case
> Choose the pronoun in the objective case to complete each sentence. Then, identify how the pronoun is used in the sentence.
>
> EXAMPLE: The orchestra plans to join (him, he) later.
> ANSWER: him (object of infinitive)
>
> 1. To (we, us) historians, the 1920's is often known as the Roaring Twenties or the Jazz Age.
> 2. For Americans in the 1920's, the Jazz Age promised (they, them) great hope and excitement.
> 3. With stock holdings enriching (they, them), many Americans achieved wealth beyond their wildest dreams.
> 4. The independent, glamourous flappers of the 1920's are role models for some of (we, us) modern women.
> 5. Studying (they, them) holds special meaning for today's independent women.

> **Exercise 6** Supplying Pronouns in the Objective Case
> Write an objective pronoun to complete each sentence. Then, identify how the pronoun is used in the sentence.
>
> EXAMPLE: My parents gave ___?___ an antique watch for my birthday.
> ANSWER: me (indirect object)
>
> 1. My aunt questioned my sisters and ___?___ about the 1920's.
> 2. She then gave ___?___ the novel *This Side of Paradise* (1920) by F. Scott Fitzgerald.
> 3. She enjoys suggesting books to ___?___.
> 4. Between my sisters and ___?___, we have read enough books to fill a small library.
> 5. It is easy to get my aunt to start talking; it is stopping ___?___ that is sometimes hard.

⊙ Technology Tip

The spell-check function on most word-processing programs will recognize *it's* and *its* as correctly spelled words. It is up to you to recognize that *it's* means *it is* or *it has* and that *its* shows ownership.

Case • 549

Answer Key

> **Exercise 5**

1. us–object of preposition
2. them–indirect object
3. them–object of a participle
4. us–object of preposition
5. them–object of a gerund

> **Exercise 6**

The following are likely responses.

1. me–direct object
2. us–indirect object
3. us–object of preposition
4. me–object of preposition
5. her–object of a gerund

Customize for
Gifted and Talented Students

Remind students that all pronouns except *you* and *it* have a distinct objective case form. Have students invent nonsense words that could serve as objective forms of these two pronouns (*youm, yout,* and *itous* are possibilities). Then, have students use their nonsense words as parts of compound constructions in brief humorous dialogues. Let them read their dialogues aloud to the class and explain the rationale for the new words they invented.

☑ ONGOING ASSESSMENT: Monitor and Reinforce

If students miss more than one item in Exercise 5 or 6, refer them to the following for additional practice.

In the Textbook	Print Resources	Technology
Section Review, Exercise 9, Section 23.1	*Grammar Exercise Workbook,* pp.127–128	*On-Line Exercise Bank,* Section 23.1

⏱ TIME SAVERS!

Answers on Transparencies
Use the *Grammar Exercises Answers on Transparencies* for Chapter 23 to facilitate correction by students.

On-Line Exercise Bank
Have students complete the exercises on computer. The Auto Check feature will grade their work for you!

The Possessive Case

1. Emphasize that possessive personal pronouns never use apostrophes to show ownership and should not be confused with the contractions *it's*, *they're*, and *you're*. Give some examples to demonstrate the difference:

   <u>You're</u> ready to give <u>your</u> speech.

   <u>It's</u> too early to give the cat <u>its</u> food.

   <u>They're</u> trying to find <u>their</u> dog.

2. Recommend that when students have a choice between *it's* and *its*, *your* and *you're*, and *their* and *they're*, they mentally substitute the uncontracted form (*it is*, *you are*, *they are*). If this form does not make sense in the sentence, then they should use the spelling without the apostrophe.

Customize for
Less Advanced Students

Students may need review on which possessive pronouns are used alone and which precede nouns. Referring to the chart on page 544, explain that *my*, *your*, *her*, *our*, and *their* precede nouns (*my* coat); *mine*, *yours*, *hers*, *ours*, and *theirs* are used alone (the coat is *mine*); *his* is used both ways. Let students use the words in phrases.

Customize for
Linguistic Learners

Have students record in a log sentences they hear with possessive nouns and pronouns. (Examples: *Pass <u>your</u> papers to the front. Is this <u>Mr. Smith's</u> class?*) Have students underline the possessive words and write each another way. (*Pass the papers that belong to you to the front. Is this the class of Mr. Smith?*) Have students share their sentence pairs and check for correct apostrophe use.

Answer Key

Exercise 7

1. its
2. your
3. ours
4. their
5. hers
6. Their
7. You're
8. It's
9. they're
10. their

The Possessive Case

The possessive case of pronouns is used to show possession before nouns and before gerunds. Some possessive pronouns are also used by themselves.

> **KEY CONCEPT** Use the possessive case before nouns to show ownership. ■

EXAMPLES: *My* report on the Roaring Twenties is almost done.
Their suggestions have been very helpful.

> **KEY CONCEPT** Use the possessive case before gerunds. ■

EXAMPLES: *Your* asking questions made me focus.
I did not appreciate *his* writing in my book.

> **KEY CONCEPT** Use certain possessive pronouns by themselves to indicate possession. ■

EXAMPLES: That book is *hers*, not *his*.
Is this movie poster *yours* or *mine*?

Sometimes, possessive pronouns are incorrectly spelled with an apostrophe. Spellings such as *your's*, *our's*, *their's*, and *her's* are incorrect. In addition, do not confuse the possessive pronouns *its*, *your*, and *their* (which do not contain apostrophes) with the contractions *it's*, *you're*, and *they're*.

POSSESSIVE PRONOUN: Which 1920's song is your favorite?

CONTRACTION: *You're* expected to dress up for the party.

> **Exercise 7** Using Pronouns in the Possessive Case Choose the correct word in parentheses.
> 1. Each era has (it's, its) distinct fashion trends.
> 2. Have you ever thought about how (your, you're) great-grandparents may have dressed in the 1920's?
> 3. Some clothing in the 1920's was similar to (ours, our's).
> 4. Flappers wore skirts that revealed (they're, their) knees.
> 5. Those long pearl necklaces were (hers, her's).
> 6. (They're, Their) choosing to dress that way was a clear break with tradition.
> 7. (Your, You're) going to enjoy our 1920's fashion show.
> 8. (Its, It's) scheduled for next Friday evening.
> 9. I found several suits from the 1920's; (they're, their) in the closet backstage.
> 10. Back then, men often wore (they're, their) hair parted in the middle.

> **More Practice**
>
> **Grammar Exercise Workbook**
> • pp. 129–130
> **On-line Exercise Bank**
> • Section 23.1
> *Go on-line:*
> PHSchool.com
> *Enter Web Code:*
> eek-1002

Get instant feedback! Exercise 7 is available on-line or on CD-ROM.

☑ **ONGOING ASSESSMENT: Monitor and Reinforce**

If students miss more than two items in Exercise 7, refer them to the following for additional practice.

In the Textbook	Print Resources	Technology
Section Review, Ex. 10–11, Section 23.1	*Grammar Exercise Workbook,* pp.129–130	*On-Line Exercise Bank,* Section 23.1

Section Review

GRAMMAR EXERCISES 8–13

> **Exercise 8** **Identifying Case** Write the case of each of the underlined pronouns in the following sentences. Then, write its use.

1. Historians believe that studying the past will help <u>us</u> in the future.
2. In the 1920's, enterprising businessmen and <u>their</u> associates amassed fortunes.
3. Their investments in oil, railroads, and steel brought great wealth to <u>them</u>.
4. Their wealth won <u>them</u> status and fame.
5. The principal investors in the stock market were <u>they</u>.

> **Exercise 9** **Identifying Pronouns in the Objective Case** Choose the correct pronoun in parentheses to complete each sentence. Then, identify its case.

1. <u>They</u> used (their, they're) wealth to influence politicians.
2. (They, Their) having so much wealth and power made poor people jealous.
3. Bill and (me, I) read novels by some prominent writers of the 1920's.
4. The novelists wrote about rich people and sometimes criticized (they, them).
5. Our teacher said that (us, we) should learn more about the 1920's economy.

> **Exercise 10** **Revising to Correct Pronoun Usage** Revise this paragraph, correcting errors in pronoun usage.

(1) The people of the 1920's experienced many exciting events. A number of technological breakthroughs were witnessed by they. (2) Many of them thrilled at seeing new forms of entertainment. (3) Like the people of today, the people of the 1920's often spent they're Saturday afternoons at movie theaters. (4) On some of those Saturdays, them watched the films of Charlie Chaplin. (5) Its him who created the character of the little tramp with the funny walk. (6) People all around the world soon fell in love with he and his antics. (7) Two of the first international movie stars were him and Al Jolson. (8) Although Chaplin's early films did not feature dialogue, they were often accompanied by dramatic music. (9) Fortunately, Chaplin's films have survived to the present and still give many of we great enjoyment. (10) Watching them, your certain to laugh out loud.

> **Exercise 11** **Find It in Your Reading** In this passage from "A Visit to Grandmother" by William Melvin Kelley, identify at least one pronoun in each of the three cases, and tell how it is used.

She let him go, and fell back into her chair, grabbing the arms. Her hands were as dark as the wood, and seemed to become part of it.

> **Exercise 12** **Find It in Your Writing** In your portfolio, find five sentences containing pronouns in all three cases. Check that you have used the pronouns correctly. Write down each pronoun, its case, and its use in the sentence.

> **Exercise 13** **Writing Application** Imagine that you are interviewing a person who lived in the United States during the 1920's. Make a list of questions and responses from your interview. Try to use pronouns in all three cases in your transcript of the interview.

Section Review • 551

ASSESS

Section Review

Each of these exercises correlates to the teaching on case, pages 544–550. The exercises may be used for more practice, for reteaching, or for review of the key concepts presented. Answers are available in *Grammar Exercises Answers on Transparencies* in your Teaching Resources.

Answer Key

> **Exercise 8**

1. objective–direct object
2. possessive–shows ownership
3. objective–object of preposition
4. objective–indirect object
5. nominative–predicate nominative

> **Exercise 9**

1. their–possessive
2. Their–possessive
3. I–nominative
4. them–objective
5. we–nominative

> **Exercise 10**

1. . . . witnessed by them
2. correct
3. . . . their Saturday . . .
4. . . . they watched . . .
5. It's he who . . .
6. . . . with him and . . .
7. . . . were he and . . .
8. correct
9. . . . give many of us . . .
10. . . . you're certain . . .

> **Exercise 11**

Find It in Your Reading
Nominative—She; objective—him, it; possessive—her, Her

> **Exercise 12**

Find It in Your Writing
After students have located their pronouns, they might read their original sentences to partners and see if the partners agree with their case and use identifications.

> **Exercise 13**

Writing Application
When students have finished, have volunteers read the interviews aloud. Have everyone listen for correct pronoun usage.

Interest GRABBER Write this sentence on the board:

Mary delivered the flowers to Kevin.

Challenge students to think of questions using *who* and *whom* that might have prompted this sentence as an answer. Look for suggestions similar to *To whom did Mary deliver the flowers?* and *Who delivered the flowers to Kevin?* and write them on the board. Point out the relationship between *whom* and *Kevin* (both objects) and *Who* and *Mary* (both subjects). Have students create other *who/whom* statements and questions.

Activate Prior Knowledge

Write these commonly used constructions on the board: *To whom it may concern, Whom shall I say is calling?, Who's the boss around here?* Tell students to identify the one erroneous construction (*Whom shall I say is calling?*) and tell why it is wrong (as subject of the sentence, *Whom* should be *Who*).

TEACH

Step-by-Step Teaching Guide

Using *Whose* and *Who's* Correctly

1. Remind students that *whose* and *who's* are often confused. Show the difference with this example:

   Who's going, and in whose car?

2. Suggest that when choosing between *whose* and *who's*, students mentally substitute the uncontracted form (*who is*). If *who is* doesn't make sense in context, they should use *whose*.

Integrating Speaking, Listening, Viewing, and Representing Skills

Who's and Whose Read aloud this list of simple sentences that use either *who's* or *whose*. For each, have students spell aloud the correct form and explain their answer.

Whose hat is on the floor?

Who's joining us for dinner?

Do you see who's also on stage?

For whose birthday is this cake?

Special Problems With Pronouns

Choosing the correct form of a pronoun is not always a matter of choosing the form that sounds correct. For example, would it be correct to say, "I can run faster than her"? Though the sentence may sound correct to you, it is wrong because an objective pronoun (*her*) is used when a nominative pronoun (*she*) is needed. Several words are understood in the sentence, which reads, in full, "I can run faster than she (can run)."

This section will discuss two special pronoun problems: the proper uses of *who* and *whom* and the related forms *whoever* and *whomever*, as well as the use of pronouns in clauses where some words are omitted but understood.

Using *Who* and *Whom* Correctly

Knowing when to use *who* or *whom* and the related forms *whoever* and *whomever* is less confusing if you understand how the words are used.

▶ **KEY CONCEPT** *Who* and *whoever* are nominative case pronouns. *Whom* and *whomever* are objective case pronouns. ■

The chart below shows the forms of these pronouns and their uses in sentences.

Case	Pronoun	Use in Sentence
Nominative	who, whoever	Subject or Predicate Nominative
Objective	whom, whomever	Direct Object, Object of a Verbal, or Object of a Preposition
Possessive	whose, whosever	To Show Ownership

The following pages focus on the nominative and objective pronouns, as the possessive case rarely causes problems.

Note About *Whose*: Do not confuse the contraction *who's*, which means "who is," with the possessive pronoun *whose*.

POSSESSIVE PRONOUN: *Whose* satellite went into orbit?

CONTRACTION: *Who's* our first contestant tonight?

Theme: Mars

In this section, you will learn about special problems with pronouns. The examples and exercises in this section are about Mars.

Cross-Curricular Connection: Science

⏱ TIME AND RESOURCE MANAGER

Resources
Print: *Grammar Exercise Workbook*, pp. 131–132; *Grammar Exercises Answers on Transparencies*, Ch. 23; *Hands-on Grammar Activity Book*, Ch. 23
Technology: *Writing and Grammar* Interactive Text, Section 23.2; On-Line Exercise Bank, Section 23.2

Using the Full Student Edition	Using the Handbook🅷
• Work through all key concepts, pp. 552–557.	• Work through all key concepts, pp. 396–401.
• Assign and review Exercises 14–17.	• Assign and review Exercises 14–17.
• Read and discuss Grammar in Literature, p. 555.	• Read and discuss Grammar in Literature, p. 399.
• Do the Hands-on Grammar activity, p. 558.	• Do the Hands-on Grammar activity, p. 402.

The Nominative Case: *Who* and *Whoever* The nominative case is used for subjects and for predicate nominatives.

> **KEY CONCEPT** Use *who* or *whoever* for the subject of a verb. ■

EXAMPLES: *Who* is the person directing the Mars study?
I know *who* had the best science project.
He chose *whoever* volunteered for the space project.

In the last two sentences, *who* and *whoever* are the subjects of subordinate clauses. You can be sure you are using the correct case in a subordinate clause by determining the use of the pronoun. Consider the pronoun in the following sentence:

EXAMPLE: I will accept help from *whoever* will offer it.

The first step in checking the case of the pronoun is to isolate the subordinate clause. In this example, the subordinate clause is *whoever will offer it*, a noun clause acting as the object of the preposition *from*.
The next step is to see how the words in the subordinate clause are used. The verb in the clause is *will offer*; the direct object is *it*. *Whoever* is the correct pronoun because it acts as a subject and, therefore, must be in the nominative case.

> **KEY CONCEPT** Use *who* or *whoever* for a predicate nominative. ■

EXAMPLE: The culprit is *who*?

A problem may arise when the pronoun is the predicate nominative in a subordinate clause.

EXAMPLE: The police do not know *who* the culprit is.

To see whether the pronoun is correct, first isolate the subordinate clause (*who the culprit is*). Next, determine each word's use within the clause. Because this clause is inverted, put it into normal word order: *The culprit is who.* You can now see that the subject is *culprit*, the verb is *is*, and *who* is the predicate nominative of the linking verb. Because predicate nominatives require the nominative case, *who* is correct.

The planet Mars has a polar icecap.

▲ **Critical Viewing**
Write two questions about this picture using the word *who* or *whom* in each.
[Analyze]

Special Problems With Pronouns • 553

Step-by-Step Teaching Guide

Using *Who* and *Whom* Correctly

1. Students sometimes have trouble using *whom,* because they rarely hear it in informal speech. Besides changing questions into statements, students might also substitute another pronoun in the statement to check for correct case use.

2. Demonstrate this strategy with the sentences *(Who/Whom) will you notify?* and *(Who/Whom) did you speak to?* Have students

   • invert each statement:
   You will notify (who/whom).
   You did speak to (who/whom).

   • substitute another pronoun:
   You will notify them.
   You did speak to her.

   Since *them* and *her* are in the objective case, the objective form *whom* is correct in each sentence.

Integrating Workplace Skills

Whoever and Whomever Explain to students that the pronouns *whoever* and *whomever* are useful for communicating to large groups of people. These pronouns are used to compose public messages in the business world. (Example: *Whoever wishes to attend the conference should contact the event coordinator promptly.*) Have students write sentences that use the pronoun *whoever* to address a large group of co-workers, using the example as a model. Then, have them share their sentences with the class.

Integrating Writing

Who, Whom, Whoever, Whomever Have students write a dialogue that might ensue when a police officer questions a suspect. Have them use *who, whom, whoever,* and *whomever* in at least one question each.

Critical Viewing

Analyze Sample responses: Who has seen Mars' polar icecap?; To whom will credit be given for photographing it?

☑ **ONGOING ASSESSMENT: Prerequisite Skills**

If students have difficulty with *who* and *whom* in clauses, you may find it necessary to review the following to assure coverage of prerequisite knowledge.

In the Textbook	Print Resources	Technology
Clauses, Section 20.2	*Grammar Exercise Workbook,* pp. 75–80	*On-Line Exercise Bank,* Section 23.2

Step-by-Step Teaching Guide

Who Clauses

1. Students may need more practice with *who* clauses used as objects.

2. Present these examples and have students explain (1) the use of the clause, and (2) the use of the underlined word in each:

   I am waiting for <u>whoever</u> is going now. (object of preposition; subject of clause)

   I want to know <u>who</u> it is. (object of verbal; predicate nominative in clause)

Customize for
Less Advanced Students

To help students use *whom* as the object of a preposition, have students write a list of common prepositions (*for, to, at, with*). Then, ask them to compose original sentences using *whom* and *whomever* with at least five of these prepositions. Work with them to make sure they understand sentences in which *whom* and the preposition are separated, as in *I saw the woman whom we had traveled with.*

The Objective Case: *Whom* and *Whomever* The objective case of these pronouns is used for direct objects of verbs, objects of verbals, and objects of prepositions.

▶ **KEY CONCEPT** Use *whom* and *whomever* for the direct object of a verb or the object of a verbal. ■

In this example, *whom* is the object of the infinitive *to see.* Check the pronoun's case by mentally rewording the sentence.

EXAMPLE: *Whom* did you expect to see?
(You did expect to see *whom*?)

Pronouns in the objective case also occur in the subordinate clauses of complex sentences.

EXAMPLES: We asked *whom* they chose to go into space.
You can select *whomever* you want.

To see whether the correct pronouns have been used, first isolate the subordinate clause (*whom they chose, whomever you want*). Next, put the clauses in normal word order: *they chose whom; you want whomever.* It now becomes clear that the subjects are *they* and *you* and that the correct direct objects are *whom* and *whomever.*

▶ **KEY CONCEPT** Use *whom* or *whomever* for the object of a preposition. ■

Whom is the object of a preposition in both examples below.

EXAMPLES: From *whom* did you receive the message?
Whom did you receive the message from?

If the pronoun is used to connect the clauses of a complete sentence, it is necessary to check the pronoun's case more carefully. Look at these two sentences with adjective clauses.

EXAMPLES: I spoke to the astronaut with *whom* we had dined.
I spoke to the astronaut *whom* we had dined with.

In the first sentence, the objective pronoun immediately follows its preposition, *with.* In the second sentence, the pronoun and the preposition are separated by many words. To check the case, isolate the subordinate clause: *whom we had dined with.* Next, put the clause in the normal word order: *We had dined with whom.* The clause has a subject (*we*), a verb (*had dined*), and a prepositional phrase (*with whom*). *Whom* is the correct pronoun because the objective case is required for the object of a preposition.

More Practice

Grammar Exercise Workbook
• pp. 131–132
On-line Exercise Bank
• Section 23.2
  Go on-line:
  PHSchool.com
  Enter Web Code:
  eek-1002

GRAMMAR IN LITERATURE

from **Making History With Vitamin C**

Penny Le Couteur and Jay Burreson

Notice the use of who in the following excerpt.

The word *scurvy* is said to be derived from Norse, the language of the seafaring Viking warriors *who*, starting in the ninth century, raided the Atlantic coast of Europe from their northern homelands in Scandinavia.

▶ **Exercise 14** Using *Who* and *Whom* Correctly in Questions and Clauses Choose the correct pronoun in each sentence, and identify the case of the pronoun.

1. (Who, Whom) has not wondered whether there is life on other planets?
2. From (who, whom) can we learn about plans to send a satellite to Mars?
3. The person most likely to be able to answer that question is (who, whom)?
4. If you could take a trip to Mars, (who's, whose) the person you would like most to accompany you?
5. Someday, such a trip may become possible. In the meantime, (whoever, whomever) is interested in Mars can learn more about it from books, magazines, and the Internet.

▶ **Exercise 15** Revising to Correct the Use of *Who* and *Whom* Revise the following sentences to correct errors in the use of *who* and *whom*. If a sentence is correct, write *correct*.

1. Cherie asked whomever she saw about the reddish planet in the sky.
2. Indeed, Mars is close enough to us that it is visible to whoever wants to search for it even without a telescope.
3. To who did you remark that it takes 687 Earth days for Mars to revolve around the sun?
4. Whom did you ask?
5. In whose book did you see a photograph of Mars?

▼ **Critical Viewing** Use *who* in a sentence about astronauts on Mars. Use *whom* in a sentence about the people watching them. **[Draw Conclusions]**

Special Problems With Pronouns • 555

Grammar in Literature

1. Have a student read aloud the excerpt from "Making History with Vitamin C."
2. Ask students to isolate the subordinate clause *(who, starting in the ninth century, raided the Atlantic coast of Europe from their northern homelands in Scandinavia).*

More About the Writer

Penny Le Couteur (b. 1943) and Jay Burreson (b. 1942) are chemists and longtime friends. She teaches chemistry and he runs a high-tech company. Together, they have written a book called *Napoleon's Buttons* that examines connections between chemical structures and historical episodes. Each chapter looks at a different molecule and its role in history.

Answer Key

▶ **Exercise 14**

1. Who—nominative
2. whom—objective
3. who—nominative
4. who's—contraction (who—nominative)
5. whoever—nominative

▶ **Exercise 15**

1. correct
2. correct
3. To whom . . .
4. correct
5. correct

Critical Viewing

Drawing Conclusions Sample responses: _Who_ was the first to travel to Mars?; _Whom_ did that person leave behind on Earth?

☑ **ONGOING ASSESSMENT: Monitor and Reinforce**

If students miss more than one item in Exercise 14 or 15, refer them to the following for additional practice.

In the Textbook	Print Resources	Technology
Section Review, Ex. 18–19, Section 23.2	*Grammar Exercise Workbook,* pp. 131–132	*On-Line Exercise Bank,* Section 23.2

Pronouns in Elliptical Clauses

1. Statements like *He is as lazy as me* or *I was more excited than her* may sound correct to students because the *as* or *than* before the pronoun seems to function as a preposition. Point out that in constructions like these, *as* and *than* are actually subordinate conjunctions introducing a new, though not fully stated clause.

2. Ask students to define *elliptical clause* in their own words (a clause in which words are understood but not actually stated).

3. Use the examples at the bottom of the page to make the point that students need to consider meaning when deciding which pronoun to use in an elliptical construction.

Customize for
Logical/Mathematical Learners

To provide a deeper understanding of possible logical meanings in elliptical clauses, write the following on the board: *She was more interested in his singing than (they, them, theirs).* Note that this sentence might be completed by a nominative, objective, or possessive pronoun. Challenge students to defend each of the three possible answers. Have student volunteers write the complete sentence, including omitted words, for each variation. Ask students to explain the logical meaning of the sentence.

Integrating Vocabulary Skills

Elliptical Explain that *elliptical* is derived from the Greek word *elleipein*, meaning "come short; leave out." A related word is the name of the punctuation mark *ellipsis* (. . .). Have students look up *ellipsis* in a dictionary and tell how the meanings of the two words are related.

23.2

Use Pronouns Correctly in Elliptical Clauses

In an *elliptical clause*, some words are omitted because they are understood. Sentences with elliptical clauses are often used to draw comparisons. Such sentences are usually divided into two parts connected by *than* or *as: Fran is smarter than he*, or *Tom is as happy as I*. In selecting the case of the pronoun, you must know what the unstated words are.

▶ **KEY CONCEPT** In elliptical clauses beginning with *than* or *as*, use the form of the pronoun that you would use if the clause were fully stated. ■

The case of the pronoun depends upon whether the omitted words belong before or after the pronoun. In the examples below, the omitted words are supplied in brackets.

WORDS LEFT OUT AFTER PRONOUN:	Jo is as interested in space exploration as *he.* Jo is as interested in space exploration as he [is].
WORDS LEFT OUT BEFORE PRONOUN:	We gave Scott the same telescope as *her.* We gave Scott the same telescope as [we gave] her.

If the omitted words come *after* the pronoun, use a nominative pronoun because it is the subject of the omitted verb. If the omitted words come *before* the pronoun, use an objective pronoun because the pronoun will be an object, generally the direct object or indirect object of the omitted verb or the object of a preposition.

Often, the entire meaning of the sentence depends on the case of the pronoun. Compare, for example, the meaning of the following sentences when the nominative pronoun is changed to an objective pronoun.

WITH A NOMINATIVE PRONOUN:	Stan taught us more about the solar system than *she.* Stan taught us more about the solar system than she [did].
WITH AN OBJECTIVE PRONOUN:	Stan taught us more about the solar system than *her.* Stan taught us more about the solar system than [he taught] her.

Always follow the steps in the chart on the next page when you choose a pronoun in an elliptical clause.

Technology Tip

You can learn more about space exploration by visiting various government Web sites. Type *space program* or *NASA* into your browser.

 STANDARDIZED TEST PREPARATION WORKSHOP

Grammar and Usage Many standardized tests require students to draw upon their knowledge and understanding of elliptical clauses to revise usage errors. Use the following example to demonstrate.

The Kelsey and the Clyde families purchased the property jointly, but the purchase required John Kelsey to mortgage his farm for nearly its entire value. <u>*This made the investment more dangerous for the Kelseys than they.*</u>

How would one rewrite the underlined sentence?

A Change *more dangerous* to *much more dangerous.*

B Change *they* to *them.*

C Change *Kelseys* to *Kelsey's.*

D Correct as is.

The correct answer is **B.** The sentence contains the elliptical clause *than (it was for) them.* In this clause, the objective form of the pronoun is required because the pronoun is used as an object of a preposition.

CHOOSING A PRONOUN IN ELLIPTICAL CLAUSES

1. Consider the choices of pronouns: nominative or objective.
2. Mentally complete the elliptical clause.
3. Base your choice on what you find.

Exercise 16 Identifying the Correct Pronoun in Elliptical Clauses Rewrite each sentence, choosing one of the pronouns in parentheses and correctly completing the elliptical clause.

EXAMPLE: She is more knowledgeable about satellites than (I, me).

ANSWER: She is more knowledgeable about satellites than I am.

1. Astronauts who have traveled to outer space probably know more about Mars and the solar system than (we, us).
2. The desire to explore new frontiers is more pressing to them than (we, us).
3. Much of the exploration of Mars has been undertaken by machines that can travel far longer in outer space than (we, us) humans.
4. These machines are accurate and efficient; however, they aren't as expressive or emotional as (we, us) humans.
5. The desire to be an astronaut is much greater in (she, her) than (he, him).

Exercise 17 Using the Correct Pronoun in Elliptical Clauses Complete each sentence by choosing an appropriate pronoun and completing the elliptical clause.

EXAMPLE: Joanne writes more often than ___?___.

ANSWER: Joanne writes more often than I do.

1. Young children think about Mars more often than ___?___.
2. I wish I had as much imagination as ___?___.
3. The possibility of living on other planets seems more real to them than ___?___.
4. I don't think I'm nearly as imaginative as ___?___.
5. According to this science-fiction writer, problem-solving skills are more highly developed in Martians than ___?___.

More Practice

Grammar Exercise Workbook
• pp. 131–132
On-line Exercise Bank
• Section 23.2
  Go on-line:
  PHSchool.com
  Enter Web Code:
  eek-1002

Interactive Textbook

Get instant feedback! Exercises 16 and 17 are available on-line or on CD-ROM.

Exercise 16
1. we (do)
2. (it is to) us
3. we humans (can)
4. we humans (are)
5. her than (in) him

Exercise 17
Allow slight variation in response.

1. we do
2. they do
3. it seems to us
4. they are
5. they are developed in us

☑ ONGOING ASSESSMENT: Monitor and Reinforce

If students miss more than one item in Exercise 16 or 17, refer them to the following for additional practice.

In the Textbook	Print Resources	Technology
Section Review, Ex. 20, Section 23.2	*Grammar Exercise Workbook,* pp. 131–132	*On-Line Exercise Bank,* Section 23.2

⏱ TIME SAVERS!

Answers on Transparencies Use the *Grammar Exercises Answers on Transparencies* for Chapter 23 to facilitate correction by students.

On-Line Exercise Bank Have students complete the exercises on computer. The Auto Check feature will grade their work for you!

Hands-on Grammar

Teaching Resources: Hands-on Grammar Activity Book, Ch. 23

1. If you wish to do this activity in class, be prepared with scissors and construction paper. Assign students to small groups.

2. Go through the directions and the samples with the whole class. Suggest that students create their sentences with compound direct objects and predicate nominatives.

3. Have students supply appropriate pronouns for the sample sentences (for example, *Bill and he, Mrs. Simmons and I.*) Then have students create their own sentences and work with them in their groups.

Find It in Your Reading

Students may either find their own nonfiction narratives or work with some from their literature texts.

Find It in Your Writing

Have students work individually with sentences from their own writing. They can then share the results within their groups.

Hands-on Grammar

Pronoun Fold-Over

Cut construction paper into strips that are each about an inch wide. Then, write sentences on each strip. Each sentence should contain half of a compound predicate. Leave a blank in each compound predicate where a pronoun would appear.

With a group of classmates, fold over each strip so that the first part of the compound predicate is hidden. Only the blank where the pronoun will appear should show. Hiding the first half of the compound predicate should help the members of your group identify which pronoun case to use to complete each sentence. Write down the pronouns in the blank spaces. Then, share your answers with classmates.

Use these sentences to create additional strips:

The only ones who attended were Bill and ___?___.

The winners were Mrs. Simmons and ___?___.

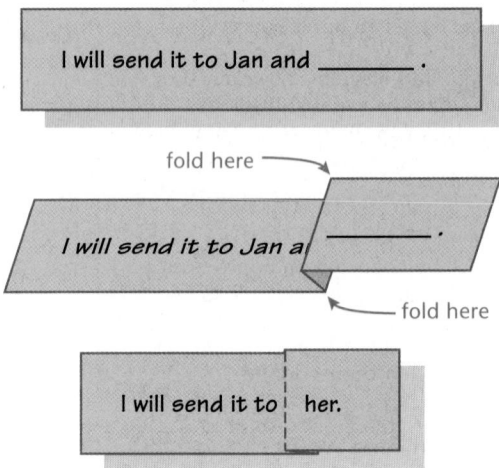

To extend this activity, create strips with sentences in which you leave out the first word of a compound subject.

Find It in Your Reading Find five sample sentences containing compound predicates or compound subjects in a work of narrative nonfiction. Include these sentences in the strips you make.

Find It in Your Writing Try the activity above with five sentences from a piece of your own writing.

Section 23.2 Section Review

GRAMMAR EXERCISES 18–23

Exercise 18 Using *Who* and *Whom* in Questions Choose the pronoun in parentheses that completes each question.

1. The first person to walk in space was (who, whom)?
2. From (who, whom) did we learn about the atmosphere on Mars?
3. Do you know (who, whom) is preparing a science project on Mars?
4. Is that the person (who, whom) I should interview?
5. With (who, whom) should I check my facts before I submit my paper?

Exercise 19 Using *Who* and *Whom* Correctly in Clauses Write the subordinate clause in each sentence. Then, identify how the form of *who* or *whom* is used.

1. I wonder (whose, who's) idea it was to name Mars after the Roman god of war.
2. The person was clearly someone (who, whom) knew a lot about mythology.
3. (Whoever, Whomever) gave Mars its name felt that the planet's red color was symbolic of blood and war.
4. No matter (who, whom) we asked, we could not find out how the names of Mars' moons were chosen.
5. I forget from (who, whom) we learned that Phobos and Deimos were sons of Ares, the Greek god of war.

Exercise 20 Using Pronouns Correctly in Elliptical Clauses Rewrite each sentence, choosing the correct pronoun and completing the elliptical clause.

1. Ancient people may have been more imaginative than (we, us).
2. Space was more a world of mystery for them than (you and I, you and me).

3. We modern people no longer believe, as (they, them), that Earth is the center of the universe.
4. We now know far more about outer space and the solar system than (they, them).
5. The concept of space exploration is far more familiar to us than (they, them).

Exercise 21 Find It in Your Reading Explain why the playwright used *who* instead of *whom* in this sentence from *Invasion From Mars* by Howard Koch.

. . . Incredible as it may seem, both the observations of science and the evidence of our eyes lead to the inescapable assumption that those strange beings who landed in the Jersey farmlands tonight are the vanguard of an invading army from the planet Mars.

Exercise 22 Find It in Your Writing Look through your portfolio and find at least five sentences in which you have used *who* or *whom*. Check to see that you used the pronouns correctly.

Exercise 23 Writing Application Imagine that you have met an alien life form. Write questions that you would ask. Use some of the following pronouns and phrases in your questions. Include at least two elliptical clauses in your questions.

1. more advanced than [pronoun]
2. whoever
3. as smart as [pronoun]
4. whom
5. than [pronoun]

Section Review • 559

Each of these exercises correlates to a section of the chapter on pronoun usage, pages 544–557. The exercises may be used for more practice, for reteaching, or for review of the key concepts presented. Answers for all chapter exercises are available in *Grammar Exercises Answers on Transparencies* in your Teaching Resources.

Answer Key

Exercise 24

1. We–nominative;
   what–nominative;
   that–nominative; us–objective
2. who–nominative;
   them–objective
3. our–possessive;
   what–nominative
4. we–nominative
5. us–objective
6. whoever–nominative;
   them–objective
7. it–nominative
8. us–objective
9. Our–possessive
10. We–nominative;
    they–nominative; their–possessive

Exercise 25

The following are likely responses.

1. they–predicate nominative
2. he–subject
3. They–subject
4. who–subject of clause;
   it–subject of clause
5. I–subject

Exercise 26

The following are likely responses.

1. me–indirect object
2. us–object of preposition
3. him–object of a verbal
4. whom–object of preposition
5. him–object of a verbal

Exercise 27

The following are likely responses. Others are possible.

1. its
2. It's
3. their
4. they're
5. You're
6. It's
7. There's
8. theirs
9. whose
10. Who's

Chapter 23 Chapter Review

GRAMMAR EXERCISES 24–32

Exercise 24 Identifying Case On your paper, write each pronoun you find in this paragraph. Then, tell whether it is *nominative*, *objective*, or *possessive*.

(1) We humans have wondered for many centuries what exists in the universe that surrounds us. (2) People who gaze into the night sky may wonder if beings on other planets are staring back at them. (3) In recent years, our efforts to learn what lies on other planets have begun to bear fruit. (4) In 1971, we Americans gained much information about Mars from the *Mariner 9* spacecraft, a robot probe. (5) That year, *Mariner 9* orbited Mars and sent us photographs of that mysterious planet. (6) The photographs impressed whoever saw them. (7) American scientists sent another satellite to Mars in 1997, and it was an even bigger success. (8) *Pathfinder* sent us Earthlings more than 16,000 photographic images of the surface of Mars. (9) Our attempts to land on Mars again in 1999 have proved less successful. (10) We on Earth lost touch with two Martian landers as they approached their destinations.

Exercise 25 Adding Nominative Pronouns to Sentences On your paper, write a nominative pronoun to complete each sentence below. Then, tell its use.

1. The first people to examine my science project on Mars were ___?___.
2. My father and ___?___ arrived soon after the exhibition hall opened.
3. ___?___ praised my model of Mars and its two orbiting moons.
4. Everyone ___?___ saw the project thought ___?___ deserved an *A*.
5. After my presentation, my brother and ___?___ went out with our parents to celebrate.

Exercise 26 Adding Objective Pronouns to Sentences On your paper, rewrite each sentence, adding an objective pronoun in the blank. Then, tell its use.

1. My older brother gave ___?___ a lesson on astronomy.
2. Although we share few other hobbies between ___?___, he insists that I learn about space exploration.
3. Challenging ___?___ is useless.
4. He is the one person against ___?___ I can never win an argument.
5. To appease ___?___, I agreed to read a book on colonizing Mars.

Exercise 27 Adding Possessive Pronouns or Contractions to Sentences On your paper, rewrite each sentence, supplying a possessive pronoun or a contraction to fill the blank.

1. Earthlings could not live comfortably on Mars because ___?___ atmosphere is too dense with carbon dioxide.
2. ___?___ a fact that the average temperature on Mars is –80˚F.
3. Through ___?___ study of photographs taken by telescope, scientists have discovered craters on Mars.
4. The scientists believe ___?___ the result of meteor landings on the planet.
5. ___?___ probably wondering whether we on Earth will ever travel to Mars.
6. ___?___ a question that may be answered in the near future.
7. ___?___ a major study of life on Mars being conducted currently.
8. Astronomers have studied photographs taken by a Martian lander. The findings in this book are ___?___.
9. I wonder ___?___ idea it was to put this photo of Mars on the cover.
10. ___?___ going to purchase the book?

Exercise 28 Revising to Correct Errors in the Use of *Who* and *Whom* and Nominative and Objective Pronouns Revise this paragraph, correcting errors in pronoun usage.

(1) Two astronomers who have studied Mars have now published their findings. The scientists are named Wendy Smith and William Yung. (2) Him and her are scientists who we respect. (3) Their research is certain to impress whomever reads their book. (4) My brother and I showed it to whomever him and me saw in the college library. (5) The person to who the book is dedicated was my favorite professor.

Exercise 29 Using Pronouns in Elliptical Clauses Change each underlined pronoun from the objective to the nominative, and vice versa. Be sure to complete each elliptical clause.

1. Janice enjoys seeing movies about Mars more than <u>I</u>.
2. She is more fascinated by outer space than <u>he</u>.
3. She spends more time visiting museums than <u>them</u>.
4. She believes that space beings can talk with each other better than <u>us</u>.
5. I think she would enjoy being the friend of a Martian more than <u>I</u>.

Exercise 30 Revising to Use Pronouns to Eliminate Repetition Revise this passage, inserting pronouns where appropriate to eliminate repetition. In addition, correct any errors in pronoun usage.

Mars has two moons. The two moons' names are Phobos and Deimos. Phobos is the larger moon. Phobos is also closer to Mars than Deimos is. The name *Phobos* comes from Greek mythology. Phobos was the son of Ares, the Greek god of war.

Deimos was Phobos' brother. My sister read an interesting fact about he. My sister told the fact to me. The orbits of Mars and Phobos may lead to Mars and Phobos crashing into each other in 50 million years.

My brother told my sister that my brother was not worried about the crash. "I don't plan to be around in 50 million years," my brother said.

Some scientists believe that Phobos and Deimos started out as asteroids. Jupiter pushed Phobos and Deimos toward Mars. Then, Phobos and Deimos began to orbit Mars.

Exercise 31 Writing Application Imagine that you are part of a crew traveling to Mars. Describe yourself and the other space travelers. Use pronouns in all three cases in your paragraph, and include either *who* or *whom* in at least one sentence. Underline the pronouns that you use.

Exercise 32 CUMULATIVE REVIEW Verb Usage and Pronoun Usage Rewrite this paragraph, correcting any errors.

(1) On Halloween night 1938, many Americans were tuned to they're radios. (2) What they heared frightened they and they're friends. (3) It will have been a radio dramatization of a play about an invasion by Martians. (4) Whom could have thought it was real? (5) Hundreds of people called the police, who's phones didn't stop ringing. (6) Some people packed suitcases and begun evacuating their homes. (7) The broadcast had putted some people into a state of panic. (8) Others listened to the broadcast more carefully than them. (9) They would realize that the events aren't real. (10) They may just have set down and had a good laugh.

Answer Key

Exercise 28

1. correct
2. He and she; whom
3. whoever
4. whomever he and I saw
5. whom

Exercise 29

1. (she enjoys seeing) me
2. (she is fascinated by) him
3. they (do)
4. we (can)
5. (she would enjoy being the friend of) me

Exercise 30

Answers will vary; a sample is given.

Mars has two moons whose names are Phobos and Deimos. Phobos is the larger moon. It is also closer to Mars than Deimos is. The name *Phobos* comes from Greek mythology. Phobos was the son of Ares, the Greek god of war. Deimos was Phobos' brother. My sister read an interesting fact about him. She told it to me. The orbits of Mars and Phobos may lead to their crashing into each other in 50 million years.

My brother told my sister that he was not worried about the crash. "I don't plan to be around in 50 million years," he said.

Some scientists believe that Phobos and Deimos started out as asteroids. Jupiter pushed them toward Mars. Then, they began to orbit it.

Exercise 31

Writing Application
When students have finished, ask for volunteers to read their paragraphs aloud. Have classmates listen for correct pronoun usage.

Exercise 32

Cumulative Review

1. their radios
2. heard, them, their
3. It was
4. Who
5. whose
6. began
7. put
8. they
9. realized, weren't
10. sat

☑ **ONGOING ASSESSMENT: Assess Mastery**

Use the following resources to assess student mastery of pronoun usage.

In the Textbook	Print Resources	Technology
Chapter Review, Ex. 24–32 Standardized Test Preparation Workshop	*Formal Assessment,* Ch. 23	*Writing and Grammar* Interactive Text, Ch. 23, Chapter Review; *On-Line Exercise Bank,* Sections 23.1–2

Lesson Objectives

1. To demonstrate control over grammatical elements
2. To recognize appropriate English usage within the context of a written passage

---

Pronoun Usage

Teaching Resources: Standardized Test Preparation Workbook, pp. 45–46

1. Review the three cases of pronouns with the students, and have them give examples of these pronouns used in context. Review the answers and explanations for the test items, being sure that students understand why the correct choice is correct and the others are not.

2. Have the students complete Practice 1 and Practice 2.

3. Although in a real test situation students will be required to mark their answers on a bubble sheet, you may have them number a piece of paper and write their answers. Alternatively, for a quick practice, you may call on students to answer the items orally.

Standardized Test Preparation Workshop

Pronoun Usage

Standardized tests measure your knowledge of the rules of standard grammar, such as correct pronoun usage. Some questions may test your ability to use the three cases of personal pronouns correctly. When answering these questions, determine what type of pronoun is needed in the sentence—*nominative*, *objective*, or *possessive*. Also, consider the rules for special problems with pronouns, such as use in *compound structures*, *appositives*, *elliptical clauses* and the use of *who* and *whom*, before choosing a pronoun. The following test item will give you practice with the format of questions that test your knowledge of pronoun usage.

Test Tip

Before choosing a pronoun for an elliptical clause beginning with *than* or *as,* mentally complete the clause using an objective or a nominative pronoun. Base your choice on the pronoun that does not change the meaning of the sentence.

Sample Test Items

	Answers and Explanations
Directions: Read the passage, and choose the letter of the word or group of words that belongs in each space. Yes, the surprise party you heard about for Larry and ___(1)___ is true. So you and ___(2)___ can't tell anyone.	

1 A I
  B her
  C she
  D we
	The correct answer is *B*. Since the sentence requires a word that is the object of a preposition, an objective case pronoun is the correct choice. Therefore, the pronoun *her* best completes the compound object of the preposition *for*.

2 F he
  G I
  H me
  J we
	The correct answer is *G*. Because the missing pronoun is part of a compound subject, the nominative *I* is correct.

 TEST-TAKING TIP

Tell students to read silently the entire passage in a test item before choosing responses for questions. As they read, they should think about pronouns that could fill in the blanks. This process will help students develop a sense of the topic so they can identify the appropriate pronouns more easily.

Answer Key

▶ **Practice 1**

1. C
2. J
3. C
4. G
5. A

▶ **Practice 2**

1. B
2. H
3. D
4. F
5. B

▶ **Practice 1** **Directions:** Read the passage, and choose the letter of the word or group of words that belongs in each space.

It has always been ___(1)___ policy to accept returns within 90 days. A refund for any item returned after 90 days must be approved by ___(2)___ in writing. It is ___(3)___, the customer's, responsibility to seek written approval for the refund. Otherwise, ___(4)___ cannot give you a guarantee. The manager, Mrs. Rajani, would be happy to speak with you regarding this matter. Please feel free to contact ___(5)___.

1 **A** their
   B her
   C our
   D his

2 **F** he
   G we
   H him
   J us

3 **A** our
   B you
   C your
   D his

4 **F** they
   G we
   H he
   J you

5 **A** her
   B we
   C she
   D they

▶ **Practice 2** **Directions:** Read the poem, and choose the letter of the word or group of words that belongs in each space.

If you were ___(1)___,
And I were you,
With ___(2)___ would ___(3)___
Be talking to?
If our garden were ___(4)___
And their garden were ours,
Which of ___(5)___
Would plant the flowers?

1 **A** me
   B I
   C she
   D they

2 **F** what
   G who
   H whom
   J whose

3 **A** him
   B me
   C us
   D we

4 **F** theirs
   G their
   H they
   J them

5 **A** we
   B us
   C her
   D him

Customize for
ESL Students

After students complete Practice 1, have them replace the pronouns with nouns so that they understand that pronouns and nouns are interchangeable.

In-Depth Lesson Plan

	LESSON FOCUS	PRINT AND MEDIA RESOURCES
DAY 1	**Subject and Verb Agreement** Students learn and apply agreement concepts covering singular and plural subjects and compound subjects. (pp. 566–569/H406–409)	*Writing and Grammar* Interactive Text, Section 24.1; *On-line Exercise Bank,* Section 24.1 **Teaching Resources** *Grammar Exercise Workbook,* pp. 133–136; *Grammar Exercises Answers on Transparencies,* Ch. 24
DAY 2	**Subject and Verb Agreement** *continued* Students learn and apply concepts covering confusing subjects, subjects of linking verbs, collective nouns, indefinite pronouns, and amounts and measurements. (pp. 570–576/H410–416)	**Teaching Resources** *Grammar Exercise Workbook,* pp. 137–138; *Hands-on Grammar Activity Book,* Ch. 24
DAY 3	**Pronoun and Antecedent Agreement** Students learn and apply agreement concepts covering personal pronouns and antecedents, agreement in number, indefinite pronouns, and reflexive pronouns. (pp. 577–579/H417–419)	*Writing and Grammar* Interactive Text, Section 24.2; *On-line Exercise Bank,* Section 24.2 **Teaching Resources** *Grammar Exercise Workbook,* pp. 139–142
DAY 4	**Special Problems With Pronoun Agreement** Students learn and apply agreement concepts covering vague, ambiguous, and distant pronoun references. (pp. 580–583/H420–423)	**Teaching Resources** *Grammar Exercise Workbook,* pp. 143–144
DAY 5	**Review and Assess** Students review the chapter and demonstrate mastery of agreement concepts. (pp. 584–585)	*Writing and Grammar* Interactive Text, Ch. 24, Chapter Review **Teaching Resources** *Formal Assessment,* Ch. 24

Accelerated Lesson Plan

	LESSON FOCUS	PRINT AND MEDIA RESOURCES
DAY 1	**Subject and Verb Agreement** Students cover subject-and-verb-agreement concepts as determined by the Diagnostic Test. (pp. 566–576/H406–416)	*Writing and Grammar* Interactive Text, Section 24.1; *On-line Exercise Bank,* Section 24.1 **Teaching Resources** *Grammar Exercise Workbook,* pp. 133–138; *Grammar Exercises Answers on Transparencies,* Ch. 24
DAY 2	**Pronoun and Antecedent Agreement** Students cover pronoun and antecedent concepts as determined by the Diagnostic Test. (pp. 577–583/H417–423)	*Writing and Grammar* Interactive Text, Section 24.2; *On-line Exercise Bank,* Section 24.2 **Teaching Resources** *Grammar Exercise Workbook,* pp. 139–144
DAY 3	**Review and Assess** Students review the chapter and demonstrate mastery of agreement concepts. (pp. 584–585)	*Writing and Grammar* Interactive Text, Ch. 24, Chapter Review **Teaching Resources** *Formal Assessment,* Ch. 24

Options for Adapting Lesson Plans

FEATURES

Extend coverage with the Grammar in Literature feature (p. 567/H407) and the Standardized Test Preparation Workshop (p. 586).

TECHNOLOGY

Students can use *Writing and Grammar* Interactive Text to complete the exercises interactively on computer. They can complete additional exercises in the *On-line Exercise Bank:* The Auto Check feature will grade their work. Go On-line: PHSchool.com Use Web Code: eek-1002

Writing and Grammar Handbook Alignment

Page numbers in Step-by-Step Teaching Guides in this Teacher's Edition refer to pages from the full student text. Handbook page references, indicated with this icon Ⓗ, are provided in Time and Resource Manager boxes and at the bottom of each Teacher's Edition page.

INTEGRATED SKILLS COVERAGE

Grammar in Literature
SE p. 567/Ⓗ407

Writing
Find It in Your Writing SE pp. 574, 576, 583/Ⓗ414, 416, 423
Writing Application SE pp. 576, 583, 585/Ⓗ416, 423
Grammar and Style SE p. 566/Ⓗ406

Viewing and Representing
Critical Viewing SE pp. 564, 568, 570, 577, 579, 581/Ⓗ404, 408, 410, 417, 419, 421

Workplace Skills ATE pp. 572, 581

Real-World Connection ATE p. 581

Vocabulary Skills ATE pp. 571, 579

ASSESSMENT SUPPORT

Standardized Test Preparation Workshop SE p. 586; ATE pp. 568, 581

Standardized Test Preparation Workbook, pp. 47–48

Formal Assessment, Ch. 24

MEETING INDIVIDUAL NEEDS

Less Advanced Students ATE pp. 566, 587. See aslo Ongoing Assessments ATE pp. 567, 569, 570, 572 573, 578, 579, 580, 582.

More Advanced Students ATE p. 570

ESL Students ATE p. 578

Linguistic Learners ATE p. 568

BLOCK SCHEDULING

Pacing Suggestions
For 90-minute Blocks
• Administer the Diagnostic Test to students to determine instructional coverage.
• Have students complete the necessary exercises in class. Use the Hands-on Grammar activity to provide a change of pace.

Resources for Varying Instruction
• *Writing and Grammar* Interactive Text A 90-minute block provides an ideal opportunity for students to work on the computer.

Professional Development Support
• *How to Manage Instruction in the Block* This teaching resource provides management and activity suggestions.

MEDIA AND TECHNOLOGY

For the Student
• *Writing and Grammar* Interactive Text, Ch. 24
• *On-line Exercise Bank,* Sections 24.1–2

For the Teacher
• Teacher**EXPRESS** CD-ROM

WRITING AND GRAMMAR ON-LINE

Interactive Text (On-line or on CD-ROM)
• Easily navigable instruction with on-line supporting resources
• Self-scoring exercises and diagnostic tests

Companion Web Site PHSchool.com
• On-line Exercise Bank (use Web Code eek-1002)

See the Go On-line! feature, SE p. iii.

LITERATURE CONNECTIONS

Grammar In Literature selection from *Prentice Hall Literature, Penguin Edition,* Grade 10:
from "The Censors," Luisa Valenzuela, SE p. 567/Ⓗ407

Lesson Objectives

1. To demonstrate control over grammatical elements such as subject-verb agreement, pronoun-antecedent agreement, verb forms, and parallelism

2. To understand and use correct subject-verb agreement with compound subjects and when interrupters separate subject and verb

3. To understand and use correct subject-verb agreement with confusing subjects, such as those in inverted sentences or following linking verbs, and those that are collective nouns, names of works, or indefinite pronouns

4. To use pronouns that agree with their antecedents in number, person, and gender

5. To recognize and avoid vague, ambiguous, or unclear pronoun antecedents

6. To demonstrate control over grammatical elements such as subject and verb agreement and pronoun and antecedent agreement

7. To evaluate writing for both mechanics and content

8. To analyze the characteristics of clearly written texts, including the patterns of organization, syntax, and word choice

Critical Viewing

Describe Sample response: The wind feels intensely strong. The sound it makes is deafening.

Chapter 24 Agreement

Tornado Bahamas, Winslow Homer

When you speak, you automatically use words that agree with other words. You might say, for example, "The twister moves fast." You know you must add an -*s* to *move* when the subject is *twister* to make the verb agree with the subject.

Agreement is the match—the "fit"—between words or grammatical forms. Because grammatical agreement is not always obvious, you need to study some sentences more closely than others.

In the first section of this chapter, you will learn to make a subject agree with its verb. The second section focuses on agreement between pronouns and their antecedents.

▲ **Critical Viewing**
Describe how you think the wind would sound and feel if you were in the scene depicted above. Use verbs that agree with the subjects in your sentences. [Describe]

☑ **ONGOING ASSESSMENT: Diagnose**

If students miss more than one item in any category, direct them to the relevant pages of the textbook and assign exercises for practice and review.

Agreement	Diagnostic Test Items	Teach	Practice	Section Review	Chapter Review
Skill Check A					
Verbs with Singular and Plural Subjects	A 1–2, 4	p. 566/Ⓗ406	Ex. 1–3	Ex. 8	Ex. 27
Verbs with Compound Subjects	A 3, 5–6	pp. 568–569/ Ⓗ408–409	Ex. 4	Ex. 8	Ex. 28
Confusing Subjects	A 7–15	pp. 570–573/ Ⓗ410–413	Ex. 5–7	Ex. 9–12	Ex. 28–29

Diagnostic Test

Directions: Write all answers on a separate sheet of paper.

Skill Check A. Choose the verb in parentheses that agrees with the subject of each sentence.

1. Thunderstorms (is, are) dangerous because of lightning.
2. If the right conditions (exists, exist), thunderstorms can become tornadoes.
3. Nebraska and Kansas, located in the region known as Tornado Alley, (has, have) been hit by many tornadoes.
4. A tornado in a southeastern state—such as Florida, South Carolina, or Georgia—(is, are) often caused by a hurricane.
5. A tornado or a hurricane (is, are) a frightening weather phenomenon.
6. Tornadoes occur when cold, dry polar air and warm, moist tropical air (meets, meet).
7. Each occurrence of a tornado (is, are) studied by a team of scientists.
8. The team (examines, examine) the atmospheric conditions and the damage caused by the tornado.
9. On the Internet, there (is, are) photos showing how tornadoes form.
10. Mathematics (is, are) important to scientists who must use formulas to determine the dimensions and speed of a tornado.
11. Two thirds of a town in Kansas (was, were) destroyed during one tornado.
12. Most of the damage could be fixed, but some buildings (was, were) damaged beyond repair.
13. Every one of the townspeople (has, have) been helping to rebuild.
14. Many (believes, believe) that within a year, much of the damage will be mended.
15. One hundred thousand dollars (is, are) the cost of the repairs.

Skill Check B. Choose the correct pronoun in each sentence.

16. John and Pam are studying earth science, a subject (you, they) need for a career in weather forecasting.
17. One of John's favorite teachers is (his, their) physics teacher.
18. Both John and Alfredo will be taking (his, their) tests today.
19. Every student feels (he or she, they) will do well on the test.
20. After I study for a test, I want to reward (me, myself).

Skill Check C. Revise the following sentences to correct problems in pronoun reference.

21. Alfredo told John he was sure he'd pass the test.
22. When the boys entered the classroom he each sat down.
23. On the test, they asked how tornadoes are formed.
24. Nearly every tornado gets their force from strong vertically spinning winds.
25. John and myself knew almost all the answers.

Skill Check A

1. are
2. exist
3. have
4. is
5. is
6. meet
7. is
8. examines
9. are
10. is
11. was
12. were
13. has
14. believe
15. is

Skill Check B

16. they
17. his
18. their
19. he or she
20. myself

Skill Check C

Answers may vary slightly; samples are given.

21. Alfredo told John he was sure John would pass the test.
22. When the boys entered the classroom, each sat down.
23. On the test, the questions asked how tornadoes are formed.
24. Nearly every tornado gets its force from strong, vertically spinning winds.
25. John and I knew almost all the answers.

☑ ONGOING ASSESSMENT: Diagnose *continued*					
Agreement	Diagnostic Test Items	Teach	Practice	Section Review	Chapter Review
Skill Check B					
Personal Pronouns	B 16–20	pp. 577–579/ ⊞417–419	Ex. 16–17	Ex. 21	Ex. 30
Skill Check C					
Reflexive Pronouns	C 25	p. 580/⊞420	Ex. 18	Ex. 22	
Special Problems in Pronoun Agreement	C 21–24	pp. 580–581/ ⊞420–421	Ex. 19–20	Ex. 23	Ex. 31
Cumulative Reviews				Ex. 13–15, 24–26	Ex. 32–33

⏱ **TIME SAVERS!**

Answers on Transparencies Use the *Grammar Exercises Answers on Transparencies* for Chapter 24 to facilitate correction by students.

🖥 **On-Line Exercise Bank** Have students complete the Diagnostic Test on computer. The Auto Check feature will grade their work for you!

Interest GRABBER Ask students whether they can tell you what the term *agreement* might refer to in English grammar. Ask them what kind of words they think need to agree (*nouns, pronouns, and verbs*) and why (*to make sense, they must all be either singular or plural*).

Activate Prior Knowledge

Ask students to supply a list of nouns and pronouns, telling you which are singular and which are plural. Try to elicit some collective nouns and indefinite pronouns.

TEACH

Step-by-Step Teaching Guide

Singular and Plural Subjects

1. Remind students that both nouns and verbs can be either singular or plural. In a sentence, the subject and verb must match in number; that is what is meant by *agreement*.

2. Ask students how they can tell whether a verb is singular or plural in number (test it with a singular subject and a plural one). Give these examples: *Joe swims* (singular); *Joe and Ann swim* (plural). Practice this test with different verbs.

3. Once students read the second key concept, ask them to identify kinds of phrases and clauses that might intervene between a subject and a verb in a sentence. Then, examine the examples.

Customize for
Less Advanced Students

Give these students a handout of a passage from a book, magazine, or newspaper article. Ask them to identify all the simple subjects and label them *singular* or *plural*. Then, have them form original sentences with each subject, using their own verbs or verbs you give them, to see whether they can use the correct form.

Answer Key

Exercise 1

1. leave / 2. use / 3. race / 4. roars / 5. is

Section 24.1
Subject and Verb Agreement

For a subject and verb to agree, both must be singular or both must be plural. In this section, you will learn how to distinguish between singular and plural subjects, how to make verbs agree with compound subjects, and how to deal with problems of agreement with special subjects.

Singular and Plural Subjects

When making a verb agree with its subject, you need to identify the subject and determine its number.

▶ **KEY CONCEPTS** A singular subject must have a singular verb. A plural subject must have a plural verb. ■

SINGULAR SUBJECT AND VERB: <u>Thunder</u> usually <u>follows</u> lightning.

PLURAL SUBJECT AND VERB: <u>We</u> <u>are</u> about to get our umbrellas.

▶ **Exercise 1** Making Verbs Agree With Their Subjects
Choose the verb in parentheses that agrees with the subject of each sentence.
1. Tornadoes (leaves, leave) a trail of destruction.
2. Meteorologists (uses, use) special instruments to measure the speed of tornado winds.
3. Tornado winds (races, race) at around 240 miles per hour.
4. In just a few minutes, a twister (roars, roar) past.
5. In that brief period, it (is, are) able to level buildings.

▶ **KEY CONCEPT** A phrase or clause that interrupts a subject and its verb does not affect subject-verb agreement. ■

EXAMPLES: The <u>destruction</u> of tornadoes <u>is</u> devastating.
The community <u>members</u> who experience the devastation <u>help</u> each other.

In the first example, the singular subject *destruction* takes the singular verb *is*. Even though the plural noun *tornadoes* is closer to the verb, it is the object of a preposition and does not affect subject and verb agreement. In the second sentence, the plural subject *members* agrees with the plural verb *help* even though they are separated by an adjective clause that causes the singular noun *devastation* to be closer to the verb.

Theme: Wind

In this section, you will learn about subject and verb agreement. The examples and exercises in this section are about tornadoes and hurricanes.

Cross-Curricular Connection: Science

⚙ Grammar and Style Tip

Remember that in grammar, the concept of number refers to the two forms of a word: singular and plural. Singular words indicate one; plural words indicate more than one.

🕐 TIME AND RESOURCE MANAGER

Resources
Print: *Grammar Exercise Workbook,* pp. 133–138; *Grammar Exercises Answers on Transparencies,* Ch. 24
Technology: *Writing and Grammar* Interactive Text, Section 24.1; *On-Line Exercise Bank,* Section 24.1

Using the Full Student Edition	Using the Handbook🅗
• Work through all key concepts, pp. 566–573. • Assign and review Exercises 1–7. • Read and discuss Grammar in Literature, p. 567. • Do the Hands-on Grammar activity, p. 574.	• Work through all key concepts, pp. 406–413. • Assign and review Exercises 1–7. • Read and discuss Grammar in Literature, p. 407. • Do the Hands-on Grammar activity, p. 414.

GRAMMAR IN LITERATURE

from **The Censors**
Luisa Valenzuela

The subjects and the verbs agree in the following excerpt. The subjects are printed in red and the verbs in blue.

He knows that *they examine, sniff, feel,* and *read* between the lines of each and every letter, and *check* its tiniest comma and most accidental stain. *He knows* that all *letters pass* from hand to hand and *go* through all sorts of tests in the huge censorship offices and that, in the end, very *few continue* on their way.

> **Exercise 2** Making Separated Subjects and Verbs Agree

Choose the verb in parentheses that agrees with the subject of each sentence.

1. A tornado occurring over a lake or an ocean (is, are) a waterspout.
2. A waterspout with winds of less than 50 miles per hour usually (lasts, last) longer than a tornado does.
3. A ship's crew members sailing on the ocean (fears, fear) waterspouts.
4. Water around waterspouts (churns, churn).
5. Small vessels caught in a storm (tosses, toss) violently from side to side.

> **Exercise 3** Correcting Subject and Verb Agreement

Revise the following passage, correcting all errors in subject-verb agreement. Not every sentence contains an error.

Scientists from the National Weather Service gathers weather information from all parts of the country. If the information indicates a tornado, a warning of severe weather conditions are issued. The movements of the tornado shows where it will strike. People living in that area evacuate. Putting storm cellars under homes also provide an excellent source of shelter. On hearing news of a tornado, members of a family heads for the shelter. Often, a supply of water and canned goods is kept there. When the powerful winds of the tornado passes, the people feel safe leaving the shelter. Usually, a broadcast on radio or TV announce the all-clear. What signs of the storm's fury remains?

> **More Practice**

Grammar Exercise Workbook
• pp. 133–134
On-line Exercise Bank
• Section 24.1
  Go on-line:
  PHSchool.com
  Enter Web Code:
  eek-1002

Interactive Textbook

Get instant feedback! Exercises 1, 2, and 3 are available on-line or on CD-ROM.

Subject and Verb Agreement • 567

Subjects Joined by *and*

1. Remind students that the coordinating conjunction *and* is frequently used to create compound subjects. Explain that the conjunction *and* functions like a plus sign (+) in mathematics, causing an addition of the parts in the compound subject. Therefore, a compound subject joined with an *and* is nearly always plural.

2. Explain to students the few exceptions to this rule. Have them read the second group of examples on this page and explain the logical reasons for each of these being singular (even though it is modified by compound nouns used as adjectives, *equipment* remains singular; the words *each* and *every* identify only one at a time).

Customize for
Linguistic Learners

Ask students to read aloud a synopsis (one they have already written or one they write for this exercise) of a chapter in a book or a scene from a play they are studying. Tell them to pay close attention to subject-verb agreement. Have them read their synopses aloud, and ask other students to listen for instances of agreement and to decide whether these are correct.

Critical Viewing

Speculate Possible answers: The sky is dark. The winds are raging.

24.1

Compound Subjects

A compound subject has two or more subjects, usually joined by *or* or *and*. Use the following rules when making compound subjects agree with verbs.

Subjects Joined by *and* Only one rule applies to compound subjects connected by *and:* Whether the parts of the compound subject are all singular, all plural, or mixed, the verb is usually plural.

▶ **KEY CONCEPT** A compound subject joined by *and* is generally plural and must have a plural verb. ■

TWO SINGULAR SUBJECTS:	A <u>thunderstorm</u> and a <u>tornado</u> <u>hit</u> the town.
TWO PLURAL SUBJECTS:	<u>Thunderstorms</u> and <u>tornadoes</u> <u>appear</u> on the radar screen.
A SINGULAR SUBJECT AND A PLURAL SUBJECT:	Luckily, the <u>tornado</u> and the <u>thunderstorms</u> often <u>miss</u> our area.

There are two exceptions to this rule. If the parts of a compound subject are thought of as one item or the word *every* or *each* precedes the compound subject, then the verb is singular. Note the number of the subjects and verbs in the following examples:

EXAMPLES: The best <u>detection</u> and specialized tornado <u>equipment</u> <u>is</u> Doppler radar.
<u>Each</u> <u>tornado</u> and <u>thunderstorm</u> <u>demonstrates</u> nature's power.
<u>Every</u> weather <u>center</u> and <u>emergency network</u> in the United States <u>issues</u> warnings for severe weather.

Singular Subjects Joined by *or* or *nor* When both parts of a compound subject connected by *or* or *nor* are singular, a singular verb is required.

▶ **KEY CONCEPT** Two or more singular subjects joined by *or* or *nor* must have a singular verb. ■

EXAMPLE: A <u>tornado</u> or <u>hurricane</u> <u>causes</u> terrible damage.

▲ **Critical Viewing** Imagine that you are the person who took this picture. Write two sentences, one with a singular subject and one with a plural subject, that describe this situation. Make sure that each verb agrees with its subject. **[Speculate]**

✎ STANDARDIZED TEST PREPARATION WORKSHOP

Grammar and Usage Many standardized tests require students to correct errors in compositions. Use the following to demonstrate.

Neither the students reading their books nor the teacher correcting papers <u>were looking out the window</u>, so they didn't notice the storm approaching.

What is the correct form of the underlined phrase in this passage?

A is looking out the window
B are looking out the window
C was looking out the window
D Correct as is

The correct answer is **C**. When a compound subject is connected by *or* or *nor*, the verb agrees with the subject closer to it (*teacher*) in both number and case.

Plural Subjects Joined by *or* or *nor* When both parts of a compound subject connected by *or* or *nor* are plural, a plural verb is required.

KEY CONCEPT Two or more plural subjects joined by *or* or *nor* must have a plural verb. ■

EXAMPLE: Neither <u>tornadoes</u> nor <u>hurricanes</u> <u>cause</u> as many deaths as lightning storms.

Subjects of Mixed Number Joined by *or* or *nor* If one part of a compound subject is singular and the other is plural, the verb agrees with the subject that is closer to it.

KEY CONCEPT If one or more singular subjects are joined to one or more plural subjects by *or* or *nor*, the subject closest to the verb determines agreement. ■

EXAMPLES: Neither <u>David</u> nor my <u>parents</u> <u>are frightened</u> by thunderstorms.
Neither my <u>parents</u> nor <u>David</u> <u>is frightened</u> by thunderstorms.

Exercise 4 Choosing Verbs That Agree With Compound Subjects Choose the verb in parentheses that agrees with the subject of each sentence.

1. *Cyclone* and *typhoon* (is, are) other names for a type of storm that North Americans call a hurricane.
2. Meteorologists and other scientists (describes, describe) hurricanes as rotating storms from the tropical ocean.
3. Dull-red sunsets or a high barometric reading (predicts, predict) a potential hurricane brewing at sea.
4. In modern times, the radio or television (allows, allow) people to learn about a hurricane before it strikes.
5. Both strong winds and heavy rainfall (is, are) typical during hurricanes.
6. Late summer and early fall (is, are) hurricane season.
7. A moist, tropical region at high risk for hurricanes (is, are) the Caribbean Islands.
8. Neither Hurricane Andrew nor Hurricane Mitch (was, were) a mild hurricane.
9. Either Hurricane Camille or Hurricane Mitch (holds, hold) the record for the lowest barometric pressure ever recorded.
10. During one hurricane, four adults and a child (was, were) trapped in a building, but they were safely rescued in the end.

More Practice

Grammar Exercise Workbook
• pp. 135–136
On-line Exercise Bank
• Section 24.1
Go on-line:
PHSchool.com
Enter Web Code:
eek-1002

interactive Textbook

Get instant feedback! Exercise 4 is available on-line or on CD-ROM.

Subjects Joined by *or* or *nor*

1. Explain to students that the rule for the coordinating conjunctions *or* and *nor* is very different from the rule for *and*. Tell students that the use of *or* or *nor* emphasizes each member of the compound subject, either one of which may make the sentence true, rather than requiring them to be taken as a group, as the word *and* would.

2. Have students read the key concept and the example on the bottom of page 568. Explain that since *tornado* and *hurricane* are each singular, the conjunction makes the verb singular because *or* establishes an "either one or the other" context.

3. Direct students to the first key concept on this page and demonstrate that the two plural subjects require a plural verb.

4. Point out that subjects of mixed number joined by *or* or *nor* are the trickiest. Tell students that whichever subject is closest to the verb determines the number of the verb. Use the examples to demonstrate the two options.

Answer Key

Exercise 4

1. are
2. describe
3. predicts
4. allows
5. are
6. is
7. is
8. was
9. holds
10. were

✓ ONGOING ASSESSMENT: Monitor and Reinforce

If students miss more than two items in Exercise 4, refer them to the following for additional practice.

In the Textbook	Print Resources	Technology
Section Review, Ex. 8, Section 24.1	*Grammar Exercise Workbook,* pp. 135–136	*On-Line Exercise Bank,* Section 24.1

⏱ TIME SAVERS!

Answers on Transparencies Use the *Grammar Exercises Answers on Transparencies* for Chapter 24 to facilitate correction by students.

On-Line Exercise Bank Have students complete the exercises on computer. The Auto Check feature will grade their work for you!

Inverted Sentences

1. Ask students to recall inverted sentences (hard-to-find subjects, interrogative sentences, sentences beginning with *here* and *there*). Remind them that the subject follows the verb in these sentences.

2. Point out that the rules of subject-verb agreement still apply in these situations. One way to check for proper agreement is to reword the sentences so that the subject comes first.

3. Have students read the note about *there's* and *here's*. Be sure they understand that these are contractions involving a singular verb, *there is* and *here is*, and are, therefore, incorrect when a plural verb is needed (*there are, here are*).

Critical Viewing

Describe Sample response: There is a jagged streak of lightning cutting through the sky.

Answer Key

▶ **Exercise 5**

1. There's
2. was
3. glow
4. is
5. are

Customize for
More Advanced Students

Ask students to search through books, magazines, and other periodicals for examples of confusing or hard-to-find subjects. Have them make lists of about ten such sentences that they find, leaving a blank for the verb in each case. Have the students exchange lists with each other and fill in the blanks.

24.1

Confusing Subjects

Some kinds of subjects have special agreement problems:

Inverted Sentences Foremost among confusing subjects are the hard-to-find subjects that come after the verbs. A sentence in which the subject comes after the verb is said to be inverted. Subject and verb order is usually inverted in questions.

▶ **KEY CONCEPT** A verb must still agree in number with a subject that comes after it. ■

EXAMPLE: At the top of the hill <u>are</u> two light-
          ning <u>rods</u>.
          (Two lightning rods are at the top of
          the hill.)

Check to make sure the verb agrees with the subject by mentally rewording the sentence so that the subject comes first.

The words *there* and *here* often signal an inverted sentence. These words never function as the subject of the sentence.

EXAMPLES: There <u>are</u> the satellite <u>photos</u> of the hurricane.
           Here <u>is</u> the revised <u>information</u> on the storm.

Note About *There's* and *Here's*: Both of these contractions contain the singular verb *is: there is* and *here is*. They should not be used with plural verbs.

CORRECT: There<u>'s</u> only one <u>hurricane</u> expected this week.
          There <u>are</u> two <u>hurricanes</u> expected next week.

▶ **Exercise 5** Making Subjects and Verbs Agree in Inverted Sentences Choose the item in parentheses that agrees with the subject of each sentence.
1. (There's, There're) usually a series of warnings before a hurricane.
2. Causing the greatest losses (was, were) Hurricane Floyd.
3. On the radar (glows, glow) traces of a hurricane track.
4. Where on these radar screens (is, are) the eye of the hurricane?
5. Here (is, are) the flashlights and candles in case the lights go out during the storm.

▲ Critical Viewing
Write a sentence beginning with the word *there* that describes this photograph. **[Describe]**

▶ **More Practice**

Grammar Exercise Workbook
• pp. 137–138
On-line Exercise Bank
• Section 24.1
  Go on-line:
  PHSchool.com
  Enter Web Code:
  eek-1002

✓ **ONGOING ASSESSMENT: Monitor and Reinforce**

If students miss more than one item in Exercise 5, refer them to the following for additional practice.

In the Textbook	Print Resources	Technology
Section Review, Ex. 9, Section 24.1	*Grammar Exercise Workbook,* pp. 137–138	*On-Line Exercise Bank,* Section 24.1

Subjects of Linking Verbs Subjects with linking verbs may also cause agreement problems.

▶ **KEY CONCEPT** A linking verb must agree with its subject, regardless of the number of its predicate nominative. ■

EXAMPLES: The strong <u>winds</u> <u>are</u> one reason we expect a tornado.
One <u>reason</u> we expect a tornado <u>is</u> the strong winds.

In the first example, the plural verb *are* agrees with the plural subject *winds*, although the predicate nominative *reason* is singular. In the next example, the singular subject *reason* takes the singular verb *is*, although the predicate nominative *winds* is plural.

Collective Nouns Collective nouns—such as *audience*, *class*, *club*, and *committee*—name groups of people or things.

▶ **KEY CONCEPTS** A collective noun takes a singular verb when the group it names acts as a single unit. A collective noun takes a plural verb when the group it names act as individuals with different viewpoints. ■

SINGULAR: The weather <u>club</u> <u>plans</u> to track the tornado.
PLURAL: The weather <u>club</u> <u>have</u> split the responsibilities of tracking the tornado.

Nouns That Look Like Plurals Some nouns that end in *-s* appear to be plural but are actually singular in meaning. For example, nouns that name branches of knowledge, such as *civics* and *economics*, and those that name single units, such as *molasses* or *mumps*, take a singular verb.

▶ **KEY CONCEPT** Use singular verbs to agree with nouns that are plural in form but singular in meaning. ■

SINGULAR: <u>Physics</u> <u>requires</u> skill in mathematics.
The <u>news</u> today <u>reports</u> good weather.

When words such as *ethics*, *politics*, and *acoustics* do not name branches of knowledge but indicate characteristics, their meanings are plural. Similarly, such words as *eyeglasses*, *pliers*, and *scissors*, though they name single items, generally take plural verbs.

PLURAL: The <u>acoustics</u> in the weather center <u>are</u> terrible.
The <u>scissors</u> <u>are</u> in the top drawer.

Subject and Verb Agreement • 571

Subjects of Linking Verbs; Nouns That Look Like Plurals

1. Remind students that a *predicate nominative* is a noun or pronoun that follows a linking verb and renames, identifies, or explains the subject of the sentence.

2. Emphasize that the predicate nominative is not the subject and can differ in number from it. Use the examples to demonstrate that the verb must still agree with the subject despite the number of the predicate nominative.

3. Have students recall and define *collective nouns* and remind them that although these nouns always look singular, their meaning can be singular or plural. A collective noun refers to a number of people, places or things that can operate as one cohesive unit or as individuals.

4. Be sure students understand why *club* can be singular or plural depending on its context. Show similar contexts using words such as *committee, family,* and *group*.

5. Tell students that some nouns ending in *-s* are not plural and are considered plural-looking nouns. Since they are singular in meaning, they require singular verbs. Explain that a main category of these nouns is branches of knowledge or study (*mathematics, economics, athletics*).

Integrating Vocabulary Skills

Hard-to-Find Subjects In certain cases (in sentences using collective nouns and plural-sounding nouns), it may be difficult to determine what verb form the subject takes. Have students make a list with three headings: plural, collective, and plural-sounding. Ask them to find as many examples of each as they can. Have them define unfamiliar words and then form sentences using these words as both simple and compound subjects in original sentences.

Step-by-Step Teaching Guide

Indefinite Pronouns

1. Have students provide a definition of *indefinite pronouns* (pronouns used to refer to persons, places, or things, often without specifying which ones). Remind students that indefinite pronouns can be singular or plural. Use the lists beneath the first key concept as a review.

2. Explain that indefinite pronouns follow the regular rules of subject-verb agreement.

3. Remind students that some indefinite pronouns can be singular or plural depending on their *antecedents* (nouns or other words for which pronouns stand). Use the examples to demonstrate.

Integrating Workplace Skills

Descriptive Writing Tell students that descriptive writing is important in journalism and that agreement is essential for clear, accurate reporting. Ask students to imagine that they are television news reporters describing an accident, burglary, or some other dramatic situation. Have them describe the event clearly for viewers in a brief written passage. Ask some students to read their passages aloud, and ask listeners to identify subjects and verbs and decide whether they agree.

Answer Key

> **Exercise 6**

1. has / 2. was / 3. find / 4. are / 5. research

Step-by-Step Teaching Guide

Titles of Creative Works and Names of Organizations

1. Tell students that some titles and proper names can be plural, but since they always represent one single unit, they are treated as singular and take singular verbs.

2. To reinforce this idea, have students read the key concept and examples at the bottom of this page.

Indefinite Pronouns Some indefinite pronouns are always singular, some are always plural, and some may be either singular or plural. Prepositional phrases that interrupt the subject and verb do not affect agreement.

> **KEY CONCEPTS** Singular indefinite pronouns take singular verbs. Plural indefinite pronouns take plural verbs. ∎

SINGULAR:	anybody, anyone, anything, each, either, every, everybody, everyone, everything, neither, nobody, no one, nothing, somebody, someone, something
PLURAL:	both, few, many, others, several

SINGULAR:	Everyone on the rescue squad has left for the day.
PLURAL:	Many of the houses were damaged during the storm.

> **KEY CONCEPT** The pronouns *all, any, more, most, none,* and *some* usually take a singular verb if the antecedent is singular, and a plural verb if it is plural. ∎

SINGULAR:	Some of the area is ruined due to the hurricane.
PLURAL:	Some of the cars are beyond repair

> **Exercise 6** Making Verbs Agree With Indefinite Pronouns
Choose the item in parentheses that agrees with the subject of each sentence.

1. Everyone studying tornadoes (has, have) learned some amazing facts.
2. Using a computer program, each of us (was, were) assigned an imaginary tornado to track.
3. Many (finds, find) the assignment exciting and informative.
4. A few in the class (is, are) frightened by the strength of the twister.
5. Some of the students (researches, research) the effects of tornadoes in certain areas of the country.

Titles of Creative Works and Names of Organizations

Plural words in the title of a creative work or in the name of an organization do not affect subject-verb agreement.

> **KEY CONCEPT** A title or the name of an organization is singular and must have a singular verb. ∎

EXAMPLES:	*Dealing With Severe Weather Conditions* is a useful reference.
	Weather Services is a helpful agency.

☑ ONGOING ASSESSMENT: Monitor and Reinforce

If students miss more than one item in Exercise 6, refer them to the following for additional practice.

In the Textbook	Print Resources	Technology
Section Review, Ex. 9, Section 24.1	*Grammar Exercise Workbook,* pp. 137–138	*On-Line Exercise Bank,* Section 24.1

Amounts and Measurements Most amounts and measurements, although they appear to be plural, actually express single units or ideas

KEY CONCEPT A noun expressing an amount or measurement is usually singular and requires a singular verb. ■

EXAMPLES: <u>Two hundred million dollars</u> <u>is</u> the cost in property damage from the tornado.
<u>Two miles</u> <u>was</u> our distance from the tornado.
<u>Three quarters</u> of the town <u>was destroyed</u>.
<u>Half</u> of the trees <u>were uprooted</u>.

In the first three examples, the subjects take singular verbs. *Two hundred million dollars* is one sum of money; *two miles* is a single distance; and *three quarters* is one part of a town. In the last example, *half* refers to a number of individual trees and therefore takes a plural verb.

Exercise 7 Making Verbs Agree With Confusing Subjects
Choose the item in parentheses that agrees with the subject of each sentence.
1. Tornadoes (is, are) a good reason for extreme caution.
2. Each tornado (has, have) unique characteristics.
3. Most (looks, look) like a funnel.
4. Many (approaches, approach) without warning.
5. One sign of approaching turbulent weather (is, are) thunder clouds.
6. Experiencing the most tornadoes (is, are) the middle of the country.
7. Each year, a series of tornadoes (causes, cause) damage to the region of the United States known as Tornado Alley.
8. *Beware the Twisters* (is, are) a book about the destruction caused by tornadoes.
9. In 1968, three million dollars (was, were) the cost of the damage caused by a tornado that passed through Tracy, Minnesota.
10. All meteorologists in the agency (rates, rate) tornadoes.
11. Physics (is, are) a science meteorologists use to measure a tornado.
12. At the center of a tornado (appears, appear) areas of low pressure.
13. (There's, There are) lots of activity in the tornado's core.
14. Some areas of a tornado (is, are) illuminated by lightning.
15. The news occasionally (contains, contain) reports about people who have seen the core, or center, of a tornado.

More Practice

Grammar Exercise Workbook
• pp. 137–138
On-line Exercise Bank
• Section 24.1
Go on-line:
PHSchool.com
Enter Web Code:
eek-1002

interactive Textbook

Get instant feedback! Exercises 6 and 7 are available on-line or on CD-ROM.

Step-by-Step Teaching Guide

Amounts and Measurements

1. Have students read the key concept. Explain that most amounts and measurements end in *-s*, which makes them appear plural. Amounts and measurements are composed of many pieces, but the resulting single quantity is usually considered singular.

2. As they examine each example, have students look for other words in each sentence that help explain why each amount is singular (*cost, distance, town*—all singular).

3. Finally, ask students to offer an explanation for the plural verb in the final example. Be sure they understand that the *half* is referring to a specific number of trees and that, logically, half of a plural number is still more than one.

Answer Key

Exercise 7

1. are
2. has
3. look
4. approach
5. is
6. is
7. causes
8. is
9. was
10. rate
11. is
12. appear
13. There's
14. are
15. contains

☑ **ONGOING ASSESSMENT: Monitor and Reinforce**

If students miss more than two items in Exercise 7, refer them to the following for additional practice.

In the Textbook	Print Resources	Technology
Section Review, Ex. 9–12, Section 24.1	*Grammar Exercise Workbook,* pp. 137–138	*On-Line Exercise Bank,* Section 24.1

⏲ **TIME SAVERS!**

🗐 **Answers on Transparencies** Use the *Grammar Exercises Answers on Transparencies* for Chapter 24 to facilitate correction by students.

💻 **On-Line Exercise Bank** Have students complete the exercises on computer. The Auto Check feature will grade their work for you!

Hands-on Grammar

Teaching Resources: Hands-on Grammar Activity Book, Ch. 24

1. If you wish to do this activity in class, be prepared with scissors, cardboard, tape, and paper clips. Have students work in pairs, and give each pair the needed materials.

2. Work through the directions with the class so that all students can see how to construct and use the wheel.

3. To work with the sentences in step 7, be sure students understand that they will have to create new small circles. Subjects in these sentences: *vase, vase, crumbs, crumbs.*

Find It in Your Reading

You might ask students to evaluate the inverted sentences they find. Would any sound better in natural order?

Find It in Your Writing

Have students discuss their new inverted sentences with their partners.

24.1

Hands-on Grammar

Inverted-Sentence Wheel

Practice inverting sentences and finding the subject.

1. Cut out a cardboard circle with a diameter of 5". Make four holes in it, as shown in the illustration. They should be about 1/4" from the edge of the circle.
2. Cut out four smaller cardboard circles—1" to 1-1/2" in diameter. Make a small hole in each circle.
3. Unfold four paper clips, as shown. Put the paper clips through the holes in the big circle, and then attach a small circle to the other end of each paper clip.
4. Tape a paper circle, 3-1/2" in diameter, to the middle of the large circle. That is the verb wheel.
5. On one of the small cardboard circles, write *two marbles*. Write *under the table* on the circle that is opposite. Then, write *the marble* on another small cardboard circle. On the opposite circle, write *under the table*. On the paper circle in the center, write the verbs *are* and *is* twice, as shown.
6. Turn the wheel so that a verb is upright. Then, read the sentence from top circle to bottom circle. Which is the subject? Spin the wheel so that the other verb is upright and read the sentence. Has the subject changed place in the sentence?

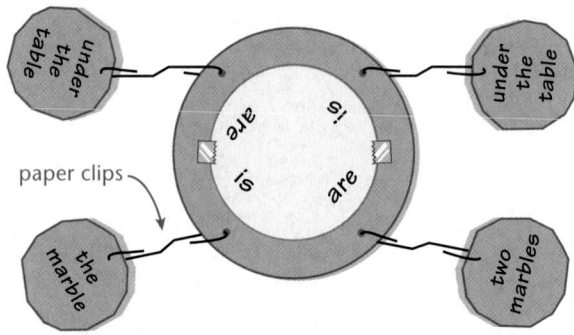

paper clips

7. Illustrate the following sentences with your wheel:
   On the table is the vase.   *Cookie crumbs are under the table.*
   The vase is on the table.   *Under the table are cookie crumbs.*

Find It in Your Reading In a story or textbook that you are reading, find other examples of sentences with inverted word order. Illustrate those sentences on your wheel.

Find It in Your Writing Review a piece of writing from your portfolio. If you have used inverted word order in any of your sentences, check to be sure that the verb agrees with the subject.

574 • Agreement

⏱ **TIME SAVERS!**

✋ **Hands-on Grammar**
Use the Hands-on Grammar activity sheet for Chapter 24 to facilitate this activity.

Section Review

GRAMMAR EXERCISES 8–15

▶ **Exercise 8** **Making Subjects Agree With Their Verbs** Choose the verb in parentheses that agrees with the subject of each sentence.

1. Rain during thunderstorms (falls, fall) quite rapidly.
2. Loud claps of thunder (shakes, shake) the house.
3. Lightning bolts (flashes, flash) across the sky.
4. Heavy rains or fast-melting snow (causes, cause) floods in many parts of the world.
5. Either too much rain or too much snow (makes, make) the level of rivers rise.
6. Rising rivers (means, mean) trouble.
7. Towns in the flood zone (is, are) in great danger.
8. A city or vacation spot located near the ocean (is, are) in danger of a tidal wave.
9. People (evacuates, evacuate) these areas before the storm hits.
10. Neither the Western Hemisphere nor the Eastern Hemisphere (is, are) immune to flooding.

▶ **Exercise 9** **Choosing Verbs for Inverted Sentences and Indefinite Pronouns** Choose the verb in parentheses that agrees with the subject of the sentence.

1. In the spring months (begins, begin) tornado season.
2. Most (occurs, occur) at this time of year due to weather patterns.
3. Often at the end of a hot, humid day (appears, appear) the thunderclouds.
4. Each cloud that produces tornadoes (is, are) different from regular clouds.
5. (Does, Do) people hear any thunder?
6. There (is, are) often rumbles of thunder before a tornado hits.

7. Each of the dark clouds (seems, seem) ready to burst.
8. At the bottom of the cloud (twists, twist) rounded cloud masses.
9. Everybody in the shelters (fears, fear) the powerful funnel.
10. Some of the most violent winds (uproots, uproot) trees and even overturn railroad cars.

▶ **Exercise 10** **Choosing the Correct Linking Verb** Choose the verb in parentheses that agrees with the subject of the sentence.

1. Severe weather conditions (is, are) a threat.
2. In Florida, one reason for building strong houses (is, are) hurricanes.
3. Hurricanes in early fall (is, are) a danger in the Southeast.
4. The responsibility of meteorologists (is, are) weather alerts.
5. These warnings (is, are) the key to saving lives during such storms.

▶ **Exercise 11** **Making Verbs Agree With Confusing Subjects** Choose the verb in parentheses that agrees with the subject of the sentence.

1. The news (includes, include) many stories of severe storms.
2. Tornadoes (represents, represent) one type of weather disaster.
3. In 1977, in the Midwest, there (was, were) millions of dollars of destruction from a tornado that lasted seven hours.
4. About 340 miles (was, were) the distance traveled by this tornado.
5. Most tornadoes (does, do) not last that long.

Section Review • 575

☑ **ONGOING ASSESSMENT: Assess Mastery**

Use the following resources to assess student mastery of subject-verb agreement.

In the Textbook	Technology
Chapter Review, Ex. 27–29	*Writing and Grammar* Interactive Text, Section 24.1, Section Review; *On-Line Exercise Bank,* Section 24.1

▶ Exercise 11

6. is
7. fears
8. occurs
9. call
10. are
11. is
12. reach
13. were
14. causes
15. has

▶ Exercise 12

Physics <u>plays</u> an important role in predicting the weather.

The science of weather studies and predictions <u>is</u> called meteorology.

Both atmospheric occurrences and geographic location <u>affect</u> weather forecasts.

Each of the weather forecasts <u>depends</u> on complex technology.

Atmospheric pressure or wind <u>requires</u> careful measurement.

Twelve hours <u>is</u> the amount of advance time needed for short-range forecasts.

For long-range predictions, mathematics <u>creates</u> important numerical models.

These models, along with a supercomputer, <u>make</u> accurate forecasts possible.

Neither the computers nor the math truly <u>predicts</u> the weather.

There <u>are</u> sometimes sudden changes in weather patterns.

▶ Exercise 13

Find It in Your Reading
she scratches—singular; tosses—singular; snares—singular

▶ Exercise 14

Find It in Your Writing
Have students exchange papers to check each other's work.

▶ Exercise 15

Writing Application
Sentences will vary; samples are provided.

1. <u>All</u> of the trees <u>are blowing</u> in the wind.
2. <u>Thunder</u> and <u>lightning</u> <u>are</u> <u>frightening</u> everyone.
3. <u>All</u> of the tornadoes <u>were</u> destructive.
4. <u>One</u> of the houses <u>has lost</u> its doors and windows.
5. <u>Two thirds</u> of the town <u>is</u> in a shambles.

Section Review Exercises cont'd.

6. *Tornadoes* by Michael Allaby (is, are) a reference book on the subject.
7. Another natural disaster nearly everyone (fears, fear) is a tsunami.
8. A tsunami is a series of waves that (occurs, occur) in an ocean or other large body of water.
9. Most people in North America (calls, call) tsunamis *tidal waves*.
10. Earthquakes on the sea floor (is, are) a major cause of tsunamis.
11. About 12 to 23 inches (is, are) the height of the typical tsunami when it begins at sea.
12. As they approach the shore, some tsunamis (reaches, reach) a height of 100 feet.
13. There (was, were) several destructive tsunamis during the 1990's.
14. Sometimes, politics (causes, cause) a delay in aid to the regions that are affected by tsunamis.
15. Not one of the towns (has, have) received money to make repairs.

▶ Exercise 12 Revision Practice:
Agreement Copy the paragraph on a separate sheet of paper. Revise it to correct all errors in subject-verb agreement.

Physics play an important role in predicting the weather. The science of weather studies and predictions are called meteorology. Both atmospheric occurrences and geographic location affects weather forecasts. Each of the weather forecasts depend on complex technology. Atmospheric pressure or wind require careful measurement. Twelve hours are the amount of advance time needed for short-range forecasts. For long-range predictions, mathematics create important numerical models. These models, along with a supercomputer, makes accurate forecasts possible. Neither the computers nor the math truly predict the weather. There's sometimes sudden changes in weather patterns.

576 • Agreement

▶ Exercise 13 Find It in Your
Reading Read the following excerpt from Pat Mora's poem "Uncoiling." Then, write all the verbs that agree with the subject, and indicate whether they are singular or plural.

With thorns, she scratches
    on my window, tosses her hair
    dark with rain,
snares lightning, cholla, hawks,
    butterfly
swarms in the tangles.

▶ Exercise 14 Find It In Your
Writing Review a draft from your portfolio, written in the present tense. Underline each subject once and each verb twice. Make sure your subjects and verbs agree.

▶ Exercise 15 Writing Application
Use each of the items below as the subject of a sentence. Provide verbs for each sentence that agree with the subjects provided. Underline all the subjects once and all the verbs twice.

1. All of the trees
2. Thunder and lightning
3. All of the tornadoes
4. One of the houses
5. Two thirds of the town
6. Storms at sea
7. The path of most hurricanes
8. Spaghetti and meatballs
9. Rain or snow
10. Neither he nor she

---

6. <u>Storms</u> at sea <u>are</u> often violent.
7. The <u>path</u> of most hurricanes <u>is</u> hard to predict.
8. <u>Spaghetti and meatballs</u> <u>is</u> my least favorite meal.
9. <u>Rain</u> or <u>snow</u> <u>is</u> surely on the way.
10. Neither <u>he</u> nor <u>she</u> <u>will admit</u> being wrong.

Pronoun and Antecedent Agreement

Section 24.2

Antecedents are the nouns (or the words that take the place of nouns) for which pronouns stand. In this section, you will learn how to make a pronoun agree with its antecedent.

Agreement Between Personal Pronouns and Antecedents

The following rule is the basis for pronoun and antecedent agreement:

▶ KEY CONCEPT A personal pronoun must agree with its antecedent in number, person, and gender. ■

The grammatical number of a pronoun indicates whether it is *singular* or *plural*. *Person* indicates whether the pronoun is first person (the one speaking), second person (the one spoken to), or third person (the one spoken about). Some nouns and pronouns also indicate *gender*—masculine, feminine, or neuter.

In the following example, the pronoun *his* and the antecedent *Byron* are both singular, in the third person, and masculine.

EXAMPLE: *Byron* completed *his* trip to India.

Agreement in Number Making personal pronouns agree with their antecedents in number is usually a problem only when the antecedent is a compound.

▶ KEY CONCEPT Use a singular personal pronoun with two or more singular antecedents joined by *or* or *nor*. ■

EXAMPLE: Neither *Tim* nor *Ike* liked *his* flight to India.

Theme: India

In this section, you will learn about pronoun and antecedent agreement. The examples and exercises in this section are about the culture and history of India.

Cross-Curricular Connection: Social Studies

▼ Critical Viewing The Taj Mahal was built by Shah Jahan as a mausoleum for his favorite wife. Write two sentences describing the Taj Mahal. Make sure that your personal pronouns agree with their antecedents. **[Describe]**

Pronoun and Antecedent Agreement • **577**

PREPARE and ENGAGE

☼ Interest GRABBER Ask students whether these sentences make sense. Have them suggest corrections:

The girl's brother is taller than he is.
The boy's uncles are known for his generosity.
Carl is going to Brazil, where you will hear Portuguese spoken.

Help students recognize the literal meanings of these sentences. (The brother is taller than himself, the uncles are known for the boy's generosity, and you will hear Portuguese when Carl goes to Brazil).

Activate Prior Knowledge

Ask students to offer descriptions or facts about a place they have visited or read about. Write some of the sentences containing pronouns and antecedents on the chalkboard. Ask students to point out all the pronouns on the chalkboard and the word each pronoun is referring to.

TEACH

Step-by-Step Teaching Guide

Agreement Between Personal Pronouns and Antecedents

1. Explain that number (singular or plural), gender (masculine, feminine, or neuter), and person (first, second, or third) are the three variables in pronoun-antecedent agreement.

2. Look at the first example. Be sure students understand that *his* agrees with its antecedent, *Byron*, in number, gender, and person.

3. Explain that just as in subject-verb agreement, when the coordinating conjunctions *or* or *nor* connect two singular antecedents, a singular pronoun is required.

continued

Critical Viewing

Describe Sample response: The Taj Majal is a beautiful, exotic building. Shah Jahan must have loved his wife very much to build it for her.

Agreement Between Personal Pronouns and Antecedents

continued

4. Explain that the coordinating conjunction *and* produces a plural that requires a plural pronoun.

5. Explain that in the second key concept the word *shift* refers to an incorrect change in either gender or number that occurs between the antecedent and the pronoun.

Customize for
ESL Students

Explain that certain nouns in English are masculine or feminine only when they specifically refer to either males or females. This is unlike a language such as Spanish or French, in which nouns that are neuter in English, like *book* or *window*, are masculine or feminine. Ask students to think of as many masculine and feminine nouns in English as they can. Then give them a list like the *bride's dress, a letter from Anna, the son's book*, and ask them to fill in the correct pronoun for each noun (*her dress, a letter from her, his book*).

Language Highlight

While it is acceptable to use the generic masculine pronoun to replace nouns of unspecific gender, writers often choose to reword their sentences. Explain that one solution is to use a *he or she* construction; another is to rephrase the item to make it plural.

Answer Key

> **Exercise 16**

1. their / 2. her / 3. its / 4. her / 5. their

24.2

> **KEY CONCEPT** Use a plural personal pronoun with two or more antecedents joined by *and*. ∎

EXAMPLE: *Darlene and Carol* liked *their* flights to India.

Agreement in Person and Number A personal pronoun and its antecedent will not agree if there is a shift in either person or number in the second part of the sentence.

> **KEY CONCEPT** When dealing with pronoun-antecedent agreement, take care not to shift either person or gender. ∎

SHIFT IN PERSON:	*Michelle* is studying Hindi, a language *you* will find useful while living in India.
CORRECT:	*Michelle* is studying Hindi, a language *she* will find useful while living in India.
SHIFT IN NUMBER:	Either *Tim* or *Ed* brought *their* map.
CORRECT:	Either *Tim* or *Ed* brought *his* map.

Note About *Generic Masculine Pronouns:* Historically, a masculine pronoun (*he, his, him, himself*) has been used to refer to a singular antecedent whose gender is not specified. Today, however, many writers prefer to use both the masculine and feminine pronouns (*he or she, him or her, his or her, himself or herself*) instead of the generic masculine form. When using two pronouns becomes awkward, rewrite the sentence.

> **KEY CONCEPT** When gender is not specified, use both the masculine and the feminine pronouns or rewrite the sentence. ∎

EXAMPLES: A *guest* might thank *his or her* host with a gift.
Guests might thank *their* host with a gift.

> **Exercise 16** Supplying Personal Pronouns to Agree With Their Antecedents Choose the correct pronoun in each sentence.

EXAMPLE: Visitors to India need ___?___ passports.
ANSWER: their

1. Marge and Susan took ___?___ vacation in India last month.
2. Marge decided to spend ___?___ time touring Agra.
3. The Taj Mahal is well known for ___?___ beauty.
4. Neither Marge nor Susan forgot ___?___ camera.
5. Susan told me that both of them missed ___?___ families.

Interactive Textbook

Get instant feedback! Exercises 16 and 17 are available on-line or on CD-ROM.

> **More Practice**

Grammar Exercise Workbook
• pp. 139–140
On-line Exercise Bank
• Section 24.2
Go on-line:
PHSchool.com
Enter Web Code:
eek-1002

☑ ONGOING ASSESSMENT: Monitor and Reinforce

If students miss more than one item in Exercise 16, refer them to the following for additional practice.

In the Textbook	Print Resources	Technology
Section Review, Ex. 21, Section 24.2	*Grammar Exercise Workbook,* pp. 139–140	*On-Line Exercise Bank,* Section 24.2

Agreement With Indefinite Pronouns

When you write a sentence with a personal pronoun that has an indefinite pronoun as its antecedent, make sure that the two pronouns agree. (See page 572 for indefinite pronouns.)

▶ **KEY CONCEPTS** Use a singular personal pronoun when the antecedent is a singular indefinite pronoun. Use a plural personal pronoun when the antecedent is a plural indefinite pronoun. ■

SINGULAR: *One* of the men rode *his* elephant.
PLURAL: *All* of the men rode *their* elephants.

With an indefinite pronoun that can be either singular or plural, agreement depends on the word to which the indefinite pronoun refers. In the first example below, the pronoun *some* refers to the singular noun *village*. In the second example, *some* refers to the plural noun *villagers*.

EXAMPLES: *Some* of the village had lost *its* charm.
              Some of the villagers expressed *their* displeasure.

▶ **Exercise 17** Making Personal Pronouns Agree With Indefinite Pronouns Choose the correct pronoun in each sentence.

1. Many visitors to India begin (his, their) vacations in Bombay.
2. All of the students enjoyed (his or her, their) visit to that city.
3. One of Bombay's best features is (its, their) pleasant climate.
4. Some of the city's appeal is (its, their) blend of old and new.
5. Both students knew (his, their) trip would be great.
6. Neither of them had developed (his or her, their) photographs of the city.
7. One of the girls finally let me see (her, their) pictures.
8. Every Indian city has (its, their) own charm.
9. Both Bombay and New Delhi face challenges because of (its, their) large populations.
10. However, either Bombay or New Delhi will delight and surprise (its, their) visitors.

▼ **Critical Viewing**
Write a sentence about this picture using this phrase: *Neither the boy nor his elephant . . .*
[Infer]

Pronoun and Antecedent Agreement • **579**

Agreement With Indefinite Pronouns

1. Explain to students that indefinite pronouns (pronouns used to refer to persons, places, or things, often without specifying which ones) can serve as antecedents of personal pronouns.

2. Have students read the key concept. Be sure they understand that indefinite and personal pronouns must agree in number. Therefore, it is important to determine whether the indefinite pronoun is singular or plural.

3. Use the examples to demonstrate how the indefinite pronoun *some* is singular or plural depending on the word to which it refers.

Integrating Vocabulary Skills

Collective Nouns Help students become comfortable using collective nouns as subjects and as antecedents. Give students the following collective nouns and ask them to use each in original sentences, once using the collective noun as a singular subject and once as a plural subject:

| jury | troop | flock |

Then, have students expand their sentences so that they use a pronoun to rename the collective noun within the same sentence. Be sure they follow all the correct rules of subject-verb and pronoun-antecedent agreement.

Critical Viewing

Infer Sample response: Neither the boy nor his elephant seems out of place.

Answer Key

▶ **Exercise 17**

1. their
2. their
3. its
4. its
5. their
6. his or her
7. her
8. its
9. their
10. its

☑ **ONGOING ASSESSMENT: Monitor and Reinforce**

If students miss more than two items in Exercise 17, refer them to the following for additional practice.

In the Textbook	Print Resources	Technology
Section Review, Ex. 21, Section 24.2	*Grammar Exercise Workbook,* pp. 141–142	*On-Line Exercise Bank,* Section 24.2

Using Reflexive Pronouns

1. Have students explain the function of *reflexive pronouns* (used to add information to a sentence by pointing to a noun or pronoun usually near the beginning of a sentence).

2. Use the examples so that students become familiar with correct and incorrect uses of reflexive pronouns. Be sure they are able to locate the antecedent.

3. Explain that reflexive pronouns should not be used to replace personal pronouns and that people frequently misuse *myself* when they mean *I* or *me.* Tell students that a reflexive pronoun should never be the subject of a sentence, even in a compound.

Answer Key

> **Exercise 18**

1. I (replaces *myself*)
2. he (replaces *himself*)
3. I (replaces *myself*)
4. correct
5. us (replaces *ourselves*)

Four Special Problems in Pronoun Agreement

1. Explain to students that an unclear antecedent can cause confusion in sentences.

2. Once students read the key concept, ask them to identify the pronoun that is unclear (*they*) and then ask who this pronoun refers to (its antecedent is not stated). Ask students to think of another pronoun that might be used vaguely, as in this example:

   When we first saw the Rocky Mountains, you can't believe how majestic they seemed!

3. Point out that pronouns such as *you* often invite unclear references. These should be eliminated or else their antecedents added.

continued

24.2

Using Reflexive Pronouns

Reflexive pronouns end in *-self* or *-selves* and refer to an antecedent earlier in the sentence.

> **KEY CONCEPT** A reflexive pronoun must agree with an antecedent that is clearly stated. ■

POOR: The tour guide brought the good news to Peter and *myself.*

CORRECT: The tour guide brought the good news to Peter and *me.*

> **Exercise 18** Correcting Misuse of Reflexive Pronouns
Correct the sentences that misuse reflexive pronouns. If a sentence contains no error, write *correct.*
1. Karen and myself studied India in our social studies class.
2. Tom said that Paula and himself had learned about India.
3. It was Billy and myself who remembered that Gandhi was assassinated in 1948.
4. During the fight for independence, Gandhi wore simple garments he had spun himself.
5. The results were a surprise to the teachers and ourselves.

Four Special Problems in Pronoun Agreement

When you use personal pronouns, make sure that they have antecedents that are clearly defined. Problems can occur when the antecedent is unstated or unclear or when the personal pronoun refers to the wrong antecedent.

> **KEY CONCEPT** A pronoun must agree with an antecedent that is either clearly stated or clearly understood. ■

VAGUE: The *movie* about India was disappointing because *they* never made the characters seem realistic.

CLEAR: The *movie* about India was disappointing because *it* never made the characters seem realistic.

CLEAR: The movie about India was disappointing because *the director* never made the characters seem realistic.

In the preceding example, the meaning of the sentence is vague because there is no antecedent for the pronoun *they.* The sentence can be made clear by replacing *they* with a personal pronoun or a noun that agrees with the antecedent *movie.*

580 • Agreement

> **More Practice**

Grammar Exercise Workbook
• pp. 141–142
On-line Exercise Bank
• Section 24.2
Go on-line:
PHSchool.com
Enter Web Code:
eek-1002

Get instant feedback! Exercise 18 is available on-line or on CD-ROM.

☑ **ONGOING ASSESSMENT: Monitor and Reinforce**

If students miss more than one items in Exercise 18, refer them to the following for additional practice.

In the Textbook	Print Resources	Technology
Section Review, Ex. 22, Section 24.2	*Grammar Exercise Workbook,* pp. 141–142	*On-Line Exercise Bank,* Section 24.2

> **KEY CONCEPT** A personal pronoun should always refer to a single, obvious antecedent. ■

AMBIGUOUS: I put a postcard in the book, but I lost *it*.

CLEAR: I put a postcard in the book, but I lost the book.
I can't find the postcard that I put in the book.

In the first example, the pronoun *it* is ambiguous because *it* can refer to either *postcard* or *book*.

> **KEY CONCEPT** A personal pronoun should always be close enough to its antecedent to prevent confusion. ■

DISTANT: Charlie asked Ralph questions about the map of India. Ralph tried to help, but, even more confused, he asked the teacher.

CLEAR: Charlie asked Ralph questions about the map of India. Ralph tried to help him, but, even more confused, Charlie asked the teacher.

In the example above, the pronoun *he* is too far from its antecedent, *Charlie*. The passage is much clearer if the word *Charlie* is repeated. You could also reword the passage to move the pronoun closer to its antecedent.

> **KEY CONCEPT** Use the personal pronoun *you* only when the reference is truly to the reader or the listener. ■

INCORRECT: During colonial rule in India, you weren't allowed the same privileges as many British citizens.

CORRECT: During colonial rule in India, Indian citizens weren't allowed the same privileges as many British citizens.

▲ **Critical Viewing**
Write two or three sentences describing some of the carving on this tenth-century Indian temple. Use *they* and *it* in your sentences and make sure that the antecedents are clear. **[Describe]**

Pronoun and Antecedent Agreement • 581

4. Read the ambiguous examples aloud and ask students to identify what the pronoun *it* refers to (either the *postcard* or the *book*). Ask students to explain how each "clear" example is better.

5. Another problem occurs when a pronoun is written too far from its antecedent, allowing some other word to appear to be the intended antecedent. Have students read the examples and explain why the pronoun *he* is not used effectively.

6. Point out that the personal pronoun *you* is frequently misused. Have students read the incorrect example. Explain that the phrase *you weren't* could also be replaced by *one wasn't* if a singular correction was necessary.

Integrating Workplace Skills

Travel Guides Pronouns may be found in descriptive writing like that used in travelogues. Have students write articles for travel magazines designed to attract tourists to a particular destination. Ask them to include nouns relating language, climate, local customs, and places of interest, as well as hints for the potential tourist, and then to use pronouns to rename the nouns.

Real-World Connection

In the real world, clarity in agreement is essential for such tasks as filling out accident reports or personal statements on job applications. Discuss how writing personal statements in the first person eliminates some of the variables for pronoun and antecedent agreement.

Critical Viewing

Describe Sample response: The intricate carvings on this temple make <u>it</u> look very exotic. The carvings are in stone and <u>they</u> appear very realistic.

🖊 STANDARDIZED TEST PREPARATION WORKSHOP

Grammar and Usage Many standardized tests require students to correct errors in a passage. Use the following to demonstrate.

Movies such as Serpico *and* The Godfather *continue to be cited by students of the medium. Many <u>consider it to be the best film ever made.</u>*

What is the correct way to write the underlined portion?

A Correct as is
B consider this movie to be the best film they ever made
C consider them to be the best film ever made.
D consider *The Godfather* to be the best film ever made.

The correct answer is **D**. The pronoun *it* was written with an unclear antecedent (*Serpico* or *The Godfather*). The pronoun must be replaced with one of the movies to make the reference clear.

Answer Key

24.2

Exercise 19 Recognizing Proper Usage

Identify the sentence in each pair that better follows the conventions of English usage of pronouns. Explain your choices.

1. (A) The film we watched about India was informative because it explained Hinduism, Buddhism, Islam, and other religions.
   (B) The film we watched about India was informative because they explained Hinduism, Buddhism, Islam, and other religions.
2. (A) The next time it is shown, you should see it.
   (B) The next time they show it, you should see it.
3. (A) India has one of the largest Muslim populations in the world, even though they are a minority in it.
   (B) India has one of the largest Muslim populations in the world, even though Muslims are a minority there.
4. (A) Jane told Andrea that Indonesia has the largest Muslim population in the world, but Andrea wanted to confirm the information.
   (B) Jane told Andrea that Indonesia has the largest Muslim population in the world, but Andrea wanted to confirm it.
5. (A) Each of the students completed their assignment on the culture of India.
   (B) Each of the students completed his or her assignment on the culture of India.

Exercise 20 Correcting Special Problems in Pronoun Agreement

Revise the following paragraph, correcting all errors in pronoun and antecedent agreement.

Mohandas K. Gandhi led Indians to independence from British rule. It made him famous. He promoted passive resistance, which you can use to change society. Sit-ins and boycotts are often involved in it. Gandhi was soon joined in his struggle by Jawaharlal Nehru. He was a much younger man. Gandhi taught passive resistance; he believed it would win them their freedom. When Gandhi became the leader of the Indian National Congress, he persuaded them that they needed to adopt his plan. Under this plan, one way you resisted British rule was by not paying your taxes. They also did not attend British schools or courts. Many of them gave up good jobs because they had to deal with the British. Gandhi and his followers believed passionately in the movement for independence, and they achieved it—especially when millions of Indians had joined it.

More Practice

Grammar Exercise Workbook
• pp. 143–144
On-line Exercise Bank
• Section 24.2
Go on-line:
PHSchool.com
Enter Web Code:
eek-1002

interactive Textbook

Complete the exercises on-line! Exercises 19 and 20 are available on-line or on CD-ROM.

✓ ONGOING ASSESSMENT: Monitor and Reinforce

If students have difficulty with Exercise 19 or 20, refer them to the following for additional practice.

In the Textbook	Print Resources	Technology
Section Review, Ex. 23, Section 24.2	*Grammar Exercise Workbook,* pp. 143–144	*On-Line Exercise Bank,* Section 24.2

Section 24.2 Section Review

GRAMMAR EXERCISES 21–26

Exercise 21 Supplying Personal Pronouns That Agree With Their Antecedents Use an appropriate personal pronoun to complete each sentence.

1. We heard the ancient story of Rama from ___?___ Indian friend Ved.
2. Rama was loved by the people of the kingdom for ___?___ kind nature.
3. Sadly, Dasrath, Rama's father, had to send ___?___ son into exile.
4. While in exile, Rama worried about ___?___ wife Sitia.
5. Hanuman, a flying monkey general, found Sitia and told ___?___ that help was on the way.
6. Each region of India has ___?___ own fashions.
7. Some Indian women like colorful skirts that swirl as ___?___ walk.
8. An Indian may wear ___?___ traditional clothes every day.
9. Most women in India wear ___?___ saris every day.
10. Red is the color of joy and celebration, so brides usually wear ___?___.

Exercise 22 Using Reflexive Pronouns Correctly Rewrite each sentence, correcting the misused reflexive pronouns. If a sentence contains no error, write *correct*.

1. Ms. Shinh prepared ourselves and her other class to study Indian history.
2. Andy and myself reviewed the notes about the Indus valley.
3. Neither Anna nor Liz gave herself enough time to study.
4. This book on Sanskrit, India's ancient language, is meant for myself, not John.
5. Manita told the class that her sister and herself had come from New Delhi.

Exercise 23 Revising to Eliminate Errors in Pronoun Agreement Rewrite these sentences, correcting any vague pronoun-antecedent agreement.

1. During the 1700's, the British came to India to trade with the Indians, but they ended up ruling them.
2. The British built a railway system in India that linked parts of it.
3. The British told the Indians that the improvements were important to them.
4. In 1947, after years of protest, they finally won their freedom from them.
5. In 1950, India became a republic with a constitution; it is still in force.

Exercise 24 Find It in Your Reading Read this excerpt from Rabindranath Tagore's "The Cabuliwallah"; then, list each pronoun and its antecedent. List the narrator as the antecedent of "I."

I cannot tell what my daughter's feelings were at the sight of this man, but she began to call him loudly. Ah, I thought, he will come in, and my seventeenth chapter will never be finished!

Exercise 25 Find It in Your Writing Review a piece of your writing, and be sure that all the personal pronouns have clear antecedents. If you find pronouns with vague or missing antecedents, make the necessary revisions.

Exercise 26 Writing Application Write five sentences about a country you have studied. Include at least five pronouns, and provide clear antecedents.

Section Review • 583

☑ **ONGOING ASSESSMENT: Assess Mastery**

Use the following resources to assess student mastery of pronoun-antecedent agreement.

In the Textbook	Technology
Chapter Review, Ex. 30–31	*Writing and Grammar* Interactive Text, Section 24.2, Section Review; *On-Line Exercise Bank*, Section 24.2

CHAPTER REVIEW

Each of these exercises correlates to a section of the chapter on agreement, pages 566–583. The exercises may be used for more practice, for reteaching, or for review of the key concepts presented.

Answer Key

Exercise 27

1. command
2. is
3. is
4. are
5. are

Exercise 28

1. does
2. are
3. drops
4. are
5. is
6. have
7. works
8. there're
9. wants
10. are

Exercise 29

1. live
2. is
3. live
4. illustrates
5. is
6. are
7. are
8. is
9. come
10. keeps

Exercise 30

1. his
2. they
3. her
4. his
5. its
6. he; his
7. their
8. their, them
9. her
10. his or her

584

Chapter 24 Chapter Review

GRAMMAR EXERCISES 27–33

Exercise 27 **Making Separated Subjects and Verbs Agree** Choose the verb in parentheses that agrees with the subject of each sentence.

1. Old people in India (commands, command) great respect.
2. White hair on old people (is, are) considered a sign of age and wisdom.
3. Each of the children (is, are) taught from a young age to respect their elders.
4. Often, children from a middle-class or wealthy home (is, are) spoiled for as long as possible.
5. Younger siblings in a large family (is, are) watched by older brothers or sisters.

Exercise 28 **Making Verbs Agree With Their Subjects** Choose the verb in parentheses that agrees with the subject of each sentence.

1. Hustle and bustle (does, do) not always rule an Indian's life.
2. Leisure time and entertaining (is, are) important, too.
3. Often, family members or a friend (drops, drop) by unexpectedly for a visit.
4. Neither food nor beverages (is, are) denied those who arrive.
5. Either a homemade sweet or a spicy treat (is, are) customarily offered.
6. Only about half of India's villages (has, have) electricity.
7. Anyone living in one of these villages (works, work) hard for a living.
8. (There's, There're) farmers who use oxen to plow their fields.
9. Although almost every one of the village farmers (wants, want) a tractor, many cannot afford one.
10. Both the practicing of old traditions

and an attention to the daily routine (is, are) a part of village life.

Exercise 29 **Revising Sentences to Eliminate Errors in Subject-Verb Agreement** Rewrite each sentence to correct errors in subject-verb agreement.

1. More than one billion people lives in India.
2. A popular image of India are its bustling cities.
3. However, the majority of Indians lives away from urban centers.
4. Ilay Cooper's *Arts and Crafts of India* illustrate a number of traditional works from the countryside.
5. The slopes of a hill or the bottom of a valley are home to many villagers.
6. Both warmth and affection is shown to dear friends.
7. Indians believe that simplicity and modesty is admirable qualities in a person.
8. Great wealth or intelligence are not a reason to boast.
9. Offering help and giving support to someone in need comes naturally to most Indians.
10. Neither monsoon rains nor a light shower keep Indians from celebrating independence day on August 15.

Exercise 30 **Making Personal Pronouns Agree With Their Antecedents** Write an appropriate personal pronoun to complete each sentence.

1. My uncle wrote to me about ___?___ visit to India.
2. He met an Indian family, and ___?___ invited him to dinner.
3. The wife made ___?___ own fresh bread, called *naan*.

4. The husband said that ___?___ wife's *naan* was the best.
5. She also served *laddoo*, a sweet that gets ___?___ flavor from cardamom seeds.
6. My uncle said that on entering most Indian homes, ___?___ had to take off ___?___ shoes.
7. He also learned that in traditional families, parents arrange ___?___ children's marriages.
8. Young people count on ___?___ parents to make a good match for ___?___.
9. When a woman gets married, she may go to live with ___?___ husband's family.
10. My uncle noticed that an Indian child is respectful toward ___?___ parents.

Exercise 31 Revising to Eliminate Errors in Agreement Rewrite each sentence, making the change indicated in parentheses and adjusting other parts of the sentence as necessary to maintain agreement.

1. All Indian students are taught to respect their teachers. (Change "All Indian students" to "Each Indian student.")
2. Every student rises when his or her teacher walks into the room. (Change "his or her" to "their.")
3. Most city schools require their students to wear uniforms. (Change "require" to "requires.")
4. Few children dare to misbehave in school. (Change "Few children" to "Almost no child.")
5. One of the boys had to have his parents meet with the teacher. (Change "One" to "Two.")
6. Nearly all students want to have their parents send them to school. (Change "Nearly all students" to "Nearly every student.")
7. Some of the girls have to care for their younger brothers. (Change "have" to "has.")

8. Many schools teach their students three languages: English, Hindi, and a regional language. (Change "Many schools" to "Almost every school.")
9. Each student spends many hours at his or her studies. (Change "Each student" to "We.")
10. I am going to enjoy my Hindi class next year. (Change "I" to "You.")

Exercise 32 Writing Application In approximately ten sentences, write a dialogue among three people discussing their first day in a new school. Use both nouns and pronouns to clarify who says what to whom, and underline every pronoun and its antecedent. In addition, underline every subject and verb. Be sure that all agree.

Exercise 33 CUMULATIVE REVIEW Verb Usage, Pronoun Usage, and Agreement Rewrite the following paragraph, correcting errors in verb and pronoun usage and subject-verb and pronoun-antecedent agreement.

How many of you has read Tagore's story "The Cabuliwallah"? It took place in Calcutta, India, where you will find many interesting stories. It was about a young girl who makes friends with a man much older than her. He is a peddler who comes to their house. The girl was Mini, and the man is Rahmun, and the friendship between her and him lasts just a short time. Mini and her father found that Rahmun is a person who they like. Each of his quaint jokes amuse them. However, one day Rahmun will have been arrested, and they send him away. At the time of his' return eight years later, he has been almost forgotten by Mini's father and herself.

Answers may vary; samples are given.
1. Each Indian student is taught to respect his or her teachers.
2. Students rise when their teacher walks into the room.
3. A city school requires its students to wear uniforms.
4. Almost no child dares to misbehave in school.
5. Two of the boys had to have their parents meet with the teacher.
6. Nearly every student wants to have his or her parents send him or her to school.
7. One of the girls has to care for her younger brother.
8. Almost every school teaches its students three languages. . . .
9. We students spend many hours at our studies.
10. You are going to enjoy your Hindi class next year.

Writing Application
Have students work in groups of three. When they are finished, ask each group to perform its dialogue for the class.

Cumulative Review
Answers may vary; a sample is given.

How many of you <u>have</u> read Tagore's story "The Cabuliwallah"? It <u>takes</u> place in Calcutta, India, where <u>one</u> can find many interesting stories. <u>The story is</u> about a young girl who makes friends with a man much older than <u>she</u>. He is a peddler who comes to <u>her</u> house. The friendship between <u>the girl</u>, Mini, and <u>the man</u>, Rahmun, lasts just a short time. Mini and her father <u>find</u> that Rahmun is a person <u>whom</u> they like. Each of his quaint jokes <u>amuses</u> them. However, one day Rahmun <u>is</u> arrested, and <u>he is sent</u> away. At the time of <u>his</u> return eight years later, <u>Mini and her father have almost forgotten him</u>.

✓ **ONGOING ASSESSMENT: Assess Mastery**

Use the following resources to assess student mastery of agreement.

In the Textbook	Print Resources	Technology
Chapter Review, Ex. 27–33 Standardized Test Preparation Workshop	*Formal Assesment*, Ch. 24	*Writing and Grammar* Interactive Text, Ch. 24, Chapter Review; *On-Line Exercise Bank*, Sections 24.1–2

Lesson Objectives

1. To demonstrate control over grammatical elements such as subject-verb agreement
2. To recognize appropriate English usage within the context of a written passage

Step-by-Step Teaching Guide

Making Words Agree

Teaching Resources: Standardized Test Preparation Workbook, pp. 47–48

1. Review the Test Tip on this page and discuss the explanation for the answers in the Sample Test Item. Use the explanation to review the rules for agreement with singular and plural subjects.

2. Have students complete Practices 1 and 2 on page 587. You may wish to provide students with standardized test answer sheets to practice the mechanics of marking in answers.

3. When students have finished, analyze the answer choices, making sure that students understand why one is correct and the others are not.

Standardized Test Preparation Workshop

Making Words Agree

Your knowledge of the rules of subject and verb agreement is frequently tested on standardized tests. When checking a sentence for errors, first identify the subject. Next, identify the type of subject: singular, plural, or compound. Then, apply the rules of agreement to make sure that the verb in the sentence agrees with the subject.

The following questions will give you practice with different formats used for items that test knowledge of subject-verb agreement.

Sample Test Item	Answers and Explanations

Directions: Identify the underlined words and phrases in the following sentence that contain an error.
 	
Josh and his sisters remembers the words
    (A)   (B)   (C)
 	
to the song. No errors.
  (D)   (E)
	The correct answer is *B*. The compound subject of the sentence is *Josh and his sisters*. When singular and plural subjects are joined by *and*, the verb is plural. Therefore, *B*, *remembers*, the singular form of the verb, contains the error.

Choose the revised version of the following sentence that eliminates all errors in grammar, usage, and mechanics. Josh and his sisters remembers the words to the song. **A.** Josh, nor his sisters remembers the words to the song. **B.** Neither Josh and his sisters remember the words to the song. **C.** Neither Josh nor his sisters remember the words to the song. **D.** Either Josh or his sisters remember the words to the song.	The correct answer is *C*. The compound subject of the sentence is *neither Josh nor his sisters*. When singular and plural subjects are joined by *or* or *nor*, the verb must agree with the subject closest to it. In this case, the subject *sisters* is plural, so the plural verb *remember* should be used in the sentence.

✎ TEST-TAKING TIP

Remind students to find the subject first. If the parts of the subject name more than one thing, use a plural verb.

If the subject is difficult to locate, encourage students to mark out any prepositional phrases, since the object of a preposition cannot be the subject of the sentence. Eliminating possibilities that are certainly wrong makes the subject easier to recognize.

Answer Key

> **Practice 1**

1. B
2. C
3. B
4. E
5. C

> **Practice 2**

1. B
2. H

Customize for
Less Advanced Students

Use the sample test item to model how to approach subject-verb agreement questions. First, identify the subject of the sentence. For compound subjects, decide whether the conjunction makes the subject singular or plural. Then, make sure the verb matches the number of the subject.

> **Practice 1**   **Directions:** Identify which underlined words and phrases in each of the following sentences contains an error.

1 The days is becoming shorter as
    (A)   (B)
December approaches. No error
  (C)   (D)   (E)

2 The dog with the brown spots
    (A)   (B)
become nervous during a thunder
    (C)   (D)
storm. No error
      (E)

3 Grandpa play golf just like a pro.
    (A)   (B)   (C)   (D)
No error.
 (E)

4 Either Pamela or Sofia tallies the
    (A)   (B)   (C)
votes every week. No error.
  (D)   (E)

5 Jorge and Leora only speaks
   (A)   (B)   (C)
Spanish with their mother.
            (D)
No error.
 (E)

> **Practice 2**   **Directions:** Choose the revised version of each numbered sentence that eliminates all errors in grammar, usage, and mechanics.

1 As long as humans has walked the Earth, herbs have been used for both medicinal and healing purpose.

A As long as humans has walked the Earth, herbs have been used for both medicinal and healing purposes.

B As long as humans have walked the Earth, herbs have been used for both medicinal and healing purposes.

C As long as humans having walked the Earth, herbs having been used for both medicinal and healing purpose.

D As long as humans have walked the Earth, herbs has been used for both medicinal and healing purposes.

2 To this day, many medicines is derived from some type of plant. One of the most commonly used medicines, aspirin, originally come from white willow or willow bark.

F To this day, many medicines is derived from some type of plant. One of the most commonly used medicines, aspirin, originally comes from white willow or willow bark.

G To this day, many medicines are derived from some type of plant. One of the most commonly used medicines, aspirin, originally come from white willow or willow bark.

H To this day, many medicines are derived from some type of plant. One of the most commonly used medicines, aspirin, originally came from white willow or willow bark.

J To this day, many medicines is derived from some type of plant. One of the most commonly used medicines, aspirin, originally came from white willow or willow bark.

In-Depth Lesson Plan

	LESSON FOCUS	PRINT AND MEDIA RESOURCES
DAY 1	**Degrees of Comparison** Students learn and apply the three degrees of comparison using both regular and irregular forms. (pp. 588–595/H424–431)	*Writing and Grammar* Interactive Text, Section 25.1; *On-line Exercise Bank*, Section 25.1 **Teaching Resources** *Grammar Exercise Workbook*, pp. 125–128; *Grammar Exercises Answers on Transparencies*, Ch. 25
DAY 2	**Making Clear Comparisons** Students learn and make logical comparisons, understand absolute modifiers, and do the Hands-on Grammar activity. (pp. 596–601/H432–437)	*Writing and Grammar* Interactive Text, Section 25.2; *On-line Exercise Bank*, Section 25.2 **Teaching Resources** *Grammar Exercise Workbook*, pp. 129–134; *Hands-on Grammar Activity Book*, Ch. 25
DAY 3	**Review and Assess** Students review the chapter and demonstrate mastery of modifiers indicating comparisons. (pp. 602–603)	*Writing and Grammar* Interactive Text, Ch. 25, Chapter Review **Teaching Resources** *Formal Assessment*, Ch. 25

Accelerated Lesson Plan

	LESSON FOCUS	PRINT AND MEDIA RESOURCES
DAY 1	**Degrees of Comparison** Students learn and apply the three degrees of comparison using both regular and irregular forms. (pp. 588–595/H424–431)	*Writing and Grammar* Interactive Text, Section 25.1; *On-line Exercise Bank*, Section 25.1 **Teaching Resources** *Grammar Exercise Workbook*, pp. 125–128; *Grammar Exercises Answers on Transparencies*, Ch. 25
DAY 2	**Making Clear Comparisons; Review and Assess** Students learn and make logical comparisons, understand absolute modifiers, review the chapter, and demonstrate mastery of the concepts. (pp. 596–603/H432–437)	*Writing and Grammar* Interactive Text, Ch. 25, Section 25.2 through Chapter Review; *On-Line Exercise Bank*, Section 25.2 **Teaching Resources** *Grammar Exercise Workbook*, pp. 129–134; *Formal Assessment*, Ch. 25

Options for Adapting Lesson Plans

HOMEWORK

Have students complete any section of the chapter for homework.

FEATURES

Extend coverage with the Grammar in Literature feature (p. 594/H430) and the Standardized Test Preparation Workshop (p. 604).

TECHNOLOGY

Students can use *Writing and Grammar* Interactive Text to complete the exercises interactively on computer. They can complete additional exercises in the *On-line Exercise Bank:* The Auto Check feature will grade their work. Go On-line: PHSchool.com Use Web Code: eek-1002

Writing and Grammar Handbook Alignment

Page numbers in Step-by-Step Teaching Guides in this Teacher's Edition refer to pages from the full student text. Handbook page references, indicated with this icon Ⓗ, are provided in Time and Resource Manager boxes and at the bottom of each Teacher's Edition page.

INTEGRATED SKILLS COVERAGE

Grammar in Literature
SE p. 594/Ⓗ430

Writing
Find It in Your Writing SE pp. 600, 601/Ⓗ436, 437
Writing Application SE p. 601/Ⓗ437
Grammar and Style SE p. 591/Ⓗ427

Spelling Skills
SE pp. 592, 598; ATE p. 591/Ⓗ428, 434

Viewing and Representing
Critical Viewing SE pp. 588, 593, 594, 597, 598, 599/Ⓗ424, 429, 430, 433, 434, 435

Vocabulary Skills
ATE p. 598

Real-World Connection
ATE p. 599

Workplace Skills
ATE p. 597

ASSESSMENT SUPPORT

Standardized Test Preparation Workshop SE p. 604; ATE pp. 595, 600

Standardized Test Preparation Workbook, pp. 49–50

Formal Assessment, Ch. 25

MEETING INDIVIDUAL NEEDS

Less Advanced Students ATE pp. 588, 591, 605. See also Ongoing Assessments ATE pp. 588, 591, 592, 593, 594, 598, 599.

ESL Students ATE pp. 591, 593

Gifted and Talented Students ATE p. 593

BLOCK SCHEDULING

Pacing Suggestions
For 90-minute Blocks
• Administer the Diagnostic Test to students to determine instructional coverage.
• Have students complete the necessary exercises in class. Use the Hands-on Grammar activity to provide a change of pace.

Resources for Varying Instruction
• *Writing and Grammar* **Interactive Text** A 90-minute block provides an ideal opportunity for students to work on the computer.

Professional Development Support
• *How to Manage Instruction in the Block* This teaching resource provides management and activity suggestions.

MEDIA AND TECHNOLOGY

For the Student
• *Writing and Grammar* **Interactive Text,** Ch. 25
• *On-line Exercise Bank,* Sections 25.1–2

For the Teacher
• **Teacher EXPRESS** CD-ROM

WRITING AND GRAMMAR ON-LINE

Interactive Text (On-line or on CD-ROM)
• Easily navigable instruction with on-line supporting resources
• Self-scoring exercises and diagnostic tests

Companion Web Site PHSchool.com
• On-line Exercise Bank (use Web Code eek-1002)

See the Go On-line! **feature, SE p. iii.**

LITERATURE CONNECTIONS

Grammar In Literature selection from *Prentice Hall Literature, Penguin Edition,* Grade 10:

from *The American Idea,* Theodore H. White, SE p. 594/Ⓗ430

Lesson Objectives

1. To recognize and use the three degrees of comparison: positive, comparative, and superlative

2. To recognize and form comparative and superlative forms of regular and irregular adjectives and adverbs

3. To use comparative and superlative degrees correctly

4. To make logical comparisons using modifiers

5. To demonstrate control over grammatical elements

6. To analyze the characteristics of clearly written texts, including the pattern of organization, syntax, and word choice

Critical Viewing

Identify Possible answers: There are *more* stringed instruments than brass or woodwind. Stringed and percussion instruments are the *most* well represented types.

Chapter 25 Using Modifiers

Adjectives and adverbs are important parts of speech that help writers make their sentences livelier, clearer, and more interesting and complete. What modifiers could a writer use to describe the sound of an unusual stringed instrument such as a sitar, a lute, or a hurdy-gurdy? The different sounds of these instruments make their music unique and colorful. Similarly, a carefully chosen adjective or adverb often turns an ordinary sentence into a superior one.

Modifiers are also important because they are used to make comparisons. For instance, if you wanted to compare the wide range of instruments in the world, you might use various forms of adjectives and adverbs to show similarities and differences in their sizes, shapes, and sounds.

In the first section of this chapter, you will learn rules for writing the forms of adjectives and adverbs used to make comparisons. In the second section, you will learn how to avoid a number of common usage problems involving comparisons.

▲ **Critical Viewing** Compare the number of different types of musical instruments in the picture. Use the word *more* or *most* in your comparison. **[Identify]**

588 • Using Modifiers

✓ ONGOING ASSESSMENT: Diagnose					
If students miss more than one item in each category, direct them to the relevant pages of the text and assign exercises for practice and review.					
Using Modifiers	**Diagnostic Test Items**	**Teach**	**Practice**	**Section Reviews**	**Chapter Review**
Skill Check A					
Degrees of Comparison	A 1–5	p. 590/⊞426	Ex. 1	Ex. 6–7	Ex. 23
Skill Check B					
Comparative and Superlative Forms	B 6–10	p. 591/⊞427	Ex. 2–3	Ex. 8	Ex. 23–24

Diagnostic Test

Directions: Write all answers on a separate sheet of paper.

Skill Check A. Identify the degree of each underlined modifier as *positive, comparative,* or *superlative.*

1. The sitar is the <u>most prominent</u> musical instrument in India.
2. It is <u>more difficult</u> to play than a guitar.
3. The <u>earliest</u> sitars were crafted more than 800 years ago.
4. It may take twenty years of practice to become a <u>skillful</u> sitar player.
5. My neighbor plays the instrument <u>more competently</u> than I do.

Skill Check B. Write the comparative and superlative form of each modifier.

6. rhythmic
7. loud
8. classical
9. quietly
10. far

Skill Check C. Write the appropriate form of the underlined modifier to complete each sentence.

11. The lute is <u>more difficult</u> to play than the mandolin, but the sitar is the __?__ of all to play.
12. The musical traditions of northern and southern India contain <u>many</u> similarities but even __?__ differences.
13. In general, Western musicians have taken <u>little</u> interest in Indian music and even __?__ in Korean music.
14. The untrained musicians played <u>badly</u> in the morning and even __?__ in the afternoon when they were tired.
15. Some scales are <u>simple</u> to play, and this one is the __?__ of all.

Skill Check D. Write the appropriate comparative or superlative degree of the modifiers in parentheses.

16 A hurdy-gurdy produces a (strong) sound than a lute.
17. Compared to the hurdy-gurdy and the lute, a sitar has the (distinctive) sound.
18. This pumpkin must be (dry) before it can be used to make a sitar.
19. The sitar has the (many) frets of all stringed instruments.
20. Of Sandra, Jacques, and me, I handle the instrument the (confidently).

Skill Check E. Rewrite each sentence, correcting the unbalanced or illogical comparison.

21. Ensembles of classical musicians are more common in India than amateur musicians.
22. The sitar's chords are more varied than the tambura.
23. The Yugoslavian tambura has a longer neck than any lute.
24. It resembles an Indian instrument more than any stringed instrument from Eastern Europe.
25. The Turks introduced this instrument in Yugoslavia, Greece, and everywhere in Europe.

Using Modifiers • 589

Diagnostic Test

Each item in the diagnostic test corresponds with a concept covered in a specific section in the using modifiers chapter. This will enable you to tailor instruction to the particular needs of your students. See "Ongoing Assessment Diagnose" below for further details. Answers for the Diagnostic Test and all chapter exercises are available in *Grammar Exercises Answers on Transparencies* in your Teaching Resources.

Skill Check A

1. superlative
2. comparative
3. superlative
4. positive
5. comparative

Skill Check B

6. more rhythmic; most rhythmic
7. louder; loudest
8. more classical; most classical
9. more quietly; most quietly
10. farther, farthest

Skill Check C

11. most difficult
12. more
13. less
14. worse
15. simplest

Skill Check D

16. stronger
17. most distinctive
18. drier
19. most
20. most confidently

Skill Check E

21. than ensembles of amateur musicians
22. than the tambura's (*or* than those of the tambura)
23. than any other lute
24. than any other stringed instrument from Eastern Europe
25. and everywhere else in Europe

✓ ONGOING ASSESSMENT: Diagnose *continued*

Using Modifiers	Diagnostic Test Items	Teach	Practice	Section Reviews	Chapter Review
Skill Check C–D					
Regular and Irregular Comparative and Superlative Forms	C 11–15 D 16–20	pp. 592–594/ 🅷428–430	Ex. 4–5	Ex. 8–9	Ex. 23–25
Skill Check E					
Unbalanced and Illogical Comparisons	E 21–25	pp. 596–598/ 🅷432–434	Ex. 13–16	Ex. 17–19	Ex. 26–28
Cumulative Reviews and Applications				Ex. 10–12, 20–22	Ex. 29–30

Section 25.1 Degrees of Comparison

Most adjectives and adverbs have three forms, called *degrees,* that are used to modify and make comparisons.

Recognizing Degrees of Comparison

Each of the three degrees of comparison has a name: the *positive,* the *comparative,* and the *superlative.*

▶ **KEY CONCEPT** Most adjectives and adverbs have three different forms to show degrees of comparison—the *positive,* the *comparative,* and the *superlative.* ■

There are different ways to form the *comparative* and *superlative* degrees of adjectives and adverbs. Notice, for example, how the forms of the adjectives and adverbs in the following chart are changed to show the degrees of comparison.

DEGREES OF ADJECTIVES		
Positive	Comparative	Superlative
simple	simpler	simplest
impressive	more impressive	most impressive
good	better	best
DEGREES OF ADVERBS		
soon	sooner	soonest
impressively	more impressively	most impressively
well	better	best

▶ **Exercise 1** Recognizing Degrees of Comparison Identify the degree of each underlined modifier.

EXAMPLE: Josef is the <u>best</u> player in the orchestra.
ANSWER: superlative

1. The accordion is a <u>small</u>, hand-held instrument.
2. It resembles an <u>earlier</u> German instrument, the handaoline.
3. Cyril Demian invented an <u>early</u> accordion in 1829.
4. The <u>oldest</u> accordions had only ten melody buttons.
5. Modern accordions have <u>more</u> melody and bass buttons.
6. These enable it to produce the <u>widest</u> range of notes.
7. The piano accordion is the <u>most familiar</u> type of accordion.
8. <u>Pianolike</u> keys are on the right side of the instrument.
9. Many people like the accordion <u>better</u> than the concertina.
10. The concertina has been used <u>most often</u> in folk music.

590 • Using Modifiers

Regular Forms

Modifiers can be either regular or irregular, depending on how their comparative and superlative degrees are formed. Two rules govern the formation of regular modifiers. The first rule applies to modifiers with one or two syllables.

KEY CONCEPTS Use *-er* or *more* to form the comparative degree and *-est* or *most* to form the superlative degree of most one- and two-syllable modifiers. ■

The more common method for forming the comparative and superlative degrees of one- and two-syllable modifiers is to add *-er* and *-est* to the modifier rather than to use *more* and *most.*

EXAMPLES: loud   louder   loudest
             shiny   shinier   shiniest

More and *most* are used with one- and two-syllable modifiers when adding *-er* and *-est* would sound awkward.

EXAMPLES: famous   more famous   most famous

The comparative and superlative degrees of all adverbs that end in *-ly*, regardless of the number of syllables, are formed with *more* and *most.*

EXAMPLES: evenly   more evenly   most evenly

KEY CONCEPT Use *more* and *most* to form the comparative and superlative degrees of all modifiers with three or more syllables. ■

EXAMPLES: difficult   more difficult   most difficult

Note About Comparisons With *Less* and *Least:* *Less* and *least,* the opposite of *more* and *most,* are also used to form the comparative and superlative degrees of most modifiers.

EXAMPLES: tall   less tall   least tall
             hopeless   less hopeless   least hopeless
             ambitious   less ambitious   least ambitious

Exercise 2 Writing Sentences Using Degrees of Comparison Write sentences using the modifiers and degrees given below. Use *less* or *least* in one or more sentences.

1. charming (comparative)
2. funny (comparative)
3. bold (superlative)
4. beautifully (superlative)
5. educated (comparative)

⚙ Grammar and Style Tip

When choosing the degree of a modifier, be careful to avoid excessive exaggerations, which may hurt your writing. Try not to use a superlative modifier when all you really need is one in the comparative degree.

Degrees of Comparison • 591

Step-by-Step Teaching Guide

Regular Forms

1. Explain that students may hear *more* and *most* used with adjectives that generally take endings (that bell looks *more shiny* than this one). Such usages should be avoided in formal writing.

2. To give students more practice using *less* and *least,* have them combine the words with the other modifier examples on this page.

Integrating Spelling Skills

Degrees of Comparison List these situations in which a spelling change occurs when *-er* and *-est* are added:

one-syllable adjectives ending with a single consonant preceded by a single vowel: *fat, fatter, fattest*

adjectives ending in a consonant and *y: busy, busier, busiest*

Tell students to check a dictionary if they are unsure of any such spellings.

Customize for ESL Students

Students may not have a good enough sense of English sound to decide which two-syllable adjectives should take *more* and *most* and which should take endings. Encourage them to use the dictionary and to record their findings in a vocabulary or spelling notebook.

Answer Key

Exercise 2

Answers will vary; samples are given.

1. He is *less charming* than his brother.
2. Was my story *funnier* than hers?
3. The *boldest* candidate beat the other two in the election.
4. Which room in the house was designed *most beautifully?*
5. The *more educated* applicant of the two received the job.

☑ ONGOING ASSESSMENT: Monitor and Reinforce

If students have difficulty with Exercise 1 or 2, refer them to the following for additional practice.

In the Textbook	Print Resources	Technology
Section Review, Ex. 6–7, Section 25.1	*Grammar Exercise Workbook,* pp. 145–146	*On-Line Exercise Bank,* Section 25.1

> **Exercise 3** Supplying Comparative and Superlative Modifiers Write each sentence on your paper. Use the form that is specified in parentheses for the underlined modifier.

EXAMPLE: That is one of the <u>small</u> instruments I have ever seen. (superlative)

ANSWER: That is one of the smallest instruments I have ever seen.

1. Some types of bagpipes are <u>simple</u> than others. (comparative)
2. I learned that the Highland pipe can play <u>many</u> notes. (comparative)
3. The Irish *uilleann* pipe is the <u>complicated</u> version. (superlative)
4. As you may know, bagpipes are played <u>often</u> in Scotland (superlative)
5. Some Irish pipers play <u>expressively</u> than Scots pipers. (comparative)

Irregular Forms

The comparative and superlative degrees of a few commonly used adjectives and adverbs are formed in unpredictable ways.

> **KEY CONCEPT** The irregular comparative and superlative forms of certain adjectives and adverbs must be memorized. ■

Notice in the following chart that the form of some irregular modifiers differs only in the positive degree. The modifiers *bad, badly,* and *ill,* for example, all have the same comparative and superlative degrees (*worse, worst*).

IRREGULAR MODIFIERS		
Positive	**Comparative**	**Superlative**
bad	worse	worst
badly	worse	worst
far (distance)	farther	farthest
far (extent)	further	furthest
good	better	best
ill	worse	worst
late	later	last *or* latest
little (amount)	less	least
many	more	most
much	more	most
well	better	best

▶ **KEY CONCEPTS** *Bad* is an adjective. Do not use it to modify an action verb. *Badly* is an adverb. Do not use it after a linking verb. ■

INCORRECT: Keith plays the bassoon *bad*.

CORRECT: Keith plays the bassoon *badly*.

INCORRECT: Keith feels *badly*.

CORRECT: Keith feels *bad*.

Note About *Good* and *Well*: Like *bad*, *good* is an adjective and cannot be used as an adverb after an action verb. It can, however, be used as an adjective after a linking verb.

INCORRECT: Jennifer plays the oboe *good*.

CORRECT: This oboe seems *good*.

Well is generally an adverb. Like *badly*, it can be used after an action verb.

CORRECT: Jennifer plays the oboe *well*.

When *well* is used to mean "healthy," it is an adjective. Thus, *well* can also be used after a linking verb.

CORRECT: Jennifer should be *well* soon.

▶ **Exercise 4** **Forming Comparative and Superlative Degrees of Irregular Modifiers** Write the appropriate form of the underlined modifier to complete each sentence.

EXAMPLE: My singing is <u>bad</u> today, but it was ___?___ yesterday.

ANSWER: worse

1. Your voice sounds <u>good</u>, but a kazoo makes it sound ___?___.
2. I play it <u>better</u> when I hum, but you say it is ___?___ when you talk into the kazoo.
3. Kazoos are used <u>little</u> as a children's toy, ___?___ in blues music, and ___?___ in a classical orchestra.
4. Usually it sounds <u>much</u> like buzzing, but sometimes it sounds ___?___ like quacking.
5. My harmonica-playing sounds <u>bad</u> and my kazoo-playing sounds ___?___, but my zobo playing is certainly the ___?___.

▲ **Critical Viewing**
Compare this oboe to a flute in at least three different ways. Which modifiers would you use? **[Compare and Contrast]**

Degrees of Comparison • **593**

4. The word *good* is so commonly used in speech after action verbs that some students may be surprised to find out that this usage is incorrect. Emphasize that *good* should never follow an action verb in writing.

5. Ask why *Keith feels bad* is correct (*the word* bad *follows linking verbs*). Then, review the list of linking verbs that *good* and *bad* can correctly follow. Besides *feel*, these include verbs such as *seem, sound, taste,* and *smell*. Have students create sample sentences using these verbs with *good* and *bad*.

Customize for
Gifted and Talented Students

Depending on the context, both *feel well* and *feel good* are correct constructions. Have students use this information to create an amusing dialogue using *feels good, feels well,* and *feels bad* with various subjects.

Customize for
ESL Students

Many and *much* may be confusing because their comparative and superlative forms are the same. Explain that *many* is used with plural words designating things that can be counted: *many hours. Much* is used with quantities that can't be counted: *much time.* Have students tell which word should modify each of these: *money, dollars, coins, love.*

Critical Viewing

Compare and Contrast Students might think of words such as *larger, heavier,* and *more melancholy.*

Answer Key

▶ **Exercise 4**

1. better
2. best
3. less, least
4. more
5. worse, worst

☑ **ONGOING ASSESSMENT: Monitor and Reinforce**

If students have difficulty with Exercise 4 or 5, refer them to the following for additional practice.

In the Textbook	Print Resources	Technology
Section Review, Ex. 8–9, Section 25.1	*Grammar Exercise Workbook,* pp. 147–148	*On-Line Exercise Bank,* Section 25.1

Grammar in Literature

1. Have a volunteer read this passage aloud. Students should follow along, noting each highlighted modifier.

2. For the first modifier, ask its part of speech (adjective) and its degree (superlative). Then, ask for its other two degrees (*well, better*).

3. Repeat this procedure with the remaining modifier (*greatest*, adjective, superlative, *great, greater*).

More About the Writer

Theodore H. White (1915–1986) is viewed as one of the finest political reporters of the twentieth century. He studied Chinese history and Asian languages at Harvard University and then became *Time* magazine's correspondent in eastern Asia. He gained fame writing about the election of John F. Kennedy in *The Making of the President, 1960*.

Connections With Literature

Theodore H. White's *The American Idea* can be found in *Prentice Hall Literature, Penguin Edition*, Grade 10.

Answer Key

Exercise 5

Expect some variation in response.

1. best
2. more
3. least
4. farther
5. better
6. badly
7. less
8. more
9. well
10. least

Critical Viewing

Judge Students might mention its straight-edged shape, its small sound hole, and its thin neck.

25.1

GRAMMAR IN LITERATURE

from **The American Idea**
Theodore H. White

Note the regular modifier in blue and the irregular modifier in red in the following passage. Both are in the superlative degree.

By the time Jefferson drafted his call, men were in the field fighting for those new-learned freedoms, killing and being killed by English soldiers, the *best*-trained troops in the world, supplied by the world's *greatest* navy.

Exercise 5 Supplying Irregular Modifiers Write an appropriate degree of an irregular modifier to complete each sentence. Use the chart on page 592 if you need help.

EXAMPLE: Suffering from a throbbing headache, the musician is not feeling ___?___ today.

ANSWER: well

1. This store has the ___?___ selection of antique instruments in the state.
2. I have been able to find ___?___ nineteenth-century English woodwinds here than in a store in England.
3. The price I was quoted for a five-key clarinet was the ___?___ of all the stores I visited.
4. Even though I had to travel ___?___ to get here than to a local store, it was worth the trip.
5. This bassoon, made in 1880, has a ___?___ sound than a modern bassoon.
6. I wish that I did not play the bassoon so ___?___.
7. I have received ___?___ training on the instrument than my sister.
8. She has been taking lessons for ___?___ years than I.
9. She can play at least seven instruments very ___?___.
10. Yet she is not the ___?___ bit conceited.

More Practice

Grammar Exercise Workbook
• pp. 147–148
On-line Exercise Bank
• Section 25.1
Go on-line:
PHSchool.com
Enter Web Code:
eek-1002

▼ **Critical Viewing**
What qualities of this instrument make it seem older than a guitar? Use modifiers in your answers. **[Judge]**

☑ **ONGOING ASSESSMENT: Assess Mastery**

Use the following resources to assess student mastery of degrees of comparison.

In the Textbook	Technology
Chapter Review, Ex. 23–25	*Writing and Grammar* Interactive Text, Section 25.1, Section Review; *On-Line Exercise Bank*, Section 25.1

Section 25.1 *Section Review*

GRAMMAR EXERCISES 6–12

▶ **Exercise 6** Recognizing Modifiers
Underline the modifier in these phrases.

1. most common lyre
2. played more skillfully
3. larger instrument
4. earliest versions
5. more decorated style

▶ **Exercise 7** Recognizing Degrees of Comparison Identify the degree of each underlined modifier.

1. You will have a <u>better</u> understanding of the Chinese *qin* if you know about zithers.
2. Zithers are among the <u>most common</u> stringed instruments in the world.
3. The *qin*'s strings are stretched over a <u>curved</u> board.
4. It features several melody strings and even <u>more numerous</u> accompaniment strings.
5. The *qin* is <u>more traditional</u> in China than a lute or a fiddle.

▶ **Exercise 8** Forming the Comparative and Superlative Degrees
Rewrite the underlined modifier in the degree indicated in parentheses.

1. The stronger the vibrations of the player's lips, the <u>loud</u> the sound from a horn. (comparative)
2. The <u>simple</u> type of horn is made from an <u>animal</u> horn. (superlative)
3. These instruments are <u>commonly</u> used in religious rituals. (superlative)
4. Horns made from shells are <u>little</u> used as musical instruments. (comparative)
5. Adding finger holes on the side gives it a <u>wide</u> range of notes. (comparative)

▶ **Exercise 9** Revising to Eliminate Errors in Modifiers Revise this paragraph, eliminating errors in forms and degrees of modifiers.

The *sheng* is one of the more old Chinese instruments. It is more popularist in China. It has a low pitch than the *chi*. Chinese instruments are used often in religious ceremonies than on other occasions. Archaeological digs have unearthed some of the better musical artifacts ever found.

▶ **Exercise 10** Find It in Your Reading Identify the degree of the underlined modifiers in this passage from R. K. Narayan's "Like the Sun."

. . . He felt very <u>unhappy</u> that he could not speak <u>more soothingly</u>. Truth, he reflected, required as much strength to give as to receive.

▶ **Exercise 11** Find It in Your Writing Look through your writing portfolio for examples of sentences containing modifiers in the comparative or superlative degree. You might also rewrite some of your sentences that contain positive modifiers so that they express comparisons.

▶ **Exercise 12** Writing Application Write five sentences of your own using the modifier and degree given below.

1. deep (superlative)
2. talented (comparative)
3. musical (superlative)
4. well (positive)
5. highly (comparative)

Section Review • 595

✎ STANDARDIZED TEST PREPARATION WORKSHOP

Grammar and Usage Many standardized tests require students to recognize and solve common modifier problems. Use the following example to demonstrate.

Which sentence contains a modifier error?

A It was the bottom of the ninth inning, and the situation could not have been worser.

B The home team, which had the worst record in the league, was losing by four runs.

C There were only two players left who hadn't batted: one, a pitcher, had a batting average of .179; the other's average was worse, .015.

D The coach had a choice: Who would be a better clutch hitter?

The correct answer is **A**. *Worser* is a nonstandard form. To correct this error, use the word *worse*.

Interest GRABBER Draw on the board an outline of a huge bicycle and next to it a smaller stick figure of a girl. Under the drawings write, "Karen's bicycle was much bigger than Jo." Ask students what they think was really intended by this sentence (*that Karen's bicycle was much bigger than Jo's*), and have them reword the sentence appropriately.

Activate Prior Knowledge

Write these sentences on the board and have students explain what, if anything, is wrong with each one.

Her shoes fit more better than mine did. (double comparison: more better)

Jo has more books than any girl I know. (illogical comparison: Jo is a girl that I know.)

TEACH

Step-by-Step Teaching Guide

Using Comparative and Superlative Degrees

1. Tell students they will often hear incorrect uses of comparatives and superlatives in informal speech.

2. Present these sentences and have students point out the problem:

   Which did you like best, the book or the play? (best *should be* better)

   This is most definitely not my car. (Nothing is being compared.)

Answer Key

▶ Exercise 13

1. earliest   4. best
2. brighter   5. more
3. more difficult   comfortably

Section 25.2

Making Clear Comparisons

In this section, you will learn the correct uses of the comparative and superlative degrees. You will also learn how to change an illogical comparison into a logical comparison.

Using Comparative and Superlative Degrees

There are two simple rules that govern the use of the comparative and superlative degrees:

▶ KEY CONCEPTS Use the comparative degree to compare two people, places, or things. Use the superlative degree to compare three or more people, places, or things. ■

Notice in the examples below that specific numbers need not be mentioned. The context of the sentence indicates whether two or more than two things are being compared.

COMPARATIVE: Oil paintings are *more effective* than watercolors. My sketch is *more detailed* than his.

SUPERLATIVE: We bought the *most expensive* painting of all. This exhibit has the *largest* number of early works in the city.

Note About *Double Comparisons:* Do not add both *-er* and *more* or *-est* and *most* to a regular modifier. In addition, do not add any of these endings or words to an irregular modifier.

INCORRECT: That sailboat is *more faster* than the other. John's technique is *more better* than mine.

CORRECT: That sailboat is *faster* than the other. John's technique is *better* than mine.

▶ Exercise 13 Supplying the Comparative and Superlative Degrees Write the appropriate comparative or superlative degree of the modifier in parentheses.

EXAMPLE: Alfred is the (young) of all the students.
ANSWER: youngest

1. Mary Cassatt was one of the (early) American Impressionists.
2. She used (bright) colors than many of her contemporaries.
3. Her revolutionary style in an art world dominated by men made it (difficult) for her to get her work displayed.
4. Mary Cassatt's (good) works are of families, especially mothers and daughters.
5. She lived (comfortably) in France than in the United States.

Theme: The Art of Mary Cassatt

In this section, you will learn the correct uses of the comparative and superlative degrees of adjectives and adverbs. The examples and exercises in this section are about the art of American painter Mary Cassatt.

Cross-Curricular Connection: Art

Interactive Textbook

Get instant feedback! Exercise 13 is available on-line or on CD-ROM.

▶ More Practice

Grammar Exercise Workbook
• pp. 149–150
On-line Exercise Bank
• Section 25.2
Go on-line:
PHSchool.com
Enter Web Code:
eek-1002

⏱ TIME AND RESOURCE MANAGER

Resources
Print: *Grammar Exercise Workbook,* pp. 149–152; *Grammar Exercises Answers on Transparencies,* Ch. 25
Technology: *Writing and Grammar* Interactive Text, Section 25.2; *On-Line Exercise Bank,* Section 25.2

Using the Full Student Edition	Using the Handbook 🄷
• Work through all key concepts, pp. 596–598.	• Work through all key concepts, pp. 432–434.
• Assign and review Exercises 13–16.	• Assign and review Exercises 13–16.
• Do the Hands-on Grammar activity, p. 600.	• Do the Hands-on Grammar activity, p. 436.

Making Logical Comparisons

Some comparisons are illogical—they do not make good sense. In order to write logical comparisons, you must make sure you do not mistakenly compare two unrelated items and that you do not unintentionally compare something with itself.

Balanced Comparisons Sometimes, when you are in a hurry, you may compare two or more unrelated items. It is then necessary to rephrase the sentence so that the comparison is properly balanced.

▶ **KEY CONCEPT** Make sure that your sentences compare only items of a similar kind. ■

Because an unbalanced comparison is illogical, it may be unintentionally humorous. The way the examples below are written, the paintings of an artist are being compared not to paintings but to another artist.

UNBALANCED:	We prefer Auguste Renoir's paintings to Mary Cassatt.
CORRECT:	We prefer Auguste Renoir's paintings to Mary Cassatt's.
UNBALANCED:	Critics considered the *paintings of Mary Cassatt* to be more emotional than *James Whistler.*
CORRECT:	Critics considered the *paintings of Mary Cassatt* to be more emotional than *those of James Whistler.*

Child in a Straw Hat, Mary Cassatt

▶ **Critical Viewing** Write three statements about this painting that include the word *than*. **[Analyze]**

Making Clear Comparisons • 597

Step-by-Step Teaching Guide

Making Logical Comparisons

1. Explain to students that in most cases, unbalanced comparisons can be corrected in one of two ways: with a phrase such as *than that of* or *than those of,* or with a possessive.

2. Have students correct each example sentence on the page in the alternative way from what is shown. *(We prefer Auguste Renoir's paintings to those of Mary Cassatt; Critics considered the paintings of Mary Cassatt to be more emotional than James Whistler's).*

Integrating Workplace Skills

Radio Commentators Point out that radio sports announcers must rely on careful verbal descriptions to compensate for a lack of visual support. Explain that these announcers often use comparisons to make descriptions clear. Have students describe scenes from sporting events they have recently witnessed and compare events within the scene, using logical and balanced comparisons.

Critical Viewing

Analyze Possible responses: The little girl looks lonelier than a child should. The painting is more than a century old. Her hat seems larger than she needs.

ONGOING ASSESSMENT: Monitor and Reinforce

If students miss more than one item in Exercise 13, refer them to the following for additional practice.

In the Textbook	Print Resources	Technology
Section Review, Ex. 17–18, Section 25.2	*Grammar Exercise Workbook,* pp. 149–150	*On-Line Exercise Bank,* Section 25.2

Exercise 14

Allow some variation in response.

1. than her earlier color use
2. than those of her fellow painters
3. Seurat's
4. than her later paintings
5. than an Expressionist's
6. to that of a studio
7. than Picasso posed his
8. than by that of France
9. than America's
10. than that of Europeans

Critical Viewing

Compare Students might mention the colors and the presence of thoughtful young girls.

Step-by-Step Teaching Guide

Other and *Else* in Comparisons

1. Tell students that in deciding whether they need *other* or *else* in a comparison, they first need to determine whether the individual or item is part of the group it is being compared with. Present these examples:

   Ice skating is more enjoyable than any winter sport.

   Ben Franklin accomplished more in his life than any European.

2. Have students explain why the first example is incorrect and the second one is correct.

Integrating Vocabulary Skills

Compare, Contrast, Collate The word *compare* is similar in meaning to *contrast* and *collate;* however, these three words have slightly different connotations. *Compare* means to show the relative value of things by bringing out either similar or divergent qualities; *contrast* emphasizes the differences between or among things; *collate* implies very careful and minute examination to show points of agreement or divergence. Ask students to use each word in a sentence.

25.2

▶ **Exercise 14** **Making Balanced Comparisons** Rewrite each sentence, correcting the unbalanced comparison.

EXAMPLE: Cassatt's paintings were as detailed as Degas.
ANSWER: Cassatt's paintings were as detailed as Degas's.

1. Cassatt's later use of color was more vibrant than earlier.
2. Some of her works were more successful than her fellow painters.
3. Degas's friendship was more meaningful to her than Seurat.
4. Cassatt's earlier paintings were more relaxed than later.
5. An Impressionist's brush strokes are looser than an Expressionist.
6. Cassatt preferred outdoor light to a studio.
7. She posed her subjects more realistically than Picasso.
8. Her woodcuts were more influenced by Japanese art than France.
9. For Cassatt, Europe's artistic community was more accepting than America.
10. Americans' appreciation for modern art was less developed than Europeans.

***Other* and *Else* in Comparisons** An illogical comparison can also be caused by failing to use the words *other* or *else.*

▶ **KEY CONCEPT** When comparing one within a group to the rest of the group, make sure that your sentence contains the word *other* or the word *else.* ■

Adding *other* or *else* in this type of comparison will prevent comparing something with itself. For instance, because Monet was an Impressionist, he cannot be compared to all Impressionists. He must be compared to all *other* Impressionists. Similarly, since Elizabeth works in the studio, she cannot be compared to *anyone* in the studio; she must be compared to *anyone else.*

ILLOGICAL: Monet's paintings became *more popular than those of any* Impressionist.

LOGICAL: Monet's paintings became *more popular than those of any other* Impressionist.

ILLOGICAL: Elizabeth has worked in the art studio *longer than anyone.*

LOGICAL: Elizabeth has worked in the art studio *longer than anyone else.*

Ballerine, Edgar Degas

▲ **Critical Viewing** What similarities do you see between this painting by Edgar Degas and the one by Mary Cassatt on page 597? **[Compare]**

💡 **Spelling Tip**

When making comparisons, don't confuse the word *than* with the word *then. Then* is an adverb that shows time. *Than* is a conjunction that links items in a comparison.

✓ ONGOING ASSESSMENT: Monitor and Reinforce

If students have difficulty with Exercise 14, 15, or 16, refer them to the following for additional practice.

In the Textbook	Print Resources	Technology
Section Review, Ex. 19, Section 25.2	*Grammar Exercise Workbook,* pp. 151–152	*On-Line Exercise Bank,* Section 25.2

▶ **Exercise 15** Revising *Other* and *Else* in Comparisons
Revise each sentence, correcting the illogical comparison.

EXAMPLE: Richard is more talented than anyone in class.
ANSWER: Richard is more talented than anyone else in class.

1. Mary Cassatt produced more prints than any American artist of her time.
2. Her printmaking was more influenced by the art of Japan than that of any country.
3. When Cassatt and several artist friends attended an exhibition of Japanese prints in Paris, she was more impressed than anyone in the group.
4. Cassatt returned to the exhibit more often than anyone.
5. She began to concentrate on printmaking more than on any art form.

▶ **Exercise 16** Writing Clear Comparisons Rewrite each sentence on your paper, completing the comparison in a balanced and logical way.

EXAMPLE: Sherilyn's paintings of horses are more realistic than ___?___.
ANSWER: Sherilyn's paintings of horses are more realistic than Barry's.

1. For many people, yellow creates a happier feeling than any ___?___.
2. Many people prefer orange paint to blue because they feel orange is ___?___ than blue.
3. I have always considered green to be the ___?___ color of all.
4. Compared to green, black is a ___?___ and ___?___ color.
5. I believe purple is ___?___ than either red or blue.
6. I prefer the color ___?___ more than anyone ___?___ in ___?___.
7. The ___?___ color of all is ___?___.
8. If I were going to choose the ___?___ color of all for my room, it would be ___?___.
9. People who wear red clothes are ___?___ than people who wear black clothes.
10. I feel the ___?___ comfortable when I am wearing ___?___ clothes.

More Practice

Grammar Exercise Workbook
• pp. 150–151
On-line Exercise Bank
• Section 25.2
  Go on-line:
  PHSchool.com
  Enter Web Code:
  eek-1002

▼ **Critical Viewing**
Make some comparisons of yellow to other colors. Use *-er*, *more*, *-est*, or *most* in your comparisons.
[Compare and Contrast]

Making Clear Comparisons • 599

Answer Key

▶ **Exercise 15**

1. than any other American artist of her time
2. than that of any other country
3. than anyone else in the group
4. than anyone else
5. than on any other art form

▶ **Exercise 16**

The following are possible responses.

1. other color
2. bolder
3. prettiest
4. darker, more somber
5. richer
6. brown, else, my art class
7. most exciting, magenta
8. best, tan
9. more noticeable
10. most, colorful

Critical Viewing

Compare and Contrast Students will probably include terms such as *brighter, livelier,* and *more noticeable* in their comparisons.

Real-World Connection

In the art world, most works are judged through a process of comparison. Since artists incorporate earlier styles and techniques, their works are frequently compared to those which preceded them. For example, a critique of a painting includes close analysis and comparison of elements such as color, composition, brush strokes, texture, use of light, density of paint, subject matter, and patina. Discuss with students ways of comparing two paintings, using comparison phrases accurately and effectively.

⏱ **TIME SAVERS!**

🎞 **Answers on Transparencies**
Use the *Grammar Exercises Answers on Transparencies* for Chapter 25 to facilitate correction by students.

💻 **On-Line Exercise Bank**
Have students complete the exercises on computer. The Auto Check feature will grade their work for you!

Hands-on Grammar

Teaching Resources: Hands-on Grammar Activity Book, Ch. 25

1. If you do this activity in class, you may wish to supply students with scissors, markers, and colored paper.

2. Direct students' attention to the sample sentences near the bottom of this page. Ask them to explain why the word *other* is needed in "I like Miami better than any other city." (It shows that Miami is a city. The writer is comparing the city of Miami to other cities.)

3. Ask students whether or not *other* is needed in the following comparisons.

   > *Chris likes basketball better than any sport.* (*Other* is needed because basketball is a sport.)

   > *Chris likes basketball better than homework.* (*Other* is not needed.)

Find It in Your Reading

If the comparisons are incorrect, have students explain the error and then propose a way to fix it.

Find It in Your Writing

Have students exchange papers with partners to check for errors in comparisons.

Hands-on Grammar

Comparison Flip Test

Use a Comparison Flip Test to learn when the word *other* is needed to complete a comparison. First, print this partial sentence across the middle of a sheet of paper: *I like* [leave 1-1/2" space] *better than . . .*

Next, cut out six 3" squares, and draw a 1" x 1-1/2" rectangle in from the middle of the left edge. On each rectangle, print a different category with the word *any*. Examples: *any city, any food, any sport,* and so on. Around the rectangle, print five examples of the category— five cities, five foods, and so on. Then, cut out the rectangles, turn them over, and print *any other* plus the category. (See illustration.)

Now, cut out six 1-1/4" squares. On one side of each, print one example of one of the categories: *Miami, pizza,* and so on. On the other side, print something that is different from or opposite the category: *the country, plain water,* and so on. Then, do the flip test.

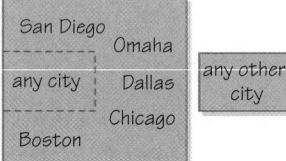

Place the 3" square at the end of your sentence, and fit the rectangle appropriate to the category in the cut-out section. Then, in the space between the words *I like* and *better than,* place the 1" square that corresponds to the category. If the item showing on the 1" square matches the category of items on the 3" square, you must flip the rectangle so that the *any other* side is facing up, because you are comparing something with others in the same category. If the item showing on the 1" square does not match the category, flip the rectangle so that the *any* side is facing up. Go on making comparisons by changing categories and flipping squares and rectangles to see when you need *any other* or when just *any* makes sense.

Find It in Your Reading Look in ads for "better than," "faster than," "more than," and so on, and see if the comparisons are correct.

Find It in Your Writing Review a piece of your writing to be sure your comparisons are logical and complete. Correct any that are not.

600 • Using Modifiers

✍ STANDARDIZED TEST PREPARATION WORKSHOP

Grammar and Usage Many standardized tests require students to recognize and solve common modifier problems. Use the following example to demonstrate.

Which sentence contains a modifier error?

A Dr. Jones is considered by his peers to be greater than any other heart surgeon.

B He has performed the most heart operations of anyone in the entire country.

C An operation involving the heart is more dangerous than tonsils.

D Many years of training are required to become the best, and Dr. Jones is the best.

The correct answer is **C**. This sentence is a poorly balanced comparison. Correct the error by balancing the comparison: *An operation involving the heart is more dangerous than one involving the tonsils.*

Section 25.2 Section Review

GRAMMAR EXERCISES 17–22

▶ **Exercise 17** Using Comparative and Superlative Forms Correctly Choose the correct comparative or superlative form in each sentence.

1. Which painter do you like (better, best), Degas or Renoir?
2. Of all Impressionist painters, I consider Pissaro the (more, most) interesting.
3. Renoir was a (more intense, more intenser) artist than many of his peers.
4. However, the scenes he painted are often the (more, most) cheerful of all.
5. Of Degas, Cassatt, and Renoir, Degas was the (older, oldest).
6. He was also the (more, most) original of the three.
7. Of his paintings of horses and ballerinas, which do you prefer (more, most)?
8. Cassatt painted (slower, more slower) than Degas.
9. Of the work of all Impressionists, her paintings seem (more, most) peaceful.
10. Cassatt's paintings are much admired, but her prints are even more (famous, famouser).

▶ **Exercise 18** Supplying Correct Degrees of Modifiers Write the appropriate comparative or superlative degree of the modifier in parentheses.

1. Renoir focused on light (well) than many of the other Impressionists.
2. He used light to make skin, fabrics, and textures the (brilliant) parts of his paintings.
3. Renoir earned (much) money by painting portraits than by any other means.
4. His subjects are the (expressive) of all the Impressionists.
5. Renoir suffered for many years from arthritis, and at the end of his life it grew even (bad).

▶ **Exercise 19** Revising to Clarify Comparisons Revise each sentence to correct unbalanced or illogical comparisons.

1. Degas's focus was more on people than Renoir.
2. The techniques he used in painting ballet dancers were more sophisticated than his fellow painters.
3. His sketches of horse racing came earlier than dancers.
4. Cassatt was friendlier with Degas than anyone in the Impressionist group.
5. Cassatt's paintings were more inventive than any woman painter of her time.

▶ **Exercise 20** Find It in Your Reading In this excerpt from "What Makes a Degas a Degas?" is the author using a comparative or superlative modifier? What is he comparing?

The results of Degas's experiments could have been executed much more quickly had he used pastels instead of oils. What Degas wanted, however, was to make paint look spontaneous.

▶ **Exercise 21** Find It in Your Writing Look through your portfolio for examples of comparisons. Check to see that your comparisons are clear and logical.

▶ **Exercise 22** Writing Application Write a comparison of the work of two painters, musicians, or actors. Make sure that you use comparative and superlative modifiers correctly and that your comparisons are clear.

ONGOING ASSESSMENT: Assess Mastery

Use the following resources to assess student mastery of modifier usage.

In the Textbook	Print Resources	Technology
Chapter Review, Ex. 23–28 Standardized Test Preparation Workshop	*Formal Assessment*, Ch. 25	*Writing and Grammar* Interactive Text, Section 25.2, Section Review; *On-Line Exercise Bank*, Section 25.2

ASSESS and CLOSE
Section Review

These exercises correlate to the instruction on clear comparisons, pages 596–600. The exercises may be used for more practice, for reteaching, or for review of the key concepts presented. Answers for all chapter exercises are available in *Grammar Exercises Answers on Transparencies* in your Teaching Resources.

Answer Key

▶ **Exercise 17**

1. better
2. most
3. more intense
4. most
5. oldest
6. most
7. more
8. slower
9. most
10. famous

▶ **Exercise 18**

1. better
2. most brilliant
3. more
4. most expressive
5. worse

▶ **Exercise 19**

Allow some variation in wording.

1. Renoir's
2. than those of his fellow painters
3. than his sketches of dancers
4. than with anyone else in the Impressionist group
5. than those of any other woman painter of her time

▶ **Exercise 20**

Find It in Your Reading
More quickly is a comparative modifier comparing Degas's speed with pastels to his speed with oils.

▶ **Exercise 21**

Find It in Your Writing
Have students pay special attention to comparisons requiring *other* or *else*, as these are easily overlooked.

▶ **Exercise 22**

Writing Application
When students have finished, have them exchange papers with a partner and check the correctness of the comparisons in each other's work.

Answer Key

Exercise 23

1. superlative
2. comparative
3. superlative
4. positive
5. comparative
6. comparative
7. superlative
8. positive
9. positive
10. comparative

Exercise 24

1. farther
2. less
3. more
4. better
5. worse

Exercise 25

1. best
2. more active
3. later
4. earliest
5. more difficult, more satisfying

Exercise 26

Allow some variation in wording.

1. than that of Medieval times
2. than Francesco Landini's *or* than that of Francesco Landini
3. than that of composers from France
4. than that of vocal music
5. than those of Vivaldi and other composers
6. than any other European city
7. than anywhere else
8. than Salieri's *or* than those of Salieri
9. than with anything else
10. than any other composer's *or* than those of any other composer

GRAMMAR EXERCISES 23–30

> **Exercise 23** Recognizing Positive, Comparative, and Superlative Degrees
Identify the degree of each underlined modifier.

1. The harp is one of the <u>oldest</u> instruments.
2. Today's harps are <u>more</u> sophisticated than ancient ones.
3. Impressionists considered the harp to be the <u>most expressive</u> instrument.
4. With the harp, it was <u>easy</u> to create rippling tones that sounded like water.
5. Composer Claude Debussy gave the harp a <u>greater</u> role within the orchestra.
6. His style was <u>more modern</u> than that of many of his contemporaries.
7. <u>Most</u> of Debussy's innovations dealt with harmonies.
8. A <u>dreamy</u> quality characterized his compositions.
9. Debussy created chamber works <u>late</u> in his career.
10. *Nocturnes* is one of his <u>more widely</u> known compositions.

> **Exercise 24** Forming Irregular Comparative and Superlative Degrees
Write the correct form of the underlined modifier to complete each sentence.

1. The fame of many modern composers has spread <u>far</u>, but Debussy's has spread even ___?___.
2. Béla Bartók was influenced <u>little</u> by Franz Liszt and even ___?___ by Richard Strauss.
3. Bartók studied <u>many</u> Turkish songs and even ___?___ Hungarian songs.
4. Bartók's violin concertos are <u>good</u>, but his string quartets are ___?___.
5. When first performed, this concerto was greeted <u>badly</u> by critics and even ___?___ by the audience.

> **Exercise 25** Supplying the Comparative and Superlative Degrees
Write the appropriate degree of the modifier in parentheses.

1. Gregorian chants are the (good) known of all types of Medieval music.
2. Pope Gregory I was (active) in the composition of church music than earlier religious leaders.
3. Early forms of chant involved just a melody line, while (late) forms involved a two-part harmony.
4. This two-part harmony was the (early) step toward the development of multi-part music in Europe.
5. Multi-part harmonies were (difficult) to compose but (satisfying) to hear than simple melodies.

> **Exercise 26** Revising to Eliminate Errors in Comparisons Revise each sentence to correct unbalanced or illogical comparisons.

1. The music of the Renaissance was smoother than Medieval times.
2. John Dunstable's style was more graceful than Francesco Landini.
3. The influence of composers from Holland was greater than France.
4. In the seventeenth century, the popularity of instrumental music was greater than vocal music.
5. Johann Sebastian Bach's compositions were more sophisticated than Vivaldi and other composers.
6. In the eighteenth century, Vienna was more important as a classical music center than any European city.
7. More classical composers gathered in Vienna than anywhere.
8. The works of Haydn and Mozart are better known than Salieri.
9. Giuseppe Verdi's operas were more

concerned with human relationships than anything.
10. Richard Wagner created operas that were longer and more dramatic than any composer.

> **Exercise 27** Revising Sentences to Eliminate Errors With Modifiers

Revise the following sentences, correcting any errors in the use of modifiers. If a sentence is correct, write *correct*.

1. I have been studying the oboe for a long time than anyone in my family.
2. I think the oboe has a more clearer sound than any instrument.
3. Compared to a bassoon, an oboe is lighter and higher pitched.
4. My cousin is the more talented of the three musicians in my family.
5. He plays the clarinet smoothlier than anyone else I have ever heard.
6. He played few wrong notes as a child and even few today.
7. He has been practicing two compositions and plans to perform the one he knows the most thoroughly.
8. The first time I tried the piece, I played it badly, but now I can play it better.
9. Performing my own composition at the festival has been my most exciting musical experience ever.
10. I received a warm reception than anyone who performed at the festival.

> **Exercise 28** Revising a Paragraph to Eliminate Errors With Modifiers

Revise the following paragraph, correcting any errors in the usage of modifiers.

Jean Sibelius from Finland is his country's famousest composer. He is more linked to Finnish nationalism than anyone. Born in 1865, Sibelius took up the violin early than any instrument. He thought at first about becoming a violinist, but he was most interested in composing. Sibelius's early compositions were more influenced by Russian composers than Finland. By the time he reached his thirties, however, Sibelius had developed an original style than before. Turning to Finnish themes, he created his more memorable work. By 1900, Finns were intent on becoming independent from Russia than in previous years. Sibelius's *Finlandia* debuted that year and created more controversy in Finland than any composition. Despite being banned by the Czar of Russia, *Finlandia* soon became the important symbol of Finnish independence.

> **Exercise 29** Writing Application

Imagine that you are a music reviewer for a magazine. Write a brief article comparing three different songs or albums. Use comparative and superlative forms of modifiers in your review and make sure that your comparisons are clear and logical.

> **Exercise 30** CUMULATIVE REVIEW Correcting Errors in Verb, Pronoun, and Modifier Usage and Agreement Rewrite the following paragraph, correcting errors in usage and agreement.

(1) The first instrument I ever play was the triangle. (2) My kindergarten teacher ask the other kids and I to choose instruments from a collection that was setting in the back of the room. (3) The others choosed drums or horns, but I pick the triangle. (4) I seen it shining brightly than the other instruments. (5) I was also impress by it's shape and tone. (6) While the triangle is an easy instrument to play, they are hard to play good. (7) There is many ways to play a triangle, but I knew only one way to play—loud. (8) I striked the instrument over and over without any sense of rhythm. (9) Certainly no one in the class played louder than me. (10) After much practice, us musicians learned to play together better.

Answer Key

> **Exercise 27**
1. . . . for a longer time than anyone else in my family.
2. . . . has a clearer sound than any other instrument.
3. correct
4. . . . most talented . . .
5. . . . more smoothly . . .
6. . . . even fewer today.
7. . . . the one he knows more thoroughly.
8. correct
9. . . . the most exciting . . . I've ever had.
10. . . . a warmer reception than anyone else . . .

> **Exercise 28**
Allow some variation in wording.
1. most famous composer
2. than anyone else
3. earlier than any other instrument
4. but he was more interested in composing
5. than by those from Finland
6. a more original style than before
7. his most memorable work
8. more intent on becoming independent
9. than any other composition
10. the most important symbol

> **Exercise 29**
Writing Application
When students have finished, have them work in groups to listen to and critique each other's compositions, pointing out any modifier errors as well.

> **Exercise 30**
Cumulative Review
1. played
2. asked the other kids and me . . . that was sitting in the back. . . .
3. chose . . . I picked
4. I saw it . . . more brightly
5. impressed by its
6. . . . to play, it is hard to play well
7. There are . . . triangle, but I . . . loudly
8. I struck
9. no one else . . . than I (did)
10. . . . we musicians learned to play together well.

Step-by-Step Teaching Guide

Standard English Usage: Using Modifiers

Teaching Resources: Standardized Test Preparation Workbook, pp. 49–50

1. Remind students how to form comparatives and superlatives: for words of three or more syllables, use *more* or *most* and the modifier. For most one- or two-syllable words, add *-er* or *-est*.

2. Briefly review the comparative and superlative forms of irregular modifiers such as *good, well, bad, badly, much, many, far,* and *little.* Encourage students to study the chart on page 592.

3. Have students complete the practice tests on page 605. Review their answers and address any questions they have. Make sure they understand why question 4 in Practice 1 and question 5 in Practice 2 take modifiers in the positive form. (The sentences do not contain any comparisons.)

Standardized Test Preparation Workshop

Standard English Usage: Modifiers

Standardized test questions often measure your ability to use modifiers correctly. This may be done by testing your ability to choose the correct form of comparison to complete a sentence. Use the following strategies to help you determine which form to use in a sentence:

- If no comparison is being made, use the **positive form** of the modifier.

- If one thing or action is compared to another thing or action, use the **comparative form** of the modifier—ending in *-er* or preceded by *more.*

- If one thing or action is being compared to more than one other thing or action, use the **superlative form** of the modifier—ending in *-est* or preceded by *most.*

- Be aware that some modifiers have **special forms,** such as *good, bad, much,* and *many.*

Test Tip

Be careful not to choose a double comparison, such as *more younger* to complete a sentence. The correct form is *younger.*

Sample Test Items	Answers and Explanations

Directions: Read the passage, and choose the word or group of words that belongs in each space.
 	
Although San Diego is a growing city; it is still much ____(1)____ than Los Angeles. Its climate is one of the ____(2)____ in the United States.
 	
1 A more small
  B most small
  C smaller
  D smallest
	The best answer is *C.* San Diego is being compared to one other city, so a comparative form is needed. Because *small* is a short word, its comparative is formed simply by adding *-er.*

2 F more beautiful
  G beautifuller
  H beautifullest
  J most beautiful
	The best answer is *J.* San Diego's climate is being compared to all United States climates; therefore, a superlative form is needed. Because *beautiful* is a three-syllable word, *most* is used to form the superlative. Note that choices *G* and *H* are neither correct forms nor proper words.

604 • Using Modifiers

TEST-TAKING TIP

Encourage students to read the test questions, with the answer choices inserted in the blanks, aloud to themselves. Often, they will be able to eliminate answer choices because they simply don't sound right. For example, in question 1 of Practice 2, the word *interestinger* sounds wrong. It can be eliminated immediately.

Remind students to carefully read the words immediately before the blanks. Sometimes, the word *more* or *most* will already be provided. If this is the case, students should not choose an answer choice that includes one of those words.

> **Practice 1** **Directions:** Read the passage, and choose the word or group of words that belongs in each space.

Fifteen museums make San Diego's Balboa Park one of the nation's ___(1)___ cultural complexes. Its Spanish Revival buildings remind visitors of an ___(2)___ era. The buildings were ___(3)___ decorated than had been seen previously. Two international expositions held in San Diego were ___(4)___ to the park's development. It now offers the ___(5)___ entertainment opportunities in the city.

1 A larger
   B more large
   C largest
   D large

2 F earliest
   G earlier
   H more early
   J most early

3 A more highly
   B highlier
   C highliest
   D most highly

4 F most crucial
   G crucialer
   H more crucial
   J crucial

5 A more diverse
   B diversest
   C most diverse
   D diverser

> **Practice 2** **Directions:** Read the passage, and choose the word or group of words that belongs in each space.

Almost nothing could be ___(1)___ than a day at the San Diego Zoo. I know I had one of the ___(2)___ times ever! The zoo is acknowledged as one of the ___(3)___ in the entire world. As famous as the zoo is for the variety of exhibits, it has often received even ___(4)___ recognition for its work with endangered giant pandas. The birth of a baby panda at the zoo was a ___(5)___ achievement.

1 A interestinger
   B more interesting
   C interestingest
   D most interesting

2 F goodest
   G best
   H better
   J good

3 A most fine
   B finer
   C finest
   D more fine

4 F more great
   G greater
   H greatest
   J great

5 A more significant
   B most significant
   C significant
   D less significant

Answer Key

> **Practice 1**
1. C
2. G
3. A
4. J
5. C

> **Practice 2**
1. B
2. G
3. C
4. G
5. C

Customize for
Less Advanced Students
Remind students that they use and hear positive, comparative, and superlative modifiers in conversation each day. They probably use most of them correctly. Therefore, they should feel confident about questions that test this concept.

605

Chapter 26 Time and Resource Manager

In-Depth Lesson Plan

	LESSON FOCUS	PRINT AND MEDIA RESOURCES
DAY 1	**Negative Sentences** Students learn to recognize double negatives and to form negative sentences correctly. (pp. 608–611/H440–443)	*Writing and Grammar* Interactive Text, Section 26.1; *On-line Exercise Bank*, Section 26.1 **Teaching Resources** *Grammar Exercise Workbook*, pp. 153–154; *Grammar Exercises Answers on Transparencies*, Ch. 26
DAY 2	**Common Usage Problems** Students learn to avoid common mistakes, such as nonstandard usage (e.g., *irregardless*) and easily confused words (*accept/except*), and practice correct usage. (pp. 612–618/H444–450)	*Writing and Grammar* Interactive Text, Section 26.2; *On-line Exercise Bank*, Section 26.2 **Teaching Resources** *Grammar Exercise Workbook*, p. 155
DAY 3	**Common Usage Problems** *continued* Students learn to avoid common mistakes, such as nonstandard usage (e.g., *like/as*) and easily confused words (e.g., *then/than*), practice correct usage, and do the Hands-on Grammar activity. (pp. 619–623/H451–455)	**Teaching Resources** *Grammar Exercise Workbook*, p. 156; *Hands-on Grammar Activity Book*, Ch. 26
DAY 4	**Review and Assess** Students review the chapter and demonstrate mastery of common usage problems. (pp. 624–625)	*Writing and Grammar* Interactive Text, Ch. 26, Chapter Review **Teaching Resources** *Formal Assessment*, Ch. 26

Accelerated Lesson Plan

	LESSON FOCUS	PRINT AND MEDIA RESOURCES
DAY 1	**Negative Sentences; Common Usage Problems** Students cover double negatives, properly formed negative sentences, and common usage problems. (pp. 608–618/H440–450)	*Writing and Grammar* Interactive Text, Sections 26.1–2; *On-line Exercise Bank*, Sections 26.1–2 **Teaching Resources** *Grammar Exercise Workbook*, pp. 153–155; *Grammar Exercises Answers on Transparencies*, Ch. 26
DAY 2	**Common Usage Problems; Review and Assess** Students complete the study of common usage problems, then review the entire chapter and demonstrate mastery of the concepts. (pp. 619–625/H451–455)	*Writing and Grammar* Interactive Text, Ch. 26, Section 26.2 through Chapter Review; *On-line Exercise Bank*, Section 26.2 **Teaching Resources** *Grammar Exercise Workbook*, pp. 155–156; *Hands-on Grammar Activity Book*, Ch. 26; *Formal Assessment*, Ch. 26

Options for Adapting Lesson Plans

HOMEWORK

Have students complete any section of the chapter for homework.

FEATURES

Extend coverage with the Standardized Test Preparation Workshop (p. 626).

TECHNOLOGY

Students can use *Writing and Grammar* Interactive Text to complete the exercises interactively on computer. They can complete additional exercises in the *On-line Exercise Bank:* The Auto Check feature will grade their work. Go on-line: PHSchool.com Use Web Code: eek-1002

Writing and Grammar Handbook Alignment

Page numbers in Step-by-Step Teaching Guides in this Teacher's Edition refer to pages from the full student text. Handbook page references, indicated with this icon **H**, are provided in Time and Resource Manager boxes and at the bottom of each Teacher's Edition page.

INTEGRATED SKILLS COVERAGE

Writing
Find It in Your Writing SE pp. 611, 622, 623/**H**443, 454, 455
Writing Application SE pp. 611, 623, 625, 629/**H**443, 455
Grammar and Style SE p. 616/**H**448

Spelling
SE p. 608/**H**440; ATE p. 617

Viewing and Representing
Critical Viewing SE pp. 606, 609, 614, 617/**H**438, 441, 446, 449

Technology SE p. 613/**H**445

Vocabulary ATE pp. 609, 619

Language Highlight ATE p. 618

Real-World Connection ATE p. 610

ASSESSMENT SUPPORT

Standardized Test Preparation Workshop SE p. 626; ATE p. 626

Standardized Test Preparation Workbook, pp. 51–52

Formal Assessment, Ch. 26

MEETING INDIVIDUAL NEEDS

Less Advanced Students ATE p. 627. See also Ongoing Assessments ATE pp. 610, 614, 618, 621.

More Advanced Students ATE pp. 620, 627

ESL Students ATE pp. 610, 619

Logical/Mathematical Learners ATE p. 609

Linguistic Learners ATE p. 620

BLOCK SCHEDULING

Pacing Suggestions
For 90-minute Blocks
• Administer the Diagnostic Test to students to determine instructional coverage.
• Have students complete the necessary exercises in class. Use the Hands-on Grammar activity to provide a change of pace.

Resources for Varying Instruction
• *Writing and Grammar* Interactive Text A 90-minute block provides an ideal opportunity for students to work on the computer.

Professional Development Support
• *How to Manage Instruction in the Block* This teaching resource provides management and activity suggestions.

MEDIA AND TECHNOLOGY

For the Student
• *Writing and Grammar* Interactive Text, Ch. 26
• *On-line Exercise Bank*, Sections 26.1–2

For the Teacher
• **Teacher**EXPRESS™ CD-ROM

WRITING AND GRAMMAR ON-LINE

Interactive Text (On-line or on CD-ROM)
• Easily navigable instruction with on-line supporting resources
• Self-scoring exercises and diagnostic tests

Companion Web Site PHSchool.com
• On-line Exercise Bank (use Web Code eek-1002)

See the Go On-line! feature, SE p. iii.

▶ **Lesson Objectives**

1. To recognize double negatives and to write negative sentences correctly

2. To recognize and avoid common usage problems with troublesome words and expressions

3. To proofread writing for appropriateness of organization, content, style, and conventions

4. To demonstrate control over grammatical elements

5. To evaluate writing for both mechanics and content

Critical Viewing

Distinguish Sample response: Marie Curie had <u>no</u> modern equipment. She had <u>barely</u> any open space on which to work.

Chapter 26 Miscellaneous Problems in Usage

Throughout history, women have achieved stunning success in many different fields. For example, Hildegard von Bingen delighted contemporaries with her writings and musical compositions in the twelfth century, and Amelia Earhart became a flying sensation in the twentieth century. These women strove for excellence in their chosen fields, and their successes inspire others.

Success in many fields requires, among other things, accurate and effective use of language. In this chapter, you will study some usage problems that have not been presented earlier. In the first section of this chapter, you will learn how to form negative sentences correctly. In the second section, you will study troublesome words and expressions.

▲ **Critical Viewing**
Marie Curie, pictured above, is renowned for her research in radioactivity. Use negative sentences to compare her laboratory to modern laboratories with which you are familiar. **[Distinguish]**

606 • Miscellaneous Problems in Usage

☑ **ONGOING ASSESSMENT: Diagnose**

If students miss more than one item in any category, direct them to the relevant pages of the textbook and assign exercises for practice and review.

Miscellaneous Problems in Usage	Diagnostic Test Items	Teach	Practice	Section Reviews	Chapter Review
Skill Check A					
Negative Sentences	A 1–5	pp. 608–609/ ⊞440–441	Ex. 1–3	Ex. 4–6	Ex. 20

Diagnostic Test

Directions: Write all answers on a separate sheet of paper.

Skill Check A. Choose the word in parentheses that makes each sentence negative without forming a double negative.

1. In earlier times, people assumed that women couldn't do (nothing, anything) outside the domestic sphere.
2. They thought women didn't have (no, any) leadership abilities.
3. It was also believed that women (had, hadn't) scarcely the strength or intelligence of their male counterparts.
4. Susan B. Anthony (was, wasn't) but one woman we remember for her achievements.
5. She (was, wasn't) hardly the only person to work for women's suffrage, but only Anthony is commemorated on U.S. currency.

Skill Check B. Choose the correct expression to complete each sentence.

6. Oftentimes, girls weren't (learned, taught) the same skills and lessons as boys.
7. Rather (than, then) science, math, or literature, girls studied cooking, sewing, and caring for the family.
8. (Being that, Because) they were often denied learning opportunities, their successes are that much more remarkable.
9. Women often had to make (their, there) own opportunities.
10. In ancient Egypt, Hatshepsut ruled as regent (due to, because of) her stepson's young age.
11. Within a few years, she had herself crowned pharaoh (so, so that) she could rule in her own right.
12. In more recent times, Marie Curie won an unprecedented (too, two) Nobel Prizes.
13. Her work, (which, who) dealt with radiation, advanced scientific research in the field of radioactivity.
14. Elizabeth I of England (adapted, adopted) to the requirements of sovereignty with strength and resolve.
15. (Beside, Besides) leading in peacetime, she also proved herself a strong leader in wartime.
16. In the twentieth century, Rosa Parks, an African American living in the South, refused to move (further, farther) back in the bus so that a white person could sit up front.
17. She inspired thousands and had a powerful (affect, effect) on the civil rights movement.
18. Eileen Collins (already, all ready) knew how to fly before she became an astronaut.
19. Harriet Tubman guided slaves (among, between) bondage in the South and freedom in the North.
20. (Them, Those) women, and many others, have inspired countless generations to strive to achieve their own dreams.

Miscellaneous Problems in Usage • 607

ONGOING ASSESSMENT: Diagnose continued

Miscellaneous Problems in Usage	Diagnostic Test Items	Teach	Practice	Section Reviews	Chapter Review
Skill Check B					
Common Usage Problems 1–15	B 14, 17–19	pp. 612–614/ 444–446	Ex. 10	Ex. 13–16	Ex. 21–23
Common Usage Problems 16–30	B 8, 10, 15–16	pp. 615–617/ 447–449	Ex. 11		
Common Usage Problems 31–45	B 6–7, 9, 11–13, 20	pp. 618–621/ 450–453	Ex. 12		
Cumulative Reviews and Applications				Ex. 7–9, 17–19	Ex. 24–25

TIME SAVERS!

Answers on Transparencies Use the *Grammar Exercises Answers on Transparencies* for Chapter 26 to facilitate correction by students.

On-Line Exercise Bank Have students complete the Diagnostic Test on computer. The Auto Check feature will grade their work for you!

Write the following on the board:

There will not be no homework tonight.

Ask students what the sentence means. (By using negatives incorrectly, the sentence literally means homework *will* be given.) Point out that using double negatives can cause confusion or convey the wrong—even opposite—meaning.

Activate Prior Knowledge

Challenge students to suggest sentences with double negatives that they have heard in movies. Write some of these on the board. (Example: *Badges? Badges? We don't need no stinking badges.*) Underline the negative words and ask students to analyze what the sentence is saying.

TEACH

Step-by-Step Teaching Guide

Recognizing Double Negatives

1. Ask a student to read aloud the examples of double negatives and the corrections in the chart.

2. Have students point out the negative words in each sentence.

3. Show students how to correct double negatives by changing one negative word to a positive word.

4. Brainstorm for other pairs of negative and positive words (*nowhere/somewhere; never/ever; nobody/somebody*).

Answer Key

Exercise 1

1. could
2. anywhere
3. anything
4. some
5. ever

Section 26.1

Negative Sentences

At one time, it was correct to use several negative words in one sentence. It was correct, for example, to say, "Father *didn't* tell *nobody nothing.*" Today, however, only one negative word is used to make the entire sentence negative. The above sentence can be restated correctly in one of three ways: "Father *didn't* tell anybody anything," "Father told *nobody* anything," or "Father told *nothing* to anybody."

Recognizing Double Negatives

A **double negative** is the use of two negative words in a sentence when only one is needed.

▶ **KEY CONCEPT** Do not write sentences with double negatives. ■

The following chart gives examples of double negatives and the two ways each can be corrected.

CORRECTING DOUBLE NEGATIVES	
Double Negatives	**Corrections**
She *couldn't* fix *nothing.*	She *couldn't* fix *anything.* She could fix *nothing.*
Ellen *didn't* have *no* training.	Ellen *didn't* have *any* training. Ellen had *no* training.
She *wouldn't* ask *no one* for help.	She *wouldn't* ask *anyone* for help. She asked *no one* for help.

▶ **Exercise 1** Avoiding Double Negatives Choose the word in parentheses that correctly completes each sentence.

1. No one (couldn't, could) tell Marie Curie that women were inferior in science.
2. She grew up in Poland, not (nowhere, anywhere) close to France, where she did her most famous work.
3. Marie wasn't as interested in (nothing, anything) as much as she was in radioactivity.
4. She and her husband won the 1903 Nobel Prize for Physics, but not without (no, some) help from Antoine Becquerel, who shared the award.
5. A woman hadn't (never, ever) before won a Nobel Prize.

Theme: Notable Women

In this section, you will learn to form negative sentences correctly. The examples and exercises in this section are about admirable women throughout history.

Cross-Curricular Connection: Social Studies

💡 **Spelling Tip**

To make a helping verb negative, just add *n't* to the end of the verb or follow it with the word *not.* Watch out for some exceptions: *Can't* and *won't* lose some letters when put into the negative form, and *cannot* is spelled as one word.

▶ **More Practice**

Grammar Exercise Workbook
• pp. 153–154
On-line Exercise Bank
• Section 26.1
Go on-line:
PHSchool.com
Enter Web Code:
eek-1002

⏰ TIME AND RESOURCE MANAGER

Resources
Print: *Grammar Exercise Workbook,* pp. 153–154; *Grammar Exercises Answers on Transparencies,* Ch. 26
Technology: *Writing and Grammar* Interactive Text, Section 26.1; *On-Line Exercise Bank,* Section 26.1

Using the Full Student Edition	Using the Handbook Ⓗ
• Work through all key concepts, pp. 608–609. • Assign and review Exercises 1–3.	• Work through all key concepts, pp. 440–441. • Assign and review Exercises 1–3.

Forming Negative Sentences Correctly

Negative sentences are formed correctly in one of three ways:

Using One Negative Word: The most common way to make a sentence negative is with a single negative word—such as *no, not, none, nothing, never, nobody,* or *nowhere*—or with the contraction *n't* added to a helping verb.

KEY CONCEPT Do not use two negative words in the same clause. ■

Using two of these negative words in the same clause will create a double negative.

DOUBLE NEGATIVE: She *wouldn't never* learn that by herself.

CORRECT: She *wouldn't* ever learn that by herself.
She *would* never learn that by herself.

Using *But* in a Negative Sense: When *but* means "only," it usually acts as a negative.

KEY CONCEPT Do not use *but* in its negative sense with another negative. ■

DOUBLE NEGATIVE: He *hadn't but* one hero.

CORRECT: He had *but* one hero.
He had *only* one hero.

Using *Barely, Hardly,* and *Scarcely:* These words have a negative sense and should not be used with other negative words.

KEY CONCEPT Do not use *barely, hardly,* or *scarcely* with another negative. ■

DOUBLE NEGATIVE: She *hadn't barely* mastered the new language.

CORRECT: She had *barely* mastered the new language.

DOUBLE NEGATIVE: He *couldn't hardly* see beyond that hill.

CORRECT: He could *hardly* see beyond that hill.

DOUBLE NEGATIVE: It *hadn't scarcely* started to rain.

CORRECT: It had *scarcely* started to rain.

▲ **Critical Viewing**
Marie Curie is admired for her research in radioactivity, among other things. Write several sentences about a person whom you admire. Use the words *but, barely, hardly,* and *scarcely* in your sentences. **[Support]**

Negative Sentences • 609

Step-by-Step Teaching Guide

Forming Negative Sentences Correctly

1. Have students read the first key concept, the double negative, and the corrections. Remind students that only one negative word should be used to write a negative clause.

2. Read the second key concept aloud and point out that *but* in this context acts as a negative.

3. Have students read the third key concept, the double negatives, and the corrections. Ask students to offer additional sentences that correctly use *barely, hardly,* and *scarcely.*

Customize for
Logical/Mathematical Learners

Write −5(−6)=30 on the board. Recall with students that when you multiply two negative numbers, the answer is positive. Similarly, when you use two negative words together in a sentence, the result may have a positive meaning. Write the following on the board:

I didn't see nothing.

Have students correct this double negative (*I didn't see anything*) and offer more examples.

Integrating Vocabulary Skills

Connotations and Denotations
Tell students that negative ideas are conveyed in other ways besides using words like *no* and *not.* Explain that some words have negative connotations—that is, they suggest negative ideas that go beyond their denotations, or literal meanings. As examples, give the words *scrawny* and *pry.* Have students check their denotations in a dictionary; then discuss the negative connotations of each word. Ask students to think of other words that have negative connotations.

Critical Viewing

Support Sample response: Hardly anyone works harder than my father. He barely relaxes at all, even on weekends.

Grammar and Usage Many standardized tests require students to recognize a double negative in the context of a passage. Use the following to demonstrate.

(A) *Paul wasn't sure he could complete his assignment on time.* (B) *He had never had so much trouble researching a theme.* (C) *He couldn't find nothing about his topic on the Internet or in the library.* (D) *Finally, Paul asked his teacher if he could change his topic.*

Which sentence in the above passage contains an error?

The correct answer is **C**. This sentence contains a double negative: the words *couldn't* and *nothing* are used in the same clause. To correct the sentence, eliminate or change one of the negative words.

Customize for
ESL Students

Students often have difficulty understanding the precise meanings of contractions that include the word *not*. Put two columns on the board, one headed *Word Pair* and the other headed *Contraction*. Help students write the contractions for each word pair.

Word Pair	Contraction
do not	don't
cannot	can't
will not	won't
are not	aren't

Answer Key

Exercise 2

1. anything
2. could
3. ever
4. was
5. knows

Exercise 3

Answers will vary; samples are given.

1. Born into slavery, Harriet Tubman was never supposed . . .
2. She didn't have any . . .
3. . . . but she scarcely took any time . . .
4. Harriet didn't think anybody . . .
5. She felt she had but one . . .
6. No one was able to stop her . . .
7. She would let no one turn back . . .
8. Tubman didn't ever stop fighting . . .
9. She hardly restricted herself . . .
10. . . . couldn't abide any injustices.

Real-World Connection

To report complicated information, newspaper articles sometimes use sentences with several negative ideas. Present the following:

The committee opposed the bill that would have made the strike illegal.

Ask students whether the committee favored the strike. Identify the negative concepts and wording: (*bill makes strike illegal; opposing bill makes strike legal*). Finally, rewrite the sentence: *"The committee believed the strike should be legal."*

▶ **Exercise 2** Avoiding Problems With Negatives Choose the word in parentheses that makes each sentence negative without creating a double negative.

EXAMPLE: There (isn't, is) scarcely a more famous female aviator than Amelia Earhart.

ANSWER: is

1. Amelia Earhart hardly liked (anything, nothing) as much as flying.
2. Nobody (could, couldn't) keep her on the ground.
3. Before she became the first woman to break the speed record while crossing the Atlantic alone, some people thought women wouldn't (ever, never) be good pilots.
4. That (was, wasn't) but one aviation record that Earhart broke.
5. She disappeared during an attempt to fly around the world, and to this day no one (doesn't know, knows) for certain what happened on that last flight.

▶ **Exercise 3** Revising Sentences to Correct Double Negatives Rewrite each sentence, correcting the double negative.

EXAMPLE: Harriet Tubman didn't allow nothing to stop her from helping others.

ANSWER: Harriet Tubman allowed nothing to stop her from helping others.

1. Born into slavery, Harriet Tubman wasn't never supposed to enjoy the freedom of her white masters.
2. She didn't have no real childhood.
3. When still a young woman, she escaped to the North, but she didn't scarcely take any time to enjoy her new freedom.
4. Harriet didn't think nobody should be a slave.
5. She felt she didn't have but one choice: to return to the South to guide others to freedom.
6. No one wasn't able to stop her, and she never lost one person on her eighteen trips on the Underground Railroad.
7. She wouldn't let no one turn back once they had started.
8. Tubman didn't never stop fighting for freedom: During the Civil War, she served as a nurse, scout, and spy for the Union army.
9. She didn't hardly restrict herself to just one cause: She also fought for women's rights, raised money for schools for black people, and established a home for poor and elderly black people.
10. Harriet Tubman couldn't abide no injustices.

610 • Miscellaneous Problems in Usage

▶ **More Practice**

Grammar Exercise Workbook
• pp. 153–154
On-line Exercise Bank
• Section 26.1
  Go on-line:
  PHSchool.com
  Enter Web Code:
  eek-1002

Complete the exercises on-line! Exercises 2 and 3 are available on-line or on CD-ROM.

✓ ONGOING ASSESSMENT: Monitor and Reinforce

If students have difficulty with Exercise 1, 2, or 3, refer them to the following for additional practice.

In the Textbook	Print Resources	Technology
Section Review, Ex. 4–6, Section 26.1	*Grammar Exercise Workbook,* pp. 153–154	*On-Line Exercise Bank,* Section 26.1

Section 26.1 Section Review

GRAMMAR EXERCISES 4–9

Exercise 4 Avoiding Double Negatives Choose the word in parentheses that makes each sentence negative without forming a double negative.

1. In the 1840's, medical schools didn't want (nothing, anything) to do with female applicants.
2. Elizabeth Blackwell (would, wouldn't) never give up, however, and on her thirtieth try, she was accepted by Geneva College.
3. She (had, hadn't) barely gotten her degree when she traveled to Europe to gain practical experience in hospitals.
4. When she returned, no one in the medical community (would, wouldn't) trust her.
5. She wouldn't acknowledge (no, any) resistance and opened a hospital to serve poor women and children.

Exercise 5 Revising Sentences to Avoid Problems With Negatives Rewrite each sentence, correcting the double negative.

1. Aung San Suu Kyi didn't promote no violence in her struggle for freedom from the military government in Burma.
2. Her father, who was assassinated when Aung San Suu Kyi was only two, didn't want no one to live under oppression, and she continued his struggle.
3. While living in India, she didn't ignore none of the methods and teachings of Mohandas Gandhi, the nonviolent protest leader.
4. She couldn't hardly win a military battle, so she gave speeches, visited the people, and started a new political party based on democratic ideals.
5. The government couldn't do nothing to stem her popularity, so they placed her under house arrest for more than ten years.

Exercise 6 Revising a Paragraph to Correct Double Negatives Rewrite the following, correcting all double negatives.

When she wasn't barely a teenager, Joan of Arc heard the voices of saints. They told her that no one but she couldn't rid France of the invading English. First, she convinced the French king that she wasn't telling no lies when she claimed she could restore his kingdom. Charles VII believed he hadn't but one choice: to trust Joan. It didn't take scarcely ten days to break the English siege of Orleans. The English couldn't do nothing to defeat her. Joan wouldn't take no rest until Charles VII was crowned at Rheims. She didn't allow nobody to attack the king as she led him through enemy territory. In Paris, however, she couldn't do nothing to prevent her own capture. The English didn't want no more trouble from Joan, so they sentenced her to death.

Exercise 7 Find It in Your Reading
Locate an article on a famous woman in a newspaper, a magazine, or one of your textbooks. Find at least two examples of negative sentences. Explain why the negatives are used correctly.

Exercise 8 Find It in Your Writing
In your own writing, find five examples of negative words. Check to make sure that you have not included any sentences with double negatives.

Exercise 9 Writing Application
Write about a woman whom you admire. Include three negative sentences. Be sure to avoid double negatives and to form all negative sentences correctly.

Section Review • **611**

✓ ONGOING ASSESSMENT: Assess Mastery

Use the following resources to assess student mastery of negative sentences.

In the Textbook	Technology
Chapter Review, Ex. 20	On-Line Exercise Bank, Section 26.1

Interest GRABBER As you read to the class these sentences, repeat the underlined portions and ask students to spell them:

Baby Lucy was <u>already</u> awake at 6:00 A.M. on Christmas Day.

For <u>a while</u> she did not come downstairs.

The whole family was awake <u>except</u> me.

Then write the correct words on the board. Point out that these words are often confused with other words that sound alike (*all ready, already; a while, awhile; except, accept*).

Activate Prior Knowledge

Write the following on the board and ask students to fill in the blanks with either *between* or *among*:

The three bears fought ___ themselves for the bowls of porridge. (among)

Mama bear placed her bowl ___ the other two. (between)

Students should recall the rule: use *between* with two things, use *among* with three or more.

TEACH

Step-by-Step Teaching Guide

Usage Problems 1–12

1. Remind students that *a* is used before consonant sounds and *an* is used before vowel sounds.

2. Point out that words beginning with *h, o,* or *u* may have either a consonant or vowel sound.

3. Ask students to practice using *accept* and *except* by writing a sentence containing both words (*I accept all assignments except the last one*).

4. Write the following sentence on the board to show the difference between the words *adapt* and *adopt*:

   The couple adopted the child and then had to adapt to their new lifestyle.

   Then, ask students to define the two verbs in their own words.

continued

Common Usage Problems

This section presents an alphabetical list of forty-five usage problems that sometimes cause confusion in writing and speaking.

▶ **KEY CONCEPT** Study the items in this glossary, paying particular attention to similar meanings and spellings. ∎

(1) a, an The article *a* is used before consonant sounds; *an* is used before vowel sounds. Words beginning with *h, o,* or *u* can have either a consonant sound or a vowel sound.

(2) accept, except *Accept* is a verb meaning "to receive." *Except* is a preposition meaning "other than" or "leaving out."

VERB: Settlers of the western frontier *accepted* the harsh realities of frontier life.

PREPOSITION: They easily found all the natural resources they needed *except* water and wood.

(3) adapt, adopt *Adapt* means "to change." *Adopt* means "to take as one's own."

EXAMPLES: Easterners quickly learned to *adapt*. Newcomers *adopted* the customs of neighbors.

(4) affect, effect *Affect*, almost always a verb, means "to influence." *Effect* may be used as a noun or as a verb. As a noun, it means "result." As a verb, it means "to bring about" or "to cause."

VERB: Natural disasters *affected* the farmers' success.

NOUN: Settlers knew the *effects* of nature and tried to combat them.

VERB: The tractor *effected* a drastic change in farming.

(5) ain't *Ain't* was originally a contraction of *am not*, but it is no longer considered standard English.

(6) all ready, already *All ready*, two separate words used as an adjective, is an expression meaning "ready." *Already*, an adverb, means "even now" or "by or before this time."

ADJECTIVE: The cowboys were *all ready* for the cattle drive.

ADVERB: Many of them had *already* driven cattle north.

612 • Miscellaneous Problems in Usage

Theme: Westward Expansion

In this section, you will learn about forty-five common usage problems. The examples and exercises in this section are about the people who took part in the westward expansion of the United States during the 1800's.

Cross-Curricular Connection: Social Studies

⏱ TIME AND RESOURCE MANAGER

Resources
Print: *Grammar Exercise Workbook,* pp. 155–156; *Grammar Exercises Answers on Transparencies,* Ch. 26
Technology: *Writing and Grammar* Interactive Text, Section 26.2; *On-Line Exercise Bank,* Section 26.2

Using the Full Student Edition	Using the HandbookⒽ
• Work through all key concepts, pp. 612–621. • Assign and review Exercises 10–12. • Do the Hands-on Grammar activity, p. 622.	• Work through all key concepts, pp. 444–453. • Assign and review Exercises 10–12. • Do the Hands-on Grammar activity, p. 454.

(7) all right, alright *Alright* is a nonstandard spelling. Make sure you use the two-word form.

NONSTANDARD: Business was *alright* if the town was located near some form of transportation.

CORRECT: Business was *all right* if the town was located near some form of transportation.

(8) all together, altogether *All together* means "together as a single group." *Altogether* means "completely" or "in all."

EXAMPLES: Cowhands had to work *all together* to transport cattle over long distances.
They would fail *altogether* if they worked alone.

(9) among, between Both of these words are prepositions. *Among* always implies three or more. *Between* is generally used only with two things.

EXAMPLES: Cows were branded so that the owners could pick out their cows from *among* a crowd.
Cowboys could transport the cows *between* the ranch and the railroad.

(10) anxious This adjective implies uneasiness, worry, or fear. Do not use it as a substitute for eager.

LESS ACCEPTABLE: The cowboys were *anxious* to reach the next town.

PREFERRED: The cowboys were *eager* to reach the next town.
The ranchers were *anxious* about cattle thieves.

(11) anywhere, everywhere, nowhere, somewhere Never end these adverbs with an *-s.*

NONSTANDARD: At first, ranchers didn't use fences, so cattle could wander *anywheres.*

CORRECT: At first, ranchers didn't use fences, so cattle could wander *anywhere.*

(12) as to *As to* is awkward. Replace it with *about.*

NONSTANDARD: Miners had no worries *as to* the land.

CORRECT: Miners had no worries *about* the land.

 **Technology Tip**

If you are using the spell-check feature of a word-processing program, keep in mind that it will not pick up as errors words such as *all right, alright, all together,* and *altogether.*

Common Usage Problems • **613**

Step-by-Step Teaching Guide continued

5. Explain to students that both *affect* and *effect* can be verbs with different meanings ("to influence" and "to cause," respectively). Tell them that only *effect* can be a noun meaning *result.*

6. Remind students that although *ain't* was once a proper contraction of *am not,* it is no longer a standard English word. Tell students to avoid it in their speech and writing.

7. Tell students that *all ready* is two words used as an adjective to refer to people or things, while *already* is an adverb used to refer to time. In order to practice using these words, ask students to write a sentence with both words. (Example: *The baseball player, already dressed in his uniform, was all ready to play.*)

8. Explain to students that there is no such word as *alright;* the proper spelling is two distinct words.

9. Read aloud the definitions of *all together* and *altogether.* Give students sentences to complete with the correct word. (Examples: *Are we going to drive ___ [all together]?; I am ___ [altogether] finished with my homework.*)

10. Point out the distinction that *among* is used when the object of the preposition is three or more things whereas *between* is used when the object of the preposition is two things. Suggest that students remember it is possible to stand between two other people, but it is not possible to stand equally between three people in a row.

11. Explain to students that *anxious* has an almost negative connotation, which means it is not synonymous with *eager,* a word that has a positive connotation. Ask students to write two sentences using the two words. Have students read aloud their sentences and explain why they chose each adjective.

12. Remind students that the words *anywhere, everywhere, nowhere,* and *somewhere* are never ended with an *–s.*

13. Point out to students that *as to* is an awkward use of language and can easily be replaced in writing and speech by the word *about.*

Usage Problems 13–21

1. Explain to students that the word *at* never follows the word *where*. (Example: *Where's the dog at?* should be written *Where's the dog?*) Tell students to solve this usage problem by eliminating the word *at*.

2. Ask students the part of speech of *awhile* (adverb). Then, ask if they know the parts of speech of the two words *a while* (article, noun). Tell them that the words *a while* usually follow the prepositions *for* or *after*.

3. Explain that *bad* is an adjective and *badly* is an adverb. Ask students to identify these words' different meanings in their own words. Then ask students to write original sentences using *bad* and *badly* properly.

continued

Answer Key

> **Exercise 10**

1. a while
2. adopted
3. between
4. about
5. altogether
6. bad
7. already
8. accept
9. isn't
10. effect

Critical Viewing

Speculate Responses will vary. Before students begin, have them brainstorm for ways to use *bad* and *badly* in description and dialogue.

26.2

(13) at Do not use *at* after *where*. Simply eliminate it.

NONSTANDARD: They didn't care *where* they were *at* as long as they found precious metals.

CORRECT: They didn't care *where* they were as long as they found precious metals.

(14) awhile, a while *Awhile* is an adverb that means "for a while." It is never preceded by a preposition. *A while* is an article and a noun, usually used after prepositions such as *for* or *after*.

ADVERB: The miners stayed *awhile* and worked the mine.

NOUN: After *a while*, a boom town would grow up to serve the needs of the miners.

(15) bad, badly *Bad* is an adjective that means "incorrect," "ill," or "undesirable." *Badly* is an adverb that means "in a bad way" or "poorly."

ADJECTIVE: Miners papered their walls with newspapers to insulate themselves from a *bad* winter.

ADVERB: Compared to today's insulation, the paper worked *badly*.

> **Exercise 10** Avoiding Usage Problems 1–15 Choose the correct expression to complete each sentence.
> 1. For (awhile, a while) ships and stagecoaches were the only means to deliver mail from the East to California.
> 2. In 1860, a California senator and a Missouri businessman (adapted, adopted) a plan to provide faster mail delivery.
> 3. The pony express delivered mail (among, between) St. Joseph, Missouri, and Sacramento, California.
> 4. At first, no one had any idea (as to, about) the exact time it would take a rider to travel from Missouri to California.
> 5. The service employed about eighty riders (altogether, all together) to deliver the mail.
> 6. Riders endured (bad, badly) weather and the threat of attacks by Indians.
> 7. After a rider covered at least 75 miles, he reached a station where another rider was (all ready, already) waiting.
> 8. The new rider would (accept, except) the leather saddlebag and continue along the route.
> 9. The fate of the pony express (ain't, isn't) a happy one.
> 10. The new transcontinental telegraph had a major (affect, effect) on the pony express, quickly shutting it down.

614 • Miscellaneous Problems in Usage

▲ **Critical Viewing** Using the words *bad* and *badly*, write a movie scene using this photograph as inspiration. **[Speculate]**

> **More Practice**

Grammar Exercise Workbook
• pp. 155–156
On-line Exercise Bank
• Section 26.2
Go on-line:
PHSchool.com
Enter Web Code:
eek-1002

Get instant feedback! Exercise 10 is available on-line or on CD-ROM.

☑ **ONGOING ASSESSMENT: Monitor and Reinforce**

If students miss more than two items in Exercise 10, refer them to the following for additional practice.

In the Textbook	Print Resources	Technology
Section Review, Ex. 13–16, Section 26.2	*Grammar Exercise Workbook,* pp. 155–156	*On-Line Exercise Bank,* Section 26.2

(16) because Do not use *because* after the word *reason*. Say "The reason . . . that" or reword the sentence.

NONSTANDARD: *The reason* miners moved so often is *because* they were always searching for a major strike.

CORRECT: *The reason* miners moved so often is *that* they were always searching for a major strike.
Miners moved so often *because* they were always searching for a major strike.

(17) being as, being that Do not use either expression. Use *because* or *since* instead.

(18) beside, besides *Beside* means "close to" or "at the side of." *Besides* means "in addition to."

EXAMPLES: Tombstone, Arizona, developed *beside* a mine.
Besides mines, towns were started near transportation centers and major shipping points.

(19) bring, take *Bring* means "to carry from a distant place to a nearer one." *Take* means the opposite: "to carry from a near place to a more distant place."

EXAMPLES: Cowboys would *bring* cattle over thousands of miles to a town with a train station.
The trains would then *take* the cattle to the East, where they would be sold for food.

(20) different from, different than *Different from* is preferred.

LESS ACCEPTABLE: A transportation town was *different than* a mining town because it was usually more permanent.

PREFERRED: A transportation town was *different from* a mining town because it was usually more permanent.

(21) doesn't, don't *Doesn't* is the correct verb form for third-person singular subjects. *Don't* is used with all other subjects.

NONSTANDARD: A town *don't* thrive without townspeople.
It *don't* seem very prosperous.
He *don't* want to stay if there is no work.

CORRECT: A town *doesn't* thrive without townspeople.
It *doesn't* seem very prosperous.
He *doesn't* want to stay if there is no work.

Common Usage Problems • **615**

Step-by-Step Teaching Guide continued

4. Tell students that the word *because* and the word *reason* have similar meanings; therefore, they should not be used in the same sentence.

5. Point out that the "Correct" examples on this page have replaced *because* with *that* or removed the word *reason*.

6. Explain that the expressions *being that* and *being as* are not standard uses of language. Tell students that the subordinating conjunctions *because* and *since* are better choices in their speech and writing.

7. Ask students to compose two sentences containing an adverb clause beginning with *because* or *since* that provides a reason supporting an idea in the main clause.

8. Explain that *beside* means "close to" (at the side of) and *besides* means "in addition to." Tell students that both words are prepositions, but *besides* can be an adverb as well. Suggest that students remember *beside* is a shorter word and therefore is closer to the <u>side</u> of the other words in the sentence.

9. Remind students that *bring* means "to carry from a farther position to a closer one." *Take* means "to carry from a closer position to a farther one." Suggest that students remember the phrases *bring in* and *take out*.

10. Explain that *different than* is a less acceptable way of saying *different from*. Point out that the word *than* is used independently when making comparisons in different situations (*That transportation town is more permanent than this mining town*).

11. Write the contractions *doesn't* and *don't* and then ask the class what subjects take these two verbs (third person singular—*he, she, it*—takes *doesn't*). Point out that every other subject (*I, you, we, you, they*) takes the contraction of *do not*.

Usage Problems 22–30

1. Ask students to name the part of speech of the word *done* (verb—past participle of *to do*). Remind students that when the main verb in a sentence is a past participle, it should always follow a helping verb.

2. Explain that the phrase *due to* has the same meaning as *caused by*. *Due to* should be used only in sentences in which *caused by* can be substituted without changing the meaning. (*My inability to do the homework was due to the difficulty of the lesson.*)

3. Tell students that *farther* is a word referring to distance while *further* refers to extent. Remind them that the word *far*, which refers to distance, is in *farther*. Have students write brief sentences for both words.

4. Explain that *fewer* and *less* are adjectives, but they can modify different things. *Fewer* refers to objects that can be counted (numbers), while *less* refers to things that are uncountable (amount). Have students offer the right words for the following sentences:

   The Cowardly Lion had ___ courage than Dorothy. (less)

   This line is for people buying ten items or ___. (fewer)

5. Review the irregular verb *to go* and ask students to identify the principal parts *gone* (past participle) and *went* (past). Explain that *gone* is the form used with a helping verb. Have students practice forming these tenses correctly. (*I went to the candy store. I have gone to the candy store.*)

6. Explain that *in* and *into* are prepositions but *in* refers to a location while *into* refers to movement. Have students fill in the blanks:

   I got ___ my car which was sitting ___ the driveway. (into, in)

   At the shopping mall ___ the next town, I pulled ___ a parking spot. (in, into)

continued

26.2

(22) done *Done*, the past participle of *do*, should always follow a helping verb.

NONSTANDARD: Merchants *done* the job of supplying farmers, miners, and cowhands.

CORRECT: Merchants *have done* the job of supplying farmers, miners, and cowhands.

(23) due to *Due to* means "caused by" and should be used only when the words *caused by* can logically be substituted.

NONSTANDARD: *Due to* the lack of natural resources, towns were often established in groups.

CORRECT: The establishment of towns in groups was *due to* the lack of natural resources.

(24) farther, further *Farther* refers to distance. *Further* means "to a greater degree or extent" or "additional."

EXAMPLES: The *farther* away a town was from transportation, the harder it was for people to get supplies.
The area around Virginia City, Nevada, was *further* developed to supply resources to the city.
Virginia City needed *further* support to survive.

(25) fewer, less *Fewer* is used with objects that can be counted. *Less* is used with qualities or quantities that cannot be counted.

EXAMPLES: *fewer* stagecoaches, *fewer* horses, *fewer* supplies
less land, *less* wood, *less* communication

(26) gone, went *Gone* is the past participle of *go*. It should be used as a verb only with a helping verb. *Went* is the past tense of *go* and is never used with a helping verb.

NONSTANDARD: Easterners *gone* west to find a better life.
They *could have went* to a major eastern city to make a better life for themselves.

CORRECT: Easterners *had gone* west hoping to find a better life.
Easterners *went* west to find a better life.
They *could have gone* to a major eastern city to make a better life for themselves.

(27) in, into *In* refers to position. *Into* suggests motion.

POSITION: People often traveled west *in* wagons.
MOTION: They loaded their supplies *into* a covered wagon.

616 • Miscellaneous Problems in Usage

✿ Grammar and Style Tip

Vary your vocabulary to make your writing more interesting. Explore new words and expressions, but always check for correct usage.

◇ STANDARDIZED TEST PREPARATION WORKSHOP

Grammar and Usage Many standardized tests require students to recognize and solve common usage problems. Use the following example to demonstrate.

Which of the following sentences contains a common usage error?

A James felt bad because he missed the game.

B He was all ready to go when he realized his car was out of gas.

C He should have went to the gas station the day before.

D The reason James missed the game is that he was careless.

The correct answer is **C**. *Went* is the past of *go* and is never used with a helping verb. *Gone*, the past participle of *go*, should be used with the helping verb *have*. The sentence should read: *"He should have gone to the gas station the day before."*

(28) irregardless Putting *ir-* on this word makes it a double negative. Use *regardless* instead.

NONSTANDARD: People settled in the West, *irregardless* of the dangers.

CORRECT: People settled in the West, *regardless* of the dangers.

(29) just When you use *just* to mean "no more than," place it right before the word or phrase it logically modifies.

LESS ACCEPTABLE: Since there was little wood, houses were *just* made of sod.

PREFERRED: Since there was little wood, houses were made of *just* sod.

(30) kind of, sort of These expressions should not be used to mean "rather" or "somewhat."

NONSTANDARD: Travel was *kind* of slow.

CORRECT: Travel was *rather* slow.

▼ **Critical Viewing**
Write a description of this painting, correctly using one of the two words listed in each of the usage problems 24–27. **[Interpret]**

Common Usage Problems • 617

7. Explain to students that *irregardless* is not a real word. Tell students to avoid this common error in their speech and writing by using the word *regardless*.

8. Tell students that the word *just*, when used as an adverb, should be placed directly before the word it is modifying. (Example: *You will need* just *your paper today.*) Explain that this helps to avoid confusion for the reader or listener.

9. Explain to students that the expressions *kind of* and *sort of* are informal ways of saying *rather* or *somewhat*. Tell them that these informal expressions should not be used in formal writing.

Integrating Spelling Skills

Slang Point out to students that the expressions *kind of* and *sort of* are both informal expressions used in American English. Ask where we encounter these expressions (more often in oral communication than in written). Tell students that *kinda* and *sorta* are incorrect spellings (abbreviated and combined) of these nonstandard expressions used in informal writing or dialogue. Ask students to think of other words that are combined or shortened when they are written in order to replicate the pronunciation (*gotta, wanna, nothin'*). Remind students that these are slang pronunciations and incorrect spellings and help them identify the correct spellings (*have to, want to, nothing*).

Critical Viewing

Interpret Responses will vary. Sample sentences: The family got <u>into</u> the coach and traveled <u>farther</u> than they had ever <u>gone</u> before. There are <u>fewer</u> people in the coach than in the background.

Answer Key

Step-by-Step Teaching Guide

Usage Problems 31–37

1. Explain that *lay* requires a direct object and that *lie* never takes a direct object. Ask students to write sentences using both verbs. (Example: *After I* laid *my bag on the chair, I* lay *down on the bed.*)

2. Ask students to explain in their own words the difference between the two verbs *learn* and *teach* (We learn; you teach).

continued

Language Highlight

The English language did not exist 2,000 years ago. Nearly 1,500 years later, English existed primarily in England; today English is used by 750 million to one billion people. Of the 2,700 languages spoken in the world, English has the richest vocabulary—one-half million (500,000) words, without counting technical and scientific words. Its closest rival is German, with 185,000 words. English is more widely spoken and written than any other language has ever been.

26.2

> **Exercise 11** Avoiding Usage Problems 16–30 Choose the correct expression to complete each sentence.
> 1. Pony express riders carried the mail (irregardless, regardless) of bad weather, rough terrain, or danger.
> 2. They (gone, went) about 75 miles a day.
> 3. Teenagers (did, done) much of the riding.
> 4. They were chosen (due to, because of) their light weight.
> 5. Horses traveled (fewer, less) miles per day than the riders.
> 6. The mail was carried (in, into) special leather saddlebags.
> 7. (Beside, Besides) letters, pony express riders also carried small packages.
> 8. The mail traveled much (farther, further) in a day with the pony express than on a ship or stagecoach.
> 9. The service (just lasted, lasted just) a year and a half.
> 10. The reason it closed down is (that, because) the transcontinental telegraph service had opened for business two days earlier.

(31) lay, lie *Lay* means "to put or set (something) down." Its principal parts—*lay, laying, laid,* and *laid*—are usually followed by a direct object. *Lie* means "to recline." Its principal parts—*lie, lying, lay,* and *lain*—are never followed by a direct object.

LAY: *Lay* the luggage on top of the stagecoach.
The driver is *laying* the bags in the back compartment.
The passengers *laid* their handbags on the seats.
The bags were jostled about and no longer rested where the driver had *laid* them.

LIE: Passengers had to sleep in the stagecoach and were not able to *lie* down.
The handbag is *lying* on the floor at her feet.
The child *lay* down across her parents' laps.
She had *lain* there throughout the night.

(32) learn, teach *Learn* means "to acquire knowledge." *Teach* means "to give knowledge to."

EXAMPLES: A person *learned* many different skills in order to survive in the West.
Settlers *taught* newcomers how to manage in the new terrain.

☑ ONGOING ASSESSMENT: Monitor and Reinforce

If students miss more than two items in Exercise 11, refer them to the following for additional practice.

In the Textbook	Print Resources	Technology
Section Review, Ex. 14–18, Section 26.2	*Grammar Exercise Workbook,* pp. 155–156	*On-Line Exercise Bank,* Section 26.2

(33) leave, let *Leave* means "to allow to remain." *Let* means "to permit."

NONSTANDARD: Cowboys *leave* the cattle wander over great tracts of land.
They *let* calves with the mothers, even if the father belongs to a different herd.

CORRECT: Cowboys *let* the cattle wander over great tracts of land.
They *leave* calves with the mothers, even if the father belongs to a different herd.

(34) like *Like* is a preposition and should not be used in place of the conjunction *as*.

NONSTANDARD: Crime in the West was widespread, *like* it was in the East.

CORRECT: Crime in the West was widespread, *as* it was in the East.

(35) of Do not use the preposition *of* in place of the verb *have*. *Of* after *outside*, *inside*, *off*, or *atop* is also undesirable in formal writing. Simply eliminate it.

NONSTANDARD: A single sheriff would *of* watched over a group of towns.

CORRECT: A single sheriff would *have* watched over a group of towns.

LESS ACCEPTABLE: One judge held court *inside* of a restaurant.
PREFERRED: One judge held court *inside* a restaurant.

(36) only Be sure to place *only* in front of the word you mean to modify.

EXAMPLES: *Only* one cowboy wanted to go to town today. (No one else wanted to go to town.)
One cowboy *only* wanted to go to town. (He did not want to do anything else.)

(37) seen *Seen* is a past participle and can be used as a verb only with a helping verb.

NONSTANDARD: The judge *seen* a number of criminals.
CORRECT: The judge *has seen* a number of criminals.

Learn More

To learn how your mastery of English usage is tested on standardized tests, see the Standardized Test Preparation Workshop for this chapter on pages 626–627.

Step-by-Step Teaching Guide continued

3. Explain that *leave* means "to allow to remain" while *let* means "to permit."
4. Tell students that *like* is a preposition and cannot replace *as*, a subordinating conjunction.
5. Explain to students that *of* is a preposition and cannot replace the verb *have*. The preposition *of* cannot be part of a verb phrase.
6. Ask students to identify the error in the following sentence:
   The book is <u>inside</u> of a desk.
7. Explain that *only* is an adverb that should be placed before the word it modifies. Using the examples, ask students to explain how moving *only* to a different position changes the meaning.
8. Tell students that *seen* is a past participle; it needs a helping verb.

Customize for ESL Students

Put the following chart on the board.

Present	Past	Perfect
do	did	have done
go	went	have gone
lay	laid	have laid
lie	lay	have lain

Remind students that these verbs do not form past and past perfect tenses in the regular way. Ask students to change these sentences to past and perfect tenses.

I do my homework.
I go to school.
He lays the book on the desk.
He lies on the bed.

Point out that when *lay* asks the question *What?* it always gets an answer (He lay what? He lay the book). *Lie* never does.

Integrating Vocabulary Skills

Expressions Ask students to define the verb *to let* ("to permit, to allow"). Then, ask them to think of expressions that use *let* (*let alone, let me know, let it go, let me in, let down, let on, let up*). Ask how the definition of *to let* works in these expressions.

451Ⓗ • **619**

Usage Problems 38–45

1. Explain that *set* is a verb meaning "to put" and that it usually requires a direct object; *sit* is a verb meaning "to be seated" and is never followed by a direct object. Review the principal parts of each verb.

2. Ask students to identify the part of speech of the word *so* (coordinating conjunction). Explain that it should not be used in place of the expression *so that*.

3. Ask students to complete these sentences:

    Grammar is harder ___ punctuation. (than)

    We learned punctuation and ___ capitalization. (then)

4. Ask students to complete the following sentence:

    The speaker ___ visited their class taught them science, ___ was their favorite subject. (who, which)

    Ask students to explain their answers.

5. Write on the board:

    They're all there in the classroom, but their books are closed.

    Ask students to identify the parts of speech of the underlined words (contraction of the words *they are*, adverb, possessive pronoun).

continued

Customize for
Linguistic Learners

Have students write brief paragraphs about a recent after-school activity, addressing as many of the usage problems as they can. Ask a student volunteer to read aloud. Have students listen and identify the potential usage problems and decide if each is handled correctly. (For some problems, the speaker will have to spell words out loud.)

Customize for
More Advanced Students

Ask students to generate a list of the usage errors they think they most frequently make. Prompt students to think about problems they encounter in their own writing or errors they have seen while reading. (Possible words: *your/you're; allot/a lot; can/ may; emigrate/immigrate*)

26.2

(38) set, sit *Set* means "to put (something) in a certain place." Its principal parts—*set, setting, set,* and *set*—are usually followed by a direct object. *Sit* means "to be seated." Its principal parts—*sit, sitting, sat,* and *sat*—are never followed by a direct object.

SET:	*Set* the tools in the barn.
	He is *setting* the plow in the backyard.
	His wife *set* the food on the table.
	She had *set* the plates out earlier.
SIT:	They brought a rocking chair from the East to *sit* in.
	She is *sitting* in it right now.
	She *sat* in it whenever they stopped.
	Her mother had *sat* in that chair before her.

(39) so *So* is a coordinating conjunction. It should be avoided when you mean "so that."

LESS ACCEPTABLE:	Townsfolk formed vigilante groups *so* they could enforce the law as they saw fit.
PREFERRED:	Townsfolk formed vigilante groups *so that* they could enforce the law as they saw fit.

(40) than, then Use *than* in comparisons. *Then,* an adverb, usually refers to time.

EXAMPLES:	The telegraph was faster *than* the pony express.
	The transcontinental telegraph was installed, and *then* the pony express went out of business.

(41) that, which, who Use these relative pronouns correctly. *That* and *which* refer to things; *who* refers only to people.

EXAMPLES:	The wagon *that* carried the food for a cattle drive was called the chuck wagon.
	The person *who* took care of the extra horses on a cattle drive was called a wrangler.

(42) their, there, they're *Their,* a possessive pronoun, always modifies a noun. *There* can be used either as an expletive at the beginning of a sentence or as an adverb. *They're* is a contraction of *they are.*

PRONOUN:	Farmers spent all *their* time working the land.
EXPLETIVE:	*There* are many obstacles to a good harvest.
ADVERB:	The fields over *there* will be planted tomorrow.
CONTRACTION:	*They're* deciding what crops to plant this year.

620 • Miscellaneous Problems in Usage

(43) them Do not use *them* as a substitute for *those.*

NONSTANDARD: *Them* horses are extremely fast.
CORRECT: *Those* horses are extremely fast.

(44) to, too, two *To*, a preposition, begins a phrase or an infinitive. *Too*, an adverb, modifies adjectives and other adverbs. *Two* is a number.

PREPOSITION: *to* the homestead, *to* the miner
INFINITIVE: *to* dig, *to* plow
ADVERB: *too* dry, *too* quickly
NUMBER: *two* fields, *two* cows

(45) when, where Do not use *when* or *where* directly after a linking verb. Do not use *where* in place of *that.*

NONSTANDARD: A barn raising is *when* farmers could socialize with their neighbors.
A general store is *where* they got supplies.
He heard *where* the square dance was held after harvest time.
CORRECT: A barn raising allowed farmers to socialize with their neighbors.
A farmer could get supplies at a general store.
He heard *that* the square dance was held after harvest time.

▶ **Exercise 12** Revising a Paragraph to Correct Usage Problems 31–45 Rewrite the following paragraph, correcting the errors in usage. Not every sentence contains an error.

(1) Even though life in the West was difficult, settlers would leave some time to enjoy themselves. (2) Homesteaders often combined they're work and play. (3) They might travel too a neighbor's farm to help with harvesting a crop or husking corn. (4) A barn raising was when farmers could do some work and have some fun. (5) The men at a house or barn raising were divided into teams so the work would go faster and be more fun. (6) The teams would lie down the floor together and then each take responsibility for building a different wall. (7) This was a good way to learn newcomers some of the skills needed to survive in the West. (8) Women might set with their neighbors at a quilting bee. (9) Traveling vaudeville shows would set up outside of several towns each year. (10) One farmer seen the famous performers Buffalo Bill, Annie Oakley, Edwin Booth, and Laura Keene.

More Practice

Grammar Exercise Workbook
• pp. 155–156
On-line Exercise Bank
• Section 26.2
Go on-line:
PHSchool.com
Enter Web Code:
eek-1002

interactive **Textbook**

Get instant feedback!
Exercise 12 is available on-line or on CD-ROM.

Common Usage Pronouns • 621

Step-by-Step Teaching Guide continued

6. Ask students to listen as you read aloud the sentence *If you'll go too I'll make two trips out to the car.* Have students define the underlined words.

7. Review linking verbs with students. Explain that *when* and *where* should not follow linking verbs. Also, remind students that *where* should not replace *that.*

Integrating Vocabulary Skills

Comparisons Tell students that the word *to* is also used in certain comparisons. Explain that they should use the word *to* when making an analogy (pointing out similarities between two disparate things) and *with* when comparing things in the same category. Examples:

The poet compared life ___ a candle. (to)

How do you compare a trumpet ___ a tuba? (with)

Have students list items that can be compared and, from these lists, create statements using *to* and *with*.

Answer Key

▶ **Exercise 12**

1. Correct
2. . . . combined <u>their</u> work . . .
3. . . . <u>to</u> a neighbor's farm . . .
4. Farmers could do some work and have some fun <u>at a barn raising</u>.
5. . . . <u>into</u> teams so <u>that</u> . . .
6. The teams would <u>lay</u> . . .
7. . . . good way to <u>teach</u> . . .
8. Women might <u>sit</u> with . . .
9. . . . set up <u>outside</u> several . . .
10. One farmer <u>saw</u> . . .

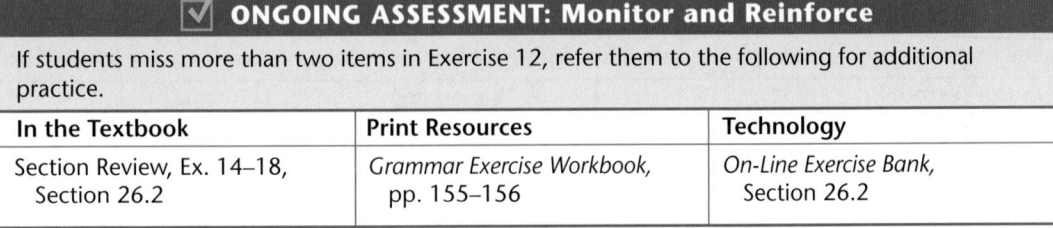

☑ **ONGOING ASSESSMENT: Monitor and Reinforce**

If students miss more than two items in Exercise 12, refer them to the following for additional practice.

In the Textbook	Print Resources	Technology
Section Review, Ex. 14–18, Section 26.2	*Grammar Exercise Workbook,* pp. 155–156	*On-Line Exercise Bank,* Section 26.2

⏱ **TIME SAVERS!**

🖨 **Answers on Transparencies** Use the *Grammar Exercises Answers on Transparencies* for Chapter 26 to facilitate correction by students.

🖥 **On-Line Exercise Bank** Have students complete the exercises on computer. The Auto Check feature will grade their work for you!

Hands-on Grammar

Teaching Resources: Hands-on Grammar Activity Book, Ch. 26

1. If you wish to do this activity in class, be prepared with scissors and index cards. Have students work in pairs, and give each pair ten or more index cards.

2. Have students work on their illustrations with a partner. When they have finished, have volunteers explain their illustrations and compare with those of other students.

3. Have students look through the other usage notes in the chapter and come up with several more that they feel they can illustrate. Again, compare their completed work with that of others.

Find It in Your Reading

Emphasize to students that the more samples they find and record, the stronger will be their sense of correct usage.

Find It in Your Writing

Before students write their own sentences on the cards, have their partners check the sentences for correct usage.

26.2

Hands-on Grammar

Illustrating Usage Problems on Index Cards

Work on common usage problems by creating illustrations that represent each word's proper usage. In the examples below, *in* and *into* are illustrated with paper airplanes and garbage cans showing that *in* refers to position and *into* suggests motion. *Bring* and *take* are illustrated with drawings and arrows showing that *bring* means "to carry from a distant place to a nearer one," while *take* means "to carry from a near place to a more distant one."

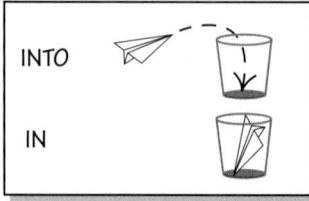
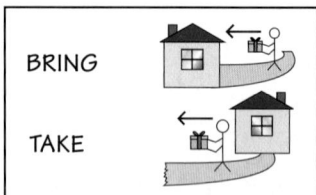

Each of the ten word pairs below represents a common usage problem. Using the common-usage glossary on pages 612–621, illustrate each word. Don't worry about making detailed drawings—just make sure they clearly illustrate the main difference between the proper usage of the two words. Use one index card for each word pair, and use the same side of the index card to illustrate both words.

After you have completed your illustrations, practice the correct usage of each word. Working with a partner, take turns selecting index cards at random, studying the illustrations, and forming sentences that use each word correctly. Refer to the common-usage problems glossary to check your answers.

1. among, between
2. fewer, less
3. lay, lie
4. beside, besides
5. leave, let

6. that, which, who
7. set, sit
8. learn, teach
9. accept, except
10. farther, further

Find It in Your Reading In textbooks or magazines, find examples of the words above used correctly in sentences. Write the example sentences on the backs of the appropriate index cards.

Find It in Your Writing Look through pieces of writing in your writing portfolio for examples of the words above used correctly in sentences. Write the example sentences on the back of the appropriate index cards. If you cannot find examples of any of the words, challenge yourself to write new sentences on the backs of the cards using the words correctly.

☑ **ONGOING ASSESSMENT: Assess Mastery**

Use the following resources to assess student mastery of common usage problems.

In the Textbook	Technology
Chapter Review, Ex. 21–24	*On-Line Exercise Bank*, Section 26.2

Section 26.2 Section Review

GRAMMAR EXERCISES 13–19

Exercise 13 Supplying *a* or *an* Correctly Complete each expression with *a* or *an*.

1. occurrence
2. usual amount
3. heirloom
4. urban outfit
5. hard-packed trail

Exercise 14 Avoiding Usage Problems Choose the correct expression to complete each sentence.

1. Life in the West favored those who could (adapt, adopt) to many jobs.
2. A well-rounded man could (except, accept) any kind of job to survive.
3. If he were paid (bad, badly) at one occupation, he could move on to another.
4. He could move about freely (like, as) the birds did.
5. George Jackson, (who, which) is credited with discovering gold in the Rockies, also worked as a roustabout, farmhand, miner, and businessman.
6. Buffalo Bill Cody is a famous jack-of-all-trades, (too, two).
7. After his father died when Bill was eleven, he worked for (awhile, a while) as a messenger for a freight company.
8. (Being as, Because) war broke out in 1861, Bill joined the Union army.
9. In 1872, Bill embarked on a career very (different from, different than) any of his previous occupations.
10. As a showman, he traveled much (further, farther) than ever before.

Exercise 15 Revising Sentences to Correct Usage Errors Rewrite each sentence, correcting the error in usage.

1. The life of a cowboy was kind of lonely.
2. On long cattle drives, cowboys spent all day setting in the saddle.

3. They had to keep the cattle altogether for the entire ride.
4. On these drives, cowboys laid down under the stars to go to sleep.
5. At home on the range, cowboys just didn't watch over the cattle.
6. They also would of had to do repairs.
7. The installation of fences effected relations with the ranchers' neighbors.
8. Tension between cattle ranchers and farmers was all ready strained.
9. Everyone was anxious to help.
10. Range wars erupted everywheres across the West.

Exercise 16 Writing Sentences Using Troublesome Words Correctly use each word in an original sentence.

1. accept
2. further
3. like
4. which
5. altogether
6. just
7. awhile
8. lay
9. set
10. effect

Exercise 17 Find It in Your Reading In a newspaper, find five examples of words discussed in this section. Explain why each is used correctly.

Exercise 18 Find It in Your Writing In your own writing, find three examples of words discussed in this section. Check to make sure that your usage of the words is correct. If not, revise your work.

Exercise 19 Writing Application Write an essay telling what you would and would not like about life in the Old West. Be sure to avoid all the usage errors described in this section.

Section Review • 623

Each of these exercises correlates to a section of the chapter on miscellaneous problems in usage, pages 606–623. The exercises may be used for more practice, for reteaching, or for review of the key concepts presented.

Answer Key

Exercise 20

1. anywhere
2. ever
3. any
4. are
5. any
6. has
7. can
8. any
9. could
10. becomes

Exercise 21

1. Further
2. than
3. badly
4. taught
5. eager
6. Besides
7. has seen
8. who
9. their
10. adapted
11. effects
12. isn't
13. rather
14. different from
15. Those

GRAMMAR EXERCISES 20–25

▶ **Exercise 20** **Avoiding Double Negatives** Choose the word in parentheses that makes each sentence negative without forming a double negative.

1. Today's ranchers and their families aren't (nowhere, anywhere) near as isolated as their counterparts in the Old West.
2. A hundred years ago, cowboys didn't (never, ever) go to town except on paydays.
3. Because we have automobiles, we don't have to wait for (no, any) special opportunities.
4. In addition, the roads (aren't, are) rarely in as poor condition as they were in the past.
5. Now children can ride buses to school; they don't have to stay home (any, no) more.
6. With advances in technology, no one (doesn't have, has) to rely solely on his or her own resources.
7. Nothing (can, can't) replace horses, but alternatives like jeeps and helicopters are sometimes used as well.
8. Since the 1940's, the price of land has risen, so ranchers can't waste (none, any) of their land.
9. They (could, couldn't) scarcely afford to leave any parcel of land unused.
10. They rotate the grazing fields so that no field (doesn't become, becomes) exhausted of all nourishment.

▶ **Exercise 21** **Avoiding Usage Problems** Choose the correct expression to complete each sentence.

1. (Farther, Further) settlement of western lands and the growth of transportation and communication ended the period of time called the Old West.

2. No time in our history is more exciting (than, then) this one.
3. However, some legends that (bad, badly) distorted history sprang up.
4. Pecos Bill, for example, supposedly (learned, taught) broncos how to buck.
5. Many who had lived in the West were (anxious, eager) to capture its essence for posterity.
6. (Besides, Beside) his many other classics, Mark Twain wrote a novel about his experiences as a reporter in the West.
7. Anyone who (seen, has seen) the paintings of Frederic Remington can easily imagine the frontier.
8. The Old West has influenced many artists (who, which) grew up after the heyday.
9. Thomas Hart Benton and Georgia O'Keeffe have used western backgrounds in (their, they're) paintings.
10. Filmmakers and novelists have (adopted, adapted) the tales of the Old West for their own stories.
11. *Oklahoma!*, one of the most popular American musicals, recounts the (affects, effects) of the range wars between ranchers and homesteaders.
12. There (isn't, ain't) any way to single out the most famous writers of westerns, but Louis L'Amour and Larry McMurtry are two of the most popular.
13. Western movies were (kind of, rather) popular from the 1920's through the 1950's.
14. Works in the 1990's portrayed a West (different from, different than) that seen in older works.
15. (Them, Those) later works, like the movies *Unforgiven* and *Dances With Wolves,* often showed the West in a less heroic light.

☑ **ONGOING ASSESSMENT: Assess Mastery**

Use the following resources to assess student mastery of miscellaneous usage problems.

In the Textbook	Print Resources	Technology
Chapter Review, Ex. 20–24 Standardized Test Preparation Workshop	*Formal Assessment,* Chapter 26	*On-Line Exercise Bank,* Chapter 26

> **Exercise 22** Revising Sentences to Correct Usage Problems Rewrite each sentence, correcting the error in usage.

1. Being as westerns were very popular in the first half of the twentieth century, many actors became famous by playing cowboys.
2. When taken altogether, there were quite a few men who became famous as television and movie cowboys.
3. Clint Eastwood, John Wayne, Gene Autry, and Roy Rogers are between the most famous cowboy stars.
4. Gene Autry was all ready a successful singer of cowboy songs when he made his first movie.
5. He became a popular actor due to his roles as a singing cowboy.
6. Even though he did alright as an actor and singer, he decided to branch out into business, too.
7. He wasn't only successful as an actor; his businesses did well, too.
8. Roy Rogers was another popular movie cowboy who became a successful businessman, to.
9. Rogers's wife, Dale Evans, played an heroine in many of his movies.
10. Them two were quite a pair.

> **Exercise 23** Revising a Paragraph to Correct Double Negatives and Other Usage Problems Rewrite the following paragraph, correcting all fifteen usage errors.

(1) Three years after the transcontinental telegraph made the pony express obsolete, post office officials established they're first railway post office. (2) Clerks sorted mail while traveling into special train cars. (3) Towns could erect posts besides a train track and hang their mail in a pouch from the top. (4) Catcher arms attached to the train cars would snatch the mail bags off of the posts. (5) This was quicker then stopping to pick up the mail. (6) Too deliver mail, the clerks would toss mail sacks onto the train platforms of a town. (7) Letters and packages could be sent anywheres in the United States. (8) The airplane was the next advance to effect the postal system. (9) At first, mail who was sent by air was more expensive. (10) The plan to deliver mail via guided missile failed all together on its first attempt. (11) Irregardless, the post office continued to experiment with new ways to improve service. (12) In the 1970's, private mail services were established so people could choose how to send their parcels. (13) The reason private services started is because the rates for the government's postal services had continued to rise. (14) In the latter half of the twentieth century, computer technology adopted to send messages electronically from one computer to another for personal use. (15) E-mail has almost eliminated private correspondence, like the telegraph eradicated the pony express.

> **Exercise 24** Using Troublesome Words Correctly Write twenty sentences —two sentences for each of the following pairs of words. Be sure the words are used correctly.

1. badly, bad
2. than, then
3. all together, altogether
4. farther, further
5. affect, effect
6. adopt, adapt
7. lie, lay
8. learn, teach
9. set, sit
10. gone, went

> **Exercise 25** Writing Application
Imagine that you live in the Old West. Write a letter describing the place and your experiences to someone who has never been there.

> **Exercise 22**

1. **Since** westerns were . . .
2. When taken **all together**, . . .
3. . . . **among** the most . . .
4. Gene Autry was **already** . . .
5. . . . popular actor **because of** . . .
6. Even though he did **all right** . . .
7. He wasn't successful **only** as . . .
8. . . . successful businessman, **too**.
9. . . . played **a** heroine . . .
10. Those two . . .

> **Exercise 23**

1. . . . established **their** first . . .
2. . . . traveling **in** special train cars.
3. . . . posts **beside** a train track . . .
4. . . . mail bags **off** the posts.
5. . . . quicker **than** stopping. . .
6. **To** deliver mail, the clerks . . .
7. . . . could be sent **anywhere** . . .
8. . . . to **affect** the postal system.
9. . . . mail **that** was sent by air . . .
10. . . . missile failed **altogether** . . .
11. **Regardless**, the post office . . .
12. . . . established **so that** people . . .
13. . . . services started is **that** . . .
14. . . . technology **adapted** to send. . .
15. . . . correspondence, just **as** the telegraph . . .

> **Exercise 24**

Answers will vary; samples are given.

1a. He drove so **badly** on his test that the instructor failed him.
1b. It was a **bad** day for him indeed.
2a. She received a higher grade **than** I (received).
2b. She studied hard and **then** received a high grade.
3a. They were **all together** in the library.
3b. That explanation is **altogether** unconvincing.
4a. Jill's house is **farther** from here than Melanie's is.
4b. We will talk **further** about usage problems in class tomorrow.
5a. Cloudy weather **affects** my mood.
5b. What **effect** does the weather have on you?
6a. We will **adopt** a puppy from the shelter.
6b. It will soon **adapt** to living with us.
7a. **Lie** down if you don't feel well.
7b. **Lay** your books on the table near the bed.
8a. I want to **learn** how to swim.
8b. Will you please **teach** me?

continued

Answer Key continued

> **Exercise 24**

9a. Please **set** the table for dinner.
9b. Let Harry **sit** next to Dad.
10a. Have you **gone** to the new skating rink?
10b. Yes, I just **went** yesterday.

> **Exercise 25**

Writing Application
Before students write, brainstorm for ways to use some of the words discussed in this chapter in describing life in the Old West.

Step-by-Step Teaching Guide

Standard English Usage

Teaching Resources: Standardized Test Preparation Workbook, pp. 51–52

1. Choose several commonly problematic areas of usage to review with students. Some of these might include *accept/except, affect/effect, between/among, good/well, fewer/less,* and *who/whom.*

2. Go over the Sample Test Item and discuss reasons for correct answers.

3. As you review Practices 1 and 2, discuss methods that will help students choose the correct answer. Point out that context is essential in choosing appropriate descriptive words, as in Practice 1, Item 1. In other sentences, it may be important to note verb tense or subject number.

Standardized Test Preparation Workshop

Standard English Usage

Standardized tests frequently test your mastery of standard English usage. Some items focus on choosing the correct word to fill in a blank; others may test your ability to avoid or correct double negatives.

The following questions will give you practice with a format that is used to assess your understanding of standard English usage.

Test Tip

When looking for the best word or group of words to complete a sentence, read the whole sentence, trying each answer choice in turn.

Sample Test Item	Answer and Explanation

Directions: Read the passage, and choose the word or group of words that belongs in the space. Mark the letter for your answer.
 	
 When I was on the trip, I never went ___(1)___ that didn't interest me.
 	
 1 **A** everywhere
    B nowhere
    C anywhere
    D no place
	
	 The correct answer is *C*. The word *anywhere* completes the sentence according to the conventions of standard English usage and makes sense in the space. This choice also avoids a double negative, which would be created by using *nowhere*.

TEST-TAKING TIP

Tell students that when they are testing response choices in sentences, they should eliminate at once any response that they are sure is incorrect. If they are undecided about a response, they should try rereading the sentence with each possible choice and choose the one that sounds the most fluid in context.

▶ **Practice 1** **Directions:** Read the passage, and choose the word or group of words that belongs in each space.

Michael was __(1)__ to marry Janine as soon as they could arrange it. He was __(2)__ to settle down, have children, and grow old with her. This desire was no __(3)__ the wishes of his best friend, George. __(4)__ for George, there was no longer __(5)__ to share his dream.

1 A anxious
  B desirous
  C most eager
  D eager

2 F already
  G all ready
  H unready
  J readier

3 A different from
  B different than
  C different
  D different then

4 F Accept
  G Expect
  H Except
  J Excepting

5 A no one
  B anyone
  C nobody
  D anything

▶ **Practice 2** **Directions:** Read the passage, and choose the word or group of words that belongs in each space.

When he was a younger man, Michael had __(1)__ higher expectations for himself. It wasn't just __(2)__ who could turn a block of wood into a rocking horse with a set of carving tools. He knew he could succeed as an artist, and Janine knew it __(3)__. __(4)__ that, he vowed to love her forever. Nothing could __(5)__ change his mind about her.

1 A kind of
  B sort of
  C somewhat
  D somewhere

2 F everyone
  G someone
  H no one
  J anyone

3 A two
  B too
  C to
  D besides

4 F Because of
  G Because
  H Being
  J Since

5 A never
  B not
  C ever
  D evermore

CUMULATIVE REVIEW

Each of these exercises reviews concepts taught in the chapters on verb usage, pronoun usage, agreement, adjective and adverb usage, and miscellaneous problems in usage. The exercises may be used for more practice, for review of the key concepts presented, or for assessment of student mastery of the major concepts.

Answer Key

> **Exercise A**

1. was – past, active; who – nominative; his – possessive
2. He – nominative; who – nominative; publish – present, active
3. are – present, passive [are named]; him – objective
4. had been – past perfect, passive [had been eliminated]; them – objective
5. consists – present, active
6. has been – present perfect progressive, active [has been growing]; its – possessive; are – present, passive [are protected]
7. are – present, passive [are covered]; their – possessive
8. their – possessive; have – present perfect, active
9. it – nominative; stands – present, active
10. its – possessive; grows – present, active
11. it – nominative; has been – present perfect, passive [has been cut]
12. its – possessive; that – nominative
13. were – past, passive [were identified]; its – possessive
14. are – present, passive [are protected]; they – nominative
15. It – nominative; stands – present, active

> **Exercise B**

1. contains, lowest
2. Much, lies
3. hottest
4. measures, less
5. many, are
6. is, almost
7. rises, maximum
8. eastern, is
9. form, higher
10. lowest, are
11. are
12. largest

continued

628

Cumulative Review

USAGE

> **Exercise A** Using Verbs and Pronouns Choose the correct word or group of words that makes each sentence correct. For each verb or verb phrase, label its tense and voice. For each pronoun, identify its case.

1. Sequoyah (was, is) a Native American (who, whom) was also known by (his, its) English name, George Guess.
2. (He, It) developed a system of writing for the Cherokees (who, that) could then (published, publish) books and newspapers.
3. The giant sequoia trees and Sequoia National Park in California (is, are) named after (he, him).
4. Many species (had been, are being) eliminated by the glaciers, and now only three of (it, them) survive.
5. The Petrified Forest in Arizona (consisted, consists) of extinct species.
6. The giant sequoia (has been, had been) growing on the Sierra Nevada mountains, where most of (their, its) groves (is, are) protected in national parks.
7. The branches (are, had been) covered by (their, its) scalelike leaves.
8. By counting (their, its) rings, we know that some trees (had, have) lived for thousands of years.
9. The General Sherman Tree is in Sequoia National Park, and (he, it) (stands, has been standing) approximately 275 feet tall.
10. The coast redwood, similar to (its, his) cousin the giant sequoia, (grew, grows) to great sizes.
11. Unlike most conifer trees, (it, they) produces sprouts after it (has been, will be) cut down.
12. The dawn redwood is a deciduous tree, a characteristic that distinguishes it from (its, their) relatives (who, that) are evergreen trees.

13. Fossil specimens of the dawn redwood (are, were) identified in 1941, and some in (its, their) family were found afterward in China.
14. Ancient redwood trees (are, were) protected in Redwood National Park, and (they, it) include the world's tallest tree.
15. (It, They) (was standing, stands) close to 370 feet tall.

> **Exercise B** Making Words Agree Choose the correct word or group of words that makes each sentence correct.

1. Death Valley (contains, contain) the (lower, lowest) point in the Western Hemisphere.
2. (Much, More) of the valley (lies, lie) below sea level.
3. This area is also one of the (hot, hottest) regions in the world.
4. Yearly rainfall (measure, measures) (less, least) than 2 inches.
5. Sand and dust storms that last for (many, more) hours (is, are) common.
6. The valley (is, are) (almost, most) entirely enclosed by mountains.
7. The Panamint Range to the west (rises, rise) to a (maximum, most maximum) altitude at Telescope Peak.
8. On the (most eastern, eastern) side (is, are) the Amargosa Range.
9. Sand and salt (forms, form) the (high, higher) portions of the valley.
10. The (low, lowest) parts of the valley floor (is, are) salt flats.
11. The valley and surrounding mountains (is, are) included in Death Valley National Park.
12. It is the (larger, largest) contiguous park of all national parks in the United States.

13. There (is, are) (most, more) than 900 plant species there.
14. Desert shrubs and grasses (grows, grow) (sparsely, more sparsely) on the slopes around the valley floor.
15. A (few, less) species of desert reptiles (live, lives) in Death Valley.

Exercise C Revising a Paragraph to Eliminate Errors in Agreement Rewrite the following paragraph, correcting any errors in agreement.

The Appalachian Mountains runs along the eastern part of North America. It have different names in different places. For example, the Green Mountains, Alleghenies, Blue Ridge, and Great Smokies is all part of the Appalachian Mountains. The Appalachians are lowest and least rugged than the Rocky Mountains. The most high Appalachian peak is Mt. Mitchell in North Carolina, which is 6,684 feet. Still, early settlers had a hardest time crossing this heavily forested mountains.

Exercise D Revising Sentences to Correct Miscellaneous Problems in Usage Rewrite the following sentences, correcting negative sentences and other common usage problems.

1. The Sierra Nevada mountain range is in California accept for a small part in Nevada.
2. Being that Mount Whitney is the highest point in the continental United States, it is the highest point in the Sierra Nevadas.
3. Mount Whitney isn't hardly the only notable mountain of the High Sierra.
4. Williamson peak rises further than North Palisade, Russell, and Tyndall peaks.
5. These peaks lay along the western part of the southeastern portion of the range.

6. There isn't but one block of the Earth's crust in the Sierra Nevada.
7. Kings Canyon National Park has a higher canyon wall then any others in the United States.
8. Devils Postpile National Monument isn't nothing more than one notable rock formation.
9. Muir Woods National Monument ain't located in the Sierra Nevada mountains.
10. Yosemite National Park contains a most unique region of the range.

Exercise E Revising a Paragraph to Correct Usage Errors Rewrite the following paragraph, correcting the usage errors.

Juan Cabrillo was a Portuguese explorer whom served Spain. He travel to Mexico with Hernán Cortés. Once they're, he than sailed northward in the Pacific Ocean. In 1542, he will discover San Diego Bay. After leaving them, he discovered islands including the Channel Islands. Much years later, Alcatraz Island was discovered by Juan Manuel de Ayala. Santa Catalina, San Clemente, and San Nicolas ain't inside the national park. The park contains San Miguel, Santa Rosa, Santa Cruz, Anacapa, and Santa Barbara, to. There aren't but animals and birds living on the islands. Them include brown pelicans, seals, and sea lions.

Exercise F Writing Application
Write a description of the geographic features that make up the region in which you live. Make your writing interesting by varying your sentence lengths and structures. Try to avoid sentence errors and common usage problems. Be sure that the words in your sentences follow rules of agreement and that your modifiers are used correctly.

Cumulative Review • **629**

In-Depth Lesson Plan

	LESSON FOCUS	PRINT AND MEDIA RESOURCES
DAY 1	**Using Capitals for First Words** Students learn and apply concepts covering capitals for first words in sentences, quotations, lines of poetry, and the words *I* and *O*. (pp. 630–634/H456–460)	*Writing and Grammar* Interactive Text, Ch. 27; *On-line Exercise Bank*, Ch. 27 **Teaching Resources** *Grammar Exercise Workbook*, pp. 157–158; *Grammar Exercises Answers on Transparencies*, Ch. 27
DAY 2	**Using Capitals for Proper Nouns** Students learn and apply concepts covering capitalization of proper nouns. (pp. 635–638/H461–464)	**Teaching Resources** *Grammar Exercise Workbook*, pp. 159–160
DAY 3	**Using Capitals for Proper Adjectives and Titles** Students learn and apply concepts covering capitalization of proper adjectives and titles and do the Hands-on Grammar activity. (pp. 639–643/H465–469)	**Teaching Resources** *Grammar Exercise Workbook*, pp. 161–162; *Hands-on Grammar Activity Book*, Ch. 27
DAY 4	**Review and Assess** Students review the chapter and demonstrate mastery of capitalization concepts. (pp. 644–645)	*Writing and Grammar* Interactive Text, Ch. 27, Chapter Review; *On-line Exercise Bank*, Ch. 27 **Teaching Resources** *Formal Assessment*, Ch. 27

Accelerated Lesson Plan

	LESSON FOCUS	PRINT AND MEDIA RESOURCES
DAY 1	**Using Capitals for First Words and Proper Nouns** Students cover capitalization concepts as determined by the Diagnostic Test. (pp. 630–638/H456–464)	*Writing and Grammar* Interactive Text, Ch. 27; *On-line Exercise Bank*, Ch. 27 **Teaching Resources** *Grammar Exercise Workbook*, pp. 157–160; *Grammar Exercises Answers on Transparencies*, Ch. 27
DAY 2	**Using Capitals for Proper Adjectives and Titles** Students cover capitalization concepts as determined by the Diagnostic Test. (pp. 639–643/H465–469)	**Teaching Resources** *Grammar Exercise Workbook*, pp. 161–162
DAY 3	**Review and Assess** Students review the chapter and demonstrate mastery of the concepts. (pp. 644–645)	*Writing and Grammar* Interactive Text, Ch. 27, Chapter Review **Teaching Resources** *Formal Assessment*, Ch. 27

Options for Adapting Lesson Plans

HOMEWORK

Have students complete any section of the chapter for homework.

FEATURES

Extend coverage with the Standardized Test Preparation Workshop (p. 646).

TECHNOLOGY

Students can use *Writing and Grammar* Interactive Text to complete the exercises interactively on computer. They can complete additional exercises in the *On-line Exercise Bank:* The Auto Check feature will grade their work. Go On-line: PHSchool.com Use Web Code: eek-1002

Writing and Grammar Handbook Alignment

Page numbers in Step-by-Step Teaching Guides in this Teacher's Edition refer to pages from the full student text. Handbook page references, indicated with this icon ⒣, are provided in Time and Resource Manager boxes and at the bottom of each Teacher's Edition page.

INTEGRATED SKILLS COVERAGE

Writing
Find It in Your Writing SE p. 643/⒣469
Writing Application SE p. 645/⒣465
Grammar and Style SE p. 639

Viewing and Representing
ATE pp. 639, 641
Critical Viewing SE pp. 630, 633, 634, 638, 639, 640/⒣456, 459, 460, 464, 465, 466

Speaking and Listening
ATE p. 639

Vocabulary
ATE p. 640

Real-World Connection
ATE p. 637

ASSESSMENT SUPPORT

Standardized Test Preparation Workshop SE p. 646; ATE pp. 637, 640

Standardized Test Preparation Workbook, pp. 53–54

Formal Assessment, Ch. 27

MEETING INDIVIDUAL NEEDS

Less Advanced Students ATE pp. 633, 647. See also Ongoing Assessments ATE pp. 634, 638, 639, 641, 642.

More Advanced Students ATE pp. 632, 647

ESL Students ATE pp. 635, 642

Spatial Learners ATE p. 635

BLOCK SCHEDULING

Pacing Suggestions
For 90-minute Blocks
• Administer the Diagnostic Test to students to determine instructional coverage.
• Have students complete the necessary exercises in class. Use the Hands-on Grammar activity to provide a change of pace.

Resources for Varying Instruction
• *Writing and Grammar* **Interactive Text** A 90-minute block provides an ideal opportunity for students to work on the computer.

Professional Development Support
• *How to Manage Instruction in the Block* This teaching resource provides management and activity suggestions.

MEDIA AND TECHNOLOGY

For the Student
• *Writing and Grammar* Interactive Text, Ch. 27
• *On-line Exercise Bank,* Ch. 27

For the Teacher
• **Teacher EXPRESS** CD-ROM

WRITING AND GRAMMAR ON-LINE

Interactive Text (On-line or on CD-ROM)
• Easily navigable instruction with on-line supporting resources
• Self-scoring exercises and diagnostic tests

Companion Web Site PHSchool.com
• On-line Exercise Bank (use Web Code eek-1002)

See the Go On-line! feature, SE p. iii.

▶ *Lesson Objectives*

1. To place capitals correctly at the beginnings of sentences, quoted sentences, new sentences after colons, and some lines of poetry
2. To identify and capitalize all proper nouns, including names of people, geographical and place names, specific events and time periods, and groups of all kinds
3. To identify and capitalize all proper adjectives
4. To place capitals correctly in all titles including personal titles (social, business, military, and government), titles showing personal relationships, titles of works, and of some courses of study
5. To evaluate writing for both mechanics and content
6. To analyze the characteristics of clearly written texts, including the patterns of organization, syntax, and word choice
7. To produce legible work that shows correct use of the conventions of capitalization

Critical Viewing

Describe Sample response: I would use capitalization at the beginning of each sentence, as well as for the name of the mountain and the country in which it is located.

Chapter 27 Capitalization

Although you wouldn't remember it, you probably started using capital letters when you learned the alphabet. Without your realizing it, capital letters most likely continue to catch your attention when you look at advertisements, headlines, and road signs, among other things. Capital letters also serve an important role in writing. Through capitalization, writers indicate important words or signal a new thought.

Many rules govern the use of capitalization. This chapter will introduce you to the most widely accepted rules, showing you when and where to capitalize letters in your writing.

▲ **Critical Viewing**
In what ways would you use capitalization if you were writing a description of this mountain? **[Describe]**

630 • Capitalization

☑ ONGOING ASSESSMENT: Diagnose

If students miss more than one item in any category, direct them to the relevant pages of the textbook and assign exercises for practice and review

Capitalization	Diagnostic Test Items	Teach	Practice	Chapter Review
Skill Check A				
Recognizing Proper Nouns and Adjectives	A 1–5	pp. 635–639/Ⓗ461–465	Ex. 3–6	
Skill Check B				
Capitalizing First Words	B 6–15	pp. 632–633/Ⓗ458–459	Ex. 1–2	Ex. 9, 11
Capitalizing Proper Nouns and Adjectives	B 6–15	pp. 635–639/Ⓗ461–465	Ex. 3–6	Ex. 10–12
Capitalizing Titles of People and Things	B 11, 12, 15	pp. 640–642/Ⓗ466–468	Ex. 7–8	Ex. 13–14

Diagnostic Test

Directions: Write all answers on a separate sheet of paper.

Skill Check A. Copy each of the underlined words below, and tell whether it is a *proper noun* or a *proper adjective*.

1. the <u>Swiss</u> countryside
2. the <u>Rocky Mountains</u>
3. <u>Yellowstone National Park</u>
4. the <u>Australian</u> continent
5. explorer <u>David Livingstone</u>

Skill Check B. Write the words that should be capitalized in each of the following sentences.

6. the himalayas of asia are the highest mountain range in the world.
7. they are located between the indus river and the brahmaputra river.
8. these majestic mountains were formed millions of years ago when the indian subcontinent collided with the eurasian landmass.
9. the majority of the greatest peaks can be found in the countries of tibet, nepal, and india.
10. the tallest himalayan peak is mt. everest, which is situated approximately 80 miles from nepal's capital of kathmandu.
11. it was named for sir george everest, a british surveyor who was the first to establish its location and height.
12. the enormous mountain was successfully scaled in 1953 by members of an expedition led by col. john hunt of great britain.
13. on may 29, 1953, edmund hillary of new zealand and a nepalese guide, tenzing norgay, were the first men to stand on the summit.
14. since that time, everest has been climbed by several international teams, including the italians, the japanese, and, in 1963, an american expedition.
15. for more information on this region of the world, read the books *geography of the himalayas* and *in exile from the land of snows*.

Skill Check C. Proofread the following paragraph, and correct all errors in capitalization.

Few people can claim to have stood on top of the world—And only one man can claim to have been there first. That person is sir Edmund Hillary. although he shares the glory of his achievement with his climbing partner, tenzing norgay, hillary was the first person to reach the Summit of mount Everest in nepal, 29,028 feet above Sea Level—the highest spot on earth. Hillary has said of himself, "i've moved from being a child who dreamed a lot and read a lot of books about adventure, to actually getting involved in things like mountaineering. . . ." These are humble words for a man who has climbed the swiss alps and conquered eleven different peaks of more than 20,000 Feet in the himalayas of tibet and nepal.

Capitalization • 631

Diagnostic Test

Each item in the Diagnostic Test corresponds to a specific section in the capitalization chapter. This will enable you to tailor instruction to the particular needs of your students. See "Ongoing Assessment: Diagnose" below for further details. Answers for the Diagnostic Test and all chapter exercises are available in *Grammar Exercises Answers on Transparencies* in your Teaching Resources.

Skill Check A

1. proper adjective
2. proper noun
3. proper noun
4. proper adjective
5. proper noun

Skill Check B

6. The, Himalayas, Asia
7. They, Indus River, Brahmaputra River
8. These, Indian, Eurasian
9. The, Tibet, Nepal, India
10. The, Himalayan, Mt. Everest, Nepal's, Kathmandu
11. It, Sir George Everest, British
12. The, Col. John Hunt, Great Britain
13. On, May, Edmund Hillary, New Zealand, Nepalese, Tenzing Norgay
14. Since, Everest, Italians, Japanese, American
15. For, *Geography, Himalayas, In, Exile, From, Land, Snows*

Skill Check C

Changed words are underlined.

Few people can claim to have stood on top of the world—<u>and</u> only one man can claim to have been there first. That person is <u>Sir</u> Edmund Hillary. <u>Although</u> he shares the glory of his achievement with his climbing partner, <u>Tenzing Norgay</u>, <u>Hillary</u> was the first person to reach the <u>summit</u> of <u>Mount</u> Everest in <u>Nepal</u>, 29,028 feet above <u>sea</u> <u>level</u>—the highest spot on earth. Hillary has said of himself, "<u>I've</u> moved from being a child who dreamed a lot and read a lot of books about adventure, to actually getting involved in things like mountaineering. . . ." These are humble words for a man who has climbed the <u>Swiss</u> <u>Alps</u> and conquered eleven different peaks of more than 20,000 <u>feet</u> in the <u>Himalayas</u> of <u>Tibet</u> and <u>Nepal</u>.

☑ ONGOING ASSESSMENT: Diagnose *continued*

Capitalization	Diagnostic Test Items	Teach	Practice	Chapter Review
Skill Check C				
Capitalizing First Words	C 1, 3, 4	pp. 632–633/ 🗄458–459	Ex. 1–2	Ex. 9, 11
Capitalizing Proper Nouns	C 3, 5	pp. 635–638/ 🗄461–464	Ex. 3–5	Ex. 10–11
Capitalizing Proper Adjectives	C 5	p. 639/🗄465	Ex. 6	Ex. 12
Capitalizing Titles of People	C 2	pp. 640–641/ 🗄466–467	Ex. 7	Ex. 13
Cumulative Reviews and Applications			Ex. 15–16	

PREPARE and ENGAGE

 Interest GRABBER Write on the board:

in english class, we are studying romeo and juliet.

It Is A Play By William Shakespeare.

Ask students what is wrong with these sentences (one has no capitals; the other has too many) and ask for a volunteer to correct them. Based on their corrections, ask students to speculate on the functions of capital letters (to start a sentence, to tell the formal name of something).

Activate Prior Knowledge

Have students volunteer some names of places they have visited, people they admire, movies they like, and so on. Write these on the board but omit all capitals. Ask students to tell you where the capitals should be used and why they are using them.

TEACH

Step-by-Step Teaching Guide

Capitals for First Words in Sentences

1. Let students know that capitalizing the first word in a sentence helps to clarify meanings and signal new ideas.

2. Point out that the rule for *I* and *O* is an exception. Remind students that incomplete sentences, phrases, or lists are not capitalized, even when they follow a colon.

3. Add that the remainder of a sentence following a semicolon or a dash is *not* capitalized.

continued

Customize for
More Advanced Students

Have students search their writing for examples of fragments and ask them their intent in using them. Discuss how writers sometimes use fragments to produce certain effects. Ask them to search for examples and then speculate on the writer's reasons for using them. Point out that fragments, even when used for emphasis, should not be used in formal writing.

Using Capitals for First Words

Capital letters work as a visual clue to the reader by making certain words stand out more prominently on a page.

Sentences

Always signal the start of a new idea by capitalizing the first word in a sentence.

▶ **KEY CONCEPT** Capitalize the first word in declarative, interrogative, imperative, and exclamatory sentences. ■

Note that each of the following sentences is complete. Each contains both a subject and a verb and makes sense by itself.

DECLARATIVE: Alberto visited the Grand Canyon last summer.
INTERROGATIVE: Did you mail the monthly bills?
IMPERATIVE: Get a stamp out of the drawer.
EXCLAMATORY: This letter says I've won a trip to Niagara Falls!

▶ **KEY CONCEPT** Capitalize the first word in interjections and incomplete questions. ■

EXAMPLES: Fantastic! Ouch! Darn!

EXAMPLES: When? For Maria? How much?

▶ **KEY CONCEPT** Capitalize the first word of a complete sentence following a colon. If a list follows a colon, it is not a complete sentence and, therefore, no capital letter is used. ■

SENTENCE
FOLLOWING COLON: We saw what was in the valley: It was a beautiful waterfall.
LIST FOLLOWING COLON: The mail carrier delivered our mail: two letters, a package, and a card.

Quotations

▶ **KEY CONCEPT** Capitalize the first word in a quotation if the quotation is a complete sentence. ■

EXAMPLE: "Mountains are earth's undecaying monuments."
                                    —Nathaniel Hawthorne

632 • Capitalization

Theme: Geography

In this chapter, you will learn about capitalization. The exercises and examples are about geography.

Cross-Curricular Connection: Geography

⏱ TIME AND RESOURCE MANAGER

Resources
Print: *Grammar Exercise Workbook*, pp. 157–162; *Grammar Exercises Answers on Transparencies*, Ch. 27
Technology: *Writing and Grammar* Interactive Text, Ch. 27; *On-Line Exercise Bank*, Ch. 27

Using the Full Student Edition	Using the Handbook Ⓗ
• Work through all key concepts, pp. 632–642. • Assign and review Exercises 1–8. • Do the Hands-on Grammar activity, p. 643.	• Work through all key concepts, pp. 458–468. • Assign and review Exercises 1–8. • Do the Hands-on Grammar activity, p. 469.

Even when the quotation appears with a "he said/she said" expression, a capital letter is still used to begin the quotation.

EXAMPLE: "It's awfully hot in the canyon," the man said.

If a "he said/she said" expression occurs in the middle of quoted material that is one continuous sentence, only the first word of the quotation gets a capital letter.

EXAMPLE: "If you visit her," Liz said, "please tell me."

If a "he said/she said" expression sits between two complete sentences, both sentences receive capital letters.

EXAMPLE: "Our family vacations are great fun!" Arleen exclaimed. "We are going camping this year."

When a portion of a quotation that is not a complete sentence is contained within a longer sentence, do not capitalize the first word of the quoted part of the sentence.

EXAMPLE: Mark Twain, who saw pony express riders in action, said that a rider was "usually a little bit of a man."

If the quoted fragment shifts to the beginning of the sentence, the first word should then be capitalized.

EXAMPLE: "Usually a little bit of a man" is the way Mark Twain described a Pony Express rider.

Poetry

KEY CONCEPT Capitalize the first word in each line of most poetry even if the line does not begin a new sentence. ■

EXAMPLE: Falling upon earth,
Pure water spills
From the cup ——Bashō

I and O

These words always require capitalization.

KEY CONCEPT Capitalize *I* and *O* throughout a sentence. ■

EXAMPLES: "Eureka! I have found it."—Archimedes
"O Romeo, Romeo! Wherefore art thou Romeo?"
——Shakespeare

▲ Critical Viewing
What are three different capitalization rules that you might use in writing about this waterfall?
[Connect]

Capitalization • 633

Critical Viewing

Connect Possible answer: Capitalize (1) first words of sentences, (2) first words of interjections, and (3) the words *I* and *O*.

Step-by-Step Teaching Guide continued

4. Remind students that "he said/she said" expressions can interrupt one complete sentence or come between two different sentences.

5. Give students additional examples that require capital letters:

   "later today," said Mary, "we can go to the station. we will buy our tickets."

   Mary said, "later today we can go to the station. we will buy our tickets."

   "later today we will go to the station," said Mary. "we will buy our tickets."

Step-by-Step Teaching Guide

Capitals for First Words in Poetry

1. Point out that new sentences sometimes begin in the middle of a line of poetry; these should be capitalized.

2. Have students look for poems with sentences that begin in the middle of a line and bring them to class (some of Robert Frost's longer poems are good possibilities). Discuss the capitalization in their samples.

Customize for
Less Advanced Students

These students may need to focus on and practice recognizing special situations where the first words of internal structures should be capitalized. Provide examples from magazines or newspapers that demonstrate the following:

• Independent clause following a colon (but not a semicolon)

• Beginning of a quoted sentence (even if it is preceded by a comma)

• Quoted sentences, exclamations, or other phrases within longer quotations

27

More Practice

Grammar Exercise Workbook
• pp. 157–158
On-line Exercise Bank
• Chapter 27
Go on-line:
PHSchool.com
Enter Web Code:
eek-1002

▶ **Exercise 1** Using Capitals for First Words Copy the following items, adding the missing capitals. Some items may require more than one capital letter.

1. central Australia is home to Ayers Rock.
2. my teacher said, "surprisingly, Ayers Rock is the largest single rock formation in the world."
3. wow! the red sandstone monolith rises 1,143 feet above the surrounding terrain.
4. seventy million years ago, the rock appeared much different from the way it does today: it was a small island surrounded by an inland sea.
5. did you know that Ayers Rock is called Uluru by the aboriginal people of Australia?

▶ **Exercise 2** Writing a Postcard Using Capital Letters for First Words Imagine that you are on a trip to Australia or another distant tourist destination. Write a postcard to a friend, describing some of your experiences. Use each of the rules for capitalizing first words at least once in your postcard.

▼ **Critical Viewing** If you were to write a few sentences describing the Australian landscape shown here, what would you write? What capitalization rules would you use? **[Describe]**

634 • Capitalization

Using Capitals for Proper Nouns

A **proper noun** is a noun that names a specific person, place, or thing.

> **KEY CONCEPT** Capitalize all proper nouns, including each part of a person's name. ■

The given or first name, the initials standing for a name, and the surname or last name all receive capital letters.

EXAMPLES: Chester Worth, Maria A. Lopez

If a surname begins with *Mc, O',* or *St.,* the letter following it is capitalized.

EXAMPLES: McGregor, O'Mara, St. John

The capitalization of names beginning with *de, D', la, le, Mac, van,* or *von* will vary.

EXAMPLES: De Mello, de Mello

> **KEY CONCEPT** Capitalize the proper names of animals. ■

EXAMPLES: Rin-Tin-Tin, Sylvester, Fido

> **KEY CONCEPT** Capitalize geographical names. ■

Capitalize the names of streets, towns, cities, counties, states, provinces, countries, continents, valleys, mountains, rivers, and oceans. If a place can be found on a map, you should normally capitalize it.

EXAMPLES: Strokes Avenue, Galapagos Islands, Red Sea

The sun and the moon are not capitalized.
When a compass point is used simply to show direction, it is not capitalized. A specific location is capitalized.

EXAMPLES: We headed northwest.
My cousin lives in the Southwest.

> **Exercise 3** **Capitalizing Names** Write the names below on a separate sheet of paper, inserting capital letters where appropriate.
> 1. sydney, australia
> 2. hawaiian islands
> 3. the pacific northwest
> 4. mr. ed
> 5. lassie

Capitalization • **635**

Step-by-Step Teaching Guide

Capitals for Proper Nouns

1. Explain that names that are proper nouns are always capitalized.
2. Remind students that the proper names of animals and pets are also capitalized.
3. Explain to students that if a place can be found on a map, it should be capitalized.
4. Point out that words like *river, mountain,* and *avenue* are capitalized only when parts of proper nouns.
5. Use this example: The main words are capitalized in discussing *the Allegheny River* and the *Ohio River,* but not *the Allegheny and Ohio rivers.*

Answer Key

> **Exercise 3**

1. Sydney, Australia
2. Hawaiian Islands
3. the Pacific Northwest
4. Mr. Ed
5. Lassie

Customize for
ESL Students

Students' first languages may follow capitalization rules different from those in English. Ask students where they have seen capital letters outside of school (store signs, books, newspapers). Place these examples into groups on the board according to the rules students will encounter in this chapter (first words, proper nouns, proper adjectives, titles of works). Label each group and be sure students recognize what each group has in common. Have students add real-life examples to each of these groups as they work through the chapter.

Customize for
Spatial Learners

Assign each student the name of a geographical entity—a river, mountain, nation, or sea. Have students use maps or atlases to find their place. Then ask students to create a sentence describing its location in relation to other places they find on maps. (Example: *The Italian Riviera is in the northwest section of Italy.*) Have students write their sentences on the board and ask the class to determine whether each is correctly capitalized.

Step-by-Step Teaching Guide

Capitals for Specific Structures

1. Have students offer additional examples of the names of structures that must be capitalized (Examples: the *Bennington Monument*, the *Whitney Museum*).

2. Remind students that words like *monument* and *museum* are capitalized only when they are parts of proper nouns.

3. Mention that the specific names of bridges, such as *Golden Gate Bridge*, are also capitalized.

Step-by-Step Teaching Guide

Capitals for Specific Events and Times

1. Explain to students that a wide variety of historical periods, events, documents, dates, and holidays are capitalized.

2. Point out that even though days and months are capitalized, seasons are not.

3. Tell students that the name of a season is capitalized only when it is part of a proper noun naming a specific event (*Fall Formal, Winter Carnival*).

▶ **KEY CONCEPT** Capitalize the names of monuments, buildings, and meeting rooms. ■

The following chart shows examples of monuments, buildings, and meeting rooms:

SPECIFIC PLACES	
Monuments and Memorials	Washington Monument, Lincoln Memorial
Buildings	Smithsonian Institution, Superdome, the Actors' Conservatory Theater
School and Meeting Rooms	Room 20B, Laboratory C, Oval Office

Do not capitalize the words *theater, hotel,* and *university* unless they are part of a proper name.

EXAMPLES: The theater is one of the oldest buildings in town.
The Fallon House Theater is in an old ghost town.

The word *room* is capitalized only if it refers to a specific room and is combined with a name, letter, or number.

EXAMPLE: The geology exam will be given in Room 46.

▶ **KEY CONCEPT** Capitalize the names of specific events and periods of time. ■

SPECIAL EVENTS AND TIMES	
Historic Events	Stone Age
Historic Periods	War of 1812
Documents	Gettysburg Address, Homestead Act
Days and Months	Monday, April
Holidays and Religious Days	Labor Day, Good Friday
Special Events	Kentucky Derby

▶ **KEY CONCEPT** Do not capitalize the seasons. ■

EXAMPLE: We felt a winter chill in the air as we reached the mountaintop.

> **KEY CONCEPT** Capitalize the names of various organizations, government bodies, political parties, nationalities, and languages. ■

SPECIFIC GROUPS AND LANGUAGES	
Clubs	Rotary Club, Lynbrook Speech Club, Lions Club
Organizations	League of Women Voters, American Cancer Society, United Farm Workers
Institutions	University of Miami, Marymount General Hospital
Businesses	Fresh Food Corporation, Unlimited Knowledge, Inc.
Government Bodies	Senate of the United States, Houses of Parliament, Department of Defense
Political Parties	Republicans, Whigs
Nationalities	American, French, Russian, Mexican
Languages	English, Spanish, French, Yiddish

> **KEY CONCEPT** Capitalize references to religions, deities, and religious scriptures. ■

Each religion has a set of words referring to the important and sacred beliefs it holds. The major religious groups to which you are likely to refer in your writing include Christianity, Judaism, Buddhism, Islam, Confucianism, and Hinduism.

CHRISTIANITY: God, Lord, Father, Son, Holy Spirit, Bible, books of the Bible (Exodus, Kings, Romans)

JUDAISM: God, Lord, Prophets (Moses, Abraham), Torah, Talmud

EASTERN RELIGIONS: Buddhism (Buddha, Tripitaka); Islam (Allah, Koran); Hinduism (Brahma, Vedas)

This list is not complete. Other religious references that you encounter must also be capitalized. These include any pronoun references made to the deity in Christian or Jewish writings.

When writing about mythological gods and goddesses, capitalize the proper names of gods and goddesses, but do not capitalize the words *god* and *goddess*.

EXAMPLES: the god Pluto, the goddess Athena

Capitalization • 637

Step-by-Step Teaching Guide

Capitals for Specific Groups and Languages

1. Let students know that this is a very broad category with many examples.

2. Have students read the examples in the chart and then provide additional names from their own knowledge.

Step-by-Step Teaching Guide

Capitals for Religious References

1. Point out that each religion has its own specific names, scriptures, and other elements that are capitalized.

2. Encourage students to check their dictionaries for spelling and capitalization of unfamiliar words.

3. Add one more example:

    My favorite Greek god is Apollo, the god of poetry and music.

Explain that the names of mythological gods are capitalized, but not the words *god* and *goddess*.

Real-World Connection

Most applications for colleges and jobs require applicants to use capitalization correctly. Ask students where on an application they are most likely to write capitals (in addresses, titles of positions, names and titles of personal references, etc.). Explain that the use of correct capitalization is an important indicator of learning. Discuss with students other places where proper capitalization is especially important for making good impressions in the real world (Examples: cover letters, letters to the editor, address on letters).

STANDARDIZED TEST PREPARATION WORKSHOP

Mechanics Many standardized tests require students to identify errors in a passage. Use the following example to demonstrate.

The largest desert in the world, the Sahara, is located in the Northern part of Africa.

What kind of error is in this sentence?

A Spelling error

B Capitalization error

C Punctuation error

D No error

The correct answer is **B.** The word *Northern* should not be capitalized. Regions of a country or continent are only capitalized when indicating a specific location, not a general direction.

Capitals for Awards and Specific Types of Craft

1. Tell students to capitalize both the proper names and nicknames of awards (Examples: *an Academy Award, an Oscar*).

2. Tell students that the specific names of all air, land, sea, and space craft are proper nouns and are capitalized. Ask for additional examples of each type.

3. Remind students that the word *the* preceding an award or craft is never capitalized.

Answer Key

Exercise 4

1. The Sahara stretches 3,200 miles across the northern portion of Africa.
2. The desert begins at the Atlantic Ocean and extends to the Red Sea.
3. The northern edge of the desert terminates in the Atlas Mountains, a dramatic scene that has been photographed from satellites such as Landsat.
4. During the Ice Age, North Africa was a land of shallow lakes and rich vegetation.
5. By the time of the Roman Empire, the region had completely turned to desert.

Exercise 5

(1) The Sahara is the largest desert in the world. (2) The desert covers large sections of several countries, including Morocco, Algeria, Tunisia, Libya, and Egypt. (3) Although the desert is generally flat, the snow-capped Mount Tahat rises above the swirling sands of the central Sahara. (4) A small group of nomadic Muslims, people called Bedouins, travel throughout the desert. (5) The majority of the desert population, however, is confined to cities, such as Luxor, Ghat, and Reggane.

Critical Viewing

Speculate Possible answers: *Africa, Saudi Arabia.*

▶ **KEY CONCEPT** Capitalize the names of awards. ■

Notice in the following examples that the word *the* is not capitalized.

EXAMPLES: the Kevin E. Morris Scholarship; the Nobel Peace Prize; the Academy Awards; the Oscar; Eagle Scout

▶ **KEY CONCEPT** Capitalize the names of specific types of air, sea, space, and land craft. ■

When capitalizing the names of air, sea, space, and land craft, do not capitalize the word *the* preceding a name unless the word is part of the official name.

AIR: Boeing 747   SPACE: *Sputnik I*
SEA: *Lusitania*   LAND: the Model T

▶ **Exercise 4** Using Capitals in Sentences With Proper Nouns
Copy the following sentences, adding the missing capitals.
  1. The sahara stretches 3,200 miles across the northern portion of africa.
  2. The desert begins at the atlantic ocean and extends to the red sea.
  3. The northern edge of the desert terminates in the atlas mountains, a dramatic scene that has been photographed from satellites such as landsat.
  4. During the ice age, north africa was a land of shallow lakes and rich vegetation.
  5. By the time of the roman empire, the region had completely turned to desert.

▶ **Exercise 5** Proofreading to Correct Errors in the Capitalization of Proper Nouns Rewrite this paragraph, adding or eliminating capital letters where appropriate.
    (1) The Sahara is the largest desert in the World. (2) The Desert covers large sections of several countries, including morocco, algeria, tunisia, libya, and egypt. (3) Although the desert is generally flat, the snow-capped mount Tahat rises above the swirling sands of the central sahara. (4) A small group of Nomadic muslims, people called bedouins, travel throughout the desert. (5) The majority of the Desert Population, however, is confined to cities, such as luxor, ghat, and reggane.

▶ **More Practice**

Grammar Exercise Workbook
• pp. 159–160
On-line Exercise Bank
• Chapter 27
Go on-line:
PHSchool.com
Enter Web Code:
eek-1002

Get instant feedback! Exercises 4, 5, and 6 are available on-line or on CD-ROM.

▲ **Critical Viewing** What proper nouns might apply to this picture? **[Speculate]**

☑ **ONGOING ASSESSMENT: Monitor and Reinforce**

If students miss more than one item in Exercise 4 or 5, refer them to the following for additional practice.

In the Textbook	Print Resources	Technology
Chapter Review, Ex. 10–11	*Grammar Exercise Workbook,* pp. 159–160	*On-Line Exercise Bank,* Ch. 27

Using Capitals for Proper Adjectives

A proper noun used as an adjective or an adjective formed from a proper noun is called a *proper adjective*.

▶ **KEY CONCEPT** Capitalize most proper adjectives. ■

EXAMPLES: Swiss government, American people, Gothic style

Proper adjectives used in popular expressions are exceptions.

EXAMPLES: french fries, venetian blinds

Adjectives referring to culture or climate that derive from capitalized terms for regions are also generally lowercase.

EXAMPLES: arctic wind (but *the Arctic*), western pioneers (but *the West*)

▶ **KEY CONCEPT** Capitalize brand names used as adjectives. ■

EXAMPLES: Timetrue watches, Hercules luggage

▶ **KEY CONCEPT** Do not capitalize prefixes attached to proper adjectives unless the prefix refers to a nationality. ■

EXAMPLES: pre-Mayan architecture, Indo-European

▶ **KEY CONCEPT** In a hyphenated adjective, capitalize only the proper adjective. ■

EXAMPLE: Spanish-speaking Americans

▶ **Exercise 6** Using Capital Letters for Proper Adjectives Copy the sentences and add any missing capitals.
1. The european continent is dominated by the massive peaks of the Alps.
2. They were formed millions of years ago as a result of a collision between the eurasian and african landmasses, which forced the rock to rise.
3. Today, the Alps exist within the borders of France, Switzerland, Italy, and Austria.
4. french-speaking, german-speaking, and italian-speaking peoples inhabit the area.
5. The tallest of the Alps are taller than the tallest of the Rocky Mountains of the american West.

✿ Grammar and Style Tip

Sometimes, proper nouns can function as proper adjectives: a *New Zealand* citizen, the *Niagara Falls* area.

▼ **Critical Viewing**
What is a proper adjective you might use in describing this ship? [**Describe**]

Capitalization • **639**

Step-by-Step Teaching Guide

Using Capitals for Proper Adjectives

1. Write a brief list on the board to help students distinguish between proper adjectives and proper nouns used as adjectives:

   Shakespeare festival (proper noun used as proper adjective)

   Victorian novel (proper adjective formed from proper noun)

2. Ask students to think of more examples for each key concept.

Answer Key

▶ **Exercise 6**

1. The European continent is dominated by the massive peaks of the Alps.
2. They were formed millions of years ago as a result of a collision between the Eurasian and African landmasses . . .
3. Correct
4. French-speaking, German-speaking, and Italian-speaking peoples . . .
5. The tallest of the Alps are taller than the tallest of the Rocky Mountains of the American West.

Critical Viewing

Describe Possible answers: <u>American</u> navy, <u>Pacific</u> Ocean, <u>Philippine</u> Islands

Integrating Speaking and Listening Skills

Proper Nouns and Adjectives
Ask students to each write a list of five proper nouns and five proper adjectives. Have volunteers read aloud words on their lists. Have another student write the words on the board with the proper capitalization and label the words PN (proper noun) or PA (proper adjective). Then, ask a volunteer to use each word aloud in a sentence.

☑ ONGOING ASSESSMENT: Monitor and Reinforce

If students miss more than one item in Exercise 6, refer them to the following for additional practice.

In the Textbook	Print Resources	Technology
Chapter Review, Ex. 12	*Grammar Exercise Workbook*, pp. 159–160	*On-Line Exercise Bank*, Ch. 27

Capitals for People's Titles

1. Ask students to suggest additional examples of people whose titles might be capitalized (Examples: *Doctor, Major, Judge*). Then have students write sentences demonstrating when the titles should and should not be capitalized. (Examples: *I saw Doctor Newman on Tuesday. I went to the doctor on Tuesday. Doctor Newman, my throat hurts.*)

continued

Critical Viewing

Connect Likely response: Supreme Court Justice Thurgood Marshall.

Language Highlight

The rules of English were not as standardized in the fifteenth, sixteenth, seventeenth, and eighteenth centuries as they are today. During that time, writers were encouraged to capitalize not only all words that started sentences and all proper names, but also any common nouns that they felt to be important. By the early eighteenth century, writers frequently capitalized nouns simply for emphasis. Later in the century, grammarians resisted the practice of indiscriminate capitalization on the grounds that it detracted from the use of capitals as a means of conferring distinction.

Integrating Vocabulary Skills

Metonymy Define *metonymy* for students (a figure of speech in which the name of one thing is used in place of that of another associated with it). Although metonymy may use common nouns (a room full of *suits* is actually crowded with business executives), point out that many proper nouns are also used in this manner. For example, the noun *White House* is used to mean *the President* or *the government*; and *Madison Avenue* has long meant the advertising industry as a whole. Can students suggest additional examples of metonymy using proper nouns?

Using Capitals for Titles

Capital letters are used to indicate titles of people and works of art and literature.

Titles of People Titles used before names and in direct address require capitalization.

▶ **KEY CONCEPT** Capitalize a person's title when it is used with the person's name or when it is used in direct address in place of a person's name. ■

TITLE:	Professor Scott gave an interesting lecture.
IN PLACE OF A NAME:	Your lecture, Professor, was very interesting.
GENERAL REFERENCE:	My history professor is late.

The titles of government officials may require capitalization in certain cases.

▶ **KEY CONCEPT** Capitalize titles of government officials when they are followed by a proper name or when used in direct address. ■

In the United States, titles such as supervisor, mayor, governor, congressman, congresswoman, senator, judge, and ambassador are used for different government officials. Officials of other countries also have titles. All of these are capitalized when they are used before a proper name or in direct address. General references, however, usually omit the capital.

PRECEDING A PROPER NAME:	Mayor Martin Hanley will speak.
IN DIRECT ADDRESS:	Will you speak tonight, Mayor?
IN A GENERAL REFERENCE:	The mayor works on the budget.

▶ Critical Viewing This illustration depicts a former justice of the Supreme Court, Thurgood Marshall. How would you use capitals when writing his name and title? **[Connect]**

640 • Capitalization

◈ STANDARDIZED TEST PREPARATION WORKSHOP

Mechanics Many standardized tests require students to recognize correct uses of capitalization. Use the following example to demonstrate.

Even as a child, James believed in the American dream that anyone could grow up to be president of the United States.

Which of the words in the above sentence should be capitalized?

A dream

B president

C the

D Correct as is

The correct answer is **B.** The titles of certain high government officials are capitalized even in a general reference when not followed by a proper name or used in direct address.

▶ **KEY CONCEPT** Capitalize titles of certain high government officials if they refer to the incumbent even when the titles are not followed by a proper name or used in direct address. ■

EXAMPLES: The President returned from his trip early.
He will meet with the Queen of England today.
The Supreme Court of the United States has eight justices and a Chief Justice.

▶ **KEY CONCEPT** Capitalize important words in compound titles, but not prefixes and suffixes added to the title. ■

EXAMPLES: Lieutenant Governor, ex-Senator Jorgenson

▶ **KEY CONCEPT** Capitalize titles showing family relationships when they refer to a specific person unless they are preceded by a possessive noun or pronoun. ■

EXAMPLES: Did Uncle John find this stone in the cave?
Anne's uncle climbed Mount Everest.

▶ **KEY CONCEPT** Capitalize abbreviations of titles before and after names. ■

The most common abbreviations found before and after names include *Mr., Mrs., Ms., Jr.,* and *Sr.*

EXAMPLES: Mr. Kevin Peterson, Jr.,   Mrs. Ann Sikorski

▶ **Exercise 7** Using Capitals for Titles of People Copy the sentences below that need capitals, adding the missing capitals. If a sentence does not need additional capitalization, write *correct.*

1. While exploring northeastern Wyoming in 1875, a team of surveyors led by colonel Richard Dodge discovered an unusual rock formation, which they named Devil's Tower.
2. Several years after its discovery, senator Francis Warren campaigned to protect it.
3. In 1906, president Theodore Roosevelt, jr., designated Devil's Tower as the first national monument.
4. A popular destination for rock climbers, Devil's Tower was first scaled in 1893 by mr. William Rogers and mr. Willard Ripley.
5. In the 1990's, secretary of the interior Bruce Babbitt banned rock climbing at the site during June.

▶ **More Practice**

Grammar Exercise Workbook
• pp. 161–162
On-line Exercise Bank
• Chapter 27
Go on-line:
PHSchool.com
Enter Web Code:
eek-1002

interactive
Textbook

Get instant feedback!
Exercise 7 is available on-line or on CD-ROM.

If students miss more than one item in Exercise 7, refer them to the following for additional practice.

In the Textbook	Print Resources	Technology
Chapter Review, Ex. 13	*Grammar Exercise Workbook,* pp. 161–162	*On-Line Exercise Bank,* Ch. 27

Step-by-Step Teaching Guide continued

2. Have students explain why family titles may be capitalized in some sentences but not in others. (*Grandpa Phil gave me this truck. Ed's grandfather drove us home.*)
3. Have students suggest abbreviations of titles not specified on this page (Examples: *Hon., Esq., Ph.D., M.D.*). Point out that these abbreviations are capitalized whether they are placed before or after their proper nouns.

Answer Key

▶ **Exercise 7**

1. While exploring northeastern Wyoming in 1875, a team of surveyors led by Colonel Richard Dodge discovered an unusual rock formation, which they named Devil's Tower.
2. Several years after its discovery, Senator Francis Warren campaigned to protect it.
3. In 1906, President Theodore Roosevelt, Jr., designated Devil's Tower as the first national monument.
4. A popular destination for rock climbers, Devil's Tower was first scaled in 1893 by Mr. William Rogers and Mr. Willard Ripley.
5. In the 1990's, Secretary of the Interior Bruce Babbitt banned rock climbing at the site during June.

Integrating Viewing and Representing Skills

Headlines Some newspaper headlines seem to pay little attention to the rules of capitalization. Ask students to search for examples of both overuse and underuse of capitalization in print media, including advertisements. Discuss why such uses do not conform to the rules of capitalization and, for each, ask students why the rules may have been broken (to achieve special emphasis, for dramatic effect). Point out that only when the rules of capitalization are fully understood should they be broken or manipulated for special purposes.

Step-by-Step Teaching Guide

Capitals for Titles of Things

1. Remind students that adjectives, adverbs, nouns, pronouns, and verbs are always capitalized in titles of works.

2. Give students these examples to capitalize, and have them identify the parts of speech of all words:

   For Whom the Bell Tolls (preposition, pronoun, article, noun, verb)

   A Tale of Two Cities (article, noun, preposition, adjective, noun)

   "A Passionate Shepherd to His Love" (article, adjective, noun, preposition, pronoun, noun)

   "Night and Day" (noun, conjunction, noun)

   Bang the Drum Slowly (verb, article, noun, adverb)

3. Remind students that even though it is a small word, *is* is a verb and should always be capitalized in titles.

Customize for
ESL Students

Ask students to list either their favorite or least favorite books, television shows, or movies. Have them write a brief paragraph about their choices and about why they like or dislike them. Instruct students to leave out all capital letters. Have students exchange papers and copyedit each other's paragraphs, introducing correct capitalization.

Answer Key

⏱ TIME SAVERS!

📄 **Answers on Transparencies**
Use the *Grammar Exercises Answers on Transparencies* for Chapter 27 to facilitate correction by students.

💻 **On-Line Exercise Bank**
Have students complete the exercises on computer. The Auto Check feature will grade their work for you!

▶ **KEY CONCEPT** Capitalize the first word and all other key words in the titles of books, periodicals, poems, stories, plays, paintings, and other works of art. ■

BOOK:	*Heart of Darkness*
PERIODICAL:	*Better Homes and Gardens*
POEM:	"Flower in the Crannied Wall"
STORY:	"A Visit to Grandmother"
PLAY:	*How to Succeed in Business Without Really Trying*
PAINTING:	*The Artist's Daughter With a Cat*
SONG:	"This Land Is Your Land"

As you look at the preceding examples, there are a number of things to notice. First, articles—the words *a*, *an*, and *the*—are capitalized only when they are the first word of the title. Second, conjunctions and prepositions shorter than four letters are capitalized only when they are the first word in the title. Third, adjectives, nouns, pronouns, verbs, and adverbs are all considered key words and are always capitalized. When capitalizing a subtitle, the same rule is used.

EXAMPLE: *Language: A Reflection of People and Culture*

▶ **KEY CONCEPT** Capitalize titles of courses when the courses are language courses or when the courses are followed by a number. ■

WITH CAPITALS: Latin II, English, California History 1A
WITHOUT CAPITALS: mathematics, history, home economics

▶ **Exercise 8** **Capitalizing Titles of Things** Write the following titles, adding the missing capitals. Underline the titles that are printed in italics.

EXAMPLE: Play: *fiddler on the roof*
ANSWER: <u>Fiddler on the Roof</u>

1. class: psychology 101
2. newspaper: *the new york times*
3. painting: *starry night*
4. statue: *the thinker*
5. story: "the lottery"

▶ **More Practice**

Grammar Exercise Workbook
• pp. 161–162
On-line Exercise Bank
• Chapter 27
Go on-line:
PHSchool.com
Enter Web Code:
eek-1002

Get instant feedback! Exercise 8 is available on-line or on CD-ROM.

☑ ONGOING ASSESSMENT: Monitor and Reinforce

If students miss more than one item in Exercise 8, refer them to the following for additional practice.

In the Textbook	Print Resources	Technology
Chapter Review, Ex. 14	*Grammar Exercise Workbook*, pp. 161–162	*On-Line Exercise Bank*, Ch. 27

Hands-on Grammar

Capitalization Card

Create a capitalization reference card that you can keep in your notebook, and refer to it any time you are unsure of a capitalization rule. Start by reviewing the chapter and noting all of the different types of items that are capitalized. Then, draw lines on a piece of paper to divide it into squares. Draw as many squares as you need to cover each of the types of items that are capitalized. Use both sides of the card. Categories might include countries, cities, and corporations.

List the categories in alphabetical order in the boxes you've created. Add examples beneath each of the categories. Once you've finished, keep the card you have created in your notebook.

BOOK TITLES All Creatures Great and Small	BUILDING NAMES Space Needle	BUSINESSES Prentice Hall
CITIES Miami, Florida	CLUBS Rotary Club	COUNTRIES England

Find It in Your Reading Look through your history book to find examples of words that fit into the various categories. Then, as you continue reading in various subjects, add other examples you come across.

Find It in Your Writing Consult your capitalization card whenever you are working on a piece of writing and are unsure about a capitalization rule.

Rules for Capitalization • 643

Hands-on Grammar

Teaching Resources: Hands-on Grammar Activity Book, Ch. 27

1. If you wish to do this activity in class, you might provide scissors and construction paper for students. Have students work in pairs, and give each pair the needed materials.

2. Have students do the activity individually, or assign partners if some students need help.

3. In some classes, you may want to work with the whole group to determine categories for cards.

Find It in Your Reading

Besides textbooks, students might also list examples they find in other nonfiction books. (Do not recommend using periodicals, however, as capitalization rules in these often vary.)

Find It in Your Writing

Students could add examples from their writing to their cards, especially items needing capitalization that they use frequently.

Answer Key

> **Exercise 9**

1. The Japanese . . .
2. Were you aware . . .
3. The article made this observation: Mount Fuji has been dormant for hundreds of years; the last . . .
4. "The cone-shaped mountain rises 12,387 feet above sea level," the geologist explained. "Because it is so cold at this altitude, . . .
5. Its head reaches above the clouds,/It surveys the mountains all around;/It hears the thunder far below—/Fuji, O highest of mountains!
   —traditional Japanese song

> **Exercise 10**

1. Victoria Falls
2. Africa, Zambia, Zimbabwe
3. January, April, Batoka Gorge
4. November, David Livingstone, Presbyterian
5. London Missionary Society, Zambezi River

> **Exercise 11**

(1) David Livingstone named the enormous waterfall he discovered after Queen Victoria, the reigning monarch of England. (2) The founder of the British South Africa Company, Cecil Rhodes, arranged for the construction of a bridge that spans the gorge directly in front of the falls. (3) Rhodes, who also founded the De Beers Mining Company, is perhaps best known for instituting the Rhodes Scholarship at Oxford University. (4) Today, tourists wishing to visit the falls can stay at the Masuwe Lodge or the Masaka Sun Hotel, both of which have Western foods such as Bubbles cola and Smith cookies. (5) Other points of interest in the area include Victoria Falls National Park and Livingstone Game Park.

> **Exercise 12**

1. Arctic
2. Apollo
3. Irish, Norse
4. Scandinavian, Celtic
5. Icelandic, pro-Norwegian

GRAMMAR EXERCISES 9–16

> **Exercise 9** Using Capitalization With First Words Copy the following items, adding the missing capitals. Some items may require more than one capital.

1. the Japanese island of Honshu is dominated by Mount Fuji, the tallest mountain in the country.
2. were you aware that the mountain, which many people consider sacred, is actually an extinct volcano?
3. the article made this observation: mount Fuji has been dormant for hundreds of years; the last eruption occurred in 1707.
4. "the cone-shaped mountain rises 12,387 feet above sea level," the geologist explained. "because it is so cold at this altitude, Mount Fuji's peak is usually covered with snow."
5. its head reaches above the clouds, it surveys the mountains all around; it hears the thunder far below— fuji, o highest of mountains!
   —traditional Japanese song

> **Exercise 10** Using Capitals for Proper Nouns Copy the following items, adding the missing capitals.

1. The largest waterfall in the world is victoria falls.
2. It is located in africa, along the border of zambia and zimbabwe.
3. Between january and april, nearly 75 million gallons of water flow into batoka gorge every minute.
4. This waterfall was discovered in november 1855 by david livingstone, a minister of the presbyterian church.
5. Livingstone, who had been sent to the region by the london missionary society, stumbled upon the falls while following the zambezi river.

> **Exercise 11** Proofreading: Correcting Errors in Capitalization of First Words and Proper Nouns Revise the following paragraph, adding and removing capitals as needed.

(1) David Livingstone named the enormous waterfall He discovered after queen Victoria, the reigning monarch of england. (2) the founder of the british south africa company, cecil Rhodes, arranged for the construction of a bridge that spans the Gorge directly in front of the falls. (3) rhodes, who also founded the de beers mining company, is perhaps best known for instituting the rhodes scholarship at Oxford university. (4) Today, Tourists wishing to visit the falls can stay at the masuwe lodge or the Masaka Sun hotel, both of which have western foods, such as bubbles cola and smith cookies. (5) other points of interest in the area include Victoria Falls national park and Livingstone game park.

> **Exercise 12** Using Capitalization With Proper Adjectives Copy the sentences below that need capitals, adding the missing capitals. If a sentence does not need additional capitalization, write *correct*.

1. Iceland is a large island that lies 500 miles off the northwest coast of Scotland, just south of arctic waters.
2. The island's remarkably diverse environment, a combination of volcanoes, glaciers, and hot springs, is so unusual that the apollo astronauts trained there for their lunar landings.
3. Although Iceland was discovered by irish explorers in the eighth century, norse adventurers were the first to

inhabit the island.
4. Over time, the island was settled by various scandinavian and celtic groups.
5. Because of these affiliations, most icelandic people are very pro-norwegian.

Exercise 13 Using Capitalization With Titles of People
Copy the sentences below that need capitals, adding the missing capitals. If a sentence does not need additional capitalization, write *correct*.

1. In 1923, superintendent Doane Robinson, head of the South Dakota Historical Society, began planning the massive stone monument known as Mount Rushmore.
2. Initially, Robinson envisioned that the carving would contain the images of notable western figures, such as general George Custer and chief Sitting Bull.
3. The artist who was hired to create the carving, Gutzon Borglum, persuaded Robinson to feature four famous presidents instead.
4. By 1925, senator Peter Norbeck and congressman William Williamson had secured permission for Borglum to begin working in Haney National Forest.
5. On June 15, 1927, president and mrs. Calvin Coolidge participated in the formal dedication of the site; however, it would take Borglum more than Fourteen years to complete the monument.

Exercise 14 Capitalizing Titles
Copy the following titles, and add capitals where necessary. Underline titles that are printed in italics.

1. book: *into thin air*
2. play: *the glass menagerie*
3. magazine: *national geographic*
4. song: "sound of silence"
5. poem: "if—"

Exercise 15 Proofreading: Applying All the Rules of Capitalization
Copy the following paragraph, correcting each error in capitalization.

One of the greatest natural wonders of north America is Niagara falls. It is situated on the Niagara river, about halfway between lake Erie and lake Ontario. The river actually forms part of the United States-canadian border. Niagara falls consists of two waterfalls, the Horseshoe Falls and the American Falls. The Horseshoe is on the Canadian Side of the border in the province of ontario. The American falls is on the united states side in the state of New York. Niagara falls was formed about 12,000 years ago, after the last great ice sheet melted from the region. Indian Tribes lived in the Niagara falls area long before the first europeans arrived. The name *Niagara* comes from the Iroquois Indian word *Onguiaahra*, meaning "the strait." The first written account of the falls was published in 1683. Louis Hennepin, a roman catholic missionary who traveled with the French Explorer René-Robert Cavelier, wrote, "these waters foam and boil in a fearful manner. they thunder continually."

Exercise 16 Writing Application
Use the following directions to write five sentences of your own, using capitals wherever necessary.

1. Write a sentence in which you name the title of a book and its author.
2. Write a sentence that includes the names of two different states and their capitals.
3. Write a sentence about a famous battle and the two sides that participated in it.
4. Write a sentence about the day of the week and the month.
5. Write a sentence that names two of your favorite songs.

Chapter Review • 645

Answer Key

✓ ONGOING ASSESSMENT: Assess Mastery

Use the following resources to assess student mastery of capitalization.

In the Textbook	Print Resources	Technology
Chapter Review, Ex. 9–16	*Formal Assessment,* Ch. 27	*Writing and Grammar* Interactive Text, Ch. 27, Chapter Review; *On-Line Exercise Bank,* Ch. 27

Lesson Objectives

1. To produce legible work that shows accurate spelling and correct use of the conventions of punctuation and capitalization

2. To proofread writing for appropriateness of organization, content, style, and conventions

3. To produce error-free writing in the final draft

Step-by-Step Teaching Guide

Proofreading

Teaching Resources: Standardized Test Preparation Workbook, pp. 53–54

1. Explain to students that they should proofread passages on tests just as they proofread their own writing: by looking carefully for one type of error at a time. For example, they might look for spelling errors during the first reading, capitalization errors during the next reading, and so on.

2. Remind students to pay close attention to the way the passage is numbered. In this passage, each sentence has its own number. Sometimes, though, single sentences have two or more numbers. Failure to notice this can result in needless errors.

3. Have students answer the practice questions on page 647. Go over their answers and address any questions they have. If necessary, review the relevant chapters in this book.

Standardized Test Preparation Workshop

Proofreading

Standardized tests often measure your understanding of the rules of capitalization. One way in which tests do this is by giving you a passage to proofread and identify the types of errors, including capitalization, spelling, and punctuation. The following sample items will help you practice proofreading for errors.

Sample Test Items	Answers and Explanations
Directions: Read the passage and decide which type of error, if any, appears in each underlined section. On the day after the incident, the organization released the following comments: "<u>it is</u> (1) <u>our firm belief that we took all of the necessary measures to ensure our passengers'</u> <u>safety. Valueright airlines is relieved that no</u> (2) <u>one was injured.</u>"	

1   A   Spelling error
     B   Capitalization error
     C   Punctuation error
     D   No error
	The correct answer for item 1 is *B*. The word *It* should be capitalized, since it begins a complete sentence following a colon.

2   F   Spelling error
     G   Capitalization error
     H   Punctuation error
     J   No error
	The correct answer for item 2 is *G*. The word *airlines* should be capitalized, since it is part of the company's name.

✎ TEST-TAKING TIP

Tell students to read the passage twice before choosing "No error." Often, as we read, our minds correct errors for us without our noticing. For this reason, it is always smart to read passages slowly and more than once.

Remind students that many of these questions do not require them to explain or fix errors; they simply have to recognize them. If students don't know an answer, but are pretty certain something doesn't look right, chances are they're right.

Answer Key

> **Practice 1**

1. B (Mountains)
2. G (National Weather Service)
3. C (winter, avalanches)
4. G (areas)
5. A (skiers)

> **Practice 2**

1. B (*The, The*)
2. G (*King*)
3. C (*Hamlet*)
4. G (title character)
5. B (father's)

> **Practice 1** **Directions:** Read the following passage and decide which type of error, if any, appears in each underlined section.

The Rocky mountains received two feet of
(1)
snow Monday. The national weather service
　　　　　　(2)
has warned that additional snow could be

coming later in the week. Given the
　　　　　　　　　(3)
tremendous amount of snow that has fallen

this winter; avalanches are expected in

certain Areas. Skiers have been warned
(4)　　　　　(5)
not to venture into restricted areas under

any circumstances.

1 **A** Spelling error
   B Capitalization error
   C Punctuation error
   D No error

2 **F** Spelling error
   G Capitalization error
   H Punctuation error
   J No error

3 **A** Spelling error
   B Capitalization error
   C Punctuation error
   D No error

4 **F** Spelling error
   G Capitalization error
   H Punctuation error
   J No error

5 **A** Spelling error
   B Capitalization error
   C Punctuation error
   D No error

> **Practice 2** **Directions:** Read the following passage and decide which type of error, if any, appears in the underlined section.

Shakespeare's great tragedies include *the*
(1)
Tragedy of Macbeth, the Tragedy of Romeo

and Juliet, and *king Lear.* Many scholars
(2)
consider "Hamlet" to be his finest work,
(3)
however. In this great tragedy, the Title
　　　　　　　　　　　　　　　(4)
Character struggles with questions about

the meaning of life as he looks to avenge
　　　　　　　　　　　(5)
his Father's death.

1 **A** Spelling error
   B Capitalization error
   C Punctuation error
   D No error

2 **F** Spelling error
   G Capitalization error
   H Punctuation error
   J No error

3 **A** Spelling error
   B Capitalization error
   C Punctuation error
   D No error

4 **F** Spelling error
   G Capitalization error
   H Punctuation error
   J No error

5 **A** Spelling error
   B Capitalization error
   C Punctuation error
   D No error

Customize for
Less Advanced Students

Review the capitalization rules with students. They will be familiar with many of the basic rules, such as capitalizing the first word of a sentence. For this reason, you might want to focus on the trickier rules, such as geographical and place names, specific events and times, and the names of various groups.

Customize for
More Advanced Students

In question 3 of Practice 2, *Hamlet* should be italicized because it is the name of a play. Tell students not to panic if they see a title whose genre they don't know. If they read carefully, they will notice that the passage almost always reveals the genre of the work. In this question, *Hamlet* is referred to as a tragedy, which students will understand is one of Shakespeare's plays, not one of his sonnets. Therefore, it takes italics or underlining, not quotation marks.

Chapter 28 · Time and Resource Manager

In-Depth Lesson Plan

	LESSON FOCUS	PRINT AND MEDIA RESOURCES
DAY 1	**End Marks and Commas** Students learn and apply concepts relating to periods, question marks, exclamation marks, and commas. (pp. 650–670/H472–492)	*Writing and Grammar* Interactive Text, Sections 28.1–2; *On-line Exercise Bank*, Sections 28.1–2 **Teaching Resources** *Grammar Exercise Workbook*, pp. 163–170; *Grammar Exercises Answers on Transparencies*, Ch. 28
DAY 2	**Semicolons and Colons** Students learn and apply concepts relating to semicolons and colons and do the Hands-on Grammar activity. (pp. 671–681/H493–503)	*Writing and Grammar* Interactive Text, Section 28.3; *On-line Exercise Bank*, Section 28.3 **Teaching Resources** *Grammar Exercise Workbook*, pp. 171–174; *Hands-on Grammar Activity Book*, Ch. 28
DAY 3	**Quotation Marks and Underlining** Students learn and apply concepts relating to quotation marks, underlining, and italics. (pp. 682–697/H504–519)	*Writing and Grammar* Interactive Text, Section 28.4; *On-line Exercise Bank*, Section 28.4 **Teaching Resources** *Grammar Exercise Workbook*, pp. 175–180
DAY 4	**Dashes Through Apostrophes** Students learn and apply concepts relating to dashes, parentheses, brackets, hyphens, and apostrophes. (pp. 698–722/H520–543)	*Writing and Grammar* Interactive Text, Sections 28.5–6; *On-line Exercise Bank*, Sections 28.5–6 **Teaching Resources** *Grammar Exercise Workbook*, pp. 181–190
DAY 5	**Review and Assess** Students review the chapter and demonstrate mastery of punctuation concepts. (pp. 722–729)	*Writing and Grammar* Interactive Text, Ch. 28, Chapter Review **Teaching Resources** *Formal Assessment*, Ch. 28

Accelerated Lesson Plan

	LESSON FOCUS	PRINT AND MEDIA RESOURCES
DAY 1	**End Marks and Commas** Students cover end marks and commas as determined by the Diagnostic Test. (pp. 650–670/H472–492)	*Writing and Grammar* Interactive Text, Sections 28.1–2; **Teaching Resources** *Grammar Exercise Workbook*, pp. 163–170; *Grammar Exercises Answers on Transparencies*, Ch. 28
DAY 2	**Semicolons Through Underlining** Students cover concepts relating to semicolons, colons, quotation marks, underlining, and italics as determined by the Diagnostic Test. (pp. 671–697/H493–519)	*Writing and Grammar* Interactive Text, Sections 28.3–4; **Teaching Resources** *Grammar Exercise Workbook*, pp. 171–180
DAY 3	**Dashes Through Apostrophes; Review and Assess** Students cover concepts relating to dashes, parentheses, brackets, hyphens, and apostrophes as determined by the Diagnostic Test. They then review the chapter and demonstrate mastery of the concepts covered. (pp. 698–721/H520–543)	*Writing and Grammar* Interactive Text, Ch. 28, Section 28.5 through Chapter Review *On-line Exercise Bank*, Sections 28.5–6 **Teaching Resources** *Grammar Exercise Workbook*, pp. 181–190; *Formal Assessment*, Ch. 28

Options for Adapting Lesson Plans

FEATURES

Extend coverage with the Grammar in Literature features (pp. 657, 663, 675, 690, 712/H479, 485, 497, 512, 534) and the Standardized Test Preparation Workshop (p. 726).

TECHNOLOGY

Students can use *Writing and Grammar* Interactive Text to complete the exercises interactively on computer. They can complete additional exercises in the *On-line Exercise Bank:* The Auto Check feature will grade their work. Go on-line: PHSchool.com Use Web Code: eek-1002

Writing and Grammar Handbook Alignment

Page numbers in Step-by-Step Teaching Guides in this Teacher's Edition refer to pages from the full student text. Handbook page references, indicated with this icon ⊞, are provided in Time and Resource Manager boxes and at the bottom of each Teacher's Edition page.

INTEGRATED SKILLS COVERAGE

Grammar in Literature SE pp. 657, 663, 675, 690, 712/⊞479, 485, 497, 512, 534

Writing
Find It in Your Writing SE pp. 653, 670, 680, 681, 697, 711, 722/⊞475, 492, 502, 503, 519, 533
Writing Application SE pp. 653, 670, 681, 697, 711, 722, 725, 729/⊞475, 492, 503, 519, 533
Grammar and Style SE pp. 656, 684, 693, 699/⊞478, 506, 515, 521
Writing Skills ATE p. 659

Spelling Skills SE pp. 705, 709/⊞527, 531

Viewing and Representing Skills
Critical Viewing SE pp. 648, 650, 655, 660, 665, 667, 673, 675, 676, 679, 683, 685, 686, 688, 692, 695, 701, 703, 707, 708, 713, 718, 721/⊞470, 472, 477, 482, 487, 489, 495, 497, 498, 501, 505, 507, 508, 510, 514, 517, 523, 525, 529, 530, 535, 540, 543

Speaking and Listening Skills ATE pp. 683, 727

Vocabulary Skills ATE pp. 672, 689, 701, 713

Technology Skills SE p. 694/⊞516

Real-World Connection ATE p. 652

ASSESSMENT SUPPORT

Standardized Test Preparation Workshop SE p. 726; ATE pp. 656, 683

Standardized Test Preparation Workbook, pp. 55–56

Formal Assessment, Ch. 28

MEETING INDIVIDUAL NEEDS

Less Advanced Students ATE pp. 651, 661, 691, 716, 727. See also Ongoing Assessments ATE pp. 652, 655, 658, 659, 662, 663, 668, 679, 684, 688, 691, 695, 700, 703, 707, 709, 716, 718, 721.

More Advanced Students ATE p. 682

Gifted and Talented Students ATE p. 699

ESL Students ATE pp. 713, 720

Spatial Learners ATE p. 719

BLOCK SCHEDULING

Pacing Suggestions
For 90-minute Blocks
• Administer the Diagnostic Test to students to determine instructional coverage.
• Have students complete the necessary exercises in class. Use the Hands-on Grammar activity to provide a change of pace.

Resources for Varying Instruction
• *Writing and Grammar* Interactive Text A 90-minute block provides an ideal opportunity for students to work on the computer.

Professional Development Support
• *How to Manage Instruction in the Block* This teaching resource provides management and activity suggestions.

MEDIA AND TECHNOLOGY

For the Student
• *Writing and Grammar* Interactive Text, Ch. 28
• *On-line Exercise Bank,* Sections 28.1–6

For the Teacher
• Teacher**EXPRESS** CD-ROM

WRITING AND GRAMMAR ON-LINE

Interactive Text (On-line or on CD-ROM)
• Easily navigable instruction with on-line supporting resources
• Self-scoring exercises and diagnostic tests

Companion Web Site PHSchool.com
• On-line Exercise Bank (use Web Code eek-1002)

See the Go On-line! **feature, SE p. iii.**

LITERATURE CONNECTIONS

Grammar in Literature selections from *Prentice Hall Literature, Penguin Edition,* Grade 10:

from "Morte d' Arthur," Alfred, Lord Tennyson, SE pp. 657/⊞479

from *A Connecticut Yankee in King Arthur's Court,* Mark Twain, SE p. 675/⊞497

from "Arthur Becomes King of Britain," T. H. White, SE p. 663, 690/⊞485, 512

from "Tepeyac," Sandra Cisneros, p. 712/⊞534

Lesson Objectives

1. To understand basic and other uses of end marks
2. To understand the use of commas with compound sentences, series, adjectives, introductory material, and parenthetical and nonessential expressions
3. To understand the uses of semicolons and colons
4. To understand the use of quotation marks and underlining in direct quotations, titles, and special situations
5. To understand the functions of dashes, parentheses, hyphens, and apostrophes
6. To produce legible work that shows the correct use of the conventions of punctuation
7. To proofread for punctuation within the context of a written passage

Critical Viewing

Compare Students may say that musical notation, like punctuation, indicates speed, pauses, and ends of ideas.

Chapter 28 Punctuation

▲ **Critical Viewing** How is the musical notation in this piece like punctuation in a sentence? [**Compare**]

When Beethoven wrote the "Moonlight Sonata" more than 150 years ago, he included in his music not only the notes he wanted played but also *how* he wanted them played. Through the use of accepted music notation, he left precise instructions on the tempo, the mood he wanted to convey, the loudness and softness, and the rests. By following Beethoven's instructions, today's musicians are able to play that piece almost exactly as Beethoven played it himself.

Just as a composer must do more than set down notes on paper, a writer must do more than set down words on paper. Just as a composer must tell musicians how to play the music, so a writer must tell readers how the words are to be read. To give the reader this information, a writer uses a set of standard marks called *punctuation*.

648 • Punctuation

✓ ONGOING ASSESSMENT: Diagnose

If students miss more than one item in each category, direct them to the relevant pages of the textbook and assign exercises for practice and review.

Punctuation	Diagnostic Test Items	Teach	Practice	Section Reviews	Chapter Review
Skill Check A					
End Marks	A 1–5	pp. 650–652/H472–474	Ex. 1–2	Ex. 3–4	Ex. 73
Skill Check B					
Commas with a Series	B 7	pp. 654–657/H476–479	Ex. 8–10	Ex. 16–17	Ex. 74
Commas with Introductory Material	B 6, 8	p. 659/H481	Ex. 11	Ex. 18	Ex. 74
Commas for Other Uses	B 9–10	pp. 660–667/H482–489	Ex. 12–15	Ex. 19–21	Ex. 74

Diagnostic Test

Directions: Write all answers on a separate sheet of paper.

Skill Check A. Write the following sentences, using proper end marks to punctuate them.

1. Did Beethoven write the "Moonlight Sonata" in 1801
2. Oh Wasn't it called the Piano Sonata No 14
3. It is only sixteen minutes long
4. What a great figure-skating performance was choreographed to that sonata
5. Play the "Moonlight Sonata" on the piano

Skill Check B. Write the following sentences, inserting commas where necessary.

6. When I was in third grade I first heard the song "Moondance."
7. My mother thinks "Blue Moon" "Moon River" and "It's Only a Paper Moon" are better songs.
8. "Obviously when we bought the album" said Larry "we knew there would be many famous songs."
9. I hope the album will arrive in Albany New York before June 21 2001.
10. I wanted to share my favorite song "Shine On Harvest Moon" with them.

Skill Check C. Write the following sentences, inserting colons and semicolons where necessary.

11. Van Gogh painted my two favorite pieces *Starry Night* and *Sunflowers.*
12. *The Night Sky* is not very realistic nevertheless it is beautiful.
13. *The Sleeping Gypsy* is dominated by a few subjects the lion, the gypsy, and the moon.
14. Michelle's birthstone is a diamond Debra's is an opal.
15. Warning If taken internally, consult a physician immediately.

Skill Check D. Write the following sentences, inserting quotation marks where necessary.

16. Have you ever been to the Prado? he asked.
17. It is filled with wonderful Spanish art, he continued.
18. Goya, Velázquez, and El Greco he said are all there.
19. Perhaps you should take me there, I suggested.
20. Have you read The Road Not Taken by Robert Frost?

Skill Check E. Write the following sentences, inserting apostrophes, hyphens, and dashes where necessary.

21. My favorite book growing up I still like to read it every now and then! was *Goodnight Moon.*
22. I scored twenty five points in my last basketball game.
23. Have you ever spent much time with a two year old?
24. It is my oldest sisters favorite movie.
25. Really, I havent seen it yet.

Punctuation • 649

Each item in the Diagnostic Test corresponds to a specific section in the punctuation chapter. This will enable you to tailor instruction to the particular needs of your students. See "Ongoing Assessment: Diagnose" below for further details. Answers for the Diagnostic Test and all chapter exercises are available in *Grammar Exercises Answers on Transparencies* in your Teaching Resources.

Skill Check A

1. . . . in 1801?
2. Oh! . . . No. 14?
3. . . . long.
4. . . . sonata!
5. . . . piano.

Skill Check B

6. . . . third grade, I first . . .
7. . . . "Blue Moon," "Moon River," and . . .
8. "Obviously, when we bought the album," said Larry, "we . . ."
9. . . . Albany, New York, before June 21, 2001.
10. . . . song, "Shine on Harvest Moon," with them.

Skill Check C

11. . . . pieces: <u>Starry Night</u> and <u>Sunflowers.</u>
12. . . . realistic; nevertheless, it . . .
13. . . . subjects: the lion, . . .
14. . . . diamond; Debra's . . .
15. Warning: If taken . . .

Skill Check D

16. "Have . . . Prado?" he asked.
17. "It is . . . art," he continued.
18. "Goya, Velasquez, and El Greco," he said, "are all there."
19. "Perhaps . . . there," I suggested.
20. Have you read "The Road Not Taken" by Robert Frost?

Skill Check E

21. . . . growing up—I still . . . then!—was <u>Goodnight Moon.</u>
22. I scored twenty-five points . . .
23. . . . with a two-year-old?
24. . . . my oldest sister's . . .
25. Really, I haven't seen it yet.

✓ ONGOING ASSESSMENT: Diagnose *continued*

Punctuation	Diagnostic Test Items	Teach	Practice	Section Reviews	Chapter Review
Skill Check C					
Semicolons and Colons	C 11–15	pp. 671–678/Ⓗ493–500	Ex. 25–28	Ex. 29–30	Ex. 75
Skill Check D					
Quotation Marks	D 16–20	pp. 682–696/Ⓗ504–518	Ex. 34–41	Ex. 42–44	Ex. 76
Skill Check E					
Other Punctuation	E 21–25	pp. 698–710/Ⓗ520–532 pp. 712–721/Ⓗ 534–543	Ex. 48–54, 61–66	Ex. 55–57, 67–69	Ex. 77–78
Cumulative Reviews and Applications				Ex. 5–7, 22–24, 31–33, 45–47, 58–60, 70–72	Ex. 79–81

Write the following words on the board and ask students to punctuate them so they form two intelligible sentences: *That that is is that that is not is not. (That that is, is. That that is not, is not.)*

Activate Prior Knowledge

Ask students to recall the different functions, or types, of sentences (interrogative, imperative, declarative, exclamatory). Have them define each type and offer examples of each that they've said or heard in the past few hours.

TEACH

Step-by-Step Teaching Guide

Using the Period

1. Write on the board: *Run from the monster! Run three laps.* Explain that the first is an urgent imperative requiring an exclamation mark, but the second is a mild imperative requiring a period.

2. Make sure students understand the difference between a direct and indirect question. Have them rephrase the following direct question as an indirect question: *Where did you go, Darren? (I asked Darren where he went.)*

Language Highlight

The literal meaning of the word *punctuate* is "to mark off with little pricklings." The word is derived from the Latin verb *pungere* meaning "to prick." A more obvious derivation from this Latin root is the word *puncture*, which we understand to mean "a small hole," but which is really defined as "a pricking." The word *punctual* has a mathematical definition as "the nature of a point," but it is more commonly used in reference to timing. Surprisingly, *pungent* has the same root and is specifically defined as "pricking to taste or smell."

Critical Viewing

Speculate Possible answer: My, the Earth looks enormous! How bright it is!

Section 28.1 End Marks

Just as every sentence must begin with a capital letter, so it must end with an end mark. The three end marks are the *period* [.], the *question mark* [?], and the *exclamation mark* [!]. These marks clearly indicate to a reader that he or she has arrived at the end of a thought. End marks also indicate the emotion or tone of a sentence. In this section, you will have the opportunity to review the more common uses of end marks and to study some of their other functions.

Basic Uses of End Marks

The period has three basic uses:

▶ **KEY CONCEPT** Use a period to end a declarative sentence, a mild imperative, and an indirect question. ■

A *declarative sentence* is a statement of fact or opinion.

STATEMENT OF FACT:	The moon is a satellite of the Earth.
STATEMENT OF OPINION:	The moon looks pretty tonight.

An *imperative* gives a direction or command. An imperative often begins with a verb.

MILD IMPERATIVE: Look through the telescope.

Some declarative sentences include an *indirect question.*

DIRECT QUESTION:	Is the moon smaller than the Earth?
INDIRECT QUESTION:	I asked whether the moon was smaller than the Earth.

◀ **Critical Viewing**
This is a view of the Earth from the moon. Imagine that you are standing on the moon, and write two exclamatory sentences about the view. **[Speculate]**

⏱ TIME AND RESOURCE MANAGER

Resources
Print: *Grammar Exercise Workbook,* pp. 163–164; *Grammar Exercises Answers on Transparencies,* Ch. 28
Technology: *Writing and Grammar* Interactive Text, Section 28.1; *On-Line Exercise Bank,* Section 28.1

Using the Full Student Edition	Using the HandbookⒽ
• Work through all key concepts, pp. 650–652. • Assign and review Exercises 1–2.	• Work through all key concepts, pp. 472–474. • Assign and review Exercises 1–2.

► **KEY CONCEPT** Use a question mark to end a direct question, an incomplete question, or a statement intended as a question. ■

A *direct question* demands an answer; it stands as a direct request. All direct questions must end with a question mark.

DIRECT QUESTIONS: Did you see the full moon?
                        How far away is the moon?

In some cases, only a portion of the question is written out and the rest is simply understood. When this occurs, place a question mark at the end of the incomplete question.

INCOMPLETE QUESTIONS: Where? What color? How much?

Sometimes, a question is phrased as if it were a declarative sentence. Use a question mark to show that the sentence is a question.

STATEMENTS INTENDED   You saw that?
AS QUESTIONS: The Earth has one satellite?

Because some sentences express a great amount of emotion, another end mark was developed—the exclamation mark.

► **KEY CONCEPT** Use an exclamation mark [!] to end an exclamatory sentence, a forceful imperative sentence, or an interjection expressing strong emotion. ■

An *exclamatory sentence* shows strong emphasis or emotion. Use an exclamation mark at the end of an exclamatory sentence.

EXCLAMATORY SENTENCES: A man landed on the moon!
                        That shuttle cost millions of dollars!

A strongly worded imperative that demonstrates forcefulness or strong emotion will also take an exclamation mark.

STRONG IMPERATIVE: Don't touch those wires!

Strong interjections should also be followed by an exclamation mark.

STRONG INTERJECTIONS: Breathtaking! Ouch! Oh!

Sometimes, a strong interjection may appear before a short exclamatory sentence. If this occurs, you may use either a comma or an exclamation mark after the interjection.

WITH A COMMA: Goodness, that thunder was loud!
WITH AN
EXCLAMATION MARK: Goodness! That thunder was loud!

End Marks • 651

Using the Question Mark

1. Direct students' attention to the examples of incomplete questions. Point out that these words depend on context for the rest of their meaning. However, they are still questions, so they require question marks.

2. Write on the board: *Do we live on the Earth?* Ask students to convert this direct question into a statement intended as a question (*We live on the Earth?*) and an indirect question (*I asked whether we live on the Earth*).

Customize for
Less Advanced Students

Emphasize that incomplete questions should be used only in context; in other words, the writer must include enough information elsewhere so that the reader is able to fill in the missing parts of the question. For example, *"What kinds?"* should occur in the context of a discussion about types of things, such as the following:

"What are you putting in the soup?"

"Vegetables."

"Oh. What kinds?"

Using the Exclamation Mark

1. Remind students that the verb *to exclaim* means "to cry out" and that the exclamation mark brings emotion and intensity to a statement, as if it were being cried out.

2. Remind students that interjections can appear before a sentence, in which case they require their own end marks, or as introductory material, in which case they require commas.

473 Ⓗ • 651

Answer Key

Exercise 1

1. The moon's diameter is about one fourth the size of the Earth's.
2. Is it true that there is no atmosphere on the moon?
3. The moon travels around the Earth at approximately 2,300 miles per hour.
4. That is really fast!
5. The pull of gravity is only one-sixth that of the Earth's.
6. Did you see the footage on television of Neil Armstrong's moon landing?
7. You can see only half the moon's entire surface at any one time.
8. Is there a new moon tonight?
9. Look! There's a full moon!
10. When the moon is full, it is farther away from the sun than it is when it is a new moon.

Step-by-Step Teaching Guide

Other Uses of End Marks

1. Have students read the list of abbreviations with periods. Ask them to identify what each abbreviation stands for.
2. Explain that when one of these abbreviations falls at the end of a sentence, an additional period is never required, but a question mark or exclamation mark may be added.

Answer Key

Exercise 2

1. When I was ten, I was 4 ft. 9 in. tall.
2. Did they arrive at 9:00 A.M. or P.M.?
3. Mr. Roth is our band teacher.
4. We have a holiday in honor of Martin Luther King, Jr.
5. Watch out, Capt. Reid! That coffee cup is leaking!

Real-World Connection

Explain to students that *Mrs.* refers to a woman who is married; *Miss* refers to an unmarried woman; and *Ms.* is a title without reference to marital status. If in doubt when writing, *Ms.* is usually a safe choice.

28.1

Exercise 1 Using the Period, Question Mark, and Exclamation Mark Copy the following items, adding the necessary periods or question marks.
1. The moon's diameter is about one fourth the size of the Earth's
2. Is it true that there is no atmosphere on the moon
3. The moon travels around the Earth at approximately 2,300 miles per hour
4. That is really fast
5. The pull of gravity is only one-sixth that of the Earth's
6. Did you see the footage on television of Neil Armstrong's moon landing
7. You can see only half the moon's entire surface at any one time
8. Is there a new moon tonight
9. Look There's a full moon
10. When the moon is full, it is farther away from the sun than it is when it is a new moon

Other Uses of End Marks

KEY CONCEPT Most abbreviations end with a period. ■

ABBREVIATIONS WITH PERIODS:	Mrs.	Jr.	Ave.	Capt.	Wash.
	M.D.	R.N.	A.M.	ft.	
ABBREVIATIONS WITHOUT PERIODS:	FBI	FL	kg	L	

KEY CONCEPT Use a period after numbers and letters in outlines. ■

EXAMPLE:
   I. Our Solar System
     A. Earth
       1. moon
     B. Pluto
       1. Charon

Exercise 2 Proofreading for End Marks Proofread the following sentences, inserting end marks where necessary.
1. When I was ten, I was 4 ft 9 in tall
2. Did they arrive at 9:00 A.M. or P.M.
3. Mr Roth is our band teacher
4. We have a holiday in honor of Martin Luther King, Jr
5. Watch out, Capt Reid, that coffee cup is leaking

Learn More

For an abbreviations reference, see Abbreviations on page 880.

Interactive Textbook

Get instant feedback! Exercises 1 and 2 are available on-line or on CD-ROM.

More Practice

Grammar Exercise Workbook
• pp. 163–164
On-line Exercise Bank
• Section 28.1
Go on-line:
PHSchool.com
Enter Web Code:
eek-1002

☑ **ONGOING ASSESSMENT: Monitor and Reinforce**

If students have trouble with Exercise 1 or 2, refer them to the following for additional practice.

In the Textbook	Print Resources	Technology
Section Review, Ex. 3–4, Section 28.1	*Grammar Exercise Workbook,* pp. 163–164	*On-Line Exercise Bank,* Section 28.1

Section 28.1 Section Review

GRAMMAR EXERCISES 3–7

Exercise 3 Using End Marks Copy all of the following sentences, adding all necessary end marks.

1. Early observers thought that the dark spots on the moon were oceans
2. This is why they are called *mares*, the Latin word for "sea"
3. Are there oceans on the moon
4. No, there are not
5. The moon is so bright tonight
6. There are mountains and craters on the moon
7. The highest ranges have peaks almost as tall as the Himalayas
8. What is the origin of the moon's craters
9. Some craters show signs of being volcanic in origin
10. Most resulted from impacts with meteorites or asteroids

Exercise 4 Proofreading to Correct End Marks On a separate sheet of paper, copy the following passage. Proofread the passage, correcting and adding end marks as needed.

In the mid-twentieth century, people began to travel in space On April 12, 1961, a cosmonaut from the USSR made a single orbit around the Earth Alan B Shepherd completed a 300-mile flight, but John H Glenn, Jr was the first person from the United States to orbit the Earth. Glenn orbited the Earth on Feb 20, 1962 Wow That must have been a thrill

Since then, many spaceflights have been launched from the John F Kennedy Space Center in Florida Who would have believed how far the technology would advance. Today, astronauts from the United States and cosmonauts from the former Soviet Union often work together on research Have you ever seen a picture of the space station in which they work It's quite a feat of engineering

Exercise 5 Find It in Your Reading Read the following from "Leiningen Versus the Ants." Tell why you think the writer uses an exclamation mark.

The Brazilian rose heavily to his feet. "I've done my best," he gasped. "Your obstinacy endangers not only yourself, but the lives of your four hundred workers. You don't know these ants!"

Exercise 6 Find It in Your Writing Look through your portfolio. Find examples of sentences that you have ended with a period, a question mark, or an exclamation mark. Explain why you used each mark.

Exercise 7 Writing Application Write sentences of your own using the following directions.

1. Write a question about schoolwork, and then rephrase it as an indirect question.
2. Write a declarative sentence about something you like.
3. Rewrite your declarative sentence so that it can end with an exclamation mark.
4. Write a strong imperative you have heard from your teacher.
5. Write a statement intended as a question to get information from a friend about a book he or she has read.

Section Review • 653

ASSESS

Section Review

Each of these exercises correlates to the instruction on end marks. These exercises may be used for more practice, for reteaching, or for review of the key concepts presented. Answers for all chapter exercises are available in *Grammar Exercises Answers on Transparencies* in your Teaching Resources.

Answer Key

Exercise 3

1. . . . oceans.
2. . . . for "sea."
3. Are there oceans on the moon?
4. No, there are not.
5. The moon is so bright tonight!
6. . . . craters on the moon.
7. . . . as tall as the Himalayas.
8. . . . of the moon's craters?
9. . . . volcanic in origin.
10. . . . meteorites or asteroids.

Exercise 4

1. in space.
2. around the Earth.
3. Alan B. Shepherd
4. John H. Glenn, Jr.,
5. Feb. 20, 1962.
6. Wow!
7. been a thrill!
8. John F. Kennedy
9. in Florida.
10. advance? or advance!
11. on research.
12. they work?
13. engineering. or engineering!

Exercise 5

Find It in Your Reading
Sample answer: He wants to convey the extreme danger that the ants may cause.

Exercise 6

Find It in Your Writing
If students cannot find examples of question marks or exclamation points, challenge them to change some statements into either questions or exclamations and add the appropriate marks.

Exercise 7

Writing Application
Answers will vary. Have students exchange papers and check that the sentences adhere to the directions.

Commas

Write these three sentences on the board:

> I read the book and then I saw the movie.
>
> I read the book, then I saw the movie
>
> I read the book, and saw the movie.

Ask students which of the above statements has an error in punctuation (they all do). Elicit that the first is a compound sentence requiring a comma before the conjunction; the second is a comma splice, or run-on, which can be fixed with a semicolon; and the third should not have a comma before *and* because this conjunction joins two verbs, not two clauses.

Activate Prior Knowledge

Ask students to make a list of rules, in their own words, for using commas. Have them share their rules. Be sure they cover introductory material, essential and nonessential expressions, series of items or adjectives, dates, and quotations.

TEACH

Step-by-Step Teaching Guide

Commas With Compound Sentences

1. Have students try to recall the coordinating conjunctions (*and, but, or, nor, for, so, yet*). Explain that these can be used to combine two independent clauses when preceded by a comma.

2. Remind students that, when they use a comma and a coordinating conjunction, both halves of the sentence must be independent clauses and related in meaning.

3. Be sure students understand the differences between a compound sentence and compound subjects, verbs, prepositional phrases, and subordinate clauses. Ask them where they might be tempted to place commas in these sentences and reinforce the reasons that commas are not needed.

The comma [,] tells the reader to take a short pause before continuing the sentence.

The comma is used more than any other internal punctuation mark. As a result, many errors are made in its use. This section presents rules to help you use the comma correctly—to separate basic elements and to set off added elements in sentences.

Commas With Compound Sentences

A compound sentence is two or more independent clauses joined by one of the following coordinating conjunctions: *and, but, for, nor, or, so,* or *yet.* A comma is needed to separate the independent clauses.

▶ **KEY CONCEPT** Use a comma before the conjunction to separate two independent clauses in a compound sentence. ■

Always check to make sure that you have written two complete sentences joined by a coordinating conjunction before you insert a comma.

EXAMPLES: We read about Mexico, and then we wrote our report on it.

Storm clouds were gathering overhead, so we brought the lawn chairs inside.

The most common error that writers make with this rule is to insert a comma automatically when they see a conjunction. Remember, however, that coordinating conjunctions can also join compound subjects, compound verbs, prepositional phrases, and clauses. When they are used in one of these ways, no comma is required.

COMPOUND SUBJECT: The parents and the teachers meet tonight.

COMPOUND VERB: Tourists swim and play sports when they visit Mexico.

TWO PREPOSITIONAL PHRASES: I hit the golf ball into the water and then into a sand trap.

TWO SUBORDINATE CLAUSES: My brothers enjoy books only if they are relatively short and only if they offer a lot of action.

⏱ TIME AND RESOURCE MANAGER

Resources
Print: *Grammar Exercise Workbook,* pp. 165–170; *Grammar Exercises Answers on Transparencies,* Ch. 28
Technology: *Writing and Grammar* Interactive Text, Section 28.2; *On-Line Exercise Bank,* Section 28.2

Using the Full Student Edition	Using the Handbook🄷
• Work through all key concepts, pp. 654–667. • Assign and review Exercises 8–15. • Read and discuss Grammar in Literature, pp. 657, 663.	• Work through all key concepts, pp. 476–489. • Assign and review Exercises 8–15. • Read and discuss Grammar in Literature, pp. 479, 485.

Exercise 8 **Using Commas in Compound Sentences** If a comma is needed in one of the following sentences, write the word before the comma, the comma, and the conjunction following the comma. If no comma is needed, write *correct*.

EXAMPLE: I practice my Spanish daily but I still make mistakes.

ANSWER: daily, but

1. Mexico's full name is the United Mexican States and it is known as *Estados Unidos Mexicanos* in Spanish.
2. The capital is Mexico City and it is also Mexico's largest city.
3. The United States is to Mexico's north and Belize and Guatemala are to its south.
4. The Tropic of Cancer goes through Mexico so the area to the south can be extremely hot.
5. In parts of the country, the temperature can go as high as 120 degrees Fahrenheit yet as low as 32 degrees Fahrenheit.
6. Some southern parts of Mexico can receive up to sixty inches of rain a year but most of the country is much drier.
7. It is hotter in Monterey than in Mexico City but not much hotter.
8. The wide temperature range gives Mexico an extremely varied plant life but rainfall affects it, too.
9. The north is desertlike but cacti grow there and yucca and mesquite as well.
10. Wolves are found in the north and in the mountain forests, along with bears and jaguars.

More Practice

Grammar Exercise Workbook
• pp. 165–170
On-line Exercise Bank
• Section 28.2
Go on-line:
PHSchool.com
Enter Web Code:
eek-1002

Interactive Textbook

Get instant feedback! Exercise 8 is available on-line or on CD-ROM.

◄ **Critical Viewing** Make a statement about the contrast between rural and urban areas of Mexico. Use two independent clauses. Identify where you would place the comma. Then, revise the sentence so that a comma is not required. **[Analyze]**

Answer Key

▶ **Exercise 8**

1. States, and
2. City, and
3. north, and
4. Mexico, so
5. correct
6. year, but
7. City, but (elliptical construction)
8. life, but
9. desertlike, but
10. correct

Critical Viewing

Analyze Possible response: Urban areas of Mexico have many cars and tall buildings, but many rural parts of the country offer a more traditional life.

Possible revision: Urban areas of Mexico have many cars and tall buildings; many rural parts of the country offer a more traditional life.

☑ **ONGOING ASSESSMENT: Monitor and Reinforce**

If students miss more than two items in Exercise 8, refer them to the following for additional practice.

In the Textbook	Print Resources	Technology
Section Review, Ex. 16, Section 28.2	*Grammar Exercise Workbook*, pp. 165–166	*On-Line Exercise Bank*, Section 28.2

⏱ **TIME SAVERS!**

🗂 **Answers on Transparencies** Use the *Grammar Exercises Answers on Transparencies* for Chapter 28 to facilitate correction by students.

💻 **On-Line Exercise Bank** Have students complete the exercises on computer. The Auto Check feature will grade their work for you!

Commas With Series

1. Explain that commas in compound sentences are used to connect elements, but here commas are used to separate elements.

2. Have students read the three examples beneath the key concept, locating the three words, phrases, and clauses in each series. Have students write their own sentences using words, phrases, and clauses in a series.

3. Point out that this book consistently uses a comma after the next to last item in a series. This is called the *serial comma*.

4. Have students think of more examples of pairs of items that don't need commas (e.g., *salt and pepper, peanut butter and jelly, macaroni and cheese*).

Commas With Adjectives

1. Ask students to define *coordinate adjectives* (adjectives of equal rank, or importance, modifying the same noun). Explain that such adjectives, even if there are only two of them, should be separated by commas.

2. Have students write two sentences: one with coordinate adjectives and one with cumulative adjectives.

Commas With Series and Adjectives

Series Whenever a series of words, phrases, or clauses occurs in a sentence, you will need to insert commas.

▶ **KEY CONCEPT** Use commas to separate three or more words, phrases, or clauses in a series. ■

WORDS:	I read the articles, extracts, and books for my final exam.
PREPOSITIONAL PHRASES:	Mexico had been ruled by the Spanish, by the Mexicans, and by the French.
CLAUSES:	The bank filled quickly with people who transferred their accounts, who cashed checks, and who opened safe-deposit boxes.

Some writers omit the last comma in a series. This is permissible as long as the writer follows a consistent pattern. In your own work, however, you will find that the full use of commas generally works better. This is especially true in those cases where the last comma is needed to prevent confusion.

CONFUSING:	Streams of people, honking geese and souvenir vendors swarmed outside the hotel.
ALWAYS CLEAR:	Streams of people, honking geese, and souvenir vendors swarmed outside the hotel.

Commas are not needed when all the items in a series have already been separated by conjunctions (usually *and* or *or*).

EXAMPLE:	I cut and chopped and diced onions until I cried.

Commas should also be avoided within pairs of items that are used together so frequently that they are thought of as a single item. Notice in the following example that commas separate the pairs but not the items in the pairs.

EXAMPLE:	I asked for ham and eggs, coffee and cream, and bread and butter.

Grammar and Style Tip

When showing a contrast, use opposing series of adjectives to create parallel structure.

⚒ STANDARDIZED TEST PREPARATION WORKSHOP

Grammar and Usage Many standardized tests require students to solve problems with punctuation marks. Use the following example to demonstrate.

Which of the following sentences contains an error in comma usage?

A Inspector Mills would probably not find any useful evidence but he had to examine all the files.

B The detective could find two reasons for the burglary: the victim was universally disliked, and the victim was enormously wealthy.

C The three suspects, who were well known by the entire neighborhood, were called in for an interview.

D Miss Thompson claimed she had been reading in her room, the butler said he had been working in his study, and Dr. Edwards refused to account for his whereabouts.

The correct answer is **A**. The sentence requires a comma before *but* because it is a compound sentence.

GRAMMAR IN LITERATURE

from Morte d'Arthur

Alfred, Lord Tennyson

In the following passage, commas are used to separate the names of guests at a Christmas celebration listed as items in a series.

> At Francis Allen's on the Christmas eve—
> The game of forfeits done—the girls all kissed
> Beneath the sacred bush and passed away—
> The parson Holmes, the poet Everard Hall,
> The host, and I sat round the wassail bowl, . . .

Adjectives Use commas to divide adjectives of equal rank. Such adjectives are called *coordinate adjectives.*

> **KEY CONCEPT** Use commas to separate **coordinate adjectives**—adjectives of equal rank. ■

To determine whether adjectives in a sentence are of equal rank, ask yourself two questions: First, can you put an *and* between the adjectives and still have the sentence retain its exact meaning? Second, can you switch the adjectives and still have a sentence that sounds grammatically correct? If the answer to the two test questions is yes, you have adjectives of equal rank and a comma should be placed between them.

EXAMPLES: The country's wild, beautiful scenery is an attraction for tourists.

She left detailed, precise instructions for the substitute.

In these examples, *wild* and *beautiful* and *detailed* and *precise* qualify as coordinate adjectives.

> **KEY CONCEPT** Do not use commas to separate **cumulative adjectives**—adjectives that must stay in a specific order. ■

EXAMPLES: Colonial Mexico had rigid social classes.

In a few short hours, we will be finished.

Try putting an *and* between these adjectives or changing their order. The sentences do not make sense. These adjectives must stay in the order in which they are written. Therefore, no comma is used to separate them.

Commas • 657

Step-by-Step Teaching Guide

Grammar in Literature

1. Have a student read the passage aloud. Ask students what they think is the largest number of items that could be linked together with commas in a series. (There is no absolute limit; the limit is that too many items might cause the reader to lose track of what the series is listing.)

2. Ask what would happen if the author had not used commas in this long series. (Readers would find it difficult to determine where one item ends and the next begins.)

More About the Writer

Alfred, Lord Tennyson (1809–1892) wrote prolifically from the age of fifteen. "Morte d'Arthur" is an excerpt from his *Idylls of the King,* a set of twelve narrative poems based on the Arthurian legends made popular by Sir Thomas Malory in the late fifteenth century.

Connections With Literature

Alfred, Lord Tennyson's "Morte d'Arthur" can be found in *Prentice Hall Literature, Penguin Edition,* Grade 10.

1. Reptiles found in Mexico include turtles, iguanas, rattlesnakes, and lizards.
2. correct
3. Corn, cotton, fruits, wheat, beans, coffee, tomatoes, and rice are grown in Mexico.
4. Natural resources in Mexico include petroleum, silver, copper, gold, lead, and zinc.
5. Plant and animal life vary with climatic zone, altitude, and precipitation.
6. Mexican culture is a mix of Native American, North American, and Spanish influences.
7. Native American groups included the Maya, the Aztec, and the Toltec.
8. Evidence suggests that a hunting people existed in 13,000 B.C., that crop cultivation developed around 8,000 B.C., and that the first major civilization in Mexico was the Olmec.
9. correct
10. The Spaniards heard of the Aztecs' wealth, wanted to take their gold, and sent a large invading army in 1519.

1. spicy, hot food
2. cumulative
3. cumulative
4. hot, humid climate
5. cumulative
6. cumulative
7. bleak, arid landscape
8. rich, complex history
9. cumulative
10. cumulative

▶ **Exercise 9** Separating Items in a Series Copy each sentence that needs commas, adding the necessary commas. For sentences that need no commas, write *correct*.

EXAMPLE: Mexican cooking uses tomatoes chilies and lots of spices.

ANSWER: Mexican cooking uses tomatoes, chilies, and lots of spices.

1. Reptiles found in Mexico include turtles iguanas rattlesnakes and lizards.
2. Both sea and game birds are numerous.
3. Corn cotton fruits wheat beans coffee tomatoes and rice are grown in Mexico.
4. Natural resources in Mexico include petroleum silver copper gold lead and zinc.
5. Plant and animal life vary with climatic zone altitude and precipitation.
6. Mexican culture is a mixture of Native American North American and Spanish influences.
7. Native American groups included the Maya the Aztec and the Toltec.
8. Evidence suggests that a hunting people existed in 13,000 B.C. that crop cultivation developed around 8000 B.C. and that the first major civilization in Mexico was the Olmec.
9. The Aztecs reached the height of their power by the fifteenth century and were intellectually and artistically advanced.
10. The Spaniards heard of the Aztecs' wealth wanted to take their gold and sent a large invading army in 1519.

▶ **Exercise 10** Using Commas With Adjectives For each of the following phrases, write *cumulative* if the adjectives are cumulative and require no comma. If the adjectives are equal in rank, write the adjectives, inserting the comma.

EXAMPLE: a vivid beautiful scene
ANSWER: a vivid, beautiful scene

1. spicy hot food
2. several distinct cultural groups
3. rigid social classes
4. hot humid climate
5. earliest advanced civilizations
6. small native minority
7. bleak arid landscape
8. rich complex history
9. varied native fauna
10. distinctive regional character

☑ **ONGOING ASSESSMENT: Monitor and Reinforce**

If students miss more than two items in Exercise 9 or 10, refer them to the following for additional practice.

In the Textbook	Print Resources	Technology
Section Review, Ex. 17–18, Section 28.2	*Grammar Exercise Workbook,* pp. 165–166	*On-Line Exercise Bank,* Section 28.2

Commas After Introductory Material

> **KEY CONCEPT** Use a comma after an introductory word, phrase, or clause. ■

KINDS OF INTRODUCTORY MATERIAL		
Words	Introductory Words	No, I will not go to Mexico with you.
	Nouns of Direct Address	Cindy, could you hold this picture of Mexico?
	Common Expressions	Of course, we can get that printed for you.
	Introductory Adverbs	Obviously, the student had tried. Hurriedly, she hid the present she had wrapped.
Phrases	Prepositional Phrases	In the deep recesses of the couch, I found the watch I had lost.
	Participial Phrases	Jumping over the fence, the horse caught its back hoof.
	Infinitive Phrases	To get to the appointment on time, the man left early.
Clauses	Adverb Clauses	When the steaks were medium rare, we took them off the grill.

> **Exercise 11** **Proofreading for Commas After Introductory Material** Copy the following passage on a separate sheet of paper. Add commas after introductory material as needed.

When the Spaniards decided to conquer Mexico they appointed Hernán Cortés to lead the army. Soon after landing in Mexico Cortés found someone who could speak Aztec. Having learned of discord in the Aztec Empire Cortés convinced some natives to join him. At the time that all of this was happening Montezuma was the leader of the Aztec Empire. During his march to the Aztec capital Cortés was in communication with Montezuma. Reaching the capital in November of 1519 Cortés took Montezuma hostage. In the following year Cortés had to return to the coast of Mexico. In his absence his deputy mistreated and killed many Aztecs. After Cortés returned from the coast a battle was fought in which Montezuma was killed. Taking the capital in 1521 the Spaniards ultimately ended Aztec power.

> **More Practice**

Grammar Exercise Workbook
• pp. 167–168
On-line Exercise Bank
• Section 28.2
  Go on-line:
  PHSchool.com
  Enter Web Code:
  eek-1002

Commas • 659

Step-by-Step Teaching Guide

Commas After Introductory Material

1. Explain to students that introductory material can consist of a single word, a phrase, or a clause.

2. Direct students' attention to the chart and ask them why such structures might be written at the beginnings of sentences (to modify a word at the beginning of the main clause, to achieve variety in sentence structure).

Integrating Writing Skills

Sentence Structure Remind students that they can use all of the constructions in the chart on this page to add variety to their sentence structures when they write.

Answer Key

> **Exercise 11**

(1) When the Spaniards decided to conquer Mexico, they . . . (2) Soon after landing in Mexico, Cortés . . . (3) Having learned of the discord in the Aztec Empire, Cortés . . . (4) At the time that all this was happening, Montezuma . . . (5) During his march to the Aztec capital, Cortés . . . (6) Reaching the capital in November of 1519, Cortés . . . (7) In the following year, Cortés . . . (8) In his absence, his . . . (9) After Cortés returned from the coast, a battle . . . (10) Taking the capital in 1521, the Spaniards . . .

☑ ONGOING ASSESSMENT: Monitor and Reinforce

If students have difficulty with Exercise 11, refer them to the following for additional practice.

In the Textbook	Print Resources	Technology
Section Review, Ex. 18, Section 28.2	*Grammar Exercise Workbook,* pp. 167–168	*On-Line Exercise Bank,* Section 28.2

⏱ TIME SAVERS!

Answers on Transparencies
Use the *Grammar Exercises Answers on Transparencies* for Chapter 28 to facilitate correction by students.

On-Line Exercise Bank
Have students complete the exercises on computer. The Auto Check feature will grade their work for you!

Commas With Parenthetical Expressions

1. Explain that parenthetical information can be removed from a sentence without changing its essential meaning.

2. Discuss the different examples of parenthetical expressions offered on this page. Point out that many conjunctive adverbs function as *transitions* because they help move the reader from one idea to another.

3. Show students that parenthetical expressions are punctuated depending on their location in a sentence: one comma for those at the beginning or end of a sentence; two commas for those in the middle.

Critical Viewing

Describe Possible answer: The steps, by the way, were covered in grass.

28.2

Commas With Parenthetical and Nonessential Expressions

Commas are often used within a sentence to set off parenthetical and nonessential expressions.

Parenthetical Expressions A parenthetical expression is a word or phrase that interrupts the general flow of a sentence. Study the following list of common parenthetical expressions.

NOUN OF DIRECT ADDRESS:	Don, Mrs. Burke, my son, sweetheart
CONJUNCTIVE ADVERBS:	also, besides, furthermore, however, indeed, instead, moreover, nevertheless, otherwise, therefore, thus
COMMON EXPRESSIONS:	by the way, I feel, in my opinion, in the first place, of course, on the other hand,
CONTRASTING EXPRESSIONS:	not that one, not there, not mine

▲ **Critical Viewing** In a sentence about the condition of these ruins, include a parenthetical comment about the grass. **[Describe]**

▶ **KEY CONCEPT** Use commas to set off parenthetical expressions. ■

Two commas are used to enclose the entire parenthetical expression when the expression is located in the middle of the sentence.

NOUN OF DIRECT ADDRESS:	We will go, Marge, as soon as your father arrives.
CONJUNCTIVE ADVERB:	The boys, therefore, decided to go to Acapulco.
COMMON EXPRESSION:	The flowers, in my opinion, have never looked healthier.
CONTRASTING EXPRESSIONS:	It was here, not there, that we found the answer.

If one of these expressions is used at the end of the sentence, however, only one comma is necessary.

EXAMPLE: We will go as soon as your father arrives, Marge.

Essential and Nonessential Expressions Because commas are used only with nonessential expressions, writers must learn to distinguish between essential and nonessential material. (The terms *restrictive* and *nonrestrictive* are sometimes used to refer to the same types of expressions.)

An *essential* expression is a word, phrase, or clause that provides essential information in a sentence: information that cannot be removed without changing the meaning of the sentence. In the following example, the clause following *boy* tells *which* boy the writer means. Thus, it provides essential information in the sentence.

▶ **KEY CONCEPT** Do not use commas to set off essential expressions. ■

EXAMPLES: The boy who is holding the book is going to Mexico.

The famous dramatist Ben Jonson wrote these comedies.

Because the clauses in the sentences above are essential expressions, they are not set off with commas.

Nonessential expressions provide additional, but not essential, information in a sentence. If you remove nonessential material from a sentence, the remaining sentence will still contain all the necessary information required by the reader.

EXAMPLES: Joe Warren, who is holding the book, is going to Mexico.

Ben Jonson, a famous dramatist, wrote these comedies.

In the first example, the boy is specifically named, and the information contained in the clause provides only an additional fact. Thus, this clause is nonessential.

Once you have decided whether or not an expression is essential, you can apply this rule:

▶ **KEY CONCEPT** Use commas to set off nonessential expressions. ■

When applying this rule, be alert for three types of word groups: appositives, participial phrases, and adjective clauses. They often serve as either essential or nonessential expressions. Check them carefully to avoid committing comma errors. Study the chart on the next page until you feel confident that you can tell the difference between essential expressions and nonessential expressions.

🕐 Learn More

To learn more about essential and nonessential expressions, see Chapter 20.

Commas • 661

Commas With Nonessential Expressions

1. Have students define the word *essential* (necessary). Point out that this adjective can be applied to words, phrases, and clauses that cannot be removed from a sentence without changing its meaning.

2. Write on the board: *My friend who is wearing a purple shirt will meet Jon at the gate. Caroline, who is wearing a purple shirt, will meet Jon at the gate.* Have students explain why the underlined material is essential in the first sentence but not in the second. (In the first sentence, the underlined material is necessary because it specifies which friend will meet Jon at the gate.)

Customize for
Less Advanced Students

If students are having difficulty determining whether an expression is essential or nonessential, tell them to rewrite the sentence, omitting the expression. If the meaning of the sentence has changed, the expression is essential.

1. The first Spanish viceroy of Mexico, Antonio de Mendoza, was appointed in 1535.
2. This appointment, it appears, established a Spanish colonial government in Mexico for almost three hundred years.
3. Moreover, the Spaniards had sixty-one viceroys in Mexico.
4. Mexico, you know, was called New Spain then.
5. A series of expeditions, adding land to Spain's territory, increased the power of Spain in the Americas.
6. correct
7. The viceregal system was not, in fact, always a fair one.
8. Native Americans, who were supposed to be free, were treated like slaves.
9. The most powerful institution in colonial Mexico was, in all probability, the Roman Catholic Church.
10. The people who occupied positions of power were from the Spanish-born minority, who enjoyed power out of proportion to their numbers.

28.2

ESSENTIAL AND NONESSENTIAL EXPRESSIONS

Appositive	Essential	My friend Joanne went to the University of Indiana.
	Nonessential	Joanne, my friend, went to the University of Indiana.
Participial Phrase	Essential	The teacher wearing a blue dress took the students on the field trip.
	Nonessential	Mrs. Goff, wearing the blue dress, took the students on the field trip.
Adjective Clause	Essential	The hotel that we enjoyed the most had three swimming pools and lighted tennis courts.
	Nonessential	The Royal Tahitian Hotel, which was our favorite, had three swimming pools and lighted tennis courts.

> Exercise 12 Setting Off Parenthetical Expressions

Copy each of the following sentences, inserting any commas necessary to set off parenthetical expressions. If no change is necessary, write *correct*.

EXAMPLE: The Spanish conquest of Mexico was in fact quite complex.

ANSWER: The Spanish conquest of Mexico was, in fact, quite complex.

1. The first Spanish viceroy of Mexico Antonio de Mendoza was appointed in 1535.
2. This appointment it appears established a Spanish colonial government in Mexico for almost three hundred years.
3. Moreover the Spaniards had sixty-one viceroys in Mexico.
4. Mexico you know was called New Spain then.
5. A series of expeditions adding land to Spain's territory increased the power of Spain in the Americas.
6. New Spain included present-day Texas and New Mexico and California.
7. The viceregal system was not in fact always a fair one.
8. Native Americans who were supposed to be free were treated like slaves.
9. The most powerful institution in colonial Mexico was in all probability the Roman Catholic Church.
10. The people who occupied positions of power were from the Spanish-born minority who enjoyed power out of proportion to their numbers.

More Practice

Grammar Exercise Workbook
• pp. 167–168
On-line Exercise Bank
• Section 28.2
  Go on-line:
  PHSchool.com
  Enter Web Code:
  eek-1002

Get instant feedback! Exercises 12 and 13 are available on-line or on CD-ROM.

✓ ONGOING ASSESSMENT: Monitor and Reinforce

If students miss more than two items in Exercise 12, refer them to the following for additional practice.

In the Textbook	Print Resources	Technology
Section Review, Ex. 19, Section 28.2	*Grammar Exercise Workbook,* pp. 167–168	*On-Line Exercise Bank,* Section 28.2

▶ **Exercise 13** Distinguishing Between Essential and Nonessential Expressions If one of the following sentences contains an essential expression needing no additional commas, write *essential.* If the sentence contains a nonessential expression, copy the sentence and add the necessary commas.

EXAMPLE: Those who tried to institute reforms sometimes succeeded but more often failed.

ANSWER: essential

(1) Spain attempted reforms which proved largely ineffectual to help the condition of Native Americans. (2) Their failure due to the fact that distance made enforcement difficult kept the Native Americans in misery. (3) The inefficiency and corruption that were so prevalent in the colonial government greatly disturbed Spain. (4) Spain tried reforms in the eighteenth century that could not eliminate the problem. (5) Resentment of the Mexican-born population which was inflamed by European ideas of freedom continued to grow. (6) The most immediate and perhaps most important cause of the Mexican War for Independence was the occupation of Spain by Napoleon. (7) Independence which took more than ten years to achieve was formally proclaimed in August 1821. (8) Peace long missing in Mexico did not last long. (9) Mexico a country that was not used to democracy continued to have problems. (10) Antonio Lopez de Santa Anna who was elected president in 1833 was to have an impact on both Mexico and the United States.

GRAMMAR IN
LITERATURE

from **Arthur Becomes King of Britain**
T. H. White

In the following sentence, notice that the phrase which he did not read *is nonessential and the phrase* on the pommel *is essential. The writer sets off the nonessential phrase (highlighted in blue italics) with commas.*

He saw the golden letters, *which he did not read,* and the jewels on the pommel, flashing in the lovely light.

Commas • 663

Exercise 13
1. Spain attempted reforms, which proved largely ineffectual, to help the condition of Native Americans.
2. Their failure, due to the fact that distance made enforcement difficult, kept the Native Americans in misery.
3. essential
4. essential
5. Resentment of the Mexican-born population, which was inflamed by European ideas of freedom, continued to grow.
6. The most immediate, and perhaps most important, cause of the Mexican War for Independence was the occupation of Spain by Napoleon.
7. Independence, which took more than ten years to achieve, was formally proclaimed in August 1821.
8. Peace, long missing in Mexico, did not last long.
9. Mexico, a country that was not used to democracy, continued to have problems.
10. Antonio Lopez de Santa Anna, who was elected president in 1833, was to have an impact on both Mexico and the United States.

Step-by-Step Teaching Guide

Grammar in Literature

Students will recognize that *which he did not read* is set off with commas. Ask them why. (It is nonessential; it is not needed to explain that he did not read the *letters*.)

☑ **ONGOING ASSESSMENT: Monitor and Reinforce**

If students miss more than two items in Exercise 13, refer them to the following for additional practice.

In the Textbook	Print Resources	Technology
Section Review, Ex. 20, Section 28.2	*Grammar Exercise Workbook,* pp. 167–168	*On-Line Exercise Bank,* Section 28.2

⏱ **TIME SAVERS!**

Answers on Transparencies
Use the *Grammar Exercises Answers on Transparencies* for Chapter 28 to facilitate correction by students.

On-Line Exercise Bank
Have students complete the exercises on computer. The Auto Check feature will grade their work for you!

Commas With Locations, Dates, and Titles

1. Have students read the first key concept. Explain that locations can have two or three parts, all of which are divided by commas.

2. Explain that dates also have two or three parts. Explain that expressions with prepositions such as *September of 2007* or *June 11 in 1974* do not require commas.

3. Explain that in a sentence, an abbreviated title is set off from the rest of the sentence with a comma. Be sure students understand that it is correct to use a period followed by a comma.

28.2

Other Uses of the Comma

Commas are used in the following situations:

With Locations Whenever you are citing a specific place, check to see whether a comma is required.

> **KEY CONCEPT** When a geographical name is made up of two or more parts, use a comma after each item. ■

EXAMPLES: I traveled from Taos, New Mexico, to Tijuana, Mexico.
This cheese was shipped from Montigny, Moselle, France, by my friend Robert.

With Dates Dates containing numbers require commas.

> **KEY CONCEPT** When a date is made up of two or more parts, use a comma after each item except in the case of a month followed by a day or a month followed by a year. ■

EXAMPLES: On Friday, April 17, we will have a special meeting.
We will discuss the class trip to Monterey on November 11, 2001.
February 1980 was one of the wettest months on record.

If the parts of a date have already been joined by prepositions, no comma is needed.

EXAMPLE: The city's new mass-transit system ran its first train on June 11 of 1974.

With Titles Use a comma with titles that follow a name.

> **KEY CONCEPT** When a name is followed by one or more titles, use a comma after the name and after each title. ■

EXAMPLE: I noticed that Jeremy McGuire, Sr., is a partner in this firm.

A similar rule applies with some business abbreviations:

EXAMPLE: She worked for Heller and Ramirez, Inc., for a year.

With Addresses Addresses consisting of two or more parts need commas to separate the parts.

▶ **KEY CONCEPT** Use a comma after each item in an address made up of two or more parts. ■

EXAMPLE: Katie Wedel's new address is 160 11th Street, Anytown, Missouri 63131.

If this address were on an envelope, most of the commas would be omitted.

> Mahoney
> 260 Broadway
> Anytown, NY 10960
>
> stamp
>
> Katie Wedel
> 160 11th Street
> Anytown, MO 63131

Avoid using commas if prepositions join parts of an address.

EXAMPLE: Katie Wedel lives on 11th Street in Anytown.

With Salutations and Closings You will need to use commas in the openings and closings of many letters.

▶ **KEY CONCEPT** Use a comma after the salutation in a personal letter and after the closing in all letters. ■

SALUTATIONS: Dear Rupert,   Dear Aunt Dolly,
CLOSINGS: Sincerely,   In appreciation,

▶ **Critical Viewing** What punctuation is used on this sign? In what situation would a comma be required with this street name? [Apply]

Commas • 665

Step-by-Step Teaching Guide

Commas With Addresses, Salutations, and Closings

1. Use the example to demonstrate that each line on an envelope is separated by a comma when converted to a sentence.

2. Be sure students understand that inserting the items from an address into prepositional phrases eliminates the need for commas.

3. Point out that in letters, salutations and closings are additional elements that should be set off from the rest of the text with commas. They are usually set apart spatially, too.

Critical Viewing

Apply Possible answer: A period appears after the abbreviation of street. In a statement giving a full address, a comma would be required after the street address.

28.2

Commas With Numbers, Omissions, and Direct Quotations

1. Explain that there is an exception to the number rule: numbers that are used for reference rather than amount. Have students think of examples of numbers without commas (social security number, Library of Congress catalog number, telephone numbers).

2. Have students supply the omitted word (*walked*) from the example of elliptical statements. Explain that, just as apostrophes signal the missing letters in a contraction, commas can signal the missing word or words in an elliptical construction.

3. Read the examples of commas used to set off direct quotations. Explain that they are not used with indirect quotations, such as *She said the line for tickets would be extremely long.*

With Numbers Certain numbers also need commas.

▶ **KEY CONCEPT** With numbers of more than three digits, use a comma after every third digit from the right. ■

EXAMPLES: The projected complex would house 1,245 people.
The company has sold 498,362,719 jelly beans.

There are several exceptions to this rule: ZIP Codes, phone numbers, page numbers, serial numbers, years, and house numbers do not have commas.

ZIP CODE:	26413
TELEPHONE NUMBER:	(612) 555-3702
PAGE NUMBER:	page 1047
HOUSE NUMBER:	18364 Lamson Road
SERIAL NUMBER:	173 55 2007

With Omissions Sometimes, you will purposely omit a word or phrase from a sentence; this omission results in an elliptical sentence. For clarity, you should insert a comma where the words have been left out.

▶ **KEY CONCEPT** Use a comma to indicate the words left out of an elliptical sentence. ■

In the following example, the omitted word is clearly understood. The comma serves as a visual clue to the reader that an omission exists.

EXAMPLE: The man walked quickly and the woman, slowly.

With Direct Quotations Commas also set off direct quotations.

▶ **KEY CONCEPT** Use commas to set off a direct quotation from the rest of the sentence. ■

EXAMPLES: The guest asked, "Do you know of any nearby grocery stores that are open all night?"
"If you don't mind a little drive," the host said, "you will find one about three miles down the road."
"Oh, that will be perfect," the guest replied.

ⓘ Learn More

For a more detailed explanation of punctuating quotations, see Section 28.4.

For Clarity You will occasionally run across a sentence structure that may be confusing without a comma. By inserting a comma, you can reduce the confusion and prevent misreading.

▶ **KEY CONCEPT** Use a comma to prevent a sentence from being misunderstood. ■

UNCLEAR:	She studied French and Mayan art.
CLEAR:	She studied French, as well as Mayan art.

Note About the *Careless Use of Commas:* Generally, you should not use a comma unless you have a rule clearly in mind. Study the following examples of the careless overuse of commas, and avoid such use in your own writing.

MISUSED WITH ADJECTIVE AND NOUN:	The Mexican, Aztecs came from farther north.
CORRECT:	The Mexican Aztecs came from farther north.
MISUSED WITH COMPOUND SUBJECT:	We watched as the man, and woman executed some fancy dance steps.
CORRECT:	We watched as the man and woman executed some fancy dance steps.
MISUSED WITH COMPOUND VERBS:	The dancers leaped, and twirled around the stage.
CORRECT:	The dancers leaped and twirled around the stage.
MISUSED WITH PREPOSITIONAL PHRASES:	The dancers bowed to the audience, and to the conductor.
CORRECT:	The dancers bowed to the audience and to the conductor.
MISUSED WITH SUBORDINATE CLAUSES:	I won't forget that you gave me the ticket, and that I thoroughly enjoyed the performance.
CORRECT:	I won't forget that you gave me the ticket and that I thoroughly the performance.

▶ Critical Viewing Use the verbs *wears* and *dances* in a sentence about this sculpture of an Aztec warrior. Does your sentence require a comma? Why or why not? [**Analyze**]

Commas for Clarity

1. Have students explain how the model sentence at the top of this page might be misinterpreted (*French* and *Mayan* could both be adjectives modifying *art*).

2. Remind students that with so many comma rules to follow, it is easy to make a mistake. Read through each example of misused commas and discuss why the error may have been made and how to correct it.

3. Remind students to use this chapter as a reference for comma use when they do writing assignments for any of their classes.

Critical Viewing

Analyze Possible answer: The warrior <u>wears</u> an elaborate headdress as he <u>dances</u>. No comma is required because the clause *as he dances* is essential.

Answer Key

Exercise 14

1. On April 21, 1836,
2. San Jacinto, Texas.
3. California, so in 1846, they declared
4. Mexico and, in 1847, Mexico City
5. of 1848,
6. February 2, 1848.
7. "Santa Anna," according to the encyclopedia, "was
8. Again, Mexico . . . dissension and, in 1854, a revolution
9. correct
10. Díaz, a general,

Exercise 15

Answers may vary slightly; samples are given.

1. Díaz led a rebellion in 1871 and in 1877 to become leader of Mexico.
2. He fought and struggled to gain power.
3. He rebelled against President Juárez and against his successor, Tejada.
4. correct
5. Emiliano Zapata and Pancho Villa refused to recognize Madero's authority.
6. correct
7. correct
8. Mexico and the United States began to work more closely.
9. Leaders searched for ways to improve Mexico's economic prosperity and the prosperity of all its citizens.
10. correct

> **Exercise 14** Using Commas in Other Situations Copy the following sentences, adding the necessary commas.
> 1. On April 21 1836 the Mexicans were defeated by Texans.
> 2. The Texans' victory occurred at San Jacinto Texas.
> 3. America had territorial ambitions in Texas and California so in 1846 they declared war on Mexico.
> 4. United States troops occupied northern Mexico and in 1847 Mexico City.
> 5. In February of 1848 a large part of Mexican territory became part of the United States.
> 6. This loss occurred on February 2 1848.
> 7. "Santa Anna" according to the encyclopedia "was compelled to resign after the war."
> 8. Again Mexico suffered internal dissension and in 1854 a revolution.
> 9. June 1863 saw French troops reach Mexico and cause the current government officials to flee.
> 10. Porfirio Díaz a general was dictator of Mexico from 1877 to 1911.

> **Exercise 15** Correcting the Careless Use of Commas
> Some of the commas have been used incorrectly in the following sentences. Rewrite each sentence, removing any incorrect commas. Write *correct* if the sentence requires no additions or alterations.

> EXAMPLE: I knew that I was right, and that Chichén Itzá was Mayan.
>
> ANSWER: I knew that I was right and that Chichén Itzá was Mayan.

> 1. Díaz led a rebellion in 1871, and in 1877, to become leader of Mexico.
> 2. He fought, and struggled to gain power.
> 3. He rebelled against President Juárez, and against his successor, Tejada.
> 4. After ruling for over thirty years, he lost power to Francisco Madero.
> 5. Emiliano Zapata, and Pancho Villa refused to recognize Madero's authority.
> 6. Madero's assassination, rival leaders, and foreign intervention all contributed to turmoil in Mexico.
> 7. Finally, things began to improve in the twenties.
> 8. Mexico, and the United States, began to work more closely.
> 9. Leaders searched for ways to improve Mexico's economic prosperity, and the prosperity of all its citizens.
> 10. The country, like all countries, still has problems, but it is struggling to solve them.

668 • Punctuation

> **More Practice**
>
> Grammar Exercise Workbook
> • pp. 169–170
> On-line Exercise Bank
> • Section 28.2
> *Go on-line:*
> PHSchool.com
> *Enter Web Code:*
> eek-1002

Get instant feedback! Exercises 14 and 15 are available on-line or on CD-ROM.

☑ ONGOING ASSESSMENT: Monitor and Reinforce

If students miss more than two items in Exercises 14 and 15, refer them to the following for additional practice.

In the Textbook	Print Resources	Technology
Section Review, Ex. 21, Section 28.2	*Grammar Exercise Workbook,* pp. 169–170	*On-Line Exercise Bank,* Section 28.2

Section Review

GRAMMAR EXERCISES 16–24

Exercise 16 Using Commas in Compound Sentences If a comma is needed in one of these sentences, write the word before the comma, the comma, and the word after the comma. If no comma is needed, write *correct*.

1. Mexico is a federal republic and it has jurisdiction over several islands.
2. The Sierra Madre contains the highest peaks in Mexico and it is a volcanic range.
3. Mexico is not exempt from earthquakes nor are they always mild.
4. A serious earthquake struck and killed more that 7,000 people in 1985.
5. The country is also prone to hurricanes and these can be quite devastating.

Exercise 17 Separating Items in a Series Copy each sentence that needs commas, inserting them as required. If no comma is needed, write *correct*.

1. Mexico can be roughly divided into the *tierra caliente tierra templada* and *tierra fría.*
2. In English, this means "the hot land" "the temperate land" and "the cold land."
3. The climate is governed by latitude and elevation.
4. The country includes coastal plains a central plateau and volcanic peaks.
5. Some of Mexico's rivers are the Grijalva the Usumacinta and the Conchos.

Exercise 18 Proofreading for Commas With Series, Adjectives, and Introductory Material Copy the following passage on a separate sheet of paper. Add or delete commas as needed.

When people think of Mexico today they think of its tourist attractions. These attractions include ancient ruins beautiful beaches rural villages and exciting urban areas. Obviously there is much to see in Mexico.

In order to reach Acapulco you must travel quite far south. Historically it is both a good harbor port and a tourist resort. Tourists flock to Acapulco to relax to enjoy the sun and to visit the interesting historical sites.

Exercise 19 Setting Off Parenthetical Expressions Copy each of the following sentences, inserting commas as necessary.

1. Mexico City the capital is also the cultural center of the country.
2. Octavio Paz a Mexican writer won the prestigious Nobel Prize for Literature in 1990.
3. Mayans and Aztecs in fact were highly advanced in art and science.
4. Mayans it is said excelled at painting and sculpture.
5. Mexican folk arts such as weaving and pottery are world renowned.

Exercise 20 Distinguishing Between Essential and Nonessential Expressions If a sentence contains an essential expression needing no commas, write *essential*. If it contains a nonessential expression, insert the commas where needed.

1. Mexico City is home to several museums that display the country's past.
2. The National Museum of Anthropology which is in Mexico City is devoted to Mayan and other artifacts.
3. The National Historical Museum which is in Chapultepec Castle is concerned with Mexico's history since the Spanish conquest.

Section Review • 669

ASSESS

Section Review

Each of these exercises correlates to the instruction on commas, pages 654–667. These exercises may be used for more practice, for reteaching, or for review of the key concepts presented. Answers for all chapter exercises are available in *Grammar Exercises Answers on Transparencies* in your Teaching Resources.

Answer Key

Exercise 16

1. republic, and
2. Mexico, and
3. earthquakes, nor
4. correct
5. hurricanes, and

Exercise 17

1. Mexico can be roughly divided into the *tierra caliente, tierra templada,* and *tierra fría.*
2. In English, this means "the hot land," "the temperate land," and "the cold land."
3. correct
4. The country includes coastal plains, a central plateau, and volcanic peaks.
5. Some of Mexico's rivers are the Grijalva, the Usumacinta, and the Conchos.

Exercise 18

1. When people think of Mexico today, they . . .
2. . . . ruins, beautiful beaches, rural villages, and . . .
3. Obviously, there . . .
4. In order to reach Acapulco, you . . .
5. Historically, it is . . .
6. . . . relax, to enjoy the sun, and . . .

Exercise 19

1. Mexico City, the capital, is also . . .
2. Octavio Paz, a Mexican writer, won . . .
3. Mayans and Aztecs, in fact, were . . .
4. Mayans, it is said, excelled
5. . . . arts, such as weaving and pottery, are . . .

Exercise 20

1. essential
2. . . . Anthropology, which is in Mexico City, is . . .
3. essential

continued

Answer Key continued

Exercise 20

4. essential
5. essential
6. essential
7. Architecture, so popular with Native Americans, is . . .
8. essential
9. . . . dances, which predate the Spanish conquest, still . . .
10. Mexico, where sports are popular, has . . .

Exercise 21

1. Mexico's area is approximately 756,066 square miles.
2. I told my pen pal that my address is 23 Deer Park Lane, Omaha, Nebraska 27103.
3. She said, "I will write to you very soon."
4. He studied Aztec and Mayan culture.
5. Spanish and other languages are spoken in Mexico.
6. Some of Mexico's peaks are almost 19,000 feet high.
7. correct
8. correct
9. Mexico and the United States share a common border.
10. He is going to Acapulco, Mexico, for his vacation this year.

Exercise 22

Find It in Your Reading
1. morning,—introductory phrase
2. tower,—introductory clause
3. afterward,—introductory adverbs
4. air,—nonessential participial phrase
5. eleven,—introductory phrase
6. vultures,—nonessential participial phrase
7. flocks,—before nonessential participial phrase
8. 20,000—numbers with more than three digits
9. times,—after nonessential participial phrase
10. sample,—introductory participial phrase

Exercise 23

Find It in Your Writing
Challenge students to add cumulative and coordinate adjectives to appropriate places in their writing if they cannot find any examples.

Exercise 24

Writing Application
Have students exchange papers and check for errors in comma use.

670 • 492

Section Review Exercises cont'd.

4. Another museum that has an important archaeological collection is in Yucatan.
5. Mexico is a country whose cultural glory is not all in the past.
6. Some Mexican actors who have achieved world fame are Cantinflas and Dolores Del Rio.
7. Architecture so popular with Native Americans is still a flourishing art.
8. A group of dancers that specializes in Mexican folk dances tours the world.
9. Some folk dances which predate the Spanish conquest still survive today.
10. Mexico where sports are popular has hosted the Olympic Games and the World Cup.

Exercise 21 Other Uses of Commas Remove incorrectly used commas or add them where necessary.

1. Mexico's area is approximately 756066 square miles.
2. I told my pen pal that my address is 23 Deer Park Lane Omaha Nebraska 27103.
3. She said "I will write to you very soon."
4. He studied Aztec, and Mayan culture.
5. Spanish, and other languages, are spoken in Mexico.
6. Some of Mexico's peaks are almost 19000 feet high.
7. Mayans were famous for their architecture and for their sculpture.
8. Europeans are the smallest minorities in Mexico.
9. Mexico, and the United States share a common border.
10. He is going to Acapulco Mexico for his vacation this year.

Exercise 22 Find It in Your Reading Explain the reason for each of the commas in the following excerpt from "Work That Counts" by Ernesto Ruelas Inzunza.

670 • Punctuation

. . . At eight this morning, as Jeros and I climbed the observation tower, about forty-five Swainson's hawks were just taking off from the nearby canyon where they had spent the night. Shortly afterward, we saw hundreds of them turning circles in the thermal columns of hot air, effortlessly gaining altitude. By eleven, the Swainson's had joined smaller numbers of broad-winged hawks and turkey vultures, forming long streams of migrants. Such large flocks, totaling more than 20,000 birds at times, can take up to thirty minutes to pass overhead. Resembling myriad moving organisms in a plankton sample, the raptors filled our binoculars' field of view. We watched the avian river continue north until it disappeared.

Exercise 23 Find It in Your Writing In your portfolio, look for examples of cumulative and coordinate adjectives. Make sure that you have used commas correctly in each example.

Exercise 24 Writing Application Write five sentences of your own using the following instructions.

1. Use at least three adjectives to describe your best friend.
2. Write a compound sentence with two independent clauses, each containing information about a place you would like to visit.
3. Write a sentence listing at least three things you like about the place where you live.
4. Write your address as it would appear on an envelope and in a sentence.
5. Write a sentence about a movie you have seen in which a character uses the expression *by the way.*

Section 28.3
Semicolons and Colons

The semicolon [;] is a punctuation mark that serves as the happy medium between the comma and the period. It signals the reader to pause longer than for a comma but to pause without the finality of a period. The colon [:] is used primarily to point ahead to additional information. It directs the reader to look farther.

The first part of this section will cover the rules that govern the use of semicolons. The second part will present the ways in which you can use colons.

Using the Semicolon

The semicolon is used to separate independent clauses that have a close relationship to each other. A semicolon is also used to separate independent clauses or items in a series that already contain a number of commas.

Using the Semicolon With Independent Clauses
Semicolons are most often used between independent clauses.

▶ **KEY CONCEPT** Use a *semicolon* to join independent clauses that are not already joined by the conjunction *and, but, for, nor, or, so,* or *yet.* ∎

Two sentences joined by a conjunction need a comma before the conjunction.

EXAMPLE: My mother works in a school, but she does not teach.

Because the semicolon is stronger than the comma, it replaces both the comma and the conjunction. Notice in the following example that the second independent clause of two clauses joined by a semicolon starts with a lowercase letter. Do not use a capital following a semicolon unless the word following a semicolon would call for a capital in any position.

EXAMPLE: My mother works in a school; she does not teach.

Do not use a semicolon to join unrelated independent clauses. Use a semicolon to join only those that are closely related.

INCORRECT: My aunt and uncle have five children; it will snow today.

CORRECT: My aunt and uncle have five children; they have two boys and three girls.

Theme: Friends and Relations

In this section, you will learn about semicolons and colons. The examples and exercises are about friends, relatives, neighbors, and acquaintances.

Cross-Curricular Connection: Social Studies

Semicolons and Colons • 671

⏱ **TIME AND RESOURCE MANAGER**

Resources
Print: *Grammar Exercise Workbook,* pp. 171–174; *Grammar Exercises Answers on Transparencies,* Ch. 28; *Hands-on Grammar Activity Book,* Ch. 28
Technology: *Writing and Grammar* Interactive Text, Section 28.3; *On-Line Exercise Bank,* Section 28.3

Using the Full Student Edition	Using the Handbook🄗
• Work through all key concepts, pp. 671–678.	• Work through all key concepts, pp. 493–500.
• Assign and review Exercises 25–28.	• Assign and review Exercises 25–28.
• Read and discuss Grammar in Literature, p. 675.	• Read and discuss Grammar in Literature, p. 497.
• Do the Hands-on Grammar activity, p. 680.	• Do the Hands-on Grammar activity, p. 502.

Semicolons With Conjunctive Adverbs and Transitional Expressions

1. Tell students that when a semicolon is used to connect independent clauses, it is sometimes followed with a conjunctive adverb or a transitional expression that helps to connect ideas logically. Remind students that the adverb or transition will be followed by a comma to set it off from the rest of the clause, just as other introductory material is set off.

2. Have students explain the meanings that various conjunctive adverbs add to sentences (for example, *thus* means "in this manner").

3. Give students practice grouping conjunctive adverbs and transitions according to purpose. For instance, expressions that show chronology might be *first, second,* and *last,* while others help to arrange ideas in order of importance: *at the very least, even more,* and *primarily.*

Integrating Vocabulary Skills

Transitional Expressions Have students brainstorm for a list of transitional words and expressions. They can transfer the list to a poster and hang it in the room to use as a reference. Remind them that transitions are needed to link paragraphs as well as to link sentences.

Sometimes, the independent clauses will share a similar structure as well as a similar meaning.

EXAMPLE: Before today, my uncle was out of work; tomorrow, he starts a new job.

Notice that both sentences center around a shared subject—work. The sentences are also similar to each other in structure. This is a situation in which to use a semicolon.

Occasionally, independent clauses may set up a contrast:

EXAMPLE: My sister excels at art; I can barely draw a straight line.

So far, the discussion has concentrated on using a semicolon to join two independent clauses. However, if there are more than two independent clauses, you can still use semicolons:

EXAMPLE: Joe's grandparents were not born in this country; they emigrated here from Italy; they settled comfortably in Boston.

Independent clauses also need a semicolon when they are joined by a conjunctive adverb or a transitional expression.

▶ **KEY CONCEPT** Use a semicolon to join independent clauses separated by either a conjunctive adverb or a transitional expression. ■

Conjunctive adverbs are adverbs used as conjunctions to connect independent clauses. Common conjunctive adverbs are *accordingly, also, besides, consequently, furthermore, however, indeed, instead, namely, nevertheless, otherwise, similarly, therefore,* and *thus.* Transitional expressions are expressions that connect one independent clause with another. Transitional expressions include *as a result, at this time, first, for instance, in fact, on the other hand, second,* and *that is.*

CONJUNCTIVE ADVERB: A cloudless blue sky dawned that morning; nevertheless, rain was expected.

TRANSITIONAL EXPRESSION: We needed to fit the whole family around the dinner table; as a result, Dad pulled out the extra leaf.

Because words used as conjunctive adverbs and transitions can also interrupt one continuous sentence, use a semicolon only when there is an independent clause on each side of the conjunctive adverb or transitional expression.

INCORRECT: The team was; consequently, disqualified.

CORRECT: The team was, consequently, disqualified.

Using the Semicolon to Avoid Confusion The semi-colon can also be used to avoid confusion in sentences that contain other internal punctuation; for example, two independent clauses that contain their own internal punctuation.

▶ **KEY CONCEPT** Use semicolons to avoid confusion when independent clauses already contain commas. ■

When a sentence consists of two independent clauses joined by a coordinating conjunction, the tendency is to place a comma before the conjunction. However, when one or both of the sentences also contain commas, a semicolon may be used before the conjunction to prevent confusion.

EXAMPLE: My cousins borrowed my favorite album, a recording of a jazz concert; but they returned it safely.

The semicolon also helps avoid confusion in a series of items containing their own internal punctuation. A series generally has several items separated only by commas.

▼ Critical Viewing
Do you think the boys in the picture are friends or relatives? Explain your answer. **[Speculate]**

Snap the Whip, Winslow Homer

Semicolons and Colons • **673**

Critical Viewing

Speculate Possible answer: The boys seem to be friends rather than relatives because they are close to the same age and playing a schoolyard game that seems to resemble Crack the Whip. Maybe the building behind them is a schoolhouse.

Step-by-Step Teaching Guide

Semicolons to Avoid Confusion

1. Explain to students that a semicolon can replace a comma before a coordinating conjunction if one or both of the independent clauses contain commas.

2. Similarly, explain to students that a semicolon can be used to separate items in a series if any of the items already contain commas.

3. Use the Grammar in Literature excerpt on page 675 to illustrate how a semicolon is used to punctuate items in a series. Show students that using only commas would have caused confusion.

28.3

> **KEY CONCEPT** Use a semicolon between items in a series if the items themselves contain commas. ∎

EXAMPLE: We visited the Averills, who live in Wisconsin; the Wilsons, friends in Michigan; and the Garcias, former neighbors now living in North Dakota.

You will use the semicolon in a series most commonly when the items contain either nonessential appositives, participial phrases, or adjective clauses.

APPOSITIVES: I sent notes to Mr. Nielson, my science teacher; Mrs. Jensen, my history instructor; and Mrs. Seltz, my coach.

PARTICIPIAL PHRASES: I developed a terrible headache from listening to my cat, meowing at the door; my dog, howling at the neighbors; and my sister, babbling on the phone.

ADJECTIVE CLAUSES: The car that I bought has spare tires, which are brand new; a stereo, which has just been installed; and a great engine, which has been newly tuned.

Notice that commas are used to separate the nonessential material from the word or words to which they refer or that they modify. The semicolons separate the complete items in the series.

> **Exercise 25** Using the Semicolon With Independent Clauses Decide where a semicolon is needed in each of the following sentences. Write the word that goes before the semicolon, the semicolon, and the word that goes after it.

EXAMPLE: I once had a red yo-yo my sister had a green one.
ANSWER: yo-yo; my

1. Genealogy is the history of the descent of a family from an ancestor the family tree gives information about the family.
2. The earliest known ancestor is placed at the top of a family tree direct descent can be traced easily.
3. Genealogy is a very popular pastime it can also be a challenging profession.
4. Genealogy is useful in the validation of wills it can ensure the fair distribution of property if a dispute occurs.
5. One practical use of genealogy is found in the medical field physicians can search genealogical records for family histories of unusual diseases.

> **More Practice**
>
> **Grammar Exercise Workbook**
> • pp. 171–172
> **On-line Exercise Bank**
> • Section 28.3
> *Go on-line:*
> PHSchool.com
> *Enter Web Code:*
> eek-1002

Get instant feedback! Exercises 25 and 26 are available on-line or on CD-ROM.

GRAMMAR IN LITERATURE

from A Connecticut Yankee in King Arthur's Court

Mark Twain

Twain uses a semicolon before the conjunction to avoid confusion. Because this sentence contains two independent clauses with internal punctuation,

You shall remain king over all your dominions, and receive all the glories and honors that belong to the kingship; but you shall appoint me your perpetual minister and executive, and give me for my services one percent of such actual increase of revenue over and above its present amount as I may succeed in creating for the state.

▼ Critical Viewing
How do semicolons prevent words from becoming as jumbled as these birthday candles? **[Connect]**

> **Exercise 26** Using Semicolons With Internal Punctuation

Copy each sentence, adding semicolons where they are needed to avoid confusion. Also, add necessary commas.

EXAMPLE: For my mother's birthday I baked cookies which were made with raisins muffins which were made with dates and a cake.

ANSWER: For my mother's birthday, I baked cookies, which were made with raisins; muffins, which were made with dates; and a cake.

1. Jane heard loud poorly played piano music the shouts of her sisters Mary Tina and Carol and the television announcer's voice.
2. The dinner table laden with food looked inviting and the happy hungry family sat down eagerly to the birthday dinner.
3. On the table were turkey which was made with gravy noodles which were cooked in butter and ham which was baked with honey and five vegetables.
4. Jane's family had invited several neighbors—Mr. Jensen who lived next door Laura Wilson Jane's friend and Mr. and Mrs. Wilson Laura's parents.
5. Air travel was a topic of conversation among Mr. Jensen an airline pilot Laura a model-plane enthusiast and Mr. and Mrs. Wilson airline customer-service agents.

Semicolons and Colons • 675

Grammar in Literature

1. Have students identify the parts of speech that are connected by semicolons in this excerpt. (independent clause; independent clause)

2. Remind them that a comma usually precedes a coordinating conjunction to join independent clauses, but in this case, the semicolon helps avoid confusion because the items in the series already contain commas.

More About the Writer

Mark Twain (1835–1910) is the pen name of Samuel Langhorne Clemens, one of American's greatest writers. In 1870, Twain married and settled in Hartford, Connecticut. It was here that he wrote his two classic novels— *The Adventures of Tom Sawyer* and *The Adventures of Huckleberry Finn*—and several other bestsellers.

Connections With Literature

A longer excerpt from *A Connecticut Yankee in King Arthur's Court* can be found in *Prentice Hall Literature, Penguin Edition,* Grade 10.

Answer Key

> **Exercise 26**

1. loud, poorly played piano music; the shouts of her sisters Mary, Tina, and Carol; and
2. table, laden with food, looked inviting; and the happy, hungry
3. turkey, which was made with gravy; noodles, which were cooked in butter; and ham, which was baked with honey;
4. Mr. Jensen, who lived next door; Laura Wilson, Jane's friend; and Mr. and Mrs. Wilson, Laura's parents.
5. Mr. Jensen, an airline pilot; Laura, a model-plane enthusiast; and Mr. and Mrs. Wilson, airline customer-service agents.

Critical Viewing

Connect Possible answer: Semicolons help to keep ideas in order in a reader's mind.

☑ ONGOING ASSESSMENT: Monitor and Reinforce

If students miss more than one item in Exercise 25 or 26, refer them to the following for additional practice.

In the Textbook	Print Resources	Technology
Section Review, Ex. 29–30, Section 28.3	*Grammar Exercise Workbook,* pp. 171–172	*On-Line Exercise Bank,* Section 28.3

Colons as Introductory Devices

1. Explain to students that a colon can be placed at the end of an independent clause to introduce something (usually a list or another clause) that logically completes the thought of the first clause.

2. Tell students that when colons introduce a series of items, those items may be separated by commas or by semicolons, depending on the complexity of the items. Emphasize that often the word or phrase ending the independent clause implies that a list will follow (*as follows* or *such as these*).

3. Write on the board: *I packed everything I needed for my trip: shoes, a dress, and my ticket.* Have students reword the sentence so that a colon would not be required. (*I packed everything I needed for my trip, including shoes, a dress, and my ticket.*)

Critical Viewing

Speculate Possible answer: The gift in the box might be one of the following items: candy, a bracelet, a small radio, or a book.

Using the Colon

The colon acts mainly as an introductory device. It is also used in several special situations.

Using Colons as Introductory Devices To use the colon correctly as an introductory device, you must be familiar with the different items it can introduce.

▶ **KEY CONCEPT** Use a colon before a list of items following an independent clause. ■

EXAMPLE: We must bring the following items to the family reunion: potato salad, a grill, and a blanket.

As shown in this example, the independent clause before a list often includes a phrase such as *the following* or *the following items.* You should familiarize yourself with these phrases, because they often indicate the need for a colon. Of course, you should not depend on these phrases alone to signal the need for a colon. The most important point to consider is whether or not an independent clause precedes the list. If it does, use a colon.

EXAMPLE: I bought my father several gifts: a shirt, a tie, and a pair of shoes.

Colons can also be used to introduce certain quotations:

▶ **KEY CONCEPT** Use a colon to introduce a quotation that is formal or lengthy or a quotation that does not contain a "he said/she said" expression. ■

Often, a formal quotation requiring a colon will consist of more than one sentence. However, your best guideline for inserting a colon should be the formality of the quotation. The more formal the quotation, the more likely you will need a colon. Do not use a colon to introduce a casual quoted remark or dialogue, even if more than one sentence is used.

COLON: The speaker began with these words: "I have never been so honored in all my life."

COMMA: As Ann left the room, she called, "I really must hurry. I don't want to be late."

▲ Critical Viewing
Finish this statement: *The gift in the box might be one of the following items . . .* Where will you place the colon? Where will you use commas? **[Speculate]**

EXAMPLES: Dad walked angrily to the door and then turned:
"Your excuses are weak. You have gone too far
this time."

Teresa stood up slowly: "I think I'll go home. It's
been a long day."

A colon can also serve as an introductory device for a sentence that either amplifies or summarizes what has preceded it:

KEY CONCEPT Use a colon to introduce a sentence that summarizes or explains the sentence before it. ■

EXAMPLES: The garage attendant provided me with one piece
of advice: He said to check my water level often
until I could get my car in for the needed repairs.

His tuna casserole lacked a rather vital ingredient: He forgot the tuna!

Notice that a capital letter follows the colon because the words following make a complete sentence.

KEY CONCEPT Use a colon to introduce a formal appositive that follows an independent clause. ■

Using a colon, instead of a comma, to introduce an appositive that follows an independent clause gives additional emphasis to the appositive.

EXAMPLE: I missed one important paragraph lesson: writing
the topic sentence.

When you are using colons in sentences, always check to be sure that an independent clause comes before the colon.

INCORRECT: We decided to: see an old movie.

CORRECT: We decided to see an old movie: *An American in
Paris.*

INCORRECT: Our tour took us by: the rose gardens, the
Japanese park, and the hanging gardens.

CORRECT: Our tour took us by some beautiful spots: the
rose gardens, the Japanese park, and the hanging gardens.

Other Uses of the Colon

1. Point out that a capital letter follows a colon when it introduces a complete sentence.

2. Have students provide a definition of an appositive (a noun or pronoun placed next to another noun or pronoun to identify, rename, or explain it). Emphasize that the appositive should be capitalized only if it is a proper noun, proper adjective, or independent clause.

3. Direct students' attention to the incorrect and correct examples to help them understand how and when to use this technique. Point out the dramatic effect of the colon.

Special Uses of the Colon

1. Have students read the chart on special uses of the colon.

2. Explain that in these situations the colon either introduces more information (titles and subtitles, labels, warnings) or provides clarity (separating numbers such as time and page or volume numbers).

28.3

Although an independent clause must precede a colon, it is not necessary that the words following the colon be an independent clause. An appositive composed of a word or short phrase may, for example, follow a colon.

EXAMPLES: From the jeep, I looked out over the dry grass and saw the king of beasts: a lion.

I have the best friend in the world: my sister.

You could successfully argue that a comma would also be appropriate where the colon is inserted. However, the colon provides a slightly more dramatic effect.

Special Uses of the Colon The colon has several specialized functions that you will probably encounter in your reading and writing:

Among the special situations that require the use of a colon are references to time, volume and page numbers, chapters and verses in the Bible, book subtitles, business letter salutations, and labels that are used to introduce important ideas. Study the examples that are given in the following chart; it shows how the colon is used in each of these special situations.

SPECIAL SITUATIONS REQUIRING COLONS	
Numerals Giving the Time	5:22 A.M. 7:49 P.M.
References to Periodicals (Volume Number: Page Number)	*Forbes 4:8*
Biblical References (Chapter Number: Verse Number)	Genesis 1:5
Subtitles for Books and Magazines	*Fixing Hamburger: One Hundred Ways to Prepare Delicious Meals*
Salutations in Business Letters	Dear Mr. Biggs: Ladies: Dear Sir:
Labels Used to Signal Important Ideas	**Warning:** Cigarette smoking can be hazardous to your health. Note: This letter must be postmarked no later than the tenth of this month.

> **Exercise 27** Understanding the Use of the Colon Copy the following sentences, adding colons where necessary. Capitalize the first word if a complete sentence follows the colon.

1. I have one project for myself this summer to chart my family tree.
2. To begin, I will need some important information my mother's maiden name, my grandparents' dates of birth and marriage, and the year the family came to America.
3. Before long, I will have found just what I need my grandfather's birth certificate.
4. It is time to do the research off to City Hall!
5. My grandmother gave me sound advice "know your roots."
6. My sister scorned the advice and my project "why do all that work?"
7. There is a simple explanation for my sister's attitude she is too young to understand.
8. I have found all of the papers I need birth and death certificates, marriage licenses, and immigration records.
9. I made a startling discovery my great-grandparents were born in China!
10. I am proud of my work this summer the genealogical search for my ancestry.

> **Exercise 28** Using Colons for Special Writing Situations
Copy each of the following items, adding the necessary colons. Underline any titles that appear in italics.

1. My family tree is entitled "The Gens One Hundred Years and Growing."
2. I used an interesting book for my research, *Finding Your Roots Tracing Your Family History.*
3. There was also a helpful article in *Time* 147 34.
4. I began my research at 8 30 A.M. today.
5. I carefully hurried past a sign that read "Warning Stairs may be slippery."

▶ **Critical Viewing** In a sentence about this picture, use a colon to set off a list of interesting features of this building on Ellis Island. **[Describe]**

More Practice

Grammar Exercise Workbook
• pp. 173–174
On-line Exercise Bank
• Section 28.3
Go on-line:
PHSchool.com
Enter Web Code:
eek-1002

Semicolons and Colons • **679**

1. I have one project for myself this summer: to chart my family tree.
2. To begin, I will need some important information: my mother's maiden name, my grandparents' dates of birth and marriage, and the year the family came to America.
3. Before long, I will have found just what I need: my grandfather's birth certificate.
4. It is time to do the research: Off to City Hall!
5. My grandmother gave me sound advice: "Know your roots."
6. My sister scorned the advice and my project: "Why do all that work?"
7. There is a simple explanation for my sister's attitude: She is too young to understand.
8. I have found all of the papers I need: birth and death certificates, marriage licenses, and immigration records.
9. I made a startling discovery: My great-grandparents were born in China!
10. I am proud of my work this summer: the genealogical search for my ancestry.

> **Exercise 28**

1. My family tree is entitled "The Gens: One Hundred Years and Growing."
2. I used an interesting book for my research, *Finding Your Roots: Tracing Your Family History.*
3. There was also a helpful article in *Time* 147:34.
4. I began my research at 8:30 A.M. today.
5. I carefully hurried past a sign that read "Warning: Stairs may be slippery."

Critical Viewing

Describe Possible answer: The building has several interesting features: the three gables in the roof, the three arches in the facade, the towers with ornate domes, and the decorative stonework.

☑ **ONGOING ASSESSMENT: Monitor and Reinforce**

If students miss more than two items in Exercise 27 or 28, refer them to the following for additional practice.

In the Textbook	Print Resources	Technology
Section Review, Ex. 29–30, Section 28.3	*Grammar Exercise Workbook,* pp. 173–174	*On-Line Exercise Bank,* Section 28.3

Hands-on Grammar

Teaching Resources: Hands-on Grammar Activity Book, Ch. 28

1. Remind students that semicolons can be used to connect clauses, but both must be independent clauses. Point out that *we were tired* and *it cannot be denied* are independent clauses because they both contain complete thoughts.

2. Discuss which versions of the sample sentences are clearer. Make sure students support their answers with specific reasons.

3. If both versions are equally clear, suggest that students consider varying sentence structure. If the selection contains a lot of sentences joined by commas and conjunctions, they might try using a semicolon to vary the rhythm.

Find It in Your Reading

For sentences with semicolons, ask students to name the conjunction that would have connected the clauses most clearly. This will illustrate whether the relationship between the clauses is clear.

Find It in Your Writing

Have students exchange papers with partners and evaluate each other's use of semicolons. Sometimes, it is hard for a writer to tell whether he or she has successfully communicated this type of relationship.

28.3

Hands-on Grammar

Semicolon Connections

Often, the choice between using a conjunction or a semicolon to connect clauses is a stylistic one. Explore the effects of each choice with the following activity.

Write the following sentence on a strip of colored paper. Cut on either side of the subordinating conjunction. Turn over the piece you have cut, and write a large semicolon on the other side of the piece. Next, flip the card to read the sentence with the subordinating conjunction; then, with the semicolon. Determine which version gives an indication of the relationship between events.

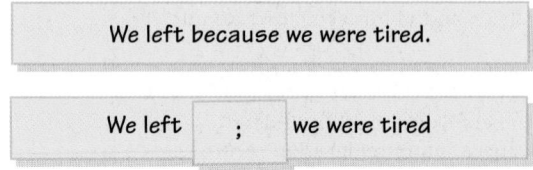

Write and cut sentence strips using the conjunctions *therefore, if, after, unless, as,* and *where.* (For this activity, place the subordinate clause at the end of the sentence rather than at the beginning.) Discuss with a partner how the meaning of the sentence is affected when you change the conjunction to a semicolon.

Next, complete sentence strips for compound sentences that contain coordinating conjunctions. Cut the coordinating conjunctions out to make flip sections with semicolons on the other side. (Keep the comma that precedes the conjunction with the conjunction rather than with the sentence.) Again, discuss with a partner when a semicolon is more effective and when the comma and conjunction are more effective.

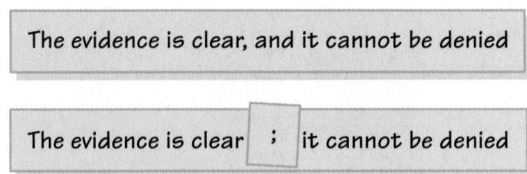

Find It in Your Reading Look for compound and complex sentences in a short story. Use the Semicolon Connections activity to evaluate the author's choice of conjunction or semicolon.

Find It in Your Writing Look for compound and complex sentences in your writing. Identify one place where you have used a semicolon to connect clauses. If you cannot find one, challenge yourself to revise at least one sentence to include one.

680 • Punctuation

✋ **Hands-on Grammar**
Use the Hands-on Grammar activity sheet for Chapter 28 to facilitate this activity.

☑ ONGOING ASSESSMENT: Assess Mastery

Use the following resources to assess student mastery of semicolons and colons.

In the Textbook	Technology
Chapter Review, Ex. 75	*Writing and Grammar* Interactive Text, Section 28.3, Section Review; *On-Line Exercise Bank,* Section 28.3

Section 28.3 Section Review

GRAMMAR EXERCISES 29–33

Exercise 29 Using Semicolons and Colons Correctly Copy each of the following sentences, adding semicolons and colons where necessary.

1. Many Americans wish to discover their roots most families can be traced back to the time of their arrival.
2. Tracing the family's country of origin is usually difficult it can also become expensive.
3. My mother gave me a book, *Tracing Your Irish Ancestors A Few Simple Steps.*
4. She would like me to learn more about the place our family came from County Kerry in Ireland.
5. Genealogical research in Britain and Ireland is relatively easy records are well kept and accessible.
6. Other records may have been lost language is often a barrier.
7. We will be visiting relatives in Ireland next summer It is a place I can't wait to see!
8. I know exactly where to start my research the library.
9. The library opens at 10 00 Saturday morning.
10. It closes at 3 00 P.M.

Exercise 30 Revising to Combine Sentences With Semicolons and Colons
On a separate sheet of paper, revise the following paragraph. Use semicolons and colons as appropriate to combine clauses or to set off lists.

Genealogy is a major hobby around the world. Its popularity is increasing in the United States. The great surge in interest here started in the 1930's. Then, it increased somewhat after World War II. People engage in genealogical research for a variety of reasons. Some are curious. Some hope to establish a legal right to property, which may require proof of family connections. Some seek membership in lineage societies, which are becoming increasingly popular.

On a family tree are listed the names of relatives. The relatives listed include the following parents, grandparents, great-grandparents and so on. Information is recorded for each person on the tree. The information usually recorded is as follows date and place of birth, marriage, death, and names of children.

Exercise 31 Find It in Your Reading Read the following excerpt from "The Way to Rainy Mountain," and tell why the author used a semicolon in this case.

. . . They could find no buffalo; they had to hang an old hide from the sacred tree.

Exercise 32 Find It in Your Writing In a selection in your writing portfolio, find two related independent clauses that are linked by a comma and coordinating conjunction. Rewrite the sentence so that the clauses are joined by a semicolon instead.

Exercise 33 Writing Application Interview an older member of your family. In a detailed, well-developed essay, tell an interesting story about your family or describe one of your family's time-honored traditions. If you use direct quotations, remember to punctuate your work correctly. Use at least three semicolons and three colons in your essay.

Section Review • 681

ASSESS

Section Review

Each of these exercises correlates to the instruction on semicolons and colons, pages 671–678. These exercises may be used for more practice, for reteaching, or for review of the key concepts presented. Answers for all chapter exercises are available in *Grammar Exercises Answers on Transparencies* in your Teaching Resources.

Answer Key

Exercise 29

1. Many Americans wish to discover their roots; most families can be traced back to the time of their arrival.
2. Tracing the family's country of origin is usually difficult; it can also become expensive.
3. My mother gave me a book, *Tracing Your Irish Ancestors: A Few Simple Steps.*
4. She would like me to learn more about the place our family came from: County Kerry in Ireland.
5. Genealogical research in Britain and Ireland is relatively easy; records are well kept and accessible.
6. Other records may have been lost; language is often a barrier.
7. We will be visiting relatives in Ireland next summer: It is a place I can't wait to see!
8. I know exactly where to start my research: the library.
9. The library opens at 10:00 Saturday morning.
10. It closes at 3:00 P.M.

Exercise 30

(1) Genealogy is a major hobby around the world; its popularity is increasing in the United States. (2) The great surge in U.S. interest started in the 1930's; then, it increased somewhat after World War II. (3) People engage in geneological research for a variety of reasons: some are curious; some hope to establish a legal right to property, which may require proof of family connections; some seek membership in lineage societies, which are becoming increasingly popular. (4) On a family tree are listed the names of relatives: parents, grandparents, great-grandparents, and so on. (5) The information
continued

Answer Key continued

Exercise 30

usually recorded for each person on the tree is as follows: date and place of birth, marriage, death, and the names of children.

Exercise 31

Find It in Your Reading
The author uses a semicolon to connect independent clauses that center around a shared idea.

Exercise 32

Find It in Your Writing
Remind students to make sure the two clauses being linked by the semicolon are both independent clauses.

Exercise 33

Writing Application
When they finish, have students exchange papers and check for errors in the use of colons and semicolons.

Write the following examples on the board and ask a student to explain why quotation marks are needed in the first sentence but not in the second.

- *The animal trainer explained, "All wild animals should be treated with caution."*

- *The animal trainer explained that all wild animals should be treated with caution.*

Students should recognize that the second sentence does not quote the trainer's exact words, but the general meaning of his words. This is called an indirect quotation.

Activate Prior Knowledge

Have students brainstorm for a list of all the uses of quotation marks (direct quotations, around titles of shorter works, and so on). Then, have them do the same for underlining (titles of books, plays, periodicals, long poems, foreign words).

TEACH

Step-by-Step Teaching Guide

Direct Quotations

1. Explain to students that quotation marks help distinguish a speaker's precise spoken words from the other information in a passage. Remind them that quotation marks are always written in pairs to establish the beginning and end of someone's speech.

2. Have students read the example of a direct quotation. Be sure they see that the period lies within the quotation marks and that the first letter of the sentence is capitalized.

Customize for
More Advanced Students

Prepare outlines of situations appropriate for dialogue, including suggestions for characters and settings. Example: *You take your little brother to the zoo, where you discuss the lion exhibit.* Ask students to choose partners and prepare a written dialogue that might take place in that situation. Make sure they use quotation marks correctly.

Quotation Marks and Underlining

Writers try to provide support for their ideas and arguments. Direct quotations can provide that support. They can also make short stories and novels more interesting. Learn the rules for the use of quotation marks. This section will discuss the use of underlining as well as quotation marks to indicate different types of titles, names, and words.

Direct Quotations

This section will take a close look at direct quotations to help clarify any uncertainties you may have regarding the way to punctuate them.

▶ **KEY CONCEPT** A direct quotation represents a person's exact speech or thoughts and is enclosed in quotation marks [" "]. ■

DIRECT QUOTATION: "High school is closer to the core of the American experience than anything else I can think of."—Kurt Vonnegut, Jr.

Do not confuse direct quotations with indirect ones.

▶ **KEY CONCEPT** An indirect quotation reports only the general meaning of what a person said or thought and does not require quotation marks. ■

INDIRECT QUOTATION: Kurt Vonnegut, Jr., wrote that being in high school was a true part of the American experience.

An indirect quotation rephrases someone else's words. The words are not the exact words of the speaker. In a direct quotation, the words of the speaker are quoted exactly.

All direct quotations must be indicated by quotation marks. There are various ways a writer may present a direct quotation. One way is to quote an uninterrupted sentence. Another way is to present a quoted phrase within an otherwise complete sentence. Writers may also use an introductory, concluding, or interrupting expression with a quotation.

To enclose a sentence that is an uninterrupted direct quotation, double quotation marks [" "] are placed around the quoted material. Of course, each complete sentence of any quotation begins with a capital letter.

EXAMPLE: "The past is but the beginning of a beginning."
—H. G. Wells

682 • Punctuation

Theme: Science Fiction

In this section, you will learn about using quotation marks, italics, and underlining. Many of the examples and exercises are about science fiction.

Cross-Curricular Connection: Literature

⏱ TIME AND RESOURCE MANAGER

Resources
Print: *Grammar Exercise Workbook*, pp. 175–180; *Grammar Exercises Answers on Transparencies*, Ch. 28
Technology: *Writing and Grammar* Interactive Text, Section 28.4; *On-Line Exercise Bank*, Section 28.4

Using the Full Student Edition	Using the Handbook🄗
• Work through all key concepts, pp. 682–696. • Assign and review Exercises 34–41. • Read and discuss Grammar in Literature, p. 690.	• Work through all key concepts, pp. 504–518. • Assign and review Exercises 34–41. • Read and discuss Grammar in Literature, p. 512.

Sometimes, you will insert only a quoted phrase into a sentence. You must set off this fragment with quotation marks also. Notice in the following examples that the first word of a phrase or fragment is capitalized only when it falls at the beginning of a sentence or when it would be capitalized regardless of its position in a sentence.

EXAMPLES: In writing about history, H. G. Wells called it "a race between education and catastrophe."

"A race between education and catastrophe" is the way H. G. Wells referred to history.

Generally, you will wish to add a "he said/she said" expression to a quotation to show who is speaking. Use the following rule for a "he said/she said" expression that comes before the quotation.

▶ **KEY CONCEPT** Use a comma or colon after an introductory expression. ■

INTRODUCTORY   H. G. Wells wrote, "The past is
EXPRESSION: but the beginning of a beginning."

If you do not use a "he said/she said" expression in your introduction to a quotation or if the introductory phrase takes a more formal tone, use a colon instead of a comma before the quotation.

EXAMPLE: The professor held up a book: "Today, we will discuss Jules Verne's work *Around the World in Eighty Days*."

▶ **KEY CONCEPT** Use a comma, a question mark, or an exclamation mark after a quotation followed by a concluding expression. ■

CONCLUDING   "The past is but the beginning
EXPRESSION: of a beginning," wrote Wells.

▲▼ **Critical Viewing** Use these pictures to illustrate a scientific principle. **[Connect]**

Critical Viewing

Connect Students may state that warm air is less dense than cool air, causing a hot-air balloon to rise.

Step-by-Step Teaching Guide

Quotation Marks With Commas

1. Explain that conversational tags are always separated from quotations either by commas or by a colon.

2. Use the examples to point out that, when a comma or colon follows an introductory conversational tag, this punctuation does not go inside the quotation marks.

3. Use the example at the bottom of the page to illustrate a conversational tag that follows a quotation; point out that in this case, the comma is placed inside the final quotation mark.

Integrating Listening Skills

Dialogue Challenge students to write a passage of dialogue from dictation. Choose a passage with several short exchanges and read it to the class. As you read, students should write down what they hear, paragraphing and punctuating it as accurately as they can. Discuss their work.

Step-by-Step Teaching Guide

Conversation Tags With Quoted Phrases

1. Explain to students that a conversational tag that falls within quoted material is called an interrupting expression. Use the example to demonstrate the proper use of punctuation in this situation.

2. Remind students that interrupting expressions always fall at natural breaks: between two phrases, clauses, or sentences.

3. Be sure students note that, when a period is placed at the end of an interrupting conversational tag, the period precedes the next quotation mark.

Answer Key

Exercise 34

1. "Mr. Phileas Fogg lived, in 1872, at No. 7, Saville Row, Burlington Gardens."—Jules Verne
2. Correct
3. One of his questions was, "Was Phileas Fogg rich?"
4. "You are a Frenchman, I believe?" asked Phileas Fogg. "And your name is John?"
5. Then, the new servant responded, "Jean, if monsieur pleases."
6. Correct
7. "He must have traveled everywhere, at least in the spirit."—Jules Verne
8. "You are well recommended to me; I hear a good report of you," said Phileas Fogg.
9. Correct
10. "I have a natural aptness for going out of one business into another," confided Jean Passepartout.

When a direct quotation is interrupted by a "he said/she said" expression, quotation marks enclose both parts of the quotation.

▶ **KEY CONCEPT** Use a comma after part of a quoted sentence followed by an interrupting expression. Use another comma after the expression. ■

INTERRUPTING EXPRESSION: "The past," wrote Wells, "is but the beginning of a beginning."

Two quoted sentences may also be interrupted.

▶ **KEY CONCEPT** Use a comma, question mark, or exclamation mark after a quoted sentence that comes before an interrupting expression. Use a period after the expression. ■

EXAMPLE: "What does writing teach?" Ray Bradbury asked. "First and foremost, it reminds us that we are alive."

▶ **Exercise 34** **Indicating Direct Quotations** Copy each sentence that needs quotation marks, adding the necessary marks. If no quotation marks are needed, write *correct*.

EXAMPLE: Mary Shelley wrote I beheld the wretch—the miserable monster whom I had created.

ANSWER: Mary Shelley wrote, "I beheld the wretch—the miserable monster whom I had created."

1. Mr. Phileas Fogg lived, in 1872, at No. 7, Saville Row, Burlington Gardens.—Jules Verne
2. Verne wrote that Phileas Fogg was an Englishman.
3. One of his questions was Was Phileas Fogg rich?
4. You are a Frenchman, I believe, asked Phileas Fogg, and your name is John?
5. Then, the new servant responded, Jean, if monsieur pleases.
6. Mr. Fogg told him that the name Passepartout was preferable.
7. He must have traveled everywhere, at least in the spirit.—Jules Verne
8. You are well recommended to me; I hear a good report of you, said Phileas Fogg.
9. Then, Fogg told Passepartout that his watch was four minutes slow.
10. I have a natural aptness for going out of one business into another, confided Jean Passepartout.

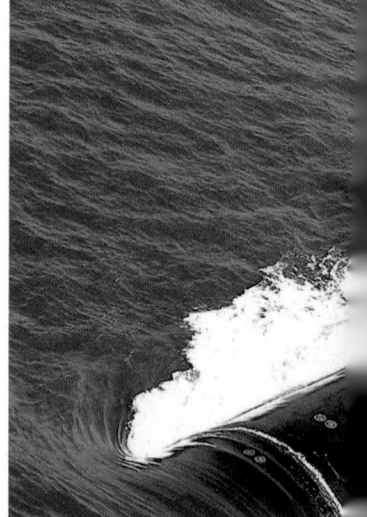

✓ ONGOING ASSESSMENT: Monitor and Reinforce

If students miss more than two items in Exercises 34 or 35, refer them to the following for additional practice.

In the Textbook	Print Resources	Technology
Section Review, Ex. 42, Section 28.4	*Grammar Exercise Workbook,* pp. 175–176	*On-Line Exercise Bank,* Section 28.4

> **Grammar and Style Tip**
>
> Vary the way you indicate the speaker of a quotation. Sometimes, introduce the quotation with an indication of the speaker; sometimes, indicate the speaker following the quotation; and sometimes, interrupt the quotation.

> **Exercise 35** **Indicating and Capitalizing Quotations** Copy the following sentences, making the necessary corrections in punctuation and capitalization. In two of the sentences, the quote has been underlined so that you can identify it.

EXAMPLE: space—the final frontier announced Captain Kirk these are the voyages of the starship *Enterprise*.

ANSWER: "Space—the final frontier," announced Captain Kirk. "These are the voyages of the starship *Enterprise*."

1. <u>the year 1866 was marked by a strange event</u> begins Verne's *20,000 Leagues Under the Sea*.
2. sea-going ships have been encountering an 'enormous thing' Verne continues a long spindle-shaped object.
3. this was described as <u>infinitely larger and quicker than a whale.</u>
4. but it did exist said Verne's narrator there was now no denying the fact.
5. some characters in the book said that they would not believe it existed unless they had seen it . . . with their own scientific eyes.
6. as for dismissing it as a myth wrote Verne this was no longer possible.
7. the monster came into fashion in all the big cities said the narrator.
8. it was sung about in cafes continued the narrator jeered at in the newspapers, acted out in the theaters.
9. the 'monster subject' inflamed people's minds.—Jules Verne
10. after some encounters with ships, the narrator said the problem took on a different complexion.

> **More Practice**

Grammar Exercise Workbook
• pp. 175–176
On-line Exercise Bank
• Section 28.4

Go on-line:
PHSchool.com
Enter Web Code:
eek-1002

▼ **Critical Viewing**
With a partner, exchange two or three sentences about this picture. Write down what was said. Use capitals and quotation marks as needed. **[Apply]**

> **Exercise 35**

1. "The year 1866 was marked by a strange event," begins Verne's *20,000 Leagues Under the Sea*.
2. "Sea-going ships have been encountering an 'enormous thing,'" Verne continues, "a long spindle-shaped object."
3. This was described as "infinitely larger and quicker than a whale."
4. "But it did exist," said Verne's narrator. "There was now no denying the fact."
5. Some characters in the book said that they would not believe it existed unless they had seen it ". . . with their own scientific eyes."
6. "As for dismissing it as a myth," wrote Verne, "this was no longer possible."
7. "The monster came into fashion in all the big cities," said the narrator.
8. "It was sung about in cafes," continued the narrator, "jeered at in the newspapers, acted out in the theaters."
9. "The 'monster subject' inflamed people's minds."—Jules Verne
10. "After some encounters with ships," the narrator said, "the problem took on a different complexion."

Critical Viewing

Apply Possible answer:
"That submarine," Jim said, "is huge. Look at how small the men on its deck seem."

"Yes," Jon agreed. "What do you think that white railing is for?"

"Well," Jim mused, "maybe it's a safety line for being on deck when the waves are high."

⏱ **TIME SAVERS!**

🗏 **Answers on Transparencies**
Use the *Grammar Exercises Answers on Transparencies* for Chapter 28 to facilitate correction by students.

🖵 **On-Line Exercise Bank**
Have students complete the exercises on computer. The Auto Check feature will grade their work for you!

Other Punctuation Marks With Quotation Marks

1. Have students read the first key concept and use the examples to demonstrate that commas and periods always lie within quotation marks when they come before a conversational tag or at the end of a sentence.

2. Explain that the rule is different for semicolons and colons, which always lie outside of quotation marks.

3. Have students copy these rules into their notebooks for easy reference.

28.4

Other Punctuation Marks With Quotation Marks

Whether to place punctuation inside or outside the quotation marks presents a problem for some writers. Four basic rules, once learned, will help clear up most of the confusion.

▶ **KEY CONCEPT** Always place a comma or a period inside the final quotation mark. ∎

EXAMPLES: "I enjoy Jack Finney's work," said Elaine.

"The future," C. S. Lewis believed, "is something which everyone reaches at the rate of sixty minutes an hour."

Note in the second example that the quotation is split, but this makes no difference in the placement of the comma. It still goes inside the quotation marks.

▶ **KEY CONCEPT** Always place a semicolon or colon outside the final quotation mark. ∎

EXAMPLES: One repair person said, "I can't do it for less than eighty dollars"; another indicated he could fix it for half that price!

She listed the ingredients for "an absolutely heavenly salad": spinach, mushrooms, hard-boiled eggs, and bacon.

▶ **KEY CONCEPT** Place a question mark or exclamation mark inside the final quotation mark if the end mark is part of the quotation. ∎

EXAMPLES: The reader asked, "How will the story end?"

The TV announcer exclaimed, "You just won the $10,000 jackpot!"

▶ **KEY CONCEPT** Place a question mark or an exclamation mark outside the final quotation mark if the end mark is not part of the quotation. ∎

EXAMPLES: Did you hear that speaker when he said, "Just use your imagination to write science fiction"?

I was thrilled when they said, "And for president, Debbie Schmidt"!

With question marks and exclamation marks, only one mark is needed. In the following, the quotation is a question and the sentence is a statement. No period, however, is needed.

EXAMPLE: My mother asked, "Did you feed the animals?"

▶ **Exercise 36** **Adding Other Punctuation Marks** Copy the following sentences, adding any needed commas, colons, semicolons, or end marks.

EXAMPLE: The young child shouted gleefully, "I believe in time travel"

ANSWER: The young child shouted gleefully, "I believe in time travel!"

1. Was it in *The Time Machine* that H. G. Wells wrote, "The Time Traveller, for so it will be convenient to speak of him"
2. He asked, "You have all heard what they have to say about this Fourth Dimension"
3. "The thing the Time Traveller held in his hand was a glittering metallic framework," wrote Wells, "scarcely larger than a small clock, and very delicately made"
4. The Time Traveller said "It is my plan for a machine to travel through time"
5. The Psychologist in *The Time Machine* exclaimed, "Of all the wild, extravagant theories"
6. The narrator said, "I am absolutely certain there was no trickery" then the time machine vanished.
7. Then, the Medical Man asked, "Do you seriously believe that that machine has travelled into time"
8. "Into the future or the past," responded the Time Traveller, "I don't, for certain, know which"
9. Did you believe it when the Time Traveller said, "I intend to explore time"
10. The characters agreed, "None of us quite knew how to take it"

▶ **More Practice**

Grammar Exercise Workbook
• pp. 177–180
On-line Exercise Bank
• Section 28.4
   Go on-line:
   PHSchool.com
   Enter Web Code:
   eek-1002

Interactive Textbook

Get instant feedback! Exercise 36 is available on-line or on CD-ROM.

Step-by-Step Teaching Guide

Quotation Marks With Question Marks and Exclamation Marks

1. Remind students that if both the quotation and the sentence require a question mark or an exclamation mark, only one such end mark is used. It should be placed inside the quotation marks.

2. Have students write examples of quotations that contain question marks or exclamation marks. Make sure they properly punctuate them.

Answer Key

▶ **Exercise 36**

1. Was it in *The Time Machine* that H.G. Wells wrote, "The Time Traveller, for so it will be convenient to speak of him"?
2. He asked, "You have all heard what they have to say about this Fourth Dimension?"
3. "The thing the Time Traveller held in his hand was a glittering metallic framework," wrote Wells, "scarcely larger than a small clock, and very delicately made."
4. The Time Traveler said, "It is my plan for a machine to travel through time."
5. The Psychologist in *The Time Machine* exclaimed, "Of all the wild, extravagant theories!"
6. The narrator said, "I am absolutely certain there was no trickery"; then the time machine vanished.
7. Then, the Medical Man asked, "Do you seriously believe that that machine has travelled into time?"
8. "Into the future or the past," responded the Time Traveller, "I don't, for certain, know which."
9. Did you believe it when the Time Traveller said, "I intend to explore time"?
10. The characters agreed, "None of us quite knew how to take it."

✎ STANDARDIZED TEST PREPARATION WORKSHOP

Grammar and Usage Many standardized tests require students to revise errors in punctuation. Use the following to demonstrate.

Choose the answer below that shows how the underlined portion of the following passage should be punctuated.

"Well, at least it can't be any <u>worse sighed Joe. Last year, I got a case of poison ivy that lasted for weeks.</u>

A worse," sighed Joe. Last year, I got a case of poison ivy that lasted for weeks!

B worse." sighed Joe. "Last year, I got a case of poison ivy that lasted for weeks!"

C worse," sighed Joe. "Last year, I got a case of poison ivy that lasted for weeks!"

D worse," sighed Joe. "Last year, I got a case of poison ivy that lasted for weeks"!

The correct answer is **C**. In this case, a comma is needed before the interrupting expression. The next sentence continues a direct quotation and should be punctuated as such, including placing the exclamation mark inside the closing quotation marks.

28.4

▶ **Exercise 37** Adding Quotation Marks and Other Punctuation Marks Copy the following sentences, adding the necessary quotation marks and punctuation.

EXAMPLE: Did you say Let's meet after the first showing of *Somewhere in Time*?

ANSWER: Did you say, "Let's meet after the first showing of *Somewhere in Time*"?

1. Does Mary Shelley's *Frankenstein* begin I am by birth a Genevese
2. So soon as the dazzling light vanished says the narrator the oak had disappeared
3. He acknowledges that Destiny was too potent
4. Her immutable laws had decreed my utter and terrible destruction said the Monster
5. He added It is with considerable difficulty that I remember the original era of my being
6. Did you realize who spoke the lines A strange multiplicity of sensations seized me
7. I saw, felt, heard, and smelt all at the same time continued the Monster
8. By degrees he said I remember, a stronger light pressed upon my nerves
9. Upon spotting the village, he exclaimed How miraculous did this appear
10. The teacher asked Do you know who the Monster is

◀ **Critical Viewing** What information might this girl be reading that would surprise or amaze someone from the nineteenth century? **[Deduce]**

688 • Punctuation

Quotation Marks in Special Situations

Several special situations may occur when you write direct quotations. These include dialogues, quotations of more than one paragraph, and quotations within other quoted material.

First, consider the use of quotation marks when writing a dialogue—a direct conversation between two or more people. Use quotation marks to enclose the directly quoted conversation, and begin a new paragraph for each change of speaker.

> **KEY CONCEPT** When writing dialogue, begin a new paragraph with each change of speaker. ■

EXAMPLE: The station attendant shouted from behind the hood, "You're a quart low on oil, Mrs. Lowell. Would you like me to put some in for you?"

"Yes, thank you," she replied.

"What kind of oil do you use in the car?"

In cases where one quotation consists of several paragraphs of quoted material, remember the following rule:

> **KEY CONCEPT** For quotations longer than a paragraph, put quotation marks at the beginning of each paragraph and at the end of the final paragraph. ■

EXAMPLE: "Experts are noticing a change in the types of food Americans are buying. More fast foods, such as TV dinners and canned meals, are being purchased by food shoppers.

"Many people who used to spend a great deal of time preparing meals now work outside their homes. Researchers conclude that this is the reason more fast foods are being purchased.

"People need well-balanced meals. They now buy meals that can be prepared quickly. Thus, people today must spend more time at work and less time in the kitchen."

Occasionally, you may need to indicate a quotation contained within another quotation.

> **KEY CONCEPT** Use single quotation marks for a quotation within a quotation. ■

EXAMPLE: The fund-raiser concluded, saying, "As we try to raise money for this worthy cause, let us not forget that old English proverb that says, 'Where there's a will, there's a way.' "

Quotation Marks in Special Situations

1. Have students provide a definition of dialogue (a conversation between two or more people). Point out that a new paragraph begins with every change of speaker.

2. As you examine the second key concept, point out that a speaker's words can be longer than one paragraph of quoted material. Use the example to demonstrate the correct placement of punctuation and quotation marks in this situation.

3. Remind students that the same key on their computer keyboard functions as an apostrophe and a single quotation mark. Remind them that although these marks look alike, they have very different uses.

Integrating Vocabulary Skills

Dialogue, Monologue As you examine quotation marks used in dialogue, introduce students to the term *monologue* and ask them whether they recognize any word parts in it (the prefix *mono-* means "one" or "single"). Explain that a monologue is a long speech or series of statements by one person.

Grammar in Literature

1. Have two students read the dialogue, one taking the part of Sir Ector and one taking the part of the Wart. Ask them to explain how they knew which character was speaking (change of paragraph, use of quotation marks, conversation tags, instructional text between dialogue).

2. Be sure they notice and understand the placement of the commas in relation to the quotation marks. Point out, for instance, that the first quoted statement is interrupted by a conversational tag requiring commas before and after the tag.

More About the Writer

T. H. White (1906–1964) was born in India when it was still a British colony. After attending Cambridge University in England, White became first a teacher, and then a writer. The four-part novel *The Once and Future King,* a comic retelling of the King Arthur legends, is his most famous work.

Connections With Literature

T. H. White's "Arthur Becomes King of Britain" can be found in *Prentice Hall Literature, Penguin Edition,* Grade 10.

Answer Key

▶ **Exercise 38**

(1) "Science fiction is not a modern invention," said the speaker. "These subjects have been written about since ancient times. What is the oldest example of science fiction that you can recall?"

(2) Tara raised her hand and said, "*The Twilight Zone* is pretty old."

(3) "Yes," agreed the speaker. "Can anyone think of any books?"

(4) "I used to read Jules Verne's books like *From the Earth to the Moon,*" said Michael.

(5) "Jules Verne wrote a great deal of early science fiction," said the speaker enthusiastically. "Other books were *Journey to the Center of the Earth* and *Off on a Comet.*"

(28.4)

GRAMMAR IN
LITERATURE

from **Arthur Becomes King of Britain**
T. H. White

Notice how the dialogue in the following passage is punctuated. How can you tell who is speaking?

"Sir," said Sir Ector, "I will ask no more of you but that you will make my son, your foster-brother, Sir Kay, seneschal of all your lands."

Kay was kneeling down too, and it was more than the Wart could bear.

"Oh, do stop," he cried.

▶ **Exercise 38** Proofreading for Punctuation and Capitalization The following dialogue has no paragraphing, quotation marks, capitalization, or punctuation. Each number indicates a new speaker. Copy the dialogue, starting new paragraphs and adding the necessary quotation marks, capitalization, and punctuation.

(1) science fiction is not a modern invention said the speaker these subjects have been written about since ancient times what is the oldest example of science fiction that you can recall (2) tara raised her hand and said *the twilight zone* is pretty old (3) yes agreed the speaker can anyone think of any books (4) i used to read jules verne's books like *from the earth to the moon* said michael (5) jules verne wrote a great deal of early science fiction said the speaker enthusiastically other books were *journey to the center of the earth* and *off on a comet* (6) what about *star trek* said someone (7) yes *star wars* is my favorite another voice exclaimed (8) one at a time said the speaker attempting to control the crowd these are all great examples they are all similar because they are about the future and scientific and technological developments (9) another speaker added science fiction began in ancient times and still continues today ray bradbury said the whole history of mankind is nothing but science fiction he also said that science fiction is a combination of our dreams and our accomplishments (10) how do you feel about science fiction do you enjoy it asked tara

---

(6) "What about *Star Trek*?" said someone.

(7) "Yes, *Star Wars* is my favorite!" another voice exclaimed.

(8) "One at a time," said the speaker, attempting to control the crowd. "These are all great examples. They are all similar because they are about the future and scientific and technological developments."

(9) Another speaker added, "Science fiction began in ancient times and still continues today. Ray Bradbury said, 'The whole history of mankind is nothing but science fiction.' He also said that science fiction is a combination of our dreams and our accomplishments."

(10) "How do you feel about science fiction? Do you enjoy it?" asked Tara.

Underlining and Other Uses of Quotation Marks

In printed material, italics and quotation marks are used to set some titles, names, and words apart from the rest of the text. In handwritten or typed material, italics are not available, so underlining is used instead. Quotation marks, on the other hand, are used in both printed and handwritten materials.

This section gives rules for using underlining and quotation marks as well as rules for titles and names that require neither.

Underlining You should use underlining in your writing or typing to highlight titles of long written works and other major artistic works. You will also need to indicate certain names and foreign expressions by underlining them. In addition, you can use underlining to indicate words you want to emphasize.

> **KEY CONCEPT** Underline or italicize the titles of long written works and the titles of publications that are published as a single work. ■

Following are examples of titles you should underline:

TITLES OF WRITTEN WORKS THAT ARE UNDERLINED	
Titles of Books	<u>Dune</u> by Frank Herbert
Titles of Plays	<u>A Raisin in the Sun</u> by Lorraine Hansberry <u>The Man Who Came to Dinner</u> by Moss Hart
Titles of Periodicals	<u>Galaxy Science Fiction</u> <u>Journal of American History</u>
Titles of Newspapers	<u>The New York Times</u> the Palm Beach <u>Post</u> the Chicago <u>Sun-Times</u>
Titles of Long Poems	<u>Idylls of the King</u> by Alfred, Lord Tennyson <u>Gilgamesh</u>

Notes About *Newspaper Titles:* The portion of the title that should be underlined will vary from newspaper to newspaper. *The New York Times* should always be fully capitalized and underlined. Other papers, however, can usually be treated in one of two ways: *The Los Angeles Times* or the Los Angeles *Times*. Unless you know the true name of a paper, choose one of these two forms and use it consistently.

1. Remind students that in handwriting, underlining serves the same function as italics in printed or typewritten documents.
2. Use the chart to help students recognize and remember the kinds of titles that are underlined by explaining that these are works that are single, full-length publications such as books, plays, and magazines. Have them think of more examples of each.
3. Have students read the Notes About Newspaper Titles. Ask them to find out the exact name of their school and local newspapers.

Customize for
Less Advanced Students

Write on the board titles of some novels, short stories, poems, television series, single television episodes, magazines, and magazine articles that most students will know. Have them decide whether each needs underlining or quotation marks. Explain that underlining creates a stronger emphasis than quotation marks; works that are underlined are usually published by themselves, not as parts of other publications. Explain that shorter works are usually published as parts of larger works and are written inside quotation marks.

ONGOING ASSESSMENT: Monitor and Reinforce

If students have difficulty with Exercise 38, refer them to the following for additional practice.

In the Textbook	Print Resources	Technology
Section Review, Ex. 42, Section 28.4	*Grammar Exercise Workbook,* pp. 177–178	*On-Line Exercise Bank,* Section 28.4

28.4

Many media presentations and pieces of artwork also require underlining.

▶ **KEY CONCEPT** Underline the titles of movies, television and radio series, paintings, sculpture, and lengthy works of music. ■

MOVIE:	It's a Wonderful Life, dir. Frank Capra
SERIES:	NOVA, PBS
PAINTING:	The River, Claude Monet
SCULPTURE:	The Minute Man, Daniel Chester French
MUSIC:	The Water Music, George Friedrich Handel

▼ **Critical Viewing** In a research paper about Charles Lindbergh and this plane, how would you set off the name of the plane? **[Apply]**

KEY CONCEPT Underline the names of individual air, sea, space, and land craft. ■

AIR:	the <u>Spirit of St. Louis</u>
SEA:	the S.S. <u>Seagallant</u>
SPACE:	<u>Millenium Falcon</u>
LAND:	the <u>De Witt Clinton</u>

If a *the* precedes the name, do not underline or capitalize it because it is not considered part of the official name. Note also that a specific name given to a group of vehicles (for example, the Explorer spaceships) is capitalized but not underlined.

KEY CONCEPT Underline foreign words not yet accepted into English. ■

EXAMPLES: It is <u>verboten</u> to leave the building without permission. (German: forbidden)

Everyone said that the <u>coq au vin</u> was delicious. (French: chicken cooked in wine)

Because the process of accepting words and phrases into the English language is a continuous one, you cannot always be certain whether a phrase is still considered foreign. Check those doubtful phrases in the dictionary. If the word or phrase is not in the dictionary, you can generally consider it foreign. If it is in the dictionary, it will either be labeled with the name of the foreign language, in which case you should underline it, or it will be given standard treatment as an English word, in which case you should not underline it.

Certain other words need underlining because they are being used in a special way.

KEY CONCEPT Underline numbers, symbols, letters, and words used to name themselves. ■

NUMBERS:	When I say the number <u>three</u>, you start running.
SYMBOLS:	Is that an <u>!</u> at the end of that sentence?
LETTERS:	Is that first letter a <u>G</u> or an <u>S</u>?
WORDS:	She wrote the word <u>fluid</u>, but she meant <u>fluent</u>.

⚙ Grammar and Style Tip

In much formal writing, numbers are written out as words. In newspaper articles—especially sports articles—numerals are often used. When you are writing, use one method of presentation for numbers. Do not switch back and forth between numerals and spelled-out words

Step-by-Step Teaching Guide

Underlining

1. Ask students to think of additional examples of each category listed in the first key concept.

2. Ask students to think of additional words from foreign languages and to use these in sentences. Have them check a dictionary to help them decide whether these words should be underlined.

3. Have students read the third key concept on this page. Remind them that numbers, symbols, letters, and words can be used as nouns and should be distinguished with underlines for clarity.

Underlining for Emphasis

1. Tell students that underlining can be used to stress certain words in a sentence. Explain that this is grammatically acceptable, but it does suggest that punctuation has been used in place of words that might be more expressive.

2. Remind students to try to convey emphasis through word choice before depending on underlining.

Answer Key

▶ **Exercise 39**

1. The movie <u>Planet of the Apes</u> was released in 1968.
2. Reviews were published in <u>The New York Times</u> and many other papers.
3. The <u>Planet of the Apes</u> soundtrack was by Jerry Goldsmith.
4. Charlton Heston wrote about starring in the movie in <u>An Actor's Life</u>.
5. He had a small role in the sequel <u>Beneath the Planet of the Apes</u>.
6. Rod Serling, creator of <u>The Twilight Zone</u> series, wrote the screenplay for <u>Planet of the Apes</u>.
7. correct
8. The magazine <u>Starlog</u> has published many articles about the series.
9. The word <u>apes</u> was used to include the many species in the movies.
10. The surprise ending of the first movie was greeted as a true <u>coup de théâtre</u>.

28.4

▶ **KEY CONCEPT** Underline words that you wish to stress. ∎

EXAMPLE: We will need a <u>minimum</u> of six dollars for the trip.

Although the underlining of the word in this example clarifies the meaning of the sentence, do not overdo underlining for emphasis. In most cases, you should rely on precise word selection to convey your meaning and emphasis.

▶ **Exercise 39** Underlining Titles, Names, and Words Write and underline titles, names, or words that require underlining. If a sentence needs no correction, write *correct*.

1. The movie Planet of the Apes was released in 1968.
2. Reviews were published in The New York Times and many other papers.
3. The Planet of the Apes soundtrack was by Jerry Goldsmith.
4. Charlton Heston wrote about starring in the movie in An Actor's Life.
5. He had a small role in the sequel Beneath the Planet of the Apes.
6. Rod Serling, creator of The Twilight Zone series, wrote the screenplay for Planet of the Apes.
7. We thought we could see the movie in Radio City Music Hall.
8. The magazine Starlog has published many articles about the series.
9. The word apes was used to include the many species in the movies.
10. The surprise ending of the first movie was greeted as a true coup de théâtre.

Quotation Marks With Titles

Quotation marks are used to set off certain titles.

▶ **KEY CONCEPT** Use quotation marks around the titles of short written works. ∎

SHORT STORY:	"Nightfall" by Isaac Asimov
CHAPTER FROM A BOOK:	"Five Days in a Mine" from *Kids With Courage*
SHORT POEM:	"Mowing" by Robert Frost
ESSAY TITLE:	"Style" by Maya Angelou
ARTICLE TITLE:	"How to Organize Your Life"

More Practice

Grammar Exercise Workbook
• pp. 179–180
On-line Exercise Bank
• Section 28.4
Go on-line:
PHSchool.com
Enter Web Code:
eek-1002

Interactive Textbook

Get instant feedback! Exercises 39 and 40 are available on-line or on CD-ROM.

Technology Tip

When writing about a particular work, use the search feature of a word-processing program to help you find every instance of the title. Make sure that you have correctly used quotation marks or underlining to set off the title.

▶ **KEY CONCEPT** Use quotation marks around the titles of songs, episodes in a series, and parts of a long musical composition. ■

EPISODE:	"The Iran File" from *60 Minutes*
SONG TITLE:	"Swing Low, Sweet Chariot"
PART OF A LONG MUSICAL COMPOSITION:	"E.T. Phone Home" from *E.T., The Extra Terrestrial* soundtrack

Occasionally, you may refer to a title of one long work contained in a larger work. Singly, each title would require underlining; when used together, another rule applies:

▶ **KEY CONCEPT** Use quotation marks around the title of a work that is mentioned as part of a collection. ■

| EXAMPLE: | "Plato" from *Great Books of the Western World* |

▶ **Exercise 40** **Using Quotation Marks With Titles** From each of the following sentences, copy the title and enclose it in quotation marks.

| EXAMPLE: | The story Euphio Effect is about the addictive quality of television. |
| ANSWER: | "Euphio Effect" |

1. The short poem Ozymandias by Shelley addresses some science-fiction themes.
2. Swift wrote science fiction and essays like A Modest Proposal.
3. Edgar Allan Poe ventured into science fiction with stories like The Tell-Tale Heart.
4. Bradbury's short story There Will Come Soft Rains was set thirty-five years into the future.
5. The Day the World Ended is the opening chapter of one of Kurt Vonnegut's books.

▲ **Critical Viewing** What type of musical composition might this orchestra be playing? Would you use underlining or quotation marks when writing the title of such a work? **[Speculate]**

Quotation Marks With Titles

1. Explain to students that quotation marks are used around the titles of shorter works, including those that are pieces of a larger work (songs, episodes, chapter titles).

2. Remind students that an exception to this rule occurs when full-length works are included in larger anthologies or other types of collections. In this case, the largest work takes the underline and the titles within the collection are written inside quotation marks.

Answer Key

▶ **Exercise 40**

1. "Ozymandias"
2. "A Modest Proposal"
3. "The Tell-Tale Heart"
4. "There Will Come Soft Rains"
5. "The Day the World Ended"

Critical Viewing

Speculate Possible answer: <u>Peer Gynt Suite</u> would be underlined.

☑ **ONGOING ASSESSMENT: Monitor and Reinforce**

If students have difficulty with Exercise 39, 40, or 41, refer them to the following for additional practice.

In the Textbook	Print Resources	Technology
Section Review, Ex. 43–44, Section 28.4	*Grammar Exercise Workbook,* pp. 179–180	*On-Line Exercise Bank,* Section 28.4

⏱ **TIME SAVERS!**

📄 **Answers on Transparencies** Use the *Grammar Exercises Answers on Transparencies* for Chapter 28 to facilitate correction by students.

💻 **On-Line Exercise Bank** Have students complete the exercises on computer. The Auto Check feature will grade their work for you!

Titles Without Underlining or Quotation Marks

1. Tell students that, in addition to the other rules they just learned, there are still some titles that do not require any underlining or quotation marks.

2. Point to the examples beneath each key concept and then have students provide additional examples of religious works and government reports. Explain that these are all capitalized because they are proper nouns but are not punctuated further.

Answer Key

1. "Binary Sunset"; <u>Star Wars: A New Hope</u>
2. <u>Close Encounters of the Third Kind</u>
3. "Here They Come!"; <u>Star Wars</u>
4. <u>Shadows of the Empire</u>; <u>The Empire Strikes Back</u>; <u>Return of the Jedi</u>
5. "Han Solo and The Princess"
6. "Leia Through the Trilogy"
7. "A Jedi Knight"; <u>Amazing Stories</u>
8. "My Time With Yoda"
9. <u>The Prisoner of Chillon</u>
10. "Dream Within a Dream"

28.4

Titles Without Underlining or Quotation Marks

Some titles require neither underlining nor quotation marks.

▶ **KEY CONCEPT** Do not underline or place in quotation marks the names of the Bible, its books, divisions, or versions or other holy scriptures, such as the Koran. ■

EXAMPLE: He received a Bible as a gift.

▶ **KEY CONCEPT** Do not underline or place in quotation marks the titles of government charters, alliances, treaties, acts, statutes, or reports. ■

EXAMPLES: the Declaration of Independence
                         Civil Rights Act

▶ **Exercise 41** Punctuating Different Types of Titles Copy the titles, enclosing them in quotation marks or underlining them. If neither quotation marks nor underlining is needed, write *correct.*

1. I listened to the Binary Sunset track on the Star Wars: A New Hope soundtrack.
2. A different soundtrack also includes music from Close Encounters of the Third Kind.
3. Here They Come! is an exciting piece from Star Wars.
4. Shadows of the Empire is a book set between the movies The Empire Strikes Back and Return of the Jedi.
5. Han Solo and The Princess is a short romantic composition by John Williams.
6. My essay Leia Through the Trilogy will have to be revised after the release of the first trilogy.
7. Nick submitted the poem A Jedi Knight to Amazing Stories for publication.
8. It was the source of the chapter My Time With Yoda in the book we are trying to write.
9. I thought we could model it after a long poem like Byron's The Prisoner of Chillon.
10. He thought a short poem like Poe's Dream Within a Dream was more inspiring.

▶ **More Practice**

Grammar Exercise Workbook
• pp. 179–180
On-line Exercise Bank
• Section 28.4
Go on-line:
PHSchool.com
Enter Web Code:
eek-1002

Get instant feedback! Exercise 41 is available on-line or on CD-ROM.

☑ ONGOING ASSESSMENT: Assess Mastery

Use the following resources to assess student mastery of quotation marks and underlining.

In the Textbook	Technology
Chapter Review, Ex. 76	*Writing and Grammar* Interactive Text, Section 28.4, Section Review; *On-Line Exercise Bank,* Section 28.4

Section 28.4 Section Review

GRAMMAR EXERCISES 42–47

> **Exercise 42** Punctuating
Quotations Copy the following sentences, adding the appropriate quotation marks and other punctuation marks. Quoted phrases are underlined.

1. I thought C. S. Lewis wrote only children's books said Ryan
2. In a letter about <u>The Lion, the Witch, and the Wardrobe,</u> Lewis wrote <u>Let us suppose that there were a land like Narnia</u>
3. A frequent question is <u>Why is my set of Narnia books numbered in the wrong order</u>
4. So perhaps it does not matter very much in which order anyone reads them—C. S. Lewis
5. He wrote many scholarly essays about a variety of topics the teacher explained

> **Exercise 43** Punctuating
Different Types of Titles Copy the titles, enclosing them in quotation marks or underlining them.

1. Kurt Vonnegut's book Welcome to the Monkey House includes the short story A Long Walk to Forever.
2. Some of the stories were originally published in magazines like The Atlantic Monthly or The Magazine of Fantasy and Science Fiction.
3. In 1970, he wrote a play called Happy Birthday, Wanda June.
4. The New York Times called Vonnegut "a laughing prophet of doom."
5. In his novel Cat's Cradle, the chapter called Nice, Nice, Very Nice introduces the reader to one of Bokonon's songs.

> **Exercise 44** Using Quotation
Marks and Underlining Copy the following sentences, adding the appropriate quotation marks and properly punctuating any titles. The quoted phrase is underlined.

1. Roger Ebert writes <u>E.T. is a movie full of surprises</u>
2. It is a variation of the story The Wizard of Oz
3. During the movie, E.T. watches an episode of Tom and Jerry and reads the Buck Rogers comic strip.
4. He also watches an old science-fiction movie called This Island Earth.
5. During the movie, Gertie hears the bedtime story Peter Pan.

> **Exercise 45** Find It in Your
Reading Look through several movie, music, and book reviews to find examples of different kinds of titles and how they are set off. Then, look in these reviews for direct quotations and how they are punctuated. Copy the titles and quotations on a separate sheet of paper. Note the source of each.

> **Exercise 46** Find It in Your
Writing Find a selection in your portfolio that has quoted material in it. Make sure that you have punctuated correctly with quotation marks.

> **Exercise 47** Writing Application
Write a brief descriptive paragraph about your favorite science-fiction story. Include a quotation from one of your favorite characters. Be sure to properly punctuate your titles and quotations.

ASSESS

Section Review

Each of these exercises correlates to the instruction on quotation marks and underlining, pages 682–696. These exercises may be used for more practice, for reteaching, or for review of the key concepts presented. Answers for all chapter exercises are available in *Grammar Exercises Answers on Transparencies* in your Teaching Resources.

Answer Key

> **Exercise 42**

1. "I thought C. S. Lewis wrote only children's books," said Ryan.
2. In a letter about <u>The Lion, the Witch, and the Wardrobe,</u> Lewis wrote, "Let us suppose that there were a land like Narnia."
3. A frequent question is "Why is my set of Narnia books numbered in the wrong order?"
4. "So perhaps it does not matter very much in which order anyone reads them."—C. S. Lewis
5. "He wrote many scholarly essays about a variety of topics," the teacher explained.

> **Exercise 43**

1. <u>Welcome to the Monkey House;</u> "A Long Walk to Forever"
2. <u>The Atlantic Monthly;</u> <u>The Magazine of Fantasy and Science Fiction</u>
3. <u>Happy Birthday, Wanda June</u>
4. <u>The New York Times</u>
5. <u>Cat's Cradle;</u> "Nice, Nice, Very Nice"

> **Exercise 44**

1. Roger Ebert writes, "<u>E.T.</u> is a movie full of surprises."
2. It is a variation of the story <u>The Wizard of Oz.</u>
3. During the movie, E.T. watches an episode of <u>Tom and Jerry</u> and reads the <u>Buck Rogers</u> comic strip.
4. He also watches an old science-fiction movie called <u>This Island Earth.</u>
5. During the movie, Gertie hears the bedtime story <u>Peter Pan.</u>

> **Exercise 45**

Find It in Your Reading
You may want to bring to class some reviews for your students to search through.

continued

Answer Key continued

> **Exercise 46**

Find It in Your Writing
Have students repeat the exercise with underlined material.

> **Exercise 47**

Writing Application
If students do not read science fiction, they may write about a story in a different genre.

PREPARE and ENGAGE

Interest GRABBER Write this sentence on the board: *Twenty two foot snakes writhed in the pit.* Ask the class how many snakes were in the pit. (The answer could be *twenty snakes that are each two feet long* or *any number of snakes that are twenty-two feet long.*) Explain to students that a hyphen is needed to clarify the intended meaning.

Activate Prior Knowledge

Write the following on the board so that it runs into the right edge of the board: *Because of the snowy weather, the game was can.* Ask, "What do you do when you can't fit the whole word on the line?" (Answers can include placing the word *canceled* on the next line or using a hyphen to divide it at the end of the line (*canceled*). Continue by asking, "How do you know where to divide the word?" (between syllables)

TEACH

Step-by-Step Teaching Guide

Dashes

1. Explain to students that the dash is not to be confused with the hyphen. Hyphens are used within words while dashes are used between words.

2. Similar to the comma, the dash can set off interrupting words, phrases, and clauses from the rest of a sentence, but the dash is a more dramatic device that adds emphasis to the interrupter.

3. Be sure students notice that question marks (and exclamation marks) can fall within dashes. Point out also that the first word of such an interrupter is never capitalized unless it is a proper noun or adjective.

Section 28.5 · Dashes, Parentheses, and Hyphens

Commas, dashes, and parentheses all perform a similar function—that of separating certain words, phrases, and clauses from the rest of the sentence. To use these marks effectively, a writer must become acquainted with their different qualities. The comma is the most common mark and, therefore, draws the least attention to itself. The dash sets off material more dramatically. Parentheses set off technical or explanatory material clearly from the rest of the sentence.

This section will focus on the uses of the dash, parentheses, and hyphens, giving you rules to follow in using them.

Dashes

The dash, a long horizontal mark made above the writing line [—], functions to set off material in three basic ways:

▶ **KEY CONCEPT** Use dashes to indicate an abrupt change of thought, a dramatic interrupting idea, or a summary statement. ■

In the following chart, examples illustrate the three basic uses of the dash.

USES OF THE DASH	
To indicate an abrupt change of thought:	I cannot believe how many free throws my brother missed—oh, I don't even want to think about it!
To set off interrupting ideas dramatically:	The slam dunk—which must be the most spectacular shot in basketball—makes a great addition to any highlight film. Next Saturday—do you have to work that day?—we want you to play basketball with us.
To set off a summary statement:	Point guard, shooting guard, small forward, power forward, and center—deciding which of these positions to play took me a full five minutes. To see his jersey hanging from the rafters—this was his greatest dream.

It may help you to know that words such as *all*, *these*, *this*, and *that* frequently begin a summary sentence preceded by a dash.

698 • Punctuation

Theme: Basketball

In this section, you will learn about using dashes, parentheses, and hyphens. The examples and exercises are about basketball, past and present.

Cross-Curricular Connection: Physical Education

⏱ TIME AND RESOURCE MANAGER

Resources
Print: *Grammar Exercise Workbook*, pp. 181–186; *Grammar Exercises Answers on Transparencies*, Ch. 28
Technology: *Writing and Grammar* Interactive Text, Section 28.5; *On-Line Exercise Bank*, Section 28.5

Using the Full Student Edition	Using the Handbook🄷
• Work through all key concepts, pp. 698–710. • Assign and review Exercises 48–54.	• Work through all key concepts, pp. 520–532. • Assign and review Exercises 48–54.

Although nonessential appositives and modifiers are usually set off with commas, dashes are sometimes used.

▶ **KEY CONCEPT** Use dashes to set off a nonessential appositive or modifier when it is long, when it is already punctuated, or when you want to be dramatic. ■

APPOSITIVE: The cause of her happiness—winning the lead in the school play—pleased her parents.

MODIFIER: The drum major—who wore a white hat, a gold cape, and blue boots—led the band at the game.

Notice how the examples in the following charts each meet at least one of the three criteria in the rule.

USING DASHES WITH NONESSENTIAL APPOSITIVES	
Reasons for Use	**Examples**
Length	The selfish player—an egomaniac more concerned with his own statistics than his team—will not pass the ball.
Internal Punctuation	Some of the players on the team—for example, Karen, Susan, and Maria—always play well under pressure.
Strong Emphasis	The upsets—three games against superior teams—were totally unexpected.

Nonessential modifiers are generally set off only when they have internal punctuation or when strong emphasis is desired.

USING DASHES WITH NONESSENTIAL MODIFIERS	
Internal Punctuation	The coach—who, for some reason known only to himself, decided to take the star player out of the game—has no fans.
Strong Emphasis	Lara's three-point shot—which she has mastered so well that even a professional could take lessons from her—is helping us beat formidable teams.

You may recall that a parenthetical expression consists of words or phrases that are inserted into a sentence but have no essential grammatical relationship to it. Parenthetical expressions are often enclosed by dashes.

⚙ Grammar and Style Tip

Use dashes sparingly. As an alternative to commas, they can add emphasis and variety to your writing. If overused, however, they will lose their impact.

Step-by-Step Teaching Guide

Dashes With Nonessential Expressions

1. Have students provide a definition of *nonessential expression* (additional information that can be removed without changing the meaning of a sentence).

2. Remind students that they have learned to set off these expressions with commas. Explain that dashes are preferred when the nonessential expression is long or already punctuated.

Customize for
Gifted and Talented Students

Have students write five sentences about the topic below. Tell them to try to use dashes, parentheses, and hyphens at least one time each: *You have been asked for items representative of your interests and personality to be included in a time capsule. Explain what you would like to put into the capsule.*

Dashes, Parentheses, and Hyphens • **699**

Dashes With Parenthetical Expressions

1. Tell students that, similar to commas, dashes can be used to set off parenthetical expressions. Explain that dashes are preferred when the expression is long or already punctuated.

2. Remind students that question marks and exclamation marks may be inside the dashes. Explain that sometimes only one dash is necessary when the nonessential expression or parenthetical expression falls at the beginning or end of a sentence.

3. Tell students that dashes are usually written as longer marks than hyphens. Point out that some word processing programs require two hyphens typed in sequence, which the program then elongates into one mark.

Answer Key

▶ **Exercise 48**

1. The rules of basketball—I don't even want to think how many there are!—have changed over the years.
2. Basketball—enjoyed by people all over the world—was invented in 1891 by James Naismith in Springfield, Massachusetts.
3. To create a game suited for indoor play—this was Naismith's goal.
4. Naismith thought his game—such a fantastic game!—would be appropriate for indoor play in the wintertime.
5. Many star basketball players—for example, Dr. J, Oscar Robertson, and Michael Jordan—often practiced a skill until they could execute it flawlessly.

28.5

▶ **KEY CONCEPT** Use dashes to set off a parenthetical expression when it is long, already punctuated, or especially dramatic. ■

Short parenthetical expressions do not need dashes.

EXAMPLE: I will, I think, go.

If the parenthetical expression is long or contains its own punctuation, you may want to set it off with dashes:

EXAMPLE: Their amazing winning streak—they won by two points Monday, by one point yesterday, and by one point today—cannot last long.

Use dashes if the parenthetical expression is a question or an exclamation:

EXAMPLE: After Karen hit the improbable shot at the buzzer—can you believe the ball swooshed in?—the fans carried her away on their shoulders.

Enclose a parenthetical expression in dashes if you want it to stand out from the rest of the sentence:

EXAMPLE: At the first practice of the season—the coach actually told us that we would hate every minute of every practice—he made us run for two hours.

Although the dash has many uses, be careful not to overuse it. Using an occasional dash adds sentence variety and interest; putting dashes in too often will make your thoughts seem confused and disjointed.

▶ **Exercise 48** **Using the Dash** On your paper, copy the following sentences, adding one or two dashes in each.

1. The rules of basketball I don't even want to think how many there are! have changed over the years.
2. Basketball enjoyed by people all over the world was invented in 1891 by James Naismith in Springfield, Massachusetts.
3. To create a game suited for indoor play this was Naismith's goal.
4. Naismith thought his game such a fantastic game would be appropriate for indoor play in the wintertime.
5. Many star basketball players for example, Dr. J, Oscar Robertson, and Michael Jordan often practiced a skill until they could execute it flawlessly.

▶ **More Practice**

Grammar Exercise Workbook
• pp. 181–182
On-line Exercise Bank
• Section 28.5
Go on-line:
PHSchool.com
Enter Web Code:
eek-1002

Interactive Textbook

Get instant feedback! Exercise 48 is available on-line or on CD-ROM.

☑ **ONGOING ASSESSMENT: Monitor and Reinforce**

If students miss more than one item in Exercise 48, refer them to the following for additional practice.

In the Textbook	Print Resources	Technology
Section Review, Ex. 55, Section 28.5	*Grammar Exercise Workbook,* pp. 181–182	*On-Line Exercise Bank,* Section 28.5

Parentheses

Parentheses set off supplementary material not essential to the understanding of the sentence. Though not as dramatic as the dash, parentheses are the strongest separator you can use.

Rules for Using Parentheses The following rules will help you determine when using parentheses is appropriate:

KEY CONCEPT Use parentheses to set off asides and explanations only when the material is not essential or when it consists of one or more sentences. ■

Note that you can take out all the material in parentheses in the following examples without altering the meaning:

EXAMPLES: The coaches will look at each player's skills (passing, shooting, and rebounding) when deciding which players to recruit for the all-star team. Nancy perfected her passing (only after years of practice) and will now start as her team's point guard.

We will pick up the new uniforms tomorrow. (The salesperson promised that she would have them ready.) By tomorrow night, we should be wearing our new jerseys.

KEY CONCEPT Use parentheses to set off numerical explanations such as dates of a person's birth and death and around numbers and letters marking a series. ■

EXAMPLES: James Naismith invented the game of basketball at the request of Luther H. Gulick (1865–1918), who was his employer.

One half of the team's members (6) caught the flu just before the championship game.

You need to raise at least twenty thousand dollars ($20,000) to send the team to play the exhibition game in China.

Go to the sporting goods store and pick up these items: (1) basketball, (2) water bottle, (3) towels, and (4) bandages.

Who played in the NBA first: (a) Larry Bird, (b) Nate Archibald, or (c) Shaquille O'Neal?

In following these rules, be careful not to overuse parentheses. As with the dash, overuse can lead to choppy, unclear prose—something every good writer wants to avoid.

▼ **Critical Viewing** Use a parenthetical comment about a nonessential element in a statement about this picture. **[Describe]**

Dashes, Parentheses, and Hyphens • 701

Step-by-Step Teaching Guide

Rules for Using Parentheses

1. Explain to students that parentheses are another strong way of setting off nonessential material from a sentence. Point out that the material within parentheses is used to add useful information such as dates, specific data, and other important observations for readers.

2. Explain that nonessential asides and explanations can also be placed within parentheses, especially if this material is one or more sentences in length. Use the examples on this page to demonstrate types of information within parentheses.

3. Direct students' attention to the examples and have them explain the reason for each number in parentheses (birth/death; appositive number; appositive number; series; multiple-choice list).

Integrating Vocabulary Skills

Parentheses The word *parentheses* is derived from the Greek word *parentithenai* meaning "to put beside." Be sure students understand that by definition, ideas and information that are *parenthetical* are separate from, derive from, amplify, or otherwise relate in a nonessential way to a main idea.

Critical Viewing

Describe Possible answer: The pick-up basketball game (amid palm trees) looks like a great way to spend the afternoon.

Capitalizing and Punctuating with Parentheses

1. Tell students that this page outlines specific rules governing the mechanics of writing with parentheses.

2. Have students read the rules. Remind them that various punctuation marks can be part of the material within the parentheses, but any punctuation marks belonging with the main sentence must be placed outside of the parentheses.

28.5

Capitalizing and Punctuating With Parentheses

Several guidelines will help you punctuate and capitalize the material in parentheses.

KEY CONCEPT When a phrase or declarative sentence interrupts another sentence, do not use an initial capital or end mark inside the parentheses. ■

EXAMPLE: A frankfurter (my grandmother tasted one for the first time last summer) provides a delicious snack at a basketball game.

However, if the sentence is exclamatory or interrogative, the rule changes.

KEY CONCEPT When a question or exclamation interrupts another sentence, use both an initial capital and an end mark inside the parentheses. ■

EXAMPLE: College basketball games (These have featured some remarkable personalities!) reach millions of viewers every March through television.

There is another rule for sentences between sentences:

KEY CONCEPT With any sentence that falls between two complete sentences, use both an initial capital and an end mark inside the parentheses. ■

EXAMPLE: We drove to the high-school basketball championship. (It took more than five hours.) The high level of play surpassed our expectations.

Apply this rule for commas, semicolons, colons, and end marks:

KEY CONCEPT In a sentence that includes parentheses, place any punctuation belonging to the main sentence after the parenthesis. ■

EXAMPLES: Our shooting guard had an amazing season (averaging 45 points per game)!

The powerful center set several scoring records (22, to be exact), and he helped his team capture three championship titles.

More Practice

Grammar Exercise Workbook
• pp. 183–184
On-line Exercise Bank
• Section 28.5
Go on-line:
PHSchool.com
Enter Web Code:
eek-1002

Exercise 49 Using Parentheses On your paper, copy the following sentences, adding the necessary parentheses.

EXAMPLE: Pete Maravich Have you ever seen him play? displayed remarkable passing skills.

ANSWER: Pete Maravich (Have you ever seen him play?) displayed remarkable passing skills.

1. Michael Jeffrey Jordan Wasn't he the greatest basketball player ever? was born on February 17, 1963, in Brooklyn, New York.
2. After a stellar high-school career it must have been spectacular Jordan earned an athletic scholarship to attend the University of North Carolina.
3. Jordan He had such an amazing career! played the guard position at the University of North Carolina.
4. When did Jordan first win a college championship: a 1982, b 1983, or c 1984?
5. Jordan left college after his junior year. He was that good! He then began his career as a professional basketball player.

Exercise 50 Using Capitals and Punctuation With Parentheses On your paper, copy each sentence, making the necessary changes in capitalization and punctuation. If no corrections are needed, write *correct*.

EXAMPLE: When I finished the workout (what a tough one it was) I took a shower.

ANSWER: When I finished the workout (What a tough one it was!), I took a shower.

1. Shooting (do you know how to shoot a jump shot?) is one of the most important skills in basketball.
2. You can improve your jump shot (It's one of basketball's most effective offensive weapons!) only by practicing.
3. The jump shot (It's the most commonly used shot in competitive basketball today) takes much practice to perfect.
4. Your shooting form (So much depends on your mechanics.) is extremely important.
5. Maybe you can become a better shooter (you'd better hope so!) with practice.

▼ Critical Viewing
Add a parenthetical statement to the following sentence:
One of the players is my neighbor. [Apply]

Dashes, Parentheses, and Hyphens • 703

Hyphens With Numbers

1. Have students read the first key concept. Explain that numbers below twenty-one and above ninety-nine do not require hyphens when they are written out.

2. Give students practice distinguishing fractions used as nouns (in *one quarter of a dollar*, the prepositional phrase modifies the noun *quarter*) and those used as adjectives (in *one-quarter acre*, the fraction modifies the noun *acre*).

Hyphens With Word Parts

1. Have students provide a definition of *prefix* (one or more syllables that can be added at the beginning of a word to form a new word) and *suffix* (one or more syllables that can be added at the end of a word to form a new word).

2. Explain that when prefixes come before proper nouns or proper adjectives, hyphens are needed. Remind students that certain prefixes (*all-*, *ex-*, and *self-*) and a suffix (*-elect*) are always used with hyphens.

Hyphens

The hyphen is often mistaken for the dash. You should note that the hyphen is shorter than the dash.

Hyphens are used to divide certain numbers and parts of words, to join some compound words, and to divide words at the ends of lines. This section will focus on the rules governing the appropriate use of the hyphen.

With Numbers Some numbers written out as words require hyphens to separate the parts of the number:

▶ **KEY CONCEPT** Use a hyphen when writing out the compound numbers *twenty-one* through *ninety-nine*. ■

EXAMPLE: The star of the team scored *forty-seven* points!

▶ **KEY CONCEPT** Use a hyphen with fractions used as adjectives. ■

EXAMPLE: The recipe calls for *one-half* cup of mushrooms.

In the preceding example, the fraction functions as an adjective. If it were used as a noun, the hyphen would then be omitted.

EXAMPLE: *Three fourths* of the junior varsity team came to the practice.

With Word Parts Some word parts require the use of a hyphen:

▶ **KEY CONCEPT** Use a hyphen after a prefix that is followed by a proper noun or an adjective. ■

EXAMPLE: The school's basketball season started in *mid-September*.

▶ **KEY CONCEPT** Use a hyphen in words with the prefixes *all-*, *ex-*, and *self-*, and in words with the suffix *-elect*. ■

EXAMPLES: all-star   self-addressed
                 ex-teacher   senator-elect

Always check to make sure that a complete word joins the prefix or suffix. When these prefixes and suffixes combine with only part of a word, no hyphen is needed.

INCORRECT: ex-ecutive
CORRECT: executive

With Compound Words Hyphens are used with some compound words:

▶ **KEY CONCEPT** Use a hyphen to connect two or more words that are used as one word unless the dictionary gives a contrary spelling. ∎

The use of hyphens in compound words is a matter of changing style. The dictionary should always be your authority on this matter. Three examples, hyphenated in most dictionaries, follow.

EXAMPLES: merry-go-round   crow's-feet   off-season

▶ **KEY CONCEPT** Use a hyphen to connect a compound modifier that comes before a noun. ∎

EXAMPLES: The clouds cast a *grayish-blue* tint on the water.
             The *well-prepared* team played with confidence.

If a compound modifier comes after the noun, however, the hyphen is dropped.

BEFORE: We got the pizza from an *all-night* deli.
AFTER: A deli open *all night* delivered the pizza.

If, however, the dictionary shows the compound modifier with a hyphen, the word remains hyphenated regardless of its position in the sentence.

EXAMPLES: We water-skied behind a *jet-propelled* boat.
             Our ski boat was *jet-propelled*.

▶ **KEY CONCEPT** Do not use hyphens with compound modifiers that include words ending in *-ly* or with compound proper adjectives or compound proper nouns acting as adjectives. ∎

INCORRECT: The *badly-damaged* car sat in the body shop.
CORRECT: The *badly damaged* car sat in the body shop.
INCORRECT: The *North-American* continent has many mountains.
CORRECT: The *North American* continent has many mountains.

💡 Spelling Tip

Most words that end in *ball*—for example, *baseball, basketball, football,* and *volleyball*—describe a particular sport. They are spelled without a hyphen or a space.

Hyphens With Compound Words

1. Have students provide a definition of *compound word* (two or more words used together to indicate a specific meaning).

2. Remind students to check their dictionaries for the accepted methods of writing compound words; point out that no universal rules exist for writing compound words.

3. Without including hyphens, write on the board: *heavy-duty boots; South African vacation; poorly prepared speaker; jack-of-all-trades.* Have students insert hyphens in the proper places and explain their choices.

Hyphens for Clarity

1. Explain to students that, as with all punctuation marks, one of the main functions of the hyphen is to ensure clarity. Explain that hyphens are essential when letters appear in confusing combinations or with unusual and unfamiliar word combinations.

2. Looking at the examples in the first key concept, explain how the hyphen converts one word into a new word. Demonstrate that these words (particularly *co-op* and *coop*) are pronounced differently and have entirely different meanings.

3. Have a volunteer read the two examples in the second key concept and explain the difference between *new home-owner* and *new-home owner*.

Answer Key

▶ **Exercise 51**

1. all-star
2. self-proclaimed
3. correct
4. mind-boggling
5. ex-marine
6. awe-inspiring
7. twenty-six; twenty-seven
8. all-time
9. self-assurance
10. non-English-speaking

28.5

For Clarity Certain letter combinations may cause a reader to misread a passage. Inserting a hyphen can prevent this.

▶ **KEY CONCEPT** Use a hyphen within a word when a combination of letters might otherwise be confusing. ■

EXAMPLES: co-op   versus   *coop*
           re-lay   versus   *relay*

Unusual combinations of words can also be made clearer with hyphens.

▶ **KEY CONCEPT** Use a hyphen between words to keep the reader from combining them erroneously. ■

EXAMPLES: a new *car-buyer*   versus   a *new-car* buyer
           three-point margins versus   three *point-margins*

▶ **Exercise 51** Using Hyphens in Numbers, Word Parts, and Words On your paper, rewrite the sentences, adding necessary hyphens. Use a dictionary when in doubt. If no hyphen is needed, write *correct*.

EXAMPLE: The politician congratulated the senator elect.
ANSWER: The politician congratulated the senator-elect.

1. The history of basketball is filled with many all star players.
2. Some players have been self proclaimed stars; some have been legitimate stars.
3. Many players have become famous because of their offensive ability.
4. Moses Malone—a powerful center with a body like a tank—became famous because of his mind boggling rebounding.
5. Although he was not an ex marine, he often appeared to possess the posture of a soldier.
6. He displayed awe inspiring prowess when going after rebounds.
7. He routinely grabbed twenty six or twenty seven rebounds in a game when others felt lucky to grab ten.
8. He quickly set all time rebounding records.
9. Moreover, from the beginning of his career, he displayed the self assurance of a veteran.
10. Not surprisingly, he won numerous fans, including thousands from the non English speaking world.

▶ **More Practice**

Grammar Exercise Workbook
• pp. 185–186
On-line Exercise Bank
• Section 28.5
Go on-line:
PHSchool.com
Enter Web Code:
eek-1002

Get instant feedback! Exercises 51 and 52 are available on-line or on CD-ROM.

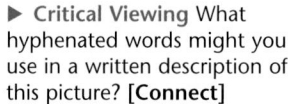 **Exercise 52** **Using Hyphens to Avoid Ambiguity** On your paper, copy the sentences, adding hyphens to make each sentence clear.

EXAMPLE: We had to relay the wood floor.

ANSWER: We had to re-lay the wood floor.

1. The coaches who attended the awards ceremony were dressed so neatly that it was obvious that they had repressed their suits for the event.
2. The organizers decided to repair presenters and coaches.
3. Unfortunately, one of the coaches could not resign a promising point guard for his team.
4. The point guard was semi literate and had failed his classes.
5. Another coach was elated about a twelve year old boy he had spotted playing at a local playground.
6. The boy was apparently a selftaught basketball prodigy who played as if he were nineteen years old.
7. When I asked him how to prepare for next season, he gave me a selfhelp book on strength training.
8. The coauthor of the book is a famous sportswriter from the Midwest.
9. The writer claims that basketball is considered to be a semiinfectious disease in her state.
10. After I left the ceremony, I could not reenter the arena because I no longer had my standing room ticket.

▶ **Critical Viewing** What hyphenated words might you use in a written description of this picture? **[Connect]**

Dashes, Parentheses, and Hyphens • 707

Exercise 52
1. re-pressed
2. re-pair
3. re-sign
4. semi-literate
5. twelve-year-old
6. self-taught
7. self-help
8. co-author
9. semi-infectious
10. standing-room

Critical Viewing

Connect Possible answers: backboard paint, cloud-strewn sky, out-of-focus branches

---

✓ **ONGOING ASSESSMENT: Monitor and Reinforce**

If students miss more than one item in Exercise 51 or 52, refer them to the following for additional practice.

In the Textbook	Print Resources	Technology
Section Review, Ex. 57, Section 28.5	*Grammar Exercise Workbook,* pp. 185–186	*On-Line Exercise Bank,* Section 28.5

Using Hyphens at the Ends of Lines

1. Write these words on the board: *affirmation; excitement; enthusiasm.* Have students practice breaking them into syllables. Have them use a dictionary to check their work.

2. Write these words on the board: *swiftly; hopeful; outdoors.* Have students suggest where to place hyphens. Remind them that, if a suffix is composed of only two letters, it should not be separated from the root word.

continued

Critical Viewing

Apply Possible answer: back/board, bas/ket/ball, over/shoot

28.5

Using Hyphens at the Ends of Lines

"To divide or not to divide?" This question comes up again and again when a writer reaches the end of a line of writing. In such a situation, you must decide whether to put one last word on the line, drop the word down to the next line, or divide it. The decision should be based on certain rules. The most important rule is the one regarding syllables.

▶ **KEY CONCEPT** If a word must be divided, always divide it between syllables. ■

If you are in doubt about how to divide a word into syllables, check a dictionary. It will show, for example, that the word *intricately* has four syllables, *in tri cate ly,* and it can be divided as in the following example:

EXAMPLE: The coach's plan was a model of intri-
                       cately plotted teamwork.

Always place the hyphen at the end of the first line—never at the start of the next line.

INCORRECT: The fans and players will continue to sup
                          -port this coach as long as he wins.
CORRECT: The fans and players will continue to sup-
                          port this coach as long as he wins.

Prefixes and suffixes provide a natural place for division.

▶ **KEY CONCEPT** If a word contains word parts, it can almost always be divided between the prefix and the root or the root and the suffix. ■

PREFIX: ex-tend   out-side   mis-fortune
SUFFIX: hope-less   four-some   fif-teen

If the suffix is composed of only two letters, however, avoid dividing the word between the root and suffix.

▶ **Critical Viewing** Identify three multisyllable words based on this picture. Between what letters in each word could you use a hyphen at the end of a line? [**Apply**]

In addition to avoiding a two-letter suffix, there are a number of other words that should not be divided. Be on the lookout for one-syllable words that sound like two-syllable words or look as if they are long enough to be two syllables. Do not divide them.

INCORRECT:	lod-ge	clo-thes	thro-ugh
CORRECT:	lodge	clothes	through

Each of these examples consists of only one syllable; therefore, dividing them is inappropriate. You will also need to watch divisions that result in a single letter standing alone.

▶ **KEY CONCEPT** Avoid dividing a word so that a single letter stands alone. ■

INCORRECT:	stead-y	a-ble	e-vict
CORRECT:	steady	able	evict

▶ **KEY CONCEPT** Avoid dividing proper nouns and proper adjectives. ■

The following divisions have traditionally been considered undesirable.

INCORRECT: We recently hired Sylvia Rodri-
guez.
I just finished eating a Mexican banana.

You may occasionally need to divide a word that already contains a hyphen.

▶ **KEY CONCEPT** Divide a hyphenated word only after the hyphen. ■

If you use the word *apple-pie* as an adjective, you would hyphenate it. When dividing the word at the end of a line, divide it only at the hyphen.

INCORRECT: Plans for a strong team appeared to be in apple-pie order.

CORRECT: Plans for a strong team appeared to be in apple-
pie order.

Spelling Tip

The spell-check feature in most word-processing programs will not recognize uncommon family names and may highlight them as incorrect. Double-check your spelling of proper nouns.

3. Remind students that before dividing a shorter word, they should always make sure that it actually contains more than one syllable. Remind students not to divide multi-syllable words in a way that would leave a single letter on one line.

4. Have students read the second key concept and point out that dividing proper nouns and adjectives is best avoided.

5. Write on the board: *atone, theme, emote, ex-husband, Scandinavian.* Have students suggest the proper places for a hyphen.

☑ **ONGOING ASSESSMENT: Monitor and Reinforce**

If students have difficulty with Exercise 53 or 54, refer them to the following for additional practice.

In the Textbook	Print Resources	Technology
Section Review, Ex. 57, Section 28.5	*Grammar Exercise Workbook,* pp. 185–186	*On-Line Exercise Bank,* Section 28.5

Step-by-Step Teaching Guide

Hyphens at the Ends of Pages

1. Emphasize to students that a word should not be divided at the end of a page.

2. Point out that periodicals sometimes divide a word so that part of it appears on one page and the rest appears on the page where the article continues, sometimes many pages away. Explain that this is not proper style but that periodicals sometimes encounter strict space restraints and break this rule for such a purpose.

Answer Key

▶ Exercise 53

1. correct
2. ev-ery
3. sister- or sister-in-
4. popula-tion
5. basket-
6. like
7. power-
8. domi-
9. Chamberlain
10. Knickerbockers

▶ Exercise 54

Encourage students to consult their dictionaries to be sure of where to hyphenate words they are unsure of.

▶ **KEY CONCEPT** Avoid dividing a word so that part of the word is on one page and the remainder is on the next page. ■

Often, chopping up a word in this way will confuse your readers or cause them to lose their train of thought.

▶ **Exercise 53** Using Hyphens to Divide Words In the sentences below, if a word has been divided correctly, write *correct*. If not, divide the word correctly or write it as one word if it cannot be divided.

EXAMPLE: Have you given much tho-
             ught to this problem?

ANSWER: Have you given much thought to this problem?

1. Do you want to play basketball with my team-
   mates?
2. We play basketball ever-
   y Saturday morning.
3. The star of our team (Did you know we had a star?) is my sister-in-law.
4. Do you know how much of the world's population enjoys playing basketball?
5. Millions of people enjoy watching or playing basketball.
6. Some people like to play basketball indoors; others like playing outdoors.
7. Basketball has long been dominated by powerful centers.
8. Wilt Chamberlain was one of basketball's most dominant centers.
9. Did you and your friends know that Wilt Chamberlain once scored 100 points in a professional game?
10. He did so against the New York Knicker-
    bockers in 1962.

▶ **Exercise 54** Using Hyphens in Written Work On a piece of looseleaf paper with the margins marked, copy a paragraph from your social studies textbook. Use the margin guidelines to keep the margins of your report even. Break words as necessary to stay within the margin guidelines.

More Practice

Grammar Exercise Workbook
• pp. 185–186
On-line Exercise Bank
• Section 28.5
  Go on-line:
  PHSchool.com
  Enter Web Code:
  eek-1002

Complete the exercises on-line! Exercises 53 and 54 are available on-line or on CD-ROM.

☑ ONGOING ASSESSMENT: Assess Mastery

Use the following resources to assess student mastery of dashes, parentheses, and hyphens.

In the Textbook	Technology
Chapter Review, Ex. 77	*Writing and Grammar* Interactive Text, Section 28.5, Section Review; *On-Line Exercise Bank*, Section 28.5

Section 28.5 Section Review

GRAMMAR EXERCISES 55–60

> **Exercise 55** **Using the Dash** On your paper, copy the following sentences, adding one or two dashes in each.

1. Basketball which has long been thought to be an urban game is extremely popular in the suburbs.
2. Modern players are much more muscular it's rare to see a lanky player anymore than players from the past.
3. This does not mean that basketball is a game only for giants thank goodness!
4. People of average height less than six feet tall have had basketball careers.
5. Tyrone "Muggsy" Bogues who enjoyed a stellar career at Wake Forest University in the late 1980's and went on to play professionally stands just five feet three inches tall.

> **Exercise 56** **Using Parentheses** On your paper, rewrite the following sentences using the necessary parentheses and capitalization.

1. Earvin Johnson did you know that he was called Magic Johnson? was one of the best point guards in basketball.
2. Johnson My dad saw him play was born in 1959 in Lansing, Michigan.
3. He starred as the point guard perhaps the most important position on the team of the Michigan State team.
4. By the time he retired in 1991, he had won numerous All-Star honors 12.
5. When did Magic Johnson first lead his professional team to a world championship: a 1980, b 1981, or c 1982?

> **Exercise 57** **Using Hyphens in Numbers, Word Parts, and Words** Rewrite the sentences that need hyphens. Use a dictionary when in doubt. If no hyphen is needed, write *correct*.

1. Wilt Chamberlain was one of the most intimidating players in basketball.
2. He was a perennial allstar during his long professional basketball career.
3. An ex high school standout, he enjoyed a stellar college career at the University of Kansas.
4. Chamberlain played for three seasons with the University of Kansas team— that university had well trained teams.
5. During his long career, he demon strated great self discipline.

> **Exercise 58** **Find It in Your Reading** Explain the use of hyphens in the excerpt from "Rare Air: Michael on Michael."

. . . And teams played me one-on-one at North Carolina. They never double-teamed me.

> **Exercise 59** **Find It in Your Writing** Look through your portfolio. Find examples of hyphens, parentheses, and dashes you have used. Explain why you used each mark.

> **Exercise 60** **Writing Application** Imagine that a talent scout has come to watch you play a sport. Write five sentences that you would want to say following the game. Use the guidelines below.

1. Use ex-teacher in a question.
2. Use the word second-class in a sentence about the sport.
3. Use a dash to set off a statement.
4. Use parentheses to set off an interrupting idea.
5. Use the dash to indicate an abrupt change of thought.

Section Review • 711

Interest GRABBER

Write the following examples on the board. Ask students to explain which one is correct, and why.

The coat is hers.

The coat is her's.

(The first form is correct. An apostrophe is not used with the possessive form of personal pronouns.)

Activate Prior Knowledge

Ask students to explain the difference between these two sentences:

The student's grades are high.

The students' grades are high.

(The first refers to one student; the second refers to more than one. This is indicated by the position of the apostrophe.)

TEACH

Step-by-Step Teaching Guide

Grammar in Literature

1. Have a student read the excerpt aloud. Point out the contraction and have students give the words that have been combined (*would have*).

2. Ask students to suggest ways of rewording the sentences with possessives so the apostrophes would not be needed (the hand of Abuelito, the mother of La Muñeca).

More About the Writer

Sandra Cisneros (b. 1954) was born to a Mexican father and a Mexican American mother. She spent her childhood shuttling between Chicago and Mexico City. Cisneros attended the prestigious Writers' Workshop at the University of Iowa. Her first novel, the autobiographical *The House on Mango Street,* was a commercial and critical success, earning her the American Book Award in 1985.

Connections With Literature

"Tepeyac" by Sandra Cisneros can be found in *Prentice Hall Literature, Penguin Edition,* Grade 10.

Section 28.6 Apostrophes

Insects comprise the largest class of animals on the planet. They are social animals, and they are extremely organized. So, too, are the rules governing apostrophes.

Though the apostrophe ['] is classified as a punctuation mark and not as a letter, its misuse can result in the misspelling of many words. The apostrophe serves two purposes: to show possession and to indicate missing letters. In most cases, you must place the apostrophe between the letters of the word, not before or after it. Thus, misplacement of the apostrophe leads to spelling errors. This section will provide you with rules so that you can use the apostrophe correctly.

Theme: Bugs

In this section, you will learn about the use of apostrophes. The exercises and examples are about insects and other bugs.

Cross-Curricular Connection: Science

GRAMMAR IN LITERATURE

from **Tepeyac**
Sandra Cisneros

Some of the apostrophes in this excerpt indicate possession. These words are highlighted in blue italics. The apostrophe in the red italic word indicates the missing letters in a contraction.

I take *Abuelito's* hand, fat and dimpled in the center like a valentine, and we walk past the basilica, . . . Past the very same spot where long ago Juan Diego brought down from the *cerro* the miracle that has drawn everyone, . . . past La *Muñeca's* mother watering her famous dahlias . . . .

Who *would've* guessed, after all this time, it is me who will remember when everything else is forgotten, . . .

712 • Punctuation

⏱ TIME AND RESOURCE MANAGER

Resources
Print: *Grammar Exercise Workbook,* pp. 187–190; *Grammar Exercises Answers on Transparencies,* Ch. 28
Technology: *Writing and Grammar* Interactive Text, Section 28.6; *On-Line Exercise Bank,* Section 28.6

Using the Full Student Edition	Using the Handbook🅷
• Work through all key concepts, pp. 712–721.	• Work through all key concepts, pp. 534–543.
• Assign and review Exercises 61–66.	• Assign and review Exercises 61–66.
• Read and discuss Grammar in Literature, p. 712.	• Read and discuss Grammar in Literature, p. 534.

Apostrophes With Possessive Nouns

An apostrophe must be used to indicate possession or ownership with nouns.

With Singular Nouns As shown in the examples, the following rule applies to most singular nouns:

> **KEY CONCEPT** Add an apostrophe and *s* to show the possessive case of most singular nouns. ■

EXAMPLES: The wing of the *insect* becomes the *insect's* wing.

The sections of the *ant* become the *ant's* sections.

The mandibles of the *cockroach* become the *cockroach's* mandibles.

The legs of the *centipede* become the *centipede's* legs.

The eye of the *fly* becomes the *fly's* eye.

The forelegs of a *mantis* become a *mantis's* forelegs.

When a singular noun ends in *s*, as in the last example, you can still follow this style in most cases. Ancient and classical names are the exception.

EXAMPLE: Zeus' thunderbolt.

With Plural Nouns Showing possession with plural nouns ending in *s* or *es* calls for a different rule:

> **KEY CONCEPT** Add an apostrophe to show the possessive case of plural nouns ending in *s* or *es*. ■

EXAMPLES: The wings of the *bees* become the *bees'* wings.
The tracks of the *caterpillars* become the *caterpillars'* tracks.
The larvae of the *moths* become the *moths'* larvae.

▲ Critical Viewing In a complete sentence that contains the possessive of *insect,* identify and describe three features of this insect. [Describe]

Apostrophes • 713

Critical Viewing

Describe Possible answer: This picture shows in detail the insect's jointed forelegs, its antennae, and its compound eyes.

Step-by-Step Teaching Guide

Apostrophes With Singular and Plural Possessive Nouns

1. Explain to students that one of the main purposes of apostrophes is to show possession (ownership).

2. Tell students that the addition of an *apostrophe* and an *–s* to the end of a singular noun is the most common method for writing the possessive form.

3. Remind students that this rule can be modified slightly with singular nouns ending in *–s*. In this case, the *apostrophe –s* combination may be awkward so just an apostrophe can sometimes suffice.

4. Ask students to recall that many regular nouns are made plural by adding an *–s* or an *–es*. Point out that the most common method of making these nouns possessive is adding a final apostrophe without an additional *s*.

5. Have students think of nouns that become plural without an *es* or *s* (*children, oxen, mice, geese*). Explain that these plural nouns are made possessive by adding an *apostrophe –s*, just as singular nouns are made possessive.

Customize for
ESL Students

Have students take turns making up sentences that use the possessive case of their classmates' names. Students can use the first names to practice singular possessives and surnames to practice plural possessives (*Leon's brother Alex is the Zubkos' oldest son*).

Integrating Vocabulary Skills

Apostrophe Tell students that the noun *apostrophe* has another definition. Originally, the Greek roots *apo* (*from*) and *strephein* (*to turn*) formed the Greek word apostrophe meaning "a turning away from the audience to address one person," and this meaning was associated with the theater. In modern English *apostrophe* means "words addressed to a person or thing, whether absent or present, generally in an exclamatory digression in speech or literature."

Step-by-Step Teaching Guide

Apostrophes With Possessive Compound Nouns

1. Remind students that some nouns are compound, which means that they are made up of more than one word.

2. Explain that to make these nouns possessive, students must simply follow the rules they have already learned for singular and plural nouns: adding an *apostrophe –s* or just an *apostrophe*.

3. Write on the board without the apostrophes: *the fire engine's siren; the commander-in-chief's briefcase; the soap opera's ending.* Have students make these terms possessive by adding apostrophes in the correct locations.

Step-by-Step Teaching Guide

Apostrophes With Expressions

1. Have students provide a definition for the word *sake* (a cause; behalf). Point out that this is frequently used in possessive expressions. Direct students' attention to the example given to demonstrate this usage.

2. Ask students for additional phrases about time and amount that reflect ownership (*a year's pay, two weeks' suspension, a dollar's value*).

Not all plural nouns end in *s* or *es*, however. Another rule will help you form the possessive case of these nouns:

> **KEY CONCEPT** Add an apostrophe and *s* to show the possessive case of plural nouns that do not end in *s* or *es*. ■

EXAMPLES: The books of the *men* become the *men's* books.

The songs of the *people* become the *people's* songs.

With Compound Nouns Sometimes, you will find that a noun showing ownership consists of several words.

> **KEY CONCEPT** Add an apostrophe and *s* (or just an apostrophe if the word is a plural ending in *s*) to the last word of a compound noun to form the possessive. ■

This rule refers to names of businesses and organizations, names with titles, and hyphenated compound nouns.

APOSTROPHES WITH COMPOUND NOUNS	
Businesses and Organizations	The Good Earth's menu the Lions Clubs' motto
Names With Titles	the Secretary of Defense's visit Edward VIII's abdication
Hyphenated Compound Nouns Used to Describe People	my father-in-law's glasses the secretary-treasurer's pen

With Expressions Involving Time and Amounts If you use possessive expressions involving time or amounts, you will need to use an apostrophe.

> **KEY CONCEPT** To form possessives involving time or amounts, use an apostrophe and *s* or just an apostrophe if the possessive is a plural ending in *s*. ■

TIME: a day's journey   six years' time

AMOUNT: one quarter's worth   fifty cents' worth

To Show Joint and Individual Ownership When two nouns are involved, take care to show ownership accurately.

▶ **KEY CONCEPT** To show joint ownership, make the final noun possessive. ■

EXAMPLES: Roger and Jeremy's ant farms
(They share the same ant farms.)
the husband and wife's car
(They share one car.)

▶ **KEY CONCEPT** To show individual ownership, make each noun possessive. ■

EXAMPLES: Roger's and Jeremy's ant farms
(Each has his own ant farm.)
the husband's and wife's cars
(Each owns a separate car.)

Checking Your Use of the Rules Often, confusion results over the application of the various rules because writers forget to determine whether they are writing about a singular noun or a plural noun. First, determine whether the owner is singular or plural. Then, consider the word before the apostrophe you are going to add. If you place the apostrophe correctly, the letters to the left of the apostrophe should spell out the owner's complete name. Look at the checking technique in this chart:

CHECKING THE USE OF APOSTROPHES		
Incorrect	**Explanation**	**Correction**
Jame's car	The owner is not *Jame*, but *James*.	James's car
one boys' book	The owner is not *boys*, but *boy*.	one boy's book
two girl's lunches	The owner is not *girl*, but *girls*.	two girls' lunches

Apostrophes to Show Joint and Individual Ownership

1. Explain to students that *joint* means "shared by more than one." Tell students that when two nouns engage in joint ownership, only the final noun takes the possessive form.

2. Have students define *individual ownership*. Point out that when individual ownership is demonstrated, each noun must be made possessive because each possesses separately.

3. Write on the board: *Aunt Mary, Uncle Andy, and Bridget gifts; the women and children organizations; James and Marilyn grandchildren.* Have students make these terms individual possessives and then joint possessives.

28.6

Exercise 61 **Using Apostrophes With Single-Word Possessive Nouns** Copy the underlined nouns, which may be singular or plural, putting them into the possessive form when necessary. For sentences that do not require possessive forms, just write the underlined word.

EXAMPLE: <u>Insects</u> sizes can vary tremendously.
ANSWER: Insects'

1. The <u>insects</u> class is the largest in the world.
2. The <u>class</u> distribution is all over the world.
3. Insects outnumber all other animal <u>species</u>.
4. Some <u>moths</u> wingspans can be twelve inches.
5. A stick <u>insect</u> length can also be twelve inches.

Exercise 62 **Using Apostrophes With Compound Nouns** Copy the underlined nouns, putting them into the possessive form.

EXAMPLE: I share my <u>sister-in-law</u> fear of insects.
ANSWER: sister-in-law's

1. <u>Life-cycle</u> lengths vary from insect to insect.
2. The <u>seventeen-year locust</u> maturation period is from thirteen to seventeen years.
3. The <u>jaws</u> function in an insect is to crush food.
4. Some insects live in a highly organized society, with the <u>leader</u> role being taken by the queen.
5. My <u>entomological society</u> rules for membership are strict.

Exercise 63 **Using Apostrophes to Show Joint and Individual Ownership** From each of the following sentences, copy the underlined words, changing them to show joint or individual ownership as the instructions indicate.

1. <u>Plant and insect</u> relationships are often necessary to the plant. (joint)
2. <u>Bee and ant</u> organizations are quite complex. (individual)
3. <u>Wasps and termites</u> social interactions are also quite unique. (individual)
4. Some <u>wasps and flies</u> maturation period is a matter of days. (individual)
5. Certain insects live by one of two methods; <u>parasitism and predation</u> features are quite different. (individual)

More Practice

Grammar Exercise Workbook
• pp. 187–188
On-line Exercise Bank
• Section 28.6
Go on-line:
PHSchool.com
Enter Web Code:
eek-1002

Interactive Textbook

Get instant feedback! Exercises 61, 62, and 63 are available on-line or on CD-ROM.

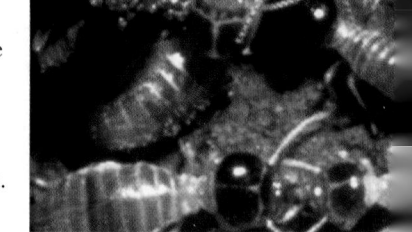

☑ ONGOING ASSESSMENT: Monitor and Reinforce

If students miss more than one item in Exercise 61, 62, or 63, refer them to the following for additional practice.

In the Textbook	Print Resources	Technology
Section Review, Ex. 67–68, Section 28.6	*Grammar Exercise Workbook,* pp. 187–188	*On-Line Exercise Bank,* Section 28.6

Apostrophes With Pronouns

Some pronouns showing ownership require an apostrophe:

> **KEY CONCEPT** Use an apostrophe and *s* with indefinite pronouns to show possession. ■

EXAMPLES: another's   nobody's   one's
           anyone's   someone's everybody's

If you form a two-word indefinite pronoun, add the apostrophe and the -*s* to the last word only.

EXAMPLES: nobody else's   one another's

Possessive personal pronouns do not need an apostrophe.

> **KEY CONCEPT** Do not use an apostrophe with the possessive forms of personal pronouns. ■

With the words *yours, his, hers, theirs, its, ours,* and *whose,* no apostrophe is necessary. These already show ownership.

EXAMPLES: Looking at the butterfly collections, I decided *yours* far outdistanced the other entries.
           Its beautiful colors drew everyone's notice.

Pay special attention to the possessive forms *whose* and *its* because they are easily confused with the contractions *who's* and *it's.* Just remember that *whose* and *its* show possession.

PRONOUNS: *Whose* wallet is this?

           Its chimes rang out clearly.

Who's and *it's,* on the other hand, are contractions of the words *who is* and *it is.* They both require apostrophes to indicate the missing letters.

CONTRACTIONS: *Who's* responsible for naming insects?

               It's up to whoever discovers a new species to name it.

▼ Critical Viewing
What possessive pronoun would you use to refer to the colony of these insects? [Apply]

Apostrophes • **717**

Step-by-Step Teaching Guide

Apostrophes With Pronouns

1. Have students define *indefinite pronouns* (pronouns referring to people, places, or things, often without specifying which ones).

2. Point out that indefinite pronouns, unlike personal pronouns, do not have their own possessive forms; they require apostrophes to show ownership.

3. Write on the board the following sentences: *Who's* going to the movie? *Whose* movie is this? Ask students to explain the meaning of the underlined words.

Critical Viewing

Apply Possible answer: their colony

Answer Key

28.6

Exercise 64 Proofreading for Correct Use of Apostrophes

On a separate sheet of paper, rewrite each sentence. Correct any errors in the use of apostrophes.

EXAMPLE: That hive is her's.
ANSWER: That hive is hers.

1. A parasite finds it's nourishment in other living creatures.
2. A social hierarchy is usually led by a queen, and all the offspring are her's.
3. Workers are usually male, and their's is the responsibility to keep the society going.
4. Some ants take over others colonies and use them for workers.
5. The eyes of an insect are on its head.
6. Some insect societies are almost as complex as our's.
7. My fear of insects is greater than yours.
8. I thought this was your ant farm, but it must be some-one's else.
9. An insect has a nervous system who's center is a nerve cord running from the head to the abdomen.
10. An insect's heart is not as complicated as your's or mine's.

▼ Critical Viewing
Identify two possessive nouns suggested by this picture. What possessive pronouns could take the place of these nouns?
[Apply]

718 • Punctuation

☑ **ONGOING ASSESSMENT: Monitor and Reinforce**

If students miss more than two items in Exercise 64, refer them to the following for additional practice.

In the Textbook	Print Resources	Technology
Section Review, Ex. 69, Section 28.6	*Grammar Exercise Workbook,* pp. 187–188	*On-Line Exercise Bank,* Section 28.6

Apostrophes With Contractions

The meaning of a contraction is implied by its name. It is a word contracted in size by the removal of some letter or letters and the insertion of an apostrophe to indicate the missing letters. This leads to the following basic rule for contractions:

▶ **KEY CONCEPT** Use an apostrophe in a contraction to indicate the position of the missing letter or letters. ■

Contractions With Verbs Verbs are often used in a contracted form. Look at the following chart, noticing how often these verb contractions are used in common speech patterns.

COMMON CONTRACTIONS WITH VERBS		
Verbs with *not*	are not = aren't do not = don't	was not = wasn't were not = weren't
Pronouns with *will*	I will = I'll you will = you'll	she will = she'll they will = they'll
Pronouns and nouns with the verb *be*	I am = I'm you are = you're	who is = who's Mark is = Mark's
Pronouns with *would*	I would = I'd he would = he'd	we would = we'd they would = they'd

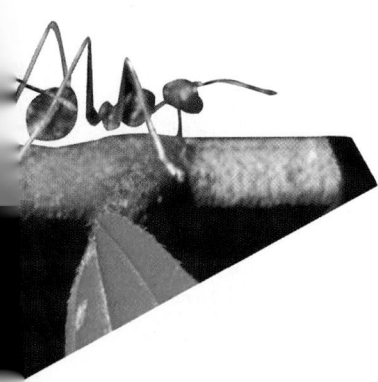

One special contraction changes letters as well as drops them: *Will not* becomes *won't* in the contracted form.

Try to avoid most verb contractions in formal writing. They tend to make your style more informal than you may wish.

INFORMAL: He's promised that he'll hide the beetle if we're still afraid of it.

FORMAL: He has promised that he will hide the beetle if we are still afraid of it.

Contractions With Years In writing about years, insert an apostrophe in places where a number is left out.

EXAMPLES: Decathlon Champion of '75
the snowstorm of '03

Step-by-Step Teaching Guide

Apostrophes With Contractions

1. Explain to students that a contraction is a word shortened in speech or spelling. Apostrophes are used to hold the place of the missing words or letters.

2. Be sure students know how these words differ: *they're, there,* and *their; you're* and *your; its* and *it's;* and *who's* and *whose.* Explain that these are called homonyms.

3. Remind students that contractions should not be used in formal speech and writing since they are informal in style.

4. Have students read the passage about contractions with years. Point out that the dropping of the millennium and century numbers is effective only when the year can be understood or made obvious by the context.

Customize for
Spatial Learners

Write the word *CANNOT* on a long strip of paper. Fold the paper so that only *CANT* shows. Hand the folded paper to a student and ask him or her to unfold it to reveal the full word. Ask what is still missing (the apostrophe following the *–n*). Do the same for *DO NOT* (*won't* is an exception that will not work with this activity), *COULD NOT,* and other contractions. This is a visual representation of the contraction (making shorter) of a word.

Rules for Apostrophes With Contractions

1. Tell students that another type of contraction is the abbreviation of words from different languages, most notably expressions with *of the, of,* or *the.* Have students read the examples on the page and provide more examples that they have heard or seen.

2. Have students read aloud the examples for contractions with dialogue. Discuss how the flavor of the words is enhanced by the changes in pronunciation created by the use of apostrophes. Explain that this is an effective way to express different dialects of the same language in written work.

Customize for
ESL Students

Many languages show possession by using their word for *of.* For example, to identify a hat that belongs to Bill, they would say (in their own words) "the hat of Bill." There is not always an equivalent to the possessive form of English. Point out that in English the apostrophe and an s *('s)* indicates the same relationship between owner and object as the "of" of their language.

Answer Key

▶ **Exercise 65**

1. don't
2. have not
3. They have
4. can't
5. do not
6. They're
7. won't
8. wouldn't
9. insect is
10. it is

28.6

Contractions With *o', d',* and *l'* These letters followed by the apostrophe make up the abbreviated form of the words *of the* or *the* as spelled in several different languages.

EXAMPLES: o'clock   d'Angelo
             O'Sullivan   l'Abbé

   As you can see, these letters and apostrophes are combined most often with surnames.

Contractions With Dialogue When writing dialogue, you may want to keep the flavor of the speaker's individual speaking style. Therefore, use any contractions the speaker might use. You may also want to include a regional dialect or a foreign accent. Because speech often includes pronunciations with omitted letters, you should insert apostrophes to show those changes.

EXAMPLES: C'mon—aren't you comin' fishin'?
             'Tis a fine spring morn we're havin'.
             That li'l ant is aworkin' hard!

   As with most punctuation, overuse reduces the effectiveness and impact, so watch the overuse of the apostrophe with contractions—even in dialogue.

▶ **Exercise 65**   Apostrophes With Contractions If a contraction is underlined in the following paragraph, write the original two words. If two words are underlined, write the contraction they would form.

EXAMPLE: <u>Aren't</u> people who study insects called
            entomologists?
ANSWER: Are not

   (1) Insects <u>do not</u> have lungs but a network of tubes to carry air through the body. (2) They are invertebrates, which means that they <u>haven't</u> got a backbone. (3) <u>They've</u> been found on land and in most types of water. (4) Insect predators <u>cannot</u> live without feeding on other insects. (5) Most species <u>don't</u> grow in the same way people do. (6) <u>They are</u> able to reach adulthood by metamorphosis. (7) Insects that are scavengers <u>will not</u> eat living plants or animals. (8) Some parasitic insects are so small that you <u>would not</u> be able to see them without a microscope. (9) An <u>insect's</u> often distinguished by its three body parts. (10) My friend studies insects and says that <u>it's</u> an interesting field.

▶ **More Practice**

Grammar Exercise Workbook
• pp. 189–190
On-line Exercise Bank
• Section 28.6
  Go on-line:
  PHSchool.com
  Enter Web Code:
  eek-1002

Get instant feedback! Exercises 65 and 66 are available on-line or on CD-ROM.

Special Uses of the Apostrophe

An apostrophe is also used to show the plural of numbers, symbols, letters, and words used to name themselves.

KEY CONCEPT Use an apostrophe and *s* to write the plurals of numbers, symbols, letters, and words used to name themselves. ∎

EXAMPLES:
There are two *8*'s in that number.
You need two more *?*'s.
Her *b*'s and *d*'s all look the same.
A's and *an*'s cause confusion.

Exercise 66 Using the Apostrophe in Special Cases Copy the following sentences, adding an apostrophe and an *s* to numbers, symbols, letters, and words whenever necessary. Underline all items in italics.

EXAMPLE: On my last report card, I got all *A* and *B*.
ANSWER: On my last report card, I got all <u>*A*</u>'s and <u>*B*</u>'s.

1. On my two papers on insects, I got *95*.
2. I might get *100* on my next papers.
3. I spelled beetle with too many *e*.
4. I must have written twenty *entomology* in that paper.
5. People in their *20* generally have a lot of energy.
6. Europeans put an extra line in their *7* to show that they are different from their *1*.
7. Insect abdomens are segmented into *10* or *11*.
8. Insect legs are usually arranged in *2*.
9. Is it all right to use *&* in my paper, or should I spell out the word?
10. She is allergic to bees, so she has two *Rx* in case she gets a bee sting.

▶ Critical Viewing Describe the appearance of this bug. What possessive noun did you use? [Apply]

Apostrophes • 721

Special Uses of the Apostrophe

1. Tell students that the special use of apostrophes applies to making plural numbers, symbols, letters, and words that name themselves.

2. Ask students to look in magazine and newspaper articles for other examples of numbers, symbols, letters, and words that name themselves.

Answer Key

Exercise 66

1. <u>*95*</u>'s
2. <u>*100*</u>'s
3. <u>*e*</u>'s
4. <u>*entomology*</u>'s
5. <u>*20*</u>'s
6. <u>*7*</u>'s; <u>*1*</u>'s
7. <u>*10*</u>'s; <u>*11*</u>'s
8. <u>*2*</u>'s
9. <u>*&*</u>'s
10. <u>*Rx*</u>'s

Critical Viewing

Apply Possible answer: The light spots on the *beetle's* back resemble the number *8*'s shape.

☑ **ONGOING ASSESSMENT: Monitor and Reinforce**

If students miss more than two items in Exercise 65 or 66, refer them to the following for additional practice.

In the Textbook	Print Resources	Technology
Section Review, Ex. 69, Section 28.6	*Grammar Exercise Workbook,* pp. 189–190	*On-Line Exercise Bank,* Section 28.6

🕐 **TIME SAVERS!**

Answers on Transparencies Use the *Grammar Exercises Answers on Transparencies* for Chapter 28 to facilitate correction by students.

On-Line Exercise Bank Have students complete the exercises on computer. The Auto Check feature will grade their work for you!

Section Review

Each of these exercises correlates to the instruction on apostrophes, pages 712–721. These exercises may be used for more practice, for reteaching, or for review of the key concepts presented. Answers for all chapter exercises are available in *Grammar Exercises Answers on Transparencies* in your Teaching Resources.

Answer Key

▶ **Exercise 67**

1. insect's
2. heart's
3. correct
4. Environment's
5. brother-in-law's

▶ **Exercise 68**

1. antennae's and eyes'
2. Butterflies' and moths'
3. Compound eyes' and simple eyes'
4. butterflies'
5. flies'

▶ **Exercise 69**

1. His
2. yours
3. whose
4. its
5. It's
6. Whose
7. o'clock
8. James's
9. Nobody's
10. theirs

▶ **Exercise 70**

Find It in Your Reading

planter's—shows singular possession
hadn't—contraction of *had not*
he'd, he'd—contraction of *he would*

▶ **Exercise 71**

Find It in your Writing
Remind students to pay extra attention to *who's, whose, it's,* and *its.*

▶ **Exercise 72**

Writing Application
Have students exchange papers with a partner and correct one another's work.

Section
28.6 Section Review

GRAMMAR EXERCISES 67–72

▶ **Exercise 67** Using Apostrophes With Single-Word and Compound Possessive Nouns Put each underlined word into the possessive if necessary. If not, write *correct.*

1. An <u>insect</u> circulatory system is quite simple.
2. The <u>heart</u> function is to keep the body cavity filled with blood.
3. The <u>walls</u> of the heart contract to force the blood out.
4. The <u>Department of the Environment</u> concerns about the loss of habitats are well founded.
5. My <u>brother-in-law</u> hobby is butterfly collecting.

▶ **Exercise 68** Using Apostrophes to Show Ownership Put each of the underlined words in the correct possessive form as indicated in parentheses.

1. The <u>antennae and eyes</u> function is to send stimuli to the insect's brain. (individual)
2. <u>Butterflies and moths</u> physical characteristics are similar. (individual)
3. <u>Compound eyes and simple eyes</u> uses in an insect are different. (individual)
4. <u>Moths and butterflies</u> metamorphoses are complete metamorphoses. (joint)
5. Some <u>beetles and flies</u> form of metamorphosis is known as hypermetamorphosis. (joint)

▶ **Exercise 69** Using Apostrophes Correct the use of apostrophes in the underlined words.

1. <u>His'</u> butterfly collection is quite extensive.
2. I believe <u>your's</u> is quite interesting, too.

3. A lepidopterist is someone <u>who's</u> interest is butterflies and moths.
4. A butterfly spends <u>it's</u> larval stage as a caterpillar.
5. <u>Its</u> very hungry during this stage.
6. <u>Who's</u> bug cage is that?
7. At 7 <u>oclock</u>, the fly will lay her eggs.
8. <u>Jame's</u> cricket has six legs.
9. <u>Nobodys</u> butterfly hatched early.
10. It is nothing compared to <u>their's</u>.

▶ **Exercise 70** Find It in Your Reading Read the following excerpt from "Leiningen Versus the Ants." Explain the use of each apostrophe.

. . . The planter's chin jutted; they hadn't got him yet, and he'd see to it they never would. While he could think at all, he'd flout both death and the devil.

▶ **Exercise 71** Find It in Your Writing Look through your portfolio. Find examples of apostrophes in contractions and for possession. Make sure that you used apostrophes correctly.

▶ **Exercise 72** Writing Application Write five sentences of your own using the following guidelines.

1. Write a sentence that distinguishes *who's* from *whose.*
2. Write two sentences that distinguish joint and individual ownership using forms of *my friend and I.*
3. Write a sentence using *will not* as a contraction.
4. Write a sentence using the possessive of *complete sentence.*

722 • Punctuation

☑ ONGOING ASSESSMENT: Assess Mastery

Use the following resources to assess student mastery of punctuation.

In the Textbook	Print Resources	Technology
Chapter Review, Ex. 78–80 Standardized Test Preparation Workshop	*Formal Assessment,* Ch. 28	*Writing and Grammar* Interactive Text, Ch. 28, Chapter Review; *On-Line Exercise Bank,* Ch. 28

Chapter 28 Chapter Review

GRAMMAR EXERCISES 73–81

Exercise 73 Using End Marks

Write the proper end mark for each of the following sentences.

1. What beautiful colors on those dragonflies
2. Are there fossils of damselflies and dragonflies
3. The tiny openings in their outer skeletons are called spiracles
4. Hey Those compound eyes are enormous
5. Look at that dragonfly warming in the sun

Exercise 74 Using Commas

Rewrite the following sentences, adding commas where necessary.

1. Where there are hollow trees honeybees make their hives.
2. Beekeepers used to keep bees in baskets but now they use wooden boxes.
3. Bees store nectar honey and pollen in honeycombs.
4. The queen the drone and the worker make up the three castes in the honeybee community.
5. During their six weeks of life worker bees build the honeycomb clean the hive feed the young and defend the colony.
6. They are armed with straight barbed stingers.
7. The worker bees produce royal jelly a protein-rich substance from special glands.
8. This is fed to the larvae but after the first three days larvae are fed bee bread a mixture of pollen and honey.
9. Queen bees however are fed royal jelly for the duration of their development.
10. The stages of development that make up the complete metamorphosis are egg larva pupa and adult.
11. The worker bees use small soft lumps of wax to build the honeycomb.
12. Returning to the hive bees use either the round dance or the wagging dance to communicate.
13. Bees use different movements to communicate distance direction and location of food.
14. Pollen baskets filled by bees using small brushes on their hind legs carry pollen.
15. The study of insects which I find fascinating is called entomology.

Exercise 75 Using Semicolons and Colons Rewrite the following sentences, adding semicolons and colons where necessary.

1. Fireflies are actually beetles they are not really flies.
2. The light flashes steadily It is a code that sends messages.
3. Other insects use their sense of smell to find mates however, fireflies use light.
4. Each species seems to have its own signal it can be recognized by all members of the group.
5. A code is a complicated combination of speed and brightness It is like a visual Morse Code.
6. Carnivorous fireflies are found in one genus Photuris.
7. They will mimic the signals of other species as a result, they attract unsuspecting prey.
8. Female fireflies lay their eggs soon after mating at this time, they fly to damp areas near water.
9. Eggs pass from the insect's body through a tube the ovipositor.
10. There are several varieties of fireflies the pyralis, the insect-eating fireflies, and the glowworms.

CHAPTER REVIEW

These exercises correlate to the concepts taught in the chapter on punctuation. The exercises may be used for more practice, for reteaching, or for review of the key concepts presented.

Answer Key

Exercise 73

1. dragonflies!
2. dragonflies?
3. spiracles.
4. Hey! . . . enormous!
5. sun.

Exercise 74

1. Where there are hollow trees, honeybees make their hives.
2. Beekeepers used to keep bees in baskets, but now they use wooden boxes.
3. Bees store nectar, honey, and pollen in their honeycombs.
4. The queen, the drone, and the worker make up the three castes in the honeybee community.
5. During their six weeks of life, worker bees build the honeycomb, clean the hive, feed the young, and defend the colony.
6. They are armed with straight, barbed stingers.
7. The worker bees produce royal jelly, a protein-rich substance, from special glands.
8. This is fed to the larvae, but after the first three days, larvae are fed bee bread, a mixture of pollen and honey.
9. Queen bees, however, are fed royal jelly for the duration of their development.
10. The stages of development that make up a complete metamorphosis are egg, larva, pupa, and adult.
11. The worker bees use small, soft lumps of wax to build the honeycomb.
12. Returning to the hive, bees use either the round dance or the wagging dance to communicate.
13. Bees use different movements to communicate distance, direction, and location of food.
14. Pollen baskets, filled by bees using small brushes on their hind legs, carry pollen.
15. The study of insects, which I find fascinating, is called entomology.

continued

Answer Key continued

Exercise 75

1. Fireflies are actually beetles; they are not really flies.
2. The light flashes steadily: It is a code that sends messages.
3. Other insects use their sense of smell to find mates; however, fireflies use light.
4. Each species seems to have its own signal; it can be recognized by all members of the group.
5. A code is a complicated combination of speed and brightness: It is like a visual Morse Code.
6. Carnivorous fireflies are found in one genus: Photuris.
7. They will mimic the signals of other species; as a result, they attract unsuspecting prey.
8. Female fireflies lay their eggs soon after mating; at this time, they fly to damp areas near water.
9. Eggs pass from the insect's body through a tube: the ovipositor.
10. There are several varieties of fireflies: the pyralis, the insect-eating fireflies, and the glowworms.

Exercise 76

1. Did Muhammad Ali say, "Float like a butterfly; sting like a bee"?
2. In his book The Lord of the Flies, William Golding wrote, "Ralph wept for the end of innocence."
3. Golding's play The Brass Butterfly was published in 1958.
4. "Isn't Papillon, the French word for butterfly, the name of a movie starring Steve McQueen and Dustin Hoffman?" I asked.
5. Robert Schumann, himself a composer of works including Papillons, exclaimed about Chopin, "Hats off, gentlemen—a genius!"
6. Puccini's opera, Madame Butterfly, was initially a failure until he revised it.
7. "I didn't know 'The Flight of the Bumble Bee' is a song from an opera called Tsar Saltan," said Steve.
8. "Rudolf Friml was an American composer," he added, "who wrote the operetta called The Firefly."
9. "Really!" exclaimed my sister. "My favorite book is The Very Lonely Firefly."
10. "Also, A Bug's Life and Beetlejuice are two of my favorite movies," she told me.

Exercise 77

1. Butterflies and moths (Did you know they make up an order called Lepidoptera?) have many similarities and differences.
2. Some of their habits—for example, flying by day or flying by night—distinguish the two groups of insects.
3. Most butterflies are brightly colored while many moths are dull colored.
4. Butterflies have scale-covered wings.
5. Moths rest with their wings flattened—at least, some of them do.
6. The bodies of butterflies and moths have three main divisions: (1) head, (2) thorax, and (3) abdomen.
7. The body parts are made form a material called chitin (pronounced kite-in).
8. Moth antennae—they can sometimes be hair-like and sometimes feather-like—differ from butterfly antennae, which

---

Chapter Review Exercises cont'd.

Exercise 76 Using Quotation Marks and Underlining Copy the following sentences, using capitalization, punctuation marks, quotation marks, and underlining where appropriate. Quoted phrases are underlined so that you will know where they begin and end.

1. Did Muhammad Ali say float like a butterfly, sting like a bee
2. In his book The Lord of the Flies, William Golding wrote ralph wept for the end of innocence
3. Golding's play The Brass Butterfly was published in 1958.
4. Isn't Papillon, the French word for butterfly, the name of a movie starring Steve McQueen and Dustin Hoffman I asked
5. Robert Schumann, himself a composer of works including Papillons, exclaimed about Chopin hats off, gentlemen—a genius
6. Puccini's opera, Madame Butterfly, was initially a failure until Puccini revised it.
7. I didn't know The Flight of the Bumble Bee is a song from an opera called Tsar Saltan said Steve.
8. Rudolf Friml was an American composer he added who wrote the operetta called The Firefly.
9. Really exclaimed my sister my favorite book is The Very Lonely Firefly
10. Also, A Bug's Life and Beetlejuice are two of my favorite movies she told me.

Exercise 77 Using Dashes, Parentheses, and Hyphens Copy the following sentences, adding dashes, parentheses, and hyphens where necessary.

1. Butterflies and moths Did you know they make up an order called Lepidoptera? have many similarities and differences.
2. Some of their habits for example, flying by day or flying by night distinguish the two groups of insects.

724 • Punctuation

3. Most butterflies are brightly colored while many moths are dull colored.
4. Butterflies have scale covered wings.
5. Moths rest with their wings flattened at least, some of them do.
6. The bodies of butterflies and moths have three main divisions: 1 head, 2 thorax, and 3 abdomen.
7. The body parts are made from a material called chitin pronounced kite-in.
8. Moth antennae they can sometimes be hairlike and sometimes featherlike differ from butterfly antennae which have a knob at the ends.
9. The butterfly proboscis which is used to feed on nectar in the flowers remains coiled up under the head.
10. Of the types of butterflies and moths 160,000 more than three quarters are moths.

Exercise 78 Using Apostrophes Write the proper form of the word or words that require apostrophes in the following sentences. If a sentence is correct, write correct.

1. These insects usually lay thousands of eggs.
2. Butterflies and moths larvae contain the cells that produce adult insects.
3. A caterpillars first meal is its own eggshell.
4. It contains nutrients essential to the insects growth.
5. All caterpillars skin is very flexible.
6. The caterpillars head contains a brain and sense organs.
7. A hawkmoths caterpillar feeds on the bed straw plant.
8. The goat moths caterpillar lives in an apple tree, eating the trees wood for almost four years.
9. Moths dont eat holes in your clothes; their larvae do.
10. The caterpillars spinnerets produce silk threads, which make up the cocoon.

---

have a knob at the ends.
9. The butterfly proboscis—which is used to feed on nectar in the flowers—remains coiled up under the head.
10. Of the types of butterflies and moths (160,000), more than three quarters are moths.

Exercise 78

1. correct
2. Butterflies' and moths'
3. caterpillar's
4. insect's
5. caterpillars'
6. caterpillar's
7. hawkmoth's
8. goat moth's; tree's
9. don't
10. caterpillar's

Answer Key

Exercise 79 Proofreading Sentences for Punctuation Copy the following sentences, and use all of the rules of punctuation to add or correct the punctuation marks. Quoted phrases are underlined so that you will know where they begin and end.

1. In Lewis Carrolls, Alices Adventures in Wonderland, the Caterpillar says <u>I don't see</u>
2. The pupa the third, major stage in a butterfly or moths life transforms the caterpillar into an adult
3. A butterfly pupa chrysalis seems life-less, in fact extensive changes are tak-ing place: within the cocoon
4. Inside the shell the caterpillar is as Ben Franklin wrote, <u>snug / As a bug in a rug</u>
5. Cocoons change in order to survive They adapt their color and size to blend in with the surroundings
6. While the flambeaus chrysalis is rugged looking an owl butterflys appearance resembles a fragile dead leaf
7. Do the giant swallowtail once called the Orange Dog and the great mormon look like pieces of wood
8. The head; wings; abdomen; and thorax can be seen through the chrysalis Did you know some are bright pink while they develop over several weeks
9. Arthur Twidles illustrations including one called A Collector at Work decorate his book "Beautiful Butterflies of the Tropics".
10. The term butterfly may come from the butter colored fly; the name for one of the first butterflies to appear each spring in Europe
11. Moses Harris published an early work on butterflies The Aurelian in 1766
12. Butterflies are protected by law: Some countries forbid collecting and scien-tists must obtain a permit in order to study rare species

13. Moths that cannot see red light are attracted to smelly sugary liquids and will feed at night
14. Male butterflies and day flying moths are brightly colored but the females are much duller
15. <u>Remember</u> as James Gleick wrote <u>a butterfly stirring the air today in Peking can transform storm systems next month in New York</u>

Exercise 80 Proofreading a Passage for Punctuation and Capitalization On a separate sheet of paper, copy the following passage. Correct capitalization and punctuation.

have you ever considered an insect for a pet? most people—and i used to agree with them—would rather walk, over hot coals, than spend time in a room with a bug. mr. janus, my science teacher; changed my mind. My Science Class at lakeview high school in northridge, pennsylvania, raised monarch butterflies. monarchs fly south to mexico in early november. mr. janus used to say, "not all insects are nasty, biting creatures. the butterfly is a graceful and delicate thing" My whole class enjoyed the project and we learned a lot from Mr. Janus.

Exercise 81 Writing Application Write a summary of a movie or a book you have recently enjoyed. Include one or two direct quotations as well as the title of the work and the titles of similar works.

Answer Key

Exercise 79

1. In Lewis Carroll's <u>Alice's Adventures in Wonderland</u>, the Caterpillar says, "I don't see."
2. The pupa, the third major stage in a butterfly's or moth's life, transforms the caterpillar into an adult.
3. A butterfly's pupa (chrysalis) seems lifeless; in fact, extensive changes are taking place within the cocoon.
4. Inside the shell, the caterpillar is, as Ben Franklin wrote, "snug / As a bug in a rug."
5. Cocoons change in order to survive: They adapt their color and size to blend in with the surroundings.
6. While the flambeau's chrysalis is rugged looking, an owl butterfly's appearance resembles a fragile, dead leaf.
7. Do the giant swallowtail—once called the Orange Dog—and the great mormon look like pieces of wood?
8. The head, wings, abdomen, and thorax can be seen through the chrysalis (Did you know some are bright pink?) while they develop over several weeks.
9. Arthur Twidles's illustrations, including one called "A Collector at Work," decorate his book <u>Beautiful Butterflies of the Tropics</u>.
10. The term <u>butterfly</u> may come from the "butter-colored fly," the name for one of the first butterflies to appear each spring in Europe.
11. Moses Harris published an early work on butterflies, <u>The Aurelian</u>, in 1766.
12. Butterflies are protected by law: Some countries forbid collecting, and scientists must obtain a permit in order to study rare species.
13. Moths that cannot see red light are attracted to smelly, sugary liquids and will feed at night.
14. Male butterflies and day-flying moths are brightly colored, but the females are much duller.
15. "Remember," as James Gleick wrote, "a butterfly stirring the air today in Peking can transform storm systems next month in New York."

continued

Answer Key continued

Exercise 80

Have you ever considered an insect for a pet? Most people—and I used to agree with them—would rather walk over hot coals than spend time in a room with a bug. Mr. Janus, my science teacher, changed my mind. My science class at Lakeview High School in Northridge, Pennsylvania, raised monarch butterflies. Monarchs fly south to Mexico in early November. Mr. Janus used to say, "Not all insects are nasty, biting creatures. The butterfly is a graceful and delicate thing." My whole class enjoyed the project, and we learned a lot from Mr. Janus.

Exercise 81

Writing Application
Collect students' work and identify any problem areas that you will need to review.

Standardized Test Preparation Workshop

Revising, Editing, and Proofreading

Standardized tests often include items that measure your ability to revise, edit, and proofread. These sections may be set up as individual items, or you may be given a hypothetical peer-review situation. The following items will give you practice with both formats.

Sample Test Items	Answers and Explanations

Directions: Choose the best way to write each underlined section. If the underlined section needs no change, mark the choice "Correct as is."
 	
 "Look" she called, "up there"!
 (1)
 	
 1 A "Look she called, "up there."
     B "Look," she called, "up there!"
     C "Look"! she called "up there."
     D Correct as is
	The correct answer is *B*. As a part of the direct quotation, the exclamation mark belongs before the quotation mark. All other punctuation in this passage is correct.

Directions: You have been asked to read and critique a classmate's essay. Read the essay, and think about the suggestions you would make. Then, answer the multiple-choice questions that follow.
 	
 1 The science teacher directed the students;
 2 parents, and other guests to look at the
 3 migrating birds.
 	
 1 What is the BEST change to make to line1?
     A Capitalize *science*.
     B Change the semicolon to a comma.
     C Delete the semicolon.
     D Change *students* to *student's*.
	The correct answer is *B*. Items in this series should be separated by commas, not semicolons.

> **Practice 1** **Directions:** Choose the best way to write each underlined section. If the underlined section needs no change, mark the choice "Correct as is."

Last call for flight 1233 to Washington
(1)
D.C announced the ticket agent, "The
(2)
345 PM. flight to Washington, D.C. will be

leaving the gate immediately"!

1 A "Last call for flight 1233 to Washington D.C" announced the ticket agent.

B "Last call for flight 1233 to Washington, D.C" announced the ticket agent.

C "Last call for flight 1233 to Washington, D.C.," announced the ticket agent.

D Correct as is

2 F "The 3:45 PM flight to Washington, D.C., will be leaving the gate immediately!"

G "The 3:45 P.M. flight to Washington, D.C., will be leaving the gate immediately!"

H "The 3:45 PM flight to Washington, D.C., will be leaving the gate immediately!"

J Correct as is

> **Practice 2** **Directions:** After having each student write an essay about a cultural event, your English teacher has asked the class to exchange papers and critique each other's essays. You have received Beth's essay. As you read her composition, think about what suggestions you would make. Then, answer the multiple-choice questions that follow.

1 Joy Brandt of the Carolina Book Festival
2 announced "The nominees this year are
3 among the best ever we are very excited
4 to have such distinguished candidates".

1 What is the BEST way to rewrite lines 1–4?

A Joy Brandt, of the Carolina Book Festival, announced, The nominees this year are among the best ever." We are excited to have such distinguished candidates."

B Joy Brandt, of the Carolina Book Festival, announced, "The nominees this year are among the best ever. We are excited to have such distinguished candidates".

C Joy Brandt, of the Carolina Book Festival, announced, "The nominees this year are among the best ever. We are excited to have such distinguished candidates."

D Joy Brandt, of the Carolina Book Festival, announced, The nominees this year are among the best ever. We are excited to have such distinguished candidates."

Answer Key

> **Practice 1**

1. C
2. G

> **Practice 2**

1. C

Customize for
Less Advanced Students

To prepare for test questions on revising, proofreading, and editing, have students proofread each other's papers frequently in class. This way, they will be accustomed to using their proofreading skills on work other than their own. In addition, they will hone skills that they can then apply to their own writing.

Integrating Speaking and Listening Skills

Tell students that one way to spot run-on sentences is to read them aloud, listening for the natural stops that signify where one sentence ends and another begins. If these stops are not signaled by punctuation (semicolon or comma and conjunction), the sentence is probably a run-on.

Each of these exercises reviews concepts taught in the chapters on capitalization and punctuation. The exercises may be used for more practice, for review of the key concepts presented, or for assessment of student mastery of the major concepts.

Answer Key

Exercise A

1. James Russell Lowell, *The Atlantic Monthly*
2. Before, American Civil War
3. George Washington Cable, South, Confederate
4. In New Orleans, Louisiana, New Orleans *Times-Picayune*
5. Cable's, Creole, French, Spanish, *Scribner's Magazine*, United States, Great Britain
6. His, *Old Creole Days, The Creoles, Louisiana*
7. Joel Chandler Harris, Uncle Remus
8. He, *The Countryman*, southern
9. The, Brer Rabbit
10. Harris's, African American, southeastern United States
11. Francis Hopkinson Smith
12. The, *Colonel Carter, Cartersville*, Confederacy
13. Kate Chopin, Louisiana's Cajun, Creole
14. Two, *Bayou Folk, A Night, Acadie*
15. Her, *The Awakening*

Exercise B

1. state: Maine.
2. collection, *The Country of the Pointed Firs,* . . . 1896?
3. Hey! . . . *Deephaven: A Country Doctor* and *The Life of Nancy.*
4. Albany, New York; however, . . . California.
5. Camp," . . . Flat," . . .edited, *Overland Monthly?*
6. literature; . . . towns.
7. connections, . . . Krefeld, Germany; subsequently, . . . Glasgow, Scotland.
8. write, . . . stories: . . . Hamlin's."
9. Joaquin Miller, . . . Miller, . . . Native Americans, . . . newspaper, . . . judge, . . . poetry.
10. Yes. . . . California, . . . poetry.

Cumulative Review

MECHANICS

Exercise A | Using Capitalization

Copy all the items in the following sentences that require capitalization, adding the missing capitals.

1. james russell lowell was the editor of the magazine *the atlantic monthly.*
2. before and after the american civil war, he called for stories emphasizing local color.
3. george washington cable, a writer from the south, had served in the confederate army.
4. in new orleans, louisiana, he began to write for the new orleans *times-picayune* newspaper.
5. cable's stories about creole life, descendants from the french or spanish settlers, in scribner's magazine, made him famous in the united states and great britain.
6. his novels include *old creole days* and *the creoles of louisiana.*
7. joel chandler harris created the character of uncle remus.
8. he learned local dialects working on *the countryman*, a newspaper published by a southern plantation owner.
9. the stories contain animals like brer rabbit that act like humans.
10. harris's stories provide a record of oral african american folk tales from the southeastern united states.
11. francis hopkinson smith was both a painter and a writer.
12. the book *colonel carter of cartersville* presents a picture of life in the confederacy.
13. kate chopin depicted louisiana's cajun and creole cultures.
14. two of her short-story collections, *bayou folk* and *a night in acadie*, were published in the 1890's.
15. her last novel, *the awakening*, was both her most famous and most controversial.

Exercise B | Using End Marks, Commas, Semicolons, and Colons

Write the following sentences, inserting end marks, commas, semicolons, and colons where necessary.

1. Sarah Orne Jewett wrote short stories about people in a New England state Maine
2. Was her most famous collection *The Country of the Pointed Firs* written in 1896
3. Hey I also enjoyed *Deephaven A Country Doctor* and *The Life of Nancy*
4. Bret Harte was born in Albany New York however he moved to California
5. Did he write "The Luck of Roaring Camp" "The Outcasts of Poker Flat" and "Plain Language from Truthful James" for the magazine he edited *Overland Monthly*
6. These are classics of regional American literature his works are noted for their tales of life in mining towns
7. Through connections he became a United States consul in Krefeld Germany subsequently he was transferred to Glasgow Scotland
8. While in these positions he continued to write including two successful stories "An Ingénue of the Sierras" and "A Protégée of Jack Hamlin's"
9. Joaquin Miller the pen name of Cincinnatus Hiner Miller lived with Native Americans edited a newspaper became a judge and wrote poetry
10. Yes He settled in California and he incorporated the local color of the American West into his poetry

▶ Exercise C Using All the Rules of Punctuation Write the following sentences, inserting end marks, commas, semicolons, colons, quotation marks, underlining, dashes, parentheses, hyphens, and apostrophes where necessary.

1. The book whose full title is Poems of Sidney Lanier, Edited by His Wife contains works previously published in magazines like The Century Magazine Scribner's Magazine and Lippincott's Magazine
2. Sidney Laniers 1842 1881 best known poem is The Marshes of Glynn
3. Is that the poem written in 1879 that reads Beautiful glooms, soft dusks in the noon-day fire
4. After serving in the Confederate army performing as a flutist in a Baltimore Maryland orchestra and lecturing on English literature Lanier became renowned for his poetrys musical quality
5. Yes Lanier certainly lived his life in a different fashion from that of another famous poet of that era Emily Dickinson
6. Emily Dickinson Can you believe that most of her poetry wasnt published until four years after her death was born in Amherst Massachusetts
7. Her poems have very personal and profound they are include the themes of love death and immortality.
8. Didnt Dickinson 1830 1886 live her life mostly in seclusion
9. Most of Dickinsons poems are numbered rather than named and No 254 reads 'Hope' is the thing with feathers—
10. A three volume edition of her letters to friends was published in 1955 more than seventy years after her death

▶ Exercise D Proofreading Dialogue for Capitalization and Punctuation On a separate sheet of paper, rewrite the following dialogue, inserting the proper capitalization, punctuation, and indentation. (Each new speaker is indicated by an asterisk.)

* hey joanna have you ever heard of the humorists christine asked *dont you mean comedians replied joanna *no ted was telling me about writers like josh billings petroleum v nasby and artemus ward *well joanna commented their names certainly are funny. they were all very creative pseudonyms used by the writers who satirized people and politics using local dialects *that sounds very effective joanna said were these pieces written in *yes these writers were able to influence public opinion interrupted christine nasbys writing was published in newspapers like the *findlay jeffersonian* and the *toledo blade* *were these normal articles or opinions *Christine explained david ross locke wrote letters from the character nasby, an adopted persona during the civil war the letters helped the side of the north after the war he turned his attention to causes like temperance and womens rights *can we still read any of this writing today joanna asked *nasby's letters were published in books like *the nasby papers* and there is also the collection called *josh billings, his sayings* *carlos who had just entered the room asked hey are you talking about artemus ward the character created by charles farrar browne *not yet said christine but that is a similar story ward was a traveling showman who wrote with horribly incorrect spelling and grammar

▶ Exercise E WRITING APPLICATION
Write a brief first-person narrative that includes dialogue in which you and a friend discuss a book, a movie, or a television show that was made in America. Be sure to follow all the rules of capitalization and punctuation.

Answer Key continued

▶ Exercise D

Carlos, who had just entered the room, asked, "Hey, are you talking about Artemus Ward, the character created by Charles Farrar Browne?"

"Not yet," said Christine, "but that is a similar story. Ward was a traveling showman who wrote with horribly incorrect spelling and grammar."

▶ Exercise E

When students complete their narratives, have them exchange with a partner to be sure punctuation and capitalization are correct. Encourage students to refer to the textbook if they disagree about a particular rule.

▶ Exercise C

1. *Poems of Sidney Lanier, Edited by His Wife* . . . *The Century Magazine, Scribner's Magazine,* and *Lippincott's Magazine.*
2. Lanier's (1842–1881) . . . best-known "The Marshes of Glynn."
3. poem, written in 1879, that reads, "Beautiful glooms, soft dusks in the noon-day fire"?
4. army; . . . Baltimore, Maryland, orchestra; . . . literature; . . . poetry's musical quality.
5. Yes, . . . era, Emily Dickinson.
6. (Can you . . . wasn't . . . death?) . . . Amherst, Massachusetts.
7. (how very . . . they are) . . . love, death, and immortality.
8. Didn't Dickinson (1830–1886) . . . seclusion?
9. . . . Dickinson's . . . numbered, rather than named, and No. 254 reads "'Hope' is the thing with feathers—."
10. three-volume . . . 1955, . . . death.

▶ Exercise D

"Hey, Joanna, have you ever heard of the 'humorists'?" Christine asked.

"Don't you mean 'comedians'?" replied Joanna.

"No, Ted was telling me about writers like Josh Billings, Petroleum V. Nasby, and Artemus Ward."

"Well," Joanna commented, "their names certainly are funny."

"They were all very creative pseudonyms used by the writers who satirized people and politics using local dialects."

"That sounds very effective." Joanna said, "Were these pieces written in—"

"Yes, these writers were able to influence public opinion," interrupted Christine. "Nasby's writing was published in newspapers like the *Findlay Jeffersonian* and the *Toledo Blade.*"

"Were these normal articles or opinions?"

Christine explained, "David Ross Locke wrote letters from the character Nasby (an adopted persona) during the Civil War. The letters helped the side of the North. After the war, he turned his attention to causes like temperance and women's rights."

"Can we still read any of this writing today?" Joanna asked.

"Nasby's letters were published in books like *The Nasby Papers,* and there is also the collection called *Josh Billings: His Sayings.*"

continued

Sentence Diagraming Workshop

Subjects, Verbs, and Modifiers

To diagram a sentence with just a subject and a verb, draw a horizontal line, place the subject on the left, the verb on the right, and then draw a vertical line to separate the subject from the verb.

                         S   V
EXAMPLE: Kathleen laughed.

Kathleen	laughed

When you diagram adjectives, place them on slanted lines directly below the nouns or pronouns they modify. Similarly, place adverbs on slanted lines directly below the verbs, adjectives, or other adverbs they modify.

               ADV   ADJ   ADJ   ADV   ADV
EXAMPLE: Quite hesitant, my sister did not answer quickly.

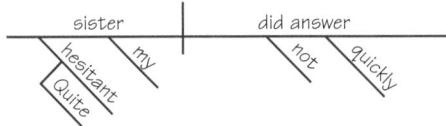

Orders and directions whose subjects are understood to be *you* are diagramed in the usual way, with parentheses around the understood subject. Inverted sentences also follow the usual subject-verb order in a diagram. The capital letter shows which word begins the sentence.

                    ORDER   QUESTION
EXAMPLES: Stand up.   How are you?

(you)	Stand		you	are
-------	-------		-----	-----
	up			How

Usually when *there* or *here* begins a sentence, it will function as an adverb modifying the verb. In this case, it should be diagramed on a slanted line below the verb.

Sometimes, however, *there* is used simply to get the sentence started. In this case, it is an expletive. Diagram an expletive by placing it on a short horizontal line above the subject. Diagram interjections and nouns of direct address in the same way.

EXAMPLES:

EXP
There was a storm.

INT   N of DA
Alas, my friend, you lost.

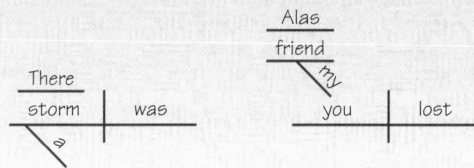

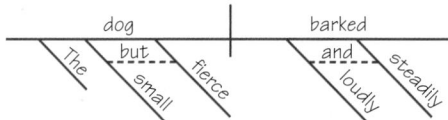

> **Exercise 1** Diagraming Subjects, Verbs, and Modifiers

Correctly diagram each sentence.
1. Mr. Ricardo, come here.
2. The ship wandered quite aimlessly.
3. Swallows soared overhead.
4. The beautiful white waterfall thunderously cascaded down.
5. There should be a parade today.

Adding Conjunctions

Conjunctions are diagramed on dotted lines drawn between the words they connect. In the example, coordinating conjunctions are used to join both adjectives and adverbs.

EXAMPLE:

CONJ   CONJ
The small but fierce dog barked loudly and steadily.

Conjunctions that connect compound subjects and compound verbs are also written on dotted lines drawn between the words they connect. Notice in the example on the next page how the horizontal line of the diagram is split so that each part of a compound subject or verb appears on a line of its own. Notice also the position of the correlative conjunctions *neither* and *nor.*

Sentence Diagraming Workshop • 731

Answer Key

> **Exercise 1**

1.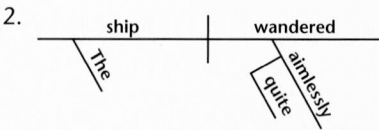

2.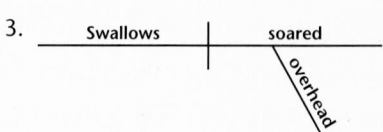

3.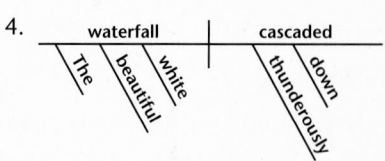

4.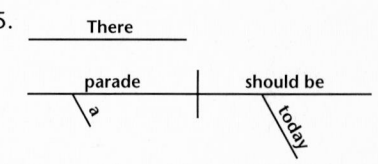

5.

Answer Key

Exercise 2

1.

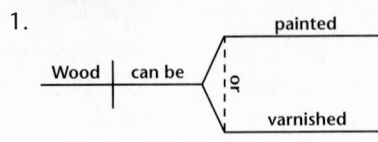

2.

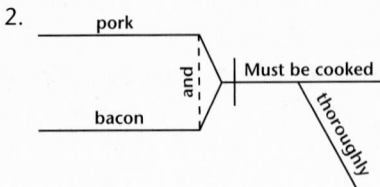

3.

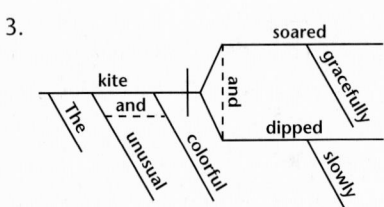

4.

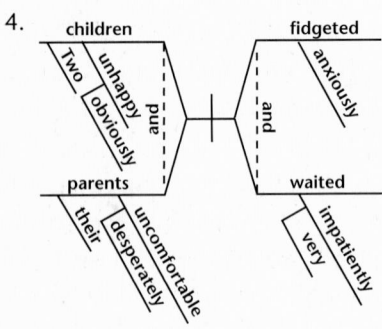

5.

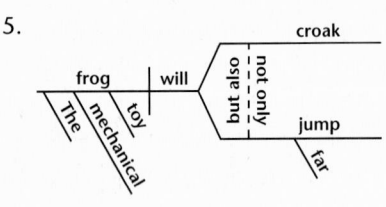

CONJ   CONJ   CONJ

EXAMPLE: Neither Amanda nor Lisa wrote or called.

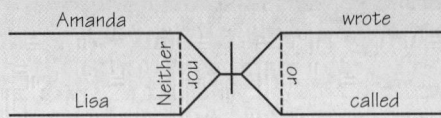

When a modifier modifies both parts of a compound subject or verb, however, it is placed under the main line of the diagram. In the example below, the adverb *confidently* modifies both parts of the compound verb, so it is placed under the main line.

ADV   ADJ   ADJ

EXAMPLE: Confidently, the children and their parents

              ADV   ADV

walked in and sat down.

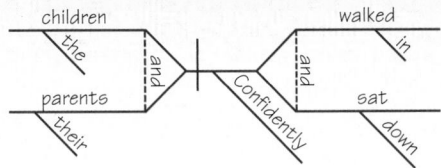

Exercise 2 Diagraming Sentences With Conjunctions

Correctly diagram each sentence.

1. Wood can be painted or varnished.
2. Must pork and bacon be cooked thoroughly?
3. The unusual and colorful kite soared gracefully and slowly dipped.
4. Two obviously unhappy children and their desperately uncomfortable parents fidgeted anxiously and waited very impatiently.
5. The mechanical toy frog will not only croak but also jump far.

Complements

In a diagram, a direct object is positioned on the main horizontal line after the verb. A short vertical line is added to separate it from the verb. An indirect object is placed on a horizontal line extended from a slanted line directly below the verb.

                         DO   IO   DO

EXAMPLES: Sue wore a gold chain.   I gave Ted advice.

Because an objective complement helps complete the meaning of a direct object, they are placed side by side. A short slanted line is added to separate the direct object from the objective complement.

EXAMPLE:
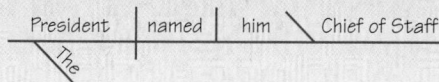
The President named him Chief of Staff.

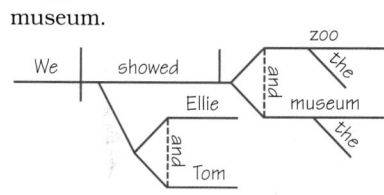

Both predicate nominatives and predicate adjectives are also placed on the main horizontal line after the verb. A short, slanted line is used to separate them from the verb.

EXAMPLES:
My dog is a spaniel.   We felt grouchy.

As the following example shows, compound complements are diagramed by splitting the lines on which they appear. Conjunctions are placed on dotted lines drawn between the words they connect.

EXAMPLE:
We showed Ellie and Tom the zoo and the museum.

Exercise 3 Diagraming Complements Correctly diagram each sentence.
1. The irritable little boy pushed his food away.
2. This remarkable but true story taught Sally and me something.
3. His shy and cautious manner gave June and me courage.
4. The fresh, clean mountain air felt wonderful.
5. Her husband is a friend and a companion.

Answer Key

▶ **Exercise 3**

1.
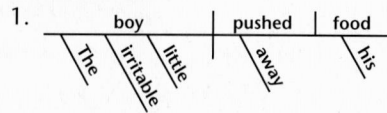

2.
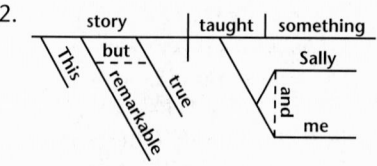

3.
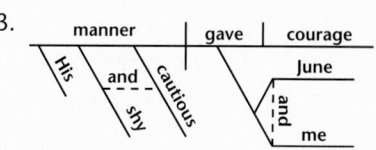

4.
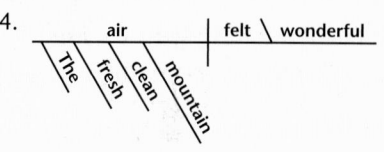

5.
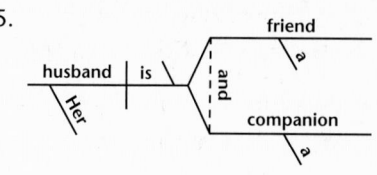

Answer Key

> **Exercise 4**

1.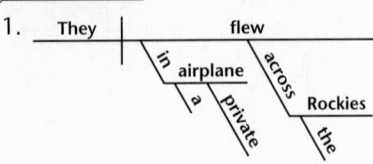

2.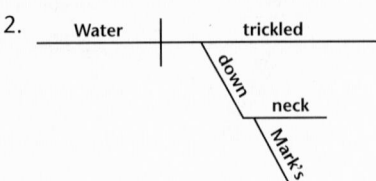

3.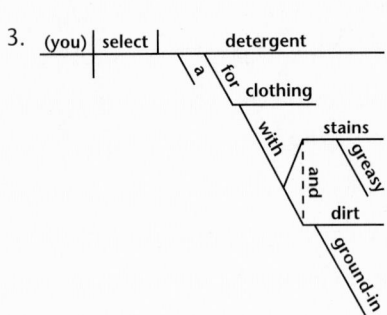

4.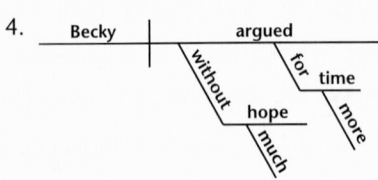

5.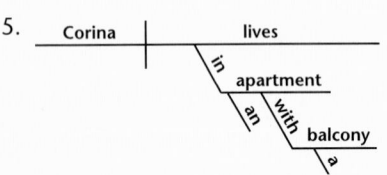

Prepositional Phrases

The diagram for a prepositional phrase has a slanted line for the preposition and a horizontal line for the object of the preposition. Modifiers are placed on slanted lines below the horizontal line. Adjective phrases are placed directly below the noun or pronoun they modify. Adverb phrases are placed directly below the verb, adjective, or adverb they modify.

EXAMPLE: The child *with the red ball* skipped *up the hill.*

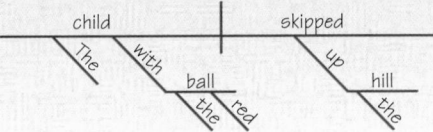

An adjective phrase that modifies the object of the preposition of another prepositional phrase goes below the other phrase.

EXAMPLE: I had salad *with pineapple in it.*

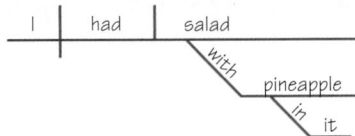

A prepositional phrase with a compound object is diagramed in the same way as the other compound parts of a sentence. The following example shows an adjective phrase that modifies a direct object.

EXAMPLE: We need a house *with three bedrooms and a den.*

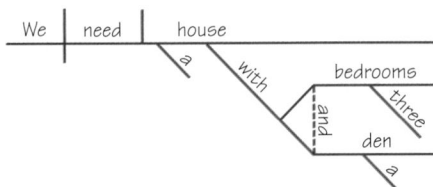

Exercise 4 Diagraming Prepositional Phrases Correctly diagram each sentence.

1. They flew in a private airplane across the Rockies.
2. Water trickled down Mark's neck.
3. Select a detergent for clothing with greasy stains and ground-in dirt.
4. Without much hope, Becky argued for more time.
5. Corina lives in an apartment with a balcony.

Appositives and Appositive Phrases

An appositive is placed in parentheses beside the noun or pronoun it identifies, renames, or explains. Any adjectives or adjective phrases included in an appositive phrase are placed directly beneath the appositive.

APPOSITIVE PHRASE

EXAMPLE: Harriet Danby, *her friend for many years*, is a lawyer.

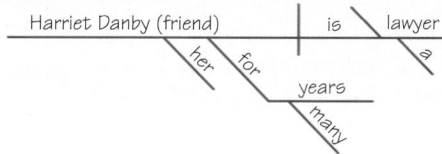

Exercise 5 Diagraming Appositives and Appositive Phrases Correctly diagram each sentence.

1. Gladys was a pianist, a very talented performer.
2. I know the author of that book, one of the top bestsellers.
3. The rat, a rodent, has one pair of upper incisors.
4. Mario prepared the meal, a lavish feast with six courses.
5. Their staircase, a spiral flight of steps, needs repair.

Participles and Participial Phrases

Because participles act as adjectives, they are placed directly beneath the noun or pronoun they modify. Unlike adjectives, however, participles are positioned partly on a horizontal line that extends from the slanted line. An adverb or adverb phrase that modifies a participle is placed below it. When a participle has a complement, the complement is also placed in its normal position, on the horizontal line with the participle, separated from the participle by a short vertical line. See the example on the next page.

Sentence Diagraming Workshop • 735

Exercise 5

1.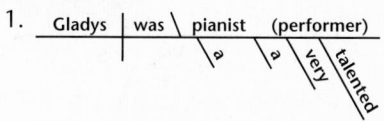

2.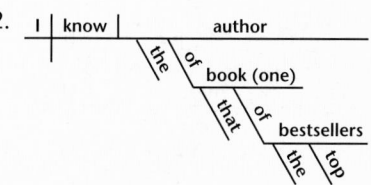

3.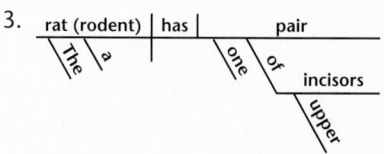

4.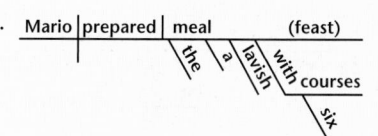

5.

Answer Key

1.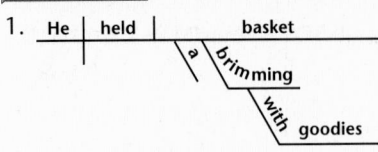

2.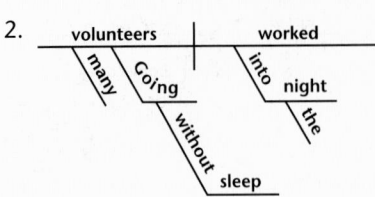

3.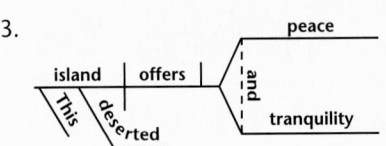

4.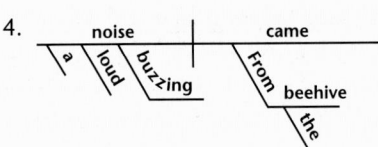

5.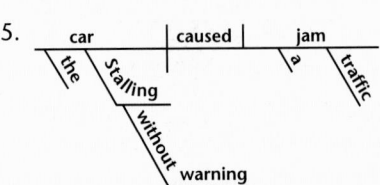

EXAMPLE: *Carefully reviewing books for children,* Russell stays busy.

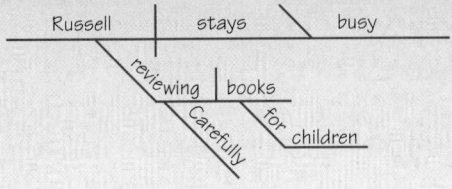

▶ **Exercise 6** Diagraming Participles and Participial Phrases
Correctly diagram each sentence.
1. He held a basket brimming with goodies.
2. Going without sleep, many volunteers worked into the night.
3. This deserted island offers peace and tranquillity.
4. From the beehive came a loud buzzing noise.
5. Stalling without warning, the car caused a traffic jam.

Gerunds and Gerund Phrases

A gerund that acts as a subject, direct object, or predicate nominative is diagramed on a pedestal above the main horizontal line of the diagram. Modifiers and complements that are part of a gerund phrase are added to the diagram in the usual way. Notice the shape of the line on which the gerund rests.

EXAMPLE: The lease forbids *keeping any pets on the premises.*

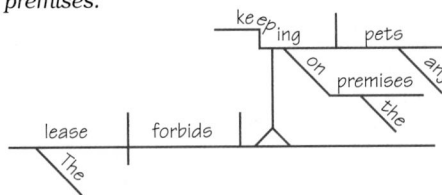

A gerund or gerund phrase that acts as an indirect object or an object of a preposition is placed on a line slanting down from the main horizontal line.

EXAMPLE: His lecture gave *traveling to South America* new dimensions.

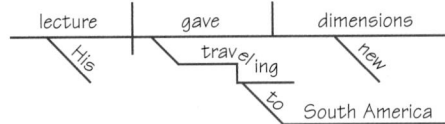

A gerund or gerund phrase that acts as an appositive is placed on a pedestal, in parentheses, next to the noun or pronoun it accompanies. The example below shows a diagram containing an appositive modifying a direct object.

GERUND PHRASE

EXAMPLE: We mastered one sport, *playing tennis.*

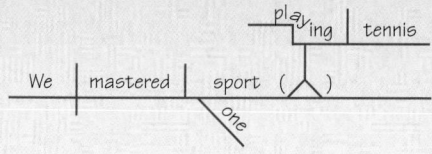

Exercise 7 Diagraming Gerunds and Gerund Phrases
Correctly diagram each sentence.
1. His favorite activity was hiking through the woods.
2. Achieving the position of senator will be very difficult.
3. Their ability to harmonize made songwriting exciting.
4. Clark's fear, injuring his elbow, kept him on the bench.
5. All of Jill's friends like helping her with her projects.

Infinitives and Infinitive Phrases

Infinitives and infinitive phrases can act as nouns, adjectives, or adverbs. An infinitive acting as a noun is generally diagramed on a pedestal just as a gerund is, but the line on which the infinitive rests is simpler.

INFINITIVE PHRASE

EXAMPLE: She wanted *to show us her stamp collection.*

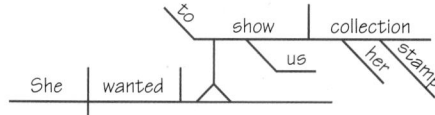

If an infinitive phrase has a subject, add it at the left.

INFINITIVE PHRASE

EXAMPLE: We asked her *to stay.*

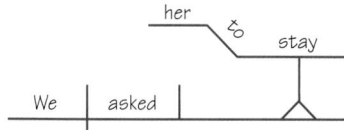

Sentence Diagraming Workshop • 737

Answer Key

▶ Exercise 7

1.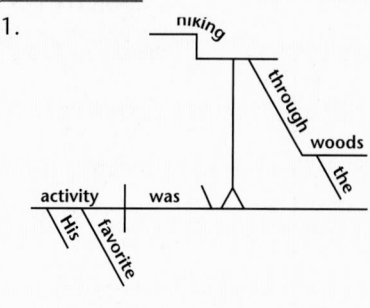

2.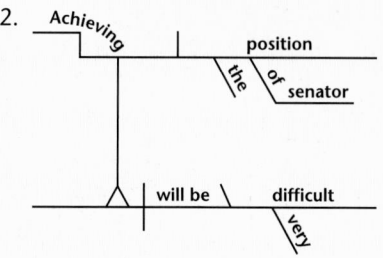

3.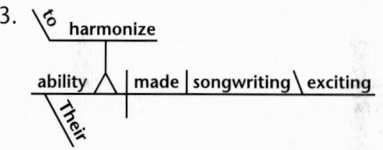

4.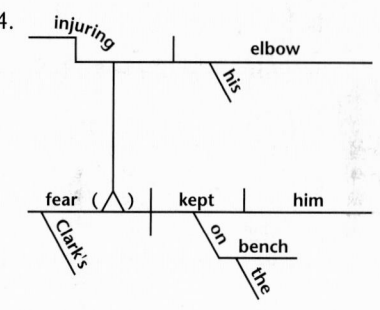

5.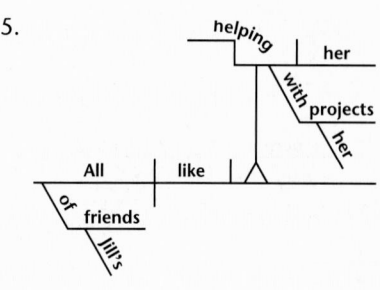

Answer Key

1.

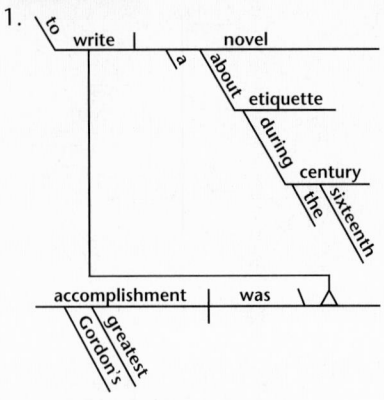

2.

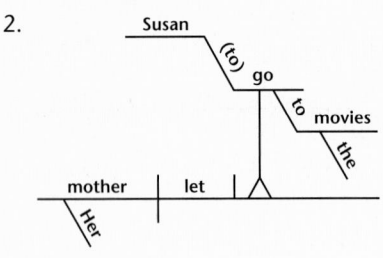

3.

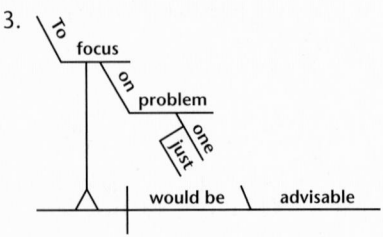

4.

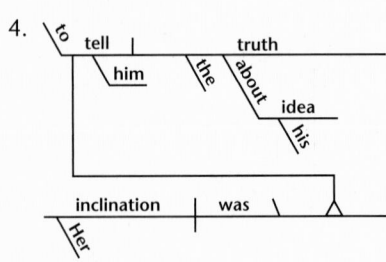

5.

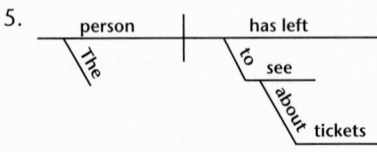

An infinitive acting as an adjective or adverb is diagramed much as a prepositional phrase is.

INFINITIVE

EXAMPLE: Beth was proud *to try.*

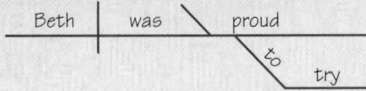

When an infinitive in a sentence does not include the word *to*, add it to the sentence diagram in parentheses.

INFINITIVE PHRASE

EXAMPLE: Clancy helped me *climb the ladder to the attic.*

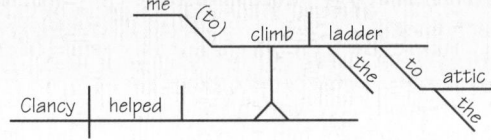

Exercise 8 Diagraming Infinitives and Infinitive Phrases

Correctly diagram each sentence.
1. Gordon's greatest accomplishment was to write a novel about etiquette during the sixteenth century.
2. Her mother let Susan go to the movies.
3. To focus on just one problem would be advisable.
4. Her inclination was to tell him the truth about his idea.
5. The person to see about tickets has left.

Compound Sentences

To diagram a compound sentence, just diagram each independent clause separately. Then, join them at the verbs with a dotted line on which the conjunction or semicolon is placed.

INDEPENDENT CLAUSE

EXAMPLE: *A gentle breeze blew across the lake,* and

INDEPENDENT CLAUSE

the raft floated inland.

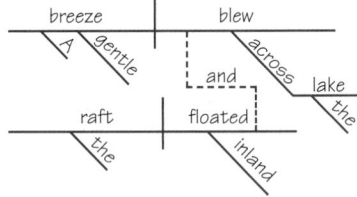

> **Exercise 9** Compound Sentences Diagram each sentence.
> 1. His temperature is high, but he remains alert.
> 2. Should I plant this cherry tree in that corner, or would you prefer it near the fence?
> 3. The steak was perfect, and the salad was excellent, but the dessert was too sweet.
> 4. Joan has little sense of her own worth; she never asserts herself.
> 5. Yesterday, we cleaned the attic and filled boxes with useless items; later, we went to the dump.

Complex Sentences

Complex sentences have an independent clause and one or more adjective, adverb, or noun clauses. Each clause is placed on a separate horizontal line.

Adjective Clauses To diagram a sentence with an adjective clause, first diagram the independent clause. Then, diagram the adjective clause beneath it. Connect the two clauses with a dotted line that extends from the modified noun or pronoun in the independent clause to the relative pronoun or relative adverb in the adjective clause. The position of the relative pronoun changes depending on its function in the adjective clause. In the following example, the relative pronoun is acting as the direct object of the adjective clause.

ADJECTIVE CLAUSE
EXAMPLE: My friend *whom you met yesterday* just called.

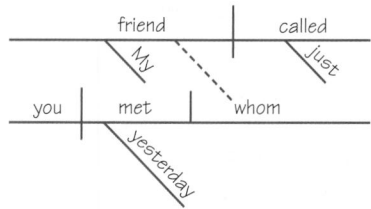

When a relative pronoun acts as an object of a preposition or as an adjective or when a clause is introduced by a relative adverb, the dotted line must be bent to connect the clauses.

ADJECTIVE CLAUSE
EXAMPLE: I need time *when I can study*.

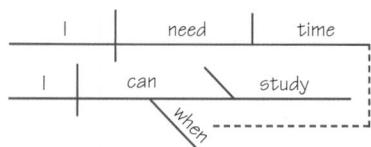

Sentence Diagraming Workshop • **739**

1.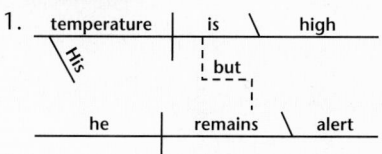

2.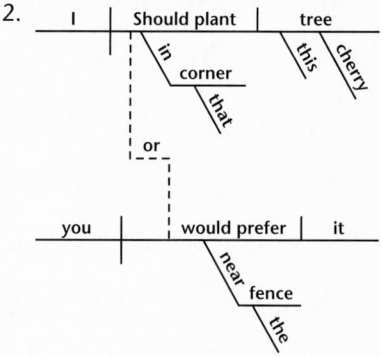

3.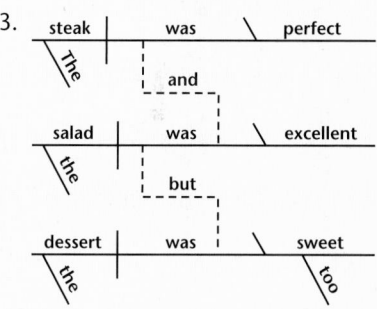

4.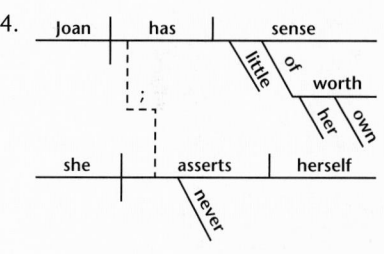

5.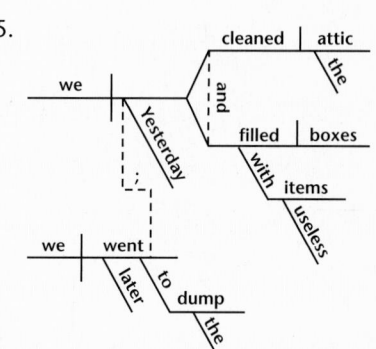

Adverb Clauses The main difference between a diagram for an adjective clause and one for an adverb clause is that the subordinating conjunction for an adverb clause is written on the dotted line. This line extends from the modified verb, adjective, adverb, or verbal in the main clause to the verb in the adverb clause.

ADVERB CLAUSE

EXAMPLE: To look *before you leap* is good advice.

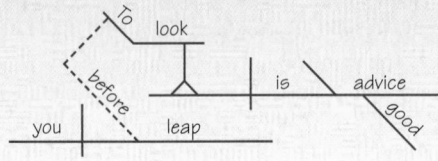

Noun Clauses When diagraming a sentence with a noun clause, first diagram the independent clause. Then, place the entire noun clause on a pedestal extending upward from the position the noun clause fills in the sentence. Notice that the pedestal meets the noun clause at the verb.

NOUN CLAUSE

EXAMPLE: *Whatever you decide* is fine with me.

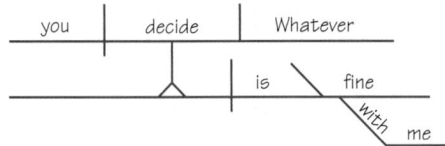

When an introductory word in a noun clause has no function in the clause, it is written alongside the pedestal.

NOUN CLAUSE

EXAMPLE: The question, *whether Jonas is truly sorry,* will be revealed in the next episode.

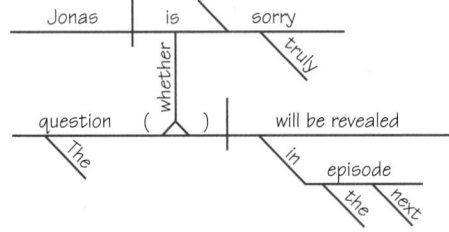

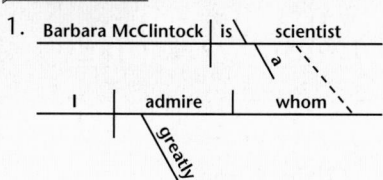

1.

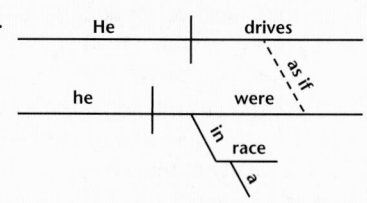

2.

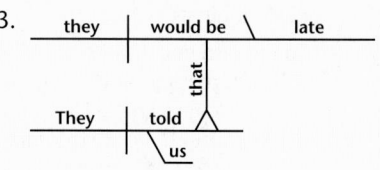

3.

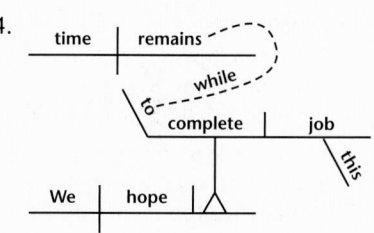

4.

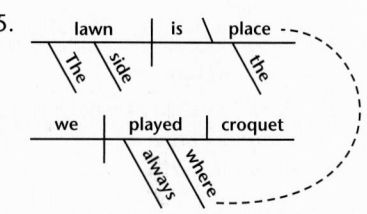

5.

continued

Exercise 10 | Diagraming Complex Sentences Correctly diagram each sentence.

1. Barbara McClintock is a scientist whom I greatly admire.
2. He drives as if he were in a race.
3. They told us that they would be late.
4. We hope to complete this job while time remains.
5. The side lawn is the place where we always played croquet.

Compound-Complex Sentences

To diagram a compound-complex sentence, begin by diagraming and connecting each of the independent clauses just as you would if you were diagraming a compound sentence. Then, diagram and connect each subordinate clause.

ADVERB CLAUSE

EXAMPLE: *When we bought our microwave oven,* we considered that brand, but we decided *that it was too expensive.*

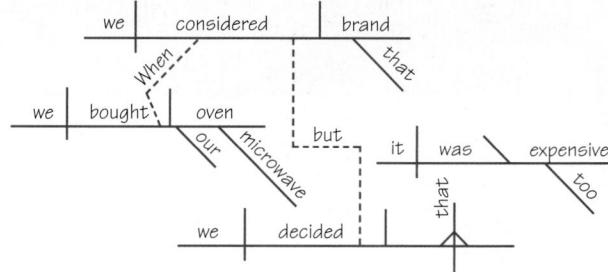

Exercise 11 | Diagraming Compound-Complex Sentences

Correctly diagram each sentence.

1. Because it rained, we missed the game that had been scheduled, but we still had a good time.
2. We waited until the plane landed, and then we rushed to the gate where the passengers would enter.

Answer Key continued

Exercise 11

1.

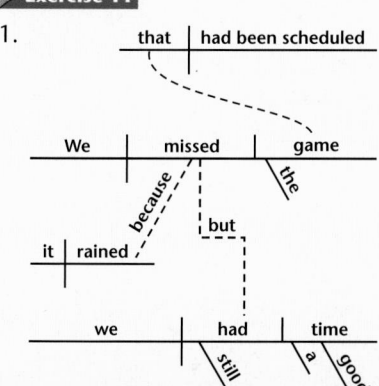

2.

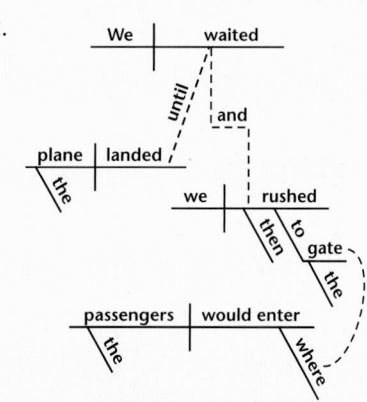

► *Objectives*

1. To develop critical listening and effective speaking skills and apply them to various types of presentations

2. To understand and evaluate visual images and messages in a variety of media

3. To produce visual images, messages, and meanings that communicate with others

4. To expand vocabulary through reading and listening and by developing skills in using context, word structure, word origins, and reference tools to determine word meanings

5. To develop and apply reading strategies for a variety purposes and texts

6. To develop study and research skills and become familiar with reference tools and the resources of libraries and the Internet

7. To develop skills in taking tests in various formats

8. To learn and apply specific communication and procedural skills of the workplace, including problem-solving and managing time and money

The Library, 1960, Jacob Lawrence, National Museum of American Art, Washington, D.C.

PART

3

Academic and Workplace Skills

Academic and Workplace Skills • **743**

Responding to Fine Art

The Library by Jacob Lawrence

Use this work of art to start a discussion about the definition of academic and workplace skills.

1. Have students examine the painting on pages 742–743. You might use the following questions to prompt discussion:

   Is the library in the city or in a small town? Who are the people pictured? What kinds of tasks are they engaged in?

   Might the scene pictured be a place of business as well as a library? What kind of business might it be? Which details in the picture suggest answers to these questions?

2. Students might suggest that the characters are studying for school assignments, simply reading for pleasure, or working. Ask them to explain why and how writing is important in the workplace. What are some other skills that are necessary for success in almost every workplace? Which skills do students hope to improve?

About the Artist

Jacob Lawrence (b. 1917) is a distinguished African American artist known for his paintings of the daily lives of black people and of episodes from African American history. His bright, highly graphic style highlights the drama in his scenes. An early influence was Diego Rivera, who also used simple forms and bright colors to paint the lives of ordinary people. Lawrence has produced several series of paintings showing the lives and accomplishments of those who struggled to free slaves, including Harriet Tubman, Toussaint L'Ouverture, and Frederick Douglass.

In-Depth Lesson Plan

	LESSON FOCUS	PRINT AND MEDIA RESOURCES
DAY 1	**Speaking and Listening Skills** Students learn key elements of speaking in a group discussion, speaking in public, and preparing, presenting, and evaluating a speech. (pp. 744–748/⊞546–550)	**Teaching Resources** *Academic and Workplace Skills Activity Book,* pp. 1–2
DAY 2	**Speaking and Listening Skills** *continued* Students learn to listen critically and ask different types of questions. (pp. 749–751/⊞551–553)	**Teaching Resources** *Academic and Workplace Skills Activity Book,* p. 3
DAY 3	**Viewing Skills** Students interpret maps and graphs and view media and fine art critically. (pp. 752–757/⊞554–559)	**Teaching Resources** *Academic and Workplace Skills Activity Book,* pp. 4–7
DAY 4	**Representing Skills** Students create graphic organizers, use formatting, and plan a multimedia presentation. (pp. 758–761/⊞560–563)	**Teaching Resources** *Academic and Workplace Skills Activity Book,* pp. 8–10
DAY 5	**Representing Skills** *continued* Students produce a video and learn about performing and interpreting. (pp. 762–763/⊞564–565)	**Teaching Resources** *Academic and Workplace Skills Activity Book,* pp. 11–12; *Formal Assessment,* Ch. 29

Accelerated Lesson Plan

	LESSON FOCUS	PRINT AND MEDIA RESOURCES
DAY 1	**Speaking and Listening Skills** Students learn about key elements of effective speaking and listening skills. (pp. 744–751/⊞546–553)	**Teaching Resources** *Academic and Workplace Skills Activity Book,* pp. 1–3
DAY 2	**Viewing Skills** Students interpret maps and graphs and view media and fine art critically. (pp. 752–757/⊞554–559)	**Teaching Resources** *Academic and Workplace Skills Activity Book,* pp. 4–7
DAY 3	**Representing Skills** Students cover use of graphic organizers, work with multimedia, and learn about performing and interpreting. (pp. 758–763/⊞560–565)	**Teaching Resources** *Academic and Workplace Skills Activity Book,* pp. 8–12; *Formal Assessment,* Ch. 29

Options for Adapting Lesson Plans

HOMEWORK

Have students complete any stage of the chapter for homework.

FEATURES

Extend coverage with the Standardized Test Preparation Workshop (p. 764).

Writing and Grammar Handbook Alignment

Page numbers in Step-by-Step Teaching Guides in this Teacher's Edition refer to pages from the full student text. Handbook page references, indicated with this icon **H**, are provided in Time and Resource Manager boxes and at the bottom of each Teacher's Edition page.

INTEGRATED SKILLS COVERAGE

Viewing and Representing
Critical Viewing, SE pp. 744, 746, 752, 753, 754/**H**546, 548, 554, 555, 556
ATE p. 750

Research Skills
SE pp. 748, 752, 757/**H**550, 554, 559

Technology Skills
SE pp. 747, 749, 751, 757, 759, 760, 761/**H**549, 551, 553, 559, 561, 562, 563
ATE p. 752

Vocabulary Skills ATE p. 755

Real-World Connection ATE p. 746

Workplace Skills
ATE p. 752

ASSESSMENT SUPPORT

Standardized Test Preparation Workshop SE p. 764; ATE p. 756

Standardized Test Preparation Workbook, pp. 57–58

Formal Assessment, Ch. 29

MEETING INDIVIDUAL NEEDS

Less Advanced Students ATE pp. 746, 762, 765. See also Ongoing Assessments ATE pp. 750, 759.

More Advanced Students ATE pp. 749, 754, 761, 765

ESL Students ATE pp. 748, 751, 763, 765

Linguistic Learners ATE p. 760

Spatial Learners ATE pp. 747, 757

BLOCK SCHEDULING

Pacing Suggestions
For 90-minute Blocks
• Have students complete the Speaking and Listening Skills sections in a single period.
• Focus one class period on Viewing and Representing Skills. Allow an additional period for student presentations.

Resources for Varying Instruction
• *Academic and Workplace Skills Activity Book,* pp. 1–12

Professional Development Support
• *How to Manage Instruction in the Block* This teaching resource provides management and activity suggestions.

MEDIA AND TECHNOLOGY

For the Teacher
• **Teacher**EXPRESS™ CD-ROM

WRITING AND GRAMMAR ON-LINE

Interactive Text (On-line or on CD-ROM)
• Easily navigable instruction with interactive Revision Checkers
• Full use of e-rater™, the essay-scoring system (on-line only)

Companion Web Site PHSchool.com
• Scoring rubrics with models (use Web Code eek-1001)

See the Go On-line! **feature, SE p. iii.**

Lesson Objectives

1. To use informal, standard, and technical language effectively to meet the needs of purpose, audience, occasion, and task

2. To communicate effectively in conversations and group discussions

3. To use language and rhetorical strategies skillfully in informative and persuasive messages

4. To make informed, accurate, truthful, and ethical presentations

5. To demonstrate proficiency in critical, empathic, appreciative, and reflective listening

6. To represent information in a variety of ways, such as graphic organizers

7. To evaluate and critique the persuasive techniques of media messages, such as glittering generalities, logical fallacies, and symbols

8. To use a variety of forms and technologies such as videos to communicate specific messages

9. To present interpretations by telling stories, performing original works, and interpreting poems and stories for a variety of audiences

Critical Viewing

Infer Students' responses should reflect an understanding of the characteristics of a good listener.

Chapter 29 Speaking, Listening, Viewing, and Representing

▲ **Critical Viewing**
Which of these students is speaking? Which is listening most attentively? Explain your choices. **[Infer]**

Speaking, listening, viewing, and representing are all unique forms of communication used for conveying and receiving information. Speaking and listening both use language to represent ideas. Therefore, understanding language is the key to developing good speaking and listening skills.

Forms of viewing and representing also use language to convey information, but always in combination with visual representations. Learning how to interpret these visual representations and seeing how they work with language to present meaning is the first step in improving your viewing and representing skills.

All together, speaking, listening, viewing, and representing are the building blocks of communication and of one's view of the world.

744 • Speaking, Listening, Viewing, and Representing

⏱ TIME AND RESOURCE MANAGER

Resources
Print: *Academic and Workplace Skills Activity Book*, pp. 1–3

Using the Full Student Edition	Using the Handbook Ⓗ
• Cover pp. 744–751 in class. • Have students work in groups on Exercise 1. • Work through Public Speaking and Critical Listening as a group. • Have students do Exercises 2–8 in class.	• Cover pp. 546–553 in class. • Have students work in groups on Exercise 1. • Work through Public Speaking and Critical Listening as a group. • Have students do Exercises 2–8 in class.

Section 29.1 Speaking and Listening Skills

In school, good speaking and listening skills are essential for success. Learning how to take part in group discussions and how to give a well-prepared oral presentation are two activities that require good speaking skills.

Critical listening skills are important also. Learning how to become a critical listener will enable you to understand and evaluate the most important points in a speaker's message.

Speaking in a Group Discussion

In school, you will most likely participate in a number of *group discussions*, or informal meetings used to openly discuss ideas. These group discussions will focus on subjects you are studying or activities being planned. To get the most from a group discussion, you have to learn to participate in it.

Communicating Effectively Effective communication means thinking before speaking. Plan the points you want to make and how you will express them. Organize these points in a logical order. Think of examples or supporting facts to illustrate your points. Also, remember to speak clearly, pronouncing words slowly and carefully.

Asking Questions Get in the habit of asking questions. Asking questions can help you clarify your understanding of another speaker's ideas. Questions can also be used to call attention to possible errors in the speaker's points or areas of confusion.

Making Relevant Contributions The information or ideas you choose to contribute should be related to the topic being discussed. When you do contribute, clearly show how your ideas are connected to the topic.

▶ **Exercise 1** Policy Discussion With three to five other students, hold a fifteen-minute group discussion about the benefits and drawbacks of a particular school policy. After the discussion, write a brief journal entry about how you used the strategies above as you participated.

▶ **More Practice**

Academic and
Workplace Skills
Activity Book
• p. 1

☑ ONGOING ASSESSMENT: Diagnose

Use one of the following options to diagnose students' current levels of proficiency in speaking and listening.

Option 1 Have students make a list of critical listening strategies. If they have trouble thinking of strategies other than taking notes, they might need extra support in this area.	**Option 2** Show students an advertisement from a magazine and ask them to list at least two persuasive techniques it uses. If students have difficulty with this exercise, they might need extra support in critical viewing skills and evaluating persuasive techniques.

PREPARE and ENGAGE

Interest GRABBER Have one student make a simple sketch. Without allowing the class to look at the drawing or ask questions, have that student tell the class how to recreate the drawing in their own notebooks. Ask students what would make the activity easier (knowing a title for the drawing, being able to ask questions, or to see the drawing).

Activate Prior Knowledge

Ask students to remember when they had a good discussion with someone or listened to a good speech. What made these experiences memorable, understandable, or positive? Refer students to the elements of a good discussion on this page.

Step-by-Step Teaching Guide

Speaking in a Group Discussion

Teaching Resources: Academic and Workplace Skills Activity Book, p. 1

1. Point out that group discussions are a common part of life. Classroom discussions, club meetings, and planning committees are a few examples.

2. Ask students how the guidelines given in the text can contribute to the success of a discussion, particularly in more formal situations, where something needs to be accomplished. (Students may note that each item listed helps ensure that everyone knows key information, and that the group keeps moving towards its goal.)

3. Emphasize that good manners and patience also contribute to the success of group discussions.

Answer Key

▶ **Exercise 1**

At the completion of the exercise, ask students for feedback on the discussions. Which strategies were most helpful? You may wish to have a few volunteers share their journal entries.

Understanding Different Types of Speeches

Teaching Resources: Academic and Workplace Skills Activity Book, p. 2

1. Refer students to the list of types of speeches on page 746. Read the characteristics of each type of speech aloud or have a student read them.

2. After reading about each type of speech, ask students for examples. (A history lecture is often an informative speech; a political speech is often persuasive; stand-up comedy, entertaining; and a toast, extemporaneous.)

Critical Viewing

Deduce Answers will vary, but students may observe that the business attire, the microphone, and the attentive listener seem to indicate that this is a prepared speech.

Customize for
Less Advanced Students

Work through Exercise 2 as a group, encouraging and prompting students as necessary to help them succeed at the task.

Answer Key

> **Exercise 2**

Ask students to share topic and audience pairings that they have come up with for each category.

Real-World Connection

Help students identify situations in which they might use each type of speech in their everyday lives. (Students might deliver informative or persuasive speeches in classes; they might give an entertaining or an extemporaneous speech at a wedding or birthday party.)

29.1

Speaking in Public

Giving a presentation in front of an audience is *public speaking*. By learning more about speeches and speechmaking, you can improve your public-speaking skills.

Understanding Different Types of Speeches

There are four kinds of speeches: informative, persuasive, entertaining, and extemporaneous. To make your speech more effective, use language—informal, standard, or technical—that suits your purpose and is appropriate for the audience.

▷ **KEY CONCEPT** Choose the kind of speech you will give and the language you will use by thinking about your purpose and what your audience is like. ■

- An **informative speech** explains an idea, a process, or an object. Facts must be presented in a clear, organized way. Also, in an informative speech, technical language may be used to more accurately describe the topic.

- A **persuasive speech** is usually spoken in standard English; it tries to make the audience agree with the speaker's position or to take some action. Opinions need to be supported by statements or facts.

- An **entertaining speech**, spoken both in standard and informal language, offers the audience an enjoyable experience. Entertaining passages may be included in other kinds of speeches to offer variety or to provide emphasis.

- An **extemporaneous speech** is an informal speech given to suit an occasion, event, or audience and does not rely on a prepared manuscript but on the speaker's knowledge and ability to improvise.

▲ Critical Viewing
Do you think this athlete is giving a prepared speech or an extemporaneous speech? Explain. [Deduce]

> **Exercise 2** Listing Speech Topics and Audiences List two possible topics and the intended audience for each of the four types of speeches discussed on this page.

Preparing and Presenting a Speech

Once you know what kind of speech you will give and have chosen an appropriate topic, you will need to gather and organize information and practice your speech before you present it.

KEY CONCEPT To prepare your speech, research your topic, cite reliable sources, and organize your thesis. ■

Gather Valid Proof From Reliable Sources Research the subject using the library or other reliable sources to find valid proof, or conclusive evidence, to support your claims. Research is especially important when preparing an informative or persuasive speech.

Use Appropriate Appeals to Support Your Arguments The evidence you use to support your claims should be appropriate to your topic. For example, if you are writing a persuasive speech on the benefits of a healthy diet, it would be appropriate to research and cite evidence from nutritional experts, but not from the founder of a fast-food chain.

Present a Clear Thesis To help you organize and develop your thesis, make an outline. Begin your outline with any necessary background material. Arrange information in a rational sequence. Include logical points to support your message. Then, transfer this information to index cards to which you can refer while presenting your speech.

KEY CONCEPT When presenting your speech, use rhetorical forms of language and verbal and nonverbal strategies. ■

Use Rhetorical Strategies Let the audience know your important points by repeating key words and phrases. Keep your speech lively and interesting by using active verbs and colorful adjectives. Create a sense of rhythm in your speech through the use of parallel phrases or parallel series of words.

Use Verbal and Nonverbal Strategies Vary the pitch of your voice and the rate at which you speak, and use movements, gestures, and facial expressions to emphasize key points of your message.

Exercise 3 **Presenting a Persuasive Speech** Prepare a persuasive speech on a topic that interests you. Follow the steps on this page to prepare and present your speech to your classmates.

⊚ Technology Tip

Practice your speech by recording it on an audio- or videotape. Play it back to analyze how you sound and look. Use the evaluation tips on page 748 to discover ways to improve your speech and delivery.

▶ **More Practice**

Academic and Workplace Skills Activity Book
• p. 2

Preparing and Presenting a Speech

1. Emphasize to students the importance of choosing a topic that interests them. If they are bored with the topic, their audience will be, too.

2. Point out that several of the keys to a good speech are the same as those for a good essay: an attention-grabbing introduction, a clear main idea and good supporting points, and a strong conclusion.

3. Encourage students to avoid writing out their speeches word-for-word. Notes or outlines will allow them to interact with the audience. Explain that note cards are a common way for speakers to keep track of their ideas: they write a key point at the top of each card, with supporting details or memorable quotes below.

4. Tell students that many people who do a lot of public speaking practice their speeches. Sometimes, they talk to a mirror, watching their gestures. Other times, they might use a tape recorder to make sure their voices are contributing to the message.

Answer Key

▶ **Exercise 3**

Suggest that students review the chapters on persuasive writing. Many of the strategies there will contribute to strengthening their persuasive speeches. If there is not enough time for every student to present a speech to the whole class, you might want to divide the class into small groups and have group members present their speeches to their groups.

Customize for
Spatial Learners

Some students will benefit from making graphic representations of the information in their speeches. They can make their speeches clearer and more compelling by including these graphics on flip charts, transparencies, or handouts.

Evaluating a Presentation or Performance

1. Point out to students that a presentation or performance is only effective if the audience understands the main idea of the presentation.

2. Explain that tone of voice, inflection, clarity, and other qualities of the speaker's voice help make presentations easier to understand.

3. If possible, show students a few short video clips of dramatic readings or other presentations by a variety of speakers. Have the class work together to evaluate these presentations using the checklists in the text.

4. Point out that students can also use these checklists to remind them of the skills they should practice before making their own presentations.

Customize for
ESL Students

Some students may be at a disadvantage when making or evaluating presentations, since they may struggle with understanding the words. Possible solutions might include making presentations in small groups or handing out transcripts of the speeches so students can follow along. Also, you might want to evaluate them on how well they support their points, rather than on their diction.

Answer Key

> **Exercise 4**

Point out to students that this evaluation process is something like a more formalized peer-review session. It is intended to point out the speaker's strengths and weaknesses, and to help students to develop and improve their speaking skills. Emphasize the importance of making useful suggestions. You may want to collect the reviews first (have students write their names on them), so that you can make certain that they performed the task with tact.

Evaluating a Presentation or Performance Evaluate works by your peers. These include presentations, such as original essays or narratives. They also include performances, such as interpretations of poetry and individual or group performances of scripts. The main purpose of the evaluation is to determine which techniques and skills were successful and which need more work. A secondary purpose is to apply the successful techniques and skills to improve your own presentations and performances.

▶ **KEY CONCEPT** An effective speaker uses verbal and non-verbal techniques to gain and hold an audience's attention. ■

TIPS FOR EVALUATING A SPEECH

- Did the speaker introduce the topic clearly?
- Did the speaker support main ideas with appropriate details?
- Did the speaker establish eye contact?
- Did the speaker's gestures and movements reinforce the message?
- Did the speaker project loudly enough?
- Did the speaker vary voice, pitch, and speaking rate?
- Did the speaker pronounce all words clearly and correctly?

Improving Your Own Presentations and Performances When you evaluate another speaker's presentation or delivery, you identify the reasons you, as a listener, did or did not find the presentation effective. Keep these reasons in mind as you practice your next presentation. If you found your attention wandering because the speaker never varied his or her position or made eye contact, then be sure to vary your position as you speak and to make eye contact with your audience.

▶ **Exercise 4** Evaluating a Presentation or Performance
Use the suggestions on this page to evaluate a presentation or performance given in class. Comment on the skills that the person used effectively, and give specific examples of how the skills were used. Be tactful in pointing out any problems the speaker displayed. Give your completed evaluation to the person.

🗊 Research Tip

Ask your librarian for help in finding information on giving presentations, such as speeches or dramatic performances. Also, look for presentations and performances on audio- and videotape, and study the techniques used by the presenters or performers.

Listening Critically

There's a lot more to listening than just hearing words. Listening involves active participation. Listening critically involves evaluating and making judgments about what you hear.

▶ **KEY CONCEPT** A critical listener takes an active role in the information he or she hears. ■

Learning the Listening Process One reason to become a better listener is to acquire new ideas and information on which to build your knowledge. Understanding the listening process will bring you one step closer to becoming a critical listener.

Focus Your Attention Give the speaker your undivided attention so you can fully understand the information you hear. If you are planning to attend a formal presentation or speech on a particular topic, acquire more information about the topic before attending. This will increase your interest and make it easier for you to focus your attention.

Interpret the Information When you are listening to a speaker, you have to analyze what you are hearing. Some information will be more important than other information. It is up to you to be selective in what you will try to remember. Use the following suggestions to guide you:

- Listen for words and phrases that are emphasized or repeated.
- Test your understanding of important statements by rephrasing them in your own words.
- Take notes and summarize ideas in writing.
- Be alert to nonverbal signals, such as tone of voice, gestures, and facial expressions. Often, body language is as important a part of the communication process as verbal language.
- Find a meaningful pattern in which to combine present and past information.

Respond to the Speaker's Message After the speaker has finished speaking, respond to the information you heard. Think about whether you feel the speaker has made valid points and supported them well. Jot down questions you still have after listening. If possible, ask questions to clarify the speaker's message.

▶ **Exercise 5** Using the Listening Process Apply the listening strategies on this page to a lecture by your teacher or a presentation or a performance by one of your peers.

⊙ Technology Tip

To improve your ability to interpret information, listen to tape recordings of classroom lectures. Ask your teachers for permission before taping. Practice your listening skills, using the techniques on this page, while you play the tapes at home.

▶ **More Practice**

Academic and Workplace Skills Activity Book
- p. 3

Speaking and Listening Skills • **749**

Step-by-Step Teaching Guide

Listening Critically

Teaching Resources: Academic and Workplace Skills Activity Book, p. 3

1. Explain to students that an important aspect of effective listening is knowing one's own weaknesses. For example, if one is easily distracted, sitting closer to the speaker might help. Let students know that listening, like most things, gets easier with practice.

2. Point out that taking notes is a good way to stay focused. Taking notes requires thinking about what is important and trying to jot down key ideas. This keeps the mind on the topic.

3. Suggest that students develop a few codes they can use while taking notes, such as stars or question marks. These can help point them to key ideas or important questions.

Answer Key

▶ **Exercise 5**

Ask students to compare summaries of a speaker's message. Were they similar or different?

Customize for
More Advanced Students

Encourage students to listen to a more formal presentation, possibly a recording of a historic speech, a story on tape, or a current-events program. Have them take notes on the presentation, write a summary, and then share what they learned with the class.

Using Different Types of Listening

1. Ask students where, outside of the classroom, they would use each type of listening?

2. Point out that one can use more than one type of listening at a time. For example, one could be empathic and still want to ask reflective questions at the end of a presentation.

Asking Different Types of Questions

1. Have students give additional examples of each type of question:

   Open-ended: *What things did you like best about the movie?*

   Closed: *Did you like the ending of the movie?*

   Fact: *Who played the main character in the movie?*

2. Ask students to reflect on when each type of questioning would be most effective. (Example: Open-ended questions can be best for getting a friend to open up about a subject.)

Integrating Viewing and Representing Skills

Have students make a pie graph to represent the use of different types of questions. Ask several students to record the types of questions asked during class discussions and create pie graphs to show the percentage of questions of each type. Discuss the results, including which types of questions were most and least common and why this was so.

29.1

Using Different Types of Listening Part of being a critical listener is knowing how to adjust your listening according to the situation. There are four main types of listening: *critical, empathic, appreciative,* and *reflective.*

Types of Listening		
Type	**How to Listen**	**Situation**
Critical	Listen for facts and supporting details to understand and evaluate the speaker's message.	Informative or persuasive essays, class discussions, announcements
Empathic	Imagine yourself in the other person's position, and try to understand what he or she is thinking.	Conversations with friends or family
Appreciative	Identify and analyze aesthetic or artistic elements, such as character development, rhyme, imagery, and descriptive language.	Oral presentations of a poem or short story and dramatic performances
Reflective	Ask questions to get information, and use or reflect on the speaker's responses to form new questions.	Class or group discussions

Asking Different Types of Questions Use different types of questions to get the information you want to know.

- An **open-ended** question allows the person you are asking to make choices about the kinds of information used in the response. Use follow-up questions to clarify specific points. An example of an open-ended question is "Why are you the best candidate for class president?"

- A **closed** question leads to a specific response and must be answered with a yes or a no. Sometimes, you may want to explore the reasons for the answer by asking an open-ended follow-up question.

- A **fact** question is aimed at getting a particular piece of information and must be answered with facts: "How many votes did you receive in the election?" Follow-up questions may help you pinpoint the source of information.

750 • Speaking, Listening, Viewing, and Representing

✓ ONGOING ASSESSMENT: Monitor and Reinforce

To help students become more familiar with the types of questions, try the following strategies.

Option 1 Have students label a sheet of paper *Open-ended, Closed,* and *Fact.* Then, have them look through their literature, science, or social studies books to find two or three questions of each type, and list them on the sheet of paper. Discuss their findings.	**Option 2** Model an interview for students, stopping to identify the type of question being asked at each step. Make certain the "interviewee" is prepared with appropriate answers to demonstrate to students which types of questions elicit which kinds of information.

Exercise 6 Using Different Types of Listening For one week, keep a "listening log." Jot down examples of ways you have used each of the types of listening. Remember that you may use more than one type of listening for the same situation.

Exercise 7 Using Different Types of Questions Work with a classmate on this exercise. Have your classmate choose a topic in which he or she is interested and knowledgeable. Then, ask two open-ended, two closed, and two fact questions to learn about that topic. Record the person's responses, and then switch roles.

Evaluating Your Listening Improve your listening skills by evaluating them. Use the following strategies to guide you:

Rephrase and Repeat Statements Test your understanding of the speaker's statements by rephrasing and then repeating them. If necessary, ask questions to improve your paraphrase.

Compare and Contrast Interpretations Compare your interpretation of a speaker's message with that of a classmate's. Before discussing with your classmate, jot down a brief summary of the speech or presentation and any questions you have. Then, compare your notes with your partner's.

Research Points of Interest or Contention Use the library or other references to learn more about the topic or to check questionable facts in the speaker's presentation.

Exercise 8 Evaluating Your Listening Skills Working with another classmate, use the skills listed above to evaluate how well you listen to a lecture by a teacher, a presentation by a classmate, or a story told by one of your friends. Afterward, write an evaluation describing how well you listened and the areas in which you need to improve.

Technology Tip

Practice your critical listening skills by listening to campaign speeches at school and in local elections and by listening to commentary on current events on television.

Answer Key

> **Exercise 6**

At the end of the week, discuss in class which types of listening students used most often. Did they find that keeping track of listening affected their listening?

> **Exercise 7**

Have students share some of what they learned from their partners.

Customize for
ESL Students

Some students may have difficulty recording their classmates' responses while listening. If this is the case, have them tape-record the responses. Allow them to play back the tape as much as needed.

Step-by-Step Teaching Guide

Evaluating Your Listening

1. Ask students how they know whether they have listened well. What might they be able to do or repeat after listening?

2. Ask students to think about times they talked to individuals or groups. What would they expect their audience or listeners to be able to do to show that they have listened well?

Answer Key

> **Exercise 8**

Discuss in class what students learned. Ask them what steps a person might take to improve his or her listening skills.

Interpreting Maps

Teaching Resources: Academic and Workplace Skills Activity Book, p.4

1. Ask students to apply what they have read about interpreting maps to this map of the European Union.

2. Ask the class to agree on the purpose of the map. (The purpose is to show when each country entered the European Union.)

3. Ask students to read the written information on the map, such as the title, captions, labels, scale, and symbols. Have them relate how this information might help them "read" the map. (Example: The map shows the longitude and latitude to give an accurate sense of how far away from each other the countries are.)

Integrating Technology Skills

Have students do an Internet search for different types of atlases and maps available on the Internet. Suggest they search first for maps and atlases in general, and then specify places for which they want maps, such as countries or continents, or even for the moon. Have them report on some of the advantages of consulting maps on the Internet. (Maps on the Internet might be more current and are updated often.)

Integrating Workplace Skills

Tell students that people who design maps for a living are called *cartographers*. Ask students why the skills of cartographers are important. (Travelers need current information about roads. Students need accurate information about countries' names and borders.) Ask students what skills they think a cartographer would need to possess (artistic ability, attention to detail, knowledge of geography).

Critical Viewing

Analyze The map shows when countries entered the European Union and where they are located.

Viewing Skills

Visual representation is an important and effective way to communicate. Television programs, textbooks, Web sites, and works of art are common types of media that use images to add to your view of the world. In this section, you will learn how to interpret information from visual sources.

Interpreting Maps and Graphs

Finding information in maps and graphs involves understanding the features contained within them.

▶ **KEY CONCEPT** Determine your purpose for reading the map or graph, and then find the information to fulfill this purpose. ■

Maps A *map* can show climate, population density, changes over historical periods, battles in a war, the relative heights of landforms, or weather patterns, among many other types of information. To interpret a map, (1) determine the type and purpose of the map; (2) read the title, captions, and labels, and examine the distance scale and other symbols; (3) relate the information on the map to any written information accompanying it.

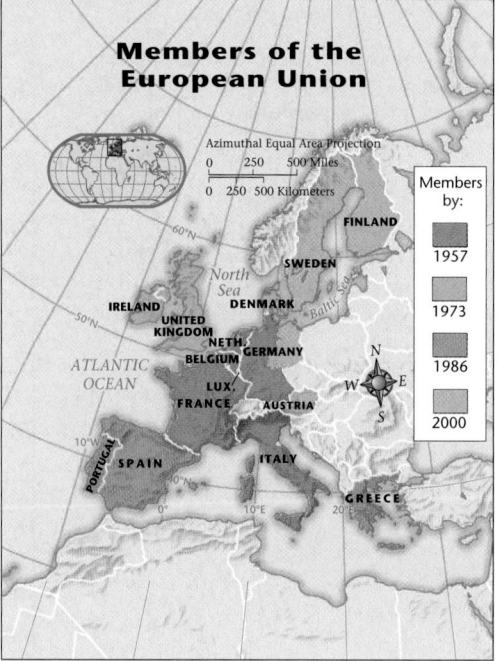

Members of the European Union

◀ **Critical Viewing**
What is the purpose of this map? **[Analyze]**

🔖 Research Tip

Browse through atlases to see the many uses that maps have. Note the features of each map and the various symbols used to communicate information.

⏱ TIME AND RESOURCE MANAGER

Resources
Print: *Academic and Workplace Skills Activity Book*, pp. 4–7

Using the Full Student Edition	Using the Handbook 🅷
• Read and discuss pp. 752–757.	• Read and discuss pp. 554–559.
• Give students time in class to complete Exercises 9–11.	• Give students time in class to complete Exercises 9–11.
• Discuss students' results from the exercises.	• Discuss students' results from the exercises.

Graphs

Graphs present numerical information in visual form and compare two or more sets of related information. Study the following three types of commonly used graphs.

Line Graph A *line graph* shows changes over a period of time. A line connects points, which appear as dots at intersections on the graph. Each dot represents a number or a quantity of something. To interpret a line graph, (1) read the labels to see what the data represent and the time interval for which the data are being recorded, (2) read both the horizontal axis (left-to-right line) and the vertical axis (bottom-to-top line) that make up the two axes of the graph, and (3) compare and contrast the data.

Bar Graph A *bar graph* compares and contrasts quantities. The height or length of each bar shows what numbers it represents. To interpret a bar graph, (1) match the label of each bar on the horizontal axis to the number that the bar reaches on the vertical axis, (2) note the labels to see what each bar represents and why the two bars are being compared, and (3) compare and contrast the data.

Temperature in Siberia, Russia

(Line graph showing temperature in °F on the vertical axis from 0 to 80, and months J F M A M J J A S O N D on the horizontal axis labeled "Month.")

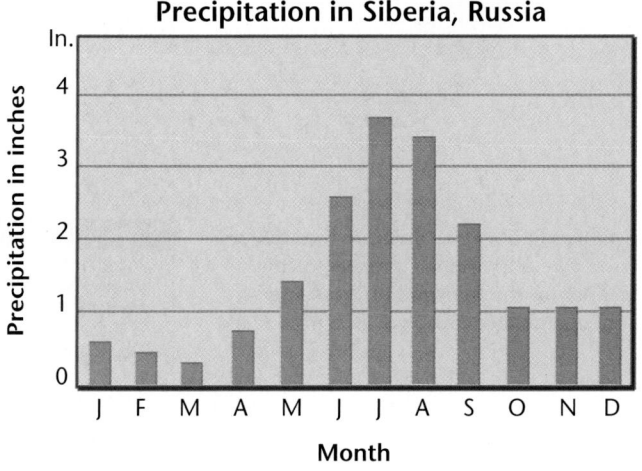

Precipitation in Siberia, Russia

(Bar graph showing precipitation in inches on the vertical axis from 0 to 4, and months J F M A M J J A S O N D on the horizontal axis labeled "Month.")

◀▲ **Critical Viewing**
What can you learn about Siberia from these two graphs? **[Synthesize]**

Step-by-Step Teaching Guide

Line Graphs and Bar Graphs

Teaching Resources: Academic and Workplace Skills Activity Book, p. 5

1. Have students read the labels on the line graph to see what information is being related.

2. Ask students to name the type of information on each axis. (The horizontal axis shows the months, the vertical axis shows the temperature in Siberia.)

3. Have students compare and contrast the information on the graph. Prompt discussion by asking the following questions:

   Which is the coldest month?

   Which is the warmest month?

   Which months seem to have almost the same temperatures?

4. Ask students to imagine other types of information for a line graph (test scores over time, product sales, sports statistics).

5. Refer students to the bar graph. Have students match the label of each bar on the horizontal axis to the number that the bar reaches on the vertical axis.

6. Ask students to read the labels to see what each bar represents (the amount of precipitation in Siberia in each month).

7. Have students compare and contrast the data. Which month has the most precipitation? Which has the least?

8. Ask students to compare and contrast the bar and line graph. Which month would they recommend for visiting Siberia? Why? Which would be the worst time to visit? Why?

Critical Viewing

Synthesize Students may comment on growing seasons, crops, travel, and other weather-related issues.

Pie Graphs

1. Have students look at the numbers that accompany the parts of each pie graph, and match the parts to the key to see what each represents.

2. Discuss the four pie graphs by asking students to compare them. Which country has the largest percentage of its labor force in each category? Which has the smallest? What conclusions can they draw about each country?

3. Ask students to imagine what other kind of information they might find on a pie graph. (Pie graphs could be made about an organization's ethnic and gender makeup, about the chemical composition of the earth's atmosphere, about how money is invested, or about the percentage of students who play on the school's different sports teams.)

4. Note that pie graphs always show the relationships of parts to a whole.

Answer Key

> **Exercise 9**

Responses will vary. Ask students why each type of graph might have been chosen for the information it shows.

Customize for
More Advanced Students

Some students will be able to take Exercise 9 one step further. After writing an explanation of the information presented and drawing conclusions, have these students convert the information from one of the graphs into the format of another. For example, they might show the information from one of the pie graphs on page 754 as a bar graph.

Critical Viewing

Identify Because the graphs show percentages and not total number of workers, students should recognize that the graphs do not indicate which country has the largest labor force in any category. Norway has the largest *percentage* of its labor force working in agriculture.

Pie Graph A *pie graph* shows the relationship of parts to a whole. The graph is a circle that represents 100 percent of something. Each part stands for a portion, or percentage, of the whole. To interpret a pie graph, (1) look at the numbers that go with each part, (2) match the parts to the key to see what each represents, and (3) use the numbers and parts to make comparisons.

THE LABOR FORCE IN SELECTED WESTERN EUROPEAN COUNTRIES

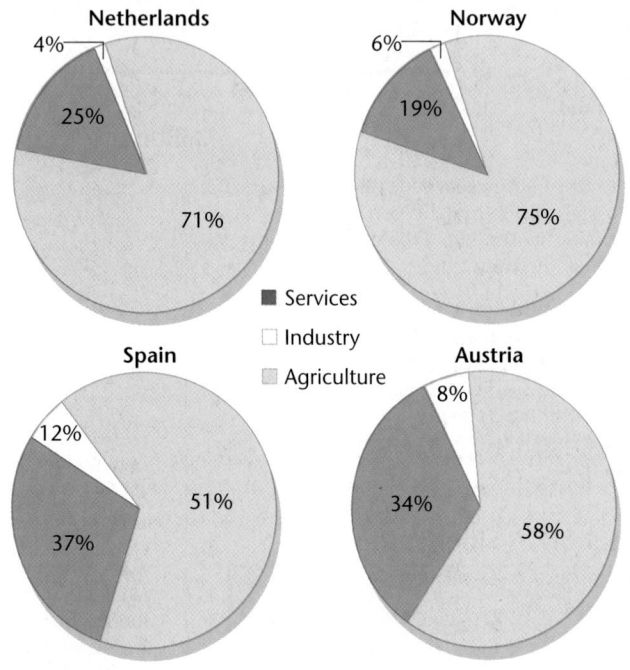

◀ **Critical Viewing**
Which country has the largest agricultural labor force? **[Identify]**

> **Exercise 9** Reading Information Visually Use the tips you have just read to interpret the map and the graphs in this section. Write an explanation of the information presented in each. Then, decide what conclusions can be drawn from them.

> **More Practice**

Academic and Workplace Skills Activity Book
• pp. 4–5

Viewing Information Media Critically

To be an informed consumer of information, it is important that you learn to critically evaluate what you see and hear in the media. Applying critical viewing skills to the various forms of news media will help you to understand events and issues and to formulate your own opinions.

▶ **KEY CONCEPT** Learn to identify and evaluate the different kinds of information found in nonprint media. ■

Recognizing Kinds of Information Media Much of the information you receive comes to you from visual media, particularly television. The quality and relevance of this information depends on the type of program being viewed.

The following chart describes several forms of nonprint information media.

NONPRINT INFORMATION MEDIA			
Form of News Media	Topic(s)	Coverage and Content	Point of View
Nightly News	Current events or news	Brief summaries illustrated by video footage	Presents information objectively
Documentary	One topic of social interest	Story shown through narration and video footage	Expresses controversial opinions
Interview	Topics of social interest	Conversation of questions and answers	Presents opinions of interviewee
Television Newsmagazine	Covers a variety of topics	Feature with hosts and footage, meant to entertain and inform	Emphasizes stories that grab a viewer's attention
Commercial	Products, people, and ideas	Short message of images and slogans	Presents information to sell something or to persuade

Viewing Skills • 755

Step-by-Step Teaching Guide

Viewing Information Media Critically

Teaching Resources: Academic and Workplace Skills Activity Book, p. 6

1. Remind students that they receive information from a variety of media every day and that it is important to be able to think critically about that information.

2. Direct students to the chart of Nonprint Information Media. Ask students which of these forms they see regularly.

3. Discuss the topics these forms of media cover. Point out the second column of the chart and ask students to think of specific examples of each.

4. Explain that when viewers are looking for information, they should consider media that cover the content adequately for their purpose. (Someone writing a research paper needs Using the Full Student Edition, while someone wanting to know the day's international events might need brief nightly news summaries.)

5. Explain that critical viewers must consider the point of view presented within each medium. Point out that no news program, advertisement, or other medium is free of bias. The viewer must always be aware of the fact that simply omitting some information can change the impression given. That is why critical viewing and fact checking are important.

Integrating Vocabulary Skills

Explain to students that *media* is the plural of *medium*, a word derived from Latin. A number of Latin derivatives form plurals by adding *-a* or *-ia* to the root. Ask students to think of other such plurals ending in *a* (*criteria, data,* and *phenomena*).

Evaluating and Critiquing Persuasive Techniques

1. After reviewing the definitions of *glittering generalities* and *bandwagon appeals*, have students think of examples they have seen or heard in persuasive speeches, editorials, and advertising. Ask students why these techniques are so common in advertising.

2. After reinforcing students' understanding of symbols, ask them to think of animal symbols that are associated with particular car models. What qualities are associated with these animal symbols? What other products can they think of that are advertised by means of symbols?

Deconstructing Information From the Media

1. Prompt students with the following questions:

   What does it take to prove that something is true?

   When proving something, which is more important to use, fact or opinion?

2. Students should understand that facts and unbiased information are important to proving something.

Answer Key

▶ **Exercise 10**

If the exercise will be done in class, you may want to show a videotape of several commercials or hand out magazines. Have students share what they write about persuasive techniques.

29.2

Evaluating and Critiquing Persuasive Techniques

When you view any form of media, you should be aware of persuasive techniques used to misrepresent information and possibly distort your understanding of a message or an event.

Glittering generalities are lofty, broad statements that seek to appeal to a wide audience. The statement, "The best is yet to come if we all do our part" "glitters" with positive words and ideas, but it offers no real insight. Note glittering generalities, and examine them to find out what they really mean.

Bandwagon appeals are statements that use a form of peer pressure as their support. A bandwagon appeal suggests that you should take a certain action or think in a certain way because many others do.

Symbols are images that stand for or embody the qualities of another thing. For example, an advertisement for a car may include symbols of wealth, power, and prestige in addition to showing the actual car. Including these symbols suggests that the car is also a symbol of these qualities and that owning the car will make you feel wealthy, powerful, and important.

Deconstructing Information From the Media First, determine the kind of media program you are watching. Then, use your knowledge of persuasive techniques combined with the following strategies to deconstruct—break down into pieces—the images and language of the media you are viewing.

- Be aware of the purpose and limitations of the program you are watching. Find out who wrote or sponsored the program.
- Separate **facts** (proven statements) from **opinions** (beliefs). Use resources to check questionable information.
- Watch for **bias**—presenting a subject from one point of view.
- Note the kinds of images shown and their emotional impact.
- View the complete program before reaching your own conclusions about issues, people, and information.

 Exercise 10 Identifying Persuasive Techniques in Advertisements Find examples of glittering generalities, bandwagon appeals, and symbols in advertising. Choose your examples from electronic and print media. Write a brief explanation of the persuasive technique used in each advertisement.

🔵 **Learn More**

For more information about methods of persuasion, see Chapter 7. For information on how advertisements persuade, see Chapter 8.

▶ **More Practice**

Academic and Workplace Skills Activity Book
• p. 6

✎ STANDARDIZED TEST PREPARATION WORKSHOP

Fact and Opinion Standardized tests may require students to distinguish between fact and opinion.

Ernest Hemingway was the most influential American writer of the twentieth century. He lived from 1899 to 1961 and often drew on his experiences in wartime and as a fisherman, hunter, and bullfight enthusiast. Two of his novels are The Sun Also Rises *and* A Farewell to Arms.

Which statement is an opinion?

A Hemingway lived from 1899 to 1961.

B Hemingway was the most influential American writer of the twentieth century.

C Hemingway wrote the novels *The Sun Also Rises* and *A Farewell to Arms.*

D Hemingway was a fisherman, hunter, and bullfight enthusiast.

Students should recognize that statement **B** is an opinion. Choices **A**, **C**, and **D** are statements of fact.

Interpreting Fine Art

Paintings, drawings, sculpture, and photographs are all examples of fine art. To enrich your understanding and enjoyment of these works, you must interpret the various elements that make up the artwork.

KEY CONCEPT In works of art, meaning is communicated through elements of design. ■

Interpreting Elements of Design To help you interpret a work of art, consider the following questions:

- Does the work present definable objects or is it abstract—not showing any particular objects?

- What shapes, lines, and colors do you see?

- What mood, theme, or message does the work convey?

- Which areas are darkest, and which are lightest? What does the contrast of light and dark areas suggest?

- How do all the individual elements work together to create a feeling or an idea?

Exercise 11 Responding to Fine Art Interpret the painting *Dancers, Pink and Green*, by Edgar Degas, by answering the questions listed above. Write your answers in a notebook, along with any other observations. Share your impressions in an open discussion with your classmates.

📕 **Research Tip**

Spend some time in the library viewing books and slides of fine art. Which artists and works of art do you prefer? Make notes in your journal about why they appeal to you.

Dancers, Pink and Green, Edgar Degas, Metropolitan Museum of Art

💿 **Technology Tip**

Great art museums are waiting for you on the Internet. Enter the name of the museum in a search engine to find the URL (address) of the museum's Web site.

Viewing Skills • 757

Interpreting Fine Art

Teaching Resources: Academic and Workplace Skills Activity Book, p. 7

1. Point out to students that, while learning more about art can help them appreciate it more, there is also a degree to which preferences are involved. Not everyone will like the same art.

2. Explain that there are two levels for appreciating art. There is the objective level, which includes knowing facts about the artist, the period, the techniques, the subject, and the medium. Then, there is the subjective level, which includes how one reacts personally to the style, colors, mood, or subject of the work because of individual experiences, emotions, beliefs, or ideas.

3. Review the guidelines in the text for interpreting elements of design. Ask students which of these seem objective and which seem subjective.

Customize for
Spatial Learners

Some students may enjoy making a response to Degas with artwork of their own. Have them create their own pictures of dancers in whatever color they choose. Then, have them use the questions listed on this page to discuss their own work as well as Degas's.

Answer Key

▶ **Exercise 11**

To extend the lesson, you may wish to invite an art teacher from your school or community to speak about this painting or others by Degas.

Creating Visual Aids

Teaching Resources: Academic and Workplace Skills Activity Book, p. 8

1. Discuss with students the types of visual aids they have seen. This may include the graphs and maps in this lesson. Ask them why they think visual aids are useful. (Students may note that such aids show the relationships between elements, they seem more concrete, and so on.)

2. As you work through the material on the page, point out that the page itself is a good illustration of how text organization is a type of visual aid. As a class, develop a concept map or idea web on the board using the headings and subheadings on pages 758–759.

3. Discuss with students why different types of visual aids work with different text structures or organizational strategies. (Just as images convey different things, so do different writing strategies; visuals need to show that.)

4. Point out that, if students have created outlines, they have created a visual aid designed to help them organize information for themselves.

5. Have students search for graphics in textbooks, newspapers, and magazines. Discuss how effective these graphics are, how they support the text, and what types of information are conveyed. Encourage students to consider what types of reports they might write that would benefit from these types of graphics.

Section 29.3

Representing Skills

Graphic organizers, multimedia presentations, and performances are ways in which you can express yourself to the world. In this section, you will learn how to prepare your own visual representations.

Creating Visual Aids

For large amounts of information or complex ideas, it is helpful to organize the material into a visual aid, such as a graphic organizer, map, or diagram. These visual aids can also help you present information to others and to organize and remember information when you study.

▶ **KEY CONCEPT** Graphic organizers make information easier to comprehend and remember. ■

Use these strategies to construct your own visual aid:

- **Use Text Descriptions** Note the headings and subheadings that are used to organize the text. You can use headings to develop a concept map or an idea web, which will present these categories in visual form.

- **Determine the Text Structure** Consider the structure of the text when you choose a visual aid to display the information. For texts that show comparison and contrast, a Venn diagram may be the best choice. A flowchart is a good way to display cause-and-effect relationships. Problems and solutions can be shown in charts or diagrams. Main ideas and supporting details lend themselves to an outline. Chronological events can be represented on a timeline.

- **Identify Your Purpose** Is the purpose of the visual aid to help you study or to present information to others? Your answer will determine what information to include and which visual aid to use. Visual aids used for studying can be simple webs, charts, tables, or outlines. Visual aids used for presentations should be designed with an audience in mind. They should be appealing to the viewer and easy to understand.

- **Study Effective Graphics** Notice the effective use of graphics in textbooks, newspapers, and magazines. How are these graphics used to support the information in the text? For example, a graph may show information to support a viewpoint or to prove an argument.

🔁 Learn More

For more information about text structures, see the following "Exposition" chapters: "Comparison and Contrast," Chapter 9; "Cause and Effect," Chapter 10; "Problem and Solution," Chapter 11.

⏱ TIME AND RESOURCE MANAGER

Resources
Print: *Academic and Workplace Skills Activity Book*, pp. 8–12

Using the Full Student Edition	Using the Handbook🅗
• Read and discuss pp. 758–763 in class. • Have students work on Exercise 12 and then share their graphic organizers. • Divide students into small groups to work on Exercises 13–15.	• Read and discuss pp. 560–565. • Have students work on Exercise 12 and then share their graphic organizers. • Divide students into small groups to work on Exercises 13–15.

Following are descriptions of various types of visual aids and examples of how they are used.

Charts, Graphs, and Tables These visual aids can be used to present survey statistics, results of experiments or research, and other complex information. A table outlining a feudal society, for example, would show the people occupying the highest ranks (kings, emperors, and lesser rulers) at the top and those of lower ranks (merchants, peasants, and craftsmen) at the bottom.

Diagrams, Maps, and Illustrations These drawings show the features of an object, place, or process. For example, you might make a drawing, like the one below, of how a volcano erupts.

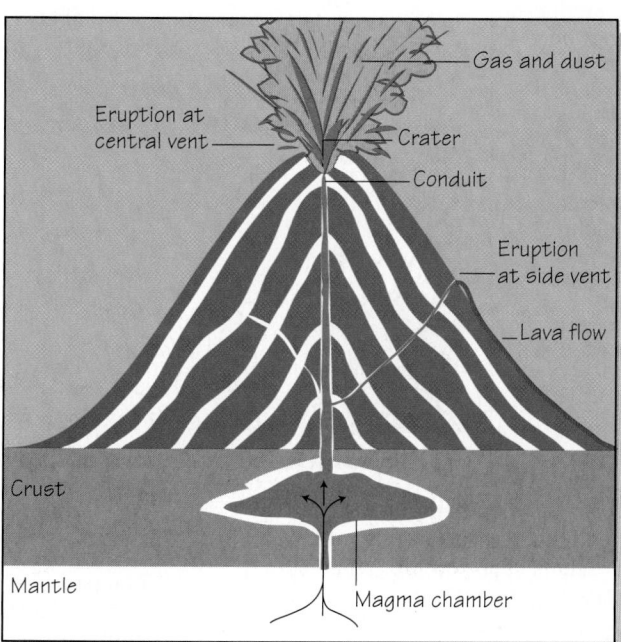

Technology Tip

Explore the table, graph, and graphics features on a computer, including changing text into graph and table form, merging text and pictures, and drawing capabilities.

Charts, Graphs, and Tables

1. Point out that graphs are visual aids such as the bar graphs, pie graphs, and line graphs covered earlier in the chapter. Tables are lists of data, such as tables for calculating taxes or determining mileage (show examples, if possible).

2. Explain that charts are generally more complex, such as a weather chart, which combines graphics of weather patterns overlapping a map of the affected region. Charts generally show variable items, such as temperature, sales, and so on.

Diagrams, Maps, and Illustrations

1. Ask students why they think maps, diagrams, and illustrations can help readers. (Visual media can show readers things they would not be able to see otherwise, for example, the cutaway view of a volcano. They can help readers understand things in relation to others, such as one country's proximity to another; they can share images that are outside a person's experience or that add to the text.)

2. Discuss what students can learn about volcanoes simply from a picture like the one in the text.

3. Encourage students to think of the types of writing that might benefit from illustrations, maps, or diagrams.

Exercise 12 **Creating Visual Aids From Textbooks** Choose a chapter from your math, science, or social studies textbook. Make a graphic organizer to represent a concept or group of facts in the chapter. Explain why you chose that particular type of visual aid and how it helps to clarify the information.

More Practice

Academic and Workplace Skills Activity Book
• p. 8

Representing Skills • 759

Answer Key

Exercise 12

If students need help getting started, ask them to show or bring in a social studies or science textbook they are currently using.

☑ **ONGOING ASSESSMENT: Monitor and Reinforce**

If you notice that your students have difficulty transferring information to visual aids, try one of the following options.

Option 1 With highlighters, have students mark the key words and phrases contained in the written information. When students transfer the information to a visual aid, allow them to begin by using only the words or phrases highlighted. This will ensure that their visual aids do not become cluttered and confused with unnecessary information.

Option 2 Have students find good examples of the type of visual aid they would like to create in magazines or newspapers. To create their own visual aid, have them start by replacing the words and pictures in the examples with their own information. This will help students create visual aids with effective formats.

Using Formatting

Teaching Resources: Academic and Workplace Skills Activity Book, p. 9

1. Explain to students that formatting refers to the way text is presented on the page. Word processors provide a variety of formatting choices, including font (style of typeface), spacing of text, and graphics. These formats can also be created by hand.

2. Point out how the information in the bulleted list applies to the advertisement in the text. Ask students to identify the different print styles and explain how each one helps highlight information.

3. Ask students to describe the spacing and positioning of the text. They should notice centered text, indented text, and bulleted text. They should also notice that care has been taken in the order of presentation.

4. Ask students to find the visuals in the advertisement. Are they only decorative or do they add to the meaning of the ad? Explain.

Answer Key

> **Exercise 13**

Encourage students to use any kind of computer software programs to create their brochures. If computers are not readily available, or have limited capabilities, suggest that students improvise. Hand-letter headings, type the body text, and then add pictures from magazines or draw borders by hand.

Customize for
Linguistic Learners

After students have chosen topics for their brochures, have them think about their presentations in terms of a speech or a story-telling session. Point out that the title would get the largest type, while the details might be placed in a bulleted list. Suggest that they relate the information orally, and note which elements they emphasize with tone or voice or voice inflection. This might help them decide which elements to highlight visually.

29.3

Using Formatting

There are many formatting techniques on most word processors that can aid you in making visual representations like the flyer shown here. Remember that the features you use should match the purpose of the text.

- Type styles have different effects on the viewer. Letters and characters can be italic (slanted), bold (dark type), or a combination of the two. They can also be shadowed or outlined and printed in a range of colors.

- Different effects can be produced by indenting and spacing the text. Information can be presented in bulleted lists or, when information has to appear in a certain order, numbered lists.

- Parts of the text can be shaded or colored for effect or to call attention to the information. Borders can be added to make information stand out or for decoration.

- Graphics can be added to attract the viewers and to give them an idea of what kind of information they can expect to read.

Have Rake, Will Travel
Buried in Autumn Leaves?

HARD-WORKING, DEPENDABLE
HIGH-SCHOOL STUDENT WILL RAKE YOUR LAWN

- Have own rake and leaf blower
- Will rake leaves from lawn and shrubbery
- Will bag leaves and take them to curb
- Reasonable rates
- Satisfaction guaranteed
- Available most weekdays 3:15 P.M. – 6:30 P.M. and weekends

Call or e-mail
Tom Wilson
Tel. 101-555-3377 or
twilson@rakeleaves.com

> **Exercise 13** Using Formatting to Design a Brochure

Use the tips on formatting and design to prepare a flyer or brochure that promotes a school sport or club. When your flyer is complete, ask a classmate to evaluate your use of various formatting and design features.

⊙ **Technology Tip**

Consult the software manual, Help feature, or toolbar to explore the possibilities for formatting, using the software on your computer.

Working With Multimedia

Some kinds of information are most effectively presented with sounds and visuals. When preparing a multimedia presentation, consider using an overhead projector, a slide projector, a video-tape player, or an audiocassette player. These can enhance your presentation with still images, moving images, recorded voices, music, graphic organizers, and art.

Giving a Multimedia Presentation Although almost any kind of media can be used in a multimedia presentation, you should consider the topic, the audience, and the available equipment before you choose which media to use.

Use the following suggestions to help you prepare and give a multimedia presentation:

- Outline your oral report, and decide which parts will be more effective if presented through visual and aural media.
- Choose forms of media that suit your topic. If your topic is American life during World War II, you might play popular music of that time as a background and show slides of women workers in defense industries to illustrate the changes in society resulting from the war.
- Use media selections evenly throughout your presentation, not just at the beginning or end.
- Make sure all visual images can be seen by the entire audi-ence. Small images can be photocopied and enlarged before being shown on an overhead projector.
- Rehearse your presentation with the multimedia equipment. Become familiar with making adjustments to the equipment.
- Before the presentation, double-check your equipment to make sure everything is in working condition.
- Have a backup plan in case your equipment fails. You might have copies of illustrations or graphic organizers to give to the audience.

> **Exercise 14** Preparing and Giving a Multimedia Presentation Look through some of your past speeches and reports. Choose one, and prepare a plan for enhancing it with multimedia selections. Outline your presentation, including the media you will use and the order of presentation. Practice a few times, and then present it to your classmates.

⊙ Technology Tip

Use a search engine to find Web sites with graphics you can print or download and use in your multi-media presentation.

> **More Practice**
>
> **Academic and Workplace Skills Activity Book**
> • p. 10

Representing Skills • 761

Producing a Video

Teaching Resources: Academic and Workplace Skills Activity Book, p. 11

1. After students read page 762, have them suggest a time line for the video production process. Record their responses on the board. (Students may mention developing the story, writing a shooting script, creating storyboards, selecting locations, casting actors, rehearsing, planning the shooting schedule, videotaping the action, and editing.)

2. Point out that camera angles and shooting techniques are used during videotaping, but most of these are planned during the shooting script stage. Tell students to plan, but to remain flexible; sometimes good ideas arise during shooting.

3. If the school has a video recorder, try to give students an opportunity to practice zooming and panning, so they can get the feel of these techniques.

4. Find out what facilities are available at school, in case students do not have access to their own video equipment.

5. You might ask someone from a video service to talk to students about how they set up shots, create effects, or select locations, and how editing helps.

Answer Key

▶ **Exercise 15**

Consider grouping videos by topic or type (narrative or documentary, for example) and showing two or three at a time. This will demonstrate the flexibility of the medium and may help students think of other ways to handle a topic.

Customize for
Less Advanced Students

If students are having difficulty handling all the production stages, have them work in groups, sharing the work at each stage, so that the final product is a group effort.

762 • 564 Ⓗ

29.3

Producing a Video

Video cameras allow individuals to record their experiences and express their ideas through the medium of film. In addition to operating the camera, video artists must learn to edit the tape to produce the effects they want.

▶ **KEY CONCEPT** A video can inform, entertain, persuade, or serve all three purposes. ■

Making a Video The process of making a video is similar to making a film, although on a smaller scale. First, you must write out a story or list of scenes meant to convey a message. This document is the beginning of a *shooting script*. Include descriptions of settings, narration or dialogue between characters, and costumes and props needed. Decide on *camera angles*, or positions, for each shot or sequence of shots.

Use the shooting script to make a *storyboard* that illustrates a clear sequence of events. A storyboard looks like a cartoon strip, with each important shot planned and illustrated.

Select locations for shooting, and get permission to use them. Cast the roles, and rehearse. Write out a shooting schedule listing each scene, when and where it will be shot, and who is in it. Film the scenes, and store the video in a safe place.

Edit the video to produce the effect you want. You might cut to make action happen more quickly, to move from one location to another, or to insert flashbacks or new material. You may also decide to reshoot some scenes.

Tips for Videotaping

- Hold the camera steady. Learn to use all the features of the equipment.

- Use shooting techniques such as **panning** (moving the camera to the left or right), **zooming** (adjusting from a distant to a close view or from a close view to a distant one), **fading** (increasing or decreasing image intensity), and **cutting** (moving directly from one shot to another).

- Be sure to shoot enough film. It is always easier to cut than to reshoot.

▶ **Exercise 15** Producing a Video Produce a five-minute documentary or story video. You may work with a partner. Write out a shooting script. On your storyboard, plan the scenes you will shoot. Then, select locations, cast actors, rehearse, and film your video. After editing, present your video to your classmates.

▶ **More Practice**

Academic and Workplace Skills Activity Book
• p. 11

Performing or Interpreting

In an oral interpretation, the performer communicates his or her personal conception of a written work.

KEY CONCEPT Performers use voice and gestures and their own personal insights to communicate the meaning of a text. ■

Preparing a Performance or Interpretation It is best to choose a poem or story that has personal meaning for you and that you think the audience will appreciate. Write the text out and highlight the ideas and phrases you wish to emphasize. Decide on the mood you wish to achieve. Experiment with different ways of reading the text aloud to achieve the desired effect. Use tone of voice and pitch to express emotions. Use gestures and other body language to convey meaning and mood. Set the scene through background music, props, and costumes, if appropriate. Rehearse in front of a mirror and then before friends and family. Ask for their feedback to improve your performance.

Exercise 16 Interpreting a Poem Choose a poem you would like to interpret for an audience. Make notes on key words and ideas and the emotions and meanings you wish to convey. Practice reading the poem aloud and get feedback from listeners. Then, interpret the poem for your class.

> **More Practice**
> Academic and
> Workplace Skills
> Activity Book
> • p. 12

Reflecting on Your Speaking, Listening, Viewing, and Representing

Review the skills covered in this chapter. Write a journal entry evaluating your experiences using these skills. Use the following questions as a starting point:

- How might effective speaking and listening benefit me in the different areas of my life—school, work, hobbies, friends, and family?

- How have I improved my ability to critically evaluate information from the media?

- What have I learned from producing visual presentations and/or interpreting literature through performing?

Representing Skills • 763

☑ ONGOING ASSESSMENT: Assess Mastery

Use one of the following strategies to assess mastery of speaking, listening, viewing, and representing skills.

Self-Assessment Ask students to reflect on what they've learned in the chapter. Have them write down the most useful strategy they learned for each of the four major skills.	**Teacher Assessment** You may wish to assign one of the exercises in the chapter as a "final exam" for the chapter. Assess students' presentations and their skills as critical viewers of their classmates' presentations.

Step-by-Step Teaching Guide

Performing or Interpreting

Teaching Resources: Academic and Workplace Skills Activity Book, p. 12

1. To practice expressing emotion, give students a simple phrase, such as "I'm not going," and have different students express it showing anger, surprise, sadness, and enthusiasm. Have students analyze how tone of voice and stressing different words changes the emotion of the phrase.

2. Urge students to look up the pronunciation and meaning of any words that are unclear. This will help them convey the emotion they are aiming for.

Answer Key

> **Exercise 16**

Encourage students to pick a poem that has particular value or meaning to them. Their performance will become more enjoyable for them and for the audience.

Customize for
ESL Students

Allow students to perform a poem in their first language. Ask students to state the topic in English. After the reading, have the class comment on the performers' expressiveness.

ASSESS and CLOSE

Step-by-Step Teaching Guide

Reflecting

Teaching Resources: Formal Assessment, Ch. 29

1. Use one of the assessment options provided in the chart below.

2. You may also wish to use the following assessment options:

   • review the Standardized Test Preparation Workshop on pp. 764–765 and have students complete the practice items.

   • administer the Chapter 29 assessment from *Formal Assessment* in the Teaching Resources to measure students' grasp of the concepts presented.

Lesson Objectives

1. To draw inferences such as conclusions and support them with text evidence
2. Use text organizers such as graphic features to locate information
3. To describe how elements are communicated through elements of design

Step-by-Step Teaching Guide

Interpreting Graphic Aids

Teaching Resources: Standardized Test Preparation Workbook, pp. 57–58

1. Tell students to examine a graphic aid before reading the questions that relate to it. This will make the questions more clear, because students will know what the questions are referring to.

2. Review the sample item. Point out that students need to combine information in the text with information in the graph to get the answer. For example, they learn in the text that sailors had meat and some vegetables in their diet, so it seems likely that fruits were lacking.

3. Have students examine the chart on page 765. Ask them to predict one question that might be asked about it.

4. Have students complete the practice test. Remind them to refer to the chart as often as necessary.

5. When they finish, check to see which items, if any, gave students difficulty. Discuss the answers.

Standardized Test Preparation Workshop

Interpreting Graphic Aids

Items that measure your ability to read not only text but also visuals are included on some standardized tests. Interpreting graphic aids means understanding the visual representation of information. You use this skill to read textbooks, news articles, directions, and surveys. On a test, a chart, map, or graph, as well as text on a particular topic, may be provided. The graphic often presents statistical information or shows categories of information that can be compared or measured. The text often provides context or shows the significance of the information.

The items that follow will give you practice with a format in which these items might appear. To respond to the questions or sentence completions, read and analyze both the graphic aid and the text.

Test Tip

Before answering the question, look at the visual and the text. Then, evaluate the answer choices to locate the one that is correct according to the information from both sources.

Sample Test Item	Answer and Explanation
Directions: Read the passage on the next page. Answer the question below. 1 What types of foods were probably missing from a sailor's diet? **A** vegetables **B** meat **C** fruits **D** bread	The correct answer is C. The text explains that many sailors contracted the disease scurvy. The chart tells you that a deficiency of citrus fruits causes scurvy. By putting together the information from the chart and the text, you can draw the conclusion that the sailors were probably not getting enough fruit.

764 • Speaking, Listening, Viewing, and Representing

✦ TEST-TAKING TIP

Tell students that when a test requires that they interpret a chart or graph, they should read the title, headings, and footnotes; look for a key if there are symbols; and pay attention to how the chart or graph is organized. They should then refer to it as they read the test items.

Students might feel intimidated by charts and graphs because they often contain specialized information. Remind them that the purpose of a chart or graph is to make complicated or detailed information easier to understand and remember. If they review the chart or graph carefully, they should be able to interpret it.

Practice **Directions:** Read the passage and answer the questions that follow.

Vitamins are chemical compounds that the human body requires in small amounts in order to maintain good health. Vitamins are a factor in the way the body converts food into energy and living tissue. Although some of the vitamins needed can be produced by the body itself, most must be supplied by a person's diet.

Each vitamin has such specific uses that one cannot replace another. The continued absence of just one vitamin can cause a vitamin deficiency disease. For example, before the connections between diet and health were completely understood, sailors often suffered from scurvy. Although plenty of salted meat was stocked on board and some vegetables were even included in a sailor's diet, the difficulties in carrying fresh foods for long journeys presented many dietary problems. In 1753, however, James Lind, a Scottish doctor, discovered which foods would prevent scurvy. The British navy followed his advice and adjusted the daily rations of sailors. Because the foods Lind recommended contained the vitamin necessary to prevent scurvy, it has become a rare disease in modern times.

Vitamin Sources and Functions

Vitamin	Source	Function	Deficiency Disease
A	green and yellow vegetables	promotes bone growth and vision	night blindness
B_1	grains, liver, legumes	metabolizes carbohydrates	beriberi
C	citrus fruits, potatoes, tomatoes	aids immunity, helps connective tissue growth	scurvy
D	milk, yeast	regulates bone formation	rickets, bowlegs

1 What foods, in addition to citrus fruits, would Lind have recommended that sailors take on board for long voyages?

 A apples
 B bananas
 C beans
 D potatoes

2 Of what other vitamin might sailors have had a deficiency?

 F Vitamin A
 G Vitamin B
 H Vitamin C
 J Vitamin D

3 Which foods help a person metabolize carbohydrates?

 A breads
 B milk
 C water
 D lemons

Answer Key

Practice

1. D
2. F
3. A

Customize for
Less Advanced Students

Students sometimes feel that all of the answer choices in a multiple choice question look reasonable. To avoid this problem, encourage them to answer the question before looking at the answer choices. If their own answer matches one of the answer choices on the test, it is probably correct. Also, they can usually confirm their answer by referring to the graphic aid or chart.

Customize for
More Advanced Students

Ask students to think of other ways that the information in the graph could be presented. Suggest that they consider different graphic aids, illustrations, or other creative ways to convey this information.

Customize for
ESL Students

Make certain that students understand all the words in the passage and graph. For example, the connection between *grains* and *bread* in Question 3 may not be readily apparent to non-fluent English speakers.

In-Depth Lesson Plan

	LESSON FOCUS	PRINT AND MEDIA RESOURCES
DAY 1	**Developing Vocabulary** Students learn strategies for developing vocabulary, such as wide reading, context clues, connotation and denotation, and analogies. (pp. 766–771/H566–571)	**Teaching Resources** *Academic and Workplace Skills Activity Book,* pp. 13–16
DAY 2	**Studying Words Systematically; Studying Word Parts and Origins** Students learn and apply strategies for studying vocabulary words. (pp. 772–777/H572–577)	**Teaching Resources** *Academic and Workplace Skills Activity Book,* pp. 17–21
DAY 3	**Improving Your Spelling** Students learn strategies for improving spelling, such as keeping a spelling notebook, studying problem words, and applying spelling rules. (pp. 778–782/H578–582)	**Teaching Resources** *Academic and Workplace Skills Activity Book,* pp. 22–24
DAY 4	**Improving Your Spelling** *continued* Students learn strategies for improving spelling words with confusing endings and for proofreading carefully. (pp. 783–787/H583–587)	**Teaching Resources** *Academic and Workplace Skills Activity Book,* pp. 25–28; *Formal Assessment,* Ch. 30

Accelerated Lesson Plan

	LESSON FOCUS	PRINT AND MEDIA RESOURCES
DAY 1	**Developing Vocabulary** Students learn and apply strategies for developing vocabulary. (pp. 766–771/H566–571)	**Teaching Resources** *Academic and Workplace Skills Activity Book,* pp. 13–16
DAY 2	**Studying Words Systematically; Studying Word Parts and Origins** Students learn and apply strategies for studying vocabulary words. (pp. 772–777/H572–577)	**Teaching Resources** *Academic and Workplace Skills Activity Book,* pp. 17–21
DAY 3	**Improving Your Spelling** Students learn and apply strategies for improving spelling and for proofreading carefully. (pp. 778–787/H578–587)	**Teaching Resources** *Academic and Workplace Skills Activity Book,* pp. 22–28; *Formal Assessment,* Ch. 30

Options for Adapting Lesson Plans

HOMEWORK

Have students complete any of the exercises for homework.

FEATURES

Extend coverage with the Standardized Test Preparation Workshop (p. 788).

TECHNOLOGY

Students may use the Internet to conduct independent research. Have them print out their completed work.

Writing and Grammar Handbook Alignment

Page numbers in Step-by-Step Teaching Guides in this Teacher's Edition refer to pages from the full student text. Handbook page references, indicated with this icon **H**, are provided in Time and Resource Manager boxes and at the bottom of each Teacher's Edition page.

INTEGRATED SKILLS COVERAGE

Viewing and Representing
Critical Viewing SE pp. 766, 769, 770, 777, 779, 781, 784/
H566, 569, 570, 577, 579, 581, 584

Technology Skills
SE pp. 770, 776/**H**570, 576

Research Skills
SE pp. 768, 772, 780/**H**568, 572, 580

Listening Skills
ATE pp. 769, 774

Workplace Skills
ATE p. 787

Real-World Connection ATE p. 772

ASSESSMENT SUPPORT

Standardized Test Preparation Workshop SE p. 788; ATE p. 770

Standardized Test Preparation Workbook, pp. 59–60

Formal Assessment, Ch. 30

MEETING INDIVIDUAL NEEDS

Less Advanced Students ATE pp. 768, 776, 785, 789. See also Ongoing Assessments ATE pp. 771, 776.

More Advanced Students ATE pp. 771, 782

ESL Students ATE pp. 769, 773, 775, 777, 789

Gifted and Talented Students ATE p. 783

Spatial Learners ATE p. 780

Linguistic Learners ATE pp. 775, 785

Intrapersonal Learners ATE p. 778

BLOCK SCHEDULING

Pacing Suggestions
For 90-minute Blocks
• Have students complete the strategies for developing vocabulary and studying words in a single period.
• Focus one class period on spelling strategies and proofreading carefully.

Professional Development Support
• *How to Manage Instruction in the Block* This teaching resource provides management and activity suggestions.

MEDIA AND TECHNOLOGY

For the Teacher
• **Teacher**EXPRESS™ CD-ROM

WRITING AND GRAMMAR ON-LINE

Interactive Text (On-line or on CD-ROM)
• Easily navigable instruction with interactive Revision Checkers
• Full use of e-rater™, the essay-scoring system (on-line only)

Companion Web Site PHSchool.com
• Scoring rubrics with models (use Web Code eek-1001)

See the Go On-line! **feature, SE p. iii.**

► *Lesson Objectives*

1. To expand vocabulary through wide reading, listening, and discussing

2. To rely on context to determine meanings of words and phrases, such as denotation and connotation

3. To recognize synonyms, antonyms, and homophones

4. To read and understand analogies

5. To use reference material, such as a dictionary or thesaurus, to determine precise meaning and usage

6. To learn techniques for remembering the meanings of new words

7. To apply meanings of prefixes, roots, and suffixes in order to comprehend vocabulary

8. To research word origins as an aid to understanding meanings, derivations, and spellings as well as influences on the English language

9. To practice careful proofreading

10. To recognize problem words and learn techniques to improve spelling

Critical Viewing

Infer While some students may prefer studying alone, most students will probably recognize that studying in a group offers the opportunity to hear words pronounced by others, to discuss meanings, and to practice using new words in conversation.

Chapter 30 Vocabulary and Spelling

▲ **Critical Viewing** Is working in a group such as this one helpful in building vocabulary? Why or why not? **[Infer]**

You encounter new words in many ways. You see new words in textbooks or in the reading you do for pleasure. In addition, you hear new words in conversations, in the classroom, and on radio and television.

Learning different ways to expand your vocabulary and improve your spelling are some of the most useful skills you can acquire. No matter how large your vocabulary is, you can always increase your knowledge of word meanings and spellings. The best way to build these skills is to work on remembering and using new words. This task requires some patience, but it is not as difficult as you may think—and the rewards of being able to read, write, and speak more successfully are well worth the effort.

766 • Vocabulary and Spelling

⏱ **TIME AND RESOURCE MANAGER**

Resources
Print: *Academic and Workplace Skills Activity Book*, pp. 13–16

Using the Full Student Edition	Using the Handbook🄷
• Cover pp. 766–771 in class.	• Cover pp. 566–571 in class.
• Discuss types of context. Do Exercise 1 in class and share results.	• Discuss types of context. Do Exercise 1 in class and share results.
• Assign Exercises 2–3 for homework.	• Assign Exercises 2–3 for homework.
• Do Exercise 4 in class, creating a test sentence for each pair of capitalized words.	• Do Exercise 4 in class, creating a test sentence for each pair of capitalized words.

Developing Your Vocabulary

Section 30.1

In today's era of communication, words are a fundamental tool. The more words you have to choose from, the more ideas and feelings you can express. Trying to write or speak with a limited vocabulary is like trying to paint a picture with a limited number of colors.

To increase your vocabulary, you must first have a desire to expand your knowledge of word meanings, as well as a commitment to studying new words. Following are a number of helpful techniques that you can use:

Reading, Listening, and Discussing

Most of the words that we use every day we learned when we were children, just by keeping our eyes and ears open.

▶ **KEY CONCEPT** The most common ways to increase your vocabulary are listening, reading, and taking part in conversations. ■

Hearing and Using New Words There was a time when you did not know even the simplest words. You had to learn the meaning of *mother* and *father*, *run* and *walk*, *hot* and *cold*, *in* and *out*. First, you heard the words spoken. Then, you learned to repeat them. Eventually, you were able to put the new words together and use them in conversation.

Listening and discussing are still excellent ways to expand your vocabulary. When you talk to other people, follow discussions in class, watch television, hear literature on audiocassettes, or listen to the radio, be alert to unfamiliar words. Find out the meaning by using a dictionary or by asking. (Never be embarrassed to ask what a word means; it shows that you are listening and that you want to learn.) Whenever possible, try to use the new words in conversation.

Reading Extensively In general, people use a wider variety of words when they write than when they speak. Therefore, you can expand your vocabulary by reading even more than you can by listening.

The more you read, the more you will be introduced to new words. You will also encounter familiar words used in new, unfamiliar ways. To expand your vocabulary, try to read as extensively as possible: A wide variety of sources and subjects means a wide variety of words. Textbooks, newspapers, magazines, novels, and articles on the Internet can all be rich sources of vocabulary.

Vocabulary and Spelling • **767**

Recognizing Context Clues

Teaching Resources: Academic and Workplace Skills Activity Book, p. 13

1. Point out that, while the term *context* is defined as "the words surrounding a word," students can often take advantage of a larger context. Often, thinking about the subject being read (science or history) contributes to the process of determining a word's meaning.

2. Ask students how they can tell which words in a sentence give important clues to the unfamiliar words. (They can read the sentence closely to discover how other words relate to the unfamiliar word.)

3. Write the following sentences on the board and have the class work to find context clues and guess the meanings of the words *spinnaker* and *pellucid*.

   The spinnaker billowed in the wind, and soon the boat was gaining speed. (type of sail)

   When I went diving on the reef, I was amazed by how far I could see in the pellucid water. (clear)

4. Remind students that it is wise to confirm a meaning discovered by context by checking a dictionary, when possible.

Customize for
Less Advanced Students

Allow students to work in pairs on Exercise 1. As they read each sentence, have them jot down underlined words as well as other important words that give clues to meaning. Let students discuss possible word meanings and then check words in a dictionary.

Answer Key

> **Exercise 1**

1. hostile feelings
2. ravenous, eating much
3. gloomy, sullen
4. lack of energy
5. still, quiet, without movement

30.1

Recognizing Context Clues

When you come across an unfamiliar word, you may be able to guess its meaning by examining its context. The context of a word is determined by the other words in the sentence or the passage surrounding it.

A knowledge of the different types of context clues can help you use them effectively.

▶ **KEY CONCEPT** Use context clues to determine the meaning of unfamiliar words. ■

TYPES OF CONTEXT CLUES	
Clue	**Example**
Key words in the sentence that give the word's meaning	*Mountains* and *tall* buildings scare me because I have <u>acrophobia</u>. (Italicized words suggest height. <u>Acrophobia</u> must mean "fear of high places.")
Comparisons; contrasts; synonyms; antonyms	One cat is *courageous* and *loves* adventure; the other is <u>timorous</u> and hides under the sofa. (<u>Timorous</u> must mean "fearful.")
Words or phrases that follow a word closely and rename or define it	<u>Bonsai</u>, *the art of growing trees in small pots*, is well known in Japan. (The italicized phrase provides the correct meaning.)

▶ **Exercise 1** Recognizing Context Clues Use context clues to determine the meaning of each underlined word. Check your answers in a dictionary.

1. Gloria's <u>animosity</u> could be seen in her unfriendly expression and hostile tone of voice.
2. After his eight-mile run, Mel was <u>voracious</u> and ate everything in the refrigerator.
3. The newcomer appeared to be <u>morose</u>, but later her spirits lifted.
4. Sitting for a long time watching a lot of television can reduce your energy, resulting in a feeling of <u>lethargy</u>.
5. Moving not a muscle, the actor playing the victim was able to remain <u>inert</u>.

🔲 Research Tip

Find a current newsmagazine, and select five unfamiliar words. Guess their meanings according to their context, and check your answers in a dictionary.

▶ **More Practice**

Academic and Workplace Skills Activity Book
• pp. 13–14

Denotation and Connotation

Context can help you determine a word's exact meaning. Knowing the denotations and connotations of a word can help you discriminate between different shades of meaning.

> **KEY CONCEPTS** The **denotation** of a word is its literal definition. Its **connotations** include the ideas, images, and feelings that are associated with the word. ∎

A definition of *dictator* is "a ruler with absolute power and authority." That is the denotation of the word. However, what comes into your mind when you hear the word *dictator*? You may think of ideas such as injustice and cruelty. You may picture specific images, such as an iron fist or a specific historic figure, such as Joseph Stalin. You may even feel emotions, such as fear and anger. All of these are connotations associated with the word *dictator*. As you strengthen your vocabulary, be aware of both positive and negative connotations of the words you use.

> **Exercise 2** Discriminating Between Denotation and Connotation Read each pair of sentences below. For each pair, write a sentence explaining the different connotations of the underlined words. Use a dictionary to help you.
> 1. John was <u>unaware</u> of the recent events in Asia.
>   John was <u>ignorant</u> of the recent events in Asia.
> 2. The <u>slim</u> model walked gracefully down the ramp.
>   The <u>skinny</u> model walked gracefully down the ramp.
> 3. The <u>uninvited</u> guests arrived at three o'clock.
>   The <u>unexpected</u> guests arrived at three o'clock.
> 4. That store carries a lot of <u>cheap</u> clothing.
>   That store carries a lot of <u>inexpensive</u> clothing.
> 5. The fans <u>crowded</u> around their favorite movie star.
>   The fans <u>swarmed</u> around their favorite movie star.

▼ Critical Viewing
Write two sentences describing this picture. In one, use words with a positive connotation; in the other, try to be neutral. **[Interpret]**

Developing Your Vocabulary • **769**

Step-by-Step Teaching Guide

Denotation and Connotation

Teaching Resources: Academic and Workplace Skills Activity Book, p. 14

1. Ask students to explain the difference between *denotation* and *connotation*. (*Denotation* is the word's actual meaning. *Connotation* includes ideas, images, and feelings that people associate with the word.)
2. Point out that, not only can context help a reader determine a word's meaning, but the connotation of a word, once determined, can help the reader determine the writer's tone, shedding light on the whole passage.
3. Explain that, often, connotation is more subtle than the images conjured up by words such as *dictator*.
4. Tell students that, in many cases, experience and context are the only ways to determine subtle differences between words with similar meanings (such as *profuseness* and *prodigality*), but generally the dictionary will be their greatest ally, giving both definitions and, in many cases, synonym studies.

Integrating Listening Skills

Encourage students to listen carefully to news reporters. Since reporters are expected to be objective, they can rarely use denotation to express their opinions, so they may rely on connotation to relate their feelings and thoughts on issues or people. Students might enjoy sharing any examples they discover.

Customize for
ESL Students

Some students may have greater difficulty recognizing connotation. Have them work in pairs with more fluent students, and allow them to discuss connotations of the words.

Critical Viewing

Interpret Answers will vary, but may include words such as *stylish* (positive) or *sleeveless* (neutral).

Answer Key

> **Exercise 2**

Answers will vary; examples are given.
1. *Unaware* connotes that John hadn't heard the news; *ignorant* connotes that he has little or no knowledge of the subject.
2. *Stubbornly* connotes willfulness; *steadfastness* connotes constancy.
3. *Uninvited* suggests that the guests may have been unwelcome; *unexpected* suggests that the arrival of the guests was a happy surprise.
4. *Cheap* suggests poorly made; *inexpensive* suggests good bargains.
5. *Crowded around* connotes a few people and orderly behavior; *swarmed around* connotes many more people and, perhaps, a frenzy.

Recognizing Related Words

Teaching Resources: Academic and Workplace Skills Activity Book, p. 15

1. Ask students to define *synonym, antonym,* and *homophone.*

2. Point out that synonyms and antonyms, besides helping students remember meanings, can also liven up their writing. For example, instead of repeating that someone is smart, they could use synonyms such as *intelligent, learned, erudite, bright,* or *gifted.*

3. Put a word such as *nice* on the board and have students brainstorm for synonyms. Repeat for antonyms.

4. Explain to students that homophones are not related words, and will not help them discover meaning, but they can confuse people. They are a common trap for writers, who might mistakenly use the wrong word because it sounds right (*they're, their, there; steak, stake; sheer, shear*).

5. Let students work through the word pairs in Exercise 3. After students identify each word pair as synonyms, antonyms, or homophones, have students use each word in a sentence.

Answer Key

> **Exercise 3**

1. homophones
2. antonyms
3. homophones *and* antonyms
4. homophones
5. synonyms
6. synonyms
7. synonyms
8. antonyms
9. synonyms
10. antonyms

Critical Viewing

Infer Answers will vary, but may include the idea that recording words helps one remember meanings.

Recognizing Related Words

Discovering how words relate to other words is a good way to increase your vocabulary.

▶ **KEY CONCEPTS** **Synonyms** are words that are similar in meaning. **Antonyms** are words that are opposite in meaning. **Homophones** are words that sound alike but have different meanings and spellings. ■

Synonyms It is often easier to remember a one-word synonym for a word than to remember a long dictionary definition. For example, you may be able to remember the word *attain* by remembering its synonym, *achieve.*

Antonyms Remembering antonyms in pairs may help you to recall each word's meaning. For example, *happy* is the antonym of *sad.*

Homophones Knowing that certain words sound alike but have different meanings and spellings can help you use their correct forms in writing. For example, make sure that you know the difference between the homophones *stationery* (writing material) and *stationary* (not moving).

▶ **Exercise 3** Recognizing Related Words Using a dictionary, identify each pair as either *synonyms, antonyms,* or *homophones.*

1. lead/led
2. rustic/refined
3. raze/raise
4. whether/weather
5. irk/annoy
6. insurrection/revolt
7. defer/delay
8. random/deliberate
9. ample/plentiful
10. vertical/horizontal

▶ Critical Viewing What subject do you think this student is studying? How will writing vocabulary words in a notebook help him expand his vocabulary? **[Infer]**

770 • Vocabulary and Spelling

Technology Tip

Do an on-line search, and find five new pairs of homophones. Add any unfamiliar words to your notebook.

✎ STANDARDIZED TEST PREPARATION WORKSHOP

Antonyms Standardized test questions may require students to recognize antonyms.

1. Which word is an antonym of *frustrate*?

A thwart   C abet

B baffle   D block

Students should recognize that **C**, *abet,* is the antonym because it means "encourage by aid or approval." A, B, and D are all synonyms of frustrate.

Using Related Words in Analogies

Working with analogies strengthens your vocabulary by increasing your understanding of connections between word meanings. Analogies are often found on standardized tests.

KEY CONCEPT An **analogy** is some similarity between things that are otherwise unlike. Analogy problems present pairs of words that have some relationship to each other. ■

Look at the following analogy, and see whether you can find the pair of words whose relationship is the most similar to the capitalized pair:

EXAMPLE: HINGES : DOOR ::
              a. roof : chimney
              b. rock : atom
              c. keyboard : organ
              The answer is *c.*

The key to solving analogies is to understand what the relationship is between the capitalized words. In this example, the relationship between the capitalized words is *part to whole—hinges* are part of a *door.* A *roof* is not a part of a *chimney.* A *rock* is not a part of an *atom.* (Although an *atom* is part of a *rock,* the words appear in a different order from the capitalized pair.) A *keyboard,* however, is a part of an *organ.*

There are other common analogy relationships. They include *type* (crocodile : reptile), *defining characteristic* (white : snow), *instrument* (knife : cut), *degree* (afraid : terrified), *sequence* (summer : autumn), and *proximity* (sidewalk : street).

Exercise 4 **Working With Analogies** First, identify the analogy relationship expressed in the capitalized pair. Then, choose the lettered pair that best expresses this relationship.
  1. INTRODUCTION : SPEECH ::
     a. preface : book b. speaker : audience c. scene : act
  2. HUMOR : COMEDIAN ::
     a. finish line : runner b. intelligence : genius c. lecture : teacher
  3. PAINTER : STUDIO ::
     a. sculpture : painting   b. judge : court c. writer : essay
  4. GEOMETRY : MATHEMATICS ::
     a. botany : science b. shape : number c. theorem : equation
  5. NEARBY : ADJOINING ::
     a. ocean : shore b. perpendicular : parallel   c. noisy : stentorious

More Practice

Academic and Workplace Skills Activity Book
• pp. 15–16

Developing Your Vocabulary • 771

Using Related Words in Analogies

Teaching Resources: Academic and Workplace Skills Activity Book, p. 16

1. Point out to students that they have probably encountered the term *analogy* before. Speakers and writers often say or write, "Let me give you an analogy," and then they embark on a story that illustrates their point.

2. Make sure students understand the definition of *analogy.* Then, discuss the meanings of the common analogy relationships identified in the text. Ask students for examples.

3. Emphasize that analogies should be as precise as possible. For example, *paw* is part of a dog and *head* is part of a human, so it seems like a part-to-whole analogy. However, *paw* is not analogous to the *head*—it would more closely parallel the hand.

Customize for
More Advanced Students

Challenge students to write their own analogy exercises to illustrate each analogy relationship. After checking the analogies yourself, have them write the analogies on the board for others to solve.

Answer Key

Exercise 4

  1. part-to-whole, a
  2. defining characteristic, b
  3. worker and workplace, b
  4. type, a
  5. degree, c

☑ **ONGOING ASSESSMENT: Monitor and Reinforce**

If you observe that students are having difficulty with Exercises 3–4, try the following strategies.

| **Option 1** Have students work in pairs on Exercise 3, using a dictionary to define the words and a thesaurus to find synonyms. Encourage them to look up words they find in the thesaurus to determine different connotations of the synonyms. | **Option 2** Ask students to suggest pairs of words in the format "X is to Y. . .," and have volunteers complete the phrase by suggesting an appropriate analogy: ". . . as A is to B." Then, have them explain why the two pairs are analogous. |

Using Resource Materials

Teaching Resources: Academic and Workplace Skills Activity Book, p. 17

1. Stress that, for effective communication, it is important to be precise in selecting words. Dictionaries make this possible.

2. Point out the four types of information found in most dictionary entries: pronunciation, part of speech, meaning, and etymology (word origins).

3. Write a few words on the board (possibilities: *scrooge, laser, algebra, scaloppine, jodhpurs*) and have students look them up. Ask volunteers to read the definitions and relate the words' etymologies. For unfamiliar words, you may also ask students to use the pronunciation guide to pronounce the word.

4. Explain that a thesaurus provides words that are similar in meaning to the word that is looked up.

5. Stress the importance of looking up in a dictionary any unfamiliar words students find in a thesaurus. This will help them avoid the embarrassment of using an inappropriate word.

Real-World Connection

Point out that many occupations require frequent use of both the dictionary and the thesaurus. Any occupation in which instructions or explanations are given might require these references. Workers in fields such as advertising and politics also use these references when writing persuasive arguments.

Answer Key

> **Exercise 5**

Have volunteers present the information they find about these words. Encourage the class to contribute any additional information they found that is not mentioned during presentations. Each presenter should comment both on what he or she found in the indicated references and on how the two uses are similar or different.

Section 30.2

Studying Words Systematically

Using Resource Materials

Two of the most valuable resource tools are a dictionary and a thesaurus. A dictionary is most helpful when you are reading; a thesaurus is most useful when you are writing.

▶ **KEY CONCEPTS** Use a dictionary to find the meaning, spelling, pronunciation, and origin of words. Use a thesaurus to expand the meaning of words. ■

Using a Dictionary It is a good idea to keep an unabridged (complete) dictionary nearby.

• Study the pronunciation given in parentheses after the word.

• Become aware of the part of speech (*n., v., adj.*). The meaning of a word can change depending upon its usage.

Using a Thesaurus A thesaurus gives a list of words similar in meaning to the one you know. (For example, if you look up *give* in a thesaurus, you might find *grant, contribute, tip, remit, fork over,* and *donate.*) Be sure to check a dictionary to see whether your substitute has the correct connotation.

Learning About Etymologies Understanding word origins can help you understand words even if you have never seen them before. The English language adopts words from a variety of sources.

• English borrows or adopts words from other languages, especially Latin and Greek. (Examples: *Drama* is a Greek word. *Tycoon* is borrowed from China and Japan.)

• Words can change meaning over time and through usage. (Example: The word *dear* used to mean "expensive.")

• Words can be invented, or coined, to serve new purposes. (Example: The words *paperbacks* and *quiz* are coined.)

• Words can be shortened. (Example: The word *flu* is short for *influenza.*)

▶ **Exercise 5** Using Vocabulary Reference Aids Look up each of the following words in the references indicated. Compare and contrast the information found in each source.
1. streak (dictionary, science textbook glossary)
2. annex (social studies textbook glossary, dictionary)
3. durability (dictionary, thesaurus)
4. grow (science textbook glossary, on-line thesaurus)

772 • Vocabulary and Spelling

🔖 **Research Tip**

Find five unfamiliar words. Look them up in a thesaurus. Then, look them up in a dictionary to determine differences in their meanings. Add the new words to your notebook.

▶ **More Practice**

Academic and Workplace Skills Activity Book
• pp. 17–18

⏱ TIME AND RESOURCE MANAGER

Resources
Print: *Academic and Workplace Skills Activity Book,* pp. 17–18

Using the Full Student Edition	Using the Handbook🄷
• Cover pp. 772–773 in class. • Give students time to complete Exercise 5 in class. • Assign Exercise 6 as homework. Let students share their results in class.	• Cover pp. 572–573 in class. • Give students time to complete Exercise 5 in class. • Assign Exercise 6 as homework. Let students share their results in class.

Remembering Vocabulary Words

To make a word part of your vocabulary, study its definition, use it in your writing and speaking, and review it to make sure that you really understand its meaning.

▶ **KEY CONCEPT** Use one or more review techniques to remember the meanings of new words. ■

Using a Vocabulary Notebook Keep a notebook for vocabulary words. Divide your page into three columns: the *words* you want to learn; hints or *bridge words* that help you remember their meanings; and their *definitions*. Test yourself by covering either the second or third column.

VOCABULARY NOTEBOOK

Word	Bridge	Definition
ornithology	oriole	study of birds
oscillate	pendulum	swing back and forth
effervescent	soda	bubbly

Making Flashcards On the front of an index card, write a *word* you want to remember and the *bridge word*. On the back, write the *definition*. Test yourself by flipping through the cards. Enter any difficult words in your vocabulary notebook. As you master the meanings, remove these cards and add new ones.

Using a Tape Recorder Record your vocabulary words. Leave a ten-second space after each word, followed by the definition and a short sentence using the word. Replay the tape. Fill in the blank space with the definition and a sentence. Replay the tape until you can give the information easily.

▶ **Exercise 6** Adding New Words to Your Vocabulary Identify five difficult words from one of your textbooks. Enter the words and their definitions in your vocabulary notebook. Study the words using one of the above methods. Then, test yourself by using each word in a sentence. Check your answers and correct them.

Remembering Vocabulary Words

Teaching Resources: Academic and Workplace Skills Activity Book, p. 18

1. Explain that writing things down has been shown to be one of the most effective ways of learning and remembering something.

2. Another effective tool for remembering things is finding or creating a clue or trigger idea that helps you remember things.

3. Point out that a vocabulary notebook combines two effective memory techniques: writing down and creating a clue.

4. Ask students whether they have ever used flashcards or a tape recorder as a memory aid. Why would these be helpful? (Repetition is very important in processing information into long-term memory.)

Customize for
ESL Students

Let students know that, as they build their vocabulary lists, they may include the translation of the word into their first language as the bridge word. However, the definition should be in English, to help them start thinking of words in context.

Answer Key

▶ **Exercise 6**

Have each student offer one word and its definition in class. You may want to have each student record the words on the board so that the rest of the class can see the correct spelling in case they wish to record the words themselves. Encourage students to look up any words they record, to reinforce the meaning and possibly find other applications.

Recognizing Word Roots

Teaching Resources: Academic and Workplace Skills Activity Book, p. 19

1. Ask students to explain in their own words why it is valuable to know the meanings of word parts. (It helps with understanding and helps increase vocabulary.)

2. Draw students' attention to the chart in the text. Have students describe how the meaning of the root relates to the definition of the word. Permit them to use dictionaries if necessary.

3. Point out that examples of roots that can stand alone can be found in the prefix chart on page 775 (*join* of *adjoin, fluent* of *effluent*).

4. If the dictionaries you use in class do not spell out the derivations of words (Old English vs. OE), show students where they can find a list of the abbreviations used.

5. Demonstrate to students how knowing both the root and the prefix can help them determine meaning. For example, using *-phil* from the list, show how students might guess that *Philadelphia* and *bibliophile* might have to do with loving something (*Philadelphia*: City of Brotherly Love; *bibliophile*: book lover).

6. Have students look up the elements of *egress* and *progress* to further illustrate how this works. Then, have them guess what *ingress* means ("to enter").

Integrating Listening Skills

Encourage students to make a list of words they hear or see in the next day or two that have the roots listed in the chart. Have them also jot down the context in which each word was used. Let students share these words in class.

Studying Word Parts and Origins

In addition to learning new words, you can improve your vocabulary by learning about *word structure,* or the parts that make up a word.

The three word parts that can combine to form a word are a root (such as *-duc-* in pro*duc*tion), a prefix (such as *pro-* in *pro*duction), and a suffix (such as *-tion* in produc*tion*). Many of these word parts come to us from Latin, Greek, and Anglo-Saxon languages.

Recognizing Word Roots

The **root** of a word contains its basic meaning. Learning to recognize the most common word roots in English is the foundation of developing your vocabulary.

▶ **KEY CONCEPT** The **root** of a word carries the basic meaning of the word. ■

In some words, especially shorter words, the root may stand alone. In either case, knowing roots can help you figure out the meanings of unfamiliar words.

Roots have come into the English language from many sources, especially from Latin and Greek. (In the chart below, Latin and Greek roots are identified by the letters *L* and *G*). In the first column below, additional spellings of the roots are indicated in parentheses.

TEN COMMON ROOTS

Root and Origin	Meaning	Examples
-cap- (-capt-, -cept-, -ceipt-) [L.]	to take, seize	*cap*able, *capt*ivate, ac*cept*, re*ceipt*
-chor- (-cho-) [Gr.]	to dance, sing	*chor*eography, *choir*
-duc- (-duce-, -duct-) [L.]	to lead	pro*duce*, re*duce*, con*duct*
-fer- [L.]	to bring, carry	trans*fer*, in*fer*ence
-graph- [Gr.]	to write	auto*graph*
-path- [Gr.]	to feel, suffer	sym*path*y, anti*path*y
-phil- [Gr.]	to love	*phil*osophy
-puls- (-pel-) [L.]	to drive	*puls*ate, pro*pel*
-tend- (-tens-, -tent-) [L.]	to stretch	dis*tend*, ex*tens*ion, ex*tent*
-vid- (-vis-) L.	to see	e*vid*ent, *vis*ion

⏱ TIME AND RESOURCE MANAGER

Resources
Print: *Academic and Workplace Skills Activity Book,* pp. 19–21

Using the Full Student Edition	Using the Handbook Ⓗ
• Cover pp. 774–777 in class. • Give students time to complete Exercises 7–12 in class. • Provide an opportunity for students to share their findings for each exercise.	• Cover pp. 574–577 in class. • Give students time to complete Exercises 7–12 in class. • Provide an opportunity for students to share their findings for each exercise.

> **Exercise 7** Using Roots to Define Words Using the chart on the previous page, select the definition that matches the word. Consult a dictionary if necessary.

1. pathos
2. reception
3. telegraph
4. impulse
5. tendency

a. a system for sending messages
b. a driving force
c. an inclination to act in a particular way
d. arousing pity or sorrow
e. a social function for receiving guests

> **Exercise 8** Finding Common Roots Look up each pair of words below in a dictionary, paying close attention to the word's root, shown in italics. Then, write the basic meaning of the root shared by each pair of words.

1. *spec*imen, in*spect*
2. con*vene*, in*ventor*
3. *ten*ure, de*tain*
4. pro*ceed*, suc*cess*
5. con*vert*, di*version*

Using Prefixes

A **prefix** is one or more syllables at the beginning of a word.

> **KEY CONCEPT** The *prefix* appears before the word root and adds to its meaning. ■

Learning Prefixes Learn the meanings and origins of the prefixes below. Additional spellings are given in parentheses. The abbreviations *L*, *Gr*, and *AS* mean Latin, Greek, and Anglo-Saxon, the origins from which the prefixes have come. Notice that some prefixes take more than one form—as shown in parentheses—but still have the same meaning.

TEN COMMON PREFIXES		
Prefix and Origin	**Meaning**	**Examples**
ad- (ac-, af-, al-, ap-, as-, at-) [L.]	to, toward	*ad*join, *af*fix, *ac*knowledge
com- (co-, col-, con-, cor-) [L.]	with, together	*col*laborate, *cor*respond
dis- (di-, dif-) [L.]	away, apart	*dis*connect, *dif*fuse
epi- [Gr.]	on, outside, among	*epi*taph, *epi*center
ex- (e-, ec-, ef-) [L.]	forth, from, out	*ec*centric, *ef*fluent
in- (il-, im-, ir-) [L.]	in, into, on, toward	*in*dent, *ir*rigate
mis- [AS]	wrongly	*mis*calculate
mono- [Gr.]	one, alone	*mono*tonous
non- [L.]	not	*non*essential
syn- [Gr.]	together with	*syn*chronize

> **More Practice**
> Academic and Workplace Skills Activity Book
> • pp.19–20

> 🖋 **Spelling Tip**
> Don't confuse the prefix *ante-*, meaning "before," with the prefix *anti-*, meaning "against."

Customize for
Linguistic Learners

Have each of two groups of linguistic learners construct another exercise for matching words from the roots chart with their definitions. When the exercises are completed, let each group solve the other's exercise and share their results with the class.

Customize for
ESL Students

Have students work on Exercise 8 in pairs. Ask them, once they know what the words mean, to write short sentences using the words, to reinforce meaning.

Answer Key

> **Exercise 7**

1. d   4. b
2. e   5. c
3. a

> **Exercise 8**

1. to look at or see, spy
2. to come upon or come together
3. to hold
4. to go
5. to turn

> **Step-by-Step Teaching Guide**

Using Prefixes

Teaching Resources: Academic and Workplace Skills Activity Book, p. 20

1. Point out that even the word *prefix* has a prefix: *pre-*, which means "before in rank or time." This indicates that a prefix is fixed (attached) to the front of a word. Suggest that students add this to their lists of prefixes, along with its opposite: *post-*, as in *postscript*.

2. Have students explain how the meanings of the prefixes in the chart relate to the definitions of the words. (Using dictionaries is acceptable.)

3. In class, brainstorm for other words using prefixes on the chart (*admit, congress, dissolve, epigram*), or for other prefixes that students know (*pro-, anti-, re-*).

4. Encourage students to add other prefixes to the list as they find them.

Customize for
Less Advanced Students

For Exercise 9, let students work with partners. Each person can figure out the meaning of five words and then trade lists and use a dictionary to check his or her partner's definitions.

Answer Key

Exercise 9

1. to name to or select for an office
2. to give or furnish something
3. skin or outer covering
4. to turn aside, direct away from
5. to move out or away
6. to put in a wrong place
7. to light up
8. a single lens
9. to bring together, combine
10. words or actions that have no meaning or are absurd

Exercise 10

1. *ab- (a-, abs-)*: Latin—away, from, from off, or down, as in *abdicate.*
2. *in- (il-, im-, ir-)*: Latin—no, not, or without, as in *incorrect.*
3. *inter-*: Latin—between or among, as in *international.*
4. *non-*: Latin—not or the opposite of, as in *nonlinear.*
5. *un-*: from Greek and Latin—not, lack of, or the opposite of, as in *uncontrollable.*

Step-by-Step Teaching Guide

Understanding Suffixes

Teaching Resources: Academic and Workplace Skills Activity Book, p. 21

1. Review the definition of *suffix* and emphasize that suffixes change both the word form and the part of speech.

2. Have students look at the examples in the chart and identify the original form of the word to which a suffix was added (for example, reliable/rely; activate/ active; clarify/clear). Have them name the part of speech of the original words.

▶ **Exercise 9** Defining Words With Prefixes Using your knowledge of prefixes, figure out the meaning of each word below. Then, check your answers in a dictionary.

1. *ap*point
2. *con*tribute
3. *epi*dermis
4. *di*vert
5. *e*migrate
6. *mis*place
7. *il*luminate
8. *mono*cle
9. *syn*thesize
10. *non*sense

▶ **Exercise 10** Defining Prefixes and Prefix Origins Using a dictionary, write the definition of each prefix and its origin. Then, provide an example of a word using each prefix.

1. ab- (a-, abs-)
2. in- (il-, im-, ir-)
3. inter-
4. non-
5. un-

Understanding Suffixes

A **suffix** is a syllable or group of syllables added to the end of a word root to form a new word. Note that a suffix often alters the part of speech.

▶ **KEY CONCEPT** The *suffix* is added to the end of the root and can change its meaning or part of speech. ■

Learning Suffixes Suffixes are unique in that they can change both word forms and parts of speech. In the first column, additional spellings are in parentheses. Note: *L, Gr,* and *AS* mean Latin, Greek, and Anglo-Saxon.

TEN COMMON SUFFIXES		
Suffix and Origin	**Meaning and Examples**	**Part of Speech**
-able (-ible) [L.]	capable of being: *reliable*	*adjective*
-ate [L.]	to make: *activate*	*verb*
-fy [L.]	to cause, become: *clarify*	*verb*
-ist [Gr.]	a skilled person: *violinist*	*noun*
-ize (-ise) [Gr.]	to make: *improvise*	*verb*
-less [AS.]	without: *ageless*	*adjective*
-ly [AS.]	in a certain way: *hourly, harshly*	*adjective or adverb*
-ness [AS.]	state of: *laziness*	*noun*
-or [L.]	quality of: *error*	*noun*
-tion (-ion,-sion, -ation) [L.]	the action of; state of being: *action*	*noun*

○ Technology Tip

Search for an on-line Web site that provides more information on Latin, Greek, and Anglo-Saxon suffixes. Find five new words, and add them and their definitions to your vocabulary notebook.

✓ ONGOING ASSESSMENT: Monitor and Reinforce

If you observe that students are having difficulty with Exercises 9–12, try one of the following strategies.

Option 1 Give students classroom time to work on dictionary skills. You may want to review how words are alphabetized (check the first letter, then move to the second letter of the word, etc.). Then, suggest words and have students look them up, offering assistance to any who appear to be having difficulty.

Option 2 Divide the class into pairs and have partners work through a difficult exercise together.

Exercise 11 Defining Suffixes For each suffix, write its definition and origin. Use a dictionary to assist you.

1. -esque
2. -ism
3. -ous (-ious)
4. -ity
5. -or
6. -ant (-ent)
7. -ful
8. -ment
9. -ance (-ence)
10. -ade

Exercise 12 Using Suffixes to Form Words Add the correct suffix to each underlined word to form a new word that will complete each sentence below. In your notebook, write each new word and its part of speech.

1. A person who <u>conforms</u> is usually called a ___?___.
2. People who are unable to <u>help</u> themselves are considered to be ___?___.
3. When you cause something to become <u>active</u>, you ___?___ it.
4. To cause an activity to become <u>legal</u> is to ___?___ it.
5. When someone gives the <u>glory</u> to someone else, they ___?___ that person.
6. One who <u>mediates</u> a controversy between people or groups is called a ___?___.
7. The quality of loving one's country like a <u>patriot</u> is called ___?___.
8. If you give a lot of <u>thought</u> to other people's feelings, you are said to be ___?___.
9. An action intended to <u>punish</u> someone is called a ___?___.
10. If it is possible to <u>break</u> something, that item should be considered ___?___.

◀ Critical Viewing
Think of some words with suffixes that this photograph calls to mind. [Interpret]

Studying Word Parts and Origins • **777**

Customize for ESL Students

After students have looked up and recorded meanings, origins, and parts of speech for each suffix, encourage them to brainstorm for words that have these endings. If they have trouble thinking of examples, suggest words, and have them look the words up. Ask students to use these words in sentences, to reinforce learning.

Answer Key

> **Exercise 11**

1. *-esque*: French—forms adjectives; means like or in the style of, as in *Romanesque*.
2. *-ism*: Greek—forms nouns; means the act or practice of___ing (*baptism* is the act of baptizing) or quality of being a___ (*heroism* is quality of being a hero).
3. *-ous (-ious)*: Latin—forms adjectives; means having, full of, or characterized by, as in *beauteous*.
4. *-ity*: Latin—forms nouns; means state, character, or an instance of, as in *ability*.
5. *-or*: Latin— forms nouns; means a person or thing that ___s, as in *inventor* (person who invents) or *accelerator* (thing that accelerates).
6. *-ant (-ent)*: Latin—forms adjectives; means has, shows, or does, as in *defiant*; also used to form nouns meaning a person or thing that, as in *occupant*.
7. *-ful*: Old English—forms adjectives; means full of or characterized by, as in *joyful*; also used to form nouns meaning the quantity that fills, as in *handful* or *cupful*.
8. *-ment*: Latin—forms nouns; means the act, art or process of, as in *enchantment*.
9. *-ance (-ence)*: Latin—forms nouns; means the act or process of ___ing, as in *continuance*; also means a thing that ___s, as in *hindrance*.
10. *-ade*: French—forms verbs; means the act of ___ing, as in *blockade*; also forms nouns meaning result or product, as in *lemonade*.

continued

Answer Key continued

> **Exercise 12**

1. conformist; noun
2. helpless; adjective
3. activate; verb
4. legalize; verb
5. glorify; verb
6. mediator; noun
7. patriotism; noun
8. thoughtful; adjective
9. punishment; noun
10. breakable; adjective

Critical Viewing

Interpret Possibilities might include *patriotic* or *patriotism, traditional*, and *symbolic*. Students may suggest other words.

More Practice
Academic and Workplace Skills Activity Book
• p. 21

Keeping a Spelling Notebook

Teaching Resources: Academic and Workplace Skills Activity Book, p. 22

1. Remind students that writing things down is one of the keys to remembering them.

2. Show students how they can keep a record of difficult words they discover, as well as aids for remembering the words.

3. Suggest that students start their lists with words in this lesson that give them difficulty, but continue with words they find misspelled in future work. They can use either a sheet of paper or the form in the activity book.

4. Point out that the spelling rules in this chapter can be used in the memory aid column of this chart.

5. Tell students that they do not need to have misspelled something to include it in the notebook. If a word is simply tricky, they can list it along with its memory aid and just leave the "misspelled" column blank.

6. Give students some time to begin their spelling notebooks.

Customize for
Intrapersonal Learners

Encourage students to develop their own tips and techniques for building vocabulary and remembering how to spell words. Then, after they have had some time to build up the lists in their spelling notebooks, ask students to share with the class their tips for recording misspelled words and remembering correct spellings.

Improving Your Spelling

When it comes to spelling, English is one of the most difficult languages in the world. In some languages, such as Italian or French, spelling tends to follow a few basic rules. In English, however, there are many exceptions to almost every spelling rule. As a result, the same sound might be spelled in different ways. For example, the words *so, hoe, dough, flow, sew,* and *beau* all rhyme. In addition, the same combination of letters might be pronounced different ways, as in the words *dough, rough, through,* and *bough.*

Despite this difficulty, it is important to learn to spell correctly. Careless spelling tends to indicate either that you do not know how to spell or that your writing is careless. Someone reading your writing may be less than favorably impressed, and the value of your efforts to communicate is diminished. By using a strategy that includes practice and some simple rules, you can improve your spelling and thereby have a positive effect on all of your writing.

Keeping a Spelling Notebook

You can reduce spelling errors if you keep track of and study words that are especially difficult for you. The best place to do this is in a special section of your notebook.

▶ **KEY CONCEPT** Make a personal spelling list of difficult words; enter it in your notebook; and keep it up to date. ■

Setting Up Your Spelling Notebook Prepare a page with four columns. In the first column, record the incorrectly spelled words as you wrote them. In the second column, record the correct spelling. In the third column, enter the dates when you practiced the word. In the fourth column, write hints that help you remember the correct spelling.

PERSONAL SPELLING LIST

Misspelled Words	Correct Spelling	Practice Dates	Memory Aids
artic	arctic	4/11	no art in arctic
seperate	separate	4/11, 4/18	separate means apart and both have two A's.

⏱ TIME AND RESOURCE MANAGER

Resources
Print: *Academic and Workplace Skills Activity Book,* pp. 22–28

Using the Full Student Edition	Using the Handbook🄷
• Review pp. 778–787 in class. • Focus on steps for reviewing problem words and ask students to create a personal spelling list in their notebooks. • Discuss spelling rules and work on developing memory aids. • Have students complete Exercises 14–22 in class.	• Review pp. 578–587 in class. • Focus on steps for reviewing problem words and ask students to create a personal spelling list in their notebooks. • Discuss spelling rules and work on developing memory aids. • Have students completed Exercises 14–22 in class.

> **Exercise 13** Selecting Words for a Personal Spelling List
Look over all of the writing you have done in the last month.
Record any of your misspelled words on your list.

Studying Problem Words

Some words may be difficult for you to spell because you
seldom use them. Others you may repeatedly misspell. A systematic study can help you correct both kinds of mistakes.

KEY CONCEPT To study problem words, use several
steps: Look, say, listen, write, and repeat.■

STEPS FOR REVIEWING PROBLEM WORDS

1. *Look* at each word carefully to notice the arrangement or
   pattern of the letters. Try to see the word in your mind.
2. *Pronounce* each syllable of the word to yourself.
3. *Write* the word, and check its spelling in a dictionary.
4. *Review* your list until you can write each word correctly.

> **Exercise 14** Working With Problem Words In each of
the following sentences, select the word in parentheses that
is spelled correctly. After you complete the exercise, add to
your spelling notebook the correct spellings of any words you
spelled incorrectly.
1. The (pronunciation, pronunciation) of some words is
   difficult.
2. The thunder and (lightening,
   lightning) terrified us.
3. The (personnel, personal) office
   has job information.
4. I hate to fill out (questionnaires,
   questionaires).
5. Who is (responsible, respons-
   able) for this messy room?
6. The (defendant, defendent)
   might be innocent or guilty.
7. Can you draw (parallel, paralel)
   lines without a ruler?
8. What kind of (mileage, milage)
   does your car get?
9. Your (appearance, appearence)
   will affect your job search.
10. The hotel can (accommodate,
    accomodate) 250 guests.

> **More Practice**
Academic and
Workplace Skills
Activity Book
• pp. 22–23

▼ Critical Viewing
Identify two words
associated with this
picture that might
cause spelling difficul-
ties. Explain why.
[Connect]

Improving Your Spelling • **779**

Answer Key

> **Exercise 13**

Check to make certain students have
begun their lists. You may want to
have students share words they
found that they think others will have
trouble spelling.

Step-by-Step Teaching Guide

Studying Problem Words

*Teaching Resources: Academic and
Workplace Skills Activity Book, p. 23*

1. Have students review the Steps for
   Reviewing Problem Words. Ask
   them to explain how completing
   each step can lead to helping
   them spell the word. (Looking at
   the arrangement of letters can
   help students memorize the word.
   Pronouncing the word helps them
   hear how it sounds and see how it
   is spelled. Writing the word and
   checking it in a dictionary helps
   them visualize and spell the word.
   Reviewing the word helps to fix it
   in their minds.)

2. Explain that definitions and
   word origins may also assist in
   remembering how a word is
   spelled. For example, *complement*
   means "complete," and both
   have two *e*'s.

3. Refer students back to the item
   on homophones to demonstrate
   an additional reason that it is
   necessary to be careful with
   spelling.

Answer Key

> **Exercise 14**

1. pronunciation
2. lightning
3. personnel
4. questionnaires
5. responsible
6. defendant
7. parallel
8. mileage
9. appearance
10. accommodate

Critical Viewing

Connect Depending on how familiar
students are with the elements
pictured, or with hotels in general,
possible suggestions might include
limousine, *concierge*, and *bellhop*.

Developing Memory Aids

1. After students have read the text, discuss why these two memory aids can be helpful. (They provide an easier word to remember).

2. Ask students to share any memory aids they have used to remember spelling or anything else. This can be examples of the two aids here or any other aids they have developed.

3. To give students some experience using these aids, have students suggest some words that are difficult to spell (they may refer to their spelling notebooks). Write the words on the board (as many examples as you feel are helpful) and have the class brainstorm for either words within words or associations that can help with remembering these words.

Customize for
Spatial Learners

For Exercise 15, invite students to use drawings to help them associate the correct spelling with a word. The drawings may take the form of icons or some other visual representation. Let these students share their drawings with the class.

Answer Key

▶ Exercise 15

Answers will vary. Ask students to share some of their strategies with the class.

30.4

Developing Memory Aids

You may find the correct spelling of some words especially difficult to learn. This is often true of words that do not follow any set rules. However, many of these words can be mastered by using memory aids.

▶ **KEY CONCEPT** Creating and using memory aids can help you remember the correct spelling of words that you find especially difficult to learn. ■

Using Words Within Words as a Memory Aid One useful memory aid is to look for a shorter, more familiar word within the harder one. Then, use both words to compose a sentence that you will be able to remember:

EXAMPLES:	bulletin	Watch for the *bullet* in the *bullet*in.
	vegetables	Did you *get* the ve*get*ables from the market?
	friend	You will be my fri*end* to the *end*.

Using Association as a Memory Aid Associate the trickiest part of the problem word with a related word that you already know how to spell.

EXAMPLES:	cellar	A cell*ar* is often d*ar*k. (Both words contain *ar*.)
	medicine	This medic*ine* will help you feel f*ine* (both words end in *ine*.)
	clientele	Clien*tele* means a group of customers. Customers often order what they want on the *tele*phone. (Both words contain *tele*.)

▶ **Exercise 15** Developing Memory Aids Create memory aids for the ten words listed below. Then, choose five difficult words from your own spelling notebook, and find a memory aid for each one. Write the hints in your notebook to help you remember the correct spelling.

1. restaurant
2. raspberry
3. cushion
4. sophomore
5. cinnamon
6. tortoise
7. rehearse
8. comedy
9. environment
10. oyster

🔲 Research Tip

Choose five words from a dictionary that would be difficult words for you to spell. Add them to your notebook, and develop a memory aid for each one.

▶ More Practice

Academic and Workplace Skills Activity Book
• pp. 24–25

Applying Spelling Rules

The spellings of some words must be learned by memorization. However, the correct spelling of other words can be learned without too much difficulty by using spelling rules. For example, some words follow certain rules about how to form plurals, how to add prefixes and suffixes, or when to use *ie* or *ei*.

Plural Forms

The plural form of a noun is the form that indicates "more than one." Plural forms can be either *regular* or *irregular*.

Regular Plurals As a general rule, you can just add -*s* to the end of a word to form a regular plural. With certain regular plurals, however, you may have to choose whether to add -*s* or -*es*. Occasionally, you may also have to change a letter or two in the singular form of the word.

1. Form the plurals of words ending in *s*, *ss*, *x*, *z*, *sh*, or *ch* by adding -*es* to the base word:

   circus + -*es* = circuses   mass + -*es* = masses
   fox + -*es* = foxes   fizz + -*es* = fizzes
   dish + -*es* = dishes   finch + -*es* = finches

2. Form the plurals of words ending in *y* or *o* preceded by a vowel by adding -*s* to the base word:

   donkey + -*s* = donkeys   toy + -*s* = toys
   trolley + -*s* = trolleys   birthday + -*s* = birthdays
   stereo + -*s* = stereos   studio + -*s* = studios

3. To form the plurals of words ending in *y* preceded by a consonant, change the *y* to *i* and add -*es*. For most words ending in *o* preceded by a consonant, add -*es*. (Exceptions to this rule are musical terms ending in *o*; form these plurals by simply adding -*s*.):

   baby + -*es* = babies   fly + -*es* = flies
   veto + -*es* = vetoes   hero + -*es* = heroes
   cello + -*s* = cellos   alto + -*s* = altos

4. To form the plurals of some words ending in *f* or *fe*, change the *f* or *fe* to *v* and add -*es*. For words ending in *ff*, always add -*s*:

   knife + -*es* = knives   shelf + -*es* = shelves
   half + -*es* = halves   elf + -*es* = elves
   gulf + -*s* = gulfs   proof + -*s* = proofs
   chef + -*s* = chefs   tariff + -*s* = tariffs

▲ **Critical Viewing**
Think of some ways that you can study spelling rules with other students.
[Support]

Improving Your Spelling • 781

Step-by-Step Teaching Guide

Regular Plurals

Teaching Resources: Academic and Workplace Skills Activity Book, p. 24

1. Write the following words on the board and ask the class to identify which of the four rules applies and what the spelling of the plural would be: *Hero, knife, valley, candy, ash, cameo, soprano, ax. (3/heroes, 4/knives, 2/valleys, 3/candies, 1/ashes, 2/cameos, 3/sopranos, 1/axes)*

2. Divide the class into four groups. Have each group create a short exercise with five or six words (words should fit one of the four variations or the general "add an -*s*" rule). Have each group give its exercise to another group (you may want to pick a general direction, such as clockwise), and have that group create plurals. Have the exercises move to a third group, which will check the answers. Finally, the exercise should return to the original group, and they can check to make sure their answers are what they expected when they wrote them down.

3. Ask students to identify any words for which they are unsure of the plurals. Have a volunteer look up the word or spell its plural based on one of the rules. (You may need to intervene if it's an irregular word, and simply have the word looked up rather than allowing students to guess.) Write both the singular and plural on the board.

Critical Viewing

Support Have students share their ideas with the class. You may wish to create a list of suggestions on the board, and then have students meet in groups to try some of the suggestions. Encourage students to use other opportunities to help each other improve spelling skills.

Irregular Plurals

1. After students have reviewed the chart, ask them to name the most effective way to remember irregular plurals (memorize them).

2. Remind students that if they don't remember an irregular plural, the next most important thing to remember is that they can always look it up.

3. Give students a few minutes to study the chart. Then, have them close their books, and ask volunteers to spell the plural of words you name from the chart.

Customize for
More Advanced Students

Challenge students to find additional irregular plurals. Encourage them to try other grammar texts at the library or ask librarians or friends for input. Have them share their findings with the class. Students may also want to look up the etymologies of some of the irregular verbs, to discover whether there are any patterns.

Answer Key

> **Exercise 16**

1. oxen	11. sheaves
2. loaves	12. geese
3. taxes	13. crises
4. chiefs	14. blocks
5. cries	15. hunches
6. deer	16. beliefs
7. alleys	17. brushes
8. stews	18. potatoes
9. classes	19. volcanoes
10. jellies	20. hearts

30.4

Irregular Plurals Irregular plurals are not formed according to the rules on the previous page. If you are unsure of how to form a plural, check a dictionary. You will usually find the spelling of an irregular plural listed right after the pronunciation of the word. If no plural form is given in the dictionary, add *-s* or *-es* to the singular form. Below is a list of common irregular plurals:

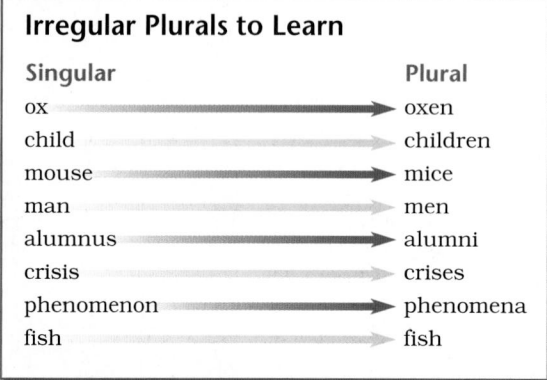

Irregular Plurals to Learn

Singular	Plural
ox	oxen
child	children
mouse	mice
man	men
alumnus	alumni
crisis	crises
phenomenon	phenomena
fish	fish

Forming the Plurals of Compound Words: To form the plural of a compound word that is written as two or more separate or hyphenated words, make the word that is being modified plural by adding *-s* or *-es* to the singular form. For example, *rule of order* becomes *rules of order*, and *mother-in-law* becomes *mothers-in-law*.

> **Exercise 16** Forming Plurals Write the plural for each of the nouns listed below. Consult a dictionary if you need to confirm your answers.

1. ox	11. sheaf
2. loaf	12. goose
3. tax	13. crisis
4. chief	14. block
5. cry	15. hunch
6. deer	16. belief
7. alley	17. brush
8. stew	18. potato
9. class	19. volcano
10. jelly	20. heart

Prefixes and Suffixes

A prefix is one or more syllables added at the beginning of a word to form a new word. A suffix is one or more syllables added to the end of a word.

KEY CONCEPTS Adding a prefix to a word does not affect the spelling of the original word. Adding a suffix often involves a spelling change in the word. ■

Adding Prefixes When a prefix is added to a word, the spelling of the word root remains the same.

• This rule also pertains to words with double letters (*dis-* + satisfy = dissatisfy).

• A prefix may change to aid pronunciation when it is added, but the root stays the same (*ad-* becomes *al-* before *locate* to form *allocate*; *in-* becomes *ir-* before *reverent* to form *irreverent*).

Exercise 17 Spelling Words With Prefixes Form words by combining roots with prefixes. You may have to change the form of the prefix. Check a dictionary.

1. *ad-* + portion
2. *de-* + activate
3. *com-* + respond
4. *in-* + migrate
5. *ex-* + fervescent
6. *pre-* + eminent
7. *co-* + operate
8. *mis-* + speak
9. *ad-* + fluent
10. *un-* + necessary

Adding Suffixes Some words require spelling changes when adding suffixes. The following three lists summarize the major kinds of spelling changes that can take place when a suffix is added.

Spelling Changes in Words Ending in *y*: Use the following rules for spelling changes of words ending in *y*, paying careful attention to the rules' exceptions:

1. When adding a suffix to words that end in *y* and are preceded by a consonant, change *y* to *i*. Most suffixes beginning with *i* are the exception to the rule.

   rely + *-able* = reliable   friendly + *-ness* = friendliness
   rely + *-ing* = relying   fly + *-ing* = flying

2. For words that end in *y* and are preceded by a vowel, make no change when adding most suffixes. A few short words are the exceptions.

   joy + *-ous* = joyous   employ + *-ment* = employment
   day + *-ly* = daily   pay + *-ed* = paid

▶ **More Practice**
Academic and Workplace Skills Activity Book
• pp. 24–25

Improving Your Spelling • 783

Step-by-Step Teaching Guide

Prefixes

Teaching Resources: Academic and Workplace Skills Activity Book, p. 25

1. After students study the item on spelling with prefixes in the text, you may want to review what they have already learned about prefixes earlier in the chapter.

2. Emphasize that, although adding a prefix does not affect the spelling of the original word or root, many prefixes change their own spelling when joined to roots.

3. You may want to work through Exercise 17 as a class. If you have students do it independently, review the answers in class.

Customize for
Gifted and Talented Students

After students have successfully added prefixes to the words, have them write a definition in their own words for each newly-formed word, comparing what its parts mean with the definition of the word. Then, ask them to use each word in an original sentence.

Step-by-Step Teaching Guide

Suffixes

Teaching Resources: Academic and Workplace Skills Activity Book, p. 25

1. Ask students to study carefully the three types of spelling changes that occur when adding suffixes. As with prefixes, you may want to review with the class what they have already learned about suffixes earlier in this chapter.

2. Point out to students that, in item 2 in this first group, adding *-ed* makes a verb past tense. The example given, *pay/paid*, is an irregular verb. Ask students to think of other irregular verbs that change this way (*lay/laid, say/said*).

Answer Key

▶ **Exercise 17**

1. apportion
2. deactivate
3. correspond
4. immigrate
5. effervescent
6. preeminent
7. cooperate
8. misspeak
9. affluent
10. unnecessary

Suffixes *continued*

1. Divide the class into six groups. Explain that each group will be responsible for "teaching" and giving examples of one of the six types of spelling changes that occur when suffixes are added.

2. Give students class time to plan what they will say. Explain that they are simply responsible for explaining the rule and giving appropriate examples other than the ones in the text.

3. Let each group make its presentation to the class. Encourage students to make notes in their spelling notebooks about any ideas or examples that they find particularly helpful.

Critical Viewing

Apply Adverbs that describe the rowing might include *orderly, powerfully, rhythmically.* Have students identify the suffix rules for the specific adverbs they choose.

Answer Key

> **Exercise 18**

1. fascination
2. luckily
3. lobbyist
4. swimmer
5. ceaseless
6. controllable
7. conference
8. courageous
9. alphabetic
10. appliance

30.4

Spelling Changes in Words Ending in *e*: Use the following rules for spelling changes of words ending in *e*, paying careful attention to the rules' exceptions:

1. For words ending in *e*, drop the *e* when adding a suffix beginning with a vowel. The major exceptions to this rule are (1) words ending in *ce* or *ge* with suffixes beginning with *a* or *o*, (2) words ending in *ee*, and (3) a few special words.

   love + *-able* = lovable   thrive + *-ing* = thriving
   manage + *-able* = manageable   sane + *-ity* = sanity
   agree + *-able* = agreeable   see + *-ing* = seeing
   dye + *-ing* = dyeing   be + *-ing* = being

2. For words ending in *e*, make no change when adding a suffix beginning with a consonant. A few special words are the exceptions.

   peace + *-ful* = peaceful   brave + *-ly* = bravely
   argue + *-ment* = argument   true + *-ly* = truly

Doubling the Final Consonant Before Suffixes: Use the following rules for cases in which a final consonant may or may not change, paying careful attention to the rules' exceptions:

1. For words ending consonant + vowel + consonant in a stressed syllable, double the final consonant when adding a suffix beginning with a vowel. The major exceptions to this rule are (1) words ending in *x* or *w* and (2) words in which the stress changes after the suffix is added.

   mud + *-y* = mud´dy   submit + *-ed* = submit´ted
   mix + *-ing* = mixing   row + *-ing* = rowing
   refer´ + *-ence* = ref´erence   confer´+ *-ence* = con´ference

2. For words ending consonant + vowel + consonant in an unstressed syllable, make no change when adding a suffix beginning with a vowel. There are no major exceptions to this rule.

   angel + *-ic* = angelic   final + *-ize* = finalize
   hammer + *-ed* = hammered   person + *-al* = personal

> **Exercise 18** Spelling Words With Suffixes Using the rules given above, write the correct spelling for the words below. Check your answers in a dictionary.

1. fascinate + *-ion*   6. control + *-able*
2. lucky + *-ly*   7. confer + *-ence*
3. lobby + *-ist*   8. courage + *-ous*
4. swim + *-er*   9. alphabet + *-ic*
5. cease + *-less*   10. apply + *-ance*

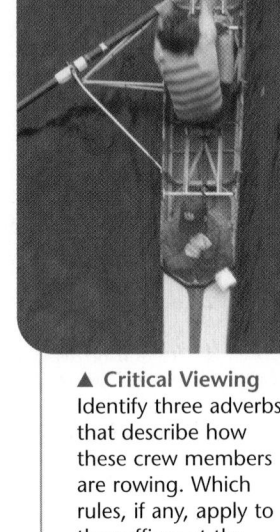

▲ **Critical Viewing** Identify three adverbs that describe how these crew members are rowing. Which rules, if any, apply to the suffixes at the ends of the adverbs? **[Apply]**

Spelling *ie* and *ei* Words and Words Ending in *-cede*, *-ceed*, and *-sede*

Words containing *ie* and *ei*, and words with the endings *-cede*, *-ceed*, and *-sede* often prove troublesome to spell.

For most words containing *ie* or *ei*, you can use the traditional rule: "Place *i* before *e* except after *c* or when sounded like *a*, as in *neighbor* or *weigh*." For words that are exceptions to this rule as well as for words ending in *-cede*, *-ceed*, and *-sede*, it is often best to memorize the correct spellings.

ie and ei Words The *ie* and *ei* rule applies to many words, but like most rules, it has exceptions.

Exceptions for ie words: *counterfeit, either, foreign, forfeit, heifer, height, heir, leisure, neither, seismology, seize, seizure, sheik, sleight, sovereign, their, weird*

Exceptions for ei words: *ancient, conscience, efficient, financier, sufficient*

> **Exercise 19** Spelling *ie* and *ei* Words Fill in the blanks by inserting the missing letters. Check your work in a dictionary.
> 1. ach __?__ ve
> 2. bel __?__ f
> 3. dec __?__ ve
> 4. sl __?__ gh
> 5. s __?__ zure
> 6. rec __?__ pt
> 7. effic __?__ nt
> 8. h __?__ ress
> 9. r __?__ gn
> 10. rel __?__ ve

Words Ending in *-cede*, *-ceed*, and *-sede* The best way to handle words that end with these suffixes is to memorize the correct spelling. The words ending in *-cede* are *accede, concede, intercede, precede, recede, secede*. The three words endings in *-ceed* are *exceed, proceed, succeed*, and the only word ending in *-sede* is *supersede*.

> **Exercise 20** Working With Words Ending in *-cede*, *-ceed*, or *-sede* Complete the word for each sentence below by filling in the blanks with *-cede*, *-ceed*, or *-sede*.
> 1. No repairs can be done until the waters re __?__.
> 2. To reach the drive-in, pro __?__ down Elm Avenue.
> 3. The senator refuses to con __?__ defeat.
> 4. We would like to ac __?__ to your proposal if we can.
> 5. The new regulations super __?__ the old ones.

> **More Practice**
> Academic and Workplace Skills Activity Book
> • pp. 26–27

Improving Your Spelling • 785

Spelling *ie* and *ei* Words and Words ending in *-cede*, *-ceed*, and *-sede*

Teaching Resources: Academic and Workplace Skills Activity Book, p. 26

1. Before students refer to this section, write the rule on the board:

   Place i *before* e *except after* c *or when sounded like* a, *as in* neighbor *or* weigh.

2. Ask how many students are familiar with the rule and use it regularly.

3. Explain that, though there are many rules that can help with spelling, for the exceptions to the *ie/ei* rule, along with words ending in *-cede*, *-ceed*, and *-sede*, the only way to learn them is by memorizing them.

4. Encourage students to list these tricky words in their spelling notebooks.

5. Allow class time for students to practice these spellings, perhaps with partners, before assigning the exercises.

Customize for
Less Advanced Students

Review the spelling for the words in Exercise 19 the day after the lesson is initially taught. This will provide students with more study time. Make sure any words with which students have difficulty are noted in their spelling notebooks.

Customize for
Linguistic Learners

For Exercise 20, ask students to make up other sentences for the target words. Let them write the sentences on the board, using blanks for the target words. Have other students fill in the blanks, spelling the words correctly.

Answer Key

> **Exercise 19**
> 1. achieve
> 2. belief
> 3. deceive
> 4. sleigh
> 5. seizure
> 6. receipt
> 7. efficient
> 8. heiress
> 9. reign
> 10. relieve

> **Exercise 20**
> 1. recede
> 2. proceed
> 3. concede
> 4. accede
> 5. supersede

Other Confusing Endings

Teaching Resources: Academic and Workplace Skills Activity Book, p. 27

1. Explain that one of the things that makes these spellings so confusing is that often there are related words that sound similar but are spelled differently. For example, *rarefy* and *rarity* or *liquid* and *liquefy*. (It's why using the dictionary is vital.)

2. Point out that for the *-ance/-ence* words, it may be easier to remember which to use if students notice that there are other, shorter forms of the words given. For example, while *radiance* and *patience* may be difficult to remember, *radiant* and *patient* may be easier. The vowel doesn't change between the two endings. Likewise, for *presence* one must be *present*, something with *resonance* must *resonate*, etc. While this memory aid does not always apply, it may help with some of the words. Remind students to apply the memory aids they've learned.

3. Encourage students to record words for which memorization is recommended in their spelling notebooks, along with any other of the words on these pages that regularly give them trouble.

Answer Key

Exercise 21

1. courteous
2. cautious
3. convertible
4. unforgettable
5. liquefy
6. irresistible
7. hypocrisy
8. correspondence
9. strenuous
10. gorgeous

30.4

Other Confusing Endings

In certain instances, suffixes may sound alike.

▶ **KEY CONCEPT** Learn to distinguish between similar word endings that can cause errors. ■

COMMON WORDS ENDING IN *-able* and *-ible*

acceptable	memorable	accessible	eligible
believable	peaceable	digestible	incredible

COMMON WORDS ENDING IN *-ance* and *-ence*

acquaintance	radiance	convenience	patience
appearance	resonance	correspondence	presence

COMMON WORDS ENDING IN *-sy*

autopsy	curtsy	epilepsy	hypocrisy
biopsy	ecstasy	fantasy	idiosyncrasy

COMMON WORDS ENDING IN *-efy*

liquefy	putrefy	rarefy	stupefy

COMMON WORDS ENDING IN *-uous*, *-eous*, and *-ious*

ambiguous	gorgeous	conscious
continuous	courteous	contagious

▶ **Exercise 21** **Writing Words With Confusing Endings** Fill in the blanks below. Consult a dictionary if necessary.

1. court __?__ s
2. caut __?__ s
3. convert __?__ ble
4. unforgett __?__
5. liqu __?__ fy
6. irresist __?__ ble
7. hypocr __?__ y
8. correspond __?__ ce
9. stren __?__ s
10. gorg __?__ s

Proofreading Carefully

Often, spelling errors are merely the result of writing quickly to try to get your thoughts down on paper. Get into the habit of proofreading everything you write, to eliminate careless errors.

▶ **KEY CONCEPT** Review everything you write, and proofread for spelling errors. ■

There are a number of different proofreading skills. To discover the proofreading methods that work best for you, use a variety or combination of strategies.

PROOFREADING STRATEGIES

- Proofread your work by slowly reading it aloud or silently to yourself.
- Proofread only one line at a time. Use a ruler or other device to focus on the line you are proofreading and to cover up the lines you are not proofreading.
- Read backward, from the last word to the first. This forces you to focus only on the words themselves.
- Consult a dictionary when you come across a word that you suspect is spelled incorrectly.
- Check the spelling of proper nouns.

▶ **Exercise 22** Proofreading Carefully Find the misspelled word, and correct it. Use a dictionary if necessary.
 1. He is quite cheerfull about the unpleasant task.
 2. We need your assistence for several moments.
 3. Although there were several qualified contestants, they were all farely certain of the outcome.
 4. She has the abilety to do several things equally well.
 5. After all that work, a peice of pie would taste delicious.
 6. The exhausted speaker aksed for a glass of water.
 7. The monkys ran around the cage, begging for bananas.
 8. Our friends incisted that we spend a few more hours and stay for dinner.
 9. The package arrived on Wensday; we found that strange because we expected it on Friday.
 10. Although many people don't realize it, penguins exhist only in the Southern Hemisphere.

▶ **More Practice**
Academic and Workplace Skills Activity Book
- p. 28

┌───┐

Reflecting on Your Vocabulary, Spelling, and Proofreading Skills

Ask yourself the following questions to think about the way you learn vocabulary and spelling words:

- Do I have more trouble with pronunciations or meanings?
- Which types of spelling words are hardest for me?
- What kinds of errors do I usually make?

└───┘

Improving Your Spelling • **787**

Step-by-Step Teaching Guide

Using Context to Determine Meaning

Teaching Resources: Standardized Test Preparation Workbook, pp. 59–60

1. Remind students that context has several layers: the words in the same sentence as the unknown word, the ideas of the paragraph in which the word appears, and the larger context of what the student already may know, either about the topic of the paragraph or about the parts of the word.

2. Go through the sample test items and answers with students. Point out that details can be important in tests, such as noting that the questions refer to the underlined words. In question 1, this is important because the word *thread* appears twice in the sentence.

3. Remind students that answers should reflect the meaning of the word as it is used in the sentence. Often, a different definition of the word will be included in a list of possible responses, but it will not be the right meaning for the context.

4. Assign the two practice tests, and go over the answers with students.

Standardized Test Preparation Workshop

Using Context to Determine Meaning

Many standardized tests have questions that are designed to evaluate your ability to determine the meaning of a word. You will be given a written passage. Several words will be underlined. You will need to use the context of the passage to select the correct meaning of the word.

The following sample items will provide practice answering these types of questions.

Sample Test Items	Answers and Explanations
Directions: Read the passage. Then, read each question that follows the passage. Decide which is the best answer to each question. To begin a cross-stitch project, <u>thread</u> an embroidery needle with the proper color thread. Then, referring to your <u>pattern</u>, create your picture with a series of stitched *x*'s.	
1 In this passage, the word *thread* means— A fine cotton string B main point C pass through D line	The correct answer for item 1 is *C*. Although the other choices offer correct definitions for *thread*, in this context, *thread* is a verb. The only choice that describes the act of putting thread through the eye of a needle is *pass through*.
2 The word *pattern* in this passage means— F blueprint G design H model J precedent	The correct answer for item 2 is *G*. The word *pattern* refers to a set of written directions accompanied by a diagram of an artistic project. The correct choice, *design*, implies something artistic. Although choice *F*, *blueprint*, is a synonym, it is not the best choice because this word usually refers to detailed plans for building projects.

788 • Vocabulary and Spelling

✐ TEST-TAKING TIP

Tell students that reading the whole passage for the general sense is often the only way to get a feeling for what is being said. If only one sentence is read, it is possible that an answer will be wrong because the choice is being made based on a context that does not include enough information.

Suggest that, if they have a general sense of the passage but are still having difficulty picking the correct answers, students try this strategy. First, they should eliminate any obviously wrong answers. Then, they should scan once more for clues. Finally, they should substitute possible answers in the sentence to see whether they make sense.

Practice 1 **Directions:** Read the passage. Then, read each question that follows the passage. Decide which is the best answer to each question.

The latest systems sold at HOTSHOT Computers are virtually virus proof. Three high school students started the company in a basement with castoff equipment they salvaged from schools, businesses, or anyone who was upgrading and getting rid of old equipment. Since the company issued its IPO on Wall Street just three months ago, stock prices have tripled!

1 In this passage, the word *systems* means—
  A living organisms
  B approaches to problem solving
  C set of computer equipment
  D orderliness

2 The word *virus* in this passage means—
  F a germ that causes illness in humans
  G a program that invades and causes damage to another computer program
  H an insect
  J a computer program that solves medical dilemmas

3 Here, the expression *castoff* means—
  A untied, as a boat from its dock
  B thrown away
  C removed, as a cast from a healed limb
  D used

4 Here, the word *upgrading* means—
  F improving
  G earning a higher grade in a computer course
  H climbing a steep rock
  J advancing

Practice 2 **Directions:** Read the passage. Then, read each question that follows the passage. Decide which is the best answer to each question.

Imagine the tedious task of cartography in the days before satellites, or even aerial photography! Humans have long recognized the need for maps, for navigation as well as for defining boundaries and borders, and have spent hours measuring and drawing out lakes, rivers, and mountains. Although most early maps were primitive, we must admire the elbow grease it took to complete the painstaking work of map-making.

1 In this passage, the word *tedious* means—
  A highly technical
  B wearisome
  C fascinating
  D fun-filled

2 The word *cartography* in this passage means—
  F carefully drawn primitive cartoons
  G the task of creating graphs
  H calligraphy
  J the science of making maps

3 In this passage, the word *navigation* means—
  A steering
  B a close relative to the crocodile
  C direction-finding
  D charting a course on the sea

4 In this passage, the expression *elbow grease* means—
  F an early chemical used to preserve maps
  G an ointment used to soothe the aching muscles of early cartographers
  H the ink used to draw maps on parchment
  J very hard work

Answer Key

▶ Practice 1
1. C
2. G
3. B
4. F

▶ Practice 2
1. B
2. J
3. C
4. J

Customize for
Less Advanced Students

Before assigning the practice tests, you may want to review page 768 with students to remind them of what they have learned about using context clues to determine meaning. After they have completed the practice tests, encourage them to look up the words tested to make certain they know what they mean and to reinforce the meaning. Suggest that, if any of the words were new to them, they write them in their vocabulary notebooks.

Customize for
ESL Students

If the examples given are too advanced, offer simpler passages and test words that are more common. Point out that learning how to use context to determine meaning is valuable when learning a new language, and worth practicing, even if it seems difficult. Encourage students to adapt the strategies to their own needs, to help them broaden their English vocabularies. Underscore the importance of using a dictionary and recording words in their vocabulary notebooks.

In-Depth Lesson Plan

	LESSON FOCUS	PRINT AND MEDIA RESOURCES
DAY 1	**Reading Methods and Tools** Students study textbook features and learn strategies for reading textbooks. (pp. 790–797/⊞588–595)	**Teaching Resources** *Academic and Workplace Skills Activity Book,* pp. 30–34
DAY 2	**Reading Nonfiction Critically** Students learn strategies for reading, analyzing, and evaluating nonfiction. (pp. 798–803/⊞596–601)	**Teaching Resources** *Academic and Workplace Skills Activity Book,* pp. 35–38
DAY 3	**Reading Literary Writing** Students learn strategies for reading and analyzing fiction, drama, and poetry. (pp. 804–807/⊞602–605)	**Teaching Resources** *Academic and Workplace Skills Activity Book,* pp. 39–42
DAY 4	**Reading From Varied Sources; Chapter Review** Students learn strategies for reading various sources such as journals, newspapers, speeches, and electronic texts. Students review the concepts presented in the chapter. (pp. 808–809/⊞606–607)	**Teaching Resources** *Academic and Workplace Skills Activity Book,* p. 43; *Formal Assessment,* Ch. 31

Accelerated Lesson Plan

	LESSON FOCUS	PRINT AND MEDIA RESOURCES
DAY 1	**Reading Methods and Tools; Reading Nonfiction Critically** Students learn strategies for reading and analyzing textbooks and other nonfiction materials. (pp. 790–803/⊞588–601)	**Teaching Resources** *Academic and Workplace Skills Activity Book,* pp. 30–38
DAY 2	**Reading Literary Writing; Reading From Varied Sources** Students learn strategies for reading literary writing and other print and electronic texts. (pp. 804–809/⊞602–607)	**Teaching Resources** *Academic and Workplace Skills Activity Book,* pp. 39–43; *Formal Assessment,* Ch. 31

Options for Adapting Lesson Plans

HOMEWORK

Have students conduct independent library research.

FEATURES

Extend coverage with the Standardized Test Preparation Workshop (p. 810).

Writing and Grammar Handbook Alignment

Page numbers in Step-by-Step Teaching Guides in this Teacher's Edition refer to pages from the full student text. Handbook page references, indicated with this icon 🅷, are provided in Time and Resource Manager boxes and at the bottom of each Teacher's Edition page.

INTEGRATED SKILLS COVERAGE

Viewing and Representing
Critical Viewing SE pp. 790, 793, 799, 803, 808/🅷588, 591, 597, 601, 606
ATE pp. 790, 793, 799, 803, 808

Real-World Connection
ATE p. 796

Research Skills
SE pp. 797, 800, 804, 805/🅷595, 598, 602, 603

Technology Skills
SE pp. 794, 798, 806/🅷592, 596, 604

Speaking and Listening Skills
SE p. 807/🅷605; ATE p. 795

ASSESSMENT SUPPORT

Standardized Test Preparation Workshop, SE p. 810; ATE p. 797

Standardized Test Preparation Workbook, pp. 61–62

Formal Assessment, Ch. 31

MEETING INDIVIDUAL NEEDS

Less Advanced Students ATE pp. 792, 805, 811. See also Ongoing Assessments ATE pp. 795, 802, 807.

More Advanced Students ATE p. 797

ESL Students ATE pp. 794, 807

Spatial Learners ATE pp. 799, 801

Linguistic Learners ATE p. 803

Bodily/Kinesthetic Learners ATE p. 806

BLOCK SCHEDULING

Pacing Suggestions
For 90-minute Blocks
- Have students review the Reading Methods and Tools section and complete Exercises 1–5 in a single period.
- Focus one class period on Reading Nonfiction Critically. Allow an additional period for Reading Literary Writing and Reading From Varied Sources.

Resources for Varying Instruction
- *Academic and Workplace Skills Activity Book,* pp. 30–43

Professional Development Support
- *How to Manage Instruction in the Block* This teaching resource provides management and activity suggestions.

MEDIA AND TECHNOLOGY

For the Teacher
- **TeacherEXPRESS™** CD-ROM

WRITING AND GRAMMAR ON-LINE

Interactive Text (On-line or on CD-ROM)
- Easily navigable instruction with interactive Revision Checkers
- Full use of e-rater™, the essay-scoring system (on-line only)

Companion Web Site PHSchool.com
- Scoring rubrics with models (use Web Code eek-1001)

See the Go On-line! feature, SE p. iii.

Lesson Objectives

1. To establish a purpose for reading, such as to discover, interpret, and enjoy

2. To use text organizers such as overviews, headings, and graphic features to locate and categorize information

3. To use study strategies such as skimming, scanning, and outlining to better understand texts

4. To construct images such as graphic organizers based on text descriptions and text structures

5. To analyze text structures such as compare and contrast for how they influence understanding

6. To evaluate the credibility of information sources, including how the writer's motivation may affect that credibility

7. To recognize logical, deceptive, and/or faulty modes of persuasion in texts

8. To draw inferences and support them with text evidence and experience

9. To analyze literary elements for their contribution to meaning

10. To read in various sources such as diaries, journals, textbooks, newspapers, letters, speeches, and electronic texts

Critical Viewing

Speculate The girl appears to be scanning a dictionary to obtain information about a specific word. She might be doing homework or studying for a test.

Chapter 31 Reading Skills

There are no other skills that are more essential to your success in life than reading skills. Throughout your years in school and throughout your life, you will read a wide variety of materials—from textbooks to newspapers to pamphlets to novels to road signs. It is important for you to be able to read all of these materials with a high level of comprehension and retention. In this chapter, you will learn skills and strategies that will help you increase your level of comprehension and become a more effective and efficient reader.

▲ **Critical Viewing**
What type of reading do you think this girl is doing? On what do you base your answer? **[Speculate]**

790 • Reading Skills

⏱ TIME AND RESOURCE MANAGER

Resources
Print: *Academic and Workplace Skills Activity Book*, pp. 30–34

Using the Full Student Edition	Using the Handbook ⓗ
• Read and discuss pp. 790–797. • Have students work in groups on Exercise 1. • Work through Using Reading Strategies, Outlining What You Read, and Using Graphic Organizers as a class. • Assign Exercises 2–5 to be done in class.	• Read and discuss pp. 588–595. • Have students work in groups on Exercise 1. • Work through Using Reading Strategies, Outlining What You Read, and Using Graphic Organizers as a class. • Assign Exercises 2–5 to be done in class.

Section 31.1 Reading Methods and Tools

The way in which you approach reading can vary widely, depending on the nature of the piece of writing. However, there are certain skills and strategies that you can apply to virtually anything you read.

Reading Textbooks

At least 80 percent of the reading you do for school involves textbooks. If you are able to get the most out of the textbooks you read, you will almost certainly improve your performance in school.

▶ **KEY CONCEPT** Use study aids when reading textbooks to help you understand what you are reading and to remember it better later. ■

Textbook Sections The material in a textbook is structured so that you can read it and learn it easily. Unlike most other books, textbooks include reading aids to help you make the best use of the books. Following are descriptions of these special sections:

Table of Contents This section shows how the book is organized by listing units and chapters with their page numbers. It offers a quick overview of the book.

Preface or Introduction Located before or after the table of contents, these features state the author's purpose in writing the book and may give suggestions for using the book.

Index This section alphabetically lists all topics covered in the book and the pages on which they can be found, making it possible to locate information quickly.

Glossary The glossary lists in alphabetical order all the specialized words and terms used in the book and defines them clearly.

Appendix This feature can include such things as charts, lists, documents, or other material related to the subject of the book. An appendix can serve as an immediate reference source.

Bibliography A bibliography lists books and articles that the author has used or referred to in writing the book. Many of the entries may be useful for follow-up study or for research projects.

Front of the Book

Front of the Book

Back of the Book

Back of the Book

Back of the Book

Reading Skills • 791

Textbook Features

Teaching Resources: Academic and Workplace Skills Activity Book, p. 31

1. Have students choose a chapter in a textbook and write down all of the headings and subheadings in it. Point out that these headings offer an outline of what will be covered in the chapter.

2. Ask students why it is helpful to read the overview of a textbook chapter. (Overviews help to focus reading by making the reader aware of the important points to come.)

3. Remind students to skim the chapter questions before reading a chapter. This will help them read more actively, as they will be searching for specific information as they read.

4. Have students choose a picture and caption in one of their textbooks and explain in writing how it enhances the text.

Customize for
Less Advanced Students

Remind students that an easy way to find the answer to a textbook question is to use headings and subheadings. Rather than scanning an entire chapter, students should use the headings to identify which section the answer will be in. Then, they can scan just that section.

Answer Key

> **Exercise 1**

Answers will vary according to the type of textbook that students choose. Students might work on this exercise in small groups or pairs.

31.1

Textbook Features

Textbooks also have a number of other features designed to help you find and review material:

Titles, Headings, and Subheadings These divide the material into manageable segments. They are printed in large, boldfaced type, often in different colors. Main topics have larger headings, and subtopics have smaller ones. By scanning the headings, you can get a quick idea of the topics being covered. You can then focus on topics with which you are having difficulty or on those that your teacher has identified as being important.

Overviews The chapters in textbooks often begin with an overview, objectives, outline, or a summary of what will be covered. These features help you to preview and review what is being covered.

Questions and Exercises Most textbooks include questions or exercises at the ends of sections or chapters. Previewing the questions and exercises before you read will help you focus your reading on the most important concepts and details. After reading, answer the questions to check your understanding.

Pictures, Captions, and Graphics Pictures can add to your understanding of the ideas in the text. Look for captions that explain the content of the pictures and connect them to the reading. Use graphics, such as maps and charts, to help you understand complex concepts.

> **KEY CONCEPT** Use titles, headings, and subheadings; overviews; questions and exercises; pictures, captions, and graphics to help you thoroughly comprehend the material. ■

> **Exercise 1** Examining a Textbook Choose one of your textbooks, and use it to answer the following questions:
> 1. Use the table of contents to identify the organization.
> 2. If there is a preface, does it explain the author's purpose in writing the book? If so, what is the purpose?
> 3. What are two specific terms found in the index?
> 4. Use the glossary to find the definitions of the two terms you found in the index.
> 5. If there is an appendix, what information does it contain?
> 6. Explain the format of any questions and exercises.
> 7. Find a chart, and explain the concept it conveys.
> 8. Identify at least three pictures you find useful, and explain why you think the publisher chose them.
> 9. What features appear at the beginning of each chapter?
> 10. Identify at least three different levels of headings.

Using Reading Strategies

Strong readers use various reading strategies to help them comprehend and critically examine what they're reading. In addition, they vary their reading style according to the content.

Vary Your Reading Style

> **KEY CONCEPT** Adjust your reading style to suit your purpose in reading. ■

Skimming Skimming a text means to look it over quickly to get a sense, or a general idea, of its contents. Look for highlighted or bold type, headings, and topic sentences. Use skimming to preview, review, and locate information.

Scanning Scanning involves looking through a text to find specific information. Look for words related to your topic or purpose for reading. Use scanning to research, review, and find information.

Close Reading Close reading refers to reading carefully to take in all of the main ideas and to understand the relationships among those ideas. Use this technique whenever you are reading material in your textbooks for the first time.

▲ **Critical Viewing**
Based on her posture, what type of reading style do you think this girl is using? Why? **[Analyze]**

> **Exercise 2** **Varying Your Reading Style** Choose a nonfiction book. Skim it in its entirety. Write down what you have learned. Then, scan it until you come across an interesting section. Read that section closely, and take detailed notes.

Use Question-Answer Relationships (QARs)

Understanding how questions are written can help you to answer them. There are four general types of questions. Learning to identify these types will help you to answer questions more easily. You can also improve your reading skills by asking and answering these types of questions as you read:

1. **Right There** This type of question deals with answers that are right there in the text, usually in one or two paragraphs or sentences.
2. **Think and Search** The answer to this type of question is in the text, but you need to think about the question's answer and then search for evidence to support it.
3. **Author and You** These questions call on you to consider what the author says and connect it to what you know.
4. **On Your Own** The answers to these questions are not in the text. They require you to draw on your experiences.

Reading Methods and Tools • **793**

Step-by-Step Teaching Guide

Vary Your Reading Style

Teaching Resources: Academic and Workplace Skills Activity Book, p. 32

1. To illustrate the three types of reading styles, write on the board the following reasons for reading a cookbook: finding some recipes for cookies, finding out how long it takes to bake cookies, and finding step-by-step instructions for baking cookies.

2. Ask students to describe how each person would read the cookbook. (Students should recognize that the person actually baking cookies needs to read closely, the person finding out how long it takes to bake cookies needs to scan several cookie recipes, and the person simply finding a few recipes needs to skim through the dessert section.)

3. Have students generate a list of more situations in which each reading style is appropriate.

Answer Key

> **Exercise 2**

You may ask students to bring in a nonfiction book the day before actually working on this exercise.

Critical Viewing

Analyze The girl's posture suggests that she is relaxed and comfortable. Her facial expression suggests that she is absorbed in the book. She is probably scanning to find information.

Step-by-Step Teaching Guide

Using Question-Answer Relationships (QARs)

1. Read and discuss the four types of questions with students. Have them explain which type they find most easy and most difficult, and why.

2. Have students label each of the questions in Exercise 1 according to type. Have them share their answers.

Use the SQ4R Method

1. Ask whether students have ever read something for school and then quickly forgotten the material. Have them share their experiences.

2. Explain that the SQ4R method will help them retain information and get the most out of their reading.

3. Read through the SQ4R method or have a prepared student read it. Ask students to compare this method with the reading styles they learned earlier: skimming, scanning, and close reading. They should see that step 1 requires skimming, step 2 requires close reading, and step 3 requires scanning.

Customize for
ESL students

While practicing the SQ4R method, allow ESL students to use textbooks written in their first language. This way, they can focus on the reading styles rather than worrying about unfamiliar textbook jargon.

Answer Key

> **Exercise 3**

Have students work on this exercise in pairs. If several students have chosen the same textbook and chapter, ask them to exchange papers and compare their findings.

31.1

Use the SQ4R Method

To get the most out of your textbook, use the SQ4R method, a guided reading approach that involves these six skills:

1. **Survey** Preview the material you are going to read, focusing on chapter titles, headings, overviews, summaries, objectives, and questions or exercises.
2. **Question** Write down a question about each heading.
3. **Read** As you read, search for the answers to the questions that you have posed.
4. **Recite** Orally or mentally, recite the questions and their answers.
5. **Record** Take notes to further reinforce information in your mind. Include a list of main ideas and major details.
6. **Review** Review the material on a regular basis.

> **KEY CONCEPT** Use the SQ4R method to guide your reading and to help you recall information later. ■

THE SQ4R METHOD

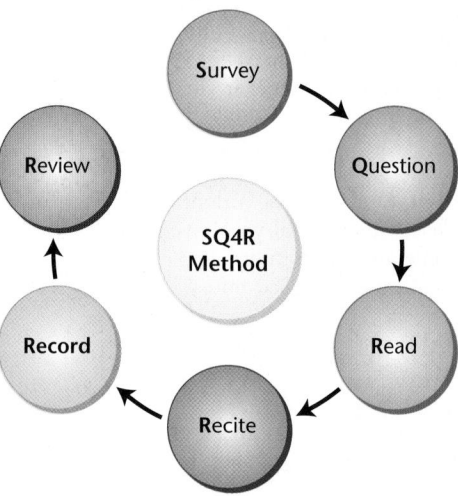

> **Exercise 3** **Using the SQ4R Method** Use the SQ4R method to study a chapter in one of your textbooks. Then, write a brief review of the ways in which using SQ4R helped. Note information that you might have missed if you had not been using SQ4R, and explain how the overall use of SQ4R affected your understanding of the material.

💿 **Technology Tip**

Use the SQ4R method when you visit new Web pages for research purposes. The notes that you record will guide you and save you time when you return to the Web page for more information.

Outlining What You Read

An **outline** is a structured list of information. The information is arranged according to main ideas, major details, and supporting details. Outlines are an excellent study tool that can help you prepare for tests and quizzes on information in your textbooks.

KEY CONCEPT Make an outline as you read to keep track of important information and ideas. ■

Follow these steps to make an outline:

- Use Roman numerals for main ideas. Use capital letters for major details. Use Arabic numerals for supporting details.
- Use indentation to indicate importance. Main ideas begin at the left. Items begin farther to the right as they become less important.
- Never place a single item under any main idea. Always place two or more items or none at all.

The example below illustrates a formal outline on the magician Jean-Eugène Robert-Houdin:

SAMPLE OUTLINE

I. The magician Robert-Houdin ———————— Main idea
   A. Robert-Houdin in 1880's ———————— Major detail
      1. Developed rules for performing tricks ——⎤
      2. Created many new tricks ——————⎦— Supporting details
   B. Tools of the magician ———————— Major detail
      1. Skill with hands ⎤
      2. Secret devices ⎟
      3. Misdirects people's attention ⎟— Supporting details
      4. Encourages false conclusions ⎦

Exercise 4 **Making an Outline** Using an assigned chapter of a textbook, make an outline of one section. Give your outline at least two main ideas. Then, test the effectiveness of your outline by sharing it with a schoolmate who has not read the chapter. See whether the schoolmate can answer the chapter review questions using the outline alone. If not, you may have left some key concepts out of your outline.

Outlining What You Read

Teaching Resources: Academic and Workplace Skills Activity Book, p. 33

1. Explain to students that outlining is another technique that will help them understand and remember what they read.

2. Ask students to apply what they have learned about the features of textbooks to the outline form. Explain that main ideas will often be expressed in titles and overviews. Details will often be expressed in headings and subheadings, within the text, and in pictures, captions, and graphics.

3. For practice in making an outline, have students complete Exercise 4.

Integrating Speaking and Listening Skills

Remind students that outlines are not only helpful for organizing written texts; they can be helpful for organizing speeches and other oral presentations, too. Explain that when giving a speech, it is often better to work from an outline than from a copy of the speech. Outlines encourage the speaker to look at the audience and think about what he or she is saying, rather than reading directly as if from a script.

Answer Key

Exercise 4

You may wish to have students exchange outlines with another class in your Language Arts department.

☑ ONGOING ASSESSMENT: Monitor and Reinforce

If students are having trouble making an outline, try one of the following strategies.

Option 1 Review with students the concept of topic sentences. Explain that they can often find the main idea of a paragraph in its first or last sentence. The other sentences should contain elaboration or supporting details.	**Option 2** Students might feel more comfortable with a web diagram, which, like an outline, also shows the way details in a selection are organized around a few main ideas. Point out that the center of the web is the most important idea, and the ideas lessen in importance as they branch away from the center.

Using Graphic Organizers

Teaching Resources: Academic and Workplace Skills Activity Book, p. 34

1. Have students identify topics that are often arranged in chronological order (examples: history, biography, and autobiography).

2. Have students practice making a timeline by arranging the main events in their own lives.

3. Explain that when a piece of writing is divided clearly into main parts and subtopics, a cluster diagram or web is often useful.

4. Have students transform the outline on page 795 into a cluster diagram. They should see that the main idea, major details, and supporting details in the outline correspond with the topic, related ideas, and supporting details in the cluster diagram.

Real-World Connection

Explain to students that people use graphic organizers at home and in the workplace to help them organize information. For example, calendars offer a visual representation of time. To-do lists show people what they've accomplished and what they have left to do. Can students think of other examples of graphic organizers that are used on a daily basis?

31.1

Using Graphic Organizers

Graphic organizers are an effective reading aid. They can help you sort out main topics and key details as well as identify relationships among the details. When choosing what organizer to use, consider the type of organization the author uses.

Analyze Chronological Order

When the events in a piece you are reading are presented in chronological order, or the order in which the events occur, you will probably find a **timeline** most effective. Use the top of the timeline to name the event, and use the bottom to indicate the elapsed time. Look at the sample below.

TIMELINE

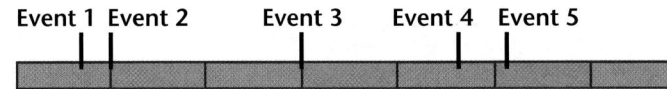

Time intervals (years, months, days, minutes)

Chart Main Points and Subtopics

When a piece of writing is divided clearly into main points and subtopics, you will probably want to use a **cluster diagram,** also known as a **web.** Begin by writing your topic in the center of a sheet of paper. Circle that topic. Then, write down any subtopics, and draw circles around them, making the circles large enough to add supporting details. Link the related ideas to the main topic with lines, and list the supporting details.

CLUSTER DIAGRAM

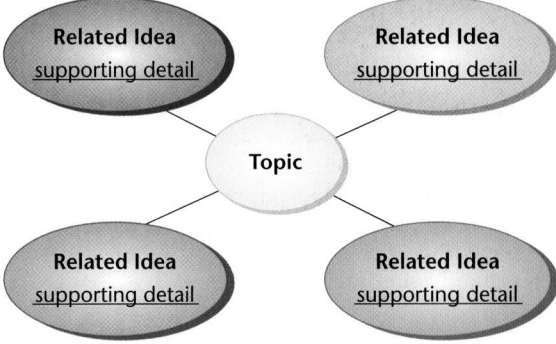

Analyze Comparison-and-Contrast Structure

Writers often make comparisons between two or more subjects. A **Venn diagram** is probably the most effective graphic organizer to help you sort out the details of such comparisons. In addition, a Venn diagram can help you make comparisons between two or more pieces of writing—a task that you will often be asked to do in school or on standardized tests.

To make a Venn diagram, draw overlapping circles. In the overlapping sections of the circles, write the subjects' shared characteristics. In the other sections of the circles, write their differences. Note that the Venn diagram below would be used for three subjects.

VENN DIAGRAM (3 Subjects)

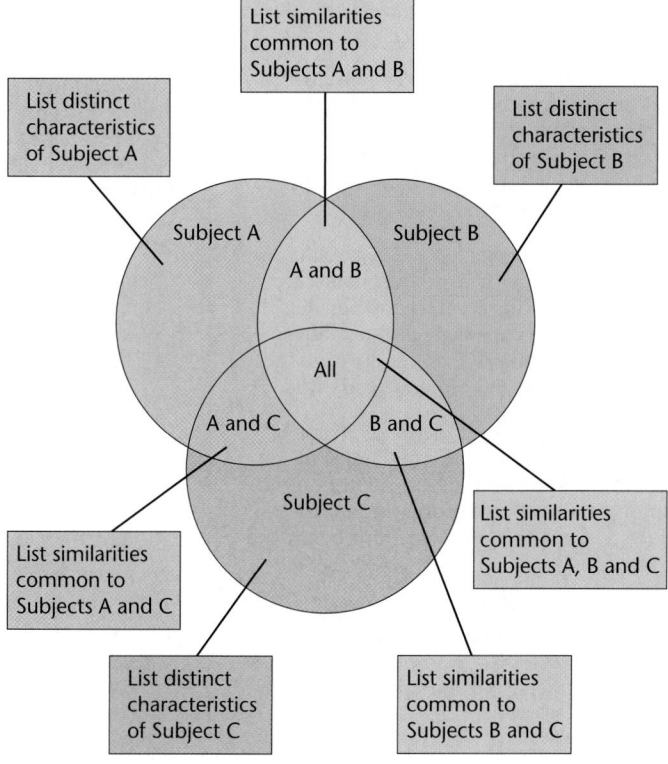

List similarities common to Subjects A and B

List distinct characteristics of Subject A

List distinct characteristics of Subject B

Subject A
Subject B
A and B
All
A and C
B and C
Subject C

List similarities common to Subjects A and C

List similarities common to Subjects A, B and C

List distinct characteristics of Subject C

List similarities common to Subjects B and C

> **Exercise 5** Using Graphic Organizers Read a chapter from one of your textbooks or a work of literature. Then, use a Venn diagram, a timeline, or a cluster diagram to organize information from the text.

Research Tip

Discover more types of graphic organizers and variations on cluster diagrams and Venn diagrams by reviewing your textbooks. Note how information is organized and relationships are shown on the graphic organizers that you find. Use them to guide you as you create your own.

Analyze Comparison-and-Contrast Structure

1. Draw a Venn diagram on the chalkboard. Label the entire diagram "After-school Activities." Label each circle with a popular after-school activity. (Examples: sports, clubs, or jobs.) Have students put their initials in the part of the diagram that describes what they like to do after school.

2. Remind students that writing their initials in the center space means they enjoy all three activities. Make sure they understand the meanings of the other six spaces and that they write their initials in the correct one.

Customize for
More Advanced Students

Have students use a Venn diagram to compare and contrast all three graphic organizers. Have them share their findings with the class. They should find that certain organizers work better than others for certain types of writing. (Example: Timelines work best for chronological events and Venn diagrams work best for comparing and contrasting.)

Answer Key

> **Exercise 5**

Ask volunteers to place their diagrams or timelines on the chalkboard or on a transparency for the entire class to see.

STANDARDIZED TEST PREPARATION WORKSHOP

Organize and Plan Standardized tests may require students to answer questions about how to organize their notes. Have them read the following outline for a report about a summer vacation.

My Summer Vacation
I   Leave for Camp
II Arrive at Lake Taquoia Camping Grounds
III Pack Up Tents
IV Unpack and Set Up Tents

V Spend Three Days Having Fun
VI Leave for Home

Which heading is out of order?

A I   C II
B III   D V

Students should recognize that **B** is the correct answer. "Pack Up Tents" should appear just before "Leave for Home."

Analyzing and Evaluating Nonfiction

Teaching Resources: Academic and Workplace Skills Activity Book, p. 35

1. Ask students to comment on the following saying: "Don't believe everything you read." Do students think this statement is true or false? Why?

2. Explain to students that even nonfiction contains the author's opinion and bias. Good readers read nonfiction critically using the strategies on this page.

3. Read the first two strategies aloud or have a student read them. Explain that they are examples of things that authors imply in nonfiction. It is up to the reader to make these connections.

4. Explain that the next four strategies are ways in which readers can evaluate the author's work. These strategies help readers know which parts of a piece of writing to question.

5. Have students practice using these strategies by asking them to read a newspaper or magazine account of a controversial event. Have them form judgements about the article by recognizing the author's purpose or bias, evaluating the writer's points or statements, evaluating the author's credibility, and recognizing persuasive techniques.

Section 31.2

Reading Nonfiction Critically

Over the course of your life, you'll probably read more non-fiction than any other type of writing. Nonfiction refers to writing that has a basis in fact. Newspaper reports, reference books, and history texts are all examples of nonfiction.

Analyzing and Evaluating Nonfiction

When you read nonfiction, it is important not only to grasp the writer's main ideas and key points, but to evaluate critically the accuracy and reliability of what you read. Use a variety of reading strategies to examine, evaluate, and form judgments about what you read.

Make Inferences Nonfiction writers are generally more direct than fiction writers in making their key points. However, that doesn't mean that some information isn't left out of a typical nonfiction work. To grasp ideas that are either only hinted at or left out, you need to make inferences, or draw conclusions, based on the information the author *does* provide.

Make Generalizations When a writer provides a related set of facts and details on one topic, you can often make generalizations about that topic. For example, if an author tells numerous stories about people who experienced hardships settling in a new land, you might make the generalization that many people who came to the land faced similar hardships.

Recognize the Author's Purpose or Bias A writer's purpose, or reason for writing, can influence the choice of details and presentation of material. In addition, writers often present an issue with their own bias—their outlook on an issue or topic. Try to identify a writer's purpose, and be on the lookout for details that suggest bias.

Evaluate the Strength of the Evidence and the Writer's Credibility Check to see that a writer thoroughly supports the points with facts, examples, and details. Also, check to see that a writer has expertise or has done thorough research on the topic.

Recognize Persuasive Techniques Be on the lookout for appeals to your emotions. Make sure a writer offers sound evidence before accepting his or her position.

Judge the Writer's Work When you read many works by the same writer, try to draw some overall conclusions about the quality of his or her work.

Internet Tip

Treat the information you find on the Internet the same way you would treat any nonfiction book: Critically analyze and evaluate the material using the strategies presented on this page.

⏱ TIME AND RESOURCE MANAGER

Resources:
Print: *Academic and Workplace Skills Activity Book, pp. 35–38*

Using the Full Student Edition	Using the Handbook🄷
• Read and discuss pp. 798–803 in class.	• Read and discuss pp. 596–601 in class.
• Have students work on Exercises 6–9 in class.	• Have students work on Exercises 6–9 in class.
• Have students share their answers.	• Have students share their answers.

Distinguishing Fact From Opinion

Don't just assume that every piece of nonfiction you read is reliable. Often, information that is presented as being the truth is simply the writer's opinion.

KEY CONCEPT To help you evaluate the reliability of what you read, be careful to distinguish facts from opinions. ■

A statement of fact can be verified, or proved true, by experimentation, records, or personal observation. A statement of opinion cannot be proved true; before it can be accepted, it must be validated, or supported, with satisfactory sources or facts. An opinion may be based on facts, but an opinion is *not* a fact.

FACT: To put a satellite in space, a rocket must travel fast enough to escape the Earth's gravity.

OPINION (feeling): Space travel is too dangerous.

OPINION (judgment): A mechanical flaw in a spacecraft could threaten an astronaut's life.

OPINION (prediction): In the next decade, humans will colonize the moon.

Verify facts and validate opinions to determine whether the material you are reading is reliable.

Exercise 6 Analyzing Fact and Opinion Statements First, identify each of the following statements as *fact* or *opinion*. Then, analyze whether each fact statement is *true* or *false*, and analyze whether each opinion statement is *valid* or *invalid*.

1. Abraham Lincoln was the greatest president the United States has ever had.
2. Our team is sure to win the baseball game next week.
3. The blue whale is the largest animal ever to inhabit Earth.
4. The Supreme Court has eleven justices.
5. We will have snow tomorrow because a cold front is approaching.

Exercise 7 Analyzing Facts and Opinions in a Magazine Look through a newsmagazine. Write down five examples of facts. Then, find at least two examples of opinions. Tell whether the opinions are backed by facts.

▼ Critical Viewing Based on her expression, do you think this girl agrees or disagrees with what she is reading? [Infer]

Reading Nonfiction Critically • 799

Inductive and Deductive Reasoning

Teaching Resources: Academic and Workplace Skills Activity Book, p. 37

1. Have students make graphic organizers to illustrate the difference between inductive and deductive reasoning. (Example: For deductive reasoning, they might draw an upside down triangle to show the movement from a broad, general idea to specific, narrow ideas. For inductive reasoning, they might draw the opposite.)

2. Ask students whether the following is an example of inductive or deductive reasoning. Then, have them explain whether or not it is valid, and why.

   Fact 1: *Nick has taken cooking classes for the past five years.*

   Fact 2: *Nick often cooks meals for his friends and families without being asked.*

   Conclusion: *Nick enjoys cooking.*

   (Students should identify the example as inductive reasoning. It is valid because the evidence suggests that Nick is an avid chef.)

3. Have students think of more examples of inductive and deductive reasoning.

Logical Fallacies

Teaching Resources: Academic and Workplace Skills Activity Book, p. 37

1. Read and discuss the section on logical fallacies.

2. Challenge students to think of examples of each type of fallacy. Here are some examples:

   Hasty Generalization: *Since the girls in this class like chocolate better than vanilla, all girls like chocolate better than vanilla.*

   Circular Reasoning: *The boys in this class like vanilla because girls like chocolate and boys like vanilla.*

Applying Modes of Reasoning

When you read critically, you draw conclusions about what you read. These conclusions need to be sound and logical.

▶ **KEY CONCEPT** Think logically to draw valid conclusions. ■

Inductive and Deductive Reasoning

When you think logically, you use *reasoning* to lead to or support a conclusion. Two main forms of reasoning are *inductive* and *deductive*.

Inductive Reasoning Inductive reasoning involves drawing an overall conclusion, or making a generalization, from a set of specific facts. A valid generalization is a statement supported by evidence that holds true in a large number of cases. The more evidence you have, the more reliable your generalization will be.

Deductive Reasoning When you use deductive reasoning, you move from the general to the specific. For example, if you learn that everyone who works at a certain company has excellent health benefits, then you can deduce that someone you know who works there has excellent health benefits.

Logical Fallacies

A logical fallacy occurs when the rules of logic are not followed. Two types of logical fallacies are hasty generalizations and circular reasoning.

Hasty Generalization A hasty generalization is a statement that is made about a large number of cases or a whole group on the basis of a few examples, without taking into account exceptions or qualifying factors. Look at this example:

VALID: Every homeroom in our school has more girls than boys, so there are more girls than boys in our school.

HASTY: There are fifteen girls and ten boys in my homeroom, so there must be more girls than boys in our school.

Circular Reasoning Circular reasoning, also called *begging the question*, occurs when a person restates a general statement as if it were a fact without supplying supporting evidence.

🗂 Research Tip

To understand the use of generalizations, research the published results of polls and surveys. Note the conclusions drawn from the results, and determine whether the generalizations are hasty or valid.

Other Forms of Reasoning

Analogies An analogy is a comparison between two unlike things that are in some way similar. A *complete analogy* is one that names the specific ways in which two things are similar. An *incomplete analogy* is one that simply states one thing is like another without offering the specifics.

COMPLETE: The cell is like a factory—it processes raw materials, produces energy, and discharges wastes.

INCOMPLETE: The human body is like a machine.

The first analogy is complete because it compares particular functions that actually are similar. The second is incomplete because it fails to acknowledge ways in which the body is *not* like a machine.

RECOGNIZE COMPLETE/INCOMPLETE ANALOGIES

1. How are the two things being compared essentially different?
2. How are the two things alike? Is the comparison logical?
3. What is the truth that the comparison tries to show?

Cause and Effect A cause-and-effect sequence is one in which something is caused by one or more events that occurred before it. When one event happens immediately after another, people sometimes conclude that the first event caused the second event. An unrelated sequence is one in which the first event did not cause the second event. In many cases, events can occur one after the other *without* signifying a cause-and-effect relationship.

▶ **Exercise 8** Analyzing Forms of Reasoning First, identify the form of reasoning (inference, generalization, analogy, or cause and effect) used in each of the following statements. Then, tell whether each conclusion is valid or invalid.

1. If you leave the lights of a car turned on, the battery will run down.
2. The atom is like a miniature solar system.
3. The two meals I got on the plane were not good, so all airline food must be terrible.
4. Luis has been elected class president for the past three years, so he must be a real leader.
5. When the available supply of a product increases, the price usually goes down.

Other Forms of Reasoning

1. Have students make the incomplete analogy on this page complete. (Example: The human body is like a machine because it does work and needs fuel to operate correctly.)

2. Have students complete the following analogy: "Reading is like opening a gift because." Then, have them determine whether their analogies are complete by subjecting them to the three questions listed on this page.

3. Have students choose an event they learned about in history class this year. Then, have them trace the list of causes and events that led to it.

4. If possible, have students arrange these causes and events in a graphic organizer that shows the relationships among them.

Customize for
Spatial Learners

Some students will benefit from creating a chart for Exercise 8. Have students fold their papers to create four columns. Label the columns "Inference," "Generalization," "Analogy," and "Cause and Effect." Have students list each statement in the correct column and then write whether the conclusion is valid or invalid.

Answer Key

▶ **Exercise 8**

1. cause and effect, valid
2. analogy, valid
3. generalization, invalid
4. inference, valid
5. cause and effect, valid

Identify an Author's Purpose

1. Copy the left side of the chart on the chalkboard. Have students think of examples of writing that have these purposes. (Examples: History texts inform, cookbooks instruct, movie reviews offer opinions, advertisements sell things, and novels entertain.)

2. If there are types of writing for which students cannot think of examples, either provide your own or ask students to find examples by looking through newspapers and magazines.

Evaluate the Use of Language

Teaching Resources: Academic and Workplace Skills Activity Book, p. 38

1. Give students an example of a fact. (Example: *One student scored 70% on the test.*) Then, give an example of how language can color that fact. (Example: *The slacker squeaked by with a 70% on the test.*)

2. Ask students to discuss ways in which language changes the way facts are interpreted. Have they ever thought carefully about how to say something so that their audience responds a certain way?

3. As you read, have students give examples of each use of language. You might have them rephrase the fact in step 1 above in each style.

4. If students cannot think of examples, either provide your own or ask them to find examples in newspapers and magazines.

31.2

Identifying an Author's Purpose and Evaluating Language Use

Identify an Author's Purpose

To read critically, you must also determine why the material was written. Is the author trying to inform you, persuade you, or simply entertain you?

IDENTIFYING AN AUTHOR'S PURPOSE IN WRITING	
Purpose	**Informational Clues**
To inform:	Series of factual statements that are verified by records or personal observation
To instruct:	Sequential development of an idea or a process
To offer an opinion:	Presentation of an issue with a predominant point of view backed up by valid authority
To sell:	Persuasion designed to sell an idea or a product
To entertain:	Narration of an event in a humorous way; often used to lighten a serious topic

Evaluate the Use of Language

Learning to understand and evaluate the various ways in which words are used is an important part of becoming a critical reader.

Connotation and Denotation As you read critically, you must be sensitive to the author's tone, or attitude toward the topic. Tone can be expressed using words with *connotative*, or implied, meanings that differ from the *denotative*, or literal, meanings. Connotations can affect a person emotionally and cause a particular response to the material. The following three statements are similar, yet each gives a different impression of the event described.

DENOTATION: The speaker walked quickly up to the lectern.

CONNOTATION: The speaker strode confidently up to the lectern.

CONNOTATION: The speaker stumbled clumsily up to the lectern.

☑ **ONGOING ASSESSMENT: Monitor and Reinforce**

If students have trouble understanding the difference between connotation and denotation, use the following strategy.

Have students choose a simple word, such as *happy*. Ask them to look in the thesaurus and write down a list of as many synonyms as possible for the word (examples: *pleased, contented, cheerful, enraptured, ecstatic*). Ask students whether describing someone as *happy* is the same as describing him or her as *ecstatic*. They should note that although the words have the same basic meaning, they vary in degree and tone. They have similar denotations, but very different connotations.

Irony Irony refers to a contrast between perception and reality; between what is said and what is actually meant.

Understatement When an idea is played down or treated casually, it is considered to be an understatement.

Inflated Language and Jargon Inflated language refers to writing that sounds very scholarly or is filled with scientific or technical terms or overly long phrases. One type of inflated language is called jargon. Jargon is the specialized vocabulary used by people in a particular field. In its place, it is useful, but jargon is often misused to impress the reader or to conceal meaning.

Euphemism A euphemism is a word or phrase used to replace words that may be considered offensive.

Slanting Slanting is the writing of a passage so that it leans toward one point of view. Choosing words with either positive or negative connotations is one type of slanting. Another type of slanting is presenting only one side of an issue by leaving out important facts that would support another point of view.

| SLANTED STATEMENT: | Management offered the union a salary increase of only 7 percent. |
| MORE BALANCED STATEMENT: | Management offered a 7-percent salary increase plus an expanded benefits package, including profit sharing. |

▶ **Exercise 9** Applying Critical Reading Skills Analyze this passage for statements of fact and opinion, forms of reasoning, author's purpose, and use of language.

Nowadays, it is impossible to drive down any street for more than a few minutes without passing at least one jogger, clad in colorful shorts and expensive running shoes, and usually panting or even gasping for air. The death from a heart attack of Jim Fixx, a fellow slave to the exercise mania, seems not to have deterred these fanatical amateur athletes. Millions of dollars are spent each year in fashionable exercise salons run by sharp entrepreneurs. If you could manage to stop one of the victims long enough to ask why he is putting himself through such torture, he would probably mumble something about the heart being a muscle that needs exercise. There is no medical evidence for this. It is true that exercise is a good thing, but overexercising is too much of a good thing. In fact, victims of the physical fitness craze may actually be harming themselves. Doctors report seeing many more injuries to joints, muscles, and tendons. And, of course, there is always the risk of a heart attack during violent exercise.

▶ **Speaking and Listening Tip**

A speaker's tone of voice or facial expression is often a clue that he or she is using irony or understatement.

▼ **Critical Viewing**
What types of connotations might the words have in a description of this runner? **[Speculate]**

Customize for
Linguistic Learners
Students might find it easier to recognize irony and understatement if they hear it. Read aloud a few examples of each and guide them to pay close attention to your tone of voice.

Answer Key

▶ **Exercise 9**

In their analyses, students may find some facts (Fixx's death from a heart attack; millions of dollars spent in exercise salons; many more exercise-related injuries), an overgeneralization ("it is impossible to drive . . . without passing at least one jogger"), and an abundance of negatively slanted words ("slave," "mania," "fanatical," "sharp entrepreneurs," "torture," "craze," "violent exercise"). All these elements are shaped to the author's purpose of deriding the fitness boom.

Critical Viewing

Speculate Students may cite words with positive connotations, such as *fit, limber, flexible,* and so on.

Analyzing and Evaluating Fiction

Teaching Resources: Academic and Workplace Skills Activity Book, p. 39

1. Read aloud the strategies for analyzing and evaluating fiction, or have a prepared student read them.

2. To practice these strategies, distribute copies of a well-known fable or fairy tale, such as "The Tortoise and the Hare."

3. Have students read the fable aloud. What is their purpose for reading it?

4. Next, have them ask questions about it. What do they think will happen to the brazen hare? To the steady tortoise?

5. Have students make personal connections with the characters. Which do they identify with more, and why?

6. Finally, have them analyze the fable. Do they agree with the idea that "slow and steady wins the race"? Does the story sufficiently illustrate this idea? Have they witnessed examples of this in real life?

Section 31.3

Reading Literary Writing

Although you will most often read literature for pleasure, you will get more out of what you read if you apply the strategies that follow. The reading strategies on this page can be applied to any type of literature. On the pages that follow, you'll find specific strategies for reading short stories and novels, drama, poetry, and epics and legends.

Analyzing and Evaluating Fiction

Establish a Purpose for Reading Before you begin, establish a purpose for reading to focus your thoughts. For example, you might read simply for enjoyment, or you might read to learn something about the exotic setting of a novel, or you might read to learn lessons you can apply to your life.

Ask Questions As you read, ask questions: *Why* did the character do this? *When* are the events taking place? *What* are the consequences of these events? Look for answers to these questions as you work your way through the piece.

Reread or Read Ahead When you are unsure what is happening or if the meaning of a sentence or a paragraph is unclear, reread it. At times, you may also find it helpful to read ahead to find more information and to make connections.

Make Personal Connections You will increase your understanding and enjoyment if you connect the characters and events to your own experiences. Consider what you would do and how you would feel if you were taking part in the action.

Read Aloud Read aloud to hear the sounds of the words. This technique is especially effective for poetry, in which sound is just as important as meaning.

Analyze When you analyze, you try to determine the meaning behind events and the characters' actions. Works of literature usually convey a theme, or a central message about life. Most themes are conveyed indirectly, so you may need to do some analyzing to grasp the message.

Respond As you read, think about how the characters and events make you feel, and explore the associations that they bring to mind. When you have finished reading, take some time to reflect and to consider what the work means to you. This may help you decide whether to read other works by that author.

🔲 Research Tip

Published literary criticisms reflect one writer's or a group of writers' critical readings of a work of literature. Review several books that contain literary criticisms to see how professional writers apply the critical thinking skills you are learning to use.

804 • Reading Skills

🕐 TIME AND RESOURCE MANAGER

Resources
Print: *Academic and Workplace Skills Activity Book*, pp. 39–43

Using the Full Student Edition	Using the Handbook🄷
• Cover pp. 804–807 in class.	• Cover pp. 602–605 in class.
• Assign Exercises 10–12 to be done in class.	• Assign Exercises 10–12 to be done in class.
• Work through the Step-by-Step Teaching Guides for Reading From Varied Sources.	• Work through the Step-by-Step Teaching Guides for Reading From Varied Sources.
• Take the class to the school library to complete Exercise 13.	• Take the class to the school library to complete Exercise 13.

Reading Fiction

Following are some strategies for reading fiction:

Predict As you read, ask yourself what might happen next. Base your predictions on what you know about the characters and setting as well as on clues the author provides.

Connect to Your Own Experiences To help you understand how the characters feel, compare their experiences to those you've had in your own life.

Envision the Setting and the Action Use details from the story to create a picture in your mind, as if you were watching the story unfold on the big screen. You might even use a chart like this one to list important details of a scene and to identify the importance of the scene to the story.

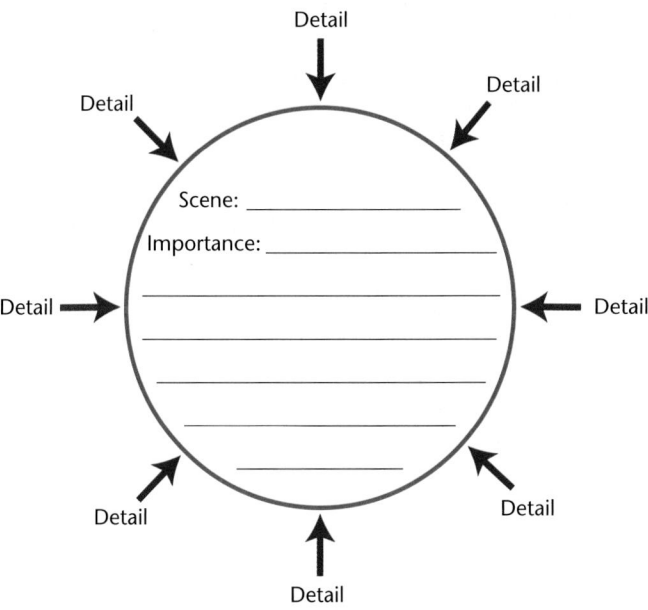

Draw Inferences and Conclusions Writers don't always tell you everything directly. Sometimes, you have to make inferences, or draw conclusions, by considering the underlying meaning of details that the writer includes or doesn't include.

> **Exercise 10** **Reading Short Stories** Read a short story. Apply all of the strategies above. When you have finished, write a brief explanation of how you used each strategy.

🔲 Research Tip

You can view film versions of stories, novels, epics, and legends for an understanding of historical context. Be aware, however, that the historical information you see may not be completely accurate and may reflect the filmmakers' interpretations.

Step-by-Step Teaching Guide

Reading Fiction

Teaching Resources: Academic and Workplace Skills Activity Book, p. 40

1. To practice these strategies, refer students to a short story they recently read as a class.

2. Ask students how they envision the setting of the story. What do the characters look like? How do the characters act?

3. Next, ask them to connect the story to their own experience. Have they ever faced a situation or challenge similar to the one confronting the main character in the story?

4. Ask students to draw conclusions about the story. What message does the story convey?

5. Finally, ask them to speculate what might happen beyond the written end of the story.

Customize for
Less Advanced Students

Making predictions is a useful strategy because it encourages students to read on and find out whether their predictions were correct. In addition, it helps them pay close attention to details because knowing the details can help them make more accurate predictions.

Answer Key

> **Exercise 10**

You may wish to provide small groups with the same short story. Assign a different scene to each group.

Reading Drama

Teaching Resources: Academic and Workplace Skills Activity Book, p. 41

1. Ask students to compare and contrast seeing a play and reading a play. Students should note when you read a play, you must imagine the way the characters and setting look. When you see it, the actors and directors do this work for you.

2. Explain that reading a play can be more difficult, but that using reading strategies can help the play come alive.

3. Choose a play you read in class this year. Have students reread one of the scenes and write a summary of it.

4. Discuss the author's stage directions, including scenery, lighting, and the movement of the actors. How are these elements important?

5. Ask students to connect the play to its historical context. They might need to do some research in the library or on the Internet.

Customize for
Bodily/Kinesthetic Learners

Students might gain a better understanding of the scene in Exercise 11 if they see it performed. Have bodily/kinesthetic learners prepare and act out the scene for the class, making sure to account for the stage directions. Have students discuss what they learned from the performance that they did not notice while reading.

Answer Key

> **Exercise 11**

Ask volunteers to read aloud a few pages of the play they selected, paying attention to stage directions and how the characters should be speaking.

31.3

Reading Drama

The key difference between dramas and other forms of literature is that dramas are meant to be performed. As a result, the story unfolds and the characters are revealed through dialogue and action—there are no long passages of description and no direct revelations about how characters feel. Stage directions indicate when and how the actors move and sometimes suggest lighting and sound effects.

Envision the Action Remember that dramas are meant to be performed rather than read. As you read, try to envision how the play would look if it were being performed on stage. Use the stage directions to help you see in your mind the action taking place and to visualize the costumes.

Connect the Play to Its Historical Context
Sometimes, the time in which a play is set can have a dramatic impact on how the characters act and can shape the message the play conveys. Look in the stage directions for information about the time in which the play is set.

Summarize Most dramas are broken into acts or scenes. Pause between acts or scenes to review in your mind the action that has taken place. Make a chart like the one below. List the act, and identify the scenes, characters, and conflict. Then, briefly summarize the events.

Act I: _____

   Scene I: _____

     Characters: _____

     Conflict: _____

▶ **Exercise 11** Reading Drama Read the first act of a play in your textbook or in another collection. Explain the play's setting, including its historical context. Tell how the stage directions and characters' comments and actions enabled you to envision the scene. Then, summarize the conflict and the events that occurred in the act.

⊙ Technology Tip

You can find performances of many plays on videotape. Once you have finished reading a play, try to find a recorded performance. Watch the video, and compare and contrast the impact of watching it with that of reading it.

Reading Poetry

Reading poetry is unlike reading other types of literature because it is a very distinctive kind of writing—it differs in its appearance, its use of language, and its sound. Poets' imaginative use of language can sometimes make a poem seem complex or hard to understand. Using specific strategies can help you to understand and appreciate poetry.

Identify the Speaker When you read a poem, you are hearing the voice of the poem's speaker. The speaker is not necessarily the poet, although it can be. The speaker may be a character created by the poet. Determine who you think is "telling" the poem, and try to determine his or her perspective on the situation in the poem.

Envision Images Use your senses to experience the pleasures of a poem. For instance, *see* the image of a storm scattering red autumn leaves and *hear* the sound of the wind howling.

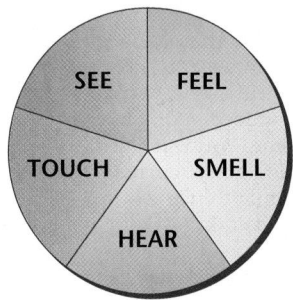

Read According to Punctuation Keep in mind that even if a poem is shaped to fit a particular rhythm and rhyme, a poem's words are usually put together and punctuated as sentences. When you read a poem, don't stop at the end of each line unless a punctuation mark stops you.

Listen to the Poem One of the things that distinguishes poetry from prose is its sound. Poetry is meant to be read aloud; by doing so, you will hear the music of the poet's words.

> **Exercise 12** **Reading Poetry** Select a poem from your textbook. Read the poem aloud, according to its punctuation, and listen to its sound. Then, write a brief description of the poem in which you identify the speaker, describe three images or figures of speech, and describe the poem's sound.

▶ Speaking and Listening Tip

To appreciate how listening to poetry differs from reading it, attend a local poetry reading. If this isn't possible, find recordings of poetry. Compare and contrast the effect of listening to a poem with the effect of reading one.

Step-by-Step Teaching Guide

Reading Poetry

Teaching Resources: Academic and Workplace Skills Activity Book, p. 42

1. Refer students to a poem in their literature anthology, copy a short lyric poem on the board, or display one on transparency.

2. Ask students to listen to the rhythm and to the sounds of the words.

3. Next, have students respond to the imagery in the poem. What does the poet want them to see? Hear? Sense?

4. Ask students who is speaking in the poem. Remind students to avoid the natural impulse to routinely assume that the poet is the speaker. In almost all cases, it is more accurate to refer to the "speaker" in the poem rather than to the poet.

5. Conclude by asking students to share the titles of favorite poems they have read recently.

Customize for
ESL Students

Some students may have difficulty with the figurative language of poetry. Before having them complete Exercise 12, check to make sure they understand the basic meaning of the poem.

Answer Key

> **Exercise 12**

After students complete their descriptions, have volunteers share them with the class.

☑ ONGOING ASSESSMENT: Monitor and Reinforce

If students have difficulty reading and understanding poetry, try the following strategy.

Paraphrasing is often a helpful technique. Suggest that students draw a two-column chart in their notebooks, labeling the left side "Author's Words" and the right side "My Own Words." Tell them to keep their notebooks open to this chart as they read a poem. When they encounter a line they don't understand, have them write it in the left-hand column. Next to it, in the other column, have them translate the line into their own words. They can work with classmates to decipher the lines they don't understand.

Reading From Varied Sources

Today, there are more sources of reading material than ever before. Not only can you read books, magazines, newspapers, and other forms of printed material, but you can also read an almost unlimited amount of material on the Internet. The following are just a few of the sources from which you can choose. When selecting a source, consider your purpose for reading, along with any time constraints with which you're faced.

Read Diaries, Letters, and Journals Diaries, letters, and journals are a great source for firsthand accounts of historical events. Use them to discover how it felt to be part of an event in which you are interested or as primary source material in a research paper. As you read, remember that diaries and journals present a single perspective—the writer's—of the events. To find a balanced point of view, look at several diaries and journals.

Read Newspapers Newspapers are probably the best source for up-to-date information on issues and events. When you are writing a research paper on a historical event, you may want to use newspapers to capture the way information about the event was presented to people at that time. You will also want to use newspapers when you are writing about current events. Beyond school, you'll probably continue to use newspapers as a means of keeping up with current events. Although newspapers are one of the most objective sources, be on the lookout for any words or choices of details that suggest a bias.

Read Speeches Transcripts of speeches can be another excellent source for learning about historical or current events. Keep in mind that a speech that you are reading was originally written to be presented orally to an audience. Also, consider that a speech presents a single point of view—that of the speaker. Many speeches, such as political speeches, have a persuasive purpose. As a result, speakers often carefully choose words and details to achieve a specific effect. Try to avoid being swayed by appeals to emotion or charged language. Instead, see how effectively the speaker has backed up his or her key points with facts, statistics, and other types of support.

"GIVE ME LIBERTY, OR GIVE ME DEATH !"

▼ **Critical Viewing**
This painting shows Patrick Henry delivering his famous "Give Me Liberty or Give Me Death" speech. What can you tell about his delivery based on the painting? **[Analyze]**

Read Electronic Texts The main type of electronic texts that you will encounter are Web pages. There is an incredible amount of information on the Web, and the amount is growing every day. Some of the information is reliable and objective; some is biased or targeted toward a specific audience. When you read material on the Internet, do so with a critical eye. Determine the purpose behind the material. Often, you will discover that the material has a persuasive purpose. Check whether any points made in a text on the Web are thoroughly supported by facts and details. Also, evaluate the credibility of the source.

> **Exercise 13** **Reading Varied Sources** Find at least one example of each of the sources mentioned on these pages. Read the material carefully. Then, write a brief summary of each piece. Follow your summary with an evaluation of the reliability of the material. How well has the author supported his or her main points? Is the author credible? Why or why not? Would you recommend the material to others? Explain.

Reflecting on Your Reading

After a week of applying reading skills and strategies for both nonfiction and fiction works, think about the experience of using them. Use these questions to direct your reflection:

- Which sections of the books that I read did I find most useful?

- How has varying my reading style affected my reading time?

- Which graphic organizers have I used to process and understand information from my reading?

- How do the steps of the SQ4R method help me obtain more complete information and understanding?

- How have critical reading skills helped me to analyze and evaluate the material I read?

- Which strategies for reading fiction did I find most useful? Which strategies did I find most difficult to use?

Jot down your responses and ideas in a journal or notebook. If you like, compare your thoughts and ideas with those of a partner.

Reading Electronic Texts

1. Ask students to discuss their experiences using the Internet. Which Web pages have given them valid and useful information? Which have not?

2. Explain that Web pages must be read critically just like any other type of writing. Students should determine the purpose behind the material, look for information that is supported by facts and details, and evaluate the credibility of the source.

3. To practice reading Web pages critically, either print a particular page or have students choose a page to print. Ask students to write a critical summary of the page, including its purpose, its sources, and its credibility.

Answer Key

> **Exercise 13**

Ask students which of the sources was the easiest to access or find. Then, ask which one was the most enjoyable to read.

ASSESS and CLOSE

Assessment

1. After students answer the Reflecting on Your Reading questions, have them discuss their answers in small groups.

2. Remind students to use this chapter as a reference when they need strategies for reading a challenging text in any of their classes or for pleasure.

3. You may wish to administer the Chapter 31 assessment from *Formal Assessment* in the Teaching Resources to measure students' grasp of the concepts presented.

Lesson Objectives

1. To draw inferences such as conclusions, generalizations, and predictions and support them with text evidence and experience

2. To monitor one's own reading strategies and to make modifications when understanding breaks down

3. To identify main ideas and their supporting details

Step-by-Step Teaching Guide

Make Inferences and Predictions

Teaching Resources: Standardized Test Preparation Workbook, pp. 61–62

1. Explain that even though the answers to these questions will not be directly stated in the text, the text will contain all the information necessary for inferring answers to every question. Students don't need background knowledge about the topic at hand.

2. Have students complete the sample test items. Have them write out an answer to question 2. They might use details from the passage that illustrate the author's respect toward the elderly. Have volunteers share their answers.

3. Have students complete the practice exercises on page 811. If they have trouble remembering which character is which, they might make notes about Mr. Manaby, the new assistant, and the other employees as they read.

4. Discuss their answers and address any questions they might have.

Standardized Test Preparation Workshop

Make Inferences and Predictions

The reading sections of standardized tests often measure your ability to make inferences. For these types of questions, a reading passage will be supplied. The answer to the question will not be directly stated in the material you use. You will need to put together clues from the text to arrive at the correct answer. Some questions will require you to make inferences or predictions about characters' actions or probable plot events. Other questions will ask you to make inferences about the author's purpose or point of view. You may be asked to respond by choosing from among several choices or by responding in writing.

Look at the following sample items:

Test Tips

- If you are given a specific amount of space in which to write an answer, plan your points carefully before you begin writing.
- Approach multiple-choice reading questions the same way you'd approach short-answer items.

Sample Test Items

Sample Test Items	Answers and Explanations
Directions Read the passage. Then, answer the questions that follow the passage. From "A Celebration of Grandfathers," Rudolfo Anaya "Buenos dias le de Dios, abuelo." God give you a good day, grandfather. This is how I was taught as a child to greet my grandfather, or any grown person. It was a greeting of respect, a cultural value to be passed on from generation to generation, this respect for the old ones. The old people I remember from my childhood were strong in their beliefs, and as we lived daily with them we learned a wise path of life to follow. They had something important to share with the young, and when they spoke, the young listened.	
1. The author opens the story with a Spanish quotation to A impress readers with his knowledge of Spanish. B establish a cultural context for the work. C explain the essay's title. D teach readers a Spanish quotation.	The answer for item 1 is *B*. By opening with a quotation in the language of his childhood, the author gives readers a taste of the culture in which he was raised.
2. Answer the following question. Base your answer on "A Celebration of Grandfathers." In what ways has the author's attitude toward the elderly changed or remained the same since he was a child? Support your answer with details from the passage	Your answer should consist of a paragraph that includes a topic sentence and details from the passage that support it.

810 • Reading Skills

TEST-TAKING TIP

Suggest that students skim the questions before reading the passage. This way, as they read, they will know which information is important. If they are permitted to write in the test booklet, encourage them to underline important passages so they will be easy to find later.

Remind students to use quotations from the text to support their answers. The passage is right in front of them, and they can refer to it as often as necessary to find appropriate quotations. If they can't find any relevant quotes, they might consider changing their answer.

▶ **Practice 1** **Directions:** Read the passage. Then, answer the questions that follow the passage.

From "Sonata for Harp and Bicycle," Joan Aiken

. . . ."No one is allowed to remain in the building after five o'clock," Mr. Manaby told his new assistant, showing him into the little room that was like the inside of a parcel. "Why not?"

"Directorial policy," said Mr. Manaby. But that was not the real reason.

Gaunt and sooty, Grimes Buildings lurched up the side of a hill toward Clerkenwell. Every little office within its dim and crumbling exterior owned one tiny crumb of light—such was the proud boast of the architect—but toward evening the crumbs were collected as by an immense vacuum cleaner, absorbed and demolished, yielding to an uncontrollable mass of dark that came tumbling through windows to take their place. Darkness infested the building like a flight of bats returning willingly to roost.

"Wash hands, please. Wash hands, please," the intercom began to bawl in the passages at a quarter to five. Without much need of prompting, the staff hustled like lemmings along the corridors to green- and blue-tiled washrooms that mocked with an illustration of cheerfulness the encroaching dusk.

❶ Mr. Manaby could best be described as
  A a man who is friendly and outgoing.
  B a man who does not like his job.
  C a man who expects rules to be followed.
  D a clean and tidy man.

❷ Which sentence BEST describes the author's attitude toward the employees of Grimes Buildings?
  F She admires their dedication.
  G She is amused by their unquestioning obedience.
  H She is impressed by their superior intelligence.
  I She is saddened by their cruelty.

❸ The reaction of the employees to the intercom announcement indicates that
  A they are used to the announcement.
  B they resent the announcement.
  C they are surprised by the announcement.
  D they don't understand the announcement.

❹ What can you predict based on the opening dialogue?
  F The new assistant will fit in well.
  G The new assistant will have a fight with Mr. Manaby.
  H The new assistant will break the intercom.
  I The new assistant will stay in the building after five o'clock.

❺ When the author says the little room is like the inside of a parcel, she means that
  A the room is square.
  B the room is filled with paper.
  C the room is small.
  D the room is closed.

❻ Which word BEST describe the assistant's reaction to Mr. Manaby's statement that everyone must leave by five o'clock?
  F curious
  G timid
  H amused
  I sad

▶ **Practice 2** **Directions:** Answer the following question. Base your answer on "A Sonata for Harp and Bicycle."

READ THINK EXPLAIN What is the main impression the author gives of Grimes Buildings? Use details from the excerpt to explain your answer.

▶ **Practice 1**
1. C
2. G
3. A
4. I
5. C
6. F

▶ **Practice 2**

Answers will vary. Students should note that the building is stark and dreary. They might use details such as "gaunt and sooty," "dim and crumbling," "uncontrollable mass of dark," and others to support their answers.

Customize for
Less Advanced Students

If students have difficulty with making a prediction in question 4, help them find clues on which to base their predictions. Point out that the new assistant is the only employee who questions company policies; the other employees follow them like "lemmings." This suggests that he might consider breaking one of the rules.

LESSON FOCUS	PRINT AND MEDIA RESOURCES
DAY 1 — **Basic Study Skills** Students develop a study plan and take notes in outline and summary form. (pp. 812–814/H608–610)	**Teaching Resources** *Academic and Workplace Skills Activity Book,* pp. 44–45
DAY 2 — **Reference Skills** Students gather information using a variety of library resources, including electronic catalogs and other non-print materials. (pp. 815–819/H611–615)	**Teaching Resources** *Academic and Workplace Skills Activity Book,* pp. 46–48
DAY 3 — **Using Dictionaries** Students survey a dictionary's contents and review various types of dictionaries. (pp. 820–823/H616–619)	**Teaching Resources** *Academic and Workplace Skills Activity Book,* p. 49
DAY 4 — **Using Other References** Students consult encyclopedias, atlases, and almanacs as well as electronic and media resources such as videos, CD-ROMs and the Internet. (pp. 824–827/H620–623)	**Teaching Resources** *Academic and Workplace Skills Activity Book,* pp. 50–52
DAY 5 — **Test-Taking Skills** Students learn to budget time while taking tests and how to approach various types of questions on standardized tests such as the SAT and ACT. (pp. 828–831/H624–627)	**Teaching Resources** *Academic and Workplace Skills Activity Book,* pp. 53–54; *Formal Assessment,* Ch. 32

Accelerated Lesson Plan

LESSON FOCUS	PRINT AND MEDIA RESOURCES
DAY 1 — **Basic Study and Reference Skills** Students review the full array of reference resources available to them, as well as strategies for organizing their study. (pp. 812–823/H608–619)	**Teaching Resources** *Academic and Workplace Skills Activity Book,* pp. 44–49
DAY 2 — **Test-Taking Skills** Students work independently to review the use of reference tools such as videotape and the Internet, and review test-taking skills and strategies. (pp. 824–831/H620–627)	**Teaching Resources** *Academic and Workplace Skills Activity Book,* pp. 50–54; *Formal Assessment,* Ch. 32

Options for Adapting Lesson Plans

HOMEWORK

Have students conduct independent library research.

FEATURES

Extend coverage with the Standardized Test Preparation Workshop (p. 832)

TECHNOLOGY

Students may use the Internet to conduct independent research. Have them print out their completed work.

Writing and Grammar Handbook Alignment

Page numbers in Step-by-Step Teaching Guides in this Teacher's Edition refer to pages from the full student text. Handbook page references, indicated with this icon H, are provided in Time and Resource Manager boxes and at the bottom of each Teacher's Edition page.

INTEGRATED SKILLS COVERAGE

Research Skills
SE pp. 819, 824/H615, 620

Technology Skills
SE pp. 813, 814, 816, 819, 820, 823, 826, 827/H609, 610, 612, 615, 616, 619, 622, 623

Spelling Skills
ATE p. 824

Workplace Skills
ATE pp. 814, 816

Viewing and Representing
Critical Viewing, SE pp. 812, 816, 818, 825/H608, 612, 614, 621
ATE p. 829

Vocabulary Skills
ATE p. 817

Real-World Connection
ATE pp. 820, 827

ASSESSMENT SUPPORT

Standardized Test Preparation Workshop SE p. 832; ATE p. 822

Standardized Test Preparation Workbook, pp. 63–64

Formal Assessment, Ch. 32

MEETING INDIVIDUAL NEEDS

Less Advanced Students ATE pp. 822, 833. See also Ongoing Assessments ATE pp. 818, 825.

More Advanced Students ATE pp. 815, 820, 823, 833

ESL Students ATE pp. 814, 818, 821, 826

Gifted and Talented Students ATE pp. 819, 825

Logical-Mathematical Learners ATE p. 813

Interpersonal Learners ATE p. 831

Musical Learners ATE p. 825

Spatial Learners ATE p. 816

BLOCK SCHEDULING

Pacing Suggestions
For 90-minute Blocks
• Have students review the extensive Reference Skills section in a single period.
• Focus one class period on Test-Taking Skills. Give students a half-hour sample ACT or SAT test.

Resources for Varying Instruction
• *Academic and Workplace Skills Activity Book,* pp. 44–54

Professional Development Support
• *How to Manage Instruction in the Block* This teaching resource provides management and activity suggestions.

MEDIA AND TECHNOLOGY

For the Teacher
• **TeacherEXPRESS** CD-ROM

WRITING AND GRAMMAR ON-LINE

Interactive Text (On-line or on CD-ROM)
• Easily navigable instruction with interactive Revision Checkers
• Full use of e-rater™, the essay-scoring system (on-line only)

Companion Web Site PHSchool.com
• Scoring rubrics with models (use Web Code eek-1001)

See the Go On-line! feature, SE p. iii.

▶ *Lesson Objectives*

1. To use study strategies such as skimming and scanning, note taking, outlining, and using study-guide questions to better understand texts

2. To use writing to discover, organize, and support what is known and what needs to be learned about a topic

3. To use writing as a study tool to clarify and remember information

4. To produce summaries of texts by identifying main ideas and their supporting details

5. To represent information in a variety of ways such as graphics, conceptual maps, and learning logs

6. To compile information from primary and secondary sources in systematic ways using available technology

7. To use reference materials such as glossaries, dictionaries, thesauruses, and available technology to determine precise meanings and usage

8. To locate appropriate print and nonprint information using text and technical resources, including databases and the Internet

9. To read and understand analogies

Critical Viewing

Analyze Students may say that reading can be done anywhere, but note taking or serious research might require a different setting.

Chapter 32 Study, Reference, and Test-Taking Skills

◀ **Critical Viewing**
What type of school-work would and would not be appropriate to do in the setting shown here? Why? **[Analyze]**

Learning how to improve your study, reference, and test-taking skills will make your schoolwork easier and prove to be a valuable asset throughout your education. The first two sections of this chapter will show you how to improve your general study habits and how to research specific information in printed and electronic forms. The final section will discuss strategies that you can use to improve your performance on tests.

⏲ **TIME AND RESOURCE MANAGER**	
Resources **Print:** *Academic and Workplace Skills Activity Book,* pp. 44–45	
Using the Full Student Edition	**Using the Handbook Ⓗ**
• Cover pp. 812–814 in class. Ask students to describe what they think is an effective study plan. • Review the various aspects of the three-point study plan. • Have students complete Exercises 1–2 in class.	• Cover pp. 608–610 in class. Ask students to describe what they think is an effective study plan. • Review the various aspects of the three-point study plan. • Have students complete Exercises 1–2 in class.

Section 32.1 Basic Study Skills

As with most other things, the more you think out and plan how you study, the more effective your studying will be. Develop a systematic approach to studying that includes how and where you study and how you record what you learn.

Developing a Study Plan

Good study habits begin with a strong study plan. The purpose of a study plan is to help you make the best use of the time available to you for doing your assignments. Your study plan should include setting up a study area, establishing a study schedule, and keeping a study notebook.

▶ **KEY CONCEPT** Use a *three point study plan* to manage your time and keep track of your assignments. ■

USING A STUDY PLAN

STUDY AREA
1. Set up a well-lit study area free from distractions.
2. Equip the area with work materials: pens, paper, ruler, dictionary.

STUDY NOTEBOOK
1. List assignments and include their due dates.
2. List long-term assignments in steps.
3. Check off assignments as you complete them.

STUDY SCHEDULE
1. Block out periods of time in which you have fixed activities.
2. Plan to study 2–3 hours a day, in 30–45 minute periods.
3. Study your hardest subject first.

▶ **Exercise 1** **Evaluating Your Study Plan** Identify which area of your study plan you need to improve most: setting up a study area, making a study schedule, or keeping a study notebook. Work to improve that skill for one week, and then evaluate your progress.

Technology Tip

You can use a software time-management program to help you set up and keep track of your study schedule.

Basic Study Skills • 813

Customize for
Logical/Mathematical Learners

Ask students why they think the study plan is displayed in the form of a triangle (to emphasize its three equally important points). Ask them what shapes they might use to display their current study methods. Have them draw and label diagrams like the one on this page and share them in small groups.

PREPARE and ENGAGE

Interest GRABBER Invite a recent graduate of your school to share his or her studying experiences with the class. The speaker should address the similarities and differences between studying in high school and studying in college. The speaker might also discuss the ways he or she learned to overcome difficulties to become a better student and test taker. Give students the chance to ask questions.

Activate Prior Knowledge

Provide several large sheets of chart paper and colored markers for the class. Invite students to form small groups and jot down their own advice for successful studying, information gathering, and test taking. Once the charts are filled with ideas, invite a reporter from each group to share the ideas with the class.

Step-by-Step Teaching Guide

Developing a Study Plan

Teaching Resources: Academic and Workplace Skills Activity Book, p. 44

1. Some students might already use some form of a study notebook. Have volunteers share their notebooks with the class.

2. Give students time to ask questions about all three points of the study plan. Some of them may want advice on time management, ideas for study areas, or examples of ways to organize their study notebooks.

Answer Key

▶ **Exercise 1**

After students have worked on improving the identified study area for one week, ask them to reassess their study skills. If necessary, meet with them individually to go over their study plans.

Taking Notes

Teaching Resources: Academic and Workplace Skills Activity Book, p. 45

1. Discuss the modified outline form with the class. Ask students to name other note-taking formats they use. (Students might mention writing notes in the margins, highlighting, writing summaries, and so on.)

2. After you explain the modified outline form to students, have them use it to take notes on the topic at hand: "Taking Notes."

3. On the board or on an overhead projector, share and discuss a possible version of a modified outline for this section of the chapter.

Integrating Workplace Skills

Have groups of students role-play a common workplace situation. Ask one student to play the role of a supervisor relating information about a pay increase to another student playing an employee. Have the employee take notes on this information in outline form. Afterward, have the employee use these notes to reconstruct the information for a group of colleagues.

Customize for
ESL Students

Some students are more comfortable writing in their first languages than in English. You may want to encourage them to take notes in the language of their greatest fluency, especially when taking notes on information presented rapidly, such as an oral presentation.

Answer Key

▶ **Exercise 2**

After students have completed their outlines and summaries, have them share the results in class. Alternatively, they might discuss their results with a partner.

32.1

Taking Notes

Notes are an important study tool. Not only will you need them to study, but the very act of writing information down helps you retain it. Divide your notebook by subject, and take notes on what you learn in class and read in your textbooks.

▶ **KEY CONCEPT** Keep an organized notebook in which you take notes while listening or reading. ■

Modified Outline Because there is not enough time to write everything down, you should take notes on only the most important information. One of the fastest ways to take notes is by using a *modified outline form*, in which you list main ideas at the margin, indent to show major details, and indent further for supporting details, if necessary.

PASSAGE:

Silicon Chips are engraved with hundreds of electronic circuits. These chips are small enough to pass through the eye of a needle, yet they can store 64,000 pieces of information. They are already at work in the digital watch, the pocket calculator, and the microwave oven.

SAMPLE MODIFIED OUTLINE

Silicon Chips ⟶ Main idea
1. Engraved with hundreds of ⟶ Major details
   electronic circuits
2. Extremely small,
   yet store 64,000 pieces of information
3. Used in digital watches,
   calculators, microwave ovens

Summaries A summary is an excellent tool to help you review material. It is a restatement of key ideas in your own words. Written summaries are usually arranged in paragraphs. You can use a summary to capture main ideas from a piece you've just read or a lecture you've just heard. You can also summarize a modified outline you've developed.

▶ **Exercise 2** Developing a Modified Outline and a Summary Develop a modified outline and a summary of a chapter from one of your textbooks.

814 • Study, Reference, and Test-Taking Skills

● Technology Tip

If you have steady access to a computer and are a strong keyboardist, you may want to record and store some of your notes on computer. Make sure that you back up your notes on a separate disk and that you keep a hard copy.

☑ ONGOING ASSESSMENT: Diagnose

Use one of the following options to diagnose students' current level of proficiency in studying and test-taking skills.

Option 1 Tell students to imagine they have to take a test on everything they've learned in English class in the last month. Ask them to create a written study plan for this test. Collect and review their plans. Students who have trouble organizing their time will need extra support in study skills.

Option 2 Have students choose an author they've read and enjoyed this year. Have them make a list of every resource they can think of for learning more about this author and his or her works. Students who have difficulty naming more than one or two resources will need extra support with reference skills.

Section 32.2 — Reference Skills

The recent revolution in electronic media has made more kinds of information available than ever before. Virtually every kind of printed reference now has an electronic equivalent, either on CD-ROM or on-line or both. At public or school libraries, you can often find all these sources: fiction and non-fiction books, audiocassettes, videocassettes, periodicals (newspapers, magazines, and scholarly journals), reference works in printed and electronic form, information on micro-film, and computer access to the Internet.

Finding Library Resources

Some library resources *circulate*—that is, you can borrow them for a fixed period of time. Others are for *reference* only and must be used at the library. Some materials are displayed on *open stacks*, or shelves, where you get them yourself; others are stored on *closed stacks* open only to library staff, who will bring you the material when you request it.

Using the Library Catalog The catalog shows whether the library owns a work. Use the catalog to help you find works by specific authors or on particular subjects. The catalog also clarifies whether a book is fiction or nonfiction and gives call numbers of nonfiction works so that you can locate them on the shelves.

> ▶ **KEY CONCEPT** Use the library catalog— in *card*, *printed*, or *electronic* form—to find important information about the materials that a library stocks. ■

Card Catalog Each work in a library has an *author card* and *title card*; each nonfiction book also has at least one *subject card*. Cards are filed alphabetically in small drawers, with author cards alphabetized by last names and title cards alphabetized by the first words of the titles, excluding *A, An,* or *The.*

CARD CATALOG (AUTHOR CARD)	
306.209C Collins, Gail	call number / author
Scorpion Tongues	title
New York:	city of publication
William Morrow, 1998	publisher, / publication date
322 p; index	number of pages / index
United States—Politics	subject

Step-by-Step Teaching Guide

Using the Library Catalog

Teaching Resources: Academic and Workplace Skills Activity Book, p. 46

1. Discuss the purpose and structure of library catalog listings. Point out that the texts of printed card listings and electronic listings are essentially the same in form and structure.

2. Provide students with several books from your school or local library. Challenge them to construct a listing for one of these books. You may have to review the places in the book, such as the spine, copyright page, or book jacket, where relevant information might be found.

3. As an extension activity, you may wish to have students retrieve detailed information about a list of titles you provide. (Examples: call number, publisher, and so on.)

Customize for
More Advanced Students

Have students choose a research topic they are interested in and compile a preliminary bibliography from the library catalog. Remind students that they can find catalog listings organized by subject as well as by author and title.

⏱ TIME AND RESOURCE MANAGER

Resources
Print: *Academic and Workplace Skills Activity Book,* pp. 46–52

Using the Full Student Edition	Using the Handbook⒣
• Give students time in class to work on Exercises 3–10. Allow students to work either alone or in pairs. Encourage them to consult the librarian when they have questions.	• Give students time in class to work on Exercises 3–10. Allow students to work either alone or in pairs. Encourage them to consult the librarian when they have questions.

32.2

Electronic Catalog Most libraries now keep an electronic catalog, an on-line database or a CD-ROM that you access from special library computer terminals. Usually, you can find a book's catalog entry by typing in its title, key words in the title, its author's name, or (for nonfiction) an appropriate subject. Electronic catalogs usually indicate whether the book is available or has been checked out. Often, the catalog will also indicate whether the book is available from other local libraries through an inter-library loan system.

Printed Catalog A printed catalog is a booklet that lists each work alphabetically by author, by title, and (for nonfiction) by subject.

> **Exercise 3** Using the Library Catalog Visit your school or local library, and use the catalog to answer these questions.
> 1. What kind of catalog does the library use?
> 2. Who wrote *The Red Badge of Courage*? Is this book fiction or nonfiction?
> 3. What are the titles, subjects, and call numbers of three nonfiction books by Annie Dillard?
> 4. What are the titles, authors, and call numbers of three books about nutrition published since 1998?
> 5. What are the titles, authors, and call numbers of two nonfiction books about space exploration?

Finding Books on Library Shelves Libraries generally separate fiction (made-up stories) from nonfiction (factual material). Nonfiction includes two smaller groups often shelved separately: biographies (real-life people's stories) and reference works (works to which you refer for information and which must be used at the library).

▶ **KEY CONCEPT** Find fiction arranged alphabetically by authors' last names and nonfiction arranged by call number. ■

Fiction Books of fiction are shelved in a special section alphabetized by authors' last names. In the library catalog and on its spine, the book may be labeled *F* or *FIC*, followed by one or more letters of the author's last name; for example, *FIC Cis* may appear on a novel by Sandra Cisneros.

▶ **KEY CONCEPT** Find nonfiction on the shelves by using the call numbers. ■

Nonfiction Works of nonfiction are assigned number-letter codes, called *call numbers*, based on their content. The call numbers are placed on the spine of each book, and the books are arranged in number-letter order on the shelves—for example, 216.1, 216.2, 216.41A, 216.41G, 216.42B, 217.1. To find a nonfiction book, look it up in the library catalog to learn its call number and then follow number-letter order to locate the book on the shelf.

Most public libraries assign call numbers according to the **Dewey Decimal System,** which divides all knowledge into ten main groups numbered from 000 to 999. The following chart shows the number spans for these ten content areas.

MAIN CLASSES OF THE DEWEY DECIMAL SYSTEM	
Number	Subject
000–099	General Works (encyclopedias, periodicals, etc.)
100–199	Philosophy
200–299	Religion
300–399	Social Sciences
400–499	Languages
500–599	Science
600–699	Technology (applied science)
700–799	Arts and Leisure
800–899	Literature
900–999	History

Finding Books on Library Shelves

Teaching Resources: Academic and Workplace Skills Activity Book, p. 47

1. Discuss the main classes of the Dewey Decimal System. Ask students to consider why this classification system is useful. (It can direct a reader to the exact place on a library shelf where they can find a particular book.)

2. Show students a range of books taken from your school or local library. Cover their Dewey Decimal classification numbers and challenge students to guess which of the main classes they would fall into based on title and subject.

3. Once students have made their predictions, show them the actual classification numbers for each book.

4. Make sure students understand the differences between how fiction and nonfiction are organized.

Integrating Vocabulary Skills

Some students may be unfamiliar with the terms that name the main classes of the Dewey Decimal System. To ensure that students have a general understanding of the meanings of *Philosophy, Social Sciences, Technology (applied sciences),* and other terms, provide some examples of books in these categories, and then have students try to come up with some examples for each category on their own.

Finding Books on Library Shelves *continued*

5. Ask students why they think some books are kept in special sections (possible response: to make them more readily available to those who are interested in them).

6. Ask students whether they are familiar with the Library of Congress. If not, you may want to explain that this government office is responsible for keeping track of all the books and magazines published in the United States.

7. Some books include Library of Congress information on the copyright page. If you have a book that shows this information, point it out to students.

Critical Viewing

Speculate The librarian may be helping the student locate information in a special reference work.

Answer Key

> **Exercise 4**

1. after
2. after
3. reference
4. *Moby-Dick* by Melville, *The Bluest Eye* by Morrison, *The Joy Luck Club* by Tan, *Ethan Frome* by Wharton
5. 518.1K, 518.1P, 518.6C, 519.3B, 519.6A
   Science

Customize for ESL Students

Take students to the library and work with them to find books that they might find to be of special interest or importance. (Example: bilingual dictionaries, pictorial dictionaries, and works published in languages other than English.)

32.2

Special Sections In the Dewey Decimal System, *biographies* are often not assigned call numbers but instead are shelved in a special section alphabetized by the last names of their subjects (the people they are about). In the library catalog and on the book's spine, a biography may be labeled *B* or *BIO*, followed by one or more letters of the subject's last name; for example, *BIO Ein* may appear on a biography of Albert Einstein.

Reference works usually have their own special section—and an *R* or *REF* before their call numbers. Many libraries also have special sections for young-adult books (often labeled *YA*) and children's books (usually labeled *J* or *JUV* for *juvenile*).

The **Library of Congress System,** unlike the Dewey Decimal System, is organized letter-number. In the Library of Congress System, the call numbers begin with letters. The main classes are designated by a single letter; combinations of two letters designate the subclasses. The letter designations are followed by a numerical notation, from 1 to 9999, which can be further subdivided:

MAIN CLASS:	H	Social Sciences
SUBCLASS:	HF	Commerce, Marketing, Advertising
DIVISION:	5717	Business Communication

> **Exercise 4** **Finding Fiction and Nonfiction** In your notebook, answer the following questions.

1. To find fiction by Ralph Ellison on a library shelf, would you look before or after fiction by George Eliot?
2. For a nonfiction work with call number 310.3R, would you look before or after of a work with call number 310.2J?
3. For a book with call number R032.1B, would you look in the reference, biography, or fiction section?
4. Arrange this fiction in the order that you would find them on library shelves: *Moby-Dick* by Herman Melville, *The Bluest Eye* by Toni Morrison, *Ethan Frome* by Edith Wharton, and *The Joy Luck Club* by Amy Tan.
5. Arrange these call numbers in the order that you would find them on library shelves: 519.3B, 518.1P, 518.6C, 518.1K, 519.6A. What is the general subject or content area of books with these call numbers?

▲ Critical Viewing
What type of assistance do you imagine that the librarian is providing for the girl in this photograph? [Speculate]

☑ ONGOING ASSESSMENT: Monitor and Reinforce

To give students extra practice in locating library materials and using note-taking strategies, try the following strategy.

Ask students to choose a subject they would like to learn more about. Have them find a nonfiction book about this subject in the school or local library. Then, have them read the first few chapters and take notes in the modified outline form. When they finish reading, have them review their notes and fill in any information that is needed to make the outline clearer.

Using Periodicals and Periodical Indexes

A *periodical* is a newspaper, magazine, or similar publication issued at regular intervals. Such publications are good sources of up-to-date information. To find out which periodicals a library carries, look up the title in the card catalog.

Periodical Indexes To find which periodicals contain articles on a particular subject, consult a periodical index. Issued regularly in printed or electronic form, these indexes contain *citations* that tell you where and when an article was published. They also may contain *abstracts*, or brief summaries, of the articles. In addition, many electronic indexes provide the *full text*, or complete article, for some articles cited.

KEY CONCEPT Use articles from periodicals for up-to-date information and periodical indexes to locate the articles. ■

Some indexes—such as the *Readers' Guide to Periodical Literature*—cover articles from many periodicals; others, such as *The New York Times Index*, cover articles from only one publication. Look at this sample *Readers' Guide* entry.

SAMPLE READERS' GUIDE ENTRY

subject heading ——————[	**HORSEMANSHIP**
See also	
cross-references ——————[	Polo
	Rodeos
subheading ⌐	**Competition** article topic clarified in brackets
title of article ⌐	A show of hooves [pony club rally].
	illustrated
author ⌐ J.B. Banks ⌐   *National Geographic World*   v288 no 4
name of periodical ⌐	volume and number⌐
pages ——————[p. 12–15   date   ⌐ Ag 1999

Exercise 5 **Using Periodicals** Visit a school or local library to answer these questions.

1. What daily newspapers does the library carry?
2. Find an article in a current magazine that provides information you could use in an essay.
3. Use a periodical index to find four citations for articles on women in sports. Also, list the subjects you looked under.
4. Use a periodical index to find an article on a subject you are studying. Read the article, and share your findings.
5. Using a periodical index, find an article about someone you admire. Read the article, and then write a summary.

Technology Tip

Many newspapers and magazines now have free Internet Web sites where you can read current editions at no cost.

Research Tip

Find citations in an electronic index by typing in the subject, the author's name, or a key word in the title of the article. Find citations in printed indexes by looking up the subject or author.

Step-by-Step Teaching Guide

Using Periodicals and Periodical Indexes

Teaching Resources: Academic and Workplace Skills Activity Book, p. 48

1. Discuss with students what type of information they might look for in periodicals as opposed to other resources. (Students may cite up-to-date information on subjects that change frequently, such as medical research or current events.)

2. Walk students through the sample *Readers' Guide* entry. Help them identify the subject, title of the periodical, title of the article, author, and page number for the article cited.

Customize for *Gifted and Talented Students*

Invite students to use periodicals and periodical indexes to write a short bibliography on a topic of particular interest to them. Provide these students with guidance on how to create a bibliography in proper citation format. Encourage students to teach the rest of the class about proper bibliography format by showing them their own bibliographies.

Answer Key

Exercise 5

After students complete the exercise, you may want to have them discuss their experience in class. Ask volunteers to read their findings or summaries from items 4 and 5.

Using Dictionaries

Teaching Resources: Academic and Workplace Skills Activity Book, p. 49

1. Have volunteers read aloud the descriptions of types of dictionaries to the class. Discuss the differences among unabridged, abridged, and specialized dictionaries.

2. Ask students which of these dictionaries they've used. What type of information were they looking for?

3. Show students the kinds of dictionaries available in your classroom and in the school library. You may also want to encourage them to check a local library to find out whether the dictionaries available are different or more numerous.

Real-World Connection

As our world changes, dictionaries continue to change. Words such as "Internet," "AIDS," and "condominium" did not exist fifty years ago, but were added to the dictionary as they were added to our vocabulary. Encourage students to research words that have been added to the dictionary in the last twenty years. They might want to check the Internet or periodical index, or ask a librarian for guidance. Have them share some examples of new words and of words that are no longer in use.

Customize for
More Advanced Students

Encourage students to find information on the Oxford English Dictionary (OED), and have them share what they discover with the class. (The OED is the only dictionary that really attempts to include every word in the English language. It is many volumes long.)

32.2

Using Dictionaries

A *dictionary* is a collection of words and their meanings, along with other information about words, such as their parts of speech and pronunciations.

▶ **KEY CONCEPT** Use a dictionary to find information about words, such as spelling, pronunciation, and parts of speech. ■

English-Language Dictionaries An *unabridged* dictionary of the English language attempts to cover all the words in the language, including those no longer in use, and gives detailed information on each word's history. An *abridged* English-language dictionary, which is shortened for everyday use, is the kind of dictionary that most people have in their homes and offices.

Specialized Dictionaries These dictionaries are limited to words of a particular type (for example, slang) or words in a particular field (for example, legal or literary terms). They also include *foreign-language dictionaries*, which are two-part dictionaries that give English equivalents of words in a particular foreign language and vice versa.

Dictionary Organization Dictionaries are available in both printed and electronic form. In printed dictionaries, entry words are arranged in *alphabetical order*. To speed your search for a word, use the **thumb index,** a series of right-hand notches that makes it easier to thumb alphabetically through a dictionary. Each notch, labeled *A, B, C,* and so on, shows the section of entries for words that start with that particular letter.

Also use the **guide words,** two large words at the top of each dictionary page that show the first and last entry words on the page. All other entry words on the page fall alphabetically between these two guide words. For instance, if the guide words are *rider* and *rift,* the words *ridge* and *rife* will also be on that page; however, the word *right* will not be there.

💿 **Technology Tip**

Abridged electronic dictionaries are now available in a computerized form resembling pocket calculators. Foreign-language dictionaries in this form can be quite convenient for travelers.

In **electronic dictionaries,** you usually find a word simply by typing the word and having the dictionary search the dictionary database.

Dictionary Entries Dictionary entries contain a wealth of information about words and their use. Here is an example:

```
                    DICTIONARY ENTRY
Pronunciation ─────────── Inflected Forms ──────
Primary Stress ──────┐    Part of Speech ─┐
Word Entry ─┐        │                    │
Syllabification ─┐   pret•ty (prit´ē; often purt´ē) adj. -ti•er, -ti•est
Etymology ───┐   [ME. prati < OE. prættig, crafty < prætt, a
             craft, trick] 1. Pleasing or attractive in a
             dainty, delicate or graceful way rather than
             through striking beauty, elegance, grandeur,
             or stateliness 2. a) fine; good; nice: often
Numbered ───── used ironically [a pretty fix] b) adroit; skillful
Definitions    [a pretty move] 3. [Archaic] elegant 4. [Archaic
               or Scot.] brave; bold; gallant 5. [Colloq.]
Usage Label ── considerable; quite large [a pretty price] —adv.
Part of Speech 1. fairly; somewhat [pretty sure]: sometimes,
               by hyperbole, quite or very [pretty angry] 2.
               [Colloq.] prettily [to talk pretty] —n., pl. -ties
               pretty persons or things —vt. -tied,
               -ty•ing to make pretty (usually with up)
Derived ────── —SYN. SEE BEAUTIFUL —sitting pretty [Slang]
Words          in a favorable position —pret´ti•ly adv.
               —pret´ti•ness n. —pret´ty•ish adj.
```

Entry Word With Syllabification The word being defined appears in dark print at the start of the entry. From it you can confirm the word's spelling and usually learn how to break it into syllables (if the word has more than one syllable). Dashes, dots, or spaces usually show the syllables.

Pronunciation Usually appearing in parentheses or brackets immediately following the entry word, the pronunciation shows how to say the word and uses accent marks (´) to show which syllable or syllables to stress. To understand the symbols in the pronunciation, you need to consult the dictionary's *pronunciation key.* When you consult the key that follows the pronunciation of *pretty*, you see that the *e* sounds like the *i* in *is* and the *y* sounds like the first *e* in *even.*

Dictionary Entries

1. Divide students into four groups and assign each group two of the elements of a dictionary described on pages 821–822.

2. Give each group at least one dictionary. Have them read the descriptions of their assigned elements and then look in the dictionary to find two or more examples of each. Have them make short presentations to the class about their concepts.

3. As the groups make their presentations, ask the following questions:

   Syllabification: *How can you tell when a word has a hyphen in it?* (The hyphen is indicated by a long dash, not a short dash or dot.)

   Pronunciation: *How can you tell how to interpret the pronunciation symbols?* (Dictionaries always include a pronunciation key, sometimes on every page, but at the very least in the beginning of the dictionary.)

continued

Customize for
ESL Students

You may want to have students use bilingual dictionaries for this exercise. Etymology may not be included, but the other elements should be.

Part of speech: *Why would the same word be labeled as a noun and as an adjective?* (Many words can be used as more than one part of speech. Have students list some examples.)

Plurals and Inflected Forms: *When does the dictionary show plural forms?* (Plurals are shown when they are formed irregularly.)

Etymology: *What is the meaning of these abbreviations: OE* (Old English), *ME* (Middle English), *fr.* (from, not French), *F* (French), *Gk* (Greek), *and L* (Latin)?

Definition and Example: *Is the first definition given used more frequently than the second or third definitions?* (Not necessarily; they are simply different definitions.)

Usage Labels: *Should writers avoid using words marked* Obs. *or* Colloq.? *Why?* (They should avoid using these words in formal writing. These words are no longer widely used or they are too informal.)

Field Labels: *Why would an ordinary word be labeled* Chem.? (It has a different meaning in the field of chemistry. You may want to suggest examples of this, such as *element* or *periodic.*)

Idioms and Derived Words: *Why is it necessary to define idioms if the entry word has already been defined?* (The meaning of the entry word often changes in an idiom.)

Customize for
Less Advanced Students

You may want to provide students with highlighted copies of the dictionary pages that include the words needed to answer Exercise 6. This will enable them to spend more time examining the dictionary features and less time trying to locate the entries themselves.

Answer Key

> **Exercise 6**

1. C, should be *hypocrisy*
2. *-mat-*
3. Arabic, *al-jabr*
4. Answers will vary.
5. yes, *nastily*

Part-of-Speech Label The dictionary uses abbreviations to show how a word functions in a sentence—as a noun (*n*), a transitive verb (*vt*), an intransitive verb (*vi*), an adjective (*adj*), an adverb (*adv*), or another part of speech.

Plurals and Inflected Forms The dictionary shows irregularly formed plurals and verb tenses and will show inflected forms, such as comparative and superlative modifiers, if there is anything unusual about their spellings.

Etymology Information about the word's origin and history also appears in brackets, parentheses, or slashes near the start or end of the entry. It often uses abbreviations for languages, all explained in the dictionary's key to abbreviations and symbols (at the front of most printed dictionaries).

Definition and Example The meanings of the entry word are numbered if there is more than one, and sometimes examples are included to illustrate their uses in phrases or sentences.

Usage and Field Labels Some definitions have labels showing how or where they are used. For instance, definitions labeled *Archaic (Arch)*, *Obsolete (Obs)*, or *Rare* are not widely used today. Those labeled *Colloquial (Colloq)* or *Slang* are not considered standard English. Those labeled *British (Brit)* or *Scottish (Scot)* are not much used in America. Those labeled with particular field names—*Electronics (Elec)*, for example, or *Music*—are not much used outside their field. American dictionaries also use a symbol (such as a star) to show whether a particular word or definition is mainly used in America.

Idioms and Derived Words The end of an entry may list and define *idioms*, or expressions, in which the entry word appears. It may also list *derived words*—words formed from the entry word—along with their part of speech.

 Exercise 6 Understanding Dictionary Entries Use a dictionary to answer these questions.
1. Which of these words is NOT spelled correctly?
   a. accommodate **b.** definite **c.** hypocrasy **d.** rendezvous
2. In the word *phlegmatic*, which syllable is stressed?
3. What is the origin of the word *algebra*?
4. Identify two meanings of the word *parade*.
5. Is there an adverb derived from *nasty*? If so, what is it?

✎ STANDARDIZED TEST PREPARATION WORKSHOP

Definitions Standardized tests often require students to recognize the definitions of words in context. Provide students with opportunities to practice this skill.

Read the sentence below. Choose the word that best defines the italicized word as it is used in this context.

> Sitting alone in the park, she sighed as she contemplated the *moving* novel she was reading.

A action-packed   **C** dynamic

B touching   **D** thrilling

Students should recognize that the correct answer is **B**. Context clues, such as *sighed*, *contemplated* and *alone,* suggest that the book put the reader in a thoughtful or meditative mood. In this case, *moving* is an adjective. It does not relate to the idea of physical motion.

Using a Thesaurus

A *thesaurus* is a specialized dictionary providing extensive lists of *synonyms*, or words with similar meanings, and often some *antonyms*, or words with opposite meanings.

KEY CONCEPT A thesaurus is one of the most useful writing tools, because it can help you to avoid the repetition of words and to make your language as precise as possible. ■

In a thesaurus, words may be arranged alphabetically or they may be grouped by theme. When the arrangement is thematic, you first have to look up the word in the index to find out in which thematic grouping its synonyms will appear. When the thesaurus is arranged alphabetically by word, you simply look up the word as you would in any dictionary.

THESAURUS ENTRY

Part of Speech ——
Entry Word —— ⌐— Synonyms grouped by
               └ shared part of speech
      MELODY—*n.* melody, euphony, mellifluence,
Synonyms —— ⌐ air, tune, carillon, measure, lay, song,
        └ chime, aria, run, chant.
Part of Speech ┐ *adj.* melodious, melodic.
for related   ⌐ euphonious; sweet, mellow, mellifluous,
forms of word │ mellifluent, sweet-sounding, dulcet; lyric,
Synonyms for ——│ songful; clear, silvery, silver-tongued, full-
related forms └ toned, deep-toned, rich, resonant, ringing.
Cross-references ⌐ See also HARMONY, MUSIC, SINGING,
to other entries └ SOUND, SWEETNESS. *Antonym*—See
Cross-reference —— HARSH.
to antonym

Exercise 7 Using a Thesaurus Use a thesaurus to find appropriate synonyms for the words in italics. For each sentence, explain whether the synonym you have identified is more effective than the original word.
1. After two workers left, the shop advertised for new *workers.*
2. The manager *managed* the search.
3. He *ran* several interviews over a two-week period.
4. The last applicant seemed very *brainy.*
5. The manager was also pleased by her *pleasant* manner.

◉ Technology Tip

Many of the word-processing programs provide an on-line thesaurus. To use this feature, simply enter a word and you will be given a list of synonyms.

Using a Thesaurus

1. Point out that a thesaurus is helpful for finding alternative ways of expressing an idea.

2. Ask students why they might want to have more than one way to express a particular idea or concept (variety adds richness and interest to writing).

3. Choose a word and challenge students to name as many synonyms as they can. Then, look up the same word in a thesaurus and list the synonyms on the board. Have students note the ones that they did not think of.

4. Remind students that it is always important to check any word they find in a dictionary if they are not familiar with it. Not all synonyms have the same connotation.

5. Encourage students to choose a word from a selection in their portfolios that could be replaced with a richer or more colorful synonym. Have them use a thesaurus to find replacement words and then share the "before" and "after" versions of their sentences.

Customize for
More Advanced Students

A thesaurus can be a useful tool for students who wish to develop and expand their vocabulary. Challenge students to take a piece of recent writing from their portfolios and underline from five to ten commonly used words. Have them look in the thesaurus for more precise replacements for each word. Encourage them to record any new or unfamiliar words they encounter in their personal vocabulary notebooks.

Using Other Reference Works

Teaching Resources: Academic and Workplace Skills Activity Book, p. 50

1. Have students read and summarize the section on Using Other Reference Works.

2. Ask students what types of research projects or schoolwork might take them to the listed reference works.

3. Discuss how a book of quotations might help a student. (In addition to enhancing a report with a relevant quotation, it can help students identify writers who wrote on specific topics, or lead them to further works by favorite authors.)

4. Ask students what other people, besides students, might rely on these reference books. (Newspaper reporters might rely on almanacs and biographical references. Travel planners may rely on atlases and maps. A director might look up a play in the *Play Index*.)

Integrating Spelling Skills

Point out to students that they can use a thesaurus as a spelling resource. If they know the meaning of a word, but are unsure of its spelling, they can look up another word with a similar meaning and note the list of associated words, which will probably include the word in question. Remind students of the importance of correct spelling when using electronic databases.

32.2

Using Other Reference Works

Most libraries have all kinds of useful *reference works*, or resources to which you refer for information instead of reading them in their entirety. Such works are usually found in the reference section of the library. Most libraries will not allow you to check out reference works, so you must look at them while on site.

▶ **KEY CONCEPT** Reference works are a good source for learning general information about a topic or as a starting point for a research project. ■

SOME GENERAL ENCYCLOPEDIAS	SOME SPECIALIZED ENCYCLOPEDIAS
Encyclopædia Britannica *The World Book Encyclopedia* *Grolier's Multimedia Encyclopedia* *Compton's Pictured Encyclopedia*	*Van Nostrand's Scientific Encyclopedia* *Health Reference Center* *Encyclopedia of the Arts* *Grove's Dictionary of Music & Musicians* *The Baseball Encyclopedia*

Encyclopedias An *encyclopedia* is a collection of articles on different subjects. Encyclopedias list articles alphabetically by subject and usually span several volumes, with letters on the spine showing which subjects each volume contains; for example, a volume labeled *Ma to Mi* may contain an article on Maine but not Montana. Not all topics have their own article, but an alphabetical index, usually in a separate volume, tells you in which articles particular topics are covered.

A *general encyclopedia* collects articles offering basic information on a great many subjects. A *specialized encyclopedia* collects more complex or detailed articles in a particular field.

Almanacs These annual publications (updated more frequently in some electronic versions) offer factual information on a wide range of subjects, including history, geography, government, weather, science, industry, sports, and entertainment. In printed almanacs, the index may be in the back or the front.

🔲 Research Tip

Encyclopedias can help you gather background information to get started on a research project. However, they should not be one of your main sources of information. Instead, you should rely on nonfiction books, interviews, and reliable Internet resources.

Biographical References These works provide brief life histories of famous people, usually listed alphabetically by last name. Some biographical references, such as *Current Biography* or *Webster's Biographical Dictionary*, cover people from many walks of life; others, such as *Contemporary Authors* or *The International Who's Who of Women*, cover people in specific fields or areas.

Literary Indexes The library catalog lists books and other full-length publications, but to find a shorter work, you need to consult a literary index. A *literary index* tells you in which *anthologies*, or collections, shorter works of literature are found. Examples include *Granger's Guide to Poetry, Poem Finder*, the *Short Story Index*, the *Play Index*, and the *Essay Index*.

Books of Quotations Looking for a snappy quotation to use in a report? Trying to learn who first said an oft-quoted remark? You can perform either task with a *book of quotations*, which lists famous remarks and tells you who said them and where. Examples include *Bartlett's Book of Quotations, The Oxford Dictionary of Quotations*, and *Gale's Quotations*.

Atlases and Electronic Map Collections *Atlases* or *electronic map collections* contain maps and geographical information based on them. They also may include statistics about population, climate, agriculture, industry, natural resources, and so forth. In printed atlases, maps often have a numbered and lettered grid; to find a particular place on a map, you look it up in an alphabetical list called a *gazetteer*, which refers you to the area on the grid that the place appears.

▼ Critical Viewing What type of reference book would you use to find out what type of flowers these are and to gather information about them? [Connect]

Exercise 8 Using Other Reference Works Use printed or electronic reference works to find answers to these questions. Indicate the type of reference you used.
1. In what year was the city of Wichita, Kansas, founded?
2. What is Elizabeth Blackwell's claim to fame?
3. What is the highest dam in the United States?
4. Which countries border Mexico?
5. Find a quotation about nature from any work by Ralph Waldo Emerson. Include the name of the work.

Reference Skills • 825

Customize for
Musical Learners

As an additional exercise, students can search library audio and video holdings to locate recordings, scores, and books about favorite music and musicians. Point out that libraries often provide headphones to listen to music on-site, or lending privileges that allow borrowers to take out recordings. Have these students teach the rest of the class how these resources work.

Critical Viewing

Connect Answers may vary, but will likely include encyclopedias, botany references, or field guides.

Answer Key

▶ **Exercise 8**

1. The beginnings of the community of Wichita, Kansas date to 1868, and Wichita was incorporated as a city on July 21, 1870.
2. Elizabeth Blackwell was the first woman to be awarded an M.D. degree, which she received in 1849.
3. Hoover Dam is the highest concrete arch dam in the U.S. It is 726 feet high.
4. Countries bordering Mexico are the United States, Guatemala, and Belize.
5. Answers will vary.

Customize for
Gifted and Talented Students

You may want to suggest that students do further research on one of the topics listed. In particular, the Wild West history of Wichita and the landmark accomplishment of Elizabeth Blackwell may be of interest.

☑ ONGOING ASSESSMENT: Monitor and Reinforce

If you observe that students are having difficulty completing Exercise 8, try one of the following options.

Option 1 Before they answer each question, have students identify in writing the type of information requested. For example, Question 1 requires a date and Question 2 requires biographical information. Students can then reread the description of each resource and determine which one offers the type of information they need.

Option 2 Work with students to decide which resource they should use to answer each question. Help them also to figure out which key words they should use. For example, in Question 3, they would search under the key word "dam." Then, take them to the library to find the answers.

Find and Evaluate Information on the Internet

Teaching Resources: Academic and Workplace Skills Activity Book, p. 51

1. Tell students to check search engines and Internet Service Provider home pages for tips and ideas for searching the Web successfully. Some search engines offer an "advanced search" option, or give suggestions on how to narrow a search.

2. Ask the class to compile a list of useful tips for finding information on the Internet. Have them write their tips on a poster for the classroom.

3. You may want to record students' responses on a chart and offer these suggestions as a handout to students as they do Exercise 9.

4. On another poster, have students make a list of sites they've found helpful for doing research for school. These sites might include on-line reference works, historical documents, reading guides for novels, and many other types of information.

Customize for
ESL Students

Point out that some Web browsers contain a "translate this page" feature. This feature allows them to translate a Web page from English to various other languages. This might help them conduct research on topics with many specialized vocabulary words with which they are unfamiliar.

Using the Internet and Other Media Resources

Find and Evaluate Information on the Internet

Through the Internet, you can access a virtually unlimited amount of information without ever leaving your desk. Because so much information is available, however, it is easy to get lost on the Web. For this reason, it is essential to know how to find information quickly on the Web and to critically evaluate the information you do find.

▶ **KEY CONCEPT** The Internet provides a wealth of information on just about any topic. However, the information must be critically evaluated. ■

Locating Appropriate Web Sites The information on the Web is offered through thousands of individual Web sites, each of which has its own address, or URL (Universal Resource Locator). These sites usually consist of several Web pages of text, graphics, and sometimes audio or video displays. Use these tips to help you find appropriate sites:

- If you know a reliable Web site and its address (URL), simply type the address into your Web browser.

- If you don't know a particular Web site, use an Internet search engine to find the information. Use general search engines to search for a key term. Use other search engines to search in specific fields or categories.

- Also, consult reference librarians familiar with the Internet or Internet coverage in established library journals (such as *Booklist* and *The Library Journal*) for information on useful, reliable reference Web sites.

Evaluating Web Sites Since almost anyone can create a Web site, not every Web site provides useful or reliable information. Once you find a Web site, evaluate its reliability by considering the following:

- Identify who set up the site. Is the organization or individual who set it up an authority on the topics covered?

- Be on the lookout for **bias,** the presentation of a single point of view on a topic. If a site does represent a single position on a topic, it is essential that all of the arguments that are presented are backed up by facts and examples.

- Check to see that the information is up to date. What clues can you find that suggest when the site was last updated?

- Compare the information presented on the topic to information presented on other related sites.

◉ Technology Tip

You often can print a Web page or download it onto a disk. On a home computer, you can also highlight and copy text and paste it into a file in your word-processing program.

Exercise 9 Using the Internet On a library, school, or home computer, use the Internet to do this research:

1. Go to the U.S. Postal Service Web site, **www.usps.gov**, to learn the ZIP Code for 146 K St., Washington, D.C.
2. Find the official Web site for the Metropolitan Museum of Art in New York City and from it find the museum hours.
3. Choose a topic for a science paper. List names and URLs of four Web sites that you think can help you.
4. Find the text of the poem "To Helen" by Edgar Allan Poe. Be sure to record the name and URL.
5. From a reliable source, find out about Lyme disease and how to prevent it. Record source information.

Use Other Media Resources

In addition to the Internet, there are a wide range of other media resources that you can use for research. These include videos, CD-ROMs, and electronic databases. You can probably find many of these resources at your local or school library.

Video Resources Videos, such as the ones below, can be an excellent reference tool and a key part of a multimedia report.

- **News Programs** provide up-to-date information on key events and issues and can offer insights into how people responded to major events at the time they happened.
- **Documentaries** can offer in-depth information on a wide range of specific topics.

CD-ROM References Most of the print references mentioned earlier in this chapter are also available on CD-ROM. For example, there are a wide range of CD-ROM encyclopedias that provide text information, photographs, video, and audio. In addition, there are CD-ROM atlases and map programs that you can use to find information about geographical regions. To use a CD-ROM reference, you simply need to type in key words and the program will take you to your topic.

Electronic Databases Electronic databases provide large collections of data on specific topics. The databases allow you to sort and examine the information in a variety of ways. You can usually find the sort feature of a database in the menu bar. To conduct a search, type in one or more key words.

Exercise 10 Using Media Resources Choose a topic that interests you. Conduct research on that topic, using two different media resources. Present your findings to the class.

 **Technology Tip**

Electronic maps often have "zoom in" and other features in which you simply click the mouse to enlarge or change the area shown.

 **Technology Tip**

Remember that in electronic database searches, one wrong letter can result in failure. Be sure to type carefully and spell everything correctly. If you aren't sure of a spelling, try several variations.

Reference Skills • 827

Taking Tests

Teaching Resources: Academic and Workplace Skills Activity Book, pp. 53–54

1. Discuss students' experience with taking tests. Have they ever been helped by reading all the directions? Have they ever been hurt by not reading them? How might previewing help them?

2. Point out that planning ahead can help with these strategies. Suggest that students ask ahead of time, if possible, what is permitted during the test (such as using scratch paper or penalties for guessing). If they cannot ask before a test, suggest that students take both scratch paper and a list of questions with them to the test, so they can make sure they understand the guidelines.

3. Encourage students to take instructions seriously and be as neat as possible. If a test is scored by machine, answers may be misread if spaces are not filled in as directed. Human scorers may not be able to read illegible handwriting and may be negatively influenced by sloppy work.

4. Explain to students that they should proofread only if they have enough time at the end of the test. Point out that it would be unwise to reread a section if they still have several pages to cover.

5. Remind them that adequate study during the year, a good night's sleep before the test, and a little planning will make test taking a less stressful and more successful process.

6. Ask students to suggest any other test-taking strategies that they have found to be effective.

Section 32.3

Test-Taking Skills

In this section, you will learn some strategies to improve your performance on tests and to deal with the different kinds of questions they often contain.

Taking Tests

Objective tests are those in which each question has a single correct answer. To prepare for such tests, carefully study the material that the test will cover. Be sure to arrive at the test on time, well rested, and with all the equipment you were told to bring—pencils, pens, and so on.

▶ **KEY CONCEPT** When taking a test, divide your time into three steps—previewing, answering, and proofreading. ■

PREVIEW THE TEST

1. Put your name on each sheet of paper you will hand in.
2. Look over the entire test to get an overview of the types of questions and how they are arranged.
3. Find out whether you lose points for incorrect answers. If you do, do not guess at answers.
4. Decide how much time you must spend on each section of the test.
5. Plan to devote the most time to questions that are hardest or worth the most points.

ANSWER THE QUESTIONS

1. Answer the easy questions first. Put a check next to harder questions, and come back to them later.
2. If permitted, use scratch paper to jot down your ideas.
3. Read each question at least *twice* before answering.
4. Supply the single best answer, giving only one answer to a question unless the instructions say otherwise.
5. Answer all questions on the test unless you are told not to guess or there is a penalty for wrong guesses.
6. Do not change your first answer without a good reason.

PROOFREAD YOUR ANSWERS

1. Check that you have followed directions completely.
2. Reread test questions and answers. Make sure that you have answered all of the questions.

828 • Study, Reference, and Test-Taking Skills

⏱ TIME AND RESOURCE MANAGER

Resources
Print: *Academic and Workplace Skills Activity Book*, pp. 53–54

Using the Full Student Edition	Using the Handbook🄷
• Read and discuss pages 828–831 with the class. • Give students time in class to complete Exercises 11–12. • If possible, bring in examples of each type of question from old class tests or standardized tests. Have students practice answering the type of question that gives them the most trouble.	• Read and discuss pages 624–627 with the class. • Give students time in class to complete Exercises 11–12. • If possible, bring in examples of each type of question from old class tests or standardized tests. Have students practice answering the type of question that gives them the most trouble.

Answering Different Kinds of Questions

Although the content of tests varies greatly, the types of questions that appear on these tests are fairly similar. This section will inform you about different types of test questions and specific strategies for answering them.

▶ **KEY CONCEPT** Improve your test scores by learning about different kinds of questions and the strategies for answering them. ■

True-or-False Questions True-or-false questions ask you to identify whether or not a statement is accurate.

- If a statement seems true, be sure that it is all true.
- Pay special attention to the word *not*, which often changes the whole meaning of a statement.
- Take note of the generalizing words *all, always, never, no, none,* and *only.* They often make a statement false.
- Take note of the qualifying words *generally, much, many, most, often, sometimes,* and *usually.* They often make a statement true.

Multiple-Choice Questions This kind of question asks you to choose from four or five possible responses.

- Try to answer the question before reading the choices. If your answer is one of the choices, select that choice.
- Eliminate obviously incorrect answers, crossing them out if you are allowed to write on the test paper.

Matching Questions Matching questions require that you match items in one group with items in another.

- Count each group to see whether any items will be left over.
- Read all the items before you start matching.
- Match the items you know first, and then match the others. If you can write on the paper, cross out items as you use them.

Fill-in Questions A fill-in question asks you to supply an answer in your own words. The answer may complete a statement or it may simply answer a question.

- Read the question or incomplete statement carefully.
- If you are completing a statement, look for context clues that may signal the answer. Pay special attention if the word *an* appears right before the missing word, which indicates that the missing word begins with a vowel sound.

Step-by-Step Teaching Guide

Answering Different Kinds of Questions

1. Explain to students that careful reading is one of the key skills to successful test taking. Often, as in the case of true-or-false questions, only one or two words in a sentence make it incorrect.

2. Remind students that if any part of a statement is false, the whole statement should be marked *false*.

3. Point out that eliminating wrong answers in multiple-choice tests improves students' odds of finding the right answer. On a test where they are not penalized for guessing, they can often improve their scores by making educated guesses.

4. Point out that once all known words are matched in a matching-question test, knowledge of roots, prefixes, and suffixes may help students identify additional matches.

5. For fill-in questions, it is essential that penmanship be as clear as possible. If a grader cannot read the answer, he or she may mark it as wrong.

6. Review each of the strategies. Encourage students to write these strategies in their notebooks, and suggest that they add any ideas of their own.

Integrating Viewing and Representing Skills

Encourage students to make a poster or visual reference that color codes the varieties of test questions discussed in this section. This will help students familiarize themselves with the various kinds of questions.

Analogies

1. Emphasize that the first step in answering an analogy question is figuring out the relationship between the first set of words.

2. Have a volunteer read aloud the common analogy patterns on page 830. Ask students to suggest additional examples of each pattern.

3. Tell students that the correct answers in analogy questions will be the same parts of speech as the original set of words. (Example: if the first set is a noun and a verb, the answer will be a noun and a verb.)

4. Work with students on the example analogy at the top of page 830. Point out that **c.** is incorrect because the words are in the wrong order. For it to be correct, it would have to read *flower: daisy*. Point out that in analogies, the words in the correct answer will match the order of the original words.

5. Give students time to complete Exercise 11 on their own. When they finish, have them share and discuss their answers.

Short-Answer and Essay Questions

1. As with other questions, careful reading is needed when responding to questions that require writing.

2. Remind students that clear penmanship is always important for written responses.

3. For essay questions, point out that responding is much like writing a paper. A little planning, possibly with a brief outline or other graphic organizer, can make these responses stronger.

32.3

Analogies An *analogy* is a special type of multiple-choice question that often appears on vocabulary and reading tests. Analogy items usually provide a pair of words and ask you to choose another pair that expresses a similar relationship.

EXAMPLE: FURNITURE : CHAIR ::

a. food : meat   **c.** daisy : flower
b. wall : window   **d.** olive : green

In the preceding example, the answer is *a*. The relationship between the pairs of words is *kind*. A chair is a *kind* of furniture, and meat is a *kind* of food. Notice that the sequence of the words matters. The following chart lists common analogy relationships:

COMMON ANALOGY RELATIONSHIPS	
Relationship	**Example**
Shared quality (synonyms)	impetuous : rash
Lack of a quality (antonyms)	enthusiasm : boredom
Degree (greater to lesser / lesser to greater)	guffaw : giggle / whisper : scream
Part to whole / Whole to part	drawer : desk / house : room
Kind (specific to general / general to specific)	salamander : lizard / dog : poodle
Sequence	arrest : trial
Location or proximity	knee : calf
Device	wrench : plumber

Short-Answer Questions Short-answer questions call on you to write one or more sentences in which you provide certain information. Before you respond to a short-answer question, look carefully at the question. Identify key words, such as *explain, compare,* and *identify.* When you answer the question, provide only the information called for through the key words. Be as direct and concise as possible.

Essay Questions On many standardized tests and tests you take in school, you will be called on to write one or more essays. Sometimes, you are given a choice of prompts to which you can respond. In other instances, you are given only a single prompt. Look for key words in the prompt or prompts to determine exactly what information you are being asked to provide. Take a few minutes to gather facts, examples, and other types of details you can include in your essay. Devote most of your time to drafting your essay. However, try to allow a little time to make revisions in your work.

⟳ Learn More

Having a strong vocabulary will help you answer analogy questions. For more on developing your vocabulary skills, see Chapter 30.

> **Exercise 11** Completing Analogies For each item, choose the letter of the pair of words that expresses the relationship most like the relationship of the words in capital letters. Also, indicate the type of relationship.
>   1. MANGO : FRUIT ::
>   **a.** vegetable : corn **b.** peas : beans **c.** zucchini : vegetable
>   2. JOY : ECSTASY ::
>   **a.** admiration : love **b.** life : hope **c.** happiness : sorrow
>   3. FOREWORD : EPILOGUE ::
>   **a.** appetizer : dessert **b.** team : spirit **c.** introduction : book
>   4. THERMOSTAT : HEAT ::
>   **a.** watt : light **b.** scale : weight **c.** temperature : thermometer
>   5. CONCEIT : MODESTY ::
>   **a.** anger : fury **b.** vitality : sloth **c.** kindness : virtue

> **Exercise 12** Understanding the Various Types of Test Questions Using a subject you are studying in one of your classes, prepare an objective test on the material. Write five true-or-false questions, five multiple-choice questions, five matching questions, and five fill-in questions. Exchange papers with another student, and take that student's test, writing your answers on a separate sheet of paper. Exchange again, and grade the test.

Reflecting on Your Study, Reference, and Test-Taking Skills

Consider the methods you have learned for improving study skills, the reference works available for improving your research skills, and the strategies for improving your test-taking skills. Answer the following questions in a journal entry:

- What changes should I make in my study area or schedule?
- What changes should I make to take notes effectively?
- Which reference materials seem the most useful to me?
- Which reference materials do I feel I need to learn more about?
- How can I budget my time more effectively when taking tests?
- What new strategies should I adopt for different kinds of test questions?

Test-Taking Skills • 831

Customize for
Interpersonal Learners

Give students time to discuss the chapter in small groups before they write their journal responses. What ideas were new? Which skill in the chapter seemed the most valuable? This will help to refresh students' memories about the entire chapter.

Answer Key

> **Exercise 11**

1. c
2. a
3. a
4. b
5. b

> **Exercise 12**

You may want to pair students based on similar strengths, so that, for example, a student who excels in math is not trading papers with a student with much weaker skills. After papers are scored, ask students what they thought of the experience of trying to write good questions.

ASSESS and CLOSE

> **Step-by-Step Teaching Guide**

Assessment

Teaching Resources: Formal Assessment, Ch. 32

1. Encourage students to search out some of the guidebooks currently available that give samples of standardized tests. Suggest that they use these to practice their test-taking skills.

2. In addition to student reflection on the chapter, you may wish to use the following assessment options:

   - review the Standardized Test Preparation Workshop on pp. 832–833 and have students complete the practice tests.

   - administer the Chapter 32 assessment from *Formal Assessment* in the Teaching Resources to measure students' grasp of concepts presented.

Lesson Objectives

1. To establish a purpose for reading
2. To respond to informational and aesthetic elements in texts
3. To identify main ideas and supporting details
4. To draw conclusions from information gathered

Constructing Meaning from Informational Texts

Teaching Resources: Standardized Test Preparation Workbook, pp. 63–64

1. Explain to students what is meant by informational texts: nonfiction writing that is intended to provide information. Point out that most of the types of writing taught in this book, such as description and exposition, are informational.

2. Review the three ways to construct meaning from informational texts on this page. Tell students that most of these points are similar to skills they have developed while learning to write and present their own ideas.

3. Have students read the passage and answer the question in the sample test item, and then review the explanation for the correct answer.

4. Assign the two practice tests and go over the answers with students.

Standardized Test Preparation Workshop

Constructing Meaning From Informational Texts

Most standardized tests will have questions designed to evaluate your reading skills. You will be given a passage to read. Following will be several questions that test your ability to construct meaning from the information provided in the passage. When answering these types of questions, you will be required to do the following:

- Distinguish between facts and nonfacts, or opinions.
- Identify the stated or implied main idea of a section of the passage.
- Choose the best summary—a brief, clear restatement of the subject and main ideas.

The following sample item will give you practice answering these types of questions.

Test Tip

The main idea of short passages is frequently, but not always, found in the first sentence.

Sample Test Item	Answer and Explanation
Directions: Read the passage. Then, read each question that follows the passage. Decide which is the best answer to each question. In 1928, T. S. Eliot became a devout member of the Church of England, after becoming a British citizen the previous year. These changes preceded radical changes in the focus of Eliot's writing, as evidenced by his exploration of religious themes in "Ash Wednesday" and "Four Quartets."	
1 Which of the following is an OPINION expressed in the passage? **A** T. S. Eliot wrote "Ash Wednesday." **B** T. S. Eliot was a British citizen. **C** The Church of England existed in 1928. **D** T. S. Eliot disliked Americans.	The correct answer is *D*. All the other choices are documented facts about Eliot's life and works. Although the reader might infer that Eliot disliked Americans based on his change in citizenship, the reader cannot enter Eliot's mind to know how he felt about Americans.

832 • Study, Reference, and Test-Taking Skills

TEST-TAKING TIP

In tests, as in other writing, paragraphs sometimes have no stated main idea. Therefore, especially when taking a test, urge students to read a passage in its entirety before answering questions, as the main idea is sometimes implied.

Remind students that as with all multiple-choice tests, they are wise to read all the answers following each item. Often, an answer is not completely wrong, but is not the best answer, because it leaves out important details or does not really sum up the idea of the passage completely or clearly. It may even be a true statement, but not the right answer for the question being asked. Careful reading of the text needs to be followed by careful reading of the questions and the possible answers.

Practice 1 **Directions:** Read the passage. Then, read each question that follows the passage. Decide which is the best answer to each question.

Frederic Remington is considered the best, and certainly the most popular, painter and sculptor of the Old West. Born in New York State, he first traveled west—to Montana in 1881—not as an artist but to seek his fortune, possibly in gold mining. In 1883, he traveled west again to try his hand at sheep ranching in Kansas. Later, he tried to make his fortune as part owner of a Kansas City saloon. All these ventures met with failure. It was in the latter part of the 1880's and early 1890's that Remington became a successful artist.

1 Which of the following is an OPINION expressed in the passage?

A Frederic Remington is the best sculptor of the Old West.

B Remington was born in New York.

C Remington failed as a saloon owner.

D Remington spent time as a sheep rancher.

2 What is the main idea of the passage?

F Remington loved the West.

G Remington was a huge failure.

H Remington tried many careers but found success as an artist.

J Remington loved gold mining.

Practice 2 **Directions:** Read the passage. Then, read each question that follows the passage. Decide which is the best answer to each question.

Two basic forms of music dominated the Harlem Renaissance: blues and jazz. The roots of blues and jazz are in the work songs, spirituals, and shouts of southern slaves. These slave songs, in turn, had their roots in the music of Africa. The pattern of theme and variation and the rhythmic counterpoint common in blues and jazz are elements in west African music. The blues, specifically, evolved after the Civil War, expressing the hardships and struggles of African Americans during Reconstruction. As Langston Hughes described the blues: "The music is slow, often mournful, yet syncopated, with a kind of marching bass behind it that seems to say, 'In spite of fate, bad luck, these blues themselves, I'm going to get on! I'm going to get on!'"

1 Which of the following is an OPINION stated in the passage?

A The roots of blues and jazz are found in the music of the Reconstruction period.

B The pattern of theme and variation common in blues and jazz are elements in west African music.

C The blues evolved after the Civil War.

D Blues and jazz music were Langston Hughes's favorite form of music.

2 What is the main idea of the passage?

F Langston Hughes loved the blues and jazz.

G The music of the Harlem Renaissance reflects the style of west African music and the sorrowful, yet hopeful music of African Americans both before and after the Civil War.

H Hughes wrote jazz and blues music for the Harlem Renaissance.

J West African music was a highly specialized type of music adopted by the musicians of the Harlem Renaissance.

Standardized Test Preparation Workshop • 833

Answer Key

Practice 1

1. A
2. H

Practice 2

1. D
2. G

Customize for
Less Advanced Students

Tell students not to worry if they don't know much about Remington or the Harlem Renaissance. Walk them through the passages, showing them how context clues can help them answer the questions. They don't need background knowledge about the subjects.

Customize for
More Advanced Students

Suggest that when reading informational texts independently, students practice picking out the main idea or writing brief summaries of the ideas covered.

In-Depth Lesson Plan

	LESSON FOCUS	PRINT AND MEDIA RESOURCES
DAY 1	**Working With People; Learning Teamwork** Students learn skills for successful interactions in interviews, meetings, and group discussions. (pp. 834–838/H628–632)	**Teaching Resources** *Academic and Workplace Skills Activity Book,* pp. 55–56
DAY 2	**Moving Toward Goals; Solving Problems and Thinking Creatively** Students learn strategies for setting and achieving goals and for problem solving. (pp. 839–841/H633–635)	*Writing and Grammar* **Interactive Text,** Ch. 11
DAY 3	**Managing Time and Money** Students learn strategies for managing time and money. (pp. 842–843/H636–637)	**Teaching Resources** *Academic and Workplace Skills Activity Book,* pp. 57–58
DAY 4	**Applying Math and Computer Skills** Students learn to apply math and computer skills to practical situations. (pp. 844–845/H638–639)	**Teaching Resources** *Academic and Workplace Skills Activity Book,* pp. 59–60; *Formal Assessment,* Ch. 33

Accelerated Lesson Plan

	LESSON FOCUS	PRINT AND MEDIA RESOURCES
DAY 1	**Working With People; Learning Teamwork; Moving Toward Goals; Solving Problems and Thinking Creatively** Students learn skills for successful interactions with others and for setting and achieving goals. (pp. 834–841/H628–635)	*Writing and Grammar* **Interactive Text,** Ch. 11 **Teaching Resources** *Academic and Workplace Skills Activity Book,* pp. 55–56
DAY 2	**Managing Time and Money; Applying Math and Computer Skills** Students learn strategies for managing time and money and for applying math and computer skills to practical situations. (pp. 842–845/H636–639)	**Teaching Resources** *Academic and Workplace Skills Activity Book,* pp. 57–60; *Formal Assessment,* Ch. 33

Options for Adapting Lesson Plans

HOMEWORK

Have students complete any of the exercises for homework.

FEATURE

Extend coverage with the Standardized Test Preparation Workshop (p. 846).

TECHNOLOGY

Students may use the Internet to conduct independent research. Have them print out their completed work.

Writing and Grammar Handbook Alignment

Page numbers in Step-by-Step Teaching Guides in this Teacher's Edition refer to pages from the full student text. Handbook page references, indicated with this icon **H**, are provided in Time and Resource Manager boxes and at the bottom of each Teacher's Edition page.

INTEGRATED SKILLS COVERAGE

Research Skills
SE pp. 839, 843/**H**633, 637

Speaking and Listening
SE p. 835/**H**629

Workplace Skills
ATE pp. 837, 843

Viewing and Representing
Critical Viewing, SE pp. 834, 836, 838, 844/**H**628, 630, 632, 638

Real-World Connection ATE p. 844

ASSESSMENT SUPPORT

Standardized Test Preparation Workshop, SE p. 846; ATE p. 845

Standardized Test Preparation Workbook, pp. 65–66

Formal Assessment, Ch. 33

MEETING INDIVIDUAL NEEDS

Less Advanced Students ATE pp. 836, 847. See also Ongoing Assessments ATE pp. 836, 843.

More Advanced Students ATE p. 840

ESL Students ATE pp. 838, 843, 845, 847

Intrapersonal Learners ATE pp. 839, 842

Linguistic Learners ATE pp. 841, 845

Spatial Learners ATE pp. 837, 841

BLOCK SCHEDULING

Pacing Suggestions
For 90-minute Blocks
• Have students complete the Working With People and Moving Toward Goals sections in a single period.
• Focus one class period on Managing Time and Money and Applying Math Skills. If possible, bring students to the computer lab for the Computer Skills section.

Resources for Varying Instruction
• *Academic and Workplace Skills Activity Book,* pp. 55–60

Professional Development Support
• *How to Manage Instruction in the Block* This teaching resource provides management and activity suggestions.

MEDIA AND TECHNOLOGY

For the Teacher
• Teacher**EXPRESS** CD-ROM

WRITING AND GRAMMAR ON-LINE

Interactive Text (On-line or on CD-ROM)
• Easily navigable instruction with interactive Revision Checkers
• Full use of e-rater™, the essay-scoring system (on-line only)

Companion Web Site PHSchool.com
• Scoring rubrics with models (use Web Code eek-1001)

See the Go On-line! **feature, SE p. iii.**

▶ Lesson Objectives

1. To learn communication and teamwork skills appropriate for business
2. To use prewriting and creative thinking strategies to generate ideas and solve problems
3. To practice making, listening to, and evaluating a variety of oral presentations
4. To write and ask clear questions for a variety of purposes and respond appropriately to the questions of others
5. To use verbal and nonverbal strategies to communicate effectively
6. To practice planning and development of personal and professional goals
7. To utilize time management and money management strategies
8. To apply math skills to a range of practical situations
9. To use technology to gather and process information

Critical Viewing

Connect Many careers require workers to use computers and to interact with others. Students might mention accountants, librarians, lawyers, Web designers, and many others.

Chapter 33 Workplace Skills and Competencies

▲ **Critical Viewing**
Identify a career that requires the computer and interpersonal skills these students are demonstrating. **[Connect]**

Many skills that make you a successful student also help to make you a valuable employee when you begin a career. In addition to writing and speaking effectively, listening attentively, and reading carefully, you will benefit from knowing how to communicate well with others and how to accomplish tasks efficiently and creatively.

This chapter will help you improve skills you already have and develop new ones in several important areas. You will learn strategies for effective interaction, goal setting, and problem solving. In addition, you will learn how to manage your time and money wisely and how to apply math and computer skills to the workplace.

834 • Workplace Skills and Competencies

⏱ TIME AND RESOURCE MANAGER

Resources
Print: *Academic and Workplace Skills Activity Book*, p. 55

Using the Full Student Edition	Using the Handbook🄷
• Cover pp. 834–836 in class. • Have students complete Exercises 1–2 in class. • Encourage students to compose a list of interview questions for Exercise 1. • You may want to record the interviews and role-playing exercises so the students can view them.	• Cover pp. 628–630 in class. • Have students complete Exercises 1–2 in class. • Encourage students to compose a list of interview questions for Exercise 1. • You may want to record the interviews and role-playing exercises so the students can view them.

Working With People

Whether you pursue a career as a salesperson, researcher, contractor, or train conductor, you will be expected to interact effectively with people. The way you speak and interact with supervisors, co-workers, clients, or the general public will influence their impression of you and the company you represent. This section will help you to further develop skills needed for communicating in one-on-one and group situations.

Learn to Communicate One on One

In the workplace, you may need to interact in one-on-one situations involving people you know only on a professional level or people you don't know at all. The first of these one-on-one situations is the job or college interview: Performing effectively during an interview can help you get into the college of your choice, land a job, or advance in the workplace.

Interviewing Interviews are the most formal type of one-on-one communication. In addition to sharing information about training, strengths, weaknesses, and interests, interview candidates must also present a positive first impression.

▶ **KEY CONCEPT** A job or college interview requires preparation, professional conduct, and follow-up work. ■

Keys to a Successful Interview

Before the Interview

- Bring copies of your résumé and names of references with you.
- Review the key points of your background and experience so you will be prepared to answer questions.
- Research the employer or college, and prepare questions that demonstrate your knowledge and interest.
- Dress neatly.

During the Interview

- Be respectful and polite at all times.
- Listen carefully, and respond directly to each question.
- Smile, and maintain eye contact.
- Thank the interviewer for his or her time, and ask when a decision will be made.

After the Interview

- Send a follow-up letter, restating your interest and thanking the interviewer for his or her time.
- When the deadline for a decision arrives, call to check your status.

▶ **Speaking and Listening Tip**

Use your experiences outside of school to practice professionalism. Request information from store clerks and telephone operators as if you were in a work environment. Discuss with a partner how communicating in this way affects the way people respond to you.

Interest GRABBER Ask students to imagine that they have been asked to hire a new employee for a store where they work. What kinds of experience, behaviors, and communication styles would they look for in a candidate? What characteristics might tell them a candidate could be problematic? Brainstorm with students using a two-column chart labeled "Might Hire" and "Won't Hire."

Activate Prior Knowledge

Have students think back to political election debates they have seen on television or in person. What communications do students remember seeing? How might they apply the most effective skills to work and school situations in their own lives?

TEACH

Step-by-Step Teaching Guide

Learn to Communicate One on One

1. After students read the text, ask them why making a good first impression is important. (They may not get a second chance.)

2. Have students identify the elements that make a good first impression, the things that continue to build on that impression, and the things that confirm the good impression. (*First impression*: being on time, being appropriately dressed and well groomed; *Continue*: being polite and respectful, being prepared, maintaining eye contact, listening carefully and responding as directed; *Confirm*: thanking interviewer, follow-up letter.)

3. Ask students why they think each element is important. (Being on time and being appropriately dressed establishes conscientiousness; being prepared shows high motivation and competence; and writing a follow-up letter shows professionalism and motivation.)

Step-by-Step Teaching Guide

Interacting Successfully

Teaching Resources: Academic and Workplace Skills Activity Book, p. 55

1. After students review the guidelines, point out that many of the items are useful for communicating in any situation.

2. Discuss the principles of successful interaction by asking questions such as these:

   What are some nonverbal messages that people send? (Students may cite smiles, frowns, playing with hair, crossed arms.)

   Why is using slang inappropriate with an employer or counselor? (Slang would indicate lack of respect; lack of professionalism.)

3. If possible, use a videotape of an interview to provide a concrete illustration of these principles.

Critical Viewing

Deduce Their smiles and relaxed posture suggest that these students are having a positive interaction.

Answer Key

Exercise 1

Have students research their "dream job" to determine the educational and work experiences needed to obtain it.

Exercise 2

Have groups perform their role-plays for the class so they can see various ways of approaching each situation.

Customize for
Less Advanced Students

Provide students with coaching before doing Exercise 1. Give them a list of the questions they can expect from the "reporter" (and supply the "reporter" with these questions), and then have them write their responses on note cards. In this way, students will be able to focus on speaking skills without having to worry about content.

Interacting Successfully In school or in the workplace, you will have conferences with others to discuss your performance and your plans for the future. In addition, you may have meetings with colleagues to get a job done. Whether you need to organize a project, solve an unexpected problem, or deal with customers, your ability to interact respectfully may mean the difference between success and failure.

▶ **KEY CONCEPT** To interact effectively in school and work situations, treat others with respect, listen carefully, and do not hesitate to communicate your thoughts and concerns. ■

Guidelines for Successful Interaction

- **Be sensitive to verbal or nonverbal messages** you receive from other people. Know when you need to be serious and when you can be casual or humorous.
- **Listen carefully,** and ask questions if necessary.
- **Find common ground**—similar interests or experiences that connect you to the other person.
- **Respect differences,** and accept that others may have different backgrounds, abilities, and opinions.
- **Use language that is appropriate** in tone, style, and complexity for your audience. For example, you may use slang with friends but not with an employer.
- **Avoid finger pointing;** instead, look for a positive resolution to problems rather than a person to blame.

▶ **Exercise 1** Interviewing for a Position With another student, choose a job you would like to pursue. Then, for a group, role-play a job interview for that position. The interviewer should ask questions to prompt the interviewee to describe his or her qualifications. After the role-play is over, ask the group to point out the strengths and weaknesses you demonstrated as a candidate.

▶ **Exercise 2** Interacting With Others in Various Situations
With other students, role-play the following situations. In each case, discuss what you learned from the experience.
1. Two students: a new student asks a coach about joining a team in midseason.
2. Four students: a salesperson is helping a customer who cannot make a decision; others are growing impatient as they wait for assistance.
3. Two students: an employee asks a supervisor for a raise.

836 • Workplace Skills and Competencies

▶ **More Practice**
Academic and Workplace Skills Activity Book
• p. 54

▼ Critical Viewing
Are these students having a positive or a negative interaction? On what do you base your answer? **[Deduce]**

☑ ONGOING ASSESSMENT: Monitor and Reinforce

To give students more information and experience in interviews and successful interaction, try one of the following strategies.

Option 1 Suggest that students talk to adults who have conducted interviews. What was their best experience? Their worst? What mistakes have they seen applicants make? What things have impressed them? What advice would they offer someone going for an interview?	**Option 2** Suggest that students watch interview shows on television or find a book on effective interviewing, and then get together with another student and practice interviewing each other. Alternatively, they might want to ask an adult they know (teacher or parent) to work with them.

Learning Teamwork

Team efforts are critical to success in many arenas outside of sports. For example, you may use teamwork to develop a group project with fellow students, participate in a town committee, or work on a job-based project team. Group interaction requires basic communication skills and the ability to anticipate or avoid conflicts among the many personalities involved. To work successfully as a team, members must be willing to listen and be respectful of one another's opinions and roles.

Conducting Meetings and Group Discussions Effective meetings or group discussions will help a team work well together. Participants can take specific roles to keep the group focused. Ideally, these roles should be rotated each meeting:

- A **facilitator** guides the discussion and encourages the interaction of all group members.
- A **note-taker** records key points and distributes meeting minutes or notes after the meeting.
- A **timekeeper** keeps track of the time allotted to a topic.

KEY CONCEPT For a group to work effectively, all members must be organized, focused on the task at hand, and aware of their responsibilities. ■

The following chart shows some of the other ground rules for an effective meeting:

GROUND RULES FOR A MEETING OR DISCUSSION

- ☑ Establish a time limit, and begin and end on time.
- ☑ Assign roles, including facilitator, timekeeper, and note-taker.
- ☑ Use a flip chart to record key points.
- ☑ When trying to make plans or find solutions, allow time for brainstorming—the free exchange of ideas.
- ☑ Make sure everyone participates.

Exercise 3 Using Group Roles Working with five classmates, choose a group facilitator, a timekeeper, and a note-taker. Then, begin a fifteen-minute discussion about the impact on students of one of the following areas: volunteering, the Internet, after-school jobs, or sports. Have the rest of the class evaluate your teamwork.

⚜ Challenge

Often, the group establishes an *agenda* that lists the order of the topics being discussed. If new issues or questions are raised during the discussion that cannot be solved during the allotted time, all of the people involved should plan to meet again.

Meetings and Group Discussions

1. Once students have read this page, invite them to share accounts of meetings and group discussions in which they have taken part, such as class meetings, club meetings, or team meetings.

2. Define and discuss the roles of facilitator, notetaker, and timekeeper. Ask students what they think might happen if these roles are not filled in an important meeting. (People get off track, not everything is covered, and there is no way to distribute what was said to people who weren't there.)

3. Review the ground rules, and then give students time to prepare for and complete Exercise 3.

Answer Key

Exercise 3

Assign student groups, or invite students to form their own groups. Give groups a few minutes to get organized and select a topic. Supply a clock or watch for the timekeeper as each group starts its discussion.

Customize for
Spatial Learners

Have students make illustrations or find photographs in books or magazines that can serve as discussion starters. In talking about the pictures and the thoughts they trigger, the speakers can use visual stimuli to inspire additional ideas that enrich their discussion.

Integrating Workplace Skills

Refer the notetaker in each group to the instruction on taking meeting minutes in Chapter 15. Have notetakers use these guidelines to formally prepare the notes they take.

Workplace Skills and Competencies • 837

⏱ TIME AND RESOURCE MANAGER

Resources
Print: *Academic and Workplace Skills Activity Book*, p. 56

Using the Full Student Edition	Using the Handbook🄷
• Cover pp. 837–839 in class.	• Cover pp. 631–633 in class.
• Have students work on Exercises 3–7.	• Have students work on Exercises 3–7.
• Provide students with tapes of recorded discussions, or have students choose a scheduled broadcast discussion, such as an interview show, to watch for Exercise 5.	• Provide students with tapes of recorded discussions, or have students choose a scheduled broadcast discussion, such as an interview show, to watch for Exercise 5.

Participating Effectively

1. Have students read the text and review the tips for effective participation.

2. Remind students that these guidelines apply to meetings where groups come together as equals and where teamwork is a goal. There will be times in business when they will be expected to listen closely without sharing perspectives or offering criticism.

3. Ask students why it is important to stay focused on a topic and to help other people stay focused. (When many people talk, it is easy to go off on tangents. Time for meetings is limited; therefore, the discussion topics need to be directed.)

4. Have students discuss how one can give and receive criticism gracefully, and why it is important.

Critical Viewing

Interpret The students are sitting on desks and exchanging ideas in a conversational manner.

Customize for
ESL Students

Suggest that students view or listen to discussions in their first languages as well as in English when completing Exercise 5. Cable channels or videotapes may be options if your area does not have television or radio programming in a range of languages.

Answer Key

▶ **Exercise 4**

Have students use computer software to create an agenda. Then, have them distribute it to group members or display it on an overhead projector during the meeting.

▶ **Exercise 5**

Ask students to name the most important participation strategy they learned from evaluating this discussion.

33

Participating Effectively Assuming roles and setting ground rules are good first steps toward running an effective meeting or discussion. However, the success of a meeting or discussion ultimately rests on the effective participation of each group member. To participate effectively in these situations, be prepared to make suggestions, be open to the ideas of others, and give and accept constructive criticism.

▶ **KEY CONCEPT** A good participant contributes ideas and constructive criticism and allows others to do the same. ■

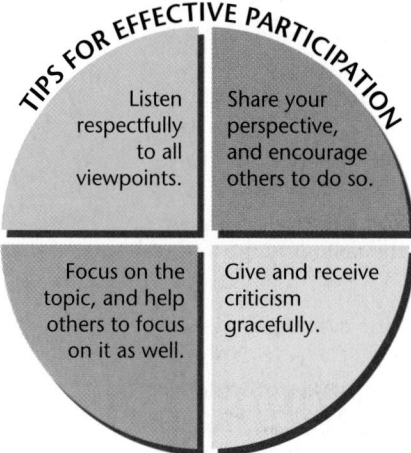

TIPS FOR EFFECTIVE PARTICIPATION

Listen respectfully to all viewpoints.	Share your perspective, and encourage others to do so.
Focus on the topic, and help others to focus on it as well.	Give and receive criticism gracefully.

▲ **Critical Viewing** What details of this photograph suggest that the students shown are meeting informally? **[Interpret]**

▶ **Exercise 4** Conducting a Meeting Form a committee with a group of classmates. Assign roles, and set an agenda for a meeting in which you will identify a goal you would all like to see accomplished, such as building a new park in your community. Then, work together at your meeting to lay out plans for how this goal might be accomplished. When your meeting is complete, list contributions each group member made to the plan.

▶ **Exercise 5** Analyzing a Group Discussion Using the tips outlined above, evaluate a televised round-table discussion. In your notebook, describe what you have witnessed. Refer to the strategies for effective participation to explain how the group did or did not work well together.

838 • Workplace Skills and Competencies

Moving Toward Goals

Thoughtful planning is a key to success in school, the workplace, and other areas of life. When you plan and set goals, you give yourself a better chance of achieving them.

▶ **KEY CONCEPT** Goals should be specific and include a clear timeline for completion. ■

Personal and Professional Goals

Some goals are *personal*—for example, making a sports team or improving your reading speed. Other goals are *professional*, because they focus on accomplishments in school or your work life. Getting into college, finishing a project on time, and earning a promotion are professional goals.

Because goals can conflict with each other, it is useful to identify all the goals you are working to achieve. You can then decide which are most important. You'll find that your priorities can shift over time. For example, when schoolwork includes final exams, you may let your academic goals override some of the other goals you are working to achieve.

Setting and Achieving Goals A vague goal like "exercising more" is hard to track. Set a specific goal, such as "exercising twice a week," and then make an action plan to outline the steps for achieving it. Assign a time for completion, and be ready to adjust your goals if necessary. A chart such as the one below can help you track your progress.

GOALS CHART

GOAL	STEPS NEEDED TO ACHIEVE IT	PROGRESS
A. ____	1. _____	_____
	2. _____	_____
	3. _____	_____
B. ____	1. _____	_____
	2. _____	_____
	3. _____	_____

▶ **Exercise 6** Developing a Goals Chart Develop a goals chart. Include at least one personal and one professional goal, and chart your progress as you work toward achieving them.

▶ **Exercise 7** Devising an Action Plan Devise an action plan for earning money to buy a new stereo system. Include the steps needed to achieve the goal, the time frame for completing each step, and the resources required for each step.

▢ Research Tip

To help plan your career goals, investigate fields of interest at the career center of a local college.

More Practice

Academic and Workplace Skills Activity Book
• p. 55

Personal and Professional Goals

Teaching Resources: Academic and Workplace Skills Activity Book, p. 56

1. Provide students with a model goal in which they are likely to have an interest. (Example: prepare for college entrance exams.)

2. As a class, fill in the Goal, Steps Needed to Achieve It, and Progress sections of the Goals Chart on the board.

3. As students try to think of goals, suggest that they look at the want ads in the paper to identify jobs they would like to pursue, talk to school counselors about necessary qualifications for college, and think about how they would like to improve themselves, their habits, or their health.

Answer Key

▶ **Exercise 6**

Before they create their charts, have volunteers share some of their goals. This will help spark ideas for students whose goals are not clearly defined.

▶ **Exercise 7**

Remind students to be realistic when calculating their daily expenses. Otherwise, their action plans will not work.

Customize for
Intrapersonal Learners

Have students write a journal entry about changes they would like to see in their lives. Encourage them to start thinking about manageable, concrete steps they can take to achieve goals gradually over time. This will help students generate goals to include in their charts.

Learning to Solve Problems

1. Explain to students that, while they occasionally have a brilliant idea that simply resolves a problem, this is the exception. Most of the time, they need a reliable method of solving problems. The steps explained here are used widely by corporations as well as by individuals.

2. Point out that identifying and stating the problem precisely is a key task. A vaguely defined problem will probably generate vague, ineffective solutions.

3. Ask students to suggest other possible solutions to the example in the text and evaluate them.

4. Encourage students to use some of the prewriting techniques they've encountered in their writing lessons as they list possible solutions. They might use the prewriting strategies in the Exposition section of the *Writing Lab* CD-ROM.

Answer Key

Exercise 8

Have students meet in small groups with others who chose the same problem. Give them time to brainstorm for a list of solutions. Then, have them evaluate the solutions on their own.

Customize for
More Advanced Students

Challenge students to look up and read about other problem-solving techniques in the library or on the Internet. Have them choose an interesting technique and use it to solve a problem in Exercise 8. Then, have them evaluate the new technique and share their findings with the class.

Solving Problems and Thinking Creatively

As you work to achieve your personal and professional goals, you are bound to meet unexpected problems. Knowing how to face these problems calmly and devise workable solutions can help you stay on track to meet the goals you have set. To master this skill, you need a strategy for outlining problems and analyzing their solutions. For particularly difficult problems, you must also learn to think creatively to generate a number of possible solutions with which to work.

Learning to Solve Problems Most problems can be solved by using a systematic strategy that will allow you to analyze the problem and define a solution more clearly.

▶ **KEY CONCEPT** Solving a problem requires a thorough understanding of what's wrong, a number of possible solutions, and a careful review of each one. ∎

Use the following steps to solve problems more efficiently, minimize setbacks, and move forward.

STEPS IN PROBLEM SOLVING

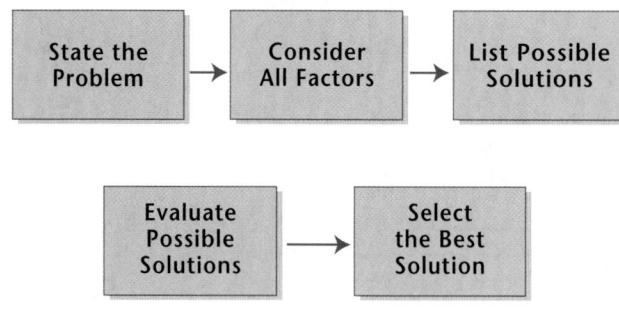

▶ **Exercise 8** Solving Problems Using the steps outlined above, identify at least two possible solutions for one of the following problems. Then, choose the best solution.
1. A student can't master a concept in math class.
2. A store manager realizes she may be losing business because cashier lines are too long on weekends.
3. A baby can choke on the small pieces of some of his older brother's games, but the older boy enjoys playing with these games.

840 • Workplace Skills and Competencies

Learn More

For more instruction about problem-and-solution writing, see Chapter 11.

⏱ TIME AND RESOURCE MANAGER

Resources
Technology: *Writing and Grammar* Interactive Text, Ch. 11

Using the Full Student Edition	Using the Handbook Ⓗ
• Cover pp. 840–841 in class, discussing the steps in problem-solving and creative-thinking tasks. • Give students time to complete Exercises 8–9 in class.	• Cover pp. 634–635 in class, discussing the steps in problem-solving and creative-thinking tasks. • Give students time to complete Exercises 8–9 in class.

Thinking Creatively You can use creative thinking to come up with possible solutions for a difficult problem. All you have to do is open your mind to ideas that are new, different, and sometimes unconventional.

> **KEY CONCEPT** Creative thinking requires openness to unusual approaches from which to draw new ideas. ■

If a star pitcher was slated to appear in the championship game but also wanted to go to a friend's birthday celebration scheduled for the same time, creative thinking might help. While standard problem solving might encourage the athlete to split time between both events, creative thinking might generate a more appealing idea: The athlete could videotape a message and ask his friend to wait until the party to play the tape.

CREATIVE THINKING SUGGESTIONS

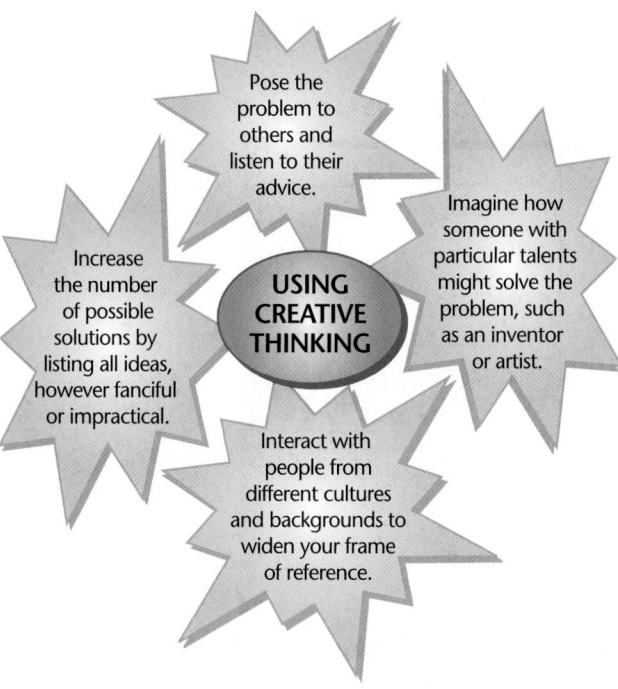

Pose the problem to others and listen to their advice.

Imagine how someone with particular talents might solve the problem, such as an inventor or artist.

Increase the number of possible solutions by listing all ideas, however fanciful or impractical.

USING CREATIVE THINKING

Interact with people from different cultures and backgrounds to widen your frame of reference.

> **Exercise 9** **Using Creative Thinking** Use creative thinking to offer two more suggestions to the problems identified in Exercise 8.

Thinking Creatively

1. Point out that creative thinking involves looking at problems in new ways or recombining familiar elements using fresh styles and approaches. You may want to cite the example of the chemist who discovered the ring-structure of the benzene molecule after having a dream about a snake forming a hoop shape.

2. Review the creative thinking suggestions depicted on the chart in the text. Have students offer examples of when they have used these approaches or seen them used by others.

Answer Key

> **Exercise 9**

Since one solution is already given, you may wish to brainstorm for others in class, to demonstrate to students how many solutions are possible. Point out that good solutions account for specific circumstances and reflect the personalities of the people involved. You may then wish to pose another dilemma for students to creatively resolve on their own.

Customize for
Linguistic Learners

There are numerous books and videotapes now available on how to think more creatively or how to kick start the creative process. If students are interested in pursuing this topic, suggest that they consult books in the library and share their findings with the class.

Customize for
Spatial Learners

Often, a difficult verbal problem can be solved by using visual means to imagine a solution. Provide students with blank paper, markers, and colored pencils. Invite them to draw a two-panel before-and-after scene showing the problem described in Exercise 8 and its resolution. Have students use their drawings to explain how the problem was solved.

Managing Time

Teaching Resources: Academic and Workplace Skills Activity Book, p. 57

1. Point out that experts say it is important to use time *effectively*, rather than merely *efficiently*. This means that one should do more complex tasks when one is fresh, and repetitive tasks, like filing papers, when one has less energy.

2. Explain that "must do" items should be added to the calendar first, with "would like to do" items added next.

3. Ask students how a big job such as writing a research paper could be made more manageable through thoughtful scheduling. (Students could block out time for research, drafting, and editing on separate days.)

4. Discuss how students might set priorities for their to-do lists. (Items with deadlines, with consequences, or that involve duties or a promise should get highest priority.)

Customize for
Intrapersonal Learners

Increasingly, technology has allowed people to work from home and set their own work and living schedules. Invite students to consider the schedule they would devise for themselves if they were able to work at home. Have them consider when they feel most comfortable working, waking, sleeping, and spending time with friends and family.

Answer Key

> **Exercise 10**

If students do not find the to-do list helpful, have them try a different time-management strategy. They can evaluate it after a week.

Managing Time

Although different careers require different abilities, most work situations present workers with tasks that need to be completed according to tight deadlines. In addition to the major projects you are assigned to complete, you often have to address unexpected problems and emergencies. In that case, your ability to manage your time effectively will play a critical role in determining your success.

Managing Your Time Proper time management takes planning and the ability to decide which of your goals and activities are most important. Budgeting your time well helps ensure that important projects are accomplished, time is free for other activities, and hasty decisions are prevented.

> **KEY CONCEPT** Manage your time effectively by keeping a calendar marked with appointments and key events, preparing daily or weekly "to-do" lists, prioritizing your tasks, and breaking up large tasks into manageable portions. ■

SAMPLE CALENDAR AND TO-DO LIST

To-Do List

1. Practice reading lines from play
2. Buy birthday present
3. Renew membership at gym
4. Write e-mail to my pen pal

Mon 9:30 Meeting with teacher

Tues

Wed 3:00–5:00 Drama auditions

Thur 7:00–10:00 Baby-sit

Fri

Sat 7:30 Katie's birthday party

Sun

> **Exercise 10** Managing Your Time Record your schedule for a week. Include a daily to-do list, with activities and appointments ranked according to importance. At the end of the week, evaluate how effectively this system worked for you.

842 • Workplace Skills and Competencies

⏱ TIME AND RESOURCE MANAGER

Resources
Print : *Academic and Workplace Skills Activity Book*, pp. 57–58

Using the Full Student Edition	Using the Handbook Ⓗ
• Cover pp. 842–843 in class. • Share examples of real-life calendars and to-do lists with students. You can also find and share examples of typical household budgets taken from books or magazine articles about personal finance. • Give students time to complete Exercises 10–11 in class.	• Cover pp. 636–637 in class. • Share examples of real-life calendars and to-do lists with students. You can also find and share examples of typical household budgets taken from books or magazine articles about personal finance. • Give students time to complete Exercises 10–11 in class.

Managing Money

The strategies of money management are simple: Spend less than you make to allow for the unexpected; treat your savings account like a bill to be paid rather than a place to put "extra" money; and plan your expenditures. Setting and sticking to a budget ensures that you will have money for what you need and want.

▶**KEY CONCEPT** To manage money wisely, track your spending, set financial goals, and make a plan to meet these goals. ∎

Developing a Budget A budget helps you manage money efficiently by tracking *credit*, or incoming money (in black), and noting *debits*, or expenses (in red). When a budget is balanced, credit and debit are equal. If debit exceeds credit, the budgeter must make choices about cutting spending or increasing income. When credit exceeds debit, the budget reveals a savings or a profit. Look at this example:

SAMPLE BUDGET

STUDENT GOVERNMENT MONTHLY BUDGET			
	INCOME	REGULAR EXPENSES	PROJECTED EXPENSES
Snack sale	200.00		
Alumni donations	50.00		
Savings for class gift		20.00	
Purchase of snacks for sale		75.00	25.00
Security deposit on tickets and chairs for dance			100.00
Total	250.00	95.00	125.00

▶**Exercise 11** **Managing a Budget** Develop a budget for someone who earns $200 a month, spends $10–20 per week on entertainment, $5 per week on snack foods, $20 per month on gifts, and puts $50 per month in a savings account.
1. How long will it take this person to save $400 without using money from the savings account?
2. Make a recommendation for cutting expenses.

🔖 Research Tip

You can find easy-to-understand guides to managing your time and money at your local library.

▶**More Practice**

Academic and Workplace Skills Activity Book
• pp. 57–58

☑ ONGOING ASSESSMENT: Monitor and Reinforce

To help familiarize students with the different types of budgets, try one of the following options.

Option 1 Have students discuss budgets with someone who has experience in setting a personal, household, or business budget. Before they talk to this individual, have students prepare a list of questions that they would like to have answered.

Option 2 At the library or bookstore, find examples of budgets or guides to budgeting that you can share with the class. Alternatively, encourage students to search out these books and bring to class sample budgets and a list of helpful tips.

Step-by-Step Teaching Guide

Managing Money

Teaching Resources: Academic and Workplace Skills Activity Book, p. 58

1. Discuss why it might be useful to limit spending for nonessentials (to avoid debt, to save for emergencies or special occasions).

2. Encourage students to make a list of expenses, and then have them identify items as essential or nonessential and explain their choices.

3. Invite students to share their successful experiences in saving money. What were some of the techniques they used?

4. Encourage students to create budgets for themselves, taking into consideration all the things on which they spend money.

Answer Key

▶ **Exercise 11**

If no other expenses occurred, the individual would have between $30 to $70 left at the end of each month. Hence, it would take between six and thirteen months to save $400. Ask students where the individual might cut back to save $400 sooner (entertainment or snack foods, but never savings).

Integrating Workplace Skills

Explain to students that it is not just individuals who need to create budgets. Corporations of all sizes have a wide range of budgets and plan their spending several years ahead.

Customize for *ESL Students*

Prior to assigning Exercise 11, review the definitions of the following terms with students: *income, expenses, paycheck, savings,* and *budget.* Encourage students to write definitions of these useful words in their vocabulary notebooks.

Applying Math Skills

Although there are many ways to apply your math skills to everyday life, this section addresses three of the most common ways: those used in the workplace, in shopping, and in the analysis of statistics.

> **KEY CONCEPT** Math skills are necessary to manage money properly, to make wise purchases, and to evaluate certain types of information. ■

Following are three areas in which math will prove useful:

1. **Succeeding in the Workplace** You may need to use your math skills while at work. For example, contractors often set rates based on the materials they need plus a fee for the hours they will work. Office managers often need to balance a budget, buy supplies, and calculate payroll. Whatever job you do, a knowledge of your own pay rate will help you determine your ability to afford items you may want to purchase.

2. **Making Wise Purchases** When you are faced with multiple choices in a competitive market, use unit prices to calculate the most economical buys. For example, when you do the math, you may see that a "buy one, get one free" sale doesn't offer the bargain you had originally imagined.

3. **Analyzing Statistics** Business reports, daily newspapers, and other sources of information often use statistics to support certain points of view. Knowing how to weigh the value of those numbers helps you to make informed judgments.

> **Exercise 12** Using Math Skills to Decide Whether or Not to Accept a Job
A neighbor has offered you and a friend $350 to paint her house. From your past painting experience, you realize that it will take five eight-hour days to complete the job, six gallons of paint at $25 per gallon, and the purchase of $50 in painting materials.

1. What is the total cost of supplies?
2. What is your hourly wage on this job?
3. Identify one other factor that might influence your decision.
4. Would you accept this job? Explain your answer.

▼ Critical Viewing How can a knowledge of math skills help you as you consider purchasing CDs? **[Connect]**

844 • Workplace Skills and Competencies

Applying Computer Skills

With computers common in many workplaces, employers in a variety of fields expect new workers to have computer skills. Consider improving your skills to increase your opportunities in the workplace.

▶ **KEY CONCEPT** A knowledge of your computer means the ability to enter information accurately, format text, use a variety of software, and access Internet information. ■

Following are a few ways to make the most of a computer:
1. **Practice your keyboarding skills.** Being an accurate and quick keyboarder gives you more time to focus on other tasks. A good typing speed is 45 words per minute, but remember that accuracy is more important than speed.
2. **Learn how to format.** You can use fonts, bullets, and other features to organize and emphasize information. Consider learning a variety of programs to help you apply your skills in any working environment.
3. **Use the thesaurus and spell-check tools.** To make your work professional and accurate, get in the habit of using a word processor's language functions. For example, with a click of a mouse, you can find just the right word or catch errors you may have missed while proofreading.
4. **Learn to use the Internet.** With a teacher's guidance, discover the wealth of information available at your fingertips.

▶ **Exercise 13** Working With Computers Complete these activities:
1. Find an application that creates charts or graphs, and use the computers Help menu to create one.
2. Conduct interviews to find out how computers enhance the workplace of several people you know.

▶ **More Practice**
Academic and Workplace Skills Activity Book
• pp. 59–60

ⓘ Learn More

The Media and Technology Skills activities in Chapters 1–3 offer instruction to help you improve your computer skills.

Reflecting on Your Workplace Skills and Competencies

To reflect on your workplace skills and competencies, consider the job you most want to pursue. Then, jot down your responses to these questions:

• What skills are most important in the job or career you want to pursue?

• What skills should you improve? Why?

✎ **STANDARDIZED TEST PREPARATION WORKSHOP**

Problem Solving Standardized text questions often require students to solve mathematical problems based on textual information. Provide students with opportunities to practice this skill.

Two trains are approaching Topeka, Kansas, from opposite directions. The Century Express is traveling from the west at 87 miles per hour. The City of Denver is coming from the east at 66 miles per hour. In one hour, approximately how many miles closer are these two trains?

A 21 miles   C 66 miles
B 87 miles   D 153 miles

Students should recognize that **D** is the correct answer. Since both trains are nearing Topeka from opposite directions, they can calculate the decrease in distance between the two by adding the distance each train can travel in one hour.

Step-by-Step Teaching Guide

Applying Computer Skills

Teaching Resources: Academic and Workplace Skills Activity Book, p. 60

1. Arrange for a demonstration of a commonly used word processing program. Encourage prepared and knowledgeable students to contribute tips and information.

2. Have students suggest a topic for researching on the Internet. Then, in the school library or other facility that has access to the Internet, allow students time to do the search. Compare the resources they found.

Answer Key

▶ **Exercise 13**

For the first activity, suggest that students create a chart for managing time or money. For the second, have students practice their keyboarding skills by typing a summary of what they learned in their interviews.

Customize for
ESL Students

The Internet provides a way to inexpensively obtain news and information from a range of cultures and languages. Encourage English language learners to find and share information on the Internet that reflects their heritages and languages.

ASSESS AND CLOSE

Step-by-Step Teaching Guide

Assessment

Teaching Resources: Formal Assessment, Chapter 33

1. Have students answer the Reflecting questions independently and then share their answers in small groups.

2. For assessment, use the following options:

   • review the Standardized Test Preparation Workshop on pages 846–847 and have students complete the practice exercises.

   • administer the Chapter 33 assessment in *Formal Assessment* to measure students' grasp of the concepts presented.

Lesson Objectives

1. To establish a purpose for reading, such as to discover, interpret, and enjoy

2. To locate appropriate print and non-print information using text and technical resources, including databases and the Internet

3. To use text organizers to locate and categorize information

4. To draw conclusions from information gathered

Step-by-Step Teaching Guide

Reading Informational Texts

Teaching Resources: Standardized Test Preparation Workbook, pp. 65–66

1. Have students meet in small groups and make a list of texts they frequently read. Have them share their answers and compile a class list.

2. Students might have strategies for reading some of these texts efficiently. If so, have them share their ideas with the class.

3. Have students answer the sample test item. Ask them more questions about it, such as "Where do you sign up to be a volunteer?" and "Who should sign up to take the class?" Explain that in most cases, the answers will be directly stated in the text.

4. Have students complete the practice questions on page 847. Address any questions they have.

Standardized Test Preparation Workshop

Reading Informational Texts

Some standardized tests assess your ability to read real-world texts, such as flyers, brochures, and advertisements. Often, this involves carefully following a sequence of steps or directions. The following sample test item will give you practice in answering these types of questions.

Test Tip

When a reading passage is presented, read it carefully, and then review it as you choose the answers to the questions.

Sample Test Item

Directions: Read the passage, and answer the question that follows.

Do you know the ins and outs of exploring the Web?

Come share your knowledge as a volunteer for Tech Literacy. As a volunteer, you will teach basic computer skills as well as every aspect of Internet use—from turning on the computer to setting up bookmarks.

If you are interested, sign up at your local library. If you know anyone who might be interested in taking the class, have them call

1-800-555-TECH

1 Based on this advertisement, which of the following would you teach first?

 A using search engines

 B how to use a computer mouse

 C using the Help key

 D creating Internet bookmarks

Answer and Explanation

The correct answer is *B, how to use a computer mouse.* Because the class will first teach basic instruction, one of the first things taught would be using a computer mouse.

✏ TEST-TAKING TIP

Remind students that all CD-ROMS work differently. Even if students are familiar with many CD-ROMS, they must read the test information carefully because the CD-ROM described here might have a unique way of functioning.

Remind students, too, that they can refer to the passage and illustration as often as necessary while answering the questions. There is no need to memorize the information or to make guesses.

> **Practice 1** **Directions:** Read the passage, and answer the questions that follow.

Jonah has to write a report on the life and times of Anton Chekhov. After beginning with an encyclopedia and then reading a few brief biographies, Jonah asked the librarian to help him find a source that would provide him with biographical, historical, and literary information. She suggested that he use a program called *AuthorWorks* CD-ROM. After finding a computer, he began to read the following pages from the user manual.

The Author Directory

The main menu, in the form of an author directory, offers you the following choices:

- Click on Guided Tour to see a demonstration of the features and contents of *AuthorWorks*.
- Click on Contents to see a listing of topics about each author. Click on any topic to take you into the program.
- Click on Index to see a list of the articles available. Then, click on any article title to take you to the article.
- Click on Projects for a directory of sample projects for each author.
- Click on an author to explore his or her life and work. A video provides an author overview. Spoken excerpts from the author's works follow. You can play each excerpt by clicking on the highlighted arrows on the Menu Bar.

To return to the Author Directory at any time, select Author Directory from the GO menu.

Whenever you want to exit from the program, select EXIT from the FILE menu.

---

1 If Jonah wants to find out more about the personal life of an author, he should click on—

A Works

B Times

C arrow keys

D the author

2 Where did Jonah first look for information?

F concise biographies

G encyclopedias

H history books

J CD-ROMs

3 If Jonah wanted to find specific articles on the author, he would choose—

A Works

B Projects

C Index

D Contents

4 If Jonah wanted to know more about what is contained in *AuthorWorks*, he should click on —

F an author

G Guided Tour

H Contents

J Index page

5 If Jonah wanted to go back to the Author Directory at any time, he would—

A click anywhere on the screen

B click on the Back button

C use the GO menu

D click on the arrows

6 To exit the program—

F click on the Stop icon

G choose control & Q

H choose EXIT from FILE menu

J click arrow in left corner

Answer Key

> **Practice 1**

1. D
2. G
3. C
4. G
5. C
6. H

Customize for
Less Advanced Students

Tell students not to panic if they encounter an information source, such as a CD-ROM or an Internet page, with which they are unfamiliar. They simply need to read carefully to become familiar with the text. All of the answers are provided somewhere in the graphic or the written description.

Customize for
ESL Students

Have students practice reading informational texts by providing examples of flyers and notices from around the school. Help them learn words commonly used in such texts, such as *location, volunteer, membership,* and more.

Interest GRABBER Invite students to describe the types of newspaper or magazine articles they have read and the different subjects the articles addressed. Then ask, "What was your purpose in reading these articles?" Encourage students to think about purposes for reading (to glean information, for enjoyment).

Discuss what makes an article interesting or fun to read. Ask, "What must you be able to do in order to become engrossed in an article?" Guide students to realize that they must be able to understand, or *comprehend*, what they read.

Tell students to read a newspaper or magazine article and write a brief summary of it. Encourage them to convey interesting or entertaining points.

Activate Prior Knowledge

Have student volunteers read aloud their article summaries. Discuss the reading skills they have learned that allow them to understand and enjoy what they read. List each skill on the board as it is suggested (e.g., vocabulary skills, context clue skills, comparing skills, cause-and-effect skills, idiom skills, punctuation and capitalization skills, and so on). Point out to students that they have already mastered a wide variety of skills that will help them do well on the reading comprehension and other parts of the new SAT® and the ACT® tests.

Test Preparation Handbook

Preparing for the New SAT® and the ACT®

The new SAT® and the ACT® are standardized tests. They are designed to help colleges compare the abilities of prospective students from all over the world. As a tenth grader, you may feel that college is in the distant future. However, if you are serious about attending college, chances are you will take the new SAT®, the ACT®, or both. Now is the perfect time to begin preparing for these tests.

This Test Preparation Handbook will focus on the Writing Section of the new SAT® and the Writing Test of the ACT®. Colleges use the results of the writing sections to find out if students are prepared for the kind of writing expected of them in college.

The Writing Section

The writing sections on both the new SAT® and the ACT® include a timed essay. On the new SAT®, students are given twenty-five minutes to write an essay in response to a prompt. On the ACT®, students are given thirty minutes to do so. This Test Preparation Handbook introduces you to the structure of both new SAT® and ACT® prompts. By studying this section carefully, you can prepare effectively for this part of the exams.

In addition to the twenty-five-minute timed essay, the new SAT®'s Writing Section contains three types of multiple-choice questions on grammar and usage. This Test Preparation Handbook will introduce you to each type of grammar and usage question that appears on the new SAT®. It will also be helpful to those preparing for the ACT®, because the same topics are addressed in the English Section of that exam.

CONTENTS

848 • Test Preparation Handbook

✎ TEST-TAKING TIP

Ask students, "How many of you have taken a standardized test?" Most students have probably taken state assessment tests. Some may have taken the PSAT® test. Invite volunteers to describe how taking such tests differs from ordinary classroom tests (the test booklet, the answer sheet and how it is filled in, and so on). Explain that the new SAT® and the ACT® use a similar format, so students should have no trouble understanding what to do. If some students are not familiar with the answer sheet format, create a simple one on the board and show them how to fill in the circles correctly.

Reading Comprehension Questions

Both the new SAT® and the ACT® test your ability to understand what you read. Although reading comprehension is not a part of the writing sections of either exam, this section will introduce you to the types of reading comprehension questions you are likely to encounter on the new SAT® and ACT®. Reading Comprehension questions typically test three reading skills:

- Vocabulary in Context: These questions test your ability to understand what a word means from the way it is used in a sentence or passage.

- Finding Information in the Text: These questions test your ability to understand the basic information stated in a text.

- Extended Reasoning: These questions test your ability to infer meaning from a text. You should expect questions that ask about the passage's main idea and details, the author's logic and attitude, and the implications of the author's statements.

The following section contains one example of each type of reading passage presented on the new SAT®. These include the following passages:

Short passages	These passages can be as short as one hundred words and are followed by two questions.
Long passages	These passages can be as long as eight hundred words and are followed by as many as thirteen questions.
Paired passages	These pairs consist of two passages and are followed by questions that ask about each passage, as well as questions that ask you to compare and contrast the paired passages.

Please note that on the new SAT® or the ACT®, these passages will be followed by at least two questions. In this Test Preparation Handbook, only one question for each reading passage will be presented along with steps to answer the question. It is a good idea to practice further by completing reading comprehension questions from old SAT® or ACT® tests. Your teacher can help you to identify books that contain practice tests. Finally, another excellent way to prepare for the Reading Comprehension section of these exams, and for college, is to read widely and often.

Test Preparation Handbook • 849

1. To introduce the format of long passage reading comprehension questions on the new SAT® and the ACT®.

2. To review inferring the meaning of unfamiliar words.

3. To teach strategies for identifying and using context clues.

Step-by-Step Teaching Guide

Strategies for Identifying Vocabulary in Context

1. Review and discuss the strategy of inferring word meanings with students. Inform students that inferences are educated guesses made by using their prior knowledge to identify indirect meanings in a text. Explain that the term *context* refers to the words, phrases, and sentences that surround an unfamiliar word.

2. Guide students through the steps identified on the student page.

3. Ask students if they have any questions about finding the general meaning of the passage.

4. Read aloud the directions as students follow along. Ask students to read the passage silently.

5. Point out that the directions and the sample test question do not explicitly instruct students to use context clues and do not identify where the target word appears in the passage. Focus students' attention on the phrase *most nearly means* in the question. This phrase tells students that they are looking for an approximate, rather than an exact, meaning. Explain that these are cue words that suggest using context clues.

continued

Reading Comprehension

Long Passage

The passage below tells about the reign of Queen Elizabeth I of England.

 **STRATEGY** **Vocabulary in Context:** When you encounter an unfamiliar word in a test passage, make inferences about its meaning by looking for context clues in the surrounding words.

▶ **Sample Test Question**

Directions: Read the passage carefully. Then, answer the question.

Queen Elizabeth I

1　　When Queen Elizabeth I ascended the throne, the English people were deeply divided in terms of religion. Years earlier, Elizabeth's father, King Henry VIII, had established the Church of England with himself as its head.

5　　He required the English people to join the Church of England, rather than remain in the Catholic Church. This directive created great unrest throughout England, which was almost entirely Catholic at the time.

　　Elizabeth took a humane and compassionate view of her
10　divided people. She was willing to allow individuals a share of privacy in their religious convictions as long as they showed outward obedience to her as queen. She is famous for saying, "I will not make windows into men's souls," by which she meant that she was unwilling to invade the
15　privacy of her subjects. Her main concern was for peace and order within her realm.

　　Elizabeth's strategy for dealing with difficult situations was often to delay in addressing them. Some of her contemporaries criticized this approach, for it seemed to
20　lack the decisiveness necessary in a leader. However, this technique actually revealed a keen understanding of how power works. For as long as she delayed in making a decision, she held power over the people vying for each side of an argument. By delaying her decision, she delayed
25　losing the loyalty of the people on the other side of the argument. Often enough, the situation resolved itself before she addressed it. When that happened, Elizabeth won because she had not sided with one group over another. As a result, she successfully <u>retained</u> the loyalty of
30　both sides. Through this strategy of indecision, Elizabeth remained in power through extremely turbulent times.

Integrating Vocabulary Skills

Explain that knowledge of prefixes and word roots can support a reader's use of context in figuring out the meaning of an unfamiliar word. Have students identify the prefix in the word *retained* (re-) and tell how other words with the shared root—*contain, maintain, obtain*—seem to have related meanings. Direct them to check their ideas in a dictionary. They will find that all the words share a Latin root meaning "to hold."

QUESTION: The word *retained* (line 29) most nearly means

A   lost

B   ignored

C   sought

D   kept

E   relinquished

STEPS

1. **Carefully read the passage to be sure you understand its general meaning.** Then, read the question. Reread the sentence containing the target word *retained*. Use the context clues, such as *successfully* and *loyalty of both sides*, to help you think about what the word might mean. From these context clues, you can tell that the word *retained* has a positive meaning in the sentence.

2. **Find context clues in the sentences surrounding the target word.** Reread the sentences before and after the sentence containing the target word. Notice that these sentences tell us that Elizabeth resisted choosing sides in an argument and that this technique helped her to avoid losing the loyalty of one group of people by siding with another party. This context helps the reader to understand that *she successfully retained the loyalty of both sides* means that she avoided losing the loyalty of a group of people. Therefore, *retain* must mean something along the lines of "kept."

3. **Review the answer choices.** If you are unsure about which answer choice to select, substitute each answer choice for *retain* in the sentence. Choices A, B, and E do not make sense within the sentence or the passage. Choice C, *sought*, is incorrect because Elizabeth's approach was a passive one and the word *sought* suggests a more active pursuit of the loyalty of both sides than the passage suggests. Choice D, *kept*, most nearly defines the target word because it makes sense within the context of the sentence. The passage tells us that Elizabeth was concerned with losing the loyalty of one of the sides in an argument. Therefore, it makes sense that her strategy allowed her to successfully *retain* or *keep* the loyalty of both sides. The answer to the question is choice D.

Reading Comprehension • 851

Step-by Step Teaching Guide continued

6. Discuss how the word *successfully* in line 29 implies that *retained* has a positive meaning in the sentence. Explain that *loyalty* has a positive connotation that also gives a clue that retained has a positive meaning.

7. Have volunteers substitute the incorrect answer choices and read aloud the resulting sentences. Explain that choice D, *kept*, is correct because it can be substituted for *retained* without changing the meaning of the sentence.

Customize for
Less Advanced Students

Tell students that the context for an unknown word may be positive or negative. Ask students to identify words and phrases with positive connotations in the last three sentences of the reading passage (*won, successfully, loyalty, remained in power*). Help them to see that the word *retained* is likely to have a positive meaning in this context. To help students better grasp the concept of positive and negative connotations, discuss which of the words in this list imply a positive meaning. Discuss which have a negative meaning: scent/odor; skinny/slim; inexpensive/cheap; and strong-willed/pig-headed. Ask students to use each word in a pair in the same sentence and note how the sentence meaning changes.

Customize for
Gifted/Talented Students

Ask students to decode additional words as they read. For example, what can they infer about the meaning of the word *vying* in line 23? What part of speech is it? Help students to conclude that it serves as a verb because it is something that *people* are doing. Point out that the phrase *each side of an argument* implies that people are presenting or arguing for one side or the other. Have students jot down their inferences, as well as the passage clues and facts on which they are based.

✎ TEST-TAKING TIP

Explain that in a multiple-choice test, students should think of their own correct answer before reading the answer choices. In the sample passage, the context suggests that *retained* means "held onto." The test taker would quickly see that choice D, *kept*, is closest in meaning to "held onto."

Give students practice in decoding an unfamiliar word. Direct them to the word *convictions* in the second paragraph of the passage. Ask them to jot down an idea of what the word means.

Then, provide this question and these answer choices:

The word *convictions* in this context most nearly means

A   accusations   B   beliefs

C   guilt   D   ceremonies

E   churches

Have students evaluate their success in determining that the correct answer is B, *beliefs*.

1. To introduce the format of paired reading passage comprehension questions on the new SAT® and the ACT®.

2. To review making inferences in paired reading passages.

3. To teach strategies for understanding suggested and implied meanings.

Step-by-Step Teaching Guide

Strategies for Making Inferences

1. Review the strategy for making inferences with students. Point out that students should approach reading comprehension questions by first looking for stated, or explicit, answers in the passage. Explain that when an answer is not readily apparent in the text, students should look for implied or suggested meanings. Remind students that *state* means to put forth in words, while *imply* means to express indirectly.

2. Read aloud the directions along with students. Point out that the directions do not specify whether the answer is stated or implied.

3. Guide students through the steps identified on student page 853.

4. Explain that reading both passages before reading the question allows students to form unbiased initial impressions. After reading the question and answer choices, explain that the phrase *general statement* cues students to infer an implied, thematic meaning that connects both passages.

5. Have students answer the question and articulate their reasoning using support from the text. Discuss why the incorrect answer choices can be eliminated. Point out that these types of questions often include answer choices that seem correct but only apply to one passage. Stress that choice A is correct because it can be inferred from both passages.

Reading Comprehension

Paired Reading Passages

The passages below come from two novels. In both passages, an important male character is introduced. The first passage is from the novel *Pride and Prejudice* by Jane Austen. The second passage is from the novel *Wuthering Heights* by Emily Brontë.

 **STRATEGY** **Make Inferences:** If the answer to a question is not plainly stated in a selection, look beyond the details and information to understand the suggestions and implications of the author's words.

▶ **Sample Test Question**

Directions: Read both passages. Then, answer the question based on what is stated or implied in the paired passages.

Passage 1

> Mr. Bingley had soon made himself acquainted with all the principal people in the room; he was lively and unreserved, danced every dance, was angry that the ball closed so early, and talked of giving one himself at Netherfield. Such amiable qualities must speak for themselves.

Passage 2

> His figure was enveloped in a riding cloak, fur collared and steel clasped; its details were not apparent, but I traced the general points of middle height and considerable breadth of chest. He had a dark face, with stern features and a heavy brow; his eyes and gathered eyebrows looked ireful and thwarted just now; he was past youth, but had not reached middle-age; perhaps he might be thirty-five. I felt no fear of him, and but little shyness. Had he been a handsome, heroic-looking young gentleman, I should not have dared to stand thus questioning him against his will, and offering my services unasked. I had hardly ever seen a handsome youth; never in my life spoken to one.

Integrating Writing Skills

Tell students that writers offer descriptive details, like those in the sample passages, so that readers can form sharp mental pictures. Another purpose is to help readers make inferences about the person who is described and the person who is doing the describing. Have students make a list of the adjectives and descriptive phrases in the two passages (*lively, unreserved, angry that the ball closed so early; middle height, considerable breadth of chest, dark face, stern features, heavy brow, gathered brow, ireful and thwarted, past youth, not handsome or heroic-looking*). Ask students to write a description of a person that creates a clear mental image and allows the reader to make inferences about the person. They may describe someone they know or a fictional person.

QUESTION: Both passages support which general statement?

A People form judgments about others based on their behavior and appearance.

B Physical attractiveness tends to make a person intimidating and unapproachable.

C Social interactions are structured by a complicated set of rules one must follow.

D Many people who appear mean-spirited are kind, once you get to know them.

E Cowardly people often mask their insecurity by acting confident and outspoken.

S T E P S

1. **Carefully read the passages to be sure you understand the general meaning of each passage.** As you read the second passage, think about the ways in which the second passage is similar to and different from the first.

2. **Read the question.** With the question in mind, reread the passages. As you reread the passages, ask yourself what the two passages have in common. Passage 1 describes the activities of Mr. Bingley at a ball. Passage 2 describes the narrator's reactions to a man he has met for the first time. Both passages depict the forming of an impression of a person.

3. **Review the answer choices.** Look for an answer choice that reflects an implication of *both* passages. Choice B may appear correct, but this idea is only present in Passage 2. Likewise, choice C is only implied by Passage 1. Choices D and E are inferences that are not supported by either passage. On the other hand, choice A contains an inference that could be drawn from both passages, *People form instant judgments about others based on outward appearances.* Therefore, the answer to the question is choice A.

Reading Comprehension • 853

Ask students to brainstorm for reasons that passages might be paired on a reading test. Have them list their ideas. Possibilities include: showing similarities or differences in characters, author's style, or another element; contrasting fiction and nonfiction; or comparing and contrasting two genres on the same topic. Then, encourage students to decide which of their reasons applies to these two sample passages. Students should defend their responses. Students may suggest the passages on page 852 are two contrasting examples of fiction.

Integrating Vocabulary Skills

Tell students that the words *imply* and *infer* and *implication* and *inference* are often confused. Ask students to explain the meaning of the sentence "Authors imply and readers infer." *Imply* means to add information without stating it directly. *Infer* means to determine such information based on existing text. Then, ask students to come up with their own sentence using the words *implication* and *inference*.

⏱ TIME SAVERS!

On-line Exercise Bank
Have students complete the exercises on computer. The Auto Check feature will grade their work for you.

🖌 TEST-TAKING TIP

Explain that it is sometimes helpful to read the questions on a standardized test before reading the passage. That way, students can focus their reading on the specific information they need, rather than spending time absorbing other details. Other ways to focus reading during a standardized test include underlining or circling main ideas during reading and using the title of the passage to find clues to the general message or theme of the passage.

Lesson Objectives

1. To introduce the format of short passage reading comprehension questions on the new SAT® and the ACT®.

2. To review finding the main idea of an informational passage.

3. To teach strategies for identifying and applying main ideas.

Step-by-Step Teaching Guide

Strategies for Finding the Main Idea

1. Review and discuss the strategy for finding the main idea of a passage with the students. Explain that the phrase *general meaning* is similar to but less specific than *main idea*.

2. Read the directions and the sample test question along with the students.

3. Guide students through the steps identified on student page 855.

4. Point out that the question following the passage does not ask students to identify the main idea of the passage. Explain that this is a multistep question that requires students to find the main idea in order to make an inference.

5. Have students articulate the passage's main idea, using support from the passage. Review that a topic sentence expresses the main idea of a paragraph and reinforces the passage's overall message. Define supporting details as examples, reasons, and other evidence. Remind students that concluding sentences reinforce the topic sentence, or main idea. Students should see that the main idea of this passage is in the first sentence.

6. Emphasize the importance of carefully reading all of the answer choices, as they often contain similar ideas and language. Explain that choices A and C are incorrect because they imply a sympathetic attitude that is not supported by the topic sentence or concluding sentences. Explain that choice B is correct because it is supported by the main idea of the passage.

Reading Comprehension

Short Passage

The passage below describes how immigrant children growing up at the turn of the century entertained themselves.

 **STRATEGY** **Find the Main Idea:** To identify the main idea of a passage, read the passage carefully to make sure you understand its general meaning. Then, pay special attention to its first and last sentences. These sentences often communicate the main idea of a selection.

▶ Sample Test Question

Directions: Read the passage carefully. Then, answer the question shown.

> ### Children's Play Long Ago
>
> Long before television and video games, children played games using simple, everyday objects. In the early 1900's, immigrant children who were growing up in America's crowded cities were especially resourceful. A ball, a stick, some bottle caps, and a piece of chalk were all that were needed for a summer of fun.
>
> While the boys played in the streets, the girls claimed the sidewalks. Hopscotch and jumping rope were great favorites. Games that involved clapping and rhyming were delightfully simple. They required no more equipment than a good memory and a fast pair of hands. The idea that expensive equipment or special skills were necessary in order to have fun would never have occurred to the immigrant children who grew up on the city streets of America!

QUESTION: The author would most likely agree with which one of the following statements?

A   An earlier generation of children missed out because they were born before the invention of television and video games.

B   It is remarkable how creative and resourceful the immigrant children of the early 1900's were.

C   Immigrant children were unfortunate because they grew up in crowded cities at the beginning of the twentieth century.

D   The games of immigrant children were hard to learn.

E   Today, immigrant children do not live in overcrowded cities.

854 • Test Preparation Handbook

◇ TEST-TAKING TIP

Tell students that in a timed test they must work efficiently and should quickly locate the information needed to answer a question. Point out that the sample question asks about the author's viewpoint. The author has not only provided information about immigrant children's games of the past but has also given an opinion about those games.

Ask students to locate words and phrases in the passage that reveal the author's viewpoint. (Possibilities include: *especially resourceful, summer of fun, great favorites, delightfully simple.*) Then, have students scan the answer choices and identify the one (answer choice B) that matches the positive words and phrases.

STEPS

1. **Carefully read the passage to be sure you understand its general meaning.** Then, read the question. This type of question is really testing your ability to make an inference based on your understanding of the author's main idea.

2. **Pay attention to the first sentence of the passage.** Notice that the first sentence of the passage states that children from long ago played games using simple objects. The other sentences in the first paragraph reinforce this main idea.

3. **Pay attention to the last sentence of the passage.** Notice that it echoes the first paragraph's main idea and extends it by adding that children long ago could not have imagined requiring anything fancy in order to have fun. The rest of the second paragraph supports the point made in the final sentence. Now that you have identified the main idea of each paragraph, you can determine the main idea of the passage: Children long ago used simple objects and their imaginations to entertain themselves.

4. **Review the answer choices.** Look for the choice that reflects an understanding of the author's *overall* message. Choices A and C suggest that the author feels sorry for the children mentioned in the selection. There is nothing in the passage to support this idea, so choices A and C are incorrect. Choices D and E reflect inferences that are not clearly supported by the text. Choice B, *It is remarkable how creative and resourceful the immigrant children of the early 1900's were*, is correct. The author would agree with this statement because it reflects the main idea of his writing. Therefore, the answer to the question is choice B.

Reflecting on Reading Comprehension

Now that you have worked through the Reading Comprehension section, answer the following questions about your reading and test-taking skills.

- Which types of strategies or questions were you already familiar with?

- Which types of strategies or questions did you find challenging?

Once you have identified areas that you need to work on further, ask your teacher for help in finding materials that can help you improve your skills.

Integrating Vocabulary Skills

Tell students that if they come across an unfamiliar word in a test passage, they should pause only long enough to decide if they need to know the word. If they understand the general sense of the sentence, they may skip the word and read on. If the word seems important, they should reread and read on to see whether the context offers help.

Direct students to the word *resourceful* in the first paragraph and to the word *hopscotch* in the second paragraph. Ask them whether it is important to understand the meaning of either or both words. (The word *resourceful* is significant, but the word *hopscotch* is not.) Have students point to clues in the context that help them define *resourceful*.

Customize for
ESL Students

Read aloud the sample passage for students. Ask questions that help them paraphrase each sentence. For example, after reading aloud the first sentence, ask, "What did children play with before they had television and video games?" Help students decide whether each sentence states a main idea or gives supporting details. After discussing the passage, ask students: "How does the author feel about the games that these children played?" Guide students to see that words like *delightful* and *great favorite* indicate the writer liked the game.

ASSESS

Ask questions to help students summarize what they have learned about these three kinds of reading comprehension questions found on standardized tests. Use questions in parentheses below to guide discussion:

1. Vocabulary in Context (What is meant by context? Why is it useful to substitute each answer choice for the target word in the sentence?)

2. Making Inferences (What is the difference between directly stated information and an inference? How can you tell that a test question is requiring you to make an inference?)

3. Finding the Main Idea (What parts of a paragraph or passage are most likely to point you to a main idea? What should you look for to determine an author's main point or opinion?)

For further practice, direct students to practice tests, which are available in school libraries, public libraries, and on the World Wide Web. The ExamView questions in the On-line Exercise Bank also offer practice opportunities.

Write these sentences on the board and then read each aloud. Ask students whether either "sounds wrong."

1. The team with the young players is winning.

2. One of the teams have young players.

Students should recognize that the second sentence sounds wrong. Have them explain what is wrong and how to correct it. Tell students that each sentence has a singular subject and therefore needs a singular verb. *(One of the teams has young players.)* Explain that grammar questions in standardized tests often focus on lack of agreement in number between subjects and verbs, as well as on other usage problems.

Activate Prior Knowledge

Ask students to read the introductory paragraph on page 856 to find and list three singular verbs and three plural verbs. Have them identify the singular and plural subjects that agree with the verbs. Verbs (with subjects in parentheses) may include: singular—*(technique) does, (it) is, (section) introduces;* plural—*(SAT and the ACT) include, (questions) feature, (students) find, (rules) are, (you) prepare, (people) can, (they) hear, (they) read,(you) have.*

Customize for
ESL Students

The use of the inflection *-s* can cause confusion because it marks both a plural noun and a singular verb. Give students practice with the distinction by having them add *-s* to either the noun or the verb in a sentence to show agreement. They may copy and correct these sentences, and then create more:

Six dog play. (Six dogs play.)

One dog play. (One dog plays.)

The wind blow hard. (The wind blows hard.)

These breeze blow gently. (These breezes blow gently.)

Grammar

The new SAT® and the ACT® include multiple-choice grammar questions. These questions typically feature sentences and paragraphs that require corrections or revisions. Many students find grammar difficult. However, by focusing on the grammar and usage rules that are most often tested, you can prepare yourself to succeed on these types of questions.

Some people can spot grammar and usage errors easily. These people can spot errors because they *hear* the errors as they read. This technique does not work for everyone. If you have a tendency to make grammar and usage errors, it is best to use a systematic approach for answering these questions. This section introduces a step-by-step process for answering common multiple-choice grammar questions.

Faulty Subject-Verb Agreement

▶ **RULE**   A singular subject must have a singular verb. A plural subject must have a plural verb.

▶ **Sample Test Question**

Directions: Read the sentence carefully. Identify the sentence error from the underlined options. If there is no error, select choice E.

> When the theater lights flickered, the audience
>   A   B
> were reminded of the impending start of the performance.
>   C   D
> No error
>   E

QUESTION: What is the error in the sentence?

  A   When

  B   lights flickered

  C   were reminded

  D   impending start

  E   No error

STEPS

1. **Read the sentence carefully.** Focus your attention on the underlined words or phrases.

A Word to the Wise
Agreement
When a verb and a subject are in agreement, they are in harmony. A subject and a verb must agree in order to make sense together.

TIP: Be careful with subjects that are indefinite pronouns. *Each, either, everyone, someone,* and *no one* are always singular subjects. *Few, both, many,* and *several* are always plural subjects.

✎ TEST-TAKING TIP

Caution students to pay special attention to forms of the verb *be,* especially *are, is, was, were.* Have students list these verbs and write a singular or plural pronoun and a singular or plural noun before each. Remind students that if any underlined portion of a sentence contains one of these verbs, they should look for the subject of the sentence or the clause and check for agreement in number.

2. **Ask yourself: "Does any underlined word or phrase sound wrong?"** If one word or phrase definitely sounds wrong to you, you have probably identified the error in the sentence.

3. **If no words or phrases sound wrong to you, ask yourself: "Does any underlined word or phrase violate a grammar or usage rule that I have learned?"**

4. **Identify the subject of the sentence.** The subject is *audience*. Notice that the word *audience* is a collective noun. A collective noun is always singular. It must be paired with a singular verb in a sentence.

5. **Identify the verb in the sentence.** The verb in the sentence is *were reminded*, which is plural.

6. **Check for subject-verb agreement.** The subject, *audience*, is singular, but the verb, *were reminded*, is plural. Therefore, the subject and verb do not agree in this sentence. In order for the verb to agree with the subject, it should be written in singular form: *was reminded*.

7. **Review the answer choices.** The verb, *were reminded*, is the error in the sentence. Therefore, the answer to the question is choice C.

Faulty Verb Tense

▶ **RULE** The tense of a verb shows the time an action takes place. Verb tense must make sense within the context of its sentence.

▶ **Sample Test Question**

Directions: Read the sentence carefully. Identify the sentence error from the underlined options. If there is no error, select choice E.

The Royal Library at Alexandria <u>will have educated</u> generations
      A   B

of <u>scholars</u> before it was <u>mysteriously</u> destroyed. <u>No error</u>
    C   D   E

QUESTION: What is the error in the sentence?

  A The Royal Library
  B will have educated
  C scholars
  D mysteriously
  E No error

FOR REVIEW

To review subject-verb agreement in greater depth, see Chapter 24, Section 1.

A Word to the Wise

Verb

The word *verb* comes from the Latin word *verbum*, which means "word."

Grammar • 857

Language Highlights

The Latin word for *word* is *verbum*. This is the source of *verb* and other English words *verbose*, *verbal*, *verbalize*, *verbatim*, *verbiage*, *proverb*, and *adverb*. Challenge students to use the word *word* (or a form of *word*) in a definition of each Latin-based word. Then, suggest that they check the definition of each term in a dictionary.

⚹ **TEST-TAKING TIP**

Explain that grammar questions on standardized tests often focus on faulty forms of irregular verbs. Students should pay special attention to a verb formed with *has, had,* or *have* and a past participle. Direct students to choose irregular verbs from Chapter 22, Section 1, and write sample items for classmates to identify as correct or incorrect. (Example: *The birds have flew south for the winter.*)

Lesson Objectives

1. To introduce questions in which students choose to revise, or accept as correct, the underlined portions of a sentence.

2. To review identifying and correcting faulty subject-verb agreement.

3. To identify and correct faulty verb tense.

4. To review pronoun case and fauly pronoun case.

5. To teach approaches for identifying and correcting a grammatical error.

Step-by-Step Teaching Guide

Strategies for Identifying Faulty Subject-Verb Agreement

1. Review the rule for identifying and correcting faulty subject-verb agreement.

2. Explain that a multiple-choice format is used for all grammar questions in the new SAT® and the ACT®. Read aloud the directions.

3. Guide students through the steps identified on student pages 856–857.

4. Read aloud the question with the students. Point out that the subject in the sentence is the collective noun *audience*. Caution students to pay careful attention when the subject is a collective noun. Remind them that a collective noun usually names a single group and requires a single verb.

5. Point out the importance of evaluating each answer choice A–D before selecting choice E, No error. Invite volunteers to come to the board and write sentences that have collective nouns as the subject.

6. Note that collective nouns are usually treated as singular because they refer to a group (*My family was united on this issue*). Discuss rare instances when collective nouns might be treated as plural because they refer to the individuals that make up the group (*My family often fight among themselves*).

Strategies for Identifying Faulty Verb Tense

1. Review the rule regarding verb tense. Remind students that verb tense must be consistent and logical.

2. Guide students through the steps identified on student page 858.

3. Read aloud the question as the students follow along. Ask students to identify the tense of the two verbs *will have educated* and *destroyed*. Point out that a future perfect tense verb could never logically precede a verb in the past tense. Ask students to explain why. Direct them to read choices A–E to locate the correct choice (answer choice B).

4. Explain that many sentences contain two or more verbs in different tenses, so students need to be proficient in using all six verb tenses. Review the placement of past perfect tense verbs before past tense verbs.

5. Explain that when two verbs are in the past tense, the action that is further back in time is in the past perfect tense. Then, reinforce using the context of the sentence to locate the verb in the wrong tense. For additional practice, suggest that students read sentences in other texts and identify the tense of the verbs.

Strategies for Identifying Faulty Pronoun Case

1. Review the rule regarding pronoun case. Emphasize that students should follow such rules when identifying grammar errors. Tell students that the test items are developed according to grammar rules, not informal usage.

continued

Grammar

STEPS

1. **Read the sentence carefully.** Focus your attention on the underlined words or phrases.

2. **Ask yourself: "Does any underlined word or phrase sound wrong?"** If one word or phrase definitely sounds wrong to you, you have probably identified the error in the sentence.

3. **If no words or phrases sound wrong to you, ask yourself: "Does any underlined word or phrase violate a grammar or usage rule that I have learned?"** Notice that there are two verbs in the sentence. The first verb, *will have educated*, is in the future perfect tense. The second verb, *was destroyed*, is in the past tense.

4. **Check that the tense of the verbs makes sense within the structure of the sentence.** The words *before it was mysteriously destroyed* make it clear that the library no longer exists. It is impossible that the library *will have educated* people if it *was destroyed* long ago. Therefore, the use of the future perfect tense, *will have educated*, does not make sense in the sentence.

5. **Review the answer choices.** The verb *will have educated* is the error in the sentence. The verb should be *had educated*. Therefore, the answer to the question is choice B.

Faulty Pronoun Case

▶ **RULE** Case is the form of a noun or pronoun that indicates its use in a sentence. A pronoun must be in the correct case for its function in a sentence.

▶ **Sample Test Question**

Directions: Read the sentence carefully. Identify the sentence error from the underlined options. If there is no error, select choice E.

After hearing the lecture by the environmentalist,
    A

several teachers and us organized a recycling program
    B   C

at our school. No error
  D   E

FOR REVIEW

To review verb tenses in greater depth, see Chapter 22, Section 1.

A Word to the Wise
Case

Case is the form of a noun or pronoun that indicates its use in a sentence. The three cases of nouns and pronouns are the nominative, the objective, and the possessive.

Language Highlights

As the English language has developed over time, some simplifying of cases has occurred. English used to have two more pronouns for speakers and writers to distinguish: *thee* and *thou*. Have students use a dictionary to find each word and identify its case. Point out that today the objective pronoun *whom* is disappearing from everyday speech, although test takers may still be expected to recognize its correct use in the objective case.

⏱ TIME SAVERS!

 On-line Exercise Bank
Have students complete the exercises on computer. The Auto Check feature will grade their work for you.

QUESTION: What is the error in the sentence?

A   After hearing

B   several teachers and us

C   recycling

D   at our school

E   No error

STEPS

1. **Read the sentence carefully.** Focus your attention on the underlined words or phrases.

2. **Ask yourself: "Does any underlined word or phrase sound wrong?"** If one word or phrase definitely sounds wrong to you, you have probably identified the error in the sentence.

3. **If no words or phrases sound wrong to you, ask yourself: "Does any underlined word or phrase violate a grammar or usage rule that I have learned?"** Notice that the subject of the sentence, *several teachers and us*, seems awkward.

4. **Check the pronoun case in the subject of the sentence.** Notice that the pronoun *us* is in the objective case. As part of the compound subject of the sentence, *us* should be in the nominative case, that is, *we*. Although awkward-sounding, the subject would be grammatically correct if written *several teachers and we*. (It would, however, be more elegant to write *we organized a recycling program with several teachers.*) The error in the sentence is the faulty pronoun case, *us*. Therefore, the answer to the question is choice B.

> **FOR REVIEW**
>
> To learn about pronoun case in greater depth, see Chapter 23, Section 1.

---

2. Guide students through the steps identified on the student page 859.

3. Review with students the three cases for nouns or pronouns: nominative, objective, and possessive. Invite students to list the appropriate forms on the board under each case. For example, nominative pronouns are *I, he, she, we, they,* and *it*; objective are *me, him, her, us, them,* and *it*; possessive are *my, his, her, our, their,* and *its*.

4. Read aloud the question with the students. Reinforce their understanding of pronoun case. Ask students to explain why the compound subject *teachers and us* must be in the nominative case. In order to make the error more obvious, reread the sentence, using only the pronoun as the subject: *us organized a recycling program.* Have students read this revised sentence with the nominative case pronoun, *we*.

Customize for
Less Advanced Students

Ask students to use their own words to tell why the underlined phrase *several teachers and us* is incorrect in the sample question. Help them to see that these words are the subject of a clause and need to be in the nominative case. Ask students to write another sentence beginning with the subject *Several teachers and we*. Ask volunteers to write their sentences on the board.

Explain that *several teachers and us* would be correct in a different sentence, and offer this example: *The recycling program was started by several teachers and us.* Point out that the underlined words in this sentence are in the objective case because they follow the preposition *by*. Ask students to compose another sentence in which *several teachers and us* is used correctly. Have volunteers share their sentences by writing them on the board or reading them aloud.

⬦ TEST-TAKING TIP

Remind students that they will be provided with an answer sheet on most standardized tests and that they must mark their answers carefully on it. A common error students can avoid is marking the correct answer in the space for a different item. One way to guard against this problem is to mark the answer first in the test booklet, to note the number of the item and to mentally pair that number and the answer, as in, "17A," and then to find the space for item 17 on the answer sheet and mark A. By marking their answer in the test booklet, students also have an advantage when proofreading their answers during any remaining time they might have.

1. To introduce questions in which students choose to revise, or accept as correct, the underlined portions of a sentence.

2. To review pronoun-antecedent agreement.

3. To teach methods for identifying faulty pronoun-antecedent agreement.

Step-by-Step Teaching Guide

Strategies for Identifying Faulty Pronoun-Antecedent Agreement

1. Review the rule regarding pronoun-antecedent agreement.

2. Read aloud the directions. Remind students that the directions require them to locate an error in the sentence or determine that the sentence is correct as presented. Explain that reading the sentence twice—once without regard to the underscores, and again with the underscored words and phrases in mind—helps them focus on any grammatical errors.

3. Guide students through the steps identified on the student page.

4. Point out that the words separating a pronoun from its antecedent can cause confusion.

5. Emphasize the importance of identifying the number, person, and gender of a noun in order to establish antecedent agreement. Help students locate the compound subject *director* and *actor*, joined by *neither/nor*. Remind students that errors often occur in sentences constructed with compound pronoun elements. Review the rules regarding antecedents for pronouns joined by *and/or* and *neither/nor*. Note that in these cases, the pronoun should agree with the closest antecedent. In the sample question, the pronoun should agree with *actor*.

6. Invite volunteers to write sentences with faulty pronoun-antecedent agreement for the class to correct.

Grammar

Faulty Pronoun-Antecedent Agreement

► **RULE** A pronoun must agree with its antecedent in person, number, and gender.

► **Sample Test Question**

Directions: Read the sentence carefully. Identify the sentence error from the underlined options. If there is no error, select choice E.

Surprisingly, neither the director <u>nor the actor</u> had
  A   B

<u>previously</u> won an award <u>for their work</u>. <u>No error</u>
  C   D   E

QUESTION: What is the error in the sentence?

  A   Surprisingly,

  B   nor the actor

  C   previously

  D   for their work

  E   No error

S T E P S

1. **Read the sentence carefully.** Focus your attention on the underlined words or phrases.
2. **Ask yourself: "Does any underlined word or phrase sound wrong?"** If one word or phrase definitely sounds wrong to you, you have probably identified the error in the sentence.
3. **If no words or phrases sound wrong to you, ask yourself: "Does any underlined word or phrase violate a grammar or usage rule that I have learned?"** Notice that the subject of the sentence is *neither the director nor the actor*. This construction makes the subject singular.
4. **Identify any pronouns in the sentence.** The pronoun in the sentence is *their*. It refers to the antecedent, *neither the director nor the actor*.
5. **Check for pronoun-antecedent agreement.** The antecedent is singular. Therefore, the pronoun that refers to it must also be singular. However, the pronoun *their* is plural. This pronoun is an error.
6. **Review the answer choices.** The faulty pronoun case represented by the use of *their* is the error in the sentence. Therefore, the answer to the question is choice D.

A Word to the Wise
Antecedent

The word *antecedent* comes from the Latin words *ante*, which means "before," and *cedere*, which means "to go." Therefore, *antecedent* means "that which comes before." An antecedent is a noun that comes before a pronoun. The pronoun refers to it and must match it in person, number, and gender.

TIP: If a sentence doesn't sound right to you, check to see if the awkwardness is caused by faulty pronoun-antecedent agreement. Remember to check the words that link two or more antecedents.

FOR REVIEW

To learn about pronoun-antecedent agreement in greater depth, see Chapter 24, Section 2.

Customize for
Gifted/Talented Students

Have students assume that in the sample test question, the director is female and the actor is male. How would students rewrite the sentence to make it error-free? (. . . won an award for *his* work.) Tell students to check for errors by crossing out all words from *neither* through *nor* and check for agreement. In the sample, this would be "Surprisingly, ~~neither the director nor~~ the actor had previously won an award for their work." The error in agreement becomes clear.

✎ TEST-TAKING TIP

Tell students to pay special attention to possessive pronouns in test questions about usage. Review the possessive pronouns: *his, her, hers, its, my, mine, your, yours, their, theirs.*

Remind students that if a possessive pronoun is in an underlined part of a test question, they should check that it agrees with the noun it refers to. They should remember that apostrophes should not be used in possessive pronouns, and belong only in contractions.

Shifts in Pronoun Person

RULE When using a pronoun to refer to an antecedent more than once in a sentence, use the same pronoun. A shift in pronoun person creates confusion.

Sample Test Question

Directions: Read the sentence carefully. Identify the sentence error from the underlined option. If there is no error, select choice E.

When the seniors took their class trip to Quebec, they discovered that
<u>A</u>   <u>B</u>
you needed extra time to pass through customs. No error
<u>C</u>   <u>D</u>   <u>E</u>

QUESTION: What is the error in the sentence?

  A   When the seniors
  B   to Quebec
  C   you needed
  D   to pass through customs
  E   No error

S T E P S

1. **Read the sentence carefully.** Focus your attention on the underlined words or phrases.
2. **Ask yourself: "Does any underlined word or phrase sound wrong?"** If one word or phrase definitely sounds wrong to you, you have probably identified the error in the sentence.
3. **If no words or phrases sound wrong to you, ask yourself: "Does any underlined word or phrase violate a grammar or usage rule that I have learned?"**
4. **Identify the subject of the sentence.** The subject of the sentence is *the seniors*.
5. **Identify the pronouns in the sentence.** There are three: *their*, *they*, and *you*. Notice that they all refer to the antecedent *the seniors*.
6. **Check for pronoun-antecedent agreement.** The pronouns *their* and *they* correctly refer to *the seniors*. However, the pronoun *you* is incorrectly used. Because the pronoun refers to the seniors, the pronoun should be *they*.
7. **Review the answer choices.** The error in the sentence is the choice of the pronoun *you*. Therefore, the answer to the question is choice C.

TIP: If a sentence sounds correct to you, look closely at the pronouns used. Errors in pronoun-antecedent agreement are common in everyday spoken language and may not stand out when you hear a sentence in your mind.

FOR REVIEW

To learn about pronoun choice in greater depth, see Chapter 24, Section 2.

Language Highlights

Writers of fiction often write with a first-person or a third-person narrator. Inexperienced writers may inadvertently shift pronouns, but careful writers are consistent in their point of view. Have students find a work of fiction told from a first-person point of view and a work told from a third-person point of view. Ask volunteers to read aloud random passages so that listeners can identify each pronoun person.

⏱ TIME SAVERS!

💻 **On-line Exercise Bank**
Have students complete the exercises on computer. The Auto Check feature will grade their work for you.

Lesson Objectives

1. To introduce questions in which students choose to revise, or accept as correct, the underlined portions of a sentence.
2. To identify and correct shifts in pronoun person.
3. To teach how to identify a shift in pronoun person in a sentence.

Step-by-Step Teaching Guide

Strategies for Identifying Shifts in Pronoun Person

1. Review the rule regarding pronoun person. Discuss the importance of maintaining consistent pronoun number, person, and gender in a sentence.
2. Ask a volunteer to read aloud the directions and sample question.
3. Guide students through the steps identified on the student page.
4. Analyze the use of the pronouns *their, they*, and *you* to replace the plural noun *seniors*. Point out the shift from third person to second person. Have students explain how that shift occurred. Review the correct use of first-, second-, and third-person singular and plural pronouns.
5. Explain that pronoun shifts often involve the second-person pronoun *you*. Clarify that *you* is used only when the reference is to the reader or the listener.
6. To provide additional practice, write sentences with faulty pronoun shifts on the board and challenge students to correct the error. Examples:

   When *Sue and Jacob* asked about the class trip, *they* learned that *you* had to put down a deposit by Friday. (*You* is a faulty pronoun shift that should be changed to *they*.)

   If people watch what *they* eat, *you* can lose weight. (*You* is a faulty pronoun shift that should be changed to *they*.)

Lesson Objectives

1. To introduce questions in which students choose to revise, or accept as correct, the underlined portions of a sentence.

2. To review using parallel grammatical structure in comparisons.

3. To guide students in identifying faulty parallelism.

Strategies for Identifying Faulty Parellism

1. Review the rule of parallel structure in comparisons. Remind students that unbalanced comparisons can make a sentence illogical.

2. Read aloud the directions and sample question with students.

3. Guide students through the steps identified on the student page.

4. Clarify that symphonies by certain composers are being compared. Ask students why the comparison of *symphonies* to *Joseph Haydn* is unbalanced and illogical.

5. Emphasize faulty comparisons must be rephrased with parallel or equivalent grammatical elements to make them balanced and logical. Comparisons must be complete as well as balanced.

6. Invite volunteers to write faulty comparison sentences on the board. Challenge students to identify the comparison, and then, to rephrase the sentence to correct the error. Suggest they use nouns and terms learned in science class. For example, write on the board: *The coloring of some insects is as brilliant and beautiful as birds.* Help students note that coloring is being compared to birds. To correct the comparison, they might reword to read: *The coloring of some insects is as brilliant and beautiful as the coloring of birds.*

Grammar

Faulty Parallelism

> **RULE** When one thing is compared to another in a sentence, both items should be grammatically parallel or equivalent, that is, equal in structure.

> **Sample Test Question**

Directions: Read the sentence carefully. Identify the sentence error from the underlined options. If there is no error, select choice E.

<u>My music teacher</u> told me <u>that she</u> enjoys
      A   B
<u>Ludwig van Beethoven's</u> symphonies <u>more than Joseph</u>
        C   D
<u>Haydn.</u> <u>No error</u>
             E

QUESTION: What is the error in the sentence?
  A   My music teacher
  B   that she
  C   Ludwig van Beethoven's
  D   more than Joseph Haydn
  E   No error

S T E P S

1. **Read the sentence carefully.** Focus your attention on the underlined words or phrases.
2. **Ask yourself: "Does any underlined word or phrase sound wrong?"** If one word or phrase definitely sounds wrong to you, you have probably identified the error in the sentence.
3. **If no words or phrases sound wrong to you, ask yourself: "Does any underlined word or phrase violate a grammar or usage rule that I have learned?"** Notice that the sentence compares *Ludwig van Beethoven's symphonies* to *Joseph Haydn*. A comparison must be made between two grammatically equal elements. It is illogical to compare the music of Beethoven to the person of Joseph Haydn. In order to be grammatical, the sentence should compare *Ludwig van Beethoven's symphonies* to *the symphonies of Joseph Haydn.*
4. **Review the answer choices.** The error in the sentence is the unparallel comparison. Therefore, the answer to the question is choice D.

A Word to the Wise
Parallel

The word *parallel* means "having comparable or identically structured parts." It comes from the Greek roots *-para-*, which means "beside," and *-allos-*, which means "one another."

> **FOR REVIEW**
> To learn about comparisons in greater depth, see Chapter 25, Section 2.

TEST-TAKING TIP

Emphasize that usage problems with comparisons may involve faulty parallelism, as in the sample test question. Standardized test questions may also focus on usage problems with comparative and superlative forms.

Remind students that a double comparison is incorrect, and ask for an example (Examples: *most fastest, more better*). Also, ask students to write sentences that correctly use the words *good/better/best* and *bad/worse/worst.* (Examples: The restaurant's soup is good (bad). My aunt's soup is better (worse) than the soup at the restaurant. My mom makes the best (worst) soup I've ever eaten.)

Faulty Word Choice

RULE Words that are spelled similarly or sound alike can be easily confused. Such words often have very different meanings.

Sample Test Question

Directions: Read the sentence carefully. Decide whether it is correct or whether it needs to be revised. If no revision is necessary, select choice E.

Harvey was surprised that such an imminent scholar could be so verbose and pretentious.

QUESTION: What is the correct way to rewrite the sentence?

A Pretentious and verbose though he was, Harvey was surprised that such an imminent scholar could be.

B Harvey was surprised that such an eminent scholar could make such an obvious mistake.

C Such an imminent scholar should not be so verbose or pretentious, thought Harvey with something like surprise.

D Harvey was surprised that such an eminent scholar could be so verbose and pretentious.

E No revision necessary

STEPS

1. **Read the sentence carefully.**
2. **Ask yourself: "Does the sentence sound wrong?"**
3. **Notice that this sentence has three difficult vocabulary words: *imminent*, *verbose*, and *pretentious*.** Using a knowledge of roots, you can tell that *verbose* might mean "wordy" and *pretentious* might mean "someone who likes to pretend." *Imminent* looks and sounds like *eminent*, which means "of high rank." However, *imminent* means "coming soon." *Eminent* fits the context of the sentence perfectly but *imminent* does not.
4. **Review the answer choices.** Choices A and C misuse the word *imminent*. Choice B replaces the word *imminent* with *eminent* but changes the meaning of the second half of the sentence. Choice D replaces *imminent* with *eminent*. Therefore, choice D is the answer to this question.

TIP: If you are not sure that a word is being used correctly in a sentence, try replacing it with its definition. If the new sentence does not make sense, then you have found an error.

FOR REVIEW

To learn about word choice in greater depth, see Chapter 10, Section 4.

Grammar • 863

Lesson Objectives

1. To introduce questions in which students choose to revise, or accept as correct, the underlined portion of a sentence.
2. To identify and correct faulty word choice.
3. To help students evaluate whether a sentence contains a word choice error.

Step-by-Step Teaching Guide

Strategies for Identifying Faulty Word Choice

1. Review the rule for accurate word choice.
2. Read aloud the directions with the class. Remind students to pay close attention to directions in multiple-choice questions.
3. Guide students through the steps identified on the student page.
4. Point out the difficult vocabulary words and ask students to define each word. Discuss the misuse of the word *imminent* for *eminent*.
5. Stress that word accuracy is particularly important on standardized tests. Tell students to read a sentence carefully to detect similar, but incorrect, words.
6. Review these strategies for identifying faulty word choice:

   examine prefixes, roots, and suffixes for clues to word meanings;

   study the context of a word to determine its meaning;

   look for homonyms and analyze correct usage of such commonly confused words.
7. Have students brainstorm for commonly confused words: *complement/compliment, canvas/canvass, cereal/serial, principal/principle, pedal/peddle, discreet/discrete, liable/libel, then/than*. Ask volunteers to write original sentences on the board using each pair of words correctly.

Customize for
ESL Students

Review with students that some words are easy to confuse because they look similar and may sound the same or only slightly different. Provide a few commonly confused words from this list:

Commonly Confused Words: *accept/except; adapt/adopt; angel/angle; cease/seize; council/counsel; desert/dessert; expect/suspect; formally/formerly; of/off; quite/quit/quiet; recent/resent; through/thorough/though*

Then, ask students to pair up and make a chart in which each word meaning is shown in words and pictures.

Language Highlights

Words that are commonly confused often share a root meaning. In the sample test item, the word *imminent*, meaning "about to happen," comes from a Latin root meaning "to jut out." The same Latin root appears in *eminent*, meaning "outstanding." Encourage students to invent a mnemonic to distinguish words that have similar spellings and sounds. They might recall, for example, that an *imminent* event is one that is *impending*.

1. To introduce questions in which students choose to revise, or accept as correct, the underlined portion of a sentence.

2. To review correct sentence structure and avoid mixed constructions.

3. To evaluate whether a sentence is a mixed construction and to correct the error.

Step-by-Step Teaching Guide

Strategies for Identifying Mixed Constructions

1. Refer to the rule that explains that well-written sentences have a clear structure with words carefully placed to form logical simple, compound, and complex sentences.

2. Read aloud the directions along with the students.

3. Guide students through the steps identified on the student page.

4. Read aloud the sample question. Students should recognize that while the underlined words form a complete sentence on their own, they do not make sense with the beginning part of the sentence (not underlined). Guide students to understand that this sentence incorrectly combines two sentences: *In 2003, New Hampshire lost a landmark.* and *The Old Man of the Mountain crumbled to the side of Cannon Mountain.* The conjunction *when* has been omitted from the sample sentence.

5. Review the three kinds of sentence structure explained on the student page as students look for sentence errors. Note that when two sentences are combined incorrectly, they result in a mixed construction. Describe the role of punctuation and coordinating conjunctions in properly joining two sentences.

6. Invite volunteers to write pairs of related sentences on the board. Challenge the class to combine them correctly to avoid mixed constructions. Suggested sentence pairs:

James realized it was late./

Grammar

Mixed Constructions

▶ **RULE** Every word in a sentence has a role to play, such as subject, verb, conjunction, or modifier. A single word cannot play more than one role in a sentence. Run-on sentences can sometimes be mixed constructions.

▶ **Sample Test Question**

Directions: Read the sentence carefully. Decide whether the underlined portion is correct or needs to be revised.

> In 2003, New Hampshire lost <u>the Old Man of the Mountain crumbled from the side of Cannon Mountain.</u>

QUESTION: What is the correct way to write the underlined words?

  A the Old Man of the Mountain when it crumbled from the side of Cannon Mountain.

  B the Old Man of the Mountain. Because it crumbled from the side of Cannon Mountain.

  C the Old Man of the Mountain crumbling from the side of Cannon Mountain.

  D crumbled from the side of Cannon Mountain.

  E No revision necessary

S T E P S

1. **Read the sentence carefully.** Focus your attention on the underlined words or phrases.

2. **Ask yourself: "Does any underlined word or phrase sound wrong?"** If one word or phrase definitely sounds wrong to you, you have probably identified the error in the sentence. Notice that the author seems to have started a new sentence *(the Old Man of the Mountain crumbled from the side of Cannon Mountain)* halfway through writing another sentence *(In 2003, New Hampshire lost).*

3. **Ask yourself: "Does any underlined word or phrase violate a grammar or usage rule that I have learned?"** The sentence is confusing because there is no conjunction to make the connection clear between the first part of the sentence and the second. As a result, this sentence is a mixed construction.

864 • Test Preparation Handbook

James rushed home. (When James realized it was late, he rushed home.)

Ellen wanted to watch her favorite program. /Ellen finished her homework right after supper. (Because Ellen wanted to watch her favorite program, she finished her homework right after supper.)

 TEST-TAKING TIP

Tell students that if they recognize an underlined portion of a sentence as incorrect, they should ask themselves, "What does the writer seem to be saying?" Then, they should try to come up with their own simple revision before looking at the answer choices. They may find an answer choice that comes close to their own revision. Ask students how they might have revised the underlined portion of the sentence in the sample question before looking at the answer choices.

4. **Review the answer choices.** Choice B divides the sentence into two sentences; however, the second sentence is a fragment. Choice C has the same mixed construction error as the sample sentence, with a different verb tense. Choice D places two verbs, *lost* and *crumbled* next to each other, which does not make sense. Choice A divides the sentence into an independent clause and a subordinate clause by adding *when it*. Therefore, the answer to the question is choice A.

Sentence Fragments

> **RULE**   A sentence fragment is a group of words with end punctuation that either does not have a subject or a verb or does not express a complete thought. Sentence fragments are a common error.

> **Sample Test Question**

Directions: Read the sentences carefully. Decide whether the underlined portion is correct or needs to be revised.

Joshua Tree National Park is one of the best places to see spring <u>flowers in bloom. Even though it is located</u> in the California desert.

QUESTION: What is the correct way to write the underlined words?

  A   flowers in bloom. Happily, located

  B   flowers in bloom, even though it is located

  C   flowers in bloom, when it is located

  D   flowers in bloom. Regardless of whether it is located

  E   No revision necessary

S T E P S

1. **Read the sentence carefully.** Focus your attention on the underlined words or phrases.

2. **Ask yourself: "Does any underlined word or phrase sound wrong?"** If one word or phrase definitely sounds wrong to you, you have probably identified the error in the sentence.

3. **If no words or phrases sound wrong to you, ask yourself: "Does any underlined word or phrase violate a grammar or usage rule that I have learned?"**

> **FOR REVIEW**
>
> To review sentence structure in greater depth, see Chapter 21, Section 4.

A Word to the Wise
Fragment

The word *fragment* comes from the Latin *fragere,* meaning "to break." A fragment is a broken piece of something.

Grammar • 865

Lesson Objectives

1. To introduce questions in which students choose to revise, or accept as correct, the underlined portion of a sentence.

2. To identify sentence fragments.

3. To evaluate whether a sentence is a fragment and to correct the error.

> **Step-by-Step Teaching Guide**

Strategies for Identifying Sentence Fragments

1. Review the rule regarding sentence fragments. Remind students that a sentence requires a subject and a verb, and expresses a complete thought.

2. Read aloud the directions along with students.

3. Guide students through the steps identified on student pages 865–866.

4. Read aloud the sample question. Encourage students to watch for phrases or clauses that are not complete sentences and cannot stand by themselves. Point out that the second group of words punctuated as a sentence is a fragment because it does not express a complete thought, even though it has a subject, a verb, and end punctuation. Help students understand that by adding the fragment to the preceding sentence, the fragment is eliminated.

5. Invite volunteers to write their own sentence and fragment on the board. Challenge the class to correct the fragments. Example: *Fran loves her dog, Mac. Because he is a good companion.* (Fran loves her dog, Mac, because he is a good companion.)

6. Explain that in sentences that express a command, the subject of a sentence can be understood. For example, *"Come!"* is a complete sentence, with the subject *you* implied.

1. To introduce questions in which students choose to revise, or accept as correct, the underlined portion of a sentence.

2. To review comma use in a compound sentence.

3. To review semicolon use with independent clauses.

4. To review correct paragraph structure.

5. To identify faulty punctuation, such as incorrect comma and semicolon use.

6. To evaluate whether sentences in a paragraph progress and connect logically.

Step-by-Step Teaching Guide

Strategies for Identifying Faulty Punctuation: Comma Use

1. Review the rule for using a comma before a conjunction in a compound sentence.

2. Ask a volunteer to read aloud the directions.

3. Guide students through the steps identified on student pages 866–867.

4. Read aloud the question with students. Ask students to identify the subtle differences between the multiple-choice answers. Discuss the incorrect punctuation marks. Point out that only choice D separates two complete thoughts with a comma and a conjunction in the correct order.

continued

Customize for
Less Advanced Students

Have students use the conjunctions *and* and *but* to build a variety of sentences. Ask students to work together to write five different sentences that include the clause *doctors practice medicine* from the sample test question. Then, use their sentences to discuss compound sentences and comma use.

Grammar

4. **Notice that "Even though it is located in the California desert" is not a sentence.** It is a sentence fragment.

5. **Review the answer choices.** Identify the answer choice that correctly joins the sentence fragment to the preceding sentence. Choices A and D simply reproduce a sentence fragment. Choice C does not make sense. Choice B correctly uses a comma before the conjunction *even though* to join the fragment to the preceding sentence. This solution is both grammatically correct and logical. Therefore, the answer to the question is choice B.

Faulty Punctuation: Comma Use

▶ **RULE** A comma must be used before a conjunction to separate two clauses in a compound sentence.

▶ **Sample Test Question**

Directions: Read the sentence carefully. Decide whether the underlined portion is correct or needs to be revised.

You may think that all doctors practice <u>medicine but any person with a Ph.D.</u> may use the title "Doctor."

QUESTION: What is the correct way to write the underlined words?

A medicine: but any person with a Ph.D.

B medicine; but any person with a Ph.D.

C medicine but, any person with a Ph.D.

D medicine, but any person with a Ph.D.

E No revision necessary

S T E P S

1. **Read the sentence carefully.** Focus your attention on the underlined words or phrases.

2. **Ask yourself: "Does any part of the sentence look or sound wrong?"** If one word or phrase definitely sounds wrong to you, you have probably identified the error in the sentence.

3. **If no words or phrases sound wrong to you, ask yourself: "Does any underlined word or phrase violate a grammar or usage rule that I have learned?"** Notice that the sentence is a compound sentence. The conjunction *but* correctly joins the two clauses within the sentence.

866 • Test Preparation Handbook

Sentence fragments are often subordinate clauses. To review subordinate clauses in greater depth, see Chapter 20, Section 2.

A Word to the Wise
Conjunction

The word *conjunction* comes from the Latin word *conjunctio*, which means "joining." A conjunction is a word that joins ideas within a sentence. Some examples of conjunctions are *and*, *but*, *as*, and *because*.

◇ TEST-TAKING TIP

Tell students to ask themselves these questions when they see a sentence with the words *and*, *but*, or *or* in a grammar test:

Does the conjunction connect independent clauses? *If yes, use a comma.*

Does the conjunction *and* or *or* separate items in a series? *If yes, use a comma.*

Does the conjunction start a sentence? *If yes, the sentences may need to be combined.*

Have students find sentences with the conjunctions *and, but*, or *or* in textbooks. Then, ask volunteers to choose a sentence to present to classmates as a test item, correctly written or with an introduced error.

4. **Check the punctuation of the sentence.** A comma should be placed before a conjunction to join the two clauses. This sentence does not contain a comma before the conjunction *but*. This omission is the error in the sentence.

5. **Review the answer choices.** Choices A and B can be eliminated as correct choices because they do not use a comma before the conjunction. Choice C places a comma *after* the conjunction, which is incorrect. Choice D correctly places a comma before the conjunction. Therefore, the answer to the question is choice D.

Faulty Punctuation: Semicolon Use

RULE A semicolon can be used to connect two independent clauses that are similar or contrasting in meaning.

▶ Sample Test Question

Directions: Read the sentence carefully. Decide whether the underlined portion is correct or needs to be revised.

You can drive all the way to mile zero on <u>U.S. Highway 1, the road ends</u> in Key West, Florida.

QUESTION: What is the correct way to write the underlined words?

A   U.S. Highway 1? The road ends

B   U.S. Highway 1 the road ends

C   U.S. Highway 1; the road ends

D   U.S. Highway 1 "the road ends

E   No revision necessary

S T E P S

1. **Read the sentence carefully.** Focus your attention on the underlined words or phrases.

2. **Ask yourself: "Does any underlined word or phrase look or sound wrong?"** If one word or phrase definitely sounds wrong to you, you have probably identified the error in the sentence.

3. **If no words or phrases sound wrong to you, ask yourself: "Does any underlined word or phrase violate a grammar or usage rule that I have learned?"**

Grammar • 867

FOR REVIEW

To learn about comma use in greater depth, see Chapter 28, Section 2.

Step-by Step Teaching Guide continued

5. Remind students that a compound sentence is two complete thoughts, or independent clauses, joined by a comma and a conjunction.

6. Review the difference between a compound subject or verb and a compound sentence. Emphasize that a comma is not used with compound subjects or verbs.

7. Invite volunteers to write related pairs of independent clauses on the board. Challenge the class to combine them correctly, using a comma and a coordinating conjunction (e.g., *and, but, or*). Example:

   Clauses—Sisters Lisa and Jenn loved each other. They disagreed about many things.

   Compound sentence—Sisters Lisa and Jenn loved each other, but they disagreed about many things.

Step-by-Step Teaching Guide

Strategies for Identifying Faulty Punctuation: Semicolon Use

1. Review the rule for semicolon use when joining independent clauses.

2. Read aloud the directions as students follow along.

3. Guide students through the steps identified on student pages 867–868.

4. Examine the sample question. Point out the comma that joins the two independent clauses in the underlined portion of the sentence. Have students explain why this is incorrect (when two independent clauses are joined with a comma, there must also be a conjunction).

5. Instruct students to look for the choice that correctly joins the independent clauses with a semicolon. Answer choice C is correct.

continued

Language Highlights

As its prefix *semi-* (which means "half") suggests, a semicolon resembles half a colon; it also has a function halfway between a comma and a period. Most independent clauses separated by a semicolon could also be written correctly as separate sentences, but a conjunction would be needed if a comma replaced the semicolon.

Have students rewrite the sample test sentence as two separate sentences. Then, have them rewrite the sentence with a comma and a conjunction replacing the semicolon. Ask students if they agree that the semicolon is the best option. Ask students to explain their responses.

6. Emphasize that the semicolon is used to connect two independent clauses similar in structure and meaning. Remind students that it replaces both the comma and the conjunction when it joins two independent clauses.

7. Invite volunteers to write two short sentences describing their bedroom on the board. Have the class combine these short sentences into one compound sentence joined by a semicolon. Example:

> My bedroom is small. There is barely room for a bed and a dresser. My bedroom is small; there is barely room for a bed and a dresser.

Strategies for Identifying Paragraph Structure

1. Review the rule about basic paragraph structure.

2. Read aloud the directions with students.

3. Guide students through the steps identified on student page 869.

4. Remind students that the main idea of a paragraph is often stated in the topic sentence. Point out that additional facts support, develop, or explain the idea expressed in the topic sentence. Discuss the importance of placing this support in logical sequence.

continued

Grammar

4. **Notice that the sentence contains two independent clauses.** The sentence incorrectly joins the independent clauses *You can drive all the way to mile zero on U.S. Highway 1* and *the road ends in Key West, Florida* with a comma. The comma should be replaced with a semicolon in order to make the sentence correct.

5. **Review the answer choices.** Look for the choice that correctly joins the independent clauses with a semicolon. Choices A incorrectly adds a question mark to the end of the first independent clause. Since there is nothing in the way the clause is written to suggest that it is a question, choice A is incorrect and can be eliminated. Choice B uses no punctuation at all between the clauses, which is incorrect. Choice D uses a quotation mark, which is also incorrect. Choice C places a semicolon *between the two clauses*. Therefore, the answer to the question is choice C.

Paragraph Structure

> ▶ **RULE**   A paragraph should consist of a topic sentence and supporting sentences. Each sentence should follow logically from the last.

> ▶ **Sample Test Question**

Directions: Read the passage carefully. Then, answer the question that follows.

> **(1)** Elmer Samuel Imes changed the scientific community's view of quantum theory. **(2)** Imes's research showed that quantum theory could be used to solve many important problems. **(3)** Other scientists finally understood that quantum theory was valid. **(4)** The scientific community owes a great deal to Elmer Samuel Imes's contribution.

FOR REVIEW

To learn about semicolon use in greater depth, see Chapter 28, Section 3.

TIP: When evaluating paragraphs, identify the topic sentence and look for sentences that do not support it.

✎ TEST-TAKING TIP

Tell students that they may need to evaluate a paragraph for clarity on a test. Suggest that they read the paragraph as an editor would. Explain that an editor asks, "Is anything confusing me? Are the ideas connected? Does something seem to be missing?" By asking those questions while reading the paragraph, students may anticipate the part of the paragraph that will be targeted in the question and may improve their efficiency in choosing the correct revision.

Step-by Step Teaching Guide
continued

QUESTION: In context, what is the best revision to the underlined portion of sentence 3 (reproduced below)?

<u>Other scientists finally understood</u> that quantum theory was valid.

    A   At the time, scientists knew

    B   Scientists other than Imes generally understood

    C   In fact, other scientists finally understood

    D   Because of Imes's work, other scientists finally understood

    E   No revision necessary

S T E P S

1. **Read the paragraph carefully.** Then, read the question. Focus your attention on the underlined words or phrases. Ask yourself if this portion of the sentence needs to be revised in order to make its relevance to the topic sentence clearer.

2. **Identify the topic sentence of the paragraph.** The topic sentence in this paragraph is *Elmer Samuel Imes changed the scientific community's view of quantum theory.*

3. **Ask yourself if sentence 3 follows logically from sentence 2.** Notice that there seems to be a gap in logic between the two sentences. The relationship between Imes's research and other scientists finally understanding the validity of quantum theory is unclear.

4. **Review the answer choices.** Choices A, B, and C do not revise the sentence in such a way as to explain *why* the scientists understood. Choice D uses the phrase *Because of Imes's work* to make the cause-and-effect relationship between two sentences clear. Therefore, the answer to the question is choice D.

FOR REVIEW

To review paragraph development and structure in greater depth, see Chapter 3, Section 2.

5. Encourage students to read a passage critically and identify its organizational structure.

6. Point out the cause-and-effect organization of the sample passage. Draw a flowchart on the board, showing the main idea and each supporting fact. Guide students to understand that a gap exists between the scientific research and its validity.

7. Have students review the answer choices. Instruct students to look for the choice that makes the relationship between the two sentences clear. Answer choice D is correct.

8. For additional practice in paragraph structure, invite a volunteer to write a topic sentence about an issue in your school. Challenge other students to write supporting sentences. As a class, combine the sentences into a logical sequence without any gaps.

Customize for
Gifted/Talented Students

Invite groups of four or five students to create a paragraph together. Have one student write a topic sentence on a piece of paper and then read it aloud. Have another student add a sentence that follows logically from the first and then read aloud both sentences. Each remaining student should add a sentence and then read aloud all the sentences. One student in each group should be responsible for writing a concluding sentence. Remind students that each sentence must follow logically from the last and support the topic sentence. When appropriate, students should use transitions to make the paragraph flow smoothly.

Language Highlights

The word *paragraph* comes from the Greek *paragraphein*, "to write beside." Before text was broken into separate blocks with indented first lines, a mark in the margin or in the text signaled the reader that a new idea was being introduced. Today, editing or formatting, we still use a symbol (¶) to signal the start of a new idea.

✏ TEST-TAKING TIP

Remind students of the importance of remaining calm while taking a test. When students come across an item that is difficult, sometimes they panic and make a random guess. Instead, students should remember to use the strategies for success they have already learned, such as eliminating answer choices they are sure are wrong. In this case, students might look for clues in the question. The words *in context* tell students that any revision probably relates to other parts of the paragraph, which provide the context for the sentence under discussion.

⏱ TIME SAVERS!

🖥 **On-line Exercise Bank**
Have students complete the exercises on computer. The Auto Check feature will grade their work for you.

1. To introduce questions in which students choose to revise, or accept as correct, the underlined portion of a sentence.

2. To review the use of transitional words and phrases to improve paragraph flow.

3. To evaluate whether a test passage needs revision based on the use of transitions.

Step-by-Step Teaching Guide

Strategies for Identifying Transitions Within a Paragraph

1. Review the rule for transitions. Remind students that transitions improve paragraph clarity.

2. Guide students through the steps identified on the student page.

3. Read aloud the passage with students. Ask students to identify the topic sentence and the two supporting sentences. Point out that the paragraph flows from Dickinson's unusual techniques, to her disregard for standard punctuation, to her use of dashes.

4. Discuss how a transition would connect her dislike of standard punctuation and her preference for dashes. Guide students to understand that the phrase *for example,* in choice D, logically transitions the reader from the idea in sentence 2 to its example in choice D, sentence 3.

5. Explain that stilted, choppy sentences can often be improved by effectively using transitions. Remind students to read passages critically to identify lack of clarity that can be improved with the use of transitions.

6. Read aloud the list of transition words in the Tip. Offer examples of other transitional phrases: *for example, on the other hand, even so.*

7. Write a topic sentence about a familiar literature selection on the board. Example: *My favorite books bring readers into a world that differs greatly from the real world.* Invite volunteers to write supporting sentences that include transitional words or phrases.

Grammar

Transitions Within a Paragraph

> **RULE** Transition words and transitional phrases make the connections between sentences clear. They also improve the flow of a paragraph.

> **Sample Test Question**

Directions: Read the passage carefully. Then, answer the question below.

> **(1)** Emily Dickinson used unusual techniques in her poetry. **(2)** She did not follow the standard rules of punctuation. **(3)** Dickinson used dashes to separate ideas in many of her poems.

QUESTION: In context, which is the best revision to the underlined portion of sentence 3 (reproduced below)?

Dickinson used dashes to separate ideas in many of her poems.

A   You will also find that she used dashes

B   However, Dickinson used dashes to separate ideas

C   Separate ideas she did with the use of dashes

D   For example, Dickinson used dashes to separate ideas

E   No revision necessary

S T E P S

1. **Read the paragraph carefully.** Then, read the question. Focus your attention on the underlined words or phrases. Notice that while it is it reasonably clear that sentence 3 states an example of a practice explained in sentence 2, the flow of the paragraph is rather awkward.

2. **Review the answer choices for the best revision.** A transition is needed in order to make the connection between sentences 2 and 3 clearer. Choice A does not have a transition, so it can be eliminated. Choice B contains the transition *however,* which does not make sense within the context of the paragraph. Choice C does not have a transition and rephrases the sentence in an oddly formal style that does not fit with the rest of the paragraph. Choice D uses a transitional phrase, *For example,* to indicate that what follows is an example of something described in the preceding sentence. Therefore, the answer to the question is choice D.

870 • Test Preparation Handbook

A Word to the Wise
Transition

The word *transition* comes from the Latin word *transitio,* meaning "change." A transition signals a change from one thought or idea to another.

TIP: Review common transitional words and phrases by category:

Causes: *Since, if, because, as soon as,* and *until*

Effects: *Therefore, consequently, as a result, subsequently,* and *then.*

> FOR REVIEW

To review transition words in greater depth, see Chapter 3, Section 2.

> **TEST-TAKING TIP**

Tell students that when they are looking over answer choices that show complete sentences, they should immediately eliminate any choices that seem ungrammatical. Ask students to identify the answer choice in the sample test item that should be immediately eliminated (choice C).

Writing

Introduction to the New SAT® and ACT® Writing Tests

This section will introduce you to the demands of the new SAT® essay and the ACT® essay respectively. You will read a sample prompt for each test and a student essay written for each prompt. By studying each prompt and essay, you can become familiar with what is expected of you on the essay section of either test.

The first thing to notice is that both tests require you to write a *point-of-view* or *persuasive* essay. In this type of essay, you are presented with an issue and asked to present your opinion on it. Your point of view must be clearly stated. Furthermore, you must support your argument with examples from current events, history, science, literature, and your own experience. The aim of the essay is to persuade the reader that your point of view is sound, logical, and wise. For this reason, it is always a good idea to show that you can see the other side of the issue you are discussing. When you acknowledge a point of view opposite to your own, you show maturity and the ability to reason and judge. You also strengthen your argument by showing that it is the result of careful consideration.

The Ingredients of a Persuasive Essay

Look at the table shown. It lists the ingredients of a successful persuasive or point-of-view essay.

TIP: The ACT® and the new SAT® have different time limits. The ACT® has a thirty-minute time limit for the essay while the SAT® has a twenty-five minute time limit.

Every point of view essay must contain . . .	Strategies
a clear position on the issue.	Read and reread the essay prompt. Be sure you understand what the prompt means. Then, decide your position on the issue.
three examples to support your position.	While outlining your essay, come up with at least three examples to support your position. If possible, vary the sources of your examples. For example, use one example from your personal life, another from a book you've read, and another from history.
a counterexample.	Think of one argument that someone might use if they were arguing against your position. Discuss your position with regard to this argument. Show why you find this argument weak compared to your own point of view.
clear transitions.	Make the logic of your essay clear by using transition words or phrases that show the relationship between one idea and another. Transition words include *therefore, for this reason, however,* and *in conclusion.*
a strong conclusion.	Wrap up your essay with a strong, confident closing statement.

Writing • 871

PREPARE AND ENGAGE

Interest GRABBER Ask students whether they think it is possible for someone who holds a particular opinion to have a change of heart. Talk about real-life incidents in which people may or may not change their point of view. Examples might include choosing a candidate in an election, being a fan of a particular recording artist, having a favorite restaurant, and so on. Explain that a point-of-view or persuasive essay should present strong arguments that will influence a reader to agree with the writer's opinion. The job of the essay writer is to be clear, logical, and convincing. Using some of the real-life examples, discuss reasons that might cause people to change their minds.

Activate Prior Knowledge

Ask students where they have read persuasive writing, and how they could tell it was designed to persuade. Encourage them to offer ideas about how a persuasive essay differs from other persuasive forms, such as advertisements, movie reviews, or letters to the editor.

Customize for *ESL Students*

Direct students to follow along on the chart as you read aloud each essay ingredient and its strategy. Review any words that might cause confusion, such as *position, prompt, counterexample, transition, and conclusion.* Be sure students can explain these terms in their own words and understand how the terms relate to writing a persuasive essay.

🖊 TEST-TAKING TIP

Emphasize two critical qualities that test examiners look for in persuasive essays: organization and voice. Because logical support is essential in this kind of essay, the writer must clearly connect the statement of opinion with supporting facts and examples. The writer's voice should also come through—in word choice and sentence variety. Also point out that persuasive essays are expected to be somewhat formal. The language should be natural but not too casual and should not contain slang expressions.

▶ Lesson Objectives

1. To introduce the use of charts and outlines in planning a timed essay.

2. To review strategies for planning a persuasive essay.

3. To teach methods for developing and structuring a persuasive essay in five minutes.

Strategies for Planning the Persuasive Essay

1. Review the strategy for planning a persuasive essay. Explain how students should provide at least three examples to support a position.

2. Guide students through the steps identified on the student page. Stress the importance of carefully reading the essay prompt and the assignment to find the two sides of the issue and the type of support required.

3. Explain how students can complete a chart to show pros and cons of an issue and then use it to create an outline for the position they choose.

4. Remind students that a counterexample is one that contradicts their position. To illustrate, suggest several positions related to students' experiences, such as the value of homework or early bedtimes, and invite volunteers to offer counterexamples.

5. Review the persuasive essay prompt on page 874. Invite a volunteer to create a sample chart on the board. Have students brainstorm for pro and con arguments and examples to fill in the chart. Ask the class to choose a position. Then, discuss which counterexample on the chart students would include in their essay. Stress that including a counterexample, and arguing against it, strengthens their position.

6. Emphasize that skipping the planning step for an essay can result in a disjointed argument.

Writing

Planning the Persuasive Essay

 **STRATEGY** Spend five minutes planning the essay before you begin to write. Make sure your outline includes at least three examples to support your argument.

STEPS

1. **Read the prompt and the assignment twice carefully.** Make sure you understand the issue presented in the prompt.

2. **Consider both sides of the argument.** To get started thinking critically, imagine what a person might say to prove each side of the issue. Use a graphic organizer like this one to capture your ideas.

PRO	CON
1.	1.
2.	2.
3.	3.

3. **Choose your position on the issue.** Review the chart you've completed and decide which side of the argument you will develop in your essay.

4. **Support your argument with at least three examples.** A strong essay will support each main point with an example.

5. **Include a counterexample in your outline.** Jot down the strongest argument you would make if you had to argue against the position you have chosen. In your essay, you will acknowledge the strength of this counterexample, but explain why it is not persuasive enough to make you choose the opposing point of view on the issue.

6. **Consult your outline as you write your essay.** Use it as a checklist to make sure you cover your main points and examples.

TIP: If you are given thirty minutes to complete an essay, plan to spend

- five minutes planning.
- fifteen minutes drafting.
- five minutes revising and editing.
- five minutes proofreading.

FOR REVIEW

To review planning a point-of-view essay, see Chapter 7, Section 2.

Discuss methods of outlining a position. Generate a simple outline with students in which the title states the essay position; list three examples from the pro side of the chart and one counterexample from the con side of the chart.

Integrating Writing Skills

Using students' suggestions, list issues being debated nationally or locally. Choose one, and ask students to make a PRO/CON chart summarizing the arguments on each side. Have students use this chart to create an outline for a persuasive essay on a timed test. Invite students to share and compare their outlines.

Supporting an Argument With Examples

PREP **STRATEGY** It is best to draw from a wide range of examples to support your position in a persuasive essay.

Essay prompts often ask students to support their position with examples. It is wise to pay attention to the *kinds* of examples a prompt calls for. If a prompt asks you to draw examples from a range of sources, do not draw all of your examples from one type of source. Instead, draw one example from your reading, one example from your studies (for example, history or science), and one example from your personal experience and observations.

Many students are unsure about what types of examples they can draw from a particular source. Look at the chart shown to learn more about the kinds of examples you might use in an essay.

If a prompt asks for examples from . . .	Follow this strategy for identifying strong examples.
your reading	Use your knowledge of literature to cite examples of plot lines and characters that are relevant. For example, if you are writing an essay about the individual's responsibility to society, you might cite a novel about a character who ignores his responsibility to society and what happens to him.
your studies	Use your knowledge of history or science to cite examples that are relevant. For example, if you are writing an essay about the individual's responsibility to society, you might cite the ideas in Thomas Paine's *The Rights of Man.*
your own experience	Use events that have happened to you or your family to cite relevant examples. For example, for an essay about the individual's responsibility to society, you might write about your own experience dealing with obligations to society.
your observations	Use insights into the topic from events or people you have observed. You might address your observations about social trends or about things happening in your neighborhood.

Writing • 873

665H • 873

Lesson Objectives

1. To introduce the use of a wide variety of examples in a timed essay.
2. To review strategies for supporting a persuasive position.
3. To teach methods for supporting a point of view with appropriate and varied examples.

Strategies for Supporting an Argument with Examples

1. Discuss the strategy of supporting an argument with examples. Explain that relying on one type of support in a persuasive essay can result in an unbalanced argument. Students must read directions and essay prompts carefully to determine the types of examples required in the scoring rubric.

2. Guide students through the chart on the student page. Tell students that most standardized test essays require support from their reading, studies, experiences, and observations. Explain that the term *cite* means "to quote or use as proof or support." Clarify that the phrase *your studies* refers to academic knowledge other than literature. Distinguish *observations*, or insights, from *experiences*, or events in which students have participated.

⏱ TIME SAVERS!

On-line Exercise Bank Have students complete the exercises on the computer. The Auto Check feature will grade their work for you.

✎ TEST-TAKING TIP

Explain that the prompts for persuasive essays tend to be general, so students can expect to be able to draw from a variety of reading and content areas. To prepare for an unknown prompt, they may find it helpful to memorize a list of works of literature, famous people, historical events, and current issues to retrieve sources readily as they quickly plan their essay.

Lesson Objectives

1. To introduce the format of a timed ACT® essay prompt.
2. To review strategies for writing a persuasive essay.
3. To teach methods for stating and supporting a point of view and creating a focused, logical argument.

Step-by-Step Teaching Guide

Strategies for The ACT® Writing Test

1. Review with students the rule that defines a persuasive essay. Explain that persuasive writing is tested on the new SAT® and the ACT® because it demonstrates reasoning ability.

2. Read aloud the directions.

3. Guide students through the steps for studying a model ACT® essay on the student page.

4. Emphasize that the sample writing prompt presents an issue that reasonable people may disagree about—which means that students must show their ability to weigh two sides of an issue and articulate a well-reasoned point of view.

5. Read the model essay on student page 875 aloud with students. Explain that studying models is helpful because it illustrates the features of a successful essay. Discuss students' impressions of the essay. Read the call outs and point out that they indicate things an examiner would notice.

6. Guide students through the steps for writing the ACT® essay identified on the student page.

7. To prepare students to respond to the sample writing prompt, invite a volunteer to make a PRO/CON chart on the board to help students identify possible arguments and counterexamples. Explain that *contradict* means "to express the opposite of." Remind students that a counterexample contradicts, or expresses the opposite position, and balances their point of view.

8. Ask students to create a simple outline using examples and a counterexample from the chart.

Writing

The ACT® Writing Test

> **RULE**   A persuasive essay presents the writer's point of view on an issue and supports this view with convincing arguments, examples, or details. It may even encourage readers to take action.

Directions: You have thirty minutes to write an essay on the topic assigned below.

Sample Writing Prompt

Many historians argue that it is irrelevant to study the personal lives of historic figures. They claim that one should focus on how these men and women changed the course of history. Other historians argue that learning about the private lives of historic figures gives us a richer understanding of their accomplishments and motivations. What value, if any, is there in learning about the personal lives of historic figures?

Assignment: In your essay, take a position on this question. You may write about either one of the two points of view given, or you may present a different point of view on this question. Use specific reasons and examples to support your position.

Studying a Model ACT® Essay

Here are some steps to follow to learn from a model essay.
- **Read the prompt and the assignment carefully.** Make sure you understand the issue at hand.
- **Read the model essay.** Decide whether the student does a good job of persuading you, the reader, that his point of view is valid and well thought out.
- **Read the call-outs.** Find out what an examiner might notice about the essay.

Writing the ACT® Essay

S T E P S

1. **After you have read the model essay, try out the prompt on this page yourself.** Give yourself thirty minutes to respond to the prompt.
2. **Make a short outline of what you will write.** Take time to think your plan through carefully as it will drive your essay. This step should take no longer than five minutes.
3. **As you draft, follow your outline to stay on task.**
4. **Allow for five minutes to proofread your essay.** Use the technique on page 878 to proofread your essay.
5. **Once the essay is complete, use the criteria on this page to judge your essay.**

TIP: The ACT® Writing Test is optional. It features a persuasive essay that must be completed within thirty minutes. If you take this exam, you will be asked to write an essay explaining your point of view on an issue.

How to succeed on the ACT® Writing Test

1. State a clear position on the issue.
2. Focus on the topic throughout the essay.
3. Support your position with examples.
4. Show logical reasoning through a well-organized essay.
5. Use standard written English.

FOR REVIEW

To review writing persuasive essays in greater depth, see Chapter 7.

---

9. Remind students to begin their essays by clearly stating their position on the issue addressed in the prompt. Tell students to follow their outline. Stress the importance of effective introductions and conclusions, as well as the use of transition words.

Drafting Tip

Tell students to use their five minutes of prewriting/planning time as effectively as they can to lay out the organization of their paragraphs. With just thirty minutes to produce a final essay, their first draft cannot be a rough one; it must be close to a final draft. However, with an outline in place, students can concentrate on developing coherent paragraphs.

Model Essay

The personal lives of historic figures are of no importance. They may be interesting, in the way that gossip is interesting. However, gossip—talking about people behind their backs—is not a worthwhile activity. In the same way, talking or reading or writing about the personal lives of historic figures is trivial. The fact that someone had a happy or unhappy life doesn't meaningfully add to the historic nature of his or her accomplishments.

Take Benjamin Franklin, for example. He apparently had an unhappy marriage. Does this change his involvement in the writing of the Constitution? Or in the writing and printing of *Poor Richard's Almanac*? Or his ambassadorship to France? It does not. Much has been made about Franklin's poor background. However, Franklin accomplished great things regardless of his difficult start in life. It is more interesting to focus on the impact of what he achieved than to get bogged down in his personal life story.

Sometimes the details of a historic figure's life story are used to make him or her seem more admirable. For example, Abraham Lincoln's poor family background has been used to make him seem more extraordinary. The truth is that what makes Lincoln's achievements admirable is that they are truly historical. By that I mean that his actions changed the course of history. So they are admirable on their own; we don't need to add his personal story to make them admirable.

In other instances, the details of a historic figure's life story are used to make a historic figure seem less admirable. For example, historians have researched many aspects of President Kennedy's life story that detract from his reputation. Many books have been written on this subject. However, this information does not change how Kennedy governed the nation. What made Kennedy a great president were the actions that he took as our leader. The choices he made in his private life are separate from that.

There are occasions when I can understand why a historic figure's personal life might be relevant to his or her professional life. For example, Thomas Jefferson, who was largely responsible for our Constitution (which declares all men to be free), had slaves. This is a major and disturbing contradiction. In this case, I can see some value in learning more about Jefferson's personal life. But even in this context, I think the crucial historical fact is that Jefferson's constitution got it right even if his personal life was misguided. And because the constitution contains the principle of freedom for all, it eventually helped ensure that all men and women were free in the United States.

In conclusion, I believe that historic figures ought to be judged for the actions they took that changed the course of history. Their personal lives only provide an interesting, but ultimately unimportant, insight into those public actions.

Strong and clear position on the issue.

The student writes an engaging concluding sentence that elaborates on the main idea of the first paragraph.

The student supports his argument with a reference to a historical figure.

The student further supports his argument by including another example from history.

The essay acknowledges the other side of the issue and introduces the counterexample of Thomas Jefferson.

The student effectively uses his counterexample to reinforce his original argument.

The student ends this polished essay with a concise concluding paragraph in which he powerfully sums up his argument.

Writing • 875

Teaching from the Model

1. Reread aloud the first and last sentences of the opening and concluding paragraphs. Ask students to summarize a pattern. (The writer repeats his position using different language.)

2. Then, ask a volunteer to read aloud the first and last sentence of each body paragraph. Ask these questions: *Why is each first sentence an effective introduction to the paragraph? How does each sentence relate to the writer's point of view?*

3. Note that the first sentence of paragraphs 2, 3, and 4 leads the reader into the example discussed in the paragraph, but the writer relates the example to his overall position in the last sentence of these paragraphs. Explain that the first sentence in paragraph 2— *Take Benjamin Franklin, for example*—introduces the discussion of Franklin's life, but does not clarify the relationship to the position that his personal life is of no importance historically. The last sentence of the paragraph—*It is more interesting to focus on the impact of what he achieved than to get bogged down in his personal life story*—clearly relates this example to the author's position.

4. Point out that the writer opens paragraph 5 by presenting his counterexample in relation to his overall position—*There are occasions when I can understand why a historic figure's personal life might be relevant to his or her professional life.* The writer then refutes the counterexample.

Customize for
Gifted/Talented Students

Have students cover the call outs and evaluate the model essay for its organization and voice. What do they think the writer did most effectively? Are there any improvements they might make? Suggest that students rewrite one paragraph to incorporate their own ideas for improving organization and voice.

1. To introduce the format of a timed new SAT® essay prompt.

2. To review strategies for writing a persuasive essay.

3. To teach methods for stating and supporting a point of view and creating a focused, logical argument.

Step-by-Step Teaching Guide

Strategies for the New SAT® Essay

1. Review with students the rule that defines elements of persuasive essays. Explain that reasons, examples, and details are ways of supporting and reinforcing a point of view.

2. Read aloud the directions. Note that the time frame for writing a new SAT® essay (twenty-five minutes) is shorter than for the ACT®.

3. Examine the sample prompt with students. Remind them that the prompt presents an issue that can be successfully argued from either side.

4. Guide students through the steps for studying the model essay on student page 877.

5. Read the model essay aloud with students. Discuss their initial impressions of the essay. Point out that the call outs highlight the strengths of the essay's argument, which an examiner would likely notice.

6. Read the SAT/ACT Prep note on student page 876 with students. Explain that it features elements from the rubric that examiners use to determine a score. Emphasize that half of the elements focus on the strength of the argument and half focus on the quality of the writing.

Writing

The New SAT® Essay

The new SAT® essay must be completed in twenty-five minutes. The writing prompt presents an issue. You must develop a position on the issue and write a short essay that develops and supports your point of view.

▶ **RULE** A persuasive essay opens with a statement of the writer's point of view on a topic, provides reasons why this point of view is valid, and supports these reasons with examples or details. The intent of a persuasive essay is to use a sound argument to convince the reader that the writer's point of view about a topic is valid or correct.

Directions: You have twenty-five minutes to write an essay on this issue. Think carefully about the issue presented in the following excerpt and assignment below.

Sample Writing Prompt

Increasingly, people seem to be reluctant to fulfill their obligations as members of society. More and more people tend to live their lives as though their convenience is more important than any other consideration.

Assignment: Does the existence of society depend upon people's willingness to occasionally place society's best interests before their individual concerns?

Model Essay

A society is a network of people bound to one another by their relationships and shared interests. In order for a society to function, there has to be cooperation between members. That means that occasionally the members of a society must place the needs of society before their own concerns.

Members of a society can address their personal concerns a lot of the time. For example, weekends offer free time. Some of the time, however, members of a society must honor their obligations to one another. Whether or not they want to, they must work together to help society function. They must put the needs of society before their own needs.

Even children must put their own wishes aside. Most children would prefer not to go to school. They'd rather stay home and play. However, children must go to school because that's the way the next generation of the society will be prepared to contribute to society when they are older. Adults must go to work so that they can earn money and take care of their families, pay taxes, and provide services that help other members of society. We don't get to do what we want all the time, but we do get the benefit of being a member of a community or a society.

> The essay opens by stating a clear point of view that directly addresses the prompt.

> The student illustrates her point with a strong example from her observations.

New SAT® PREP ACT®

To write the new SAT® essay successfully, your essay should

- develop a point of view on the issue.

- use logical reasoning and appropriate examples.

- be well-organized and focused.

- demonstrate good language skills and appropriate vocabulary.

- use a variety of sentence lengths.

- have relatively few errors of grammar, punctuation, or spelling.

Teaching from the Model

1. Remind students that the first paragraph of a persuasive essay must clearly show the writer's point of view on an issue. •

2. Tell students to reread the question in the sample writing prompt and the model essay opening paragraph. Ask, "What does the writer do to show he or she is focusing on the assigned question?" Explain that it is fine to introduce an essay by paraphrasing or restating the question. Point out that by adding related ideas, a writer shows that he or she is not merely copying.

When people opt out of some of these expectations, by not paying taxes or by not voting or by not going to work, society suffers. I have noticed this play out in my own experience. At our school, the PTA is barely active. The purpose of the PTA is to support the school in various ways. However, if parents don't contribute their time and energy, the school is deprived of resources and assets. That is the situation at my school, where we had to cancel our annual trip to Washington, D.C., due to lack of funds. In this way, the individual choices of members of society have a large impact.

> The student supports her point with a strong example from her experience.

There is no clearer example of this problem than in the statistics regarding voting. Just half of eligible voters vote for the President of the United States. That means that half of the population doesn't care about the future of the country. It also means that their own needs and wishes are not reflected by the leadership of the country. With so little participation in the voting process, it is little wonder that there are so many problems in society. Voting for effective leaders is one of the best ways to deal with major social problems. But if people cannot even be bothered to vote, then that is perhaps the biggest social problem of all because it means that half the population is not serious about improving their nation and society.

> The student includes an example from current events to strengthen her argument.

To conclude, society depends entirely on the cooperation of individuals. People must be willing to look beyond their own concerns and act for the greater good.

> The student closes the essay with a strong and polished statement that reiterates her main point.

Revising Tip

Tell students that when they have completed a draft, they should reread it to *hear* the sentences, fix any awkward spots, and make sure that sentence length varies. Ask students to point out some short sentences in the model essay. Examples: second paragraph—*For example, weekends offer free time;* third paragraph—*They'd rather stay home and play;* fourth paragraph—*At our school, the PTA is barely active.* Point out that these short sentences create emphasis and help hold reader interest by varying the pace and rhythm of the writing. In addition, students should pay special attention to transition words that introduce new examples, counterexamples, causes, and conclusions. Have students identify transition words in the model essay. These include *for example, however, in this way,* and *to conclude.*

Studying the Model Essay

Here are some steps to follow in order to learn from the model essay.

- **Read the prompt and the assignment carefully.** Make sure you understand the issue at hand.

- **Read the sample essay.** Decide whether the student does a good job of persuading you, the reader, that her point of view is valid and well thought out.

- **Read the call-outs.** Find out what an examiner might notice about the essay. Pay attention to the elements of the essay that are noted, such as clear and strong introductions and conclusions and the use of many types of examples.

1. To introduce the format of a timed new SAT® essay prompt.

2. To review strategies for writing a persuasive essay.

3. To teach methods for stating and supporting a point of view and creating a focused, logical argument.

4. To present techniques for proofreading timed writing essays.

Step-by-Step Teaching Guide

Strategies for Writing the New SAT® Essay

1. Guide students through the steps identified on the student page.

2. Review the sample writing prompt on student page 876.

3. Remind students that they have twenty-five minutes to plan, draft, revise, and proofread their essay.

4. Tell students to make connections with their prior knowledge and experiences related to the issue.

5. Ask a volunteer to make a PRO/CON chart on the board to help students organize arguments and counterexamples. Remind students that a counterexample contradicts, or expresses the opposite position, and balances their point of view.

6. Ask students to create a simple outline using examples and a counterexample from the chart.

7. Remind students to begin their essays by clearly stating their position on the issue addressed in the prompt and to follow their outline.

8. Introduce the proofreading acronym CUSP presented on the student page, and encourage students to review their writing to make their work error-free.

9. When students have completed their practice essays, have them check the chart of ingredients on student page 871 and the SAT/ACT Prep note on student page 876 as they evaluate their work.

Writing

Writing the SAT® Essay

S T E P S

1. **Now that you have read a model essay, try out the prompt on page 876 yourself.** Give yourself twenty-five minutes to respond to the prompt.

2. **Make a short outline of what you will write.** Take time to think your plan through carefully as it will drive your essay. This step should take no longer than five minutes.

3. **As you draft, follow your outline to be sure you stay on task.** Allow about about thirteen minutes for drafting and two minutes for revising your essay.

4. **Allow for five minutes to proofread your essay.** Use the technique below to proofread your essay in five minutes or less.

5. **Once the essay is completed, use the criteria on page 871 to evaluate your essay.**

FOR REVIEW
To review writing persuasive essays in greater depth, see Chapter 7.

Proofreading in Five Minutes

 **STRATEGY** On a timed essay, spend five minutes proofreading your essay. Since you don't have a lot of time, use the acronym *CUSP* to remember to check the following elements:

C = Capitalization: check that every sentence begins with a capital letter and that proper nouns begin with capital letters. Make sure that no words begin with capital letters unnecessarily.

U = Usage: check that your grammar and word choice are correct.

S = Spelling: check that all words are correctly spelled.

P = Punctuation: check that there are no missing or unnecessary punctuation marks.

Finally, check that your essay is neatly presented. If your writing is illegible, try to make it clearer. Check that any inserted words or sentences are neatly indicated.

878 • Test Preparation Handbook

Customize for
Less Advanced Students

To guide students in proofreading, read aloud one paragraph from the model essay as a dictation exercise. After students have written the paragraph, direct them to reread three times—for capitalization, spelling, and punctuation. Students may then compare their proofread and corrected versions with the original.

Proofreading Tip

Explain that proofreading one's own writing is challenging because all writers have a tendency to see what they intended to write instead of what is actually on the page. By checking for each kind of error methodically, rather than just rereading the whole essay, students will be more likely to find spots that need fixing.

Reflecting on Test Preparation

Now that you have reached the end of the Test Preparation Handbook, take some time to think about what aspects of test preparation were most challenging for you. Use these tips to get your ideas started.

1. Quickly flip through the pages of the Test Preparation Handbook and jot down reading, grammar, and writing topics that represent a challenge for you.

2. Once you have identified a particular problem area or areas, work through the textbook chapter on the topic. Then, review the Test Preparation Handbook so that you can learn strategies for answering questions on those topics in exams.

3. Ask your teacher for help in building your skills and accessing old standardized tests that you can use for practice.

As a tenth grader, you have a good amount of time to prepare for success on the new SAT® or the ACT®. Use this time wisely so that you can do your very best on these tests.

ASSESS

Ask students the following questions to help them sum up what they have learned about preparing for standardized tests:

1. What are three important things to remember about writing a persuasive essay on a standardized test?

2. What kinds of usage errors will you be expected to identify and fix on standardized tests?

3. What are two strategies to use when answering questions about reading passages on standardized tests?

For further review, direct students to practice tests, which are available in school libraries, public libraries, and on the World Wide Web. The ExamView questions in the On-line Exercise Bank also offer practice opportunities.

✎ TEST-TAKING TIP

Suggest that students bring a watch or sit where they can see a clock while taking a timed test. If neither option is available, tell them to request that the test proctor note the time remaining on the board every five minutes. This will allow students to keep to the schedule of five minutes for planning, fifteen or twenty minutes for writing and revising, and five minutes for proofreading their work.

Citing Sources and Preparing Manuscript

The presentation of your written work is important. Your work should be neat, clean, and easy to read. Follow your teacher's directions for placing your name and class, along with the title and date of your work, on the paper.

For handwritten work:

- Use cursive handwriting or manuscript printing, according to the style your teacher prefers. The penmanship reference below shows the accepted formation of letters in cursive writing.
- Write or print neatly.
- Write on one side of lined $8\frac{1}{2}$" x 11" paper with a clean edge. (Do not use pages torn from a spiral notebook.)
- Indent the first line of each paragraph.

- Leave a margin, as indicated by the guidelines on the lined paper. Write in a size appropriate for the lines provided. Do not write so large that the letters from one line bump into the ones above and below. Do not write so small that the writing is difficult to read.
- Write in blue or black ink.
- Number the pages in the upper right corner.
- You should not cross out words on your final draft. Recopy instead. If your paper is long, your teacher may allow you to make one or two small changes by neatly crossing out the text to be deleted and using a caret [^] to indicate replacement text. Alternatively, you might make one or two corrections neatly with correction fluid. If you find yourself making more than three corrections, consider recopying the work.

PENMANSHIP REFERENCE

For word-processed or typed documents:

- Choose a standard, easy-to-read font.
- Type or print on one side of unlined $8\frac{1}{2}$" x 11" paper.
- Set the margins for the side, top, and bottom of your paper at approximately one inch. Most word-processing programs have a default setting that is appropriate.
- Double-space the document.
- Indent the first line of each paragraph.
- Number the pages in the upper right corner. Many word-processing programs have a header feature that will do this for you automatically.

- If you discover one or two errors after you have typed or printed, use correction fluid if your teacher allows such corrections. If you have more than three errors in an electronic file, consider making the corrections to the file and reprinting the document. If you have typed a long document, your teacher may allow you to make a few corrections by hand. If you have several errors, however, consider retyping the document.

For research papers:

Follow your teacher's directions for formatting formal research papers. Most papers will have the following features:

- Title page
- Table of Contents or Outline
- Works-Cited List

Sybil Luddington: Female Paul Revere

Megan Mahoney
Language Arts
3rd Period
March 26, 20- -

Table of Contents

.... 6
.... 10
.... 12
.... 15

Cited

Incorporating Ideas From Research

Below are three common methods of incorporating the ideas of other writers into your work. Choose the most appropriate style by analyzing your needs in each case. In all cases, you must credit your source.

- **Direct Quotation:** Use quotation marks to indicate the exact words.
- **Paraphrase:** To share ideas without a direct quotation, state the ideas in your own words. While you haven't copied word-for-word, you still need to credit your source.
- **Summary:** To provide information about a large body of work—such as a speech, an editorial, or a chapter of a book— identify the writer's main idea.

Avoiding Plagiarism

Whether you are presenting a formal research paper or an opinion paper on a current event, you must be careful to give credit for any ideas or opinions that are not your own. Presenting someone else's ideas, research, or opinion as your own—even if you have rephrased it in different words—is *plagiarism*, the equivalent of academic stealing, or fraud.

You can avoid plagiarism by synthesizing what you learn: Read from several sources and let the ideas of experts help you draw your own conclusions and form your own opinions. Ultimately, however, note your own reactions to the ideas presented.

When you choose to use someone else's ideas or work to support your view, credit the source of the material. Give bibliographic information to cite your sources of the following information:

- Statistics
- Direct quotations
- Indirectly quoted statements of opinions
- Conclusions presented by an expert
- Facts available in only one or two sources

Crediting Sources

When you credit a source, you acknowledge where you found your information and you give your readers the details necessary for locating the source themselves. Within the body of the paper, you provide a short citation, a footnote number linked to a footnote, or an endnote number linked to an endnote reference. These brief references show the page numbers on which you found the information. To make your paper more formal, prepare a reference list at the end of the paper to provide full bibliographic information on your sources. These are two common types of reference lists:

- A **bibliography** provides a listing of all the resources you consulted during your research.
- A **works-cited list** indicates the works you have referenced in your paper.

Choosing a Format for Documentation

The type of information you provide and the format in which you provide it depend on what your teacher prefers. These are the most commonly used styles:

- **Modern Language Association (MLA) Style** This is the style used for most papers at the middle-school and high-school level and for most language arts papers.
- **American Psychological Association (APA) Style** This is used for most papers in the social sciences and for most college-level papers.
- ***Chicago Manual of Style*** (CMS) **Style** This is preferred by some teachers.

On the following pages, you'll find sample citation formats for the most commonly cited materials. Each format calls for standard bibliographic information. The difference is in the order of the material presented in each entry and the punctuation required.

MLA Style for Listing Sources

Book with one author	Pyles, Thomas. *The Origins and Development of the English Language.* 2nd ed. New York: Harcourt Brace Jovanovich, Inc., 1971.
Book with two or three authors	McCrum, Robert, William Cran, and Robert MacNeil. *The Story of English.* New York: Penguin Books, 1987.
Book with an editor	Truth, Sojourner. *Narrative of Sojourner Truth.* Ed. Margaret Washington. New York: Vintage Books, 1993.
Book with more than three authors or editors	Donald, Robert B., et al. *Writing Clear Essays.* Upper Saddle River, NJ: Prentice-Hall, Inc., 1996.
A single work from an anthology	Hawthorne, Nathaniel. "Young Goodman Brown." *Literature: An Introduction to Reading and Writing.* Ed. Edgar V. Roberts and Henry E. Jacobs. Upper Saddle River, NJ: Prentice-Hall, Inc., 1998. 376–385. [Indicate pages for the entire selection.]
Introduction in a published edition	Washington, Margaret. Introduction. *Narrative of Sojourner Truth.* By Sojourner Truth. Ed. Washington. New York: Vintage Books, 1993. v–xi.
Signed article in a weekly magazine	Wallace, Charles. "A Vodacious Deal." *Time* 14 Feb. 2000: 63.
Signed article in a monthly magazine	Gustaitis, Joseph. "The Sticky History of Chewing Gum." *American History* Oct. 1998: 30–38.
Unsigned editorial or story	"Selective Silence." Editorial. *Wall Street Journal* 11 Feb. 2000: A14. [If the editorial or story is signed, begin with the author's name.]
Signed pamphlet	[Treat the pamphlet as though it were a book.]
Pamphlet with no author, publisher, or date	*Are You at Risk of Heart Attack?* n.p. n.d. [n.p. n.d. indicates that there is no known publisher or date]
Filmstrips, slide programs, videocassettes, DVDs, and other audiovisual media	*The Diary of Anne Frank.* Dir. George Stevens. Perf. Millie Perkins, Shelley Winters, Joseph Schildkraut, Lou Jacobi, and Richard Beymer. 1959. DVD. Twentieth Century Fox, 2004.
Radio or television program transcript	"Washington's Crossing of the Delaware." Host Liane Hansen. Guest David Hackett Fischer. *Weekend Edition Sunday.* Natl. Public Radio. WNYC, New York City. 23 Dec. 2003. Transcript.
Internet	"Fun Facts About Gum." NACGM site. National Association of Chewing Gum Manufacturers. 19 Dec. 1999. <http://www.nacgm.org/consumer/funfacts.html>. [Indicate the date of last update if known and the date you accessed the information. Content and addresses at Web sites change frequently.]
Newspaper	Thurow, Roger. "South Africans Who Fought for Sanctions Now Scrap for Investors." *Wall Street Journal* 11 Feb. 2000: A1+ [For a multipage article that does not appear on consecutive pages, write only the first page number on which it appears, followed by a plus sign.]
Personal interview	Smith, Jane. Personal interview. 10 Feb. 2000.
CD (with multiple publishers)	Simms, James, ed. *Romeo and Juliet.* By William Shakespeare. CD-ROM. Oxford: Attica Cybernetics Ltd.; London: BBC Education; London: HarperCollins Publishers, 1995.
Article from an encyclopedia	Askeland, Donald R. "Welding." *World Book Encyclopedia.* 1991 ed.

APA Style for Listing Sources

The list of citations for APA is referred to as a Reference List and not a bibliography.

Book with one author	Pyles, T. (1971). *The Origins and Development of the English Language* (2nd ed.). New York: Harcourt Brace Jovanovich, Inc.
Book with two or three authors	McCrum, R., Cran, W., & MacNeil, R. (1987). *The Story of English.* New York: Penguin Books.
Book with an editor	Truth, S. (1993). *Narrative of Sojourner Truth* (M. Washington, Ed.). New York: Vintage Books.
Book with more than three authors or editors	Donald, R. B., Morrow, B. R., Wargetz, L. G., & Werner, K. (1996). *Writing Clear Essays.* Upper Saddle River, New Jersey: Prentice-Hall, Inc. [With six or more authors, abbreviate second and following authors as "et al."]
A single work from an anthology	Hawthorne, N. (1998) Young Goodman Brown. In E. V. Roberts, & H. E. Jacobs (Eds.), *Literature: An Introduction to Reading and Writing* (pp. 376–385). Upper Saddle River, New Jersey: Prentice-Hall, Inc.
Introduction to a work included in a published edition	[No style is offered under this heading.]
Signed article in a weekly magazine	Wallace, C. (2000, February 14). A vodacious deal. *Time, 155,* 63. [The volume number appears in italics before the page number.]
Signed article in a monthly magazine	Gustaitis, J. (1998, October). The sticky history of chewing gum. *American History, 33,* 30–38.
Unsigned editorial or story	Selective Silence. (2000, February 11). *Wall Street Journal,* p. A14.
Signed pamphlet	Pearson Education. (2000). *LifeCare* (2nd ed.) [Pamphlet]. Smith, John: Author.
Pamphlet with no author, publisher, or date	[No style is offered under this heading.]
Filmstrips, slide programs, and videotape	Stevens, G. (Producer & Director). (1959). *The Diary of Anne Frank.* [Videotape]. (Available from Twentieth Century Fox) [If the producer and the director are two different people, list the producer first and then the director, with an ampersand (&) between them.]
Radio or television program transcript	Broderick, D. (1999, May 23). The First Immortal Generation. (R. Williams, Radio Host). *Ockham's Razor.* New York: National Public Radio.
Internet	National Association of Chewing Gum Manufacturers. Available: http://www.nacgm.org/consumer/funfacts.html [References to Websites should begin with the author's last name, if available. Indicate the site name and the available path or URL address.]
Newspaper	Thurow, R. (2000, February 11). South Africans who fought for sanctions now scrap for investors. *Wall Street Journal,* pp. A1, A4.
Personal interview	[APA states that, since interviews (and other personal communications) do not provide "recoverable data," they should only be cited in text.]
CD (with multiple publishers)	[No style is offered under this heading.]
Article from an encyclopedia	Askeland, D. R. (1991). Welding. In *World Book Encyclopedia.* (Vol. 21 pp. 190–191). Chicago: World Book, Inc.

CMS Style for Listing Sources

The following chart shows the CMS author-date method of documentation.

Book with one author	Pyles, Thomas. *The Origins and Development of the English Language,* 2nd ed. New York: Harcourt Brace Jovanovich, Inc., 1971.
Book with two or three authors	McCrum, Robert, William Cran, and Robert MacNeil. *The Story of English.* New York: Penguin Books, 1987.
Book with an editor	Truth, Sojourner. *Narrative of Sojourner Truth.* Edited by Margaret Washington. New York: Vintage Books, 1993.
Book with more than three authors or editors	Donald, Robert B., et al. *Writing Clear Essays.* Upper Saddle River, New Jersey: Prentice-Hall, Inc., 1996.
A single work from an anthology	Hawthorne, Nathaniel. "Young Goodman Brown." In *Literature: An Introduction to Reading and Writing.* Ed. Edgar V. Roberts and Henry E. Jacobs. 376–385. Upper Saddle River, New Jersey: Prentice-Hall, Inc., 1998.
Introduction to a work included in a published edition	Washington, Margaret. Introduction to *Narrative of Sojourner Truth,* by Sojourner Truth. New York: Vintage Books, 1993. [According to CMS style, you should avoid this type of entry unless the introduction is of special importance to the work.]
Signed article in a weekly magazine	Wallace, Charles. "A Vodacious Deal." *Time,* 14 February 2000, 63.
Signed article in a monthly magazine	Gustaitis, Joseph. "The Sticky History of Chewing Gum." *American History,* October 1998, 30–38.
Unsigned editorial or story	*Wall Street Journal,* 11 February 2000. [CMS states that items from newspapers are seldom listed in a bibliography. Instead, the name of the paper and the relevant dates are listed.]
Signed pamphlet	[No style is offered under this heading.]
Pamphlet with no author, publisher, or date	[No style is offered under this heading.]
Filmstrips, slide programs, and videotape	Stevens, George. (director). *The Diary of Anne Frank.* 170 min. Beverly Hills, California: Twentieth Century Fox, 1994.
Radio or television program transcript	[No style is offered under this heading.]
Internet	[No style is offered under this heading.]
Newspaper	*Wall Street Journal,* 11 February 2000. [CMS states that items from newspapers are seldom listed in a bibliography. Instead, the name of the paper and the relevant dates are listed.]
Personal interview	[CMS states that, since personal conversations are not available to the public, there is no reason to place them in the bibliography. However, the following format should be followed if they are listed.] Jane Smith. Conversation with author. Wooster, Ohio, 10 February 2000.
CD (with multiple publishers)	Shakespeare, William. *Romeo and Juliet.* Oxford: Attica Cybernetics Ltd.; London: BBC Education; London: HarperCollins Publishers, 1995. CD-ROM.
Article from an encyclopedia	[According to CMS style, encyclopedias are not listed in bibliographies.]

Sample Works-Cited List (MLA)

Carwardine, Mark, Erich Hoyt, R. Ewan Fordyce, and
Peter Gill. *The Nature Company Guides: Whales,
Dolphins, and Porpoises.* New York: Time-Life
Books, 1998.

Ellis, Richard. *Men and Whales.* New York: Knopf,
1991.

Whales in Danger. "Discovering Whales." 18 Oct. 1999.
<http://whales.magna.com.au/DISCOVER>

Sample Internal Citations (MLA)

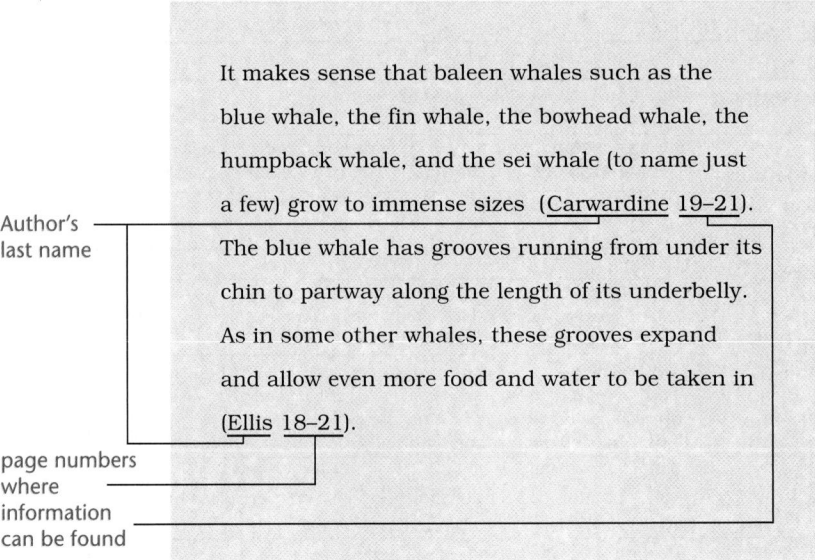

It makes sense that baleen whales such as the
blue whale, the fin whale, the bowhead whale, the
humpback whale, and the sei whale (to name just
a few) grow to immense sizes (Carwardine 19–21).

Author's last name

The blue whale has grooves running from under its
chin to partway along the length of its underbelly.
As in some other whales, these grooves expand
and allow even more food and water to be taken in
(Ellis 18–21).

page numbers
where
information
can be found

Introduction to the Internet

The Internet is a series of networks that are interconnected all over the world. The Internet allows users to have almost unlimited access to information stored on the networks. Dr. Berners-Lee, a physicist, created the Internet in the 1980's by writing a small computer program that allowed pages to be linked together using key words. The Internet was mostly text-based until 1992, when a computer program called the NCSA Mosaic (National Center for Supercomputing Applications at the University of Illinois) was created. This program was the first Web browser. The development of Web browsers greatly eased the ability of the user to navigate through all the pages stored on the Web. Very soon, the appearance of the Web was altered as well. More appealing visuals were added, and sound was also implemented. This change made the Web more user-friendly and more appealing to the general public.

Using the Internet for Research

Key Word Search

Before you begin a search, you should identify your specific topic. To make searching easier, narrow your subject to a key word or a group of key words. These are your search terms, and they should be as specific as possible. For example, if you are looking for the latest concert dates for your favorite musical group, you might use the band's name as a key word. However, if you were to enter the name of the group in the query box of the search engine, you might be presented with thousands of links to information about the group that is unrelated to your needs. You might locate such information as band member biographies, the group's history, fan reviews of concerts, and hundreds of sites with related names containing information that is irrelevant to your search. Because you used such a broad key word, you might need to navigate through all that information before you find a link or subheading for concert dates. In contrast, if you were to type in "Duplex Arena and [band name]" you would have a better chance of locating pages that contain this information.

How to Narrow Your Search

If you have a large group of key words and still don't know which ones to use, write out a list of all the words you are considering. Once you have completed the list, scrutinize it. Then, delete the words that are least important to your search, and highlight those that are most important.

These **key search connectors** can help you fine-tune your search:

AND: narrows a search by retrieving documents that include both terms. For example: *baseball AND playoffs*

OR: broadens a search by retrieving documents including any of the terms. For example: *playoffs OR championships*

NOT: narrows a search by excluding documents containing certain words. For example: *baseball NOT history of*

Tips for an Effective Search

1. Keep in mind that search engines can be case-sensitive. If your first attempt at searching fails, check your search terms for misspellings and try again.

2. If you are entering a group of key words, present them in order, from the most important to the least important key word.

3. Avoid opening the link to every single page in your results list. Search engines present pages in descending order of relevancy. The most useful pages will be located at the top of the list. However, read the description of each link before you open the page.

4. When you use some search engines, you can find helpful tips for specializing your search. Take the opportunity to learn more about effective searching.

Other Ways to Search

Using On-line Reference Sites *How*
you search should be tailored to *what* you
are hoping to find. If you are looking for
data and facts, use reference sites before
you jump onto a simple search engine. For
example, you can find reference sites to
provide definitions of words, statistics
about almost any subject, biographies,
maps, and concise information on many
topics. Some useful on-line reference sites:

    On-line libraries
    On-line periodicals
    Almanacs
    Encyclopedias

You can find these sources using subject
searches.

Conducting Subject Searches As you
prepare to go on-line, consider your subject
and the best way to find information to suit
your needs. If you are looking for general
information on a topic and you want your
search results to be extensive, consider the
subject search indexes on most search
engines. These indexes, in the form of category and subject lists, often appear on the
first page of a search engine. When you
click on a specific highlighted word, you will
be presented with a new screen containing
subcategories of the topic you chose. In the
screen shots below, the category *Sports &
Recreation* provided a second index for
users to focus a search even further.

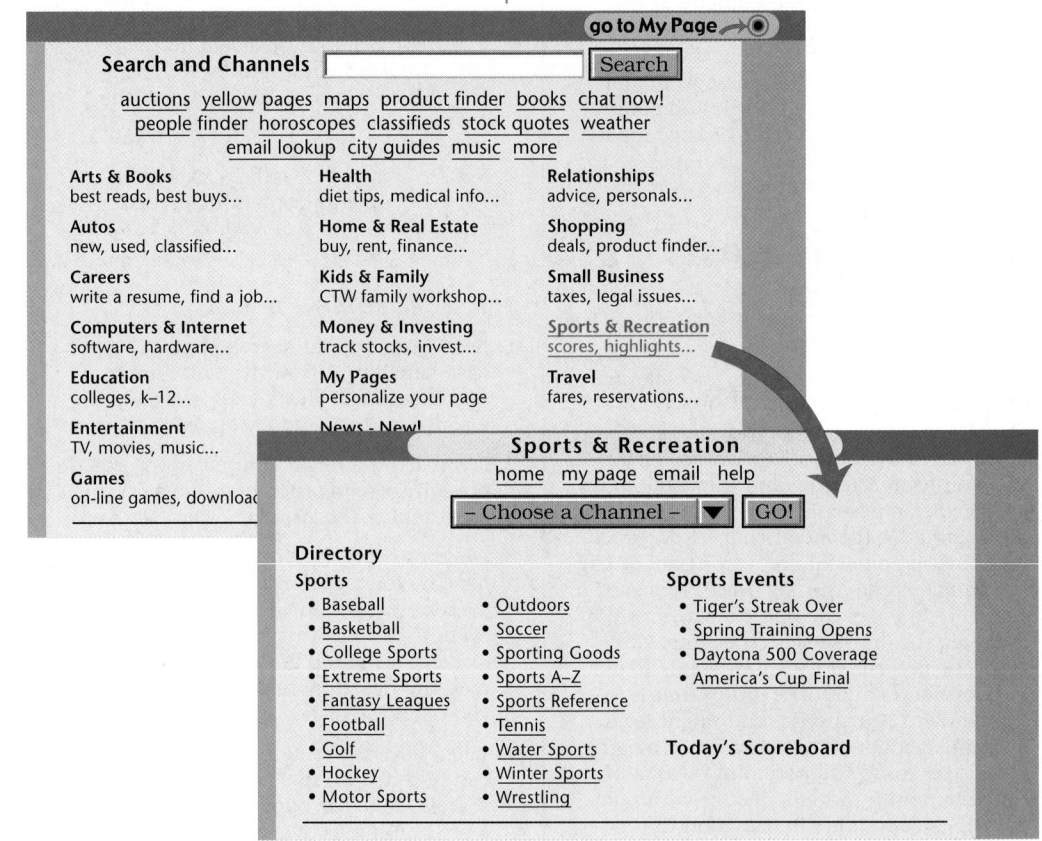

Evaluating the Reliability of Internet Resources

Just as you would evaluate the quality, bias, and validity of any other research material you locate, check the source of information you find on-line. Compare these two sites containing information on the poet and writer Langston Hughes:

Site A is a personal Web site constructed by a college student. It contains no bibliographic information or links to sites that he used. Included on the site are several poems by Langston Hughes and a student essay about the poet's use of symbolism. It has not been updated in more than six months.

Site B is a Web site constructed and maintained by the English Department of a major university. Information on Hughes is presented in a scholarly format, with a bibliography and credits for the writer. The site includes links to other sites and indicates new features that are added weekly.

For your own research, consider the information you find on Site B to be more reliable and accurate than that on Site A. Because it is maintained by experts in their field who are held accountable for their work, the university site will be a better research tool than the student-generated one.

Tips for Evaluating Internet Sources

1. Consider who constructed and who now maintains the Web page. Determine whether this author is a reputable source. Often, the URL endings indicate a source.

   - Sites ending in *.edu* are maintained by educational institutions.
   - Sites ending in *.gov* are maintained by government agencies (federal, state, or local).
   - Sites ending in *.org* are normally maintained by nonprofit organizations and agencies.
   - Sites with a *.com* ending are commercially or personally maintained.

2. Skim the official and trademarked Web pages first. It is safe to assume that the information you draw from Web pages of reputable institutions, on-line encyclopedias, on-line versions of major daily newspapers, or government-owned sites produce information as reliable as the material you would find in print. In contrast, unbranded sites or those generated by individuals tend to borrow information from other sources without providing documentation. As information travels from one source to another, the information has likely been muddled, misinterpreted, edited, or revised.

3. You can still find valuable information in the less "official" sites. Check for the writer's credentials and then consider these factors:

   - Don't let official-looking graphics or presentations fool you.
   - Make sure the information is updated enough to suit your needs. Many Web pages will indicate how recently they have been updated.
   - If the information is borrowed, see whether you can trace it back to its original source.

Respecting Copyrighted Material

Because the Internet is a relatively new and quickly growing medium, issues of copyright and ownership arise almost daily. As laws begin to govern the use and reuse of material posted on-line, they may change the way that people can access or reprint material.

Text, photographs, music, and fine art printed on-line may not be reproduced without acknowledged permission of the copyright owner.

Glossary of Internet Terms

attached file: a file containing information, such as a text document or GIF image, that is attached to an e-mail message; reports, pictures, spreadsheets, and so on transmitted to others by attaching these to messages as files

bandwidth: the amount of information, mainly compressed in bits per second (bps), that can be sent through a connection within a specific amount of time; depending on how fast your modem is, 15,000 bits (roughly one page of text) can be transferred per second

bit: a binary digit of computerized data, represented by a single digit that is either a 1 or a 0; a group of bits constitutes a byte

bookmark: a feature of your Web browser that allows you to place a "bookmark" on a Web page to which you wish to return at a later time

browser: software designed to present material accessed on the Web

bulletin-board system: a computer system that members access in order to join on-line discussion groups or to post announcements

case-sensitivity: the quality of a search engine that causes it to respond to upper- or lowercase letters in different ways

chat room: informal on-line gathering sites where people share conversations, experiences, or information on a specific topic; many chat rooms do not require users to provide their identity, so the reliability or safety of these sites is uncertain

cookie: a digitized piece of information that is sent to a Web browser by a Web server, intended to be saved on a computer; cookies gather information about the user, such as user preferences, or recent on-line purchases; a Web browser can be set to either accept or reject cookies

cyberspace: a term referring to the electronic environment connecting all computer network information with the people who use it

database: a large collection of data that have been formatted to fit a certain user-defined standard

digerati: a slang term to describe Internet experts; an offshoot of the term *literati*

download: to copy files from the Internet onto your computer

e-mail: electronic mail, or the exchange of messages via the Internet; because it is speedier than traditional mail and offers easier global access, e-mail has grown in popularity; e-mail messages can be sent to a single person or in bulk to a group of people

error message: a displayed communication or printout that reports a problem with a program or Web page

FTP site (file transfer protocol): a password-protected server on the Internet that allows the transfer of information from one computer to another

GIF (Graphic Interchange Format): a form of graphics used on the Web

graphics: information displayed as pictures or images instead of text

hits: items retrieved by a key word search; the number tracking the volume of visits to a Web site

home page: the main Web page for an individual or an organization, containing links to subpages within

HTML (HyperText Markup Language): the coding text that is the foundation for creating Web pages

interactivity: a quality of some Web pages that encourages the frequent exchange of information between user and computer

Internet: a worldwide computer network that supports services such as the World Wide Web, e-mail, and file transfer

JPEG (Joint Photo Experts Group, the developers): a file format for graphics especially suited to photographs

K: a measurement of file size or memory; short for "Kilobyte," 1,000 bytes of information (see *bit*)

key word: search term entered into the query box of a search engine to direct the results of the search

link: an icon or word on a Web page that, when clicked, transfers the user to another Web page or to a different document within the same page

login: the procedure by which users gain access to a server or a secure Web site; usually the user must enter a specific user name and password

modem: a device that transfers data to a computer through a phone line. A computer's modem connects to a server, which then sends information in the form of digital signals. The modem converts these signals into waves, for the purpose of information reception. The speed of a modem affects how quickly a computer can receive and download information

newbie: jargon used to describe Internet novices

newsgroup: an on-line discussion group, where users can post and respond to messages; the most prevalent collection of newsgroups is found on USENET

query box: the blank box in a search engine where your search terms are input

relevance ranking: the act of displaying the results of a search in the order of their relevance to the search terms

search engines: tools that help you navigate databases to locate information; search engines respond to a key word search by providing the user with a directory of multiple Web pages about the key word or containing the key word

server: a principal computer that provides services, such as storing files and providing access to the Internet, to another computer

signature: a preprogrammed section of text that is automatically added to an e-mail message

surfing: the process of reading Web pages and of moving from one Web site to another

URL (Uniform Resource Locator): a Web page's address; a URL can look like this:

http://www.phwg.phschool.com or
http://www.senate.gov/~appropriations/ labor/testimony

usenet: a worldwide system of discussion groups, or newsgroups

vanity pages: Web sites placed on-line by people to tell about themselves or their interests; vanity pages do not have any commercial or informational value

virus: a set of instructions, hidden in a computer system or transferred via e-mail or electronic files, that can cause problems with a computer's ability to perform normally

Web page: a set of information, including graphics, text, sound, and video, presented in a browser window; a Web page can be found by its URL once it is posted on the World Wide Web

Web site: a collection of Web pages that are linked together for posting on the World Wide Web

W3: a group of Internet experts, including networking professionals, academics, scientists, and corporate interests, who maintain and develop technologies and standards for the Internet

WWW (World Wide Web): a term referring to the multitude of information systems found on the Internet; this includes FTP, Gopher, telnet, and http sites

zip: a format for compressed files (files reduced in size); used to make their transmission and storage more efficient

Commonly Overused Words

When you write, use the most precise word for your meaning, not the word that comes to mind first. Consult this thesaurus to find alternatives for some commonly overused words. Consult a full-length thesaurus to find alternatives to words that do not appear here. Keep in mind that the choices offered in a thesaurus do not all mean exactly the same thing. Review all the options, and choose the one that best expresses your meaning.

about approximately, nearly, almost, approaching, close to

absolutely unconditionally, perfectly, completely, ideally, purely

activity action, movement, operation, labor, exertion, enterprise, project, pursuit, endeavor, job, assignment, pastime, scheme, task

add attach, affix, join, unite, append, increase, amplify

affect adjust, influence, transform, moderate, incline, motivate, prompt

amazing overwhelming, astonishing, startling, unexpected, stunning, dazzling, remarkable

awesome impressive, stupendous, fabulous, astonishing, outstanding

bad defective, inadequate, poor, unsatisfactory, disagreeable, offensive, repulsive, corrupt, wicked, naughty, harmful, injurious, unfavorable

basic essential, necessary, indispensable, vital, fundamental, elementary

beautiful attractive, appealing, alluring, exqui-site, gorgeous, handsome, stunning

begin commence, found, initiate, introduce, launch, originate

better preferable, superior, worthier

big enormous, extensive, huge, immense, massive

boring commonplace, monotonous, tedious, tiresome

bring accompany, cause, convey, create, conduct, deliver, produce

cause origin, stimulus, inspiration, motive

certain unquestionable, incontrovertible, unmistakable, indubitable, assured, confident

change alter, transform, vary, replace, diversify

choose select, elect, nominate, prefer, identify

decent respectable, adequate, fair, suitable

definitely unquestionably, clearly, precisely, positively, inescapably

easy effortless, natural, comfortable, undemanding, pleasant, relaxed

effective powerful, successful

emphasize underscore, feature, accentuate

end limit, boundary, finish, conclusion, finale, resolution

energy vitality, vigor, force, dynamism

enjoy savor, relish, revel, benefit

entire complete, inclusive, unbroken, integral

excellent superior, remarkable, splendid, unsurpassed, superb, magnificent

exciting thrilling, stirring, rousing, dramatic

far distant, remote

fast swift, quick, fleet, hasty, instant, accelerated

fill occupy, suffuse, pervade, saturate, inflate, stock

finish complete, conclude, cease, achieve, exhaust, deplete, consume

funny comical, ludicrous, amusing, droll, entertaining, bizarre, unusual, uncommon

get obtain, receive, acquire, procure, achieve

give bestow, donate, supply, deliver, distribute, impart

go proceed, progress, advance, move

good satisfactory, serviceable, functional, competent, virtuous, striking

great tremendous, superior, remarkable, eminent, proficient, expert

happy pleased, joyous, elated, jubilant, cheerful, delighted

hard arduous, formidable, complex, complicated, rigorous, harsh

help assist, aid, support, sustain, serve

hurt injure, harm, damage, wound, impair

important significant, substantial, weighty, meaningful, critical, vital, notable

interesting absorbing, appealing, entertaining, fascinating, thought-provoking

job task, work, business, undertaking, occupation, vocation, chore, duty, assignment

keep retain, control, possess

kind type, variety, sort, form

know comprehend, understand, realize, perceive, discern

like (adj) similar, equivalent, parallel

like (verb) enjoy, relish, appreciate

main primary, foremost, dominant

make build, construct, produce, assemble, fashion, manufacture

mean plan, intend, suggest, propose, indicate

more supplementary, additional, replenishment

new recent, modern, current, novel

next subsequently, thereafter, successively

nice pleasant, satisfying, gracious, charming

old aged, mature, experienced, used, worn, former, previous

open unobstructed, accessible

part section, portion, segment, detail, element, component

perfect flawless, faultless, ideal, consummate

plan scheme, design, system, plot

pleasant agreeable, gratifying, refreshing, welcome

prove demonstrate, confirm, validate, verify, corroborate

quick brisk, prompt, responsive, rapid, nimble, hasty

really truly, genuinely, extremely, undeniably

regular standard, routine, customary, habitual

see regard, behold, witness, gaze, realize, notice

small diminutive, miniature, minor, insignificant, slight, trivial

sometimes occasionally, intermittently, sporadically, periodically

take grasp, capture, choose, select, tolerate, endure

terrific extraordinary, magnificent, marvelous

think conceive, imagine, ponder, reflect, contemplate

try attempt, endeavor, venture, test

use employ, operate, utilize

very unusually, extremely, deeply, exceedingly, profoundly

want desire, crave, yearn, long

Commonly Overused Words • **893**

Commonly Misspelled Words

The list on these pages presents words that cause problems for many people. Some of these words are spelled according to set rules, but others follow no specific rules. As you review this list, check to see how many of the words give you trouble in your own writing. Then, read the instruction in the "Vocabulary and Spelling" chapter in the book for strategies and suggestions for improving your own spelling habits.

abbreviate	athletic	catastrophe	curious
absence	attendance	category	cylinder
absolutely	auxiliary	ceiling	deceive
abundance	awkward	cemetery	decision
accelerate	bandage	census	deductible
accidentally	banquet	certain	defendant
accumulate	bargain	changeable	deficient
accurate	barrel	characteristic	definitely
ache	battery	chauffeur	delinquent
achievement	beautiful	chief	dependent
acquaintance	beggar	clothes	descendant
adequate	beginning	coincidence	description
admittance	behavior	colonel	desert
advertisement	believe	column	desirable
aerial	benefit	commercial	dessert
affect	bicycle	commission	deteriorate
aggravate	biscuit	commitment	dining
aggressive	bookkeeper	committee	disappointed
agreeable	bought	competitor	disastrous
aisle	boulevard	concede	discipline
all right	brief	condemn	dissatisfied
allowance	brilliant	congratulate	distinguish
aluminum	bruise	connoisseur	effect
amateur	bulletin	conscience	eighth
analysis	buoyant	conscientious	eligible
analyze	bureau	conscious	embarrass
ancient	bury	contemporary	enthusiastic
anecdote	buses	continuous	entrepreneur
anniversary	business	controversy	envelope
anonymous	cafeteria	convenience	environment
answer	calendar	coolly	equipped
anticipate	campaign	cooperate	equivalent
anxiety	canceled	cordially	especially
apologize	candidate	correspondence	exaggerate
appall	capacity	counterfeit	exceed
appearance	capital	courageous	excellent
appreciate	capitol	courteous	exercise
appropriate	captain	courtesy	exhibition
architecture	career	criticism	existence
argument	carriage	criticize	experience
associate	cashier	curiosity	explanation

extension
extraordinary
familiar
fascinating
February
fiery
financial
fluorescent
foreign
forfeit
fourth
fragile
gauge
generally
genius
genuine
government
grammar
grievance
guarantee
guard
guidance
handkerchief
harass
height
humorous
hygiene
ignorant
illegible
immediately
immigrant
independence
independent
indispensable
individual
inflammable
intelligence
interfere
irrelevant
irritable
jewelry
judgment
knowledge
laboratory
lawyer
legible
legislature
leisure
liable

library
license
lieutenant
lightning
likable
liquefy
literature
loneliness
magnificent
maintenance
marriage
mathematics
maximum
meanness
mediocre
mileage
millionaire
minimum
minuscule
miscellaneous
mischievous
misspell
mortgage
naturally
necessary
negotiate
neighbor
neutral
nickel
niece
ninety
noticeable
nuclear
nuisance
obstacle
occasion
occasionally
occur
occurred
occurrence
omitted
opinion
opportunity
optimistic
outrageous
pamphlet
parallel
paralyze
parentheses

particularly
patience
permanent
permissible
perseverance
persistent
personally
perspiration
persuade
phenomenal
phenomenon
physician
pleasant
pneumonia
possess
possession
possibility
prairie
precede
preferable
prejudice
preparation
prerogative
previous
primitive
privilege
probably
procedure
proceed
prominent
pronunciation
psychology
publicly
pursue
questionnaire
realize
really
recede
receipt
receive
recognize
recommend
reference
referred
rehearse
relevant
reminiscence
renowned
repetition

restaurant
rhythm
ridiculous
sandwich
satellite
schedule
scissors
secretary
siege
solely
sponsor
subtle
subtlety
superintendent
supersede
surveillance
susceptible
tariff
temperamental
theater
threshold
truly
unmanageable
unwieldy
usage
usually
valuable
various
vegetable
voluntary
weight
weird
whale
wield
yield

Abbreviations Guide

Abbreviations, shortened versions of words or phrases, can be valuable tools in writing if you know when and how to use them. They can be very helpful in informal writing situations, such as taking notes or writing lists. However, only a few abbreviations can be used in formal writing. They are: *Mr., Mrs., Miss, Ms., Dr., A.M., P.M., A.D., B.C., M.A, B.A., Ph.D.,* and *M.D.*

The following pages provide the conventional abbreviations for a variety of words.

Abbreviations of Common Titles

Ambassador	Amb.	Lieutenant	Lt.
Attorney	Atty.	Major	Maj.
Brigadier-General	Brig. Gen.	President	Pres.
Brother	Br.	Professor	Prof.
Captain	Capt.	Representative	Rep.
Colonel	Col.	Reverend	Rev.
Commander	Cmdr.	Secretary	Sec.
Commissioner	Com.	Senator	Sen.
Corporal	Cpl.	Sergeant	Sgt.
Doctor	Dr.	Sister	Sr.
Father	Fr.	Superintendent	Supt.
Governor	Gov.	Treasurer	Treas.
Honorable	Hon.	Vice Admiral	Vice Adm.

Abbreviations of Academic Degrees

Bachelor of Arts	B.A. (or A.B.)	Esquire (lawyer)	Esq.
Bachelor of Science	B.S. (or S.B.)	Master of Arts	M.A. (or A.M.)
Doctor of Dental Surgery	D.D.S.	Master of Business Administration	M.B.A.
Doctor of Divinity	D.D.		
Doctor of Education	Ed.D.	Master of Fine Arts	M.F.A.
Doctor of Laws	LL.D.	Master of Science	M.S. (or S.M.)
Doctor of Medicine	M.D.	Registered Nurse	R.N.
Doctor of Philosophy	Ph.D.		

Abbreviations of States

State	Traditional	Postal Service	State	Traditional	Postal Service
Alabama	Ala.	AL	Montana	Mont.	MT
Alaska	Alaska	AK	Nebraska	Nebr.	NE
Arizona	Ariz.	AZ	Nevada	Nev.	NV
Arkansas	Ark.	AR	New Hampshire	N.H.	NH
California	Calif.	CA	New Jersey	N.J.	NJ
Colorado	Colo.	CO	New Mexico	N.M.	NM
Connecticut	Conn.	CT	New York	N.Y.	NY
Delaware	Del.	DE	North Carolina	N.C.	NC
Florida	Fla.	FL	North Dakota	N.Dak.	ND
Georgia	Ga.	GA	Ohio	O.	OH
Hawaii	Hawaii	HI	Oklahoma	Okla.	OK
Idaho	Ida.	ID	Oregon	Ore.	OR
Illinois	Ill.	IL	Pennsylvania	Pa.	PA
Indiana	Ind.	IN	Rhode Island	R.I.	RI
Iowa	Iowa	IA	South Carolina	S.C.	SC
Kansas	Kans.	KS	South Dakota	S.Dak.	SD
Kentucky	Ky.	KY	Tennessee	Tenn.	TN
Louisiana	La.	LA	Texas	Tex.	TX
Maine	Me.	ME	Utah	Utah	UT
Maryland	Md.	MD	Vermont	Vt.	VT
Massachusetts	Mass.	MA	Virginia	Va.	VA
Michigan	Mich.	MI	Washington	Wash.	WA
Minnesota	Minn.	MN	West Virginia	W. Va	WV
Mississippi	Miss.	MS	Wisconsin	Wis.	WI
Missouri	Mo.	MO	Wyoming	Wyo.	WY

Common Geographical Abbreviations

Apartment	Apt.	National	Natl.
Avenue	Ave.	Park, Peak	Pk.
Block	Blk.	Peninsula	Pen.
Boulevard	Blvd.	Point	Pt.
Building	Bldg.	Province	Prov.
County	Co.	Road	Rd.
District	Dist.	Route	Rte.
Drive	Dr.	Square	Sq.
Fort	Ft.	Street	St.
Island	Is.	Territory	Terr.
Mountain	Mt.		

Abbreviations of Traditional Measurements

inch(es)	in.	ounce(s)	oz.
foot, feet	ft.	pound(s)	lb.
yard(s)	yd.	pint(s)	pt.
mile(s)	mi.	quart(s)	qt.
teaspoon(s)	tsp.	gallon(s)	gal.
tablespoon(s)	tbsp.	Fahrenheit	F.

Abbreviations of Metric Measurements

millimeter(s)	mm	liter(s)	L
centimeter(s)	cm	kiloliter(s)	kL
meter(s)	m	milligram(s)	mg
kilometer(s)	km	centigram(s)	cg
milliliter(s)	mL	gram(s)	g
centiliter(s)	cL	Celsius	C

Other Commonly Used Abbreviations

about (used with dates)	c., ca., circ.	manager	mgr.
and others	et al.	manufacturing	mfg.
anonymous	anon.	market	mkt.
approximately	approx.	measure	meas.
associate, association	assoc., assn.	merchandise	mdse.
auxiliary	aux., auxil.	miles per hour	mph
bibliography	bibliog.	miscellaneous	misc.
boxes	bx(s).	money order	M.O.
bucket	bkt.	note well; take notice	N.B.
bulletin	bull.	number	no.
bushel	bu.	package	pkg.
capital letter	cap.	page	p., pg.
cash on delivery	C.O.D.	pages	pp.
department	dept.	pair(s)	pr(s).
discount	disc.	parenthesis	paren.
dozen(s)	doz.	Patent Office	pat. off.
each	ea.	piece(s)	pc(s).
edition, editor	ed.	poetical, poetry	poet.
equivalent	equiv.	private	pvt.
established	est.	proprietor	prop.
fiction	fict.	pseudonym	pseud.
for example	e.g.	published, publisher	pub.
free of charge	grat., gratis	received	recd.
General Post Office	G.P.O.	reference, referee	ref.
government	gov., govt.	revolutions per minute	rpm
graduate, graduated	grad.	rhetorical, rhetoric	rhet.
Greek, Grecian	Gr.	right	R.
headquarters	hdqrs.	scene	sc.
height	ht.	special, specific	spec.
hospital	hosp.	spelling, species	sp.
illustrated	ill., illus.	that is	i.e.
including, inclusive	incl.	treasury, treasurer	treas.
introduction, introductory	intro.	volume	vol.
italics	ital.	weekly	wkly
karat, carat	k., kt.	weight	wt.
left	L.		

Proofreading Symbols Reference

Proofreading symbols make it easier to show where changes are needed in a paper. When proofreading your own or a classmate's work, use these standard proofreading symbols.

insert	I proofred.
delete	Ip proofread.
close up space	I proof read.
delete and close up space	I proofreade.
begin new paragraph	¶ I proofread.
spell out	I proofread ⑩ papers.
lowercase	I Proofread. ⓛⓒ
capitalize	i proofread. ⓒⓐⓟ
transpose letters	I proofraed. ⓣⓡ
transpose words	I only proofread her paper. ⓣⓡ
period	I will proofread.
comma	I will proofread and she will help.
colon	We will proofread for the following errors.
semicolon	I will proofread she will help.
single quotation marks	She said, "I enjoyed the story The Invalid."
double quotation marks	She said, I enjoyed the story.
apostrophe	Did you borrow Sylvias book?
question mark	Did you borrow Sylvia's book ?/
exclamation point	You're kidding !/
hyphen	online /=/
parentheses	William Shakespeare 1564–1616

Student Publications

To share your writing with a wider audience, consider submitting it to a local, state, or national publication for student writing. Following are several magazines and Web sites that accept and publish student work.

Periodicals

Merlyn's Pen merlynspen.org

Skipping Stones P.O. Box 3939, Eugene, OR 97403
http://www.skippingstones.org

Teen Ink Box 30, Newton, MA 02461 teenink.com

On-line Publications

Kid Pub http://www.kidpub.org

MidLink Magazine http://www.ncsu.edu/midlink

Contests

Annual Poetry Contest National Federation of State Poetry Societies, Contest Chair, Kathleen Pederzani, 121 Grande Boulevard, Reading, PA 19608-9680

http://www.nfsps.com

Paul A. Witty Outstanding Literature Award International Reading Association, Special Interest Group for Reading for Gifted and Creative Students, c/o Texas Christian University, P.O. Box 297900, Fort Worth, TX 76129

Seventeen Magazine Fiction Contest *Seventeen* Magazine, 1440 Broadway 13th Floor, New York, NY 10018

The Young Playwrights Festival National Playwriting Competition Young Playwrights Inc., Dept WEB, 306 West 38th Street #300, New York, NY 10018

webmaster@youngplaywrights.org

Glossary

A

accent: the emphasis on a syllable, usually in poetry

action verb: a word that tells what action someone or something is performing (*See* linking verb.)

active voice: the voice of a verb whose subject performs an action (*See* passive voice.)

adjective: a word that modifies a noun or pronoun by telling *what kind* or *which one*

adjective clause: a subordinate clause that modifies a noun or pronoun

adjective phrase: a prepositional phrase that modifies a noun or pronoun

adverb: a word that modifies a verb, an adjective, or another adverb

adverb clause: a subordinate clause that modifies a verb, an adjective, an adverb, or a verbal by telling *where, when, in what way, to what extent, under what condition,* or *why*

adverb phrase: a prepositional phrase that modifies a verb, an adjective, or an adverb

allegory: a literary work with two or more levels of meaning—a literal level and one or more symbolic levels

alliteration: the repetition of initial consonant sounds in accented syllables

allusion: an indirect reference to a well-known person, place, event, literary work, or work of art

annotated bibliography: a research writing product that provides a list of materials on a given topic, along with publication information, summaries, or evaluations

apostrophe: a punctuation mark used to form possessive nouns and contractions

appositive: a noun or pronoun placed after another noun or pronoun to identify, rename, or explain the preceding word

appositive phrase: a noun or pronoun with its modifiers, placed next to a noun or pronoun to identify, rename, or explain the preceding word

article: one of three commonly used adjectives: *a, an,* and *the*

assonance: the repetition of vowel sounds in stressed syllables containing dissimilar consonant sounds

audience: the reader(s) a writer intends to reach

autobiographical writing: narrative writing that tells a true story about an important period, experience, or relationship in the writer's life

B

ballad: a song that tells a story (often dealing with adventure or romance) or a poem imitating such a song

bias: the attitudes or beliefs that affect a writer's ability to present a subject objectively

bibliography: a list of the sources of a research paper, including full bibliographic references for each source the writer consulted while conducting research (*See* works-cited list.)

biography: narrative writing that tells the story of an important period, experience, or relationship in a person's life, as reported by another

blueprinting: a prewriting technique in which a writer sketches a map of a home, school, neighborhood, or other meaningful place in order to spark memories or associations for further development

body paragraph: a paragraph in an essay that develops, explains, or supports the key ideas of the writing

brainstorming: a prewriting technique in which a group jots down as many ideas as possible about a given topic

C

case: the form of a noun or pronoun that indicates how it functions in a sentence

cause-and-effect writing: expository writing that examines the relationship between events, explaining how one event or situation causes another

character: a person (though not necessarily a human being) who takes part in the action of a literary work

characterization: the act of creating and developing a character through narration, description, and dialogue

citation: in formal research papers, the acknowledgment of ideas found in outside sources

classical invention: a prewriting technique in which writers gather details about a topic by analyzing the category and subcategories to which the topic belongs

clause: a group of words that has a subject and a verb

climax: the high point of interest or suspense in a literary work

coherence: a quality of written work in which all the parts flow logically from one idea to the next

colon: a punctuation mark used before an extended quotation, explanation, example, or series and after the salutation in a formal letter

comma: a punctuation mark used to separate words or groups of words

comparison-and-contrast writing: expository writing that describes the similarities and differences between two or more subjects in order to achieve a specific purpose

complement: a word or group of words that completes the meaning of a verb

compound sentence: a sentence that contains two or more independent clauses with no subordinate clauses

conclusion: the final paragraph(s) of a work of writing in which the writer may restate a main idea, summarize the points of the writing, or provide a closing remark to end the work effectively (*See* introduction, body paragraph, topical paragraph, functional paragraph.)

conflict: a struggle between opposing forces

conjugation: a list of the singular and plural forms of a verb in a particular tense

conjunction: a word used to connect other words or groups of words

connotation: the emotional associations that a word calls to mind (*See* denotation.)

consonance: the repetition of final consonant sounds in stressed syllables containing dissimilar vowel sounds

contraction: a shortened form of a word or phrase that includes an apostrophe to indicate the position of the missing letter(s)

coordinating conjunctions: words such as *and, but, nor,* and *yet* that connect similar words or groups of words

correlative conjunctions: word pairs such as *neither . . . nor, both . . . and,* and *whether . . . or* used to connect similar words or groups of words

couplet: a pair of rhyming lines written in the same meter

cubing: a prewriting technique in which a writer analyzes a subject from six specified angles: description; association; application; analysis; comparison and contrast; and evaluation

D

declarative sentence: a statement punctuated with a period

demonstrative pronouns: words such as *this, that, these,* and *those* used to single out specific people, places, or things

denotation: the objective meaning of a word; its definition independent of other associations the word calls to mind (*See* connotation.)

depth-charging: a drafting technique in which a writer elaborates on a sentence by developing a key word or idea

description: language or writing that uses sensory details to capture a subject

dialect: the form of a language spoken by people in a particular region or group

dialogue: a direct conversation between characters or people

diary: a personal record of daily events, usually written in prose

Glossary • 903

diction: a writer's word choice

direct object: a noun or a pronoun that receives the action of a transitive verb

direct quotation: a drafting technique in which writers indicate the exact words of another by enclosing them in quotation marks

documentary: nonfiction film that analyzes news events or another focused subject by combining interviews, film footage, narration, and other audio/visual components

documented essay: research writing that includes a limited number of research sources, providing full documentation parenthetically within the text

drafting: a stage of the writing process that follows prewriting and precedes revising in which a writer gets ideas on paper in a rough format

drama: a story written to be performed by actors and actresses

E

elaboration: a drafting technique in which a writer extends his or her ideas through the use of facts, examples, descriptions, details, or quotations

epic: a long narrative poem about the adventures of a god or a hero

essay: a short nonfiction work about a particular subject

etymology: the history of a word, showing where it came from and how it has evolved into its present spelling and meaning

exclamation mark: a punctuation mark used to indicate strong emotion

exclamatory sentence: a statement that conveys strong emotion and ends with an exclamation mark

exposition: writing to inform, addressing analytic purposes such as problem and solution, comparison and contrast, how-to, and cause and effect

extensive writing: writing products generated for others and from others, meant to be shared with an audience and often done for school assignments (See reflexive writing.)

F

fact: a statement that can be proved true (See opinion.)

fiction: prose writing about imaginary characters and events

figurative language: writing or speech not meant to be interpreted literally

firsthand biography: narrative writing that tells the story of an important period, experience, or relationship in a person's life, reported by a writer who knows the subject personally

five *W*'s: a prewriting technique in which writers gather details about a topic by generating answers to the following questions: *Who? What? Where? When?* and *Why?*

fragment: an incomplete idea punctuated as a complete sentence

freewriting: a prewriting technique in which a writer quickly jots down as many ideas on a topic as possible

functional paragraph: a paragraph that performs a specific role in composition, such as to arouse or sustain interest, to indicate dialogue, to make a transition (See topical paragraph.)

G

generalization: a statement that presents a rule or idea based on particular facts

gerund: a noun formed from the present participle of a verb (ending in *-ing*)

gerund phrase: a group of words containing a gerund and its modifiers or complements that function as a noun

grammar: the study of the forms of words and the way they are arranged in phrases, clauses, and sentences

H

helping verb: a verb added to another verb to make a single verb phrase that indicates the time at which an action takes place or whether it actually happens, could happen, or should happen

hexagonal writing: a technique in which a

writer analyzes a subject from six angles: literal level, personal allusions, theme, literary devices, literary allusions, and evaluation

homophones: pairs of words that sound the same as each other yet have different meanings and different spellings, such as *hear/here*

how-to writing: expository writing that explains a process by providing step-by-step directions

humanities: forms of artistic expression including, but not limited to, fine art, photography, theater, film, music, and dance

hyperbole: a deliberate exaggeration or over-statement

hyphen: a punctuation mark used to combine numbers and word parts, to join certain compound words, and to show that a word has been broken between syllables at the end of a line

I

I-Search report: a research paper in which the writer addresses the research experience in addition to presenting the information gathered

image: a word or phrase that appeals to one or more of the senses—sight, hearing, touch, taste, or smell

imagery: the descriptive language used to re-create sensory experiences, set a tone, suggest emotions, and guide readers' reactions

imperative sentence: a statement that gives an order or a direction and ends with either a period or an exclamation mark

indefinite pronoun: a word such as *anyone, each,* or *many* that refers to a person, place, or thing, without specifying which one

independent clause: a group of words that contains both a subject and a verb and that can stand by itself as a complete sentence

indirect quotation: reporting only the general meaning of what a person said or thought; quotation marks are not needed

infinitive: the form of a verb that comes after the word *to* and acts as a noun, adjective, or adverb

infinitive phrase: a phrase introduced by an infinitive that may be used as a noun, an adjective, or an adverb

interjection: a word or phrase that expresses feeling or emotion and functions independently of a sentence

interrogative pronoun: a word such as *which* and *who* that introduces a question

interrogative sentence: a question that is punctuated with a question mark

interview: an information-gathering technique in which one or more people pose questions to one or more other people who provide opinions or facts on a topic

intransitive verb: an action verb that does not take a direct object (*See* transitive verb.)

introduction: the opening paragraphs of a work of writing in which the writer may capture the readers' attention and present a thesis statement to be developed in the writing (*See* body paragraph, topical paragraph, functional paragraph, conclusion.)

invisible writing: a prewriting technique in which a writer freewrites without looking at the product until the exercise is complete; this can be accomplished at a word processor with the monitor turned off or with carbon paper and an empty ballpoint pen

irony: the general name given to literary techniques that involve surprising, interesting, or amusing contradictions

itemizing: a prewriting technique in which a writer creates a second, more focused, set of ideas based on an original listing activity. (*See* listing.)

J

jargon: the specialized words and phrases unique to a specific field

journal: a notebook or other organized writing system in which daily events and personal impressions are recorded

K

key word: the word or phrase that directs an Internet or database search

L

layering: a drafting technique in which a writer elaborates on a statement by identifying and then expanding upon a central idea or word

lead: the opening sentences of a work of writing meant to grab the reader's interest, accomplished through a variety of methods, including providing an intriguing quotation, a surprising or provocative question or fact, an anecdote, or a description

learning log: a record-keeping system in which a student notes information about new ideas

legend: a widely told story about the past that may or may not be based in fact

legibility: the neatness and readability of words

linking verb: a word that expresses its subject's state of being or condition (See action verb.)

listing: a prewriting technique in which a writer prepares a list of ideas related to a specific topic. (See itemizing.)

looping: a prewriting activity in which a writer generates follow-up freewriting based on the identification of a key word or central idea in an original freewriting exercise

lyric poem: a poem expressing the observations and feelings of a single speaker

M

main clause: a group of words that has a subject and a verb and can stand alone as a complete sentence

memoir: autobiographical writing that provides an account of a writer's relationship with a person, event, or place

metaphor: a figure of speech in which one thing is spoken of as though it were something else

meter: the rhythmic pattern of a poem

monologue: a speech or performance given entirely by one person or by one character

mood: the feeling created in the reader by a literary work or passage

multimedia presentation: a technique for sharing information with an audience by enhancing narration and explanation with media, including video images, slides, audiotape recordings, music, and fine art

N

narration: writing that tells a story

narrative poem: a poem that tells a story in verse

nominative case: the form of a noun or pronoun used as the subject of a verb, as a predicate nominative, or as the pronoun in a nominative absolute (See objective case, possessive case.)

noun: a word that names a person, place, or thing

noun clause: a subordinate clause that acts as a noun

novel: an extended work of fiction that often has a complicated plot, many major and minor characters, a unifying theme, and several settings

O

objective case: the form of a noun or pronoun used as the object of any verb, verbal, or preposition, or as the subject of an infinitive (See nominative case, possessive case.)

observation: a prewriting technique involving close visual study of an object; a writing product that reports such a study

ode: a long formal lyric poem with a serious theme

onomatopoeia: words such as *buzz* and *plop* that suggest the sounds they name

open-book test: a form of assessment in which students are permitted to use books and class notes to respond to test questions

opinion: beliefs that can be supported but not proved to be true (See fact.)

oral tradition: the body of songs, stories, and poems preserved by being passed from generation to generation by word of mouth

outline: a prewriting or study technique that allows writers or readers to organize the presentation and order of information

oxymoron: a figure of speech that fuses two contradictory or opposing ideas, such as "freezing fire" or "happy grief"

P

parable: a short, simple story from which a moral or religious lesson can be drawn

paradox: a statement that seems to be contradictory but that actually presents a truth

paragraph: a group of sentences that share a common topic or purpose and that focus on a single main idea or thought

parallelism: the placement of equal ideas in words, phrases, or clauses of similar types

paraphrase: restating an author's idea in different words, often to share information by making the meaning clear to readers

parentheses: punctuation marks used to set off asides and explanations when the material is not essential

participial phrase: a group of words made up of a participle and its modifiers and complements that acts as an adjective

participle: a form of a verb that can act as an adjective

passive voice: the voice of a verb whose subject receives an action (See active voice.)

peer review: a revising technique in which writers meet with other writers to share focused feedback on a draft

pentad: a prewriting technique in which a writer analyzes a subject from five specified points: actors, acts, scenes, agencies, and purposes

period: a punctuation mark used to end a declarative sentence, an indirect question, and most abbreviations

personal pronoun: a word such as *I, me, you, we, us, he, him, she, her, they,* and *them* that refers to the person speaking; the person spoken to; or the person, place, or thing spoken about

personification a figure of speech in which a nonhuman subject is given human characteristics

persuasion: writing or speaking that attempts to convince others to accept a position on an issue of concern to the writer

phrase: a group of words without a subject and verb that functions as one part of speech

plot: the sequence of events in narrative writing

plural: the form of a word that indicates more than one item is being mentioned

poetry: a category of writing in which the final product may make deliberate use of rhythm, rhyme, and figurative language in order to express deeper feelings than those conveyed in ordinary speech (See prose, drama.)

point of view: the perspective, or vantage point, from which a story is told

portfolio: an organized collection of writing projects, including writing ideas, works in progress, final drafts, and the writer's reflections on the work

possessive case: the form of a noun or pronoun used to show ownership (See objective case, nominative case.)

prefix: one or more syllables added to the beginning of a word root (See root, suffix.)

preposition: a word that relates a noun or pronoun that appears with it to another word in the sentence to indicate relations of time, place, causality, responsibility, and motivation

prepositional phrase: a group of words that includes a preposition and a noun or pronoun

presenting: a stage of the writing process in which a writer shares a final draft with an audience through speaking, listening, or representing activities

prewriting: a stage of the writing process in which writers explore, choose, and narrow a topic and then gather necessary details for drafting

problem-and-solution writing: expository writing that examines a problem and provides a realistic solution

Glossary • **907**

pronoun: a word that stands for a noun or for another word that takes the place of a noun

prose: a category of written language in which the end product is developed through sentences and paragraphs (*See* poetry, drama.)

publishing: a stage of the writing process in which a writer shares the written version of a final draft with an audience

punctuation: the set of symbols used to convey specific directions to the reader

purpose: the specific goal or reason a writer chooses for a writing task

Q

question mark: a punctuation mark used to end an interrogative sentence or an incomplete question

quicklist: a prewriting technique in which a writer creates an impromptu, unresearched list of ideas related to a specific topic

quotation mark: a punctuation mark used to indicate the beginning and end of a person's exact speech or thoughts

R

ratiocination: a systematic approach to the revision process that involves color-coding elements of writing for evaluation

reflective essay: autobiographical writing in which a writer shares a personal experience and then provides insight about the event

reflexive pronoun: a word that ends in *-self* or *-selves* and names the person or thing receiving an action when that person or thing is the same as the one performing the action

reflexive writing: writing generated for oneself and from oneself, not necessarily meant to be shared, in which the writer makes all decisions regarding form and purpose (*See* extensive writing.)

refrain: a regularly repeated line or group of lines in a poem or song

relative pronoun: a pronoun such as *that, which, who, whom,* or *whose* that begins a

subordinate clause and connects it to another idea in the sentence

reporter's formula: a prewriting technique in which writers gather details about a topic by generating answers to the following questions: *Who? What? Where? When?* and *Why?*

research: a prewriting technique in which writers gather information from outside sources such as library reference materials, interviews, and the Internet

research writing: expository writing that presents and interprets information gathered through an extensive study of a subject

response to literature writing: persuasive, expository, or narrative writing that presents a writer's analysis of or reactions to a published work

revising: a stage of the writing process in which a writer reworks a rough draft to improve both form and content

rhyme: the repetition of sounds at the ends of words

rhyme scheme: the regular pattern of rhyming words in a poem or stanza

rhythm: the form or pattern of words or music in which accents or beats come at certain fixed intervals

root: the base of a word (*See* prefix, suffix.)

rubric: an assessment tool, generally organized in a grid, to indicate the range of success or failure according to specific criteria

run-on sentence: two or more complete sentences punctuated incorrectly as one

S

salutation: the greeting in a formal letter

satire: writing that ridicules or holds up to contempt the faults of individuals or of groups

SEE method: an elaboration technique in which a writer presents a statement, an extension, and an elaboration to develop an idea

semicolon: a punctuation mark used to join independent clauses that are not already joined by a conjunction

sentence: a group of words with a subject and a predicate that expresses a complete thought

setting: the time and place of the action of a piece of narrative writing

short story: a brief fictional narrative told in prose

simile: a figure of speech in which *like* or *as* is used to make a comparison between two basically unrelated ideas

sonnet: a fourteen-line lyric poem with a single theme

speaker: the imaginary voice assumed by the writer of a poem

stanza: a group of lines in a poem, seen as a unit

statistics: facts presented in numerical form, such as ratios, percentages, or summaries

subject: the word or group of words in a sentence that tells whom or what the sentence is about

subordinate clause: a group of words containing both a subject and a verb that cannot stand by itself as a complete sentence

subordinating conjunction: a word used to join two complete ideas by making one of the ideas dependent on the other

suffix: one or more syllables added to the end of a word root (*See* prefix, root.)

summary: a brief statement of the main ideas and supporting details presented in a piece of writing

symbol: something that is itself and also stands for something else

T

theme: the central idea, concern, or purpose in a piece of narrative writing, poetry, or drama

thesis statement: a statement of an essay's main idea; all information in the essay supports or elaborates this idea

tone: a writer's attitude toward the readers and toward the subject

topic sentence: a sentence that states the main idea of a paragraph

topic web: a prewriting technique in which a writer generates a graphic organizer to identify categories and subcategories of a topic

topical paragraph: a paragraph that develops, explains, and supports the topic sentence related to an essay's thesis statement

transition: words, phrases, or sentences that smooth writing by indicating the relationship among ideas

transitive verb: an action verb that takes a direct object (*See* intransitive verb.)

U

unity: a quality of written work in which all the parts fit together in a complete, self-contained whole

V

verb: a word or group of words that expresses an action, a condition, or the fact that something exists while indicating the time of the action, condition, or fact

verbal: a word derived from the verb but used as a noun, adjective, or adverb (*See* gerund, infinitive, participle.)

vignette: a brief narrative characterized by precise detail

voice: the distinctive qualities of a writer's style, including diction, attitude, sentence style, and ideas

W

works-cited list: a list of the sources of a research paper, including full bibliographic references for each source named in the body of the paper (*See* bibliography.)

Index

Note: **Bold numbers** show pages on which basic definitions or rules appear.

Asides, **701**
Assessment, 304–321
  defined, **305**
  types of, **305**
  See also Rubric for Self-
    Assessment; Writing for
    Assessment
Assonance, **902**
at, **614**
Atlases, 752, 825
Attached Files, Electronic, **890**
Audiences, **902**
  choosing details for, 56, 106,
    133, 252, 284
  choosing language for, 226,
    252, 284
  choosing tone for, 106
  creating profile for, 16
  evaluating topic for, 178
  impressing, in assessment, 307
  persuading, 133, 156
  plan for identifying, 202
  purpose planner and, 82
Audiotapes, 9
  for practicing listening skills,
    749
  recording work on, 115, 747,
    748
Authors
  evaluating messages of, 222
  questioning statements by, 198
  recognizing purpose of, 50
  strategies, 3, 6, 19, 49, 77, 101,
    125, 153, 173, 197, 221,
    245, 277, 305, 323
Autobiographical Writing, 48–75
  defined, **49**, **902**
  drafting, 58–59
  editing and proofreading, 66
  model from literature, 50–53
  prewriting, 54–57
  publishing and presenting, 67
  revising, 60–65
  rubric for self-assessment, 67
  types of, 49
  See also Biographies
Awards, Names of, 638
awhile, a while, **614**

B

bad, badly, **593, 614**
Balanced Comparisons, 597
Balances, Paragraph, 20
Ballads, **902**
Bandwagon Appeals, 147, **756**

Bandwidths, Electronic, **890**
Bar Graphs, 753
barely, 609
Basic Sentence Parts, 410–439
  direct objects, **425**–428
  indirect objects, **428**–429
  objective complements, **430**
  predicates, **412**–417
  subject complements, **432**–435
  subjects, **412**–424
  test items for, 411, 438–439
  See also Effective Sentences;
    Sentences
be, 355, 529, 719
because, **615**
because, since, 211
before, 399
"begging the question," 800
being as, being that, **615**
being, having, 449
beside, besides, **615**
between, among, **613**
Bias, **902**
  in media, 756
  in nonfiction, 798
  on Web sites, 826
Bibliographies, **882, 902**
  annotated, **902**
  sample entry for, 265
  textbook, 791
Biographies, **902**
  finding, in library, 818
  firsthand, 71, **904**
  references for, 825
  See also Autobiographical
    Writing
Bits/Bytes, **890**
Blocks, Paragraph, 41
Blueprinting, 14, 54, **902**
Body, of Essays, 39
Body Paragraphs, **902**
Bookmarks, Electronic, **890**
Books
  capitalizing titles of, **642**
  citing, **691**
  finding, in library, 817–818
  punctuating titles of, 678
  See also Textbooks
"Borrowed" Words, 419, 452
Bracketing, 20
  See also Circling; Coding;
    Color-Coding; Highlighting;
    Underlining
Brainstorming, 6, **902**
bring, take, **615**
Brochures, **101**, 169

Budgets, Developing, **843**
Building Your Portfolio, 23, 25
  advertisements, 164
  anthologies, 91, 266
  assessment essays, 313
  audiotapes, 115
  book clubs, 294
  displays, 115
  e-mail, 212
  electronic essays, 188
  encouraging responses, 236
  guidance counselors, 313
  importance of, 4, 23
  Internet publications, 266
  narratives, 67
  newspapers, 143, 294
  presentations, 188, 212
  problem-and-solution essays,
    236
  storytelling, 67
  verbal sharing, 91
  Web sites, 164, 294
  See also Portfolios
Buildings, Names of, **636**
Bulletin Boards
  electronic, 301, **890**
  posting descriptions on, 115
Business Names
  apostrophes in, 714
  capitalizing, **637**
but, 397, 609, 654, 671
but, and, 61
by, buy, 163

C

Calendars, 842
Call Numbers, **817**, 818
Cameras, 9
  See also Video Cameras
Campaigns, 157
Capitalization, 630–647
  for first words, 632–634
  of parenthetical material, **702**
  of proper nouns, 342, **635**–638
  test items for, 631, 646–647
  in titles, 293, **640**–642
Captions, 792
Case-Sensitivity, Electronic, **890**
Cases, 64, **544**–551, **902**
  See also Nominative Case;
    Objective Case; Possessive Case
Catalogs
  electronic, 816
  library, **815**–816
  printed, 816

deduce, 688, 746, 836
describe, 35, 41, 43, 352, 362,
393, 398, 451, 489, 491, 493,
506, 527, 547, 564, 570, 577,
581, 630, 634, 639, 660, 679,
701, 713
distinguish, 72, 240, 272, 383,
606
draw conclusions, 555
evaluate, 144, 298, 459, 469
generalize, 51, 292
hypothesize, 270
identify, 338, 354, 372, 427,
588, 754
infer, 37, 345, 357, 445, 579,
744, 766, 770, 799
interpret, 24, 44, 68, 94, 100,
129, 148, 246, 357, 617,
769, 777, 838
make a judgment, 126, 199,
215, 249, 276, 316, 503, 594
modify, 269
reflect, 141
relate, 79, 116, 136, 181, 196,
278, 338, 448, 454, 476
respond, 341
speculate, 61, 69, 70, 76, 120,
137, 168, 198, 220, 239, 267,
295, 300, 342, 372, 457, 465,
568, 614, 638, 650, 673, 676,
695, 790, 803, 818
support, 345, 609, 781
Criticisms, Literary, 804
Cross-Curricular Connections
art, 596
fine art, 534
geography, 632
literature, 682
music, 496, 500, 590
physical education, 698
science, 370, 380, 432, 486,
552, 566, 650, 712
social studies, 340, 344, 352,
360, 392, 397, 412, 418,
425, 442, 464, 489, 520,
544, 577, 608, 612, 654, 671
Cubing, 107, 202, **903**
Cumulative Adjectives, **657**, 658
Cumulative Review
mechanics, 728–729
parts of speech, 408–409
phrases, clauses, and sentences,
516–517
usage, 628–629

Curricular Connections. *See*
Cross-Curricular Connections
Cyberspace, **890**

D

d', 720
Dance, **8**
See also Humanities, Focus on
Dangling Modifiers, **111**
Dashes, **698**–700
Databases, Electronic, 333, 827,
890
Dates, Calendar
commas with, **664**
contractions in, 719
parentheses with, **701**
Days, Names of, **636**
Declarative Sentences, **161**, **486**,
903
parentheses with, **702**
punctuating, **650**
Deductive Reasoning, 800
Degrees, Academic, 896
Degrees of Comparison, **590**–605
Deities, Capitalizing References
to, **637**
Demonstrative Adjectives, **375**
Demonstrative Pronouns, **348**,
375, **903**
Denotation, **156**, **903**
vs. connotation, **769**
in critical reading, 802
Depth-Charging, **903**
Derived Words, Dictionary, 822
Description, 100–123
defined, **101**, **903**
drafting, 110–111
editing and proofreading, 114
model from literature, 102–103
prewriting, 104–107
publishing and presenting, 115
revising, 109–113
rubric for self-assessment, 115
telling through, 85
types of, **101**
Desktop Publishing, 9
Details
choosing, for audience, 106, 284
choosing, for purpose, 53, 106,
284
circling important, 159
collecting, 227
color-coding related, 207
deleting unrelated, 60

historical, 136
order of importance for, 158
outlining, 109
underlining, 288
See also Gathering Details;
Providing Elaboration;
Supporting Details
Dewey Decimal System, **817**
Diagnostic Tests
for adjectives and adverbs, 369
for agreement, 565
for basic sentence parts, 411
for capitalization, 631
for effective sentences, 485
for modifiers, 589
for nouns, pronouns, and verbs,
339
for phrases and clauses, 441
for prepositions, conjunctions,
and interjections, 391
for pronoun usage, 543
for punctuation, 649
for usage problems, 607
for verb usage, 519
Diagraming Sentences, 730–741
adjective clauses, 739
adverb clauses, 740
appositive phrases, 735
complements, 732–733
complex sentences, 739–741
compound sentences, 738–739
compound-complex sentences,
741
conjunctions, 731–732
gerunds and gerund phrases,
736–737
infinitives and infinitive phrases,
737–738
modifiers, 730–731
noun clauses, 740
participles and participial
phrases, 735–736
prepositional phrases, 734–735
subjects and verbs, 730–731
Diagrams, 759
Dialects, 720, **903**
Dialogue, **903**
contractions in, 86, 720
developing plot with, 85
elaborating with, 59
formatting, 90
functional paragraphs with, 40
punctuating, 66, 90, **689**–690
Diaries, 808, **904**

915

Quotations
  books of, 825
  capitalizing, **632**–633
  citing for elaboration, 181
  colons with, **676**–677
  direct, 666, 882, **904**
  indirect, **682, 905**
  proofreading, 259, 264
  punctuating direct, **682**–690
  punctuating quotations within, **689**

R

Radio
  advertising on, 153
  citing series on, **692**
Ratiocination, **19, 908**
Readers' Journals, 4
Reading
  critical, for nonfiction, 798–803
  developing vocabulary through, **767**
  keeping track of, 4
  from literary writing, 804–807
  outlines for, **795**
  and replacing, 292
  sources for, 808–809
  in SQ4R method, **794**
  strategies for, **793**–794
  from textbooks, 791–792
Reading Aloud
  checking grammar and style by, 497
  checking transitions while, 186
  finding errors while, 235
  sharing short stories by, 91
Reading Comprehension in SAT/ACT, 849–855
  long passage, 850
  paired reading passages, 852
  short passage, 854
Reading Skills, 790–811
  in literary writing, 804–807
  methods and tools for, 791–797
  in nonfiction, 798–803
  question-answer relationships, 793
  sources for, 808–809
  SQ4R method (survey, question, read, recite, record, review), 794
  test questions for, 810–811, 832–833
Reading-Writing Connections
  answering readers' questions, 199

choosing details, 53
envisioning words and subjects, 102, 103
evaluating messages, 222
finding and giving context clues, 246, 249
identifying and including main points, 126, 129
identifying supporting points, 278, 281
predicting outcomes, 78, 79
providing support for messages, 223
questioning statements, 198
recognizing and using patterns, 174, 175
recognizing author's purpose, 50
using creative language, 154
Reasoning, Applying Modes of, 800–801
Reciting, in SQ4R Method, **794**
Recording, in SQ4R Method, **794**
Reference Skills
  CD-ROM references, 827
  dictionaries, **772**, 824–826
  electronic catalogs, 816
  electronic databases, 827
  Internet and media resources, 826–827
  library resources, 815–827
  note-taking, 814
  periodicals and periodical indexes, 819
  thesaurus, **772**, 823
References
  colons in, **678**
  creating and checking lists of, 264–265
  in libraries, 818
  on-line, 888
  parenthetical, **265**
  types of, **824**–825
Reflecting on Your Reading, 809
Reflecting on Your Speaking, Listening, Viewing, and Representing, 763
Reflecting on Your Study, Reference, and Test-Taking Skills, 831
Reflecting on Your Vocabulary, Spelling, and Proofreading Skills, 787
Reflecting on Your Workplace Skills and Competencies, 845
Reflecting on Your Writing
  for advertisements, 164

for assessments, 313
for autobiographical writing, 67
for cause-and-effect essays, 212
for comparison-and-contrast essays, 188
for description, 115
for persuasive essays, 143
for problem-and-solution essays, 236
for research writing, 266
for response to literature, 294
self-questioning for, 7
for short stories, 91
for writing process, 23
Reflective Essays, **908**
Reflective Listening, 750
Reflexive Pronouns
  antecedent agreement with, **580**
  defined, **346, 908**
Reflexive Writing, **12, 908**
Refrains, **908**
Regular Verbs, **523**–524
Relationships
  adding transitions for, 186
  analyzing media, 193
  cause-and-effect, 218–219
  circling to identify, 206
  clarifying with transitions, 208
  common analogy, 367, 830
  prepositions clarifying, 393
  question-answer, 793
Relative Adverbs
  adjective clauses with, **465**–466
  within clauses, 469
Relative Pronouns
  adjective clauses with, **465**–466
  clauses with, **468**
  defined, **348, 908**
Relevance Ranking, Electronic, **891**
Reliability
  evaluating, in nonfiction, 799
  of Internet resources, 889
Religions, Capitalizing References to, **637**
Reporter's Formula, **908**
Representing Skills, 758–765
Research, **908**
  creating quiz on, 241
  finding unbiased, 134
  incorporating ideas from, 882
  information sources for, 824
  investigative, 255
  for speeches, 747
  using Internet for, 252, 266, 887–889
  See also References

Index • 925

Index • 927

identifying, 399
list of, **398**
Subtopics, 796
Suffixes, **909**
  -able, 786
  adding to nouns, 370
  -ance, 142, 786
  -ball, 705
  capitalizing, **641**
  -cede, -ceed, -sede, 785
  dividing words with, **708**
  -efy, 786
  -elect, **704**
  -ence, 142, 786
  -eous, 786
  -er, -est, **591**, 592, 596
  -er, -or, 502
  hyphenating, **704**
  -ible, 786
  -ing, **455**
  -ious, 786
  -ly, **705**
  -or, -er, 502
  rules for adding, 776–777
  -self, -selves, 346, **580**
  spelling words with, 502, **783**–787
  -sy, 786
  -uous, 786
Summaries, 814, **909**
  crediting sources of, 882
  note-taking and, 818
Summary Statements, dashes in, **698**
Superlative Degree **590**–596
  test items for, 604–605
Supporting Details
  elaborating with, 309
  identifying, 137, 278, 281
  for topic sentences, 35
  See also Details; Gathering Details; Providing Elaboration
Supporting Sentences, 35
Surfing, Electronic, **891**
Surveys
  gathering details through, 227
  in investigative research, 255
  in SQ4R method, **794**
-sy, 786
Syllabification, 821
Symbols, **909**
  apostrophes in, **721**
  citing, **693**
  in media, 756

Synonyms, **770**
  in analogies, 367
  in thesaurus, 823

T

Tables, 759
Tables of Contents, 252, 791
Tag Words, 89
take, bring, **615**
Take-Home Tests, 316–317
Tape Recorders, 773
T-Charts, gathering evidence with, 134
teach, learn, **618**
Teamwork, 837
Technical Language, 746
Technology Skills in Writing, 9, 25, 169, 241, 301, 319, 845
  See also Media and Technology Skills
Television
  citing series on, **692**
  examining effects of, 217
  information media on, 755
  recording viewing habits for, 149
  See also Media and Technology Skills
Tenses. *See* Verb Tenses
Test Preparation. *See* Standardized Test Preparation Workshops; Writing for Assessment
Test-Taking Skills, 828–831
  See also Diagnostic Tests; Standardized Test Preparation Workshops
Testimonials
  including in ads, 158
  in TV commercials, 149
Testimony, Expert, 136
Tests
  computerized, 319
  open-book, **906**
  take-home, 316–317
  timed, **305**, 312
  types of, **305**, 828–830
  See also Diagnostic Tests; Standardized Test Preparation Workshops
Text-Organizers, Using to Locate Information
  glossary, 791
  graphic features, 792
  headings, 792

tables of contents, 791
textbook features, 792
textbook sections, 791
Textbooks
  appendix, 791
  chapter introduction and summary, 792
  glossary, 791
  index, 791
  pictures and captions, 792
  questions and exercises, 792
  tables of contents, 791
  titles, headings, and subheadings, 792
Texts, Electronic, 809
Textual Evidence, 136
than, then, 211, **598**, **620**
that, which, who, **620**
that, which, 235
Theater, **8**
  See also Drama; Humanities, Focus on; Performances; Plays
their, there, they're, **620**
them, **621**
Themes, **98**, **909**
  in writing process, 17
there, here, **419**–420
there, they're, their, 312
there's, here's, 570
Thesaurus, 141, 772, **823**, 845
Thesis
  developing, 310
  matching key words to, 307
  for speeches, **747**
Thesis Statements, **909**
  drafting, 286
  examples of, 39
Third-Person Pronouns, 345, 346
Thumb Indexes, 820
till, 399
Time, Expressions of
  capitalizing, **636**
  punctuating, 678, 714
  verb tenses for, 521
Time Management
  software for, 813
  tools for, **842**
  in writing process, 4, 5
Timed Tests, **305**
  checking spelling on, 312
Timed Writing Prompts
  autobiographical essay about a humorous event, 55
  cause-and-effect essay about a historical event, 201

V

Vague Words, 112
Vanity Pages, Electronic, **891**
Variety, Sentence, 160
  adding, 140
  color-coding for, 62
  creating, 311
  inverting for, 261
  writing style and, 42
Venn Diagrams, 178, 797
  See also Comparison-and-
    Contrast Order
Verb Phrases, **360**–363
Verb Tenses, **520**–533
  basic and progressive forms for,
    233, **520**
  components of, **523**–527
  conjugating, **528**–531
  faulty, 857
  fixing shifts in, 232
Verb Usage, 518–541
  active and passive voice, **534**–
    537
  tenses, **520**–533
  test items for, 519, 540–541
Verbal Phrases
  gerund, **456**–457
  infinitive, **461**
  participial, **452**–453
Verbals, **449**, **909**
  gerunds, **454**–455
  infinitives as, **458**–459
  participles, **449**–451
Verbs, **338**–339, **352**–366, **909**
  action, **352**–353, 357, **902**
  active and passive voice for, 88
  as adjectives, 377
  adverb phrases and, 444
  compound, **415**–416, 489, 654,
    667
  contractions with, **719**, 720
  helping, 360, **523**–527, 608,
    609, **904**
  identifying, 451, 455
  intransitive, **353**–354, 358, **905**
  in inverted questions, **418**
  irregular, **524**–527, 531
  linking, **355**–357, 571, **906**
  plural, 566–567
  principal parts of, **523**–527
  regular, **523**–524
  singular, 566–567
  standard usage of, 540–541
  subject agreement with, 566–
    576

  transitive, **353**–354, **909**
  vivid, 162
Video Cameras, 73, 97, 273, 762
Videotapes, 9
  creating journals with, 73
  identifying trends in, 121
  producing, 762
  producing reports on, 273
  recording presentations and
    performances on, 748
  recording speeches on, 747
  as reference tools, 827
  viewing performances on, 806
Viewing Skills
  comparing and contrasting
    newscasts, 45, 121
  comparing different media, 9,
    45, 121, 149, 193, 217
  evaluating persuasive tech-
    niques, 756
  fine art, analyzing elements, 8,
    72, 120, 272
  graphs, 753
    bar, 753
    line, 753
    pie, 754
  information media, 755–756
  maps, 752
  See also Critical Viewing Skills;
    Information Media;
    Responding to Fine Art and
    Literature; Spotlight on the
    Humanities
Vignettes, **909**
Viruses, Electronic, **891**
Visual Aids, **758**–759, 760
Vocabulary, 766–777
  development of, 767–771
  improving spelling of, 778–787
  notebooks for, 773
  systematic study for, 772–773
  test items for, 788–789
  word parts and origins in, 774–
    777
Voice
  active *vs.* passive, 87, **88**, **534**–
    537, **909**
  in good writing, 7
  See also Audiences; Purpose for
    Writing

W

Web Pages, 301, **891**
  See also Internet

Web Sites, **891**
  advertising on, 152
  art museums on, 757
  finding and evaluating, 887–
    889
  finding information at, 525
  finding new words at, 776
  government, 556
  locating and evaluating, 826
  for periodicals, 819
  student, 294
  using company, 179
  See also Internet; Search Engines
well, good, 592
went, gone, **616**
when, 398
when, where, **621**
where, 398
which, **620**
which, that, 235
who, **620**
who, whoever, **552**–553
who, whom, 552–555
whom, whomever, **552**, **554**
who's, whose, 163, 349, 552, **717**
will, 719
Word Choice, 7
  faulty, 863
  See also Revising Word Choice,
    Strategies for
Word Division, **708**–710
Word-Processing Programs
  common features of, 9
  creating flyers with, 167
  Find feature in, 187
  finding words with, 210, 211
  formatting with, 760
  organizing writing with, 58
  spell-checking with, 22, 549,
    613, 845
  thesaurus in, 823
  using Find feature of, 90
  See also Computers
Wordiness, 263
Words
  in analogies, 771
  commonly confused, 211
  commonly misspelled, 894–895
  hearing and using new, 767
  origins of, 774–777
  problem, 779
  recognizing related, 770
  systematic study of, 772–773
  within words, 780
Working With Others, 6, 835–836

The program authors would like to acknowledge the work of the following writers whose ideas have influenced the writing strategies presented in this series.

Brock, Paula. "Help Me, Quick." *R&E Journal 2* (1998): 14–16.

Burke, Kenneth. *A Grammar of Motives.* Berkeley: University of California Press, 1969.

Cooper, Charles R., and Lee Odell. *Evaluating Writing: Describing, Measuring, Judging.* Urbana, IL: National Council of Teachers of English, 1977.

Corbett, Edward P. J., and Robert J. Connors. *Classical Rhetoric for the Modern Student.* New York: Oxford University Press, Inc., 1998.

Cowan, Gregory, and Elizabeth Swan. *Writing.* New York: John Wiley, 1980.

Elbow, Peter. *Writing Without Teachers.* New York: Oxford University Press, 1973.

Emig, Janet. *The Composing Process of Twelfth Graders.* Urbana, IL: National Council of Teachers of English, 1971.

Lane, Barry. *After the End: Teaching and Learning Creative Revision.* Portsmouth, NH: Heinemann Educational Books, Inc., 1993.

Rico, Gabriele Lusser. *Writing the Natural Way.* Los Angeles: J. P. Tarcher, 1983.

Reif, Linda. *Seeking Diversity.* Portsmouth, NH: Heinemann Educational Books, Inc., 1992.

Stillman, Peter R. *Families Writing.* Cincinnati, OH: Writer's Digest Books, 1989.

Acknowledgments

Staff Credits
The people who made up the *Prentice Hall Writing and Grammar: Communication in Action* team—representing design services, editorial, editorial services, electronic publishing technology, manufacturing & inventory planning, marketing, marketing services, market research, online services & multimedia development, product planning, production services, project office, and publishing processes—are listed below. Bold type denotes the core team members.

Ellen Backstrom, Betsy Bostwick, Evonne Burgess, **Louise B. Capuano, Sarah Carroll, Megan Chill,** Katherine Clarke, Rhett Conklin, Martha Conway, Harold Crudup, **Harold Delmonte,** Libby Forsyth, Maggie Fritz, Ellen Goldblatt, Elaine Goldman, Jonathan Goldson, **Rebecca Graziano, Diana Hahn,** Rick Hickox, Kristan Hoskins, Raegan Keida, Carol Lavis, **George Lychock, Gregory Lynch,** William McAllister, Loretta Moser, Margaret Plotkin, Maureen Raymond, Gerry Schrenk, **Melissa Shustyk,** Annette Simmons, Robin Sullivan, Julie Tomasella, **Elizabeth Torjussen, Doug Utigard**

Additional Credits
Ernie Albanese, Diane Alimena, Susan Andariese, Michele Angelucci, Penny Baker, Susan Barnes, John Carle, Angelo Focaccia, Kathy Gavilanes, Beth Geschwind, Michael Goodman, Jennifer Harper, Evan Holstrom, Leanne Korszoloski, Sue Langan, Rebecca Lauth, Dave Liston, Maria Keogh, Vicki Menanteaux, Gail Meyer, Artur Mkrtchyan, LaShonda Morris, Karyl Murray, Omni-Photo Communications, Kim Ortell, Carolyn Sapontzis, Mildred Schulte, Slip Jig Image Research Services, Sunnyside, NY, Debi Taffet

Grateful acknowledgment is made to the following for copyrighted material:

Barnes & Noble Books
"Introduction to The Hunchback Of Notre Dame" from *The Hunchback Of Notre Dame* by Paul Montazzoli. Copyright © 1996 by Barnes & Noble, Inc. Reprinted by permission of Barnes & Noble, Inc.

Susan Bergholz Literary Services
From In Commemoration: One Million Volumes by Rudolfo A. Anaya from *A Million Stars By Anaya.* Copyright © by Rudolfo A. Anaya. "Tepeyac" by Sandra Cisnernos from *Vintage Cisneros.* Copyright © 2004 by Sandra Cisneros. All rights reserved.

Chana Bloch
From Pride from *The Window* by Dahlia Ravikovitch. Translated by Chana Bloch. Copyright © 1989. Reprinted by permission of Chana Bloch.

Brooks Permissions
"The Bean Eaters" by Gwendolyn Brooks from *Blacks.* Copyright © 1991 by Gwendolyn Brooks, published by Third World Press, Chicago. "Maud Martha spares the Mouse" from *Maud Martha* by Gwendolyn Brooks, copyright © 1993. Published by Third World Press, Chicago, 1993. First published by Harper and Brothers, 1953. Reprinted by consent of Brooks Permissions.

Channel One
"Growing Pains in China" by Cindy Lin from *www.channelone.com.* Reprinted by permission of Channel One.

Crown Publishers
"Damon and Pythias," from *Classic Myths to Read Aloud* by William F. Russell, copyright © 1989 by William F. Russell. Published by Crown Publishers. All rights reserved.

Bernard Edelman
From Dear America: Letters Home From Vietnam, edited by Bernard Edelman. Copyright © 1985 by The New York Vietnam Veterans Memorial Commission. Originally published by W.W. Norton & Company. Reprinted by permission of Bernard Edelman.

Harcourt, Inc.
"The Antigone of Sophocles" an English version by Dudley Fitts and Robert Fitzgerald. Copyright © 1939 by Harcourt, Inc. and renewed 1967 by Dudley Fitts.

The Barbara Hogenson Agency, Inc.
"The Dog That Bit People" from *My Life and Hard Times.* Copyright © 1933, 1961 by James Thurber.

Alfred A. Knopf, Inc.
From Swimming to Antarctica by Lynne Cox. Copyright © 2004 by Lynne Cox. All rights reserved.

The New York Times Syndication Sales Corp. Headquarters
"The Long Tale of Madonna the Iguana" from *The New York Times Magazine, Januay 16, 2000* by Linda Greenhouse. Copyright © 2000 by Linda Greenhouse. Reprinted by permission of The New York Times.

Weldon Owen Publishing
"Caring for Whales, Dolphins and Porpoises" text by Mark Carwardine from *Whales, Dolphins and Porpoises*. Copyright © 1998 by Weldon Owen Pty. Ltd. Reprinted by permission of Weldon Owen Publishing.

Oxford University Press, UK
"How Much Land Does a Man Need?" from *The Raid and Other Stories* (1999) by Tolstoy, Leo edited by Maude, Louise & Aylmer. Copyright © 1935 Oxford University Press.

G.P. Putnam's Sons
"Arthur Becomes King" Part I, Chapter XXII from *The Once and Future King* by T.H. White. Copyright © 1938, 1939, 1940, © 1958 by T. H. White renewed.

Jeremy P. Tarcher/Putnam
"Asorbic Acid" from *Napoleon's Buttons: How 17 Molecules Changed History* by Penny Le Couteur and Jay Burreson, copyright © 2003 by Micron Geological Ltd. All rights reserved.

Random House, Inc.
From A Raisin in the Sun, Act I, Scene II by Lorraine Hansberry from *A Raisin In The Sun*. Copyright © 1984 by Robert Nemiroff, as an unpublished work. Copyright © 1959, 1966, 1984 by Robert Nemiroff. All rights reserved.

Rogers, Coleridge and White, Ltd.
"Games at Twilight" from *Games at Twilight and Other Stories* by Anita Desai. Copyright © 1978 by Anita Desai. All rights reserved.

Heyden White Rostow
From The American Idea by Theodore H. White from *The New York Times Magazine, July 6, 1986*. Copyright © 1986 by Theodore H. White. All rights reserved.

David Unger
"The Censors," from *Open Doors: Stories* by Luisa Valenzuela. Copyright © translation by David Unger. All rights reserved.

University of Arizona Press
"The Figurative Tradition" from *The Pueblo Storyteller: Development of a Figurative Ceramic Tradition* by Barbara A. Babcock and Guy and Doris Monthan. Copyright © 1986 The Arizona Board of Regents. Reprinted by permission of the University of Arizona Press.

Viking Penguin, Inc.
From What Makes a Degas a Degas? by Richard Muhlberger, published by The Metropolitan Museum of Art, New York, and Viking, a Division of Penguin Putnam Books for Young Readers, copyright © 1993 by The Metropolitan Museum of Art. All rights reserved.

The Washington Post Writers Group
"But What Of The Parents Whose Son Seeks Political Asylum?" by Ellen Goodman. From *The Boston Globe, August 7, 1980* issue. Copyright © 1980, The Washington Post Writers Group. Reprinted with permission.

William K. Zinsser c/o Carol Brissie
"Two Writing Processes"(originally titled: "The Transaction") by William K. Zinsser. From *On Writing Well, Seventh Edition*, published by HarperCollins. Copyright © 1976, 1980, 1985, 1988, 1990, 1994, 1998, 2001, 2006 by William K. Zinsser. Reprinted by permission of the author.

Note: Every effort has been made to locate the copyright owner of material reproduced on this component. Omissions brought to our attention will be corrected in subsequent editions.

Photo Credits

Cover: Pearson Prentice Hall iii: PhotoEdit ix: Tony Stone Images vi: (top) LEA/ Omni-Photo Communications, Inc. (bottom) Corel Professional Photos CD-ROM™ vii: (top) Corel Professional Photos CD-ROM™ (middle) Corel Professional Photos CD-ROM™ (bottom) David Young-Wolff PhotoEdit x: ©1997, G. & M. Kohler/FPG International Corp.; xi: PhotoDisc/Getty Images, Inc.; xii: Will Hart/PhotoEdit; xiii: PhotoDisc/Getty Images, Inc.; xiv: PhotoDisc/Getty Images, Inc.; xv: F. Hoffmann/The Image Works; xvi: ©1996, Walter Bibikow/FPG International Corp.; xvii: *Federal Brigade Commanded by General Winfield Scott,* Julian Scott, Smithsonian Institution; xviii: Kunsthistorisches Museum, Antikensammlung, Vienna, Austria, ©Photograph by Erich Lessing/Art Resource, NY; xix: *Ballet Class,* Edgar Degas, Corel Professional Photos CD-ROM™; xx: (top) David Young-Wolff/PhotoEdit; (bottom) Bruce Ayres/Tony Stone Images; xxi: (top) Corel Professional Photos CD-ROM™; (bottom) Corel Professional Photos CD-ROM™; xxii: (top) Corel Professional Photos CD-ROM™; (bottom) Courtesy of the Italian Government Tourist Board; xxiii: (top) Corel Professional Photos CD-ROM™; (bottom) Courtesy of the Library of Congress; xxiv: (top) Corel Professional Photos CD-ROM™; (bottom) Corel Professional Photos CD-ROM™; xxv: (top), (middle) & (bottom) Corel Professional Photos CD-ROM™; xxvi: (top) Corel Professional Photos CD-ROM™; (bottom) ©The Stock Market/Jose L. Pelaez; xxvii: (top) Corel Professional Photos CD-ROM™; (bottom) ©The Stock Market/Tom Stewart; 1: *Femme Cousant,* Henri Lebasque, Christie's Images/SuperStock, ©2001 Artists Rights Society (ARS), New York,

ADAGP, Paris; 2: ©Sven Martson/ The Image Works; 5: Don Smetzer/Tony Stone Images; 6: David De Lossy/The Image Bank; 8: Shelley Rotner/Omni-Photo Communications, Inc.; 12: Bob Daemmrich/Stock, Boston Inc./ PictureQuest; 24: Photofest; 28: Tony Page/Tony Stone Images; 29: Kindra Clineff/Index Stock Photography, Inc.; 35: Don Spiro/ Medichrome/The Stock Shop, Inc.; 37: AP/Wide World Photos; 41: Corel Professional Photos CD-ROM™; 43: ©StockFood America/EISING; 44: Tony Freeman/PhotoEdit; 48: North Carolina Museum of Art/CORBIS; 51: Silver Burdett Ginn; 52: Tony Stone Images; 55: *Backgammon,* 1976, Jane Freilicher, oil on canvas, 38 x 44 in., From the permanent collection of the Utah Museum of Fine Arts, Acc. 1979.008; 61: LEA/ Omni-Photo Communications, Inc.; 68: Tony Stone Images; 70: Karen Huntt Mason/CORBIS; 71: Robert Ullmann/Monkmeyer; 72: Photofest; 76: Richard Hutchings/ PhotoEdit; 78: ©1997, G. & M. Kohler/FPG International Corp.; 79: (left) © StockFood America/ Mastri; (right) ©1997, G. & M. Kohler/FPG International Corp.; 81: *Students of Modelling and Painting,* Anonymous, Private Collection/Bridgeman Art Library, NYC; 85: Tony Freeman/ PhotoEdit; 92: PhotoDisc/Getty Images, Inc.; 94: Richard T. Nowitz/CORBIS; 96: *He Laid Down His Hammer and Cried,* 1944–47, Palmer C. Hayden, Museum of African American Art, Los Angeles, CA; 100: Gottlieb/Monkmeyer; 102: Tim Page/CORBIS; 105: Studio Interior, 1982, Jane Freilicher, Tibor De Nagy; 108: Kevin R. Morris/CORBIS; 113: Michelle Bridwell/PhotoEdit; 116: PhotoDisc/Getty Images, Inc.; 117: David Young-Wolff/PhotoEdit; 118: ©The Stock Market/Craig Tuttle; 120: Portrait of Dolores Olmedo, Diego Rivera, Schalkwijk/ Art Resource, NY; 121: Mark

Richards/PhotoEdit; 124: AP Photo/Jan Bauer; 126: Richard Derk/Chicago Sun-Times; 129: AP/Wide World Photos; 131: *Arrivals and Departures,* 1999, Chester Arnold, The Seven Bridges Foundation, Greenwich, CT. Photo courtesy of George Adams Gallery, New York; 136: Bill Bachman/The Image Works; 137: Tom Stack/ Tom Stack & Associates; 141: Will Hart/PhotoEdit; 144: Myrleen Ferguson/PhotoEdit; 148: *Snap the Whip,* Winslow Homer, Corel Professional Photos CD-ROM™; 152: PhotoDisc/Getty Images, Inc.; 154: Costa Rica Tourist Board; 166: Amy Etra/PhotoEdit; 168: Mitchell Gerber/CORBIS; 172: Tony Arruza/CORBIS; 174: ©The Stock Market/Jon Feingersh; 177: *Minor League,* Clyde Singer, The Butler Institute of American Art; 181: PhotoDisc/Getty Images, Inc.; 189: (left) David Young-Wolff/ PhotoEdit; (right) Amy C. Etra/ PhotoEdit; 191: Ken Karp/PH photo; 193: Photofest; 196: *The Landing of Columbus at San Salvador (Guanahani) in Bahamas,* 12 October 1492, The Granger Collection, New York; 198: ©The Stock Market/Andrew Holbrooke; 199: Bill Bachmann/PhotoEdit; 201: *Rolling Power,* 1939, Charles Sheeler, Smith College Museum of Art, Northampton, Massachusetts. Purchased, Drayton Hillyer Fund, 1940; 204: Ralph White/CORBIS; 213: F. Hoffmann/The Image Works; 214: Stephen Wilkes/The Image Bank; 215: David Young-Wolff/PhotoEdit; 216: City of Edinburgh Museums and Art Galleries/The Bridgeman Art Library, London/New York; 220: Mary Kate Denny/PhotoEdit; 222: David A. Northcott/CORBIS; 225: *Unloading the Cargo,* 1942, Ralston Crawford; 230: Corel Professional Photos CD-ROM™; 234: Will Hart; 237: Michael Newman/ PhotoEdit; 238: ©1996, Walter Bibikow/FPG International Corp.; 239: